THE INLAND FISHES
OF NEW YORK STATE

THE INLAND FISHES
OF NEW YORK STATE

By C. LAVETT SMITH

Curator — The American Museum of Natural History

Sponsored and Published by

The New York State
Department of Environmental Conservation

Mario M. Cuomo   Henry G. Williams
Governor   *Commissioner*

DEDICATION

This book is respectfully dedicated
to five who paved the way:

Samuel Latham Mitchill 1764 — 1831

James Elsworth De Kay 1799 — 1851

Tarleton Hoffman Bean 1846 — 1916

John R. Greeley 1904 — 1982

Edward C. Raney 1909 — 1984

ISBN 0-9615433-0-2

Funded By
Return
a Gift to
Wildlife
Contributions

Funds for this publication were contributed from several sources. The New York State Conservation Fund and the Federal Aid in Sport Fishing Restoration Act (Dingell-Johnson Act) supported preparation of the manuscript and original art. Printing and design costs were paid by the New York State "Return a Gift to Wildlife" program.

The Dingell-Johnson Act provides for the collection of federal excise tax on certain sport fishing tackle. The United States Fish and Wildlife Service administers the Dingell-Johnson program and distributes revenue to states for qualifying fishery projects. The Conservation Fund is derived primarily from the sale of hunting, fishing, and trapping licenses in New York. "Return a Gift to Wildlife" is a special source of revenue to the Conservation Fund that was established in 1982 to promote the welfare and understanding of New York's fish and wildlife. State taxpayers voluntarily support projects funded by "Return a Gift to Wildlife" through donations made on their state income tax returns. The Department of Environmental Conservation administers the Conservation Fund and allocates money for fish and wildlife research and management, habitat protection, and educational programs and projects.

From 1926 to 1939, a Biological Survey of New York Watersheds was conducted by the New York State Conservation Department. Annual reports published from this survey comprise the most comprehensive assessment of New York's fishery resource in print. However, after more than five decades, resource inventory data from the original Biological Survey inevitably have become outdated. Today's resource managers require up-to-date information to implement modern, scientific environmental and resource enhancement practices. In response to this problem the Department of Environmental Conservation, which incorporates the former Conservation Department, began planning in 1983 for a Second Biological Survey of New York Watersheds with funds to be provided by "Return a Gift to Wildlife" contributions.

This book represents an initial expenditure by the Second Biological Survey. Information contained herein provides current data and a historical perspective on the status and distribution of fishes in New York. Determination of Biological Survey field collection objectives will be greatly assisted by this publication.

Many individuals were involved with preparation of this text for publication. Lawrence Strait, unit leader of the Second Biological Survey, served as managing editor and production coordinator. Paul Carella, Pat Clearey, Anne Griggs, Shaun Keeler, Rodger Klindt, Jeff Liddle, Rich Preall, Ed Reed, Tim Sinnott, and Eric Siy of the Biological Survey staff assisted with the various mundane, but essential, tasks required in the publication of a large book. John Scott and Martha McEwen made a special contribution by carefully examining the reference sections.

Carl Parker, retired chief of DEC Bureau of Fisheries, reviewed the entire text and provided numerous improvements to copy.

Typesetting services were procured from the New York State Department of Education. Staff of the New York State Museum assisted with preliminary production planning and Dr. Robert Daniels, also of the museum, edited the fish distribution maps.

Frances Johansson designed the book and dust jacket. Illustrations are the work of Howard Friedman, Marilyn Fairman, Carol Gene Schleifer, Edward Kenney, Anita Cleary, and Scott Smerznak.

Dr. James Atz of the American Museum of Natural History constructed the common and scientific names, geographical names, and subjects indexes.

PREFACE

Aims and Scope

The State of New York, by reason of its history and geographic location, has one of the richest and most interesting fish faunas of any land area of comparable size in the world. Interesting, of course, is a relative term, but in this case it is a defensible one. The fishes of New York are interesting to the legions of sport fishermen whether they are accomplished anglers who ply their skills in our justly famous Beaver Kill and Batten Kill, or less dedicated fishermen out for a day's relaxation by a quiet pond. They are of interest to the committed commercial fishermen who flaunt traditional skills in the face of a hostile twentieth century and to the customers who reap the rewards of their efforts. Our fishes are interesting to the many professional fishery biologists who strive to find better ways to maintain quality fishing in our waters and to the esoteric scientists who recognize that fishes are living laboratories that can help us to better understand how living organisms work and interact with their environment. Finally, fishes are interesting to naturalists who enjoy watching and learning about the beauties of natural systems.

The book is intended as a ready reference to all the fishes that live in the inland waters of New York State. By inland, we mean the freshwaters and also the long Hudson River estuary where many marine and brackish water species live. This coverage is necessarily somewhat arbitrarily limited because the Hudson is an arm of the sea and new records will continue to accumulate as long as we study fishes there. A few species are included on the basis of very dubious older records and there are undoubtedly others that frequently enter the estuary but have escaped notice. Nevertheless, I have tried to make this book as complete as the present state of knowledge permits.

I hope that this book will serve three purposes. First, to provide a list of the species found in the state with their geographic and ecologic distributions within our boundaries. Second, to provide through keys, illustrations and descriptions, the means for identifying juvenile and adult specimens. Third, to present brief summaries of what is known of the life history and ecology of our species together with an introduction to the pertinent literature as a starting point for those who would know more about the life styles of our fishes.

Our intended audience includes both the professional biologists who, in their daily toils, deal with fishes, and those interested and interesting people who find fishes fascinating, be they fishermen, conservationists, or naturalists who simply derive pleasure from learning about the world around them.

Although the study of fishes is a highly technical subject with its own methods and vocabulary, I have tried to present this introduction in a straightforward language that can be easily understood by anyone willing to devote a little time and thought to a complex subject.

Acknowledgments

To thank all of the people who have helped make this book possible would require an additional complete book but there are some individuals who deserve special recognition. Certainly it would not have come to be had it not been for the aid and encouragement of many members of the staff of the New York State Department of Environmental Conservation. It was Howard Loeb who first encouraged me to start serious work on a Fishes of New York and later Dr. Paul Neth, Bruce Shupp and Tony Bonavist provided additional support and aided in myriad ways. Many of the biologists, hatchery personnel and support staff of the department aided by providing information and specimens. Dan Plosila, Gene Lane, Walt Keller, Norm McBride, Jim Johnson, Wayne Elliot, Bob Brandt, Larry Strait, Tom Eckert, Tom Jolliff, Bob Brewer, Dean Bouton, Eli Dietsch, Rick Colesante, and Patrick Festa were especially helpful.

Much of the data collecting and routine laboratory studies were done by graduate students and volunteers in the Department of Ichthyology at the American Museum of Natural History. Especial thanks go to Dan Cirnigliaro, Kathy Sarg, Martha Halsey, Joseph Ceasereli and Leslie Avery for the hours they spent measuring specimens. Another group of people, including Martha Halsey, Townsend Weeks and Irwin A. Levy, spent many days checking references and correcting spelling and grammar, and generally cleaning up the manuscript. Their dedication is near miraculous. Norma Feinberg prepared large numbers of X-ray plates for vertebral and other counts.

A particular kind of thanks goes to those members of our field crew who made the fishes of New York their project. Carol Schleifer, Felix Locicero, Chang Hwa Chang, Marjorie Smith, Loretta Stillman, Jerry Platt and his "Raiders" (a very special group of young biologists from the Museum of the Hudson Highlands), Chuck Keene, Director of that institution, John Waldman, several generations of fish classes from the City College of New York, Wayne Hadley and his students from the University of Buffalo, Steve Eaton and St. Bonaventure students, and many others who joined us for a day or two in the field, taught me more than I could ever teach them.

I am especially grateful to the many landowners who graciously allowed us to cross their lands to study the fish. Without their cooperation our task would have been much more difficult.

Scientists interested in fish in all parts of the state have given more than generously of their knowledge. Bob Daniels, Joe Pickett, Ed Brothers, Bob Schocknecht, Dwight Webster, Bill Flick, Steve Eaton, Allen Beebe, Paul Moccio, Eric Kiviat, Bob Schmidt, Neil Ringler, Bob Werner, Antonio Pappantoniou, George Dale, Bill Dovel, John Forney, Carl George, and Wayne Hadley deserve especial mention. My colleagues James Atz, Donn Rosen and Gareth Nelson at the American Museum have provided the intellectual stimulation and examples of high scholarship that I can only admire.

This book has been edited by Dr. Edwin L. Cooper, who graciously shared his experience with the Fishes of Pennsylvania, and guided me through the final phases of this work. His meticulous and demanding scholarship have inspired me through many tedious hours of rewriting. As an editor, he has walked the fine line of pushing me toward an acceptable level of precision while allowing me my own idiosyncrasies.

Finally, there are special colleagues who have made the study of fishes a rewarding career and to whom I owe more than I can ever express: James Tyler, who has shared many expeditions and has been a constant source of inspiration; Reeve Bailey, who provided guidance and example in the most important formative part of my career; and Ed Raney, who first introduced me to the most exciting field in the world.

Part of the art work has been made possible by a grant from the Nixon Griffis Foundation.

CONTENTS

MARINE FISHES IN THE INLAND WATERS OF NEW YORK *

see page xi

CONTENTS

LIST OF ILLUSTRATIONS

I.   Brook trout, *Salvelinus fontinalis*
II. Common shiner, *Notropis cornutus*
 Spotfin shiner, *Notropis spilopterus*
III. Redfin shiner, *Notropis umbratilis*
 Rosyface shiner, *Notropis rubellus*
IV. Eastern blacknose dace, *Rhinichthys atratulus* male
 Eastern blacknose dace, *Rhinichthys atratulus* female
 Western blacknose dace, *Rhinichthys meleagris* male
V.   Redside dace, *Clinostomus elongatus*
 Northern redbelly dace, *Phoxinus eos* female
 Pearl dace, *Semotilus margarita*
VI. Eastern sand darter, *Ammocrypta pellucida*
 Iowa darter, *Etheostoma exile*
 Spotted darter, *Etheostoma maculatum*
VII. Greenside darter, *Etheostoma blennioides*
 Rainbow darter, *Etheostoma caeruleum*
 Variegate darter, *Etheostoma variatum*
VIII. Tessellated darter, *Etheostoma olmstedi*
 Banded darter, *Etheostoma zonale*
 Channel darter, *Percina copelandi*

LIST OF TABLES

Average proportional measurements and counts of:

•

The phylogenetic order and designation of species presented in *The Inland Fishes of New York State* represents the opinion of the author and may deviate from that described in *A List of Common and Scientific Names of Fishes,* fourth edition (1980), published by the American Fisheries Society. This arrangement is not necessarily endorsed by the New York State Department of Environmental Conservation.

ICHTHYOLOGY IN NEW YORK 1

The history of any study is a fascinating mixture of factual discoveries, the synthesis of isolated facts into general theories, and the personalities of the students making the discoveries and syntheses. The study of fishes in New York has closely paralleled the development of the state, and New York has never suffered from a lack of colorful personalities in any field.

The science of ichthyology was a comparatively late development and its early practitioners were generally people who made their living in some other line of work. Most early ichthyologists were physicians but a few were merchants or statesmen who studied fishes as an avocation. Even today many ichthyologists are college faculty whose primary obligation is to teach and whose research efforts are necessarily secondary to teaching or administration.

The development of the study of any group of organisms is revealed in the names and classifications used for those organisms. This connection may not be obvious but it results from the inevitable evolution of our knowledge. The earliest efforts were to inventory the species that existed and in order to communicate this inventory the species were given names. Since it is almost inevitable that different workers sometimes will apply new and different names to species that have been described earlier, an International Code of Zoological Nomenclature sets forth the rules by which animals are to be named. Two of the most important principles of this code are that there be only one valid name for each species and that this name must be the oldest available name, that is, the first name that was applied to that particular species which was not already in use for some other species or could not be used for some other reason.

Formal zoological nomenclature began officially on 1 January 1758, because 1758 is the date of publication of the 10th edition of Carl von Linne's *Systema Naturae*. Linnaeus, as he is usually called, was a Swede who developed a workable system of classifying plants and animals in a hierarchy of classes, orders, families, genera and species with the scientific name consisting of two words, the name of its genus and the name of its species.

Names proposed before 1758 have no official recognition although, of course, Linnaeus based many of his names on terms that had been proposed by earlier students. Much of Linnaeus' knowledge of American organisms came from a large and beautifully illustrated volume by Mark Catesby entitled *The Natural History of Carolina, Florida and the Bahama Islands . . .* published in 1731. Linnaeus also received many specimens from a Dr. Alexander Garden of Charleston, South Carolina (for whom he named the gardenia). Modern fish collectors will find it interesting that Garden slit his fishes and dried them in a plant press with surprisingly good results.

While Linnaeus' 1758 volume is the starting point, there was relatively little progress in the study of North American fishes during the rest of the 18th century. Pennant, an English writer, described a few American species in his *Arctic Zoology* (1784). Some others were added in the 12th edition of the *Systema Naturae* and in the 13th edition which was revised and enlarged by Johann Frederick Gmelin. In 1792, Johann Julio Walbaum published a kind of revision of Linnaeus' work under the title *Petri Artedi renovati*. Artedi was a co-worker of Linnaeus' and was responsible for much of the fish work in the *Systema*. His name is well known to fish students as the species name of the lake herring or cisco. Artedi drowned at the age of thirty when he fell into a canal in Amsterdam late at night. Walbaum's revision also contains original descriptions of fishes that were mentioned but not formally named in a 1788 paper by Johann David Schoepf. Schoepf was an army surgeon stationed in New York during the Revolutionary War. He listed some 120 species and described about 30 in detail.

The turn of the century saw the publication of some general works that included such New York species as happened to come to their authors' attention. Lacepede, a Frenchman working in exile during the French Revolution, published a five-volume *Histoire Naturelle des Poissons,* 1798-1803. Bloch and Schneider's *Systema Ichthyologiae* appeared in 1801. Still, no one specifically addressed the North American fauna.

In 1814 there appeared a small paper that marked the beginning of the study of North American ichthyology in its own right. On January first, Dr. Samuel Latham Mitchill, a physician turned statesman, published a small tract entitled *Report, in Part, on the Fishes of New York*. This privately printed article contained the original descriptions of 49 species and listed 21 more. In 1815, Mitchill published in the Transactions of the Literary and Philosophical Society a longer article, *The Fishes of New York, Described and Arranged*. This was followed in 1818 by a supplement in the American Monthly Magazine and Critical Review and, subsequently, Mitchill published a number of shorter articles in a variety of periodicals including daily newspapers.

At about the time Mitchill was listing the fishes of New York, two other naturalists were doing the same thing in other parts of the country. Charles A. Le Sueur — later Lesueur — a French naturalist residing in Philadelphia, published a long series of papers on North American fishes, chiefly from the Great Lakes region. Simultaneously, the brilliant but erratic Constantine Samuel Rafinesque was also describing fishes from upstate New York and, later, from the Ohio River valley. Rafinesque was one of the most colorful personalities the country has ever seen. He sometimes called himself Rafinesque-Schmaltz, with the addition of his mother's name calculated to capitalize on the pro-German prejudice he felt existed at the time. His friendship with John James Audubon produced some unexpected results as Rafinesque duly described imaginary fishes conceived by Audubon. British expeditions of the time to "the northern parts of British America" collected natural history specimens and in the 1820s and 1830s Sir John Richardson published on the fishes. About this time another statesman-naturalist, DeWitt Clinton of Erie Canal fame, published some papers describing fishes from New York. (Clinton, 1815, 1822). Clinton's most lasting contribution was the original description of the spottail shiner, *Notropis hudsonius*. In 1838, Kirtland reported on the fishes of Ohio and named some New York species and, in 1839, Storer released his major work on the fishes of Massachusetts and included species that also occur in New York.

The first volume of the last major attempt to treat all of the fishes of the world in a single series was published in 1828. Under the joint authorship of Le Baron Cuvier and Achille Valenciennes, the *Histoire Naturelle des Poissons* included original descriptions by other authors as well as by Cuvier and Valenciennes. The actual work was divided between Cuvier and Valenciennes so that all of the descriptions are clearly by one author or the other, not both. Cuvier died in 1832, and volumes 10 through 22 are by Valenciennes alone.

By 1842, knowledge of the fishes of New York had progressed to the point that James E. DeKay could produce the first "fishes of New York." Published as *The Zoology of New York or The New York Fauna;. . . . Part IV. The Fishes*, DeKay's book is an excellent review of the fishes of the state as they were known at that time. If anything, DeKay erred on the side of being too inclusive and some of the species he described are merely variants of species that were already known. It is interesting that in his review of previous work on fishes of the state there is no indication that he ever heard of Rafinesque. One gets the impression that Rafinesque was too radical for DeKay.

The second half of the 19th century saw continued progress and expanded explorations. Spencer F. Baird *(Cottus bairdi* was named in his honor) and Charles Girard described many species, some of which were collected by the survey crews that were mapping routes for the transcontinental railroads. Edward Drinker Cope studied the fishes of the Appalachian drainages and, in 1876, David Starr Jordan, another New Yorker, published the first edition of his *Manual of the Vertebrates,* a guide to the identification of vertebrate animals of the eastern United States. This guide would grow through 13 editions and continue to be used by students until the early 1950s. Jordan's powerful intellect dominated the field until his death in 1931. It was during this period that ichthyologists came to fully appreciate the importance of saving specimens and the great collections of the country got their start. Jordan and his co-workers saw zoology in general and ichthyology in particular develop into modern sciences. This was the time that Darwin's concepts of evolution came into being and changed the way systematists approached their subject. Jordan and his colleagues also began to appreciate the importance of geography and undertook studies of all of the major drainages of the country. Jordan's illustrious career reached its apex with the publications of *The Fishes of North and Middle America. . . . Bulletin 47 of the United States National Museum.* Under the joint authorship of Jordan and Barton Warren Evermann, the four-volume work that appeared from 1896 through 1900 is still a standard reference on North American fishes.

The second half of the 19th century was a time when zoologists began to take classification seriously. (Here we make the distinction between describing, which is the process of announcing the discovery of a new species, and giving it a formal scientific name; identifying species, which is determining that they belong to a species that is already known; and classifying, which is arranging species in larger categories, such as genera and families.) Perhaps the dean of the 19th century classifiers was Theodore Gill. Gill worked at the U. S. National

Museum as a volunteer and seldom handled specimens except clean and dry skeletons. In his lifetime, he wrote more than 300 papers on classification and is responsible for many of the families and genera that are still used today. Gill and Cope epitomize the classifiers of their era. Where the Linnaean genera were large and all-inclusive, the pendulum had started to swing the other way and genera became smaller and more numerous.

Shortly after Jordan and Evermann's monumental *Fishes of North and Middle America* was published, there appeared another *Fishes of New York,* this time by Tarleton H. Bean (Bean, 1903). Bean's compilation lists three hundred and sixty species including saltwater forms. A number of the species he expected to be found within the state do not occur here. While Bean was making his compilation Evermann and Kendall were making surveys of Lake Champlain, Lake Ontario, and the St. Lawrence River. Their studies complemented the earlier surveys by Meek in the Cayuga Lake basin and Mather in the Adirondacks.

The next few decades saw active field work in New York. T. L. Hankinson, W. A. Dence, and C. C. Adams worked in the western and central parts of the state. In 1916, Adams and Hankinson published a preliminary report on the fishes of Oneida Lake and, in 1928, this was expanded into their classic paper *The Ecology and Economics of Oneida Lake Fishes.*

In 1930 Jordan, Evermann and Clark published a *Checklist of the fishes and fishlike vertebrates of North and Middle America north of the northern boundary of Venezuela and Colombia.* This listed current names and synonyms of all of the fishes then known. About this time, another giant was achieving full stature. Carl Hubbs of the University of Michigan, and later Scripps Institution, began to publish on the North American freshwater fishes. In 1926, Hubbs published a checklist that untangled many nomenclatural problems and this was followed by a long series of papers by Hubbs, Hubbs and Greene, Hubbs and Brown, and finally culminated in the book by Hubbs and Lagler, *The Fishes of the Great Lakes Region,* which is one of the best and most useful identification guides ever issued. In 1929, Walter Koelz published a revision of the whitefishes of the Great Lakes and brought to light many of the problems of classification of one of the most difficult groups of fishes. Whitefishes are extremely variable, and Koelz made an attempt to name all of the recognizable populations. Now, however, it seems that some of his subspecies merely reflect the effects of the environment and we are still far from a satisfactory solution to the problem of naming these variable fishes. In spite of the difficulties it raised, Koelz's study ushered in an era of revisionary studies that progressed in the 1930s

and is still flourishing today. In 1930, Hubbs published his *Materials for a Revision of the Catostomid fishes.* In 1937, Hubbs and Trautman revised the genus *Ichthyomyzon.* In 1940, Hubbs and Bailey revised the black basses and these studies have been followed by papers by Raney at Cornell, Bailey at Michigan and a host of their students including Lachner, Taylor, Gilbert, Gibbs, Collette, Miller, Jenkins, Robins, Snelson, Tsai, Suttkus, and Cole.

In 1926, the New York Conservation Department began a series of watershed surveys that have not been matched anywhere. Each summer a watershed or a combination of two watersheds was thoroughly surveyed. The survey started with the Genesee system in 1926 and finished with Long Island and Staten Island in 1939. Under the general direction of Dr. Emmeline Moore, the crews made thorough surveys, investigated special problems, and made studies of critical species. John R. Greeley prepared the fish reports, assisted by C. W. Greene for the St. Lawrence and by S. C. Bishop for the Upper Hudson and Oswegatchie-Black. These survey reports still provide the basic data for many fish management decisions in the state.

Beginning in the late 1930s, and continuing after World War II, Edward C. Raney at Cornell University and his many students turned their attention to descriptions of life history and especially to breeding behavior patterns of fishes in the state. Although there are still many species to be studied, their works have amply demonstrated the rich diversity of life styles of our local fishes.

Recently, the Hudson River estuary has become the site of some of the most comprehensive and sophisticated fishery work that has so far been attempted. Much of this effort is the result of environmental conflicts such as (1) the location of power plants which use enormous quantities of cooling water and thus greatly influence the local aquatic environments and (2) the discovery that the sediments of the upper Hudson River were heavily polluted with polychlorinated biphenyls. More recently, the controversial Westway project in New York City has necessitated intensive studies of the distribution of fishes in the New York Harbor area. Because of the complex legal issues involved, all of this fishery work has been subjected to rigorous scrutiny and quality control. The Hudson River settlement, a complex agreement between environmentalists, utilities, and governmental agencies will surely come to be recognized as a landmark effort to manage natural resources for the common good.

In the past few years, a number of authors have brought together knowledge of fishes into treatises on the fishes of individual states. Noteworthy are *The Fishes of Ohio* by M.B. Trautman, *The Freshwater Fishes of New Hampshire* by John Scarola, *The Freshwater Fishes of Connecticut* by

Whitworth, Berrien and Keller, *The Fishes of Missouri* by Pfleiger, *The Fishes of Illinois* by P. Smith, *The Fishes of Pennsylvania* by Cooper, and *The Fishes of Wisconsin* by Becker. On a national scale, *A List of Common and Scientific Names of Fishes from the United States and Canada,* by the Committee on Names of Fishes of the American Fisheries Society, is a most useful reference and the *At-las of North American Freshwater Fishes* by Lee et al. provides ranges of all of the North American species. *The Freshwater Fishes of Canada* by Scott and Crossman is an excellent compendium. All of these publications reflect the sophistication of North American ichthyology today and point the way to studies in the future.

THE STATE OF NEW YORK* 2

Location

The State of New York is shaped roughly like the letter "T" lying on its side with the top bar on the east and Long Island extending out into the Atlantic Ocean like some kind of punctuation mark. Its area is approximately 50,000 square miles. The state extends from the Atlantic Ocean northward to near the northern end of Lake Champlain and westward from the New England border to Lake Erie and the Niagara River. Its eastern edge spans from latitude 40°30′ north at Staten Island to 45°00′ at the Ca-

*Much of the information in this section is summarized from papers in Thompson (1977)

nadian border or roughly 430 miles. Its east-west span is from 73°00′ to 79°45′ west longitude or about 320 statute miles. In the western part of the state, the distance from the Pennsylvania border at 42°00′ north latitude to the Lake Ontario shore near Rochester is approximately 90 miles.

Climate

Geographers recognize five climatic zones in the state: 1. Extremely cold winters and very cool wet summers (Adirondacks), 2. Very cold winters and cool sunny summers (St. Lawrence Valley), 3. Cool snowy winters and cool wet summers (higher parts

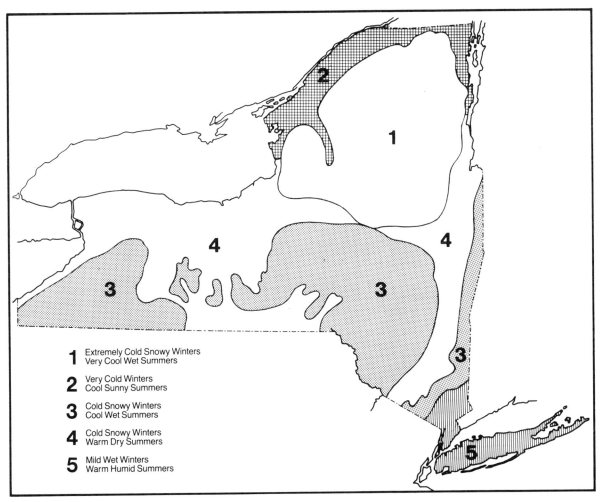

1 Extremely Cold Snowy Winters
Very Cool Wet Summers

2 Very Cold Winters
Cool Sunny Summers

3 Cold Snowy Winters
Cool Wet Summers

4 Cold Snowy Winters
Warm Dry Summers

5 Mild Wet Winters
Warm Humid Summers

Figure 1. Climactic Zones of New York

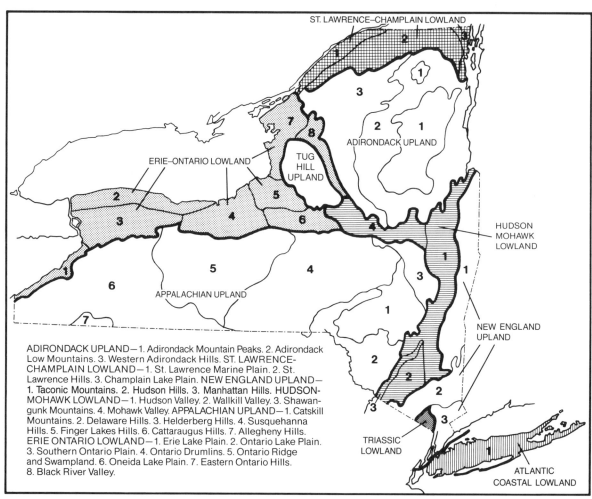

ADIRONDACK UPLAND—1. Adirondack Mountain Peaks. 2. Adirondack Low Mountains. 3. Western Adirondack Hills. ST. LAWRENCE-CHAMPLAIN LOWLAND—1. St. Lawrence Marine Plain. 2. St. Lawrence Hills. 3. Champlain Lake Plain. NEW ENGLAND UPLAND—1. Taconic Mountains. 2. Hudson Hills. 3. Manhattan Hills. HUDSON-MOHAWK LOWLAND—1. Hudson Valley. 2. Wallkill Valley. 3. Shawangunk Mountains. 4. Mohawk Valley. APPALACHIAN UPLAND—1. Catskill Mountains. 2. Delaware Hills. 3. Helderberg Hills. 4. Susquehanna Hills. 5. Finger Lakes Hills. 6. Cattaraugus Hills. 7. Allegheny Hills. ERIE ONTARIO LOWLAND—1. Erie Lake Plain. 2. Ontario Lake Plain. 3. Southern Ontario Plain. 4. Ontario Drumlins. 5. Ontario Ridge and Swampland. 6. Oneida Lake Plain. 7. Eastern Ontario Hills. 8. Black River Valley.

Figure 2. Landforms in New York

of the southern tier of counties), 4. Cold snowy winters and warm dry summers (Lake Ontario Plain and south in the Finger Lakes and Susquehanna Valley) and, 5. Mild wet winters and warm humid summers (Long Island). The Hudson-Mohawk Corridor is a kind of transition zone between the mild southeast areas and the cold higher elevations to the west (Figure 1).

The mean annual temperature in the state varies considerably, from 40.6 F in the Adirondacks to 54 F in New York City, and the growing season (frost-free days) ranges from less than 100 days in the Adirondacks to 180 in the Hudson-Mohawk Corridor and as much as 220 in eastern Long Island.

The annual precipitation is also variable. The Tug Hill Plateau and the southern Adirondacks, the southern Catskills and the southwestern parts of the Appalachian Upland all receive more than 50 inches of rain per year but the Lake Ontario and Finger Lakes regions get less than 32. In general, the higher parts of the state receive more precipitation than the lowlands. Intense precipitation (more than 3 inches in a single day) has occurred throughout the state. A number of places have had more than 6 inches and New York City has had as much as 9.55 inches in one 24-hour period. Most of the

intense storms occur between May and December, most commonly in July. Since this is the period when soil moisture is low, the impacts of these intense storms is minimized because the soil can absorb water before it is shed as run-off. This fact, together with the rather even distribution of rainfall throughout the year — most areas receive from 2 to 4 inches each month — means that stream flows are quite consistent, although droughts sometimes occur in some areas, particularly the Lake Ontario shore, the St. Lawrence Valley and the Champlain Lowland.

Of particular significance to aquatic life is the annual water surplus; i. e. the precipitation that falls minus the amount that is stored and that which is lost to transpiration and evaporation. The surplus is, therefore, the amount of water that runs off the land in the streams and it is this surplus that makes New York a land of water, and of fish. Water surplus is measured in inches of rainfall per year and ranges from somewhat less than 10 in the driest parts of the state to more than 30 in the higher regions of the Adirondacks and Tug Hill.

Landforms

The present day distribution of the fishes is a reflection of the habitats available combined with the past history of waterway connections that gave the fishes access to those habitats. Probably the most important factors that govern what kinds of habitats will be present are land elevation, which determines stream gradients and influences to a great extent local weather and climate, and the nature of the underlying rocks which affects landforms and water quality.

The most spectacular upland areas of New York are the Adirondack Mountains which occupy the northeastern part of the state. Geographers recognize three subdivisions of the Adirondacks: the central High Peaks region which is surrounded by lower mountains which are in turn flanked on their western side by the Adirondack Hills. Southwest of the Adirondacks, and separated from them by the Black River valley, is a plateau area called Tug Hill which is the snowiest place east of the Rocky Mountains, often receiving more than 225 inches of snow per year (Figure 2).

The southern half of the state is dominated by the Appalachian Upland which is really the northern terminus of the Appalachian Mountain chain. There are seven subdivisions of this region. At the eastern end, the high Catskill Mountains rise above the Hudson River valley. The Catskills are joined on the north by the Helderberg Mountains and on the south by the Delaware Hills. West of these three upland areas are the Susquehanna Hills, which are dissected by the south-flowing streams of the Susquehanna River system. Still farther west are the Finger Lakes Hills, also dissected into north-south ridges, this time by the north-flowing streams of the Finger Lakes region and by the Finger Lakes themselves. West of the Finger Lakes Hills, the Cattaraugus Hills extend to the lowlands of the Lake Erie lake plain. In the southwestern part of the state there is a semicircle of hills cut off by the bend of the Allegheny River. These are the Allegheny Hills and they are the only part of the state that was not covered by the last glacial ice sheet.

The east wall of the Hudson Valley is formed by the New England Upland. Three subdivisions are recognized in this area. The Taconic Hills, contiguous with the famous scenic mountains of Vermont and Massachusetts, extend from the southern end of Lake Champlain to the vicinity of Poughkeepsie, where they join the Hudson Highlands, a series of ridges that veer off to the southwest and are breached by the Hudson River between Cornwall and Peekskill. South of this the Manhattan Hills form the charming uplands of Westchester County and New York City.

The lowlands separating these higher areas include the St. Lawrence marine plain, which was once the floor of an arm of the sea that extended inland to eastern Lake Ontario and the Champlain

Valley. A band of low-lying hills, the St. Lawrence Hills, are the northern foothills of the Adirondacks and form a transition between the plain and the Adirondacks. At the extreme northeastern part of the state there is a triangular flat area, the Champlain lake plain, wedged in between Lake Champlain and the mountains. It pinches out a few miles south of the Canadian border. East of the mouth of the Niagara River, and extending past Rochester nearly to Sodus Bay, is the Lake Ontario Plain. A sharp escarpment divides the Lake Ontario Plain between the Niagara River and the Genesee River. East of the Genesee a band of glacial hills, the Ontario drumlins, lie between the lake plain and the Finger Lakes Hills. To the east of Sodus Bay the lake plain pinches out and the drumlin fields extend to the lake shore, giving way to the Ontario ridge and swampland at the southeast corner of Lake Ontario. South and east of the ridge and swampland zone the Oneida Lake Plain forms a connection with the western end of the Mohawk Corridor that separates the Adirondacks from the southern uplands. Similarly, the Black River valley connects the Mohawk Valley with the Ontario Hills that border the eastern shore of Lake Ontario.

There are three other subdivisions of the Mohawk-Hudson Lowland. The Hudson Valley which extends from the lower end of Lake Champlain to the Hudson Highlands; the Wallkill Valley which branches off to the southwest near Kingston and separates the highlands from the Catskills; and the Shawangunk Mountains which form the western wall of the Wallkill Valley and merge into the southern Catskills. South of the highlands, the Hudson is bordered by the Triassic Lowland representing the downshot side of the Ramapo Fault which forms the southern limit of the highlands.

Long Island is a part of the Atlantic Coastal Plain. It is divided lengthwise into a hilly northern part and a flat southern part, the former representing the terminal moraines of the Wisconsin ice sheet and the latter the outwash plain associated with those moraines.

Watersheds

Fish distribution is limited by stream-drainage patterns. Species that are confined to headwaters are essentially island species. It is not possible for them to travel downstream through the ocean or large lake and back up into the next stream, and they certainly cannot travel overland without help.

New York is made up of five major watersheds. Most of the northern part of the state is technically in the St. Lawrence basin. This includes Lake Erie and its tributaries which, being above Niagara Falls, are part of the upper Great Lakes, Lake Ontario and its tributaries, some direct tributaries of the St. Lawrence River, and Lake Champlain and its tribu-

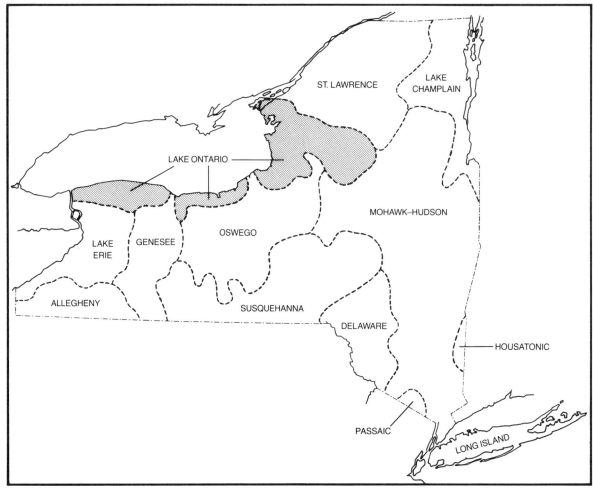

Figure 3. Watersheds of New York

taries. All of the Finger Lakes and Oneida Lake also flow into Lake Ontario through the Oswego River. The southern drainages of the state include the Hudson watershed which flows directly into the Atlantic at New York City; the two branches of the Delaware River which eventually reach the sea through Delaware Bay; the North Branch of the Susquehanna River and its western branch, the Chemung, which ultimately flows into the Chesapeake Bay; and the Allegheny River which is a tributary of the Ohio River and whose waters ultimately reach the Gulf of Mexico by way of the Mississippi River (Figure 3).

A small part of the state along the Connecticut border is drained by the Housatonic River and there are a few streams in Westchester County that flow directly into Long Island Sound. Parts of Rockland County are drained by the Passaic River that flows into the lower part of New York Harbor.

Each of the major watersheds has some distinctive fish species that do not occur in the other watersheds, or at least did not until they were introduced by modern man. The distribution patterns of our state fishes reflect the postglacial history of the region as well as the present day watershed patterns.

Habitats

The freshwater habitats of the state are conveniently grouped into those of flowing waters and those of standing waters. New York has approximately 70,000 miles of streams and more than 4,000 inland lakes, ponds, and reservoirs, in addition to parts of Lake Champlain and of Great Lakes Erie and Ontario. Eight inland lakes have more than 10,000 surface acres: Chautauqua Lake, Canandaigua Lake, Keuka Lake, Seneca Lake, Cayuga Lake, Oneida Lake, the Sacandaga Reservoir and Lake George. Together, the inland lakes total more than 740,600 acres.

Lake and pond habitats can be characterized according to depth, temperature, bottom type and shoreline type. Many fish occupy different habitats at different times of the year and at different stages in their life history. Water quality, the amount of nutrients and turbidity are also important in determining which habitats are acceptable to particular species. Some fishes make daily migrations from one habitat to another.

Stream habitats are also characterized by size (small streams are generally those with an average width of less than 10 feet and large streams are generally those whose average width exceeds 100 feet). Temperature, current speed, nature of the bottom, and character of the shoreline are other important measures of stream habitats that can be quantified to whatever degree of precision is necessary for the purpose at hand.

For the purpose of identifying fish habitats, it is convenient to consider streams as having three main parts, viz., headwater, midreach, and baselevel sections. Headwaters are the areas where the streams originate and are usually either tiny streams flowing through marshy or swampy lands, or rocky rills over eroded bedrock. Midreach streams have well defined, alternating pool and riffle sections, a riffle being a part of the stream where the surface is disturbed by the current and a pool being where the surface is calm unless disturbed by air currents. Baselevel sections are quiet larger reaches of the streams where there are no distinct riffles. Baselevel streams usually have pronounced meanders. In headwaters most of the erosion is headward, in midreach streams most of the erosion is lateral, and in baselevel streams there is considerable deposition. Undercut banks can occur in any part of the streams.

3 THE NEW YORK FISH FAUNA

Origin and Age

Historically, Europe and North America were once a single land mass and this is reflected in those species that occur on both sides of the Atlantic. The northern pike and the burbot of Europe are indistinguishable from those of North America and our yellow perch, walleye, and mudminnows have close relatives on opposite sides of the Atlantic. The suckers, some whitefishes, and possibly some lampreys seem to have a greater affinity with forms in eastern Asia, presumably having reached our area by traveling along the edge of the ice sheet during the terminal stages of Pleistocene glaciation. (Miller, 1965; Stewart and Lindsey, 1983). The affinity between North American and European marine fishes is much closer, presumably because there was a time after the continents drifted apart when individuals could still travel across the widening ocean.

The freshwater fauna of North America east of the Rocky Mountains seems to form a cohesive unit. A number of groups such as the Centrarchidae are essentially confined to this area and the few taxa whose affinities are obviously elsewhere (such as the cichlids and characins that reach their northern limit in Texas) only serve to emphasize the affinity of the remaining forms.

Since the area that is now New York State was nearly completely covered by thick ice sheets during the Wisconsin glacial period, and since there were no fish habitats under or on the glacial ice, it is apparent that our fauna can be dated from the time of the last recession of the edge of the glacier, approximately 16,000 years ago. It is also apparent that the present-day distribution of our fishes is to a very large degree associated in one way or another with the events that took place as the ice sheets advanced and retreated, beginning nearly a million years ago.

Distribution Patterns

When we examine the distributions of the fishes in New York it becomes apparent that there are five general patterns, each shared by a number of species:

1. Species that occur throughout the state, that is, in all of the major watersheds.

2. Species that are limited to the eastern part of the state.

3. Species that are limited to the western part of the state.

4. Species that occur only in the northern part of the state.

5. Species that occur in the east and west but not in the central parts of the state.

The species that live in all parts of the state (or would, were they not limited by their stringent habitat requirements) seem to be species that were able to use glacial outlets for expanding their ranges. Glacial outwash waters are not good fish habitats; they are cold, they lack nutrients and food resources as a result, and they often have high clay turbidity. Only the most tolerant and adaptable fishes were able to travel freely through glacial meltwaters.

When the glacier reached its extreme southern limit its edge was against the northern end of the Appalachian Mountains. This means that species whose ranges formerly extended across the northern states were divided into western and eastern populations. The areas south of the glacial front then served as refugia, one on the Atlantic coast and one in the Mississippi Valley. As the glaciers receded for the last time the fish were able to repopulate the glaciated areas from these refugia. The species that are still confined to either the eastern or the western parts of the states are those associated with the corresponding refugium. Since there were four major advances and many more minor shifts in the location of the glacier margin, it is not surprising that some species are limited to one region or the other, having either been eliminated on one side or the other of the Appalachians or else having evolved in their present range.

At first, it might seem that those fishes that are limited to the northern parts of the state are restricted because of their particular habitat requirements, possibly the need for lower temperatures during some part of their life cycle. When we examine the entire range of the species, however, we often find that they occupy a curved band or at least that the southern limit of their distribution forms an arc that seems to correlate very well with former glacial limits. The retreat of the glaciers was marked by periods when the location of the ice front remained stationary for considerable periods, and even advanced a short way, interspersed with periods when it retreated rapidly for considerable distances. It appears that during these stationary periods conditions became favorable and permitted some species to extend their range but they were unable to continue to follow the glacial margin while the ice was retreating rapidly.

The species that occur in both the eastern and western parts of the state are of particular interest. Some of these, such as the eastern and western blacknose dace and the johnny and tessellated darter (the johnny darter from the Mississippi refugium and the tessellated darter from the Atlantic refugium), seem to be simply cases of band-shaped distributions cut in two by the glacier. The grass (west) and the redfin (east) pickerels and the eastern and western pirate perches, however, are quite different. Their overall distribution is a ring surrounding the Appalachian Highlands with a zone of intergradation along the gulf coast. Apparently, as the glacier advanced these lowland species were able to expand their range southward rapidly enough so that they came together on the gulf coast while they were still able to interbreed. The northern populations were separated long enough so that they cannot reproduce together and thus they act as full species in the north but as subspecies in the south.

Study of the distribution patterns on an even finer scale has enabled us to trace the sequence of recolonization events, and in many cases, even the routes that have been used. For the most part such details are beyond the scope of this volume, but the reader will find much of interest in the excellent 1981 review of the Great Lakes fish fauna by Bailey and Smith.

Pleistocene Glaciation

The fish fauna of New York State is a postglacial fauna. For all practical purposes, there were no fish habitats in the state while the Pleistocene ice sheets were at their maxima and this means that all of our fishes have reached their present distributions in somewhat less than 16,000 or 17,000 years. This is not long enough for new species to form and so it also means that there are no endemic New York species; that is, there are no fishes that are found here and nowhere else.

While the fauna of North America in general is much older, the details of species distributions in the northern part of North America are the result of the climatic changes that occurred during the Pleistocene. It is generally believed that there have been at least four major advances of continental ice sheets, called the Nebraskan, Kansan, Illinoian and Wisconsin. These were separated by warm periods when the ice receded and the interglacial periods are named Aftonian, Yarmouth, and Sangamon. Each

of these stages consisted of a dynamic series of advances and retreats. The early glacial events are not well documented and it is not possible to assess their effects on the fishes that were in the region.

When the Wisconsin ice moved over New York it eliminated or reworked the deposits left by earlier glaciers and, except for a few traces in the western part of the state where the Illinoian ice sheet reached farther south than the Wisconsin, we know very little about the earlier glacial periods. However, there is a voluminous literature on the events that occurred as the Wisconsin ice sheet receded, and this is the time that is important to the fishes of New York.

Deglaciation

The flow of glacial ice was toward the south even when the front of the glacier was receding. As a result of this southward movement, huge quantities of rock and soil were deposited along the edges of the glacier as irregular hills called moraines. Still more material was deposited by meltwaters running on top of the glacier or underneath it near its edge. Some of these sediments were subsequently washed away and deposited beyond the edge of the glacier on the outwash plain, as for example the southern half of Long Island. Glaciers were effectively steered by the general topography of the land and they tended to round off east-west features and emphasize north-south topography so that the southern uplands of the state are dominated by deep north-south valleys, the best examples being the Finger Lakes where the glacier scooped out the floors of the valleys to depths that are below sea level. As the glaciers retreated from the valleys, their terminal moraines formed dams across the valleys and created lakes that remained in some cases long enough to accumulate thick layers of black peaty soil, the remains of hundreds of generations of plant life.

As the glaciers retreated, the drainage patterns changed as new outlets opened and old ones closed. The area that is now the Finger Lakes region was drained successively by the Susquehanna, the forerunner of Lake Erie, the Mohawk-Hudson Corridor, and the St. Lawrence. These patterns have given fishes rather free access to all parts of the state and raise the question of why all of the fishes do not occur throughout the state. The answer seems to be that glacial connections, and even large lakes, are not good routes for fishes to use in expanding their ranges.

Stream Capture

If, as I believe, glacial connections are not sufficient to account for the distribution patterns of most of the fishes of New York, what was the mechanism for postglacial dispersal of these fishes? In my opinion the most important means of transferring fishes from one drainage to another is stream capture.

Streams that flow down opposite sides of a ridge or mountain constantly erode their beds toward the highest point of their drainage basin. The rate of this erosion depends on a number of factors such as the nature of the underlying rocks, the relative amounts of rainfall, and the steepness of the gradient. As a result, no two streams erode at the same rate and it frequently happens that one stream will intersect another and take over (capture) the upper reaches of the second. Where this happens, the fishes that were living in the headwaters above the point of intersection are transferred to the new drainage even though they haven't moved. Most stream captures are between branches of the same stream and this will have little or no effect on the distribution except to hasten the spread of the species throughout the watershed. Occasionally, however, a stream capture will occur between tributaries of entirely different drainages.

Stream captures can often be recognized on maps as anomalies in the usual dendritic branching of the tributaries. Generally, tributaries converge downstream but, where a stream capture has occurred, the tributaries often appear to reverse their direction as they join a larger stream. Hundreds of stream capture sites are visible on New York drainage maps.

Stream captures can sometimes be placed in time sequence by considering the distributions of the fishes that have made use of them. For example the Upper Genesee River, above the falls at Portageville, has some species in common with the Allegheny that are not present in the Genesee below the falls. The Allegheny River shares some species with the Lake Erie tributaries that are not present in the Genesee drainage. For example the tonguetied minnow, *Exoglossum laurae,* occurs in the Allegheny and Upper Genesee but not in the Lake Erie tributaries whereas the rainbow darter, *Etheostoma caeruleum,* occurs in the Lake Erie streams and in the Allegheny but not in the Upper Genesee. This seems to indicate that the capture between the Upper Genesee and the Allegheny occurred before the capture between the Lake Erie tributaries and the Allegheny.

As a general rule, stream captures between small headwaters are more frequent than stream captures between the middle and lower reaches of the streams and, therefore, the preferred habitat of the fishes themselves plays an important role in the speed of their transport. This seems to be why the swallowtail shiner, *Notropis procne,* (a midreach species) is restricted to the Susquehanna whereas the bridle shiner, *N. bifrenatus,* (a headwater species) ranges much farther north.

Man and Fish

Although the native Americans made extensive use of fish in their diet, and for other purposes, it is likely that they had relatively little effect on the distribution of species. For one thing, fish were plentiful and transport was difficult so there would have been little incentive for the Indians to introduce species into areas where they did not occur naturally. For another, the human populations were well dispersed and it is doubtful if their fishing intensity was high enough to have had any lasting effects on fish populations.

The European colonists, on the other hand, were quick to recognize the value of the fisheries as a resource. As early as 1630, Dutch leaders were encouraging fishing by granting exclusive rights to anyone who discovered good fishing areas, and later steps were taken to develop fishing for fish to export to Europe. The Hudson River and the Great Lakes, as well as the larger inland waters, were fished intensively but as the population continued to grow it became apparent that the production of fish in inland waters was limited and today only the larger waters support commercial fishing. At present, high levels of chemical contaminants have restricted commercial fishing even more. Recreational fishing, on the other hand, is one of the state's most important resources, and New York's salmonid fishery is among the best in the world.

Introductions

It is a human trait to try to improve whatever is at hand. If the fishing is already good, why not try to make it better? One of the first attempts to supplement the fishery was by introducing new species. With the wisdom of hindsight it is hard to find the rationale for some of the introductions. Perhaps it was that European species were considered superior to the local fishes; possibly it was a desire for a source of familiar fish close at hand. At any rate, the carp was introduced in 1832, and it appears that the goldfish had been successfully imported even earlier. The first carp introductions were in New York by way of some ponds near Newburgh. When one considers the difficulty of bringing carp across the Atlantic on a sailing vessel, it seems that the desire for familiar food must have been strong indeed.

About 13 species of the New York fish fauna owe their presence to introductions. Some of these immigrants, such as the brown and rainbow trouts, are among our most respected game fishes. Others are considered nuisances.

Today, any planned introductions are considered very carefully. The grass carp is strictly prohibited by law and, in fact, all stocking requires a permit from the Department of Environmental Conservation. The recent introductions of Pacific salmon have created an outstanding fishery but the attempt was made only after careful consideration of the possible adverse effects such introductions might have had.

Some populations are maintained, or at least supplemented, by stocking of hatchery fishes. Stocking in itself does not alter the geographic ranges of the species, but it may have effects on other species upon which the stocked species preys or with which it competes. Since the early fish culturists were not aware of the potential problems, they did not keep extensive records and we will probably never be able to evaluate the true impact of the introduction of the brown and rainbow trouts.

Because some species that occurred in, but not throughout, New York have been introduced into areas where they did not occur naturally, it is sometimes difficult to determine just what the original distribution of the species was. There is a difference of opinion as to whether the sea lamprey was native to Lake Ontario or reached there through the Erie Canal. Those who believe it to be a canal immigrant cite the absence of early records from Ontario. Those who believe that it was native point to the absence of records from the canal or even from the Mohawk system above the Cohoes Falls. My own opinion is that it was native to Lakes Ontario and Champlain, having adapted to life in fresh water in postglacial times when the Champlain Sea gradually lost its salinity. This is more than an academic exercise. If the landlocked lamprey is a separate population that lives only in fresh water it could ultimately be eradicated. If any lampreys that come in from the sea are able to complete their life cycles in fresh water, in effect becoming landlocked lampreys in the succeeding generations, then there is no possibility of eradication as long as lampreys have access to the Great Lakes through either the New York Barge Canal or the St. Lawrence Seaway.

Management

In addition to introductions and stocking of fishes, other management practices have affected the nature of the New York fish fauna. Habitat improvement and control of undesirable species are two such techniques. Habitat improvement encompasses the building of stream deflectors and shelters designed to create pools or races that provide good gamefish habitat. Sometimes lakes and ponds that are overpopulated with stunted fish are reclaimed by removing all of the fish and restocking with species designed to produce a better balance. Such drastic measures have to be used with great care.

Habitat Changes

Many changes were produced in the waterways as the state became more populated and the forests were cleared for lumber or for agricultural use. Fortunately, for the fish populations, much of the upland area of the state proved to be unsuited for anything but subsistence agriculture and has now been returned to forest. The farsighted establishment of

the Adirondack Park has preserved many of the streams of that area. Still, modern civilization has taken its toll. The Atlantic salmon was extirpated in Lake Ontario, probably as the result of a combination of overfishing and construction of dams that denied the fish access to their spawning sites. Most recently, widespread chemical pollution has had drastic deleterious effects on fishes.

Canals *

Perhaps no part of the history of New York State is more colorful than the canal era. Late in the 18th century it became apparent that the future of New York State, and the development of the Midwest in general, would depend on the availability of efficient means of transporting people and goods inland. It was equally apparent that water transport was the most promising means of moving large quantities of bulky materials economically. Furthermore, the Mohawk Corridor was the logical place for a major canal route because the old glacial outlets had left a reasonably level pass between the Adirondack and Catskill uplands. To the south, the routes were blocked by a continuous range of the Appalachians and, to the north, the St. Lawrence was icebound for a large part of the year. After some failures in the late 1700s, serious plans for a canal route across New York were developed and, with much political difficulty, construction was begun near Rome in 1817. Before the railroads made canals obsolete, all of the major drainages in New York State were linked by water routes. Most of those canals were open for only a few years but the Erie Canal (now the New York State Barge Canal), the Champlain-Hudson Canal, and the Oswego and Seneca Canals are still functioning. Through the years, improvements to the canals have resulted in fewer and larger locks and this has made it easier for fish to pass through from one watershed to another (Figure 4).

Canals are wonderful examples of the engineer's art. They are gravity-fed and, except for opening and closing the gates and valves, require little power. They do, however, use enormous quantities of water and this meant that reservoirs and feeder canals had to be constructed to supply the canals with sufficient water at their higher points. The Glens Falls feeder canal which diverts Hudson River water to the Champlain-Hudson Canal is itself a fair-sized channel and a direct route between the upland parts of the canal and the river. Its steep gradient would seem to be a better environment for upland fishes than the slow-moving main canal.

Champlain-Hudson Canal. The first part of the Erie Canal system to be completed was the Champlain-Hudson Canal. It connects the Hudson

*Source: Whitford (1914)

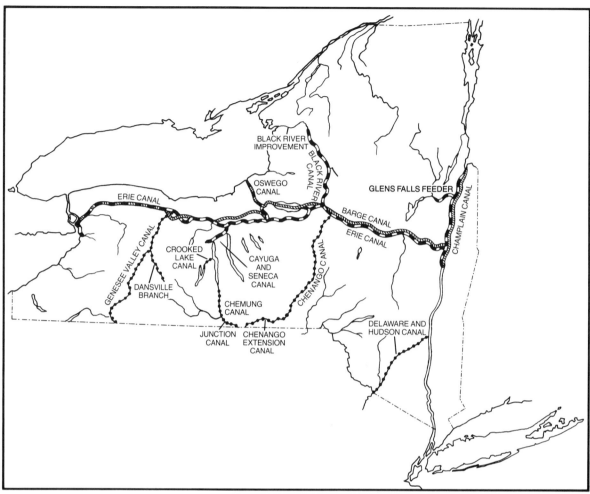

Figure 4. Canals of New York

River with the southern end of Lake Champlain and together with the Richelieu Locks provides a complete water link between the Atlantic Ocean at New York City and the St. Lawrence River. When it was first opened in 1819 it made use of short stretches of canals around falls between Fort Edward and Sandy Hill; then the canal was continuous to Whitehall. Including the Glens Falls feeder it was 76 miles long and the main canal had 26 locks with a rise of 134 feet and a fall of 54 feet northbound. The canal is still active, with 11 locks, and carries a good deal of recreational as well as commercial traffic.

Erie Canal. Construction of the Erie Canal began in 1817, and by 1825 it formed a link between the Hudson River and Lake Erie. When it opened it had 85 locks rising westbound 630 feet and falling 62. The original canal was 40 feet wide at the surface, 28 feet wide at the bottom, with a minimum depth of four feet. Its route included two long level stretches where no locks were required, one 69.5 miles long between Frankfort and Syracuse, and the other 62 miles long west of Rochester. The canal crossed major streams on aqueducts, the largest of which were across the Genesee River at Rochester

(803 feet) and across the Mohawk at Little Falls (744 feet) and Cohoes (1188 feet). In 1818, a short spur, the Chittenango Canal, was built to carry trass for manufacturing hydraulic cement for the canal locks.

In 1836, the Erie Canal was widened to a minimum of 70 feet at the surface, 52.5 feet at the bottom and 7 feet in depth. Between 1837 and 1862 it was widened again and the number of locks was reduced to 74. It was also shortened by 13.5 miles and routed through, rather than south of, Oneida Lake.

Today, the New York Barge Canal has 36 locks with usable dimensions of 300 feet length, 43.5 feet width and 13 feet minimum depth over the sills. In canalized sections of rivers it is 200 feet wide, in earth cuts 104 feet wide, and rock cuts 120 feet wide. West of Three Rivers its minimum width is 75 feet and its minimum depth is 12 feet. A spur connects Onondaga Lake with the main canal, thus providing access to the City of Syracuse.

Oswego Canal. The Oswego Canal connects the Barge Canal with Lake Ontario at Oswego, following the valley of the Oswego River from Three Rivers. The original canal was built between 1826 and

1828. In 1840, it had 14 locks with a descent to the Lake of 123 feet in 38 miles. Today, it has a fall of 118.6 feet through eight locks, and is the shortest route for vessels from Albany to the upper Great Lakes through Lake Ontario and the Welland Canal in Canada.

Cayuga-Seneca Canal. The Cayuga-Seneca Canal joins the two largest Finger Lakes with the Barge Canal. In 1840, it descended 73 feet and the total length of the system was 23 miles including a 2-mile branch to East Cayuga. Today, it has four locks with a total lift of 63.5 feet. Construction of the Cayuga-Seneca Canal was authorized in 1826 and it was opened in 1829.

Crooked Lake Canal. Crooked Lake is an old name for Keuka Lake which is the only branched Finger Lake. The canal ran from Penn Yan to Seneca Lake at Dresden. In this 7.75-mile section it had 27 locks and fell 269 feet. It was an expensive canal and an economic disaster. It was closed in 1878.

Chemung Canal. The Chemung Canal was built between 1830 and 1833 and connected the south end of Seneca Lake with the Chemung River at Elmira and continued west to Painted Post. It was 23 miles long with a total ascent and descent of 516 feet. A navigable feeder canal reached Knoxville. A 10- or 12-mile junction canal ran between Elmira and the state line but it was destroyed by a flood after 12 years of operation and never rebuilt. The Chemung Canal was abandoned in 1877.

Chenango Canal. The Chenango Canal was a more ambitious connection between the Mohawk River at Utica and the Susquehanna River at Binghamton. It was built between 1833 and 1838 and had a total length of 97 miles. There were 116 locks with a total rise of 706 feet and a fall of 303 feet. It was supplied by 19 aqueducts, with 12 dams and 17 miles of feeder canal. Seven reservoirs were built near the summit. It was abandoned in 1878.

Black River Canal. The Black River Canal between Rome and Carthage provided a second link with Lake Ontario through the rich farmland of the Black River valley. The canal ran between Rome and Lyons Falls and the water route was continued as improvements to the river itself. In its 39 miles it had 109 locks, and its total rise and fall was 1078 feet. Including the river section its total length was 85 miles. The Black River Canal opened in 1840, was completed in 1855, and closed in 1926. Just north of the Rome fish hatchery and aqueduct a series of high locks provides a good view of canal construction of that period.

Genesee Canal. The Genesee Canal was a connecting link between the Barge Canal at Rochester and the Allegheny River at Olean. It was started in 1837 and reached Mount Morris before the work was interrupted from 1842 to 1847. It reached Olean in 1856 and Portville in 1862. By this time, railroads were in direct competition with the canals and in 1878 the Genesee Canal, too, was closed. In its total length of 119 miles it had 114 locks with a total rise and fall of 1063 feet. An 11-mile branch with 83 feet of lockage connected Mount Morris with Dansville.

Delaware and Hudson Canal. The Delaware and Hudson Canal was not part of the New York State canal system but was built by private funds. It was, in fact, the first private project to cost more than a million dollars and it was built to carry coal from the mountains of eastern Pennsylvania to New York by way of the Hudson River. The canal was constructed in only 3 years. It began in Honesdale, Pennsylvania, where the coal was delivered by gravity railroads, there being no locomotives at that time. The canal ran along the Lackawaxen River to the Delaware at Lackawaxen, then along the Delaware River to Port Jervis, up the Neversink and Basher Kill to Wurtsboro, through the valleys of the Homowack Kill and Sandburg Creek to the Rondout Valley. It crossed Rondout Creek at High Falls and continued to Creek Lock where it joined the Rondout. Its total length was 107 miles and it had 107 locks, 22 aqueducts, 110 waste weirs, 16 feeder dams, 22 reservoirs, and 136 bridges. The original canal was 32 feet wide at the top, 20 feet wide at the bottom, and 4 feet deep. Later, it was deepened to 6 feet and widened to 32 feet at the bottom. The original locks were 76 feet long and 9 feet wide and in 1850 they were enlarged to 100 feet long by 15 feet wide. Also in 1850, suspension bridges were built across the Lackawaxen, Delaware, and Neversink Rivers and Rondout Creek. The one crossing the Delaware is still preserved as a historical landmark.

From 1870 to 1898, the Delaware-Hudson Canal was open 24 hours a day between High Falls and Eddyville. The canal was sold in 1898 but remained open between Eddyville and Rosendale to transport cement. It was finally closed after the 1913 boating season.

One other canal has figured prominently in the distribution of New York fishes. This is the Welland Canal in Canada which bypasses Niagara Falls and thus connects the upper and lower Great Lakes. It was first opened in 1829 and at that time was 27.5 miles long with 40 locks and a total lift of 326 feet. In 1873, the locks were enlarged to 270 feet long, 45 feet wide and 14 feet deep and their number was reduced to 25. In 1913, the Welland Canal was brought to its present condition with eight locks (only seven are lift locks) each 80 feet wide with a depth of 30 feet and a lift of 46 feet.

The St. Lawrence Seaway also has a potential effect on the ecology, if not the distribution, of our fishes. This is essentially a navigation system around rapids of the St. Lawrence River. It has seven locks each 766 feet long, 80 feet wide and 30 feet deep. Its combined lift from sea level to Lake Ontario is 246 feet. Together with the locks in the St. Marys River at Sault Ste. Marie, it gives oceangoing vessels access to Lake Superior. Already a European flatfish, *Platichthys,* has been found in Lake Erie, presumably having arrived in ballast water of a trans-Atlantic vessel.

Canals and Fish Distribution

Because canals were built across the lowest land between drainage divides and because these low passes are often the routes of glacial outlets or sites where stream capture has occurred, it is not always possible to be certain that a species has achieved its present distribution by traveling through a canal. If, however, most of the records for a species in a particular watershed are near a canal terminus, the chances are that the canal is responsible for its occurrence there. The occurrence of the species in the canal itself is additional evidence of canal transport.

Apparently, fishes frequently do not travel through canals in both directions with equal ease. The Suez Canal, for example, although a sea level canal with no locks, has resulted in 36 species from the Red Sea establishing populations in the Mediterranean but only 6 Mediterranean species have successfully colonized the Red Sea. This is currently explained on the basis that the Mediterranean fauna is less diverse and had fewer species with which the immigrants had to compete.

At present, I regard the following as instances of canal introductions:

Champlain-Hudson Canal. Recent records of the blueback herring in Lake Champlain and the silver lamprey in the Hudson River seem to be canal immigrants.

Erie Canal. Gibbs (1963) suggested that *Notropis spilopterus,* the spotfin shiner, may have moved east through the canal. Recent records of the central mudminnow and its abundance in stretches of the old Erie Canal seem to indicate canal travel. Dwight Webster (pers. comm.) has suggested that the fallfish may not have been in the Adirondacks before canals and associated waterways were constructed. Possibly the record of the satinfin shiner from a Lake Ontario tributary may be a canal introduction, although Gibbs (1963) considered it a relict population. The white bass, and possibly the gizzard shad, in the Mohawk-Hudson system also seem to be canal immigrants.

S. Smith (1970) reviewed the evidence and concluded that the alewife became established in Lake Ontario by moving through the Erie Canal and not, as others have concluded, as the result of having been planted accidentally with American shad between 1870 and 1872. According to Smith it was only possible for the alewife to become abundant after the decline of the populations of large predators, especially the Atlantic salmon and the lake trout in the 1860s. Aron and Smith (1971) postulated that the sea lamprey entered the Lake Ontario drainage through the canal, first becoming established in the Finger Lakes Cayuga and Seneca, and then moving into Lake Ontario in the 1880s. It appears, however, that most of the river herrings that move into the Mohawk each year are blueback herrings and not alewives, and there are no lamprey records from either the Canal or the Mohawk River. Therefore, I favor the hypothesis that alewives and sea lampreys are native to Lake Ontario but were present in small numbers until the decline of the predators.

Both the Erie Canal and the Welland Canal provided connections between Lake Ontario and Lake Erie but the Welland Canal is much shorter and is the most likely route for the lamprey, the alewife, and more recently the white perch, to have reached the upper Great Lakes.

Chemung Canal. Greeley (1928) recorded the swallowtail shiner from Catharine Creek and ascribed its presence there to the Chemung Canal. Snelson (1968) considered the comely shiner to have reached Seneca Lake by the same means.

Chenango Canal. Our records of the hornyhead chub and the brassy minnow in the Susquehanna drainage seem to indicate that the Chenango Canal was a dispersal route. Our series of the chub was actually collected in a section of the canal that still has water in it. The presence of the emerald shiner in Lebanon and Erieville Reservoirs could be the result of travel through canal connections, but this is a popular bait species and may have been released by fishermen.

Delaware-Hudson Canal. The comely shiner, *Notropis amoenus,* probably moved into the Shawangunk Kill through the canal (Snelson, 1971). The presence of the sand shiner, *N. stramineus,* and the satinfin, *N. analostanus,* are less certainly the result of canal transit.

Black River Canal. Greeley and Bishop (1932) and Gibbs (1963) suggest that the presence of the satinfin shiner in the Black River may have been the result of passage through the canal although there are few records of the satinfin in the Mohawk basin other than Schoharie Creek.

Scarce Fishes

Throughout the world, environmentalists are justifiably concerned about animal species that are in danger of becoming extinct, and steps have been taken to identify and protect those forms that are being threatened, particularly those whose plight is the result of human activities such as over-hunting or destruction of critical habitat. Criteria have been set up to identify species as threatened, rare or endangered and, once identified, the species in these categories can be monitored to keep track of the status of their populations and, where necessary, additional steps can be taken to protect and encourage them. These steps can range from merely prohibiting their being hunted or fished for, to the establishment of special preserves, to maintaining and breeding them in captivity.

While the State of New York has only one species (the shortnose sturgeon) that is on the Federal List of Endangered Species, there are a number of species in the state that occur in only a few localities or only in low numbers. Some of these have thriving populations elsewhere in their ranges and, therefore, are not threatened or endangered in the conventional sense but they are of special interest in our area. Some of the species on this list are potentially important sport or forage fish but most of them are small, inconspicuous, and of interest only as members of our natural environment.

Northern brook lamprey, *Ichthyomyzon fossor*. This small, nonparasitic lamprey is known only from a single locality in western New York although there are reports that it is present in Vermont tributaries of Lake Champlain.

Lake sturgeon, *Acipenser fulvescens*. Once an important commercial species, this freshwater sturgeon is now very scarce. Fishing for it is prohibited but the fact that it requires nearly two decades to reach maturity means that the populations will recover only slowly if at all. Its size alone makes it a conspicuous species and one that should be saved if it is at all possible to do so.

Mooneye, *Hiodon tergisus*. The mooneye can provide some sport fishing but it is now quite scarce in the eastern part of its range. It is of academic interest as the only local representative of a major lineage of ancient fishes.

Bigeye chub, *Hybopsis amblops*. This is a small species confined to the western part of the state. Its dependence upon clear streams makes it an excellent indicator of water quality. It appears to have become less common in our area during the last few years but because it has not been studied, it is not possible to tell whether this is the result of the lack of sampling in the right habitats, a low point in a natural cycle of abundance, or a true long-term trend.

Silver chub, *Hybopsis storeriana*. This species seems to be very scarce in Lake Erie where it was once plentiful. In our area it is confined to the lake and its decline there is probably due to wide-ranging environmental degradation.

Gravel chub, *Hybopsis x-punctata* and streamline chub, *Hybopsis dissimilis*. These species are confined to the Allegheny River in our area. They are difficult to sample and their status is not known at present. They are of interest because of their specialized habitat and limited distribution.

Pugnose shiner, *Notropis anogenus*. This tiny species is one of the rarest minnows in North America and New York is the eastern limit of its range. It has a highly specialized mouth and it closely resembles the blackchin shiner. It requires clear weedy areas in larger streams, hence is a good indicator of habitat quality.

Blackchin shiner, *Notropis heterodon*. This is another small minnow with a specific habitat requirement. It frequently occurs with the pugnose shiner. The Survey found it at a number of locations but we have collected it only in the St. Lawrence River.

Blacknose shiner, *Notropis heterolepis* . The blacknose shiner is also a species of weedy areas but it seems to be more tolerant than the two preceding species. We have collected it at a few locations but it seems less common than it was in the past.

Swallowtail shiner, *Notropis procne*. This species is limited to the southern part of the state where it occurs in moderate-sized to small streams. Our records indicate that it is becoming less common.

Redfin shiner, *Notropis umbratilis*. The redfin shiner occurs only in the Lake Erie drainage and it is still present in Tonawanda Creek. It is locally common but seems to occur at only a few sites.

Finescale dace, *Phoxinus neogaeus*. This is a northern species reaching its southern limit in the Adirondacks. It hybridizes with the redbelly dace and pure finescales are collected infrequently, although they may be present in undisturbed habitats in the more remote area of the northern part of the state.

Bitterling, *Rhodeus sericeus*. This introduced species has maintained a small population in the Bronx River for many years and this fact alone makes it worthy of further study.

Rudd, *Scardinius erythrophthalmus*. This is another introduced species that has held its own without either becoming a nuisance or going extinct. Its interactions with local native species is certainly worthy of further study.

Lake chubsucker, *Erimyzon sucetta*. This small species was recorded by the Survey from a few localities in the western Lake Ontario drainage. It has not been seen in many years but possibly still exists in the swampy wetlands west of Rochester.

Black redhorse, *Moxostoma duquesnei*. Black redhorses are apparently becoming scarce throughout much of their range.

Black bullhead, *Ictalurus melas*. The eastern tributaries of Lake Ontario are the eastern limit of the natural range of the black bullhead. We have not found any individuals from that area that are definitely black bullheads although the anal ray count of the brown bullheads in that area is almost as low as those of the black bullhead. It is possible that the black bullhead is being genetically swamped in this region where it is at the limit of its natural range. Black bullheads from the eastern part of the state, including the formerly recognized record fish from Lake Waccabuc, are probably the result of introductions.

Pirate perch, *Aphredoderus sayanus gibbosus.* The western subspecies of the pirate perch was collected at only about six localities along the south shore of Lake Ontario. We collected it at only one. The New York localities are a long way from the nearest other populations and appear to be relict populations that have been maintaining themselves since postglacial times.

Mud sunfish, *Acantharchus pomotis.* The Hackensack River is or was the northern limit of the species. We have not found it there but much of that drainage is protected by the Hackensack Water Company and it could still be maintaining a small population.

Northern longear sunfish, *Lepomis megalotis.* This species is known from only a few localities in the western part of the state and, as it frequently hybridizes with other species, it may be disappearing from our state.

Green sunfish, *Lepomis cyanellus.* The green sunfish has been successfully introduced into the Susquehanna, Hudson, Housatonic, and probably other drainages. It was said to be native to the western part of the state but it is probably not possible to identify the native populations, if they still exist.

Eastern sand darter, *Ammocrypta pellucida.* This species is scarce throughout its range but there are a few populations still surviving in New York. It has a rather specific habitat requirement.

Gilt darter, *Percina evides.* The Survey collected the gilt darter at a few localities in the Allegheny River but recent efforts to collect it there have been unsuccessful.

Bluebreast darter, *Etheostoma camurum.* The bluebreast has been taken twice in the Allegheny River in the past few years. Its distribution in the adjacent parts of Pennsylvania is scattered and it may be moving into New York from Allegheny tributaries upstream in Pennsylvania.

Spoonhead sculpin, *Cottus ricei,* and deepwater sculpin, *Myoxocephalus thompsoni.* These deepwater species have not been taken in Lake Ontario in several years and are presumed to be extinct there. The Great Lakes populations of the spoonhead are rare but the deepwater sculpin is thriving in the upper lakes.

HOW TO USE THIS BOOK **4**

Sources

The information in this book has been assembled from many sources. The distribution maps are based primarily on our own collections and specimens housed in the American Museum of Natural History. These were collected mostly between 1975 and 1982, with a few collections going back to the start of my career in the late 1940s. Some specimens collected by E.A. Mearns during the last century are still in the museum's holdings. Our records have been supplemented by examination of specimens in other collections, notably those of the New York State Museum, Cornell University, the Hadley Collection at the University of Buffalo (now in the

Buffalo Museum of Science), and the Eaton Collection at St. Bonaventure University which has recently been transferred to the American Museum. The records of the original Biological Survey have been used extensively to fill in records of lake fishes and fishes that are scarce in the state. I have also made free use of reports and files of the Department of Environmental Conservation and reports produced by consulting firms, particularly Texas Instruments and Lawler, Matusky & Skelly Engineers (LMS). In general, records without specimens are used to fill in areas where the species is expected to occur but where we have not obtained it. Unusual or unexpected occurrences are not plotted without

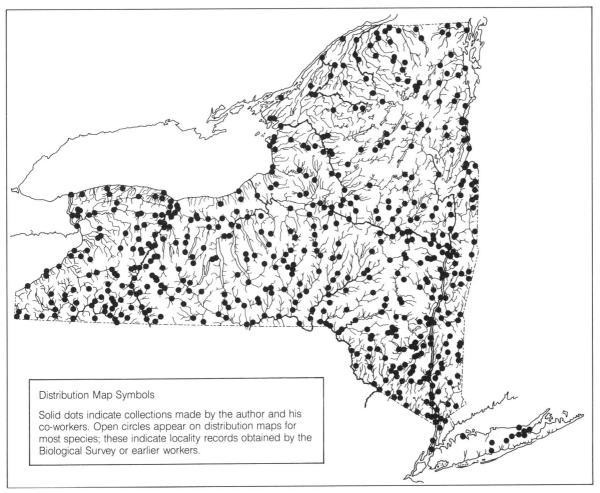

Distribution Map Symbols

Solid dots indicate collections made by the author and his co-workers. Open circles appear on distribution maps for most species; these indicate locality records obtained by the Biological Survey or earlier workers.

Figure 5. Collections

sound evidence that the data and the identification are correct (Figure 5).

All descriptions have been compared against specimens, although they have been augmented from the literature. In doing this I have made extensive use of the counts given by Trautman (1981), Scott and Crossman (1973) and, for marine fishes, Bigelow and Schroeder (1953b). I have also tried to use the latest revisions available for particular species. Information on general distribution comes from the Atlas by Lee et al. (1980) again supplemented by whatever other information I could find. I have made a conscious effort to examine original sources, but I have not examined all of the literature listed in the references sections of the accounts, especially some of the unpublished theses. The listing of the references is intended to give the user a head start on his search for more information but it is not intended to be a full bibliography. Record sizes for game fishes are taken from lists published by the International Game Fish Association, 1983 edition.

The Biological Survey

Beginning in 1926, and continuing through the summer of 1939, the New York State Conservation Department conducted thorough surveys of the aquatic environments of the state. Each summer field crews studied one or more watersheds and published the results of their investigations as a supplement to the annual report of the Department. The fish studies were under the supervision of Dr. John R. Greeley, and many of the people who worked on the survey went on to distinguished careers in ichthyology or fishery biology. The importance of these surveys, made at a time when the study of fishes was undergoing rapid development, can hardly be overstated.

Throughout this book there are numerous references to the survey reports. For convenience and brevity such references are given as "the Survey", sometimes with the name of the watershed added. Complete citations are found in the literature cited under Greeley, Greeley and Greene (1931), and Greeley and Bishop (1932, 1933). Other papers that appeared in the Survey reports are cited by author in the usual manner.

General References

There are a number of classical references that are so much a part of the working tools of ichthyology that they are seldom specifically cited. A few of the most important of these classic works are listed here.

Jordan and Evermann, 1896-1900 (North America). Jordan, Evermann, and Clark, 1930 (nomenclature). Bean, 1903 (New York). Trautman, 1981 (Ohio). Scott and Crossman, 1973 (Canada). Hildebrand and Schroeder, 1928. Hildebrand, 1963 (marine fishes in Fishes of the Western North Atlan-

tic). MacKay, 1963 (Ontario). Cooper, 1983 (Pennsylvania). Moore, 1957 (United States). Eddy, 1957 (northern fishes). Everhart, 1950 (Maine). Pfleiger, 1975 (Missouri). Bailey, 1938 (Merrimack watershed). Moyle, 1976 (California). McCabe, 1943 (western Massachussetts). Decker et al., n.d. (New York). Werner, 1980 (New York). Nelson, 1976 (second edition, 1983, world fishes). Thomson, Weed and Taruski, 1971 (Connecticut). Whitworth, Berrien and Keller, 1968 (Connecticut). Scarola, 1973 (New Hampshire). Leim and Scott, 1966 (Atlantic coast of Canada).

Hough (1958) and MacClintock and Apfel (1944) are especially useful references on the glacial history of the Northeast.

Local Fauna Studies

In addition to the monumental Biological Surveys that were conducted by the New York State Conservation Department between 1926 and 1939, there have been numerous smaller studies of particular streams and individual lakes conducted both before and after the watershed surveys. The following lists make no claim to completeness but they will prove useful guides to information on particular local waterways:

Lake Erie drainage: Hubbs and Lagler, 1964 (Great Lakes in general). Hankinson, 1923, 1924. Leach and Nepszy, 1976. Kenyon, 1979. Van Meter and Trautman, 1970.

Lake Ontario drainage: Evermann and Kendall, 1901, 1902a. Kenyon, 1979. Crossman and Van Meter, 1979.

Allegheny drainage: Dence, 1928. Kendall and Dence, 1922. Liegy, Donahue, and Eaton, 1955. Eaton, Nemacek and Kozubowski, 1982. Becker, 1982.

Oswego River drainage: Eaton and Moffett, 1971 (Canandaigua Lake). Eaton and Kardos, 1972. Finger, 1982. Clady, 1976 (Oneida Lake). Browne, 1981 (salmonid runs).

St. Lawrence River drainage: Webster and Flick, 1960 (Brandon Park). Kendall and Dence, 1929 (Cranberry Lake). Pasko, 1957 (Carry Falls Reservoir). Schiavone, 1983 (Black Lake).

Lake Champlain drainage: Evermann and Kendall, 1902b. Cobb, 1904.

Susquehanna River drainage: Denoncourt and Cooper, 1975 (Pennsylvania). Denoncourt, Hocutt and Stauffer, 1975a (Pennsylvania). Denoncourt, Robins and Hesser, 1975. Macwatters, 1983 (Otsego Lake).

Hudson River drainage: Nichols, 1913 (New York City area). Adams, Hankinson and Kendall, 1919 (Palisades Park). Perlmutter, Schmidt and Leff, 1967 (Lower Hudson). Boyle, 1968. Texas Instruments, 1975. Dovel, 1981a. Jablonski, 1974 (geology). Schmidt and Samaritan, 1984 (Bronx River).

Staten Island: Mathewson, 1959. Howells, 1981 (Arthur Kill).

Long Island: Ayres, 1843. Bean, 1891. Bean, 1899. Reismann and Nicol, 1973 (Gardiner's Island).

Ecological References

Further information on the general ecology of fishes will be found in the following references:

Kuehne, 1962 (classification of streams). Minckley, 1963 (stream ecology). Lotrich, 1973 (communities and stream order). Grossman, Moyle, and Whitaker, 1982 (community ecology). Finger, 1982. Keast, 1966 (trophic interrelationships). Keast and Webb, 1966. Small, 1975 (energy dynamics). Mendelson, 1975, Moyle, 1973. Werner and Hall, 1974, 1976, 1977, 1979. Webster, 1942 (life histories). Brett, 1944, 1956 (temperature).

Arrangement

The arrangement of families generally follows that used in the American Fisheries Society Special Publication No. 12, A List of Common and Scientific Names of Fishes from the United States and Canada, fourth edition, 1980, with one major exception. Rosen (1973a) summarized the existing evidence and concluded that the Ostariophysi are the sister group of all other euteleostean fishes. Therefore, it is necessary to place the catfishes, suckers and minnows before the salmonids and pikes, rather than after them. Even more recently it has been suggested that the pikes are not as closely related to the salmonids as has been thought and, if this is true, further rearrangement will be necessary.

All of the accounts are arranged according to a somewhat standardized format. The family accounts include general statements listing common characteristics, relationships, world distribution, number of species, and general importance.

The generic accounts also discuss the characters that unite the included species and information as to the included species, their distribution and interrelationships.

The species accounts are the most detailed. Each starts with an identification section which is intended to give the outstanding features, a suggestion as to what the species might be confused with and characteristics that will confirm the distinctions. This is followed by a description section that lists additional characteristics that will prove useful when dealing with incomplete or abnormal specimens. Proportional measurements and counts have been placed in separate tables for convenience in comparing similar species. After the description section, there is a general description of the fish's habitat followed by a listing of its geographic distribution as a

whole and in New York. The life history section contains a summary of life history data with particular emphasis on breeding habits. A listing of food and feeding habits is a brief summary of the information, but the reader should be alerted to the fact that most fishes are extremely flexible in their feeding habitats and it has not been possible to include all of the available information. A notes section includes information of special interest not falling into one of the other categories. There is a reference list intended to be only a guide and not a complete literature listing.

Finally, there is a section on names. This includes a statement about derivation of the name (mostly from Jordan and Evermann, 1896-1900, and Jaeger, 1950, with other sources used as necessary) and a list of scientific names that have been applied to the species in the literature of New York State. It must be emphasized that these lists are for New York only and, therefore, they are not full synonymies of all of the names that have ever been applied to the species. The use of this list may not be apparent to those who are unfamiliar with the scientific literature, but anyone who is gathering data on, say, the bluegill sunfish will sooner or later need to know that *Helioperca incisor* is the species that we now call *Lepomis macrochirus*.

Because the Hudson River estuary extends inland for more than 150 miles, the inland fish fauna of New York includes a substantial number of species normally limited to marine and estuarine environments. To mix these with the freshwater species makes an ungainly arrangement, and makes the keys too cumbersome for convenient use. I have, therefore, placed the marine species in a separate section. Some of these estuarine species are year-round residents; others are seasonal visitors or have only been recorded from the river a few times and must be considered strays. Anadromous species (those that come into fresh water to spawn) and the catadromous American eel, which spends most of its life in estuarine or fresh water and returns to the sea to spawn, are included with the freshwater species.

Keys to families that include both freshwater and marine species are presented in the freshwater section and not duplicated in the marine section. Anyone attempting to identify a fish from the Hudson Estuary should be sure to check both the freshwater and saltwater sections.

Counts and Measurements

Meristic (countable) and morphometric (measurable) features are often useful in identification and are especially helpful when dealing with poorly preserved or incomplete specimens, or with immature specimens that have not developed the primary characteristics of their species. For convenience in making comparisons these features are listed in table form. Whenever possible, measurements were made on five specimens from New York State. If five specimens from New York were not available, specimens from other regions were used. Counts were also made on five specimens, although these were not necessarily the same five specimens that were used for the measurements. In some cases, these observations were supplemented from the literature, particularly for those species that have been studied intensively in recent publications.

Obviously, data based on such a small sample must be used with caution. The main use of these data will be for comparisons between species. It will be apparent, for example, that the black redhorse is much more slender than other species of redhorses when one compares the body depth measurements.

All measurements are straight-line measurements between the points shown on Figure 6a; measurements were made either with dial calipers or dividers and ruler. Proportions are computed by dividing each measurement by the standard length and multiplying by 100 to give percentage values. The tables (see contents page) list only the average values to one decimal place, for the number of specimens (N) listed.

Dorsal and anal fin ray counts are principal rays unless otherwise noted, ignoring the splint-like rays at the front of the fin and counting the last ray as branched to its base (Figure 7). In other words, if the last ray branches just above or just below the body surface (the latter indicated by the bases of the last two rays being close together) it is counted as a single ray. Paired fin counts include all elements. Gill raker counts are total counts.

Vertebral counts were taken from x-rays and include the terminal half-centrum, the conical element that supports the hypural bones. For minnows, suckers, and catfishes the Weberian apparatus is not counted, and the first vertebra is that one with a neural spine just behind the Weberian complex. Vertebral numbers are total counts.

Scale counts are lateral line counts if the species

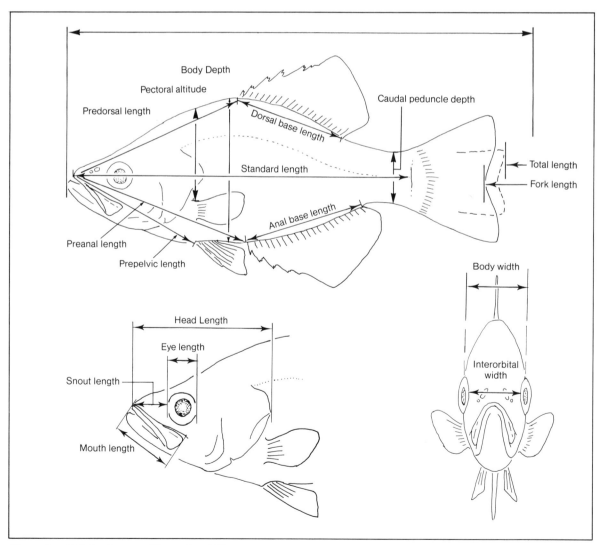

Figure 6a. Fish Anatomy and Proportional Measurements

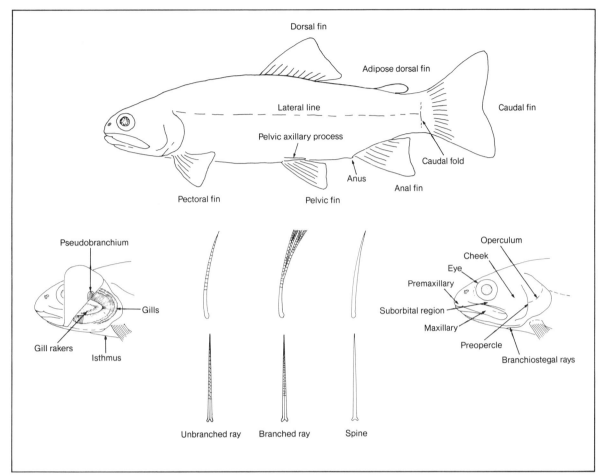

Figure 6b. Fish Anatomy and Proportional Measurements

has a lateral line, otherwise the number of diagonal rows crossing the midside between the shoulder girdle and the caudal fold. Scale rows above the lateral line are counted diagonally downward and backward from the dorsal origin to, but not including, the lateral line and the scale rows below the lateral line are counted from the anal origin upward and forward to, but not including, the lateral line.

Numbers are listed following the convention of listing extreme counts in parentheses and the "usual" counts as a range of two numbers connected by the words "or" or "to". The hyphen is reserved to indicate separated dorsal or pelvic fins or pharyngeal teeth. Spines are, as usual, indicated by Roman numerals.

Identifying Fishes

Fishes are identified using three approaches. These are not mutually exclusive nor are they redundant; they are stages in the process that leads to accurate results. First, there are illustrations with which the specimen can be compared. Second, there is a key. Third, the species accounts contain an identification and a description section. I believe that the illustrations should be used first because running the key demands considerable time and attention to detail,

and the procedure is much easier if one can recognize patently erroneous results sooner, rather than later. The key is simply a series of choices and the arrangement used here will, I hope, make it easier to keep track of where in the key one is and how one got there. The final step, comparing the specimen with the identification and description, is a check against near misses. It is an important step that should not be neglected.

Most fishes have external fertilization and, when several species spawn together, accidental cross fertilization sometimes produces hybrid individuals. In general, cross fertilization is more likely to occur between closely related species of the same genus although some intergeneric combinations are known. Hybrids are usually intermediate between the parents and are best detected by comparing them directly with specimens taken in the same place and at the same time and with the same state of preservation and degree of expansion of the pigment cells. Summaries of the literature of fish hybrids can be found in Hubbs (1955) and Schwartz (1972).

Identification of Larval Fishes

Modern fish management often requires serious consideration of the ecology of fishes throughout

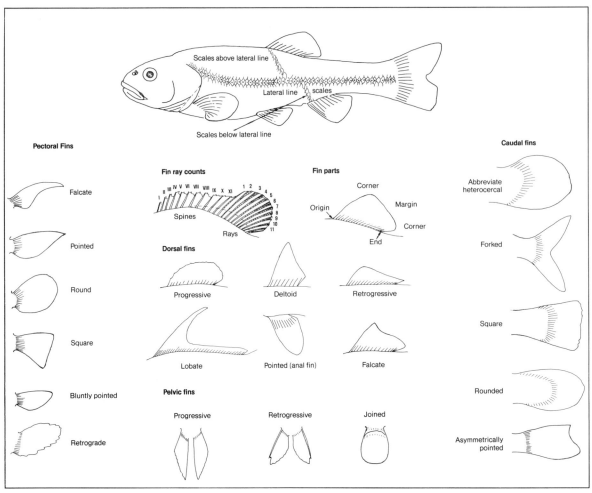

Figure 7. Counts and Descriptive Terms

their entire life history. This is particularly important when considering the potential effects of industrial plants that require large quantities of water for cooling and which may result in the discharge of heated effluent into natural waterways. In the past few years many environmental decisions have rested on considerations of the distribution and sensitivity of larval stages and biologists have devoted a tremendous effort to studies of larval fishes.

The identification of larval stages requires specialized knowledge because larval fishes have not yet developed their full complement of such characteristics as fin rays, scales, and color patterns that serve to distinguish adults.

The literature of larval fishes is quite scattered but in recent years a number of publications have appeared that gather together existing information. Some of the most useful and comprehensive are listed here to guide the reader to a starting point.

Auer, Nancy A., ed. 1982 Identification of larval fishes of the Great Lakes region with emphasis on the Lake Michigan drainage. Special publication 82-3 of the Great Lakes Fishery Commission, Ann Arbor, Michigan. 744 pp.

Fahay, Michael P. 1983 Guide to the early stages of marine fishes occurring in the western North Atlantic Ocean, Cape Hatteras to the southern Scotia Shelf. Journal of Northwest Atlantic Fishery Science 4, 423 pp.

Lippson, Alice J. and R. Lynn Moran, eds. 1974 Manual for identification of early developmental stages of fishes of the Potomac River estuary. Power Plant Siting Program, Maryland Department of Natural Resources. pp. 115-151.

U. S. Fish and Wildlife Service. 1978 Development of fishes of the mid-Atlantic Bight. An atlas of egg, larval, and juvenile stages. 6 volumes.

Wang, Johnson C. S. and Ronnie J. Kernehan. 1979 Fishes of the Delaware estuaries. A guide to the early life histories. EA Communications. Ecological Analysts, Inc. Towson, Maryland. xxxi + 410 pp.

FRESHWATER AND DIADROMOUS FISHES OF NEW YORK 5

This section includes 167 species representing 27 families currently assigned to 69 genera. Six species (three river shads, two sturgeons, and the striped bass) are anadromous, one (American eel) is catadromous, and seven (sea lamprey, alewife, rainbow smelt, threespine stickleback, ninespine stickleback, fourspine stickleback, and white perch) have both saltwater and landlocked populations. The remaining 153 species are strictly freshwater fishes.

Seven species (shorthead redhorse, pearl dace, redfin pickerel, pirate perch, banded killifish, green-side darter, and walleye) are represented by two subspecies or by a subspecies and intergrades with another subspecies. The two forms of the blacknose dace, usually considered to be subspecies, are here treated as full species.

Although ichthyologists prefer to have species arranged in phylogenetic order, it seems preferable here to arrange the species accounts alphabetically within families. Families are, of course, arranged in phylogenetic order as it is currently understood.

KEY TO FAMILIES

A. One pair of gill slits. Jaws present although mouth is sometimes sucker-like. Pectoral fins present.

B.

A'. Seven pairs of gill openings. No jaws, the mouth opening in the center of a sucker disk that has horny teeth in radiating rows or patches in adults, or mouth fringed with tentacles and shielded by a flexible hood (larvae). No paired fins. Body elongate and flexible, eel-like.

Petromyzontidae   **Lampreys, p. 31**

Sea lamprey, *Petromyzon marinus*

B. (A. A single pair of gill slits.) Tail rounded, square, or forked, the end of the body more or less symmetrical, the tail lobes nearly the same size. All fin rays clearly separated by membrane.

D.

B'. Tail strongly heterocercal, the end of the body bent upward into the base of its upper lobe. Fins like those of sharks with numerous horny rays that are not clearly separated by membrane.

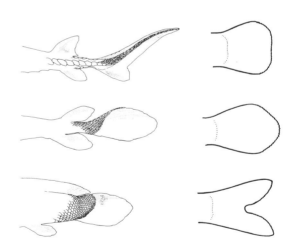

Caudal fins. Left, top to bottom: Strongly heterocercal tail of sturgeon. Moderately heterocercal tail of young gar. Abbreviate heterocercal tail of bowfin. Right, top to bottom: Square, rounded, and forked homocercal tails.

C. Body with five rows of large bony plates. Head covered with bony plates, snout conical, mouth protrusible into a short tube.

Acipenseridae   **Sturgeons, p. 43**

Lake sturgeon, *Acipenser fulvescens*

C'. Body without horny plates. Snout expanded into a spatula-shaped blade in individuals more than 100 mm long; conical in young. Mouth very large.
Polyodontidae   **Paddlefishes, p. 49**

Paddlefish, *Polyodon spathula*

D. (B. Tail not strongly heterocercal.) Body with thin scales or with no scales but never with thick, diamond-shaped scales. Jaws may, or may not, be elongated.

E.

D'. Body covered with thick, diamond-shaped scales. Jaws elongate and armed with sharp teeth. Juveniles in which the scales have not yet formed have a prominent filament above the upper lobe of the tail.
Lepisosteidae   **Gars, p. 52**

Longnose gar, *Lepisosteus osseus*

E. (D. Scales thin or absent.)   Lower jaw without a gular plate.

F.

E'. Outside of lower jaw with a short, broad, bony gular plate between the mandibles. Dorsal fin long, tail asymmetrically rounded with its upper base longer. Scales large and rectangular. A conspicuous dark spot at the upper base of the tail.
Amiidae   **Bowfins, p. 57**

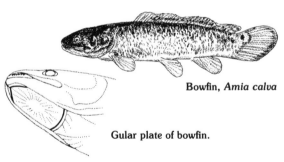

Bowfin, *Amia calva*

Gular plate of bowfin.

F. (E. Lower jaw without a gular plate.) Pelvic fins present, body of various shapes but not elongate and flexible.

G.

F'. Pelvic fins absent, body slender and flexible with the dorsal and anal fins joined to the tail by membrane so there appears to be a single fin around the end of the body.
Anguillidae   **Freshwater eels, p. 60**

American eel, *Anguilla rostrata*

G. (F. Pelvic fins present.) No strong teeth on tongue or centerline of the roof of the mouth. Nostrils in the normal position in front of the eye.

H.

G'. Tongue and roof of the mouth with large, strong teeth. Nostrils near tip of the snout. Edge of the belly behind the pelvic fins sharp and somewhat keel-like but never with modified scales forming a saw edge. Lateral line present.
Hiodontidae   **Mooneyes, p. 74**

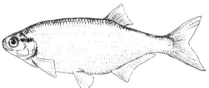

Mooneye, *Hiodon tergisus*

H. (G. No large teeth on midline of roof of mouth.) Lateral line present on the body although it does not always reach the base of the tail.

J.

H'. No lateral line present on the body although a segment of the head canal may encroach on the upper shoulder region.

I. Modified scales along the center of the belly forming a saw edge. No lateral line on body. Mouth various but never with the maxillary extending behind the preopercular margin. Snout not conical although it may bulge ahead of the upper lip.
Clupeidae   **Herrings, p. 63**

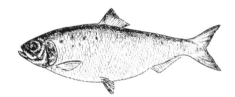

American shad, *Alosa sapidissima*

Ventral scutes of herrings.

I'. No modified scales forming a saw edge on the belly. Mouth large with the maxillary bone extending to, or beyond, the margin of the preopercle. Snout conical, extending forward in front of the mouth.
Engraulidae   **Anchovies, p. 397**

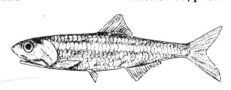

Bay anchovy, *Anchoa mitchilli*

Enlarged maxillary bone of anchovy.

J. (H. Lateral line present.) Dorsal fin with three or more true spines at the front. (These spines are sometimes quite flexible but they are neither segmented nor branched).

U.

J'. Dorsal fin without true spines although there is a single, stiff, serrated spine-like ray in catfish, carp and goldfish. Disregard any splint-like elements that are less than half as long as the first full-length ray.

Dorsal fin rays and spines. Left: First dorsal fin consisting of spines, second, with one spine followed by soft rays. Right: Fin of a minnow showing a splint-like element followed by an unbranched and branched soft rays. The last ray is branched at its base.

K. No adipose dorsal fin.

O.

K'. Adipose dorsal fin present although it is a keel-like ridge in some catfishes, which have conspicuous barbels and lack scales.

Adipose dorsal fins: Left: Keel-like adipose fin of madtom. Right: flag-like adipose of bullhead.

L. Body completely without scales. Long barbels present on snout, chin (two pairs), and end of maxillary.
Ictaluridae Bullhead catfishes, p. 76

Brown bullhead, *Ictalurus nebulosus*

L'. Scales present, no long barbels.

M. Edge of the upper jaw formed by two bones, the premaxillary anteriorly and the maxillary posteriorly. No fin spines, mouth terminal.

N.

M'. Edge of the upper jaw formed by a single bone, the premaxillary. Scales weakly ctenoid, dorsal fin with two spines at the front. Mouth inferior, teeth very fine, almost invisible. No pelvic axillary process.
Percopsidae Trout-perches, p. 259

Trout-perch, *Percopsis omiscomaycus*

Left: Margin of the upper jaw formed by the premaxillary alone. Right: Margin of the upper jaw formed by both the premaxillary and the maxillary bones.

N. (M. Edge of upper jaw supported by two bones.) Scales small, more than 80 in lateral line. Teeth small. Pelvic axillary process present.
Salmonidae Trouts, p. 207

Pelvic axillary process.

Brook trout, *Salvelinus fontinalis*

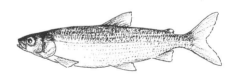

Cisco, *Coregonus artedii*

N'. Scales larger, fewer than 75 in lateral line. Teeth larger, of various sizes with large canine-like teeth on tongue. No pelvic axillary process.
Osmeridae Smelts, p. 239

Rainbow smelt, *Osmerus mordax*

O. (K. No adipose dorsal fin.) Mouth with teeth on the jaw bones (sometimes the teeth are small and hard to see but can be felt and heard by scraping a needle along the edge of the jaw.)

Q.

O'. Mouth without teeth on the jaw bones.

P. Mouth usually inferior with thick, papillose or plicate lips. Anal fin well back, the distance from its origin to the middle of the caudal base usually less than one-half the distance from the anal origin to the middle of the gill opening.

Catostomidae   **Suckers, p. 92**

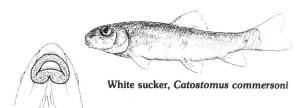

White sucker, *Catostomus commersoni*

Suctorial mouth of white sucker.

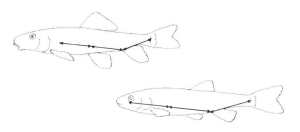

Position of the anal fin. Top: In suckers the distance from the anal fin origin to the caudal base is less than half the distance from the anal origin to the gill opening. Bottom: In minnows the anal fin is farther forward.

P'. Mouth variable in position but usually with thin lips that are not papillose or plicate. Anal fin farther forward, the distance from its origin to the middle of the caudal base greater than half the distance from the origin forward to the middle of the gill opening.

Cyprinidae   **Minnows, p. 113**

Creek chub, *Semotilus atromaculatus*

Q. (O. Mouth with teeth.) Premaxillary protractile, a groove between the upper lip and the tip of the snout.

             S.

Q'. Premaxillary nonprotractile, i.e., without a groove between the upper lip and the tip of the snout.

Left: Nonprotractile premaxillary of mudminnow.
Right: Protractile premaxillary of killifish.

R. Mouth large, the snout about equal to or longer than the postorbital head length, broad and flat with with pointed or blade-like teeth of various sizes. Body elongate but slab sided, somewhat rectangular in cross section. Tail slightly forked. Size large, the smallest species reaching at least 12 inches total length.

Esocidae   **Pikes, p. 246**

Redfin pickerel, *Esox americanus americanus*

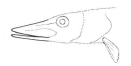

Broad elongate snout of a pike, *Esox*.

R'. Mouth small, snout shorter than the postorbital head length, snout not broad and flat. Tail rounded. Size small, seldom exceeding 5 inches total length.

Umbridae   **Mudminnows, p. 242**

Central mudminnow, *Umbra limi*

S. (Q. Mouth protractile.) Pelvic fins abdominal, originating well behind the base of the pectoral fin.

             T.

S'. Pelvic fins far forward, originating below or in front of the base of the pectoral fin. Dorsal divided into two or three sections. Chin with a single median barbel.

Gadidae   **Codfishes, p. 261**

Burbot, *Lota lota*

T. (S. Pelvic fins abdominal.) Origin of dorsal fin in front of the origin of the anal. Females with a fleshy oviducal sheath around the anterior rays of the anal fin.

Cyprinodontidae   **Killifishes, p. 264**

Banded killifish, *Fundulus diaphanus*

T'. Origin of dorsal fin behind the origin of the anal fin. Males with the anterior rays of the anal fin modified into an intromittent organ. Females without an oviducal sheath.

Poeciliidae   **Livebearers, p. 267**

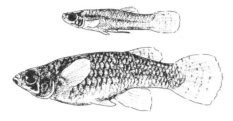

Mosquitofish, *Gambusia affinis* (male above)

U. (J. Dorsal fin with three or more true spines). Pelvic fins with one spine and five or fewer soft rays. Anus in the normal position, just anterior to the anal fin.

       V.

U'. Pelvic fins each with more than five soft rays. Anus well forward, in the throat region in adults, near or between the pelvic fins in juveniles less than one inch long.

Aphredoderidae   **Pirate perches, p. 256**

Pirate perch, *Aphredoderus sayanus*

Position of the anus in the pirate perch, *Aphredoderus*. Left: juvenile. Right: adult.

V. (U. Pelvic fins with five or fewer soft rays.) Body with scales.

       X.

V'. Body without scales although there may be large bony plates along the side.

W. Dorsal fin with 2 to 10 spines that are not connected by membrane. Caudal peduncle extremely slender. Pectoral fins small, transparent, paddle-shaped. Mouth tiny and oblique. Pelvic fins with a spine and one or two rays.

Gasterosteidae   **Sticklebacks, p. 272**

Brook stickleback, *Culaea inconstans*

W'. Dorsal spines connected by membrane. Caudal peduncle normal, not extremely slender. Pectoral fins large. Head depressed, mouth very large. Pelvic fins with one spine and three of four soft rays, body without scales.

Cottidae   **Sculpins, p. 353**

Slimy sculpin, *Cottus cognatus*

X. (V. Body more or less covered with scales.) Dorsal fin with the spiny and soft parts continuous or, if separate, close together so that the space between them is less than the length of the dorsal base.

       Y.

X'. Dorsal fins well separated, the space between them greater than the length of the base of the spiny part. First (spiny) dorsal small, with slender flexible spines. Body with a distinct silvery stripe along its side.

Atherinidae   **Silversides, p. 269**

Brook silverside, *Labidesthes sicculus*

First and second dorsal fins close together.

First and second dorsal fins well separated.

Y. (X. Dorsal fins continuous or close together.) One or two anal spines.

       Z.

Y'. Three or more anal spines.

       AA.

Z. (Y. Anal spines one or two.) Lateral line ending at the base of the tail, not continuing out to the tips of the middle rays. Head canals not greatly enlarged. Second dorsal with fewer than 15 rays.
Percidae   **Perches, p. 313**

Yellow perch, *Perca flavescens*

Walleye, *Stizostedion vitreum vitreum*

Logperch, *Percina caprodes*

Z'. Lateral line canal continuing on the caudal fin to the tips of its middle rays. Head scaled, with greatly enlarged sensory canals. Second dorsal fin with 25 or more soft rays.
Sciaenidae   **Drums, p. 351**

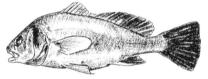

Freshwater drum, *Aplodinotus grunniens*

Enlarged head canals of freshwater drum, *Aplodinotus.*

AA. (Y'. Anal spines three or more.) Dorsal fins nearly or completely separated, longest soft ray near the front of the fin. Pseudobranchium well developed. Body color silvery, sometimes with narrow, dark, longitudinal lines or vertical bars or both.
Moronidae   **Temperate basses, p. 280**

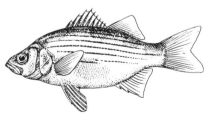

White bass, *Morone chrysops*

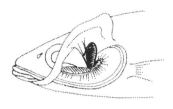

Well-developed pseudobranchium of white perch, *Morone.*

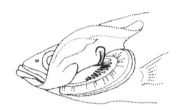

Vestigial pseudobranchium of a centrarchid.

AA'. Dorsal fins continuous but there may be a deep notch between them in some species. Longest soft rays towards the middle of the fin. Pseudobranchium small and covered with membrane, or absent. Color generally not silvery, but greenish, bronze, reddish brown, or mottled. Young with vertical bars.
Centrarchidae   **Sunfishes, p. 287**

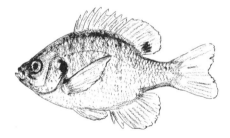

Bluegill, *Lepomis macrochirus*

Smallmouth bass, *Micropterus dolomieui*

LAMPREYS
PETROMYZONTIDAE

Lampreys are among the most primitive fishes in the world. They are modern remnants of a large group of jawless fishes that flourished in the early Paleozoic Age and were, in fact, the first vertebrates. Modern lampreys, with their parasitic food habits and complex life cycles, are extremely specialized but they also retain many of the primitive features of their ancestors. There are about 30 species and they live in the higher latitudes of both Northern and Southern Hemispheres.

Lampreys are easily recognized by their elongate shape and by their seven pairs of round gill openings. Their fins are supported by fine horny rods. There is a single nostril (naso-hypophyseal opening) in front of the eyes.

Many lampreys are parasites of other fishes. They attach to the host by means of their sucker-like mouths, then rasp through the victim's skin using strong teeth on their tongues. Sharp horny teeth on the inside of the oral disk help the lamprey to hold its position on the host's body. Some lampreys are secondarily nonparasitic. These species simply do not feed during the adult phase of their life, and they generally have fewer, less well-developed teeth on the oral disk. (Figure 8)

Lampreys all have similar life history patterns. In the spring, they move into streams to spawn, building nests by moving pebbles to form a shallow depression with a ridge of stones on the downstream edge. The eggs sink into the crevices in the gravel. The adults die after spawning. The young, called ammocoetes, drift downstream to muddy areas where they burrow into the bottom and spend much of their time with mouths exposed. During the larval stage, which may last several years, they feed by filtering particles out of the water using a fringe of fleshy tentacles surrounding the mouth. At this stage, the eyes are covered with skin and there is a fleshy hood around the mouth. As they transform into adults, the mouth becomes sucker-like, the teeth develop, and the eyes become functional. Parasitic species find hosts and continue to feed and grow; nonparasites cease to feed and their guts degenerate.

Six species of lampreys occur in New York. The parasitic sea lamprey is best known for the damage it has caused to the sport and commercial fishes in the Great Lakes. The American brook lamprey is superficially similar to the sea lamprey but it is a nonparasitic species with much reduced dentition.

Within the genus *Ichthyomyzon*, there are pairs of species that have similar morphology, but one is parasitic and the other not. Each of these pairs apparently shared a common ancestor. *Ichthyomyzon unicuspis* and *I. fossor* constitute one pair; *I. bdellium* and *I. greeleyi* make up another. Members of the same pair are difficult, if not impossible, to distinguish in the ammocoete stage.

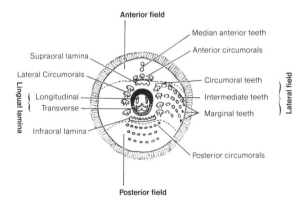

Figure 8. Mouth Parts of Lampreys

Identification of lampreys depends on coloration, dentition, and myomere (segment) counts. The teeth most useful for purposes of identification are named in the accompanying diagram. Myomeres are counted along the sides following the method of Hubbs and Trautman (1937): "The muscle bands (myomeres = myotomes), not the intermuscular septa (myocommata), were counted between the last gill opening and the cloaca. The first myomere counted is the one whose posterior septum passes distinctly and entirely behind the groove which surrounds the fringed margin of the last gill opening so as to leave a definite, though often narrow, band of muscle between the groove and the septum. The last myomere counted is the one whose lower posterior angle lies in part or wholly above the cloacal slit."

KEY TO THE SPECIES OF LAMPREYS IN NEW YORK

A. Mouth surrounded by a fleshy hood, its opening protected by a sieve of soft feather-like tentacles. No visible teeth. Eyes undeveloped or covered with thick skin so that they are not visible externally.
ammocoete larvae   **G.**

A'. Mouth surrounded by a round sucking disk, without a fleshy hood. Tentacles reduced to a fleshy fringe around the disk margin. Disk with horny teeth in patches or radiating rows. Eyes plainly visible.
adults   **B.**

Heads of adult (left) and larval lampreys (right).

B. Dorsal fin continuous, not divided into two separate fins by a deep notch, although there may be a shallow notch in the margin of the fin *.
Ichthyomyzon   **D.**

B'. Dorsal fin divided into two separate fins by a deep notch, although in breeding adults they may be close together or joined by a fleshy keel so that they appear as a single fin unless one looks closely.

C. Parasitic, mouth lined with teeth in curved, radiating rows. Size large, adults reaching lengths of more than two feet.
Petromyzon marinus   **Sea lamprey, p. 40**

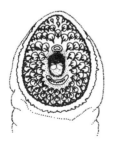

C'. Nonparasitic, mouth with a few teeth arranged in groups rather than rows. Maximum length about 10 inches.
Lampetra appendix
        American brook lamprey, p. 38

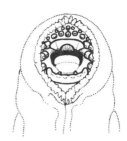

D. (B. Dorsal fin continuous.) Teeth nearest the mouth opening all with single points. Muscle segments between the last gill opening and the front of the anal slit 47 to 56, usually 49 to 52.
           F.

D'. Some (1 to 11, usually 6 to 8) of the teeth next to the mouth opening with double points. Muscle segments 55 to 62.

E. Parasitic. Disk large, its greatest diameter contained about 13.3 times in the total length. Teeth well developed.
Ichthyomyzon bdellium   **Ohio lamprey, p. 33**

E'. Nonparasitic. Disk smaller, 15.4 to 23.3 times in the total length. Teeth somewhat degenerate, especially those behind the mouth.
Ichthyomyzon greeleyi
        Mountain brook lamprey, p. 36

F. (D. Circumoral teeth with single points.) Teeth in lateral rows 5 to 8, usually 6 or 7. Disk large, wider than the gill region when expanded, about 12.5 in total length. Parasitic.
Ichthyomyzon unicuspis   **Silver lamprey, p. 37**

F'. Teeth in lateral rows 2 to 6, usually 3 to 5. Disk smaller, usually not as wide as the gill region, 20.4 to 27.7 in total length. Nonparasitic.
Ichthyomyzon fossor
       Northern brook lamprey, p. 34

G. (A. Ammocoete larvae.) Dorsal fin single *. **I.**

G'. Dorsal fin divided into two separate fins.

H. Muscle segments between gills and anus 67 to 74, average 70. Tail rounded. Rays of the tail fin dark to the edge of the fin. Lower parts of the muscle segments behind the anus grayish. Area above the gill openings nearly completely pigmented. Region beneath the eye and the lower half of the lip at least partly pigmented.
Petromyzon marinus   **Sea lamprey**

H'. Muscle segments between gills and anus 63 to 70, average 67. Tail bluntly pointed. Pigment on caudal fin limited to the bases of the rays; margin of the fin clear. Lower parts of the muscle segments behind the anus clear. Area above the gill openings pigmented only about halfway from the dorsal midline to the gill openings. Upper lip and the region below the eye devoid of pigment.
Lampetra appendix   **American brook lamprey**

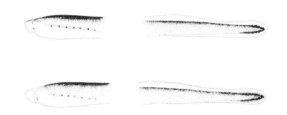

Pigmentation of larval lampreys. Top: American brook lamprey. Bottom: Sea lamprey.

I. (G. Dorsal fin single.) Muscle segments between last gill opening and anus 47 to 56. Great Lakes and Hudson River drainages.
Ichthyomyzon unicuspis and *I. fossor*

I'. Muscle segments 55 to 62. Allegheny drainage.
Ichthyomyzon bdellium and *I. greeleyi*

---

* Sea lamprey ammocoetes less than 40 mm total length have continuous dorsal fins and resemble the ammocoetes of *Ichthyomyzon* spp. At that size the two genera can be separated by myomere count (less than 65 in *Ichthyomyzon* and averaging 70.1 in *Petromyzon*). They can also be distinguished by pigmentation — the inside of the upper lip is pigmented and the tail is not in *Ichthyomyzon* whereas in the sea lamprey the tail has pigment and the inside of its lip does not.

** In New York, *I. fossor* has only been recorded from Little Buffalo Creek near Elma. Recently, it has been reported from the Vermont side of Lake Champlain.

Ichthyomyzon

The species of *Ichthyomyzon* have a single dorsal fin with only a shallow notch suggesting a division into two fins. They are uniformly colored with black pigment around the lateral line pores of large individuals of all species except *Ichthyomyzon fossor* and they occur only in the eastern part of North America, in fresh water. The lateral circumoral teeth are only slightly larger than the next teeth in each radiating row.

Ichthyomyzon unicuspis and *I. fossor* have similar myomere counts and seem to have shared a common ancestor. *I. unicuspis* is parasitic; *I. fossor* is not. Similarly, *I. bdellium* and *I. greeleyi* are morphologically similar, and *I. greeleyi* is the nonparasitic form.

Several features of dentition, including the lack of strong specialization of the circumoral teeth, have been interpreted as indicating that *Ichthyomyzon* is the most primitive genus of lampreys.

OHIO LAMPREY

Ichthyomyzon bdellium (Jordan, 1885)

Identification
The Ohio lamprey is a rather small parasitic lamprey with radiating rows of strong teeth surrounding the mouth. At least one, and usually more, of the teeth nearest the mouth have double points. The mouth is larger than that of nonparasitic species and the disk can be expanded until it is about as wide as the body. There are 53 to 62 (usually 55 to 61) muscle bands between the last gill opening and the anus.

The Ohio lamprey is closely related to the mountain brook lamprey, sharing with that species a high myomere count and bicuspid circumoral teeth.

Description
The following characteristics are taken from Hubbs and Trautman: Supraoral cusps 2 or 3, average 2.6; infraoral cusps 7 to 10, most frequently 8; teeth in circumoral row 19 to 22, most frequently 21, average 20.8; teeth in anterior row 4 or 5, usually 4, average 4.3; teeth in lateral row 7 to 10, usually 8, average 8.3; bicuspid circumorals 5 to 10, usually 8, average 7.8. Proportional measurements are given in Table 1.

Color: Dark slaty gray with a slight yellowish wash. Darker above, shading to paler below but the colors are not sharply defined. It is said to be slightly darker and more bicolored than the northern brook lamprey but definitely lighter and less bicolored than the mountain brook lamprey. The lateral line openings are unpigmented in the ammocoetes and newly transformed young but they later become surrounded with black pigment. Those of the dorsal surface usually darken first. This agrees with the condition in the silver lamprey and contrasts with the condition in the mountain and northern brook lampreys.

Size: Adults range from 124 to 259 mm.

Habitat

Most of the collections of the Ohio lamprey are from small- or moderate-sized streams but they probably spend much of their adult life in larger creeks and small rivers.

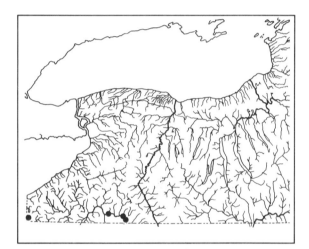

Distribution

As its name implies, the Ohio lamprey occurs in the Ohio River drainage including the Tennessee River, the Wabash River in Indiana and in Illinois, where it is probably extinct, the last specimens having been taken prior to 1918. It occurs in the Allegheny River in western Pennsylvania and New York.

Although it had not been reported earlier from New York, Dr. S. Eaton collected it near the Vandalia bridge on 6 June 1961 and Dr. R. C. Bothner collected nine specimens in the Allegheny River just above Olean on 22 September 1969. More recently, Dr. Wayne Hadley collected it near Portville on 24 October 1971 and 22 October 1972. We took one specimen in French Creek near Cutting on 24 May 1979.

Life History

The Ohio lamprey moves into small streams to spawn. Its breeding behavior has not been described but is assumed to be similar to that of other species of *Ichthyomyzon.*

Food and Feeding

Our adult specimen was attached to a large mature male river chub, *Nocomis micropogon.* It was fastened to the midline of the nape just behind the fleshy crest that develops in that species. It has also been reported to feed on redhorse suckers.

Notes

This species is most closely related to the non-parasitic mountain brook lamprey, *Ichthyomyzon greeleyi,* which it resembles in myomere count. The Ohio lamprey was first described by Kirtland (1838) from the Big Miami River, Ohio, as *Petromyzon argenteus.* Later, it was found that the true *P. argenteus* is the European species now known as *Lampetra fluviatilis,* and Jordan proposed the substitute name *bdellium* in 1885.

References

Hubbs and Trautman, 1937 (general account). Eaton et al., 1982 (New York records).

Names

The species name is from the Greek *bdella,* a leech or sucker.

Petromyzon argenteus, Kirtland, 1838: 170,197 (preoccupied)

Petromyzon bdellium Jordan, 1885: 4 (substitute name)

NORTHERN BROOK LAMPREY

Ichthyomyzon fossor
Reighard and Cummins, 1916

Identification

This is the nonparasitic relative of the silver lamprey and, like that species, it has a low myomere (segment) count: 49 to 55 between the last gill opening and the anus. Like other nonparasitic lampreys, its oral disk is not as wide as the body, it has weakly developed teeth (none of which has more than a single point) and the gut is reduced to a solid strand in the adults. It is a small species; the adults are usually 5 to 7 inches in total length.

At present, there is no certain way to distinguish the ammocoetes of this species from those of the silver lamprey, *Ichthyomyzon unicuspis,* and there is enough overlap in the segment counts so that it is not always possible to distinguish the larvae of this species from those of other lampreys in the state.

Description

The following characteristics are taken from Hubbs and Trautman: Trunk myomeres 47 to 56, usually 50-52, average 50.9; supraoral cusps 1,2, or 3, seldom 1, average 2.0; infraoral cusps 6 to 11, average 8.7, extremely blunt and often obsolete; teeth in circumoral row 15 to 25, average 20.3; teeth in anterior row 1 to 3, usually 2, average 2.2; teeth in lateral row 2 to 6, usually 4 or 5, average 4.7; bicuspid circumorals never present; disk teeth weak, blunt, conspicuous only near side of the mouth, absent or very small in the posterior part and near the edge of the disk. Proportional measurements are given in Table 1.

Color: Dark slate gray over the dorsal surface. Ventral surface of the gill region silvery and behind this the lower surface is pale gray, tinted with orange. Base of the dorsal fin light tan, iris bluish. The lateral line organs remain unpigmented throughout life.

Size: Adults range from 94 to 146 mm, average 119.

Habitat

This species seems to prefer clear water. The ammocoetes live in the slower parts of streams in muddy sand in pools and along the banks. Spawning takes place in small streams with some alternating pools and riffles.

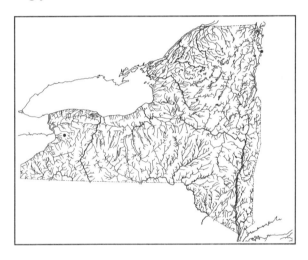

Distribution

The range of the northern brook lamprey is centered in Wisconsin and the Lower Peninsula of Michigan. It occurs in northern Illinois and Indiana with additional, apparently disjunct, populations in Manitoba, Quebec, Missouri, Kentucky, southern Ohio, western Pennsylvania and northeastern Ohio, and western New York.

The only New York records are from Little Buffalo Creek near Elma where adults were collected by Hankinson on 12 June 1928. Ammocoetes were collected at the same spot by DEC personnel in 1976 and by us on 25 May 1978. From the myomere counts, we identify these larvae as *Ichthyomyzon fossor*, although they might be *I. unicuspis*.

Life History

Leach studied the life history of this species in northern Indiana where they spawned in late May or June when the water temperatures reached 55 to 60 F.

The eggs hatched in 3 to 4 weeks and Leach estimated from laboratory studies that they remained ammocoetes for 5 years, then spent another year in

what he called a rest period during which no further growth took place. They did not feed during the last part of the rest period. Transformation took place between 20 August and 20 November when the ammocoetes were 120 to 150 mm long. They remained "immature adults" until late February when they became sexually mature. In late May, they spawned and died a few days later. During the rest period and following transformation, the ammocoetes and adults actually shrank about 10 percent of their length.

Spawning took place in water 8 to 18 inches deep over gravel and cobbles up to 6 inches in diameter. The adults used their suckers to move small stones and construct nests 3 or 4 inches in diameter and up to 4 inches deep. The actual spawning, however, took place under rocks when the mate attached to the female with his vent close to hers but without wrapping his tail around her. The pair vibrated vigorously as the eggs and sperm were released. Females contained 1,000 to 1,350 eggs. In the laboratory, the eggs stuck together as a mass but in the wild they probably adhere individually to the gravel of the nest.

Hatching began in about 12 days and for the first 2 days the newly hatched young remained in the nest. They then attempted to burrow into the bottom. Leach reported the following sizes at the end of the respective growing seasons: Age I-38mm, age II-56mm, age III-73mm, age IV-105mm, age V-125mm. Purvis showed that there was considerable variation in growth rates of northern brook lampreys in the Sturgeon River in Michigan and also suggested that some brook lampreys transform at age III without a one-year rest period.

Food and Feeding

Ammocoetes feed mostly on diatoms and other plankters including protozoans and desmids. They also eat detritus and pollen in the drift. Adults and late ammocoetes do not feed.

Notes

Hubbs and Trautman regarded this species as the nearest relative of *Ichthyomyzon unicuspis*, the silver lamprey, with which it shares a low myomere count.

References

Reighard and Cummins, 1916 (spawning; original description). Hubbs and Trautman, 1937 (systematics). Okkelberg, 1922 (life history). Leach, 1940 (life history). Vladykov, 1949 (Quebec). Purvis, 1970 (age, growth, metamorphosis).

Names

The species name, *fossor,* means digger in Classical Latin.

Ichthyomyzon fossor Reighard and Cummins, 1916:1 Mill Creek and Huron River, Michigan

Ammocoetes unicolor DeKay, 1842: 383, pl.x-ixx, fig. 250 (regarded as not positively identifiable)

Ichthyomyzon unicolor Greeley, 1929: 166 Erie-Niagara drainage

MOUNTAIN BROOK LAMPREY

Ichthyomyzon greeleyi
Hubbs and Trautman, 1937

Identification

This nonparasitic species is most similar to the parasitic Ohio lamprey, *Ichthyomyzon bdellium*, with (53) 57 to 59 (62) body segments between the last gill opening and the anus. These counts are higher than other *Ichthyomyzon* in our area. At least some of the teeth nearest the mouth are double pointed. The northern brook lamprey and the silver lamprey both have lower myomere counts and lack bicuspid teeth. The sea lamprey and the American brook lamprey have two separate dorsal fins.

This species is less specialized as a nonparasite than the other nonparasitic species of New York. Its disk is nearly as wide as the body and its teeth are quite well developed, obsolescent only near the edge of the disk, especially in the posterior field. Its degenerate gut, however, confirms that it does not feed as an adult and this serves to distinguish it from the similar Ohio lamprey.

Description

Hubbs and Trautman list the following characteristics: Trunk myomeres (55) 57 to 59 (61), average 57.9; supraoral cusps 2 to 4 average 2.8; infraoral cusps 7 to 12, usually 8 to 10, average 9.4; teeth in circumoral row 19 to 24, usually 21, average 21.5; teeth in anterior row 3 to 5, usually 4, average 4.1; teeth in lateral rows 5 to 9, most frequently 7, often 8, average 7.2; bicuspid circumorals 7 to 11, typically 8, average 8.4; transverse lingual lamina moderately to strongly bilobed; teeth rather long and sharp, more or less curved, well developed except toward the margin and in posterior field of disk.

Color: More sharply bicolored than other species of *Ichthyomyzon*, olive tan above, abruptly silvery tan below, becoming darker as spawning progresses. Iris light gray around the pupil, gray blue peripherally. Dorsal fin pale gray with yellowish cast. Ammocoetes silvery tan. Ventral lateral line organs never pigmented but the dorsal and lateral sensory organs are dark although inconspicuous because of the dark background.

Size: Total length 105 to 161, usually 100 to 150, average 128 mm.

Habitat

Apparently this nonparasitic species spends its life in creeks without moving to larger rivers. Its abundance in northwestern Pennsylvania indicates that it can tolerate a wider range of habitats than some other lamprey species.

Distribution

This species is common in northwest Pennsylvania and adjacent parts of Ohio with additional disjunct populations in the Ohio River drainage in Kentucky and West Virginia. It also occurs in the Cumberland and Tennessee Rivers in Tennessee, northern Alabama, Kentucky, and Virginia.

The only New York records are from French Creek although it occurs in the Allegheny River tributaries above and below the New York section.

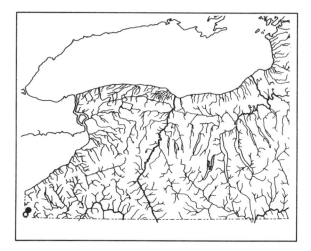

Life History

The spawning behavior of this species is similar to that of other lampreys. Raney observed spawning 19 to 26 May 1938 in the the Little Neshannock Creek near Wilmey, Pennsylvania. The water temperature was 18.9 C. Nests were built by males just above riffles where the water was about a foot deep. The nests were excavated by moving pebbles to form a depression downstream from a flat stone 6 to 12 inches in diameter. The nests were 8 to 10 inches in diameter and about 2 inches deep, with a bottom of fine gravel and sand. Once a nest was started, other males sometimes joined in the building and then later moved on to build their own nests. Nest building and spawning reached a peak about 3 pm.

Spawning occurred when a female moved over the nest and attached to a stone. The male then attached to her and they vibrated together. Usually there were five to nine lampreys per nest and spawning by one pair seemed to stimulate other pairs to spawn. Between spawning episodes, the males continued to move pebbles around the nest.

Ammocoetes reach 28 to 35 mm the first summer. Transformation takes place in the late fall or early spring but the age at transformation has not been determined.

Notes

Populations from the Upper Tennessee River in western North Carolina and Georgia were described as a separate species, *Ichthyomyzon hubbsi,* by Raney (1952b).

References
Hubbs and Trautman, 1937 (description). Raney, 1939 (spawning).

Names
This species is named for Dr. John R. Greeley, ichthyologist of the New York State Conservation Department, who collected the type.

Ichthyomyzon greeleyi Hubbs and Trautman, 1937: 93-98 French Creek, 1 mile east of Wattsburg, Pennsylvania

SILVER LAMPREY

Ichthyomyzon unicuspis
Hubbs and Trautman, 1937

Identification
The silver lamprey is a rather chunky parasitic species with well-developed teeth, a large oral disk and a low myomere count (usually 49 to 53, rarely as high as 56). None of the disk teeth have more than one point. The low myomere count is shared with the northern brook lamprey which, as a nonparasitic species, has a narrow disk and reduced dentation. All other *Ichthyomyzon* in our area have higher myomere counts and some bicuspid disk teeth.

Ammocoetes of the silver lamprey and the northern brook lamprey are similar and, in fact, there is no known way of distinguishing them.

Description
The following characteristics are from Hubbs and Trautman: Trunk myomeres (47) 49 to 52 (55), average 50.5; supraoral cusps 1 to 4, almost always 2, average 2.0; infraoral cusps 5 to 11, average 7.8; teeth in circumoral row 15 to 25, average 19.2; teeth in anterior row 2 to 4, usually 3, average 3.2; teeth in lateral rows 5 to 8, usually 6 or 7, average 6.6; bicuspid circumorals 0 to 2, very rarely 1 or 2; transverse lingual lamina moderately to strongly bilobed, very wide and strong, heavily cornified, and with numerous short denticulations.

Color: Adults are light yellow tan, lighter on the belly, gradually darkening posteriorly, not sharply bicolored. In life, the iris is blue. In newly transformed adults, the lateral line organs are unpigmented, but they all darken with increasing age. Silver lampreys darken to blue black shortly before they die.

Size: 103 to 328, average 224 mm.

Habitat
The parasitic adults live in larger streams and lakes where they find their fish hosts. Spawning takes place in moderate-sized streams where there are sand- and gravel-bottom riffles. The ammocoetes require sand and dark mud that is relatively free of clay silt.

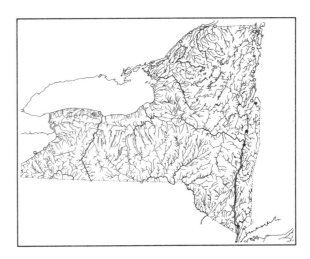

Distribution
The silver lamprey is generally distributed along the Great Lakes and in the large tributaries of the Mississippi and Ohio Rivers from Minnesota to Nebraska, Tennessee and West Virginia. There are isolated records from the Hudson Bay drainage and the Mississippi River in the State of Mississippi. According to Trautman, their abundance in Ohio decreased drastically between 1920 and 1945.

In New York State, there are records from Lakes Erie and Ontario, the St. Lawrence drainage, and Lake Champlain and its tributaries. The Survey reported it as common in Lake Champlain with spawning observed in Putnam Creek and the Lower Ausable River. We did not find it in Putnam Creek in 1978, but we did find ammocoetes of *Petromyzon* near Crown Point. It has been taken in the Hudson River near Stillwater and, recently, specimens have been collected in the Lower Hudson near Albany and Nyack. Quite probably their presence in the Lower Hudson is due to their having passed through the Champlain-Hudson Canal.

Life History
Spawning occurs in May and June when the water temperature reaches 50 F. The nests are built in shallow gravelly riffles and spawning is similar to that of the sea lamprey. At times, they share the nests of sea lampreys. The adults constantly work on the nests with short interruptions for spawning. The female attaches to a rock and the male attaches to her head, wrapping his tail around hers to bring the genital openings close together. The pair vibrates as the eggs and sperm are released; then they separate and return to nest building. The adults die when spawning is completed.

Greeley reported finding a nest in Putnam Creek on 18 June when the water temperature was 72 F. Six adults were under a large stone at the head of a riffle where the water was about 8 inches deep. Apparently, they had hollowed out a cavity as a nest. The eggs of the silver lamprey are approximately 1 mm in diameter and the average female produces 10,800 eggs. After hatching, the ammocoetes drop downstream to quiet water where they burrow into the mud. It is estimated that the larval period lasts 4 to 7 years. They transform in the fall when they are about 3 inches long. They remain in the streams over winter, then move downstream to rivers and lakes where they find hosts. After 1 or possibly 2 years as parasites, they return to the streams to spawn and die.

Food and Feeding
Ammocoetes feed on drifting plankton and detritus. Adults attack a variety of fish including trout, whitefish, smelt, pike, white sucker, black buffalo, brown bullhead, carp, rock bass, walleye, paddlefish, and even such armored species as sturgeons and gars.

Notes
Because of its low myomere count and single tooth cusps, this species is considered the most primitive member of the genus.

References
Hubbs and Trautman, 1937 (systematics). Vladykov and Roy, 1948 (biology). Trautman, 1957 (Ohio). Scott and Crossman, 1973 (general account). Reider, 1979a (Hudson River).

Names
Early authors recorded this species under the names *argenteus* and *concolor,* but Hubbs and Trautman showed that neither of these names could be used, and renamed the species *unicuspis* in reference to the single points on the circumoral teeth.

Ichthyomyzon unicuspis Greene, 1935:21 (nomen nudum)

Ichthyomyzon unicuspis Hubbs and Trautman, 1937: 53-65 Toledo, Ohio (Type: UMMZ 107040)

Ichthyomyzon concolor (Kirtland), Bean, 1903: 14-15? New York

Ichthyomyzon concolor, Greeley, 1929: 166 Erie-Niagara watershed

Lampetra

Lampetra is a large genus with about a dozen species and there is considerable difference of opinion as to how these species are related. Most specialists now regard *Lampetra* as consisting of three subgenera: *Lethenteron* (to which our single species belongs) *Entosphenus,* and *Lampetra.* Unlike *Ichthyomyzon* and *Petromyzon,* the teeth are not arranged in radiating rows and there are only a few remnant teeth on the rear of the mouth disk. *Lampetra appendix* has two dorsal fins. The genus includes parasitic and nonparasitic species but only the nonparasitic American brook lamprey occurs in our area.

AMERICAN BROOK LAMPREY

Lampetra appendix (DeKay, 1842)

Identification
The American brook lamprey is the only non-parasitic species in New York with two dorsal fins. It also has a high myomere count: (63) 64 to 70 (73). The myomere count alone will separate it from all other local species except the sea lamprey which usually has 65 to 76 myomeres. The sea lamprey, however, is parasitic and, when adult, has the disk filled with radial rows of well-developed teeth while adults of the American brook lamprey have only a few teeth in the disk: the supra- and infraorals, a row of blunt, bicuspid teeth on each side of the mouth and sometimes a single row in the posterior field.

Ammocoetes of the American brook lamprey can be distinguished from those of the sea lamprey by pigment characters given in the key.

Description
The following characters are taken from AMNH specimens from New York State: Supraoral lamina bilobed; infraoral cusps 7 or 8 blunt knobs; teeth in the circumoral row 10 or 11, usually 11; teeth in the anterior row 4 or 5, usually 5; teeth in the lateral row 3 on each side, bicuspid, with blunt cusps; posterior circumorals obsolescent or not visible.

Color: Ammocoetes are brownish above, silvery tan below with a pale yellowish brown middorsal stripe. Newly transformed adults are silvery brown to gray, somewhat bicolored, darker above than below. During spawning they become darker, turning blue black just before they die.

Size: Total lengths 169 to 200 mm, average 143 to 146 mm. Manion and Purvis (1971) found five giant female brook lampreys averaging 281 mm in a tributary of the Straits of Mackinac and concluded that these individuals must have fed parasitically after metamorphosis.

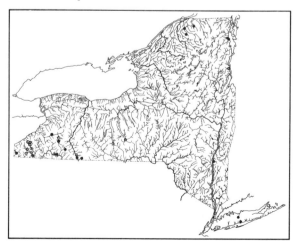

Habitat

Trautman found that in Ohio the American brook lamprey spawns in streams wider than 15 feet. In areas where it occurred with the northern brook lamprey, it spawned somewhat earlier than that species.

Distribution

The American brook lamprey occupies a broad band across the northern part of the United States and southern Canada from Manitoba and Minnesota east in the Great Lakes drainage to the St. Lawrence and New Hampshire. In the Mississippi, it reaches the Ozark Plateaus of southeastern Missouri and northern Arkansas and the Tennesee River system in northern Alabama and western North Carolina. On the Atlantic, it reaches the Roanoke River in Virginia.

Its distribution in New York is spotty. It occurs in the Allegheny drainage, the Upper Genesee system, Cattaraugus Creek in the Lake Erie drainage, the southern ends of Cayuga and Seneca Lakes, the St. Lawrence tributaries, Lake Champlain and the New York City area. Recently, it has been collected on Long Island, although the Survey did not find it there.

Life History

The classic study of lamprey life history was made by Professor Simon Henry Gage of Cornell University who worked on lampreys for more than 40 years. Professor Gage's work was summarized in the Oswego Survey report (1928) and in this paper he compared the life history of the sea lamprey with that of the American brook lamprey. The brook lamprey began its breeding activities when the water temperature reaches 50 to 54 F, which is usually late March in the western part of the state and April in the vicinity of New York. Usually, the brook lampreys were through spawning by the time the sea lampreys began their runs. Brook lamprey males began the nest building at sites upstream from the head of a riffle. Females soon joined the males and the nest building consisted of picking up pebbles with their mouths and moving them to form the rim of a shallow pit. When the female was ready to spawn, she held on to a large pebble on the upstream side of the pit with her mouth and the male attached himself to her head so that their bodies were parallel with their genital openings close together. The two vibrated together, stirring up the sand in the bottom of the pit as the eggs and milt were released. The eggs were sticky at first and adhered to sand grains so that they became covered as they sank through the cloud of disturbed sand. Spawning was repeated at intervals of 5 to 10 minutes or longer.

Brook lampreys lay all of their eggs in small batches. Those in the posterior part of the ovary ripen first. About 3,000 eggs are produced, each about 1 mm in diameter.

Professor Gage was able to confirm that all lampreys die after spawning. Their decomposing bodies are often seen along streams and the noto-chord is the last to decay so that the white string-like remains are good indications that the lampreys have spawned in the stream.

At 20 C the eggs hatch in about 9 days. In the wild, this would be unusually warm and hatching normally takes somewhat longer. After their yolk supply is gone, the young lampreys swim out of the nests and drift and swim downstream to slower waters with sandy mud bottom where they work themselves into U-shaped burrows with their heads positioned so that they can feed on particles of detritus and small organisms that drift close to the bottom.

It appears that American brook lampreys spend 4 or 5 years as ammocoetes, and that they do not grow during the last year. Beginning in July or August they transform into the adult phase. The eyes develop, the hood and tentacles shrink, and the disk with its teeth develops into the adult form. Transformation proceeds slowly over the next few months and is not fully complete until the next January or March, only a few weeks before spawning. The adults do not migrate downstream but remain in the gravel until they are ready to spawn.

Food and Feeding

The ammocoetes are filter feeders and sieve food from the water by means of the feather-like tentacles that surround the mouth. Moore and Beamish found that there was little selectivity so that the relative abundance of items in the gut was about the same as in the water and sediment samples. Diatoms were the main food and there was little change as the ammocoetes grew. Adults do not feed and in many individuals the esophagus is actually blocked by epithelial tissue.

Notes

At present, this species is placed in the subgenus *Lethenteron* in the genus *Lampetra*. Some authors consider *Lethenteron* to merit recognition as a separate genus. Hubbs and Potter believed that this species is a nonparasitic derivative of *Lampetra japonica*, which occurs in Siberia, Japan, Alaska, and northern Canada.

References

Hubbs and Potter, 1971(systematics). Vladykov, 1960 (ammocoetes). Gage, in the Oswego Survey report, 1928 (life history). Hubbs, 1925 (life cycle). Rhode, Arndt and Wang, 1976 (life history). Moore and Beamish, 1973 (feeding). Young and Cole, 1900 (nesting). Dean and Sumner, 1898 (spawning). Manion and Purvis, 1971 (gigantism). Wilson, 1955 (Lake Champlain). Surface, 1898 (Cayuga Lake). Trautman, 1957 (Ohio). Rhode in Lee et al., 1982 (nomenclature, distribution).

Names

The nomenclature of this species has long been debated. Recently, it has been called *lamotteni* or *lamottenii* which is the name given to it by Lesueur based on specimens from Madison County, Missouri. Some authors have emended the name to *lamottei* because it was based on the name Lamotte. The international rules of zoological nomenclature are vague on this point but this emendation is probably not correct.

Lesueur's description was not adequate to separate this species from the least lamprey which occurs in the same area and the name is therefore regarded as unidentifiable. The next available name is *appendix,* described by DeKay (1842) and based on specimens from Providence and the Hudson River. Recently, Vladykov and Kott (1982) have argued that DeKay's drawing fits the least lamprey better as it shows a long urogenital papilla and a low myomere count, and they argue that "Providence" might have been a town in the Allegheny drainage of New York where the least lamprey might have occurred. There are, however, no New York records of the least lamprey although it does occur downstream in the Allegheny River drainage. It seems more likely that the Providence was Providence, Rhode Island, which is in the range of the American brook lamprey and that DeKay's illustration is simply inaccurate.

The name *appendix* is Latin for "that which hangs to something."

Petromyzon lamottenii Lesueur, 1827: 9 Madison Co., Missouri

Petromyzon appendix DeKay, 1842: 381 Providence; Hudson River

Entosphenus appendix, Greeley, 1929: 166 Erie-Niagara watershed

Lampetra wilderi Gage *in* Jordan and Evermann, 1896: 13 Cayuga Lake

Entosphenus lamottenii, Hubbs and Lagler, 1964: 36-37 (distribution)

Ammocoetes branchialis, Meek, 1889: 298 Cayuga Lake basin

Petromyzon

The genus *Petromyzon* contains only a single species and it occurs on both sides of the Atlantic Ocean. There are no known nonparasitic populations. The sea lamprey has two dorsal fins and a mottled coloration and well-developed teeth arranged in radiating rows. The inner tooth of each row is much enlarged.

SEA LAMPREY

Petromyzon marinus
Linnaeus, 1758

Identification
The sea lamprey is probably the easiest of our lampreys to identify. It is the largest species, with sea-

run adults sometimes exceeding 2 feet in length and it is the only one of our species that has a mottled, rather than a uniform, countershaded, or bicolored pattern. Moribund adults of other species often have patches of fungus that give them a mottled look but this is not to be confused with the mottled color of the sea lamprey. It differs from all of the *Ichthyomyzons* in having the dorsal fin divided by a deep notch into two fins, and it has a high myomere count.

Sea lampreys are most similar to the American brook lamprey which also has two dorsal fins and a high myomere count but the brook lamprey is not parasitic and has reduced teeth, in patches rather than in curving rows, and a nonfunctional gut.

Ammocoetes less than 40 mm long do not have clearly separated dorsal fins. They can be distinguished from *Ichthyomyzon* ammocoetes by the presence of pigment on the caudal rays and the lack of pigment on the inside of the upper lip.

Description
The following characters are taken from Great Lakes specimens from Michigan and sea-run lampreys from the Delaware River in New York. Counts for Great Lakes specimens, if different, are given in parentheses: Supraoral cusps 2; infraoral cusps 7 to 9 (7 to 8); circumoral teeth 18 or 19 (11, 17 to 19); anterior circumoral 1; lateral circumoral 4-4 (3-4 or 4-4); bicuspid lateral circumorals 4-4 (3-3 or 4-4); posterior circumorals 10 or 11 (8 to 10); transverse lingual lamina bilobate with 11 to 13 points; myomeres 69 to 71 (69 to 73).

Color: Ammocoetes slaty brown, not sharply bicolored. Adult males from the Carp Lake River in Michigan were generally orange beige including the inside of the mouth, with the upper sides and dorsal surface mottled gray and dark gray. Teeth yellow. Females more gray with a yellowish green cast and fins shading to a yellow or beige margin. Lower surface of the head yellowish, iris pale gray. Teeth yellow, same color as the inside of the disk. Belly of female speckled. There is a dark gray swollen area on the ventral surface just behind the disk.

Juveniles and breeding adults: Spawning males have a prominent fleshy ridge along the middorsal line in front of the dorsal fin.

Size: Total length of adults ranges from 584 to 670 mm (292 to 425).

Habitat
The sea lamprey is an anadromous fish that spends its egg and larval periods in streams. After transformation, it moves out to sea for the parasitic phase of its life and finally returns to streams to spawn and die. Landlocked populations in the Finger Lakes and in the Great Lakes generally spend their parasitic life in deeper and colder waters below the thermocline.

Distribution
The sea lamprey occurs on both sides of the Atlantic. In Europe, it ranges from the Mediterranean to Finland and Norway and on the American side it is found from Labrador to Florida. There are conflict-

ing opinions as to whether or not the sea lamprey was native to Lake Ontario. An 1835 record seems to be the earliest notice of its presence there and some workers have taken this to indicate that it did not reach the lake until after the Erie Canal was opened in 1819-25. Lawrie, however, has reviewed the spread of the sea lamprey in the Great Lakes and accepts the view that it was native to Lake Ontario. We have been unable to find records from the upstream (western) part of the Mohawk drainage and I believe this is an indication that the species was native to Ontario and its tributaries, the Finger Lakes, and Lake Champlain. It would be interesting to know if the sea-run population is capable of completing its life cycle if denied access to salt water.

The sea lamprey was first recorded from Lake Erie in 1921, nearly a century after the Welland Canal provided access to the lakes above Niagara Falls. It was first found spawning in Michigan tributaries of Lake Erie in 1932 but it has never become abundant in Lake Erie and only six Canadian and four U.S. streams are known to have spawning runs. Cattaraugus Creek in western New York has one of the largest runs.

The sea lamprey ascends streams in Long Island and also the Hudson and Delaware Rivers. Landlocked populations occur in Lakes Champlain, Oneida, Seneca, and Cayuga. Greeley reported it from the Otselic River (Susquehanna drainage) near Whitney Point and Lisle. The Survey also reported it from the St. Regis River near Hogansburg.

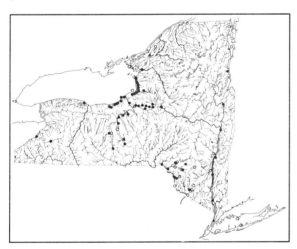

George (1981a) postulated that the falls in the Mohawk River at Cohoes and the falls in the Hudson above Troy limit upstream movement of sea lampreys, but specimens have recently been taken at Fort Edward and above the dam at Troy, suggesting that they can pass through the locks.

Life History
Because of its economic importance, the life history of the sea lamprey has been studied intensively. In general, the life history pattern is similar to that of other lampreys although they spawn somewhat later than the American brook lamprey. Spawning runs vary with location. Anadromous lampreys spawn in the Delaware River in early June and the landlocked populations begin spawning in April and continue to July or even early August in Lake Superior. The male begins the nest building by moving stones to hollow out a depression. Later he is joined by the female and the pair continues to work on the nest throughout their spawning period with brief interruptions when the spawning takes place. Females ready to spawn attach to a rock and the male attaches to her head, wrapping his body around hers as they vibrate as the eggs are released. Spawning continues for a few hours or up to 2 or 3 days until the female has released her complement of eggs. Immediately after spawning, the female drops downstream and soon dies; the male may remain on the nest for a time before he dies.

Early in the season, there is rather strict monogamy and the males defend their nests against other males but later in the season mating becomes more promiscuous with sharing of nests and mates.

Great Lakes female lampreys lay about 100,000 eggs and sea-run females, in keeping with their larger size, lay substantially more, averaging about 236,000.

Sea lamprey eggs hatch in about 2 weeks at 15 or 16 C and a few days later the larvae drift downstream to quiet water where they burrow into soft bottom.

Manion and Stauffer recognized four stages in the transformation process, characterized by, respectively: Mouth reduced, mouth fused, mouth enclosed, and mouth elongated. Changes involved eyes, snout, mouth, nasopore, gill openings, color, and total length.

Transformation takes place from July to October and the adults move downstream during the fall and spring to begin their parasitic life. Landlocked populations begin their spawning runs after 12 to 20 months at large.

For a long time, it was believed that sea lampreys remained ammocoetes for 6 or 7 years but studies on a stream in Michigan where lampreys were deliberately introduced have shown that the larval period can be as long as 14 years or possibly even longer.

Food and Feeding
Farmer and Beamish reported that in tank experiments, splake, carp, and white suckers were attacked significantly more frequently than lake whitefish, burbot, shorthead redhorse, or brown bullheads, and that walleyes were rarely parasitized by lampreys. Most attacks were on the head and the caudal peduncle below the lateral line and particularly the region behind the pectoral fins. The lampreys usually attacked the largest individuals of a species. None of the fish seemed to avoid the attacks nor did they appear to avoid fish to which the lampreys were attached.

Ammocoetes are filter feeders and diatoms are the main component of the diet with some sand grains consumed apparently accidentally. Experiments have shown little selection and the relative abundance of items in the gut is roughly the same as in samples of the water and sediments. The diet of the ammocoetes does not change as they get older.

Notes

The profound effects of the sea lamprey on the fish communities of the Great Lakes have been documented by several authors. As the sea lamprey became abundant in the Great Lakes, there was a concurrent decline in the commercial fish stocks. Whether the lamprey was the chief cause, or merely the last straw, has been debated, but its presence in large numbers certainly precluded any recovery of the overfished populations. In the 1950s a concerted effort to find a control was successful. Practical selective poisons (called TFM and Bayer 73) were developed and a program of treating the spawning sites has reduced the lamprey populations to low levels. The recovery of the fishery has been dramatic.

References

Volume 37, no. 11 of the Canadian Journal of Fisheries and Aquatic Sciences is devoted to the proceedings of an international sea lamprey symposium and has an excellent series of papers. Other papers of especial interest are: Hubbs and Pope, 1937 (Great Lakes). Applegate, 1950 (life history), 1951 (general). Applegate and Moffett, 1955 (relation to lake trout). Youngs, 1972 (predation on lake trout). Beamish, 1979 (migration and spawning). Farmer and Beamish, 1973 (predation). Lennon, 1954 (feeding mechanism; effect on hosts). Greeley, 1956b (New York). Lawrie, 1970 (distribution and spread). B. Smith, 1971 (Great Lakes). Wilson, 1955 (Lake Champlain). Manion and Stauffer, 1970 (metamorphosis). S. Smith, 1970 (effects on fish communities). Vladykov, 1960 (identification of lampreys). Moore and Beamish, 1973 (larval food). Crowe, 1975 (control program). Surface, 1898 (Cayuga Lake). Aron and Smith, 1971 (effects of canals). Manion and Smith, 1978. Gage, 1928, 1929 (life history). Lark, 1973 (early record from Lake Ontario). Wigley, 1959 (life history in Cayuga Lake). Creaser and Hann, 1929 (food of larval stages). Coventry, 1922 (breeding habits). Potter, Beamish, and Johnson, 1974 (sex ratios). Potter and Beamish, 1977 (freshwater populations). Neth and Jolliff, 1984 (New York).

Names

The generic name comes from the Greek, *petra*, stone and *myzon* to suck. *Marinus* is Latin meaning of the sea.

Petromyzon marinus Linnaeus, 1758: 230 Europe

Ammocoetes bicolor Lesueur, 1818a: 386-387 Massachusetts

Ammocoetes bicolor DeKay, 1842: 383 New York

Petromyzon americanus Lesueur, 1818a: 383-385 Massachusetts

Petromyzon americanus DeKay, 1842: 379-380 New York

Petromyzon marinus unicolor Bean, 1903 (not *Ammocoetes unicolor* of DeKay, which is unidentifiable)

Petromyzon marinus dorsatus Wilder *in* Jordan and Gilbert, 1883: 869 Cayuga Lake

Petromyzon marinus, Greeley, 1928: 95 Oswego drainage

TABLE 1
AVERAGE PROPORTIONAL MEASUREMENTS AND COUNTS OF LAMPREYS
(Ichthyomyzon, Lampetra, and *Petromyzon)*

All proportions are expressed in percentage of total length.

		Ichthyomyzon			*Lampetra*	*Petromyzon*
	unicuspis	fossor	bdellium	greeleyi	appendix	marinus
TAIL LENGTH	30.2	30.4	27.4	20.7	30.7	25.2
BODY DEPTH	8.2	7.4	7.3	7.6	6.2	7.8
EYE LENGTH	1.1	1.3	1.1	1.3	2.1	2.1
SNOUT LENGTH	9.5	5.5	8.6	7.3	6.6	9.8
DISK LENGTH	8.6	4.1	6.7	5.3	3.7	6.5
LENGTH OVER GILLS	10.1	10.4	8.9	9.8	10.5	11.7
TRUNK MYOMERES	47-55	47-56	53-62	55-61	63-73	65-76
SUPRAORAL CUSPS	1-4	1-3	2-3	2-4	2-2	—
INFRAORAL CUSPS	5-11	6-11	7-10	7-12	7-8	7-9
TEETH IN CIRCUMORAL ROW	15-25	15-25	19-22	19-24	10-11	18-19
TEETH IN ANTERIOR ROW	2-4	1-3	4-5	3-5	4-5	8-9
TEETH IN LATERAL ROW	5-8	2-6	7-10	5-9	3	3-4
BICUSPID CIRCUMORALS	0-2	0	5-10	7-11	3	3-4
DISK TEETH	Strong	Weak	Strong	Strong	Weak	Strong

From: Hubbs and Trautman, 1937.

STURGEONS

ACIPENSERIDAE

Sturgeons are large fishes with five rows of bony plates along the body, flattened or conical snouts, sculptured bony plates on the head, gill covers that do not quite cover the gill chambers, and undershot mouths that can be extended into a tube for feeding on the bottom.

Sturgeons, together with their relatives the paddlefishes, belong to a primitive group of bony fish called the Chondrostei. Among their primitive features are a strongly upturned heterocercal tail and fine horny fin rays like those of sharks. Their ad-

vanced features include barbels on the underside of the snout, the rostrum of the paddlefish, and the body armor of the sturgeons.

Sturgeons live only in the Northern Hemisphere. There are about two dozen species. Some are confined to fresh water, others are anadromous. Of the seven North American species, three occur in New York. The lake sturgeon and the shortnose resemble each other more closely than either resembles the Atlantic sturgeon.

KEY TO THE SPECIES OF STURGEONS IN NEW YORK

A. Width of mouth inside the lips slightly more than one-half the distance between the eyes. Gill rakers 17 to 27 (average 21.6). Postdorsal and preanal shields paired. Two to six bony plates at least as large as the pupil of the eye between the anal fin base and the lateral row of scutes. Viscera pale or only slightly pigmented.

Acipenser oxyrhynchus

Atlantic sturgeon, p. 47

A'. Width of mouth inside lips more than three-fifths the distance between the eyes. Gill rakers 22 to 40. Postdorsal and preanal shields in a single row. No large scutes between the base of the anal fin and the midlateral row of scutes. Viscera black.

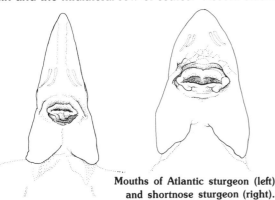

**Mouths of Atlantic sturgeon (left)
and shortnose sturgeon (right).**

B. Anal fin rays 19 to 29. Gill rakers 22 to 29, average about 25. Dorsal and lateral shields pale and contrasting with darker background color of the body.

Acipenser brevirostrum

Shortnose sturgeon, p.44

Bony plates are present along the anal fin of the Atlantic sturgeon (left) but absent in the shortnose sturgeon (right).

B'. Anal fin rays 25 to 35. Gill rakers 25 to 40, average 33. Dorsal and lateral shields about the same color as the background.

Acipenser fulvescens   **Lake sturgeon, p. 45**

Acipenser

The genus *Acipenser* is the largest genus with about 16 species in the Northern Hemisphere. Five species occur in North America, three on the Atlantic coast and two in the Pacific drainages. One other genus, *Scaphirhynchus,* with two species, occurs in the Mississippi and other gulf coast drainages. Members of the genus *Acipenser* have more or less conical snouts and terete caudal peduncles. Members of the genus *Scaphirhynchus* have depressed, shovel-shaped snouts and depressed (flattened) caudal peduncles.

SHORTNOSE STURGEON

Acipenser brevirostrum
Lesueur, 1818

Identification

The shortnose is the smallest member of the genus *Acipenser* (the only genus of sturgeons in New York), and its size does not exceed 3.5 feet. As its name implies, it has a shorter snout than the Atlantic sturgeon but older Atlantic sturgeons have relatively short snouts so the comparisons must be made between fish of the same size. At about 3 feet, the distance from the front of the eye to the tip of the snout goes into the distance from the back of the eye to the edge of the gill cover about 1.2 times, but in the Atlantic sturgeon it only goes about 0.6 times. The diameter of the eye goes into the length of the snout about 2.4 times in the shortnose, about 4.0 or 4.1 in the Atlantic. Atlantic sturgeons have a small area of cartilage between the main plates on top of the head until they are about 3 feet long but in the shortnose the plates close by the time they are about 8 inches long. Atlantic sturgeons have several bony plates, each at least as large as the pupil, along the base of the anal fin but these are not present in the shortnose.

Shortnose sturgeons resemble the lake sturgeon in having a wide mouth (inside of the gape about 65 percent of the distance between the eyes) and darkly pigmented viscera, but they differ in that the dorsal and lateral bony plates of the shortnose are light in color so that they stand out against the darker ground color of the body. In the lake sturgeons, the plates are the same color as the background.

The width of the mouth will distinguish between the Atlantic and shortnose sturgeons as small as three inches total length.

Description

Body elongate, pentagonal in cross section. Dorsal profile arched, ventral profile nearly straight. Dorsal fin far back, falcate with moderately high anterior lobe. Caudal strongly heterocercal, its upper lobe narrowly pointed, its ventral lobe prominent and bluntly rounded. Anal origin below anterior third of dorsal base. Anal fin pointed anteriorly, its margin slightly concave. Pelvics retrogressive, inserted ahead of the dorsal fin, their longest rays not reaching to the level of the dorsal origin. Pectorals retrogressive, low and horizontal. Head profile convex, snout a blunt cone, not turned up anteriorly. Barbels large. Operculum not reaching the shoulder girdle. Gill membranes broadly joined to the isthmus. Counts and proportional measurements are given in table 2.

Color: Grayish olive to brownish above, somewhat lighter ventrally. Scutes in dorsal and lateral rows pale.

Size: Koski et al. reported a specimen 932 mm standard length from the Hudson River. Vladykov and Greeley listed a 39.5-inch specimen from the Connecticut River.

Habitat

Shortnose sturgeons live in estuaries and large coastal rivers. Although they move upstream and downstream with the seasons, there is conflicting evidence as to how much, if any, of their lives they spend in the open sea. Many of the immature shortnose sturgeons remain in the river near the salt front while older fish move down to the lower estuary or possibly out to sea. In the southern part of its range, it appears that the shortnose enters the rivers only to spawn and spends the bulk of its life in coastal waters. Occasionally, the shortnose enters the freshwater parts of rivers and even lakes.

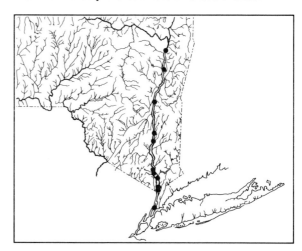

Distribution

The shortnose ranges along the Atlantic coast from the St. John River in New Brunswick to the St. Johns River in Florida. Its occurrence is spotty and only a few streams still support breeding populations. In New York, it is not rare in the Hudson River. It occurs in the Delaware River and could occasionally stray upstream to the New York section. Although it is listed as endangered, there are reliable reports of its being sold in the southern parts of its range.

Life History
Reproducing populations have been studied in the Altamaha River, Georgia, the Hudson River, New York, the Upper Connecticut River, Massachusetts, the Kennebec River in Maine and the St. John River in New Brunswick. The life history of the Delaware River population is unknown. Taubert studied spawning in the Holyoke Pool of the Connecticut River. The fish spawned over a bottom that was mostly rubble with some gravel and large rocks. Spawning took place 1-9 May 1978 when the water temperatures were 12 to 15 C and the current velocities ranged from 37 to 125 cm per second. The females spawning for the first time were 9 to 14 years old. Males in the spawning population were 10 to 26 years old. Growth marks on the pectoral fin indicated that they first spawn at an average age of 9.8 years and a second time at 14 to 20 years, with 4 to 12 years between spawnings.

Shortnose from Canada grew more slowly than those from Georgia. The Canadian fish reached lengths of 50 cm at age IX; those from Georgia reached 50 cm at age II.

Females lay 40,000 to 200,000 eggs. Hatching requires 13 days at 10 C and the newly hatched larvae average 7 mm. The larvae remain on the bottom most of the time but where the current exceeds 40 to 65 cm per second, they cannot maintain their position and may drift with the current. Population estimates are 18,000 in the St. John River, 5,400 in the Kennebec, 500 in the Holyoke Pool and between 13,000 and 30,000 in the Hudson River.

Food and Feeding
Dadswell reported that the young sturgeon eat insects and crustaceans; the older individuals eat small mollusks.

Notes
Although the Hudson River stock and some Canadian populations seem to be maintaining stable population levels, the shortnose has disappeared from much of its range and is on the Federal List of Endangered Species. Because it is much smaller than the Atlantic sturgeon, limiting the commercial catch to large fish serves to protect the shortnose. Occasionally, individual sturgeons are found with the tip of the snout notched. The cause of this"split-nose" anomaly is not known.

References
Vladykov and Greeley, 1963 (general review). Vladykov and Beaulieu, 1946 (characters). Dadswell, 1979 (population ecology, St. John River). Koski et al., 1971 (size). Gorham and McAllister, 1974 (identification and status in St. John River). Fried and McCleave, 1973 (Maine). Taubert, 1980 (life history). Dovel, 1978; 1981b (Hudson River population). McCleave et al., 1977 (movements).

Magnin, 1963 (growth). Atz and Smith, 1976 (hermaphroditism).

Names
Brevirostrum is from the Latin *brevis,* short, and *rostrum,* snout.

Acipenser brevirostrum Lesueur, 1818: 390-392 Atlantic coast

Acipenser brevirostris, DeKay, 1842: 345-346 New York

Acipenser dekayi Dumeril, 1870: 168-170 New York

Acipenser (Huso) lesueuri Valenciennes *in* Dumeril, 1870: 166-168 New York

Acipenser microrhynchus Dumeril, 1870: 164-166 New York

Acipenser (Huso) rostellum Dumeril, 1870: 173-175 New York

Acipenser (Huso) simus Valenciennes *in* Dumeril, 1870: 175-177 New York

LAKE STURGEON

Acipenser fulvescens Rafinesque, 1817

Identification
The lake sturgeon is most like the shortnose sturgeon. Both have a single row of scales in front of the anal fin, wide mouths, and dark-colored viscera. Lake sturgeons, however, have the dorsal and lateral scutes about the same color as the background whereas the shortnose sturgeon has plates that are considerably lighter than the background.

Description
Body elongate, pentagonal in cross section, its profiles equally curved. Tail strongly heterocercal with the lower lobe prominent but much smaller than the upper. Dorsal fin far back, its margin deeply concave. Anal fin origin below middle of the dorsal fin base. Anal pointed, its middle rays longest. Pelvics well in front of the dorsal origin, the tips of their rays reaching to the level of the dorsal origin. Pelvics bluntly pointed. Pectorals low, pointed, their bases horizontal. Barbels four, the longer outer pair reaching back to the upper lip. Posterior nostril large; gill covers not reaching the shoulder girdle. Gill membranes broadly joined to the isthmus. Ventral scutes disappear in old specimens. Counts and proportional measurements are given in Table 2.

Color: Large individuals are a uniform dull gray. Younger specimens are brownish gray with the lower parts of the head and body clear green.

Juveniles: Individuals less than 300 mm long are light brown with dark blotches as follows: one pair on top of the anterior part of the snout, a pair of large spots behind the pectoral fin and between the dorsal and lateral shields, a pair of smaller spots at the same level below the dorsal fin. In addition, there are prominent black spots on the top of the head, the back and sides of the body, and the underside of the caudal peduncle. The blotches start to fade when the fish are 1 to 2 feet long and are no longer visible by the time the fish reach 40 inches total length.

Size: The lake sturgeon reaches a larger size than the shortnose. The record is a 310-pound female that was 7 feet 11 inches long.

Habitat
Lake sturgeons are confined to larger lakes and rivers where they show a marked preference for clean sand, gravel, or rock bottom where food is abundant and they tend to avoid muddy areas. They move into smaller streams during their spawning runs.

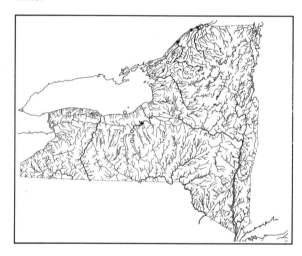

Distribution
The lake sturgeon occurs throughout most of the Northeast from Hudson Bay and its tributaries and far up the Churchill and Saskatchewan Rivers, south through the Mississippi and its larger tributaries to Arkansas and northern Alabama. In the Missouri River, it reaches eastern Nebraska. It also occurs in the Coosa River in Alabama. It ranges through the Great Lakes and down the St. Lawrence to Cape Brule.

In New York, it has been recorded from Lakes Ontario and Champlain and it was once an important commercial fish in Lake Erie. It has been taken in Cayuga Lake and in the Seneca and Cayuga Canal near Montezuma.

Life History
The lake sturgeon spawns in the spring not long after the ice disappears and sometimes even under the ice. Spawning takes place along windswept shores of rock islands or the fish move into streams to spawn in the rapids. They do not build nests but the eggs are demersal and adhesive and dark gray in color. The eggs range from 2.7 to 3.5 mm in diameter. There is a considerable variation in the

number of eggs produced but it has been estimated that a 200-pound female could lay three million eggs. At 60 to 64 F, they hatch in 5 to 8 days and by the end of the first summer the young will be 4 to 5 inches long. Cuerrier and Roussow noted that when the fish become mature their growth slows at intervals of 4 to 7 years. These periods of slow growth are reflected as bands on the otoliths and seem to indicate spawning intervals. Spawning can sometimes be delayed for 2 or 3 years after maturity. In one population, females first spawned at 14 to 23 years and males at 9 to 13 years and again 6 to 7 years later at age 15 to 19. In other populations, maturity may be delayed until the fish are 20 to 23 years old. Some individuals may reach 150 years of age.

In Lake Winnebago (Wisconsin), there is an active sport fishery for sturgeon. Four hundred to more than 3,000 are taken through the ice in February. They range from 30 to 79 inches total length. Pectoral fin rays showed good annual marks and 911 fish ranged from 1 to 82 years old. In this population, the young reached 7.1 to 8.2 inches during their first year, and at age XXXII ranged from 56 to 76 inches. Males and females grew at the same rate but the females lived longer; 96 percent of the fish more than 60 inches long were females.

Food and Feeding
The lake sturgeon feeds on insects, especially mayflies and midge larvae, and other benthic invertebrates including snails, clams, amphipods, and crayfish. It also feeds on fish and is sometimes taken on hook and line using young gizzard shad or killifish for bait.

Notes
Sturgeon were formerly so abundant that they were considered trash fish. Their long generation time and slow growth, however, has led to their decline throughout most of their range. A few populations still support viable sport fisheries in the United States and some commercial fishing in Canada. Sport fishermen occasionally take them on hook and line but most are taken by spearing through the ice.

Not only is the meat valuable but the eggs can be used to make caviar and the skin is sometimes tanned for leather. In the past, when they were abundant, they were processed for oil and the swim bladders were used for isinglass, a high-quality gelatin used for pottery cement, waterproofing, and for clarifying wine and beer.

In New York, there is presently no open season on lake sturgeons.

References
Vladykov and Beaulieu, 1946 (characters). Vladykov and Greeley, 1963 (general account). Harkness and Dymond, 1961 (life history). Trautman, 1957 (status in Ohio). Scott and Crossman, 1973 (general). Priegel and Wirth, 1971, 1975, 1978 (Wisconsin). Priegel, 1973 (Wisconsin). Probst and Cooper, 1954 (age and growth). Cuerrier and Roussow, 1957 (age and growth, St. Lawrence).

Names

The species name *fulvescens* is the Latin word for reddish yellow, tawny.

Acipenser fulvescens Rafinesque, 1817: 288 Great Lakes

Acipenser rubicundus LeSueur, 1818A: 388-390 Bean, 1903: 66-67 Great Lakes, New York

Acipenser megalaspis Dumeril, 1870: 135-137 Lake Champlain

Acipenser buffalo Dumeril, 1867: 175-176 Lake Erie at Buffalo

ATLANTIC STURGEON

Acipenser oxyrhynchus
Mitchill, 1815

Identification

The Atlantic sturgeon is the easiest to recognize of the three species of sturgeons in New York State. Its snout is long and narrow, and its mouth opening, measured inside the lips, is usually less than 60 percent of the distance between the eyes, although there is enough variation so that this character is not always reliable and should not be used by itself. There are double rows of plates behind the dorsal and anal fins in most individuals and there are two to six plates on the lower side between the anal fin base and the lateral row of plates. The viscera are not pigmented although the developing eggs are black.

Description

Body tapering, pentagonal in cross section. Dorsal profile more curved. Caudal fin strongly heterocercal with the lower lobe weakly developed. Anal origin under middle of the dorsal fin base. Anal fin bluntly pointed. Pelvic base in front of dorsal origin by about its own length. Pectoral fin retrogressive, low and horizontal. Gill membranes broadly united to the isthmus. Head and pectoral girdle with sculptured bones. Snout pointed, center of eye over tip of lower jaw. Four barbels in a transverse row across the underside of the snout. Forty percent of the snout length is ahead of the upper lip. Counts and measurements are given in Table 2.

Color: Back and upper sides brownish gray to blue black, shading to white on the belly. Dorsal shields each with the keel and point white, contrasting with the dark ground color and appearing as a row of white spots. Lateral shields similar but not as contrasting because the background of the sides is paler. Anterior edges of the pectoral, pelvic, and lower lobe of caudal white, anal entirely white. Iris golden. Intestinal tract and peritoneum white.

Size: This is the largest of our sturgeons and individuals weighing more than 200 pounds are some-times taken in the Hudson River. Specimens 14 feet long and weighing 800 pounds have been recorded and there are reports of even larger ones.

Habitat

This is an anadromous species that enters rivers and estuaries to spawn. In New York it is confined to the deeper parts of the Hudson. It is sometimes seen basking at the surface and occasionally makes spectacular jumps.

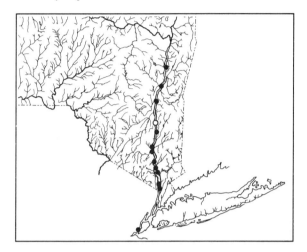

Distribution

The typical subspecies ranges from Labrador to northern Florida. In the Gulf of Mexico it is replaced by a similar form, *Acipenser oxyrhynchus desotoi* Vladykov, which ranges from St. Petersburg to the Mississippi Delta.

In New York, it is sometimes found as far upriver as Albany but young-of-the-year are rarely taken north of Hudson.

Life History

Atlantic sturgeon are anadromous. Mature males move into the river before the females, appearing in April when the water temperature reaches 42 to 43 F. Males returning for the first time are at least 12 years old and 3.5 to 6.5 feet long. They remain in the river until October or November. The females mature for the first time at 18 or 19 years when they weigh about 72 pounds. They reach the Haverstraw area about the middle of May when the water temperature is about 55 F.

Spawning apparently takes place in fresh water, just above the salt front, and the spawning fish may move upstream with the salt front as the season progresses. Spawning continues, possibly intermittently, from May to early July. During the spawning season the fish move upstream and downstream with the tide. Females seem to move continuously but the males may stop for a few hours or a day or so. Females move out of the river after spawning but the males may remain until cold weather. Larval and juvenile Atlantic sturgeons have been found from Kingston south (one 150-mm juvenile at New Baltimore) from May to July. When the water temperature drops below about 68 F the immature sturgeons begin to move downstream to congregate in deeper water in the channel between Cornwall-on-Hudson and the George Washington Bridge in water more than 25 feet deep. They remain there until the temperatures begin to rise in the spring and begin to move upstream, reaching Port Ewen by mid-April. As the river continues to warm, they move downstream again to seek temperatures of 24.2 to 24.7 C and salinities of 4.2 to 4.3 ppt.

Between their second and sixth fall, most of the immature sturgeons migrate out to sea. Tagged Hudson River sturgeons have been recaptured from Nantucket to North Carolina.

Eggs of the Atlantic sturgeon are 2.5 to 2.6 mm in diameter. An 8-foot 9-inch female weighing 352 pounds contained 3,755,745 eggs.

Food and Feeding

The Atlantic sturgeon is a bottom feeder and its stomach frequently contains mud along with worms, amphipods, isopods, midge larvae, and small fishes, particularly sand lance. In fresh waters its diet is dominated by insects, amphipods, and oligochaetes. During the spawning runs the adults eat very little.

Notes

Tag-and-recapture studies indicate that the Atlantic sturgeon spends more time in the sea and spawns farther downstream than the shortnose. Although it is still a commercial species, population levels are quite low.

This species is closely related to the European Acipenser sturio and Berg (1962) considers them to be the same species.

References

Vladykov and Greeley, 1963 (general account). Smith et al., 1980 (induced spawning). Dovel, 1978 (life history). Vladykov and Beaulieu, 1946 (Quebec). Gorham and McAllister, 1974 (identification). Brundage and Meadow, 1982 (Delaware River). Ryder, 1888 (development).

Names

The name *oxyrhynchus* is from the Greek *oxys*, sharp, and *rhynchos*, snout.

Several authors have treated the Atlantic sturgeon as a subspecies of the European *Acipenser sturio*.

Acipenser oxyrhynchus Mitchill, 1815: 462 New York

Acipenser sturio oxyrhynchus, Greeley, 1935: 88-89 Lower Hudson

Acipenser leconti Dumeril, 1867: 177-178 New York

Acipenser mitchilli Dumeril, 1870: 116-118 New York

Acipenser macrorhinus Dumeril, 1870: 137-139 New York

Acipenser milberti Dumeril, 1870: 137-139 New York

(*A. mitchilli, A. macrorhinus,* and *A. milberti* of Dumeril, 1867, are nomina nuda.)

TABLE 2
AVERAGE PROPORTIONAL MEASUREMENTS AND COUNTS OF STURGEONS
(Acipenser)

All proportions are expressed in percentage of standard length.

	brevirostrum	*fulvescens*	*oxyrhynchus*
ST. LENGTH (mm)	605	333	1252
TOTAL LENGTH	118.5	120.7	122.2
PREDORSAL	80.8	81.9	79.6
PREANAL	83.1	86.4	84.0
PREPELVIC	66.3	72.3	67.4
BODY DEPTH	16.9	15.6	13.7
BODY WIDTH	13.8	11.4	13.2
C.PED. DEPTH	4.5	3.9	4.1
HEAD LENGTH	22.7	30.9	23.3
SNOUT	7.4	16.5	8.7
EYE	2.0	2.7	1.5
MOUTH WIDTH	7.3	7.5	5.0
SNOUT TO UPPER LIP	6.1	18.3	8.5
N (sample size)	6	1	10
GILL RAKERS	13-25	25-40	16-27
SCUTES:			
DORSAL	9-13	9-17	7-11
LATERAL	25-32	29-42	24-35
VENTRAL	8-9	7-12	8-11

PADDLEFISHES
POLYODONTIDAE

Paddlefishes are specialized relatives of the sturgeons, and together with the true sturgeons, family Acipenseridae, they constitute the order Acipenseriformes. All Acipenseriformes have a largely cartilaginous skeleton, a heterocercal tail, barbels on the underside of the snout, and fine horny fin rays that are not clearly separated by membrane. While the sturgeons have bony plates on the head and body, the paddlefish has smooth skin. This and the structure of its fins led early naturalists to describe it as an aberrant kind of shark. There are only two kinds of paddlefishes in the world: *Polyodon spathula* in North America and *Psephurus gladius* in China.

Polyodon

The North American genus *Polyodon* contains only one living species. It has embedded scales on the caudal peduncle and several hundred long slender gill rakers. The gill cover is expanded into a long pointed flap. The Chinese *Psephurus* differs in having a protractile mouth and fewer and shorter gill rakers.

PADDLEFISH

Polyodon spathula
(Walbaum, 1792)

Identification
The paddlefish is unlike any other fish in North America. Its most conspicuous feature is its snout which is prolonged into a spatulate rostrum that is fully one-fifth to one-third the length of the body. Additional features are its huge mouth, fine and extremely long numerous gill rakers, smooth, scaleless skin, strongly heterocercal tail and fine horny fin rays. In the structure of its fins, it resembles the sturgeons to which it is closely related. Also like the sturgeons, the paddlefish has tiny barbels on the underside of the rostrum, well ahead of the mouth.

Description
Body short, robust, slab sided and tapering. Profiles symmetrical. Dorsal fin far back, deltoid, its margin falcate, its base three-fourths its height. Inclinator muscles extend onto vertical fin rays for about one-fourth their length. Caudal fin heterocercal but its lower lobe is well developed so that it is nearly symmetrically forked. Fulcra prominent. Anal similar to dorsal, its origin under middle of dorsal base. Pelvic insertion anterior to dorsal fin, end of pelvic base under dorsal fin origin. Pelvic retrogressive, its margin straight. Pectorals low, retrogressive with straight margins. Gill membranes joined but free from the isthmus. Flap of operculum long, extending to distal third of depressed pectoral rays. Rostrum bluntly rounded, widest one-third of its length behind its tip, supported by interlocking stellate bones. Eye far forward, over tip of upper lip. Mouth very large. Barbels tiny, thread-like and placed well ahead of the tip of the upper lip. No scales.

Counts are omitted here because both fin rays and gill rakers are difficult to count and would serve no purpose for so distinctive a fish.

Color: Bluish gray above shading to silvery white below, no conspicuous marks.

Size: The largest paddlefish on record weighed 184 pounds.

Habitat
The paddlefish is a large-water species that is confined to lakes and low-gradient sections of larger rivers.

Distribution

Paddlefish range from central Montana and Wisconsin east through the Missouri, Mississippi and Ohio Rivers to western Pennsylvania and south to the gulf coast where it lives from the San Jacinto River in Texas to the Mobile drainage in Alabama. Trautman noted that there were only two reliable records of the paddlefish in Lake Erie although fishermen reported taking them occasionally up to about 1903. Although Greene suggested that it might have entered Lake Erie through canals, Trautman considered the evidence to favor an early invasion through glacial outlets, especially the Wabash-Maumee connection.

It appears that the construction of dams that bar the adults from the spawning grounds has been responsible for its disappearance from much of its former range. From what is known of its breeding habits it appears that the paddlefish is well adapted for living in areas subject to annual flooding and that, in fact, such flooding may be essential to their successful reproduction. This would explain why the species now occurs at far fewer localities than it did previously.

The only New York record is that of Evermann and Goldsborough which was based on a photograph by R. W. Benjamin of Mayville of a 6-foot 2-inch paddlefish caught in Chautauqua Lake about 1890. That fish weighed 123.5 pounds.

Since there have been no further records, we can safely assume that the species is now extinct in New York.

The Chautauqua Lake specimen was probably 40 to 60 years old which means that it must have been hatched well before the Civil War. One can visualize this fish, and perhaps some shortnose gar, moving into Chautauqua Lake on its spawning run during unusual flood conditions in the Ohio Valley and western New York.

Life History

Purkett reported on the spawning and early development of the paddlefish in the Osage River of Missouri. Spawning occurred when the water temperature reached 50 F and the water level rose several feet. Some years when there were several periods of high water the paddlefish spawned more than once. Spawning was observed 20-22 April over a gravel bar where the water level had risen about 9 feet and the temperature was 61 F. Although the spawning procedure could not be seen because of the turbid water, occasionally a single fish would surface and vigorously agitate the water with its caudal fin. Purkett interpreted this to be the end of a spawning rush that took place mostly below the surface. Eggs and newly hatched larvae were collected in the area on 24 April after the water level had dropped about 7 feet.

Newly fertilized eggs had an adhesive surface. At 75 to 80 F, they hatched in 7 days or less. The yolk was absorbed in 2 or 3 days, after which they swam constantly. Purkett suggested that this motion served to prevent their becoming stranded by receding waters although many were so stranded.

Eggs that did not become stuck to the bottom often did not hatch. Although the embryos struggled vigorously, they were not successful at freeing themselves from the eggs.

Fertilized eggs averaged 3 mm in diameter (range 2.7 to 4.0). Newly hatched larvae were 8 to 9.5 mm long. The first development of the rostrum started when they were about 3 weeks old and a 29-day-old fish 47.9 mm long had a rostrum measuring 7.8 mm.

Robinson found ovarian egg counts ranged from 83,397 in a 47.7-inch female 15 years old to 269,043 in a 53.8-inch female 24 years old.

Robinson also found that paddlefish could be aged by year marks in the dentary bones. Growth was rapid during the first 3 years when the fish attained lengths of 8.2, 16.0 and 22.7 inches respectively. Considerable variation in growth rate has been reported. In Montana, fish from the Missouri River averaged 67.9 inches at age XXV and those from another area averaged only 51 inches at the same age.

Food and Feeding

Paddlefishes feed on plankton by swimming around with their mouths open and filtering large volumes of water through their gill rakers. The rostrum is apparently sensitive to contact and serves to detect dense swarms of plankton. Because they often live in turbid waters and have small eyes, they rely heavily on the sense of touch to navigate and locate their food. In some areas, paddlefish feed almost exclusively on crustacean zooplankton; in other areas insects dominate, and occasionally fish remains have been reported from their stomachs. Rosen and Hales found no selectivity in feeding, that is, the proportions of organisms in the stomachs were about the same as the proportions in the water column. Filter feeding develops when the fish reach 225 to 250 mm eye to fork length. Below this size, the gill rakers are undeveloped and the fish feed selectively on larger zooplankton and insects.

References

Coker, 1923 (general account). Adams, 1942 (age). Thompson, 1933 (juveniles). Allen, 1911 (breeding season and young). Kofoid, 1900 (natural history). Barbour, 1911 (juveniles). Evermann and Goldsborough, 1902 (Chautauqua Lake). Stockard, 1907 (natural history). Greene, 1935 (distribution). Trautman, 1957 (Lake Erie records). Robinson, 1967 (life history). Purkett, 1961 (life history). Dingerkus and Howell, 1976 (tetraploidy). Carlson and Bonislawsky, 1981 (fisheries). Houser and Bross, 1959 (growth and reproduction). Vasetskiy, 1971 (systematics). Rosen and Hales, 1981 (feeding).

Notes

In parts of the southern United States, this species is abundant enough to be a sport and commercial fish.

Names

Because of its color and smooth scaleless skin, the paddlefish is frequently called spoonbill cat. The name *Polyodon* comes from the Greek *poly,* many and *odont,* tooth. This is an obvious misnomer for the paddlefish has no teeth, and the author was probably referring to the gill rakers. *Spathula* is a Latin diminutive for a blade or spatula.

    Squalus spathula Walbaum, 1792: 522 (no locality)

    Proceros vittatus Rafinesque, 1820a: 87? Lake Ontario

GARS

LEPISOSTEIDAE

Gars, like the sturgeons, are quite primitive bony fishes. They are slightly more advanced than the sturgeons but more primitive than the bowfins and higher bony fishes. The most recent study of their relationships, Wiley (1976) classifies them in the division Ginglymodi which is equivalent to the Halecostomi, the group that encompasses the bowfins and the teleosts.

Seven of the eight living species are confined to North and Central America, the other lives in Cuba. Fossil gars are known from Europe, Africa, India, and North America.

Gars can be recognized by their arrow-shaped bodies, armor-like ganoid scales and elongated jaws with needle-sharp teeth. The caudal fin is abbreviate heterocercal with an upper lobe that disappears as the fish grows. Gars are the only modern fishes with opistocoelous vertebrae, that is, the centrum is convex in front and concave behind. In other fishes, the vertebral centra are concave on both faces. The fin rays are bony and separated by membrane. Gars have chambered (alveolar) swim bladders with which they can breathe atmospheric air. They also have two pairs of pseudobranchiae. They inhabit weedy shallow areas and are efficient predators but there is no convincing evidence that they are detrimental to other species.

KEY TO THE SPECIES OF GARS THAT MAY OCCUR OR HAVE OCCURRED IN NEW YORK

A. Snout extremely long and slender, its width at the nostrils less than the diameter of the eye. Postocular head length (measured from the back of the eye socket to the edge of the opercular membrane) 4.5 times or more in the total head length (tip of snout to edge of opercular membrane). Fishes less than 4 inches long have shorter snouts, the postocular head length 3.0 to 3.5 times in head length.
Lepisosteus osseus   **Longnose gar, p. 53**

A'. Snout shorter and wider, its width at nostrils 1 to 1.5 times the eye diameter. Postocular head length contained 2.9 to 3.5 times in total head length.

B. Scales smaller, 59 to 63 in lateral series from the shoulder bone to the base of the caudal fin, including the small scales at the base of the tail. Fifty to fifty-five scales in the midline between the back of the head and the dorsal fin origin. Dark spots, if present, restricted to the posterior one-third of the body. No spots on head.
Lepisosteus platostomus   **Shortnose gar, p. 55**

B'. Scales larger, 54 to 58 in lateral series. Predorsal scales 46 to 49. Dark spots all over body including top and bottom of the head.
Lepisosteus oculatus   **Spotted gar, p. 54**

Note: Shortnose gars were reported from Chautauqua Lake in the last century. Presumably, they were shortnose gar which occur in the Ohio River into which Chautauqua Lake drains, but there is a slight chance that they were spotted gar which occurs in Lake Erie, a different drainage but only 7 miles away. There are no recent records of either species from New York State.

Lepisosteus

All of the living gars are similar in appearance but Wiley has separated them into two genera, *Lepisosteus* and *Atractosteus,* on the basis of osteological features, including the fact that members of the genus *Lepisosteus* have small pear-shaped gill rakers and lack large fangs on the dermopalatine bones. All of the New York species belong to this genus. *Atractosteus,* in contrast, has blade-like gill rakers, fangs on the dermopalatines and several other skeletal specializations. The large alligator gar, a Central American species, and the Cuban gar belong to *Atractosteus.* Most ichthyologists agree that these characters indicate that the two groups of species have evolved separately but feel that they should be treated as subgenera rather than genera.

LONGNOSE GAR

Lepisosteus osseus
(Linnaeus, 1758)

Identification
It would be difficult to confuse a gar with any other fish in New York State. Its flinty-hard, diamond-shaped scales, its arrow-shaped body with the dorsal and anal fins far back, and long, slender tooth-studded jaws combine to make the gar totally unique. The needlefish that live in the Lower Hudson have similarly elongated jaws but they have small, thin scales and their fins are longer with a different shape. The longnose differs from other gars that might possibly be encountered here, the spotted gar in Lake Erie and the shortnose gar in the Allegheny River, in having a much narrower and longer snout.

Description
Body elongate, nearly terete anteriorly and slightly compressed posteriorly. Profiles symmetrical. Dorsal fin short and rather high, its margin angled with its third ray the longest. Caudal base asymmetrical the upper part longer. Upper margin of caudal fin with sharp fulcra. Small specimens (up to 245 mm) have a remnant of the upper lobe of the heterocercal tail present as a separate dorsal lobe. Caudal bluntly pointed to rounded. Anal fin a little anterior to the dorsal, the end of its base below the dorsal origin. Anal fin shape similar to that of the dorsal fin. Pelvic fins near the middle of the body, retrogressive, with convex margins. Pectorals low, their bases oblique, retrogressive with convex margins. Gill membranes broadly united across the isthmus. Eyes lateral. Jaws greatly elongated, about 2.8

times the postorbital head length, the upper overhanging the lower. Teeth caniniform, sharp. Counts and proportional measurements are give in Table 3.

Color: Olive brown to gray above, shading to white on the belly. The fins and upper parts of the body are variously spotted in the younger fish but these spots disappear with age.

Juveniles: Young less than 3 inches long have a broad brown or black stripe along the midside and a middorsal stripe of the same color. The belly is chocolate brown in these small young with a white stripe between the dark belly and the midlateral stripe. As the fish get older, the belly color fades in the midline first, leaving ventrolateral stripes that disappear later.

Size: Agassiz (1878) reported a female of 4 feet 1.5 inches in total length from Black Lake. Males tend to be somewhat smaller than females. Most specimens seen are less than 3 feet long. The maximum length is about 4.9 feet.

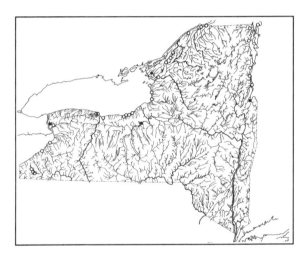

Habitat
The longnose gar occurs in lakes and the sluggish parts of larger streams, usually associated with emergent vegetation in bays. It can tolerate some current and sometimes feeds where there is considerable stream flow. Along the Atlantic coast, it occasionally enters brackish water.

Distribution
The longnose is the widest-ranging member of the family. It occurs from southern Minnesota east to southern Lake Huron, Georgian Bay to the St. Lawrence River and Lake Champlain south through the Mississippi basin to the gulf coast from the Pecos and Rio Grande Rivers and east to peninsular Florida. On the Atlantic coast, it ranges north to southern Pennsylvania and the Pennsylvania-New Jersey section of the Delaware River.

Early reports indicated that it was rather common in Cayuga Lake but the Survey found it uncommon there although they obtained specimens from the Seneca and Oswego Rivers. It was reported by the Survey from Black Lake, where it is now uncommon, the Oswegatchie River, and the Lower Raquette. It is still common in eastern Lake Ontario, Lake Champlain, and the Niagara River. The only

Allegheny records are from Chautauqua Lake. It is not known from the Hudson or the New York sections of the Delaware and Susquehanna systems.

Life History

Gars spawn in the spring and early summer, sometimes moving into the lower reaches of streams. Apparently, no nest is built despite some claims that they hollow out a crude nest depression.

The spawning of longnose gars in Black Lake was described by S. W. Garman (who else?) in Agassiz, 1878. On May 18th that year, small groups of gars moved in to spawn near headlands where granite outcrops extended into the lake. The bottom consisted of small pieces of rock 3 to 8 inches in diameter. According to Garman, single males seemed to scout the area and if they were not frightened away, small spawning groups would move into the area. A group usually consisted of one female with one to four males pressed against her sides. The groups moved back and forth several times before spawning. Garman described the spawning as "lashing and splashing the water in all directions with their convulsive movements." After a few seconds of spawning, the fish resumed swimming slowly over the area, then continued to alternate slow swimming with vigorous spawning episodes. Cold rainy weather interrupted the spawning for nearly 2 weeks, then even larger numbers of gars moved into the shallows. This time, the fish were less selective and spawned all along the shore.

The dark green eggs are rather large, 2.1 to 3.2 mm in diameter, and adhesive. Ovarian egg counts of 4,272 to 77,156 have been reported, averaging 27,830 or 3,002 eggs per pound of body weight of the female. Newly hatched young have an adhesive organ at the tip of the snout with which they adhere to vegetation above the bottom until the yolk is used up. Gars grow rapidly, reaching as much as 20.2 inches during their first year. Females grow faster and live longer; few males survive past 10 or 11 years but females may live to age XXII.

Food and Feeding

Gars are strictly carnivorous and most of their diet is fish with some crayfish and occasional insects. Other studies have shown that gars take frogs, and once a shrew, but they rarely, if ever, feed on carrion. Young gars in the aquarium glide up to their prey, then seize it with a quick sideways sweep of the jaws. Once they have secured their quarry they work it back to the mouth in stages and finally swallow it, usually headfirst.

Notes

Gar eggs are extremely toxic to humans. The flesh is considered second-rate but gars provide some sport for bow-and-arrow fishermen. Only a direct hit will penetrate the hard scales. Although they are effective and voracious predators, they are opportunistic feeders and have little deleterious effect on populations of native fishes.

References

Wiley, 1976 (classification). Suttkus, 1963 (systematics). Agassiz, 1878 (life history). Netsch and Witt, 1962 (life history). Wilder, 1877 (popular account). Mark, (1890). Lagler and Hubbs, 1940 (food). Pearson et al., 1979 (feeding). Lagler, Obrecht, and Harry, 1942 (management). Trembley, 1930 (Lake Champlain). Echelle and Riggs, 1972 (life history).

Names

The generic name of the gars is sometimes spelled *Lepidosteus,* which is grammatically correct but inadmissible under the International Code of Zoological Nomenclature. The species name, *osseus* is Latin for bony.

Esox osseus Linnaeus, 1758: 313 (after Artedi and Catesby)

Lepisosteus bison DeKay, 1842: 271 Buffalo

SPOTTED GAR

Lepisosteus oculatus (Winchell, 1864) (Hypothetical in New York)

Identification

The spotted gar is a short-nosed species most easily recognized by its color pattern which includes spots on the anterior part of the body and the underside of the head as well as on the vertical fins and the rear of the body. It is apt to be confused only with the shortnose gar which has smaller scales as well as fewer spots.

Description

General shape as in the shortnose gar. Counts and proportional measurements are given in Table 3.

Color: This is truly a spotted species with the ground color olive to nearly black above, shading to pale ventrally. Belly sometimes whitish or yellow. All fins, the upper parts of the body and all parts of the head with distinct round dark spots and blotches. Young with a broad dark brown middorsal stripe (wider than that of the longnose gar) and a midlateral stripe that is nearly straight along its upper margin. Belly chocolate brown in the smallest young. These dark areas begin to break up when the fish reaches 100 to 150 mm in total length.

Habitat

Spotted gars are characteristically found in areas where there is a profusion of aquatic plants, in the quieter parts of lakes and large streams. Along the gulf coast they occasionally enter brackish water.

Distribution

The spotted gar has not yet been reported from New York State but it does occur in western Lake Erie, where it is quite scarce. It ranges from Lake Erie south to the gulf coast and along the coast from Texas to western Florida.

Life History

Apparently, little is known of the life history of this species.

Food and Feeding

Suttkus reported that in the Lake Pontchartrain area it feeds on fishes and crustaceans, particularly the blue crab, *Callinectes sapidus*.

Notes

This is one of several fish species that occurs in the western part of Lake Erie but does not reach New York waters. Any gars suspected of being this species should be saved for positive identification and preservation as voucher specimens.

References

Wiley, 1976 (relationships). Suttkus, 1963 (general account, systematics).

Names

Oculatus comes from the Latin *oculus, eye,* and *atus,* which means provided with. Apparently, this is a reference to the spotted color pattern.

The trivial name *productus* was widely used for this species.

Lepidosteus oculatus Winchell, 1864: 183 Huron River, Michigan

Cylindrosteus productus Cope, 1865b: 86 San Antonio, Texas

SHORTNOSE GAR

Lepisosteus platostomus
Rafinesque, 1820

Identification

The shortnose gar is easily separated from the longnose by its shorter and broader snout. It differs from the spotted gar, which is also a short-nosed species, in scale counts and in color pattern, being mostly unspotted except for the vertical fins and sometimes the posterior part of the body. The spotted gar has definite spots all over including the underside of its head.

Description

Similar to longnose gar. Body elongate and slender, subterete anteriorly, compressed posteriorly. Dorsal and anal fins far back, asymmetrically rounded, the dorsal inserted behind the anal. Caudal abbreviate heterocercal with a dorsal lobe in young. Pelvic fins abdominal, pectorals low on the sides. Jaws moderately elongated, premaxillary with two rows of teeth in the outer row. Counts and proportional measurements are given in Table 3.

Color: Olive to brownish or grayish tan above, shading to yellowish tan below. Vertical fins and sometimes the posterior part of the body with sparse dark spots; head and anterior body unmarked.

Juveniles: The young have middorsal and midlateral stripes like those of juvenile longnose gars.

Size: The shortnose gar seldom exceeds 3 feet in length.

Habitat

Unlike other gars that occasionally venture into brackish water, the shortnose gar is strictly a freshwater species. It occurs in lakes and the slower-moving parts of rivers where it is less dependent on rooted vegetation than the spotted gar.

Distribution

The shortnose gar ranges throughout the Mississippi River and its larger tributaries including the Missouri River as far west as Montana, the eastern parts of South Dakota, Nebraska, Kansas, and Oklahoma. It reaches the gulf drainages of western Louisiana. Its only Great Lakes records are from Wisconsin. It occurs in the Tennessee River and ranges up the Ohio River as far as south-central Ohio. The only New York records are from Chautauqua Lake where it is said to have been abundant prior to 1898. No New York specimens are known.

Life History

Apparently, the life history of this species has not been studied.

Food and Feeding

Like the other gars, the shortnose is primarily a predator on fishes with occasional crayfish and insects.

Notes

In the late 1890s, gars were considered such a nuisance in Chautauqua Lake that a control program was initiated. Large numbers of gars were netted and killed and some of them were said to be shortnose gars. However, no specimens were saved and there is no way of checking their identity or even confirming that they were present. The nearest records for the shortnose are a long way from New York but it is possible that they existed as a disjunct population.

References
Wiley, 1976 (systematics). Suttkus, 1963 (systematics). Trautman, 1981 (Ohio). Potter, 1926 (ecology). Priegel, 1963 (dispersal).

Names
The species name is from the Greek *platys* or *platos,* meaning flat or broad, and *stoma,* mouth.

Lepisosteus platostomus Rafinesque, 1820a: 72 Ohio River

Lepisosteus platostomus, Evermann and Goldsborough, 1901: 171 Chautauqua Lake

BOWFINS
AMIIDAE

The bowfin is a uniquely North American fish that is a remnant of a primitive group of bony fishes called the Halecomorphi which is equal in rank to the modern teleosts.

Bowfins are rugged predators. They are able to breathe atmospheric air using their alveolar swim bladders and can therefore thrive in situations where there is little oxygen in the water. Their large size and complex breeding habits make them especially interesting fishes. Although they are sometimes considered a competitor of more desirable species, there is little evidence that they are detrimental to healthy populations of other species.

Amia

This is the only living genus in the family Amiidae and it contains only one species. At present, it lives only in eastern North America but fossils are known from North America, Europe and Asia.

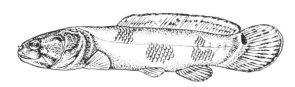

BOWFIN

Amia calva Linnaeus, 1766

Identification
The bowfin is such a distinctive fish that no other New York species is likely to be confused with it. Its most striking features are its heavy, almost cylindrical body, its slightly asymmetrical rounded tail, its long wavy dorsal fin, its bullet-shaped head with heavy plates on the cheeks, and a thick broad gular plate between the lower jaws. Overall, the bowfin has the delicacy and grace of a stick of firewood.

Juvenile bowfins might be confused with mudminnows which have a similar shape, but mudminnows have short dorsal fins and no gular plates.

Description
Body very robust, nearly terete, elongate and only slightly tapering. Dorsal fin originating over the tips of the pectoral fins and ending at the base of the caudal. Dorsal gently arched. Caudal abbreviate heterocercal, slightly asymmetrical with its ventral base in advance of the dorsal. Caudal fin asymmetrically rounded. Anal fin short, pointed, its origin under middle of dorsal base. Pelvic origin under anterior third of the dorsal base. Pelvic and pectoral fins paddle-shaped. Pectoral fins low, their bases nearly vertical. Eye small, mouth large, maxillary reaching to below posterior margin of eye. Anterior nostril tubular, gular plate large and broad. Large, superficial bones covering the space between the eye and the preopercle. Branchiostegal rays flat, gill membranes broadly overlapping. Scales large and rectangular with longitudinal rather than circular ridges. Counts and measurements are given in Table 3.

Color: The overall color is greenish, sometimes with a brownish or gray cast shading to white or yellow ventrally. There is a dark spot, larger than the eye and varying in shape, at the upper base of the tail. In breeding males, this spot is nearly black and ringed with bright yellow. In females, it is less prominent and sometimes diffuse without a prominent yellow ring. Breeding males have bright green lower fins. Juveniles are black until they reach 30 or 40 mm. Then they look like miniature, but somewhat more colorful, adults. The scales of the upper parts of the body often have darker margins which form zig-zag lines at the overlap between scale rows. The sides of the head have three dark lines bordered by pale stripes above and below. One of these stripes runs from the tip of the snout through the eye to the upper angle of the gill opening, another from the lower part of the orbit to the edge of the preopercle and the third from the tip of the lower jaw to the posterior end of the mandible. The upper end of the gill membrane has a black margin preceded by a lighter stripe that is reddish dorsally and shades to yellow ventrally.

The dorsal fin has a black margin and a central black stripe and the anal is similar. The caudal margin is black and there are two irregular transverse dusky bands. The leading edges of the pelvic fins are black. The paired fins are yellow with an orange tinge, peppered with small melanophores. Large females are often dull countershaded gray without conspicuous markings.

Size: Females tend to be larger. The IGFA all-tackle record is 21 pounds 8 ounces from South

Carolina. Trautman gives the maximum length in Ohio as 686 mm for males and 787 mm for females.

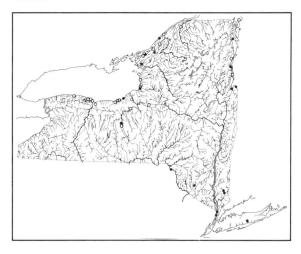

Habitat
The bowfin is generally a big-water fish. It lives in the slow parts of larger streams and in lakes where there is abundant vegetation and clear or moderately turbid water. It is very common in the southern part of the United States and less so in the North.

Distribution
Bowfins occur throughout the lowlands of eastern United States from Wisconsin to Texas, along the gulf coast to the tip of peninsular Florida and north on the Atlantic coast to southern Pennsylvania. Apparently, its occurrence in southern New York and Connecticut is due to introductions. It ranges through the Great Lakes, down the St. Lawrence and into Lake Champlain and the lower reaches of the St. Lawrence tributaries. It is known from the Seneca River and from Cayuga, Neatahwanta and Oneida Lakes where it is less common than formerly. It is scarce in the eastern part of Lake Erie. Greeley considered the record from Chautauqua Lake doubtful, possibly based on the burbot, *Lota lota*. The specimen from North Canaan Lake near Patchogue, Long Island taken in 1972 was probably the result of an introduction. There are a few records from the Delaware including a sight record from the Basher Kill.

Life History
Bowfins are spring spawners, nesting from May to early June when the temperatures are 60 to 66 F.

The classical study of the life history of the bowfin was made by Jacob Reighard who studied its courtship and nesting near Ann Arbor, Michigan. Reighard camped along the river where the bowfins were nesting and observed more than 177 nests although "no one group was followed completely through the entire cycle."

Males build saucer-shaped nests from 30 to 90 cm in diameter in water that is 30 to 60 cm deep. The central part of the depression is usually 10 to 20 cm deep. The nests are usually in quiet bays or inlets with abundant water plants and have shelter such as stumps or fallen logs. The nests are constructed by biting and tearing out leaves and stems of rooted vegetation. The nests are usually in deep mats of fibrous roots, so the lining of the nest is spongy. Most of the nest building is carried on at night. The nests are usually finished 24 to 36 hours before spawning begins, and guarded by the male. Spawning usually occurs at night, although Reighard thought that the stage of development of the eggs in some nests suggested that they had been fertilized during the day. A female ready to spawn enters the nest and the male circles her, gently biting at her snout and side. If the female is not quite ready to spawn she turns her head toward the male's tail. When she is ready, she allows the male to align his body with hers with his snout behind her pectoral fin. Spawning occurs with violent vibrations of both partners and may continue intermittently for several hours. In general, the mating is promiscuous, the male spawning with two or more females and each female laying eggs in the nests of more than one male.

The male continues to guard the nest after spawning, leaving it only for short periods. The newly laid eggs are whitish and soon darken. Hatching occurs after 8 to 10 days. The newly hatched young are colorless at first and about 7 mm long. They remain in the nest for about 9 days, at first attached to the wall of the nest by a special adhesive organ on the snout. By the time they are 12 mm long, the upper body has become very dark greenish black with a slightly lighter abdomen and the adhesive organ is no longer functional. At this stage, they form swarms and begin to feed, although some yolk still remains. They also come to the surface for air.

After they leave the nest, the young are still guarded by the male. Reighard believed they follow a scent trail left by the male as he works his way through the dense aquatic vegetation. If the male is alarmed and flees, the young remain together in a tight swarm. Later on, the male splashes when he flees and the young scatter to seek shelter in the weeds. At 30 to 32 mm, the bright colors begin to develop. The schools break up when the young are about 100 mm long.

Food and Feeding
Bowfins are predaceous and feed on nearly anything that moves from insects to crayfish, leeches, oligochaetes, frogs, and fish. Large bowfins are predominantly piscivorous but the exact diet depends on the availability of prey.

Notes
The swim bladder of the bowfin is lung-like and bowfins can breathe by gulping air at the surface, thus they can survive in waters with very low oxygen content. There is a pair of distinctive appendages on the side of the isthmus inside the gill cover. The exact homology of these structures is in doubt.

Because it is a predator, the bowfin has been considered a threat to game fishes but this is not a problem in New York. Bowfins are tenacious fighters and provide good sport on light tackle. They also provide good sport for spear fishermen and bow-and-arrow fishermen. Their soft flesh requires special treatment to make it palatable.

As the only representative of an ancient group of fishes, it deserves to be better known.

References
Dean, 1896 (larval development). Reighard, 1902; 1904 (life history). Dence, 1933 (stranded individual). Lagler and Hubbs, 1940 (food habits). Boreske, 1974 (fossil history). Trautman, 1981 (Ohio). Greeley, 1938 (Allegheny watershed).

Names
Rafinesque "corrected" the generic name to *Amiatus* because he thought that *Amia* was too short to go with the trivial name.   *Amia* is from Greek and means "a kind of tunny which ascends rivers." *Calvus* means smooth or bald.

Amia calva Linnaeus, 1766: 500 Charleston, South Carolina

Amia occidentalis DeKay, 1842: 269-270 Michigan, St. Marys River

Amia calva Reed and Wright, 1909: 393 Cayuga basin

Amia thompsoni Dumeril, 1870: 419-420 Lake Champlain

TABLE 3
AVERAGE PROPORTIONAL MEASUREMENTS AND COUNTS OF GARS AND BOWFIN
(*Lepisosteus* and *Amia*)

All proportions are expressed in percentage of standard length.

| | *Lepisosteus* | | | *Amia* |
	osseus	platostomus	oculatus	calva
ST. LENGTH (mm)	130.4	240.7	135.1	56.6
TOTAL LENGTH	120.0	121.4	124.5	121.7
FORK LENGTH	120.3	121.4	124.5	121.7
PREDORSAL LENGTH	86.6	89.5	86.3	45.7
PREANAL LENGTH	83.1	86.7	84.5	72.1
PREPELVIC LENGTH	60.7	58.0	62.4	56.0
DORSAL BASE	5.1	6.5	6.0	53.9
ANAL BASE	6.4	6.8	6.0	10.1
BODY DEPTH	7.2	10.8	9.9	19.2
BODY WIDTH	5.9	11.7	9.0	16.5
C.PED. DEPTH	4.0	6.8	6.1	13.0
PECTORAL ALT.	5.1	6.7	7.1	15.6
HEAD LENGTH	38.7	33.1	37.3	35.5
SNOUT	26.9	27.4	23.3	8.8
EYE	3.1	3.3	3.2	5.2
MOUTH LENGTH	26.2	18.3	21.8	14.4
INTERORB	4.7	6.1	5.6	10.4
N (sample size)	3	5	3	4
COUNTS:				
DORSAL RAYS	7-8	11-12	6-9	46-58
ANAL RAYS	9	12-13	7-9	9-10
PECTORAL RAYS	10-13	9-10	9-13	16-18
PELVIC RAYS	6	6	6	7-9
GILL RAKERS	20-28	17-21	15-24	17-19
VERTEBRAE	61-62	59-62	56	85-90
SCALES:				
ABOVE L. L.	6-11	10-12	10	7-9
LATERAL LINE	60-62	59-60	53-59	64-68
BELOW L. L.	5-9	10-11	9	10-12

FRESHWATER EELS

ANGUILLIDAE

The family Anguillidae includes about 15 species in temperate waters of the Atlantic and Indo-Pacific regions. They are the best known of the catadromous species, that is, they spawn in the sea but move into fresh water for most of their life. Finally, they travel back to the ocean to spawn and die.

True eels have jaws and pectoral fins but no pelvic fins. Other eel-shaped fishes in our area are the lampreys which have no jaws and no paired fins and the cusk-eel which has filamentous pelvic fins on the underside of the head.

Worldwide, there are about 21 families of eels but only 1 species occurs in local freshwaters and 1 other occasionally strays into the Lower Hudson.

In addition to their distinctive shape and the lack of pelvic fins, all eels have a distinctive larval stage called a leptocephalus. This is an elongate, compressed, transparent stage with very large anteriorly directed teeth. During part of the leptocephalus stage the gut is not functional. The leptocephalus larvae of the American eels make their way to the coastal waters where they transform into tiny eels, shrinking as they develop their final form and coloration.

Anguilla

As it is presently understood, the family Anguillidae contains only the single genus.

AMERICAN EEL

Anguilla rostrata (Lesueur, 1817)

Identification

Although there are several fishes that have eel-like shapes, the chances of confusing eels which have jaws, single gill slits, and no pelvic fins, with the eel-like members of other families is remote. Only the conger eel, which is sometimes found in the Lower Hudson, is apt to be a problem. In the conger eel,

the dorsal fin begins over the ends of the pectoral fins but in the American eel it is well behind the pectorals. The conger also lacks scales but those of the American eel are so small and deeply embedded in the skin that they are easily overlooked. The conger also reaches a much larger size than the American eels, which seldom exceed a length of 3.5 feet.

Description

Body elongate and very flexible. Dorsal and anal fins joined to the tailfin forming a continuous fin around the end of the body. No pelvic fins. Pectoral fins large, slightly asymmetrically rounded. Mouth terminal, lower jaw projecting. Gill slits short, nearly vertical, slightly longer than the width of the base of the pectoral fin. Anterior nostril at the end of a short tube, posterior nostril in front of the eye. Scales tiny, embedded, well separated in a herringbone pattern. Counts and proportional measurements are given in Table 4.

Color: Juvenile eels are grayish green dorsally, shading to white below. As they grow they become yellowish with the upper parts gray to yellow brown, the lower parts clear dark yellow. In some individuals, the demarcation is quite sharp, others are merely countershaded. Just before they begin their spawning migration, the color changes to bronze or silvery and the eye enlarges.

Size: The New York angling record is 5 pounds 13 ounces from Kiamesha Lake, taken May 1981 by LeGrande Ahlers.

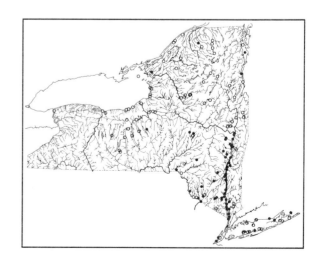

Habitat

Because of their migratory habits, eels are found from the ocean to small headwater creeks far inland. They are adept at working their way upstream over or around low falls and dams and sometimes travel overland, presumably on rainy nights. Surprisingly large individuals are sometimes found in tiny creeks while the smallest juveniles occur along the coast. Eels spend much of their time buried in gravel or mud bottoms or under rocks.

Distribution

American eels are generally distributed in Atlantic coastal rivers from Greenland south to the Gulf of Mexico, the West Indies and South America to about 5 degrees north latitude in Brazil. They move up larger rivers as far inland as Minnesota, South Dakota and Lake Superior. Trautman (1957) reviewed its occurrence in Ohio where it was first recorded in the middle 1800s after the Welland Canal was opened. Eels were stocked in southern Michigan and Ohio in the late 1800s but these would not have established breeding populations.

In New York, the eel is extremely abundant in the Lower Hudson and it also occurs inland in the St. Lawrence, the Great Lakes and their tributary streams, including the Finger Lakes. George (1981a) has noted that its abundance apparently has declined in the Adirondacks, presumably because dams now limit its access to upland areas. It is confined to the lower and middle sections of the Genesee River and does not occur above the falls at Portageville. It is rare in Lake Erie and the Susquehanna system but it is abundant in the Delaware system. The only collections made by the Survey in the Chemung drainage were from Waneta Lake although there were reports from the Chemung River, Cayuta Creek and a few other locations. It is present in Otsego and Canadarago Lakes in the Susquehanna drainage.

Life History

The American eel is our only catadromous species. Its spawning place seems to be the Sargasso Sea, a vaguely defined area southeast of Bermuda in the North Atlantic gyre. No adult eels have ever been found there but this is the area where the smallest larvae are found. Larval eels are called leptocephali and they are compressed, ribbon-shaped, and transparent except for their eyes. The leptocephali are poor swimmers but they manage to drift and swim to land in about a year. As they reach shore they transform into miniature eels called elvers or glass eels, shrinking in the process and developing their pigment over a period of a couple of weeks. As a rule, males stay near the coast in salt or brackish waters while the females move upstream. After spending several years in streams or along the coast, the maturing eels transform into silver eels with larger eyes and silvery coloration and move out to sea. Eels leaving the Chesapeake Bay are usually somewhat more mature than those leaving from Canada.

One hundred sixty-nine eels from New Jersey were aged by counting rings on their otoliths. The oldest appeared to be about 19 years old. The smallest eels were less than 20 cm long and appeared to be 3 or 4 years old. The average stay in fresh water was about 10 years.

Food and Feeding

Ogden (1970) studied the food habits of eels in eight New Jersey streams. The size of the food items increased with the size of the eels; the smallest had fed on insects and the larger eels had eaten fish and crustaceans. Mayflies, megalopterans, and caddisflies were the dominant foods in eels less than 40 cm long and the tessellated darter was the most frequently consumed fish with the white sucker being taken in smaller numbers. Some carrion was eaten but eels rarely fed on mollusks. In smaller, headwater streams, terrestrial insects such as lepidopterans were taken in large numbers.

Notes

The European eel is very similar to the American eel except that it has more vertebrae (110 to 119 in European eels; 103 to 111 in American eels). It has been suggested that this difference could be due to the greater length of the larval period for European eels and that the two are really a single species but the presence of both kinds in Canadian waters seems to refute this.

Eels are of considerable commercial importance in New York and are also frequently caught by anglers. At present, eels from the Hudson River cannot be sold commercially because of high PCB levels and fishermen complain that they are a serious predator on shad caught in their nets. Adams and Hankinson reviewed eel fishing in the Oneida River and mentioned that around the turn of the century eel skins were in demand for binding books and lining whips. Some oil from eels was used for harness grease and medicinal purposes.

Albino eels have been reported by several authors and on 17 November 1979 Tom Lake saw an albino near the Brooklyn Bridge foraging in water shallow enough so that he could see its pink eyes. He estimated it to be 24 to 30 inches long.

References

Fish, 1927 (embryology). Adams and Hankinson, 1928 (Oneida Lake). Ogden, 1970 (age and food). Hurley, 1972 (Lake Ontario). Wenner and Musick, 1974 (fecundity); 1975 (food and abundance). Brinley and Bowen, 1935 (feeding habits). Wenner, 1973 (distribution). Schmidt, 1922; 1925 (breeding grounds). Gunning and Shoop, 1962 (movements). Facey and LaBar, 1981 (Lake Champlain). LaBar and Facey, 1983 (movements in Lake Champlain).

Names

Anguilla is the Latin word for eel (from *anguis*, snake). *Rostrata* is from the Latin *rostrum*, snout.

Muraena rostrata Lesueur, 1817a: 81   Cayuga Lake

Anguilla anguilla rostrata Meek, 1889: 312 Cayuga Lake

Muraena macrocephala Lesueur, 1817a: 81 Saratoga, New York

Muraena bostoniensis Lesueur, 1817a: 81 Boston

Anguilla bostoniensis Greeley, 1928: 175 Erie-Niagara watershed

Anguilla chrysypa Rafinesque, 1817b: 120 Lake George, Lake Champlain, and the Hudson River

Anguilla chrysypa Bean, 1903: 170-174 New York

Anguilla blephura Rafinesque, 1817b: 120 Long Island

Anguilla tenuirostris DeKay, 1842: 310 New York

Anguilla punctatissima Kaup, 1856: 44 Niagara River

TABLE 4
AVERAGE PROPORTIONAL MEASUREMENTS AND COUNTS OF AMERICAN EEL AND MOONEYE *(Anguilla* and *Hiodon)*

All proportions are expressed in percentage of standard length.

	Anguilla rostrata	*Hiodon tergisus*
ST. LENGTH (mm)	113.3	207.7
TOTAL LENGTH	101.5	123.3
FORK LENGTH	—	111.9
PREDORSAL	33.2	64.1
PREANAL	43.0	67.3
PREPELVIC	—	46.7
DORSAL BASE	66.6	12.0
ANAL BASE	57.0	22.2
BODY DEPTH	6.2	32.1
BODY WIDTH	3.8	11.3
C.PED. DEPTH	1.0	10.6
PECTORAL ALT.	2.8	21.1
HEAD LENGTH	13.1	24.4
SNOUT	2.1	4.9
EYE	1.2	7.8
MOUTH LENGTH	3.3	10.5
INTERORB	1.5	6.9
N (sample size)	5	3
COUNTS:		
DORSAL RAYS	244	10-14
ANAL RAYS	206	26-29
PECTORAL RAYS	14-17	12-15
PELVIC RAYS	—	6-7
GILL RAKERS	Rudimentary	12-17
VERTEBRAE	105-110	57-58
SCALES:		
ABOVE L.L.	Embedded,	6
LATERAL LINE	not	52-57
BELOW L. L.	counted	ca.10

HERRINGS

CLUPEIDAE

The herrings are rather primitive bony fishes. They lack fin spines, they have abdominal pelvic fins, and the maxillary bones form part of the margin of the upper jaw. As a group they are silvery schooling fishes without a lateral line and with a specialized head canal system. They also have modified scales along the ventral edge of the body.

The New York fauna includes freshwater and anadromous herrings as well as strictly marine species that come into the Hudson Estuary as strays. Four species of river shads, all belonging to the genus *Alosa* are anadromous in the Hudson River. While on their spawning runs, they are sought by fishermen and the largest species, the American shad, is the object of a colorful traditional commercial fishery. American shad and hickory shad are also caught by sport fishermen.

The gizzard shad is a freshwater species that occasionally occurs in the estuarine part of the Hudson. It is distinctive in having the last ray of the dorsal fin extended as a filament and a bulbous snout overhanging the mouth. Gizzard shads have sometimes been placed in a separate family, the Dorosomatidae, but at present they are considered to be a subfamily of the Clupeidae. The name refers to a muscular modification of the stomach resembling the gizzard of a chicken.

KEY TO THE SPECIES OF HERRINGS IN NEW YORK *

A. Belly rounded and without obvious scutes although there is a single scute in the skin around the bases of the pelvic fins. Dorsal fin far forward, its base entirely in front of the pelvic fins.
Etrumeus teres   **Round herring, p. 396**

A'. Edge of belly sharp and keel-like with pointed scutes that form a saw edge. Dorsal fin base at least partly over the pelvic fins.

B. Midline of back, in front of the dorsal fin, not covered with scales. Last ray of dorsal fin prolonged into a filament. Mouth subterminal. Wall of stomach thick and gizzard-like. Juveniles with a large, conspicuous dark spot behind the upper end of the gill cover. (This spot fades in the adults.)
Dorosoma cepedianum   **Gizzard shad, p. 71**

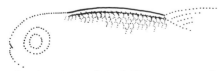

Predorsal region of gizzard shad. There are no scales in the midline.

Elongate last dorsal ray of the gizzard shad.

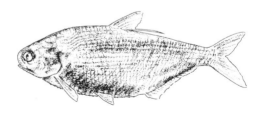

Gizzard shad, *Dorosoma cepedianum*

B'. Predorsal midline covered with scales. Last dorsal ray not elongated. Mouth terminal. Stomach not gizzard-like.

C. Middle of back, in front of dorsal fin, with a double row of modified scales. Head very large, its length about one-third the standard length. Exposed margins of scales scalloped.
Brevoortia tyrannus

                    Atlantic menhaden, p. 394

* Including marine species from the Lower Hudson River.

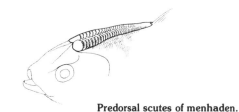

Predorsal scutes of menhaden.

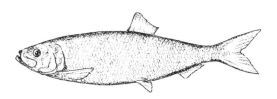

Atlantic menhaden, *Brevoortia tyrannus*

C'. Predorsal midline without modified scales. Head much shorter than one-third the standard length. Scales on sides with entire margins.

D. Origin of dorsal fin about equidistant between tip of snout and middle of caudal base. Body slender, belly scutes rather weak.
Clupea harengus   **Atlantic herring, p. 395**

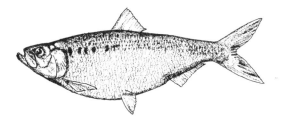

D'. Origin of dorsal fin much nearer tip of snout than middle of caudal base. Body deeper. Belly scutes prominent.

E. Lower jaw extending well beyond the tip of the upper jaw, forming a continuation of the dorsal profile when the mouth is closed. Gill rakers 19 to 21 on the lower limb of the first arch.
Alosa mediocris   **Hickory shad, p. 66**

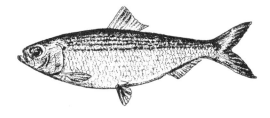

E'. Lower jaw only slightly longer than the upper, not forming a continuation of the dorsal profile. Gill rakers 26 or more on the lower limb of the first arch.

F. Lower jaw slender, its upper margin only slightly curved. Cheek deeper than long. Maxillary extending to below the posterior edge of the pupil of the eye. Gill rakers increase with age, 26 to 31 in fish

less than 8 inches long and as many as 76 in larger fish. May reach a length of 2 feet or more.
Alosa sapidissima   **American shad, p. 69**

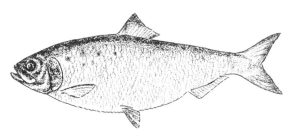

F'. Lower jaw wide, its upper margin strongly curved. Cheek longer than deep. Upper jaw short, reaching only to below middle of the eye.

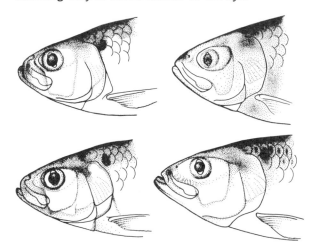

Cheek patches of *Alosa* **species. Above: (left)** *A. mediocris,* **(right)** *A. sapidissima.* **Bottom: (left)** *A. pseudoharengus,* **(right)** *A. aestivalis.*

G. Diameter of eye about equal to length of snout in fish more than 6 inches long. Peritoneum black. Gill rakers usually 44 to 50 (41 to 52) on lower limb of first arch.
Alosa aestivalis   **Blueback herring, p. 65**

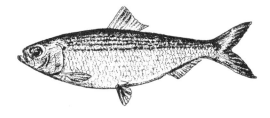

G'. Diameter of eye greater than length of snout in adults. Peritoneum pale with dusky spots. Gill rakers 38 to 44 (usually 39 to 41) on lower limb of first arch.
Alosa pseudoharengus   **Alewife, p. 67**

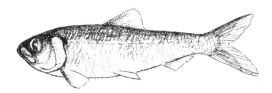

Alosa

Members of the genus *Alosa* are called shads, or, sometimes, river herrings. Most of the species are anadromous which means they move into fresh water to spawn, usually in the spring. In addition, the alewife, *Alosa pseudoharengus*, has landlocked populations that do not need to return to salt water. Like most other herrings, they are compressed silvery fishes with serrate bellies. Their dorsal fins originate closer to the tip of the snout than to the base of the tail. They have no epibranchial organs, no gizzard-like stomach, and normal scales on the predorsal area. The edges of the scales are smooth or slightly crenulate but not definitely serrate.

Four species are found in New York. A fifth species, *Alosa chrysochloris*, the skipjack herring, was listed in the Erie-Niagara Survey report because it was believed to have been in Lake Erie. However, Trautman (1981) has since reviewed the records and concluded that there is no evidence of its ever having occurred there.

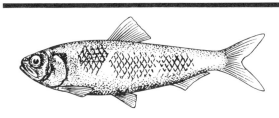

BLUEBACK HERRING

Alosa aestivalis (Mitchill, 1814)

Identification
The blueback herring is a rather slender species that most closely resembles the alewife, from which it differs in having a smaller eye and a black, rather than gray or silvery, lining of the body cavity. In life the dorsal surface of the body is blue rather than greenish. These two species can also be distinguished by the shape of the otolith which is more tapered and strongly hooked in the blueback, L-shaped in the alewife.

The American shad and hickory shad, which reach larger sizes, have the silvery patch below the eye deeper than long, whereas in the blueback and alewife it is longer than deep. The river shads have distinctive gill raker counts with only a slight overlap between the blueback and alewife. The American shad has a very high count (59 to 73 in the adult); the hickory shad has a low count (18 to 23). Bluebacks have 41 to 51; alewives have 38 to 43.

Description
Body rather elongate, conspicuously so in adults. Dorsal profile less curved than the ventral. Body deepest in front of the dorsal origin with the dorsal outline nearly straight from the deepest point to the caudal peduncle. Ventral profile more or less curved throughout. Dorsal short, its margin straight, its corners sharp. Caudal deeply forked, its lobes pointed.

Anal longer than the dorsal, its margin straight. Pelvic insertion below middle of dorsal base. Pelvics retrogressive. Pelvic axillary process well developed, about half longest ray. Pectoral fins low and horizontal. Gill membranes separate and free from the isthmus. Adipose eyelid well developed with lenticular opening. Nostrils single. Counts and proportional measurements are given in Table 5. The number of gill rakers increases with growth: at 3 to 6 inches there are 28 to 36, at 9 to 11 inches there are 38 to 44, and larger fish may have up to 52.

Color: Blue gray above, shading to silvery white on the sides and belly. There is a conspicuous dark spot behind the upper end of the gill opening and rows of small dark spots forming lines on the upper sides of the body. Neither the spot nor the lines are conspicuous in juveniles. The tip of the snout and lower jaw dusky. Peritoneum very dark.

Size: The maximum is about 15 inches total length but most of the blueback adults in the Hudson are 10 to 12 inches.

Habitat
The blueback herring is an anadromous species that moves into larger streams to spawn. It apparently travels farther inland than the other river herrings. In the Connecticut River they are stopped by dams 109 km upstream and in the Hudson they travel through locks and up the Mohawk at least to the mouth of Schoharie Creek.

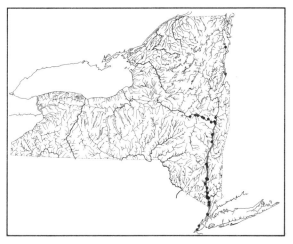

Distribution
The blueback ranges from the St. Johns River in northern Florida to Cape Breton and Prince Edward Island. The Mohawk River and Lake Champlain are its farthest inland localities. The recent discovery of young-of-the-year bluebacks in Lake Champlain suggest that it can negotiate canal locks with little difficulty. At present, landlocked populations have not been documented and there are no nearby records in the St. Lawrence to suggest that they reached Lake Champlain via a northern route.

Life History
The most complete study of the life history was

made in the Connecticut River by Loesch and Lund. Spawning runs began in mid- or late April and continued to mid-August. The fish gathered at the mouth of the river in early April when the water temperature was 4 to 9 degrees C. By the time the river temperature reached 14 C, the fish were on the spawning grounds in tributary streams and beginning to spawn. The fish move up in distinct runs separated by periods when few or no fish were in the streams. Loesch and Lund identified eleven runs betwen 31 May and 15 August and there may have been some additional, earlier runs. High temperatures (27 C) inhibited the runs.

Bluebacks appeared to prefer swift water and hard bottom for spawning while the alewives tended to select eddies and pools rather than the main streams. Spawning fish were age III through VII. Spawning groups usually consisted of one female pursued by several males. Spawning started with the group swimming in a circle with the males nudging the vent region of the female with their snouts. Swimming speed increased until the group made a dive toward the bottom, faced into the current and quivered as the sex products were released. The eggs were adhesive at first, but as they water-hardened they lost their stickiness and if the current was sufficiently strong the eggs were dispersed through the water column. Incubation required 50 hours at 72 F.

Estimates of ova production ranged from 45,800 to 349,700. Age group VI females produced the greatest number of eggs.

Food and Feeding
Like other herrings, the blueback is a planktivore whose diet consists mostly of copepods, pelagic shrimp larvae, and larval fishes.

Notes
Because the blueback is easy to confuse with the alewife, the species may be more widespread than the present records indicate.

References
Hildebrand, 1963b (general summary). Loesch and Lund, 1977 (life history). Plosila and LaBar, 1981 (presence in Lake Champlain). Cianci, 1969 (larval development). Chambers, Musick, and Davis, 1976 (larval characters). Donnermuth and Reed, 1980 (food). Marcy, 1969 (age). MacLellan, Newsome, and Dill, 1981 (recognition).

Names
The name *aestivalis* is from the Latin word for summer, *aest.*

   Clupea aestivalis Mitchill, 1815: 456 New York
   Pomolobus aestivalis Greeley, 1937: 91 Hudson River
   Alosa cyanonoton Storer, 1848: 242 Massachusetts
   Pomolobus cyanonoton Bean, 1903: 202-203 New York

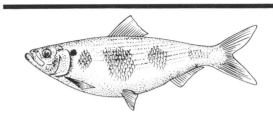

HICKORY SHAD
Alosa mediocris (Mitchill, 1815)
Identification
The hickory shad is a typical river herring with the silvery sides, ventral scutes and forward dorsal fin of that group. It is distinctive in its genus because it has fewer than 21 gill rakers on the lower limb of the first arch whereas all of the other river herrings have more than 25. The shape of the hickory shad is also distinctive. Its back is only slightly curved and the lower jaw projects forward so that its tip forms a continuation of the dorsal outline of the head and snout. The hickory shad resembles the shad in having the silvery patch below the eye deeper than long. It is intermediate in size between the large American shad and the smaller alewife and blueback herring.

Description
Body elongate and compressed, wedge-shaped in cross section. Ventral profile much more arched than the dorsal, which is only gently arched. Dorsal fin short and well forward, about equidistant between the tip of the snout and the tip of the last anal fin ray. Caudal deeply forked with pointed lobes. Anal fin low and longer than the dorsal. Pelvic insertion below the dorsal origin. Pelvic retrogressive with well-developed axillary process. Pectorals low and horizontal, retrogressive. Gill membranes separate and free from the isthmus. Lower jaw projecting. Counts and proportional measurements are given in Table 5. The number of gill rakers on the lower limb of the first arch apparently does not increase with age.

Color: Hildebrand (1963c) described Chesapeake specimens as follows: "Grayish green above, shading somewhat gradually into the iridescent silver of the sides. Nape green, side of head brassy. Tip of lower jaw dusky. Dorsal and caudal fins dusky. Anal and pelvic plain, translucent. Pectoral slightly dusky. Narrow dark lines along rows of scales on upper part; missing on specimens less than 150 mm standard length, or so, and most distinct in large examples that have lost their scales. A dark spot on the shoulder; several obscure dark spots behind it, but missing in some examples. Peritoneum pale, but with scattered dusky puncticulations." A fresh specimen from the Hudson River caught by Tom Lake agrees very well with this description except that the greenish color of the back was not obvious, presumably having been lost upon the death of the fish.

Size: The maximum size is about 24 inches, the usual size 12 to 15 inches.

Habitat
The hickory shad is a coastal marine species that occasionally moves into fresh water.

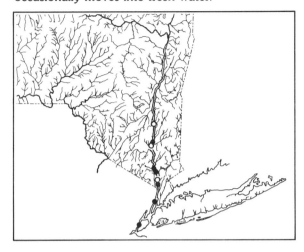

Distribution
The hickory shad ranges from the St. Johns River in Florida north to the Bay of Fundy. It is apparently fairly common in New England and from the Chesapeake to North Carolina but is scarce in between. In New York, there are a few records from the Hudson but it is not common there although fishermen like Mr. Lake occasionally get them and it may be more plentiful than the records indicate.

Life History
The life history of this species is almost unknown. Hildebrand expressed doubt that it is anadromous, pointing out that spawning fish had never been taken in fresh or salt water. Jones, Martin, and Hardy state that it runs into tidal freshwater in the Chesapeake Bay in spring (April to early June), with a smaller run in the fall, and returns to the sea soon after spawning. There is some evidence that spawning takes place between dusk and midnight. The egg range from 0.98 to 1.65 mm in diameter and hatch in 48 to 70 hours at 16 to 31 C. The eggs are demersal and weakly adhesive but their buoyancy is near neutral and they are easily carried by current and turbulent waters.

Food and Feeding
Hickory shad feed on small fish of various kinds, fish eggs and miscellaneous invertebrates including squids and crabs and other crustaceans.

Notes
The hickory shad is quite similar to the skipjack herring, *Alosa chrysochloris,* which occurs in the Mississippi watershed.

References
Hildebrand, 1963c (general summary, systematics). Mansueti, 1962 (development and life history). Jones, Martin, and Hardy, 1978 (life history summary).

Names
The name *mediocris* is Latin for ordinary, moderate, not important.

Clupea mediocris Mitchill, 1815: 450 New York

Clupea mattowacca Mitchill, 1815: 451 New York
  Clupea parvula Mitchill, 1815: 452 New York
  Clupea pusilla Mitchill, 1815: 452 New York
  Clupea viridescens DeKay, 1842: 252 New York
  Pomolobus mediocris Bean, 1903: 197-198 New York
  Alosa mattowacca DeKay, 1842: 260 New York

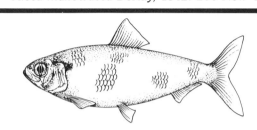

ALEWIFE

Alosa pseudoharengus (Wilson, 1811?)

Identification
Alewives are rather ordinary river herrings, lacking the modified predorsal scales and huge head of the menhaden and the undershot mouth and dorsal fin filament of the gizzard shad. Alewives are most like the blueback herring and differ from the American and hickory shads in the long, rather than deep, silvery area under the eye, smaller size, and gill raker counts which are intermediate between the very low count of the hickory shad and the very high count of the American shad. Alewives and blueback herring can be distinguished on the basis of the color of the lining of the body cavity (gray or silver in the alewife, black in the blueback), eye size (larger in the alewife) and body shape (the alewife has a deeper body). Still the resemblance is close, and some older records may be unreliable.

Description
Body compressed and wedge-shaped in cross section, thickest above midside. Ventral profile curved more than the dorsal. Body deepest ahead of the dorsal tapering to the narrow part of the caudal peduncle. Dorsal origin midway between tip of snout and end of anal base. Dorsal fin subdeltoid, its margin straight, its corners sharp. Caudal deeply forked, its shortest rays less than half the longest. Anal fin long and low, trapezoid, its margin straight. Pelvic insertion below the dorsal origin or slightly behind. Pelvics retrogressive with straight margin. Pelvic axillary process about half the longest pelvic ray. Pectorals low, retrogressive, their bases horizontal. Gill membranes separate and free from the isthmus. Counts and proportional measurements are given in Table 5.

Color: Hildebrand describes the color of alewives as "Grayish green above, sides silvery. Rows of scales on the upper part of the sides sometimes with more or less definite lines in adults. A small dark spot at shoulder, often missing in specimens less than 100 mm long. Fins all plain, slightly yellowish to green in life. Peritoneum generally pale or silvery, often with dark puncticulations and sometimes quite dusky."

Size: Sea-run alewives reach a maximum length of 15 inches, but landlocked alewives are smaller, the average size being closer to 5 inches.

Habitat

The alewife is a schooling fish that lives in open water most of the year and moves into the shallows in spring to spawn. In lakes, they tend to move inshore during the night and retreat to deeper water during the day. In Lake Ontario, Graham found them moving to water 150 to 300 feet deep in September to December and remaining there until the next March.

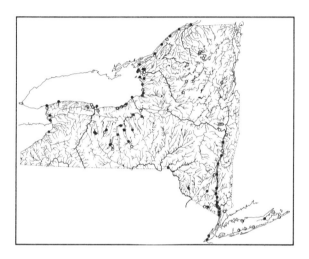

Distribution

The alewife ranges from Labrador and Newfoundland south to southern South Carolina. It has been introduced into the upper Great Lakes and inland lakes in Rhode Island, Maine, New Hampshire, Virginia, Ontario, and New York. Its presence in Lake Ontario may also be due to introduction. In New York, the species is known from the Hudson River, Oneida Lake, some ponds in the Genesee drainage, the Finger Lakes, some inland lakes in the Delaware drainage, and in the Adirondacks where it has been stocked as forage for trout. Alewives are conspicuous by their absence in Lake Champlain itself although they occur in lakes and ponds in the Champlain drainage.

Its presence in the upper Great Lakes was reviewed by Miller who concluded that the alewife is probably native to Lake Ontario but that there is no conclusive evidence that this is so. The earliest specimens and records were collected in 1873 and it has periodically become abundant there since 1890. It was first taken in Lake Erie in 1931, in Lake Huron in 1933, in Lake Michigan in 1949, and in Lake Superior in 1955. Whether it was native to Lake Ontario or not, the evidence seems to indicate that the alewife reached the upper Great Lakes via the Welland Canal.

Smith presented evidence that the alewife reached Lake Ontario through the Erie Canal some time between 1819 (when critical sections of the canal first opened) and 1873 when it was first reported. Other authors have suggested that alewives were accidentally planted with shad fry that were stocked in the lake beginning about 1870, but Smith pointed out that not enough were stocked to account for their abundance in 1873, since fish stocked as juveniles in 1870 would not have spawned until after the first reports from the lake. Large numbers of alewives were reported from Cayuga and Seneca Lakes in 1868. Smith also pointed out that alewives had access to Lake Ontario through the St. Lawrence but did not become abundant until the decline of large predators, including the Atlantic salmon and the lake trout, in the 1860s. He suggested that the predators were responsible for keeping the alewife out or at least in such low numbers that they were not reported.

The abundance of alewives in Lake Erie is also correlated with the decline of predators. When the alewives were first reported in 1931, there had already been a drastic decline in the walleye, blue pike, and sauger populations that had begun in the 1920s.

Life History

In the Finger Lakes, the alewives spawn in the shallow parts of the lake from late May or early June until August. In Lake Ontario, the spawning reaches its peak in late June or early July in the Bay of Quinte. The alewife runs in the Hudson in March and April. Spawning is by pairs or groups of three. Greeley described the spawning as a spiral whirling, ending at the surface. His observations were made in the Poesten Kill near Troy where the current was fast over gravel, sand, and stones. The water depth was about 2 feet and the temperature was 52 F. The eggs were broadcast over various types of bottom. Alewife eggs are semidemersal, slightly adhesive, but easily torn free and carried by currents. The egg diameter ranges from 0.80 to 1.27 mm. Hatching takes 3.7 days at 21.1 C, the actual time ranging from 15 days at 7.2 C to 2.1 days at 28.9 C. Spawning activity was most intense when the water temperatures were 10.5 to 21.6 C and ceased above 27.8 C.

In Lake Ontario, males mature at 1 year and 9.5 cm standard length and females at 2 years and 11.0 cm. Some anadromous males in Connecticut mature at 3 years and most are mature by age IV while females mature at age IV and V. Cayuga Lake females had egg counts of 2,180 to 10,011, Lake Ontario fish had 11,147 to 22,407 eggs, and searun alewives had averages of 102,800 in Maryland and 229,000 in Connecticut.

Food and Feeding

In Seneca Lake, Odell found alewives fed on a variety of plankton including their own eggs, microcrustaceans, gammarids, insects (especially midges during June), and some plant material. It is an opportunistic planktivore and often feeds on terrestrial insects blown off the shore.

Notes

The alewife has been introduced as a forage fish in many areas and trout, especially lake trout, feed voraciously on it. In the Great Lakes, it proved to be a better competitor than the plankton-eating ciscoes and as its predators became scarce the alewife populations increased, leading to the decline, and in some cases, extinction of the ciscoes.

Alewives have a tendency to die off in large numbers and become a nuisance, if not a health hazard, on Great Lakes beaches. Recently, the number of dead alewives has declined possibly because predation by introduced Pacific salmons has reduced the populations of alewives.

Dence reported finding the remains of alewives on the shores of Onondaga Lake near Syracuse. Unlike the mummified remains found on Lake Ontario beaches, the flesh of these fishes had been replaced by a chalky material and the central part of the body usually remained.

Otto et al. studied the temperature requirements of Lake Michigan alewives acclimated to ambient field temperature. In December and January when the lake temperature was 1 to 4 C, the alewives preferred water temperature of 11 or 12 C. The preferred temperature rose to 16 to 21 C during the warmest season. Young-of-the-year preferred temperatures of 19 to 20 C.

References

Hay, 1979 (popular account). Hildebrand, 1963b (general summary). Rothchild, 1962; 1966 (Cayuga Lake). Odell, 1934 (life history). Graham, 1956 (freshwater ecology). Otto et al., 1976 (temperature). Price, 1978 (otoliths). MacLellan et al., 1981 (recognition). Morsell and Norden, 1968 (food in Lake Michigan). Pritchard, 1929 (Lake Ontario). Durbin et al., 1979 (migration). Wilcox and Effler, 1981 (community ecology). Dence, 1956 (concretions in Onondaga Lake). Janssen, 1978 (feeding in dark). Brown, 1968; 1972 (dieoff and population biology). Cianci, 1969 (larval development). Chambers, Musick and Davis, 1976 (larval characters). Cooper, 1978b (eggs and young). Marcy, 1969 (age). O'Gorman, 1974 (predation by smelt). Smith, 1968, 1970 (species interactions). Greeley, 1935 (Mohawk-Hudson Survey).

Names

The name *pseudoharengus* is a bastardization from the Greek *pseudes*, false, and *harengus*, Middle Latin for herring.

Clupea pseudoharengus Wilson, 1811? (no page, probably Philadelphia)

Clupea vernalis Mitchill, 1815: 454 New York

Maletta venosa Valenciennes, 1847: 454 New York

Pomolobus pseudoharengus Bean, 1903: 199-201 New York

Pomolobus pseudoharengus lacustris Jordan, 1876: 265 Cayuga Lake

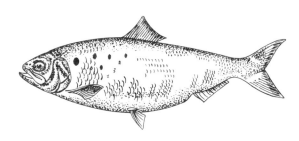

AMERICAN SHAD

Alosa sapidissima (Wilson, 1811?)

Identification

The American shad is the largest of the river herrings. It resembles the hickory shad and differs from the blueback and alewife in the shape of the silvery area behind and below the eye which is deeper than it is long. The lower jaw fits into a notch in the upper, similar to, but deeper than, the corresponding notch in the hickory shad. There is at least one, and sometimes two or three rows of dark spots behind the gill opening, more than in the other species of river herrings. Finally, adult shad have more gill rakers, 59 to 73, on the lower limb of the first arch.

Description

Body strongly compressed, deepest anterior to the dorsal fin, the ventral profile more strongly curved than the dorsal. Dorsal origin midway between the tip of the snout and the rear third of the anal fin base. Dorsal fin deltoid with straight margin and sharp corners. Caudal deeply forked with two longitudinal scaly folds on each side of its base. Anal fin low, trapezoid with sharp corners and slightly concave margin. Pelvic insertion below middle of dorsal fin base. Pelvic retrogressive with well-developed axillary process. Pectoral fins low and horizontal, retrogressive. Gill membranes separate and free from the isthmus. Mouth large and oblique, tip of lower jaw fitting into a deep notch at the tip of the upper jaw. Upper margin of the mandible gently curved without a sharp angle. Counts and proportional measurements are given in Table 5. Gill rakers increase from 26 to 43 in young to 59 to 73 in individuals more than 300 mm standard length.

Color: American shad are bright silvery on the sides shading to bluish or greenish gray above. No dark lines on scales of upper sides as in some other species but there is a definite spot behind the upper end of the gill opening and this is sometimes followed by one to three rows of spots. The lining of the body cavity is pale gray to silvery.

Size: Shad may reach more than 10 pounds in weight. The present New York State angling record is held by a 7-pound 6-ounce fish that was taken in the Delaware River 9 May 1982 by David Kobiela.

Habitat

Shad spend most of their lives at sea and only enter fresh water to spawn. Consequently, they only occur in larger streams and tributaries not blocked by dams or impassable falls. During the spring, summer, and fall, the schools are often seen near the surface but their winter habits are not known.

Distribution

The American shad is a migratory species that formerly ranged from the St. Johns River in Florida to Newfoundland and Labrador. Because of its importance as a food and game fish it was introduced to the Pacific coast in 1871. The introduction was spectacularly successful and today the shad is an important species on the west coast, where it ranges from Mexico to Kamchatka.

Greeley suggested that a landlocked population may have existed in Lake Ontario but this has not been confirmed. Old records from the mouth of the Niagara River by Dymond, Hart and Pritchard and from the eastern end of Lake Ontario may have been stocked fish (Evermann and Kendall). The shad was last reported from Lake Ontario in 1931 but it occurs in the St. Lawrence and Ottawa Rivers and stragglers may occasionally reach the lake (Radforth; Miller). Before the canals with their dams and locks were built, shad ran up the Hudson at least to the Batten Kill (Greeley and Bishop).

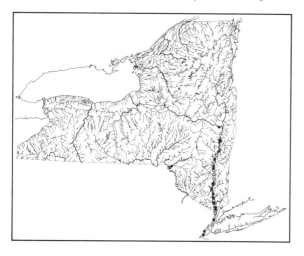

Life History

Shad spawn in the spring and begin their migrations when the water temperature reaches about 50 F. In the Hudson, the commercial fishing season opens on 15 March but the time of the run varies from year to year. In some rivers they run inland as far as 350 miles. Spawning takes place when the water temperature is 12 to 21 C. Most of the spawning is in the evening between dusk and midnight. After spawning the adults return to the sea. In the Hudson, spawning occurs from Croton north with the greatest densities from Hyde Park through the Catskill regions. Eggs have been collected as far upstream as Albany. The parents spawn in pairs and the eggs are released in the water column.

The eggs are slightly heavier than water and weakly adhesive at first. After water-hardening they are 2.5 to 5.8 mm in diameter. Incubation takes 2 days at 27 C; 17 days at 12 C. Leim found that a salinity of 7.5 ppt and temperature of 17 C was optimal for development.

Juveniles reach 1.5 to 4.5 inches their first sum-

mer and migrate to sea in the fall. Males mature at 300 to 350 mm in their fourth year and females first spawn at 400 to 430 mm in the fifth, sixth, or seventh year. Females may live as long as 10 or 11 years. Growth rates and size at maturity vary greatly with locality.

Food and Feeding

Shad are planktivores. The first year fish feed on insects and ostracods; older fish eat mysid shrimps, copepods, ostracods, amphipods, insects and fish. Apparently, the rate of feeding is reduced while they are on their spawning runs but they do feed occasionally and can be caught on artificial lures or minnows.

In salt water, mysids and copepods are dominant in the diet with other invertebrates, algae, fish eggs and fish together making up only about 10 percent of the diet.

Notes

At present, only the shad and large sturgeons can be caught commercially in the Hudson River because of chemical contamination of other species. Shad are taken in staked, anchored, or drifted gill nets. Fishing is prohibited from Friday night to Sunday morning to allow some adults to pass to the spawning grounds.

In 1980, Everett Nack and a few other fishermen began to catch shad in the river using white shad darts with red heads. The lures were cast out and allowed to sink to about 20 feet. The largest shad caught to date weighed about 5.5 pounds. There are reports of shad weighing as much as 14 pounds, and 10- to 12-pounders are taken occasionally.

References

Evermann and Kendall, 1901 (Lake Ontario). Leim, 1924 (life history). Greeley and Bishop, 1933 (Hudson River). Dymond, Hart, and Pritchard, 1929 (Lake Ontario). Hildebrand, 1963c (general summary). Jones, Martin and Hardy, 1978 (development). Cating, 1953 (age). Mansueti and Kolb, 1953 (history of the fishery). Levesque and Reed, 1972 (food). Burdick, 1954 (abundance). Greeley, 1940 (Lake Ontario). Radforth, 1944 (distribution). Miller, 1957 (distribution). Talbot, 1954 (factors in its abundance). Leggett and Whitney, 1972 (migration and temperature). Chittenden, 1973, 1974, 1976a, 1976b, (salinity tolerance and spawning grounds). Dodson and Leggett, 1973 (homing); 1974 (olfaction and vision). Gabriel et al., 1976 (fall run in Canada). Cheek, 1968 (general account). Atkinson, 1951 (feeding in fresh water). Westman et al., 1965 (Delaware River). Carscadden and Leggett, 1975 (populations). Chittenden, 1974 (Delaware River). Domermuth and Reed, 1980 (food of juveniles). Medeiros, 1974 (Hudson River fishery).

Names

The species name is from the Latin word *sapid,* meaning savory, well flavored.

Although the original description is ascribed to

Wilson, it and the description of the alewife were unsigned and there is some doubt that Wilson was the author. The date of the description is also in doubt.

Clupea sapidissima Wilson, 1811? (no page number, probably Philadelphia)

Clupea indigena Mitchill, 1815: 454 New York

Clupea alosa (non Linnaeus), Mitchill, 1814: 22 New York

Alosa praestabilis DeKay, 1842: 255-257 New York

Dorosoma

The gizzard shad belongs to a distinctive subfamily of herrings. Members of this group are characterized by having a third primary flexure in the hindgut. In the gizzard shad there are additional secondary flexures as well. The gizzard shad also has a muscular stomach but this is not unique for a similar structure occurs in the menhaden and some other herrings as well.

The subfamily Dorosomatinae consists of three tribes: Anodontostomini and Clupanodontini in the Indo-Pacific region and the Dorosomatini with five species in North America. (Nelson and Rothman, 1973). Gizzard shads are freshwater fishes although they occasionally stray into salt water.

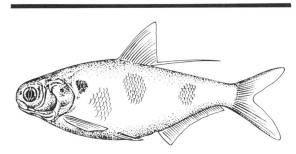

GIZZARD SHAD

Dorosoma cepedianum (Lesueur, 1818)

Identification

Not only is the gizzard the only truly freshwater herring in our state but it is also the most distinctive in appearance. Its snout is blunt and rounded and overhangs the small mouth. The last ray of the dorsal fin is drawn out into a long filament and there is a scaleless area in front of the dorsal fin. Internally, the gizzard shad has a muscular stomach like the gizzard of a fowl and it also has epibranchial organs, a pair of muscular coiled sacs behind the upper part of the gill apparatus. These serve as a food storage area. Neither the modified stomach nor the epibranchial organs are present in the river herrings.

Description

Body deep and compressed, with the ventral profile more curved than the dorsal. Dorsal fin origin closer to snout than to base of caudal. Dorsal fin deltoid, its margin concave and its last ray prolonged into a filament that is longer than the base of the dorsal fin. Caudal deeply forked. Anal fin long and low, its margin nearly straight. Pelvic fins inserted in front of the dorsal origin. Pelvics retrogressive, pelvic axillary process well developed. Pectorals low and horizontal, retrogressive. Gill membranes separate and free from the isthmus. Mouth low and slightly oblique. Adipose eyelid well developed. Predorsal midline scaleless. Ventral scutes prominent.

Counts and proportional measurements are given in Table 5. There are more than 300 gill rakers (total count) in specimens 65 mm standard length, increasing to 412 at 157 mm.

Color: Miller (1960) described the color as follows: "Silvery bluish over the back and upper sides but milky white on the abdomen and often has brassy or golden reflections from the scales. There are six to eight horizontal dark stripes along the upper sides above the level of the middle of the shoulder spot, extending from behind the head to the base of the caudal fin. The large round dark spot behind the opercle, so prominent in the young and half grown is lustrous purple. In adults, the dorsal fin is nearly uniformly dusky but darkened on its outer third; the outer two-thirds of the anal fin is dark, the basal third lighter, with melanophores sprinkled over most of the fin. The pectorals and pelvics have their outer halves darkened, paling basally. The top of the head, snout, upper jaw, and upper part of the opercle are pigmented in young and adults; the rest of the head is silvery. In young-of-the-year (up to 4.5 inches total length), the dorsal fin is sparsely but uniformly sprinkled with chromatophores; the caudal fin is similar but has more pigment cells; the anal, pectoral, and pelvic fins are almost unpigmented. A good color plate is given by Forbes and Richardson (1920, opposite p. 46)."

To this we add that the pectoral and pelvic fins of a specimen 120 mm standard length were distinctly yellow. The spot behind the head is subtriangular, straight anteriorly and bluntly pointed behind. The spot has a broad white margin along its anterior and posterior borders, which was narrower ventrally and lacking dorsally.

Size: According to Miller, gizzard shad obtains a length of 19 inches but the usual adult size is 10 to 14 inches.

Habitat

The gizzard shad is a quiet-water fish although we collected it in a rather swift stream in the Genesee drainage. It is most common in lakes and protected bays and in slow-moving rivers. It can tolerate high turbidity but it often occurs in clear water. Along the coast it ranges into brackish water with salinities up to 33 or 34 ppt and there is a Long Island record from high salinity. It is often found near the surface and the young are common around weed beds. The young school during their first year and are sometimes found well upstream in small streams.

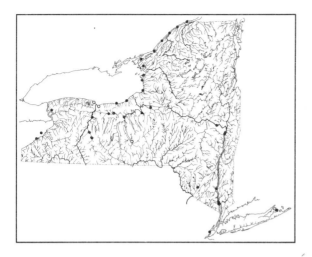

Distribution

The present distribution of the gizzard shad encompasses the Great Lakes except Lake Superior, the St. Lawrence River and south from Wisconsin and the Dakotas to Texas and New Mexico, along the gulf coast from the Rio Panuco, Mexico to central peninsular Florida. On the Atlantic coast it ranges north to Sandy Hook, New York Harbor and Long Island. Miller reviewed the distribution and noted that reports of the gizzard shad from Cape Cod and New Brunswick are unacceptable.

There is a question as to whether the gizzard shad is native to the Great Lakes or reached there through canals. After reviewing the literature, Miller concluded that the question cannot be settled but there are no records of the species in the Great Lakes before the canals were built. Miller and a few others believe that the gizzard shad is a postglacial immigrant that crossed the lowland between the Ohio and the Great Lakes tributaries through headwater swamps. Miller pointed out that gizzard shads tend to move into streams to spawn and this would make such crossings possible during spring floods when the headwaters are temporarily connected. The presence of the gizzard shad in Lake Michigan seems to be due to the Chicago River Canal and it seems to have reached Lake Ontario through the Welland or Erie Canals.

In New York, the gizzard shad occurs in the Barge Canal, the Genesee drainage, the Oswego drainage and the Mohawk and its tributaries. It occurs in the Hudson below Albany but not in Lake Champlain or the Adirondacks. Dr. Carl George has raised the interesting speculation that the Hudson River gizzard shad may be expatriates from a Mohawk population as all of the known specimens from the Lower Hudson have been subadults.

Life History

Gizzard shad spawn when the water temperature reaches 50 to 70 F, usually in April, May or June depending on location and varying from year to year. Groups of adults mill around near the surface and usually a female spawns with two males simultaneously. Spawning sometimes takes place in water as shallow as 6 to 12 inches. The eggs sink slowly and adhere to the bottom. Fertilized eggs are about 0.75 mm in diameter. Hatching occurs after 36 hours at 27 C or 95 hours at 17 C. In Lake Erie, age I females with an average standard length of 231 mm averaged 59,480 eggs and age VI females had 215,330 eggs. The highest fecundity was that of age group II which had an average standard length of 291 mm and 378,990 eggs. Young shad reach about 4 inches standard length by the end of the first summer in Indiana and Ohio. They live to age VI or VII in the North, less in the South.

Food and Feeding

Newly hatched gizzard shad feed on protozoans and entomostracans and other plankton. After a few weeks the diet changes to include phytoplankton and algae. The gizzard shad is essentially a filter feeder.

Notes

The gizzard shad is a valuable forage fish in some waters but it can overpopulate and become a nuisance if there are not enough predators to control its populations. It is of relatively little use for food but it might be a source of fish meal and oil in the larger and warmer lakes.

References

Miller, 1957 (distribution); 1960 (biology and systematics). Bodola, 1966 (life history). Nelson and Rothman, 1973 (systematics). Dew, 1973 (occurrence in Hudson River). Cooper, 1978b (eggs and young). Hickey and Lester, 1976 (Long Island record). Schmitz and Baker, 1969 (gut anatomy). George, 1983 (Lower Mohawk River).

Names

The species was named after Compte de Lacepède, a French ichthyologist who described many North American fishes.

Megalops cepediana Lesueur, 1818c:361-362 Delaware and Chesapeake Bays

Dorosoma cepedianum Greeley, 1929: 167 Erie-Niagara watershed

TABLE 5
AVERAGE PROPORTIONAL MEASUREMENTS AND COUNTS OF RIVER AND GIZZARD SHADS (*Alosa and Dorosoma*)

All proportions are expressed in percentage of standard length.

			Alosa			*Dorosoma*
	aestivalis	*mediocris*	*pseudoharengus* (Cayuga)	*pseudoharengus* (Hudson)	*sapidissima*	*cepedianum*
ST. LENGTH (mm)	85.6	213.0	104.8	230.5	385	101.4
TOTAL LENGTH	121.3	128.2	124.0	121.3	122.0	124.0
FORK LENGTH	110.8	109.0	109.3	107.9	107.1	109.7
PREDORSAL	46.5	46.5	47.5	44.4	47.2	51.4
PREANAL	75.3	75.2	75.8	76.2	73.6	67.8
PREPELVIC	51.2	51.2	52.8	48.8	49.8	49.3
DORSAL BASE	14.0	16.0	15.9	16.5	14.2	12.4
ANAL BASE	14.9	17.9	14.2	16.4	15.0	27.4
BODY DEPTH	26.5	29.1	26.7	33.1	33.9	40.0
BODY WIDTH	10.6	10.8	10.7	12.7	16.4	13.0
C.PED. DEPTH	9.4	9.1	9.1	10.3	9.8	11.4
PECTORAL ALT.	19.1	20.7	20.5	21.9	23.5	24.7
HEAD LENGTH	23.7	27.3	27.6	23.2	24.8	28.8
SNOUT	5.5	6.8	6.7	6.1	5.8	4.9
EYE	8.0	5.9	8.9	6.7	5.0	6.7
MOUTH LENGTH	10.7	12.2	12.9	11.3	12.2	6.8
INTERORB	8.7	5.3	5.3	5.1	5.7	7.0
N (sample size)	5	1	5	4	2	5
COUNTS:						
DORSAL RAYS	15-20	14-20	15-19	15-17	17-20	10-13
ANAL RAYS	16-21	19-23	15-21	17-18	19-23	25-36
PECTORAL						
RAYS	14-18	15-16	13-16	15	14-18	14-17
PELVIC RAYS	9-11	9	9-10	8-9	9	7-10
GILL RAKERS	41-52 L	18-23 L	38-43 L	36 L	59-73 L	100-400 T
VERTEBRAE	50-52	54-55	48-51	48-50	56-59	48-51
SCALES:						
TRANSVERSE*	15	16	14	14	17	20
LATERAL LINE	41-46	48-57	42-50	50	50-55	47-49
SCUTES:						
PREPELVIC	18-20	19-23	17-21	18-20	19-27	18-19
POSTPELVIC	12-17	12-17	13-16	14-15	12-15	12-13

* Transverse scale rows counted from base of pelvic fin to dorsal origin.

MOONEYES

HIODONTIDAE

Although the mooneye with its compressed silvery shape superficially resembles the herrings, it actually belongs to a distinctive group of fishes called the bony tongues (osteoglossomorpha). As this common name implies, they are characterized by a strong, toothed plate on the tongue and a corresponding set of prominent teeth on the midline of the roof of the mouth (the parasphenoid bone). The mooneye has a large eye and a very short snout. Its body is quite compressed along its ventral edge but there are no modified scales forming a saw edge as in most herrings.

Most osteoglossomorphs occur in the Southern Hemisphere and the group includes the giant arapaima of the Amazon, the aruana, *Osteoglossum bicirrhosum,* and the featherbacks of Africa and Southeast Asia. Only the mooneye and its close relative, the goldeye, *Hiodon alosoides,* live in North America.

Hiodon

This is the only genus in the family Hiodontidae. It consists of two species, the mooneye, which has 11 or 12 dorsal rays, and the goldeye, which has only 9 or 10 dorsal rays and a moderately sharp keel in front of the pelvic fins. One fossil species is known from British Columbia.

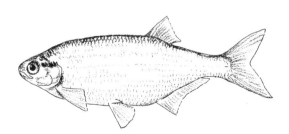

MOONEYE

Hiodon tergisus Lesueur, 1818

Identification

In general shape and appearance, the mooneye resembles the herrings from which it can be readily distinguished by the presence of a lateral line that is nearly complete, the lack of fatty tissue partly covering the eye, and the presence of large pointed teeth on the tongue and the roof of the mouth. The scales of the mooneye are firm and not as easily knocked off as those of the herrings. Mooneye have rounded, rather than saw-edged bellies, and very short snouts.

Description

Body compressed, dorsal and anal profiles nearly equally curved. Head rather short, snout quite short, eyes large. Dorsal fin placed well back on body, its origin behind the pectoral fins. Dorsal deltoid with sharp angles, its margin straight. Anal originating under middle of dorsal fin, long with sharp angles and slightly concave margin, anterior third of the fin of mature males forming an elevated rounded lobe. Caudal moderately forked with rounded lobes. Pelvics abdominal, retrogressive with convex margin and rounded corners. Pelvic axillary process well developed. Pectoral low, retrogressive, its base nearly horizontal, bluntly pointed with convex margin. Lateral line nearly complete, straight. Trautman notes that the scales above the anal base are characteristically irregular. There is a single pyloric caecum. Counts and proportional measurements are presented in Table 4

Color: Silvery, somewhat dusky above, shading to white on the belly. Eye silvery to brassy, fins pale to dusky.

Size: Trautman records this species as reaching 17.5 inches and 2 pounds 7 ounces.

Habitat

The mooneye occurs in large rivers and lakes, apparently selecting clearer waters. It has declined over much of its range and this has been attributed to silting of the habitat. Van Oosten (1961) noted that nearly all of the mooneyes taken in Lake Erie came from depths of less than 35 feet.

Distribution

The mooneye is a Mississippi Valley species whose range extends from the Red River of the North, south through the Mississippi and its larger tributaries to the gulf coast and east to the Mobile Bay drainage. It occurs in southern Lake Michigan, Lake Erie, Lake Ontario, and the St. Lawrence system including the Ottawa River and Lake Champlain.

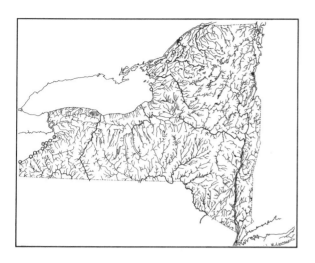

Names

Hyodon is from the Greek word *yoeides* referring to the hyoid bone which is shaped like the letter Y and *odonus* (tooth), referring to the teeth on the tongue. *Tergisus* is Latin for scoured or polished.

Hiodon tergisus Lesueur, 1818c: 364 Ohio River

Hyodon tergisus DeKay, 1842: 265 Allegheny River

Hiodon clodalis Lesueur, 1818c: 367-368 Pittsburgh

Hyodon clodalis DeKay, 1842: 266-267 Lake Erie at Buffalo

There is a semi-disjunct population in the James Bay region. New York State records are from Lakes Erie and Ontario, where they are now very scarce, the St. Lawrence, and Lake Champlain. Apparently, they are still reasonably common in Lake Champlain.

Life History

In Lake Erie, spawning occurs in April, May, and possibly early June. Greeley and Bishop (1932) reported collecting mooneye eggs in the Oswegatchie River below the Ogdensburg Dam on June 3, when the water temperature was 67 F. The eggs were among rocks in rapid current in water 2 feet deep or less. The age of the eggs was unknown but they had a thick gelatinous covering that suggested the jelly coat of a frog's egg. The yolk sac was absorbed when the hatchlings were about 13 mm total length. Females lay 10,000 to 20,000 eggs.

Van Oosten (1961) studied age and growth of commercial specimens from Lake Erie. At the end of the first summer the mooneyes averaged 4.1 inches total length and by the end of the seventh summer their average was 12.7 inches.

Food and Feeding

Mooneyes are said to feed near the surface at night and are caught on grasshoppers, minnows, or worms. Stomachs contain mostly aquatic and terrestrial insects.

Notes

The name mooneye is sometimes used by fishermen for other species such as gizzard shad, alewife, and some deepwater ciscoes. As a result, some of the earlier range statements were erroneous.

References

Trautman, 1957 (Ohio). Johnson, 1951 (biology). Glenn, 1978 (growth and diet). Van Oosten, 1961 (distribution, age and growth). Greenwood, 1977 (classification). Snyder and Douglas, 1978 (larvae).

BULLHEAD CATFISHES

ICTALURIDAE

This family is part of the Ostariophysi and its members, like the minnows and suckers, have the swim bladder connected to the ear by a chain of small bones derived from the anterior vertebrae. Catfishes, however, are less closely related to either minnows or suckers than those groups are to each other.

Worldwide, there are some 30 families of catfishes with more than 2,000 species. Only one family occurs naturally in the freshwaters of the United States; 2 of its 5 genera and 9 of its 37 species occur in New York. Catfishes live in the freshwaters of Asia, Africa, South America and Europe. Only two or three families have members that breed in salt water.

Catfishes are distinctive. Our species have four pairs of long barbels. They have no scales and there are strong serrated spine-like rays at the fronts of the dorsal and pectoral fins. In New York, the genera are *Ictalurus,* which includes the channel cat, the white cat and the bullheads, and *Noturus,* the madtoms. In a sense the madtoms are to the bullheads what the darters are to the perch — small and more diverse representatives of their respective families.

Bullheads, channel catfish, and white catfish are excellent food fish and provide interesting sport for fishermen willing to go to the trouble of using special techiques and esoteric baits.

The firm spines of the ictalurids are often preserved as fossils and the group has been studied in a historical context. Recently LeGrande (1981) studied their chromosomes and includes counts for all of the species in New York State.

KEY TO THE CATFISHES IN NEW YORK

A. Adipose dorsal fin a low, keel-like ridge, separated from the tail by only a shallow notch.
Noturus   F.

A'. Adipose fin flag-like, separated from tail by a short space.
Ictalurus

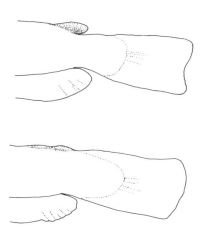

Adipose fins of catfishes. Top: Flag-like (adnexed) fin of *Ictalurus*. Bottom: Keel-like (adnate) fin of *Noturus* species.

B. Tail rounded, square, or slightly lunate but never definitely forked. Bony ridge between skull and dorsal fin with a gap that can be felt through the skin.

Bullheads, D.

B'. Tail definitely forked.

C. Tail moderately forked, the shortest rays about three-fourths the length of the longest upper rays. Anal rays, including rudiments, 25 or fewer. Color blue gray above, white below, never with conspicuous round spots.
Ictalurus catus   **White catfish, p. 78**

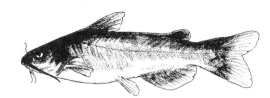

C'. Tail deeply forked, the shortest rays less than half the longest upper rays. (Less so in very large individuals for which the anal ray count is the best diagnostic character.) Young usually with definite

round black spots scattered on the sides. Anal rays 26 or more.
Ictalurus punctatus   **Channel catfish, p. 83**

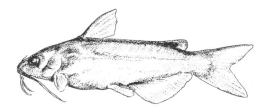

D. (B. Tail rounded, square, or lunate.) Anal rays 24 to 27. Caudal rounded. Chin barbels white.
Ictalurus natalis   **Yellow bullhead, p. 81**

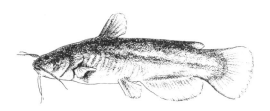

D'. Anal rays 17 to 24. Caudal square or slightly emarginate. Chin barbels gray or black.

E. Pectoral fin with strong posterior serrations. Anal rays (19) 21 to 24. Total gill rakers 15 to 24, usually 17 to 20. Jaws of almost equal length. Membranes of vertical fins dusky.
Ictalurus nebulosus   **Brown bullhead, p. 82**

E'. Pectoral fin spines with weak posterior serrations. Anal fin rays 17 to 21. Total gill rakers 13 to 16, usually 13 to 15. Membranes of vertical fins jet black, except those of the anal fin are pale for their basal third. Adults have a white vertical bar at the base of the caudal that joins the whitish belly. This is not always conspicuous.
Ictalurus melas   **Black bullhead, p. 79**

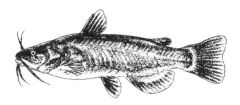

F. (A. Adipose dorsal fin keel-like.) Premaxillary tooth patches with a curved process extending backward from their posterior lateral corners. Skull very flat.
Noturus flavus   **Stonecat, p. 86**

F'. Premaxillary tooth patches rectangular, without a posterior process. Skull only moderately flat.

G. Body color distinctly blotched and speckled. Pectoral fin with very large tooth-like serrations along its posterior side.
Noturus miurus   **Brindled madtom, p. 89**

G'. Body color not blotched and only weakly countershaded, or uniform.

H. Body elongate and slender, Vertical fins with dark margins. Procurrent caudal rays only moderately developed.
Noturus insignis   **Margined madtom, p. 88**

H'. Body short and stout, tadpole-shaped. Fins without dark edges, color uniform. Procurrent caudal rays very well developed, extending forward as keels on top and bottom of caudal peduncle.
Noturus gyrinus   **Tadpole madtom, p. 87**

Ictalurus

The larger members of the Ictaluridae are now placed in the genus *Ictalurus,* although until about 1954 the bullheads, with emarginate or square tails, were assigned to the genus *Ameiurus.* The white cat, *I. catus,* however, is so nearly intermediate between the bullheads, subgenus *Ameiurus,* and the forktail catfishes, subgenus *Ictalurus* (represented in our state by the channel catfish), that two genera are unjustified. The bullheads are divided into the *catus* group (the white cat and others) and the *natalis* group which includes our brown, black, and yellow bullheads. For discussions see Taylor (1954) and Burkhead et al. (1980).

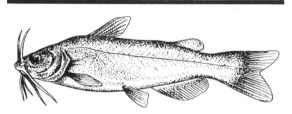

WHITE CATFISH

Ictalurus catus (Linnaeus, 1758)

Identification

The white catfish is a moderate-sized catfish with a free adipose dorsal fin. This distinguishes it from the madtoms which are small and have a keel-like adipose dorsal. It also has a forked tail which distinguishes it from the black, brown and yellow bullheads, all of which have rounded or square tails. This leaves only the channel catfish and differentiating the two is easy enough if the fish are less than about 14 inches long because the channel catfish has spots and a deeply forked tail and the white cat has no spots and a tail that is only moderately forked. However, very large channel catfish, say those that weigh more than 10 pounds, tend to have worn tails that are less deeply forked and no spots. Thus, they may look like large white cats. The best recognition feature for these large individuals is the number of anal fin rays: 22 to 25, usually 22 to 24 in the white cat, and 23 to 29, usually more than 26, in the channel cat. These counts include rudiments at the front of the fin.

Description

Body moderately elongate, head depressed, body compressed posteriorly. Dorsal fin origin midway between the pectoral and pelvic insertion. Snout to dorsal origin contained 1.5 times in the distance from dorsal origin to caudal base. Adipose dorsal short and flag-like, nearer to base of caudal than to end of the dorsal base. First soft ray of the dorsal longest, about twice the last ray. Caudal fin forked, middle rays two-thirds the longest upper rays. Caudal lobes rounded. Anal fin origin midway between the end of the dorsal base and the beginning of the adipose. Anal margin rounded, the rays increasing to the last third of the fin then decreasing. Pelvic fin inserted below the distal fourth of the depressed last dorsal ray. Pelvic pointed, the third and fourth rays the longest. Last ray three-fourths the longest. Pectoral bluntly pointed, its base low and nearly horizontal. Pectoral spine with strong serrae. Gill membranes separate. Mouth subterminal. Lateral line complete, straight. Counts and proportional measurements are given in Table 6.

Color: Gray to gray blue dorsally shading to creamy white below, sometimes with a sharp line of demarcation. Fins dusky, especially on the membranes. Chin barbels pale with some pigment near their bases. Other barbels dark. Iris pale.

Juveniles and breeding adults: Breeding adults become considerably darker than normal adults. Juveniles have neither spots nor the dark fin margins seen in juvenile channel catfish.

Size: The white catfish is smaller than the channel catfish, but the IGFA records are presently vacant. In the Hudson River their usual size is 12 to 14 inches. Fish weighing more than 6 pounds should be checked carefully because of the possibility of confusing them with channel cats. In the Santee-Cooper Reservoir (now called Lake Marion), they are said to reach 22 inches total length.

Habitat

The white catfish seems to prefer estuarine waters with some salinity although it also occurs in freshwater lakes and ponds and has been stocked in inland waters. In Ohio, Trautman (1957) noted that the white cat habitat was intermediate between that of the channel cat and the bullheads. It avoided the swifter waters of larger rivers but it did not thrive in weedy or muddy shallow ponds.

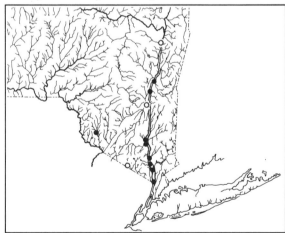

Distribution

The natural range of the white catfish is the Atlantic coast from the Lower Hudson to peninsular Florida and west along the gulf coast to the Mobile Bay drainage. It was introduced into many areas including Ohio and California. In New York it lives in the Lower Hudson and in a few inland lakes.

Life History

Spawning occurs in California in June and July when the water temperature reaches 70 F. Both sexes work at digging a nest depression 30 to 36 inches in diameter and 12 to 18 inches deep on sand or gravel bars. Pebbles are removed by carrying them in the mouth or by fanning with the body and fins. The eggs are fanned and protected by the parents, and may be covered with five or six inches of gravel. One or both parents, usually the male, guard the eggs and young. Hatching takes 6 or 7 days at 75 to 85 F and the newly hatched young gradually darken over the first 4 days until they are entirely dark except for the lower head and belly.

White catfish mature at 7 or 8 inches in their third or fourth year of life. The eggs are 4 to 4.5 mm in diameter. An 11- or 12-inch female may lay 3,200 to 3,500 eggs. In Lake Marion they reach 3.2 inches total length by the time they form their first annulus and 8.1 inches at age III, 17.2 inches at age VIII, and 22 inches at age XI.

Food and Feeding
White catfish eat a variety of fishes and fish eggs including herring, menhaden, gizzard shad, and bluegills. Aquatic insects, crustaceans, filamentous algae and other vegetable matter is consumed. In some areas, small white catfish eat midge larvae from March through October when they become large enough to eat fish. Larger fish eat midge larvae, cladocerans and fish eggs in the spring and fish during the summer and fall.

Notes
White catfish are fished for in the Lower Hudson but it is recommended that they not be eaten frequently because their flesh often contains high levels of polychlorinated biphenyls.

References
Miller in Calhoun, 1966 (summary of life history). Menzel, 1945 (fishery in Virginia). Fowler, 1917 (nesting). Kellogg and Gift, 1983 (preferred temperature).

Names
The name *catus* is Latin for cat.
Silurus catus Linnaeus, 1758: 305 (after Catesby)
Amiurus catus, Jordan, 1877d: 90-91 (misidentification; this is the brown bullhead)
Ameiurus catus, Mearns, 1898: 312 Hudson River
Villarius catus, Greeley, 1935: 95-96 Hudson River

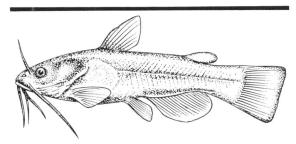

BLACK BULLHEAD

Ictalurus melas (Rafinesque, 1820)

Identification
The black bullhead is a rare species in New York and any specimens suspected of being this species should be checked carefully. It differs from the madtoms, genus *Noturus,* in having a free (adnexed) adipose dorsal fin; it differs from the channel and white catfishes in having a tail that is not forked; and it differs from the yellow bullhead in that its anal fin is much shorter and its chin barbels are spotted or gray rather than white.

The black bullhead is most like the brown bullhead, *Ictalurus nebulosus.* The two species differ in coloration. The black bullhead tends to be more sharply bicolored with the pale color of the belly extending upward as a bar at the base of the tail and onto the basal third of the anal fin. The membranes between the rays of all of the fins are darker in the black bullhead than in the brown bullhead. The brown bullhead lacks the white bar at the base of the tail and its anal fin is uniformly pigmented.

The best feature for separating these species is the gill raker count, 15 to 24, usually 17 to 20, whereas the brown bullhead has only 13 to 16. In the brown bullhead there are well-developed teeth on the posterior edge of the pectoral spine. The pectoral spine of the black bullhead is nearly smooth although small black bullheads have weak serrations. It is said that if you can pick the fish up by grasping the spine it is a brown bullhead. The anal ray count of the black bullhead is lower, 18 to 21, and the brown bullhead usually has more than 20 anal rays but, because of the overlap, this is not a surefire distinction.

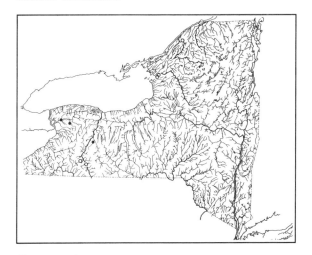

Description
Body moderately elongate, head depressed and the body progressively more compressed. Dorsal fin origin midway between the pectoral base and the pelvic insertion. Dorsal fin pointed, the last ray about 60 percent of the longest rays. Adipose fin large and flag-like. Caudal emarginate, the middle rays four-fifths the longest upper rays. Anal origin midway between the end of the dorsal base and the origin of the adipose fin. Pelvics rounded, retrogressive, last pelvic rays about two-thirds the first. No pelvic axillary process. Pectoral asymmetrically pointed, its spine nearly edentulate, its base low and nearly hor-

izontal. Lateral line nearly complete. Mouth subterminal, gill membranes separate. Counts and proportional measurements are given in Table 6.

Color: Back and upper sides very dark, often with brassy overtones. Belly abruptly lighter, white, creamy, or bright yellow. Sides not mottled. In adults the pale color of the belly extends upward as a pale bar at the base of the tail. Fin membranes dark except for the basal one-third to one-half of the anal fin. Chin barbels gray, other barbels black.

Juveniles and breeding adults: Small juveniles are jet black above and pale below. Larger juveniles are somewhat paler with dark fin margins and leading edges and have dark interradial membranes. Trautman describes breeding males as jet black above and bright yellow below.

Size: This is a rather small species, usually 8 to 10 inches long. Trautman lists a 16.8-inch specimen that weighed 2 pounds 12 ounces. A reported 8-pound fish from Lake Waccabuc is possibly a misidentification although it could have been a stocked fish. A photograph of the fish is inconclusive but does look like a black bullhead. At present, this record is not recognized by the International Game Fish Association.

Habitat
The black bullhead lives in a broad range of standing and slowly flowing waters. Like other bullheads, it is tolerant of swampy, low-oxygen conditions. Trautman reported that it is more tolerant of silt than the other species and this is reasonable in view of its wide distribution in the Great Plains region.

Distribution
The black bullhead ranges from southern Canada to Mexico and from the Rocky Mountains to the western slopes of the Appalachians. It has been stocked in areas outside its natural range.

In New York, it is said to occur in the western part of the state east to the eastern tributaries of Lake Ontario. We have only one recent record, from the Genesee drainage, and because of its close resemblance to the brown bullhead it is possible that some of the older records are erroneous. Apparently bullheads are brought into the state from suppliers in the Midwest and it is possible to find the black bullhead in almost any part of the state. There is some indication that they have been stocked in ponds in the New York City area.

Life History
The black bullhead spawns in the spring and early summer. The exact dates and length of the spawning period are variable and range from May and June to July. Forney found its spawning peak in Clear Lake, Iowa to be early July.

Spawning takes place where there is considerable vegetation. The female excavates the nest which is a depression approximately equal in diameter to her length. The nest is made by fanning and pushing objects with her snout. The spawning pairs embrace head to tail with the male clasping the female's head with his tail while his head is bent downward slightly and his mouth is open. The female quivers for about one second as the eggs are released. Then they separate, rest for a minute or so, and resume swimming with the female over the nest and butting the male away when he comes too close. Wallace (1967) noted that spawning was repeated about five times in an hour and about 200 eggs were laid during each spawning episode. Ovarian counts of 3,000 to nearly 7,000 have been reported.

Hatching takes about 5 days and the young are guarded for several weeks until they reach a length of about 1 inch. By the end of the first summer they reach about 3 inches and in North Dakota they are 4.5 to 6.7 inches at the end of the third summer and 10.1 to 12.4 at the end of the fifth summer. Growth is variable and like other bullheads they are subject to stunting. Maturity is attained at 180 to 190 mm total length and this is usually at age II + .

Food and Feeding
Young black bullheads feed in dim light with peaks of activity just before dawn and around dusk. Adults are strictly nocturnal feeders. Items consumed include a variety of immature insects, clams, snails, crustaceans, plant material, leeches and fishes.

Young bullheads take immature insects, crustaceans, and leeches.

References
Forney, 1955 (ecology). Bowen, 1931 (aggregation). Wallace, 1967 (life history). Darnell and Meierotto, 1965 (behavior). Baur, 1970 (digestion rate). Trautman, 1957 (Ohio).

Names
The name *melas* is a Greek word meaning black.

Silurus melas Rafinesque, 1820c: 51 Ohio River

Ameiurus melas, Greeley, 1927: 57 Genesee River drainage

Ictalurus melas melas, Hubbs and Lagler, 1964: 90 (distribution)

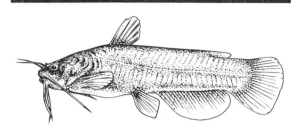

YELLOW BULLHEAD

Ictalurus natalis (Lesueur, 1819)

Identification
The yellow bullhead is the easiest to recognize of the three species of bullheads. Its size and flag-like adipose fin distinguish it from the madtoms; its round tail separates it from the channel and white catfish; and its long anal fin and white chin barbels separate it from the black and brown bullheads. The anal ray count of 24 to 27 is distinctive: black bullheads have 18 to 21, brown bullheads have 21 to 23. Generally, its color is somewhat yellowish but the young are black and white and the adults of the brown bullhead frequently have a yellowish cast.

Description
Body moderately slender, head depressed, the posterior part of the body compressed. Dorsal fin origin closer to the pectoral than the pelvic origin. Dorsal bluntly pointed, its middle rays the longest. Caudal fin round, the middle rays longer than the longest rays of the upper lobe. Anal fin elongate, its margin only slightly convex, its origin below a point a little nearer to the end of the dorsal base than to the origin of the adipose dorsal. The origin of the adipose dorsal fin is not definite. Pelvic insertion slightly behind the end of the dorsal base. Pelvic fin roundly pointed. Pectoral base horizontal, pectoral fin retrogressive, its margin convex. Gill membranes slightly united. Mouth subterminal. Counts and proportional measurements are given in Table 6.

Color: Brownish or gray above with underparts of head and belly pale yellow. Chin barbels white, other barbels pigmented. Fin membranes pale or dusky, vertical fins with darker margins. An adult from turbid waters of South Bay, Lake Champlain, was bright yellow all over.

Juveniles and breeding adults: Juveniles are jet black above with the lower parts of the head and belly white and the chin barbels white.

Size: The adults are usually 8 to 12 inches total length in New York. Trautman records an Ohio specimen of 18.3 inches that weighed 3 pounds 10 ounces. The International Game Fish Association recognizes a 3-pound fish from Nelson Lake, Wisconsin as the rod-and-reel record.

Habitat
The yellow bullhead shows a preference for ponds and streams, including small brooks where there is clear water and some vegetation. It is relatively intolerant of silt, especially if other bullhead species are present.

Distribution
The native distribution of the yellow bullhead is east of a line from South Dakota to Texas and south of a line from central Minnesota, the Great Lakes and southern New England.

In New York, it ranges through most of the state except the central Adirondacks and the northern parts of the St. Lawrence drainage.

Food and Feeding
The yellow bullhead is a generalized bottom and near-bottom feeder, heavily dependent upon the chemical senses. It feeds mostly at night and eats crustaceans, mollusks, immature aquatic insects and some fishes.

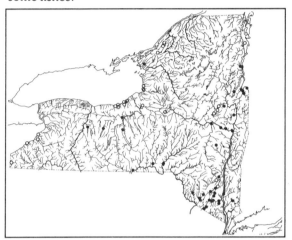

Life History
The yellow bullhead is a spring spawner and there are indications that it spawns earlier than the other two bullheads in our state. The parents prepare a nest that may be a shallow depression or a tunnel under an overhanging bank or a cavity under a log or stump. Its spawning behavior has not been reported but it can be expected to be similar to that of other bullhead species. The eggs are laid in batches of 300 to 700 and are guarded by the male through incubation and until the young are nearly 2 inches long.

Average total lengths at the end of the first summer are 1.2 to 2.6 inches, 7.1 to 9.6 at the end of the second summer, and 8.9 to 11.6 inches at the end of the fifth summer. Sexual maturity is attained at age II or III and the maximum age is about 6 or 7 years.

References
Todd, 1971 (chemical communication). Reynolds and Casterlein, 1977 (activity cycles). Fowler, 1917 (breeding). Smith and Harrow, 1903 (breeding).

Names
The name *natalis* is Latin meaning having large nates or buttocks.

Pimelodus natalis Lesueur, 1819: 154 North America

Ameiurus natalis, Greeley, 1928: 99 Oswego drainage

Ameiurus natalis natalis, Greeley, 1939: 68 Allegheny drainage

Ictalurus natalis natalis, Hubbs and Lagler, 1964: 90 (distribution)

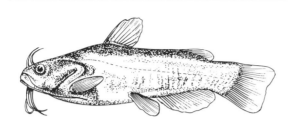

BROWN BULLHEAD

Ictalurus nebulosus
(Lesueur, 1819)

Identification

The brown bullhead is the most common member of its family in New York and is quite variable in color. It differs from the madtoms in having a flag-like adipose dorsal fin and it differs from the white and channel catfish in that its tail is not deeply forked but square or sometimes slightly emarginate. It can be separated from the yellow bullhead by its shorter anal fin which has 21 to 24 rays rather than 24 to 27. It also has dark chin barbels whereas those of the yellow bullhead are white.

The brown bullhead most resembles the black bullhead but that species has an even shorter anal fin with 17 to 21 rays, a white bar at the base of the tail and a pale area on the base of the anal fin and, perhaps most diagnostic, 13 to 16 gill rakers. The black bullhead has very weak serrations on the pectoral fin spine while those of the brown bullhead are quite large. The young of both species have fairly well-developed pectoral serrations, so this distinction may not be reliable in fish less than 4 inches long.

Description

Head and anterior body depressed, caudal peduncle somewhat compressed. Dorsal fin origin equidistant between pectoral base and pelvic insertion. Dorsal fin pointed with the third and fourth rays longest. Last dorsal ray two-thirds length of the dorsal spine. Adipose dorsal fin adnexed, inserted over the middle of the anal fin. Caudal emarginate, its middle rays equal in length to the longest rays in the upper lobe. Caudal fin corners rounded. Anal fin origin below a point between the end of the dorsal fin base and the beginning of the adipose dorsal fin. Pelvic insertion slightly behind end of dorsal base. Pelvic rounded, its third and fourth rays longest. Pectoral fin retrogressive. Its base horizontal, its margin convex. Gill membranes joined to each other across the isthmus. Mouth subterminal with the snout overhanging slightly. Counts and proportional measurements are given in Table 6.

Color: Olive to blackish above shading to pale white or yellow on the belly and underside of the head. Sides often somewhat mottled. Fins dark but not jet black as in the black bullhead. Basal third of the anal fin as dark as the rest of the fin. All barbels gray to black, the base of those of the chin sometimes slightly paler.

Size: The usual adult size is about 8 to 14 inches. The IGFA record is a 5-pound 8-ounce fish from Veal Pond, Georgia.

Juveniles and breeding adults: The juveniles are at first jet black above and white on the belly and underside of the head. Breeding adults become somewhat darker than they are at other times.

Habitat

The brown bullhead occupies a variety of habitats from the Great Lakes to small ponds and the slower parts of streams. Trautman (1957) noted that it was less dependent on vegetation than the yellow bullhead and often lived in deeper water than the other two species of bullheads.

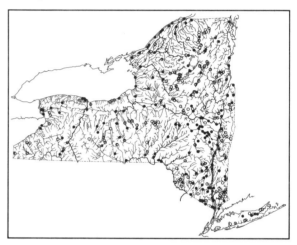

Distribution

This is an eastern species that originally ranged from southern Canada, the Great Lakes except Lake Superior, and the Red River of the North in Ontario and Manitoba south to Arkansas, northern Louisiana and Mississippi across the Appalachian Plateaus to the Atlantic coast. It is universal in New York.

Life History

Like other catfishes, the brown bullhead spawns in late May and June when the water temperature reaches 27 C. The male, sometimes aided by the female, builds a nest by clearing a small depression or cleaning a burrow under an overhanging bank or some obstruction such as a log or rock. Spawning behavior includes circling and caressing each other with their barbels. There is head-to-tail contact as the sex products are released. The eggs adhere in a creamy or pale yellow clump and are guarded or groomed by one or both parents. Hatching takes 6 to 9 days at 69 F. After they hatch, the young are guarded by the parents until they are nearly 2 inches long. Growth is rapid and the young reach 2 to 5 inches by the end of the first summer. The growth rate is variable and some populations become stunted, but "normal" growth is to 7 to 8 inches by age IV and 10 to 11 inches by age VI. Maturity is reached at age II and the usual life span is 6 or 7 years.

Food and Feeding

Raney and Webster studied the food of this species

in northern Cayuga Lake. Crustaceans made up about 60 percent of the diet and chironomids made up another 25 percent. As the fish became larger, other foods were consumed in greater quantities. Larger fish have also been reported to eat crayfish, leeches, oligochaetes, bryozoans, small fish and fish eggs, amphipods, and some plant material. Most of the feeding takes place at night.

References
Raney and Webster, 1940 (food habits). Raney, 1967 (general account). Keast and Webb, 1966 (feeding, ecology). Rigley and Muir, 1979 (sound production). Loeb, 1964 (burrowing behavior).

Names
Nebulosus is Latin for dark or clouded.

Pimelodus nebulosus Lesueur, 1819: 49 Lake Ontario

Ameiurus nebulosus, Greeley, 1927: 57 Genesee drainage

Pimelodus atrarius DeKay, 1842: 185 Wappingers Creek

Pimelodus vulgaris Thompson, 1842: 138 Lake Champlain

Ameiurus vulgaris, Evermann and Kendall, 1902b: 222 Lake Champlain

Pimelodus dekayi Girard, 1859: 160 Oswego, New York

Ameiurus nebulosus nebulosus, Greeley, 1938: 68 Allegheny-Chemung drainage

Ameiurus nebulosus marmoratus, Bean, 1903: 89 (after Holbrook; misidentification)

Ictalurus catus Mitchill, 1817: 289 Wallkill River (misidentification)

Pimelodus pullus DeKay, 1842: 182 Lake Pleasant

Amiurus catus, Jordan, 1877d: 90-91 (misidentification)

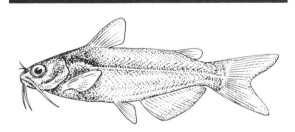

CHANNEL CATFISH

Ictalurus punctatus
(Rafinesque, 1818)

Identification
Channel catfish have deeply forked tails and this separates them from both the madtoms and the bullheads. The only species with which they can be (and often are) confused is the white catfish, which has a less deeply forked tail and fewer than 24 rays in the anal fin. Young channel catfish have distinct round spots scattered over the sides of the body. These are variable in size and number and disappear in larger adults.

Large channel catfish are sometimes mistaken for white catfish because their tails are not as deeply forked as in younger fish. Any catfish weighing more than 5 or 6 pounds is probably a channel cat but the identification should be confirmed by counting the anal rays.

Description
Body moderately elongate, somewhat compressed posteriorly. Head depressed. Profile straight to dorsal origin, which is over a point nearer to pectoral base than to pelvic insertion. Dorsal pointed with its anteriormost branched ray the longest. Last dorsal ray half the longest. Adipose dorsal fin adnexed.

Distance from origin of adipose to caudal midbase contained 1.25 times in the distance from adipose origin to end of dorsal base. Caudal deeply forked, its middle rays about half the longest upper rays. Caudal lobes pointed. Anal origin below a point midway between end of dorsal base and origin of adipose. Anal margin convex, its seventh ray longest. Pelvic insertion closer to anal origin than to pectoral base. Pelvic bluntly pointed, its third ray longest. Last ray two-thirds the third. Pectoral asymmetrically pointed; pectoral spine with strong, rather regular serrae. Mouth subterminal, lateral line complete. Gill membranes free from isthmus. Counts and proportional measurements are given in Table 6.

Color: Like that of other ictalurids, the color of the channel catfish is varied. Young 10 inches or so in length are blue gray, shading to paler on the belly with some silvery overtones. The sides usually have some distinct round spots but these are variable in number and position. There are dark edges on the vertical fins. Large fish tend to be somewhat darker.

Juveniles and breeding adults: Young are pale grayish blue with distinct black fin margins. Old fish become quite dark. Breeding males have broader heads than the females.

Size: The IGFA record is held by a 32-pound 3-ounce fish from the Satilla River in Georgia. The New York State record is 23 pounds 5 ounces, a fish taken from Oneida Lake in July 1980 by Fred Russell. Fish weighing 2 to 4 pounds are more usual.

Habitat
The channel cat is a big-water fish and also occurs in

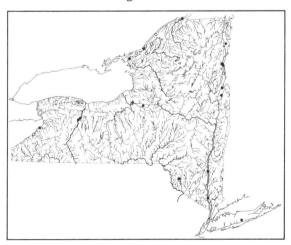

larger streams where it is able to thrive in moderate current. It can tolerate oxygen levels as low as 0.95 ppm and temperatures in excess of 90 F.

Distribution

The channel catfish is native to the central part of North America from southern Canada to Mexico. Possibly it was native to some Atlantic coast streams but it was generally absent north of southern Georgia. It has been widely introduced outside of its original range.

In New York the channel catfish occurs in the Great Lakes and Lake Champlain, Oneida Lake and the Oneida River. A 20-pound catfish from White Lake in the southern Catskills was apparently a stocked fish.

Life History

Spawning begins in the late spring when water temperatures are between 75 and 85 F. Nests are prepared by the male under logs or rocks or undercut at depths ranging from a few inches to several feet. In pond culture, old kegs or drainage tiles are provided for spawning sites. The eggs are laid during a head-to-tail clasp. Males guard the eggs and groom them until they hatch in 5 to 10 days, then guard the eggs for a time after the yolk sac stage. Young channel cats reach 2 to 4 inches fork length during the first summer and 9 or 10 inches by their fourth or fifth summer. Maturity is reached at age V to VII when they are 10 to 16 inches long. Some individuals may live for more than 25 years. Growth rates and life span vary greatly.

Food and Feeding

The channel catfish is a nocturnal feeder and depends heavily upon chemical senses to locate its food. The young feed largely on aquatic insects and other bottom-dwelling arthropods. When they reach about 100 mm standard length they become omnivorous with fish making up a large part of the diet.

Seeds and terrestrial animals, including birds, have been found in their stomachs.

Notes

Channel catfish culture is a major industry in the southern part of the United States.

References

Clemens and Sneed, 1957 (spawning and behavior). Magnin and Beaulieu, 1966 (biology). Lewis, 1976 (food). Walburg, 1975 (food). Speirs, 1952 (names). Regier, 1963c (management in farm ponds).

Names

The name *punctatus* is a Latin word *punctus*, meaning a puncture or sting, hence spotted as with punctures.

Silurus punctatus Rafinesque, 1818c: 359 Ohio River

Ictalurus punctatus, Greeley, 1928: 99 Oswego drainage

Gadus lacustris Walbaum, 1792: 144 Arctic America (actually a burbot)

Ameiurus lacustris, Evermann and Kendall, 1902c: 235 St. Lawrence River

Villarius lacustris, Greeley, 1929: 173 Lake Erie drainage

Pimelodus nigricans DeKay, 1842: 180-182 Buffalo, New York

Pimelodus catus (non Linnaeus), Mather, 1886: 37-38 Adirondacks

Pimelodus aracilis Hough, 1852: 26 Somerville, New York

Pimelodus houghi Girard, 1859: 159 (substitute name)

Pimelodus dekayi Girard, 1859: 160 Oswego, New York

Leptops olivaris (non Rafinesque), Meek, 1889: 302 Cayuga Lake

Ictalurus sp. Greeley, 1928: 99 Seneca River, near Weedsport

TABLE 6
AVERAGE PROPORTIONAL MEASUREMENTS AND COUNTS OF
BULLHEADS AND CATFISHES *(Ictalurus)*

All proportions are expressed in percentage of standard length.

	catus	punctatus	melas	natalis	nebulosus
ST. LENGTH (mm)	227.4	119.9	126.5	53.4	116.2
TOTAL LENGTH	121.3	129.7	125.5	122.2	123.8
FORK LENGTH	116.4	112.2	120.7	120.9	123.8
PREDORSAL	38.2	36.2	40.5	38.3	39.9
PREANAL	64.1	60.2	62.2	58.1	62.0
PREPELVIC	50.4	48.8	50.2	48.5	50.1
DORSAL BASE	9.9	10.7	9.3	9.2	9.6
ANAL BASE	21.7	28.7	24.1	32.0	24.6
BODY DEPTH	23.8	24.7	28.5	26.9	27.4
BODY WIDTH	22.7	20.3	19.3	21.0	20.6
C.PED. DEPTH	8.7	10.3	12.0	12.2	13.4
PECTORAL ALT.	18.0	17.8	19.1	17.2	19.1
HEAD LENGTH	29.2	26.9	29.9	29.7	30.3
SNOUT	12.8	10.7	11.1	11.2	12.3
EYE	3.8	5.6	4.8	4.4	4.2
MOUTH LENGTH	10.2	7.0	10.3	10.0	10.8
INTERORB	17.4	10.6	14.7	14.7	15.8
N (sample size)	4	5	3	5	5
COUNTS:					
DORSAL RAYS	6	6	5-6	6	6
ANAL RAYS	22-24	26-27	15-21	24-28	19-24
PECTORAL RAYS	8-9	8-9	8	7-8	7-9
PELVIC RAYS	7-8	8	8	8	8-9
GILL RAKERS	16-19	14-18	14-20	14-16	13-14
VERTEBRAE*	37-40	41-44	34-36	38-40	34-39

* Excluding Weberian apparatus.

Noturus

This is a well-defined genus united by small size and adnate adipose dorsal fins. Taylor (1969) recognizes three subgenera on the basis of pectoral fin and tooth structure. All three are represented in the New York fauna. *Noturus flavus* belongs to the subgenus *Noturus; N. gyrinus* and *N. insignis* belong to *Schilbeodes;* and *N. miurus* belongs to the subgenus *Rabida.* About 24 species are currently recognized. As early as 1907, Reed described the poison glands associated with the pectoral fins and fishermen are well aware that a puncture from the spines can be quite painful.

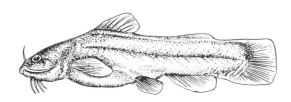

STONECAT

Noturus flavus Rafinesque, 1818

Identification
The madtoms are small catfishes that are readily distinguished from the bullheads and catfishes by their keel-like (adnate) rather than flag-like (adnexed) adipose dorsal fins. The stonecat is a rather slender species with a flat head and no distinct dark spots or blotches, and pale margins on some of the fins.

The distinctive characteristic of the stonecat is that the premaxillary tooth patch, which is rectangular in the other species, has the lateral posterior corners drawn out into triangular backward extensions. The pectoral spines of the stonecat are nearly smooth, without large serrations on the posterior edge but with a few small barbs on the front edge near the tip.

Description
Body elongate, terete anteriorly, slightly compressed posteriorly. Head depressed, flat on top. Dorsal origin to pectoral spine base contained 1.5 times in the distance from the dorsal origin to the pelvic insertion. Dorsal fin pointed, its third and fourth rays longest, one and one-half times as long as last dorsal ray. Adipose fin keel-like with a notch before the upper procurrent rays. Caudal convex, the middle rays one and one-fourth times as long as the longest upper caudal rays. Anal origin about as far behind the pelvics as the pelvics are behind the dorsal origin. Anal fin pointed, the middle rays longest, about twice the last ray. Pelvics inserted under the distal two-thirds of the depressed last dorsal ray. Pelvic fins round and paddle-like, their first and last rays about equal. Pectoral fin similarly rounded, pectoral fin spine smooth. Gill membranes separate

and free from the isthmus. Mouth subterminal. Lateral line incomplete, ending below the adipose dorsal fin. Counts and proportional measurements are given in Table 7.

Color: Generally yellowish to slate gray or olive, shading to white or pale yellow ventrally. Mental barbels white. Dorsal fin with a gray blotch on its basal third, adipose fin dark in the middle with pale ends and pale margin. Lower edge of the caudal fin cream color, distal and upper edges pale yellow. Anal and pelvic fins pale yellow, pectorals with a gray blotch at their base. A light yellow transverse elliptical spot on the body behind the posterior base of the dorsal fin.

Juveniles and breeding adults: This species has neither special juvenile nor breeding colors.

Size: Taylor reported a specimen 240 mm standard length and suggested that it might reach 250 mm. Specimens 175 to 200 mm standard length are common in collections.

Habitat
The stonecat lives in swifter parts of streams where there are cobbles or rock slabs and also in the Great Lakes where there are wave-swept shores with rocks. It is more common in larger streams.

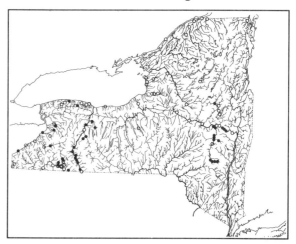

Distribution
The stonecat ranges from the St. Lawrence to the Upper Mississippi drainage and south on the western side of the Appalachians to Arkansas and the Tennessee River systems.

In New York it occurs in the Great Lakes, St. Lawrence and Allegheny River systems. It also occurs in the Upper Hudson and in Schoharie Creek.

Life History
The stonecat spawns from early June to late August. The eggs are deposited under rocks and guarded by both parents. They are opaque yellow and stick together in a clump of about 500. Each egg is 3.5 to 4 mm in diameter. Ovarian egg counts range from 767 to 1,205. The young reach 1.2 to 3.2 inches by the end of the first summer. Gilbert found fish up to 10 years old.

Food and Feeding
Stonecats feed on insects, mollusks and crayfish. Earlier studies in Lake Erie showed that they were

especially partial to mayflies but this may merely indicate that they are opportunistic feeders that were taking advantage of the most abundant and readily available food resource.

References
Taylor, 1969 (systematics). Langlois, 1954 (ecology). Gilbert, 1953 (age and growth). Greeley, 1952 (summary).

Names
The name *flavus* is the Latin word for yellow.

Noturus flavus Rafinesque, 1818d: 41 Ohio River

Pimelodus flavus, DeKay, 1842: 187

Noturus flavus, Evermann and Kendall, 1902a: 210 Lake Ontario

Schilbeodes gyrinus, Greeley, 1927: 57 Genesee River (misidentification)

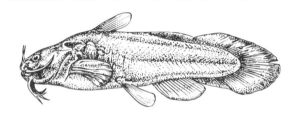

TADPOLE MADTOM

Noturus gyrinus (Mitchill, 1817)

Identification
True to its name the tadpole madtom is shaped somewhat like a tadpole, with a large head and a rather stubby body. Like other madtoms, it has a keel-like adipose dorsal fin.

The tadpole madtom has a uniform color pattern and rectangular premaxillary tooth patches. Its most prominent characteristic is the extreme development of the procurrent caudal fin rays. These are the short, unbranched rays at the front of the caudal fin. It also has no serrations on the pectoral spines.

Description
Body short, head depressed, giving the fish a distinctive tadpole-like form. Dorsal origin over a point midway between the pelvic and pectoral insertions. Dorsal fin pointed, its third and fourth rays longest. Last dorsal ray length contained 1.5 times in the dorsal spine. Adipose keel-like, without a notch in front of the procurrent caudal rays. Caudal fin bluntly pointed, the middle rays about twice as long as the uppermost branched ray. Dorsal and ventral caudal procurrent rays numerous and long. Anal fin origin below the front of the adipose dorsal fin. Anal fin rounded, its rays increasing in length to the last three which are progressively shorter. Pelvic origin below or slightly behind the end of the dorsal base. Head short, eye small, mental barbels stout, reaching the gill opening. Maxillary barbels reaching beyond the preoperculum. Pelvic fins paddle shaped. Pectoral fins pointed. Pectoral spine unarmed. Mouth terminal, lips gibbous. Lateral line ending below end of dorsal base. Head short, eye small.

Myomeres prominent on posterior half of body. Counts and proportional measurements are given in Table 7.

Color: In life this species ranges from grayish yellow to olive on the dorsal and lateral surfaces, shading to pale gray, yellow, or white on the underside of the head and belly. The fins are similar with the pelvic fins pale like the belly and the remaining fins similar to the upper parts of the body. Sometimes there is a darker submarginal band on the dorsal, anal and caudal fins. Barbels pigmented. Skin thick with a line of deep pigment on the midside of the posterior half of the body and the caudal peduncle. Myosepta are also pigmented in this region.

Juveniles and breeding adults: The tadpole madtom does not develop any special breeding structures or colors.

Size: This is a small species. The largest specimen examined by Taylor was 105 mm standard length. The species rarely exceeds 90 mm standard length.

Habitat
This is a species that is confined to dense weed beds in slow-moving waters.

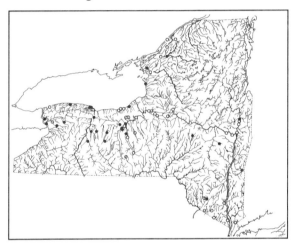

Distribution
The tadpole madtom ranges from the St. Lawrence drainage through the southern Great Lakes to western Lake Superior and the Red River of the North, south in the lowland parts of the Mississippi watershed to the gulf coast of Texas. Its range extends along the gulf coast to peninsular Florida and north on the Atlantic seaboard to the Basher Kill and the Lower Hudson.

In New York it occurs in Lake Erie, Lake Ontario, and the Oswego drainage and in the Hudson River above Albany as well as in the Delaware and Lower Hudson Valley.

Life History
The tadpole madtom is reported to spawn in July in Illinois and Iowa. Egg counts of 50 to 93 have been recorded. The eggs are laid in dark cavities, including discarded tin cans. The eggs are 3.5 mm in diameter and have a gelatinous capsule. Presumably they are guarded by one or both parents.

The calculated life span is short, probably no more than 2 or 3 years. Average back-calculated standard lengths in Minnesota were: I- 26 mm, II- 62 mm, III- 89 mm.

Food and Feeding
Reported foods include cladocerans, ostracods, gammarids, midges and debris.

Notes
Taylor, studying the tadpole madtom throughout its range, concluded that division into subspecies is not warranted although there are local differences. The tadpole madtom and the margined madtom are placed in the subgenus *Schilbeodes* which also includes other species that do not occur in New York. Members of this genus are plain colored and have no anterior serrae on the pectoral fin spines.

References
Taylor, 1969 (systematics). Hooper, 1949 (age and growth). Greeley, 1952 (summary). Menzel and Raney, 1973 (hybrids with *N. miurus)*. Mahon, 1977 (age and fecundity).

Names
The name *gyrinus* is the Greek word for tadpole.
Silurus gyrinus Mitchill, 1817: 289 Wallkill River
Schilbeodes gyrinus, E. Smith. 1898: 11-12 Hackensack River
Schilbeodes gyrinus gyrinus, Greeley, 1936: 77 Basher Kill
Noturus flavus DeKay, 1855: 61 New York (misidentification)
Noturus sialis Jordan, 1877b: 102 Ohio and White Rivers
Schilbeodes gyrinus sialis, Greeley, 1940: 76 Lake Ontario
Schilbeodes mollis, Hubbs and Raney, 1944: 25-26 (taxonomy)

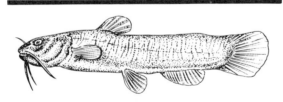

MARGINED MADTOM

Noturus insignis (Richardson, 1836)

Identification
The margined madtom is a rather slender catfish with dark edges on the dorsal and caudal fins. It clearly differs from the bullheads and catfishes in having a keel-like adipose fin and from the catfishes in having a square tail.

Among the madtoms it lacks the highly developed procurrent rays of the tadpole madtom, the projections on the tooth patches of the stonecat and the color pattern of the brindled madtom.

Description
Body elongate, caudal peduncle deep. Head depressed, body terete anteriorly, becoming somewhat compressed posteriorly. Dorsal fin rounded, its last ray two-thirds the longest. Adipose dorsal fin low and keel-like with a shallow notch at the front of the procurrent caudal rays. Caudal square, the longest upper rays slightly shorter than the middle caudal rays. Anal origin in front of the beginning of the adipose dorsal. Anal fin rounded, its rays increasing in length except for the last two or three. Pelvic insertion under middle of depressed last dorsal ray. Pelvic fin paddle shaped, the first and last rays about two-thirds as long as the middle rays. Pectoral spine with irregular serrae on the basal two-thirds of its posterior side. Mouth subterminal. Lateral line ending slightly behind the dorsal base. Counts and proportional measurements are given in Table 7.

Color: The general color is olive, slate gray or yellowish above, shading to pale cream on the lower head and belly. The chin barbels are pale, the other barbels dark. There is a bridge of pigmented skin across the belly in front of the pelvic fins. All fins lightly pigmented basally. Margins of pectoral, dorsal, anal, and caudal with a dark submarginal band and a narrow clear margin. Pelvic lightly pigmented to clear throughout. Adipose dorsal fin with a pale margin. Chin dark in front of the barbels.

Juveniles and breeding adults: There are no special features of either the breeding adults or the juveniles.

Size: Specimens more than 100 mm standard length are taken quite frequently. The largest specimen examined by Taylor came from Virginia and was 126 mm standard length.

Habitat
The margined madtom inhabits clear-water streams where it lives among rocks, boulders, or coarse gravel in riffles and moderate to swift current.

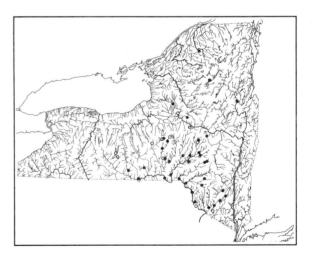

Distribution
This is an upland Atlantic drainage species that ranges from the Finger Lakes region of the Lake Ontario drainage southward through the Piedmont and Appalachian Highlands to Georgia.

In New York it occurs in the Delaware and Susquehanna drainages and in parts of the Lower Hudson and Mohawk drainages.

Life History

The nesting and spawning habits of this species seem not to have been described. Clugston and Cooper studied age and growth in Pennsylvania. They found the first young-of-the-year in 1957 and 1958 on 13 July and suggested a June spawning period. An egg count of 107 was reported.

Sexual maturity of the females occurred in the third summer (age 24 months). Males matured in the second or third summer. The maximum age was IV + and most of the growth of older fish took place in the late summer.

Food and Feeding

Insects and fish have been reported in the stomachs of the margined madtom.

Notes

This species is commonly used for bait and has probably been introduced by fishermen into some areas where it did not occur naturally.

References

Taylor, 1969 (systematics). Bowman, 1932, 1936 (life history). Rubec and Coad, 1974 (first record in Canada). Clugston and Cooper, 1960 (growth). Fowler, 1917 (breeding).

Names

The trivial name is from the Latin *insignes* meaning remarkable or extraordinary. Taylor notes that this was probably in reference to the color and the long adipose fin.

Pimelodus insigne Richardson, 1836: 132 (After Lesueur who did not give it a name; the type is MNHN Paris 3053 from Philadelphia.)

Schilbeodes insignis, Bean, 1903: 95-96 New York

Schilbeodes insignis insignis, Hubbs and Lagler, 1958: 89 (distribution)

Pimelodus lemniscatus Valenciennes *in* Cuvier and Valenciennes, 1840: 144-145 Pennsylvania

Noturus marginatus Baird *in* Cope, 1868: 237, 241

Schilbeodes marginatus, Robins and Deubler, 1955: 14, 16 Tioughnioga River

S. m. marginatus, Hubbs and Lagler, 1947: 71-73 Broome County, New York

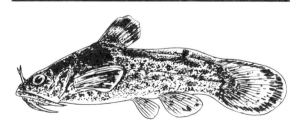

BRINDLED MADTOM

Noturus miurus Jordan, 1877

Identification

The brindled madtom has a bold color pattern of dark spots and blotches on a paler beige to white background. Like the other madtoms, it has a keel-like adipose dorsal fin. It differs from the stonecat in that its premaxillary tooth patches are rectangular, without lateral backward extensions and it lacks the highly developed procurrent caudal fin rays of the tadpole madtom. Its body is short and robust rather than elongate like that of the margined madtom. Its most distinctive feature is its pectoral fin spine which is curved with well-developed teeth on the anterior edge and huge regular curved teeth on its posterior edge. These teeth are easily visible with the naked eye if one shines a light through the fin. No other catfish in New York has such a highly specialized pectoral spine.

Description

Body rather short and robust. Head depressed, body compressed posteriorly. Dorsal origin about equidistant between pelvic insertion and pectoral base. Dorsal margin rounded, its third and fourth rays longest. Last ray slightly shorter than the spine. Adipose adnate and well developed with a deep notch before the procurrent caudal rays. Caudal fin convex, its uppermost branched rays about half the middle rays. Anal origin below beginning of the adipose dorsal fin. Anal fin rounded, its middle rays about twice as long as the last ray. Pelvic insertion under the end of the dorsal base. Pelvic fin rounded with its third and fourth rays longest, its first and last rays about equal. Pectoral retrogressive. Pectoral spine with large teeth on its posterior side and large serrations on its anterior margin. Gill membranes free from the isthmus. Lateral line decurved, ending between the pelvic insertion and the anal origin. Mouth subterminal. Counts and proportional measurements are given in Table 7.

Color: In life the ground color is white to pale tan or yellowish, shading to white on the belly. The upper parts and the sides have light and dark blotches. There are small and dispersed melanophores on the sides and larger dark areas dorsally. The top of the head is dark and there is a large saddle-shaped blotch in front of the dorsal fin, another smaller saddle behind the dorsal, and a definite saddle across the central part of the adipose dorsal fin. There is a crescent-shaped band at the base of the tail and a dark submarginal band around the tail that connects with the basicaudal band. The tip of the dorsal fin is dark. The anal, pelvic, and pectoral fins all have a few irregular dark blotches.

Juveniles and breeding adults: The brindled madtom does not develop special breeding colors.

Size: The largest specimen examined by Taylor was 88 mm standard length.

Habitat

The brindled madtom lives in the lower reaches of streams, usually below riffles and often in weedy areas. It appears to show a preference for soft bottom where there is mud or debris.

Distribution

The brindled madtom ranges from the Great Lakes through the Ohio and Mississippi basin to the gulf coast between the Mississippi and Pearl Rivers.

The brindled madtom was not collected by the Erie-Niagara Survey but it was listed on the basis of an Ohio record from Sandusky Bay. It was recorded from Oneida Lake by Adams and Hankinson but was not taken by the Survey. In the Lake Ontario watershed, the Survey recorded it from Johnson Creek, Oak Orchard Creek, and Eighteen Mile Creek, and mentioned that specimens from Salmon Creek, Long Pond Inlet, and Northrup Creek were in the University of Rochester collection. It also occurs in Cayuga Lake. In the Allegheny drainage it was taken only three times in the Cassadaga and Stillwater Creeks, and Evermann and Goldsborough obtained it in Chautauqua Lake. In 1981, we collected specimens in Stillwater Creek. In August 1975, it was thriving in Tonawanda Creek at Millersport. We collected it in Honeoye Creek in 1982 and recently it has been reported from the Mohawk River at Lock 7.

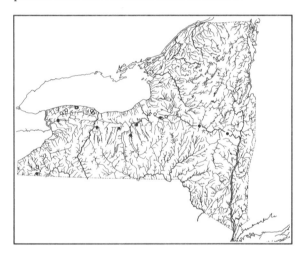

Life History
Taylor reported finding males guarding eggs and young in sunken beverage cans in the Huron River in southern Michigan. Nests were found 8-10 August 1951 and 27 July 1952. The water temperature on 10 August 1951 was 78 F. Guarding males ranged between 51 and 71 mm standard length. Their color patterns were less distinct than those of younger individuals and the head was broader and flatter. Muscles in front of the dorsal fin, on top of the head and on the cheeks were swollen. The lips and the areas around the maxillary barbels were also swollen so that the mouth appeared to have enlarged. Broods ranged from 34 eggs for a 55-mm male to 46 eggs from a 68-mm male. The eggs stick together in an irregular mass.

Food and Feeding
The food habits have not been reported.

Notes
This is the only species of the subgenus *Rabida* that occurs in New York. According to Taylor, 14 other species also belong to this subgenus. All are blotched and have the distinctive scimitar-shaped pectoral spines with small but distinct anterior serrae and large curved posterior serrae.

References
Taylor, 1969 (systematics). Burr and Mayden, 1982 (life history). Menzel and Raney, 1973 (hybrids with *N. gyrinus*). Adams and Hankinson, 1916 (Oneida Lake). Evermann and Goldsborough, 1902 (Chautauqua Lake).

Names
The name *miurus* is a Greek word meaning curtailed.

Noturus miurus Jordan, 1877a: 46 Indiana records (nomen nudum)

Noturus miurus Jordan, 1877b: 370-377 Ohio Valley and Indianapolis, White River (Lectotype selected by Taylor (1969): MNHN Paris A1308 from the White River, Indiana.)

Schilbeodes miurus, Adams and Hankinson, 1916: 118 Oneida Lake

TABLE 7
AVERAGE PROPORTIONAL MEASUREMENTS AND COUNTS OF MADTOMS *(Noturus)*

All proportions are expressed in percentage of standard length.

	flavus	*gyrinus*	*insignis*	*miurus*
ST. LENGTH (mm)	62.8	49.4	82.8	36.1
TOTAL LENGTH	123.8	124.7	120.2	124.1
FORK LENGTH	123.8	124.7	120.2	124.1
PREDORSAL	38.2	38.3	36.6	40.0
PREANAL	63.4	61.7	60.9	64.0
PREPELVIC	48.6	48.5	47.4	52.2
DORSAL BASE	12.9	11.4	10.7	13.4
ANAL BASE	21.1	18.9	20.9	23.3
BODY DEPTH	20.6	25.0	19.0	23.3
BODY WIDTH	19.1	21.9	18.2	20.3
C.PED. DEPTH	13.9	14.7	12.8	12.0
PECTORAL ALT.	13.0	17.9	11.5	18.3
HEAD LENGTH	28.7	31.1	29.0	30.9
SNOUT	11.2	11.2	9.8	11.5
EYE	4.7	3.5	5.8	6.8
MOUTH LENGTH	10.9	11.8	10.1	10.4
INTERORB	11.0	11.5	8.9	8.7
N (sample size)	5	5	5	5
COUNTS:				
DORSAL RAYS	5-7	4-7	6	5-7
ANAL RAYS	15-19	12-18	15-21	13-15
PECTORAL RAYS	9-11	5-8	7-10	8-9
PELVIC RAYS	8-10	8-10	9-10	9-10
GILL RAKERS	6-7	5-10	6-10	6-10
VERTEBRAE*	37-41	32-37	37-40	32-37

* Excluding Weberian apparatus.

SUCKERS
CATOSTOMIDAE

Suckers look very much like minnows and, in fact, they are each other's closest relatives. Both groups are members of the Ostariophysi all of which have a Weberian apparatus, a chain of small bones derived from the anterior vertebrae and connecting the swim bladder with the ear. In addition to the minnows and suckers, the catfishes, the familiar aquarium fishes called tetras, and the electric eels are ostariophysans. Minnows and catfishes have specialized pharyngeal arches and lack teeth in the mouth. In suckers, the pharyngeal teeth are comb-like or molariform and eight or more in number. Minnows have fewer pharyngeal teeth.

Suckers have fleshy lips and most species have inferior mouths. The anal fin is farther back than that of most of the North American minnows but the introduced grass carp resembles the suckers in this respect. Two groups of suckers are represented in New York. The longfinned suckers, with more than 18 rays in the dorsal fin, are represented by the carpsuckers, while all of the other species are shortfinned suckers, with 13 or fewer dorsal rays.

Catostomids are scavengers, feeding on detritus and bottom-dwelling organisms that they slurp with their vacuum-cleaner-like mouths. They run into creeks to spawn, and because some species are quite large they provide sport for spearfishermen.

The family is primarily North American with one genus in Southeast Asia and the longnose sucker which occurs in Siberia and across North America.

The currently recognized classification of the family is that of Jenkins (1970).

Catostomidae	
Subfamily Cycleptinae	
Myxocyprinus (Asia)	1 species
Cycleptus	1 species
Subfamily Ictiobinae	
Ictiobus	
(Ictiobus)	4 species
(Megastomatobus)	1 species
Carpiodes	4 species
Subfamily Catostomidae	
Erimyzontini	
Minytrema	1 species
Erimyzon	3 species
Moxostomatini	
Hypentelium	3 species
Moxostoma	
(Megapharynx)	2 species
(Scartomyzon)	8 species
(Thoburnia)	3 species
(Moxostoma)	8 species
Lagochila	1 species
Catostomini	
Catostomus	
(Catostomus)	ca. 17 species
(Pantosteus)	6 species
Deltistes	1 species
Chasmistes	3 species
Xyrauchen	1 species

KEY TO THE SPECIES OF SUCKERS IN NEW YORK

A. Dorsal fin short, with fewer than 18 rays.
D.

A'. Dorsal fin long, with more than 28 rays.

B. Mouth relatively large and oblique, length of the upper jaw nearly equal to length of snout. Subopercle widest below its middle. (Known from western Lake Erie but no definite New York records.)
Ictiobus cyprinellus **Bigmouth buffalo**

B'. Mouth small and nearly horizontal, the upper jaw much shorter than the length of the snout. Subopercle widest at its middle.

C. Tip of lower jaw without a knob-like projection. Dorsal fin with a high lobe in front, the anterior rays reaching beyond the middle of the fin base when depressed. Lateral line scales usually 36 to 40. Snout relatively long, usually contained 3 to 3.5 times in head length.
Carpiodes cyprinus **Quillback, p. 95**

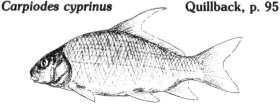

C'. Tip of lower jaw with a knob-like projection at the symphysis. Dorsal fin with a low anterior lobe, its longest rays not reaching the middle of the fin when depressed. Lateral line scales 34 to 36. Snout short, more than 3.5 times in head length. (No definite New York records.)
Carpiodes carpio   **River carpsucker**

D. (A. Dorsal fin with fewer than 18 rays.) Lateral line complete although it may be inconspicuous in juveniles.

                                                             G.

D'. Lateral line incomplete or absent.

E. Scales of the upper sides and back with black spots that form rows so the fish appears streaked. (Known from western Lake Erie but there are no definite New York records.)
Minytrema melanops   **Spotted sucker**

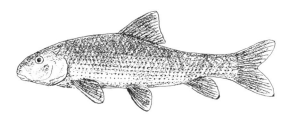

E'. Scales of the upper sides without definite spots at their bases.

F. Dorsal fin rays usually 11 or 12. Scales in lateral series 36 to 38. Dark stripe along midside present at all ages although it may be faint in larger adults.
Erimyzon sucetta   **Lake chubsucker, p. 101**

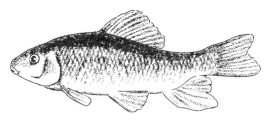

F'. Dorsal fin rays 11 to 14, usually 12. Scales in lateral series 41 to 43. Dark stripe along side continuous in young but broken into vertical bars in adults.
Erimyzon oblongus   **Creek chubsucker, p. 100**

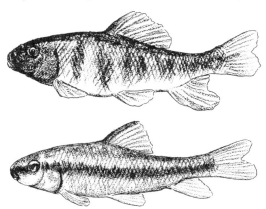

Creek chubsucker, *Erimyzon oblongus* (juvenile below)

G. (D. Lateral line complete.) Head concave between the eyes in individuals more than three inches long, flat in smaller fish. Body conspicuously marked with prominent saddle-shaped crossbands.
Hypentelium nigricans
            Northern hog sucker, p. 102

G'. Head convex between eyes. No definite saddle-shaped crossbands.

H. Scales large, fewer than 53 in the lateral line. Swim bladder with three chambers.

                                                             L.

H'. Scales small, more than 55 in lateral line. Swim bladder with two chambers.

I. Scales fewer than 80 in lateral line. Snout short.
                                                             K.

I'. Scales more than 80 in lateral line. Snout long.

J. Scales very small, more than 100 in lateral line.
Catostomus catostomus
            Longnose sucker, p. 96

J'. Scales 85 to 100 in lateral line.
Catostomus c. nannomyzon   **p. 97**

K. (I. Scales fewer than 80 in lateral line.) About 25 scale rows crossing the midline in front of the dorsal fin.
Catostomus commersoni
            White sucker, p. 98

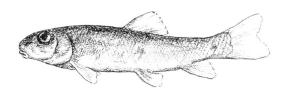

K'. About 30 scale rows crossing the midline in front of the dorsal fin.
Catostomus c. utawana   **p. 99**

L. (H. Scales large, fewer than 53 in lateral line, swim bladder with three chambers.) Scale rows around caudal peduncle 15 or 16. Margin of dorsal fin convex in adults, caudal and dorsal fin red in life. Scales with dark crescents at their bases in juveniles and adults.

Moxostoma valenciennesi

Greater redhorse, p. 111

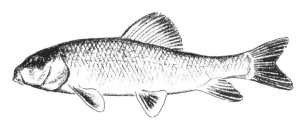

L'. Scale rows around caudal peduncle 12 or 13, usually five above and five below the lateral line.

M. Dorsal fin with 15 or 16 rays, its base long, about equal to its distance from the beginning of the predorsal scales. Dorsal fin margin convex in adults, straight in juveniles. (Tail gray in life, no dark spots at scale bases. Posterior edge of lips forming a definite angle that is obtuse in the young and becomes sharply acute in the adults. Plicae of lips of adults broken into small segments by transverse folds. Body deep, its depth about 2.8 in standard length in adults, 3.7 in young.)

Moxostoma anisurum   **Silver redhorse, p. 105**

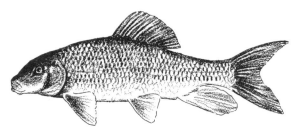

M'. Dorsal fin with 12 to 14 rays, its base shorter, about 1.25 times in predorsal distance. Body slender, its depth more than 3.8 in standard length. Dorsal fin margin straight to strongly falcate.

N. Lateral scales with definite dark spots at their bases. Tail pinkish or red in life.

P.

N'. Lateral scales without dark spots at their bases. Tail gray to orange in life.

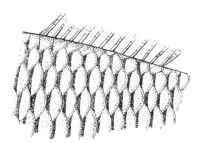

Scales of *Moxostoma macrolepidotum*, showing dark crescents at bases of scales.

O. Lateral line scales 44 to 47 (42 to 49). Pelvic fins usually with 10 rays (9 to 11). Posterior margin of lower lip nearly straight, Plicae of lower lip not broken into papillae. Dorsal fin pointed in front, its margin slightly concave. Body quite slender, its greatest depth more than 4.0 in total length.

Moxostoma duquesnei   **Black redhorse, p. 107**

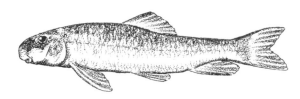

O'. Lateral line scales 42 to 44. Pelvic fin rays usually nine. Posterior margin of lips forming an obtuse angle, folds of lips not broken by transverse grooves except possibly near the corners of the mouth. Dorsal margin slightly concave. Body deeper, less than 4.0 in standard length.

Moxostoma erythrurum

Golden redhorse, p. 108

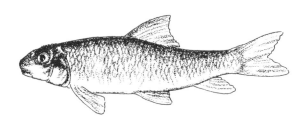

P. (N. Lateral scales with dark spots at their bases.) Posterior margin of lips nearly straight. Folds of lips not broken into papillae. Lateral line scales 42 to 47. Tail pink in life. Lower pharyngeal teeth large and molariform. Dorsal fin margin nearly straight or slightly concave. Head longer, less than 4 times in standard length. Body deeper, its depth less than 4 times in standard length. Tubercles present on snout of breeding males.

Moxostoma carinatum   **River redhorse, p. 106**

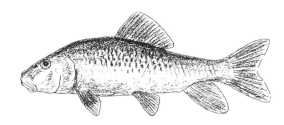

P'. Folds of lips broken into large oval papillae in larger individuals. Lateral line scales 39 to 42. Tail red in life. Lower pharyngeal teeth not enlarged and molar-like. Dorsal margin strongly concave in adults, slightly so in young. Head short, 4.3 to 5.4 times in standard length (3.5 to 4.0 in juveniles less than 3 inches total length). Body slender, its depth 3.7 to 3.9 times in standard length. No tubercles on snout of breeding males.

Moxostoma macrolepidotum

Shorthead redhorse, Q.

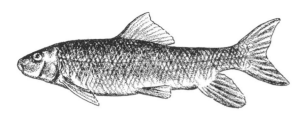

Q. Pelvic rays usually 10, often 9 on one side. Dorsal rays usually 12. Allegheny drainage.
Moxostoma m. breviceps   p. 109

Q'. Pelvic rays usually 9, sometimes 10 on one side. Dorsal rays usually 13. Great Lakes, St. Lawrence, Susquehanna and Hudson drainages.
Moxostoma m. macrolepidotum   p. 109

Carpiodes

Members of this genus have a long dorsal fin with more than 22 rays and a deep and relatively compressed body with large scales. This genus differs from the related *Ictiobus* in having two large cartilaginous areas in the top of the skull (the anterior one reduced or absent in members of the genus *Ictiobus*).

Species of *Carpiodes* also have a longer intestine, arranged in a coil, whereas the gut is in longitudinal loops in *Ictiobus*. There are three species.

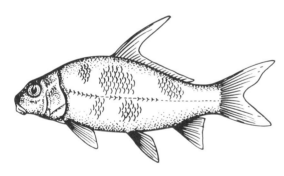

QUILLBACK

Carpiodes cyprinus
(Lesueur, 1817)

Identification
As if it weren't bad enough to have a carpsucker named *Carpiodes cyprinus* and the carp named *Cyprinus carpio,* the two even look a lot alike. Both have rather heavy bodies, large scales, and a long dorsal fin so that sometimes a close look is necessary to separate the two. The carp, however, has hard, serrated rays at the fronts of the dorsal and anal fins and suckers do not; the carp has two pairs of barbels on the upper jaw and the suckers don't; and the sucker has thick grooved lips and an inferior mouth.

Carpsuckers differ from other New York suckers in having more than 22 dorsal fin rays. Their nearest relatives are the buffalofishes, but the buffaloes have a single cartilaginous area in the top of the skull and the carpsuckers have two. (It is necessary to dissect a flap of skin from the top of the head to see this feature.) Buffaloes also have different pharyngeal arches and intestinal convolutions. Two species of buffaloes have been reported from western Lake Erie but not from New York waters.

The quillback differs from the river carpsucker, another species that occurs in the Allegheny River but has not been reported from New York, in having a high lobe at the front of the dorsal fin. This lobe is rather inconspicuous in small juveniles but it becomes higher than the length of the fin base in larger juveniles and adults.

Description
Body robust, deep and compressed, especially dorsally. Dorsal profile highly arched, ventral profile nearly straight to the anal fin, then rising to the base of the caudal rays. Dorsal origin midway between tip of snout and caudal midbase. Dorsal fin falcate with a high anterior lobe, the longest rays as much as 2 or 3 times as long as the rays at the middle of the fin. Caudal fin forked, its lobes rather slender and bluntly pointed. Anal origin midway between caudal midbase and posterior end of pelvic base. Anal falcate with high anterior lobe. Pelvic inserted below the anterior part of the dorsal fin base. Pelvic retrogressive, its anterior corner bluntly pointed and its posterior corner rounded. Pelvic axillary process undeveloped. Pectoral base low and nearly horizontal. Pectoral retrogressive, its anterior corner bluntly pointed, posterior rounded. Gill membranes broadly joined to the isthmus. Mouth inferior, snout large and blunt. Lateral line complete, nearly horizontal. Counts and proportional measurements are given in Table 8.

Color: Generally silvery tan above, shading to silvery cream color ventrally. Scales of the upper sides with narrow pigmented borders. Dorsal and caudal fins dusky. Pelvic, pectoral, and anal fins with an orange wash shading to white at the margin, white on the leading edges. Iris silvery with a suggestion of a vertical bar.

Juveniles and breeding adults: Huntsman illustrated the rather small tubercles on the sides and ventral surface of the head and noted that tubercles were also present on the first dorsal ray, the first eight or nine pectoral rays and the first two pelvic rays. Tubercles were not present on the top of the head. Females do not develop breeding tubercles.

Size: Trautman noted that this species reaches 24 to 26 inches total length but is usually much smaller. Ten or 15 inches is a common size.

Habitat
The quillback is a big-water species, most plentiful in large rivers and lakes, occasionally in moderate-sized, baselevel streams. River specimens tend to be more slender.

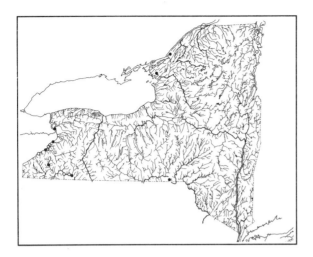

Distribution

The quillback ranges from the St. Lawrence across southern Canada and the Great Lakes to Alberta and south to Louisiana, Alabama, Mississippi, and the Florida Panhandle. On the Atlantic coast it ranges south to the Altamaha River in Georgia.

In New York it is present in Lakes Erie, Ontario and Champlain and in the Susquehanna and Allegheny Rivers.

Life History

Apparently little is known of the life history of the quillback. Spawning takes place in spring or early summer, April to July. Presumably the eggs are broadcast over sandy or muddy bottoms.

Food and Feeding

Definitive studies of the food habits of the quillback seem to be lacking. It probably feeds on immature insects and other invertebrates in the bottom sediment.

References

Bailey and Allum, 1962 (taxonomy). Vanicek, 1961 (life history). Berner, 1948 (generic characters). Huntsman, 1967 (breeding tubercles). Trautman, 1957 (general account). June, 1977 (life history).

Names

Cyprinus is from the Greek *kyprinos,* a kind of carp.

Catostomus cyprinus Lesueur, 1817d: 91 Chesapeake Bay

Labeo cyprinus, DeKay, 1842: 194

Carpiodes cyprinus, Greeley, 1929: 168 Erie-Niagara watershed

Carpiodes thompsoni Agassiz, 1850: 191 Lake Champlain

Catostomus

The two species of *Catostomus* in our area are elongate slender suckers with complete lateral lines, papillose lips, short dorsal fins, small (more than 50 in lateral line) scales, and two-chambered swim bladders. This genus contains about 22 species, most of which are found in the western parts of North America.

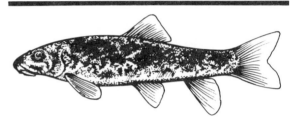

LONGNOSE SUCKER

Catostomus catostomus (Forster, 1773)

Identification

The longnose sucker most resembles the white sucker in general appearance and in having small scales and a short dorsal fin. As its common name implies it has a longer snout than the white sucker and it also has finer scales, more than 85 in the lateral line. The lips of the longnose sucker flare backward whereas in the white sucker they narrow posteriorly. The longnose sucker also has a pronounced transverse ridge on the lower jaw just inside the mouth. This ridge is less developed in the white sucker.

Description

Body slender, nearly terete anteriorly. Dorsal profile a little more arched than the ventral. Dorsal origin slightly closer to tip of snout than to caudal midbase. Dorsal retrogressive with rounded corners. Caudal forked, its lobes bluntly pointed. Anal origin slightly behind tip of depressed last dorsal ray. Anal pointed, its third and fourth rays longest. Pelvic insertion below fourth dorsal ray. Pelvic paddle shaped, its margin convex. Pelvic axillary process well developed. Pectoral base low and slightly oblique. Pectoral retrogressive, its margin straight. Gill membranes broadly joined to isthmus. Mouth inferior, lips papillose. Lateral line complete, straight. Counts and proportional measurements are given in Table 8.

Color: Longnose suckers are rather somber fish, dark gray or brownish above, white or creamy yellow below a rather sharp line of demarcation from the tip of the snout to the base of the lower caudal fin rays. The general color is often overlain with large, irregular blotches of dark gray. Adults with a broad red stripe along the midside, most intense in the breeding season but often present throughout the year. Dorsal, caudal, and pectoral fins slaty, the pectoral with an orange wash. Pelvic and anal fins pale creamy to orange.

Juveniles and breeding adults: Juveniles often have a suggestion of three spots along the sides but these are not as distinct as in the white sucker, and are frequently masked by other marblings. Breeding males develop tubercles on the anal fin, the lower lobe of the caudal and on the head.

Size: Scott and Crossman report the maximum size is about 25 inches total length.

Habitat

The longnose sucker inhabits clean, cool streams in our area and also the deeper parts of lakes. It has been reported to depths of 600 feet in Lake Superior. Scott and Crossman report that it is one of the most widespread and successful ostariophysans in northern Canada but in New York its occurrence is sporadic.

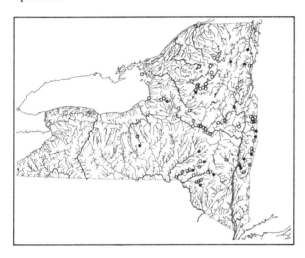

Distribution

The longnose sucker ranges across North America from the northern United States through most of Canada and Alaska to the Arctic drainages of Siberia where it occurs in the Yena, Kolyma, and Anadyr drainages.

In New York, it is common throughout the Adirondacks and east of the Hudson River, sporadic in the Mohawk and Hudson tributaries in the Catskills and in the Upper Delaware watershed. There are a few records farther west.

Life History

Longnose suckers spawn a few days earlier than the white suckers and their spawning run is shorter, as some fish begin to leave after 5 days. Spawning begins when the water temperatures reach 5 C in April or May. The spawning adults move into streams, if possible, or into the shallows of lakes if streams are not available. When ready to spawn a female moves to a group of males. Two to four males then crowd against her and clasp her with their anal fins. The group vibrates together broadcasting the eggs over the gravel. Each episode lasts only a few seconds and may be repeated 6 to 40 times an hour.

The eggs hatch in about 2 weeks and the young remain in the gravel for another 2 weeks. The eggs are about 2.8 to 3.0 mm in diameter and each female produces 17,000 to 60,000.

Longnose suckers grow rather slowly and may live to 20 years or more in the northern part of their range. Age determined from scales has been shown to be inaccurate for the white sucker and published age and growth data for the longnose may also be unreliable.

Food and Feeding

The longnose sucker is a bottom feeder that consumes a variety of invertebrates including amphipods, copepods, cladocerans, and various insects. It is commonly thought to eat trout eggs but the only record is from a situation where trout nests were superimposed so that some nests were excavated by other trout. Thus, the trout eggs may have been dead or at least exposed before they were eaten. Suckers were not seen to dig in the redds.

Notes

The longnose sucker is said to be represented by a dwarf form, *Catostomus c. nannomyzon,* in the Adirondacks and other localities in the eastern part of the state. The dwarf form is said to have larger scales but this has not been verified and the dwarfing may be a strictly environmental effect. Other subspecies have been recognized in other parts of its range.

References

Stenton, 1951 (trout eggs eaten). Geen et al., 1966 (life history). Weisel, 1962 (digestive anatomy). Harris, 1962 (growth and reproduction). Bailey, 1969 (age and growth). Nelson, 1973 (hybridization).

Names

Catostomus is from the Greek *kata,* downward, and *stoma,* mouth.

Cyprinus catostomus Forster, 1773: 155 Hudson Bay

Catostomus catostomus, Greeley, 1928: 97 Owasco Lake

Catostomus catostomus catostomus, Greeley and Bishop, 1932: 81-82 Adirondacks

Catostomus longirostris Lesueur, 1817d: 102 Vermont

Catostomus hudsonius Lesueur, 1817d: 102 Vermont

Catostomus longirostris, Mather, 1886: 33-34 Adirondacks

Catostomus nannomyzon Mather, 1886: 36 Big Moose Lake

Catostomus catostomus nannomyzon, Greeley and Bishop, 1932: 82 Big Moose Lake

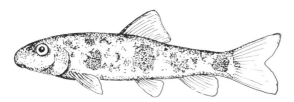

WHITE SUCKER

Catostomus commersoni
(Lacepède, 1803)

Identification
White suckers most closely resemble longnose suckers, agreeing with them in having small scales, short dorsal fins, a complete lateral line and convex interorbital region. White suckers differ from longnose suckers in having larger scales, 55 to 85 in the lateral line, lips flaring less posteriorly, a shorter snout, and less-developed ridges across the jaws. Young white suckers have three large spots along the sides that tend to be more distinct than in the longnose. White sucker scales are somewhat rectangular with radii only in the anterior and posterior fields, whereas the longnose sucker has radii in the dorsal and ventral fields as well.

Description
Body elongate, nearly terete anteriorly. Dorsal profile more arched than the ventral. Dorsal origin midway between tip of snout and caudal midbase. Dorsal fin retrogressive with blunt corners. Dorsal margin straight or slightly falcate, concave anteriorly and convex posteriorly. Caudal fin forked with bluntly pointed lobes. Anal origin well behind tip of depressed last dorsal ray, equidistant between caudal midbase and pelvic insertion. Anal base short. Anal fin pointed with rounded corners. Pelvic insertion below third dorsal ray. Pelvic axillary process distinct, fleshy. Pelvic retrogressive, with straight margin and rounded corners. Pectoral base low and nearly horizontal. Pectoral retrogressive to bluntly pointed. Gill membranes broadly connected to isthmus. Mouth inferior, lips broad and papillose. Lateral line complete, straight. Counts and proportional measurements are given in Table 8.

Color: Dark gray above, shading to white on the belly, the demarcation not as sharp as in the longnose. Scales of the upper sides and back with dusky margins. Dorsal and caudal fins gray. Pectoral gray, sometimes with an orange wash. Pelvic and anal fins pale, sometimes slightly orange.

Juveniles and breeding adults: Smaller fish have three or four irregular to round spots on each side: One above the pectoral fin, one below the dorsal, one in front of the anal fin and one on the side of the caudal peduncle. Breeding males develop tubercles on the anal fin, the lower lobe of the caudal, and the scales of the caudal peduncle, also on the lower gill cover and between the pectoral fins. Females develop some smaller tubercles. During each spawning episode the males develop a pale stripe and a red stripe on the upper sides.

Size: The usual size of adults is 10 to 20 inches. Trautman reported that Lake Erie specimens sometimes reach 25 to 28 inches total length although his largest specimen was 25 inches.

Habitat
The white sucker is nearly ubiquitous in New York and it occurs in nearly every kind of habitat from small creeks to large lakes. Beamish found that below pH 4.2 suckers stop feeding and eventually die but this is reversible if the pH is raised to 5.0. Levels of 3.0 to 3.8 were lethal in 24 hours.

White suckers frequently form large aggregations.

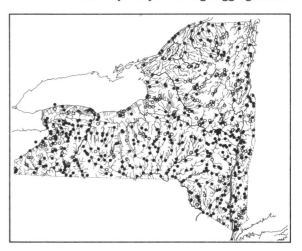

Distribution
The white sucker ranges throughout much of North America from Labrador to the Mackenzie River and south to British Columbia, New Mexico, across to northern Georgia and north on the Atlantic coast to Nova Scotia and Cape Breton Island.

Life History
Raney and Webster studied the migration of white suckers into the inlet of Skaneateles Lake during the spring runs of 1939 and 1941. The 1939 run began on 11 April when the water temperature reached 45 F and continued until 2 June. The run of 1941 began 10 April when the water temperature had increased from 42 to 54 F in a period of 5 days. Most of the migration took place at night, especially between sunset and 10 or 11 pm. Fish were trapped moving both upstream and downstream. Males lost relatively little weight during the spawning run but females lost 20 to 25 percent of their body weight. Females were larger than males — 14 to 21 inches total length. Males ranged from 12 to 18.5 inches.

A 16-inch female contained 21,800 eggs, two 19-inch females contained 36,600 and 47,800 eggs and a 20.75-inch fish contained 41,600 eggs. Eggs maintained at 60 degrees hatched in 7 days, at 65 F they hatched in 5 days, and at 70 degrees they hatched in 4 days with high mortality.

Raney noted that white suckers also spawned in a nearly isolated pool and pointed out that the ability to use a variety of different habitats for spawning is surely one factor in their wide distribution.

The classic study of the breeding behavior of the white sucker is that of Reighard. He was able to observe spawning suckers in Mill Creek, near Grand Rapids, Michigan. Spawning took place on gravel riffles and the site could be recognized by the light color of the gravel where it had been cleaned by the spawning activities of the fish. Males fed over the riffles while waiting for the females. Females remained in deep pools or under banks until they were ready to spawn. Both sexes developed light streaks across the back of the head and along the upper sides leaving a dark stripe along the midside. In males the light stripe was white; in females it was yellow. Males also tended to have white blotches on the back between the head and the dorsal fin.

When ready to spawn a female moved onto the gravel and came to rest on the bottom. Two males approached and stopped with their pectoral fins spread. Then the female moved a short distance and stopped again. After this was repeated, the males were allowed to approach closely. First they raised their dorsal fins, spread their pectorals, protruded their lower jaws and trembled slightly. Finally, they moved into contact with the female, one on each side, with their pectorals beneath her and their bodies close against hers. Their white stripes turned bright scarlet and their eyes turned red. All three fish then vibrated together with their heads moving only slightly but their bodies and tails thrashing vigorously. At this point the milt was released and presumably the eggs too, although the movement and the cloudiness caused by the milt made it impossible to see the nearly transparent eggs being released. Wherever the fins of the males overlapped the fin of the female, the two males pressed close together so there was rigid contact between the three fish. Spawning took only a short time (Reighard estimated 1.5 seconds), then the fish separated and the female continued upstream, sometimes spawning with other males a few feet away. The males resumed searching for food until another female approached. As soon as the fish separated the red stripes faded to white.

Frequently more than 2 males, sometimes as many as 10, spawned with a single female at the same time.

Reighard noted that the spawning activity attracted small fish such as blacknose dace and rainbow darters who came to feed on the eggs and material dislodged by the spawning activity.

Dence studied the life history of "dwarf" white suckers in the Adirondacks. Spawning runs began about 15 May, 3 weeks after the ice disappeared. Males outnumbered females on the spawning riffles. A 4.75-inch fish had 775 eggs; a 6-inch fish had 1,300. Young suckers reached 1.5 inches by the end of the first summer and the fish lived 6 to 9 years. The eggs of the dwarf form hatched in 8 days at 60 to 70 F.

Food and Feeding
Newly hatched suckers feed at the surface in slight current and eat protozoans, rotifers, cyclops nauplii and adult cyclops, insects, and diatoms. There is a critical period later during which they make occasional excursions to the bottom to take in some sand. Midges, cyclops, diatoms, protozoans and algae are eaten during the critical period and up to a length of 3 inches. At larger sizes, the diet changes from microscopic organisms to midges and larger insects with about 6 percent plant material and a small amount of sand. Most sucker stomachs contain a considerable amount of mucus. White suckers feed most at night. The dwarf form feeds on mayfly nymphs, chironomids, small clams, tubificids, snails, amphipods and caddisflies.

Notes
Mather described a dwarf form from the Adirondacks which was supposed to differ in having 30 rather than 25 scales before the dorsal fin and spawning later in the season. Beamish and Crossman studied the growth rates and found no evidence of any difference. They pointed out that the white suckers show great variability in size at maturity and that the "normal" white suckers in Wolf Lake (studied by Dence, 1948) were actually older females and that the females grew faster and lived longer than the males. It is suggested that the apparent difference in spawning time is a reflection of the observation that, in general, older white suckers spawn later in the season. Beamish and Crossman therefore concluded that there is no evidence that the dwarf form, *C. c. utawana*, is worthy of subspecies recognition.

References
Bigelow, 1923 (food habits). Reighard, 1920 (reproductive behavior). Nelson, 1959 (embryology of the swim bladder). Nelson, 1973 (hybridizes with longnose). Buynak and Mohr, 1978b; 1980c (larvae). Raney and Webster, 1942 (spring migration). Dence, 1948 (life history of dwarf form). Beamish and Crossman, 1977 (validity of subspecies). Beamish and Harvey, 1969 (age determination). Beamish, 1972 (pH tolerance); 1974 (growth in acidified lake); 1973 (age and growth variation). Trojnar, 1977 (egg survival at low pH). Metcalf, 1966 (distribution). Stewart, 1926 (food habits). Werner, 1979 (home range). Raney, 1943 (unusual spawning habits). Fuiman and Trojnar, 1980 (eggs). Mather, 1886 (Adirondack fishes).

Names
This species is named for Philebert Commerson, an early French naturalist whose collections were studied by Lacepède.

Cyprinus commersonii Lacepède, 1803: 503 (locality unknown)

Catostomus commersonii, Greeley, 1927: 57 Genesee watershed

Cyprinus teres Mitchill, 1815: 458 New York

Catostomus communis Lesueur, 1817d: 96, 106 Delaware

Catostomus pallidus DeKay, 1842: 200 New York

Catostomus utawana Mather, 1886: 84 Blue Mountain Lake

Erimyzon

The members of this genus have moderate-sized scales, two-chambered swim bladders, and no lateral line. The mouth is somewhat oblique and the males have a few large tubercles on the sides of the snout. Three species.

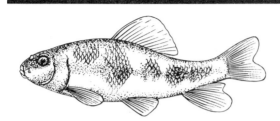

CREEK CHUBSUCKER

Erimyzon oblongus (Mitchill, 1815)

Identification

Chubsuckers are rather stubby-bodied with large scales, a short dorsal fin and no lateral line. All other suckers in New York State have fully developed lateral lines. Juveniles have a pronounced midlateral stripe and resemble minnows but they can be distinguished from minnows by the position of the anal fin and the configuration of the mouth.

Lake and creek chubsuckers are rather similar but the lake chubsucker, *Erimyzon sucetta*, has larger scales, usually fewer than 37 in a row along the midside, but sometimes as many as 40, whereas the creek chubsucker usually has 39 to 44, occasionally as few as 37. In the lake chubsucker the lateral stripe of the juveniles becomes broken into distinct bars in adults, but in the creek chubsucker the band remains visible although with pale sections that give the appearance of a series of partially connected blotches. The lake chubsucker also has fewer dorsal rays, usually 9 or 10; the creek chubsucker usually has 11 or 12.

Description

Body deep and robust, slab sided. Dorsal profile more arched than the ventral. Dorsal origin closer to snout than to caudal base, midway between tip of snout and narrowest part of the caudal peduncle. Dorsal margin convex, the fourth ray longest, the last ray only a little shorter than the first. Caudal moderately forked, its middle rays about four-fifths of the longest upper rays. Caudal lobes rounded. Anal insertion below tip of the depressed dorsal rays. First five rays of the anal fin form a lobe with the last three rays only about half as long. Pelvic insertion below third dorsal ray. Pelvic axillary process prominent, fleshy. Pelvics rounded, paddle shaped with the fourth and fifth rays longest. Gill membranes broadly joined to the isthmus. Mouth rather small, inferior; lips plicate with the lower lips meeting at an acute angle. No lateral line. Counts and proportional measurements are given in Table 8.

Color: Body dark gray above, becoming abruptly paler at midside. There is a diffuse midlateral stripe with about seven semiconnected vertical blotches of varying width that cross the midlateral stripe and encroach on the pale areas above and below the stripe. The scales in the blotches have distinct dark margins, scales of the rest of the sides are less definitely outlined. Caudal grayish, dorsal and anal gray with irregular spots at their bases and with a faint orange wash. Paired fins orange with slightly dusky margins.

Juveniles and breeding adults: Juveniles have a distinct midlateral stripe from the tip of the snout to the base of the tail. This stripe is set off from the dark back by a pale olive stripe of equal width, running from the upper edge of the eye to the base of the upper lobe of the caudal fin. Belly and lower sides abruptly silver white, dorsal and caudal fins reddish.

Adult males develop three huge tubercles in the preorbital region and smaller tubercles on the rays of the anal fin and the lower parts of the caudal peduncle. The anal fin of the male has a blunt anterior lobe.

Size: The creek chubsucker reaches about 10 inches.

Habitat

The creek chubsucker occurs in the deeper parts of moderate-sized streams, moving into smaller creeks during the spawning season. The young often occur in sizeable aggregations in darkly stained swampy streams. Trautman (1957) notes that it has disappeared from much of its former range, apparently because of its inability to tolerate silty waters.

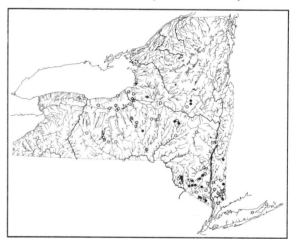

Distribution

This is a lowland species ranging from eastern Lake Ontario and Maine, south on the Atlantic slope to central Georgia. There is a gap on the gulf coast and then it ranges from Mississippi and east Texas north in the Mississippi drainage to southern Wisconsin and Michigan and western Ohio. It is reasonably common in eastern New York State from the southern Adirondacks, the Oswego and Susquehanna drainages, the Delaware and Lower Hudson watersheds and in the Peconic River on Long Island.

Life History

There seems to have been no comprehensive study of the life history of the creek chubsucker. Forney noted that individuals 5 to 7 inches long were ripe. He also found that they did not reproduce in some ponds and considered them of limited potential as a bait species.

Food and Feeding

Flemmer and Wolcott found entomostracans and about 61 percent digested vegetable material in the stomachs of 13 individuals from Tuckahoe Creek in Virginia.

References

Wagner and Cooper, 1963 (ecology). Flemmer and Wolcott, 1966 (food habits). Forney, 1957 (pond culture). Carnes, 1958 (biology).

Names

The species name is the Latin word for rather long, oblong.

Cyprinus oblongus Mitchill, 1815: 459 New York

Labeo oblongus, DeKay, 1842: 193 New York

Labeo elegans DeKay, 1842: 192-193 New York

Labeo esopus DeKay, 1842: 195-196 New York

Labeo elongatus DeKay, 1842: 394 New York

Moxostoma oblongum, Agassiz, 1855: 16-17 (nomenclature)

Catostomus tuberculatus Lesueur, 1817d: 94 Germantown, Pennsylvania

Labeo tuberculatus, DeKay, 1842: 199

Erimyzon sucetta oblongus, Greeley, 1927: 58: Genesee watershed (hypothetical)

Erimyzon oblongus oblongus, Greeley and Bishop, 1932: 82 Lake Ontario drainage

Catostomus gibbosus Lesueur, 1817d: 92 Connecticut River

Labeo gibbosus, DeKay, 1842: 194 New York

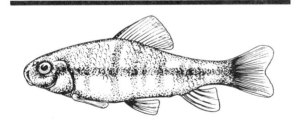

LAKE CHUBSUCKER

Erimyzon sucetta (Lacepède, 1803)

Identification

Chubsuckers differ from other species of suckers in our state in that they have no lateral line. They also have rather short deep bodies and short dorsal fins.

The creek chubsucker is quite similar to the lake chubsucker but they differ in scale size — there are 35 to 37 scales in a row along the side of the body (where the lateral line would be if it were present) in the lake chubsucker but 39 to 44 in the creek chubsucker. In both species the young have a prominent midlateral stripe but in the lake chubsucker it breaks into a series of distinct vertical bars, whereas in the

creek chubsucker it remains visible but with paler sections that separate a series of semiconnected, rather than discrete, bars or blotches.

Description

Body robust, slab sided. Profiles equally curved, with the ventral profile rising sharply at the level of the anal fin. Dorsal fin inserted well forward, the distance from the tip of the snout to the dorsal origin contained about 1.25 times in the distance from dorsal origin to base of the caudal. Dorsal margin convex, its third ray longest, corners rounded. Caudal moderately forked, its middle rays four-fifths the longest upper rays. Caudal lobes rounded. Anal origin well behind the end of the depressed dorsal. Last anal ray less than half the first. Anal margin straight, anterior corner pointed, posterior corner rounded. Pelvic inserted below third dorsal ray. No pelvic axillary process. Pelvic retrogressive, its margin convex. Pectoral low and horizontal, its corners rounded, its margin convex. Gill membranes broadly joined to the isthmus. Mouth small, inferior, lips plicate, halves of the lower lip meeting at an acute angle. No lateral line, no pyloric caeca. Counts and proportional measurements are given in Table 8.

Color: (from a specimen in the Cornell University collection). Sides with a distinct midlateral stripe above which is a pale stripe. Dorsal surface quite dark. Belly pale. Larger specimens have about eight indistinct bars that are primarily formed by intensification of the pigment along the edges of the scales. Margins of the dorsal and anal fins slightly dusky, as are the outer thirds of the pectoral and pelvic fins.

Juveniles and breeding adults: Juveniles have a continuous midlateral stripe and the anterior ray of the dorsal fin is black. Breeding males develop three large tubercles in the side of the snout and the anal fin becomes lobate.

Size: The maximum size is about 11 inches total length. The few New York specimens are all small.

Habitat

The lake chubsucker is an inhabitant of clear, highly vegetated areas of lakes and the slower-moving parts of streams. It is apparently intolerant of fast water, whereas the creek chubsucker shows a definite preference for areas with considerable current.

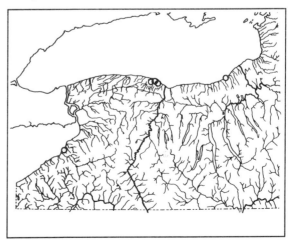

Distribution
The lake chubsucker ranges from western Lake Ontario to Wisconsin and southern Michigan south through the Mississippi Valley to Texas, and along the gulf coast to peninsular Florida, then north on the Atlantic coast to North Carolina and southern Virginia.

In New York it was reported from only a few localities in the lowland areas west of Rochester and Blind Sodus Bay. It appears not to have been collected since the Survey. Greeley also reported it from Muddy Creek near Angola in the Lake Erie drainage.

Life History
Cooper found the lake chubsucker spawned in early June in one pond and in late June and early July in another. The eggs are nonadhesive, about 2 mm in diameter, and were broadcast over vegetation. The eggs hatch in 5 to 7 days at 22.5 to 29.5 C. Each female laid 3,000 to 20,000 eggs and both sexes matured in the third summer. The average length was about 3 inches at the end of the first year, 5 inches at 2 years, 6 inches in 3 years, and 8 inches at 5 years.

Food and Feeding
Small chubsuckers feed on a variety of organisms, including copepods, cladocerans, and midge larvae from on or near the bottom.

Notes
Hubbs recognized two subspecies, *E. s. kennerlii* in the Great Lakes and the Mississippi Valley and *E. s. sucetta* on the Atlantic coast.

References
Cooper, 1936a (life history). Hubbs, 1930b (systematics). Greeley, 1929 (Erie-Niagara watershed).

Names
The name *sucetta* is from the French *sucet,* sucker.
   Cyprinus sucetta Lacepède, 1803: 606 South Carolina
   Erimyzon sucetta Bean, 1903: 105-106 New York
   Moxostoma kennerlii Girard, 1857: 171; 1859: 35 Victoria, Texas
   Erimyzon sucetta kennerlii Hubbs, 1930b: 35-37

Hypentelium

These are elongate, terete suckers with papillose lips, a concave area between the eyes, complete lateral line and two-chambered swim bladder.
Three species are currently recognized.

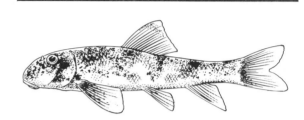

NORTHERN HOG SUCKER

Hypentelium nigricans (Lesueur, 1817)

Identification
Hog suckers are nearly round in cross section with large, prominent saddle-shaped markings, and a mouth that is distinctly tubular. Adults have broad heads that are distinctly concave between the eyes, but the interorbital region of the young is flat or even slightly convex. There are about 50 scales in the lateral line and two chambers in the rather small swim bladder.

Redhorses have larger scales and smaller heads, chubsuckers have no lateral lines and the quillback has a long dorsal fin. White and longnose suckers are more similar in shape but they have much smaller scales.

Description
Body elongate, nearly terete, dorsal profile more arched than the ventral. Head depressed, concave between the eyes in adults. Dorsal fin origin midway between tip of snout and the narrowest part of the caudal peduncle. Dorsal retrogressive, its margin slightly falcate, corners rather sharp. Caudal forked, its lobes bluntly pointed. Anal origin midway between the pelvic insertion and the caudal midbase, well behind the tip of the depressed dorsal fin. Anal base short, anal fin pointed, its third ray longest. Pelvic insertion below middle of dorsal base. Pelvic fin pointed, its fourth ray longest. Pectoral base low and nearly horizontal. Pectoral asymmetrically pointed, with falcate margin. Gill membranes broadly joined to isthmus. Mouth inferior, suctorial, on the bottom of the tubular snout. Lateral line complete, straight. Counts and proportional measurements are given in Table 8.

Color: generally grayish or brown, sometimes tawny above and silvery white below. Snout and top of head dark, almost black in some juveniles, with a dark smudge along the preopercular margin and the anterior part of the lower half of the opercle. Dorsal surface of the body crossed by four irregular bands that slope forward and downward: one before the dorsal origin, one at the middle of the dorsal, one just behind the dorsal and one over the front of the anal fin. There is also a smudge at the base of the tail. There is a spot at the front corner of the dorsal fin and an indistinct bar across the base of the caudal fin. The distal third of the caudal is dusky. Lower fins white, paired fins with irregular spots anteriorly.

Juveniles and breeding adults: Males develop tubercles on all surfaces of the body except the belly and on all of the fins. The tubercles are largest on the anal and lower parts of the caudal fins and on the caudal peduncle. Females also have tubercles but not on the dorsal fin, the sides of the body or the lower surfaces of the pectoral and pelvic fins.

Size: The hog sucker commonly reaches lengths of 7 to 14 inches and Trautman cites a 22.5-inch specimen from Kellys Island, Lake Erie.

Habitat
The hog sucker is a fish of riffles and pools of clear warm streams where there is considerable gradient. It is frequently seen over areas of flat, rocky bottom where the water is only a few inches deep. Its shape and coloration as well as its reduced swim bladder are considered adaptations for living in swift, shallow water.

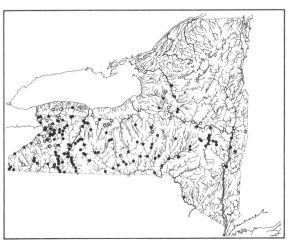

Distribution
The hog sucker is widely distributed west of the Appalachians from Louisiana and southern Mississippi to the Upper Mississippi, Missouri, Tennessee and Ohio drainages, and throughout the southern Great Lakes and in the headwaters of Atlantic coast streams from the Hudson south to Georgia.

It is common throughout western New York and in the Mohawk and Lower Hudson.

Life History
Reighard studied the reproductive behavior of this species in Michigan. Unlike the white sucker and the redhorse, the coloration of the sexes of the hog sucker is similar and there is no light stripe along the body of the breeding fish. The anal fin is longer (by 17 percent) in the male than in the female. Spawning was observed on 4 May 1904 in a small stream near Ann Arbor, about 4:30 in the afternoon. A large female entered the riffle followed by six males which were much smaller. The males pressed them-

selves against the sides and top of the female so they formed a complete mantle with only her head and tail protruding. Reighard did not observe the spawning vibration but noted that none of the males attempted to dislodge the others. He also suggested that the distribution of the tubercles indicates that it is normal for the female to be in contact with males on all sides during the spawning.

Food and Feeding
The hog sucker feeds by turning over stones in riffles to get at insect larvae and other invertebrates. It also grazes on diatoms and other organisms in the aufwuchs on the stones.

References
Reighard, 1920 (spawning). Raney and Lachner, 1946 (age and growth). Buth, 1980 (evolutionary genetics). Buynak and Mohr, 1978a (larval development).

Names
The species name is the Latin word for blackish.
Catostomus nigricans Lesueur, 1817d: 102-103 Lake Erie
Hypentelium nigricans Greeley, 1927: 57 Genesee drainage

TABLE 8
AVERAGE PROPORTIONAL MEASUREMENTS AND COUNTS OF SUCKERS
(Carpiodes, Catostomus, Erimyzon, and *Hypentelium)*

All proportions are expressed in percentage of standard length.

	Carpiodes cyprinus	*Catostomus* catostomus	*Catostomus* commersoni	*Erimyzon* oblongus	*Erimyzon* sucetta	*Hypentelium* nigricans
ST.LENGTH (mm)	144.0	77.4	103.1	135.4	51.6	77.5
TOTAL LENGTH	131.6	126.5	121.9	125.8	127.8	125.2
FORK LENGTH	117.3	118.3	115.6	120.0	121.0	116.8
PREDORSAL	53.8	53.5	51.4	48.6	47.9	47.8
PREANAL	81.9	79.1	77.6	77.5	78.6	76.0
PREPELVIC	58.5	58.0	57.7	52.1	51.3	52.5
DORSAL BASE	42.7	13.5	16.6	21.9	19.6	15.1
ANAL BASE	9.6	7.5	8.2	11.1	10.3	7.2
BODY DEPTH	40.0	20.2	22.6	31.0	29.4	20.6
BODY WIDTH	18.4	15.9	17.8	18.9	14.4	18.3
C. PED. DEPTH	14.7	10.2	10.2	10.9	10.8	9.0
PECTORAL ALT.	30.7	16.8	18.5	22.9	21.8	17.6
HEAD LENGTH	28.9	27.5	27.7	27.1	28.3	26.6
SNOUT	9.8	12.6	12.3	12.3	10.3	13.7
EYE	6.0	5.7	6.1	4.7	6.6	6.7
MOUTH LENGTH	5.7	7.5	9.7	5.8	5.2	6.7
INTERORB	11.3	10.6	14.6	12.7	11.9	12.8
N (sample size)	5	5	4	5	5	5
COUNTS:						
DORSAL RAYS	25-30	9-11	10-13	11-13	10-12	10-13
ANAL RAYS	7-9	7-9	6-8	7	7	7-8
PECTORAL						
RAYS	16-18	16-18	16-19	15-16	15-16	15-17
PELVIC RAYS	8-10	9-11	10-11	8-9	8-10	9
GILL RAKERS	25-29	23-30	20-23	24-26	31-35	21
VERTEBRAE*	34-36	42-43	42-43	35-37	31-33	39-42
SCALES:						
ABOVE L. L.	7-9	16-18	9	15**	13-14**	6-7
LATERAL LINE	35-41	98-108	53-74	41-44	35-37	46-54
BELOW L. L.	5-6	9	5-6	—	5	—

* Excluding Weberian apparatus.   ** Transverse scales counted from pelvic base to dorsal origin.

Moxostoma

Moxostoma differ from other suckers in having rather large scales, complete lateral lines and three-chambered swim bladders. Their lips are typically folded, rather than papillose, although in some species the plicae are broken into papilla-like segments by cross-striations.

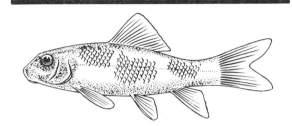

SILVER REDHORSE

Moxostoma anisurum
(Rafinesque, 1820)

Identification
The six species of redhorses that occur in New York are troublesome to identify but once learned they are not really difficult. All moxostomas are generally brassy in color, without prominent markings, and have a complete lateral line, a short dorsal fin, a rather elongate body that is not greatly compressed and large scales (fewer than 50 in the lateral line). They also have the swim bladder divided into three chambers rather than two.

The silver redhorse has 12 or 13 scales around the caudal peduncle (16 in *valenciennesi*), no dark spots at the bases of the scales (present in *macrolepidotum*, *carinatum*, and *valenciennesi*) and no enlarged lower pharyngeal teeth as in *carinatum*. The most distinctive features are the lips — they have fine folds with cross grooves and the halves of the lower lip meet at an acute angle and are often bulbous — and the long dorsal fin with 14 to 15 rays and a convex margin. In life its caudal fin is gray rather than pink or red.

Description
Body elongate but usually somewhat deeper than other species of *Moxostoma*. Dorsal profile more arched than the ventral. Dorsal fin well forward, the distance from the tip of the snout to the dorsal origin contained about 1.25 times in the distance from the dorsal origin to the middle of the caudal base. Dorsal fin retrogressive, its margin slightly falcate in young, becoming convex in adults. Caudal moderately forked, the upper lobe becoming pointed, and the lower rounded, in larger individuals. Anal origin behind tip of depressed dorsal fin. Anal fin bluntly pointed anteriorly, its margin nearly straight, its posterior corner obtuse. Pelvic origin under middle of dorsal base. Pelvic retrogressive with convex margin, bluntly angled corners. Pelvic axillary process small and fleshy. Pectoral low and horizontal, retrogressive, bluntly pointed anteriorly, and rounded

posteriorly. Mouth small, inferior, lips finely plicate with the plicae broken into small papilla-like segments. Lower lip with acute to 90 degree angle, the halves often bulbous. Lateral line complete, straight. Counts and proportional measurements are given in Table 9.

Color: Dorsally olive to brownish, shading to silvery on the sides with a yellow or golden tinge, especially in spawning adults. Pectoral, pelvic and anal fins with a red or orange tinge; dorsal and caudal fins dusky or slightly pink in some southern populations. In preserved specimens the bases of the scales sometimes show a slight darkening but not definite dark bars.

Juveniles and breeding adults: Juveniles have four irregular lateral blotches of which the first three are connected with saddle-shaped dorsal blotches. Males develop tubercles on the caudal and anal fins with smaller tubercles on the dorsal surfaces of the paired fins, the anterior ray of the dorsal fin and the head and body, especially the lower surface of the caudal peduncle. Sometimes there are also small tubercles on the lower surfaces of the paired fins. Females have small tubercles on the lower lobe of the caudal and anal fins, and minute tubercles on the head.

Size: The maximum size listed by Trautman for Ohio is 25 inches total length and 8 pounds 4 ounces.

Habitat
The silver redhorse lives in small to moderate-sized streams and large rivers where it inhabits pools with some current. It is occasionally taken in lakes and reservoirs.

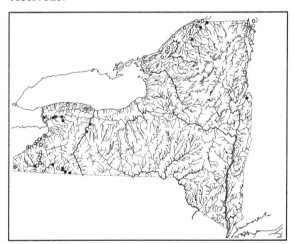

Distribution
The silver redhorse ranges through the Upper Mississippi Valley and the Ohio watersheds, the Great Lakes and Hudson Bay drainages and on the Atlantic coast from the Chowan to the Altamaha drainage. In New York State, it is found in the Allegheny, Erie, Ontario, Lower Genesee and St. Lawrence drainages, and in Lake Champlain.

Life History
Little is known of the life history of the silver redhorse. Workers in Iowa have noted that it spawns in

April or May and earlier in the south. Water temperatures at the time of spawning are reported to be about 13 C (42 F). It is said to mature at about 5 years.

Food and Feeding
The main foods are insect larvae and small mollusks.

Notes
This is the type species of the genus *Moxostoma*.

References
Meyer, 1962 (life history). Jenkins, 1970 (systematics, general summary).

Names
The name *anisurum* is from the Greek *an,* an inseparable prefix meaning not, *is,* equal, and *oura,* tail. This is an obvious reference to the fact that the lobes of the tail differ in shape in larger specimens.

Catostomus anisurus Rafinesque, 1820a: 300 Ohio River (No type designated, but Jenkins (1970) selected CU 53016 from the Ohio River near Matamora, Ohio at U.S. Lock 16 as the type.)

Moxostoma anisurum Greeley, 1928: 97 Oswego drainage.

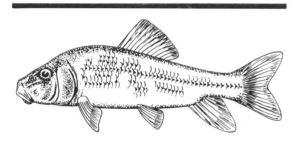

RIVER REDHORSE

Moxostoma carinatum
(Cope, 1870)

Identification
The river redhorse rather closely resembles the golden redhorse, sharing with that species a moderately long head and plicate lips with folds that are not broken by cross folds as in the shorthead and silver redhorses. Like the golden and shorthead redhorses, it has red fins in life. It differs from the golden redhorse in having dark areas at the base of the scales of the upper sides. It has larger scales than the black redhorse and only 12 scales around the caudal peduncle rather than the 15 or 16 of the greater redhorse.

The one distinctive feature of the river redhorse is that the lower six to nine teeth on each pharyngeal arch are enlarged and molar-like.

Description
(Compiled). Body rather elongate, somewhat compressed, especially in adult males. Dorsal profile more arched than the ventral. Dorsal fin margin straight or slightly concave. Caudal fin forked, the upper lobe usually longer and more pointed. Anal fin pointed or rounded. Pectoral fin asymmetrically pointed, third or fourth ray longest. Pelvic retrogressive, inserted below the anterior half of the base of the dorsal fin. Gill membranes broadly joined to the isthmus. Lips plicate, the lower lip forming a slightly to very obtuse angle. Lips very large in breeding adults. Counts and proportional measurements are given in Table 9.

Color: Olive or yellow to brassy above, shading to yellowish white ventrally. Scale bases moderately to intensely darkened. Dorsal and caudal red, brilliant in breeding adults. Lower fins red to orange.

Juveniles and breeding adults: Only the adult males develop breeding tubercles. These can be present on all of the caudal rays, all of the anal rays and occasionally on the dorsal surface of the anterior rays of the pelvic and pectoral fins. On the head there are larger tubercles on the tip and sides of the snout and on the side of the head behind the cheek. Occasionally there are smaller tubercles on the gular and dorsal surfaces of the head and nape. Usually there are no tubercles on the body or a few on the anterior scales.

Size: This is a rather large species; Jenkins noted that tuberculate males were 300 to 460 mm standard length.

Habitat
The river redhorse is a fish of larger streams and sometimes lakes. It seems to show a preference in streams for moderate to swift current and is seldom taken over silty bottom.

Distribution
The range of this species is in the Mississippi drainage from the southern Great Lakes to eastern Oklahoma and Arkansas and east in the Ohio and Tennessee River drainages. There are disjunct populations on the gulf coast and in the Lower St. Lawrence.

Recently it has been reported from the Allegheny River by Becker.

Life History
There is relatively little information about the spawning of this species except that it is a late spawner. Tuberculate males have been taken in Quebec in early June and in the Tennessee River it is reported to be the last of the redhorses to spawn. It spawns in May in Illinois. Jenkins, in Lee et al. (1980), noted that Hackney and his co-workers found that it builds a large redd and the males have a swimming display, habits that are unknown in other catostomids.

Food and Feeding
Hackney et al. reported that it fed on an introduced bivalve mollusk. Forbes and Richardson found that it fed on one-third mollusks, and two-thirds insects. Apparently the molariform teeth are an adaptation for feeding on mollusks.

References
Jenkins, 1970 (complete account). Purkett, 1958 (age and growth). Eastman, 1977 (tooth structure). Buth and Brooks, 1978 (genetics). Becker, 1982

(Allegheny River). Hackney et al., 1968 (life history). Forbes and Richardson, 1920 (general account).

Names
Carinatus is a Latin word meaning keeled.

Placopharynx carinatus Cope, 1870: 467 Wabash River

Moxostoma carinatum Becker, 1982: 36 Allegheny River in New York

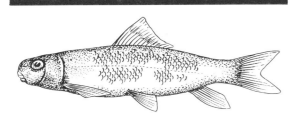

BLACK REDHORSE

Moxostoma duquesnei (Lesueur, 1817)

Identification
The black redhorse is the most slender and terete of the New York redhorses. It agrees with the greater and golden redhorses in having the lips plicate without cross grooves as in the silver and shorthead redhorses. It has no heavy molariform teeth like those of the river redhorse. The black redhorse has more scales in the lateral line (47 to 50) than any other local species of *Moxostoma*, but it has only 12 or 13 rows of scales around the caudal peduncle. Its pelvic ray count, usually 10, will help to separate it from the golden redhorse which usually has only 9 pelvic rays. Its tail is not pink in life.

Description
Body elongate, nearly terete. Dorsal profile a little more curved than the ventral. Dorsal origin over or slightly closer to the tip of the snout than to the base of the caudal. Dorsal fin retrogressive, its margin concave, its corners sharp. Caudal forked, middle rays more than two-thirds the length of the longest upper rays. Anal origin midway between caudal base and middle of the depressed anterior pelvic rays. Anal fin pointed, its middle rays longest. Last anal ray less than half the first. Pelvic fin inserted below middle of the dorsal base. Pelvic retrogressive, its last ray more than half the length of the first, its margin slightly falcate. Pelvic axillary scale well developed. Pectoral base low and nearly horizontal. Pectoral retrogressive, its margin slightly falcate. Gill membranes broadly joined to the isthmus. Lips plicate, without transverse folds. Lower lips form an obtuse angle. Lateral line complete, straight. Counts and proportional measurements are given in Table 9.

Color: Back and upper sides dusky to brownish or black, shading to silvery on the sides and belly. Large young and adults with brassy or golden overtones. Dorsal and caudal fins slate colored, tinged with red in some populations. Anal and paired fins orange or reddish especially near their anterior edges.

Juveniles and breeding adults: Juveniles have a pattern of four irregular dark lateral blotches, the anterior three connected with dark saddles. Breeding males develop tubercles on all rays of the caudal and anal fins, the anterior rays of the dorsal fin, and both surfaces of the paired fins. The head and body also have minute tubercles. Females develop tubercles on the head and body but not on the fin rays. During spawning the males develop a pinkish midlateral band below which the body is a uniform, metallic, greenish black.

Size: Usually 10 to 15 inches. The largest specimen reported by Trautman (1957) from Ohio was 17.3 inches total length.

Habitat
The black redhorse lives in moderate-sized streams and large rivers but it is not common in streams less than 10 feet wide. It seems to be intolerant of consistent silting and usually shows a preference for moderately swift streams where it lives in pools. Sometimes it occurs in lakes but they seem to be a secondary habitat. Young-of-the-year frequently occur around beds of water willow, *Justica americana*.

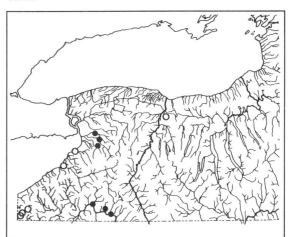

Distribution
The black redhorse occurs throughout the central part of the Mississippi Valley and the Great Lakes east to southern Lake Ontario. It is also present in the uplands of Missouri, Arkansas, and eastern Oklahoma. A distinctive race occurs in the Upper Mobile River system of the gulf coast.

In New York it is known from the Lake Erie and Ontario drainages including the Genesee and the Allegheny River systems.

Life History
The spawning was described by Bowman who studied this species in Big Piney River, Missouri. Spawning occurred in April when the water temperature was 56 to 72 F in shallows, 0.1 to 0.6 meters deep, on riffles with sand and gravel. Males jumped clear of the surface in a pool upstream from the spawning site for an hour or two before drifting onto the shoals. When they reached the shoals they estab-

lished territories 4 to 5 meters in diameter, challenging intruders by swimming at them with the fins extended. Females remained in the pool until ready to spawn, then drifted tailfirst onto the shoals. Two males then came alongside the female and clasped the posterior half of her body between them. The trio vibrated rapidly for about 2 to 4 seconds, tilting their bodies taildown during the spawning. Sometimes other males joined the spawning group. Males and females spawned repeatedly over several days. Spawning seemed to be continuous throughout the day and may have continued at night but the fish were disturbed by the investigators' lights. Ovarian egg count ranged from 1,357 for 50- to 60-gram females to 6,000 for 600- to 650-gram females.

Young-of-the-year reached 77 mm standard length by the end of their first summer and matured at ages II to V. The smallest mature males were 150 mm in the Niangua River and the smallest mature females were 170 mm. In the Big Piney River, the sizes were 200 and 210 mm, respectively. The oldest fish were IX +, 13.3 inches total length.

Black redhorse did not show strong homing tendencies. During the summer they formed loose schools in pools. In the fall they formed schools three or four layers deep and moved into deeper holes in November.

Food and Feeding

Meyer reported that the young up to 65 mm standard length fed principally on phytoplankton. Larger fish fed on aquatic insects with some cladocerans, copepods, and helminths.

Notes

The black redhorse is apparently becoming scarce in New York State.

References

Bowman, 1970 (life history). Jenkins, 1970 (general review, systematics). Kott, Jenkins, and Humphreys, 1979 (status in Canada). Meyer, 1962 (food).

Names

The name *duquesnei* is for Fort Duquesne, an old name for Pittsburgh, Pennsylvania.

Catostomus duquesnii Lesueur, 1817d: 105 Ohio River at Pittsburgh (Type in Acad. Nat. Sci. Phila., apparently lost.)

Moxostoma duquesnii Greeley, 1929: 169 Erie-Niagara watershed

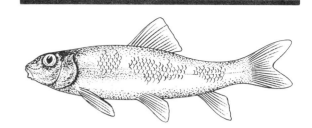

GOLDEN REDHORSE

Moxostoma erythrurum (Rafinesque, 1820)

Identification

The golden redhorse is most easily identified by the features it does not have, rather than those it does. It does not have the dark scale bases of the shorthead, river, and greater redhorses, it does not have the lip folds broken by cross grooves, as in the shorthead and silver redhorse, and it does not have the enlarged pharyngeal teeth of the river redhorse. It has a deeper body and fewer lateral line scales (42 to 44) than the black redhorse (44 to 47).

Description

Body elongate, slab sided. Dorsal profile more arched than the ventral. Dorsal origin a little nearer the tip of the snout than the base of the tail. Dorsal margin slightly falcate, its last ray less than half the first. Caudal fin forked, the middle rays two-thirds as long as the longest upper rays. Caudal lobes bluntly pointed. Anal fin origin behind tip of the depressed dorsal fin. Anal fin bluntly pointed, its third ray longest, its corners rounded. Pelvic axillary process well developed. Pelvic insertion below center of dorsal base. Pelvic fin retrogressive, its margin slightly falcate, its corners slightly rounded. Pectoral base low and almost horizontal. Pectoral asymmetrically pointed. Gill membranes broadly joined to isthmus. Mouth subterminal, lips plicate without cross folds or with a few cross folds near the corners. Eye rather large. Lateral line complete, straight. Counts and proportional measurements are given in Table 9.

Color: Dorsal region olive to brown, upper sides golden or brassy, shading to white on the belly. Scales of the back with dark margins, but no dark bars at their bases. Anal and paired fins yellowish to reddish orange in life. Dorsal and caudal olive to slate gray, sometimes reddish in the Tennessee and Mobile Bay drainages.

Juveniles and breeding adults: Juveniles have four lateral blotches, the anterior three connected by saddles. Spawning individuals of both sexes develop dark stripes and the anal and paired fins become bright salmon colored. They also develop a distinct white stripe on the upper sides and this stripe continues forward across the head above the eyes. Sometimes there are also elongate white spots above the lateral stripe. Males have tubercles developed on all fins, largest on the caudal and anal, minute on the paired fins and present only on the anterior rays of the dorsal. Males also have small to moderately large tubercles on the snout and suborbital and in large individuals also on the dorsal surface of the head and on the operculum. Body with small tubercles on the sides, somewhat larger tubercles on the nape and underside of the caudal peduncle. Females usually without tubercles, sometimes with a few tubercles on the snout and lacrimal. The fins of the males are longer than those of females.

Size: The usual adult length is 10 to 18 inches, Trautman lists a 26-inch specimen from Ohio.

Habitat

The golden redhorse prefers moderate-sized to large streams with some current. It is apparently able to tolerate a moderate amount of silting.

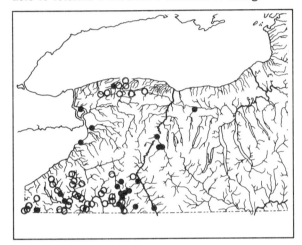

Distribution

The golden redhorse occurs in the Mississippi and southern Great Lakes drainages from western Lake Ontario to Minnesota and south to Oklahoma, Mississippi and the Mobile Bay drainage of Alabama. It occurs on the Atlantic coast from the Roanoke to the James Bay drainages.

In New York it is known from the Allegheny system and from Lakes Erie and Ontario and the Genesee both above and below the Portageville falls. It is frequently encountered in the Barge Canal.

Life History

Reighard described the breeding behavior of this species (under the name *Moxostoma aureolum*). Spawning took place in streams 30 to 40 feet wide, over gravel riffles. Reighard observed spawning on 4 April and 17 May in Mill Creek near Ann Arbor, Michigan. The males were more abundant in the spawning riffles while the females remained in the pools until ready to spawn. Spawning was initiated by the female moving slowly upstream where she was momentarily joined by five males. They soon separated and she continued to move upstream where she was joined by two males, one on each side. The males arched their bodies and turned their heads so that their sides were in close contact with the female. The dorsal fins of the males were fully erected. The three vibrated briefly, then the males

separated and the female continued upstream.

Meyer found that the golden redhorse reaches 3.3 inches total length at age I, 19.2 inches by age VII. Sexual maturity occurred at age III or IV. The oldest fish he examined was age VII.

Food and Feeding

Meyer could find no differences in food habits between the golden redhorse, the silver redhorse, and the shorthead redhorse. Individuals more than 4 inches long of all three species consumed immature chironomids, immature ephemeropterans, and immature trichopterans, along with small mollusks, oligochaetes, and some inorganic debris.

Notes

This species may be increasing in abundance as we have collected it more frequently than other species although the early Survey reports listed it only infrequently.

References

Jenkins, 1970 (summary account, systematics). Reighard, 1920 (spawning behavior). Meyer, 1962 (life history).

Names

The trivial name is from the Greek *erythros*, red, and *oura*, tail. This species however, rarely has red on the tail.

Catostomus erythrurum Rafinesque, 1820d: 305 Ohio basin (Neotype designated by Jenkins: CU 53018 from the Ohio River at Doe Run, Meade County, Kentucky, collected 1959.)

Moxostoma erythrurum Greeley, 1938: 63 Allegheny watershed

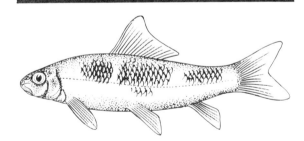

SHORTHEAD REDHORSE

Moxostoma macrolepidotum macrolepidotum (Lesueur, 1817) and *M. m. breviceps* (Cope, 1870)

Identification

The shorthead redhorse is well named for it does have a short head, contained about 4.3 to 5.5 times in the standard length. It also has distinctive lips with the folds broken by cross grooves into large papillae and the halves of the lower lip meeting in a straight line or at a very obtuse angle. The bases of the scales of the sides have definite dark bars. The river redhorse and the greater redhorse, which has more scale rows around the caudal peduncle, are the only other species in our area with dark spots at the bases of the scales, and pink tails. Neither the river redhorse nor the greater redhorse has the lip plicae broken by crossfolds.

Description
Body elongate and slab sided. Dorsal profile more arched than the ventral. Dorsal origin forward, the predorsal distance 1.5 in distance from the dorsal origin to the caudal midbase. Dorsal margin falcate, the anterior corner pointed, the posterior corner slightly rounded. Caudal forked, its upper lobe longer and more pointed than the lower. Anal origin well behind the tip of the depressed dorsal rays. Anal fin pointed, its third ray longest, its corners rounded. Pelvic insertion slightly in advance of the middle of the dorsal base. Pelvic axillary process developed. Pectoral base low and nearly horizontal. Pectoral fin asymmetrically bluntly pointed. Mouth inferior, plicate with crossgrooves, rear margin of lower lip nearly straight. Lateral line complete, straight. Counts and proportional measurements are given in Table 9.

Color: Body olive brown above, shading through brassy yellow to creamy white ventrally. Anal and paired fins orange red, caudal, especially the lower lobe, bright red. Dorsal tinged with red, sometimes completely red. Scales of the upper side with definite bars at their bases.

Juveniles and breeding adults: Breeding males have well-developed tubercles on the caudal and anal fins and minute tubercles on other fins, and on the head and body. Females have a few minute tubercles on the head and on the paired and dorsal fins.

Size: Usually adults are 14 to 18 inches. Trautman (1957) reports individuals up to 24 inches from Lake Erie.

Habitat
The shorthead redhorse apparently prefers moderate to large streams with swift water and relatively silt-free bottoms, but at times it is taken over mud and silt. It sometimes occurs in lakes.

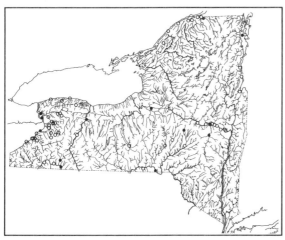

Distribution
The shorthead is widespread in the Mississippi watershed and ranges east through the Great Lakes as far as the St. Lawrence. Its western limits are in Montana and Colorado and its southern extension

is in Arkansas and northern Alabama. On the Atlantic coast, it ranges from the Hudson to the Santee, but apparently it has been extirpated from the Delaware.

Two subspecies are found in New York. *Moxostoma m. breviceps* lives in the Ohio drainage and has 10 pelvic rays and usually 12 (10 to 14) dorsal rays. The upper lobe of the caudal fin is longer than the lower and the dorsal fin is moderately to highly falcate. The typical subspecies, *Moxostoma macrolepidotum macrolepidotum,* occurs in the rest of the state (except the Delaware drainage), has 9 pelvic and usually 13 dorsal rays, caudal lobes equal or the upper slightly longer and the dorsal margin straight to moderately falcate.

Life History
Burr and Morris described the spawning behavior of the shorthead redhorse in Big Rock Creek, Illinois. Spawning took place in daylight hours (11 am to 4 pm) on 16 and 18 May 1976. The spawning site was near the edge of a sandbar on a riffle 15 to 21 cm deep. Circular depressions 40 by 55 and 50 by 90 cms were present and may have been the result of the spawning activities. At least 100 fish milled around and others were present in deeper waters (30 to 60 cm) adjacent to the riffles. Groups of three to seven fish kept together. Two males would align themselves with a female and press close to her, clamping her caudal region with their tails. A vigorous vibration was taken to be the spawning act. The group then dispersed and rejoined the others in the spawning area. No territoriality was observed. Tuberculate hog suckers, *Hypentelium nigricans*, were present on the same riffle on 17 May.

In the Des Moines River, Meyer found that the shorthead redhorse matured at age II and III. They averaged 4.55 inches total length at age I, 13.4 at age V and 25.8 at age VIII.

Buynak and Mohr described and figured the larval stages. The eggs were pale yellow, nonadhesive, and in formalin had a diameter of 3.3 mm. Hatching took place after 8 days at 15.6 C. The newly hatched larvae were 10 mm long and remained quiet for the first 5 days. They were very similar to the larvae of the hog sucker and the differences in myomere counts were too small for positive identification. In the hog sucker, there is a pigment-free area between the eyes, whereas the same area is completely pigmented in the redhorse. By the time they reach a length of 20 mm the pigment bands on the body of the hog sucker are clearly visible.

As in the hog sucker, the urostyle flexes upward shortly after hatching. In quillbacks and white suckers, however, the urostyle remains straight until they reach 9.0 and 14.7 mm, respectively.

Food and Feeding
The chief food of the shorthead redhorse is benthic insect larvae. Some algae and other debris is also ingested.

Notes
Intergrades between the subspecies *M. m. macrole-*

pidotum and *M. m. breviceps* occur in Illinois and Indiana. A third subspecies, *M. m. pisolabrum,* occurs in Kansas, Oklahoma, Missouri, and Arkansas.

References
Jenkins, 1970 (full account). Burr and Morris, 1977 (spawning). Buynak and Mohr, 1979b (larvae). Meyer, 1962 (life history).

Names
The species name is from the Greek *makros,* large, *lepis,* scale, and the New Latin suffix *ota,* having.

Catostomus macrolepidotus Lesueur, 1817d: 94-95 Delaware River

Catostomus aureolus Lesueur, 1817d: 95 Lake Erie near Buffalo

Moxostoma lesueuri Richardson, 1823a: 772 "British America"

Moxostoma aureolum Greeley, 1927: 58 Genesee drainage

Moxostoma lesueuri Greeley, 1927: 58 Genesee drainage

Catostomus oneida DeKay, 1842: 198 Oneida Lake

Ptychostomus breviceps Cope, 1870b: 478 Youghiogheny River

Moxostoma breviceps Greeley, 1938: 63 Allegheny River

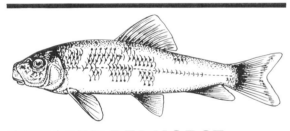

GREATER REDHORSE

Moxostoma valenciennesi
Jordan, 1885

Identification
The greater redhorse is the only New York species belonging to the subgenus *Megapharynx*. Members of this subgenus have 15 or 16 rows of scales around the caudal peduncle (usually 7 above and 7 below the lateral line) whereas members of the subgenus *Moxostoma,* to which the rest of our redhorses belong, have 12 or 13 (usually 5 above and 5 below the lateral line). The greater redhorse resembles the shorthead redhorse in having dark bars at the bases of the scales of the upper sides and pink tails in life. It is easily separated from the shorthead redhorse by its longer head and especially by the lower lip which does not have the folds broken into large papillae. The rear margins of the lower lips also meet at more of an angle in the greater redhorse.

Another species of *Megapharynx*, the copper redhorse, *Moxostoma hubbsi,* occurs in the St. Lawrence but has not been reported from New York waters. The copper redhorse has 15 or 16 rows of scales across the back by the dorsal fin origin (12 or

13 in the greater redhorse). It also has distinctive pharyngeal teeth, of which the lower six or seven are so enlarged that they occupy about half of the arch. In the greater redhorse, however, there are 12 to 30 teeth in the same lower half of the arch.

Description
Body elongate and slab sided. Dorsal profile more arched than the ventral. Dorsal origin nearer snout than base of caudal. Dorsal retrogressive, its corners angled, its margin straight or slightly convex. Caudal moderately forked, its middle rays 1.5 in longest upper rays. Upper caudal lobe slightly more pointed than the lower. Anal origin equidistant between middle of caudal base and end of dorsal fin base. Anal deltoid, retrogressive, its anterior corner bluntly pointed and its posterior corner obliquely angled. Pelvic insertion below anterior half of dorsal base. Pelvic retrogressive with straight margin and bluntly angled corners. Pectoral low and horizontal, retrogressive with pointed anterior corner and obliquely angled posterior corner. Snout blunt. Mouth inferior with plicate lips. Posterior edge of lower lip with obtuse angle. Lateral line complete, nearly straight. Body fully scaled. Counts and proportional measurements are given in Table 9.

Color: Dorsal surface coppery to olive green, shading to golden on lower sides to white on belly. Bases of scales of the upper sides with distinct dark areas. All fins with some red or orange tinge, the caudal often masked with gray.

Juveniles and breeding adults: The males have well-developed tubercles on all fins as well as on the head and body. Females have tubercles only on the fins and the lower caudal peduncle.

Size: Trautman reported 24.5 inches total length as the largest he saw in Ohio.

Habitat
The greater redhorse lives in lakes and large rivers and is seldom seen except during its spawning runs. Apparently it is not tolerant of silting or pollution.

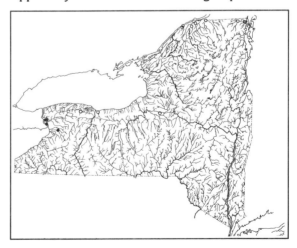

Distribution
The greater redhorse has a more restricted range than many other redhorses. It occurs in the Great Lakes, the St. Lawrence River and the Red River of the North. It also occurs in the Upper Mississippi

and the Ohio basin. In New York it lives in Lakes Erie, Ontario, Champlain and Oneida and in the St. Lawrence and Niagara Rivers.

The life history of this species has not been studied in detail. Jenkins (1970) noted that it spawned between 25 June and 8 July in 1967 and 1968 when the water temperatures were 62 to 66 F. This was soon after the spawning of the white sucker. Spawning occurred over gravel in trios consisting of one female and two males.

Food and Feeding
Rimsky-Korsakoff reported that the greater redhorse in Lake Champlain fed on midges, mollusks, plants, and miscellaneous crustaceans.

Notes
There has been considerable confusion as to the identification of the greater redhorse and records before 1930 may not be reliable.

References
Jenkins, 1970 (systematics, general account). Hubbs, 1930b (taxonomy). Legendre, 1942 (taxonomy). Rimsky-Korsakoff, 1930 (food).

Names
The name *valenciennesi* is given in honor of Achille Valenciennes, a great French naturalist of the 19th century who with Baron Cuvier produced the last comprehensive work on the fishes of the world.

Catostomus carpio Valenciennes *in* Cuvier and Valenciennes, 1844: 457 Lake Ontario (This name is preoccupied by the quillback.)

Moxostoma valenciennesi Jordan, 1885b: 73 (substitute name)

Moxostoma rubreques Hubbs, 1930b: 24-28 Ausable River, Michigan

Moxostoma rubreques Greeley, 1930: 78 Champlain drainage

TABLE 9
AVERAGE PROPORTIONAL MEASUREMENTS AND COUNTS OF REDHORSES *(Moxostoma)*

All proportions are expressed in percentage of standard length.

	anisurum	carinatum	duquesnei	erythrurum	macro-lepidotum	valenci-ennesi
ST. LENGTH (mm)	46.7	365.2	157.6	73.4	305.0	297.0
TOTAL LENGTH	129.4	126.2	128.2	127.9	122.4	123.6
FORK LENGTH	120.5	114.6	103.2	117.8	112.7	116.0
PREDORSAL	47.6	51.8	48.0	49.3	47.0	51.8
PREANAL	78.5	81.8	81.6	78.4	79.8	81.2
PREPELVIC	55.8	55.9	56.7	53.9	52.8	54.6
DORSAL BASE	24.1	17.1	15.8	19.9	17.8	20.8
ANAL BASE	11.0	8.4	5.4	7.1	10.2	8.4
BODY DEPTH	27.8	28.1	22.0	25.5	25.5	28.0
BODY WIDTH	16.4	16.3	13.3	16.3	15.9	18.0
C.PED. DEPTH	11.6	10.6	8.8	10.2	10.2	11.2
PECTORAL ALT.	21.6	21.0	16.9	19.6	18.5	22.2
HEAD LENGTH	29.9	25.6	23.2	25.7	21.5	25.6
SNOUT	11.6	11.8	10.9	10.7	9.6	12.8
EYE	8.6	4.0	4.4	7.7	4.4	4.0
MOUTH LENGTH	5.6	7.0	4.6	2.7	4.5	6.2
INTERORB	11.9	11.5	8.8	5.4	9.9	12.8
N (sample size)	5	5	5	5	5	5
COUNTS:						
DORSAL RAYS	13-17	12-14	12-14	11-14	12-14	12-14
ANAL RAYS	7	7	7	7	7	7
PECTORAL RAYS	16-20	15-19	16-18	16-18	16-17	15-19
PELVIC RAYS	9-10	9	9-10	9	9-10	9
GILL RAKERS	26-30	22	30-32	25-27	22-30	27-31
VERTEBRAE*	36-37	38	39-41	36-39	38-39	40-41
SCALES:						
ABOVE L.L.	6	6	7	5-6	6	6-7
LATERAL LINE	38-46	41-46	45-47	42-44	40-46	40-45
BELOW L. L.	4-5	5	5	4-5	4	5-6

* Excluding Weberian apparatus.

MINNOWS
CYPRINIDAE

Although the name minnow is often applied to any small fish, technically it should be reserved for members of the family Cyprinidae. Most minnows are small, but carp and goldfish are members of this family, and therefore minnows, in spite of their size. Mudminnows and killifishes are not minnows, however, because they belong to completely different families.

Minnows, suckers, and catfishes belong to a large group called the Ostariophysi, members of which have a chain of small, movable bones connecting the swim bladder with the ear. This chain of bones, together with the associated modifications of the vertebral column, is called the Weberian apparatus.

Other ostariophysans are the characins, the Old World loaches, some hillstream fishes of southeastern Asia, and the gymnotoids, the group to which the electric eel belongs. The complexity of the Weberian apparatus is so great that it is unlikely that it arose more than once; hence, all Ostariophysi must have had a common ancestor.

The family Cyprinidae is one of the largest fami-

lies of fishes and far and away the largest in New York State, where 48 species and 53 recognizable forms are present. This family contains about 275 genera and more than 1,600 species. They dominate the freshwaters of the Northern Hemisphere and occur in Africa but are replaced by other ostariophysans in South America. There are no native freshwater ostariophysans in Australia.

During the breeding season some minnows develop bright breeding colors and special skin structures called pearl organs or breeding tubercles. These are highly variable and useful for identifying and classifying the species of minnows. The fish themselves use their tubercles for nest building, fighting and courtship rituals, and for maintaining contact between the sexes during spawning. Some other groups of fishes also have breeding tubercles or other contact organs but the minnows have them especially well developed. For a review of breeding tubercles and contact organs see Wiley and Collette (1970).

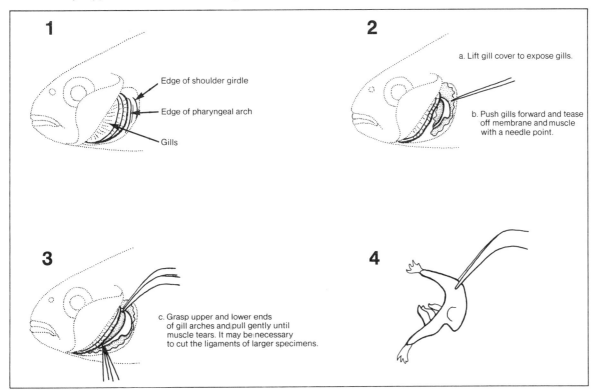

1
Edge of shoulder girdle
Edge of pharyngeal arch
Gills

2
a. Lift gill cover to expose gills.
b. Push gills forward and tease off membrane and muscle with a needle point.

3
c. Grasp upper and lower ends of gill arches and pull gently until muscle tears. It may be necessary to cut the ligaments of larger specimens.

4

Figure 9. How to Dissect Pharyngeal Teeth of Minnows

Although minnows have no teeth on the jaws, they do have highly specialized teeth on the lower pharyngeal bones, which are located just behind the gills and, in fact, are the remnants of a specialized fifth gill arch. The pharyngeal teeth are greatly enlarged and occur in one, two, or three rows. No native North American fish has more than two rows but the introduced carp has three. The inner row consists of four or five teeth that may have hooks, flat grinding surfaces or other special forms. The outer row consists of one or two smaller teeth. Some of the teeth of the carp and the grass carp have enamel ridges on the grinding surface.

Tooth counts are useful for identification of species and the accompanying diagram illustrates how to remove the teeth so that they can be cleaned and examined under a low-power microscope.

Arrangement of Species Accounts

Because there are so many species of minnows in our area, the conventional alphabetical arrangement of generic and species accounts is unsatisfactory. It is much more informative to group the genera (and species in the genus *Notropis*) so that species that are apt to be confused, or that share some common characteristics are together. The groups that I have chosen are as follows:

1. Exotic (introduced) species.
   a. Goldfish *(Carassius auratus)*
   b. Grass carp *(Ctenopharyngodon idella)*
   c. Common carp *(Cyprinus carpio)*
   d. Bitterling *(Rhodeus sericeus)*
   e. Rudd *(Scardinius erythrophthalmus)*

2. Native minnows with striking anatomical specializations.
   a. Central stoneroller *(Campostoma anomalum)* — Cartilaginous rim on lower jaw; long gut.
   b. Silverjaw minnow *(Ericymba buccata)* — Greatly enlarged head canals.
   c. Cutlips and tonguetied minnows *(Exoglossum maxillingua* and *E. laurae)* — Blade-like modification of lower jaw.
   d. Golden shiner *(Notemigonus crysoleucas)* — Fleshy keel in front of anus; deeply decurved lateral line.

3. Native species with barbels.
   Genera *Couesius, Hybopsis, Nocomis, Rhinichthys,* and *Semotilus.*

4. Native minnows without barbels.
   Genera *Clinostomus, Hybognathus, Notropis, Phoxinus,* and *Pimephales.*

KEY TO THE GENERA OF MINNOWS IN NEW YORK

(Species are given for monotypic genera)

A. Dorsal fin short, consisting of fewer than 12 rays. (The short, rudimentary rays at the fronts of the dorsal and anal fins are not counted.)

C.

A'. Dorsal fin long, with 14 or more branched rays. Dorsal and anal fins with a hard, serrated ray at the front.

Elongate dorsal fin of carp, with hardened, serrated ray at front.

B. Upper jaw with two pairs of long barbels. Lateral line scales 35 or more. Introduced. (Some individuals have only a few scales in irregular patches or no scales at all.)
Cyprinus carpio **Common carp, p. 121**

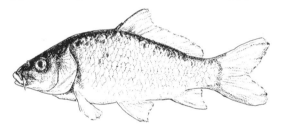

B'. Upper jaw without barbels. Scales large, 31 or fewer in the lateral line. Introduced.
Carassius auratus **Goldfish, p. 119**
(Carp and goldfish sometimes hybridize and the hybrids are intermediate with one or more small, often asymmetrical, barbels and 30 to 35 scales in the lateral line.)

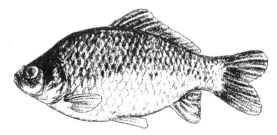

C. (A. Dorsal fin with 12 or fewer rays.) Body deep, scales 34 to 38. Lateral line very incomplete with only five or six pores. Total length less than 3 inches. Introduced.
Rhodeus sericeus **Bitterling, p. 123**

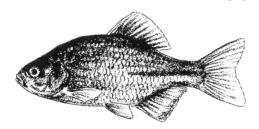

C'. Lateral line longer, with 10 or more pored scales.

D. Belly rounded, without a keel-like area in front of the anus. Lateral line straight or only moderately decurved.

F.

D'. Body rather compressed, belly with a moderately sharp keel-like area just in front of the anus. Lateral line deeply decurved.

E. Keel in front of the anus covered with scales. In life, the iris is golden with a red spot dorsally. Introduced.
Scardinius erythrophthalmus **Rudd, p. 124**

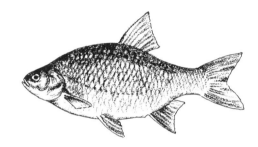

E'. Keel in front of the anus short and fleshy and not covered with scales. Native.
Notemigonus crysoleucas
Golden shiner, p. 132

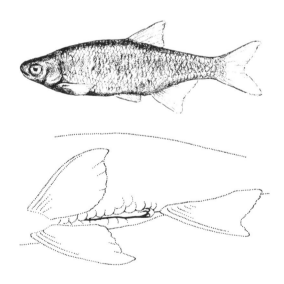

Abdominal keel of golden shiner.

F. (D. No keel in front of the anus.) Pharyngeal teeth 2,5-5,2 or 2,4-5,2, each tooth in the main row with prominent parallel ridges and grooves. Anal fin far back, the distance from the anal origin to the base of the ventral caudal rays one-third or less of the distance from the anal origin to the tip of

the snout. Eyes low on the side of the head. Introduced.
Ctenopharyngodon idella
Grass carp (White amur), p. 120

F'. Pharyngeal teeth without parallel grooves. Anal fin farther forward, the distance from the anal origin to the base of the ventral caudal rays 2.5 or fewer times in the distance from the anal origin to the tip of the snout. Eyes in the usual position, not noticeably low on the side of the head.

G. Edge of lower jaw with a raised cartilaginous rim or "rock scraper" .
Campostoma anomalum
Central stoneroller, p. 126

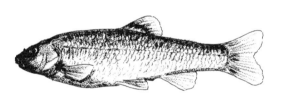

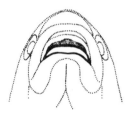

"Rock scraper" of stoneroller.

G'. Lower jaw without a raised, cartilaginous rim although it may be otherwise modified.

H. Sensory canals of head greatly enlarged with the covering bone reduced to narrow bridges that are visible through the skin and give the head, and especially the lower jaw, a honeycomb appearance.
Ericymba buccata **Silverjaw minnow, p. 127**

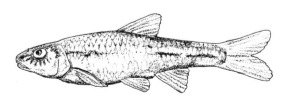

H'. Head canals not greatly enlarged, not having honeycomb appearance.

I. Lower jaw with three lobes, the middle one hard and bony, the lateral ones fleshy. In one species, the lateral lobes are poorly developed but recognizable.
Exoglossum **p. 129**

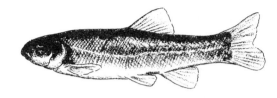

Cutlips minnow, *Exoglossum maxillingua*

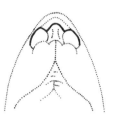

Lobate lower jaws of *Exoglossum* species.

I'. Lower jaw not lobate.

J. Maxillary barbels present, located either in a depression behind the end of the maxillary or in the groove above the posterior part of the maxillary bone
O.

J'. Barbels absent

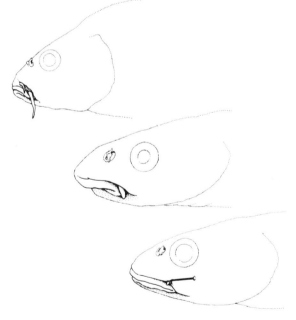

Minnow barbels. Left: Double barbels of carp. Center: Terminal barbel of longnose dace. Right: Subterminal barbel of creek chub.

K. Scales very small, more than 60 in lateral series.
N.

K'. Scales larger, fewer than 55 in lateral series.

L. Dorsal fin with a stout ray at the front that is about one-half the length of the first principal rays and separated from the latter by membrane. Adults with a distinct black spot at the front of the dorsal fin and well above its base. Predorsal scales small and irregular.
Pimephales   p. 203

Bluntnose minnow, *Pimephales notatus*

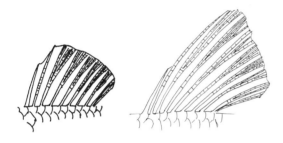

First dorsal fin rays of *Pimephales* (left) and *Notropis* (right). The splint-like element at the front is much stouter in *Pimephales*.

L'. Short ray at the front of the dorsal fin usually splint-like and closely attached to the first principal ray although there is a narrow separation in some species. Spot at front of dorsal fin, if present, close to the base of the fin.

M. Lower jaw crescent shaped. Intestine with extra loops on the right side. (In preserved specimens, these are sometimes visible through the skin.)
Hybognathus   p. 162

Brassy minnow, *Hybognathus hankinsoni*

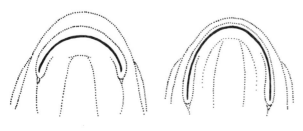

Lower jaw of *Hybognathus* (left) and *Notropis* (right).

M'. Lower jaw U-shaped. Intestine short and S-shaped, without extra loops on the right side.
Notropis   p. 166

Common shiner, *Notropis cornutus*

N. (K. Scales small, more than 60 in lateral series.) Mouth large and oblique, the upper jaw reaching to below front of the eye. Peritoneum silvery.
Clinostomus elongatus   Redside dace, p. 160

N'. Mouth smaller, the maxillary not reaching to the front of the eye.
Phoxinus   p. 199

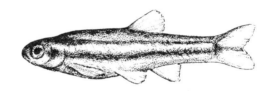

Northern redbelly dace, *Phoxinus eos*

O. (J. Barbels present.) Barbels subterminal, located in the groove above the maxillary. Sometimes difficult to see in small fish. Often, it will be necessary to open the mouth to see them.
Semotilus   p. 153

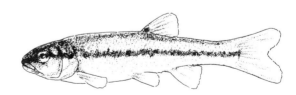

Creek chub, *Semotilus atromaculatus*

O'. Barbels terminal, located in depression behind the end of the maxillary.

P. Scales small, 55 or more in lateral line.
                                                              R.

P'. Scales larger, fewer than 55 in lateral line.

Q. Mouth large and subterminal, the snout blunt and only slightly overhanging the mouth. Eye diameter less than the length of the upper jaw. Breeding males with large, conspicuous tubercles on head.
Nocomis p. 142

R'. Upper jaw protractile, a continuous groove between the tip of the snout and the upper lip.
Couesius plumbeus Lake chub, p. 135

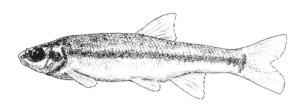

River chub, *Nocomis micropogon*

Q'. Mouth horizontal and inferior. Snout blunt and conspicuously overhanging the mouth. Eye large, its diameter greater than the length of the upper jaw.
Hybopsis p. 137

Bigeye chub, *Hybopsis amblops*

R. (P. Scales small, more than 55 in lateral line.) Upper jaw nonprotractile, the upper lip joined to the tip of the snout by a bridge of tissue (frenum).
Rhinichthys p. 147

Eastern blacknose dace, *Rhinichthys atratulus*

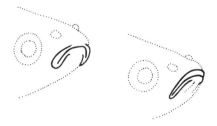

Premaxillary frenum: present in *Rhinichthys* (left), absent in *Couesius* (right).

Carassius

The goldfish belongs to the Asian genus *Carassius*. It is quite similar to the carp in general appearance but goldfish have no barbels and only a single row of pharyngeal teeth. There is at least one other species in the genus.

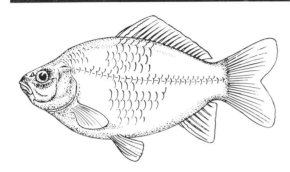

GOLDFISH

Carassius auratus (Linnaeus, 1758)

Identification
The goldfish and the carp are the only minnows in North America that have more than ten rays in the dorsal fin and hard serrated rays at the fronts of the dorsal and anal fins. They both have rather heavy bodies and large scales (fewer than 40 in the lateral line). They might be confused with the quillback or with a buffalofish but those species are suckers and do not have hard fin rays.

Carp and goldfish are easily distinguished by the fact that the carp has two pairs of barbels on the upper jaw and the goldfish has none. Carp have more than 35 scales in the lateral line and three rows of pharyngeal teeth on each side. The goldfish has fewer than 30 lateral line scales and only a single row of pharyngeal teeth on each side.

Description
Body short and robust, deepest at the dorsal origin. Caudal peduncle deep, head rather short. Dorsal fin long, slightly falcate, with a stout, hard, serrated ray at its front, preceded by one or two short splint-like rays. Caudal fin moderately short, with rounded lobes. Anal fin short, its margin convex, its first principal ray hard and serrated. Pelvics abdominal, retrogressive, rounded. Pectoral base low and horizontal. Pectorals short, retrogressive, with bluntly rounded corners. Gill membranes broadly joined but not fused to the isthmus. Mouth terminal, strongly oblique, the maxillary ending below the posterior nostril. Counts and proportional measurements are presented in Table 10.

Color: Goldfish are extremely variable in color. The natural or wild color is olive dorsally, paler below with a slight brassy sheen. Individuals that are uniform orange red or orange with black or white, or both, spots and blotches are not uncommon.

Juveniles and breeding adults: Juveniles are usu-ally olive color and assume the bright gold color later in life. Breeding males develop fine tubercles on the opercle, anterior dorsal surface of the body and on the pectoral fins.

Size: Goldfish vary greatly in size and pets kept in aquaria may never grow to more than 3 or 4 inches. In the wild, however, they commonly attain lengths of 12 to 14 inches and Trautman (1957) reports individuals up to 16 inches total length.

Habitat
Goldfish are generally confined to larger streams and lakes and ponds. They show a preference for areas with abundant vegetation and seem to be less tolerant of swift water, low temperature, siltation, and pollution than the carp.

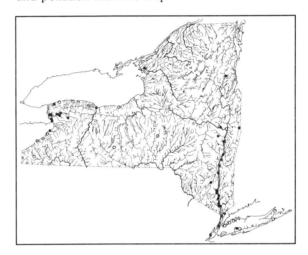

Distribution
The goldfish is a native of eastern Asia and was domesticated in China about 960 AD. It was widely introduced into North America before 1832 but the exact date of the first introductions is probably not known.

Goldfish may be found almost anywhere in New York State but flourishing, reproducing populations are found only in Lakes Erie and Ontario and in the Hudson River.

Life History
Goldfish spawn in weedy areas in May or June, when the water temperature is 77 to 85 F. Sometimes, the female and one or more males swim together over vegetation and broadcast the eggs, which are adhesive and 1.2 to 1.5 mm in diameter. Often, the eggs are deposited on algae an inch or two below the surface. Spawning groups often place their snouts against the bank as they spawn and thus deposit their eggs just below the shoreline. Hatching takes 3 to 6 days depending on temperature.

Under ideal conditions, goldfish reach about 2 to 2.5 inches fork length by the end of the first summer and mature at 100 to 185 mm standard length.

Food and Feeding
Goldfish are omnivorous feeders and consume phytoplankton as well as a variety of bottom orga-

nisms including insects, worms, mollusks, crustaceans, and aquatic vegetation.

Notes
There is a small fishery in the Hudson River where large goldfish are caught to be used for ornamental purposes. In 1979 and 1980, an epidemic of furunculosis reduced the population drastically.

Goldfish hybridize with carp and the offspring are recognizable by the presence of poorly developed and often asymmetrical barbels, intermediate scale counts, and intermediate pharyngeal tooth structure. Hybrids, however, are not found everywhere the two species occur together, and it is suspected that the genetics of their hybridizing is quite complex.

Colorful "koi carp" are often seen in ponds. These resemble bright goldfish but they are actually carp, *Cyprinus carpio*. Another common pet species is the crucian carp, *Carassius carassius*. These are not known to be reproducing in the wild in New York.

References
Hervey and Hems, 1968 (general review). Murai and Andrews, 1977 (salinity tolerance). Battle, 1940 (life history). Taylor and Mahon, 1977 (hybridization). Gerlach, 1983 (larvae).

Names
Auratus is the Latin word for rich in gold, ornamented.

Cyprinus auratus Linnaeus, 1758: 322 China, Japan

Carassius auratus Bean, 1903: 164-166 New York

Ctenopharyngodon

The grass carp belongs to a monotypic (single species) Asiatic genus. There are no barbels and no hard serrated rays in the dorsal and anal fins and the dorsal fin is short with 8 to 10 rays. (Carp and goldfish have longer dorsal fins). There are three rows of pharyngeal teeth on each arch and the teeth are strongly serrated. Grass carp have the eyes lower on the sides of the head than most other species of minnows and the anal fin is farther back than in North American minnows. Grass carp are large fish, reaching weights of more than 17 pounds.

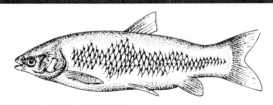

GRASS CARP

Ctenopharyngodon idella (Valenciennes, 1844)

Identification
The grass carp is an introduced species easily recog-

nized by its large size, large scales, short dorsal fin with only eight rays, and distinctive physiognomy with the eyes low on the sides of the head. Its anal fin is inserted far back on the body, more like suckers than native American minnows. The pharyngeal teeth are in two rows and those in the main row have parallel transverse grooves unlike the pharyngeal teeth of other New York species.

Dark scale margins give the grass carp a characteristic crosshatched appearance.

Description
Body elongate, nearly terete. Profiles about equally curved. Dorsal origin near the center of the body. Dorsal fin retrogressive, with pointed corners. Caudal peduncle deep, caudal fin moderately forked with bluntly pointed lobes. Anal fin short, retrogressive, deltoid, with sharp corners. Pelvic insertion below dorsal origin. Pelvic retrogressive. Pectoral base low, nearly horizontal. Head rather short. Mouth terminal, maxillary ending below front of eye. Counts and proportional measurements are given in Table 10.

Color: Dark gray above, shading to white on the belly. Scales of the upper sides with dark margins. Fins dark.

Size: Grass carp reach weights in excess of 23 pounds.

Habitat
Grass carp live in lakes, ponds, and streams. They can tolerate a wide range of environmental conditions, including brackish water so that they have been able to move between major river systems.

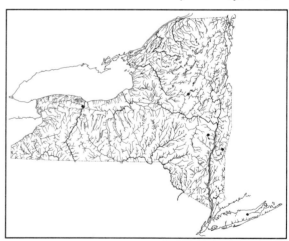

Distribution
Grass carp are native to eastern Asia from the Amur basin to the West River.

In the United States, they have been stocked since 1963 and presently range throughout much of the central United States from Ohio, Michigan and Wisconsin to Texas and Louisiana, east along the gulf coast to peninsular Florida and north to South Carolina. They have also been stocked in some areas of the Northeast and the Far West. There are several hatcheries in North Carolina and at least 115 lakes and numerous reservoirs in that state have been stocked with grass carp. Four ponds in New York are known to have been stocked from private hatcheries but, so far, no free wild fish have been caught here.

Life History
As of 1978, no natural reproduction had been documented in the continental United States. Stanley, Maley, and Sutton reviewed the environmental requirements and predicted that spawning can and probably will occur here but it will be limited to a relatively few areas. Grass carp eggs are large, about 2 to 2.5 mm unfertilized and up to 6 mm after water-hardening. Temperatures must be at least 19 C, and the optimum is between 22 and 26 C. Hatching requires 24 to 30 hours at 17 C, 18 hours at 28 C. This imposes a limit on the spawning because the semibuoyant eggs must be kept suspended in the water column by turbulent waters until they hatch. At 20 C and with an average current of 1.2 meters per second, 180 km of river would be needed and at 28 C and 0.8 m/sec about 50 km would be needed. After hatching, the larval stages must find quiet water with abundant microplankton as soon as their yolk supplies are exhausted, usually in 2 to 4 days. Ideal food production occurs in areas with dense aquatic vegetation but older grass carp feed on vegetation and thus tend to limit their own population. Juvenile grass carp are wanderers and mature adults often migrate upstream to suitable spawning sites. In Russia, grass carp mature at age VI or VII.

Grass carp grow rapidly. Fish stocked (illegally) in a Long Island pond when they were 4 to 6 inches long weighed 8 to 11 pounds when they were caught 16 months later.

Food and Feeding
Grass carp adults and larger juveniles are primarily herbivores with *Potamogeton, Elodea, Ceratophyllum* and *Najas* among the most important foods. Animal remains constitute less than 0.1 percent of the diet. There is some selection in the diet but no strong preferences.

Notes
Because of its herbivorous diet, the grass carp is considered a possible candidate for a fish to be used to control aquatic weeds in highly eutrophic environments. Much research is being conducted to evaluate this potential but because of the potential harm to aquatic environments at least 35 states, New York among them, have outlawed its importation and release.

Reference
Greenfield, 1973 (inadvisability of its introduction). The Transactions of the American Fisheries Society, volume 107, number 1 (1978), contains a special section of 16 papers on various aspects of grass carp management. Bornholdt, 1979 (literature review). Stanley, Maley, and Sutton, 1978 (habitat requirements).

Names
Idella is probably a diminutive of *ide,* a kind of European minnow.

Leuciscus idella Valenciennes *in* Cuvier and Valenciennes, 1844: 362 China

Cyprinus

The carp is a Eurasian species with two pairs of well-developed barbels and three rows of pharyngeal teeth. Like the goldfish, it has strong serrated spine-like rays at the front of the dorsal and anal fins. *Cyprinus* is the genus on which the family name Cyprinidae is based.

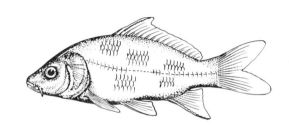

COMMON CARP

Cyprinus carpio Linnaeus, 1758

Identification
Only two species of minnows in New York State have hard serrated rays in the front of the dorsal and anal fins. They are the carp and the goldfish, both introduced species, originally native to Eurasia. Both have more than 15 rays in the dorsal fin.

Carp are distinguished from goldfish by their smaller scales, 35 to 39 in the lateral line (goldfish have fewer than 30), the presence of 2 pairs of barbels on the upper jaw (none in the goldfish), larger size and by the presence of 3 rows of teeth on the pharyngeal arch. Carp pharyngeal teeth are molariform and some have wavy dark crosslines.

At first glance, a carp might be confused with the quillback sucker but the suckers lack both barbels and serrated fin spines.

Description
Body moderately elongate, thick and slab sided. Dorsal profile more curved than the ventral. Dorsal origin about equidistant between tip of snout and base of caudal fin. Dorsal fin long, with a hard ray at the front which has a double row of teeth along its posterior margin, these teeth normally embedded in membrane. Dorsal fin retrogressive, its margin slightly concave, its corners rather sharp. Caudal moderately forked, with rounded lobes. Anal fin short, with serrated anterior ray, retrogressive, with softly angled corners. Pelvic inserted slightly behind dorsal origin. Pelvics retrogressive, with rounded corners. Pelvics low, with strongly oblique bases, retrogressive, with rounded corners. Gill membranes broadly joined to the isthmus. Opercles with radiating striations. Upper jaw with two pairs of barbels, the anteriormost shorter. Scales large and regular, reduced to a few patches, or absent. Counts and proportional measurements are given in Table 10.

Color: Carp are generally a brassy gold to brown or olive above, shading to silver, white, or yellow below. The scales of the upper sides have rather prominent dark margins with a concentration of pigment at the base of each scale.

Juveniles and breeding adults: Males tend to be darker green to gray with a dark abdomen; females are lighter with a yellowish belly. Only the males develop tubercles which are very tiny and scattered over the head and pectoral fins.

Size: The IFGA all-tackle record is 55 pounds 5 ounces from Clearwater Lake in Minnesota. The New York record is 35 pounds 4 ounces taken in Keuka Lake, May 1976 by Joseph Dewey.

Habitat

Carp are generally restricted to lakes, ponds, and larger streams. Usually, they are most abundant where there is dense aquatic vegetation, although in their feeding activities they often destroy vegetation by physically uprooting the plants, and by stirring up the bottom, making the water turbid so that light cannot reach the growing plants.

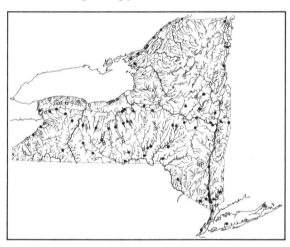

Distribution

Carp are native to Europe and temperate Asia and were one of the first fishes to be domesticated. They have been introduced into most of North America and also into many other parts of the world. They occur throughout New York State wherever suitable habitats are present.

Life History

Carp have a fairly long spawning period from late spring to early August, beginning when the water temperatures reach at least 17 C. Spawning may be interrupted if the water temperature falls below 18 C or rises above 18 C. Swee and McCrimmon studied reproduction in St. Lawrence Lake. As the water warmed, large numbers of carp congregated over shallow, weedy flats where the water was 1 to 5 feet deep. Spawning groups usually consisted of 1 to 3 females and 2 to 12 males. Males outnumbered the females and remained on the spawning beds longer. Spawning occurred only during daylight hours.

Males initiate spawning by pushing their heads against the female's side. The females respond by raising the tail and caudal peduncle, then the males move alongside the females, usually four or five males accompanying each female. The group moves along just below the surface, thrashing violently as the small, adhesive eggs are broadcast over vegetation. After spawning, the females rest for several hours while the males join other spawning groups. The eggs water-harden in 15 to 25 minutes and hatch between 55 and 114 hours later. Some females spawn a second time during the season. A 15.5-inch fish contained 36,000 eggs; a 33.5-inch female had 2,208,000. In Lake St. Lawrence, males matured at ages III and IV (14 inches); females at IV and V (17 inches).

Food and Feeding

Carp are general omnivores that feed on filamentous algae and various benthic animals including snails, annelids, midge larvae, and crustaceans. At times, they move up in the water column to feed on plant and animal materials.

Notes

Carp are abundant in some eutrophic waters and are considered detrimental because they destroy aquatic vegetation and stir up the bottom so the water is continually turbid. They are a good food fish but their feeding habits make them difficult for sport fishermen to catch. Any fisherman who accepts the challenge, however, finds the carp a worthy quarry. Considerable work has been done on control methods including experiments with hallucinogenic compounds that alter the carps' behavior so they can be more readily captured.

References

Swee and McCrimmon, 1966 (life history). McCrimmon, 1968 (Canada). Loeb, 1962 (effects of LSD). Balon, 1974 (domestication). Gerlach, 1983 (larvae). Taylor and Mahon, 1977 (hybrids). Evans, 1952 (brain patterns). Greeley and Everett, 1952 (popular summary).

Names

Cyprinus is from the Greek word for carp, *kyprinos,* possibly from *Cypris,* the word for Aphrodite or Venus, in allusion to its fecundity. *Carpio* is the Low Latin name for carp.

Cyprinus carpio Linnaeus, 1758: 329 Europe
Cyprinus carpio, DeKay, 1842: 188-190 (introduced at Newburgh, New York in 1832)

Rhodeus

The bitterling is a tiny species from Europe and Asia. It is a deep-bodied, compressed species with a very short lateral line and no barbels. There is a single row of five pharyngeal teeth on each arch. Other species may occur in Asia.

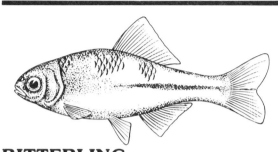

BITTERLING

Rhodeus sericeus (Pallas, 1776)

Identification
The bitterling is a stubby, compressed little fish with an obsolescent lateral line that has only four to seven pored scales. The dorsal fin is longer than that of native minnows but not as long as that of the carp or goldfish.

Description
Body deep, rhombic, compressed. Profiles evenly and equally curved. Dorsal origin nearer snout than caudal base. Last dorsal ray more then half the first. Dorsal retrogressive, its margin straight, its corners softly angled. Caudal moderately forked, with rounded lobes. Anal origin below last half of the dorsal base. Anal retrogressive, trapezoidal, with straight margin and softly angled corners. Pelvics inserted below the dorsal origin. Pelvics retrogressive, with straight margin and rounded corners. Pectorals low, with slightly oblique bases, retrogressive, with rounded corners. Gill membranes slightly joined to the isthmus, mouth small, subterminal, maxillary ending below anterior nostril. Counts and proportional measurements are given in Table 10.

Color: Freshly preserved fish are gray above, shading to silver white ventrally. The scales of the sides above a line from the anal origin to the top of the pectoral base are clearly outlined as are the rays of the caudal and pectoral fins. Dorsal membranes with dense melanophores, pelvic membranes with sparse melanophores. There is a distinct stripe on the midside of the caudal peduncle. The stripe curves slightly upward and ends in a point below the middle of the dorsal fin.

Juveniles and breeding adults: Breeding males develop rather large tubercles in a patch on each side of the snout. They become iridescent along the sides and the stripe on the side of the caudal peduncle turns bright blue. They are also blue or mauve on the top of the head and body. The dorsal and anal fins turn bright red. Females develop a tubular extension of the urogenital papilla that is nearly as long as the body.

Size: This is a small species. Adults collected in New York are 30 to 51 mm standard length.

Habitat
Our only localities are streams of rather low gradient.

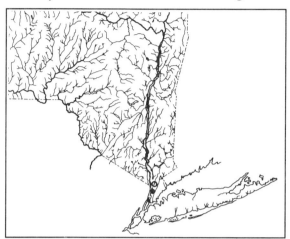

Distribution
The bitterling is an Old World species that is widespread across northern Europe to central and northeast Asia. It has been introduced into the British Isles and in New York State where it has at times been established in the Sawmill and Bronx Rivers. Dence reported that specimens had been collected in the Sawmill River near Tarrytown on 16 September 1923. Breder assumed that the species had disappeared but the Lower Hudson Survey found it well established in the Sawmill and also collected two specimens in the Bronx River. Specimens in the Cornell University collection were taken south of Ardsley and 2.5 miles north of Yonkers on 10 July 1936. Other Cornell specimens were collected between Farragut and Odell Avenues and along the Sawmill River Parkway in 1950 and 1951. We visited these localities in July 1979 but did not find any. On 4 August 1979, Dr. Robert Schmidt collected one specimen from the Bronx River between Midland Avenue and the Cross County Parkway Bridge in Bronxville. On 14 August, he and his students collected additional specimens in the same area.

Life History
The bitterling has the remarkable habit of depositing its eggs in the mantle cavity of a freshwater mussel. There the eggs develop in the folds of the gills, completely protected by the host. In a way, this is poetic justice because freshwater mussels have parasitic larvae that develop on the gills of fishes.

At the time of spawning, the tissue around the oviduct expands to form a tube that may reach to the base of the tail. Apparently, this ovipositor tube is inserted into the respiratory siphons of the mollusk and the eggs are delivered to the gills. Males release the sperm in the area to be carried to the eggs by the host's respiratory currents. After spawning, the ovipositor shrinks to its normal size.

Breder reported that bitterling kept at the New York Aquarium spawned, and the embryos developed in the American mussels *Anodonta cataracta* and *Unio complanatus*. About 100 embryos emerged in a tank containing five bitterlings and these two mollusk species. The ovipositor of one female shrank to one-third of its maximum length in 3 days after spawning and the males lost their nuptial coloration by the same time.

Notes
Schmidt et al. argued that the Bronx River population has survived continuously since the 1920s rather than having been reintroduced by aquarists discarding their surplus stock. They contend that the fact that breeding populations of the bitterling are known only from the two New York rivers suggests a single introduction sometime before 1923.

References
Dence, 1925 (Sawmill River). Myers, 1925 (Sawmill River). Bade, 1926 (introduced). Breder, 1933b (breeding in American mussels). Schmidt et al., 1981 (rediscovery). Schmidt and McGurk, 1982 (life history). Schmidt and Samaritan, 1984 (distribution).

Names
Sericeus is a Latin word pertaining to silk.
  Cyprinus sericeus Pallas, 1776: 208
  Cyprinus amarus Bloch, 1782: 52 Elbe basin
  Rhodeus amarus, Myers, 1925: 20 Sawmill River
  Rhodeus sericeus, Schmidt et al., 1981: 481-482
Bronx River

Scardinius

This is a monotypic European genus that superficially resembles our golden shiner, *Notemigonus*. It is a rather deep-bodied, moderately compressed fish with 3,5- pharyngeal teeth, no barbels and no hard serrated rays in the fins.

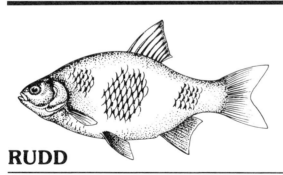

RUDD

Scardinius erythrophthalmus (Linnaeus, 1758)

Identification
The introduced rudd is a rather deep-bodied, moderately compressed minnow with a strongly decurved lateral line. It somewhat resembles the golden shiner but it has larger scales (38 to 42 in the lateral line; 44 to 54 in *Notemigonus*). It also lacks the scaleless fleshy keel in front of the anus although the belly may be somewhat sharp edged. The rudd is said to have pharyngeal tooth counts of 3,5-5,3 or 2,5-5,2 whereas the golden shiner has 5-5 teeth

and, in fact, no native North American minnows have three teeth in the lesser row.

Description
Body deep and compressed, the ventral profile more curved than the dorsal. Dorsal origin midway between the caudal base and the upper end of the preopercle. Last dorsal ray less than half the longest. Dorsal margin slightly concave, its corners angulate. Middle caudal rays about two-thirds the longest upper rays. Caudal forked, its lobes bluntly pointed. Anal origin under middle of depressed last dorsal ray (behind the dorsal base). Anal fin similar to dorsal fin, its margin concave. Pelvic insertion considerably in advance of the dorsal origin. Pelvic axillary scale small. Pelvic retrogressive, its margin slightly convex, its corners softly angulate. Pectoral base oblique, pectoral asymmetrically pointed. Gill membranes narrowly joined to the isthmus. Mouth very steep, nearly vertical. Lateral line complete, decurved. Scale radii very prominent. Counts and proportional measurements are given in Table 10.

Color: The rudd is usually illustrated as being generally golden or silvery, darker above and shading to white on the belly. The scales of the upper sides have dark crescents at their bases like those of fallfish. In life, the iris is yellow or orange with a red spot above. The dorsal and caudal fins are washed with brownish orange. The anal and pelvic fins are red, the pectorals dusky yellow.

Juveniles and breeding adults: Males are brighter colored, with gold or brassy bodies and intense red fins. The males also develop fine white tubercles over the head and body during the spawning season.

Size: The usual size of the rudd is 12 to 14 inches total length but they can weigh as much as 4 pounds. Our single specimen from New York is 280 mm standard length.

Habitat
The rudd is said to live in both still and sluggish waters. It is generally found hovering well above the bottom or near the surface.

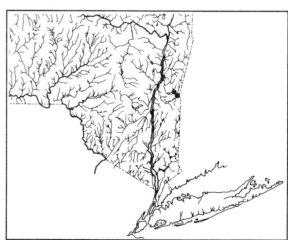

Distribution
The rudd is native to Europe where it is widely distributed except for Greece, the Iberian Peninsula,

and northern Scandinavia. It was introduced into the Roeliff-Jansen Kill and was established there in 1936. In 1968, it was taken in Copake Lake by Walter Keller of the DEC (the specimen is now AMNH no.55048) and in late August or September 1969, Wayne Elliot and DEC field crews caught two specimens below the dam at the outlet of Robinson Pond north of Copake in the Roeliff-Jansen Kill drainage.

Life History

In Europe, the rudd spawns in April or May when the water temperature reaches 18 C. The females lays 80,000 to 100,000 adhesive eggs, broadcast over vegetation. The eggs are about 1 mm in diameter and hatch in 7 to 14 days.

Food and Feeding

Rudd feed near or at the surface. Their diet includes surface and aerial insects such as water boatmen, water beetles and dipterans. They also feed on larval caddisflies, midges, copepods, ostracods, amphipods, and small amounts of plant material. Large rudd sometimes eat small fish.

Notes

Although it was introduced more than 50 years ago, it has not become abundant and there have been no studies of its biology in our waters. The rudd has also been introduced into New Jersey.

References

Cahn, 1927b (Wisconsin).

Names

The trivial name *erythrophthalmus* is from the Greek words *erythros*, red and *ophthalmos*, eye.

Cyprinus erythrophthalmus Linnaeus, 1758: 530
Scardinius erythrophthalmus, Greeley, 1937: 94
Roeliff-Jansen Kill

TABLE 10
AVERAGE PROPORTIONAL MEASUREMENTS AND COUNTS OF
INTRODUCED MINNOWS *(Carassius, Ctenopharyngodon, Cyprinus, Rhodeus,* and *Scardinius)*

All proportions are expressed in percentage of standard length.

	Carassius auratus	*Cyprinus* carpio	*Ctenopharyngodon* idella	*Scardinius* erythrophthalmus	*Rhodeus* sericeus
ST. LENGTH (mm)	114.7	110.4	562	129.5	44.5
TOTAL LENGTH	125.9	125.9	125.6	126.0	—
FORK LENGTH	116.3	114.9	109.4	114.7	118.1
PREDORSAL	51.3	54.3	51.4	59.0	52.1
PREANAL	74.9	76.3	76.7	73.5	62.6
PREPELVIC	48.2	51.2	53.2	49.5	48.3
DORSAL BASE	39.6	39.9	10.2	13.4	22.9
ANAL BASE	14.9	9.8	9.5	14.6	19.3
BODY DEPTH	38.2	38.2	26.7	33.2	34.8
BODY WIDTH	20.1	20.4	16.4	13.4	16.6
C.PED. DEPTH	16.2	13.4	13.9	10.5	10.8
PECTORAL ALT.	29.1	27.4	17.3	21.3	21.1
HEAD LENGTH	32.5	32.4	24.9	23.6	25.0
SNOUT	10.0	12.8	2.5	6.9	6.9
EYE	7.0	5.9	2.9	6.4	7.8
MOUTH LENGTH	8.5	9.1	6.2	6.2	3.0
INTERORB	12.8	12.2	13.5	9.7	6.0
N (sample size)	5	5	5	5	5
COUNTS:					
DORSAL RAYS	i,16-18	i,19-22	7-8	8-10	9-11
ANAL RAYS	i,5	i,5	8-9	10-12	8-11
PECTORAL RAYS	16-18	17-18	20	16	12-13
PELVIC RAYS	8-9	9	9	9	8
GILL RAKERS	37-44	21-27	12-15	9-11	12
VERTEBRAE*	26-27	33-34	38-39	35-36	32-33
SCALES:					
ABOVE L. L.	6-7	5	6-6	8	9-10
LATERAL LINE	25-30	35-39	39-42	40-45	35-37**
BELOW L. L.	5-6	5	4-5	4	—
PHARYNGEAL TEETH	0,4-4,0	1,1,3-3,1,1	2,5-4,2	3,5-5,3	5-5

* Excluding Weberian apparatus.   ** Four pored scales in l.

Campostoma

This is a small genus with about three species. Members of this genus feed on diatoms and other aufwuchs which they scrape off rocks using a special cartilaginous ridge on the lower jaw. The gut is extremely elongated and wound around the swim bladder.

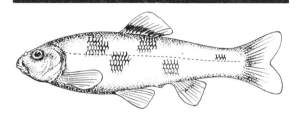

CENTRAL STONEROLLER

Campostoma anomalum
(Rafinesque, 1820)

Identification
The stoneroller is a rather undistinguished minnow that is dark gray above, often with a slight brassy or golden cast and a pale stripe along the upper side. Its body is torpedo shaped and nearly round in cross section. Its distinguishing feature in our area is the presence of a cartilaginous ridge just inside of, and protruding beyond, the lower lip. This ridge is separated from the lower lip by a definite groove.

The lining of the stoneroller's body cavity is jet black and the gut is so elongated that it is actually wound around the swim bladder. All of these distinctive features are related to its food habits.

Description
Body elongate, terete, fusiform, deepest in front of the dorsal fin. Dorsal profile more curved than ventral, especially in adult males. Dorsal fin origin slightly nearer tip of the snout than base of caudal. Dorsal retrogressive, with rounded corners and slightly convex margin. Caudal moderately forked, with rounded lobes. Anal origin below outer fourth of last dorsal ray. Anal retrogressive, with slightly convex margin, its anterior corner rounded, posterior angled. Pelvics rounded, third pelvic ray longest. Pelvic origin below dorsal origin. Pectoral base low and slightly oblique. Pectoral retrogressive, rounded. Lips thick, fleshy, the lower with a prominent cartilage ridge. Gill membranes broadly joined to the isthmus. Exposed scales rounded. Lateral line complete or nearly so, only slightly decurved anteriorly. Counts and proportional measurements are given in Table 11.

Color: Dusky gray above, shading to brassy on sides to white on the belly. In life, there is a pale golden stripe along the dorsolateral area from the back of the head to the upper base of the tail, separating a midlateral stripe from the darker dorsal area. Fins hyaline, rays outlined with melanophores. Dark regenerated scales give most individuals a mottled appearance.

Juveniles and breeding adults: Breeding males develop a warm orange cast, with bright orange bands at the bases of the dorsal, caudal, pelvic, and pectoral fins. Distal to these orange areas are black bands at the middle third of the fin, then the outer margins are paler orange. The central rays of the caudal fin have a distinct round spot in a paler dusky bar. The posterior part of the upper lip is white, with a distinct white bar from the nostrils to the center of the upper lip. A distinct black bar along the shoulder girdle. Iris deep reddish brown.

Large, white, breeding tubercles are present on the top of the head and on the scales of the upper sides as far back as the base of the tail. Not all scales have tubercles and no scales have more than one. There are also some pearl organs on the gill membranes and along the lower edge of the preopercle. Small tubercles are present on the dorsal surface of the first six pectoral rays and there are a few on the first dorsal ray.

Size: the maximum length is about 7.5 inches total length. Our largest New York specimen is 137 mm standard length.

Habitat
The stoneroller occurs in stream habitats where there are riffles and pools and considerable current. It is usually most abundant in the riffles.

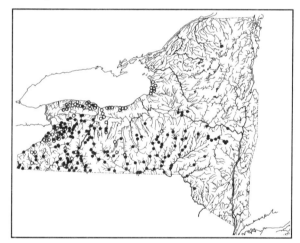

Distribution
This species is widely distributed in the central United States with only a single record from the Lake St. Clair drainage in Canada. It ranges from New York to Wisconsin and south into southern Mexico and Georgia.

In New York, it occurs in the central part of the Mohawk system west through the Great Lakes, Finger Lakes, Susquehanna and Delaware systems. There is an isolated record in the Adirondacks that is considered an introduction.

Life History
The reproductive behavior of the stoneroller was studied near Ithaca by Miller. Males became tuberculate in mid-December and spawning began in mid-April when the water temperatures ranged from 58 to 75 F. If the temperature dropped to 50 F or below, the spawning ceased. Stonerollers showed relatively

little movement and other workers have noted that if they are removed from a section of stream the populations recover quite slowly. Miller found only local movements to the spawning areas. The nests were built in areas near pools or where an overhanging bank provided shelter, usually at the head of a riffle where water was 8 to 24 inches deep, either in quiet water or in moderate to swift current. The nests were circular depressions and sometimes adjacent nests were fused so that there were large cleared areas with deeper pits. Sometimes, the stonerollers used the nests of other species such as the creek chub and the river chub. On the other hand, the stoneroller nests were sometimes preempted by other species. Males built the nests by carrying pebbles in their mouths or by swimming down into the gravel to loosen it so the current carried it downstream. Less frequently, the males simply pushed the larger pebbles to the edge of the pit with their backs and heads.

Large stonerollers spent much time chasing other fish away from the pits. These attacks were direct rushes, and sometimes short chases without the elaborate ritualistic posturing seen in some fishes. Males of the same size sometimes postured and brushed against each other until one fled. Males defended territories but the limits of the territories changed as the male visited different pits and spent a few minutes at each. When many males were present, the territorial defense was reduced and other males were permitted to come closer to the dominant male.

Females remained in small schools, a short distance from the nests, until they were ready to spawn. A female would move into the nest area and enter a pit. The male would move toward her and, if she stayed, he would press against her and spawning would occur. Sometimes, other males joined the spawning pair. Apparently, there was no clasping.

Food and Feeding
Stonerollers feed by scraping organisms off stones on the bottom and their long guts usually contain diatoms and other benthic organisms including blue-green algae and midges.

Notes
Various authors have recognized subspecies of the stoneroller and traditionally the New York populations have been assigned to the subspecies *C. a. pullum*. Ross studied the stonerollers of New York and found slight differences in scale counts that he used to differentiate populations ("races"), recognizing a fine-scaled form in the Upper Allegheny, a slightly different fine-scaled form in the Upper Genesee, and a coarse-scaled race in the Upper Susquehanna drainage with a subrace in the Fall Creek drainage of the Finger Lakes region. Trautman recognized the subspecies *anomalum* in the southern part of Ohio intergrading with *C. a. pullum* in the northern part of that state. More recent work using sophisticated biochemical techniques reveals a more complex pattern and it seems best to reserve judgment until the patterns are completely worked out. For the time being, then, only the species name is used.

References
Ross, 1958 (New York populations). Kraatz, 1923 (food habits). Kraatz, 1924 (gut anatomy). Smith, 1935 (breeding). Reed, 1958 (early life history). Miller, 1962 (life history). Buynak and Mohr, 1980a (larvae). Buth and Burr, 1978 (isozyme variability). Gunning and Lewis, 1956 (age and growth in Illinois).

Names
Anomalum is from the Greek *anomalos,* extraordinary or irregular.

Rutilus anomalus Rafinesque, 1820a: 53 Licking River, Kentucky

Campostoma anomalum Bean, 1903: 113-114 New York

Campostoma anomalum anomalum Hubbs and Lagler, 1964: 87 (distribution)

Chrondrostoma pullum Agassiz, 1854: 357 Burlington, Iowa

Campostoma anomalum pullum Ross, 1958: 1-20 New York races

Ericymba

This is a very distinctive monotypic genus, characterized by enlarged sensory canals in the superficial skull bones, particularly the suborbital and lower jaw regions. In general appearance it resembles some species of *Notropis*.

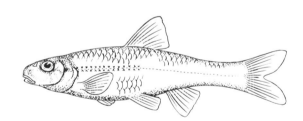

SILVERJAW MINNOW

Ericymba buccata Cope, 1865

Identification
The overall coloration of the silverjaw is a pale sandy, with silvery sides and white belly. At first glance, it looks like the sand shiner, *Notropis stramineus,* or, perhaps even more, the bigeye shiner, *Notropis dorsalis,* but a closer look soon reveals that the sensory canals of the head are greatly enlarged, with the bony covering reduced to narrow bridges. This results in a characteristic appearance of the lower jaw and suborbital regions, as if the canals were represented by a series of squarish silver patches in living specimens. In preserved specimens, the cheek and lower jaw have a honeycomb appearance. The silverjaw has a rather long snout and small eyes that are directed upward and outward.

Description

Body elongate, deepest at the dorsal origin, little compressed. Dorsal profile more curved, the bottom of the head especially flat. Dorsal origin equidistant between tip of snout and base of caudal. Dorsal fin retrogressive, with sharp corners and straight margin, trapezoidal. Caudal moderately forked, with blunt points. Anal origin below tip of depressed last dorsal ray. Anal shape similar to dorsal. Pelvic insertion below dorsal origin. Pelvic fins retrogressive, with rounded corners. Pelvic axillary process minute. Pectoral base low, moderately oblique. Pectoral retrogressive, rounded. Snout long, slightly overhanging the low, horizontal mouth. Head canals greatly enlarged. Gill membranes broadly joined to the isthmus. Eyes dorsolateral, rather small. Lateral line complete, slightly decurved anteriorly. Counts and proportional measurements are presented in Table 11.

Color: In life, the silverjaw is pale sand color above, silvery white below. The cheeks and lower jaw have distinct squarish silvery patches. Middorsal stripe narrow and distinct anterior to the dorsal fin, present but less distinct behind. Midlateral stripe diffuse anteriorly, moderately distinct behind the dorsal fin, a faint secondary pencil-line stripe above the midlateral stripe. Scales of dorsal surface with dark margins.

Juveniles and breeding adults: Wallace described the tubercles as: ". . .minute but sharp tubercles on the dorsal surface of the pectoral fins, the operculum, snout, and lateral surfaces of the chin, and along the dorsum from the occiput to the origin of the dorsal fin. Those on the pectoral fins are closely crowded on the second through the sixth or seventh ray, where they are present from the base to slightly beyond the point of branching. They are not present on the anteriormost branch of the rays. Tubercles of the head and back are more widely spaced." Wallace found the extent of tuberculation to be a good indicator of the stage of reproductive maturity.

Size: The maximum size is about 3.8 inches. Our largest New York specimens are 58.5 mm standard length.

Habitat

The silverjaw lives in small- to moderate-sized streams with sandy bottoms and is reasonably tolerant of turbidity and pollution, as long as the sand is not covered with silt.

Distribution

The silverjaw is essentially a species of the Mississippi watershed with some Atlantic slope populations in the Potomac, Lower Susquehanna, and Upper Rappahannock drainages. It is absent from the Tennessee River and the Cumberland River below Cumberland Falls and this gap divides the range into a northern segment from western New York, western Pennsylvania, West Virginia to eastern Illinois and Missouri and a southern segment that ranges from eastern Louisiana to the Florida Panhandle.

In New York State, it is known only from French Creek and Brownell Creek near Clymer. It was not found by the Survey and its abundance at both localities suggests that it is a recent immigrant.

Life History

In Indiana, Wallace found the silverjaw spawning from the end of April to at least the end of July. There was some indication of two major spawning periods each season, one in May and the second in late June or July. The early spawners were mostly 2- and 3-year-olds, the second spawning was dominated by 1- and 2-year-old fish. The reproductive behavior has not been completely described. Hankinson observed chases in water 2 or 3 inches deep but did not see the actual spawning. Hoyt described a head-standing behavior that Wallace believed was probably feeding rather than courtship or territorial threats. Hoyt found an average of 228 ova in age I fish, 762 in age II fish, and 977 in age III females. The number of ova also varied with season and size of the fish.

Food and Feeding

Schwartz reported that the silverjaw feeds on insects.

Notes

The enlarged canals seem to be an adaptation for life in turbid waters. Wallace regarded the prolonged spawning period as an adaptation to life in streams where there are periods of drought or flooding.

References

Wallace, 1971 (age and growth). Hoyt, 1971a (reproductive biology); 1971b (life history, age and growth); . Wallace, 1972; 1976 (ecology); 1973 (reproduction). Reno, 1971 (lateral line structure). Ross, 1974 (tubercles). Baker and Ross, 1981 (competition). Schwartz, 1963 (food). Hankinson, 1919 (spawning).

Names

Ericymba is from the Greek *eri*, a prefix meaning very and *cymbe*, a cup. This is in reference to the enlarged head canals. *Buccata* is from the Latin *bucca*, cheek.

Ericymba buccata Cope, 1865b: 87-88 Kiskiminetas River, 40 miles northeast of Pittsburgh

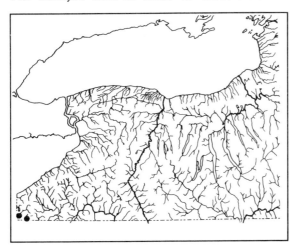

Exoglossum

There are only two species in this highly specialized genus and both occur in New York State. They are heavy-bodied, terete minnows with moderately forked tails and specialized lower jaws. One species has barbels somewhat like those of *Semotilus*; the other lacks barbels.

KEY TO THE SPECIES OF *EXOGLOSSUM* IN NEW YORK

A. Mouth highly modified, the lower jaw divided into three lobes, of which the middle is bony and the lateral ones are fleshy. No barbels.
Exoglossum maxillingua

Cutlips minnow, p. 130

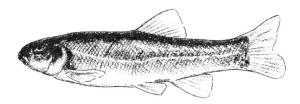

A'. Mouth less modified, the lower jaw triangular, with the central lobe tongue-like and bony and the lateral lobes scarcely developed. Usually, there is a

barbel in the groove above the upper lip, ahead of the end of the maxillary, like that of *Semotilus*.
Exoglossum laurae   Tonguetied minnow, p. 129

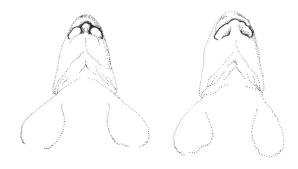

Mouths of cutlips (left) and tonguetied minnows (right).

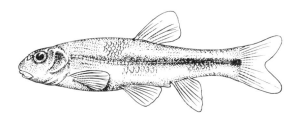

TONGUETIED MINNOW

Exoglossum laurae (Hubbs, 1931)

Identification

The tonguetied minnow closely resembles the cutlips. Both are heavy-bodied, nearly terete fishes with moderately small scales, rounded fins and an indistinct lateral stripe that ends at a distinct, but small, basicaudal spot.

The chief difference between the cutlips and the tonguetied minnow is that the lower jaw of the tonguetied minnow is more pointed, with a triangular central lobe and small lateral lobes. The lower jaw of the cutlips is definitely three-lobed with the central bony lobe only slightly longer than the fleshy lateral lobes. The tonguetied minnow often, but not always, has barbels like those of members of the genus *Semotilus,* small, and in the groove above the end of the maxillary bone. The geographic ranges are complementary: the tonguetied minnow lives in the Allegheny and Upper Genesee drainages; the cutlips lives in the Lower Genesee and drainages to the east and northeast.

Description

Body robust, elongate, and nearly terete. Dorsal profile slightly more curved than the ventral. Caudal peduncle deep. Dorsal fin origin equidistant between tip of snout and caudal base. Dorsal retrogressive, trapezoidal with rounded corners and slightly convex margin. Caudal moderately forked, its lobes bluntly pointed. Anal origin under middle of depressed last dorsal ray, similar to dorsal. Pelvic insertion below dorsal origin. Pelvic fins retrogressive, rounded. Pelvic axillary process small. Pectorals low, retrogressive, and rounded. Pectoral base somewhat oblique. Gill membranes broadly joined to the isthmus. Lateral line complete, nearly straight, rising slightly anteriorly. Body completely scaled. Premaxillaries nonprotractile, upper lips thickened posteriorly. Mouth low, horizontal. Lower jaw triangular. Barbels usually present, subterminal, sometimes slightly fimbriate. Counts and proportional measurements are given in Table 11.

Color: In coloration, the tonguetied minnow is similar to the cutlips: waxy olive or brown, often with a surface sheen of metallic lavender. Juveniles with a well-developed midlateral stripe ending in a small, round or rectangular, dark spot, followed by a dusky crescentic spot. A horizontal stripe narrower than the pupil runs from the side of the snout through the eye to the cheek, fading on both the snout and the gill cover. Scales of the dorsal region not outlined but those of the sides often have dark margins that tend to form indistinct longitudinal stripes. Some scattered dark scales are probably regenerated. The fins tend to be slightly amber in life and the caudal fin in some populations has been reported as dusky red. The peritoneum is silvery, with scattered melanophores.

Juveniles and breeding adults: Males develop minute tubercles on the pectoral fins.

Size: Hubbs reported specimens to 137 mm standard length. Our largest New York specimen is 97 mm standard length.

The tonguetied minnow lives in streams 10 to 150 feet or so wide with stony or gravelly bottom and moderately swift current.

Distribution

The tonguetied minnow occurs in three disjunct areas. The Miami and Little Miami Rivers in southwest Ohio, The New (Upper Kanawha) River of North Carolina, Virginia, and West Virginia, and the Allegheny and Upper Genesee of New York and western Pennsylvania. There is one questionable record from the Upper Monongahela.

In New York, it is present in the Allegheny and upper part of the Genesee River.

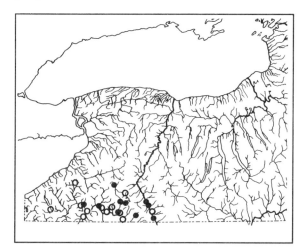

Life History

The breeding habits of the tonguetied minnow were studied by Raney in two Pennsylvania streams, the Allegheny River near Tionesta and Marvin Creek near Smethport. At the former site, spawning was observed 10 June when the water temperature was 21 C. In each case, the nests were in quiet to moderately swift water on the upstream side of some obstruction, either a log or a fairly large rock. The nests consisted of circular piles of uniformly sized gravel, with the individual pebbles about a half-inch in diameter. Each nest was 6 to 18 inches in diameter in water about 12 inches deep. The nests were 5 to 20 feet from shore in streams 30 to 70 feet wide, where there were alternating pools and riffles. The eggs were pale yellow and about 2 mm in diameter. Males guarded the nests, seeking shelter under the adjacent log or boulder when startled. From time to time, they would pick up a pebble in their mouths and deposit it in the nests, thus burying the eggs deep in the nest.

Food and Feeding

The feeding habits of the tonguetied minnow seem not to have been reported in detail.

Notes

The tonguetied minnow was described from the Upper Kanawha River in West Virginia in 1931 by Carl L. Hubbs. Trautman described *Parexoglossum hubbsi* from western Ohio. In 1941 Raney reported that *laurae* occurred in New York, in the Allegheny, and in the Genesee above the Portageville falls. It was believed that the Ohio population was a separate subspecies, *Parexoglossum laurae hubbsi,* and that Kanawha and New York populations were the typical subspecies, *P. l. laurae.* Trautman suggested that they may be indistinguishable and Gilbert and Bailey synonymized *Parexoglossum* with *Exoglossum.*

References

Trautman, 1931 (comparison with *P. hubbsi).* Raney, 1939c (spawning). Raney, 1941 (distribution). Gilbert and Bailey, 1972 (relationships). Jenkins and Lachner, 1971 (allied to *Semotilus).* Hubbs, 1931 (Kanawha River system).

Names

Exoglossum laurae is named for Laura Hubbs, wife of the describer.

Parexoglossum laurae Hubbs, 1931: 1-12 tributary of Greenbrier River, West Virginia (Type UMMZ 292413)

Parexoglossum laurae Raney, 1941: 272 New York

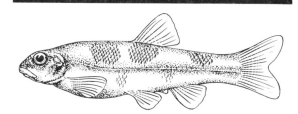

CUTLIPS MINNOW

Exoglossum maxillingua (Lesueur, 1818)

Identification

Cutlips are rather drab, heavy-bodied minnows with subdued colors and no particularly prominent markings, although some individuals have a weakly developed midlateral stripe and a small basicaudal spot. In life, they somewhat resemble the pearl dace but the two are readily distinguished by the structure of the mouth. That of the pearl dace is of the form usual in minnows but the lower jaw of the cutlips is highly specialized. It has three distinct lobes, the center one bony, the lateral lobes soft and fleshy. The lateral lobes are thicker so that the center lobe seems to be recessed.

Only the tonguetied minnow has a similar modification of the mouth but it is less highly specialized and the lower jaw is triangular in shape when viewed from below. The tonguetied minnow also frequently has subterminal maxillary barbels but these are not present in the cutlips. Both species have a distinctive waxy appearance, with olive or sometimes lavender overtones.

Description

Body elongate, nearly terete, rather stout, with the caudal peduncle deep and slightly compressed. Dorsal fin trapezoidal, retrogressive, with rounded corners and slightly convex margin. Dorsal origin midway between tip of snout and caudal base. Caudal fin moderately forked, with rounded lobes. Anal origin below the outer quarter of the depressed last dorsal ray. Anal fin similar to dorsal. Pelvic insertion below the dorsal origin. Pelvics retrogressive, with rounded corners and convex margin. Pelvic axillary process small. Pectoral base low, slightly oblique. Pectorals retrogressive, rounded. Gill membranes broadly joined to the isthmus. Mouth low and horizontal, overhung by snout. Frenum present. Lower jaw trilobate, the central lobe hard. Lateral line complete, slightly decurved. Counts and proportional measurements are given in Table 11.

Color: The cutlips is a somber fish, waxy olive to lavender above and on the sides with the belly only slightly paler. Juveniles have a prominent midlateral stripe that ends in a large round spot. This stripe becomes diffuse and disappears in fish more than 3 inches long. There is a pale yellow-olive stripe above the midlateral stripe and the lower sides are smoky olive. The fin membranes are clear but the rays of the dorsal, caudal, anal, and pectorals have dark margins. Vertical and pelvic fins sometimes show a reddish tinge. Upper half of the operculum dark, a diffuse dark area on the sides of the snout from the lip to the eye. Iris pale golden, upper lip and cheeks pale, as are the lower parts of the head. Peritoneum silvery white.

Juveniles and breeding adults: The adults do not have prominent tubercles.

Size: Our largest New York specimen is 120 mm standard length. The record size is about 5.5 inches total length.

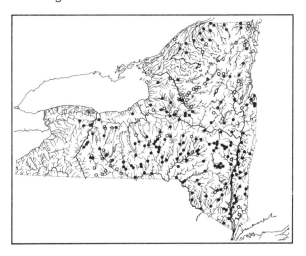

Habitat

Cutlips minnows prefer small- to moderate-sized clear creeks, usually with boulders, cobbles or gravel bottoms and little vegetation. They usually remain near the bottom of pools and often seek shelter under overhanging banks.

Distribution

The cutlips is an east coast species, ranging from the Upper St. Lawrence system and the eastern tributaries of Lake Ontario south to the Roanoke River in North Carolina and the New River drainage of West Virginia and Virginia.

In New York, it is abundant in the eastern part of the state in the Housatonic, Hudson, Delaware, Susquehanna and St. Lawrence drainages as far west as the Lower Genesee and Salmon Creek in Monroe County. It is replaced by *E. laurae* in the Upper Genesee and the Allgeheny drainage.

Life History

On 8 May 1921, T.L. Hankinson observed a cutlips building a nest in Butternut Creek just outside Syracuse. The nest was in moderately swift water 2.5 feet deep at a point where the stream was about 50 feet wide. The nest was about 10 feet from shore adjacent to, and partly under, an algae-covered piece of sheet metal. The nest consisted of fine gravel with stones of uniform size, mostly less than 0.5 inch in diameter. The pile was about 18 inches in diameter and about 3 inches high. The fish was observed bringing the gravel downstream from distances up to about 3 feet.

The breeding habits of the cutlips were studied in Catatonk Creek near Candor by Van Duzer. Beginning in late May, the males selected sites near rocks or logs and began to build their pebble nest. Early in the season, nests took about 3 days to build and were as large as 18 inches in diameter and 5 or 6 inches high. Later in the season, the nests were smaller, some less than 7 inches in diameter, and were built in a single day. The nests were roughly circular and the size of the pebbles was remarkably uniform. Apparently, the size of the mouth of the male determined the size of the pebbles that were selected. Males 5.25 inches long used pebbles ranging from 0.3 to 0.8 inch in diameter. The pebbles were carried from as much as 20 feet away and the males made 6 to 10 trips per minute at the height of their nest building. The nests were always built where there was considerable current and in water less then 2.5 feet deep. Most of the nest building occurred between 9 am and 6:30 pm. Nesting continued through 11 July.

Each of the nests studied by Van Duzer sloped rather gently on its upstream side and more steeply downstream. As the nest neared completion, the females began to approach in groups of 1 to 12 (usually 3 to 8) at a time. When a male was ready to spawn, he took up a position on the crest of the nest. A single female would then approach from the rear or side and thrust her head under the male's body at the region of the vent. Approaches were from the right and left with about equal frequency. Immediately, both curved their bodies with the female tight against the concave side of the male. Together the pair moved upstream 4 to 6 inches, vibrating as they moved. At the end of this movement, which took about 20 seconds, they dipped their bodies so that their tails nearly touched the gravel. Then they separated and the male shifted some stones and often added more to the nest before returning to the crest of the nest to signal his readiness to spawn again. When there was crowding, sometimes two or three males moved to the female but apparently only one actually spawned at a time.

The eggs were pale yellow when first laid and about 2 to 4 mm in diameter. Later, they turned opaque. Actions of the parents and the current buried the eggs nearly 3 inches deep. After breeding, the males continued to work on the nest, thus keeping it free of silt. The young remained in the nest for about 6 days after hatching and the yolk sac was visible for about 3 days.

Prespawning males were uniformly dark but became lighter once spawning began. Females had a pronounced dark midlateral stripe, like that of the juveniles, during spawning.

Food and Feeding
In general, the cutlips feeds on bottom-dwelling insects and mollusks. Dipterans and trichopterans are especially important items. Algae, detritus, and mayflies are also consumed. The diet does not change appreciably with size of the fish.

Notes
The cutlips is able to feed on the eyes of other fishes. This often occurs in bait buckets and in aquaria. In our samples, we have found the following species with missing eyes, taken in the same collections with cutlips: *Perca flavescens, Micropterus dolomieui, Lepomis gibbosus, Lepomis macrochirus, Semotilus atromaculatus, Campostoma anomalum, Exoglossum maxillingua, Catostomus commersoni, Catostomus catostomus,* and *Ambloplites rupestris.* A study of the eye-picking behavior has recently been completed by A. Pappantoniou at Fordham University.

Jenkins has suggested that the nest-building minnows belonging to the genera *Semotilus, Campostoma, Nocomis,* and *Exoglossum* may all be closely related.

References
Haase and Haase, 1975 (food habits). Hankinson, 1922 (nests). VanDuzer, 1939 (life history). Hubbs, 1931 (taxonomy). Miller, 1964 (breeding behavior). Jenkins, 1971 (relationships). Johnson and Johnson, 1982a (eye predation). Buynak and Mohr, 1980a (larvae).

Names
Maxillingua is a combination of the Latin *maxilla,* jawbone and *lingua,* tongue.

Cyprinus maxillingua Lesueur, 1817c: 85 Pipe Creek, Maryland

Exoglossum lesurianum Rafinesque, 1818e: 420 (after Lesueur)

Exoglossum annulatum Rafinesque, 1818e: 421 Hudson River

Exoglossum nigrescens Rafinesque, 1818e: 422 Lake Champlain

Notemigonus

Although the relationships of minnow genera are not well understood, many ichthyologists believe that *Notemigonus* belongs to a different subfamily, the Abraminae, than the rest of the North American minnows. Certainly, it resembles some European species of that subfamily. Its size, long anal fin, decurved lateral line and general physiognomy all suggest its relationship to *Abramis.*

Notemigonus is a monotypic genus, distinguished by the presence of a scaleless, fleshy keel in front of the anus.

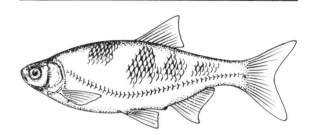

GOLDEN SHINER

Notemigonus crysoleucas (Mitchill, 1814)

Identification
The golden shiner belongs to a distinctive group of minnows sometimes considered to represent a separate subfamily called the Abraminae. It is the sole North American representative of this group and as such it is quite different from other native minnows. The golden shiner is a compressed, deep-bodied fish with a long anal fin that has a conspicuous lobe in front. Its lateral line is strongly decurved, curving well below midside and then rising again on the posterior half of the body. Adults are golden yellow to brassy with red fins. Juveniles are silvery with a definite, even, midlateral stripe.

Because of their deep compressed shape, golden shiners somewhat resemble some of the deep-bodied species of *Notropis* and they resemble even more the introduced European rudd, *Scardinius erythrophthalmus.* The golden shiner, however, has one unequivocal feature: it has a fleshy scaleless keel in front of the anus. Although small and difficult to see in small specimens, no other species in our area has this feature.

Description
Body deep and compressed, profiles equally curved or the ventral profile slightly more curved. Dorsal fin inserted behind the middle of the body, deltoid, retrogressive, its anterior corner bluntly rounded, posterior corner sharp. Dorsal margin slightly concave. Caudal fin moderately forked, with rounded lobes. Anal fin long and falcate, retrogressive, with rather sharp corners, inserted beneath end of dorsal base. Pelvics inserted anterior to the dorsal origin, retrogressive, with convex margin

and rounded corners. Pelvic axillary process moderately developed. Pectoral low, with its base slightly oblique, retrogressive, rounded. Head triangular. Mouth slightly oblique, supraterminal. Gill membrane narrowly attached to isthmus. Body completely scaled except over a fleshy keel directly in front of the anus. Lateral line complete, strongly decurved. Counts and proportional measurements are given in Table 11.

Color: Adults golden to brassy yellow with dark crescents at the scale bases. Fins with orange-yellow wash.

Juveniles and breeding adults: Juveniles are silvery, somewhat darker above with an even-width stripe along the midside. Breeding adults have bright orange lower fins. Breeding males develop fine tubercles on the dorsal surface of the head and body.

Size: Reaches about 10.5 inches total length.

Habitat
The golden shiner is a slow-water fish that thrives in ponds and the slower parts of streams. It usually occurs where there is abundant vegetation and clear water. Trautman noted that they avoid areas that are silty.

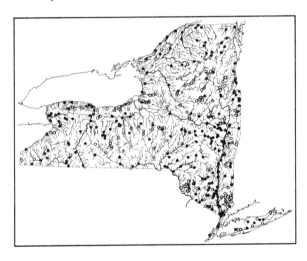

Distribution
This is a wide-ranging species that occurs throughout the United States and Canada east of the Rocky Mountains, from Saskatchewan to the Maritime Provinces and south to Texas and Florida. It appears to be absent from the higher parts of the Appalachian chain. It has been introduced west of the Rockies in California, Arizona, and Washington. It is universal in New York State, although Carl George (1981a) has suggested that its presence in the Adirondacks may be the result of introductions.

Life History
The golden shiner spawns in late spring when the water temperatures exceed 68 F. The spawning season lasts from May to August in New York, later farther north. Spawning takes place in shallow water over vegetation, including filamentous algae and rooted aquatic plants. The breeding behavior has not been described. The eggs are adhesive and simply broadcast with no nesting or parental care.

Growth is rapid and in New York they reach 53 to 74 mm by October of their first year. Maturity is usually reached at age II, although fast-growing fish may spawn during their second summer if they reach at least 64 mm total length. In Alabama, they spawn at the age of 7 months.

Food and Feeding
Golden shiners feed mainly in midwater and zooplankton forms a large part of their diet. They are croppers that swim after individual plankton organisms. Adults eat considerable filamentous algae and occasionally insects and small fishes.

Notes
This species is one of the largest and most abundant of our minnows and is raised in ponds for bait. It is an important forage fish in many of our waters.

Some ichthyologists have recognized subspecies of the golden shiner, but it is generally conceded that the variation is clinal and the use of subspecies names is unwarranted.

References
Cooper, 1936b (propagation). Hubbs, 1921a (geographic variation). Schultz, 1927 (temperature related variation). Evans, 1952 (brain pattern). Alpaugh, 1972 (lethal temperature). Lippman and Hubbs, 1969 (karyotypes). Dobie et al., 1956 (propagation). Forney, 1957 (propagation). Murai and Andrews, 1977 (effects of salinity on eggs and larvae). Keast and Webb, 1966 (feeding). Regier, 1963b (management in farm ponds). Snyder, Snyder and Douglas, 1977 (larvae). DeMonte, 1982 (spawning in bluegill nests).

Names
Notemigonus is from the Greek *notos*, back, and *gonia*, angle, in reference to the sharpness of the compressed body.

Crysoleucas is from the Greek *chrysos*, gold, and *leukos*, white.

Cyprinus crysoleucas Mitchill, 1814: 23 New York

Stilbe chrysoleucas, DeKay, 1842: 204-205 New York

Abramis crysoleucas, Bean, 1903: 132-134

Cyprinus hemiplus Rafinesque, 1817b: 121 Lakes George and Saratoga, New York

Abramis crysoleucas roseus Bean, 1902 132-134 Central Park

Notemigonus crysoleucas crysoleucas, Greeley, 1928: 97 Oswego watershed

Hemiplus lacustris Rafinesque, 1820b: 6 Lake George

Abramis versicolor DeKay, 1842: 191 Connecticut and Hudson Rivers

TABLE 11
AVERAGE PROPORTIONAL MEASUREMENTS AND COUNTS OF NATIVE MINNOWS WITH SPECIAL ADAPTATIONS (Campostoma, Exoglossum, Ericymba, and Notemigonus)

All proportions are expressed in percentage of standard length.

	Campostoma anomalum	Exoglossum laurae	Exoglossum maxillingua	Ericymba buccata	Notemigonus crysoleucas
ST. LENGTH (mm)	61.4	46.9	74.7	48.3	83.5
TOTAL LENGTH	122.6	125.5	125.9	126.2	123.3
FORK LENGTH	114.4	115.8	117.4	114.4	115.4
PREDORSAL	51.8	54.1	53.2	50.4	58.2
PREANAL	67.2	68.3	69.1	66.2	68.8
PREPELVIC	49.1	51.4	50.9	50.6	49.6
DORSAL BASE	11.4	12.2	13.0	12.2	11.7
ANAL BASE	9.2	8.6	10.5	4.7	17.0
BODY DEPTH	20.4	21.1	22.8	23.0	28.0
BODY WIDTH	15.4	16.1	18.6	15.0	13.0
C.PED. DEPTH	9.7	12.5	13.4	10.3	11.1
PECTORAL ALT.	13.5	16.2	16.6	15.4	15.4
HEAD LENGTH	25.6	26.1	25.6	26.3	23.4
SNOUT	6.8	8.6	10.3	9.9	6.6
EYE	6.7	7.8	6.2	7.2	6.8
MOUTH LENGTH	6.8	7.2	9.2	7.7	5.9
INTERORB	6.2	9.6	10.0	10.5	8.6
N (sample size)	5	3	5	5	5
COUNTS:					
DORSAL RAYS	8-9	8	8	8	7-9
ANAL RAYS	7	7	7	7-8	10-15
PECTORAL RAYS	15-18	15-17	13-16	14-16	16-18
PELVIC RAYS	8	8	8	7-9	9
GILL RAKERS	26-32	5	3-5	5-7	16-19
VERTEBRAE*	38-39	36-37	35-36	30-31	34-35
SCALES:					
ABOVE L. L.	7-8	7-8	7-8	4-5	9
LATERAL LINE	47-58	48-52	49-52	33-36	45-54
BELOW L. L.	7	6	5	3-4	3-4
PHARYNGEAL TEETH	4-4	1,4-4,1	1,4-4,1	1,4-4,1	5-5

* Excluding Weberian apparatus.

Couesius

This monotypic genus is characterized by small scales and protractile mouth. It has a well-developed barbel that is slightly anterior to the end of the maxillary but not as far forward and not flap-like as in *Semotilus*.

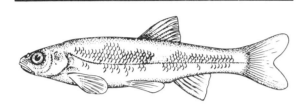

LAKE CHUB

Couesius plumbeus
(Agassiz, 1850)

Identification
The lake chub is a graceful, streamlined minnow that at first glance looks as if it might be a species of *Semotilus*. The lake chub, however, has a rather large, almost terminal barbel, whereas the barbel of *Semotilus* is small and in the groove above the upper lip, somewhat ahead of the end of the maxillary (subterminal). Four genera of minnows in our area have terminal barbels. Species of *Hybopsis* and *Nocomis* have large scales, species of *Rhinichthys* have a prominent frenum connecting the upper lip to the snout, and *Couesius* has small scales and no frenum.

Description
Body elongate, little compressed, the upper and lower profiles evenly curved, deepest in front of the dorsal fin. Dorsal deltoid, retrogressive, with rounded corners and straight margin. Caudal fin moderately forked, with rounded lobes. Anal similar to dorsal. Pelvic insertion below dorsal origin, rounded, retrogressive. Pectoral low, its base slightly oblique, retrogressive. Lateral line complete, slightly decurved. Scales smaller anteriorly. Mouth terminal, slightly oblique. Maxillary barbel terminal but at upper corner of the end of the maxillary. Gill membranes united to the isthmus. Counts and proportional measurements are given in Table 11.

Color: Silvery gray to olive above, shading to white ventrally. Midlateral stripe prominent in young only, extending from tip of snout through the eye to the base of the caudal fin. Lower sides peppered with melanophores. Dorsal scales with dark margins.

Juveniles and breeding adults: Juveniles have prominent midlateral stripes. Both sexes develop fine tubercles on the top of the head and body anterior to the dorsal origin, the sides of the head around the eye, the breast, the upper surface of the pectoral rays and on the anterior pelvic rays. Males develop some red on the snout and below the eye, on the shoulder region and at the upper part of the pectoral axil and sometimes around the pelvic fin base and the corners of the mouth. A specimen from West Canada Creek near Morehouseville collected in August 1979 had the anterior four pectoral rays thickened, each with a single row of contact organs on its dorsal surface.

Size: The lake chub reaches a length of nearly 9 inches total length.

Habitat
This species lives in streams and lakes and ponds, apparently moving into deeper water during the summer.

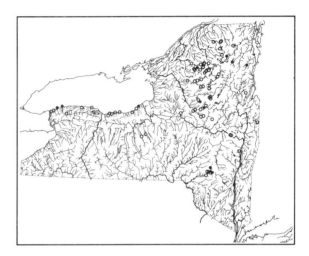

Distribution
The lake chub is a northern, periglacial species that lives in a broad band across Canada and northern United States from Nova Scotia and Labrador to British Columbia and central Alaska. It lives in northern New England, New York, Michigan and Wisconsin to Idaho, Wyoming and Colorado.

In New York, it is widely distributed in the Adirondacks and along the south shore of Lake Ontario with scattered records in the Mohawk, Hudson, and Oswego drainages. There is an isolated population in the East Branch of the Delaware near Margaretville.

George (1981a) reported that the lake chub lives in at least 30 prominent lakes in the Adirondacks and probably occurs in others.

Life History
The lake chub is an early spawner, moving into streams in April in the southern part of its range. Scott and Crossman note that the lake chub spawns at about the same time as the smelt or even earlier. McPhail and Lindsey cite J. H. Brown who observed the lake chub spawning around rocks in Saskatchewan, without guarding eggs or building a nest.

Food and Feeding
Zooplankton, aquatic insects, algae and small fishes are the chief food items.

Notes
The lake chub has a large range and some populations may be somewhat differentiated.

For a time, it was thought that all species with terminal barbels were closely related and should be placed in a single genus *Hybopsis*. Further study has not confirmed this and at present *Couesius* and *Nocomis* are recognized as separate genera.

References

Hubbs, 1942 (hybridization with pearl dace). Lindsey, 1956 (distribution). McPhail and Lindsey, 1970 (general summary). Brown, Hammer, and Koskinsky, 1970 (breeding biology). Fuiman and Baker, 1981 (larvae). Scott and Crossman, 1973 (general account).

Names

Plumbum is the Latin word for lead, referring to its silvery gray color.

Gobio plumbeus Agassiz, 1850: 366-368 Lake Superior

Ceratichthys prosthemius Cope *in* Gunther, 1868: 177 Montreal; Keweenaw Point, Lake Superior

Couesius prosthemius, Mather, 1886: 30-31 Adirondacks

Couesius plumbeus, Bean, 1903: 161-162 Adirondacks

Hybopsis

This is a rather large genus of about 17 species. Their relationships are not well understood and it is possible that the genus is polyphyletic, that is, that not all species shared a common ancestor. For the time being they are placed together because they all have rather large scales, protractile mouths, terminal barbels, and scale radii only in the posterior field.

KEY TO THE SPECIES OF *HYBOPSIS* IN NEW YORK

A. Color plain silvery, with a faint lateral band at most. Lower lobe of tail with a conspicuous white margin. Teeth 1,4-4,1.
Hybopsis storeriana   Silver chub, p. 139

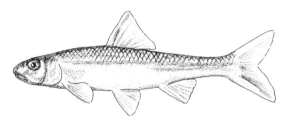

A'. Color pattern with distinct markings, either a continuous lateral stripe or a series of round or X-shaped spots.

B. Color pattern consists of a more or less distinct lateral stripe that continues around the snout (sometimes quite pale in fish from turbid waters). Teeth 1,4-4,1.
Hybopsis amblops   Bigeye chub, p. 137

B'. Color pattern consists of round or X-shaped spots on side. Pharyngeal teeth 4-4.

C. Color pattern a series of rounded spots in a row along midside. These are sometimes connected by a fainter stripe. Often, there are some X- or W-shaped spots on the back above the lateral markings.
Hybopsis dissimilis   Streamline chub, p. 138

C'. Body without a midlateral row of rounded spots. Back and sides with W- or X-shaped spots.
Hybopsis x-punctata   Gravel chub, p. 140

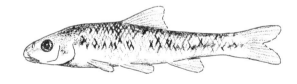

BIGEYE CHUB

Hybopsis amblops
(Rafinesque, 1820)

Identification
At first glance, the bigeye chub looks like a species of *Notropis* but this impression is quickly dispelled by the presence of a terminal maxillary barbel. The bigeye is a rather small species with a broad, dark midlateral band that continues forward on the head to the snout. It does not have X-shaped marks on the upper sides. The bigeye chub has 1,4-4,1 pharyngeal teeth, as does the silver chub (the pharyngeal teeth are 4-4 in the gravel chub and the streamline chub), but the silver chub is a larger species without a dark lateral stripe and with a conspicuous white lower edge of the caudal fin.

Description
Body elongate, nearly terete, with its dorsal profile more arched than the ventral. Dorsal fin deltoid, retrogressive, with sharp corners and straight or slightly concave margin. Caudal fin moderately forked, with pointed lobes. Anal origin below, or slightly ahead of, tip of depressed last dorsal ray. Anal deltoid, retrogressive, with sharp corners and slightly concave margin. Pelvic insertion below dorsal origin. Pelvic retrogressive, its corners rounded. Pectoral low, its base somewhat oblique, retrogressive, with pointed anterior and rounded posterior corner. Mouth low, horizontal, snout protruding beyond upper lip. Gill membranes joined to the isthmus. Eyes large, directed dorsolaterally. Barbel large. Lateral line complete, slightly decurved anteriorly. Counts and proportional measurements are given in Table 12.

Color: Pale, with a broad, rather even, midlateral stripe from the tip of the snout to the base of the tail, paler between the eye and the preopercle. No mid-dorsal stripe. Scales of the upper sides with dark edges that join to form wavy lines. Scales just above the lateral stripe with less prominent margins forming a pale stripe above the dark midlateral stripe. There is deep pigment at the base of the tail that is not separated from the midlateral stripe. All fins pale. Lips, lower parts of head and belly pale but there is deep pigment along the base of the anal fin.

Juveniles and breeding adults: There are no bright breeding colors and the tubercles are tiny and developed only on the head, breast and isthmus, and on the dorsal surface of the first nine pectoral rays.

Size: The maximum size is about 75 mm standard length.

Habitat

The bigeye chub lives in small and moderate-sized creeks with clean sand, gravel, or rocky bottoms. It often occurs in rather quiet water, but near riffles and often near aquatic vegetation. Apparently, it is intolerant of silt and Trautman documented its decline as the streams of northern Ohio became increasingly silty.

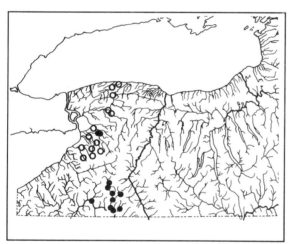

Distribution

This is a species of the Upper Mississippi basin, reaching its northeastern limit in the Allegheny and Lake Erie tributaries of New York. It ranges southwest through the Ohio and Tennessee Rivers to the Arkansas drainage in northern Arkansas and northeastern Oklahoma.

Life History

Very little seems to be known about the life history of the bigeye chub. It has been reported to spawn from April to June in Kansas and in June in Missouri.

Food and Feeding

The bigeye chub is said to feed on insects but comprehensive studies have not been reported.

Notes

Gilbert noted that, except for its barbels, this species is very similar to the species of *Notropis* and may eventually be placed in that genus.

References

Gilbert, 1978 (relationships). Trautman, 1957 (decline in Ohio).

Names

Amblops comes from the Greek *ambl*, blunt or stupid, and *ops*, eye or face. Probably blunt face was intended but the dorsally directed eyes give it a look that lends credence to the alternate derivation.

Rutilus amblops Rafinesque, 1820a: 51 Ohio River and Louisville, Kentucky

Ceratichthys hyalinus Cope in Gunther, 1868: 177 Tennessee

Erinemus hyalinus, Greeley, 1929: 170 Erie-Niagara watershed

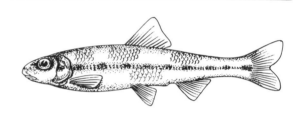

STREAMLINE CHUB

Hybopsis dissimilis (Kirtland, 1840)

Identification

The streamline chub is a graceful little minnow with a row of 10 or fewer round spots along the midside. It has a rather pointed head, a low horizontal mouth, and well-developed terminal barbels. Its nearest relative is the gravel chub, *Hybopsis x-punctata,* and the two are quite similar. Both have X- or W-shaped spots on the upper sides but only the streamline chub has the row of midlateral spots. The gravel chub and the streamline chub have 4-4 pharyngeal teeth; the other New York species of *Hybopsis,* the silver chub and the bigeye chub, have 1,4-4,1 pharyngeal teeth.

The streamline chub also has smaller scales, usually 46 to 49 in the lateral line, usually 40 to 43 in the lateral line of the gravel chub.

Description

Body elongate, little compressed, deepest in front of the dorsal origin. Profiles symmetrical. Caudal peduncle slender. Dorsal origin considerably nearer tip of snout than base of caudal. Dorsal retrogressive, its margin slightly falcate, with rounded anterior and sharp posterior corners. Caudal moderately forked, its lobes bluntly pointed, often the lower lobe shorter. Anal origin behind tip of depressed last dorsal ray. Anal retrogressive, its margin falcate, with rounded anterior and sharp posterior corners. Pelvic insertion below anterior half of dorsal base. Pelvic retrogressive, with very rounded anterior corner. Pelvic axillary process well developed.

Pectoral base low, oblique. Pectoral retrogressive, rounded. Gill membranes broadly joined to isthmus. Mouth low, horizontal, snout overhanging the upper lip. No frenum. Barbel large. Counts and proportional measurements are given in Table 12.

Color: Generally silvery to greenish olive dorsally. Scales of the upper sides with dark margins. A distinct midlateral line from the tip of the snout to the opercle, continuing on body as a series of 7 to 11 prominent round to squarish spots, the last of which is at the base of the tail. Upper sides with scattered irregular X- and W-shaped spots formed by intense pigment at the base of some scales. Predorsal stripe interrupted by three to seven light spots. Fin membranes clear, a few melanophores along the rays.

Juveniles and breeding adults: Head, including chin and gill membranes, breast, and anterior part of the body with fine tubercles. There is a single row of tubercles on the dorsal surface of first interradial membranes of the pelvic and pectoral fins.

Size: To somewhat over 4 inches total length. Our largest New York specimen is 87.5 mm standard length.

Habitat
The streamline chub lives in riffles and over bars in moderate-sized streams with coarse silt-free gravel, often near the lower ends of riffles in water 1 to 4 feet deep.

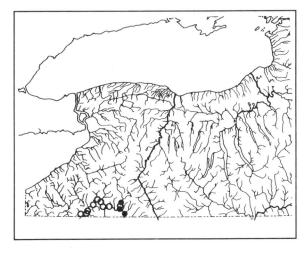

Distribution
This is a Mississippi watershed species that occurs in New York State only in the Allegheny drainage. Its overall range is the Ohio and Tennessee Rivers, from North Carolina to Indiana, Ohio, and western New York. *Hybopsis dissimilis harryi* occurs in the Ozarks of Arkansas and southeastern Missouri, replacing the typical subspecies, *H. d. dissimilis*.

Life History
This species probably spawns in May and June but its life history has not been studied.

Food and Feeding
This is apparently a sight-feeding carnivore that feeds on the bottom on aquatic insects, snails, and other bottom-dwelling organisms.

Notes
Trautman found that it was more abundant and widespread in the past, and possibly reached Lake Erie tributaries. In New York, pollution and the impoundment of the Allegheny River have eliminated its habitat below Salamanca but it is still present near Portville.

References
Hubbs and Crowe, 1956 (taxonomy). Davis and Miller, 1967 (brain pattern). Trautman, 1957 (general account).

Names
Dissimilis is Latin for unlike, not similar. Presumably, Kirtland was comparing it to other minnows of the *Luxilus* species group of *Notropis* to which it is certainly not similar.

Luxilus dissimilis Kirtland, 1840: 341-342 Mahoning River, Ohio

Erimystax dissimilis, Greeley, 1939: 65 Allegheny River

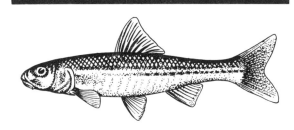

SILVER CHUB

Hybopsis storeriana (Kirtland, 1844)

Identification
The silver chub is a pale species with little pigment anywhere and a conspicuous white lower margin of the caudal fin. In the field, it looks a little like a spotfin shiner, *Notropis hudsonius,* without a caudal spot, but the silver chub has conspicuous terminal barbels. The other local species of *Hybopsis* all have prominent color markings. Like the bigeye chub, the silver chub has two rows of pharyngeal teeth.

Description
Body elongate, slightly compressed. Dorsal profile angulate, nearly straight before and behind the dorsal origin. Ventral profile evenly curved. Dorsal origin closer to the snout than to the base of the tail. Dorsal fin trapezoidal, retrogressive, with concave margin and sharp corners. Tail moderately to deeply forked with pointed lobes. Anal origin behind tip of depressed last dorsal ray. Anal similar to dorsal. Pelvic inserted below anterior fourth of dorsal base. Pelvic retrogressive, with straight outer margin, its corners rounded. Pectoral base low, oblique. Pectoral retrogressive, bluntly pointed. Mouth low and nearly horizontal. Barbel terminal. Snout protruding well beyond upper lip. Gill membranes broadly joined to isthmus. Lateral line com-

plete, nearly straight. Counts and proportional measurements are given in Table 12.

Color: Pale allover, slightly darker dorsally. Midlateral stripe absent or pale, not continued around snout. Caudal fin lightly pigmented except lower three or four rays, which are white.

Breeding adults: The males have fine tubercles on top of the head, larger ones on the side of the head, and a row of fine tubercles on the upper surface of the first pectoral rays.

Size: Trautman lists specimens up to 9.1 inches total length.

Habitat

The silver chub lives in Lake Erie at depths of 3 to 60 feet. Over most of its range, it occurs in streams where the bottom is clean sand and fine gravel. It avoids silty areas and normally inhabits pools but if the pools have silt bottoms, it moves onto riffles.

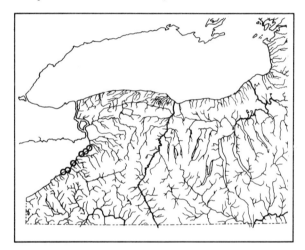

Distribution

The silver chub occurs from Lake Erie and the Allegheny and Ohio Rivers to the Red River of the North and through the Mississippi Valley to the gulf coast from the Rio Brazos to the Pascagoula drainage.

In New York, it was taken in Lake Erie by the Survey but it is scarce now. The record of Evermann and Kendall from Long Pond near Charlotte in the Lake Ontario drainage is presumed to be an error.

Life History

The spawning of the silver chub has not been described. Apparently, in Lake Erie, they spawn in open water in June or possibly late May when the water temperature reaches 20 C. Kinney found that the ovarian egg counts ranged from 2,603 to 11,555.

Food and Feeding

Young silver chubs feed on cladocerans, copepods, and chironomid larvae. In the western basin of Lake Erie, the larger chubs fed on the abundant nymphs of the mayfly *Hexagenia*. In the early 1950s, these mayflies suddenly became scarce and the chubs had to switch to other foods including midges and *Gammarus*.

Notes

Greeley (1929) reported the silver chub as common in Lake Erie and at the mouths of larger creeks. We collected it in the Bass Islands of Ohio as late as 1972, but we have not taken it in New York waters and presume that it is now rare in the eastern basin of Lake Erie. Scott and Crossman also list it as rare in Canada.

References

Kinney, 1954 (ecology). Trautman, 1957 (general account). Evermann and Kendall, 1901 (notes).

Names

The silver chub is named for David Humphreys Storer who published History of the Fishes of Massachusetts in 1839.

Rutilus Storeriana Kirtland, 1844b: 71 Lake Erie (nomen nudum)

Leuciscus Storerianus Kirtland, 1844b: 199-200 Lake Erie

Erinemus storerianus, Evermann and Kendall, 1902a: Lake Ontario (probably an error)

Erinemus storerianus, Greeley, 1929: 170 Lake Erie

Hybopsis storerianus, Greeley, 1940: 73 (after Evermann and Kendall)

GRAVEL CHUB

Hybopsis x-punctata
Hubbs and Crowe, 1956

Identification

The gravel chub is a small minnow with a terminal barbel and conspicuous X- and W-shaped marks on the upper sides. It is similar to the streamline chub but lacks the conspicuous midlateral row of large, rounded, dark spots that characterizes the streamline chub.

Description

Body elongate, nearly terete. Dorsal origin nearer tip of snout than base of tail. Dorsal retrogressive, trapezoidal, with concave margin and sharp corners. Caudal moderately forked, with pointed lobes. Anal origin below tip of depressed last dorsal ray. Anal similar to dorsal. Pelvic inserted below anterior part of dorsal base. Pelvic retrogressive, with straight margin and rounded corners, its axillary process moderate. Pectoral base low, only slightly oblique. Pectoral retrogressive, rounded. Head conical, eyes dorsolateral, mouth low and horizontal. Snout pointed and overhanging the mouth. Barbel terminal, well developed. Gill membranes broadly joined to isthmus. Lateral line complete and nearly straight. Counts and proportional measurements are given in Table 12.

Color: Generally silvery, shading from greenish or brownish above to silvery white below. Scales of the dorsal surface with dusky margins, some with intense pigment that forms X- or W-shaped marks. Sometimes, there is a weak midlateral stripe but it is never prominent. Basicaudal spot small and dark.

Juveniles and breeding adults: Males develop fine tubercles on all parts of the head and on the scales of the anterior part of the body. Our specimen, AMNH 55391, collected in the Allegheny River near Westons Mills by Steven Eaton, has large tubercles on the lower parts of the head and especially the isthmus where several tubercles form a comb-like structure between the lower ends of the gill covers.

Size: To about 4 inches total length.

Habitat
The gravel chub requires silt-free streams of moderate or large size. Trautman noted that it preferred slower water but occasionally moved into faster waters, where it spent much of its time near shelter where the current was slow.

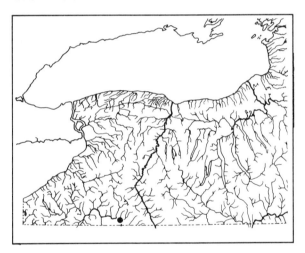

Distribution
The eastern subspecies, *Hybopsis x-punctata trautmani*, occurs in the Ohio River and its tributaries from Illinois to western New York. In New York, it occurs in the Allegheny River above Salamanca. Our specimen was collected on 20 September 1973. It also occurs in southern Ontario where it has not been seen since 1958. In Illinois tributaries of the Mississippi and from southern Minnesota to Arkansas, eastern Oklahoma, Kansas and the Ozarks, it is replaced by the typical subspecies.

Life History
The life history of the gravel chub has not been studied.

Food and Feeding.
The food habits are unknown but its similarity to other species of *Hybopsis* suggests that it has a similar diet of insects and other benthic invertebrates.

Notes
Because of its strict habitat requirements, the gravel chub is a good indicator of water quality. It was not described until 1956 and it is possible that some of the specimens Greeley called *Hybopsis dissimilis* were actually this species.

References
Hubbs and Crowe, 1956 (description). Eaton et al., 1982. Trautman, 1981 (Ohio).

Names
The species name, *x-punctata,* is Latin for X-shaped spots. *Trautmani* is named for Milton Trautman, the author of The Fishes of Ohio.

Hybopsis x-punctata trautmani Hubbs and Crowe, 1956: 1-8 Waldoning River, Ohio

Nocomis

The chubs are rather large terete fishes with large scales, terminal barbels, and a common life history pattern which involves the construction of large pebble nests. Their nest as well as their general appearance resembles that of the fallfish but the fallfish has a subterminal barbel and is placed in the genus *Semotilus*. This genus has six species and has been studied intensively by Lachner and Jenkins.

KEY TO THE SPECIES OF *NOCOMIS* IN NEW YORK

A. Suborbital region of adults wide, its minimum width greater than half the distance from the back of the eye to the edge of the gill membrane. Spot at the base of the tail inconspicuous or absent. Caudal fin of juveniles gray in life. Pharyngeal teeth 4-4. Breeding males with tubercles on top of the front of the head only (tubercle scars of large males often persist throughout the year). No conspicuous red spot behind the eye.
Nocomis micropogon   River chub, p. 144

A'. Suborbital region of adults narrower, its minimum width less than half the postorbital distance. Spot at base of tail round, blackish and conspicuous, especially in juveniles less than two inches long. Caudal fin of juveniles red in life. Pharyngeal teeth 1,4-4,1. Breeding males with tubercles extending well behind the eyes and with a conspicuous red spot behind the eye.
Nocomis biguttatus   Hornyhead chub, p. 142

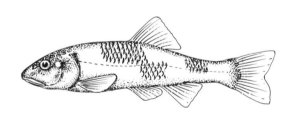

HORNYHEAD CHUB

Nocomis biguttatus
(Kirtland, 1840)

Identification
Members of the genus *Nocomis* are rather large, terete minnows with well-developed terminal barbels and a characteristic diamond pattern formed by the dark margins of the scales of the upper sides and back.

Hornyheads get their name from the prominent breeding tubercles that cover the entire top of the head of breeding males. These tubercles slough off after the breeding season but larger males may show the tubercle scars all year long. In the related river chub, the tubercles are confined to the region in front of the eyes. Juvenile hornyheads have a dark midlateral stripe that ends in a large round spot. The stripe fades as the fish get bigger, but

there is usually a trace of the spot.

Positive separation of the hornyhead and river chubs is provided by the pharyngeal teeth: 1,4-4,1 in the hornyhead; 4-4 in the river chub.

Description
Body elongate, little compressed. Profiles equally curved. Dorsal origin equidistant from tip of snout and caudal base. Dorsal retrogressive, its margin nearly straight, with rounded corners. Tail moderately forked with rounded lobes. Anal origin below middle of depressed last dorsal ray. Anal retrogressive, similar to dorsal, sometimes with last ray longer than penultimate. Pelvic inserted slightly ahead of the dorsal origin. Pelvic retrogressive, with margin slightly convex and corners rounded. Pectoral low, slightly oblique, retrogressive, rounded. Lateral line complete, nearly straight, rising anteriorly. Mouth terminal, slightly oblique. Barbel large, terminal. Counts and proportional measurements are given in Table 13.

Color: Dark olive above with the scales boldly outlined and a dark bar on the base of each scale. Sides with midlateral stripe from the preopercle to the caudal base fusing with a permanent, round, basicaudal spot. Belly pale yellow to white. Fin rays reddish in life, with dark margins.

Juveniles and breeding adults: Juveniles have bright red tails and distinct lateral stripes and basicaudal spots. Breeding males with large tubercles on the entire top of the head, from the internasal region to the occiput, and sometimes to the nape. Many of the tubercles antrorse.The total number of tubercles is 40 to 60. Breeding males develop a prominent light middorsal stripe from the occiput to the dorsal origin, and behind the dorsal to the base of the upper caudal rays. Dorsal and caudal fins red, upper pectoral rays orange and black, and outer rays of pelvic and anal edged in white. Lower lip red, upper lip black. Postocular spot scarlet in breeding males, pale at other times.

Size: Lachner reported males to 124 mm, females to 118 mm standard length. Our largest New York specimens are 118 mm standard length.

Habitat
The hornyhead lives in small- to moderate-sized streams and shows a preference for clear water with clean gravel and some sand on the bottom. Pools and riffles are usually present and sometimes long stretches of slow water. Silt and excessive turbidity are avoided. Young chubs tend to remain near algae and aquatic vegetation.

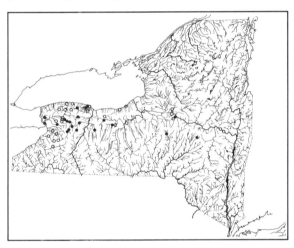

Distribution
The hornyhead is a Mississippi refugium species ranging from the Mohawk west to the Red River of the North in North Dakota and south to Iowa, Illinois, Ohio, and northwestern Pennsylvania. It occurs also in the Ozarks and scattered localities in the North and South Platte Rivers and the Kansas River in Kansas.

In New York, it is in western drainages, the Mohawk, and in the old Chenango Canal. Its presence in the Susquehanna drainage, and possibly the Mohawk, seems to be due to canal access.

Life History
The hornyhead is a spring-spawning nest builder. Spawning usually begins in May or early June when the temperature reaches 65 F. Males build the nests by carrying pebbles in their mouths and depositing them in a depression, either a natural one or one that was built by the male sweeping the area clean. Females ready to spawn move near the nests and the male interrupts his nest building to entice the

female over the nest. The pair vibrates together as the sex products are released, then the female moves off and the male continues to add pebbles to the nest. It is believed that as many as ten females may contribute eggs to a nest. The finished nest can be as large as 3 feet in diameter and 6 inches high.

Frequently, common shiner males move in and share the nests of the hornyhead. The males of the two species share the guarding of the nests, driving away other other males without interfering with each other. Hankinson noted that the common shiner usually drove away smaller fish and the hornyhead, with its heavier tubercles, took on the large invaders such as hog suckers.

The nests are usually built in areas of moderate current, often below or in riffles. Females 80 to 89 mm standard length contained 460 to 725 eggs, only part of which were released at a time. The fastest growing individuals became mature at age II + . The maximum age is IV + .

Food and Feeding
The hornyhead consumes a variety of plant and animal foods. Young fish tend to feed on filamentous algae and diatoms as well as cladocerans and aquatic insect larvae. Larger chubs feed on larger insects, annelids, mollusks, crayfish, and fish. Terrestrial insects that fall into the streams are frequently eaten.

Notes
For a time, this species and the river chub were placed in the genus *Hybopsis.* Jenkins and Lachner have argued that the seven species of *Nocomis* are closely related but distant from other minnows with terminal barbels, although possibly allied to *Semotilus.*

References
Lachner and Jenkins, 1971 (systematics). Jenkins and Lachner, 1971b (relationships). Lachner, 1950 (food). Lachner, 1952 (life history). Hankinson, 1919 (ecology). Hankinson, 1932 (breeding habits). Greeley, 1955c (popular account).

Names
The name *biguttatus* is from the Latin *bi,* two and *gutta,* a drop, hence a drop-like spot. Thus, the name means two spots.

Semotilus biguttatus Kirtland, 1840: 340-345 Yellow Creek, Ohio

Hybopsis biguttata, Hubbs and Lagler, 1964: 78 (distribution)

Luxilus (Luxilus) Kentuckiensis Rafinesque, 1820a: 48 Ohio River

Hybopsis kentuckiensis, Bean, 1903: 159-160

Nocomis biguttatus, Greeley, 1927: 60 Genesee watershed

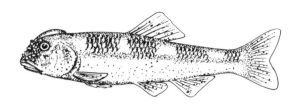

RIVER CHUB

Nocomis micropogon (Cope, 1865)

Identification

The river chub is a large, terete minnow with a deep caudal peduncle, a rather small eye, and terminal barbels. It has rather large, regular scales and those of the upper body have conspicuous dark margins, giving the fish a crosshatched appearance.

The only species the river chub can be confused with in our area is the hornyhead chub, but the hornyhead has two rows of pharyngeal teeth while the river chub has only one. Externally, the river chub has a wider space between the upper lip and the eye — more than half the distance between the back of the eye and the upper end of the gill opening. A less conspicuous spot lies at the base of the tail and there is no pale or red spot behind the eye in the hornyhead. Juvenile river chubs have gray or slightly orange tails; the caudal fins of juvenile hornyheads are bright red in life.

Adult male river chubs have breeding tubercles (or tubercle scars) on top of the head between the nostrils and the middle of the interorbital region. In the hornyhead, the entire top of the head has large tubercles or scars.

Description

Body elongate, nearly terete, with deep caudal peduncle. Dorsal origin nearer base of tail than tip of snout. Dorsal retrogressive, its margin slightly falcate, rounded anteriorly and concave posteriorly. Caudal rather shallowly to moderately forked, with rounded lobes. Anal origin below middle of depressed last dorsal ray, retrogressive, with rounded corners. Pelvic insertion slightly ahead of the dorsal origin. Pelvic retrogressive, rounded. Pelvic axillary process small. Pectoral low, with slightly oblique base. Pectoral retrogressive, rounded. Snout blunt, overhanging the mouth. Mouth large, low, and slightly oblique. Barbel large, terminal. Lateral line complete, nearly straight. Counts and proportional measurements are given in Table 12.

Color: Back greenish olive, shading to silvery white at midsides. Scales of the upper sides with conspicuous dark outlines and a vertical rectangular spot at the base of each scale. Upper half of operculum and top of head olive gray. Dorsal and caudal fin rays with dark outlines. Anal and paired fins white, sometimes tinged with yellow.

Juveniles and breeding adults: Juveniles have a conspicuous midlateral stripe that ends in a small basicaudal spot. Breeding adult males develop a large,

fleshy crest on the top of the head and large tubercles in front of the eyes, The pigment of the dorsal surface becomes more intense and the lower parts of the head and body develop a rosy-pink wash. The pectoral and anal fins become bright yellow; the dorsal and caudal fins paler yellow. The leading edges of the anal and paired fins are white. Small breeding tubercles are present on the dorsal surface of the pectoral fins.

Size: The largest male reported by Lachner was 188 mm standard length; the largest female was 127 mm. There is a 270-mm specimen in the Tulane University collection but its origin is not known.

Habitat

River chubs are found in larger creeks and rivers where the water is clear and the bottom is mostly gravel, rubble or boulders with little or no aquatic vegetation. The presence of gravel is a requirement for successful reproduction.

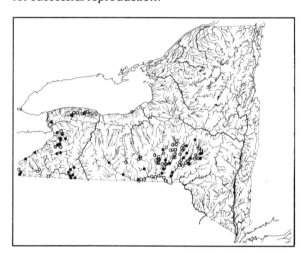

Distribution

The river chub occurs east of the Mississippi River. On the Atlantic coast, it ranges from the Susquehanna drainage of New York south to the James River in Virginia and the Upper Savannah system in Georgia. West of the Appalachians, it occurs in southern Ontario and the Lower Peninsula of Michigan to the uplands of Kentucky, Tennessee and northern Alabama. It also occurs in the Coosa system of the Mobile Bay drainage.

In New York, it lives in the Susquehanna system and west, but it is absent from the Genesee watershed.

Life History

The conspicuous nests of the river chub have been studied by a number of workers. Reighard (1943) is the classic study most often cited. Reighard worked in southern Michigan. Nest building and spawning took place from mid-April to the end of May or early June when water temperatures were 15 to 20 C. Nests are built in water 18 to 24 inches deep, sometimes as deep as 36 inches. Stones 0.25 inch to 3 or 4 inches in diameter are required.

After testing several sites, the male selects one and digs a pit by removing stones and dropping them at the sides and downstream from the nest. After the pit is 12 to 15 inches in diameter and 3 to 6 inches deep, the male begins to bring stones back, filling the pit, and then building it into a mound 6 or 7 inches high and 33 to 43 inches in diameter. These mounds are usually slightly oval, the long axis with the current. One nest contained approximately 7,000 pebbles (70.5 quarts) weighing 235 pounds. The stones were brought from distances up to 20 feet and Reighard estimated that the fish had traveled about 16 miles to accumulate the pebbles. The nest building is frequently interrupted but usually 20 to 30 hours were required to complete the nest.

When the nest is nearly finished, the approach of a female stimulates the male to dig a spawning trench in the top of the pile. This is a narrow trough about as wide as his body and one-half to two-thirds his length, deepest at its upstream end. He then lies in the trench, with his pectoral fins spread, and vibrates his body. This attracts the female who joins the male in the trough. The male presses his side against the female who may leave by swimming forward or she may raise off the bottom, allowing the male to seize her between his body and the upper surface of his pectoral fin. At this time, the eggs and milt are extruded, then the female is released and swims away downstream while the male covers the trench.

Reighard stated that although swarms of other minnows may move over the nest, the male pays little attention to them and combat even with other males of the same species is rare. Sometimes, smaller river chub males worked on the nest at the same time as the primary male, but they were not seen to spawn. Among the other species that use river chub nests for spawning are the stoneroller, *Campostoma anomalum,* the common shiner, *Notropis cornutus,* and the rosyface shiner, *N. rubellus.* Reighard noted that the other species were somewhat segregated on the nests and suggested that this made some hybrid combinations more likely than others because the milt is quickly carried downstream. Since *Notropis rubellus* usually remained downstream, the chances of its milt reaching the eggs of other species was reduced but the chances of its eggs being fertilized by other species was increased.

Lachner found egg counts of 400 to 625 in female river chubs 92 to 100 mm standard length. Males and females mature at age III + and one male was in its fifth summer.

Food and Feeding
The river chub feeds on plankton and some algae when young and progresses to larger prey. Insect larvae are a major food item.

Notes
Because other species use river chub nests for spawning, hybrids between river chubs and other species are quite common.

References
Reighard, 1943 (life history). Lachner, 1952 (general biology). Raney, 1947b (nesting). Hankinson, 1932 (nesting). Lachner, 1950 (food). Miller, 1964 (breeding behavior). Lachner and Jenkins, 1967; 1971 (systematics). Jenkins and Lachner, 1971 (relationships). Stauffer et al., 1979 (hybridization). Cooper, 1980 (development). Buynack and Mohr, 1980a (larvae).

Names
Micropogon is from the Greek *mikros,* small and *pogon,* beard, apparently in reference to the barbels.

Ceratichthys micropogon Cope, 1865a: 277 Conestoga River, Pennsylvania

Nocomis micropogon, Greeley, 1928: 97 Oswego watershed

Hybopsis micropogon, Bailey, 1951: 192

TABLE 12
AVERAGE PROPORTIONAL MEASUREMENTS AND COUNTS OF
CHUBS (*Hybopsis* and *Nocomis*)

All proportions are expressed in percentage of standard length.

| | *Hybopsis* | | | | *Nocomis* | |
	amblops	dissimilis	storeriana	x-punctata	biguttatus	micropogon
ST. LENGTH (mm)	31.2	67.2	103.8	61.7	88.0	63.5
TOTAL LENGTH	129.0	119.8	127.8	123.9	124.5	122.4
FORK LENGTH	116.0	110.1	113.4	111.5	116.3	114.8
PREDORSAL	52.9	48.9	47.8	47.2	55.3	54.1
PREANAL	64.0	67.6	70.2	68.9	68.9	68.7
PREPELVIC	47.4	49.3	49.7	49.3	51.8	53.4
DORSAL BASE	13.4	11.9	14.6	12.4	13.3	11.3
ANAL BASE	10.2	8.1	10.3	10.6	10.3	8.9
BODY DEPTH	18.7	16.9	24.6	19.2	24.4	22.6
BODY WIDTH	12.2	13.2	13.0	14.8	15.9	15.6
C.PED. DEPTH	9.0	7.3	10.3	8.6	10.7	11.2
PECTORAL ALT.	12.2	13.2	16.3	14.0	17.2	15.8
HEAD LENGTH	25.7	23.4	24.8	25.3	26.8	26.8
SNOUT	6.5	8.6	8.2	9.9	9.4	10.4
EYE	9.7	6.6	7.0	7.1	5.6	6.5
MOUTH LENGTH	9.0	6.0	7.9	6.0	6.2	8.4
INTERORB	6.5	6.4	6.8	5.6	5.1	9.1
N (sample size)	5	5	5	5	5	5
COUNTS:						
DORSAL RAYS	8	8	8	8	8	8
ANAL RAYS	7-9	7	8	6-7	7	7
PECTORAL						
RAYS	14-15	17-19	17-19	19	15-16	16-17
PELVIC RAYS	8	8-9	8-9	9	8	8
GILL RAKERS	1-4	4	5-6	7-8	8	7
VERTEBRAE*	32-33	35-37	37	34	35-37	35-36
SCALES:						
ABOVE L. L.	4-5	5-6	5	6	6	6
LATERAL LINE	35-37	43-49	38-43	43	40-48	38-43
BELOW L. L.	4	5	4-5	5	5	5
PHARYNGEAL						
TEETH	1,4-4,1	4-4	1,4-4,1	4-4	1,4-4,1	4-4

* Excluding Weberian apparatus.

Rhinichthys

The species of *Rhinichthys* are rather small slender and terete fishes with a terminal barbel and a well-developed bridge of tissue (frenum) between the tip of the snout and the upper lip. The scales are small, more than 55 in the lateral line. There are five or six species and several of these have local variant populations that have been named in the past, but at present the use of subspecies is out of fashion.

KEY TO THE SPECIES OF *RHINICHTHYS* IN NEW YORK

A. Snout long, projecting well beyond the inferior mouth. Lateral dark stripe usually diffuse on body, often well developed on side of snout. Eyes supralateral, center of pupil above level of the dark line on side of snout. Swim bladder rudimentary, extending only as far back as the base of the pelvic fin.
Rhinichthys cataractae   Longnose dace, p. 149

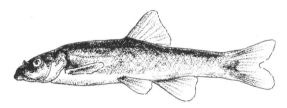

A'. Snout short, at most only slightly overhanging the terminal mouth. Lateral stripe well developed on body and on head. Eyes lateral, the center of the pupil in line with stripe on side of snout. Swim bladder well developed, extending beyond the pelvic fin base.

B. Adult males with the lateral stripe reddish orange only during the breeding season. Breeding males with pectoral fins bright orange. Caudal peduncle

relatively slender. Dark specklings on sides below the lateral band rather sparse and indistinct.
Rhinichthys atratulus
Eastern blacknose dace, p. 147

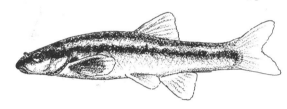

B'. Adult males with lateral band brick red throughout the year. Breeding males with little orange on the pectoral fins. Lower sides with conspicuous speckling. Caudal peduncle deeper.
Rhinichthys meleagris
Western blacknose dace, p. 150

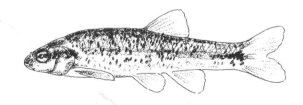

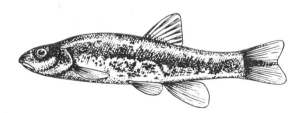

EASTERN BLACKNOSE DACE

Rhinichthys atratulus
(Hermann, 1804)

Identification
Fine scales, terminal maxillary barbels, and a frenum connecting the upper lip to the tip of the snout, are all characteristics of the members of the genus *Rhinichthys*. The blacknose daces have distinct midlateral stripes and short snouts that protrude only slightly beyond the upper lip, whereas the longnose dace

has a weak, or no, lateral stripe, and a very protuberant snout. The longnose may, however, have a distinctive stripe on the side of the snout and this stripe passes through the lower part of the eye rather than through its center. The eyes of the blacknose dace are laterally directed but those of the longnose are aimed dorsolaterally and are smaller. The blacknose dace also has a larger swim bladder that reaches at least to the level of the tip of the pectoral fin but the swim bladder of the longnose dace is shorter.

The eastern and western blacknose daces are very similar and are usually treated as subspecies, *Rhinichthys atratulus atratulus,* the eastern blacknose dace, and *R. a. meleagris,* the western blacknose dace. There is, however, little evidence that the two forms intergrade. Their geographic ranges overlap little, if any, and the males of the two forms are quite different in appearance although the females and immature males are closely similar. Until they have been studied more thoroughly, it seems best to recognize them as full species in order to keep the information about the two forms clearly separated.

Description

Body elongate, terete. Dorsal profile evenly curved, ventral profile nearly straight. Dorsal origin midway between caudal base and posterior margin of the eye. Dorsal subtrapezoidal, with slightly concave margin, its corners rounded. Caudal moderately forked, its middle rays three-fourths the upper rays. Caudal lobes blunt. Anal inserted below end of caudal base. Anal trapezoidal, its corners rounded, its margin straight. Pelvic insertion anterior to dorsal origin, pelvic retrogressive, with rounded corners and convex margin. Pelvic axillary process obsolete. Pectorals low, nearly horizontal, retrogressive, with convex margin. Head flat on ventral surface, mouth low, slightly oblique, frenum well developed. Barbel present, terminal. Upper jaw longer than lower. Snout slightly protruding. Eye small, interorbital broad. Gill membranes broadly united to the isthmus. Lateral line complete, slightly decurved anteriorly. Body fully scaled. Counts and proportional measurements are given in Table 13.

Color: Generally dark olive gray to black above, shading to silvery white below. Sides with a broad midlateral stripe from tip of snout to the base of the caudal and continuing on to the caudal rays, fading distally. Iris brassy; fin rays outlined. Top of the body with fine specklings, lower sides usually unspotted or with a few spots.

Size: The blacknose dace occasionally reaches 3.5 inches total length. Our largest New York specimens are 85 mm standard length.

Juveniles and breeding adults: Adult males have a pale gold stripe above the narrow midlateral dark stripe and bright orange on the rays of the pectoral, pelvic, and anal fins and an orange wash on the dorsal fin and the tail. Males develop small tubercles over the top of the head from the nostrils to the occiput and finer tubercles on the suborbital, cheek, and the upper half of the operculum. Tubercles are also present over the entire body including the lower surface of the caudal peduncle. Tubercles are also present on all fins except the pectorals.

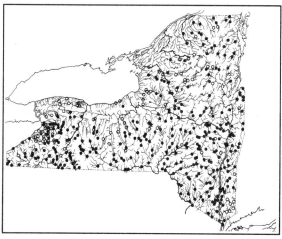

Habitat

The blacknose lives in small clear streams, often in sections where there are no other fishes. It also occurs in larger streams where there is moderate to swift current with riffles and pools. It frequently shares headwater areas with the brook trout.

Distribution

The eastern blacknose dace ranges from Nova Scotia to South Carolina and Georgia. In New York, it occurs throughout the eastern part of the state and west to the Genesee River.

Life History

Most of the observations of the breeding habitats have been made on the western blacknose dace and it appears that there are some differences in reproductive behavior. It has been reported that the eastern form defends its territory less vigorously than the western form, although there is some dispute about this.

Food and Feeding

Aquatic insect larvae are the most important food, especially midge larvae. Diatoms and desmids are taken frequently during the later part of the season.

Notes

Bartnick studied reproductive isolation between the blacknose and longnose daces. Natural hybrids between them are unknown, and must be rare, although the two species are interfertile and hybrids can be produced experimentally. The spawning seasons overlap but the longnose spawns earlier and at a lower temperature, 15 C, as compared with 19 C for the longnose in Manitoba. Bartnick believed that the separation was maintained mostly by behavioral differences. Longnose spawned in swifter water where the bottom included larger pebbles. In experimental aquaria, the blacknose females ignored longnose males and vice versa even though the males occasionally courted females of the other species. Generally, however, each species ignored or even chased the other. Blacknose territories are larger, 30 to 60 cm across, with a central station 10 to 12 cm in diameter. Blacknose chase and dart at intruders, whereas longnose butt and bite. Blacknose pair when spawning and longnose do not. Blacknose males perform a courting dance and the longnose do not.

A third form, species or subspecies, *R. a. obtusus*, occurs in the Southeast.

References

Raney, 1940a (life history). Traver, 1929 (spawning). Tarter, 1969 (comparison of breeding habits of the three subspecies). Johnson, 1982 (summer feeding ecology). Pappantoniou and Dale, 1982 (food). Bartnick, 1970 (reproductive isolation).

Names

Atratulus is Latin meaning clothed in black as for mourning.

Cyprinus atratulus Hermann, 1804: 320 "America septentrionalis"

Cyprinus atronasus Mitchill, 1815: 460 Wallkill River

Leuciscus atronasus, DeKay, 1842: 205-206

Rhinichthys a. atronasus, Hubbs and Brown, 1929: 125

Cyprinus vittatus Rafinesque, 1817b: 121 Upper Hudson

Rhinichthys atronasus, Greeley, 1927: 60 Genesee River

Rhinichthys atratulus, Hubbs, 1936: 124-125 (names)

LONGNOSE DACE

Rhinichthys cataractae
(Valenciennes, 1842)

Identification
Species of *Rhinichthys* are slender, terete fishes with terminal maxillary barbels, and a distinct frenum connecting the center of the upper lip to the snout.

Longnose dace differ from blacknose in the length of the snout. Some blacknose, however, have a slightly overhanging snout and can cause some problems if you do not have the two side by side. Longnose usually do not have a well-developed midlateral stripe although they may have a diffuse band along the side. Longnose usually have a dark stripe on the side of the snout and this line is aimed toward the lower half of the eye. In the blacknose, the stripe on the side of the snout is a forward continuation of the lateral stripe and passes through the middle of the eye. Longnose also have smaller eyes than blacknose and the eyes are directed upward more than laterally. They also have reduced swim bladders that scarcely reach beyond the tips of the pectoral fins. Some specimens from the eastern part of the state lack barbels.

Description
Body slender, terete, dorsal profile more curved than the ventral. Dorsal origin midway between caudal base and anterior nostril. Dorsal retrogressive, its margin convex to slightly falcate, its corners rather sharply angled. Caudal moderately forked, with rounded lobes. Anal inserted below middle of depressed last dorsal ray. Anal margin strongly convex, its anterior corner rounded, posterior corner bluntly angled. Pelvic insertion well ahead of the dorsal fin. Pelvic arched, its middle rays longest. Pelvic axillary process well developed. Pectoral low, the base slightly oblique. Pectoral retrogressive, rounded. Gill membranes broadly joined to the isthmus. Snout definitely overhanging the mouth. Frenum prominent. Maxillary barbel present, terminal, slightly fimbriate. Body completely scaled. Lateral line complete, nearly straight. Counts and proportional measurements are given in Table 13.

Color: Sides and back dark gray, with patches of darker scales. Sometimes with a diffuse midlateral stripe, especially on the anterior part of the body. Snout with low lateral stripe. Lower sides and belly paler, often with a golden cast. Frequently, there is a diffuse or even a distinct spot at the base of the caudal. Fin rays with distinct dark margins.

Juveniles and breeding adults: Juveniles have a definite midlateral dark stripe. Males have orange red on the lips and lower cheeks, across the isthmus, the bases of the paired and anal fins and on the midline of the belly and the caudal peduncle. There is also an orange or red wash on the dorsal and caudal fins. Small, numerous breeding tubercles are present on the head and upper body of the males.

Size: Hubbs and Lagler reported specimens as long as 7 inches from Isle Royale, Lake Superior. Our largest New York specimens are 100 mm standard length.

Habitat
Longnose dace are primarily fish of small, clear, and swift streams but they also live near the shores of larger lakes where there is considerable wave action over gravel shoals.

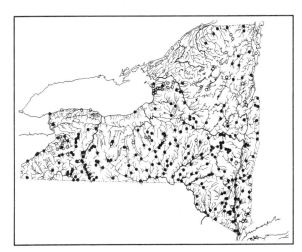

Distribution
This is an extremely wide-ranging species that lives across Canada and in the Rocky Mountains from the Mackenzie River south to northern Mexico, and from Hudson Bay and the Ungava region south to Tennessee and North Carolina but it is not in New Brunswick, Nova Scotia or Prince Edward Island.

It occurs throughout New York State.

Life History
Bartnick reported on the life history of the longnose dace from the Mink River, Manitoba. Fish were captured in October and kept in 100-gallon tanks under conditions that simulated winter conditions in pools, including covering the tanks with plywood to duplicate the low light levels under the ice. In February, the fish were placed in tanks that simulated flowing streams with rising temperatures. Field ob-

servobtions indicated that the longnose preferred areas with current velocities more than 45 cm per second with a rock bottom and with pebbles more than 5 cm in diameter. Small males guarded territories 10 to 20 cm in diameter and spent most of their time at a central station. At first, they were aggressive toward both sexes but as the season progressed they began to try to attract receptive females, with increasing aggression against males. When a female moved into a territory, the male trembled with high-frequency vibrations for 0.5 to 2 seconds, separated by periods of 0.75 to 1 second. The male pushed his snout against rocks with his body inclined at 45 to 90 degrees. When the female was ready to spawn, she moved into the territory and similarly pushed her snout against the bottom. Sometimes, the female would leave for a short time and return. Finally, the sexes came together and, pushing against the bottom parallel to each other, quivered for 1 or 2 seconds while releasing the eggs and milt. There was no detectable spawning clasp.

Eggs were spherical, 0.9 to 1.5 mm in diameter. At 21 C, the eggs hatched in 3 or 4 days and the newly hatched larvae were 5.9 mm long.

Food and Feeding
In Montana, the food consists mostly of bottom insects, especially mayflies and midges. Algae and debris make up a large part of the diet of smaller fish. Burrowing insects are seldom taken.

Notes
Longnose dace occasionally hybridize with the river chub. This hybrid has been reported from Cazenovia Creek near East Aurora and we have additional specimens from the Allegheny drainage. In West Virginia, similar fish have been named *Rhinichthys bowersi*. Recent biochemical studies indicate that the West Virginia population may actually be a separate, reproducing species since electrophoretic studies of its proteins do not show the combination of bands usually seen in hybrids.

References
Bartnick, 1970 (reproduction). Gee, 1972 (swim bladder size). Cooper, 1980 (larval development). Reed and Moulton, 1973 (age and growth). Evans, 1952 (brain pattern).Reed, 1959 (food, age and growth). Gibbons and Gee, 1972 (ecological separation). Gerald, 1966 (food). Brazo, Liston, and Anderson, 1978 (habitat). Fuiman and Loos, 1977 (development). Gee and Machniak, 1972 (lake populations). Gee and Northcote, 1963 (biology). Pappantoniou and Dale, 1982 (food). Hubbs and Lagler, 1964 (Great Lakes).

Names
Cataractae means of the cataract, in reference to the type locality, Niagara Falls.

Gobio cataractae Valenciennes *in* Cuvier and Valenciennes, 1842: 315 Niagara Falls

Rhinichthys cataractae Greeley, 1927: 60 Genesee watershed

Rhinichthys cataractae, Hubbs and Lagler, 1964: 79 (distribution)

Leuciscus nasutus Ayres, 1843: 299-302 Connecticut

Rhinichthys marmoratus Agassiz, 1850: 354

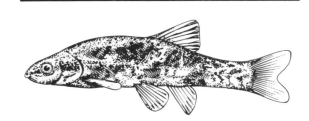

WESTERN BLACKNOSE DACE

Rhinichthys meleagris Agassiz, 1854

Identification
The western blacknose dace is so similar to the eastern blacknose that their descriptions are almost interchangeable. Both have fine scales, and a prominent dark stripe along the side from the snout to the tail, extending onto the base of the caudal fin. They also have a prominent frenum, a bridge of tissue connecting the upper lip with the snout. They also have a prominent terminal barbel at the angle of the mouth. They differ from the longnose dace in having shorter snouts and the dark line on the side of the head passing through the center of the eye rather than below it.

It is extremely difficult to tell the difference between eastern and western blacknose juveniles and females, but the males are quite distinctive. The eastern form has only fine speckling on the back and sides but the western has larger blotches, patches of dark scales, that give it a rather untidy appearance. The western males have a broad band of rust color along the midlateral stripe and this is generally present all year long, whereas the eastern males lose the reddish stripe after the breeding season. There is also a difference is shape that is best seen in the illustrations, the western blacknose dace being more humpbacked.

Description
Body elongate and terete. Dorsal profile arched, ventral profile nearly straight. Dorsal fin equidistant between midbase of caudal and the center of the eye. Dorsal margin convex, its corners rounded. Caudal moderately forked, its middle rays four-fifths the longest upper rays. Anal origin beneath the end of the dorsal base. Anal margin straight, its corners rounded. Pelvic insertion anterior to the dorsal origin. Pelvic retrogressive with convex margin. Pectoral low, retrogressive, with convex margin. Pectoral base slightly angled. Mouth low, slightly oblique. Snout slightly protuberant. Gill membranes broadly joined to isthmus. Lateral line complete. Body fully scaled. Counts and proportional measurements are given in Table 13.

Color: Dark gray above, shading to silver white

below. Midlateral stripe prominent with a reddish-brown wash in adult males. Dorsal surface and sides with irregular patches of dark scales. Fins clear, rays of dorsal and caudal fins outlined with melanophores.

Juveniles and breeding adults: Adult males have a very broad rust-colored lateral band. The breeding males develop fine tubercles on the top and sides of the head and over most of the body. Those of the lower surface of the caudal peduncle are larger than those of *R. atratulus*.

Size: This species reaches almost 4 inches total length.

Habitat
The western blacknose dace occurs in small- and moderate-sized streams.

Distribution
This species ranges from Manitoba and the Lake of the Woods region to western Lake Ontario and south to Nebraska and eastward through the northern part of the Ohio River basin.

Life History
Raney described the breeding behavior of this species in a small stream, Slippery Rock Creek, 10 miles southeast of New Castle, Pennsylvania. Spawning was observed 29-31 May 1934. The males established territories in the downstream ends of pools where the water was 4 to 8 inches deep and there was little current. Each territory was 2 feet or less in diameter with a depression in the center about 2 inches deep. Raney indicated that the fish did not dig this depression but that it was the result of repeated spawnings over the middle of the territory. Males actively defended the territories, sometimes actually fighting with invaders, if they were not intimidated by the first rushes of the defending males.

Females milled around in deeper waters until they were ready to spawn. A female then approached the male's territory and was met by males from several adjacent territories as well as smaller males that did not maintain their own territories but remained in the general area. Eventually, one male managed to chase the others away and guided the female to his territory. The pair lay side by side with the caudal peduncle of the male on top of that of the females. Spawning consisted of violent vibrations for periods of up to 2 seconds. This vibration forced the urogenital papilla of the female into the sand so that at least some of the eggs were buried. Afterward, the female returned to deeper water until she was ready to spawn again, while the male chased away other fishes that moved in to try to eat the eggs. Females spawned repeatedly but not necessarily with the same male.

Food and Feeding
Aquatic insect larvae are the most important food, especially midge larvae. Diatoms and desmids are frequently consumed during the latter part of the summer season.

Notes
Although the eastern and western forms are generally considered subspecies, there is little evidence of their intergrading and their ranges appear to be distinct.

References
Raney, 1940a (breeding behavior). Noble, 1967 (life history and ecology in Iowa). Bartnick, 1970 (reproductive isolation). Tarter, 1969 (comparative breeding habits); 1970 (food). Rollwagon and Stainken, 1980 (ectoparasites and breeding behavior).

Names
Meleagris is the Greek word for Guinea fowl, hence speckled.

Rhinichthys meleagris Agassiz, 1854: 357 Burlington, Iowa

Rhinichthys atratulus meleagris, Greeley, 1938: 65 Allegheny drainage

Rhinichthys lunatus Cope, 1865a: 278 Grosse Isle, Michigan

Rhinichthys atronasus Greeley, 1927: 60 Genesee drainage

Rhinichthys atronasus lunatus, Greeley, 1929: 170 Erie-Niagara drainage

TABLE 13
COUNTS AND AVERAGE PROPORTIONAL MEASUREMENTS OF
DACE *(Rhinichthys)*

All proportions are expressed in percentage of standard length.

	atratulus	meleagris	cataractae
ST. LENGTH (mm)	53.3	52.7	59.3
TOTAL LENGTH	121.1	122.6	123.3
FORK LENGTH	114.4	115.2	115.4
PREDORSAL	57.7	57.6	54.9
PREANAL	65.8	67.9	66.6
PREPELVIC	51.1	51.3	48.5
DORSAL BASE	9.8	11.4	12.3
ANAL BASE	8.7	9.3	10.2
BODY DEPTH	22.1	23.9	21.6
BODY WIDTH	16.0	17.3	17.2
C.PED. DEPTH	10.5	12.1	12.0
PECTORAL ALT.	14.5	16.3	15.1
HEAD LENGTH	25.2	26.4	26.3
SNOUT	8.6	9.3	10.6
EYE	5.7	5.3	5.7
MOUTH LENGTH	6.8	7.0	6.8
INTERORB	10.4	10.4	11.6
N (sample size)	5	5	5
COUNTS:			
DORSAL RAYS	8	8	8
ANAL RAYS	7	7	7
PECTORAL RAYS	13-15	15	13-14
PELVIC RAYS	8	8	8
GILL RAKERS	5-7	5-7	7-8
VERTEBRAE*	35-36	35-36	35-36
SCALES:			
ABOVE L.L.	10-12	9-10	11-13
LATERAL LINE	56-68	56-59	55-67
BELOW L.L.	7-9	7-8	8-10
PHARYNGEAL			
TEETH	2,4-4,2	2,4-4,2	2,4-4,2

* Excluding Weberian apparatus.

Semotilus

Three of the four recognized species of *Semotilus* occur in New York. They are rather large, carnivorous minnows with a characteristic flat barbel that lies in the groove above the maxillary bone, a short distance in front of the end of the maxillary bone.

KEY TO THE SPECIES OF *SEMOTILUS* IN NEW YORK

A. Scales large, about 45 in lateral line. Scales not especially crowded in front of the dorsal fin.
Semotilus corporalis   **Fallfish, p. 155**

A'. Scales smaller, 50 to 78 in lateral line

B. A prominent black spot at front of base of dorsal fin. Lateral scales 52 to 62.
Semotilus atromaculatus   **Creek chub, p. 153**

B'. No spot at base of dorsal fin. Scales 49 to 78.
Semotilus margarita   **Pearl dace, C.**

C. Scales 61 to 78 (95 percent have 63 or more).
Semotilus m. nachtriebi   **p. 157**

C'. Scales 49 to 63 (95 percent have 62 or fewer).
Semotilus m. margarita   **p. 157**

Pearl dace, *Semotilus margarita*

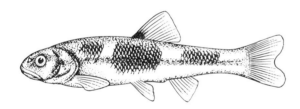

CREEK CHUB

Semotilus atromaculatus
(Mitchill, 1818)

Identification
The creek chub is an elongate, nearly terete fish with a large head and mouth, and a conspicuous spot at the front of the base of the dorsal fin. The scales are rather small on the front part of the body and become progressively larger toward the tail, for a lateral line count of 53 to 61.

Creek chubs share with other members of the genus *Semotilus* a subterminal maxillary barbel. This barbel is tiny and lies in the groove between the upper edge of the maxillary and the preorbital region, a short distance in front of the end of the maxillary. It is never large and occasionally it is absent. It is, however, an important character that unites the pearl dace, the fallfish and the creek chub. The only other species in New York that has a similar barbel is the tonguetied minnow.

Neither the pearl dace nor the fallfish has a spot at the base of the dorsal fin. The fallfish has large scales and the pearl dace has scales of uniform size along the body.

Description
Body elongate, nearly terete, profiles equally curved. Dorsal origin midway between caudal base and the rear margin of the eye. Dorsal trapezoidal, retrogressive, with slightly convex margin and rounded corners. Caudal moderately forked, with rounded lobes. Anal origin below middle of depressed last dorsal ray, anal similar in shape to dorsal. Pelvic inserted slightly ahead of the dorsal origin. Pelvic retrogressive, with convex margin and rounded corners. Pelvic axillary process not developed. Pectorals low, base slightly oblique. Pectorals retrogressive, rounded. Gill membranes broadly joined to the isthmus. Mouth terminal and oblique, large, maxillary ending below front of the eye. Lateral line complete, decurved anteriorly. Counts and proportional measurements are given in Table 14.

Color: Olive dorsally, shading to white on the belly. Juveniles have a quite regular midlateral stripe from the snout through the eye and across the cheek and opercle to the base of the tail. This stripe is widest just behind the gill opening and may expand slightly at the base of the tail. There is a much darker spot on the base of the caudal rays that is sometimes triangular. Scales of the upper sides with narrow black margins but they are small and do not

153

MINNOWS

stand out in a regular pattern. Scales below the lateral stripe are outlined only at their distal edge. The lateral stripe is obsolescent in larger individuals.

There is a conspicuous spot at the base of the first three principal dorsal rays. The rays of the dorsal and caudal fins have prominent outlines, those of the anal and paired fins are less conspicuous. Adults from dark water usually have the fin rays with very dark margins.

Juveniles and breeding adults: The juveniles have a conspicuous midlateral stripe. Breeding adults are darker and often have a brassy yellow coloration on the back and upper sides. The lower parts of the head and the belly become rosy in breeding males and the upper parts sometimes become apple green. The tail and paired fins turn yellow and a bright orange ring develops around the dorsal spot. Only the males develop breeding tubercles. Usually, there is a single row of large tubercles from the upper lip over the eye. Smaller tubercles develop on the operculum and its membrane and on the scales of the anterior parts of the body. Tubercles are also present on the rays of the pectoral, pelvic, anal, and caudal fins.

Size: The creek chub commonly reaches lengths of 6 inches or longer. The maximum size is about 12 inches total length.

Habitat

The creek chub is most abundant in small- to moderate-sized streams but is is a tolerant species that sometimes occurs in standing waters as well. Often, it is heavily parasitized with black spot disease. It requires gravel for spawning.

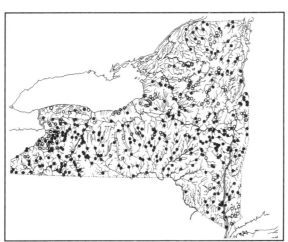

Distribution

The creek chub occurs throughout much of eastern North America from southern Canada and the Great Plains south to eastern Texas and along the gulf coast to the Florida Panhandle, and north on the Atlantic slope to the Maritime Provinces of Canada.

Life History

A classic paper on the breeding habits of the creek chub (called horned dace) earned Jacob Reighard of the University of Michigan a prize of $100 in gold when it was presented to the Fourth International Fishery Congress in Washington D.C, in September, 1908. The prize was offered by Theodore Gill for "…the best methods of observing the habits and recording the life histories of fishes, with an illustrative example."

In southern Michigan the creek chub spawns in April or May. The nests are built without help from the females and consist of a narrow gravel ridge 2 or 3 inches high and about 1 foot wide. It is constructed by moving gravel upstream so that a pit is excavated as the ridge is built. Small pebbles are carried in the mouth; larger pebbles are pushed with the lower jaw. The nest ridges are conspicuous because the clean gravel contrasts with the ooze-covered stones of the surrounding undisturbed bottom. As the building proceeds, the ridge is extended downstream and some may reach lengths of 16 to 18 feet. The pit at the downstream end is usually 2 or 3 inches deep.

As the males work on the pit, they chase away smaller males and other small fishes, often striking or "hooking" them with their large head tubercles. Sometimes, larger males approach and engage the nest builder in a ceremonial or deferred combat in which the two males swim upstream in unison for 15 or 20 feet, at the end of which they dip their heads toward each other once or twice, then separate, with the holder of the nest territory returning to his nest-building activities.

The females are smaller than the males and lack the bright colors but have their abdomens distended with eggs. At first, the females approach the nest but flee as the male approaches them. When she is ready to spawn, the female moves near the pit and holds her place as the male assumes a position a little below and behind her and often partly on his side at the bottom of the pit. The male then slips his head and pectoral fin under her head and flips her upward until she is nearly vertical. He then wraps his body around hers, holding her between his roughened opercles and pectoral fin and the tuberculate posterior part of his body. Either her ventral or dorsal side can be toward the male. The eggs are released at this time, presumably in groups of 25 to 50. The entire procedure takes only a few seconds (Reighard estimated 10 seconds) and the eggs fall to the gravel on the back slope of the ridge. The female floats briefly, then recovers and swims away to the bank or other shelter, returning later to spawn again. The male resumes moving gravel and thus covers the eggs, interrupting his task from time to time to spawn again. Spawning is promiscuous and eggs of different sizes and different stages of development can be found in a single nest.

Reighard noted that nests provide a secure haven for the eggs, but some silting can occur and destroy the nests and many nests are torn apart by other males building their nests and by fishes that root in the gravel.

Ross noted that males spending a lot of time chasing intruders spawned less frequently than those that showed less intense aggressive behavior.

Subordinate males frequently assumed a position downstream from a nesting male and simply stayed there without attempting to enter the nest or spawn. Ross termed this behavior nestwatching. Only rarely did a nestwatcher spawn when the nesting male left the nest to chase an intruder.

Food and Feeding
The creek chub is a generalized sightfeeder. Apparently, the young chubs eat planktonic organisms and switch to larger organisms as they get bigger. Insects, cladocerans, crayfishes, and small fishes are taken and at times algae and plant tissues are consumed.

Notes
Subspecies have been recognized but it has been suggested that the differences are clinal and that the use of trinomials is unwarranted. Formerly, the southeastern populations were called *Semotilus atromaculatus thoreauianus*.

Several other species have been reported to spawn in creek chub nests and hybrids between the creek chub and several other species are not unusual. Ross and Cavender (1981) analyzed the characteristics of several hybrid combinations that they were able to produce by artificial fertilization. Included were crosses with stoneroller, redside dace, hornyhead chub and blacknose dace.

References
Reighard, 1910 (life history). Greeley, 1930 (life history); 1955c (popular account). Washburn, 1948 (propagation). Leonard, 1927 (food). Evans, 1952 (brain pattern). Barber and Minckley, 1971 (food). Bailey, Winn, and Smith, 1954 (nomenclature). Evans and Deubler, 1955 (tooth replacement). Dinsmore, 1962 (life history). Miller, 1964 (breeding behavior). Sisk, 1966 (unusual spawning behavior). Moshenko and Gee, 1973 (spawning). Powles et al., 1977 (growth and fecundity). Schemske, 1974 (growth and fecundity). Ross, 1976 (behavior); 1977a (aggression); 1977b (nest building). Ross and Cavender, 1981 (hybrids). Newsome and Gee, 1978 (prey selection), Buynak and Mohr, 1979a (development). Magnan and FitzGerald, 1982 (trout interactions).

Names
Atromaculatus is from the Latin *ater*, black and *macula*, spot.

Cyprinus atromaculatus Mitchill, 1818a: 324 Wallkill River

Leuciscus atromaculatus, DeKay, 1842: 210

Leuciscus iris Valenciennes *in* Cuvier and Valenciennes, 1844: 255

Leuciscus storeri Valenciennes *in* Cuvier and Valenciennes, 1844: 255

Semotilus atromaculatus, Bean, 1903: 123-126

Semotilus atromaculatus atromaculatus, Greeley, 1929: 170-171 Erie-Niagara watershed

Semotilus corporalis Mather, 1886: 29-30 Adirondacks (misidentification)

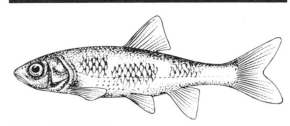

FALLFISH

Semotilus corporalis (Mitchill, 1817)

Identification
The fallfish is the largest native minnow in the northeast, occasionally reaching nearly 17 inches total length. It is a slender, nearly terete, fish with fairly large scales (43 to 50 in the lateral line). Juveniles have a distinct midlateral stripe that expands at the base of the tail into an ovoid spot which is, in turn, connected to a small darker triangular spot at the caudal base. Adults lose the dark line but have characteristic crescents at the bases of the scales of the upper body.

Like the creek chub and the pearl dace, it has a small subterminal maxillary barbel.

Description
Body elongate, terete or slightly slab sided. Dorsal profile slightly more curved than the ventral. Dorsal origin midway between caudal base and a point between the nostrils and the tip of the snout. Dorsal trapezoidal, retrogressive, with straight or slightly concave margin and rather sharp corners. Caudal moderately forked, with pointed lobes. Anal origin behind tip of depressed last dorsal ray. Anal shape similar to dorsal. Pelvic insertion slightly anterior to dorsal origin. Pelvic retrogressive, with its corners bluntly pointed. Pelvic axillary process small. Pectoral base low, slightly oblique. Pectoral retrogressive, rounded. Gill membranes joined to the isthmus. Mouth terminal, slightly oblique, maxillary ending below the front margin of the eye. Body fully scaled, lateral line complete, slightly curved anteriorly. Counts and proportional measurements are given in Table 14.

Color: Generally silvery, darker on top, shading to white on the belly. Scales of the back and upper sides with dark crescent-shaped marks at their bases. Snout and preorbital area dusky. Adults with a dark bar along the edge of the shoulder girdle. Dorsal, caudal and anterior pectoral rays with dark outlines, pelvic and anal fins white. In some habitats, the coloration is remarkably similar to that of common shiners.

Juveniles and breeding adults: The fallfish does not develop bright breeding colors but breeding males have a pinkish wash over the opercular region and the pectoral fins. Males develop tubercles on the snout and in a single row over each eye, on the operculum, the anterior sides of the body and along the anterior ray of the pectoral fins. Juveniles have a dark midlateral stripe.

Size: The fallfish may reach a size of 16 or 17 inches total length. Our largest New York specimens are 225 mm standard length.

Habitat

The fallfish is abundant in clear streams of small to moderate size. It also occurs in lakes and ponds.

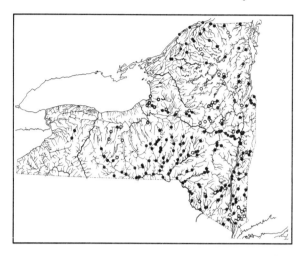

Distribution

The fallfish is an east coast species ranging from New Brunswick to the James Bay drainage and south on the eastern slopes of the Appalachians to Virginia. In New York, it occurs in the eastern drainages except Long Island. It apparently has recently been introduced into Tonawanda Creek, Lake Erie drainage, where it is locally very abundant. Its population there should be monitored as it may potentially spread throughout Lake Erie and the upper Great Lakes. Dr. D. A. Webster (pers. comm.) believes that it was originally absent from the Adirondacks and may have been established there through canals or bait-pail introductions.

Life History

Raney reported that the fallfish spawns from April to June in New York. Atkins found it spawning as early as May in Maine, and Reed reported that it spawned from 27 April to 10 June in Massachusetts. Reed noted that there was no nesting until the water temperature reached 14.4 C and that the spawning was interrupted when the temperature fell below that level.

Fallfish nests are piles of gravel and the largest seen by Reed was 4 feet in diameter although there have been reports of nests up to 6 feet across and 12 to 24 inches high. Reed also found small nests, 1 foot in diameter and 4 inches high with eggs. Pebbles in the nests weighed 1 to 168 grams. In quiet waters, the nests were round and domed, but in flowing waters they tended to have a downstream keel. Unfertilized eggs were nonadhesive and averaged 2.19 mm in diameter. Fertilized and water-hardened eggs were 2.7 mm in diameter and adhesive. Common shiners and blacknose dace often spawned on fallfish nests and Reed found a few white sucker eggs that he believed had accidentally drifted into the nests. At 17 C, the eggs hatched in

139 to 144 hours. Newly hatched larvae were 6.82 mm long and the yolk sacs were absorbed at 9 mm; the scales developed by 33 mm. Large females laid more eggs.

Ross and Reed analyzed the reproductive behavior on the nests. Two types of nests were found: single nests near banks under overhanging alder bushes, and nests in groups of two or three, 1 to 3 meters apart in midstream. Males often swam over the site for an hour before starting to dig. The nest was first excavated as a shallow pit 30 to 50 cm in diameter. The gravel removed from the pit was deposited on the upstream side. When the mound reached 10 to 20 cm in diameter, the male moved laterally and started to pick up pebbles in his mouth and carry them back to the nest. Eventually, he filled the pit and built a mound about 10 cm high. Pebbles were carried from as far as 5 meters. Nest-building males were accompanied by three to seven females and sometimes one or two non-nestbuilding males.

The nesting males defended their territories with displays, spreading the fins, arching the body, and flaring the gill covers. Sometimes, intruders were chased in a parallel swim and at times the intruders were bitten or butted.

Unlike the creek chub, the fallfish did not have a spawning clasp. Groups of fallfish aggregated over the nest, facing upstream, arching their bodies and quivering as the sex products were released. The nesting male initiated spawning, either by moving a stone into the nest or deliberately swimming to the center of the nest where he was joined by females and sometimes by non-nesting males. After spawning, the male resumed gathering pebbles and adding to the nest.

Fallfish live as long as 10 years.

Food and Feeding

Plant and animal plankton are eaten by the young until they are 35 to 40 mm long; then they shift to aquatic flies and terrestrial insects. Fallfish 1 year old and older are omnivorous, feeding on algae, fish, insects, and crayfish.

Notes

Reed noted that the other species that spawned on fallfish nests were not chased by the guarding males.

References

Wilson, 1907 (nests). Breder and Crawford, 1922 (food). Greeley, 1955c (popular account). Miller, 1964 (breeding behavior). Reed, 1971 (life history). Ross and Reed, 1978 (reproductive behavior). Raney, 1949 (nesting). Atkins, 1905 (culture). Buynak and Mohr, 1979a (larval development). Hadley and Clulow, 1979 (introduced into the Lake Erie drainage). Ross, 1983 (nesting). Victor and Brothers, 1982 (daily growth).

Names

Corporalis is from the Latin word meaning bodily. Mitchill, however, called the fish *corporal* and *corpalum* and it seems likely that the name is from the military rank, possibly in allusion to its aggressive behavior.

Cyprinus corporalis Mitchill, 1817: 289 Wallkill River, New York

Cyprinus bullaris Rafinesque, 1817b: 120 Hudson River

Semotilus bullaris, Bean, 1903: 122-123

Leuciscus nitidus DeKay, 1842: 209 Lake Champlain

Leuciscus argenteus Storer, 1839: 90 Massachusetts

Leuciscus argenteus, DeKay, 1842: 212

Leuciscus pulchellus Storer, 1839: 90 Massachusetts

Leuciscus pulchellus, DeKay, 1842: 208

Leuciscus chrysopterus DeKay, 1842: 211 New York Harbor

Leucosomus corporalis, Greeley, 1927: 97 Oswego watershed

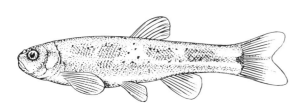

PEARL DACE

Semotilus margarita margarita (Cope, 1868) and *S. m. nachtriebi* (Cox, 1896)

Identification

The pearl dace is one of the prettiest fishes in the state. Even when it is not in breeding condition, the sides of the males have a faint pink tinge that sets off its pearly gray ground color. Usually, adults have irregular patches of dark scales that add a tasteful elegance to its dress. Pearl dace share with the creek chub and the fallfish the characteristic *Semotilus* subterminal maxillary barbel. The pearl dace has much smaller scales than the fallfish and is unlikely to be confused with it. It most resembles the creek chub but has a shorter head and lacks the conspicuous spot at the base of the front rays of the dorsal fin. Unlike the other two species of *Semotilus,* pearl dace males develop bright red flanks during the breeding season.

Description

Body elongate, terete, profiles equally curved. Dorsal origin midway between caudal base and the upper end of the preopercle. Dorsal fin retrogressive, with rounded corners and slightly convex margin. Caudal moderately forked, with bluntly pointed lobes. Anal origin below outer half of the depressed last dorsal ray. Anal shape similar to that of dorsal. Pelvic insertion well ahead of the dorsal origin. Pelvic axillary scale small. Pelvic retrogressive, rounded. Pectoral base low, somewhat oblique. Pectoral retrogressive, rounded. Gill membranes broadly attached to isthmus. Mouth terminal, oblique, gape curved. Maxillary barbel small, sometimes absent. Body completely scaled. Lateral line complete, slightly decurved anteriorly. Counts and proportional measurements are given in Table 14.

Color: Dorsum and upper sides gray or olive gray, shading to silver gray on the sides and white on the belly. Scales of the upper sides without definite dark margins. Middorsal stripe present, broad and sharply limited but not prominent, continued behind the dorsal fin. Sides with a diffuse dark stripe separated from the dark back by an irregular paler stripe. A distinct small triangular dark spot behind the caudal fold. Scattered groups of darker scales give the fish a speckled appearance. Lateral line pale and conspicuous anteriorly. Fin rays, except the posterior part of the pectoral fin, outlined with dark margins. Pelvic and anal fins somewhat lighter. Dorsal and caudal fins with orange cast. Lower lips and tip of lower jaw weakly pigmented. Upper lip and top of the head densely punctated with especially intense pigment at the medial side of the nostrils. Eye with a pale ring around the pupil, broadest ventrally. Margin of preopercle and lower part of opercle with scattered melanophores.

Juveniles and breeding adults: Adult males develop a brilliant red stripe on the lower sides from the pectoral base to the tail. The belly is white. Some individuals have red color in the prepectoral and suborbital regions as well.

Size: The largest reported individual was 6.25 inches total length.

Habitat

Pearl dace occur in small, clear, streams and in darkly stained waters of bogs and swamps. They also live in ponds and lakes.

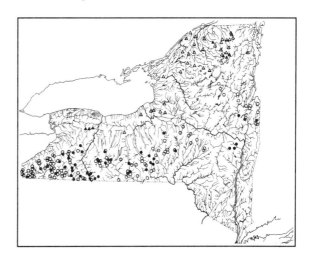

Distribution

The pearl dace lives in a wide band across Canada and northern United States from the Rocky Mountains to Labrador and Nova Scotia. There are disjunct populations in Nebraska, South Dakota, and Pennsylvania to Virginia.

Life History

The breeding of the pearl dace was reported by

Langlois from observations made in Oceana and Manistee Counties, Michigan. Spawning was observed in small streams where the current varied from weak to strong. Breeding males established territories about 8 inches in diameter over sand and gravel but avoiding shingle or humus. The closest territories were about 6 feet apart. They did not build pebble nests. Spawning occurred in June when the water temperature reached 63 to 65 F.

During the spawning season, the males spent most of their time chasing other males or trying to entice females into their territories. Adult females were somewhat larger than males (females ranged from 3.25 to 4.25 inches; males averaged 3.25). When a female was ready to spawn, she allowed the male to guide her into his territory where he slipped his pectoral fin under the anterior part of her body and threw his tail across her back behind her dorsal fin, thus pressing the back part of her body downward while raising her head until she was at about a 30 degree angle. The pair then vibrated together for about 2 seconds after which the female swam forward and out of the male's embrace, leaving the territory until she was ready to spawn again.

The eggs were small, about 0.036 inches in diameter. A 4.5-inch female contained 1,686 eggs.

Food and Feeding
Apparently, the pearl dace is an opportunistic feeder. Copepods, cladocerans, and midges have been reported as well as beetles, filamentous algae, and *Chara*.

Notes*
Two subspecies are recognized: *Semotilus m. nachtriebi* is a widespread, northern, fine-scaled form. *S. m. margarita* has a much smaller range in the East from Vermont to West Virginia. Our records suggest that *nachtriebi* is confined to the northern part of the state and those in the southern tier are *S. m. margarita*. This is the only species in the state with northern and southern populations.

References
Langlois, 1929 (breeding). Hubbs, 1942 (hybridization with *Couesius*). Bailey and Allum, 1962 (distribution). McPhail and Lindsey, 1970 (general). Fava and Tsai, 1974 (Maryland, life history). Stasiak, 1978b (food and growth). Johnson and Johnson, 1982b (feeding).

Names
The species name comes from the Greek word for pearl, *margarites*.

Leuciscus margarita Cope *in* Gunther, 1868: 346 Pennsylvania

Margariscus margarita, Greeley, 1927: 58-59 Genesee watershed

Margariscus margarita margarita, Greeley, 1930: 70 Champlain watershed

Leuciscus nachtriebi Cox, 1896: 614 Mille Lacs Lake, Minnesota

Margariscus magarita nachtriebi, Greeley, 1928: 98 Oswego drainage

Semotilus m. margarita and *S. m. nachtriebi,* George, 1981a: 53 and 54 Adirondacks

*Collection sites for *Semotilus m. nachtriebi* appear as open and closed triangles on the pearl dace distribution map (page 157). Closed triangles indicate collections by the author and his co-workers; open triangles indicate collections by the Biological Survey and earlier workers.

TABLE 14
AVERAGE PROPORTIONAL MEASUREMENTS AND COUNTS OF CHUBS, DACE, AND FALLFISH (*Semotilus* and *Couesius*)

All proportions are expressed in percentage of standard length.

	Semotilus atromaculatus	*Semotilus* corporalis	margarita	*Couesius* plumbeus
ST. LENGTH (mm)	67.7	102.9	61.1	66.9
TOTAL LENGTH	123.7	124.7	127.1	123.4
FORK LENGTH	116.6	114.4	118.3	114.5
PREDORSAL	57.1	53.9	57.0	53.5
PREANAL	69.2	70.8	71.1	67.1
PREPELVIC	52.1	51.0	52.3	49.8
DORSAL BASE	11.8	12.2	10.9	11.7
ANAL BASE	9.9	10.2	9.2	10.4
BODY DEPTH	23.1	23.7	23.3	21.2
BODY WIDTH	15.8	16.1	15.9	15.4
C.PED. DEPTH	9.9	10.0	11.7	10.6
PECTORAL ALT.	17.0	17.8	18.4	15.9
HEAD LENGTH	28.8	26.2	26.4	26.7
SNOUT	8.8	9.1	8.1	9.3
EYE	6.4	6.1	7.2	6.8
MOUTH LENGTH	9.9	8.9	7.8	7.9
INTERORB	11.6	9.7	9.1	9.2
N (sample size)	5	5	5	5
COUNTS:				
DORSAL RAYS	8	8	8	8
ANAL RAYS	8	8	8	8
PECTORAL RAYS	15-17	16-18	15-16	15-17
PELVIC RAYS	8	8	8-9	8
GILL RAKERS	9	7	4-7	7-9
VERTEBRAE*	39-40	40-41	36	36-39
SCALES:				
ABOVE L.L.	8	7	9-11	10
LATERAL LINE	53-61	43-50	49-62**	53-79
BELOW L. L.	5	5	6-8	7
PHARYNGEAL TEETH	2,5-4,2	2,5-4,2	2,5-4,2	2,4-4,2

*Excluding Weberian apparatus.   ** 62-78 in *Semotilus m. nachtreibi*

Clinostomus

Clinostomus species are slender minnows with large oblique mouths, no barbels, and a characteristic color pattern of pink or red on the anterior sides. A second species, *C. funduloides,* occurs in the middle Atlantic coastal drainages and in the Tennessee and Ohio watersheds.

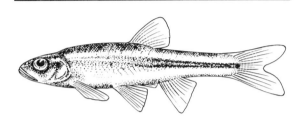

REDSIDE DACE

Clinostomus elongatus (Kirtland, 1838)

Identification
The most outstanding features of the redside dace are its large, oblique mouth and its fine scales. Its body is exquisitely streamlined and its color pattern, dark olive above with a bright pale stripe from the upper part of the eye to the base of the tail and a prominent lateral stripe on the posterior part of the body, is also diagnostic. It has no barbels.

Most adults show at least a pinkish wash on the midsides just behind the head. In breeding males, this area becomes intense red.

Description
Body elongate, streamlined, and somewhat slab sided, deepest at the dorsal fin origin. Upper and lower profiles equally curved. Dorsal origin slightly closer to the base of the tail than to the tip of the snout. Dorsal fin retrogressive, deltoid, with rounded corners and slightly convex margin. Caudal fin moderately forked, with bluntly pointed lobes. Anal deltoid, retrogressive, with rounded corners and straight margin. Pelvic insertion just ahead of the dorsal origin, pelvic axillary process small. Pelvics retrogressive, with rounded corners and convex margin. Pectorals low, with slightly oblique base, retrogressive, with rounded corners and convex margin. Gill membranes broadly joined to the isthmus. Head pointed, lower jaw projecting. Mouth terminal, large, the maxillary ending below the front of the eye. Lateral line straight and complete. Counts and proportional measurements are given in Table 19.

Color: Dark olive dorsally with a brilliant golden-green stripe from the upper corner of the eye to the upper caudal base. Midlateral stripe prominent on snout through the eye and on the side of the head, vague on the anterior side, becoming definite below the dorsal fin and continuing to the base of the tail. In life, adults of both sexes have some red color in the anterior part of the midlateral stripe. This stripe is silvery pink in females and brilliant red in males. The sides of the body also have irregular patches of dark scales. The iris is silver with a dark horizontal stripe through its middle. All fins clear, the rays of the dorsal, caudal and anterior part of the pectoral outlined with dark pigment.

Juveniles and breeding adults: The breeding males develop tubercles on the scales of their sides and over most of the head, body, and the dorsal surfaces of the pectoral and pelvic fins. These tubercles are white and stand in contrast to the dark olive color of the upper body. They are largest on the dorsal surface of the head, body, and pectoral fins. The scales of the prepectoral area have rows of tubercles along their margins that suggest the comblike structures of some species of *Phoxinus*. Females have some smaller tubercles. In general, males have longer pectoral fins.

Size: To a little more than 3 inches. The maximum lengths are 71 and 79 mm for males and females respectively.

Habitat
The redside dace is a fish of small streams where it occupies deeper pools, frequently under overhanging banks and under stumps.

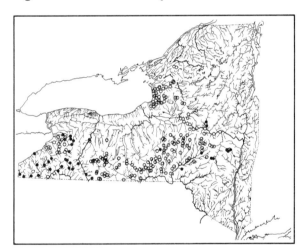

Distribution
This species occurs in a short broad band from eastern Minnesota, Wisconsin and northeastern Iowa and southeastern Michigan, Ohio and western Pennsylvania to southern Ontario and central New York, with a few scattered records in Kentucky and West Virginia.

In New York, the redside dace is found in the Erie, Ontario, Allegheny and Upper Genesee drainages, the Susquehanna, and some northern tributaries of the Mohawk in the southern Adirondacks. It appears that this species reached the Adirondacks early, before the Mohawk-Hudson outlet was open and while streams that are now Mohawk tributaries were still connected to the Great Lakes.

Life History
Koster described the spawning of the redside dace in Danby Creek, near Ithaca. Spawning occurred in late May when the water temperature was 18 C.

The only migration was a short distance from pools into a patch of gravel at the head of a riffle. Males intensified their defense of territories just before the spawning season and chased intruders by swimming next to them to guide them away. Territorial behavior diminished again as spawning began. Koster observed some spawning near the nest pit of a creek chub. A group of dace assembled downstream from the pit with the females at the side and downstream edge of the group. A female initiated spawning by leaving the group and swimming upstream. At least two, and sometimes six or more males joined her and the spawning occurred over the pit. Immediately afterward, the group broke up and the fish returned to the group. Mating appeared to be promiscuous and spawnings occurred as often as four to six times per minute although often several minutes elapsed between spawnings.

Water-hardened eggs were 1.2 to 2.4 mm in diameter and nonadhesive. Egg counts ranged from 409 to 1,526. Sexual maturity is attained in the third spring when the males are approximately 56 mm and the females 57 mm in standard length.

Food and Feeding
Koster noted that the redside dace spends much of its time near the surface, often leaping into the air in pursuit of insects. Schwartz and Norvell found that 95 percent of the diet by volume consisted of insects. Spiders, water mites, nematodes, plants, and debris made up the rest. About 77 percent of the total diet was terrestrial insects.

Notes
Bailey considered this species to be closely related to the western North American genera *Richardsonius* and *Gila,* but this has yet to be confirmed. Koster commented on a possible affinity with *Chrosomus* and *Semotilus margarita.*

References
Koster, 1939 (life history). Schwartz and Norvell, 1958 (food and growth). Evans and Deubler, 1955 (tooth replacement). Bailey, 1951 (relationships).

Names
Elongatus is the Latin word meaning lengthened, elongate.

Luxilus elongatus Kirtland, 1838: 169, 193 Mahoning River and Lake Erie

Clinostomus elongatus, Greeley, 1928: 171 Lake Erie watershed

Hybognathus

Hybognathus is a genus with about six species. They lack barbels and in general appearance are similar to the shiners but their lower jaw is crescent-shaped rather than U-shaped and there is a secondary loop in the gut, which is sometimes visible through the body wall of preserved specimens.

KEY TO THE SPECIES OF *HYBOGNATHUS* IN NEW YORK

A. Color generally brassy in life. Fins rounded, the dorsal margin straight or slightly convex. Scales on sides with 14 to 20 radii and with the circuli rounded at the basal corners of the scale. Head blunt. Maximum size about 4 inches total length.
Hybognathus hankinsoni
Brassy minnow, p. 162

A'. Color silvery in life. Fins more angulate, the dorsal margin slightly concave. Scales with 10 to 12 radii. Circuli with sharp angles at the basal corners of the scale. Head more pointed. Maximum size about 6 inches total length.
Hybognathus regius
Eastern silvery minnow, p. 163

BRASSY MINNOW

Hybognathus hankinsoni
Hubbs, 1929

Identification

At first glance, the brassy minnow looks like the common shiner but the brassy minnow has a less compressed body, a smaller eye, and the exposed parts of its scales are more rounded than diamond-shaped. The lower jaw of the brassy minnow is crescentic; that of the species of *Notropis* is U-shaped. The intestine of *Hybognathus* species has extra loops.

Distinguishing the brassy minnow from the eastern silvery minnow is more difficult. In life, the colors are diagnostic; the brassy minnow has a golden sheen, the silvery minnow is silver white. The fins of the brassy minnow are convex with rounded corners; those of the silvery minnow have sharp corners. The two species differ in the structure of the scales. Those of the brassy minnow have more numerous radii, 14 to 20 rather than 10 to 12, and the circuli are less sharply angled. The focus is farther away from the anterior edge of the scale.

The pelvic axillary process is small and fleshy in the brassy minnow, larger and more scale-like in the silvery minnow.

Description

Body elongate and slab sided. Dorsal and ventral profiles equally curved. Dorsal origin nearer tip of snout than base of caudal. Dorsal trapezoidal, retrogressive. Dorsal fin convex, with rounded corners. Caudal fin moderately forked, its lobes bluntly pointed. Anal origin behind tip of depressed last dorsal ray. Anal similar to dorsal. Pelvic insertion below anterior half of dorsal base. Pelvics retrogressive, rounded. Pectoral base low, slightly oblique. Pectorals retrogressive, rounded. Head blunt, mouth terminal, slightly oblique, snout overhanging the upper lip. Lower jaw crescentic. Lateral line complete, slightly decurved anteriorly. Gill membranes joined to the isthmus. Counts and proportional measurements are given in Table 20.

Color: Brassy olive above, shading to silvery white ventrally. Scales of the sides appear to have been dabbed with an artist's brush. Sides with dusky midlateral stripe, diffuse anteriorly but quite distinct behind middle of the dorsal fin. Scales of the upper sides with dark margins, forming two or more indistinct zig-zag stripes above the lateral stripe. Middorsal stripe intense, varying slightly in width. No pigment around anus, no stripe along base of anal. Top and sides of head punctate. A few scattered melanophores on the gular region. Rays of the vertical fins with a yellow tint and melanophores along their margins. Dorsal interradial membrane punctate. Anterior pectoral and pelvic rays outlined, posterior parts of the paired fins unpigmented.

Juveniles and breeding adults: In the breeding males, the brassy color becomes more intense and there are tiny tubercles on the middle pectoral rays.

Size: The maximum total length is about 85 mm.

Habitat

The brassy minnow is a bog species that often occurs in schools in darkly stained waters in the slower parts of creeks where the bottom is mud or organic debris and there is some vegetation. It is less common in moderate current. Immature brassy minnows congregate in shallows and vegetation and often spend the night in muskrat burrows. In the winter, they form pods in pools and deep runs, often near shelter. Some have been found buried in bottom debris.

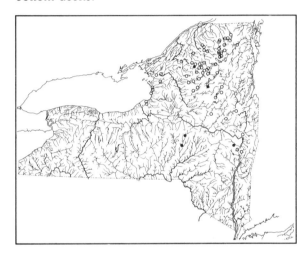

Distribution

The distribution of the brassy minnow is a curved band extending from eastern New York to eastern Colorado, Wyoming, Montana and north to southern Quebec in the East, to Saskatchewan, Alberta, and the Fraser and Peace River systems. The British Columbia populations are disjunct but are considered remnants of a once continuous distribution.

In New York, it ranges from the eastern tributaries of Lake Ontario and the Upper Hudson drainage to the St. Lawrence tributaries, exclusive of the Lake Champlain system. Specimens from the Susquehanna drainage could have been canal introductions.

Life History

Copes studied the brassy minnow in Wyoming and Wisconsin. In Wyoming, spawning was observed on 27 and 28 May and ripe adults were taken from 15 May to 18 June. Spawning occurred during the daylight hours from 11 am to 5 pm with the peak about 2 pm. Most of the spawning took place in flooded depressions and marshes. Females and unripe males swam about in schools, sometimes several thousands in a small depression. One to 15 males would approach a female near the edge of the school and she would respond by spiralling upward and jumping out of the water, which would cause the males to discontinue their pursuit, or by swimming to vegetation, whereupon one or more males would press against her and they would vi-

brate rapidly, stirring up the sediments as they released the eggs and sperm. They reached 24 to 44 mm by the end of the first summer, and matured at age I + in Wyoming and II + in Wisconsin. Annulus formation occurred in June. Few if any fish reached age V.

Food and Feeding

Copes found that 94 percent of the diet was algae, chiefly diatoms and desmids, and about about 5 percent was organic debris, with copepods, cladocerans, and dipterans making up the rest. Feeding was most intense from 1 to 3 pm and was communal, with schools of fish feeding over detritus beds and mud bottom. Other workers have found brassy minnows feeding on plankton, aquatic insects and surface drift.

Notes

The brassy minnow is uncommon in the eastern part of its range but it is one of the most abundant minnows in Wisconsin and Minnesota. It is frequently used for bait.

References

Dobie, Meehan, and Washburn, 1956 (food, ecology). Hubbs, 1951 (hybridization). Gould and Brown, 1967 (Montana). Bailey, 1954 (taxonomy, distribution). Copes, 1975 (life history).

Names

Hankinsoni is named in honor of T. L. Hankinson, who worked on New York fishes in the 1920s and who was the co-author of the classic work on the ecology of fishes in this state.

Hybognathus hankinsoni Hubbs *in* Jordan, 1929: 88 (Type locality Michigan.)

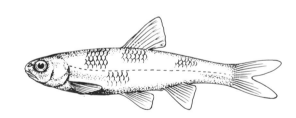

EASTERN SILVERY MINNOW

Hybognathus regius Girard, 1857

Identification

Like the brassy minnow, the silvery minnow could easily be mistaken for a species of *Notropis* but it has a crescent-shaped rather than a U-shaped lower jaw, a smaller jaw and the exposed fields of the scales are more round than those of the common shiner, which is the species of *Notropis* it most resembles. The gut of the silvery minnow is elongate and coiled on the right side.

Silvery minnows have the dorsal and anal fins with sharp corners and slightly concave margins whereas brassy minnows have more rounded fins. The best difference is probably in the structure of the scales (see illustration in key). The pelvic axillary process of the silvery minnow is large and scale-like; that of the brassy minnow is short and fleshy.

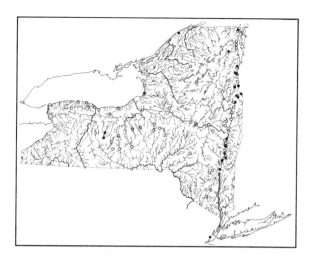

Description

Body elongate, slab sided, deepest anterior to the dorsal fin. Profiles about equally curved. Dorsal origin markedly nearer tip of snout than caudal base. Dorsal deltoid, retrogressive, with slightly concave margins and rather sharp corners. Caudal moderately forked, its lobes bluntly pointed. Anal origin behind tip of depressed last dorsal ray. Anal similar to dorsal. Pelvic insertion below anterior part of dorsal base. Pelvics retrogressive, rounded. Pelvic axillary process well developed. Pectoral fin low, its base slightly oblique. Pectoral retrogressive, rounded. Mouth subterminal, lower jaw crescentic. Gill membranes broadly joined to the isthmus. Lateral line complete, slightly decurved anteriorly. Scales with the circuli sharply angled at their basal corners, focus close to anterior edge. Counts and proportional measurements are given in Table 20.

Color: Overall color silvery, dorsal surface olive with the scales diffusely outlined with a band of large melanophores. Middorsal stripe broad and continuous from the occiput to the base of the tail. Midlateral stripe of deeper pigment, diffuse, but the top edge is sharp beginning midway between the gill opening and the level of the origin of the dorsal fin. Midlateral stripe expanded at the base of the caudal. Belly and lower half of head silvery white. Iris white. Preorbital with a bright silvery spot. Top of head punctate, with melanophores extending to the tip of the snout, upper and lower lips. Dorsal and caudal rays outlined, lower margin of caudal white. Rear edges of anal rays two and three with a single row of melanophores. Pectoral rays one through seven outlined, the rest of fin and pelvic fins white. No pigment on the periproct, no postanal stripe. *Notropis hudsonius* collected with the specimens described here (from the Muitzes Kill, collected 16 October 1979) are silvery and strongly resemble the eastern silvery minnows.

Juveniles and breeding adults: Breeding males develop a yellow tinge on the sides and lower fins. The males tend to be darker than the females.

Size: To about 120 mm total length. Our largest specimens are 103 mm standard length.

Habitat

The silvery minnow lives in lakes and larger, slow-moving streams. This is in contrast to the habitat of the brassy minnow which prefers smaller streams.

Distribution

This is an Atlantic coast species ranging from the Altamaha River to the St. Lawrence drainage. In New York, it occurs in the Hudson and St. Lawrence drainages and Lake Ontario, including the Lower Genesee and the Finger Lakes.

Life History

Raney described the spawning of this species in quiet backwaters near the mouth of Fall Creek near Ithaca, New York. Spawning occurred between 25 April and mid-May. The males concentrated along the edges of a narrow cove over decayed grasses from the previous year and grasses that were just beginning to grow. The females milled around in deep water near the center of the cove. When a female was ready to spawn, she moved toward shore whereupon 1 to 10 males approached and guided her into shallow water. Usually two, but sometimes more, males aligned themselves with the female as the group continued toward shore. Females that were not ready to spawn circled back toward the deeper water. Spawning consisted of the female and flanking males vibrating vigorously in water 2 to 6 inches deep. After spawning, the female returned to the deeper water and the males took up their station near shore waiting for another female. There was no territoriality and no fighting among the males. The eggs were demersal and nonadhesive. Hatching required 6 to 7 days at 13.3 to 20.0 C. The young reached 40 mm standard length by early August. Apparently, the faster growing fish spawned at age I but others did not reach maturity until the third summer at age II. Females 60 mm standard length contained 2,000 eggs; those 68 to 70 mm contained 3,000. The largest female examined was 96 mm and contained 6,600 eggs.

Food and Feeding

Bottom ooze and algae are the main food of the silvery minnow.

Notes

Many authors have regarded the eastern silvery minnow as a subspecies of the western silvery minnow under the name *Hybognathus nuchalis regius.* Pfleiger elevated the eastern form to species rank.

References

Raney, 1939b (spawning); 1942b (propagation). Pfleiger, 1971 (relationships). Bailey and Allum, 1962 (relationships). Malick et al., 1978 (Susquehanna).

Names

Regius is the adjectival form of the Latin *rex,* royal.

Hybognathus regius Girard, 1857: 209 Potomac River

Hybognathis nuchalis, Greeley, 1927: 58 Genesee watershed

Hybognathus nuchalis regius, Hubbs and Lagler, 1964:85 (distribution)

NOTROPIS

The genus *Notropis* encompasses the true shiners. It includes more species than any other genus in North America; 131 are currently recognized and several more are known but have not yet been formally named. It is a very diverse genus and the relationships of its species are not well known. Indeed, there is no good definition of the genus and it is based more on the absence of specializations than on the presence of any uniting characteristic. It is quite probable that further study will show that it should be broken into a number of smaller groups. Gilbert (1978) has reviewed the nomenclature of the genus and this excellent paper should be consulted by anyone interested in this genus.

Most species of the genus are rather small fishes, our common and striped shiners being comparative giants at 6 to 7 inches. All are more or less silvery and this is the reason for the name shiner. They are generally characterized as not having barbels but there are one or two exceptions and it has been suggested that some other barbeled minnows including the bigeye chub, *Hybopsis amblops*, should be placed in this genus. They have U-shaped mouths without specializations such as a cartilaginous rim, although the mouth of the pugnose shiner is tiny and nearly vertical. Most species are carnivorous with a short digestive tract and a silvery peritoneum but some have the peritoneum dark. They have relatively large scales, fewer than 55 in the lateral line, and, with an exception that appears to be a secondary development in one species, only 4 teeth in the main row on the pharyngeal arch. The patterns of breeding tubercles do not seem to be consistent.

The species of *Notropis* inhabit a variety of habitats and exhibit specializations for feeding and reproduction. Most species occur in schools or at least in aggregations.

The name *Notropis* comes from the Latin words *notus,* meaning back, and *tropis,* meaning keel. To be grammatically correct, the name should have been spelled *Nototropis* but the International Rules of Zoological Nomenclature dictate that the original spelling must stand. The word is a feminine noun and because Latin adjectives must have endings that agree with the gender of the noun they modify, all adjectival species names should have feminine endings. Most ichthyologists, however, have considered *Notropis* a masculine word and have used masculine endings. A petition to the International Commission on Zoological Nomenclature to have

Notropis declared a masculine name under the plenary powers of the commission has been accepted and *Notropis* is now officially masculine.

The species of *Notropis* are notoriously difficult to identify but in a limited area such as the state of New York the problem is not really so bad. Our species fall into four groups within which the choices are limited. These groups are only for the purposes of identification; they make no claim to indicating relationships:

1. The subgenus *Notropis* — *atherinoides, amoenus, rubellus,* and *photogenis.*
2. Deep-bodied species — *cornutus, chrysocephalus, analostanus, spilopterus,* and *umbratilis.*
3. Species with distinct black midlateral stripes — *anogenus, heterodon, heterolepis, chalybaeus, bifrenatus,* and *procne.*
4. Pallid species in which the midlateral stripe is weakly developed or absent. — *stramineus, volucellus, dorsalis,* and *hudsonius.*

The first of these groups is composed of related species with 10 or more anal fin rays. It is a natural group in that all of these species are closely related. The second group is a composite; *cornutus* and *chrysocephalus* are close relatives, *analostanus* and *spilopterus* are related to each other, and *umbratilis* stands alone. The third and fourth groups are less sharply defined and include species that may or may not be closely related. The presence of a lateral stripe is also somewhat variable because the pigment cells expand and contract so that even the conspicuous lateral stripe can disappear at times. Also, under some conditions, the pallid species may develop considerable pigment along their sides. Thus, the distinctions are not always clear and the groupings must be used with caution.

The key uses a different set of characteristics so the identification of a specimen at hand does not depend on the user placing the species in the correct group. Once a specimen has been tentatively identified, using the key, the groupings will make it relatively easy to confirm or refute the identification. Although the identification of the species of *Notropis* can be difficult, some of the species have stringent habitat requirements and this makes them excellent indicators of environmental quality. Thus, it is important to be able to identify the species correctly.

KEY TO THE SPECIES OF *NOTROPIS* IN NEW YORK

A. Mouth fairly large and oblique or horizontal.
C.

A'. Mouth tiny and nearly vertical, the maxillary not reaching past the posterior nostril.

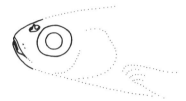

Mouth of pugnose shiner.

B. Dorsal rays nine. Teeth 5-5 or 5-4; the individual teeth with coarse serrations. Chin light, peritoneum silvery, dark pigment around the anus. (Recorded from Lake Erie but no definite New York records.)
Notropis emiliae **Pugnose minnow**

B'. Dorsal rays eight. Teeth 44, finely serrated. Chin dark, peritoneum dark, no pigment around the anus. Lake Ontario drainage and St. Lawrence. Scarce.
Notropis anogenus **Pugnose shiner, p. 185**

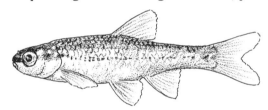

C. (A. Mouth not nearly vertical.) Scales before the dorsal fin very fine and crowded. A conspicuous concentration of pigment at the base of the anterior dorsal rays. Body compressed, similar in shape to golden shiner. Fins red in life.
Notropis umbratilis **Redfin shiner, p. 182**

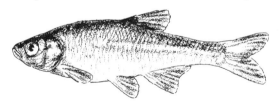

C'. Scales not especially crowded before dorsal fin. No conspicuous spot at the front of the dorsal fin base.

D. Scales firm and regular, those of the back and upper sides with narrow dark margins; diamond-shaped. Posterior interradial membranes of the dorsal fin with dark pigment.
(subgenus *Cyprinella*) **I.**

Pigment in dorsal fin of spotfin (left) and satinfin (right) shiners.

D'. Scales less firm and regularly diamond-shaped. Dorsal fin without definite pigment on posterior interradial membranes.

E. Anal rays seven to nine. **K.**

E'. Anal rays 10 to 13.

F. Middorsal stripe absent or weakly developed and diffuse. Snout blunt, contained 1.5 times in postorbital head length.
Notropis atherinoides **Emerald shiner, p. 171**

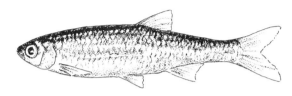

F'. Middorsal stripe well developed. Snout more pointed, about equal to postorbital head length.

G. Inner walls of nasal capsules heavily pigmented, appearing as a pair of crescent-shaped areas between the nostrils. Size large, to about 7 inches standard length. Pelvic rays 9, anal rays 10.
Notropis photogenis **Silver shiner, p. 172**

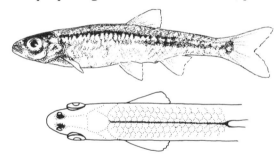

Dorsal view of silver shiner showing pigment crescents next to nostrils.

G'. No conspicuous paired spots between the nostrils. Smaller, maximum length about 4 inches. Pelvic rays seven or eight.

H. Pectoral rays 14 to 16. Anal rays usually 11. Margin of extended anal fin concave. Chin pigment with a well-defined backward extension onto the midline of the gular region.
Notropis amoenus **Comely shiner, p. 170**

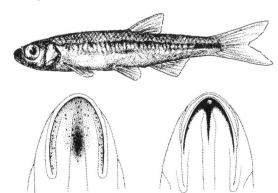

Chin pigment of rosyface (left) and comely shiners (right).

H'. Pectoral rays 13 or 14, anal rays 9 to 12, usually 10. Margin of extended anal fin straight. Chin weakly pigmented without a distinctive backward mark on the gular midline.
Notropis rubellus   **Rosyface shiner, p. 173**

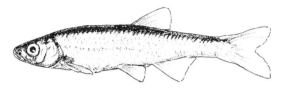

I. (D. Posterior interradial membranes with dark pigment.) Anal rays usually eight. Posterior dorsal interradial membranes clear around the pigmented areas.
Notropis spilopterus   **Spotfin shiner, p. 180**

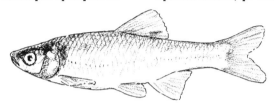

I'. Anal rays usually nine.

J. Lateral line scales 34 to 37. Pectoral rays usually 13 or 14. Dorsal interradial membranes dusted with melanophores in addition to the darkly pigmented areas.
Notropis analostanus   **Satinfin shiner, p. 176**

J'. Lateral line scales 37 or 38. Pectoral rays usually 15. (Probably does not occur in New York.)
Notropis whipplei   **Steelcolor shiner**

K. (E. Anal rays seven to nine.) Body nearly terete (round in cross section), its greatest depth 1.5 times its greatest width or less.
                                        M.

K'. Body more slab sided, its greatest depth more than 1.5 times its greatest width or more.

L. Anterior dorsolateral scales relatively large, 13 to 16 between the dorsal origin and the back of the head, in the third to sixth row above the lateral line. Dorsal surface of the body with pronounced wavy or straight lines meeting behind the dorsal fin in a series of chevron-shaped marks. Tip of chin and gular area dusky. Western part of the state only.
Notropis chrysocephalus

                              Striped shiner, p. 177

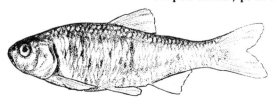

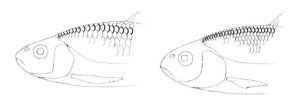

Dorsolateral scales of striped (left) and common (right) shiners.

L'. Scales small, anterior dorsolateral scale count 17 to 25. Without prominent stripes on the upper part of the body although breeding males often have wide longitudinal stripes. No pigment on the chin and gular area of specimens from the western part of the state and the Susquehanna drainage. Occurs throughout the state.
Notropis cornutus   **Common shiner, p. 178**

M. (K. Body nearly terete.) Caudal fin base with a prominent large, round black spot. Snout blunt and overhanging the mouth. (The spot is sometimes masked by silvery pigment and often obsolescent in individuals from smaller streams.)
Notropis hudsonius   **Spottail shiner, p. 194**

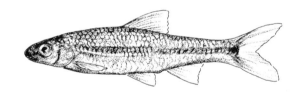

M'. No prominent spot at the base of the tail although there may be a small triangular or irregular spot at the end of the lateral pigment band.

N. Sides with a more or less regular dark stripe from the base of the tail to the shoulder girdle and continued on the head in some species.
                                        R.

N'. Sides without a longitudinal stripe or with a partial stripe from the tail to about the level of the dorsal fin. Lateral line pores sometimes pigmented.

O. Anal rays seven, teeth 4-4.
Notropis stramineus   **Sand shiner, p. 195**

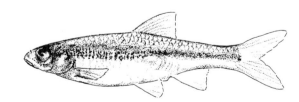

O'. Anal rays eight.

P. Anterior lateral line scales elevated, much higher than long and conspicuously higher than those in the rows above or below the lateral line. Teeth 4-4.
Notropis volucellus **Mimic shiner, p. 196**

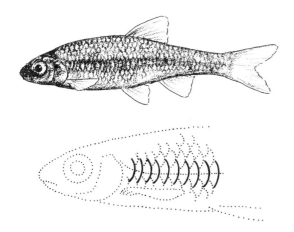

Enlarged lateral line scales of the mimic shiner.

P'. Anterior lateral line scales not elevated. Teeth 1,4-4,1. Eyes dorsolateral, lower surface of head flat. Usually there is a single row of melanophores above the midlateral pigment on the caudal peduncle.
Notropis dorsalis **Bigmouth shiner, Q.**

Q. Shape of head similar to that of *Notropis stramineus.* Genesee drainage.
Notropis d. keimi **p. 193**

Q'. Snout longer, mouth larger and head more flattened. Tail pink in life.
Notropis d. dorsalis **p. 193**

R. (N. Sides with a prominent, dark, midlateral stripe.) Anal rays seven.

U.

R'. Anal rays eight.

S. Lateral band broad, Dark pigment present inside the mouth on the oral valves and adjacent areas.
Notropis chalybaeus **Ironcolor shiner, p. 187**

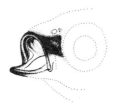

Mouth pigment of ironcolor shiner.

S'. No dark pigment inside mouth.

T. Chin and premaxillaries black. Lateral line scales with dark pigment bars that alternate with similar bars on the row above, thus producing a zig-zag pattern that is superimposed on the dusky lateral band. Teeth 1,4-4,1.
Notropis heterodon **Blackchin shiner, p. 188**

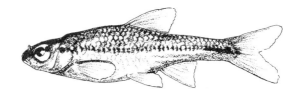

T'. Chin and upper lip without pigment but the tip of the snout is included in the black band that extends forward from the eyes. Prominent dark marks above and below the lateral line pores form a row of crescents within the lateral dark band. Teeth 4-4.
Notropis heterolepis **Blacknose shiner, p. 190**

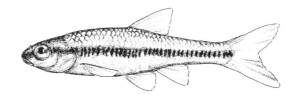

U. (R. Anal rays seven.) Lateral stripe continued forward through eye and around snout but not on chin. Dark pigment on scales in the lateral band sometimes produces a zig-zag pattern. Lateral line incomplete.
Notropis bifrenatus **Bridle shiner, p. 186**

U'. Lateral stripe weakly developed and not continued forward of the eye, although there may be a dark spot on the preorbital region.
Notropis procne **Swallowtail shiner, p. 191**

The Subgenus *Notropis*

Members of the subgenus *Notropis* are graceful, slender, and elongated fishes with 10 or more principal rays in the anal fin. (All of the other species of *Notropis* in our area have nine or fewer anal rays.) They are rather pale in color although the rosyface shiner can sometimes be quite dark and conspicuously marked. The midlateral stripe is somewhat developed on the caudal peduncle and becomes narrow or absent anteriorly. Usually, the scales of the upper sides are narrowly outlined with pigment cells. In life, they are quite transparent with a silvery band on the sides.

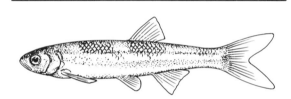

COMELY SHINER

Notropis amoenus (Abbott, 1874)

Identification

Members of this subgenus are rather slender, silvery minnows with 10 or more anal rays. They have a broad midlateral stripe on the posterior part of the body but this stripe becomes narrower anteriorly and disappears at the level of the pectoral fin. Four members of the group occur in New York waters: The emerald shiner, *Notropis atherinoides;* the silver shiner, *N. photogenis;* the rosyface shiner, *N. rubellus;* and the comely shiner, *N. amoenus.* The emerald shiner is a slab-sided fish with a short snout, the silver shiner is a larger species with a distinctive color pattern, and the rosyface develops red pigmentation on the top of the head in breeding males. The emerald shiner is thought to be the nearest relative of the comely shiner but the rosyface looks most like it and, except for the breeding males, is the species with which it is most apt to be confused. The best way to distinguish the two is the pigmentation on the midline of the lower jaw. The rosyface has a diffuse band of dark pigment cells on the midline but in the comely shiner the pigment cells are grouped into a narrow tapering line that, together with the distinct pigment on the edge of the lower lip, forms a distinctive anchor-shaped mark.

Snelson (1968) presents additional differences as follows:

	N. amoenus	*N. rubellus*
Pectoral rays	Usually 14 to 16	Usually 13 or 14
Anal rays	Modally 11, often 10 or 12	Usually 10
Body circumferential scales above lateral line	15 to 17, usually 15 except Upper Potomac River	13 to 15, usually 13 or 14 except Upper Susquehanna where 15
Body width/depth	Deeper and more compressed, D/W 1.6 to 1.7	More terete, D/W 1.4 to 1.5
Dorsal fin	Pointed, angulate	Rounded
Anal fin	Anterior rays reach beyond tip of posterior rays when depressed, margin falcate	Anterior rays reaching tip of posterior rays when depressed, or shorter, margin straight
Tubercles on pectoral fin of breeding male	Present on ray 1, bi- or tri-serial on rays 2-10 with 6 to 16 per segment	None on ray 1, 1 per segment on rays 2-8
Male breeding colors	No red	Red on parts of head and body
Pigment on gular area	Y- or V-shaped extension	Scattered or absent on midline
Anterior dorsolateral scale pigment	Scales distinctly outlined, centers of scales with little pigment	Scales weakly outlined, centers of scales with considerable pigment

Young *amoenus* have better developed pigment behind the anal fin than young *rubellus* the same size.

Description

Body slender and moderately compressed. Dorsal and ventral profiles evenly and equally curved. Dorsal fin inserted well behind the pelvic origin, nearer caudal base than tip of the snout. Dorsal fin angular but its corners not sharply pointed. Caudal lobes equal and bluntly pointed. Anal falcate, with concave margin. Pelvics retrogressive, pelvic axillary process minute. Head pointed, snout equal or nearly equal to eye diameter. Eye lateral, gill membranes somewhat joined. Lateral line complete, noticeably decurved, reaching its lowest point anterior to the pelvic fin origin. Scales crowded anterior to the dorsal fin origin. Counts and proportional measurements are given in Table 15.

Color: The comely shiner is rather pale, darker above, with the back opaque olive green in life. Dorsal scale pockets outlined with melanophores. Midside with a silvery band from the gill opening to the base of the tail. A midlateral band of melanophores is present on the caudal peduncle, becoming diffuse anteriorly, variable. Middorsal stripe developed, variably but usually stronger anterior to the dorsal fin and not present along its base. Often, the stripe is weaker behind the dorsal fin. Upper lip heavily pigmented. Gular region with a Y- or V-shaped patch in the midline. Fin rays, except those of the pelvic fin, outlined with melanophores, fin membranes immaculate.

Juveniles and breeding adults: Neither sex develops red breeding colors. Males may be darker than the females. Females lack tubercles on the fins.

Size: Snelson reported that the largest specimen he examined was 88 mm standard length.

Habitat

The comely shiner seems to prefer moderate-sized to larger streams and areas where the water is 2 feet or more deep. Lakes and reservoirs are marginal habitats and it sometimes enters smaller streams of low gradient. It tolerates a wide range of currents but seems to keep to pools and backwaters of swifter streams. In the Hudson drainage, it sometimes occurs with the rosyface shiner.

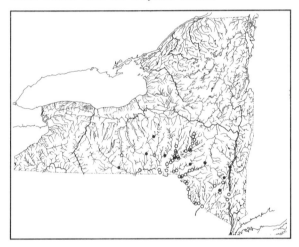

Distribution

The comely shiner lives on the Atlantic Coastal Plain and Piedmont from the Hudson River south to the Cape Fear River system in North Carolina. There is one recent collection from the Yadkin River in North Carolina and one old record from Seneca Lake in New York.

Life History

Apparently, the comely shiner spawns in late spring and summer and Snelson states that most July collections contain some males with tubercles. Its spawning behavior has not been reported.

Food and Feeding

The feeding habits of this species have not been reported but its shape and the position of its mouth suggest that it is a midwater feeder and its diet is probably similar to that of *Notropis rubellus* which feeds on aquatic and terrestrial insects.

Notes

Although this species is superficially similar to, and was for a time considered a subspecies of, the rosyface shiner, the study by Snelson indicates that it is actually more closely related to the emerald shiner.

References

Snelson, 1968 (systematics).

Names

Amoenus is the Latin word for pleasing, lovely.

Alburnus amoenus Abbott, 1874: 333-335 fig. 8 Delaware and Raritan Canal, probably Mercer County, New Jersey (Gilbert lists two specimens in the Museum of Comparative Zoology as types but Snelson believed that this is not correct and that the types have not been located if, indeed, they still exist.)

Notropis amoenus, Bean, 1903: 150-151 New York

Notropis rubellus amoenus, Greeley, 1936: 83 Delaware-Susquehanna drainages

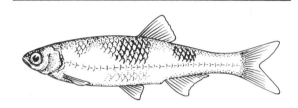

EMERALD SHINER

Notropis atherinoides Rafinesque, 1818

Identification

The emerald shiner belongs to the subgenus *Notropis,* which also includes the silver shiner, *N. photogenis,* the comely shiner, *N. amoenus,* and the rosyface shiner, *N. rubellus.* All of the species are slender minnows with no barbels and 10 or more anal fin rays.

The emerald shiner is a moderate-sized species with the shortest snout and the deepest body of the group. It never has the red pigment that characterizes breeding males of the rosyface shiner, it lacks the distinct predorsal stripe and dark crescents between the nostrils of the silver shiner, and it lacks the pigment pattern on the chin area that characterizes the comely shiner. Except during the breeding season, the emerald shiner is perhaps most apt to be confused with the rosyface from which it can be separated by the following additional characters: The emerald shiner usually has 11 anal rays, the rosyface 10; there are 23 to 25 scale rows around the body of *atherinoides* and 26 to 28 in *rubellus,* consistently 6 rows of scales above the lateral line in *atherinoides,* often 5 in *rubellus.* The dorsal fin originates over the pelvic base in *atherinoides* and behind the pelvics in *rubellus.*

Description

Body elongate, moderately compressed and slab sided. Profiles equally curved. Dorsal origin midway between caudal and center of the eye. Dorsal deltoid, retrogressive, with straight margin and softly angled corners. Caudal moderately forked, its lobes moderately pointed. Anal origin below distal quarter of depressed last dorsal ray. Anal long, retrogressive, with falcate margin, anterior corner rounded. Pelvic inserted slightly ahead of the dorsal origin. Pelvic fin retrogressive, with straight margin and rounded corners. Pelvic axillary process well developed but short. Pectoral base low, slightly oblique. Pectoral fins retrogressive, bluntly pointed. Gill membranes broadly joined to the isthmus. Mouth terminal, moderately oblique, reaching to front of eye. Lateral line complete, slightly decurved. Counts and proportional measurements are given in Table 15.

Color: Dorsal surface dusky with green or blue iridescence. Sides silvery, shading to white on the belly. Preserved specimens have a dark midlateral stripe on the posterior half of the body. This stripe narrows and disappears between the dorsal fin and the gill opening. Middorsal stripe diffuse. Scales of the upper body with dusky margins. Fins hyaline with lightly outlined rays.

Juveniles and breeding adults: Breeding males have minute tubercles on the upper surface of the pectoral fins. They do not develop bright breeding colors.

Size: In the Great Lakes, the emerald shiner attains lengths of about 5 inches. Our largest New York specimens are 106 mm standard length.

Habitat

The emerald shiner is a fish of big waters, the Great Lakes and larger rivers, such as the Niagara and the Hudson. It is a midwater or near-surface species that usually lives in large- or moderate-sized schools. In the spring, they often make vertical migrations, approaching the surface at night and retreating to deeper water during the day.

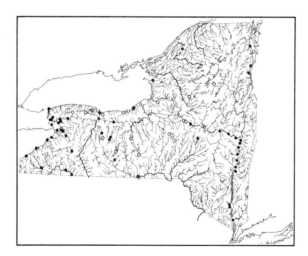

Distribution

The range of the emerald shiner is a broad band across southern Canada from Lake Champlain and the St. Lawrence to the southern part of the Northwest Territories. Its southern limit dips through the Mississippi basin to the gulf coast from Texas to Alabama. In New York, it occurs in the Great Lakes and in the Hudson-Mohawk system. A record from the Earlville Reservoir cited by Snelson may have been the result of movement through the old Chenango Canal or it could have been a bait-bucket introduction.

Life History

The emerald shiner spawns in the late spring or early summer, sometimes as late as mid-August. Water temperatures at that time are around 75 F and the eggs hatch in 24 to 32 hours. Emerald shiners rarely live through their third summer. Population numbers fluctuate and they are extremely abundant in some years, scarce in others.

Food and Feeding

The emerald shiner is a midwater plankton cropper, feeding on a variety of zooplankton with some blue-green algae and diatoms. Protozoans are important in the diet of the young-of-the-year and fish and insect larvae are taken by adults.

Notes

The emerald shiner is an important bait species when it is abundant.

References

Brigham, 1932 (life history). Flittner, 1964 (morphology, life history). Fuchs, 1967 (life history). Snelson, 1968 (systematics). Campbell and MacCrimmon, 1970 (biology). Siefert, 1972 (first food). Mendelson, 1975 (feeding). McCormick and Kleiner, 1976 (temperature tolerance). Whitaker, 1977 (seasonal changes in feeding).

Names

Atherinoides means like *Atherina*, referring to its resemblance to members of the silversides family.

Notropis atherinoides Rafinesque, 1818a: 204 Lake Erie (No types designated but the description is said to have been based on specimens collected by De Witt Clinton and deposited in the Lycaeum of Natural History.)

Notropis nitidus Kirtland, 1854b: 44-45 Rocky River near Cleveland, Ohio

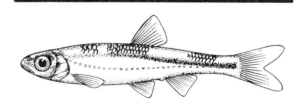

SILVER SHINER

Notropis photogenis (Cope, 1865)

Identification

The silver shiner is a large (for a shiner) slender shiner with a pointed snout and more than 10 anal rays. It looks a lot like the rosyface shiner but has a striking middorsal stripe whereas the middorsal stripe of the rosyface is diffuse. The silver shiner lacks red pigment on the head and has the origin of the dorsal fin over, rather than behind, the pelvic insertion. It also has nine pelvic rays. A distinctive mark is a concentration of pigment on the mesial side of the olfactory capsules that forms a pair of dark crescents that can be seen when the head is viewed from above. The silver shiner also has only five rows of scales above the lateral line; the emerald shiner has six, and the rosyface has five or six.

Description
Body elongate, slender, and somewhat slab sided. Profiles symmetrical. Dorsal origin slightly nearer the caudal base than tip of snout. Dorsal retrogressive, deltoid, its margin convex, its corners softly angled. Caudal moderately forked with bluntly pointed lobes. Anal inserted behind tip of depressed last dorsal ray. Anal retrogressive, deltoid, with concave margin and softly angled corners. Pelvics inserted below, or slightly ahead of the dorsal origin. Pelvics retrogressive, with straight margins. Pectoral base low, slightly oblique. Pectoral retrogressive, bluntly pointed. Gill membranes narrowly joined to the isthmus. Snout pointed, mouth oblique, terminal. Lateral line complete, slightly decurved anteriorly. Counts and proportional measurements are given in Table 15.

Color: Dorsal surface of body with a prominent narrow middorsal stripe. Midlateral stripe present but narrowing anteriorly and ending at the shoulder girdle; somewhat expanded at the caudal base. A thin dark line along the side marks the outer edge of the horizontal skeletaginous septum. Sides silvery, beginning at the top of the midlateral stripe and shading to white on the belly. A concentration of pigment above and below anterior lateral line pores. Dorsal and caudal fin rays with dark margins, other fins hyaline. Mesial wall of each nasal capsule with a concentration of pigment that is overlain by less dense and more superficial melanophores.

Juveniles and breeding adults: This species does not develop bright colors. The tubercles are microscopic and confined to the head, the anterior scales of the body, and the upper surface of the pectoral fins.

Size: Trautman lists the largest specimens as 5.2 inches total length. Our largest specimens from New York are 107 mm standard length.

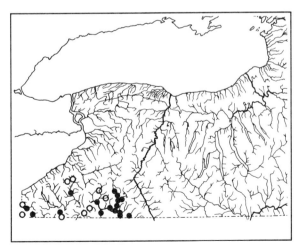

Habitat
The silver shiner occurs in clear, gravel-bottom streams where there is moderate to swift current. It is especially abundant in deep riffles and in pools below the riffles, where it usually occurs in schools.

Greeley found it in silty water in streams 2 to 3 feet deep and 15 to 60 feet wide.

Distribution
The silver shiner occurs in the Ohio and Tennessee River systems with some populations in the Lake Erie drainage of Ohio and Ontario. In New York, it is recorded only from the Allegheny watershed.

Life History
The life history of this species seems not to have been reported.

Food and Feeding
Caddisfly larvae, dipteran adults and larvae and flatworms were found in the stomachs of nine specimens from Ontario.

References
Gruchy, Bowen, and Gruchy, 1973 (Canadian records, ecology). Gilbert, 1971 (taxonomy). Gilbert in Lee et al., 1980 (distribution).

Names
Photogenis is from the Greek *phos,* light or shining, and *genys,* the cheeks, hence silver cheeks.

Squalius photogenis Cope, 1865a: 280 Youghiogheny River, Pennsylvania

Notropis photogenis, Greeley, 1938: 67 Allegheny watershed

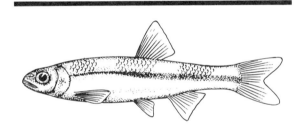

ROSYFACE SHINER
Notropis rubellus (Agassiz, 1850)

Identification
The rosyface shiner takes its name from the coloration of the breeding males which are bright red on the top of the head and the bases of the pectoral fins. It is a slender, silvery minnow with a pointed snout and 10 or 11 anal fin rays.

Three other New York species are closely related to the rosyface shiner and sometimes confused with it. They are the emerald shiner, the comely shiner, and the silver shiner. Only the rosyface has red pigment during the breeding season and it has been suggested that it might not be closely related to the others. For the present, however, *rubellus* is retained in the subgenus *Notropis* with the other three.

The silver shiner is easily separated from the rosyface by its very prominent middorsal stripe, dark crescents between the nostrils, and nine pelvic rays. The emerald shiner has a deeper and more compressed body, and a much shorter snout. The comely shiner is the most similar species and the best way to distinguish them is by the pigment on the chin area, which is diffuse on the midline in the rosyface and in a distinct tapering line in the comely shiner. Other distinguishing features are given in the account of that species.

Description

Body elongate, very streamlined and slightly slab sided. Profiles equally curved. Dorsal fin equidistant between the caudal base and the upper limb of the preopercle. Dorsal retrogressive, its margin slightly convex with rounded corners. Caudal moderately forked, with rounded lobes. Anal origin below middle of depressed last dorsal ray. Anal retrogressive, with concave margin and rounded corners. Pelvic insertion well ahead of dorsal origin. Pelvic process well developed. Pelvic retrogressive, rounded. Pectoral base low, slightly oblique. Pectorals retrogressive, rounded. Gill membranes joined to isthmus. Mouth rather large, terminal, slightly oblique. Lateral line complete, somewhat decurved anteriorly. Breast and prepectoral naked. Counts and proportional measurements are given in Table 15.

Color: (from a specimen collected 14 August 1979 in the Little Salmon River, west of Parish, NY). Upper sides yellow olive, the scales with broad marginal bands of melanophores. Middorsal line diffuse. Sides silvery, belly below line between pectoral base and pelvic origin white, ventral side of caudal peduncle white. Gill membranes and base of pectoral yellowish. Caudal membranes with yellow wash. Scales above the silvery area rather dark. Lateral line pores surrounded by melanophores, showing as a row of dots. In preserved specimens, there is a midlateral stripe on the side of the caudal peduncle which becomes narrower anteriorly and pinches out at the shoulder girdle.

Juveniles and breeding adults: Males develop tubercles on rays 2 through 8 of the pectoral fin, one tubercle per segment. Tubercles also cover the snout and lower jaw and there are a few on the upper half of the opercles and on the scales above and below the lateral line. The upper sides of the pelvic fins and the dorsal and anal fins also have some tubercles.

Pfeiffer described the breeding colors of the males at the height of the breeding season as ". . the entire snout, lips, chin, branchiostegals, and top of the head as far as the nape brick red. The opercle, belly, and lower sides as far as the anal are a lighter red. The middorsal line from head to dorsal fin is brick red mixed with the usual dark color of this area. A dark line runs from the eye to the upper angle of the opercle, around its posterior edge and there fuses with the base of the pectoral fins. A light red diffuses over the opercle, merging with a darker band of color at the posterior border. The basal two-thirds of the pectoral fins, the base and proximal halves of the pelvics, and the base of the anal are red. The basal portion of the dorsal fin is bright red." Females have the top of the head light red, as are the edges of the lips and the base of the pectorals. A

faint red covers the belly from the branchiostegals to the pelvic fins. Tubercles occur on top of the head, on the opercle, cheeks, back of and below the eye, as well as on the branchiostegals, mandibles, and a few on the dorsal scales.

Size: This is a medium-sized *Notropis*. Our largest specimens are 71 mm standard length.

Habitat

The rosyface occurs in the swifter parts of large- and moderate-sized streams, less frequently in smaller creeks.

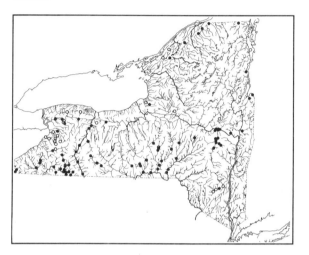

Distribution

The rosyface is widespread from Manitoba and Minnesota to the St. Lawrence drainage in Quebec and New York, south to the James River on the Atlantic coast and the Tennessee River west of the Appalachians. It also occurs in the Ozarks and in the Ouachita River in Arkansas.

In New York, it is in all major drainages except the Delaware, but it is not found in the Adirondacks.

Life History

Pfeiffer studied the life history of the rosyface shiner near Allegany, New York, in Five Mile Creek, about 200 yards above its confluence with the Allegheny River. Spawning took place on a riffle at the head of a pool. Prespawning activities consisted of schools including both sexes circling between two pools below the spawning riffles. The front of the school was mostly females, the rear mostly males. Spawning took place between 23 and 28 June when the water temperature was 76 to 84 F. The spawning area was over gravel bottom in the lower part of a riffle where the water was 1 to 3 inches deep and the stones were 0.5 to 5 inches in diameter. Depressions 5 to 12 inches in diameter served as nests.

A school of fish near the site suddenly rushed into the area, breaking the surface and thrashing about. Spawning occurred in groups of 8 to 12 individuals, the fish vibrating together over a depression for 5 or 6 seconds, then remaining quiet for 30 seconds or so, and repeating the cycle for about 5 minutes before returning to the pool. After 10 minutes, the school again moved into the riffle and repeated the process.

Pfeiffer noted some chasing activity while the fish were in the pool with two fish in contact for runs of 5 or 6 feet. He did not believe this to be pair-spawning but a ritual chase similar to that observed by Reighard for the creek chub.

One-year-old females average 600 eggs, and 3-year-olds averaged 1,175. The maximum age was 3 years. Both sexes matured at age I. Males grow faster the first year; females grow faster during the second and third years.

Food and Feeding
Aquatic and terrestrial insects made up 91 percent of the diet.

References
Pfeiffer, 1955 (life history). Reed, 1954 (hermaphroditism); 1957 (life history). Miller, 1963 (morphology, hybridization); 1964 (breeding behavior). Snelson, 1968 (taxonomy, comparison with *N. amoenus*).

Names
Rubellus is the diminutive of the Latin word *ruber*, red.

Alburnus rubellus Agassiz, 1850: 364-366 Lake Superior at Sault Sainte Marie

Notropis rubellus, Greeley, 1930: 80 Lake Champlain tributaries

Notropis rubellus rubellus, Greeley, 1936: 83 Susquehanna watershed

Alburnus rubrifrons Cope, 1865b: 85 Kiskiminitas River, Allegheny drainage, Pennsylvania

Notropis rubrifrons, Greeley, 1927: 60 Genesee watershed

Photogenis rubrifrons, Hubbs, 1930a: 430 (nomenclature)

Notropis atherinoides Meek, 1889: 308 Cayuga tributaries (misidentification)

TABLE 15
AVERAGE PROPORTIONAL MEASUREMENTS AND COUNTS OF SHINERS
(subgenus *Notropis*)

All proportions are expressed in percentage of standard length.

	amoenus	atherinoides	photogenis	rubellus
ST. LENGTH (mm)	49.3	51.4	59.0	42.4
TOTAL LENGTH	125.1	125.4	123.7	124.8
FORK LENGTH	113.8	114.2	113.2	115.3
PREDORSAL	55.4	54.9	54.2	56.8
PREANAL	66.5	66.7	67.5	66.6
PREPELVIC	47.6	48.8	50.4	50.6
DORSAL BASE	9.5	10.6	10.5	9.0
ANAL BASE	13.5	14.6	11.9	13.0
BODY DEPTH	17.7	21.9	18.1	17.2
BODY WIDTH	10.5	13.6	11.6	11.0
C.PED. DEPTH	8.5	9.7	8.1	7.4
PECTORAL ALT.	12.3	15.2	13.8	13.1
HEAD LENGTH	23.5	24.6	24.7	24.7
SNOUT	7.2	6.3	7.8	7.2
EYE	7.2	7.7	7.8	7.2
MOUTH LENGTH	7.8	3.4	7.9	4.5
INTERORB	7.0	5.1	7.7	4.5
N (sample size)	5	5	5	5
COUNTS:				
DORSAL RAYS	8	8	8	8
ANAL RAYS	10-11	10-11	10(11)	9-10
PECTORAL RAYS	15-16	14-16	15-17	12-13
PELVIC RAYS	8	8	9	8
GILL RAKERS	6-8	10-11	6-7	4-6
VERTEBRAE*	35	36-37	35-36	35-37
SCALES:				
ABOVE L. L.	6-8	6	5-6	6
LATERAL LINE	37-41	38-43	36-40	38-45
BELOW L. L.	3-4	4	4	3-4
PHARYNGEAL TEETH	2,4-4,2	2,4,4,2	2,4-4,2	2,4-4,2

* Excluding Weberian apparatus.

The Species of *Notropis* with Deep, Compressed Bodies

This group is really a complex of three unrelated lineages of species. *Notropis cornutus* and *Notropis chrysocephalus* are close relatives and belong to the subgenus *Luxilus*. They have nine anal rays, 2,4-4,2 pharyngeal teeth and deep, diamond-shaped scales that are easily dislodged. Characteristically, they have groups of dark, regenerated scales on their sides. The males develop considerable red pigment on the fins during the breeding season. The predorsal scales of these species are not outlined with pigment and the individual scales are not readily visible.

Notropis analostanus and *N. spilopterus* belong to the subgenus *Cyprinella*. This subgenus is characterized by firm diamond-shaped scales and those of the upper sides are distinctly outlined with marginal melanophores. They also have definite pigment on the posterior membranes of the dorsal fin and adults have a dark triangular bar on the shoulder region just behind the gill opening. Breeding males are steel blue with yellow lower fins.

Notropis umbratilis is a member of the subgenus *Lythrurus*. It has 11 or more anal rays and a dark spot at the base of the anterior dorsal rays. It also has small scales in the predorsal region and these scales are not outlined in dark pigment. Males have conspicuous pink fins that become bright red during the breeding season.

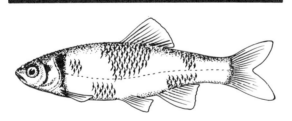

SATINFIN SHINER

Notropis analostanus (Girard, 1860)

Identification
The satinfin is a deep-bodied, somewhat compressed minnow, with firm, diamond-shaped scales that give it a "neat" appearance. It also has dark pigment on the membranes between the fifth and sixth and sixth and seventh rays of the dorsal fin. It and its relative, the spotfin, are similar in appearance but differ in that the satinfin has 9, rather than 8 anal rays and usually 36, rather than 38, lateral-line scales.

Description
Body moderately deep and slab sided. Profiles equally curved. Dorsal origin midway between caudal base and nostrils. Dorsal retrogressive, with straight margin and rounded corners. Caudal moderately forked, with rounded lobes. Anal origin below end of dorsal base. Anal similar to dorsal. Pelvic insertion in front of dorsal origin. Pelvics retrogressive, rounded. Pelvic axillary process minute. Pectoral base low, slightly oblique. Pectoral retrogressive, rounded. Snout pointed and slightly overhanging the mouth. Gill membranes broadly united to the isthmus. Mouth small, somewhat oblique. Eye rather small, lateral. Scales deep, rhombic, firm. Lateral line complete, slightly decurved anteriorly. Counts and proportional measurements are given in Table 16.

Color: Overall silver, darker above. Scales with bold dark margin. Predorsal stripe present, postdorsal stripe weaker. Midlateral band present on posterior part of body, narrow and weak anteriorly. Both lips pigmented about same gray color as top of head.

Juveniles and breeding adults: Breeding males have scattered, medium-sized tubercles on top of head and snout. Tubercles on nape smaller, diminishing to the dorsal origin. Chin with one or more rows of tubercles as large as those of the head. Scales of the body, except those of the belly, have minute tubercles, as do all of the fins. Breeding males become steel blue above with the lower fins yellow. All dorsal membranes become nearly black.

Habitat
The satinfin shows a preference for large- and moderate-sized streams although it is occasionally taken in small creeks. It is often in the tidal freshwaters of coastal rivers.

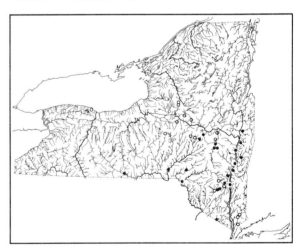

Distribution
The satinfin is an Atlantic coast species ranging from the Mohawk-Hudson to the Cape Fear River in North Carolina. In New York, it occurs in the Delaware and in the Susquehanna River and in some mid-Hudson tributaries. There are three isolated populations in the Great Lakes, one at the southern end of Cayuga Lake, one in a Lake Ontario tributary west of Rochester, and one in the Black River. These isolated populations could be remnants of former wide distributions, bait-bucket introductions or possibly canal waifs.

Life History

Gale and Buynak studied the spawning of the satin-fin in wading pools near Berwick, Pennsylvania. Single pairs were placed in pools in water 150 to 200 mm deep. Black acrylic plates separated by a 3 mm space were placed on legs so they were 40 mm off the bottom. About two-thirds of the pools were covered with styrofoam sheets for shelter. Spawning began in June and continued until mid-August when it suddenly stopped. Seven pairs spawned and the eggs were collected at 2-hour intervals. Most of the spawning occurred between 6 am and noon with the peak activity between 8 am and 10 am. The spawning pairs made several passes along the crevice before releasing their eggs and several more when the eggs were sprayed into the crevices. Each spawning session lasted less than 2 hours, during which time 6 to 634 eggs were laid. Some fish produced more eggs early in the season, others later. Individual pairs spawned in 3 to 11 sessions separated by intervals of 3 to 31 days. The total number of eggs produced ranged from 381 to 3,268.

Newly laid eggs were demersal, adhesive, and pale yellow in color. The size of the eggs ranged from 1.4 to 1.9 mm and varied significantly between females. The eggs laid early in the season were larger than those laid later on. Hatching took 6 to 8 days at 20 to 25 C. Newly hatched larvae were 5.9 mm long and began to feed in about 6 days. Stout, and Winn and Stout, noted that the males made a purring sound during courtship.

Food and Feeding

Insects, particularly dipterans and ephemeropterans, are the main food of the satinfin.

Notes

There is a distinct subspecies in the Santee River system of North Carolina and South Carolina. The populations in the Peedee River are considered by Gibbs to be intergrades.

Six specimens from Wells Creek at the village of French Creek in the Allegheny system were identified by Gibbs as *Notropis whipplei*, the Mississippi relative of the satinfin shiner. The characteristics of these specimens suggest the satinfin but Gibbs considered it less likely that they belonged to that species than to the related *whipplei*. If they really are satinfins, they may be the results of an introduction or perhaps an error in labeling. I believe it more likely that they were aberrant *Notropis spilopterus*.

Apparently, the species was formerly much more common in the Cayuga Lake basin than it is now.

References

Gibbs, 1963 (systematics). Stone, 1940 (biology). Winn and Stout, 1960 (sound production). Stout, 1975 (sound and reproduction). Gale and Buynak, 1978 (spawning).

Names

The name *analostanus* comes from the locality near which the types were collected, Analostan Island in the Potomac River, now called Roosevelt Island.

Cyprinella analostana Girard, 1860: 58-59 Rock Creek, Washington, DC

Notropis analostanus, Greeley and Bishop, 1932: 85 Black River Canal

Notropis whipplei (non Girard), Meek, 1889: 307 Cayuga Lake

Notropis whipplei analostanus, Greeley, 1935: 94 Mohawk-Hudson watershed

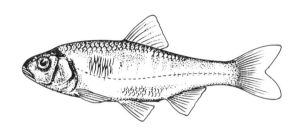

STRIPED SHINER

Notropis chrysocephalus (Rafinesque, 1820)

Identification

Two species in our state belong to the subgenus *Luxilus*, the striped shiner and the common shiner. Among features they share are large size, up to 7 inches, deep, moderately compressed body, nine anal rays, 2,4-4,2 teeth, deep deciduous scales, and dark peritoneum. They are quite similar and for many years were considered to be subspecies. In New York, they are quite distinct where they occur together, with only occasional intermediates. Elsewhere, they intergrade, with intermediate individuals that cannot be readily assigned to either species.

The chief difference between the striped shiner and the common shiner is the size of the scales of the upper front part of the body. In the striped shiner, the scales are large and easy to see because of their dark outlines but in the common shiner, the scales are smaller and lack dark margins. The size is reflected in the number of scales counted in the row halfway between the lateral line and the middle of the back, from the back of the head to the level of the origin of the dorsal fin (14 to 16 in the striped shiner, and 18 to 24 in the common shiner). Another difference is that in the striped shiner the scales of the upper side have extra pigment where the rows overlap and this produces zig-zag stripes that meet in the midline behind the dorsal fin to form a series of nested chevron-shaped marks. Such marks are sometimes present in the common shiner but less prominent.

Description

Body elongate but moderately deep and compressed. Profiles symmetrical. Dorsal origin well forward, much closer to tip of snout than to caudal base. Dorsal retrogressive, with slightly convex margin and softly angled corners. Caudal moderately forked, its lobes bluntly pointed. Anal origin below distal one-fourth of depressed last dorsal ray. Anal retrogressive, with straight margin and angled corners. Pelvic insertion below dorsal origin. Pelvics retrogressive, with convex margin and blunt corners. Pelvic axillary process small. Pectoral base low, slightly oblique. Pectoral fin retrogressive, bluntly pointed. Gill membranes slightly joined to isthmus. Mouth large, terminal, oblique and straight in profile. Scales on flanks deep and rhombic. Lateral line complete, decurved anteriorly. Counts and proportional measurements are given in Table 16.

Color: In life, the striped shiner is generally silvery, gray or olive above, shading to white below. The dark dorsal stripes are not always visible in fresh specimens. Adults develop patches of dark regenerated scales on the sides. The peritoneum is dark and visible through the body wall of preserved specimens. Chin and gular region with some pigment, more than in *N. cornutus*.

Breeding adults: Breeding males develop red on the outer parts of the fins. This starts as a narrow margin and spreads through the fin as the season progresses until the fins are mostly red during the breeding season. The head and the body take on a bluish cast with pink on the sides. The breast and the belly remain silvery with little or no pink. Females have the outer third of the fins slightly pink.

Size: This is the largest *Notropis* in our area, reaching more than 8 inches total length. Trautman reported a 9.3-inch fish from Ohio. Our largest specimens are 133 mm standard length.

Habitat
Striped shiners occur in a variety of habitats from small streams with moderate gradients to larger streams with pools and riffles. It is most common in clear, weedless areas over gravel or rubble bottom. It avoids riffles and very quiet areas and prefers deeper sections with a slight current. Usually, it is not common in lakes but in the northern part of its range it sometimes lives over gravel or rubble along windswept shores.

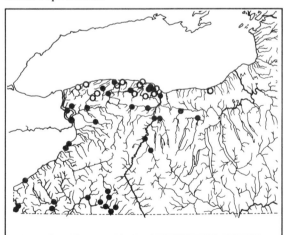

Distribution
The striped shiner is a Mississippi Valley and Great Lakes fish. It ranges from western New York and the lower Great Lakes (it is not in Lake Superior) to southeast Wisconsin and south to the Coosa River in Alabama and Georgia, and west to Arkansas and

eastern Oklahoma. In the South, *Notropis chrysocephalus chrysocephalus* is replaced by *N. c. isolepis*.

In New York, the typical subspecies occurs in the Allegheny, Lake Erie and western Lake Ontario watersheds, including the northern end of the Finger Lakes which it could have reached through the Erie Canal and Seneca Canal system.

Life History
The spawning habits of the striped shiner are essentially the same as those of the common shiner except that the striped shiner seems to spawn at higher temperature. Both species spawn over gravel in riffle areas of streams.

Food and Feeding
Aquatic insects and their larvae dominate the diet with some plant material as well. It can take food off the bottom but usually feeds in the upper part of the water column.

Notes
Hubbs (1921a) regarded the striped shiner as a subspecies of the common shiner but Gilbert treated it as a full species. Menzel concluded from a study of blood proteins of the two forms that they should be considered subspecies. We treat it as a full species because it frequently occurs sympatrically with the common shiner and is readily distinguished from that species with little or no evidence of intergradation.

References
Gilbert, 1961; 1964 (systematics). Menzel, 1976 (systematics); 1978 (hybridization). Marshall, 1939 (annulus formation). Gillen and Hart, 1980 (food competition). Kott, McCauley and Humphreys, 1980 (comparisons).

Names
Chrysocephalus is from the Greek *chryson*, gold and *kephale*, head.

Luxilus chrysocephalus Rafinesque, 1820a: 48 Kentucky

Notropis cornutus chrysocephalus, Greeley, 1927: 60 Genesee watershed

Notropis chrysocephalus chrysocephalus, Gilbert, 1964: 157-167

Notropis megalotis frontalis (non Agassiz) Meek, 1889: 307 Cayuga Lake

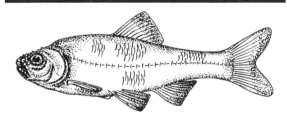

COMMON SHINER

Notropis cornutus (Mitchill, 1817)

Identification
The common shiner is large and deep bodied for a

Notropis and has large vertically elongate scales, nine anal rays, and 2,4-4,2 teeth. It has a dark peritoneum and the splint-like ray at the front of the dorsal fin is quite well developed and sometimes separated from the first principal ray by a membrane. In larger adults, there are patches of dark, regenerated scales on the sides of the body.

The common shiner slightly resembles the redfin shiner but the redfin has much smaller scales and a spot at the front of the dorsal base. It looks a little like the satinfin and spotfin shiners which are also rather compressed, deep-bodied species but they both have firm, regular scales and pigment on the posterior dorsal fin membranes.

It looks most like the striped shiner and, indeed, the two are so close that they have been considered as subspecies. They differ in color pattern, definite zig-zag stripes on the dorsal surface of the striped shiner, and in the size of the predorsal scales. Where they occur together, the striped shiner has more pigment on the chin than the common shiner but this does not hold true for populations from other parts of their ranges.

Description

Body elongate, deepest in front of the dorsal fin, slab sided to moderately compressed. Dorsal origin considerably nearer tip of snout than base of tail. Dorsal retrogressive, with straight margin and rounded corners. Caudal moderately forked, with bluntly pointed lobes. Anal origin below distal fourth of depressed last dorsal ray. Anal similar to dorsal. Pelvic insertion below dorsal origin. Pelvic retrogressive, with convex margin. Pelvic axillary process somewhat developed. Pectoral low, slightly oblique, retrogressive, bluntly pointed. Gill membranes moderately attached to isthmus. Mouth terminal, oblique. Lateral line complete, decurved anteriorly. Lateral scales deep, thin. Counts and proportional measurements are given in Table 16.

Color: Body olive dorsally, shading to silvery on the sides and white on the belly. Scales of the upper predorsal sides weakly outlined, dark segmental blood vessels sometimes visible. A prominent narrow pale stripe on third row of scales above the lateral line is pale greenish gold in life. Middorsal stripe broad and distinct, widening along the base of the dorsal fin, prominent behind the dorsal. Dorsal and caudal rays with dark outlines. Anal and pelvic fins mostly unpigmented. Pectoral with some pigment along its anterior rays.

Juveniles and breeding adults: Postlarval common shiners have two rows of large melanophores on the dorsal surface. Breeding males become brilliant with broad red bands on all fins edged by a narrow clear area. Paired fins suffused with red, with a clear margin and milky white leading edge. The base of the dorsal, caudal, and pectoral fins dusky, base of anal white. Branchiostegal membranes and lower parts of cheeks and opercula red, this color continuing on the sides of the body as a narrow red band. Middorsal stripe and a paler streak on the upper sides are silver to bright green.

Large breeding tubercles are present on the head and anterior parts of the body, and on the pectoral fins.

Size: This is a rather large species and individuals 6 to 6.5 inches in total length are not uncommon. Our largest New York specimens are 136 mm standard length.

Habitat

The common shiner lives in small- to moderate-sized streams. Trautman has suggested that it is less tolerant of silt than the striped shiner.

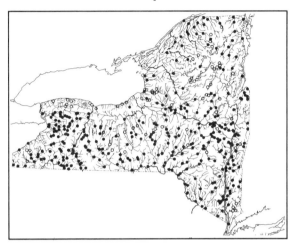

Distribution

The range of the common shiner is a broad band from the Gaspé Peninsula across southern Canada to Saskatchewan and south in the Mississippi and Ohio drainages to Kansas and Missouri, and on the Atlantic coast south to the James River. It occurs throughout New York State.

Life History

Raney described the life history of the common shiner in streams near Ithaca. Spawning begins when the water temperature reaches 60 to 65 F, usually between 1 May and 15 July (rarely as late as July). Usually, there is some movement from the wintering sites in deep pools to shallow riffles. The common shiner utilizes at least three distinct habitats for spawning and this is probably one of the reasons for its wide distribution. It appears to prefer to spawn over the nests of other species including the creek chub, fallfish, river chubs, hornyhead chub, and stonerollers. If such nests are not available, it will spawn over gravel beds, or excavate depressions in gravel or sand in running water.

Groups of males assemble in the spawning area and vie for position at the head of the site, that is, farthest upstream. Females are usually more abundant in the spawning area and not as dispersed as the males. When a female is ready to spawn, she moves upstream to a position just downstream from a male and higher in the water column. Raney suggested that the male recognizes the female by the presence of a conspicuous white area around her anal region. The female then moves down beside the male and places her snout at the anterior edge of his pectoral fin. In response, the male slips his pectoral fin under her head and throws his caudal peduncle over hers. This pushes her down with her head toward shore and her ventral surface upstream. The male flexes his body until it is in a U-shape around hers. At this time, the eggs are released, then the female straightens out and darts toward the surface. The female drifts downstream briefly, then returns to spawn again, usually with a different male. The male takes his old position on the riffle. Each spawning act takes less than 1 second and one male spawned 20 times in 10 minutes. Dominant males may hold the lead position for as long as 20 minutes, but usually they retreat downstream and rest after spawning for about 10 minutes. Raney thought that only a few eggs were laid at a time, probably less than 50. The current over the nest is slowed by the nest and the eggs drop into crevices. Other species of minnows in the area try to eat the newly released eggs and are attacked by the spawning males. The newly laid eggs are orange and 1.5 mm in diameter.

Food and Feeding
The common shiner takes a variety of food including some plant material. It usually feeds near the surface but will also feed on the bottom. Insects and insect larvae are the dominant food but other organisms from protozoans to small fishes are sometimes eaten.

Notes
Gilbert considered the striped shiner and the common shiner to be full species and I concur in this although Menzel suggested that the blood serum protein patterns indicate that they should be treated as subspecies.

References
Buynak and Mohr, 1980b (larval development). Greenfield et al., 1973 (hybridization with *Chrosomus*). Rainboth and Whitt, 1978 (biochemical systematics). Ryer, 1938 (life history). Raney, 1940b (spawning); 1940c (hybrids). Gilbert, 1964 (systematics). Fee, 1965 (life history). Menzel, 1976 (taxonomy). Page and Magnin, 1978 (biology). Cooper, 1960 (lethal oxygen levels). Ulvestad and Zar, 1977 (temperature). Gilbert, 1961 (systematics). Sheppard, 1969 (life history, Ontario). Buth, 1979 (biochemical systematics). Leonard, 1927 (food). Miller, 1964 (breeding behavior); 1968 (species). Ferguson and Noakes, 1981 (social groupings).

Names
Cornutus is the Latin word for horned, in reference to the breeding tubercles.

Cyprinus cornutus Mitchill, 1817a: 289 Wallkill River

Leuciscus cornutus, DeKay, 1842: 207-208 New York

Luxilus cornutus, Mather, 1886: 28-29 Adirondacks

Notropis cornutus cornutus, Gilbert, 1964: 140 et seq. (systematics)

Cyprinus megalops Rafinesque, 1817b: 121 Hudson River

Notropis megalops, Meek, 1889: 307 Cayuga Lake

Cyprinus melanurus Rafinesque, 1817b: 121 Hudson River

Cyprinus trivittatus Rafinesque, 1820b: 6 Fish Creek and Wallkill River

Cyprinus haematopterus Rafinesque, 1820b: 6 Hudson River

Leuciscus vittatus, DeKay, 1842: 212 Mohawk River

Leuciscus frontalis Agassiz, 1850: 368-370 Montreal River; Keweena Pond

Notropis cornutus frontalis, Greeley, 1928: 98 Oswego watershed

Notropis cornutus chrysocephalus, Greeley, 1937: 95 Lower Hudson watershed (misidentification)

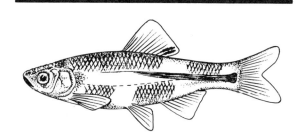

SPOTFIN SHINER
Notropis spilopterus (Cope, 1868)

Identification
The spotfin shiner is a somewhat compressed minnow with firm diamond-shaped scales and dark pigment on the last membranes of the dorsal fin. There is a gray midlateral stripe on the posterior part of the body and in large individuals, a narrow, tapering vertical bar behind the base of the pectoral fin.

The spotfin is very similar to the satinfin but the two are easily distinguished by anal fin ray count: eight in the spotfin and nine in the satinfin. The satinfin has scattered pigment throughout the dorsal fin membranes; the spotfin has clear membranes except for the definite spots at the back of the fin.

The spotfin has 37 to 39 lateral line scales; the satinfin has 35 to 37.

Description
Body moderately deep and slab sided. Profiles equally curved. Dorsal origin midway between caudal base and tip of snout. Dorsal retrogressive, with straight margin and slightly rounded corners. Caudal moderately forked, with rounded lobes. Anal origin below basal half of depressed last dorsal ray. Anal margin concave, its anterior corner rounded, posterior acute. Pelvic insertion slightly ahead of the dorsal origin. Pelvic axillary process small but distinct. Pelvic retrogressive, with convex margin and rounded corners. Pectoral base low, slightly oblique. Pectoral retrogressive, somewhat pointed. Gill membranes slightly joined to isthmus. Mouth terminal. Lateral line complete, somewhat decurved an-

teriorly. Counts and proportional measurements are given in Table 16.

Color: Generally silvery, darker above, shading to white on the belly. Scales of the back and upper side boldly margined in black, forming a regular pattern. Midlateral stripe gray, developed only on posterior part of the body. Middorsal stripe narrow, widening at the dorsal origin. A deep, narrow, dark bar on midline of lower jaw. Top of head gray to side of snout and upper part of gill cover. Upper lip darker than tip of snout. Dark bar on the shoulder in the form of a narrow inverted triangle.

Breeding adults: Breeding males develop dark pigment and become steel blue. The midlateral stripe becomes darker and widens until it occupies the middle third of the side of the caudal peduncle. Dorsal and caudal fins develop a yellowish wash; anal and paired fins become deep yellow. Anterior corners of dorsal and pelvic fins white, margin of anal fin white.

Breeding tubercles are prominent on top of the head with a separate patch on the snout. Middorsal region with smaller tubercles than those of the head, becoming even smaller in front of the dorsal fin. Lower jaw with a single row of tubercles on each side. Scales of the back and sides and the caudal peduncle with a curved row of small tubercles along the margin or each scale. Belly without tubercles. Tubercles on the upper surface of each pectoral and pelvic ray and on both sides of the rays of the dorsal, caudal, and anal fins, those of the anal fin the largest.

Size: To 4.2 inches total length. Our largest specimen is 87 mm standard length.

Habitat

The spotfin lives in lakes and in small to moderately large creeks. It appears to be quite tolerant of silty and turbid conditions. We have collected breeding males in the abandoned Erie Canal near Vischer Ferry.

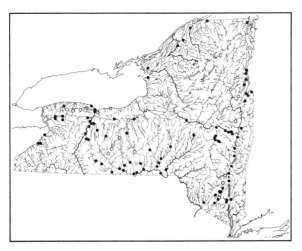

Distribution

The eastern subspecies, *N. s. spilopterus,* ranges through the Ohio River and its tributaries from the Tennessee River in northern Alabama to the Wabash in Indiana and eastern Illinois, and east to Pennsylvania and western New York in the Allegheny system. In the Great Lakes, it occurs from eastern Michigan to the St. Lawrence near Montreal and south on the Atlantic coast to the Potomac River system. In western Michigan and Wisconsin, it intergrades with *N. s. hypsisomatus,* a deeper bodied form that ranges through the Upper Mississippi system from Minnesota to northeastern Oklahoma.

In New York, it is widespread but absent from the Upper Genesee, the Adirondacks, and Tug Hill.

Life History

The spawning season in the Susquehanna River near Port Trevinton, Pennsylvania, extended from mid-June to mid-August. The spotfin spawns in horizontal crevices in rocks and logs. Spawning groups of 10 to 30 fish, usually more females than males, gather at a suitable site. The males establish territories that include one or more crevices which can be as short as 2 cm but are usually longer. Defense of the territory includes fights where one male tries to grasp the pelvic or anal fin of the other and drag it away from the site. If each fish grabs the other, they swim in a circle with increasing speed until they can no longer hang on. The fins, especially the dorsal, are erected as a display before the attack begins.

After the territory is set up, the male makes one or more display passes along the crevice, vibrating his body and extending his pectoral fins and sometimes the tail and caudal peduncle into the crevice. He then swims to a group of females and entices one female toward the crevice. Females ready to spawn make a prespawning pass along the crevice and then both partners swim along the crevice with the female slightly ahead and closer to the crevice. The fish turn on their sides if the crevice is horizontal. The presence of another male usually interrupts the spawning but occasionally a female or even another male is allowed to join the spawning pair. Males spawned in the same crevice several times with the same or with different females. Usually, the female stops spawning before the male ceases making display passes. The sight of a displaying female stimulates the male to spawn, thus the female selects the crevices in some cases.

Prespawning behavior may take an hour before spawning or only a few minutes. Spotfins are fractional spawners and spawn at intervals of 1 to 7 days, 5 days is the most common interval between spawnings. Up to three groups of eggs may be released during one spawning session. One female spawned 31 groups of eggs, each containing 10 to 97 eggs. Adults sometimes fed on eggs flushed from the crevices before they became attached to its walls.

Food and Feeding

White and Wallace found that spotfins in the Huron River, Michigan, fed near the bottom during the day and nearer the surface at dawn and dusk when the feeding was most intense. During the daylight hours, trichopterans were the most important food but at night dipterans were the dominant food. Other insects, including coleopterans, lepidopterans, and terrestrial hymenopterans were a smaller part of the diet. The major peak in stomach fullness occurred around 9 pm.

References
Hankinson, 1930 (breeding). Stone, 1940 (life history). Gibbs, 1957 (systematics). Pfleiger, 1965 (reproductive behavior). Gale and Gale, 1976 (spawning sites); 1977 (spawning). Mendelson, 1975 (feeding relationships). White and Wallace, 1973 (feeding). Snyder et al., 1977 (identification of larvae).

Names
Spilopterus is from the Greek *spilos*, spot, and *pteron*, wing or fin.

Leuciscus spilopterus Cope *in* Gunther, 1868: 254 St. Joseph River, Michigan

Notropis whipplei spilopterus, Greeley, 1929: 171 Erie-Niagara watershed

Notropis whipplei, (non Girard), Meek, 1889: 307 (part, those specimens from Cayuga Lake)

Notropis whipplei, (non Girard) Evermann and Goldsborough, 1902: 172 Chautauqua Lake tributaries

Notropis spilopterus spilopterus, Gibbs, 1957: 186 et seq. (general account)

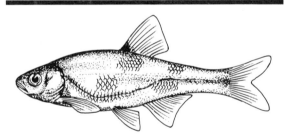

REDFIN SHINER

Notropis umbratilis (Girard, 1857)

Identification
The redfin is a deep-bodied, rather compressed species with 10 to 12 anal rays and a pronounced concentration of dark pigment at the base of the anterior rays of the dorsal fin. The scales of the predorsal area are small and do not have dark margins, so they are inconspicuous. The segmental blood vessels appear as dark lines under the skin of the upper sides in front of the dorsal fin.

Redfins are somewhat similar to the cyprinellas, the spotfin and satinfin shiners, but those species have conspicuously outlined scales and dark pigment on the last rays of the dorsal fin.

The striped shiner and the common shiner are also rather similar but in those species the dorsal fin origin is over, or in front of, the pelvic insertions, whereas the dorsal of the redfin originates behind the pelvic insertion.

It also resembles the golden shiner in its shape and long anal fin but the golden shiner has larger scales, a decurved lateral line, and a fleshy keel in front of the anus.

Description
Body deep and moderately compressed for a species of *Notropis*. Profiles equally curved. Dorsal origin midway between caudal base and front of eye. Dorsal retrogressive, with straight margin and acute corners. Caudal moderately forked, with pointed lobes. Anal insertion below middle of depressed last dorsal ray. Anal margin concave with sharp corners. Pelvic insertion anterior to dorsal origin. Pelvics retrogressive, with straight margin. Anterior corner rounded, posterior sharp. Pelvic axillary process small but distinct. Pectoral base low, oblique. Pectoral retrogressive, rather pointed. Gill membranes slightly joined to isthmus. Head pointed, mouth terminal, oblique. Breast and prepectoral naked. Lateral line complete, decurved. Counts and proportional measurements are given in Table 16.

Color: Upper sides pale olive with the individual scales not outlined and therefore not apparent. Sides silvery, shading to white below. Midlateral stripe weakly developed on caudal peduncle. Mid-dorsal stripe diffuse but expanded at the anterior of the dorsal base. Dark pigment along anal base. Fins clear, with a dark spot at the base of the anterior dorsal rays. Sometimes, the body is crossed by 4 to 11 faint, diffuse vertical bands. These are often conspicuous in breeding males.

Juveniles and breeding adults: Males become almost steel blue on the body and intense blue on top of the head. The caudal fin and anal become intense red, the dorsal and paired fins reddish. Moderate-sized tubercles are present on top and sides of head, the predorsal and upper sides of the body and on the lower jaw and cheeks. Females sometimes develop a few tubercles.

Size: To about 3.2 inches total length.

Habitat
The redfin shows a preference for streams with moderate or low gradient over sand and gravel bottom with some vegetation.

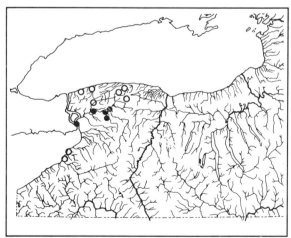

Distribution
This species reaches its northeastern limit in the Great Lakes drainages of western New York where

it is present in tributaries along the Lake Erie and Lake Ontario Plains. The subspecies *cyanocephalus* ranges from Texas and Louisiana through the eastern tributaries of the Mississippi to southeastern Minnesota and southern Ontario. Its overall range extends southwestward into the central Mississippi region where it intergrades with *N. u. umbratilis* in west-central Arkansas.

Life History

The reproductive behavior of the redfin shiner was studied in Wisconsin by Hunter and Hasler and by Hunter and Wisby. In the introduced populations they studied, the redfins spawned over nests of the green sunfish, *Lepomis cyanellus*. Male redfins defended territories over the sunfish nests, 5 to 8 cm above the bottom. Solitary males defended large territories but when several males were present the territories were smaller. Small males crowded at the periphery of the spawning areas or above the territories of the larger males. Defending males chased and butted intruders. Sometimes, two males swam parallel to each other for as much as 2 meters, butting each other as they went.

Females remained outside the clusters of territorial males. As the female approached, a male would join her and they would swim together, undulating wildly as the spawning took place. Most of the spawning took place between 10 am and 2:30 pm.

Sometimes, the shiners formed dense aggregations in which the males' territories were only slightly larger in diameter than their length. Females swam through these aggregations and spawning occurred in the midst of the males fighting and chasing each other. Aggregation occurred most frequently when the sunfish were spawning and the redfin shiners were not pursued by the male sunfishes although bluegills and other species of shiners were. Hunter and Hasler postulated that the redfin shiners were not bothered because their territories were maintained above the bottom. This suggests that the association of the shiners and the green sunfish is a normal occurrence. Milt and ovarian fluid from the sunfish attracted the shiners and triggered spawning behavior and it was suggested that the shiners depend on the presence of spawning sunfish for initiating their spawning activities.

In Ohio, Trautman found redfin shiners spawning over sand and gravel in sluggish riffles and pools with some current. Outside of the spawning season the redfins preferred pools with some vegetation.

Food and Feeding

Not reported.

Notes

This species is uncommon in New York and appears to be present in fewer localities than it was a few years ago.

References

Hunter and Wisby, 1961 (spawning). Hunter and Hasler, 1965 (reproductive behavior). Snelson and Pfleiger, 1975 (taxonomy). Snelson, 1972 (systematics).

Names

The species name *umbratilis* is from the Latin *umbratus*, shading or spreading over from *umbro*, shade. The subspecies name *cyanocephalus* is from the Greek *kyaneos*, dark blue and *kephale*, head.

Alburnellus umbratilis Girard, 1857: 193 Poteau River, Arkansas

Notropis umbratilis, Greeley, 1928: 98 Oswego watershed

Notropis lythrurus (non Jordan), Meek, 1889: 307 Montezuma

Notropis umbratilis lythrurus, Bean, 1903: 151-152 (after Meek)

Lythrurus cyanocephalus Copeland *in* Jordan, 1877a: 70-71 Wisconsin

Notropis umbratilis cyanocephalus, Greeley, 1929: 132 Erie-Niagara watershed

TABLE 16
AVERAGE PROPORTIONAL MEASUREMENTS AND COUNTS OF DEEP-BODIED SHINERS (subgenera *Luxilus, Cyprinella,* and *Lythrurus*)

All proportions are expressed in percentage of standard length.

	Luxilus		*Cyprinella*		*Lythrurus*
	cornutus	chryso-cephalus	analostanus	spilopterus	umbratilis
ST. LENGTH (mm)	82.6	79.5	58.5	73.6	42.8
TOTAL LENGTH	124.1	125.4	131.2	124.9	125.6
FORK LENGTH	114.1	114.2	121.1	113.5	114.5
PREDORSAL	50.5	49.4	56.0	53.5	54.1
PREANAL	66.1	67.7	71.3	66.7	64.5
PREPELVIC	48.0	48.8	53.7	50.9	49.4
DORSAL BASE	12.4	10.9	13.2	12.6	12.0
ANAL BASE	11.2	9.3	13.3	11.8	16.0
BODY DEPTH	26.3	25.1	26.1	25.2	25.3
BODY WIDTH	13.3	14.6	14.8	13.8	13.1
C.PED. DEPTH	9.7	9.7	12.8	11.4	10.0
PECTORAL ALT.	19.5	18.3	19.6	18.8	18.8
HEAD LENGTH	25.4	25.1	28.1	24.6	25.3
SNOUT	6.9	7.6	8.7	8.0	6.9
EYE	6.5	6.3	7.1	6.2	7.6
MOUTH LENGTH	7.2	8.2	5.4	7.4	8.1
INTERORB	8.4	8.0	5.4	8.9	7.6
N (sample size)	5	5	5	5	5
COUNTS:					
DORSAL RAYS	8	8	8	8	8
ANAL RAYS	9	(8)9	9	8	11
PECTORAL RAYS	15-17	13-14	13-15	12-13	—
PELVIC RAYS	9	8	8	8	8
GILL RAKERS	6-9	10-11	8-11	5-8	8-10
VERTEBRAE*	35-36	35-36	32-33	34-35	32-33
SCALES:					
ABOVE L. L.	7-8	7-10	6	6	7-8
LATERAL LINE	39-44	37-41	35-37	34-41	39-46
BELOW L. L.	5	4-5	4	4	4
PHARYNGEAL TEETH	2,4-4,2	2,4-4,2	1,4-4,1	1,4-4,1	2,4-4,2

* Excluding Weberian apparatus.

The Species of *Notropis* with Distinct Midlateral Stripes

Six of our species of *Notropis* have more or less distinct stripes along the sides and these stripes continue forward to the tip of the snout. In life, however, the stripes are sometimes masked with silvery pigment so they may not always be conspicuous. All of these species are rather small, terete fishes. The males of *anogenus*, *heterodon* and *bifrenatus* become bright golden during the breeding season. *N. anogenus* and *N. heterodon* are very similar except that *anogenus* has a tiny, nearly vertical mouth. *N. chalybaeus* is the darkest species and has pigment within its mouth. *Notropis heterolepis* is somewhat larger than the other species in this group and has pigment above and below the lateral line pores emphasized so that it forms a series of darker crescents within the dark lateral stripe.

Notropis procne has the least well developed midlateral stripe. Not only is it rather weakly developed on the body but it is interrupted on the side of the head behind the eye and again across the tip of the snout. *N. procne* also has 4-4 pharyngeal teeth and seven anal rays.

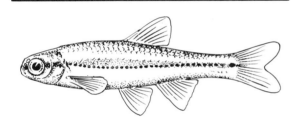

PUGNOSE SHINER

Notropis anogenus Forbes, 1885

Identification
The unmistakable feature of the pugnose shiner is its tiny mouth that is almost vertical so that the lower jaw opens like the ramp of a military landing craft.

The only other North American minnow with such a small mouth is the pugnose minnow, *Notropis emiliae*, and while that species has been recorded from the Ohio section of Lake Erie, it has never been reported from New York. The pugnose minnow has nine dorsal rays and 5-5 pharyngeal teeth whereas the pugnose shiner has eight dorsal rays and 4-4 teeth.

The pugnose is a small species with a pronounced dark midlateral stripe. It is most similar to the blackchin shiner, *Notropis heterodon*, and I have not been able to distinguish them in the field. Both have concentrations of pigment that produce a zig-zag pattern in the lateral stripe and dark pigment at the tip of the lower jaw. Under magnification, however, the mouth feature is definite and the blackchin has a more definite postanal fin and a pale peritoneum. The pugnose has an obsolescent postanal stripe and a dark peritoneum that shows through the body wall of preserved specimens.

Description
Body slender, little compressed. Profiles symmetrical. Dorsal origin midway between caudal base and front of eye. Dorsal retrogressive, deltoid, with straight margin and rounded corners. Caudal moderately forked, with rounded lobes. Anal origin behind tip of depressed last dorsal ray. Anal similar to dorsal. Pelvic insertion slightly ahead of dorsal origin. Pelvic axillary process small. Pelvic retrogressive, rounded. Pectoral base low, somewhat oblique. Pectoral retrogressive, rounded. Head blunt, mouth nearly vertical. Gill membranes slightly attached to isthmus. Lateral line complete, slightly decurved anteriorly. Eyes large, lateral. Counts and proportional measurements are given in Table 17.

Color: In life, this species is silver with the scales of the dorsal surface boldly outlined with dark pigment. Midlateral stripe even, extending from tip of snout through the eye and across the cheek and opercle to the base of the tail, with a partially separated pear-shaped spot the same width on the base of the caudal rays. There is a conspicuous unpigmented area above the lateral stripe separating it from the outlined scales of the back. Belly clear white, with the centers of the scales silvery. All fins hyaline, rays of vertical fins with dark margins. Central rays of caudal with a little more pigment forming a continuation of the midlateral stripe.

Juveniles and breeding adults: Breeding males are bright yellow above the lateral stripe, with tubercles on top of the head, the dorsal surface of the pectoral rays and sometimes on the first pelvic rays.
Size: The largest specimen reported by Trautman was 2.2 inches total length. Our largest New York specimen is 35.6 mm standard length.

Habitat
The pugnose shiner lives in dense aquatic vegetation in slow waters of larger streams.

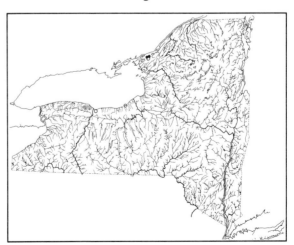

Distribution
Like the brassy minnow, *Hybognathus hankinsoni*, the pugnose shiner occurs in a narrow band from the St. Lawrence River in New York to North Da-

kota. In New York, it has been reported from Iron-dequoit Bay, Little Sodus Bay, and French Creek near Clayton, New York. In 1976 and 1983, it was collected in Eel Bay in the St. Lawrence River.

Life History
The life history has not been studied. It spawns in June and July in Michigan.

Food and Feeding
Its small mouth suggests a specialized mode of feeding but, surprisingly, this has not been studied.

Notes
The pugnose shiner has strict habitat requirements and is therefore a good indicator of environmental quality.

References
Bailey, 1959 (taxonomy, distribution). Raney, 1969 (popular summary).

Names
Anogenus is from the Greek *an*, without and the Latin *gena*, chin.

Notropis anogenus Forbes, 1885: 138-139 Fox River, Illinois

Notropis anogenus, Greeley and Bishop, 1932: 84 near Clayton, New York

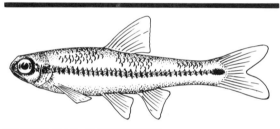

BRIDLE SHINER

Notropis bifrenatus (Cope, 1869)

Identification
The bridle shiner is a small species with a large eye and a distinct even-width stripe from the tip of the snout to the base of the tail. It has an incomplete lateral line, 4-4 pharyngeal teeth, and seven anal rays. The scales of the predorsal region are large, regular, and have distinct dark outlines.

Five other species of shiners in New York are similar but readily distinguished as follows: *Notropis anogenus*, the pugnose shiner, has a tiny, nearly vertical mouth. *Notropis procne*, the swallowtail shiner, has the midlateral stripe interrupted behind the eye. *Notropis heterodon*, the blackchin shiner, has the tip of the lower jaw pigmented and eight anal rays. *Notropis heterolepis*, the blacknose shiner, has eight anal rays and crescentic marks in the lateral line, and *Notropis chalybaeus*, the iron-color shiner, has pigment on the inside of the mouth.

Description
Body slender and elongate, the profiles equally curved. Dorsal fin inserted nearer snout than base of caudal. Dorsal deltoid, retrogressive, with straight margin and softly angled corners. Caudal moderately forked, with bluntly pointed lobes. Anal origin below tip of depressed last dorsal ray, its shape similar to that of dorsal. Pelvic inserted below anterior part of dorsal base. Pelvic axillary process small but distinct. Pelvics retrogressive, with convex margin and bluntly pointed corners. Pectoral base low, slightly oblique. Pectoral retrogressive, its corners blunt. Gill membranes narrowly joined to the isthmus. Mouth terminal, oblique. Lateral line short, ending before the dorsal origin. Counts and proportional measurements are given in Table 17.

Color: In life, the bridle shiner is transparent yellow above the midlateral stripe and silvery white below. The midlateral stripe continues forward to the tip of the snout and the center of the upper lip but does not include the lower jaw. The fins are hyaline, with the rays outlined by melanophores.

Juveniles and breeding adults: Males are bright golden dorsally and even more intense yellow on the sides below the lateral band. Females are silvery white, with some pale straw color dorsally. The dorsal and caudal fins have a yellow tinge in both sexes. Dark pigment along the edges of the dorsal scales and anterior pectoral rays becomes more pronounced in breeding males.

Size: To about 2 inches total length.

Habitat
The bridle shiner is a widespread species that lives in warm, still, or slow-moving waters of small streams and ponds and the slow parts of larger lakes and rivers. It is usually found over mud, silt, or debris and prefers areas of moderate amounts of vegetation. It is sometimes found in slightly brackish water in the southern part of its range.

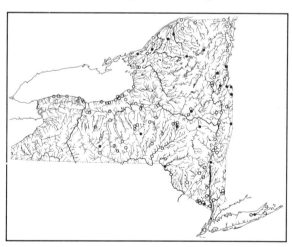

Distribution
This is an Atlantic coast species ranging from eastern New Hampshire to the Rappahannock, York, James and Chowan drainages of Virginia and the Neuse River of eastern North Carolina.

In New York, it occurs throughout the eastern part of the state and west along the south shore of Lake Ontario to west of Rochester. It occurs in the Peconic and other streams of eastern Long Island. It does not occur in or west of the Genesee.

Life History
The breeding behavior of this species was studied by Harrington. Spawning took place between 22 May and 31 July. (2 May to August at Ithaca, June and July in Connecticut). The water temperature varied between 58 and 80 F. The spawning sites were located in water about 2 feet deep in openings surrounded by dense emergent vegetation, usually over *Myriophyllum* or *Chara,* where there was no perceptible current. Spawning activity usually began before daylight and was most vigorous between 7 am and 2 pm.

Females were pursued by males, which were usually smaller. Before spawning, the females hovered nearly motionless close to the surface. The males bumped their snouts along the females' lower sides and snouts. If the female was not ready to spawn, she moved away and resumed feeding. A few days later, there were chases which appeared to be the spawning act. Usually, one male would start to chase the female and one or two other males would join the chase. Sometimes, a male would discontinue the pursuit to chase another male and sometimes a male would switch to another female. Normally, the pursuits lasted about 1 second to about 1 minute during which they covered a distance of several meters. As the chase proceeded, the males bumped the females with their snouts. The chase appeared to end in a slight curve with the female flanked by two or sometimes only one male. At times, several pursuits would be going on at once in a small area with complex interactions. Although other species such as small chubsuckers and golden shiners were chased from time to time, no regular territories were held. Spawning apparently occurred many times during the day and only a few eggs were released each time. The eggs sank to the bottom and adhered to the vegetation. Water-hardened eggs were approximately 1.5 mm in diameter and hatched in 57 hours at 75 F. The newly hatched young, about 5 mm long, remained in the vegetation at first, then began to swim in small groups. By late July, they were in schools of 100 or more and by August when they were about 22 mm standard length, they joined schools of adult fish.

Food and Feeding
Harrington reported on the food habits of 200 individuals from New Hampshire and Ithaca. Feeding is by sight and occurs only during daylight hours. Most of the feeding was observed where the water was still or there was a slight current. Food was taken from plant surfaces and the bottom; plankton organisms were taken on or near vegetation. Small insects were the most important items, constituting 36 percent of the volume and in 73 percent of the stomachs. Crustaceans made up another 24 percent of the volume. Amphipods, water mites, mollusks, and plant materials were also taken in significant quantities.

References
Harrington, 1947a (distribution, life history); 1947b (breeding); 1948a (life cycle); 1948b (food); 1955 (osteology). Jenkins and Zorach, 1970 (systematics and distribution). Hubbs and Raney, 1947 (comparisons).

Names
Bifrenatus is from the Latin *bio,* two and *frenatus,* bridled. I assume this refers to the stripes on the head that resemble a horse's bridle.

Hybopsis bifrenatus Cope, 1869a: 384-385 Schuylkill River, Pennsylvania

Notropis cayuga Meek, 1889: 305 Cayuga Lake and Fall Creek at Ithaca, New York (The type series included *bifrenatus, heterodon,* and *analostanus.* Hubbs, 1926: 41, restricted the name *cayuga* to *N. bifrenatus.)*

IRONCOLOR SHINER
Notropis chalybaeus (Cope, 1869)

Identification
The ironcolor shiner is a small minnow with a prominent midlateral stripe and large eyes. It has eight anal rays and 1,4-4,1 teeth, and an incomplete lateral line. Its most distinctive feature is the presence of pigment inside the mouth, on the oral valves, the inner sides of the jaws, and the roof and floor of the mouth.

Notropis procne and *bifrenatus* have seven anal rays and 4-4 teeth. *N. heterolepis* has a pale chin, *anogenus* has a tiny mouth, and *heterodon* has a complete lateral line and a more oblique mouth.

Description
Body elongate, somewhat slab sided. Ventral profile slightly more curved than the dorsal. Dorsal origin midway between caudal base and anterior nostril. Dorsal deltoid, retrogressive, with straight margin and angulate corners. Caudal forked, with rounded lobes. Anal origin below distal half of depressed last dorsal ray. Anal retrogressive, with concave margin and sharp corners. Pelvic origin below dorsal origin. Pelvic axillary process small. Pelvic retrogressive, its margin convex with angulate corners. Pectoral base low, slightly oblique. Pectoral retrogressive, bluntly pointed anteriorly and rounded posteriorly. Gill membranes connected to the isthmus. Mouth oblique, terminal, jaws equal. Eye large. Breast and prepectoral naked. Lateral line incomplete, slightly decurved anteriorly. Counts and proportional measurements are given in Table 17.

Color: Dark olive dorsally with the scales prominently outlined ahead of the dorsal fin, less so behind. Midlateral stripe broad, complete from tip of lower jaw and snout to base of tail. Lower sides and belly white. Fin rays distinctly outlined. Peritoneum pale. Melanophores present on oral valves, roof, and anterior part of the floor of the mouth.

Juveniles and breeding adults: Male ironcolor shiners develop an orange or rosy wash over the entire body including the dark dorsal area. The breeding colors vary with the environment; those from reddish-brown water are orange and those from clear water are rosy. The color is intense on the dorsal and caudal fins but less so on the anal and pelvic fins. Color is present on the pectoral fins and quite intense on the ventral surface of the caudal peduncle. Females and nonbreeding males may have a trace of color but it is much less intense. Breeding tubercles develop on the chin, the anterior part of the snout, and in small patches arranged in bands on the pectoral fin rays.

Size: The maximum length is slightly more than 2 inches.

Habitat

Notropis chalybaeus, like the other black-striped species of *Notropis*, is essentially a fish of slow, weedy areas, but it can tolerate a wide variety of stream habitats and is sometimes found where there is considerable current. Usually, however, it is found in deeper pools, often where the water is deeply stained and there is considerable vegetation or debris for shelter.

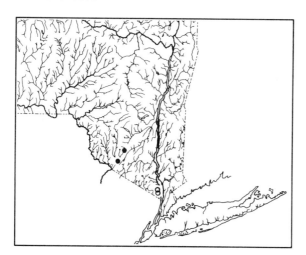

Distribution

This species has an overall distribution in the lower parts of coastal streams from southeastern New York to peninsular Florida, across the gulf coast and up the Mississippi Valley to southern Illinois, with apparently disjunct populations in northern Illinois, Iowa, Wisconsin, Indiana, and southern Michigan. This is an incomplete ring surrounding the Appalachian Highlands. Gerking suggested it entered the Tippecanoe River by glacial connections and continued to the St. Joseph River in southern Michigan.

In New York, it is common in the Basher Kill and was reported from the Hackensack River but I have not been able to verify its presence there.

Life History

Marshall studied the breeding of this species near Gainesville, Florida, where the spawning season lasted from mid-April to September. (It is likely to be much shorter in New York). The water temperature varied between 57 and 77 F during the breeding season. Most spawning occurred where there was little or no current but no nests were constructed. The males chased the females throughout the daylight hours and, in the laboratory, would resume courtship activities if the lights were turned on after dark. When a female was ready to spawn, she would allow the male to swim close to her; then, with their ventral surfaces close together, the pair would dash across the pool and separate. Marshall was not able to recover the eggs after a spawning rush. Eggs were 0.8 to 0.9 mm in diameter and hatched in 52 to 56 hours at 52 F. The newly hatched larvae were 2.3 mm long.

Food and Feeding

The ironcolor shiner locates its food by sight and feeds in the water column during daylight hours. Insects and other animal material are the main food and plant fragments found in the posterior part of the gut were undigested. Individual microcrustacea fed to captive shiners were found to have been shredded by the hooked pharyngeal teeth.

Notes

The ironcolor shiner is quite abundant in the Basher Kill, although its numbers seems to vary from year to year.

References

Marshall, 1947 (life history). Gerking, 1947 (distribution).

Names

The trivial name *chalybaeus* is a New Latin word meaning steel colored which is derived from the Greek *chalyps*, steel.

Hybopsis chalybaeus Cope, 1869a: 383-384 Schuylkill River near Conshohocken, Pennsylvania

Notropis chalybaeus, Greeley, 1936: 82 Basher Kill

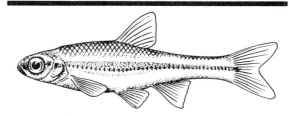

BLACKCHIN SHINER

Notropis heterodon (Cope, 1865)

Identification

The blackchin is a small shiner with a continuous midlateral stripe that continues forward across the opercles and cheeks, through the eye and around the snout and lower jaw. It has a rather large, oblique jaw, eight anal rays and 1,4-4,1 pharyngeal teeth.

In overall size and appearance, it most resembles the pugnose shiner, sharing with that species intensification of pigment on the scales of the lateral line and the row above the lateral line to form a zig-zag pattern within the midlateral stripe. The blacknose shiner has a pigmented chin and crescents, rather than zig-zags, in the lateral stripe. *Notropis procne* and *N. bifrenatus* have 4-4 teeth and seven anal rays. *N. chalybaeus* has pigment inside the mouth and a short lateral line.

Description
Body slender, somewhat slab sided. Dorsal profile more arched than ventral. Dorsal origin closer to snout than base of caudal. Dorsal deltoid, retrogressive, with straight to slightly convex margin rounded anteriorly and angulate posteriorly. Caudal moderately forked, with rounded lobes. Anal origin below outer third of depressed last dorsal ray. Anal retrogressive, with straight margin and angulate corners. Pelvic insertion below dorsal origin. Pelvic axillary process small. Pelvics retrogressive, with rounded corners and slightly convex margin. Pectoral base low, slightly oblique. Pectorals retrogressive, bluntly pointed. Gill membranes slightly joined to the isthmus. Mouth large, oblique, terminal. Lateral line complete or lacking a few scales posteriorly, slightly decurved anteriorly. Counts and proportional measurements are given in Table 17.

Color: Head and body with dark midlateral stripe with superimposed zig-zag line. Stripe interrupted at caudal fold. Back and upper sides light olive, scales of the upper sides with dark margins. A pale stripe above the midlateral stripe. Middorsal line diffuse, more intense at dorsal origin and again at middle of dorsal base, narrow behind the dorsal fin. Belly whitish with a few scattered melanophores along margins of scales of the lower sides. Posterior rim of anus darkly pigmented. Intense pigment along base of anal fin continuing on caudal peduncle as a double line ending at the base of the caudal rays. Upper side of head dusky, eye ring narrow but definite, lower side of head white. All fins with pigment along each ray.

Juveniles and breeding adults: Breeding males are bright golden yellow.

Size: To 2.8 inches total length.

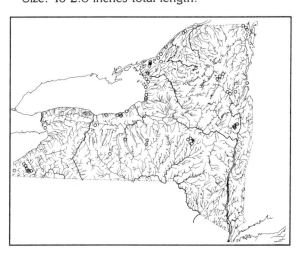

Habitat
The blackchin shiner lives in slow, clear, weedy areas of large streams and the shallow parts of lakes. It appears to be intolerant of silt and is becoming uncommon over much of its range.

Distribution
The blackchin occurs in a narrow band from Lake Champlain to Wisconsin and from the south shore of Lake Superior to northern Indiana, Illinois, and Iowa. There are a few records in the Mississippi and Susquehanna watersheds.

In New York, it is recorded from Chautauqua Lake, the Allegheny, Finger Lakes, St. Lawrence, Lake Champlain drainages, and Otsego and Canadarago Lakes in the Susquehanna watershed. We have collected it only in the St. Lawrence drainage.

Life History
There have been no intensive studies of the life history of the blackchin shiner. Specimens from the northern part of the Lower Peninsula of Michigan were in breeding color in late July.

Food and Feeding
Wilsmann compared the feeding habits of the blackchin shiner to those of the blacknose shiner, *Notropis heterolepis,* in a lake in Michigan where there was evidence that the availability of food was limiting the size of the shiner populations. The blackchin fed on a greater variety of prey and took about half its prey from open water and the other half from vegetation, the surface, and the bottom. In contrast, the blacknose shiner fed primarily on the bottom, with little prey from open water and none from the surface. Prey from the surface of vegetation was particularly important for young blacknose shiners. Wilsmann attributed the ability of the blackchin to eat a greater variety of prey to the terminal position of its mouth, whereas the blacknose has a subterminal mouth suited to feeding on the bottom or from a plant surface.

Keast noted that the blackchin feeds on cladocerans and flying midges taken from the surface of the water.

Notes
Because of its intolerance to silt and its need for dense weed beds, the blackchin is a good indicator of water quality.

References
Wilsmann, 1979 (feeding habits). Keast, 1966 (food).

Names
Heterdon is from the Greek words *heteros,* different and *odontos,* tooth.

Alburnops heterodon Cope, 1865a: 281 Lansing and Grosse Isle, Michigan

Notropis heterodon, Greeley, 1927: 59 Black Creek, Monroe County, Genesee watershed

Notropis anogenus (non Forbes), Reed and Wright, 1909: 395 Fall Creek

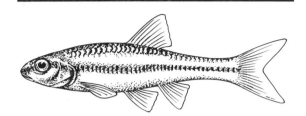

BLACKNOSE SHINER

Notropis heterolepis
Eigenmann and Eigenmann, 1893

Identification
The blacknose shiner has a complete midlateral stripe that is overlain with darker crescents and does not include the lower jaw, eight anal rays and 4-4 teeth, and an incomplete lateral line. Five other species are similar but do not have this combination of features: *anogenus, bifrenatus, chalybaeus, heterodon,* and *procne.*

Description
Body elongate, slightly slab sided. Profiles symmetrical. Dorsal origin nearer tip of snout than caudal base. Dorsal deltoid, retrogressive, its margin straight or slightly convex, its corners angulate. Caudal moderately forked, with rounded lobes. Anal origin below distal half of depressed last dorsal ray. Anal deltoid, its margin straight, its corners angulate. Pelvics inserted below dorsal origin. Pelvic axillary process very small. Pelvic fins retrogressive, with convex margin and rounded corners. Pectorals low with slightly oblique base. Gill membranes slightly joined to isthmus. Mouth subterminal, slightly oblique. Breast and prepectoral naked. Lateral line slightly decurved, incomplete. Counts and proportional measurements are given in Table 17.

Color: Head and body with olive above, shading to white below. Midlateral stripe complete from tip of snout, past caudal fold to base of caudal rays. Scales of the lateral line row with intense crescent-shaped spots that are most prominent on the anterior half of the body. Scales of upper surface with prominent dark margins, a pale stripe above the dark midlateral stripe. Middorsal stripe present, of varying width, consisting of three thin lines anterior to the dorsal fin, present but not prominent behind the fin. Posterior margin of the periproct weakly pigmented. Scattered melanophores along base of the anal fin and continuing posteriorly as a double line on the ventral side of the caudal peduncle which varies in width and terminates at the base of the anterior ventral procurrent caudal rays. All fins with melanophores along the front and back of each ray. Upper lip pigmented, lower lip white. Eye ring narrow.

Juveniles and breeding adults: Breeding males develop a yellow color at least on the upper part of the body. Breeding tubercles are minute and confined to the head.

Size: To about 3.7 inches total length. Our largest New York specimens are 44 mm standard length.

Habitat
The blacknose shiner lives in small creeks and in the weedy shallows of lakes and ponds. Like some of the other blackstripe minnows, it is becoming rare in many parts of its range due to loss of habitat and deterioriating water quality.

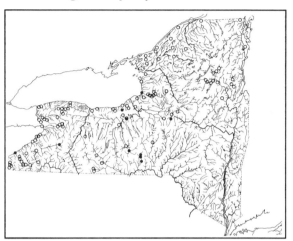

Distribution
The blacknose lives in a broad band from the Hudson Bay drainage across southern Canada to Nova Scotia. It ranges through the Great Lakes and Mississippi drainage south to Nebraska and Missouri with disjunct populations in several areas including northern Tennessee where it is said to occupy warm, clear, weedless streams.

In New York, it has been recorded from the Allegheny, Erie, Ontario and St. Lawrence drainages and from the Finger Lakes, Upper Mohawk and Susquehanna-Chemung watersheds.

Life History
The life history of the blacknose shiner has not been studied but the Survey reported females in spawning condition in the Niagara River in late July.

Food and Feeding
Wilsmann found that the blacknose fed primarily from the bottom and not at all from the surface. Small individuals fed on vegetation. Most of the feeding took place early in the morning and late in the day.

Notes
We have not found the blacknose to be common in New York State and its populations should be monitored.

References
Wilsmann, 1979 (food, competition with *N. heterodon*). Emery and Wallace, 1974 (age and growth). Hubbs, 1951 (hybridization with *Hybognathus hankinsoni*). Hubbs and Raney, 1947 (comparisons).

Names
Heterolepis is from the Greek *heteros,* different, and *lepis,* a scale.

Notropis heterolepis Eigenmann and Eigenmann, 1893: 152 Fort Qu'Applelle, Saskatchewan, Canada

Notropis cayuga Meek, 1889: 305 aberrant specimens from Montezuma (Hubbs, 1926, restricted the name *cayuga* to *Notropis bifrenatus.)*

Notropis procne Reed and Wright, 1909: 395 Cayuga Lake (misidentification)

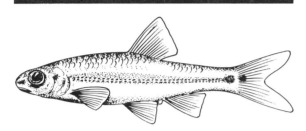

SWALLOWTAIL SHINER

Notropis procne (Cope, 1865)

Identification

The swallowtail is another of the small species of *Notropis* that has a conspicuous midlateral stripe. In this species, however, the stripe is interrupted on the side of the head behind the eye. In front of the eye, the stripe appears as a preorbital blotch, then fades across the uniformly pigmented snout. The swallowtail shiner has 4-4 teeth and seven anal rays, a combination that it shares with the bridle shiner, which has an incomplete lateral line and a continuous midlateral stripe, and the sand shiner, which lacks a complete midlateral stripe.

Description

Body elongate, somewhat slab sided anteriorly. Profiles equally curved. Dorsal origin midway between the caudal base and the tip of the snout. Dorsal retrogressive, with sharp corners and straight margin. Caudal fin moderately forked, with bluntly pointed lobes. Anal insertion slightly ahead of tip of depressed last dorsal ray. Anal retrogressive, its margin slightly concave, its corners softly angled. Pelvic insertion below dorsal origin. Pelvic axillary process developed but small. Pelvic retrogressive, rounded. Pectoral base low, slightly oblique. Pectoral retrogressive, rounded. Gill membranes narrowly joined to isthmus. Mouth subterminal, slightly oblique, snout protuberant. Breast and prepectoral area naked. Lateral line complete, slightly decurved anteriorly. Counts and proportional measurements are given in Table 17.

Color: Pale olive above with a well-developed but narrow midlateral stripe that is most intense on the operculum, interrupted behind the eye, ending as an oval spot on the side of the snout. There are intense dark spots above and below each pore in the anterior part of the lateral line. There is a definite spot at the base of the caudal rays, slightly separated from the midlateral stripe. The scales of the middorsal region have dark margins and there is a pale stripe above the dark midlateral stripe. Bases of the rays of the caudal lobes darkly outlined, forming radiating stripes. Peritoneum pale.

Juveniles and breeding adults: Males have longer pectoral and pelvic rays. In breeding males, the an-terior pectoral rays are thickened and bowed outward. Both sexes have breeding tubercles but those of the male are larger. Tubercles occur on the top, side, and underside of the head, on the body scales, the dorsal and anal fins, and the tops of the paired fins.

Size: Raney reported that this species averages about 2.25 inches and occasionally reaches 3 inches total length. Our largest New York specimens are 42 mm standard length.

Habitat

The preferred habitat of the swallowtail shiner is upland streams and small rivers. It is tolerant of sandy bottom and turbid water conditions, but it avoids deeper pools and torrential rapids. It is usually seen in schools near the bottom.

Distribution

Two subspecies are recognized. *N. p. procne* ranges from the Delaware and Susquehanna systems in New York south to the James River in Virginia. It also has been reported from Catharine Creek, the inlet to Seneca Lake, and this has been ascribed to the old Seneca Canal or possibly to a postglacial invasion at the time the Finger Lakes still drained into the Susquehanna. A third possibility is a postglacial stream capture.

The other subspecies, *N. procne longiceps* (Cope), ranges from the Roanoke River in Virginia to the Santee River in South Carolina.

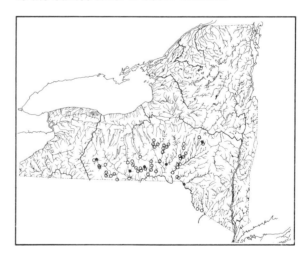

Life History

The breeding habits of the swallowtail shiner were studied by Raney in the Covington River near Washington, D.C. Spawning took place in a riffle 4 to 12 inches deep over sand and fine gravel when the water temperature was about 78 F. Males and females were about the same size but the males were darker and more active. Males guarded territories, maintaining distances of 4 to 18 inches. Courtship consisted of the male making a series of figure-eight movements over an area of clean gravel that presumably had been swept by the fish's movements. Invading males were chased with a quick rush. Females hovered downstream or at the side until ready to spawn, then moved into the male's territory and stopped within 2 to 4 inches of the male. The male then backed downstream and placed his pectoral fin beneath her head while throwing his caudal peduncle over hers. Together the pair dropped to the bottom and vibrated, stirring up sand as the eggs were laid and fertilized. After spawning, the pair separated gently and the female drifted downstream while the male returned to guarding his territory. Spawning continued after a few minutes and Raney estimated that it would take several days to deposit all of a female's complement of eggs. Yearlings averaged 33 to 39mm and 2- and 3-year-olds were 43 to 52 mm. Few fish live through the third winter.

Food and Feeding
Not reported.

Notes
Snelson considered the subspecies to be dubious.

References
Hubbs and Raney, 1947 (comparisons); 1948 (characters). Raney, 1947 (systematics, life history). Snelson, 1971 (comparisons).

Names
Procne is from the Greek *Prokne,* daughter of Pandion who was transformed into a swallow by the gods.
   Hybognathus procne Cope, 1865a: 283 Conestoga River, Pennsylvania
   Notropis procne, Bean, 1903: 138-139 New York
   Notropis procne procne, Raney, 1947: 103-109

TABLE 17
AVERAGE PROPORTIONAL MEASUREMENTS AND COUNTS OF SHINERS WITH COMPLETE BLACK STRIPES (*Notropis,* in part)

All proportions are expressed in percentage of standard length.

	anogenus	*bifrenatus*	*chalybaeus*	*heterodon*	*hetero-lepis*	*procne*
ST. LENGTH (mm)	31.6	32.5	32.1	36.3	41.0	37.4
TOTAL LENGTH	127.9	132.0	126.1	126.7	127.5	128.5
FORK LENGTH	121.3	122.8	113.6	113.8	114.7	116.0
PREDORSAL	52.6	51.7	51.4	48.7	52.3	50.8
PREANAL	64.6	66.0	65.6	64.3	66.5	68.7
PREPELVIC	48.2	50.1	48.7	47.8	49.4	49.7
DORSAL BASE	15.9	14.3	11.1	13.8	10.4	12.2
ANAL BASE	12.7	12.4	11.2	11.1	9.6	8.8
BODY DEPTH	22.8	23.3	20.8	23.9	20.1	19.0
BODY WIDTH	14.6	15.2	12.9	14.7	12.5	11.6
C.PED. DEPTH	10.1	9.2	9.5	8.3	9.8	9.3
PECTORAL ALT.	15.8	17.2	15.5	13.8	14.5	14.5
HEAD LENGTH	27.3	27.3	26.0	27.6	26.4	25.5
SNOUT	6.4	6.5	7.3	5.5	7.8	7.0
EYE	9.6	9.6	9.5	11.1	7.7	8.8
MOUTH LENGTH	3.2	4.2	7.3	5.5	5.7	7.1
INTERORB	9.6	5.2	7.8	8.3	8.0	6.8
N (sample size)	5	5	5	3	4	5
COUNTS:						
DORSAL RAYS	8	8	8	8	8	8
ANAL RAYS	8	7	8	8	8	7
PECTORAL RAYS	12-13	12	11	13-14	12-13	14
PELVIC RAYS	8	8	7	8	8	8
GILL RAKERS	6-8	6-8	7-8	6-9	6	6-7
VERTEBRAE*	32-33	32-33	30-31	32-35	31-33	31-32
SCALES:						
ABOVE L. L.	4-5	4-5	5-6	5	4	4-5
LATERAL LINE	34-37	32-36	35	34-37	33-40	35
BELOW L. L.	3-4	4	3-4	3	4	3-4
PHARYNGEAL TEETH	4-4	4-4	1,4-4,1	1,4-4,1	4-4	4-4

* Excluding Weberian apparatus.

The Pale Species of *Notropis*

In the pallid species of *Notropis* the midlateral stripe is usually only weakly developed on the posterior part of the body and becomes narrower and disappears anteriorly. *Notropis hudsonius* usually has a distinct spot at the base of the tail, *N. dorsalis* has a distinctive shape and physiognomy and *volucellus* and *stramineus* can be separated by a number of pigment and structural features. There is no reason to think that any of the members of this group are closely related to each other.

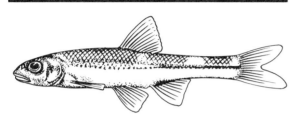

BIGMOUTH SHINER

Notropis dorsalis (Agassiz, 1854)

Identification

The bigmouth shiner is a pale species with the midlateral stripe developed only on the posterior half of the body. The bottom of its head is flat and the eyes are directed upward as well as outward and this makes it look like the silverjaw minnow or like the bigeye chub. The bigmouth, however, has neither large cavernous head canals nor barbels. It has eight anal rays and 1,4-4,1 pharyngeal teeth which separates it from the similar species of *Notropis*, notably, the sand shiner and the mimic shiner.

Another distinctive characteristic of the bigmouth is that the body narrows abruptly at the dorsal fin so that the profiles of the caudal peduncle taper more gently than in other shiners. This is perhaps less noticeable in bigmouth from the Allegheny drainage. Both the bigmouth and the sand shiner have a narrow secondary line of pigment above the midlateral band on the caudal peduncle. This line is shorter and widens slightly at its caudal end in the bigmouth.

Description

Body slender and elongate, nearly terete. Dorsal profile noticeably more arched than the ventral. Most of the taper of the posterior part of the body is at the dorsal fin. Dorsal origin midway between caudal base and tip of snout. Dorsal trapezoid, retrogressive, with straight margin and rather sharp corners. Caudal moderately forked, its lobes bluntly pointed. Anal origin below middle of depressed last dorsal ray. Anal trapezoidal, retrogressive, with straight margin, anterior corner rounded, posterior sharp. Pelvic insertion below dorsal origin. Pelvic retrogressive, rounded. Pelvic axillary process small. Pectoral base low, slightly oblique. Pectoral retrogressive, rounded. Gill membranes moderately joined to isthmus. Lower surface of head flat.

Mouth large, low, and slightly oblique. Snout overhanging the upper lip. Breast and prepectoral areas naked. Lateral line complete, nearly straight. Counts and proportional measurements are given in Table 18.

Color: Pale straw color, the dorsal scales with slightly dusky margins, and a middorsal stripe that encircles the dorsal base. Lower sides silvery, shading to white. Midlateral stripe developed posteriorly, with a narrow secondary line above it. Peritoneum pale. No postanal stripe.

Juveniles and breeding adults: Breeding males develop fine tubercles on the head, the anterior part of the body, and the upper surface of the pectoral rays. They do not have bright breeding colors.

Size: To about 3 inches total length. Our largest New York specimen is 63.5 mm standard length.

Habitat

The bigmouth occupies small creeks with moderate gradients, usually where there is sand that is not covered with silt. Its habitat, as well as its appearance, is similar to that of the silverjaw minnow.

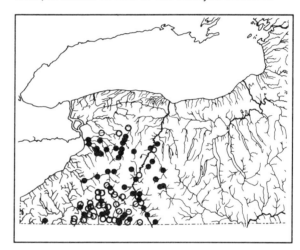

Distribution

This is a plains species ranging from Illinois to Montana and from southern Canada to Nebraska and Missouri, with disjunct populations in Wisconsin, Michigan, Ohio, western Pennsylvania and New York. In New York, it occurs in the Allegheny, Genesee, and Lake Erie drainages. We have one record from the Susquehanna drainage near Arkport, presumably the result of its having moved through the Arkport Ditch which connects the Genesee drainage and the Susquehanna system.

Life History

The life history of the bigmouth shiner seems not to have been studied. Moore suggested it might spawn in midchannel with the eggs drifting with the current but this was based on its habitat and general resemblance to another species of *Notropis*, *N. girardi*. In Illinois, it apparently spawns from May to July.

Food and Feeding

The bigmouth ingests some bottom ooze and plant material but its diet is mostly insects.

Notes

Hubbs and Lagler recognized two subspecies, *Notropis d. dorsalis* and *N. d. keimi*. They are said to differ in head proportions with *keimi* in the Allegheny, Genesee, and Oneida systems in New York, and *N. d. dorsalis* in the Lake Erie drainage. The differences are slight, and most ichthyologists do not treat *keimi* as a separate entity.

References

Gilbert and Burgess in Lee et al., 1980 (distribution and summary). Moore, 1944 (comparison with *N. girardi*). Underhill and Merrell, 1959 (variation). Hubbs and Lagler, 1964 (key). Mendelson, 1975 (feeding).

Names

The name *dorsalis* is from Middle Latin and pertains to the back.

Hybopsis dorsalis Agassiz, 1854: 358 Iowa

Notropis gilberti Jordan and Meek, 1885: 4-5 Iowa

Notropis gilberti, Greeley, 1927: 59 Genesee watershed

Notropis keimi Fowler, 1909: 533-535 Allegheny River, Pennsylvania

Notropis dorsalis dorsalis, Hubbs and Lagler, 1964: 84 (distribution)

Notropis dorsalis keimi, Greeley, 1938: 66 Allegheny watershed

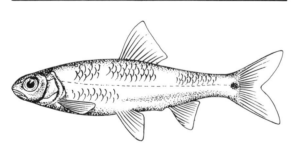

SPOTTAIL SHINER

Notropis hudsonius (Clinton, 1824)

Identification

The spottail shiner is a rather slim fish with a blunt head and subterminal mouth. It has eight anal rays and a variable pharyngeal tooth count that is most often 2,4-4,2 but can be as low as 0,3-3,1. It is usually recognizable by a large oval black spot at the base of the tail but, in large individuals, the spot is sometimes small and triangular and sometimes masked by silvery pigment. The lower margin of the caudal fin is white. There isn't any one species with which the spottail can be confused, but several species bear a superficial resemblance to it, including species of *Hybognathus, Hybopsis storeriana* and the common shiner, *Notropis cornutus.*

Description

Body elongate, terete to slab sided. Profiles equally curved. Dorsal origin much closer to tip of snout than to base of caudal. Dorsal deltoid, retrogressive, with concave margin and sharp corners. Caudal moderately forked, with bluntly pointed lobes. Anal origin below tip of depressed last dorsal ray. Anal retrogressive, with concave margin and angulate corners. Pelvic insertion below dorsal origin. Pelvic axillary scale differentiated but small. Pelvics retrogressive, with concave margin. Pectoral low, with oblique base. Gill membranes attached to isthmus. Mouth low, subterminal, slightly oblique. Snout blunt and overhanging the mouth. Breast and prepectoral area naked. Lateral line complete, decurved anteriorly. Counts and proportional measurements are given in Table 18.

Color: Upper sides olive down to the second scale row above the lateral line. Scales of the upper sides punctate with a greater concentration of melanophores along their edges. Middorsal stripe varying in width, prominent along base of dorsal fin and narrower behind the dorsal fin. Anal base with sparse melanophores continuing as a midventral line to the base of the caudal rays. Deep pigment spots above and below the lateral line pores. Caudal spot prominent, varying from almost rectangular to oval or round to triangular. Scales at the bases of the caudal lobes conspicuously outlined and the bases of the fin lobes are quite dark. The middle rays have conspicuous dark outlines for their entire length. Belly and lower surface of head, including the chin, intensely white. Upper lip with a few melanophores. Tip of snout and top of head densely stippled.

Juveniles and breeding adults: Juveniles have very conspicuous caudal spots. The adults do not develop bright breeding colors. The breeding tubercles are minute and confined to the upper surface of the head and the base of the anterior pectoral rays.

Size: The spottail reaches a maximum size of 5.8 inches total length. Our largest specimen, from the Hudson River, is 101 mm standard length.

Habitat

Spottails occur in a variety of habitats from large lakes and rivers to small streams. It seems to do best in clear waters and at times becomes quite abundant in Lake Erie, where it occurs offshore in water at least 60 feet deep.

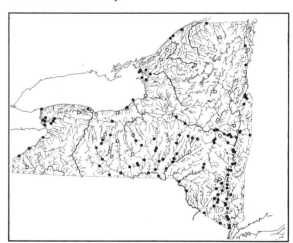

Distribution

The spottail occurs in a broad band from the Mackenzie River in northwest Canada to the St. Lawrence River and south to the Missouri drainage and southern Illinois. On the Atlantic slope, it occurs from New Hampshire to the Chattahoochee River in Georgia. In New York, it was absent from the Allegheny and Genesee Rivers, the central Adirondacks, and Long Island. E. L. Cooper has informed me that it has been introduced successfully and is now abundant in Allegheny Reservoir in Pennsylvania and is undoubtedly present in the New York part of that reservoir as well.

Life History

The life history of the spottail shiner has not been thoroughly studied. Spawning appears to take place in June or July over sandy bottom and at the mouths of streams where the ripe fish assemble in large aggregations. Ovarian egg counts range from 100 to 2,600 depending on size of the female.

Food and Feeding

The diet is variable and includes zooplankton and benthic organisms such as insect larvae, algae, and the eggs and larvae of its own species. Its undershot mouth suggests a benthic feeder.

Notes

Individuals from small streams sometimes lack a conspicuous spot and are often confused with other species of *Notropis*. Hubbs and Lagler (1964) have suggested that several forms and possibly distinct species have been placed under this name but a study by Seaman (MS thesis, Univ. of Florida) showed no consistent patterns.

The spottail is frequently used for bait although it is generally regarded as inferior to the emerald shiner.

References

Smith and Kramer, 1964 (life history). Wells and House, 1974 (life history). Peer, 1966 (size and maturity). McCann, 1959 (life history). Nursall, 1973 (behavior). Anderson and Brazo, 1978 (feeding). Dymond, 1926 (ecology). Shapiro, 1975 (bibliography). Seaman, 1968 (variation). Griswold, 1963 (food). Kellogg and Gift, 1983 (preferred temperatures).

Names

Hudsonius means from the Hudson River.

Clupea hudsonius Clinton, 1824: 49-50 Hudson River, New York

Hudsonius amarus Girard, 1857: 210 Potomac River

Leuciscus hudsonius, DeKay, 1842: 205

Notropis hudsonius hudsonius, Greeley, 1935: 94 Hudson River

Notropis hudsonius amarus, Bean, 1903: 142-143

Notropis hudsonius amarus, Greeley, 1936: 83 Delaware-Susquehanna watershed

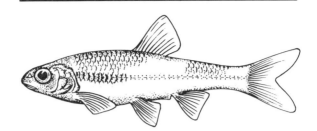

SAND SHINER

Notropis stramineus (Cope, 1865)

Identification

The sand shiner is a small, clean-looking, straw-colored minnow with rather firm scales that are distinctly outlined above the lateral line. It has seven anal rays and 4-4 pharyngeal teeth. Its midlateral band is developed only on the side of the caudal peduncle. Sand shiners are often confused with the mimic shiner but the mimic shiner has more pigment around the anus, eight anal rays, and the anterior scales of its lateral line are elevated, that is, longer from top to bottom than the scales in the rows above and below the lateral line. Sand shiners also have a narrow line of pigment, like a pencil mark, above the midlateral stripe.

Description

Body elongate, slightly slab sided. Profiles symmetrical. Dorsal origin equidistant from tip of snout to caudal base, or slightly closer to tip of snout. Dorsal retrogressive, with straight margin and angled corners. Caudal moderately forked, with blunt lobes. Anal origin below or slightly anterior to tip of depressed last dorsal ray. Anal trapezoid, retrogressive, with concave margin and rounded corners. Pelvic insertion below dorsal origin. Pelvic retrogressive, with slightly convex margin and rounded corners. Pelvic axillary process small. Pectoral base slightly oblique. Pectoral retrogressive, rounded. Gill membranes moderately attached to isthmus. Mouth subterminal, slightly oblique, gape curved. Lateral line slightly decurved anteriorly. Counts and proportional measurements are given in Table 18.

Color: In life, the upper part of the body is an almost transparent, pale, sandy color with the silver-white peritoneum clearly visible through the body wall. An interrupted middorsal line often flashes golden as the fish turns in shallow water. The horizontal septum is silvery for about 1 mm in from the body surface and is visible in living individuals. Freshly preserved specimens are olive dorsally, becoming abruptly silvery on the midside, and shading to white on the belly. The silvery area continues posteriorly as a broad stripe on the caudal peduncle where it overlies a diffuse band of melanophores. A narrow, yellow line runs along the dorsal edge of the silvery area and a thin "pencil line" of dusky melanophores immediately above this runs from the shoulder girdle to about the middle of the body. Scales of the back with dark margins. Middorsal stripe present but not prominent; anterior to dorsal fin, it consists of three parallel lines of melanophores. These become more intense just ahead of the dorsal origin, and again at the middle of the dorsal base. The postdorsal stripe is a single, ill-defined band of melanophores. The lateral line is unpigmented, but there are dark spots above and below each pore, best developed on the anterior half of the body. Scattered melanophores along the anal base continue as a diffuse midventral stripe on the caudal peduncle. Basicaudal spot not well developed; sometimes there are a few melanophores behind the basicaudal fold. Pelvic and anal fins clear; dorsal, caudal, and anterior pectoral rays with scattered melanophores.

Juveniles and breeding adults: Tubercles develop as small points on the head. The rays of the pectoral and pelvic fins become thickened with small tubercles that give them a serrated appearance.

Size: The maximum size of the sand shiner is about 3.5 inches. The largest New York specimen we have seen is 67.5 mm standard length.

Habitat

Clear water and sandy bottom are the primary requirements of the sand shiner. It occurs in moderate to large streams and in lakes where there is enough current or wave action to keep the bottom free of silt.

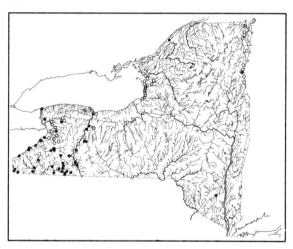

Distribution

The sand shiner is widespread in the central part of the United States and southern Canada, from Lake Champlain and the St. Lawrence River to Montana, Colorado and Texas. It is in the western drainages of New York State, the Allegheny, Lake Erie and the Genesee, as well as eastern Lake Ontario and the St. Lawrence. There is an isolated population in the Shawangunk Kill which may be introduced.

Life History

The life history of the sand shiner has not been thoroughly studied. It apparently spawns at temperatures of 21 to 37 C and has a prolonged spawning season, May through August in Kansas. Ovarian egg counts averaged 340. It is said to scatter its eggs over clean sand.

Food and Feeding

Iowa populations were found to be omnivorous, feeding on aquatic and terrestrial insects, bottom ooze and diatoms.

Notes

This species has been confused with several others so that some of the earlier literature may be unreliable. Some western populations have been separated as distinct subspecies but this is now considered doubtful. Sand shiners are sometimes used for bait.

References

Hubbs and Greene, 1928 (confusing species). Summerfelt and Minckley, 1969 (life history). Mendelson, 1975 (feeding). Starrett, 1950 (food habits). Bailey and Allum, 1962 (taxonomy). Suttkus, 1958 (taxonomy). Tanyolac, 1973 (variation and life history).

Names

Stramineus is the Latin for made of straw, probably referring to the color of the living fish.

Hybognathus stramineus Cope, 1865a: 283 Detroit River, Michigan

Notropis deliciosus (non Girard), Greeley, 1927: 59 Genesee watershed

Notropis deliciosus stramineus, Greeley, 1928: 171 Erie-Niagara watershed

Notropis blennius (non Girard), Hankinson, 1924: 31 western New York

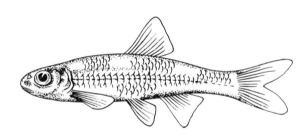

MIMIC SHINER

Notropis volucellus (Cope, 1865)

Identification

The mimic shiner is a pale species with the midlateral stripe developed only weakly on the posterior part of the body. It resembles the sand shiner and is often confused with it, but the mimic shiner has eight anal rays and the sand shiner has only seven. The mimic shiner also has the scales of the lateral line expanded vertically so that they are about 1.5 times as high as those in the row above the lateral line. In the sand shiner, the lateral line scales are only slightly higher than the scales in the row above. The mimic shiner looks a little like the bigmouth shiner but the bigmouth has eight anal rays and 1,4-4,1 teeth. Both the sand shiner and the mimic shiner have 4-4 teeth.

Description

Body elongate, only slightly slab sided. Profiles

equally curved. Dorsal origin midway between caudal base and the nostrils. Dorsal retrogressive, with straight margin and rounded corners. Anal origin below distal half of depressed last dorsal ray. Anal retrogressive, with slightly convex margin and rounded corners. Pelvic insertion slightly anterior to dorsal origin. Pelvic axillary process slightly developed. Pelvic retrogressive, with straight margin, its anterior corner softly angulate, posterior rounded. Pectoral base low, slightly oblique. Pectoral fin retrogressive, rounded. Gill membranes joined to the isthmus. Snout overhanging the mouth. Mouth subterminal, slightly oblique. Breast and prepectoral areas naked. Lateral line complete, slightly decurved, its anterior scales elevated. Counts and proportional measurements are given in Table 18.

Color: Overall silvery, grayish above, shading to white below. Scales of the upper sides conspicuously outlined. No predorsal stripe but the edges of the predorsal scales somewhat darkened. Midlateral stripe poorly developed, disappearing forward of the level of the dorsal fin. Posterior end of the stripe expanded into an ovoid enlargement with a separate triangular spot behind. Fins hyaline, the rays of the dorsal and caudal with black margins. Considerable black pigment around the anus and along the anal base. Peritoneum silvery.

Juveniles and breeding adults: breeding adults develop fine tubercles on top of the head and the upper surface of the pectoral rays.

Size: To about 3 inches total length.

Habitat

Mimic shiners live in lakes and the quieter parts of streams, often around vegetation. Trautman noted that it is more tolerant of siltation than the sand shiner although the two are similar and often found together.

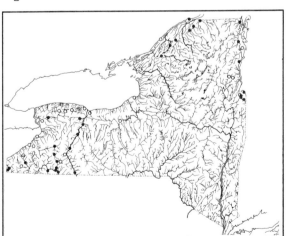

Distribution

This species is widely distributed in the central part of North America from the St. Lawrence to the Red River of the North and south to the gulf coast, with disjunct populations in Virginia and North Carolina. It occurs throughout New York State.

Life History

Black studied the life history in Shriner Lake in Indiana where the species was extremely abundant. Spawning was not observed but there were indications that it spawned at night in moderately deep water. Spawning probably takes place in aquatic vegetation with no nesting or parental care. The spawning season was June and July. Ovarian egg counts averaged 367. Spawning adults were mostly 1- and 2-year-olds and few 3-year-olds were found.

Food and Feeding

Black found entomostracans, algae and other plant debris, and midge adults and larvae to be the most frequent food items. Olmstead et al. used mimic shiners to test models of predation and found great variability in the feeding responses of individual mimic shiners and a rapid response to changing prey densities. The feeding of mimic shiners did not conform to either the predator-switching model or the direct-proportionality model.

Notes

Subspecies have been recognized but they are not clearly defined and some may be ecologically mediated variants.

References

Black, 1945 (natural history). Suttkus, 1958 (taxonomy). Olmstead et al., 1979 (feeding strategy). Malick, 1978 (distribution). Trautman, 1957 (Ohio).

Names

Volucellus is the diminutive of the Latin word *volucer,* winged or swift.

Hybognathus volucellus Cope, 1865a: 283-284 Detroit River at Grosse Isle, Michigan

Notropis volucellus volucellus, Greeley, 1928: 98 Oswego watershed

TABLE 18
AVERAGE PROPORTIONAL MEASUREMENTS AND COUNTS OF PALLID SHINERS
(Notropis, in part)

All proportions are expressed in percentage of standard length.

	dorsalis	*stramineus*	*volucellus*	*hudsonius*
ST. LENGTH (mm)	47.4	48.2	41.3	79.9
TOTAL LENGTH	126.3	125.3	125.5	128.4
FORK LENGTH	115.7	112.5	114.8	116.8
PREDORSAL	52.6	50.9	53.3	50.9
PREANAL	65.2	68.5	67.7	68.6
PREPELVIC	48.9	49.6	49.8	49.9
DORSAL BASE	10.5	12.4	11.5	14.0
ANAL BASE	9.5	9.3	10.6	11.6
BODY DEPTH	19.1	22.9	20.7	28.5
BODY WIDTH	12.5	15.8	12.7	18.0
C.PED. DEPTH	9.4	10.1	9.9	10.6
PECTORAL ALT.	14.5	16.8	16.3	17.4
HEAD LENGTH	26.1	24.5	25.4	24.0
SNOUT	8.1	7.2	7.3	7.4
EYE	7.9	7.6	8.6	7.7
MOUTH LENGTH	7.9	7.6	6.9	3.9
INTERORB	7.8	6.6	7.3	5.1
N (sample size)	5	5	5	5
COUNTS:				
DORSAL RAYS	8	8	8	8
ANAL RAYS	8-9	7	7	7
PECTORAL RAYS	14-15	13-15	12-15	12-17
PELVIC RAYS	8	8	9	8
GILL RAKERS	4-5	6-7	5-6	5-8
VERTEBRAE*	31-32	31-32	32-34	34
SCALES:				
ABOVE L.L.	5-6	5	4	5
LATERAL LINE	34-37	34-39	36-39	38-42
BELOW L.L.	4-5	4	3-4	4-5
PHARYNGEAL TEETH	1,4-4,1	4-4	4-4 variable, to 2,4-4,2	4-4

* Excluding Weberian apparatus.

Phoxinus

This genus presently consists of at least four North American and two European species. They are small fishes with tiny scales, no barbels, and bright breeding colors.

Currently, there is still a debate as to the closeness of the relationship and some evidence suggests that the finescale dace should have its own genus, for which the name *Pfrille* is available. In much of the recent literature the redbelly daces have been placed in the genus *Chrosomus*.

KEY TO THE SPECIES OF *PHOXINUS* IN NEW YORK

A. Scales very fine and difficult to count, about 90 in lateral series. Sides with a single, prominent, narrow lateral stripe, above which is a a pale stripe that is sharply delimited from the darker dorsal surface. Sometimes, the edge of this darker area suggests a second dark stripe. There is a still darker middorsal stripe but no rows of spots on the dorsal surface.
Phoxinus neogaeus　　　**Finescale dace, p. 200**

A'. Scales somewhat larger but still small and hard to count, about 80 in lateral series. Sides with two prominent longitudinal stripes and a row of conspicuous spots on each side of the very dark middorsal stripe. (These spots may be weak or absent on small specimens which, however, have both lateral longitudinal stripes distinct.)

B. Mouth with a simple downward curve so that the anterior part of the gape is nearly horizontal.

Snout slightly overhangs the lower jaw. (Does not occur in New York State.)
Phoxinus erythrogaster
　　　　　　　Southern redbelly dace

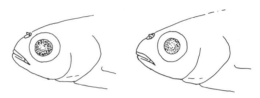

Mouth of northern (left) and southern (right) redbelly dace.

B'. Mouth nearly straight or with slight S-shaped curve so that the anterior part of the gape slopes obliquely upward. Jaws about equal, or the lower jaw slightly projecting.
Phoxinus eos　　**Northern redbelly dace, p. 199**

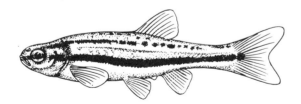

NORTHERN REDBELLY DACE

Phoxinus eos (Cope, 1862)

Identification
The redbelly dace is a small, usually rather dark minnow with tiny scales and two dark longitudinal stripes on the upper sides of its body. Its head is rather short, it has no barbels, and the lateral line ends before the origin of the dorsal fin.

The only identification problem with this species is that it is rather similar to the related finescale dace, *Phoxinus neogaeus*. This problem is further complicated by the fact that the two species frequently interbreed to form hybrids. In its pure form, the finescale dace is a stouter fish with a larger head and only one lateral stripe. The color pattern, however, is sometimes misleading and for positive identification it may be necessary to examine the viscera. The redbelly has dark viscera with two loops of the gut in addition to the primary loop. In the finescale, only the primary loop is present and the internal organs are pale. Hybrids may have any combination of gut color and pattern.

Description
Body slender, nearly terete, deepest anterior to the dorsal origin. Profiles about equally curved. Dorsal fin deltoid, retrogressive, with rounded lobes and

slightly convex outer margin. Dorsal origin slightly posterior to the middle of standard length. Caudal moderately forked, with bluntly pointed lobes. Anal origin below posterior end of dorsal base. Anal similar to dorsal. Pelvic origin anterior to dorsal origin. Pelvics retrogressive, with rounded corners. Pectorals low, retrogressive, with blunt anterior and rounded posterior corners. Mouth terminal, ending ahead of the eye, quite oblique. Gill membranes broadly joined to the isthmus. Lateral line incomplete, decurved. Counts and proportional measurements are given in Table 19.

Color: Body dark olive above, shading to silvery white on the belly, with one dark midlateral stripe running from the snout to the midbase of the caudal. A second dark stripe higher, running from the nape to behind the dorsal fin where it breaks up into irregular dark spots. There are some dark spots in the middorsal line.

Juveniles and breeding adults: Adult males have the sides below the lateral stripe brilliant red. In females, this region is yellow with a slightly greenish tinge. Males develop four or five comb-like nuptial organs on the prepectoral area and small tubercles on the lower surface of the head.

Size: Females reach at least 2.4 inches and males at least 2.1 inches.

Habitat
The redbelly dace occurs in ponds and in the slow parts of streams, often in cool, darkly stained waters of swampy northern creeks. It is occasionally taken in moderate current.

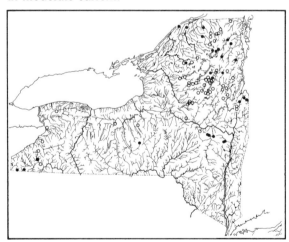

Distribution
The overall range of the redbelly dace is from Nova Scotia and Prince Edward Island west in a rather narrow curving band through southern Canada and the northern and north-central United States from New York and Pennsylvania to Michigan, Wisconsin, and north to the Peace-Mackenzie drainage of British Columbia and the Northwest Territories.

In New York, it occurs throughout the central and northern Adirondacks, with isolated populations in Vly Creek in the Hudson drainage, the Finger Lakes area, and western part of the state where we have recent records from Conewango and Brokenstraw Creeks.

Life History
The redbelly dace spawns in the spring and early summer, May to early August. Cooper suggested that at least some females spawned twice a year because he found two size classes of maturing eggs. Spawning takes place on clumps of filamentous algae. A female accompanied by one or more males would dart from one algal mass to another with a spawning embrace of 2 to 4 seconds at each one. During each spawning episode, 5 to 30 nonadhesive eggs were released and became entangled in the algal filaments. The eggs hatched in 8 to 10 days at 70 to 80 F. Maturity is reached in the second or third summer, and the fish live at least 3 years.

Food and Feeding
The diet of the redbelly dace includes much plant material, including diatoms and filamentous algae, as well as zooplankton, insects, and occasionally fish. Cooper noted that large redbellies would sometimes eat newly hatched bass fry.

Notes
Until recently, the American species, the redbelly and finescale dace, were placed in the genus *Chrosomus,* but recent work has demonstrated their close relationship to the European species of *Phoxinus.* The name *erythrogaster* was formerly used for the northern, as well as the southern, redbelly dace but they have been shown to be separate, although closely related, species. The true *erythrogaster* does not occur in New York State although it is found in southwestern Pennsylvania.

References
Cooper, 1936a (life history). Smith, 1908 (spawning). New, 1962 (hybridization). Phillips, 1969 (variation, no clines). Legendre, 1970 (hybridization). Stasiak, 1977 (hybrids). Joswiak and Moore, 1982 (species comparison). Mahy, 1972 (osteology, relationships). Tyler, 1966 (lethal temperature).

Names
Eos is the Greek word for dawn, probably an allusion to the red color.

Chrosomus eos Cope, 1862: 523 Susquehanna River

Chrosomus erythrogaster (non Rafinesque), Greeley, 1928: 99 Oswego drainage

Phoxinus eos, Stasiak *in* Lee et al., 1980: 336 (distribution)

FINESCALE DACE

Phoxinus neogaeus Cope, 1868

Identification
The finescale dace is a small, rather dark species

with very small scales (too small to count easily), a dark lateral stripe separated from the dark dorsal area by a pale stripe, a rather blunt head, and a moderately small mouth. It lacks the barbels of the longnose and blacknose daces and it is much less streamlined and has a smaller mouth than the redside dace.

The only species with which the finescale can be confused is the redbelly dace. The redbelly, however, has two dark lateral stripes and slightly larger scales. The redbelly and the finescale frequently hybridize and the hybrids may resemble one or the other parent. The best separation is on the basis of gut anatomy. The finescale has pale viscera and the gut has a simple S-curve. The redbelly has black viscera and the gut has two additional transverse loops.

Adult male finescales have the anterior rays of the pectoral fin specialized so that, at first glance, they appear abnormal. There is a constriction near the middle of the rays with a sharp bend, distal to which the segments of the first ray are enlarged and flattened. There is also a striated pad on the prepectoral area in front of the base of the fin.

Description

Body rather short and heavy, nearly terete. Profiles about equally curved. Dorsal origin behind the middle of the body. Dorsal retrogressive, with rounded corners and slightly convex margin. Caudal moderately forked, with rounded lobes. Anal similar to dorsal. Pelvic retrogressive, convex, with rounded corners, its insertion anterior to the dorsal fin. Pectorals low, retrogressive, rounded. Counts and proportional measurements are given in Table 19.

Color: Brassy brown to nearly black dorsally with a distinct midlateral stripe separated from the dark dorsum by a pale stripe that is brassy or golden in life. Often, there is a definite dark spot at the end of the lateral stripe. In some individuals, the lower edge of the dark dorsal area is emphasized but it is not separated as a distinct stripe. Lower flank white to silvery, iris brassy, side of head silvery. Fin membranes transparent, the rays of the vertical fins outlined in dark pigment.

Juveniles and breeding adults: Males have longer fins and a deeper caudal peduncle. Breeding males have four or five rows of comb-like structures in front of the pectoral fin and tubercles on the base of the anal fin and on the ventral surface of the body. The sides of the males are brilliant red below the lateral stripe. Adult males with modifications of the anterior pectoral rays as described above.

Size: The finescale is a small species, but somewhat larger than the redbelly. The maximum length is about 90 mm.

Habitat

The finescale is a northern species that does best in sluggish, darkly stained, swampy streams. It also occurs in ponds and lakes.

Distribution

The finescale ranges from Maine and New Bruns-

wick west through the northern United States and southern Canada to Hudson Bay and the Mackenzie River drainage, with disjunct populations in South Dakota and Nebraska.

New York records are mostly from the northern Adirondacks and the St. Lawrence Valley, with one record by the Survey in the Allegheny drainage.

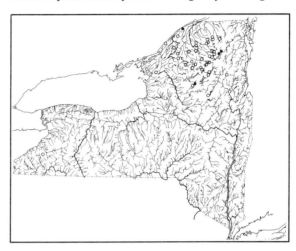

Life History

Stasiak studied the life history of the finescale in Minnesota. Spawning took place in late April and early May when the water temperature was about 15 C. Stasiak made his observations in a beaver pond where the bottom was fine silt, with fallen trees for cover and some rocks and brush. The fish also spawned in flower pots in laboratory aquariums 2 m by 1 m by 0.7 m deep.

In the wild, the sex ratio was 1.5 males to 1 female. The fish milled around in a large school and, at intervals, one or two females left the school. They were pursued by several males who chased them under shelter where the females remained for about 15 seconds and the males stayed for about 30 seconds. In the laboratory, the male could be seen to guide the female with his pectoral fin under her belly, behind her pectoral fins. The female was crowded against some object with the tail of the male over her tail so that the tubercles on his anal fin rubbed against her vent region. The female vibrated for about 10 seconds, then moved away, while the male continued to vibrate and emit milt for another few seconds. Each spawning episode resulted in the release of 30 to 40 eggs which sank to the bottom. The eggs were about 1.4 mm in diameter and hatched in 6 days at 20 C. Each female contained 784 to 3,060 eggs, depending on the size of the female.

Food and Feeding

Insects and small crustaceans have been found in the stomachs of finescale dace.

Notes

Many fish hybrids are known, including several intergeneric crosses. Usually, these are uncommon and only one or two hybrids will be taken at one locality. With *Phoxinus neogaeus* and *P. eos*, however, the situation is different and frequently all of the individuals collected at a site will be hybrids, indicating that the hybrids are fertile and that the parents are much less common, if present at all. Most of the hybrids of this combination are females. The hybrids are variable. In some collections, they resemble redbelly dace except for details of coloration. At another locality, they all have rather similar color patterns but an array of gut shape and pigment patterns.

References

New, 1962 (hybridization). Stasiak, 1977 (morphology); 1978a (life history).

Names

This species has sometimes been placed in its own genus *Pfrille,* and with the American species in the genus *Chrosomus.*

Neogaeus is from the Greek *neos,* new and *gaia,* the earth or land, hence, of the New World.

Phoxinus neogaeus Cope in Gunther, 1868: 247 New Hudson, Michigan

Pfrille neogaea, Greeley, 1930: 79 Saranac River system

Chrosomus neogaeus, Hubbs and Lagler, 1964: 80 (distribution)

Phoxinus neogaeus, Stasiak in Lee et al., 1980: 338 (distribution)

TABLE 19
AVERAGE PROPORTIONAL MEASUREMENTS AND COUNTS OF DACE
(Phoxinus and Clinostomus)

All proportions are expressed in percentage of standard length.

	Phoxinus		*Clinostomus*
	neogaeus	eos	elongatus
ST. LENGTH (mm)	32.6	42.7	58.1
TOTAL LENGTH	125.4	123.7	124.9
FORK LENGTH	116.1	—	114.1
PREDORSAL	56.7	56.4	53.0
PREANAL	65.0	65.8	67.6
PREPELVIC	50.5	50.6	49.7
DORSAL BASE	9.4	9.5	10.9
ANAL BASE	9.5	9.2	11.1
BODY DEPTH	20.7	22.6	21.5
BODY WIDTH	13.4	14.9	14.3
C.PED. DEPTH	10.0	10.2	9.8
PECTORAL ALT.	15.3	16.5	16.7
HEAD LENGTH	25.9	27.6	26.9
SNOUT	6.6	7.3	8.9
EYE	8.0	7.2	7.4
MOUTH LENGTH	6.3	9.0	12.4
INTERORB	6.9	7.9	4.1
N (sample size)	5	5	5
COUNTS:			
DORSAL RAYS	8	8	8
ANAL RAYS	8	7-8	8-9
PECTORAL RAYS	14-16	16-17	14-15
PELVIC RAYS	8	8	8
GILL RAKERS	9	11	4-6
VERTEBRAE*	33-34	33-34	37-38
SCALES:			
ABOVE L. L.	x	x	11
LATERAL SERIES	63-85	70-90	64-69
BELOW L. L.	x	x	6-7
PHARYNGEAL TEETH	1 or 2,5-4 or 2	5-5	2,5-4,2

* Excluding Weberian apparatus.   x Too small to count.

Pimephales

Four species make up the genus *Pimephales* and two of these are found in New York. They are united by color pattern, in particular a dark spot on the anterior rays of the dorsal fin, and by the fact that the small ray at the front of the dorsal fin is well developed and separated from the first principal ray by membrane. They also have a distinctive pattern of breeding tubercles and similar nesting and breeding patterns. The young are sometimes confused with species of *Notropis*.

KEY TO THE SPECIES OF *PIMEPHALES* IN NEW YORK

A. Mouth inferior, horizontal. Scales in front of the dorsal fin crowded and irregular, clearly outlined with dark pigment. Lateral line complete. Body slender, elongate, and nearly terete.
Pimephales notatus

Bluntnose minnow, p. 203

A'. Mouth terminal. Scales in front of dorsal small but not definitely outlined with dark pigment. Lateral line incomplete. Body short and deep, rather robust.
Pimephales promelas

Fathead minnow, p. 204

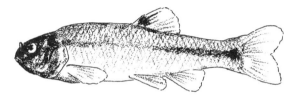

BLUNTNOSE MINNOW

Pimephales notatus
(Rafinesque, 1820)

Identification

The bluntnose is a small, pale, terete minnow with a blunt snout overhanging the low and horizontal mouth. The best field character is probably the congested appearance of the scales of the predorsal area. They are small, crowded, and irregular and they have dark margins so that they can readily be seen. Bluntnose minnows also have a narrow, rather even stripe along the sides of the body. This stripe is separated from a small but distinct spot at the base of the tail.

The bluntnose has no barbels but breeding adults have swellings at the corners of the lips that suggest barbels. Members of the genus *Pimephales* are characterized by a well-developed half-ray at the front of the dorsal fin. While this is prominent in adults and is often used in keys, the reader should be aware that in small individuals the splint is not always well developed and that some species of *Notropis* have the splint almost as well developed. The species of *Pimephales* also have a characteristic spot at the front of the dorsal fin about two-thirds of the way to the tips of the anterior rays. This is diagnostic for the genus, but it is inconspicuous or absent in small juveniles.

Bluntnose differ from fatheads in having a complete lateral line and a more elongate shape. The predorsal scales of fatheads do not have conspicuous dark margins.

Description

Body elongate, nearly terete, deepest anterior to the dorsal fin. Profiles equally curved. Dorsal origin midway between caudal base and front of eye. Dorsal retrogressive, with rounded corners. Caudal moderately forked, with rounded lobes. Anal inserted below outer one-fourth of depressed last dorsal ray. Anal fin retrogressive, its margin straight, convex, or falcate, its corners rounded. Pelvics inserted slightly ahead of the dorsal origin. Pelvic axillary process distinct but small. Pelvics retrogressive, rounded. Pectorals low, with slightly oblique base, retrogressive, rounded. Gill membranes broadly connected to the isthmus. Snout blunt, mouth low and horizontal. Gape crescentic. Breast and prepectoral area naked. Lateral line complete, slightly decurved anteriorly. Counts and proportional measurements are given in Table 20.

Color: General color pale sandy, slightly olive above, shading to white on the belly. Midlateral stripe from preorbital region (not across snout) to base of tail, where it is separated by a light space from a conspicuous basicaudal spot. Scales of back and sides down to second row below the lateral line with dark outlines. Small dark spots above and below anterior lateral line pores. Middorsal stripe present, more intense at the dorsal origin and in the middle of the dorsal fin base, diffuse postdorsally. Peritoneum black. Snout and top of head with scattered superficial melanophores, and deeper pigment in the brain membranes. A narrow, black ring around the eye. Dorsal and caudal rays with dark outlines. Anal and paired fins pale. Individuals from clear or stained waters with more pigment, often with numerous melanophores around the anus and a midventral stripe on the caudal peduncle.

Juveniles and breeding adults: Juveniles have a very conspicuous lateral stripe and basicaudal spot. Breeding males are almost black, with three rows of large tubercles across the snout. There are also small tubercles on the dorsal surface of the pectoral rays. Breeding males have the skin of the predorsal area thickened and barbel-like swellings at the corners of the mouth.

Size: Males reach about 4 inches total length, females are somewhat smaller. Our largest New York specimen is 85.5 mm standard length.

Habitat

The bluntnose lives in a variety of habitats from lakes and ponds to streams. It is able to tolerate silt and organic enrichment. It is often very abundant in weedy areas.

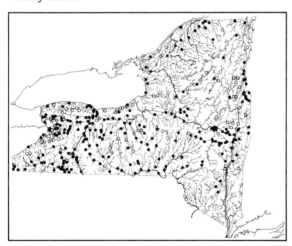

Distribution

This species ranges from Lake Champlain to the Dakotas, from southern Canada to the gulf coast in Louisiana, Alabama and Mississippi.

In New York, it is present in all watersheds except Long Island. It is rare in the Delaware and higher parts of the Adirondacks.

Life History

The bluntnose minnow spawns from the end of May to near the end of July. In Michigan, Hubbs and Cooper reported that it spawns from the latter part of May to late August. At any one locality, the spawning lasted a maximum of 7 weeks. Water temperatures range from 19 to 27 C.

The male prepared nests by excavating a cavity under a rock or some other object, sweeping with the tail and pushing stones, sticks, and other objects

with his snout. The roof of the cavity is cleaned with the spongy predorsal area and the mouth. Males isolated in aquaria prepared nests even in the absence of a female. Spawning takes place mostly at night, sometimes during the day. Males guard the nests vigorously. Single females deposit 40 to more than 400 eggs in a nest and several females may contribute so that a single nest can contain more than 2,000 eggs. A female can produce up to 2,300 eggs. Eggs were eyed in 3 to 5 days and hatched in 6 to 10 days. Newly hatched larvae were about 5 mm long. Males remove dead eggs and, if the male was removed, the embryos died in about 12 hours.

Bluntnose mature in their second summer although maturity is sometimes delayed until their third summer. Westman suggested that they may live to spawn two and sometimes three times. In New York, fewer than 10 percent of the bluntnose reach 55 mm standard length by the end of the first summer.

Food and Feeding

Keast and Webb (1966) found that the diet of the bluntnose in Lake Opinicon, Ontario, consisted of 20 to 50 percent bottom ooze, 5 to 30 percent chironomid larvae and 10 to 75 percent cladocerans.

References

Westman, 1938 (life history in New York). Hubbs and Cooper, 1936 (spawning). Keast and Webb, 1966 (feeding). Van Cleave and Markus, 1929 (life history). Kraatz, 1928 (food). Snyder, Snyder and Douglas, 1977 (larvae). Gale, 1983 (fecundity).

Names

The species name is Latin for marked, distinguished.

Minnilus notatus Rafinesque, 1820a: 47 Ohio River

Hyborhynchus notatus, Greeley, 1927: 58 Genesee watershed

Pimephales notatus, Hubbs and Lagler, 1964: 86 (distribution)

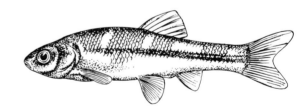

FATHEAD MINNOW

Pimephales promelas Rafinesque, 1820

Identification

The fathead minnow is a stubby, heavy-bodied fish with a small mouth and an incomplete lateral line. Like its relative, the bluntnose minnow, it has a dark spot on the anterior dorsal rays, and a stout half-ray at the front of the dorsal fin that is well separated from the first principal ray although connected by membrane. Fatheads have a dark peritoneum and conspicuous dark segmental blood vessels are visible through the skin of the upper sides in front of the dorsal fin. They differ from the bluntnose in that the scales of the predorsal area do not have conspicuous dark margins. They also differ in shape, the bluntnose being more elongate and almost round in cross section.

Description

Body stubby, slab sided. Profiles about equally curved. Dorsal origin midway between the snout and the base of the caudal. Dorsal trapezoidal with convex margin. Caudal moderately forked, its lobes bluntly pointed. Anal origin below the middle of the depressed last dorsal ray. Anal short, trapezoidal, retrogressive, with rounded corners and convex margin. Pelvic insertion below the dorsal origin. Pelvic axillary scale scarcely developed. Pelvic retrogressive, with convex margin. Pectoral base low, oblique. Pectoral retrogressive, with rounded corners. Head blunt, eye small, mouth terminal, oblique, maxillary ending before the eye. Gill membranes broadly joined to the isthmus. Body completely scaled, scales crowded before the dorsal fin. Scales of the breast and pectoral area deeply embedded. Lateral line decurved, incomplete but of variable length, sometimes ending before the dorsal fin, sometimes lacking only a few pored scales. Counts and proportional measurements are given in Table 20.

Color: Body olive to gray above, shading to straw color or white ventrally. Scales of the upper sides outlined, except not conspicuously so in the predorsal area. Midlateral stripe present, better developed in juveniles, often obsolete in large adults, of even width throughout, although light anteriorly, expanded just ahead of the caudal fold, producing a spot that is not separated from the rest of the stripe.

There is often a wedge-shaped spot behind the caudal fold and on the base of the caudal rays. Top of head black, cheeks dark olive. There is a conspicuous spot at the middle of the anterior dorsal rays and sometimes an intensification of pigment near the middle of all of the dorsal rays. Caudal rays with dark outlines. Leading edge of pectoral fins black.

Juveniles and breeding adults: Breeding males become very dark, sometimes coppery in life. There is frequently a pale ring around the body just behind the head and a pale vertical band at the level of the dorsal fin. Males develop a thick fatty pad between the nape and the dorsal origin. They also have three rows of large tubercles across the snout and smaller ones on the lower jaw. Sometimes there are small tubercles on the top of the head.

Size: the maximum size is about 90 mm. Males are usually larger than females.

Habitat

Ponds and slower streams are the preferred habitat of the fathead although they tolerate a wide range of conditions. We have often found it in rather tur-

bid waters and also in clear, but darkly stained waters at higher elevations. Its occurrence seems to be scattered but it is frequently abundant where it does occur.

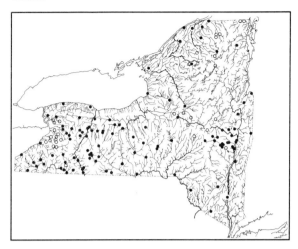

Distribution

The fathead occurs throughout most of the middle part of North America from Great Slave Lake and Hudson Bay south to Chihuahua, Mexico. It has been introduced on the Atlantic slope and also west of the Continental Divide. The fathead is a popular bait fish and its distribution has undoubtedly been altered by introductions within and close to its original range as well.

In New York, it occurs in all watersheds except Long Island.

Life History

Both the bluntnose and the fathead minnows deposit their eggs on the undersides of objects such as logs, stones, and lily pads. We have found it nesting under pieces of discarded lumber and in empty beverage cans. Usually, the nests are in water 1 to 3 feet deep. The male grooms the eggs by rubbing them with his dorsal pad. The eggs are embedded in a viscous material so they can be moved without becoming detached.

Males set up territories and prepare the nest by sweeping out a cavity if the nest is close to the bottom. Females are herded into the nest and deposit the eggs by means of a short fleshy ovipositor tube. Apparently, the eggs are laid in small batches and more than one female may contribute eggs to a nest. Females also lay eggs in more than one nest.

Fatheads have a prolonged spawning period from May to August when the water temperature is 60 to 64 or occasionally as high as 79 F. Hatching takes 6 to 9 days. Most fatheads mature at age I and few live beyond the third summer. Often, there is high mortality just after spawning.

Food and Feeding

The diet of the fathead minnow includes algae, bottom detritus, insect larvae, and zooplankton.

Notes

Although subspecies have been recognized, it has been shown that much of the variation is clinal and subspecies are probably not warranted.

The fathead is widely cultivated for bait and is also used in toxicity studies. Large chemical companies often raise their own disease-free fatheads for their screening tests.

References

Wynne-Edwards, 1932 (breeding). Smith, 1978 (seasonal changes in histology). Lord, 1927 (propagation). Markus, 1934 (life history). Flickinger, 1969 (sex determination). Coyle, 1930 (food). Mehrle and Mayer, 1975 (effects of toxaphene). Lewis, 1977 (sexual dimorphism). Vandemeer, 1966 (variation). Isaak, 1961 (life history). Tsai, 1971 (Chesapeake records). Merritt, 1972 (distri-

bution, enzymes). Smith and Murphy, 1974 (functional morphology of dorsal pad).

Names

The trivial name *promelas* is from the Greek *pro,* before, in front of, and *melas,* black. This seems to be an allusion to the very dark head of breeding males.

Pimephales promelas Rafinesque, 1820a: 53 Lexington, Kentucky

Pimephales promelas, Greeley, 1927: 58 Genesee watershed

Pimephales p. promelas, Greeley, 1928: 99 Oswego drainage

TABLE 20
AVERAGE PROPORTIONAL MEASUREMENTS AND COUNTS OF MINNOWS
(Pimephales and Hybognathus)

All proportions are expressed in percentage of standard length.

	Pimephales		Hybognathus	
	notatus	promelas	hankinsoni	regius
ST. LENGTH (mm)	52.2	47.5	51.4	50.4
TOTAL LENGTH	119.7	126.0	123.8	128.3
FORK LENGTH	111.3	116.9	115.5	115.2
PREDORSAL	51.3	54.8	49.7	51.2
PREANAL	69.4	69.4	67.3	71.2
PREPELVIC	49.5	54.3	51.3	52.4
DORSAL BASE	14.6	13.0	11.7	12.2
ANAL BASE	6.4	7.4	10.0	10.0
BODY DEPTH	21.6	29.1	22.5	24.1
BODY WIDTH	14.2	19.7	14.6	15.0
C.PED. DEPTH	9.4	13.0	10.3	10.7
PECTORAL ALT.	13.4	19.6	16.0	16.4
HEAD LENGTH	22.6	25.8	26.0	25.6
SNOUT	5.9	8.0	7.5	7.6
EYE	6.5	6.2	6.2	7.3
MOUTH LENGTH	6.2	6.4	5.7	6.6
INTERORB	7.6	10.2	9.8	7.3
N (sample size)	5	5	5	5
COUNTS:				
DORSAL RAYS	8	8	8	8
ANAL RAYS	7	7	8	8 (9)
PECTORAL RAYS	15-16	15-16	13	15-16
PELVIC RAYS	8	8	8	7-8
GILL RAKERS	9	13	8-9	10-11
VERTEBRAE*	34-36	33-34	33	33-35
SCALES:				
ABOVE L. L.	6	7	5-6	6
LATERAL LINE	42-50	41-54	36-41	38-40
BELOW L. L.	4	5	3-4	4
PHARYNGEAL TEETH	4-4	4-4	4-4	4-4

* Excluding Weberian apparatus.

TROUTS

SALMONIDAE

Members of this family are perhaps the best known of all of New York fishes. They are sometimes colorful, reach a respectable size, and are justly famed for their wariness and fighting qualities. Their flesh is highly esteemed and some species are abundant enough to be of both sport and commercial importance.

Salmonids are rather primitive fishes. They have soft fin supports, the maxillary bone forms part of the margin of the upper jaw, and they have an adipose dorsal fin and abdominal pelvic fins. The family is not a large one; at present, 9 genera and about 70 species are recognized. Originally, they were all confined to the Northern Hemisphere but several species have been introduced into the southern continents and even to the high altitudes of the tropics. Salmonids are very physical fishes. They are able to survive on insects and other invertebrate prey and thus they can thrive in habitats that contain no other fish species as long as they have cool and well-oxygenated waters.

Two groups of salmonidae are represented in our waters: The whitefishes and ciscoes of the subfamily Coregoninae, which have large scales and tend to be silvery or white in color, and the Salmoninae (trouts, chars and salmons) which have tiny scales and tend to be more colorful. Attempts to introduce a representative of a third subfamily, the Thymallinae or graylings, have not been successful. Our native species are the brook trout (our state fish), the lake trout, the Atlantic salmon, and the whitefishes. In addition, the brown trout from Europe and the rainbow trout from western North America have been successfully established here, and several species of Pacific salmons are presently being maintained by stocking and one or two species seem to have established breeding populations in a few streams.

Under artificial and even some natural conditions, many species of salmonids can interbreed. Some hybrid combinations such as the splake, a cross between the brook trout and the lake trout, are routinely used for stocking because they grow faster and have reduced fertility so that the populations are easier to control. Field identification of hybrids is sometimes difficult. Buss and Wright (1958) presented photographs of hybrid combinations that are useful for confirming the identification of suspected hybrids. The identification guide by Decker et al. (1978) will prove useful to the fisherman.

KEY TO THE SPECIES OF SALMONS, TROUTS, AND WHITEFISHES IN NEW YORK

A. Color generally silvery, white or gray. Scales large, fewer than 100 in lateral line. Mouth small, the upper jaw not reaching the level of the front of the eye. **J.**

A'. Color darker, usually with definite spots or worm-like markings. Scales small, more than 100 in lateral line. Mouth large, reaching to below the eye or beyond.

B. Anal rays 13 to 19. **G.**

B'. Anal rays 7 to 12 (not counting the small splint-like rays at the front of the fins).

C. Scales very fine, more than 190 along lateral line. Teeth in midline of roof of mouth (vomerine teeth) confined to a raised area at the front of the vomer bone. Color pattern consisting of lighter markings on a darker background. Lower fins with a conspicuous white leading edge. **F.**

C'. Scales somewhat larger, fewer than 140 along lateral line. Teeth in the midline of the roof of the mouth in one or two rows running backward toward the throat, sometimes lost in older fish. Vomer bone without a raised crest at its anterior end. Color pattern consisting of dark marks on a lighter background. Lower fins without a conspicuous white leading edge.

Vomerine teeth of brown trout (left) and brook trout (right).

D. Caudal fin deeply forked, its middle rays less than half as long as the longest rays. Teeth in the midline of the roof of the mouth lost in older individuals. Large fish are silvery with X-shaped dark marks. Tail fin with only a few spots. Juveniles have red spots between their parr marks.
Salmo salar   **Atlantic salmon, p. 228**

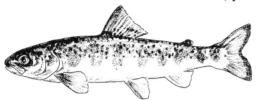

D'. Caudal fin not deeply forked, its middle rays more than half as long as the longest rays. Teeth on vomer permanent.

E. Back and sides with diffuse brownish spots. Red spots on sides often surrounded by a blue ring. Adipose fin orange in young, without a black margin. Dorsal fin origin much closer to tip of snout than to middle of caudal base. Pelvic fin insertion under posterior half of the dorsal fin base.
Salmo trutta   **Brown trout, p. 230**

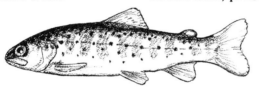

E'. Back and sides with sharply outlined spots that are also present on both lobes of the tail. Adipose fin distinctly outlined in black with a pale center. No red spots but adult males have a broad red stripe along the midsides. Dorsal fin origin about equidistant between tip of snout and middle of caudal base, slightly closer to snout in older fish. Pelvic fin originates under anterior half of dorsal base.
Salmo gairdneri   **Rainbow trout, p. 227**

F. (C. Scales very fine. Color pattern of light marks on a darker background.) Caudal fin square or slightly forked. Body with red spots. Pelvic and anal fins with a dark stripe behind the white leading edge.
Salvelinus fontinalis   **Brook trout, p. 232**

F'. Caudal fin strongly forked. Body without red spots, sides with gray or silver spots. White leading edge of lower fins not followed by a conspicuous black line.
Salvelinus namaycush   **Lake trout, p. 236**

Note: Hybrids between lake trout and brook trout, called splake, are stocked in New York. They are intermediate between the parent species and this is perhaps most obvious in the depth of the fork of the caudal fin.

G. (B. Anal rays 13 to 19.) No distinct spots on the back or caudal fin although there is usually some speckling. Gill rakers on first arch 30 to 39.
Oncorhynchus nerka   **Kokanee, p. 223**

G'. Back and tail fin with distinct spots. Gill rakers 18 to 40.

H. Black spots on back and tail large, about equal to the diameter of the eye. Gill rakers 26 to 34. Scales small, 169 to 229 in the first row above the lateral line.
Oncorhynchus gorbuscha   **Pink salmon, p. 221**

H'. Black spots on back and tail small, the largest about the size of the pupil. Gill rakers 19 to 30. Scales larger, generally fewer than 154 in the first row above the lateral line.

I. Black spots present on back and the upper lobe of the tail. Tissue at base of the teeth lightly pigmented. Pyloric caeca fewer than 100. Anal fin high, the longest rays at the front of the fin reaching more than two-thirds of the way to the end of the fin when bent back along the body.
Oncorhynchus kisutch   **Coho salmon, p. 222**

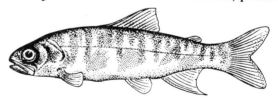

I'. Black spots present on the back and on both lobes of the caudal fin. Tissue at base of teeth black. Pyloric caeca more than 120. Anal fin low, its longest rays reaching less than two-thirds of the way to the end of the fin when depressed.
Oncorhynchus tshawytscha
          Chinook salmon, p. 224

J. (A. Color plain silvery or gray, scales large.) Mouth terminal, the snout not definitely overhanging the mouth. **L.**

J'. Mouth inferior, the premaxillaries broad and directed backward so that the snout overhangs the mouth.

K. A single flap between the nostrils. Gill rakers fewer than 20 on the first arch, short, the longest only about 1.5 times as long as the space between the bases of the neighboring gill rakers. Body little compressed, nearly round in cross section.
Prosopium cylindraceum
Round whitefish, p. 219

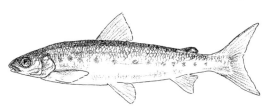

K'. Two flaps between the anterior and posterior nostrils. Gill rakers more than 21, moderately long, the longest about five times as long as the interspaces.
Coregonus clupeaformis
Lake whitefish, p. 212

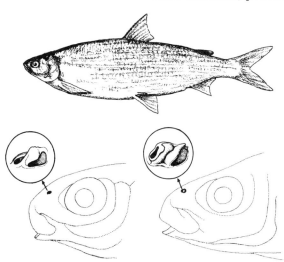

Nostrils of round whitefish (left) and lake whitefish (right).

L. (J. Mouth terminal.) Lower jaw frail and long, usually protruding beyond the upper jaw and usually with a pronounced knob at its tip. **N.**

L'. Lower jaw about equal to, or somewhat shorter than, the upper, without a knob at its tip.

M. Gill rakers more than 43 (sometimes as few as 37 in Lake Erie specimens).
Coregonus artedii
Cisco, p. 210

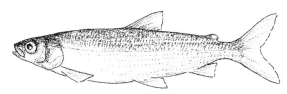

Cisco, *Coregonus artedii*

M'. Gill rakers fewer than 43 (usually fewer than 34 in Lake Erie specimens). Great Lakes only. Three deepwater species, the longjaw cisco, *C. alpenae*, from Lake Erie, the shortnose cisco, *C. reighardi*, from Lake Ontario and the shortjaw cisco, *C. zenithicus*, from Lake Ontario will key out here. These species are presumed to be extinct in New York and were so variable that their identification is uncertain. See species accounts.

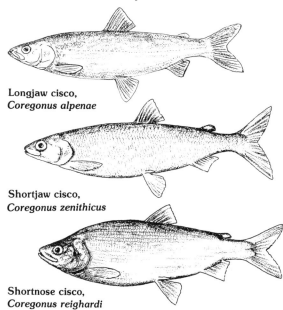

Longjaw cisco,
Coregonus alpenae

Shortjaw cisco,
Coregonus zenithicus

Shortnose cisco,
Coregonus reighardi

N. (L. Lower jaw long and frail.) Tip and anterior side of upper jaw heavily pigmented. Eye large, about 3.9 to 4.2 in head; pectoral fins long. Fall spawners (August to October.) Lateral line (41) 76 to 87 (91). Body ovate in side view, its deepest part ahead of the dorsal fin.
Coregonus kiyi
Kiyi, p. 215

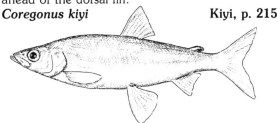

N'. Tip and anterior side of upper jaw lightly pigmented. Eye smaller, about 4 to 4.5 in head. Pectoral fins not as long. Body deep and more elliptical, deepest at middle. Spring spawners (November to March.) Lateral line scales (63) 68 to 76 (81).
Coregonus hoyi
Bloater, p. 214

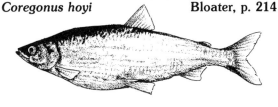

Coregonus

The genus *Coregonus* is characterized by its silvery-white coloration, adipose dorsal fin, and pelvic axillary process. There are fewer than 100 scales in the lateral line and a double flap between the nostrils. Some authorities separate the lake whitefish (the only species with a subterminal mouth) as the only American species of *Coregonus* and place all of the others in the genus *Leucichthys*.

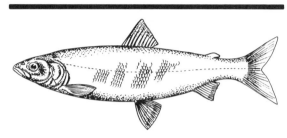

LONGJAW CISCO

Coregonus alpenae (Koelz, 1924)

Identification

The longjaw cisco is quite similar to the lake herring, *Coregonus artedii,* but has a broader back, heavier head and head parts and a blunter snout. Scott and Smith noted that gill raker counts for the longjaw cisco were 30 to 34 on the lower limb of the first arch and this provided a good separation from the lake herring which has counts of 37 to 53 in Lake Erie. In about half of the specimens, the lower jaw extends beyond the upper. Scott and Smith used a discriminant function to separate the two:

$$F = R (100 \ CR/LA)$$

Where: R = number of gill rakers;
CR = length of the center gill raker;
LA = length of the lower gill arch.

For *C. alpenae* F = 64 to 77 (average 69.2) and for *C. artedii* F = 82 to 96 (average 89.5). In Lake Erie the length of the lower gill arch is greater for *alpenae* (100 to 113, average 107) than for *artedii* (84 to 105, average 94). These lengths are expressed in thousandths of the standard length.

Description

Other than the differences noted above, this species is very similar to the cisco or lake herring.

Habitat

The specimens examined by Scott and Smith came from commercial nets and from some experimental nets fished at 33 to 34 fathoms and a trawl fished at 17 fathoms. One specimen was taken within 20 feet of the bottom in water 80 feet deep.

Distribution

This form occurs, or did occur, in the eastern basin of Lake Erie.

Life History

Scott and Smith noted that specimens taken on 11 November 1957 had pearl organs and ripe gonads, hence the species probably spawns in late Novem-

ber. Maturity is reached at least by the start of the fourth growing season. Age group III fish from 1946 ranged from 12.2 to 13.6 inches. A 1957 age IV was 13.7 inches long. Age group III from 1957 ranged from 10.2 to 12.6 (average 11.6). Specimens collected in 1957 had back-calculated lengths of 5.1 inches total length at the first annulus, 8.6 at the second, and 10.6 at the third.

Food and Feeding

The food habits of the longjaw cisco have not been reported.

Notes

Scott and Smith suggested that *Leucichthys macropterus* Bean, which is generally considered to have been an aberrant cisco, may actually have been this species. Todd, in Lee et al. (1980) stated that the species *alpenae* which was known from Lakes Michigan, Huron, and Erie, was probably not a valid species but a variant of the shortjaw cisco, *Coregonus zenithicus.* It is probably extinct throughout its range. To what extent it differed from the *zenithicus* of Lake Ontario will probably never be known.

References

Scott and Smith, 1962 (presence and biology in Lake Erie.) Todd in Lee et al., 1980 (probably not valid.) Koelz, 1931 (characters.) Jobes, 1949a (age and growth.)

Names

This species is named for the town of Alpena, Michigan.

Leucichthys alpenae Koelz, 1924: 1-8 Lake Michigan

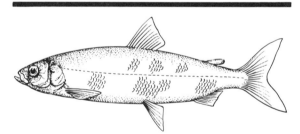

CISCO or LAKE HERRING

Coregonus artedii Lesueur, 1818

Identification

Its silvery white color, prominent adipose fin, spindle-shaped body and moderate-sized scales readily identify the cisco as a member of the whitefish complex. It differs from the lake whitefish, *Coregonus clupeaformis,* and the round whitefish, *Prosopium cylindraceum,* in that it has a terminal mouth whereas those species have the mouth slightly back on the underside of the snout.

In our waters, the only species with which the cisco might be confused are the deepwater ciscoes which belong to one, two, or three species. In Lake Erie, it is closely similar to a much rarer species which Scott and Smith (1962) identified as the longjaw cisco, *Coregonus alpenae,* but which Todd (in Lee et al. 1980) has suggested might be the shortjaw cisco, *Coregonus zenithicus*. The two can be told apart on the basis of gill raker count, usually more than 43 (rarely as few as 37) in *C. artedii*, fewer than 43 in *C. alpenae*.

In Lake Ontario the problem was more complex. Four deepwater ciscoes have been reported, all of which may now be extinct. Here too, gill rakers provide the best means of distinguishing the species. (See discussion under longjaw cisco.)

Description

Body elongate, fusiform, and relatively slender. Dorsal profile slightly more curved than the ventral. Dorsal origin midway between tip of snout and end of anal base. Dorsal deltoid with sharp corners and slightly concave margin. Adipose dorsal over rear of anal fin. Caudal fin deeply forked. Anal fin deltoid, its margin straight. Pelvic fins inserted below rear fourth of dorsal fin base, retrogressive. Pelvic axillary process well developed. Pectorals retrogressive, low and slightly oblique. Gill membranes separate and free from isthmus. Lower jaw slightly longer than the upper. Lateral line straight. Maxillary reaching to below the front half of the eye. Counts and proportional measurements are given in Tables 21 and 22.

Color: Variable. Back dusky gray to bluish, greenish or tan. Scales of back with silvery reflections; those of the sides and belly silvery white. Iris silvery. Dorsal, anal, and caudal fins with some darker pigment, usually dusky toward their margins. Pectoral and pelvic fins clear or whitish in adults.

Juveniles and breeding adults: Juveniles lack parr marks. Breeding males have pearl organs, one on each scale in the rows above and below the lateral line and on all sides of the head. Females have tubercles on the body but not on the head or fins.

Size: The maximum length of the lake herring is over 16 inches but the usual size is 8 to 12 inches. The state angling record is held by a 1-pound 8-ounce fish from Sodus Bay, Lake Ontario, caught 22 April 1982 by Michael Mannara.

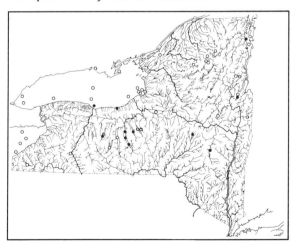

Habitat

Ciscoes are definitely lake fish and most of the time they remain below the thermocline. They tend to school in midwater. As the water cools in the fall they move into shallow areas. Ciscoes are reasonably tolerant of turbidity; there was no effect on growth or survival when young ciscoes were raised in turbidities of up to 46 formazin units. Upper lethal temperatures of 20 and 26 C. have been reported.

Distribution

The cisco is widely distributed in the northern part of North America from New England to eastern Quebec and Labrador west to the Northwest Territories, Great Bear Lake, and the Mackenzie River drainage. It reaches its southern limit in the Great Lakes and the Upper Mississippi drainage of Illinois, Wisconsin, and Minnesota.

In New York it occurs in Lakes Erie, Ontario, Champlain, Chautauqua, Oneida, the Finger Lakes, Otsego Lake, and a number of Adirondack lakes and ponds. It has been introduced into Rushford Lake in the Genesee drainage. Koelz separated the ciscoes of Lake George, Paradox Lake, and Millsite Lake in the St. Lawrence drainage as a separate subspecies, *Coregonus artedi greeleyi*, but George (1981b) noted that there have been subsequent introductions of ciscoes, not necessarily of the same stock, so it is difficult to evaluate the differences noted by Koelz.

Life History

Ciscoes spawn in the late fall when they move into waters sometimes as shallow as 10 feet. Often the spawning takes place when the ice is forming along the shores. Brown and Moffitt studied food and fecundity of ciscoes in a small lake in southern Michigan. Spawning was in progress on 14 December 1939, the night the lake froze over for the winter. Individuals were seen breaking the surface during the early evening and most of the fish taken in gill nets showed signs of having spawned. Females ranged from 5 to 9 years old and were 15.25 to 16.25 inches total length. Egg counts averaged 32,328 and other workers have found egg counts ranging from 6,000 in Lake Superior to 29,000 in Lake Erie. Development is slow, 92 days at 5.6 C and 236 days at 0.5 C. In Oneida Lake, Smith found that most ciscoes developed a false annulus that was attributed to high temperatures in late summer. There were also massive die-offs of larger fish each summer and it appeared that this was also related to high temperature. About 80 percent of the dead ciscoes had lamprey scars and this may have lessened their ability to withstand high temperatures.

Food and Feeding

Ciscoes are primarily plankton feeders throughout their lives. A study in Wisconsin revealed little selectivity although ciscoes ate few rotifers in comparison with their abundance in the environment. Insects, fish eggs, and small fish are also eaten and ice fishermen catch them using minnows for bait.

Notes

All of the whitefishes are variable and this variability is difficult to interpret. As a result, their taxonomy has been confused and is still in a state of flux. The most extensive work on ciscoes is that of Walter Koelz. In his 1931 paper, Koelz recognized a large number of subspecies, six of which he found in New York:

C. artedii albus in Lake Erie;

C. a. artedii in Lakes Erie, Ontario, Champlain, Cayuga, and Otisco;

C. a. greeleyi in Lakes George, Canandaigua, Keuka, Owasco, Skaneateles, Millsite Lake in the St. Lawrence drainage, and Paradox Lake;

C. a. huronicus in Chautauqua Lake;

C. a. hankinsoni in Oneida Lake;

C. a. osmeriformis in Seneca Lake.

Subsequent stockings may have obscured the differences between these forms which were weakly differentiated at best. Many of the observed differences may be attributable to the effects of variations in the environment. Their names are included here only to emphasize the variability of the species. In Canada the problem is even more complex and some forms are recognized as full species by some workers and as subspecies by others.

References

Lindsey and Woods (eds.), 1970 (series of papers on whitefish biology). Swenson and Matson, 1976 (effects of turbidity). Cahn, 1927a (biology). Brown and Moffitt, 1942 (fecundity and feeding). Pritchard, 1930 (Lake Ontario). Colby and Brooke, 1973 (effect of temperature on development). Engel, 1976 (food habits). Van Oosten, 1929 (life history). Koelz, 1929; 1931 (systematics). D. Smith, 1972 (age and growth in Oneida Lake). Smith, 1957 (life history in Lake Michigan). Dryer and Beil, 1964 (Lake Superior). McCormick, Jones and Syrett, 1971 (temperature requirements). Hinricks and Booke, 1975 (eggs, larval ecology). Peters and LaBar, 1980 (fecundity in Lake Champlain).

Names

The species is named in honor of Petrus Artedi, an early ichthyologist who worked closely with Linnaeus.

This is one of the few species for which the American Fisheries Society accepts alternate names of cisco and lake herring. Tullibee is a less commonly used name.

There is also disagreement about the generic name. Some authors believe that the ciscoes are sufficiently different from the lake whitefish and its relatives to be placed in a separate genus *Leucichthys*.

Coregonus artedi Lesueur, 1818b: 231-232 Lake Erie and Niagara River at Lewiston

Argyrosomus artedi, Evermann and Smith, 1896: 305-309 Great Lakes

Leucichthys artedi, Jordan and Evermann, 1911: 17-19 Great Lakes

Coregonus clupeaformis DeKay, 1842: 248 Lake Ontario (misidentification)

Leucichthys ontariensis Jordan and Evermann, 1911: 13-14 Lake Ontario

Leucichthys macropterus Bean, 1916: 25-26 Lake Erie (A "monstrosity"; may have been *C. alpenae* according to Scott and Smith, 1962: 1018.)

Argyrosomus tullibee (non Richardson), Bean, 1903: 238-240 Onondaga Lake

Argyrosomus hoyi (non Gill), Bean, 1903: 235-237 Canandaigua Lake

Leucichthys artedi artedi (Lesueur), Koelz, 1931: 330 Ontario, Hudson, and St. Lawrence drainages; Lake Champlain and Otisco and Cayuga Lakes

Argyrosomus eriensis Jordan and Evermann, 1909: 165-167 Lakes Erie and Huron

Leucichthys eriensis, Jordan and Evermann, 1911: 20-22

Leucichthys artedi huronicus Koelz, 1931: 317-319 Chautauqua Lake (doubtful)

Argyrosomus huronius Jordan and Evermann, 1909: 167-169 Lakes Erie and Huron

Leucichthys cisco huronius, Jordan and Evermann, 1911: 12-13 Lakes Michigan, Huron, and Erie

Leucichthys artedi greeleyi Koelz, 1931: 313-317 Torch Lake, Michigan; Canandaigua, Keuka, Owasco, Skaneateles, Millsite, and Paradox Lakes and Lake George

Leucichthys artedi hankinsoni Koelz, 1931: 323 Oneida Lake

Leucichthys artedi osmeriformis, Koelz, 1931: 339 Seneca Lake (not Skaneateles Lake)

Coregonus osmeriformis Smith, 1895: pl. 1 and 2 Skaneateles and Seneca Lakes

Argyrosomus osmeriformis, Bean, 1903: 230-233

Leucichthys artedi albus, Koelz, 1929: 478 Lakes Erie, Ontario, and Superior

Coregonus albus Lesueur, 1818b: 232 Lake Erie

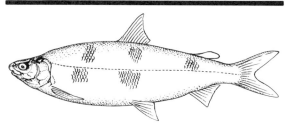

LAKE WHITEFISH

Coregonus clupeaformis (Mitchill, 1818)

Identification

The lake whitefish and the round whitefish are the only local salmonids with small, undershot mouths. All of the rest have somewhat larger, terminal mouths. The two differ in shape, the round whitefish being nearly round in cross section. Another difference is that the round whitefish has a single rather than a double flap between the anterior and posterior nostrils on each side. There is a striking and conclusive difference in the number of gill rakers. The lake whitefish has between 20 and 32 moderately long gill rakers (total count) on the first arch but the round whitefish has fewer than 20.

Description

Body elongate but variable in depth, slab sided, with the dorsal profile more curved than the ventral. First dorsal fin deltoid, retrogressive, with moderately sharp corners, and nearly straight margin. Dorsal origin midway between tip of snout and rear third of adipose fin. Adipose well developed. Caudal moderately forked, with bluntly pointed lobes. Anal fin base centered below origin of adipose fin. Anal similar in shape to dorsal. Pelvic origin below middle of dorsal base. Pelvic axillary process well developed. Pelvic retrogressive, with angled corners. Pectoral low, retrogressive, its base slightly inclined. Premaxillaries retrorse, snout overhanging the mouth. Mouth rather small, maxillary ending below anterior margin of eye. Gill membranes separate and free from the isthmus. Opercle and preopercle rounded. Counts and proportional measurements are given in Table 22.

Color: The general color is silver gray with the top of the head and body darker gray, sometimes brownish or greenish, and the belly white. Darker scale margins give the upper parts a reticulated appearance. The fins are dusky, sometimes with darker tips.

Juveniles and breeding adults: Breeding tubercles are present in both sexes but better developed in the males. They are present on all scales but best developed on the middle six or seven rows on the flanks; smaller on the back and belly. Tubercles are also present on all surfaces of the head including the branchiostegal rays, and on the anterior rays of the pectoral and pelvic fins. A few tubercles are present on the first dorsal ray.

Size: The lake whitefish commonly reaches lengths of 18 to 24 inches and weights of 2 to 6 pounds. The largest reported individual weighed 42 pounds. The New York angling record is held by a 7-pound 1-ounce fish taken by James Treadway in Eagle Lake, September 1979.

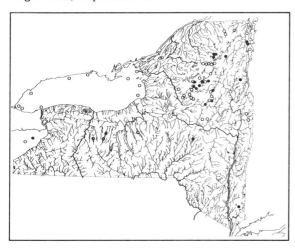

Habitat

Lake whitefish are limited to lakes and large rivers where they remain in the cooler water below the thermocline during the warmer parts of the year. They often move into shallows during the spring and again during the fall breeding season. Young whitefish occur in the shore zone during the spring but move offshore in early summer. They occur in brackish water in the Northwest Territories and in the Hudson Bay region.

Distribution

The lake whitefish ranges throughout most of Canada, Alaska and the Great Lakes, with a few populations in cooler lakes in New York and New England. It has been introduced into parts of Montana and Washington. In New York, it occurs in the Great Lakes and Lake Champlain and in the Finger Lakes, Otsego Lake, and through introductions, in the Adirondacks. Dr. Carl George has reviewed the history of the Great Lakes whitefish in the Adirondacks from the original stocking with fish from Labrador. Koelz assigned the offspring from the original stocking to the subspecies *neohantoniensis* (Prescott) and also recognized another, smaller, form, *C. c. gulliveri* Koelz, in Lake of the Woods, Blue Mountain Lake, Brantingham Lake, and possibly Chateaugay Lake.

Life History

Spawning of the lake whitefish occurs somewhat earlier than that of the cisco, usually beginning when the water temperature drops to about 46 F. Spawning generally takes place near shore in water about 25 feet deep or sometimes deeper, over rock, gravel, or sand. The details of spawning behavior have not been reported but some authors have noted that whitefish thrash around at the surface and sometimes jump clear of the water. There are indications that much of the spawning takes place at night. The eggs are demersal and slightly adhesive. The water-hardened eggs are 3.0 to 3.2 mm in diameter. Fecundity has been estimated at 8,200 to 16,000 eggs per pound of the female's weight. Development is slow and at temperatures of 33 to 43 F, hatching usually does not take place until April or May.

Food and Feeding

The lake whitefish is a bottom feeder and its primary foods are amphipods, mollusks, and insect larvae. They sometimes feed on fish eggs and small fish.

Notes

The lake whitefish is an important commercial fish and also provides some sport fishing, especially for the ice fisherman.

Koelz recognized three subspecies in New York.

References

Koelz, 1929; 1931 (taxonomy). Hart, 1930 (spawning and life history). Van Oosten and Deason, 1939 (age and growth in Lake Champlain). Price, 1940 (development). Lock, 1974 (variation). Newell, 1976 (population dynamics). Edsall and Rottiers, 1976 (temperature tolerance). Scott and Crossman, 1973 (general summary). Weisel, 1966 (juveniles). George, 1981a (Adirondacks).

Names

Clupeaformis is Latin meaning shaped like a herring.

Salmo clupeaformis Mitchill, 1818a: 321 Sault Sainte Marie

Coregonus clupeaformis, Evermann and Smith, 1896: 297-301 Great Lakes

Salmo otsego Clinton, 1822: 1-6 Otsego Lake

Coregonus labradoricus Richardson, 1836: 206 Musquaw River, Labrador

Coregonus labradoricus, Evermann and Smith, 1896: 302-305 Great Lakes

Coregonus otsego, DeKay, 1842: 248-249

Coregonus albus, Jordan and Evermann, 1911: 37-38 Lakes Erie and St. Clair (not of Lesueur which is C. artedii)

Coregonus clupeaformis clupeaformis, Koelz, 1931: 373 Great Lakes, etc.

Coregonus clupeaformis latus Koelz, 1931: 373-378 Lake Erie

Coregonus neo-hantoniensis Prescott, 1851: 343 Lake Winnepesaukee

Coregonus clupeaformis neo-hantoniensis, Koelz, 1931: 374-376 Lakes Champlain, Otsego, Chazy, Kiwassa, Clear, Eagle, and Saranac

Coregonus clupeaformis gulliveri Koelz, 1931: 380-382 Chateaugay Lake, St. Lawrence drainage

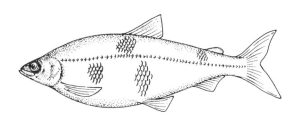

BLOATER

Coregonus hoyi (Gill, 1872)

Identification

The bloater is a deepwater species that is immediately separated from the lake whitefish and the round whitefish by its terminal mouth. It differs from the lake herring, *C. artedii*, and from all of the deepwater ciscoes in Lake Ontario, except the kiyi, in that most individuals have the lower jaw longer than the upper so that the lower jaw protrudes when the mouth is closed. Additionally, both the kiyi and the bloater have a pronounced knob at the tip of the lower jaw and the tips of the jaws are in line with the profile of the top of the head and the snout. In the other ciscoes, the tips of the jaws curve downward so that they are below a continuation of the profile of the head and snout. Bloaters and kiyis have longer fins than other ciscoes; the sum of the lengths of the longest rays of the dorsal, anal, pectoral, and pelvic fins is equal to 56 to 67 percent of the standard length.

The kiyi and the bloater are similar and difficult to tell apart and most of their characters overlap. Usually, the body of the bloater is elliptical, deepest at the dorsal fin, while that of the kiyi is deepest ahead of the dorsal. In the bloater, the longest anal ray is about as long as the base of the fin; in the kiyi, it is longer. Bloaters spawn later than kiyi, so female bloaters taken during the summer have smaller eggs than kiyis taken at the same time.

Description

Body somewhat slab sided, fusiform, deepest at the front of the dorsal fin. Upper and lower profiles about equally curved. Dorsal retrogressive, deltoid, its corners sharp, its margin straight. Dorsal origin midway between caudal base and tip of snout. Adipose fin closer to caudal base than to end of dorsal base. Caudal moderately forked, its lobes pointed. Anal fin inserted well ahead of the adipose dorsal, retrogressive, trapezoidal, with sharp corners and low lobe anteriorly. Pelvics inserted below middle of dorsal base. Pelvic axillary process well developed. Pelvic retrogressive, its anterior corner pointed, its posterior corner rounded. Pectoral low with inclined base, retrogressive, with convex margin, pointed anteriorly and rounded posteriorly. Head pointed, mouth terminal, with lower jaw projecting. Body fully scaled, head naked. Scales cycloid. Gill membranes separate and free from the isthmus. Counts and proportional measurements are given in Tables 21 and 22.

Color: Silvery white with a slightly gray tinge above the lateral line. Top of head fairly heavily pigmented. Dorsal fin tipped with black, dorsal edge of the pectoral fin with a broad dark margin, and the margin of the caudal dusky to black. Anal, pelvic, and adipose fins immaculate.

Size: The bloater is the smallest of the deepwater ciscoes and, in the 1930s, it averaged about 8 inches total length. Koelz reported that the largest bloaters he saw averaged about 277 mm standard length but the usual size was seldom more than 250 mm. Some individuals are sexually mature at 250 mm.

Habitat

In Lake Ontario, the bloater occurred at depths from 125 to 400 feet and was most abundant at 250 to 300 feet. The upper lethal temperature was 26.75 C.

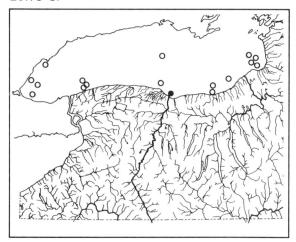

Distribution

Bloaters are, or were, found in Lakes Superior, Michigan, Huron, Nipigon, and Ontario. In Lake Ontario, it was generally distributed throughout the lake wherever the water was the right depth.

Life History

Bloaters spawn in the late fall and winter (November to January), which is later than the spawning of the kiyi. They grow more slowly than other deepwater ciscoes, reaching about 144 mm in their second summer and 255 mm in their seventh summer. A few are mature after their second summer; nearly all are mature in their third summer. The fecundity of 5-year-olds in Lake Michigan increased 22 percent from 1967-69 to 1973-75, even more from the 1950s when they were more abundant. A 241-mm female contained 3,230 eggs; a 305-mm female contained 18,678 eggs.

Food and Feeding

Pritchard found little difference in the diets of four species of ciscoes from Lake Ontario. All ate some flatworms, some mollusks and some insects but crustaceans, cladocerans, copepods, ostracods, and especially amphipods and mysid shrimps were the most important items in the diet.

Notes

A number of authors have reviewed changes in the species composition of the deepwater ciscoes. In general, the bloater, because of its small size and rather poor-quality flesh was not intensively fished. The larger mesh commercial gill nets took relatively few bloaters. Its early maturity, combined with lower fishing mortality, enabled it to thrive as the other species declined. In Lake Ontario, as in the other Great Lakes where it occurs, it gradually came to dominate the catch. In 1927, it made up 21 percent of the catch but by 1942 it accounted for 98.6 percent. Between 1900 and 1925, there was a gradual decline in the annual catch of all deepwater ciscoes but from 1925 to about 1940 the catch increased as large predators became scarce. Then, in the late 1940s, the populations began to decline rapidly and by 1960 there was no commercial fishing for any deepwater cisco in Lake Ontario. Bloater, kiyi, and shortnose ciscoes were taken by research vessels as late as 1964 but have not been found since.

References

Koelz, 1929 (taxonomy). Pritchard, 1931 (ecology in Lake Ontario). Stone, 1947 (Lake Ontario). Jobes, 1949b (age and growth, Lake Michigan). Smith, 1964 (Lake Michigan populations). Wells, 1969 (population changes). Christie, 1973 (changes in Lake Ontario); 1974 (changes in Great Lakes populations). Edsall et al., 1970 (temperature tolerance). Emery and Brown, 1978 (fecundity). Wells and Beeton, 1963 (food).

Names

The species name is in honor of Dr. P. R. Hoy of Wisconsin who collected fishes from Lake Michigan and published on the deepwater fauna of that lake. The name bloater refers to the tendency of the fish to expand when brought to the surface from deep water. This and other species are called chubs in the commercial fishery.

Argyrosomus hoyi Gill in Hoy, 1872: 99 Lake Michigan

Leucichthys hoyi, Koelz, 1929: 473-476 Lake Ontario

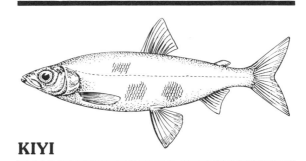

KIYI

Coregonus kiyi (Koelz, 1921)

Identification

The kiyi differs from the round whitefish and the lake whitefish in having a terminal rather than an inferior jaw. It differs from the other deepwater ciscoes, except the bloater, in that the lower jaw is longer than the upper and its tip lies in line with the profile of the top of the head and snout. In the other deepwater ciscoes, the tips of the upper and lower jaws curve downward so that they are below the extension of the upper profile. Both the kiyi and the bloater have a slight knob at the tip of the lower jaw.

The bloater and the kiyi are closely similar and difficult to distinguish as nearly all of their characteristics show some overlap. Usually, they differ in body shape. The kiyi is ovate with the body deepest anterior to the dorsal fin. The bloater is deepest at the front of the dorsal fin. The kiyi has a higher anal fin; its longest ray is longer than the anal fin base. The kiyi spawns earlier in the fall, therefore females caught in the summer have larger eggs than female bloaters taken at the same time.

Description

Body elongate, slab sided, deepest anterior to the dorsal fin. Profiles about equally curved. Dorsal origin midway between caudal base and tip of snout. Dorsal fin retrogressive, deltoid, with sharp corners. Adipose much closer to caudal base than to end of dorsal base. Caudal moderately forked, with pointed lobes. Anal origin far anterior to beginning of adipose. Anal trapezoidal, with sharp corners and a definite anterior lobe. Pelvic insertion below middle of dorsal base. Pelvic axillary process large. Pelvic fin large, retrogressive, with pointed anterior corner and rounded posterior corner. Pectoral fin low with sloping base, retrogressive, pointed anterior corner and rounded posterior corner. Mouth terminal, lower jaw projecting. Maxillary ending below front of pupil. Body completely scaled, head naked, scales cycloid. Gill membranes separate and free from isthmus. Counts and proportional measurements are given in Tables 21 and 22.

Color: (from Pritchard, 1931). Back quite dark, shading to silvery on the belly. Sides show a blue tinge. First ray of dorsal black, tips of rays with much pigment. Pectorals black on dorsal edge, adipose and occasionally pelvic fins sprinkled with black. Snout and lower jaw heavily pigmented.

Juveniles and breeding adults: Breeding tubercles are present on the head and body of males and possibly females.

Size: The kiyi is seldom larger than 200 mm standard length. In the 1930s, when several species of ciscoes were abundant in Lake Michigan, it averaged 10.2 inches (260 mm) total length. Koelz reported the maximum size seen was 263 mm standard length. It is the smallest cisco except for the bloater.

Habitat
Pritchard reported that the kiyi occurred in water 250 to 475 feet deep with its maximum abundance at about 410 feet. Apparently, it occurred throughout Lake Ontario at these depths.

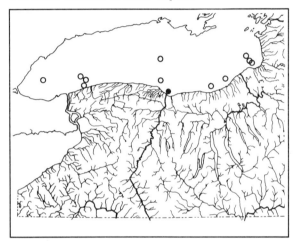

Distribution
The kiyi occurred in Lakes Superior, Huron, Michigan, and Ontario. Koelz recognized the Ontario population as a distinct subspecies based on gill raker count, 34 to 45 in *C. k. kiyi* and 41 to 48 in *C. k. orientalis* of Lake Ontario.

Life History
The kiyi spawned in fall and early winter (August to January) somewhat earlier than the bloater. Some kiyi matured at about 140 mm standard length and most were ripe in the fall of the third year when they averaged about 203 mm. Fish with two annuli averaged 178 mm, those with six annuli averaged 274 mm, and no older fish were taken.

Food and Feeding
Pritchard found plant material, flatworms, crustaceans, insects, mollusks, and eggs of unknown species in the stomachs. Amphipods (*Pontoporeia*) and mysid shrimps were the most important items in the diet.

Notes
Unlike the bloater, which increased for a time, the kiyi has shown a continuous decline, at least in Lake Michigan (comparable data are not available for Lake Ontario because the species were not separated in the records). Kiyi were last reported from Lake Ontario in 1964.

References
Koelz, 1929 (taxonomy). Pritchard, 1931(ecology in Lake Ontario). Hile and Deason, 1947 (ecology in Lake Michigan). Deason and Hile, 1947 (age and growth in Lake Michigan). Smith, 1964 (population changes in Lake Michigan). Christie, 1973 (changes in Lake Ontario). Wells, 1969 (Lake Ontario).

Names
The scientific name of this species comes from the common name used by Lake Michigan fishermen. It is variously called chub, kiyi, or waterbelly.

Leucichthys kiyi Koelz, 1921: 1-4 Lakes Michigan, Superior and Huron

Leucichthys kiyi orientalis Koelz, 1929: 445-446 Lake Ontario

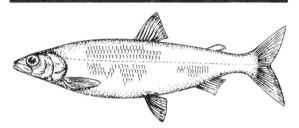

SHORTNOSE CISCO
Coregonus reighardi (Koelz, 1924)

Identification
The shortnose is said to be the most distinctive of the deepwater ciscoes of Lake Ontario. Its gill raker count is low, 30 to 43, usually 34 to 38, Its snout is short and the lower jaw is stout and short and fits inside the upper when the mouth is closed. The lower jaw also has considerable pigment and the snout is heavily pigmented. It was a spring spawner whereas *C. zenithicus* (*prognathus*) was an early winter spawner.

Description
The shortnose has short fins; the body is deepest at the middle and little compressed, its width 47 to 62 percent of the greatest depth.

This is a rather heavily pigmented species with the dorsal and caudal fins quite dusky. The other fins are clear.

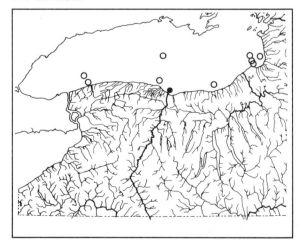

Habitat

Apparently, the species was most common in the shallow part of its depth range which was 6 to 90 fathoms.

Distribution

This deepwater cisco occurred in Lakes Huron, Michigan, and Ontario. Apparently, it is still extant only in the Georgian Bay region of Lake Huron. The last specimens from Lake Ontario were taken in 1964 and none have been seen in Lake Michigan since 1972.

Life History

The shortnose was a spring spawner with the spawning peak in April or the first 2 weeks in May. Spent fish have been found as early as January and as late as the first week of June.

Notes

Populations in Lake Superior and Lake Nipigon were considered to be a separate subspecies by Koelz but Todd and Smith (unpublished, cited by Todd in Lee et al.,1980) found that those populations were conspecific with *C. zenithicus*. Todd also cites Clarke as stating that *C. r. reighardi* may be conspecific with *zenithicus* but, if so, the Lake Ontario population, which numerous authors treated as distinct from the form called *C. prognathus* (*Leucichthys nigripinnis prognathus* according to Koelz) may be unnamed.

References

Koelz, 1929 (systematics). Pritchard, 1931 (ecology).

Names

The species is named for Jacob Reighard, a University of Michigan zoologist who did some of the classical work on the breeding behavior of freshwater fishes.

Leucichthys reighardi Koelz, 1924: 5-8 Lake Michigan (USNM 87351)

Leucichthys reighardi reighardi, Koelz, 1929 Lake Ontario

Coregonus r. reighardi, Hubbs and Lagler, 1964

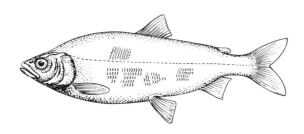

SHORTJAW CISCO

Coregonus zenithicus
(Jordan and Evermann, 1909)

Identification

In addition to the lake herring and the whitefish, four deepwater ciscoes are reported to have occurred in Lake Ontario. These are the bloater, *C.*

hoyi, the kiyi, *C. kiyi,* and two other forms which have been called *Coregonus reighardi* and *C. prognathus.* Koelz considered *C. prognathus* a subspecies of the blackfin cisco, *C. nigripinnis prognathus,* but recently Todd (1981) examined the types of *C. prognathus* and found that the type series included 3 *C. artedi,* 12 *C. hoyi,* 2 *C. kiyi,* 6 *C. reighardi* and 7 *C. zenithicus.* Todd considered the holotype to be unidentifiable and therefore rejected the name *prognathus* as a doubtful name that cannot be used for any species of whitefish.

Identification of the deepwater whitefishes is difficult at best but, unfortunately, the problem will probably not arise again because it now appears that the deepwater species have become extinct. Should it be found again, the shortjaw cisco could be recognized by its somewhat compressed shape, jaws equal in length, lower jaw rather stout without a symphyseal knob, and its gill raker count of 34 to 43.

Description

In general, the shortjaw cisco resembles the other deepwater ciscoes, but it has a terminal mouth with the jaws equal in length, the lower jaw stout with no pigment and medium pigment at the middle of the upper lip, and light pigment on the sides of the jaws. Counts and proportional measurements are given in Table 21.

Habitat

This was a deepwater form occurring at depths of 60 fathoms or more. Elsewhere, the species occurs in deeper lakes at depths of 11 to 100 fathoms, usually less than 30 fathoms.

Distribution

The shortjaw cisco occurred in Lakes Ontario, Huron and Superior and in a curved band to Great Slave Lake. Clarke and Todd *in* Lee et al. (1980) noted that presently only Lakes Superior and Nipigon have extant populations.

Life History

Pritchard found that *C. nigripinnis prognathus* spawned in January in Lake Ontario, moving inshore to water 40 to 50 fathoms deep. Assuming that he was referring to the species here called *C. zenithicus,* it would appear that the species spawned a little later than it does in other areas (November).

Food and Feeding

Mysis and *Pontoporeia* made up 95 percent of its food along with miscellaneous items such as midge larvae, fingernail clams, and debris.

Notes

Koelz (1929) reviewed the history of the fishery for what he called *Leucichthys nigripinnis prognathus.* Apparently, the fishery started in Oswego in 1875. Other fishermen joined the chase and by 1890 they were being taken in the western end of the lake out of Wilson. At first they were abundant, but by 1900 they were commercially extinct. Efforts to collect them in 1921 and 1923 were unsuccessful.

References

Pritchard, 1931 (ecology in Lake Ontario). Koelz, 1929 (taxonomy and life history). Christie, 1973 (Lake Ontario). Clarke and Todd *in* Lee et al., 1980(systematics and distribution). Van Oosten, 1937a (age and growth).

Names

The name *zenithicus* is from the French for zenith which in turn comes from the Arabic. The name actually refers to Duluth, Minnesota, the Zenith city.

Argyrosomus zenithicus Jordan and Evermann, 1909: 169 Lake Superior between Duluth and Isle Royale

Coregonus prognathus Smith, 1895: 4-13 Lake Ontario

Argyrosomus prognathus, Evermann and Smith, 1896: 314-317

Leucichthys prognathus, Jordan and Evermann, 1911: 23-24

Leucichthys nigripinnis prognathus, Koelz, 1929: 433-434

TABLE 21
COMPARISON OF DEEPWATER CISCOES *(Coregonus)* **OF LAKES ERIE AND ONTARIO**
(Compiled from various sources)

All proportions are expressed in percentage of standard length.

	alpenae[1]	reighardi	artedii	kiyi	hoyi	zenithicus
SNOUT PIGMENT	Light	Heavy	Heavy	Heavy	Light	Light
MANDIBLE	Long	Short, stout	Long	Long, frail	Long, frail	Short to long, frail
SPAWN IN	Fall	Spring	Fall	Fall	Spring	Fall
HEAD LENGTH	23.3	21.3	22.0	23.8	23.8	23.8
EYE LENGTH	5.2	5.0	5.4	5.8	5.6	x
SNOUT LENGTH	6.2	5.6	5.8	6.3	6.2	x
MOUTH LENGTH	8.6	7.7	8.0	8.8	8.9	x
BODY DEPTH	24.1	25.6	24.4	24.1	20.7	19.6-28.6
BODY WIDTH	14.2	15.0	12.6	12.4	10.4	10.4-15.6
C. PED. LENGTH	—	11.8	13.5	12.2	12.3	x
C. PED. DEPTH	7.5	7.2	7.9	7.2	6.7	x
DORSAL HEIGHT	17.0	13.0	14.4	16.1	15.7	x
ANAL HEIGHT	11.9	9.0	9.2	9.9	10.2	x
ANAL BASE	10.7	10.3	10.6	17.4	17.6	9.1-11
PECTORAL LENGTH	17.1	13.4	15.4	17.4	17.6	x
PELVIC LENGTH	17.2	13.3	15.1	16.9	15.9	x
COUNTS:						
DORSAL RAYS	10-13	8-11	9-11	9-10	9	9-11
ANAL RAYS	10-14	9-12	10-12	9-12	10-12	10-12
PECTORAL RAYS	13-16	15-17	14-17	15-17	14-16	16-17
PELVIC RAYS	10-13	10-12	10-12	10-12	10-11	10-12
GILL RAKERS	30-39	33-42	41-54	41-48	39-50	32-44
VERTEBRAE	56-59	55-58	60-63	55-58	53-57	54-58
SCALES:						
LATERAL LINE	68-83	66-86	66-89	78-83	63-82	70-88

[1] Lake Erie specimens after Scott and Smith, 1962.
Other data from Koelz, 1929, Pritchard, 1931, Hubbs and Lagler, 1964.　　　　x = data not available

Prosopium

The round whitefish is placed in a distinct genus because it has a single, rather than a double, flap between the nostrils and because of some special features of the skeleton. Juveniles have spots and parr marks.

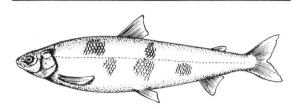

ROUND WHITEFISH

Prosopium cylindraceum
(Pallas, 1784)

Identification
The round whitefish has a distinctive torpedo-like shape and an inferior mouth somewhat like that of the lake whitefish. It differs from all of the other whitefish and ciscoes in our area in having only a single flap between the nostrils and fewer than 20 (total count) gill rakers. Juveniles have distinctive spots on the sides.

Description
Body elongate, subterete. Profiles symmetrical. Dorsal fin forward, equidistant between the tip of the snout and the end of the base of the adipose dorsal. Dorsal retrogressive. Caudal moderately forked, with angulate lobes. Anal base centered below anterior of adipose dorsal. Anal retrogressive. Pelvic insertion below middle of dorsal base. Pelvic axillary process small. Pectorals low, retrogressive, with rounded posterior corner. Pectoral base strongly oblique. Mouth inferior, small, maxillary ending below front of eye. Gill membranes separate and free from the isthmus. Counts and proportional measurements are given in Table 22.

Color: Dark olive gray or brownish above, sometimes with a greenish tinge, shading to silvery white on the sides and belly. Scales of back with dark margins. Pectoral and pelvics sometimes brownish or yellowish.

Juveniles and breeding adults: Juveniles have 7 to 13 parr marks on the sides and 1 or more additional rows of spots on the upper sides. Breeding tubercles are present on both sexes but only on the body and not on the head. Those of the male are arranged one on each scale on the five scale rows above and below the lateral line.

Size: The maximum size is around 22 inches total length.

Habitat
The round whitefish inhabits deep and cold lakes where it is most common at depths of about 150 feet, although one was taken in Lake Superior at 600 feet. In the northern part of its range, it lives in rivers and it has been taken in brackish water in Hudson Bay.

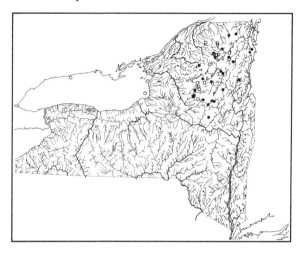

Distribution
The round whitefish occurs in deep lakes from the Genesee drainage of New York to the Bering Strait, throughout Alaska and northern Canada to the Hudson Bay drainage, and east to Labrador. It occurs in all the Great Lakes except Erie and in scattered lakes in New England. In Asia, it occurs west to the Yenisei River, and south to Kamchatka. McPhail and Lindsey noted that the range is nearly discontinuous near the Manitoba-Ontario border.

Life History
Round whitefish spawn in November and early December over gravel in water up to 48 feet deep. Males precede the females to the spawning grounds. In a New Hampshire lake, Normandeau found it spawning at depths of a few centimeters to about 2 meters over gravel and rubble where wave action and current kept the bottom free of silt. Spawning adults usually swam in pairs, occasionally in groups of four to eight. They did not feed while on the spawning grounds.

The eggs are large, 3.3 to 4.6 mm, and in the New Hampshire population the greatest number in the ovaries was 9,445. Elsewhere, counts up to 11,888 have been reported. These relatively low numbers are in keeping with the large size of the eggs. Hatching required 140 days at 36 F. They reached 3.5 to 4.3 inches during their first summer. In most populations, both sexes mature at age III or IV when they are 12 or 13 inches total length. The maximum age is 12 or 13 years.

Food and Feeding
Like the lake whitefish, the round whitefish is a bottom feeder and eats a variety of insects, mollusks, crustaceans, fish, and fish eggs.

Notes
In the past, it was believed that the Asian and North American populations represented different subspecies and the American form was designated *Prosopium cylindraceum quadrilaterale*. Koelz treated the American populations as a full species and described the Chazy Lake population as a dis-

tinct subspecies, *Prosopium quadrilaterale minor,* on the basis of its having fewer lateral line scales, fewer gill rakers, larger head, and longer fins. McPhail and Lindsey note that the two North American populations, one in the west and the other in the east, have somewhat different, although overlapping, gill raker and pyloric caeca counts. At present subspecies are not recognized.

References
Norden, 1961 (osteology and relationships). Scott and Crossman, 1973 (summary). Normandeau, 1969 (life history). Norden in Lindsey and Woods, 1970 (evolution and distribution). Jessop and Power, 1973 (age and growth). Booke, 1974 (cytotaxonomy). Armstrong et al., 1977 (life history in Lake Michigan). McPhail and Lindsey, 1970 (taxonomy).

Names
Cylindraceum is from the Greek word for cylinder, *kylendros.* Other common names are frostfish, menominee.

Salmo cylindraceus Pallas *in* Pennant, 1784: 103-104 Lena, Siberia

Coregonus quadrilateralis Richardson, 1823a: 714-716 Fort Enterprise

Prosopium quadrilaterale, Koelz, 1929: 556 Lake Ontario

Prosopium quadrilaterale minor Koelz, 1931: 382-383 Chazy Lake

TABLE 22
AVERAGE PROPORTIONAL MEASUREMENTS AND COUNTS OF CISCOES AND WHITEFISHES *(Coregonus,* in part, and *Prosopium)*

All proportions are expressed in percentage of standard length.

	Coregonus		*Prosopium*
	artedii	clupeaformis	cylindraceum
ST. LENGTH (mm)	158.0	267.7	352
TOTAL LENGTH	113.7	120.2	116.5
FORK LENGTH	115.1	108.8	108.0
PREDORSAL	51.4	48.9	45.5
PREANAL	79.2	78.7	78.4
PREPELVIC	55.7	52.1	50.0
DORSAL BASE	18.5	11.2	11.4
ANAL BASE	9.9	11.1	8.0
BODY DEPTH	24.6	24.1	25.0
BODY WIDTH	11.4	12.1	12.5
C.PED. DEPTH	7.8	8.0	6.6
PECTORAL ALT.	25.0	15.3	13.7
HEAD LENGTH	26.3	21.9	19.4
SNOUT	6.4	6.1	5.2
EYE	6.6	5.0	4.0
MOUTH LENGTH	8.3	6.3	3.7
INTERORB	6.3	6.4	5.7
N (sample size)	5	5	1
COUNTS:			
DORSAL RAYS	10-15	10-12	13
ANAL RAYS	11-13	10-14	9-13
PECTORAL RAYS	14-18	15-16	14-17
PELVIC RAYS	11-12	11	9-11
GILL RAKERS	44-64	26-28	16-18
VERTEBRAE	56-59	60-61	60-61
SCALES:			
ABOVE L. L.	8	—	—
LATERAL LINE	64-105	81-88	58-65
BELOW L. L.	8	—	—

Oncorhynchus

Pacific salmons of the genus *Oncorhynchus* have 13 or more developed anal rays and die after spawning once. There are five American species and two others in eastern Asia.

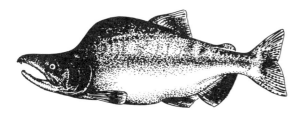

PINK SALMON

Oncorhynchus gorbuscha
(Walbaum, 1792)

Identification
The long anal fin with more than 13 rays identifies the pink salmon as a member of the Pacific salmon genus *Oncorhynchus*. It differs from the other species of that genus in having large spots on the back, upper sides, and tail. Some of these spots are elongated and almost as large as the eye. In the other species of *Oncorhynchus*, the spots are either absent or much smaller than the eye. The pink salmon also has a well-developed fatty eyelid and its fingerings lack parr marks.

Description
Body fusiform, somewhat compressed, deepest anterior to the dorsal fin. Profiles about equally curved except in breeding males. Dorsal fin retrogressive, with moderately sharp corners. Caudal moderately forked, with angulate lobes. Anal fin retrogressive, with straight margin. Pelvic retrogressive, its anterior corner bluntly pointed, its posterior corner rounded. Pelvic axillary process well developed. Pectoral low, its base oblique, retrogressive. Head conical, eye small, mouth terminal and large, maxillary reaching well beyond the eye. Premaxillaries not protractile. Gill membranes separate and free from the isthmus. Scales cycloid, body completely scaled. Teeth well developed on jaws, head and shaft of the vomer, palatines and tongue. Counts (after Scott and Crossman and McPhail and Lindsey) are given in Table 22.

Color: Bluish to greenish dorsally, shading to silvery on the sides and white ventrally. The silvery color more brilliant in individuals from the sea or larger lakes. Back, upper sides, and both lobes of the tail with large round or oval spots.

Juveniles and breeding adults: Juveniles lack the typical parr marks. Breeding males develop grossly elongate and hooked jaws and a large hump in the predorsal area. The head and back darken while the sides become pale red with brown or green blotches.

Size: Most returning adults are 17 to 19 inches long and weigh about 4 pounds. The maximum size is about 30 inches and 14 pounds.

Habitat
Pink salmon spend most of their life in the sea, returning at sexual maturity to spawn in fresh water. Spawning areas are usually in small streams with areas of fine- or moderate-sized gravel. The channel areas of some larger rivers are also used.

Distribution
The original range of the pink salmon is from San Francisco north around the coast of Canada and Alaska to the Mackenzie River, and eastern Asia from Japan to the Lena River. It has been successfully introduced into Newfoundland, but other attempts to introduce the species into Atlantic and Hudson Bay streams have been unsuccessful.

Pink salmon were introduced into Lake Superior in Thunder Bay and the Current River in 1956. Mature adults were reported from Lake Superior in 1959 and by 1971 they were reported as widespread. They were found in Lake Huron in 1969 and in Lake Michigan in 1973. In 1979, they were taken in Lakes Erie and Ontario.

Life History
In their native range, the adults move into fresh water to spawn, traveling upstream for various distances. Some spawn in tidal areas, others move upstream 40 or 50 miles and in some rivers they travel inland as much as 300 miles. In Lake Superior, the runs occur from late August to the middle of October, with the peak in late September to early October. Redds are constructed at the upstream ends of riffles in water 22 to 110 cm deep and where water velocities are 4.6 to 15.5 cm/sec and the bottom gravel consists of pebbles less than 50 mm in diameter.

As in other salmons, the female digs the redd by lying on her side and fanning away the gravel to form a pit that may be 50 cm deep and a meter long. Although males are territorial, several males may spawn with a single female. The eggs are about 6 mm in diameter and most females produce between 1,500 and 1,900. After spawning, the female guards the nest until she dies, a few days later. Hatching occurs from December to February and the young remain in the gravel until the yolk sac is absorbed, usually emerging in April or May. As soon as they leave the gravel, the young start to migrate downstream to open water. Most individuals spawn when they are 2 years old, but occasionally a fish spends an extra year at sea.

In Lake Superior, the pink salmon usually spawns in odd-numbered years but Wagner and Stauffer have collected 28 even-year spawners in streams along the south shore of Lake Superior and at least 21 of these were 3-year-olds. They appeared to be slow-growing fish and this may have contributed to their delayed maturity.

Food and Feeding
At sea, the pink salmon feeds on a variety of crustaceans, fishes, squids and pteropod mollusks. Juve-

niles on short migration may not feed or may feed on larval insects. Adults do not normally feed during their spawning runs, but in the Great Lakes they continue to feed even while they are on the spawning beds. Insects, mostly terrestrial insects, fish, and zooplankton are the main items of food while they are in the streams.

References
Wagner and Stauffer, 1980 (Lake Superior). Kwain and Laurie, 1981 (fisheries in Great Lakes). Emery, 1981 (range extension in the lower Great Lakes). Kwain, 1982 (life history). McPhail and Lindsey, 1970 (northwestern Canada and Alaska).

Names
Gorbuscha is the Russian word for humpback, in reference to the shape of the breeding males.

Salmo gorbuscha Walbaum, 1792: 69 Kamchatka

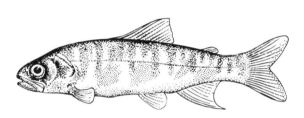

COHO SALMON

Oncorhynchus kisutch
(Walbaum, 1792)

Identification
The coho, like other Pacific salmons, has a long anal fin with 13 to 15 rays. It also has small spots on the back and upper lobe of the tail but few on the dorsal fin and none on the lower lobe of the tail. These spots are small and round like those of the chinook. Pink salmon have larger spots and kokanee have only flecks rather than well-defined spots.

Young cohos have a high lobe at the front of the anal fin and even in adults the depressed first anal ray reaches two-thirds of the way to the end of the anal base. The anal fin also has a white leading edge followed by a dusky area. Other diagnostic features are 45 to 80 pyloric caeca and uniform coloration of the adipose fin. The chinook has 135 to 185 pyloric caeca and a clear area in the adipose fin.

Description
Body slab sided and ovate with its greatest depth at the front of the dorsal fin. Profiles symmetrical. Dorsal fin retrogressive, with rounded corners. Caudal fin emarginate. Anal fin retrogressive, with a high anterior lobe. Pelvic axillary process well developed. Pelvic insertion below middle of dorsal base. Pelvic fin retrogressive, with convex margin and rounded posterior corner. Gill membranes separate and free from the isthmus. Pectorals low, retrogressive, with moderately oblique base. Mouth terminal,

large, the maxillary reaching well beyond the eye. Teeth on both jaws, vomer, palatines and tongue. Counts and proportional measurements are given in Table 23.

Color: Steel blue or greenish above, shading to silvery on the flank and white ventrally. Back and upper part of the tail with small round black spots. Scott and Crossman report that Great Lakes cohos have gray to black pigment around the teeth in the lower jaw although this area is usually pale in Pacific populations and is often cited as a useful characteristic for distinguishing between the coho and the chinook salmon.

Juveniles and breeding adults: Adult males are dark bluish green on the head and back, dark on the belly, with a red stripe on the side. The jaws become enlarged and hooked and the teeth enlarge but these changes are not as extreme as in some other species of Pacific salmon. Permanent freshwater populations generally show less dramatic changes than do sea-run cohos.

Juveniles have 8 to 12 narrow parr marks that are higher than the diameter of the eye. These parr marks are narrower than the pale interspaces and, although they are somewhat variable, the anterior ones are usually narrower than those farther back. In life, the caudal, anal, and especially the pelvic fins are orange.

Size: Coho adults usually range from 5 to 12 pounds, occasionally weighing 20 pounds or more. In New York waters, anglers commonly take fish 24 inches long and up to 8 pounds. The state record is 21 pounds 9 ounces taken August 1980 in Lake Ontario by Randy Ruchler. The IGFA world record is 31 pounds, but larger fish have been taken.

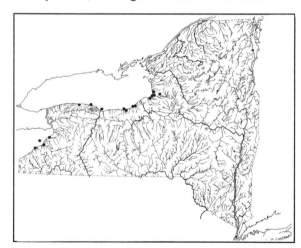

Habitat
Although the coho is an anadromous species that spends most of its life at sea, it can also live in freshwater lakes. The young remain in streams for as much as 2 years, gradually moving downstream from gravel shallows to progressively deeper pools where there is good cover.

Distribution
The coho occurs on the Pacific coast of Asia from Hokkaido to the Anadyr River and on the Ameri-

can side from Monterey Bay to Point Hope, Alaska. It has been introduced in all of the Great Lakes. In New York, there has been some natural reproduction in the Salmon River drainage of Lake Ontario and in the Cattaraugus Creek watershed of Lake Erie.

Life History

Usually, the young spend their first year in fresh water and move downstream the following March or April, but there is some variation. Some individuals move out of the streams at the end of their first summer, others spend two years in fresh waters, and still others never go to sea. Most cohos spend 18 months in the ocean and return to spawn in the fall when they are 3 or 4 years old, but some return at age II and some at age IV or V.

Spawning takes place in tributary streams and, as in other salmonids, the female digs a nest, usually in a riffle area just below a pool, while several males remain nearby. Usually, a dominant male, sometimes aided by the female, keeps other fish at a distance. When the female is ready to spawn, she enters the nest and is joined by the dominant male. Often, the spawning pair is joined by smaller males as the eggs and milt are released. After spawning, the female covers the eggs and may dig several nests and spawn several times before her death. Females lay between 1,440 and 5,700 eggs, each 4.5 to 6 mm in diameter.

In the Great Lakes, the spawning runs are in September and October. Hatching takes place in the spring and the young leave the gravel in spring.

Food and Feeding

At sea, cohos feed on euphausids, squids, and small fish. In the Great Lakes, the young fish are predominantly insect eaters but sometimes they eat large quantities of small fish. The adults eat smelts, alewives, and occasionally lampreys. In a Wisconsin lake, Engel found a seasonal progression in the coho's diet. In April and May, aquatic insects dominated; from May to July, when the fish were offshore in the epilimnion, terrestrial insects were more important. After July, when they moved into deeper waters, insects became less important and they fed more on cladocerans. After August, fish became a major component of the diet.

Notes

The coho is an excellent sport fish. They grow rapidly in the Great Lakes and 8- to 11-pound fish are common. Most cohos are caught as they assemble near river mouths before beginning their spawning runs. Snagging is permitted since the fish will die after spawning. They are also taken in the streams after they begin to move up but before they stop feeding. Baits and artificial lures are effective. The spawning run in the Salmon River near Pulaski is one of the most dramatic outdoor events in the state.

References

Buss, 1957 (general). Drahos, 1968 (popular account). Scott and Crossman, 1973 (summary).

McPhail and Lindsey, 1970 (Alaska, summary). Harney and Norden, 1972 (food habits). Engel, 1976 (food habits, Wisconsin). Johnson, 1980 (reproduction in Ontario tributaries); 1981 (food). Mikol and Hadley, 1979 (spawning in New York tributaries of Lake Erie). Brown, 1975 (sport fishery in New York). Johnson and Ringler, 1981 (ecology).

Names

Kisutch is a Russian common name for this species.
   Salmo kisutch Walbaum, 1792: 70 Kamchatka

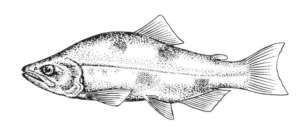

KOKANEE

Oncorhynchus nerka (Walbaum, 1792)

Identification

The kokanee is the landlocked form of the sockeye salmon. It differs from the trouts and the Atlantic salmon in that it has more than 13 or 14, rarely as few as 11, rays in the anal fin. It differs from the other species of Pacific salmons (genus *Oncorhynchus*) that have been stocked in New York in lacking definite spots on the back and tail. The back has small flecks of dark pigment but no definite spots. It also has 30 to 40 long, slender gill rakers (19 to 27 on the lower limb of the first arch).

Description

Body elongate, slab sided, deepest at the dorsal origin. Profiles symmetrical. Dorsal fin retrogressive, trapezoidal, with blunt corners. Caudal slightly forked. Anal centered below origin of adipose. Anal trapezoidal, retrogressive, its corners angulate. Pelvic insertion below posterior end of dorsal base. Pelvic axillary process well developed. Pectoral low, retrogressive, with rounded posterior corner. Pectoral base strongly oblique. Teeth strong, present on vomer, palatines, jaws and tongue. Body fully scaled. Mouth large, the maxillary extending past the eye. Counts and proportional measurements are given in Table 23.

Color: The kokanee is steel blue to greenish above, shading to silvery on the sides and white on the belly. No distinct spots.

Juveniles and breeding adults: The breeding males develop somewhat of a hump in front of the dorsal fin although it is not as extreme as in the pink salmon. They also develop hooked jaws but these, too, are less extreme than in other species. Breeding males are brilliant with reddish gray to bright red on the body, green heads and white on the lower jaw and belly. The dorsal, anal, and adipose fins are bright red, and the paired fins are red at the base but otherwise dark. Females are similarly colored but somewhat darker.

Juveniles have short parr marks whose maximum height is less than the diameter of the eye. These marks are less than half the width of the pale interspaces.

Size: Kokanee are usually less than 16 inches long and about 1 pound in weight. Sea-run sockeyes are larger, sometimes reaching 33 inches and 15 or 16 pounds.

Habitat
The kokanee is a lake fish that moves into streams to spawn. Apparently, they respond most to temperature, living at all depths during the spring and fall and only in deeper waters during the winter. In the summer, they make daily excursions inshore and into the upper layers of open water.

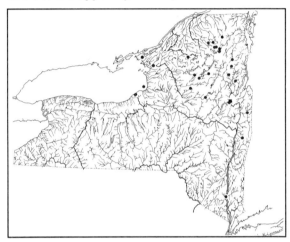

Distribution
The sockeye ranges from Hokkaido to the Anadyr River in Asia and from the Klamath River to Point Hope, Alaska. Kokanee occur throughout most of the range and also occur in Arctic Lake in the headwaters of the Mackenzie River.

The kokanee has been introduced into many lakes in North America from Wyoming to Maine. Most of these introductions have failed to establish reproducing populations. In New York, they have been introduced into several Adirondack lakes and Lake Ontario. A mature male was taken in the Hudson River near Newburgh.

Life History
Spawning takes place in the fall, the exact time varying between August and February. Usually, they move into streams but sometimes they can spawn in lakes. The females fan the gravel bottom to produce a trough-like or circular depression, turning on their sides in streams but remaining vertical when spawning in lakes. After the nest is built, the male joins the female and they lie side by side as the eggs and milt are extruded. Hatching time is dependent on water temperature and the young remain in the gravel until spring. Most spawn at age IV but a few mature at age II and some as late as age VIII.

Food and Feeding
Kokanee are primarily plankton eaters but they also consume some bottom organisms.

Notes
In many areas, kokanee provide good sport fishing. The orange-red flesh is highly rated. The kokanee is sometimes considered to be a subspecies, *O. n. kennerlyi*, but McPhail and Lindsey (1970) point out that populations of kokanee differ in gill raker count and are probably of independent origin. Recognizing all of them as one subspecies would have no biological meaning.

References
Foerster, 1968 (comprehensive account). Ricker, 1966 (ecology). Reider, 1979b (Hudson River). Buss, 1957 (general).

Names
Nerka is the Russian common name for the sockeye.

Salmo nerka Walbaum, 1792: 71 Kamchatka
Oncorhynchus nerka, Reider, 1979b: 94 Hudson River

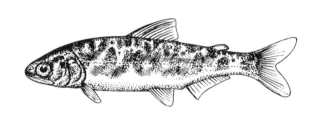

CHINOOK SALMON

Oncorhynchus tshawytscha (Walbaum, 1792)

Identification
The chinook is most similar to the coho but it has spots on the dorsal fin and on the lower, as well as the upper, lobe of the tail fin. Pink salmon have large spots and kokanee have only flecks on the back and tail. Both the chinook and the coho have pigment on the inside of the mouth but the coho often has light flesh around the base of the teeth of the lower jaw, whereas the chinook has dark gums. This difference is not reliable in Great Lakes fish, however, and for positive identification it may be necessary to dissect the fish and count the pyloric caeca: 45 to 114 in the coho; 90 to 240 in the chinook.

Description
Body elongate, slab sided, profiles symmetrical. Dorsal trapezoidal, retrogressive, with straight margins and angulate corners. Caudal slightly forked. Anal base centered below the origin of the adipose. Anal fin retrogressive. Pelvics inserted under or slightly behind middle of dorsal base. Pelvics retrogressive, pelvic axillary process well developed. Pectoral fins low, retrogressive, with rounded posterior corner. Pectoral base moderately oblique. Gill

membranes separate and free from the isthmus. Gill rakers rough and widely spaced. Lateral line nearly straight. Mouth large, terminal, the maxillary reaching beyond the rather small eye. Body completely scaled. Counts and proportional measurements are given in Table 23.

Color: Upper parts bluish or greenish, sides silvery, shading to white on the belly. Back, dorsal fin, and entire tail with small black spots. A few spots on all fins except the adipose which has a black margin and a clear center. Inside of mouth with considerable pigment, gums of lower jaw black.

Juveniles and breeding adults: Juveniles have 6 to 12 parr marks, each higher than the diameter of the eye and wider than those of the other Pacific salmon species. The anal fin of juvenile chinooks has a low anterior lobe, not as high as that of the coho and without dark pigment behind the white leading edge.

Breeding males are dark allover, olive brown to purplish. Females are somewhat lighter but neither sex develops the red color of other species.

Size: The chinook is the largest of the Pacific salmons, the IGFA record being 93 pounds. The usual size is about 33 to 36 inches total length. In New York, the record is a 47-pound fish from Lake Ontario taken in 1980 by Thomas Cossanti.

Habitat

Chinooks are anadromous with some spawning just above the tide line and others traveling as much as 1,200 miles inland.

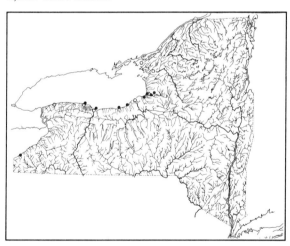

Distribution

The chinook ranges from Hokkaido to the Anadyr River and from the Ventura River in California to Point Hope, Alaska. It has been introduced in many parts of the world and there is now a spectacular fishery for chinook in Lake Ontario. At present, the run is maintained by stocking but it now appears that there is some natural reproduction in tributaries of the Salmon River in New York.

Life History

There are many races of chinooks and the time of the run varies with locality. Those that migrate farthest tend to start earlier and may appear at river mouths as early as January; those that do not travel as far run in the summer, fall, or early winter. Spawning takes place in July and August in the Yukon River, September in British Columbia, and October on Vancouver Island. In New York, the chinooks run in August and September. In keeping with their larger size, chinooks select areas with deeper water and coarser gravel than other species. Females turn on their sides to dig the redds and the nest depressions can be as much as 12 feet long. When she is ready to spawn, the female lies in the redd and the dominant male moves in next to her. After spawning, the female digs another nest upstream and covers the eggs in the process. The process is repeated, often with several males, until the female is spent. The eggs are 6 to 7 mm in diameter and a female may lay 8,000 to 13,600, although freshwater fish probably lay fewer eggs than sea-run individuals. The time to hatching depends on temperature but the young do not leave the nest until spring.

At first, they school but later they become more solitary and aggressive. In the southern part of their natural range, some individuals migrate out to sea during their first summer but in the Yukon they spend up to 2 years in fresh water before going to sea. After 2 to as long as 9 years, they return to the streams to spawn and die.

Food and Feeding

In the streams, the young chinook feed on insects, largely terrestrial insects that fall into the water. They also eat aquatic insects and crustaceans but they seldom feed on fish. At sea their diet is largely fish with invertebrates making up only about 3 percent of the diet.

Notes

The chinook is an important commercial as well as sport fish and the fact that some natural reproduction has occurred in New York is encouraging. Like other Pacific salmons, the chinook shows a remarkable ability to return to the same locality where they were hatched.

References

Johnson, 1980 (New York); 1983a, 1983b (food). Hoover, 1936b (New Hampshire).

Names

Tshawytscha is a Russian common name for this species. The chinook is also known as king salmon.

Salmo tschawytscha Walbaum, 1792: 71 Kamchatka

Oncorhynchus tschawytscha, Johnson, 1980: 549-554 New York

TABLE 23
AVERAGE PROPORTIONAL MEASUREMENTS AND COUNTS OF PACIFIC SALMONS (Oncorhynchus)

All proportions are expressed in percentage of standard length.

	gorbuscha	kisutch	nerka	tshawytscha
ST. LENGTH (mm)	N.Y.	60	218	63.2
TOTAL LENGTH	specimens	124.6	118.8	121.6
FORK LENGTH	not	113.4	111.0	111.6
PREDORSAL	available	49.0	52.3	50.0
PREANAL		70.1	72.0	70.5
PREPELVIC		53.5	53.7	55.1
DORSAL BASE		14.5	11.5	12.9
ANAL BASE		16.1	14.7	14.6
BODY DEPTH		25.7	28.9	26.7
BODY WIDTH		12.3	11.0	12.1
C.PED. DEPTH		10.1	9.6	9.6
PECTORAL ALT.		18.4	20.6	18.3
HEAD LENGTH		28.4	28.9	27.8
SNOUT		5.1	10.1	7.0
EYE		10.6	5.5	8.9
MOUTH LENGTH		16.8	17.0	14.5
INTERORB		7.2	8.7	8.5
N (sample size)		3	1	2
COUNTS:				
DORSAL RAYS	10-14	11-12	10-16	11-16
ANAL RAYS	14-19	12-17	13-19	13-18
PECTORAL RAYS	14-17	13-16	14-17	11-21
PELVIC RAYS	10-11	9-11	9-11	9-11
GILL RAKERS	16-26	21-24	25-36	31-44
VERTEBRAE	67-75	61-69	63-72	64-66
SCALES:				
ABOVE L. L.	—	24	18-19	—
LATERAL LINE	130-165	121-148	147-205	120-150
BELOW L. L.	—	22	21-19	—
PYLORIC CAECA	90-240	45-114	95-224	50-87

Salmo

The genus *Salmo* includes the Atlantic salmon, the brown and rainbow trouts, and two other species in western North America. All have rather large scales, fewer than 190 in the lateral line, and dark spots on a paler background.

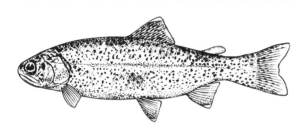

RAINBOW TROUT

Salmo gairdneri
Richardson, 1836

Identification
The rainbow trout differs from the Pacific salmons in having fewer than 13 rays in the anal fin. It differs from the brook trout and the lake trout in having a pattern of dark spots on a lighter background. Unlike the brown trout, it has no pale halos around the spots and no red spots on the sides. It also has many spots on its tail whereas the brown trout has only a few at most. It also has a conspicuous dark margin on the adipose fin.

Atlantic salmon lack the black margin on the adipose and usually have no spots on the tail. They also have smaller mouths, with the maxillary ending below the back of the eye. There is some age variation in mouth size; in fish less than 6 inches long, the maxillary reaches to below the middle of the eye in salmon and to the back of the eye in rainbows. Salmon also have a stiffer, more deeply forked, tail and weaker teeth on the shaft of the vomer.

Description
Body elongate and slab sided, deepest in front of the dorsal fin. Profiles equally curved. Dorsal fin retrogressive, its margin slightly concave. Tail slightly forked with bluntly pointed lobes. Anal fin mostly ahead of the adipose, retrogressive, with sigmoid margin. Pectoral insertion below anterior third of dorsal base. Pelvics retrogressive with convex margin. Pectoral fins low with oblique base, retrogressive, with rounded posterior corner. Gill membranes separate and free from isthmus. Mouth terminal, oblique, reaching beyond the eye. Teeth present on jaw, head and shaft of the vomer, palatines and tongue. Counts and proportional measurements are given in Table 24.

Color: Dark olive to blue green above, lighter on the sides with the belly pale yellow, gray, or white. Head, back and upper sides, dorsal and tail fins densely spotted, tail spots in radiating rows. Adipose with black spots around its margin coalescing

to form a continous black margin. No red spots on sides, but adults have a pink or red band along the sides. Anal and paired fins immaculate or with a few scattered spots. Pelvic and pectoral fins often with a red-orange wash. Anterior tips of dorsal and anal are white. Sea-run and lake-run fish are silvery, with small black spots on the back, dorsal, and caudal fins.

Juveniles and breeding adults: Breeding adults are dark and the males have a more intense red band along the sides than the females. The males also have a pointed snout and develop a hooked upper jaw, although this is not as extreme as in the Pacific salmons. Juveniles have 8 to 13 parr marks that are narrower than the interspaces. Spots on the tail do not develop until they are 5 or 6 inches long. The dorsal fin has the leading edge dark and there are 5 to 10 parr marks in the middorsal line ahead of the dorsal fin. There are dark spots above, but not below, the lateral line.

Size: The IGFA record is a 49-pound 2-ounce fish but in some streams rainbows mature at 6 to 10 inches. Steelheads (lake- or sea-run individuals) tend to be larger and usually mature when they are about 16 inches long. The New York State record is a 23-pound 5-ounce fish from Lake Ontario caught in April 1981 by James Dunn.

Habitat
Rainbows occur in medium to large streams with moderate flow and they seem to select areas with gravel or rocky bottom. They also occur in lakes but they must have access to streams if they are to reproduce. They are intolerant of temperatures above 70 F. Some rainbows are anadromous and spend much of their life at sea.

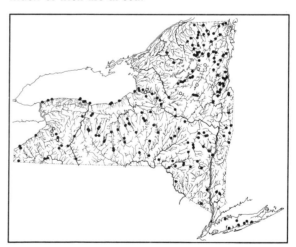

Distribution
The original range of the rainbow is the Pacific drainages from northwestern Mexico to the Kushowin River in Alaska. Rainbows also crossed the continental divide in Canada, to the Peace and Athabasca Rivers in the Mackenzie system. McPhail and Lindsey suggest that they may have crossed at more than one place. The Mexican and Colorado River populations are now disjunct but are probably relics of an orginally continuous range.

The rainbow has been introduced into many parts of the world. It appears to have been first introduced into New York in 1874 and it is now present in all parts of the state wherever there is suitable habitat. By 1900, it was established in eastern streams in Michigan, Wisconsin, Missouri, and North Carolina. It has also become established in Australia, Tasmania, New Zealand, Hawaii, South America, Europe and Asia.

Life History

Unlike the brook and brown trout, rainbows are usually spring spawners, the season lasting from January to May, usually concentrated in April. Its preferred spawning temperature is around 50 to 60 F. In Esopus Creek rainbows spawn in late March to the second week in April. In Lake Gilead there is a fall-spawning population. Spawning takes place in streams over gravel bars. The female digs a pit with her tail, turning on her side and fanning out the gravel. While she is digging, males court her by lying next to her and touching her. When she is ready, she braces herself in the pit she has dug and two males, usually one larger and one smaller than she is, lie on either side of her. All three open their mouths and Greeley believed this helps to wedge the fish into position because it catches the current and drives the fish into the bottom. The fish remain together for 5 to 8 seconds. After the eggs are released the female covers them by digging upstream from the nest. At first, this is done with a rapid vibration of the tail; slow sweeps are used later to smooth out the gravel. Most of the spawning takes place in the morning and evening and they tend to leave the nests in midday. Rainbows do not spawn at night although the females remain near the nests.

The eggs are rather large, 3 to 5 mm in diameter, and pink to orange. The number varies from 650 to more than 12,000, 400 to 2,500 per kilogram of the female's weight. Hatching takes 18 days at 15.5 C, to 101 days at 3.2 C. Growth is extremely variable, depending on temperature, food, and probably other factors as well as genetics. Some males mature as early as 9 months but most mature at age II or in their third summer. Steelheads tend to mature later than stream residents. The maximum age is 4 to 8 years. Spawning mortality is high and less than 10 percent of the females, and even fewer males, live to spawn a second time.

Food and Feeding

Rainbow trout feed on aquatic and terrestrial insects, plankton, and larger invertebrates such as gammarids and other crustaceans, snails, leeches, and small fishes, especially sculpins and shiners. Studies have shown that they feed less on dipterans than brook trout do and take slightly less of their food from the surface than either brook or brown trout. At sea, steelheads feed mainly on squids and fishes.

Notes

Under artificial conditions, rainbows can be brought into spawning condition at almost any time of year so that hybrid crosses that would not occur in nature can be produced in hatcheries. Brownbows (rainbow x brown trout) and sambows (rainbow x Atlantic salmon) are raised for stocking in some areas.

References

Summaries can be found in Scott and Crossman, 1973, Shapovalov and Taft, 1954, and Maher and Larkin, 1955. Other pertinent references are: Carlander, 1969 (age and growth). MacCrimmon, 1971, 1972 (world distribution). Hartman, 1959 (Finger Lakes). Hatch, 1957 (Finger Lakes). Sopuck, 1978 (emigration of juveniles in Cayuga Inlet). Wedemeyer, 1973 (heat stress). Kwain, 1975a and 1975b (physiology). Boreman, 1981 (Cayuga Lake). Bacon, 1954 (juveniles). Fraser, 1978 (competition). Thorgaard, 1983 (karyology). McPhail and Lindsey, 1970 (Canada, Alaska). Greeley, 1932 (spawning).

Names

The rainbow trout is named for Dr. Meredith Gairdner, a naturalist who worked for Hudson's Bay Company at Fort Vancouver and impressed Richardson, the describer, as "an able and promising young naturalist."

Salmo Gairdnerii Richardson, 1836: 221 Columbia River at Fort Vancouver

Salmo irideo Gibbons, 1855: 37-37 San Leandro Creek, California

Salmo irideus, Mather, 1886: 19-20 Adirondacks (introduced)

Salmo irideus shasta Jordan, 1894: 142 McCloud River, California

(*Salmo gairdneri irideus, Salmo irideus irideus,* and *Salmo gairdneri shasta* are combinations that appear in the literature.)

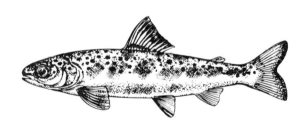

ATLANTIC SALMON

Salmo salar Linnaeus, 1758

Identification

The Atlantic salmon is most apt to be confused with the brown trout, especially when they come from big lakes or the sea, where they are both generally silvery with X-shaped markings on the back and upper sides. The tail of the salmon is more deeply forked with the middle caudal rays less than half as long as the longest upper caudal rays. In the brown trout, the middle rays are nearly two-thirds the length of the upper rays. The mouth of the salmon is smaller, the maxillary reaching to the middle of the eye in fish less than 6 inches long and to the rear of the eye or slightly beyond in larger fish. In the brown trout, the maxillary falls below the rear margin of the eye in small fish and well beyond in larger fish. The salmon has 12 branchiostegal rays; the brown trout has 10. The salmon has 11 rays in the dorsal fin; the brown trout has 9.

Vomerine teeth are weakly developed and lost from the shaft of the vomer in large salmon; they are strongly developed on both the head and shaft of the vomer of the brown trout.

There are pale halos around the dark spots of the brown trout but not those of the salmon. Juvenile salmon have a single red spot between each pair of parr marks but these are lost in the adult. Brown trout, however, have red spots at all sizes. Salmon also have longer pectoral fins than other trouts, usually longer than the depressed first dorsal ray.

Description

Body elongate, ovate, deepest at the front of the dorsal fin. Profiles symmetrical. Caudal peduncle slender. Dorsal retrogressive, with rather sharp corners. Caudal moderately forked in young, emarginate in adults. Anal retrogressive. Pelvics inserted below rear half of the dorsal base. Pelvic axillary process well developed. Pelvics retrogressive. Pectorals low with moderately oblique bases, retrogressive, their anterior corners bluntly pointed and their posterior corners rounded. Gill membranes separate and free from the isthmus. Lateral line complete and nearly straight, body completely scaled. Teeth present on jaws, vomer, palatines and tongue, becoming obsolescent on the shaft of the vomer in older fish. Counts and proportional measurements are given in Table 24.

Color: Dorsal surface olive brown to green or blue, sides and belly silvery. Large fish have scattered X-shaped marks on the upper sides and back, a few on head. Pectoral and caudal fins blackish. Salmon become darker as they move into streams on their spawning runs and darker still after spawning.

Juveniles and breeding adults: Spawning fish may develop orange or orange-red blotches on the sides. Juveniles have 8 to 11 narrow parr marks alternating with single red spots. They are best recognized by their small mouths, forked tail, and long pectoral fins.

Size: The rod and reel record for Atlantic salmon is 79 pounds 2 ounces, a fish taken in Norway in 1928. Commercially caught salmon average about 10 pounds. Landlocked salmon are smaller, but there is a report of a 44.7-pound fish from Lake Ontario and the present New York State record is 19 pounds 3 ounces from Lake George taken in August 1981 by Donald Clark.

Habitat

The salmon is an anadromous fish that moves into streams to spawn. Some populations are landlocked and able to complete their life cycle in fresh water. Landlocked salmon have been stocked in many areas, usually without establishing breeding populations.

Distribution

The Atlantic salmon occurs on both sides of the At-

lantic, from Portugal north to the Arctic Circle in Europe, in Iceland and from southern Greenland and northern Quebec south to the Connecticut River.

They were native to Lakes Ontario and Champlain but apparently did not survive the environmental changes and overfishing. In 1810, when DeWitt Clinton visited the western part of the state there were populations in Lakes Seneca, Cayuga, Onondaga, and Oneida (Webster, 1980). Salmon runs probably did not occur in the Hudson although individuals may have strayed into the Hudson from time to time. Robert Juet, who was on Hudson's third voyage, reported salmon to be abundant inside Sandy Hook on 3 September and near the Hudson Highlands on 15 September. Since Hudson was an Englishman, he should have known a salmon but it is possible that what he saw were not salmon but striped bass or even sturgeon. DeKay surmised, but without much evidence, that previous to the setting of "so many nets" the salmon may have been more numerous. Parsons reviewed the occurrence of Atlantic salmon in Lake Ontario and listed fifteen tributaries in which it spawned, from Twelvemile Creek to the Chaumont River. Parsons concluded that both anadromous and freshwater populations were present; some fish migrated down the St. Lawrence to the sea while others completed their life cycle in fresh water.

Salmon of Lake Ontario began to decline in the early 1800s. The last reports from Lake Champlain were in 1852 and in the 1870s they began to decline all along the Atlantic coast and in Lake Ontario at the same time. Mill dams and other manmade obstructions prevented them from reaching their spawning grounds and deforestation, leading to increased temperatures and silting, overfishing, and pollution were contributing causes. Sea lamprey parasitism was probably not a major factor as the lampreys only became abundant later.

Anadromous salmon were planted in Lake Ontario between 1873 and 1902, and landlocked salmon were stocked between 1878 and 1917. None of these efforts was successful and the last report of a salmon caught in Lake Ontario was in 1898.

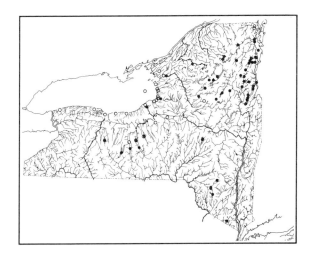

Since 1948, landlocked salmon have been planted in inland lakes and have produced fishable populations in several waters. Some natural reproduction occurs in tributaries of Lake George.

Life History

In coastal waters, salmon move into rivers in the spring and summer although they do not spawn until October or November. Landlocked salmon move into the streams in early fall. The redds are built by the female who turns on her side and fans out a depression. After spawning, the female moves upstream and fans more gravel which is carried downstream by the current and covers the eggs. The salmon spawn repeatedly until the female has deposited all of her eggs, then they drop downstream to a pool where they may rest for a few weeks before moving back to the lake or ocean, although some fish start to move downstream soon after spawning. The eggs hatch in April and the young salmon spend 2 or 3 years in streams before moving into big waters until they mature. Some males mature after only a year out of the streams but most spend 2 years in open waters. Unlike Pacific salmon, which die after spawning once, the Atlantic salmon may live to spawn several times although few live more than 9 years.

Salmon eggs are 5 to 7 mm in diameter and the females produce about 700 for each pound of body weight.

Food and Feeding

In the streams, the young salmon feed mostly on aquatic insects, with terrestrial insects contributing to the diet, especially in late summer and fall. In the sea, they feed on fish and crustaceans. Adults do not feed during their spawning runs.

Notes

The Atlantic salmon is a good example of a species that was unable to survive manmade environmental changes. Its restoration has received a good deal of attention and it has becomes something of an environmentalist's *cause célèbre*.

Much has been made of the return of the salmon to the Connecticut River and in New York State efforts are being made to encourage the salmon in Lake Champlain. In 1982, a fish ladder was opened on the Boquet River in Willsboro and it is hoped that this will make 40 miles of stream accessible to the salmon. During the first season, more than 100 salmon passed up the ladder.

References

Clinton, 1815 (distribution in Lakes Ontario and Oneida). Cheney, 1898 (not in Hudson). Greeley, 1955b (Lake George). Rostlund, 1953 (presence in Hudson). Parsons, 1973 (history in Great Lakes). Webster, 1982 (history in New York). Belding, 1940 (races). Wilder, 1947 (taxonomy). Harvey and Warner, 1970 (life history and management in Maine). Schaffer and Elson, 1975 (adaptive significance of life history variations). Netboy, 1968 (popular account). Sosiak et al., 1979 (feeding). Greeley, 1952 (identification); 1956a, 1962 (management).

Names

Salar probably comes from the Latin *salio,* to leap.

Salmo salar Linnaeus, 1758: 308 European oceans

Salmo sebago Girard, 1854a: 380 Sebago Lake, Maine

Salmo salar sebago, Mather, 1886: 13-19 (introduced)

Salmo salar ouananiche Eugene McCarthy *in* Jordan and Evermann, 1896: 487 Canada

Salmo ouananiche, Evermann and Kendall, 1902c: 238 St. Lawrence (no New York records)

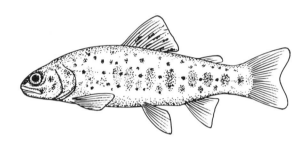

BROWN TROUT

Salmo trutta Linnaeus, 1758

Identification

The brown trout differs from the Pacific salmons in having fewer than 13 rays in the anal fin. It differs from the chars, the lake trout, and the brook trout in having larger scales and a pattern of dark spots on a light background instead of the other way around. It differs from the rainbow trout in having definite red spots on the sides, larger and more diffuse spots on the head, fewer spots on the body and few or no spots on the tail, and in lacking a black margin on the adipose fin.

The brown trout is sometimes confused with the Atlantic salmon because, in big waters, brown trout become generally silvery with only a few spots. Salmon, however, have more definitely X-shaped spots, a shorter head, smaller mouth, and a pointed tongue (the tongue of the brown trout is square). Salmon also tend to lose the teeth on the shaft of the vomer when they become larger and have more deeply forked tails.

Description

Body ovate, somewhat compressed, profiles nearly symmetrical. Dorsal retrogressive from third ray, its margin nearly straight. Caudal square, slightly forked in young. Anal retrogressive, its margin straight or slightly convex in males, falcate in females. Pelvics retrogressive, inserted below middle of dorsal base. Pelvic axillary process well developed. Pectorals low, retrogressive, their bases slightly oblique. Mouth terminal, large, end of maxillary extending well behind the eye. Well-developed teeth on jaws, palatines, vomer, and tongue. Counts and proportional measurements are given in Table 24.

Color: Olive green on the body, shading to tan or

white on the lower sides and belly. Sides of head and body with distinct, small, irregular spots most of which are surrounded with pale halos. Only a few spots on the upper part of the tail. Spots are smaller on the back and lack halos, often missing from the middorsal region. Dorsal fin with small spots. Adipose orange or with orange spots, no black margin but often with some black spots. Anterior tip of dorsal, and the leading edge of the anal white, sometimes followed by a diffuse black line. Sometimes the paired fins and the upper and lower margins of the tail have a peach-colored wash.

Juveniles and breeding adults: Juveniles have 9 to 14 short, narrow parr marks, and two or three rows of red spots, the uppermost of these along the lateral line and alternating with the parr marks.

Breeding adults become more yellowish and the males have darker lower fins.

Size: Brown trout usually reach 1 or 2 pounds in weight but can grow much larger. The world all-tackle record is 35 pounds 15 ounces from Argentina. The New York record is 22 pounds 4 ounces from Keuka Lake, caught in June, 1979 by Carson Fitzwater. One European strain reaches a very large size and an attempt is being made to establish this strain in New York.

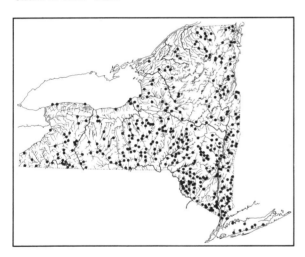

Habitat
The brown trout is primarily a stream fish but it also lives in lakes and there are some sea-run strains. It is often found in small headwater streams with brook trout, but it can tolerate higher temperatures than the brook trout and does best in streams where the summer temperatures are less than 68° F.

Distribution
The brown trout is an Old World species that originally ranged throughout Europe and western Asia from Iceland, the British Isles and Scandinavia to the Aral Sea and Afghanistan. It also occurred in the Atlas Mountains of northern Africa. It was first introduced into Michigan and New York in 1883 and has since been stocked in many parts of the world.

Life History
The brown trout spawns in fall or early winter, usu-

ally somewhat later than the brook trout, but occasionally both species use the same spawning areas at the same time. The males usually arrive first and mill around the spawning area, partially clearing the silt from the gravel before the female starts digging the pit. A female excavates a nest by lying on her side and moving her tail violently until a pit somewhat larger than she is has been fanned out. Males court the female by approaching her while she is in the nest. When she is ready to spawn, she braces herself in the nest and a male, usually larger, curves his body against hers. The pair vibrates several seconds and the eggs and milt are released. The female then covers the eggs by digging rapidly with her tail upstream of the nest. The male leaves after a few minutes but the female may work on the nest for an hour or so, finally smoothing the area with slow sweeps of her tail. Both sexes spawn repeatedly over a period of several days.

Brown trout eggs are rather small for salmonid eggs, 3.2 to 5mm in diameter, and the number produced varies with size of the female, nutrition, and location. Smaller fish average more eggs per unit of body weight than larger fish. Hatching takes 148 days at 1.9 C and 33 days at 11 C. The young fish emerge from the gravel in the spring and usually reach about 4 inches total length by the end of the first summer. Maturity is reached at age II to age IV for males, age III to age V for females, with some individuals maturing a year earlier. The maximum age is about 18 years.

Food and Feeding
Brown trout begin to feed on small bottom organisms often even before their yolk sac is absorbed. Small trout eat mostly insects, amphipods, and other crustaceans; larger fish eat more fish, tadpoles, and other larger items.

Notes
Brown trout hybridize with brook trout to produce a spectacularly colored, stubby fish usually called tiger trout.

References
Schuck, 1945 (population dynamics). Heacox, 1974 (popular account). MacCrimmon and Marshall, 1968 (distribution). MacCrimmon, Marshal and Gots, 1970 (distribution). Clary, 1972 (predation by sculpins). Clemens, 1928 (food). Reynolds and Casterlin, 1979 (temperature). Brynildson, Hacker, and Klick, 1963 (life history and management). Dumas, 1961 (eggs and young). Bacon, 1954 (larval characters). Shirvell and Dungey, 1983 (microhabitats). Haynes and Nettles, 1983 (fall movements in Lake Ontario).

Names
Trutta is the Latin word for trout.
Salmo trutta Linnaeus, 1758: 308-309 European rivers
Salmo fario Linnaeus, 1758: 309
Salmo fario, Bean, 1903: 254-257 New York (introduced)
Salmo trutta levenensis, Bean, 1903: 259-261 New York (introduced)

Salvelinus

This is the genus of the chars. All species have very small scales, more than 190 in the lateral line, and pale gray or red spots on a darker background. The genus contains five species including the brook trout and the lake trout.

BROOK TROUT

Salvelinus fontinalis (Mitchill, 1815)

Identification

Our state fish is probably the easiest species to recognize. Its most conspicuous feature is the brilliant white leading edges of the pectoral, pelvic, and anal fins. These are set off by a following black streak and the rest of the fins are red. These marks are so conspicuous that a brook trout lurking under a log can sometimes be recognized with no other clue. The brook trout has pale, wormlike markings on the dorsal surface and pale tan spots on a darker background on the upper sides. There are also brilliant red spots on the sides, many of which are surrounded by blue halos. These spots give it the local name of speckled trout.

The brook trout is a char with very fine scales (more than 200) in the row above the lateral line. Our only other char is the lake trout, which has a forked tail and lacks red spots on the sides.

Description

Body ovate, deepest anterior to the dorsal fin, moderately compressed. Dorsal profile slightly more curved than the ventral. Dorsal fin retrogressive. Caudal fin emarginate, retrogressive, with straight margin. Pelvics inserted below middle of dorsal base, retrogressive, with rounded margins. Pelvic axillary process present. Pectorals low with somewhat oblique bases, retrogressive, rounded. Head blunt, becoming pointed in breeding males. Teeth well developed on jaws, head of the vomer, palatines, and tongue. Mouth quite large, the maxillary extending well past the eye. Counts and proportional measurements are given in Table 24.

Color: Dark olive green to almost black above with paler vermiculations that break into pale tan spots on the upper sides. Dorsal fin with irregular rows of black spots. Caudal fin with vertical rows of darker spots, dark along its upper and lower margins and the tips of the rays. Lower fins with conspicuous white leading edges, followed by black lines and with the rest of the fins yellow to red. Underside of lower jaw white.

Juveniles and breeding adults: Males with the lower sides salmon to orange or red. This color is separated from the whitish belly by a dark longitudinal stripe running from the pectoral to the base of the anal fin. Females tend to be paler and lack the red lower sides of the breeding males. Hatchery-raised fish tend to be less colorful. Juveniles have eight or nine broad parr marks.

Size: The maximum size of the brook trout is variable depending on genetic makeup as well as environmental conditions. The official state record is an 8.5-pound fish from Punchbowl Pond in Sullivan County, taken in 1908 by William Keener. An unofficial record is the 14.5-pound "salter" (a brook trout that runs into the sea from a coastal stream) caught by Daniel Webster in the Carmans River on Long Island in 1827.

Habitat

Brook trout live in lakes and streams where they are limited to cold waters (below 75 F). They are often found in very small creeks as long as the temperatures are low enough. In ponds and lakes, they seek cooler depths as the surface waters warm. They also require considerable oxygen and this makes some waters with low oxygen levels below the thermocline unacceptable even if the temperatures are low enough. In some coastal streams, there are anadromous strains of brook trout.

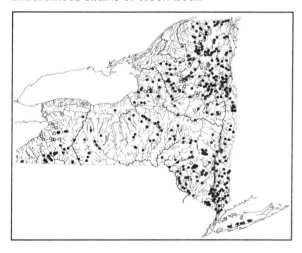

Distribution

The original range of the brook trout was North America from Hudson Bay and the Canadian Maritime Provinces south to Cape Cod and Long Island on the coast, and at higher elevations in the Appalachians south to Georgia. It ranged through the Great Lakes drainage to Minnesota, Wisconsin, northern Iowa and Illinois. It has been introduced into other parts of North America and other continents.

Life History

Brook trout are fall spawners. The timing is variable but generally extends from mid-October to early December. The spawning areas are gravel-bottom sections of large or small streams, usually near springs. Lake populations spawn in shallow gravel-bottom bays where there is some upwelling through

the gravel. Males usually outnumber the females on the spawning beds and as they swim about they stir up the silt so the current sweeps it away. The female digs the spawning pit by lying on her side and vibrating her tail rapidly. The most intense spawning activity occurs near midday. A female may spend 2 days digging the pit although she may interrupt the work and desert the nest for short periods. She is inactive at night. In nearly all cases, the size of the pit is determined by the size of the female, the pit being larger and deeper than she is. While the female is still digging the pit, the males begin to court her by approaching and touching her sides. During this courtship, both males and females defend the pit by chasing away any intruders. Usually, the male chases those that approach from downstream and the female those that come from upstream. Those that approach from the sides are attacked by the nearest partner.

When the female is ready to spawn, she moves to the bottom of the pit, spreads her pelvic fins against the gravel with her vent in the deepest part of the pit. The male moves in and curves his body so as to hold her in position. They then vibrate together for several seconds. Greeley dug up nests immediately after spawning and recovered 40 to 79 eggs. Immediately after spawning, the female begins to sweep the nest with her tail and after half an hour or so she begins to dig another pit a few inches upstream. The male remains with the female for only a few minutes after spawning. Both partners spawn repeatedly during the season.

Food and Feeding

Brook trout are voracious carnivores and feed on a wide variety of aquatic insects and other invertebrates. Because of their stream habitat they eat a lot of terrestrial insects that fall into the water. Brook trout at times feed on fish and other vertebrates such as salamanders, tadpoles, snakes and small mammals that venture, or fall, into the streams.

Notes

Normally, brook and brown trout are fall spawners and rainbows are spring spawners, but in hatcheries the spawning times can be changed by selective breeding and by manipulating temperature and day length as well as by hormone injections, so crosses that are not possible normally can be produced.

Brook trout x lake trout hybrids are called splake. They are frequently stocked in New York lakes because they grow fast and mature early. Other hybrids such as brook trout x brown trout (tiger trout) are occasionally found in the wild and can be produced in hatcheries. Three-way crosses between splake and brown trout or splake and rainbows are possible and splake can be backcrossed with brook trout. Each hybrid cross has a distinctive appearance; perhaps the most striking is the vermiculated tiger trout which is a cross between the brown trout female and the brook trout male. (For excellent photographs see Buss and Wright, 1958.)

Berst, Emery, and Spangler (1981) described in detail the reproductive habits of splake. They found acoustic signals to be used at various stages of the courtship process. A click, possibly produced by the jaws closing, was used as part of the threat signal when the fish were defending territories and thumps were also used as threats. During the spawning quiver, a prolonged burst of sound was produced.

The splake record for New York State is 11 pounds 2 ounces from Eagle Lake, taken in March, 1979 by Jeffrey Burres.

Recently, Stoneking et al. have suggested that the brook trout of the Great Smoky Mountain National Park are so different genetically that they may be a subspecies, but they did not believe that their results were definitive enough to name the southern form.

There are slight differences in local populations of brook trout and experience has shown that native fish are usually superior in terms of survival and growth in their home waters. At present, the Department of Environmental Conservation recognizes eleven strains and attempts to preserve their genetic identity in their native lakes. These are termed Heritage Strains and are named for the waters in which they occur. Some are identifiable by morphological features; others are distinguished only by biochemical or life history characteristics. The DEC also maintains two Canadian strains, Temiscamie and Assinica, and domestic brook trout that have been maintained in hatcheries for many generations. Hybrids of these sometimes have special features that make them especially suited for certain kinds of waters.

References

There is an enormous literature on the brook trout but good summaries are found in Ricker, 1932 and Carlander, 1969. Other references are: Brasch et al., 1958 (general account). Greeley, 1932 (life history, spawning behavior). McCormick et al., 1972 (effects of temperature on survival). Bridges and Miller, 1958 (general account). Webster and Eiriksdottir, 1976 (spawning sites). Gibson and Power, 1975 (habitat selection). Wilder, 1952 (anadromous and freshwater populations). Webster, 1954b (survival, sampling). Stoneking et al., 1981 (population). Flick and Webster, 1975; 1976 (ecology and management). Dunson and Martin, 1973 (survival in acidity gradient). Johnson and Webster, 1977 (avoidance of low pH). Swartz et al., 1978 (acid resistance). Brown, 1961 (behavior of fingerlings). Bacon, 1954 (juveniles). Fraser, 1978 (competition). Magnan and FitzGerald, 1982 (competition with creek chub). Estes, 1983 (bibliography). Avery, 1983 (bibliography of trout-beaver interactions)

Names

Fontinalis is the genitive of the Latin *fons*, fountain or spring and refers to the habitat of the brook trout.

Salmo fontinalis Mitchill, 1815: 435 near New York City

Salmo erythrogaster DeKay, 1842: 235-236 Indian Lake and Lake Janet

Baione fontinalis, DeKay, 1842: 244-245 Rockland County

BROOK TROUT STRAINS IN NEW YORK STATE (From Keller, 1979)

Heritage Strains

STRAIN	LOCATION	LIFE HISTORY	MORPHOLOGY	ADVANTAGE
Balsam Lake	Catskills	Mature at I +, live to III +	To 9-12 inches	
Dix Pond	Adirondacks	Live to III +	To 9 inches	
Honnedaga Lake	Adirondacks	Mature at II + (12 inches)	To 6 pounds	
Horn Lake	Adirondacks	Mature at III + (12 inches), live to IV +, lake spawners	To 16 inches	
Little Tupper Lake	Adirondacks	Mature at III +, live to V +, lake and tributary spawners	To 6 pounds	
Nate Pond	Adirondacks	Mature at III + (11.5 inches), live to VI +	To 20 inches, 4 pounds	
Stink Lake	Adirondacks	Live to III +	To 14 inches	
Tamarack Pond	Adirondacks	Mature at II +, live to III + or more, pond spawners	To 16-17 inches	
Tunis Lake	Catskills	Mature at I +, lake and tributary spawners	Maximum length 24 inches	
Windfall Pond	Adirondacks (Franklin Co.)	Mature at II +, live to V + or more, spawn in inlets and outlets	Maximum weight 4 pounds	
Windfall Pond	Adirondacks (Herkimer Co.)	Spawn in outlets or shore	To 18 inches, 3 pounds	

Canadian Strains

STRAIN	LOCATION	LIFE HISTORY	MORPHOLOGY	ADVANTAGE
Assinica	Quebec	Live to VIII +, mature at II +, require forage	To 4 pounds (10-12 in Canada)	Large size
Temiscamie	James Bay	Mature at II + or III + (15 inches), require forage fish	To 4-5 pounds (10 in Canada), brightly colored with large yellow spots	Large size, acid resistant

Hybrid Strains

STRAIN	LOCATION	LIFE HISTORY	MORPHOLOGY	ADVANTAGE
Assinica x Crown Point				Better growth and survival
Temiscamie x Crown Point				Acid tolerant, but tends to emigrate

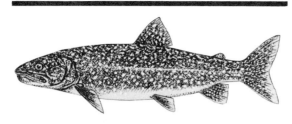

LAKE TROUT

Salvelinus namaycush
(Walbaum, 1792)

Identification

The lake trout is readily identified by its streamlined body with a distinctly forked tail and its color, a pattern of white spots on a silvery-gray background, shading to white on the belly. Its short anal fin distinguishes it from the Pacific salmons and its fine scales identify it as a char. Lake trout are related to brook trout but they are quite different. In addition to body and tail configuration, the brook trout has red spots on the sides and the lake trout does not; the lake trout has more gill rakers (16 to 26 in lake trout and 14 to 22 in brook trout), and more than 92 pyloric caeca (fewer than 55 in brook trout).

The pyloric caeca are the best identification for splake (lake trout x brook trout hybrids); there are 23 to 55 in brook trout, 93 to 208 in lake trout and 65 to 85 in splake.

Description

Body ovate, deepest in front of the dorsal fin, streamlined, slab sided. Caudal peduncle rather narrow. Profiles nearly symmetrical. Dorsal fin deltoid, its outer margin nearly straight. Adipose fin origin over rear half of anal base. Tail moderately forked, its lobes bluntly pointed. Anal short, deltoid, with slightly concave margin. Pelvics inserted below rear of dorsal base. Pelvic retrogressive, with rounded corners. Pelvic axillary process well developed. Pectorals retrogressive, with bluntly pointed anterior corner and rounded posterior corner. Pectoral base somewhat oblique. Gill membranes separate and free from isthmus. Lateral line complete, nearly straight. Body completely scaled, head naked. Mouth large, terminal, maxillary extending well past eye. Teeth well developed on jaws, head of the vomer, palatines, tongue, and basibranchial. Counts and proportional measurements are given in Table 24.

Color: Silvery gray to dark gray on back and sides, shading to silvery white on the belly and underside of the head. Back with darker areas with dense white or creamy spots that tend to be elongate or vermiculate. Pectoral, pelvic, and anal fins with white leading edges. These fins sometimes have an orange cast. No red spots.

Juveniles and breeding adults: Juveniles have 7 to 12 quite irregular and variable parr marks. The exact pattern varies from locality to locality. Adult males rarely develop the hooked jaws that characterize the breeding males of other salmonids.

Size: The largest lake trout on record was 49.5 inches long and weighed 102 pounds. It was taken in Lake Athabaska, Saskatchewan, Canada. The present New York record is 31 pounds and was taken in Follensby Pond in 1922 by Malcolm Hain. The world angling record is 65 pounds.

Habitat

In the southern part of its range, the lake trout is confined to deeper and colder lakes but in northern Canada it occurs in shallow lakes and in rivers as well. It does not enter the sea but it can tolerate slightly brackish water.

Lake trout are usually found at or near the bottom of well-oxygenated lakes. They usually occur in water about 50 F and they do not venture into warmer waters for very long, although they may make brief excursions above the thermocline. McCauley and Tait found that their preferred temperature is 17 C, nearly 2 C warmer than their usual habitat in stratified lakes. Acclimation at 5, 10, 15, and 20 C has little effect on the final preferred temperature.

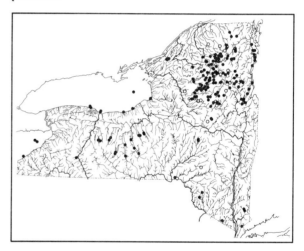

Distribution

The lake trout ranges over much of the glaciated part of North America but its distribution has unexplained gaps within that area. It is the only species of freshwater fish that occurs in Alaska and northern Canada that does not extend into Siberia.

It has been widely introduced in the Rocky Mountains and elsewhere in the United States and also in other parts of the world, including New Zealand, Sweden, and South America.

Plosila classified the distribution of the lake trout in New York as: 1) Its relict natural range which includes the border lakes Erie, Ontario, and Champlain, and the Adirondacks, the Finger Lakes, and Otsego Lake in the Susquehanna drainage. 2) Its introduced range including lakes in Sullivan, Westchester, and Putnam Counties. 3) An unclassified area in St. Lawrence and Jefferson Counties for which it could not be determined whether the populations were native or introduced. Plosila found that 121 lakes now contain lake trout. Eighty-four of these are open to public fishing; the rest are on posted preserves. Lake trout have disappeared from 34 lakes that formerly supported them; in 18 of these, the species has disappeared since the Biological Surveys of the 1930s. Habitat deterioration leading to the lowering of dissolved oxygen levels, overfishing, and pesticides have been the chief causes of their decline.

Lakes Erie and Ontario formerly supported commercial fisheries for lake trout but by 1930 few lake trout were taken in Lake Erie and the native stock there is now considered to be extinct. By 1950, the Lake Ontario population was on the verge of extinction. Although still listed as a commercial species in Lakes Erie and Ontario, commercial fishing for them is now prohibited. Inland lakes which supported only a minor commercial fishery still provide considerable sport fishing and lake trout rank eleventh in sport fishing popularity. It is the fourth most frequently sought salmonid.

Lake trout from the Finger Lakes are lighter colored and more silvery with little yellow or orange on the fins. In contrast, those from the darkly colored Adirondack waters are darker and do have orange or yellow paired fins. A study by Plosila showed that Finger Lakes lake trout do not survive well when stocked in the Adirondacks and peripheral waters. Yearlings stocked in the spring produced better results than stocking yearlings or fingerlings in the fall.

In Cayuga Lake, hatchery fish have been essential to maintaining the population for the last 50 years.

There is an active program to restore the fishing in other lakes where the habitat is still suitable.

Life History

The lake trout spawns between September and early December, the exact time varying from lake to lake. They usually spawn in lakes although some Canadian populations spawn in rivers. The spawning depths vary from 6 inches to 15 feet in some lakes to 100 or 200 feet in Seneca and Cayuga Lakes. Usually, spawning takes place over rock and rubble 1.5 to 4 inches in diameter with some larger boulders and no fine sediments. Ordinarily, the eggs drop into crevices and are protected but where the lake trout spawn over smooth bottom the eggs are subject to predation by newts and fishes including suckers, bullheads, burbot, round whitefish, and others.

Apparently, spawning is triggered by a sudden drop in temperature but it is also influenced by cloud cover and winds, and associated with fall turnover of the lakes. The spawning period lasts 5 to 20 days at any one location. The fish move onto the beds in late afternoon and remain through the early hours of darkness although a few individuals stay through the day and night. The males clean the spawning sites by twisting the tail or body over the rocks and rubbing their snouts in the crevices.

During courtship, the males develop shiny dark bands on the sides and dark areas around the head while the top of the body becomes quite pale. This is a transient color phase that disappears when the fish are killed. The male courts the female by butting her sides and brushing her vent region with his back and dorsal fin. Males reach the spawning grounds earlier in the season and usually make up 60 to 85 percent of the spawning population. Larger fish tend to spawn later than the smaller fish. The eggs are broadcast and experiments have shown that they are scattered so the average density is about 20 to 50 per square foot. Hatching takes approximately 4 months and the young remain on the spawning beds for about another month before moving into deep water in mid-May. Females produce 400 to 1,200 eggs per pound of body weight, a 32-inch fish laying about 18,000 eggs. The eggs are about 5 to 6 mm in diameter. Maturity is usually at age VI or VII when the fish are 14 to 17 inches fork length. Some tagged fish have shown a tendency to return to the same spawning grounds year after year but other populations have revealed little or no homing tendency.

Food and Feeding

Newly hatched lake trout feed on small zooplankton and as they grow their diet changes to larger zooplankton, insects, opossum shrimp, scuds, and small fish. In lakes where fish are not available, they survive on zooplankton but grow more slowly and mature earlier. Ciscoes and round whitefish are favorite prey but smelt, alewife, yellow perch, lake whitefish, sculpins, ninespine sticklebacks, troutperch, white suckers, and various minnows have been reported from lake trout stomachs. Other items include mice and shrews and even sponges.

Notes

In the lake trout, the vomerine teeth are on a raised crest that extends backward from the front part of the prevomer bone, separate from its shaft. This was previously considered sufficient difference to warrant placing the lake trout in its own genus, *Cristivomer*. There is, however, some variation and in other features the lake trout resembles other chars and is now placed with them in the genus *Salvelinus*.

References

Royce, 1951 (breeding habits). Eschmeyer, 1955 (reproduction in Lake Superior). Daly, Hacker, and Wiegert, 1962 (life history and management). Galligan, 1962 (distribution in Cayuga Lake). McCauley and Tait, 1970 (temperature preference). Youngs, 1972 (lamprey mortality). Youngs and Oglesby, 1972 (fishery in Cayuga Lake). Plosila, 1977a, 1977b (management in New York). Dean, Colquhoun, and Simonin, 1977 (toxicology). Dean et al., 1979 (Lake George). Van Oosten and Deason, 1938 (food).

Names

Namaycush is an Indian name for lake trout.

Salmo namaycush Walbaum, 1792: 68 Hudson Bay (after Pennant)

Cristivomer namaycush, Bean, 1903: 266-271 Caledonia

Salmo pallidus Rafinesque, 1817b:120 Lake Champlain
Salmo amethystus Mitchill, 1818a: 410 New York
Salmo confinus DeKay, 1842: 238-239 Lake Louise, Hamilton County
Salmo adirondacus Norris, 1865: 255 Adirondack Lakes

TABLE 24
AVERAGE PROPORTIONAL MEASUREMENTS AND COUNTS OF TROUTS AND ATLANTIC SALMON *(Salmo* and *Salvelinus)*

All proportions are expressed in percentage of standard length.

	Salmo			*Salvelinus*	
	gairdneri	salar	trutta	fontinalis	namaycush
ST. LENGTH (mm)	121.5	98.4	80.8	101.3	140.9
TOTAL LENGTH	121.6	118.8	120.8	119.7	125.0
FORK LENGTH	114.7	112.5	114.3	113.8	118.8
PREDORSAL	50.8	44.3	49.4	47.6	54.4
PREANAL	75.0	74.3	73.9	73.5	80.5
PREPELVIC	55.0	54.4	53.5	52.6	61.9
DORSAL BASE	15.0	14.7	14.9	13.7	10.6
ANAL BASE	11.6	9.4	10.0	10.5	9.2
BODY DEPTH	26.7	23.3	24.5	24.6	21.8
BODY WIDTH	13.9	12.4	14.3	14.6	13.0
C.PED. DEPTH	10.9	8.7	11.4	11.5	8.0
PECTORAL ALT.	19.2	15.9	17.8	18.6	16.0
HEAD LENGTH	28.1	24.2	28.4	27.5	28.6
SNOUT	6.4	6.4	7.3	7.4	8.1
EYE	7.0	6.5	7.4	6.7	6.7
MOUTH LENGTH	13.0	10.6	14.2	16.2	14.4
INTERORB	7.9	6.0	7.8	7.8	6.8
N (sample size)	5	5	5	5	2
COUNTS:					
DORSAL RAYS	11-13	10-13	11-14	10-14	8-10
ANAL RAYS	8-12	8-11	9-12	8-11	10
PECTORAL RAYS	11-17	14-15	13-15	11-14	12-17
PELVIC RAYS	9-10	9-10	9-10	8-10	9-11
GILL RAKERS	15-16	15-19	14-18	14-22	16-26
VERTEBRAE	62-65	59	58-59	56-60	64-66
SCALES:					
ABOVE L. L.	25	23	24	40	31-32
LATERAL LINE	100-150	109-121	120-130	110-130	116-138
BELOW L. L.	20	15	22	32	24-25
PYLORIC CAECA	27-80	40-74	30-60	23-55	93-208

SMELTS

OSMERIDAE

The family Osmeridae is a small family with about six genera and around a dozen species. They occur in the Northern Hemisphere in both the Atlantic and Pacific Oceans and most species are marine or anadromous or live near the coasts in the lower reaches of freshwater streams. They are slender fishes with an adipose fin, rough scales, large teeth on the tongue, and a silvery stripe along the side of the body.

Only one species, the rainbow smelt, *Osmerus mordax,* occurs in New York. It is anadromous in the Hudson and streams on Long Island and also has freshwater populations in the Great Lakes and in a number of inland lakes. In some areas, it is abundant enough to be a sport fish in spite of its small size. It is taken through the ice in lakes and it is caught in dip nets at night when it runs up streams to spawn.

OSMERUS

This genus is distinguished by having the opercle and subopercle smooth (without concentric striations), 3 to 8 pyloric caeca, large teeth on the tongue, 1 or 2 large canines at each side of the vomer, and 15 to 24 gill rakers on the lower half of the first arch. The maxillary extends as far back as the rear of the pupil.

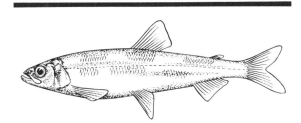

RAINBOW SMELT

Osmerus mordax (Mitchill, 1815)

Identification

The smelt is a pale, slender, elongate fish with a bright silvery stripe along the side of its body. At first glance, it might be confused with some kind of minnow but a closer look reveals the presence of an adipose fin, and large teeth in the mouth including distinctive curved canines on the tongue and the vomer.

These large teeth will distinguish the smelts from the whitefishes, which also have an adipose fin but only tiny teeth. Another difference between the smelts and the whitefishes is that smelts lack well-developed pelvic axillary processes which are characteristic of whitefishes and other salmonids. Rainbow smelt are said to smell like fresh cucumbers when alive but I have not been able to confirm this.

Description

Body slender, little compressed, slightly ovate in cross section, and deepest just in front of the origin of the dorsal fin. Dorsal and ventral profiles evenly and equally curved. Dorsal fin deltoid, its margin straight and its points rounded. Adipose fin present, adnexed. Caudal forked, Anal fin trapezoidal, its margin slightly concave. Pelvic fins abdominal, their insertion below middle of dorsal base. No pelvic axillary process. Pectoral fins low, base nearly horizontal. Gill membranes separate and free from the isthmus. Teeth present on jaws, vomer, palatine, pterygoid, tongue, and basibranchial. Scales cycloid. Lateral line incomplete. Counts and proportional measurements are given in Table 25.

Color: Pale greenish tan dorsally, shading to silvery on the sides and white below. Scales of the back outlined with pigment forming a regular network pattern. Sides sometimes with a greenish or purplish iridescence. Fins clear, rays of dorsal and caudal fins outlined with melanophores. Caudal dusky at base. Paired fins and anal fin clear.

Juveniles and breeding adults: Juveniles are clear and elongate. Breeding males develop tubercles on the head, body and fins. Females have much smaller tubercles. The anal and paired fins of males are larger than those of females.

Size: Usually adult male smelt average 7 to 8 inches total length but they can reach more than 12 inches. The largest specimen studied by McAllister (1963) was 257 mm standard length.

Habitat

Smelts are anadromous fish with landlocked populations in eastern North America where, except for their spawning period, they are confined to larger lakes. They live in the thermocline in the summer but rarely venture below 70 meters.

Distribution

The rainbow smelt occurs on the Atlantic coast from Labrador to the Delaware River in Pennsylvania. Reports of the species in Virginia are considered doubtful. It occurred naturally in freshwater lakes in Maine, New Hampshire and Canada. A closely related form, currently recognized as a subspecies by some authorities but not others, occurs in the Pacific and Arctic Oceans from Vancouver Island and Korea to the Bering Strait and from the White Sea east to Cape Bathurst. A similar species, *Osmerus eperlanus,* occurs in Europe from the mouth of the Loire River to the North and Baltic Seas.

The rainbow smelt was introduced into the upper Great Lakes several times but Van Oosten believed that it became established after a 1912 planting in Crystal Lake, Michigan. It was first reported from southern Lake Huron and Lake St. Clair in 1932 but the report by Creaser that they had been released by the Belle Isle Aquarium was denied by the curator of that institution according to Van Oosten. The smelt was first reported from near Port Dover on Lake Erie in 1935 and in June 1936 several were taken in gill nets near Vermillion, Ohio. Smelt were not recorded from Lake Ontario until 1929. Some authorities believe that the species was native to Lake Ontario but rare; others think the evidence suggests an introduction, either from the upper Great Lakes via the Welland Canal or from the Finger Lakes via the Seneca-Cayuga, Erie and Oswego Canals. Spawning runs in Lake Ontario tributaries were first noticed in the mid- to late-1940s, and a commercial fishery developed there in the 1950s. The increase in smelt in Lake Ontario coincided with the decline of the lake herring.

In New York, the smelt occurs in the Lower Hudson and Long Island streams, Lakes Erie, Ontario and Champlain, the Finger Lakes, Canadarago Lake, Neversink Reservoir, and in several Adirondack lakes including Lake George.

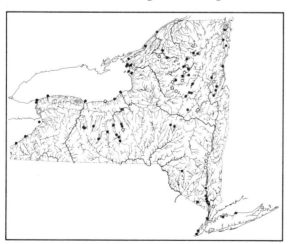

Life History

The rainbow smelt has both landlocked and anadromous populations. Even the landlocked populations, however, have the habit of migrating from their lake habitats to the streams to spawn. Spawning takes place in February or March when the wa-

ter reaches 48 F. Greene and, later, Langlois described the spawning runs of the smelt in Canandaigua and Owasco Lakes in New York and Crystal Lake in Michigan. The adult fish move into the lower reaches of creeks each evening and normally return to the lake or larger river the next morning. On cloudy days, they may remain in the stream all day. The first night, only the males moved into the stream but the next night the run included about 6 percent females and the percentage continued to increase until the run included 60 percent females on the fifth night. Females were abundant early in the evening but the males dominated toward morning.

Langlois described the spawning of one female accompanied by five males in a pocket behind a log. The female lay just off the bottom with her head between two stones about 2 inches in diameter. She moved her body slowly from side to side releasing small groups of eggs as she moved and sometimes turned on her side so that the flash of her silvery underbody could be seen from the surface. The eggs dropped to the bottom and stayed there. The males maintained a position downstream from the female with their heads at the level of the middle of her body. Langlois was unable to see the milt released.

The eggs are small, about 0.036 inches in diameter. One 232-mm female had 43,125 eggs, and Kendall found 5,893 eggs in a smelt 4 5/8 inches long. Langlois noted that the males were smaller than the females and while both sexes had tubercles, those of the male formed a keel along each scale so that they appeared rougher than the females. Males were also darker in color.

Cooper studied the development of smelt eggs from Trout Run, a Pennsylvania tributary of Lake Erie. Unfertilized eggs were 0.8 to 0.9 mm in diameter. Upon agitation after fertilization, the outer membrane turned inside out to form an adhesive stalk. Water-hardened eggs were 1 mm in diameter. Hatching took place 162 to 205 hours after fertilization at 13 to 18 C. Newly hatched larvae were 5 mm long. Cooper presented characters for separating larvae of smelt from those of gizzard shad and alewife.

Food and Feeding

Sea-run smelt feed on crustaceans, nereid worms, squid, and fish. Freshwater smelt eat *Mysis,* amphipods, aquatic oligochaetes, and aquatic insect larvae. Fish make up a relatively small part of the diet.

Notes

Apparently, two races, large and small, occur in Lake Champlain. These differ in growth rate and life span but no one has found consistent morphological differences. The large race reaches 233 mm in its third winter, the small one averages 158 mm at the same age. The small race matures after two winters; but only about a third of the large race is mature at the same age. The large race lives longer, normally to the sixth winter whereas 4 years is the normal life span of the small race. Zilliox and

Youngs noted that the small race was less abundant in 1948 and 1950 than in 1929. In 1929, large fish made up 69.7 percent of the population but in 1948 the proportion has risen to 92.8 percent and by 1950 it was 95.7 percent.

The smelt is an important commercial species in Lakes Ontario and Erie but most of the fishery is in Canadian waters where they are taken in otter trawls. In many New York waters, they are taken by dip netting during their spawning run and in Lake Champlain they are taken through the ice.

References

Kendall, 1927 (general). McAllister, 1963 (systematics). Hankinson and Hubbs, 1922 (Great Lakes). Van Oosten, 1937b, 1937c (first record and spread in Great Lakes). Creaser, 1926a, 1932 (Great Lakes). Greene, 1930 (life history). Langlois, 1935 (spawning). Zilliox and Youngs, 1958 (races in Lake Champlain). Christie, 1973 (Lake Ontario). George and Gordon, 1976 (Lake George). Bailey, 1964 (maturity). Siefert, 1972 (first food). Roecker, 1961 (popular account). Rupp, 1965 (spawning and survival). Foltz and Norden, 1977 (feeding). McKenzie, 1964 (Canadian fishery). MacCallum and Regier, 1970 (Lake Erie). Hoover, 1936a (sex ratio, spawning). Emery, 1973 (school at night). Copeman and McAllister, 1978 (effect of transplantation on morphology). O'Gorman, 1974 (predation on alewives). Cooper, 1978b (eggs and larvae). MacCrimmon, Gots, and Clayton, 1983 (Lake Erie).

Names

The word *mordax* is from the Latin *morsus*, biting. Because of the close similarity of the rainbow smelt and the Arctic smelt with the European *eperlanus*, there has been considerable debate over the scientific name. Recently, they have been called *Osmerus mordax mordax* and *O. m. eperlanus*.

 Atherina mordax Mitchill, 1815: 446 New York
 Osmerus viridescens Lesueur, 1818b: 230 Maine
 Osmerus sargenti Norris, 1868: 93 Schuylkill River, New Jersey

MUDMINNOWS

UMBRIDAE

Mudminnows are somber little fish that look a lot like cigar butts with fins. Although they are minnow-sized, the mudminnows are related to the pikes rather than to the true minnows. The family is a small one and confined to the northern part of the Northern Hemisphere. It includes the legendary Alaska blackfish, *Dallia pectoralis,* famed for its ability to survive being frozen in solid ice, the Olympic mudminnow of Oregon, the two species that occur in our area, and one species native to central Europe.

Mudminnows slightly resemble some of the killifishes (family Cyprinodontidae) but they have non-protractile jaws, that is, there is no groove between the upper lip and the tip of the snout. They are hardy little fish and very tolerant of low oxygen levels which enables them to live in areas where there is a great deal of decaying plant debris.

Umbra

Members of this genus are distinguished from the closely related genera *Novumbra* and *Dallia* by having well-developed gill rakers and a subopercle that is triangular rather than elongate.

KEY TO THE SPECIES OF MUDMINNOWS IN NEW YORK

A. Color pattern on body consisting of 10 or more regular, dark, longitudinal lines separated by pale spaces of equal width.
Umbra pygmaea   Eastern mudminnow, p. 242

A'. Color pattern consisting of rather indistinct and irregular vertical bands. No regular, longitudinal lines although in some individuals there is a single line or row of spots along the midside.
Umbra limi   Central mudminnow, p. 243

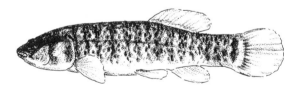

EASTERN MUDMINNOW

Umbra pygmaea (DeKay, 1842)

Identification

In general size and shape, mudminnows most resemble killifishes but they are darker in color, have their pelvic fins farther back so that most of the pelvic fin base is below the dorsal fin, and have more rounded fins than the killifishes. In both groups, most of the head is scaled but the killifishes have a protractile mouth with a groove between the snout and the upper lip whereas the mouth of the mudminnow is not protractile and only the posterior end of the maxillary is freely movable. Mudminnows

bear little resemblance to the true minnows which have forked tails and lack teeth in their mouths.

The eastern mudminnow differs from the central mudminnow in color, having a pattern of longitudinal stripes separated by narrow pale lines rather than vertical bars. Both species have a prominent black bar at the base of the tail.

Description

Body elongate, robust, nearly terete anteriorly and slab sided posteriorly. Profiles nearly equally curved. Dorsal fin progressive, with last two or three rays shorter, its margin curved with rounded corners. Dorsal origin midway between midbase of caudal and anterior part of operculum. Caudal rounded, its base slightly asymmetrical. Anal origin below middle of dorsal base. Anal fin similar to dorsal, its origin below middle of dorsal base. Pelvic origin slightly anterior to dorsal origin. Pelvic fin retrogressive, with convex margin and rounded corners. No pelvic axillary process, no membrane between last pelvic ray and body wall. Pectorals low, with their bases oblique, rounded, nearly symmetrical. Scales of a special type with longitudinal ridges at various angles. Body completely scaled, head scaled forward to the nostrils. Mouth terminal, nonprotractile. Operculum round, preoperculum with free margin only at its angle. Subopercle large, sometimes slightly dentate. Gill membranes free and separate. Lateral line absent. Teeth present on premaxillary, vomer, palatine, and dentary. Counts and proportional measurements are given in Table 25.

Color: Upper parts dark brown, shading to pale tan below and with about 10 longitudinal brown stripes separated by narrow, pale lines that are wider ventrally. A prominent black vertical bar at caudal base. Head with an oblique white bar or V-shaped area below and behind the eye. Fins pale with the rays outlined. Pectoral and pelvic fins often with a reddish wash in life.

Size: The maximum size is about 5 inches total length. Our largest specimen from New York is 94 mm standard length.

Habitat

The eastern mudminnow lives in slow parts of streams and ponds where there is dense aquatic vegetation. Like the central mudminnow, it is tolerant of low oxygen but requires shelter.

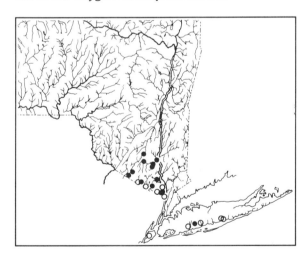

Distribution

The eastern mudminnow ranges from Long Island and the Wallkill River system in New York south along the Atlantic coast to the St. Johns River in Florida and to the Aucilla River on the Gulf of Mexico side of Florida. It has also been established in Belgium.

Life History

The general features of reproduction in this species in the New York area were described by Breder and

Rosen. Spawning takes place in early spring. Breder first found them on 10 April when the water was 57 F. The adults moved into a stream area that was covered with ice in the winter and dry in the summer. The males appeared to spread their fins in a display for the females although the details were not seen clearly. The eggs were deposited under rocks, usually in a single layer on the roof of small cavities. Another author reported that nests with lateral openings were hollowed out of dense algae. Females guarded the nests while the males remained nearby. It was not clear whether the males were guarding the nests or trying to eat the eggs.

Food and Feeding

The only reported foods of the eastern mudminnow are copepods and trichopteran larvae but they are undoubtedly generalized feeders that take a wide variety of small prey.

References

Breder and Rosen, 1966 (reproduction). Breder, 1933a (development). Poll, 1949 (introduced into Belgium). Panek, 1981 (life history, relationships). Gee, 1980 (respiration).

Names

The name *pygmaea* is Latin for small, dwarf-like.
Leuciscus pygmaeus DeKay, 1842: 214 Tappan, New York
Fundulus fuscus Ayres, 1843: 296 Brookhaven, New York

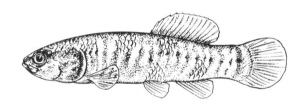

CENTRAL MUDMINNOW

Umbra limi (Kirtland, 1841)

Identification

Mudminnows resemble killifishes in size and shape and, like the killifishes, have the dorsal and anal fins far back on the body. Killifishes, however, have a protractile mouth with a distinct groove between the upper lip and the tip of the snout. Mudminnows have a nonprotractile mouth with no separation between the lip and the snout. The fins of the mudminnows, especially the tail, are less angular. Both species of mudminnows have a dark vertical bar at the base of the tail.

The central mudminnow is generally mottled with a suggestion of dark vertical bars but the eastern mudminnow has a regular pattern of alternating light and dark longitudinal lines.

Description

Body elongate, nearly terete, caudal peduncle deep. Upper and lower profiles nearly parallel and about equally curved. Caudal base slightly asymmetrical (abbreviate heterocercal). Dorsal fin arched, progressive, with its last rays shorter. Dorsal origin midway between midbase of caudal and preopercle. Caudal rounded, slightly asymmetrical. Anal similar to dorsal, its origin below middle of dorsal base. Pelvic fins abdominal, retrogressive, rounded. Pelvic origin slightly ahead of dorsal origin. No pelvic axillary process, no pelvic membrane. Pectoral fins low, retrogressive, rounded, base oblique. Head bullet shaped, mouth small and terminal, upper jaw nonprotrusible. Opercle rounded, smooth, preopercle with free margin only at its angle. Subopercle large. Body fully scaled, top of head scaled to nostrils. No lateral line. Scales of a distinctive type with longitudinal, rather than concentric, ridges at varying angles giving a cross-bedded appearance. Gill membranes separate and free from isthmus. Conical teeth present on jaws, vomer, palatines, and basibranchials. Counts and proportional measurements are given in Table 25.

Color: Generally dark brown, mottled with indistinct and irregular dark bars along the sides. Lower surfaces only slightly lighter. A definite dark vertical bar at the base of the tail, often somewhat constricted at midside. Sides of head with silvery oblique line or spot. Iris brown, fin membranes pale, sometimes with a pink or orange wash. Fin rays outlined.

Juveniles and breeding adults: The following color notes were made from a freshly preserved 27-mm specimen from Michigan: "dorsum sprinkled with melanophores which become less dense ventrally until the belly is plain greenish white. Top of head and especially the olfactory capsule densely pigmented. Middorsal stripe present, a triple line in front of the dorsal fin and a dusky line behind. Caudal bar irregular. Dorsal and caudal fins with pigment along the margins of the rays and across the segmental joints. Anal and paired fins clear with sparse melanophores along the rays. Scattered spots on the maxilla, lips and lower surface of the head.

Size: This species reaches a maximum total length of about 5 inches. The largest specimen we have from New York is 98 mm standard length.

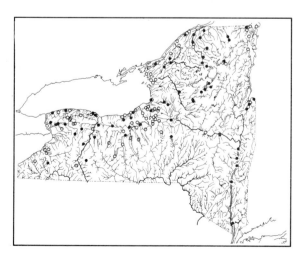

Habitat
Mudminnows live in sluggish waters where there is dense vegetation and organic debris. They are often taken in small pools in swampy woodlands. They burrow into soft flocculent bottom, especially in the winter, but it is unlikely that they hibernate as has been reported. Mudminnows taken under ice cover are usually quite active. They are able to obtain some oxygen by swallowing air into the swim bladder but they also need oxygen in the water and at times die of suffocation.

Distribution
The range of the central mudminnow centers in the Great Lakes and the Upper Mississippi drainage from the St. Lawrence to the Red River of the North in southern Manitoba, south to western Tennessee and northeastern Arkansas.

In New York, the central mudminnow occurs in the Great Lakes and in the Genesee, Oswego, St. Lawrence, Champlain and Mohawk drainages. It is especially abundant in sections of the old Erie Canal east of Fort Hunter and there are recent records in the Hudson as far south as the Montrose area and Constitution Island. This strongly suggests that this species has extended its natural range through canals.

Life History
Spawning of the central mudminnow was studied by Peckham and Dineen who made their observations near South Bend, Indiana, and also by Westman in western New York. In both areas, spawning took place in mid-April where the streams were flooded and the water temperature was about 13 C. The eggs were deposited, apparently singly, on vegetation in flooded areas. The eggs hatched in about 6 days and, as the floodwaters receded, the young moved into vegetation along the edges of the streams. Peckham and Dineen reported egg counts of 220 to 1,489, but Westman found up to 2,286 eggs in the largest females. The newly hatched prolarvae were about 5 mm long.

Applegate was unable to identify annual marks on the scales but his size-frequency data suggested that they reach 30 mm by the end of the first summer and 41 mm by the end of the second summer. Females 50 mm standard length were mature.

Food and Feeding
The central mudminnow is a carnivorous bottom feeder. Midges, copepods, ostracods, and crustaceans are the main food of the young; adults feed on insects, mostly chironomids, mayflies and caddisflies, and small mollusks. A few small fish are eaten.

Notes
The mudminnow has a justified reputation for being an extremely hardy fish, but it is said to be a poor live bait because of its somber colors and tendency to remain close to the bottom.

References
Applegate, 1943 (age and growth). Peckham and

Dineen, 1957 (life history). Westman, 1941 (life history), Ryder, 1886 (development). Gee, 1980 (respiration). Dineen and Stokely, 1954 (osteology). Panek, 1981 (relationships).

Names

The name *limi* comes from the Latin *limus,* mud.

Hydrargyra limi Kirtland, 1840: 277 northern Ohio

Hydrargira atricauda DeKay, 1842: 220 New York

Hydrargyra fusca Thompson, 1842: 137 Lake Champlain

TABLE 25
AVERAGE PROPORTIONAL MEASUREMENTS AND COUNTS OF
SMELT AND MUDMINNOWS *(Osmerus* and *Umbra)*

All proportions are expressed in percentage of standard length.

	Osmerus mordax	*Umbra* limi	*Umbra* pygmaea
ST. LENGTH (mm)	150.5	65.6	57.9
TOTAL LENGTH	117.7	120.9	125.2
FORK LENGTH	108.0	120.9	125.2
PREDORSAL	50.9	63.4	60.7
PREANAL	73.1	69.8	71.0
PREPELVIC	51.9	57.6	56.0
DORSAL BASE	9.38	19.6	20.0
ANAL BASE	14.6	11.2	9.9
BODY DEPTH	17.6	23.8	23.2
BODY WIDTH	10.7	17.4	16.1
C.PED. DEPTH	5.8	14.7	14.5
PECTORAL ALT.	12.4	17.9	16.9
HEAD LENGTH	23.8	29.9	27.6
SNOUT	6.6	7.2	6.2
EYE	5.4	8.1	7.0
MOUTH LENGTH	11.2	9.9	8.2
INTERORB	5.7	14.3	12.8
N (sample size)	5	5	5
COUNTS:			
DORSAL RAYS	8-11	13-15	13
ANAL RAYS	12-16	8-10	8
PECTORAL RAYS	11-14	14-16	14-15
PELVIC RAYS	8	6-7	6
GILL RAKERS	26-35	12-15	11-15
VERTEBRAE	59-61	35-37	35-36
SCALES:			
ABOVE L. L.	6-7	12-13*	12-13*
LATERAL LINE	62-72**	34-37	32-34
BELOW L. L.	7-8		

* Transverse count from dorsal to anal.   ** 13 to 30 pored scales.

PIKES

ESOCIDAE

The pikes and pickerels constitute a small family with one genus, *Esox,* and five species. Three of its species, *americanus, masquinongy,* and *niger* are confined to North America, *E. reicherti* lives in Siberia, and *E. lucius* occurs across the Northern Hemisphere. Pikes are closely related to the mudminnows and more distantly related to the salmonids, although they lack an adipose fin and do not look much like trout.

Pikes have slender, elongate bodies with the dorsal and anal fins set so far back they appear arrowshaped. They have a broad, rather flat, snout with a large mouth and stout teeth. In keeping with their preference for weedy habitat, they are usually green or brassy in color.

The larger species, the muskellunge, northern pike, and chain pickerel, are fine game fish but the redfin and grass pickerel are too small to be good sport fish. Pikes frequently hybridize and the tiger muskellunge or norlunge, which is a cross between the northern pike and the muskellunge, is raised in hatcheries for stocking throughout the state. Buss and Miller (1967) listed the characteristics of various esocid hybrid combinations.

The European amur pike, *Esox reicherti* Dybowski, has been stocked in a lake near Altoona, Pennsylvania (Cooper, 1983), but there are no definite records for New York State.

Esox

This is the only genus in the family.

KEY TO THE SPECIES OF PIKES IN NEW YORK

A. Cheeks and opercles both fully scaled.

C.

Cheek and gill cover scales.
Top: muskelleunge.
Center: northern pike.
Bottom: chain pickerel.

A'. Lower part of the opercles without scales.

B. Cheeks completely scaled, Branchiostegal rays 14 to 16.
Esox lucius   **Northern pike, p. 250**

B'. Lower part of cheeks without scales. Branchiostegal rays 17 to 19.
Esox masquinongy   **Muskellunge, p. 251**

C. (A. Cheeks and opercles fully scaled.) Branchiostegal rays 24 to 27 on each side. Snout long, less than 7 times in total length; 2.2 to 2.5 times in head length.
Esox niger   **Chain pickerel, p. 253**

C'. Branchiostegal rays 11 to 13 on each side. Snout shorter, more than 8.7 times in total length; 2.8 to 3.1 in head length.

D. Upper profile of snout convex. Lower fins of adults red to orange in life. More than five notched scales in the triangular area between the bases of the pelvic fins and more than five notched scales in the diagonal row of scales running upward and forward from the origin of the anal fin.

Esox americanus americanus

Redfin pickerel, p. 247

D'. Upper profile of snout slightly concave. Lower fins of adults dusky to yellow green but not orange or red in life. Fewer than five notched scales between the pelvic fin bases and fewer than five notched scales in the diagonal row above the origin of the anal fin.

Esox a. vermiculatus

Grass pickerel, p. 248

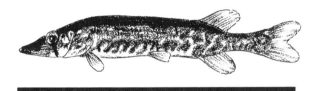

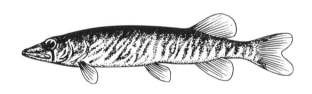

REDFIN PICKEREL

Esox americanus americanus Gmelin, 1788

Identification

An arrow-shaped body, long broad snout, and jaws with prominent canine-like teeth immediately brand the redfin as a member of the pike family. The redfin is a small species, seldom reaching 14 inches in length and its snout is short, usually shorter than the postorbital head length. Both its cheeks and its gill covers are fully scaled and it has only 11 to 13 branchiostegal rays. The northern pike and the muskellunge lack scales on the lower half of the operculum and the chain pickerel has 14 to 17 branchiostegal rays.

The redfin pickerel is very similar to the grass pickerel, although the two have complementary ranges and might be found together in the extreme northern part of the state, in the St. Lawrence and Champlain basins. The redfin has a shorter and broader snout with a convex profile. It is a darker fish with bars on the side of the body wider than the interspaces, and its fins, except the dorsal fin, are orange or red throughout the year. One of the best distinguishing features is the presence of more notched or heart-shaped scales on the sides. This is best seen in the area between the pelvic fins where

there are more than six heart-shaped scales if the fish is a redfin, up to three if the fish is a grass pickerel. Also, the redfin has more than seven notched scales in the diagonal row of scales between the dorsal and anal fins and the grass pickerel has four or fewer.

Description

A small species of *Esox* with the dorsal profile more arched than the ventral. Dorsal and anal fins far back, trapezoidal, with the margin strongly convex. Caudal moderately forked. Pelvics abdominal, rounded. Pectorals low on side with their bases nearly horizontal. Preopercle evenly curved, entire. Opercular margin smooth. Teeth present on the premaxillary, vomer, palatines, dentaries, and in patches on the tongue and basibranchials. Larger caniniform teeth present on the head of the vomer, the inner edge of the palatines and the dentaries. Gill rakers obsolescent. Counts and proportional measurements are given in Table 26.

Color: In life, the overall color is dark green or brownish above, shading to brassy or silvery white below. There is a pale middorsal stripe and also a pale midlateral stripe that is less prominent than in the grass pickerel. Below the midlateral stripe, a series of short dark bars extend downward and forward. These bars are often fused at their upper ends and diverge ventrally. Their combined area exceeds that of the pale interspaces. A prominent dark line runs from the front of the eye to the tip of the snout and a dark teardrop mark curves downward and backward. This mark is inclined about 29 degrees from the vertical but there is considerable variation in this angle.

Juveniles and breeding adults: Juveniles less than 100 mm long are quite dark above with a pronounced middorsal stripe and an indistinct midlateral pale stripe. The dark areas on the sides extend downward below the lateral stripe to the level of the pectoral fins where they meet the pale color of the belly along a fairly straight line.

Size: This is a small species reaching a total length of about 13 inches.

Habitat

The redfin pickerel lives in weedy areas of sluggish streams and in lakes and ponds. The young often

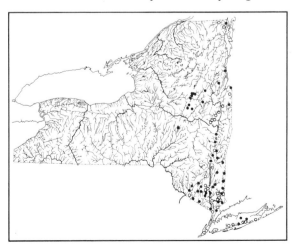

occur in water only a few inches deep. Crossman noted that the redfin pickerel often occurs with the chain pickerel and that when they live together in ponds the chain pickerel usually is the more abundant whereas in streams it is the redfin that predominates.

Distribution

Esox americanus has a ring-shaped distribution around the Appalachian Highlands. The redfin is the eastern subspecies and it occurs from northern Florida to New Hampshire and up the Hudson-Champlain corridor to the Richelieu and St. Lawrence Rivers. Populations in peninsular Florida and along the gulf coast to eastern Mississippi are intergrades.

In New York, the redfin is confined to Long Island and the eastern part of the state including Otsego Lake in the Susquehanna drainage, the Delaware system, Champlain, and Hudson drainages.

Life History

Redfin pickerel spawn early in the spring when the water temperature reaches 50 F in March or April. Spawning continues for about a month and the eggs require 12 to 14 days to hatch. Spawning often takes place on floodplains or overflow areas, along grassy stream banks and among dense vegetation. The unfertilized eggs average 1.9 mm in diameter and the ovaries usually contain three stages of developing eggs. The total counts average from 722 to 4,364 eggs, 186 to 542 of the largest size class. Growth is rapid; in North Carolina, the fish reach 92 to 129 mm fork length by the time the first annulus is formed. It is to be expected that New York fish would grow somewhat more slowly. The maximum age is about 5 to 7 years.

Food and Feeding

Redfin pickerel in Woodbury Creek in southeastern New York showed a progression in the size of the items taken from plankton, snails, crustaceans to larger insect nymphs, crayfishes, and fishes. Along with the increase in size of the prey there was a decrease in the number of items eaten. Fish more than 100 mm total length fed mainly after dawn and in late afternoon while smaller fish fed most intensively in mid-afternoon and after sunset.

Notes

Although it is too small to be a sport fish, the redfin pickerel is an important predator in many waters. Because it is difficult to distinguish from the young of other pikes, fishermen often release redfins thinking they are pike or chain pickerel. Thus, size limits intended to protect the larger species actually favor this smaller, nongame species.

References

Crossman, 1962a (life history and ecology, North Carolina). Buss, 1962 (life history). Crossman, 1966 (subspecies); 1978 (taxonomy and distribution). Chang, 1979 (food habits). Weed, 1927 (taxonomy).

Names

The trivial name *americanus* means from America.

Esox lucius (non Linnaeus) Schoepf, 1784: 26 near New York

Esox B-americanus Gmelin, 1788: 1390

Esox americanus Lacepède, 1803: 294

Esox scombrinus Mitchill, 1818a: 322 Murderers Creek

Esox fasciatus DeKay, 1842: 224 Long Island

Lucius americanus, Bean, 1903: 292-294

GRASS PICKEREL

Esox americanus vermiculatus Lesueur, 1846

Identification

The grass pickerel can be distinguished from the northern pike and the muskellunge in that both its cheeks and its gill covers are completely scaled, with at least three-fourths of each region covered with scales. It can be distinguished from the chain pickerel by its short snout and fewer (less than 15) branchiostegal rays. Adult chain pickerel are larger and have a reticulated pattern on the sides, and even small chain pickerel have more white on the sides than grass pickerel the same size.

The grass pickerel is very similar to the redfin pickerel and the two could occur together in the Lake Champlain or St. Lawrence region. The best recognition characters are the dorsal profile of the snout, convex in the redfin, concave in the grass pickerel, and the number of notched scales. The grass pickerel has fewer than 5 in the region between the bases of the pelvic fins and fewer than 10 in a diagonal row of scales above the anal fin.

The grass pickerel is lighter in color with a pronounced midlateral stripe and the combined area of the diagonal bars on the lower sides is less than the area of the interspaces.

Description

Body elongate and slab sided, sagittate, with the dorsal and anal fins far back. Dorsal profile slightly more curved than the ventral, the greatest curvature at the dorsal base. Dorsal origin a little closer to the pectoral insertion than to the middle of the caudal fold. Dorsal fin trapezoidal, its margin arched, both corners rounded. Anal similar, originating under the anterior one-fifth of the dorsal base. Caudal moderately forked, with rounded lobes. Pelvic retrogressive, with convex margin and rounded corners. Pelvic insertion midway between dorsal origin and pectoral insertion. No axillary process, no membrane between last ray and body. Pectoral fin low, its base slightly oblique, retrogressive, with rounded corners and convex margin. Body completely scaled. Head naked except for cheeks and opercles. Opercle and preopercle smooth. Lateral line complete but with many unpored scales. Teeth on vomer, palatines, premaxillary, maxillary, dentary, tongue, and basibranchials, enlarged on the premaxillary, head of the vomer and inner edge of the palatines. Gill membranes free, separate and overlapping. Gill rakers reduced to small patches of teeth. Counts and proportional measurements are given in Table 26.

Color: The color pattern is quite variable and specimens in aquaria go through a range of color changes. At rest, they are usually dark greenish above with a pronounced pale lateral stripe and pale diagonal bars on the lower sides. Suborbital bar more nearly vertical than in the redfin. A narrow dark line runs from the tip of the snout through the eye to the upper end of the gill cover. In life, the fins are dusky or washed with yellowish but not red or orange.

Juveniles and breeding adults: Juveniles less than 50 mm have a wide, pale, midlateral stripe and a dark stripe with a wavy lower edge below it. This lower area breaks into oblique bars as the fish grow.

Size: The maximum size of the grass pickerel is about 375 mm total length.

Habitat

The grass pickerel lives in heavily vegetated areas of slow-moving streams and lakes and ponds. Crossman noted that the grass pickerel occurs more often in neutral to basic, often silted, waters whereas the redfin is partial to dark, acid waters.

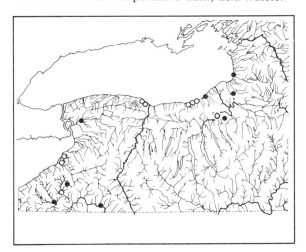

Distribution

The grass pickerel occurs west of the Appalachians from the gulf coast of Texas, Louisiana and western Mississippi north through the Mississippi drainage to the southern half of Lakes Michigan and Huron, Lake Erie and Lake Ontario, and the St. Lawrence River as far downstream as the mouth of the Ottawa River. There are isolated populations in eastern Iowa and eastern Nebraska. Intergrades with the redfin pickerel occur on the eastern Gulf Coastal Plain and in peninsular Florida.

Life History

Crossman has summarized the life history of the grass pickerel in Canada. Although its spawning behavior has not been studied carefully, it appears similar to that of other esocids. Spawning takes place in the spring when the water temperature reaches 36 to 54 F. The eggs are broadcast over vegetation near shore and in flooded areas with no parental care. The eggs are 1.5 to 2.5 mm in diameter and hatch in 11 to 15 days at 46 to 48 F. The young begin to feed actively about 2 weeks later. Growth is rapid and the young fish reach about 4 inches in total length during their first growing season. Some females have been found to have ripe eggs in August and young only 32 to 42 mm long have been taken in October. Thus, it appears that some grass pickerel spawn in the fall. Sexual maturity is reached at age II when the females average 157 mm and the males average 141 mm fork length. Grass pickerel ovaries contained nearly twice as many eggs as the ovaries of redfin pickerel the same size.

Food and Feeding

Individuals 20 to 50 mm total length fed on small invertebrates including cladocerans, amphipods, ostracods, isopods and insects especially odonates, dipterans, plecopterans, and hemipterans. At 50 to 100 mm the diet shifts to trichopterans, odonates, and crayfish. Grass pickerel more than 100 mm long eat mostly fish and crayfish, with an occasional large dragonfly.

Notes

There is one report of a hybrid between the northern pike and the grass pickerel taken in Nebraska.

References

Crossman, 1962b (life history); 1966 (systematics). Ming, 1968 (life history, Oklahoma). McNamara, 1937 (breeding and food habits). McCarraher, 1960 (hybrid with pike). Kleinert and Mraz, 1966 (life history). Buss, 1962 (life history).

Names

The name grass pickerel is recommended by the American Fisheries Society but this species is frequently called grass pike or mud pike. The subspecies name is from the Latin *vermiculatus* meaning worm-shaped, an allusion to the irregular bars on the sides.

Esox vermiculatus Lesueur in Cuvier and Valenciennes, 1846: 333 Wabash River at New Harmony, Indiana

Lucius vermiculatus, Bean, 1903: 294-296 New York

Esox americanus, (non Gmelin) Greeley, 1928: 100 Oswego drainage

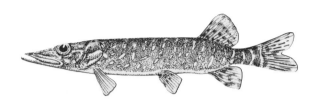

NORTHERN PIKE

Esox lucius Linnaeus, 1758

Identification

The northern pike is the second largest species in the family. It is distinguished from all other esocids by the pattern of scales on the side of the head; the cheek is fully scaled but only the top half of the gill cover has scales. There is some variation in the degree to which the gill covers are scaled but if there is any doubt the color pattern, the number of branchiostegal rays, and the number of pores on the lower jaw will provide confirmation.

Juvenile northern pike have alternating pale and dark green bars on the sides and with increasing size the pale bars break into oval cream-colored to golden spots. Some individual chain pickerel have rather similar patterns but in that species the spots are separated by a narrow network of dark lines whereas the pike has the spots in a uniform background. The muskellunge has dark markings on a light background and has only the upper parts of the cheeks and gill covers scaled.

There are three to six pores on each side of the lower jaw. The muskellunge has six to nine and the pickerels have five or fewer.

Description

Body elongate, arrow shaped, moderately compressed, at least more so than the grass and redfin pickerels. Dorsal and anal fins far back, somewhat more angulate than *Esox americanus,* with strongly convex margins. Caudal fin shallowly forked. Pelvic fins abdominal, rounded. Pectoral fins low, their bases horizontal. Gill membranes separate and overlapping. Lower jaw protruding, longer than the upper. Teeth on premaxilla, vomer, palatines, dentary, and tongue. Gill rakers reduced to sandpaper-like patches. Counts and proportional measurements are given in Table 26.

Color: Ground color dark green above, shading to white below. Upper sides flecked with gold spots at the tips of the scales.

Juveniles and breeding adults: Adults with rows of oval golden- or cream-colored spots along the sides. In juveniles, these spots are in vertical rows and in small juveniles they are fused into pale bars. Juveniles also have prominent pale middorsal stripes. The subocular bar is inconspicuous.

A color variant called the silver pike is silvery blue or green without the light spots and occurs sporadically throughout the North American range of the northern pike.

Size: The current angling record is a 46-pound 2-ounce fish from Sacandaga Reservoir that was taken 15 September 1940 by Peter Dubuc. There are reports of fish weighing 55 pounds, and European reports of fish weighing as much as 74.8 pounds.

Habitat

The northern pike occurs in the weedy parts of rivers, ponds, and lakes. Apparently, the larger fish tend to move offshore to deeper waters during the hotter parts of the summer but the young remain fairly near shore.

Distribution

Northern pike occur all across the northern part of Eurasia from France, the northern part of the Iberian Peninsula and eastern Scandinavia to Siberia, across the Bering Strait to Alaska and across the northern part of North America to eastern Canada, the Great Lakes and St. Lawrence River, and south to the northern Mississippi and Missouri drainages. It is absent from the Arctic coast of Canada, the Maritime Provinces, and the northern part of Labrador. Crossman discusses its original range and the areas where it has subsequently been introduced. In general, its distribution complements that of the chain pickerel and originally their ranges overlapped only in Quebec, New York, and Pennsylvania. It is the only esocid in arctic environments. It occurs primarily in northern New York in the St. Lawrence and Upper Hudson drainages.

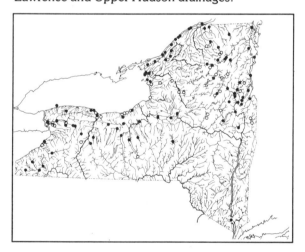

Life History

The northern pike is a spring spawner that begins its breeding activities soon after the ice disappears and the water temperatures reach 40 to 52 F. In New York, this is usually April or May. Spawning usually takes place in vegetated areas, often in marshes that will dry up by late summer. The adults move into shallow water, often less than 1 foot deep. The males precede the females and wait until the females are ready to spawn. Spawning consists of the adults swimming in pairs or triads of one female and two males. At irregular intervals, they roll so that their urogenital openings are close together and vibrate briefly as the eggs and sperm are released. Spawning usually takes place in the afternoon between 2:00 pm and 5:00 pm.

The eggs are 2.5 to 3.0 mm in diameter and quite sticky. On the average, a female produces 9,000 eggs per pound of body weight and a single female can produce more than 59,000 eggs. At 48.2 F the eggs hatch in 12 to 14 days. The young remain attached to vegetation by means of adhesive glands for 6 to 10 days, then start to feed. Growth is rapid and the young average about 6 inches by the end of the first summer. Females normally mature at age III or IV, males at II or III, later in northern Canada. In slow-growing populations, pike may live as long as 26 years. Wolfert and Miller found that in eastern Lake Ontario the growth rate was greater in the 1970s than it had been when studied by Greeley in the late 1930s. They suggested that this might be due to the greater abundance of such forage fish as alewife and smelt.

Food and Feeding

Pike are carnivorous and highly specialized for feeding individually on relatively large fishes. They are opportunistic and there is little correlation between size of the pike and size of its prey. They also feed on crayfish and other invertebrates and such vertebrates as happen to be available including frogs, mice, muskrats, and ducks.

Notes

Although it is a prized game fish, it is such an efficient predator that it can reduce populations of other fishes in some situations. In particular, it has been shown to have a detrimental effect on some muskellunge populations.

Muskellunge x northern pike hybrids, called tiger muskellunge, norlunge, or nor'lunge, are frequently stocked as game fish because of their rapid growth and low reproductive potential. The cross works either way, but Richard Colesante of the Oneida Hatchery noted that fish culturists prefer to use male pike and female muskellunge because the eggs of the muskellunge are less adhesive and do not clump as badly in the hatching jars. The present New York State record for a tiger musky is 28 pounds 9 ounces from Chenango Lake, taken in May 1982 by Walter Prindle. Natural pike x musky hybrids were reported by Cameron.

References

Crossman, 1978 (distribution). Franklin and Smith, 1963 (life history). Wolfert and Miller, 1978 (age and growth in Lake Ontario). Eddy, 1944 (hybridization). Hassler, 1969 (biology). Clark, 1950 (spawning). Siefert et al., 1973 (effects of oxygen on embryos). Williamson, 1942 (spawning). Black and Williamson, 1947 (hybrids). Embody, 1910 (ecology). Carbine, 1942 (life history). Threinen et al., 1966 (general account). Buss, 1961a (record size); 1961b (literature survey of life history data). McNamara, 1937 (breeding and food). Diana, 1979 (feeding). Cameron, 1948 (hybrids). Harrison and Hadley, 1983 (Niagara River).

Names

The species name is the Latin word for pike.
Esox lucius Linnaeus, 1758: 313 Europe

Esox estor Lesueur, 1818c: 413-414 Lake Erie at Buffalo
Lucius lucius, Bean, 1903: 298-301 New York

MUSKELLUNGE

Esox masquinongy Mitchill, 1824

Identification

The most important feature for the identification of the muskellunge is that both the cheeks and the operculum have scales on their upper halves only. In the northern pike, the cheek is fully scaled and the operculum has scales only on its upper half, and in the pickerels both the cheeks and the opercula are at least three-fourths covered with scales. In addition, the muskellunge has 6 to 9 pores on each side of the lower jaw (rarely 5 or 10 on one side) and 16 to 19 branchiostegal rays on each side.

The color of the muskellunge is more variable than that of the other species; muskies can be barred, spotted, or plain. Juvenile muskies, however, are distinctively pale tan with irregular dark areas on the upper and lower sides. All other members of the family are greenish and more or less banded when they are less than 4 inches long.

Description

Generally resembling the other esocids with the body arrow-shaped and moderately slab sided. Dorsal and anal fins far back, trapezoidal and rounded. Caudal moderately forked. Pelvic fins abdominal, rounded. Pectoral fins low and horizontal. Gill membranes free and overlapping. Teeth present on premaxillaries, vomer, palatines, dentary, tongue, and basibranchials. Gill rakers reduced to patches of denticles. Snout spatulate, lower jaw protruding. Counts and proportional measurements are given in Table 26.

Color: Color pattern extremely variable but usually consisting of dark markings on a pale green or brown background. Usually with numerous dark, vertical bars but sometimes spotted, vermiculated, or plain. Although these color differences have been construed as indicating subspecific differentiation, all of the patterns occur throughout the range of the species, hence, subspecies are no longer recognized.

Juveniles: The juvenile color pattern is distinctive. A specimen from the Cheboygan River in Michigan was pale buff with dark brown areas along the dorsolateral and ventrolateral regions. Belly white. Middorsal region pale buff with a triple red median line that was somewhat more intense behind the dorsal fin. Dorsal fin clear with a few melanophores along the rays. In a few areas, these were intensified into dark spots. Caudal similar, anal clear. Anterior rays of the pectoral fin with some dark pigment along the margins of the rays. Pelvic fin with a few melanophores on the middle rays. Iris with orange-yellow wash dorsally, otherwise dark and forming part of a dark line that passes from the snout through the eye to the upper part of the operculum. A blotch behind the eye continues across the cheek.

Size: This is the largest of the pikes and one of the largest North American freshwater fishes. The current angling record is 69 pounds 15 ounces. This fish was 64.5 inches long and was taken in the St. Lawrence River 22 September 1957 by Arthur Lawton. Most muskellunge caught by anglers are in the 30- to 46-inch range.

Habitat

The muskellunge occurs in cool lakes and large rivers, sometimes in moderately swift areas. Radio telemetry studies in Wisconsin showed that they move most when the water temperatures are 4 C to 12 C. During the summer, the fish remained in water less than 2 meters deep where the temperatures were 24 C to 27 C.

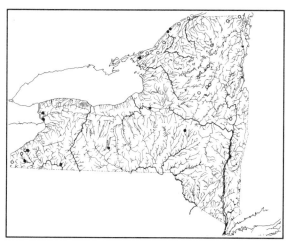

Distribution

The muskellunge occurs in southern Canada from the Red River of the North, east through the Great Lakes to the St. Lawrence River and Lake Champlain. It also occurs in the Ohio and Tennessee River systems to northern Alabama, and in the Upper Mississippi River in Wisconsin and Minnesota. The muskellunge has been introduced in several areas in Canada and along the Atlantic coast. Crossman suggested that its range may have once extended farther west.

In New York, the muskellunge occurs in the Allegheny drainage, especially in Chautauqua Lake and the Conewango Creek system. It also supports a fishery in the Niagara River and in the St. Lawrence. It also occurs in Lake Champlain and it has been introduced in other lakes including Canadarago in the Susquehanna system.

Life History

The muskellunge spawns in the spring when the water temperatures reach 10 C to 18 C (49 to 59 F). This is usually somewhat later than the spawning season of the northern pike, although the sea-

sons sometimes overlap and natural hybrids occur. Recently, Osterberg (pers. comm.) has noted that muskellunge in the St. Lawrence spawn where the current is more than 0.1 m/sec and the water is 1.3 to 4 m deep. The female is accompanied by one or two males and the group swims slowly along, occasionally rolling together as the sex products are released. The eggs sink to the bottom but they are not as adhesive as northern pike eggs. The fertilized eggs are 2.5 to 3.5 mm in diameter and each female produces 6,000 to 265,000 eggs, the average being about 120,000. Hatching takes 8 to 14 days at 53 to 63 F. The young start to feed 10 days later and by the end of the first summer they are 10 to 12 inches long. Sexual maturity is reached in 3 to 5 years and they live at least 15 years and possibly as long as 22 to 25 years.

Food and Feeding

Muskellunge are notorious carnivores. Their first food is zooplankton, but by the time they reach a length of an inch or so the diet shifts to fish. Also, they are known to take crayfish, frogs, young waterfowl, and small mammals.

Muskellunge are solitary feeders and usually ambush their prey in a quick, short rush.

Notes

There are indications that the populations of muskellunge in the St. Lawrence have declined since the construction of the St. Lawrence Seaway. It appears that the dams associated with the locks have resulted in slower currents in parts of the river and this tends to favor the northern pike which spawns in dense vegetation with little current. The earlier spawning season of the pike gives it a size advantage which lasts at least through the first growing season. Artificial hybrids, called tiger muskies or norlunge, are used for stocking areas with high fishing pressure. Because of their rapid growth and large size they provide exciting fishing and because they are infertile there is little risk of their becoming a nuisance.

References

Crossman, 1978 (taxonomy); 1977 (home range). Galat and Eipper, 1975 (feeding, juveniles). Williamson, 1942 (spawning). Black and Williamson, 1947 (hybridization with northern pike). Hourston, 1955 (color varieties). Chambers, 1904 (names). Cameron, 1948 (variant). Harrison and Hadley, 1978 (growth in Niagara River). Crossman and Goodchild, 1978 (bibliography). Panek, 1980 (management in St. Lawrence). Mooradian and Shepherd, 1973 (management in Chautauqua Lake). Bimber, 1983 (life history, Chautauqua Lake). Menz and Wilton, 1983 (economics of fishery).

Names

Chambers (1904) points out that there are several interpretations of the derivation of the name muskellunge, but it probably came from the Chippewa words *mis*, or *mas*, large, and *kenosha*, pike. The common name has many forms, among them muscalonge, maskinonge, etc.

The original description was apparently published in a periodical called the Mirror. Efforts to locate copies have been unsuccessful and the description is accepted on the basis of DeKay's 1842 summary.

Esox masquinongy Mitchill, 1824: 297 Lake Erie

Esox nobilior Thompson, 1850: 163 Lake Champlain

Esox immaculatus Garrard (not of Bean) in Weed, 1927: 30-35 (There is no indication that this is intended to be an original description.)

Esox masquinongy masquinongy, Greeley, 1934: 83 Lake Champlain

Esox ohiensis Kirtland, 1854b: 79 Mahoning River, Ohio

Lucius ohiensis, Evermann and Goldsborough, 1902: 172 Chautauqua Lake

Esox masquinongy ohiensis, Greeley, 1938: 69-70 Chautauqua Lake

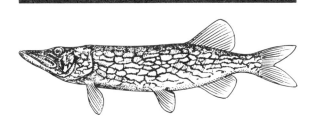

CHAIN PICKEREL

Esox niger Lesueur, 1818

Identification

Adult chain pickerel have a distinctive reticulated pattern of narrow black lines on a bright brassy or pale greenish background. It is distinguished from both the muskellunge and the northern pike in that it has fully scaled cheeks and gill covers. It is most similar to, and young individuals are most easily confused with, the redfin and grass pickerel which also have fully scaled cheeks and opercles but shorter snouts. The chain pickerel has 14 to 17 branchiostegal rays on each side; the redfin and grass pickerel have 11 to 13. The long snout of the chain pickerel is 44 to 48 percent of the head length, 12 percent of the standard length, and goes into the total length 6.8 times or less.

The dark suborbital bar of the chain pickerel is nearly vertical; those of the grass and redfin pickerels are curved backward.

Description

Body elongate, sagittate, somewhat compressed. Dorsal and anal profiles nearly equally curved. Dorsal fin originating far back, midway between the midbase of the caudal and the origin of the pelvic fin. Dorsal highly arched, with corners round. Caudal moderately forked with bluntly pointed lobes. Anal origin below anterior fourth of the dorsal base, arched, its corners rounded. Pelvic fins abdominal, slightly closer to base of first ray of the pectoral fin than to dorsal origin. Pelvic retrogressive, rounded, no pelvic axillary process, no membrane between

last ray and the body wall. Pectoral low, slightly oblique, retrogressive with convex margin and rounded corners. Scales cycloid, body completely scaled, head with only cheeks and opercles scaled. Operculum and preopercle smooth. Mouth large and terminal, without separate upper lip. Lateral line complete, but with unpored scales along its length. Teeth present on premaxillary, maxillary, vomer, palatine, tongue, and basibranchials. Canines present on vomer, inner edge of palatines, tongue, and dentary. Some of the canines flattened, with sharp edges. Gill rakers reduced to patches of denticles. Counts and proportional measurements are given in Table 26.

Color: The adult ground color is dark green or sometimes brownish above, shading to brassy on the flanks, and white ventrally. Back often marked with irregular bars and mottlings. Sides with a reticulated pattern of dark lines suggesting chain links. Fin rays outlined against clear membranes. Tip and leading edge of the anal fin often with orange wash; paired fins orange. Juveniles have a distinct pale cream to golden-tan middorsal stripe and lack the chain pattern, but have broken bars above and below a midlateral pale stripe. At a length of 200 mm, the adult pattern begins to develop. Redfin pickerel resemble juvenile chain pickerel but are darker and do not have pale bars crossing the dark area above the pale midlateral stripe.

In early January, 1980, the Department of Environmental Conservation received a specimen of chain pickerel from Shandelee Lake in the Willowemoc drainage that was uniform dark gray above and white on the belly and underside of the head. The scales of the back were broadly outlined in melanophores but the fish lacked green or brassy coloration. The fisherman who caught it reported catching two others that were smaller than the legal limit in the same lake. A similar color phase was described by Menzel and Green from Dryden Lake near Ithaca where these "blue pickerel" constituted about 0.2 percent of the population over a 6-year period.

Size: Chain pickerel are intermediate between the small redfin and grass pickerels and the larger northern pike and muskellunge. The angling record is a 9-pound 6-ounce fish, 31 inches total length, from Georgia taken in 1961. The New York record is 8 pounds 1 ounce from Toronto Reservoir caught in 1965 by John Bosland.

Habitat

The chain pickerel is, like other esocids, primarily a fish of weedy areas, but it can also live in deeper parts of lakes where there is little or no vegetation and in some regions it lives in larger streams. It can tolerate acid waters with pH 3.8, can withstand temperatures to 35 C or higher, and can survive in salinities up to 22 parts per thousand.

Distribution

The chain pickerel ranges from Nova Scotia to central Florida, along the gulf coast and up the Mississippi Valley to Missouri and southwestern Kentucky.

It has been introduced into the Lake Erie system of New York, but is native to the Finger Lakes and eastern tributaries of the Lake Ontario, Hudson, Delaware, and Susquehanna watersheds, Long Island, the Black and Oswegatchie Rivers. It apparently did not occur in the Adirondacks until it was introduced there.

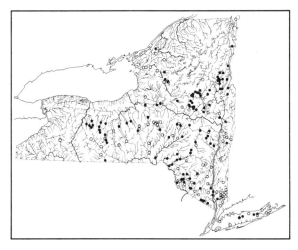

Life History
The chain pickerel is normally a spring spawner, but Miller found ripe fish in September and was able to strip the eggs and artificially fertilize them with normal hatching success. Spawning takes place when the water temperature reaches 47 to 52 F, which is usually April or May in New York. Females, accompanied by one or two males, swim along slowly, periodically rolling so that the vents are together, and vibrating as the eggs are released. Spawning continues intermittently for a day or two. The eggs are sticky and adhere to the vegetation. Hatching takes place 11 or 12 days later and the young attach to vegetation by means of an adhesive gland at the tip of the snout. They begin to feed after about a week and reach 4 or 5 inches by the end of the first summer. Sexual maturity is reached at age IV or V and few chain pickerel live more than 8 or 10 years.

Food and Feeding
Chain pickerel are predaceous, opportunistic feeders. Small pickerel feed on microcrustaceans, then insects, and by the time they reach 6 inches the diet shifts to fish and crayfish. Injured and slow-moving prey are most vulnerable and pickerel feed at night as well as during the day.

Notes
Raney reviewed the literature on hybridization between the chain pickerel and the redfin pickerel and found hybrids which were intermediate in color as well as counts and body proportions. He also identified some backcrosses between the hybrids and each of the parental species. Experimental and natural hybrids with the northern pike have also been reported.

In New York, chain pickerel x redfin pickerel hybrids have been reported from the Upper Hudson watershed, Coveville and Moses Kill, and from Valley Stream and Millburn Creek on Long Island.

References
Raney, 1942a (food and feeding). Miller, 1962 (fall spawning). Raney, 1955 (hybrids). Crossman, 1978 (taxonomy). Wich and Mullen, 1958 (compendium of life history). Underhill, 1949 (life history). Cameron, 1948 (variation). McCabe, 1958 (general summary). Crossman and Lewis, 1973 (general bibliography). Embody, 1910 (ecology, growth). Menzel and Green, 1972 (color mutant). Weed, 1927 (general account). Warner, 1973 (food in Maine lakes).

Names
Niger is Latin for black or dark and is apparently a reference to the darker coloration of the young specimens on which the description was based.

Esox reticulatus Lesueur, 1818: 414-415 Connecticut River, Massachusetts

Esox niger Lesueur, 1818c: 415-416 Saratoga Lake

Esox tridecemlineatus Mitchill, 1824: 361 Oneida Lake (reference from DeKay)

Esox tridecem-radiatus DeKay, 1842: 225-226 New York

Lucius reticulatus, Bean, 1903: 296-298 New York

TABLE 26
AVERAGE PROPORTIONAL MEASUREMENTS AND COUNTS OF PIKES *(Esox)*

All proportions are expressed in percentage of standard length.

	americanus americanus	americanus vermiculatus	lucius	niger	masquinongy
ST. LENGTH (mm)	124.3	152.5	164.3	117.1	79.6
TOTAL LENGTH	116.2	117.4	118.6	116.5	113.2
FORK LENGTH	110.2	110.6	111.1	109.1	107.9
PREDORSAL	74.7	74.4	74.6	74.3	75.0
PREANAL	74.5	75.2	77.2	74.4	75.1
PREPELVIC	52.1	53.4	56.4	53.2	58.4
DORSAL BASE	11.3	10.8	13.4	11.0	11.2
ANAL BASE	10.0	9.8	10.5	10.0	9.9
BODY DEPTH	16.7	16.6	16.0	15.7	12.1
BODY WIDTH	10.7	10.5	9.2	10.3	8.3
C. PED. DEPTH	6.8	6.8	6.5	5.8	5.3
PECTORAL ALT.	13.3	12.9	12.1	12.1	10.0
HEAD LENGTH	31.1	30.0	33.8	32.8	34.5
SNOUT	11.9	12.1	14.7	14.2	15.9
EYE	5.2	5.2	5.2	6.2	5.1
MOUTH LENGTH	14.4	14.4	15.2	14.9	14.0
INTERORB	6.6	7.7	6.6	8.1	6.4
N (sample size)	5	2	5	7	3
COUNTS:					
DORSAL RAYS	17-19	17-21	15-19	19-20	21-24
ANAL RAYS	15-18	16-17	12-15	18	21-22
PECTORAL RAYS	14	14-15	14-17	13-14	14-19
PELVIC RAYS	9	9-10	10-11	10	11-12
VERTEBRAE	50-54	49-50	61-63	52-54	66-68
SCALES:					
ABOVE L. L.	11-12	12-15	13	14	17
LATERAL LINE	100	93-118	105-148	116-118	132-167
BELOW L. L.	9-12	12-15	13	13	13

PIRATE PERCHES

APHREDODERIDAE

Although it is such a distinctive species that it is generally placed in its own family, the pirate perch is closely related to the trout-perches and to the cavefishes of the family Amblyopsidae. These three groups are united by certain features of the jaw muscles and the structure of the caudal fin (Rosen and Patterson, 1969).

The pirate perch has true spines in the dorsal fin, pelvic fins that are nearly thoracic in position, and ctenoid scales. Unlike the trout-perch, it has no adipose dorsal fin. Its most distinctive feature is the position of the anus which, in adults, is far forward on the isthmus.

There is only one living species in the family.

Aphredoderus

This is the only genus in the family.

KEY TO THE SUBSPECIES OF PIRATE PERCHES

A. Lateral line short, consisting of 5 to 20 pored scales. Scales smaller, about 55 to 60 in lateral series. Western and central New York.
Aphredoderus sayanus gibbosus
Pirate perch, p. 256

A'. Lateral line nearly complete, with more than 20 pored scales. Scales larger, about 45 to 55 in lateral series. Eastern New York and Long Island.
Aphredoderus s. sayanus
Pirate perch, p. 256

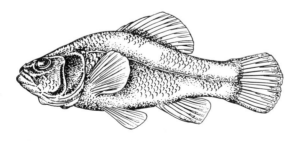

PIRATE PERCH

Aphredoderus sayanus sayanus
(Gilliams, 1824) and
A. s. gibbosus **Lesueur, 1833**

Identification

The pirate perch is a stubby, heavy-bodied, little fish with a single dorsal fin and a convex tail. Its scales are strongly ctenoid and the preopercle is strongly serrated. Its pelvic fins are thoracic; the mouth is large and terminal; and its eye is rather small.

The most distinctive feature of the pirate perch is the location of its anus and urogenital openings. In young fish, these structures are behind the pelvic fins but, as the fish grows, they position relatively farther forward until, in adults more than 2 inches long, they lie between the gill openings.

Pirate perches have spines in the dorsal, anal, and pelvic fins. Young pirate perch have one less anal spine than the adults. As the fish grow, the first ray loses its segmentation and transforms into a spine.

Description

Body short and deep, robust, little compressed. Dorsal profile rising steeply in an almost straight line to the front of the dorsal, then decreasing again in a nearly straight line to the narrow part of the caudal peduncle. Ventral profile more evenly curved. Dorsal fin margin convex, with rounded corners, its last ray more than half the first soft ray. First dorsal spine about one-third the second, and the second one-third the third. Caudal fin convex, anal fin inserted below the end of the caudal base in the western subspecies, somewhat farther forward in the eastern form. Anal fin margin convex, the last anal ray more than half the first anal ray. Anal spines graduated. Pelvic fins inserted ahead of the dorsal origin but well behind the pectoral base. Pelvics retrogressive, the last pelvic ray joined to the body by membrane for more than half its length. Pectoral fins paddle shaped, nearly symmetrical, with convex margin. Pectoral base strongly oblique. Gill membranes separate and free from the isthmus. Mouth terminal, maxillary almost reaching to below the front of the eye. Frenum present. Lower jaw projecting. Margin of preopercle serrated. Body completely covered with ctenoid scales. Cheeks and opercles scaled. Lateral line slightly arched anteriorly, complete in the eastern form, ending below the dorsal fin in the western subspecies. Counts and proportional measurements are given in Table 27.

Color: Dark, purplish brown, becoming slightly paler on the belly and with a yellowish tinge on the gill membranes. Long Island specimens have two dark lines separated by a light line on each ramus of the lower jaw. The lower jaw of the western subspecies tends to be merely punctate. The cheeks are paler, with a dark vertical bar extending from the lower part of the eye to the corner of the mouth. Also, a dark triangular area below the lower posterior part of the eye in Long Island specimens. Operculum dark centrally. Fin membranes dusky but the fin rays heavily outlined; dorsal and anal fin membranes with a clear central area in Long Island specimens. A dark vertical bar at the base of the caudal fin.

Juveniles and breeding adults: Apart from the changes in position of the anus, the juveniles are very much like the adults. There is no breeding coloration or tuberculation.

Size: Trautman reports Ohio specimens reach 4.3 inches total length. Oklahoma specimens reach 5 inches total length. Largest New York specimens are 75 mm standard length.

Habitat

The pirate perch is a fish of weedy habitats and sluggish waters. During high flows, it seeks refuge under overhanging banks and in weed beds. Trautman has noted that the western form preferred sluggish areas such as oxbows, marshes, and overflow ponds where the bottom was soft muck with much organic matter and timber debris.

Distribution

The pirate perch ranges from western Ohio and southern Michigan to Wisconsin, south through the Mississippi Valley to eastern Texas, along the gulf coast where the eastern and western subspecies intergrade, through peninsular Florida and north on the Atlantic coast to eastern Long Island.

The Survey obtained records of the western subspecies in the Lake Ontario drainage in South Bay Pond and the Salmon River and in Buttonwood Creek west of Rochester. In the Niagara drainage, they collected it in Cayuga and Bergholz Creeks. We were able to collect it only in Buttonwood Creek. The eastern form is quite common in eastern Long Island.

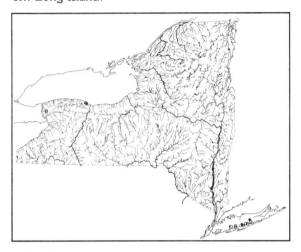

Life History

The life history of the pirate perch does not seem to have been thoroughly studied. Forbes and Richardson quoted C. C. Abbott who reported that the pirate perch spawned in May in Illinois and built a nest that was guarded by both parents. The parents also guarded the young until they were about 0.3 inch long. Murdy and Wortham stated that it spawns in April in Virginia.

Hall and Jenkins presented data on the age and growth of this species in Oklahoma. Their largest specimen was 5 inches total length; average back-calculated lengths (in mm.) were age I - 55.8, age II - 84.5, age III - 101.6, and age IV - 116.4 mm.

Shepherd and Huish obtained back-calculated lengths of 63 mm, 71 mm, and 81 mm for the first three growing seasons. Males grew faster the first year but more slowly than females during the second and third years.

Food and Feeding

Forbes and Richardson found that the pirate perch fed on insects, mostly aquatic species with a few terrestrial forms, a few amphipods, isopods, aquatic oligochaetes, and some entomostracans. Some small fishes were eaten. The diet of young after the anus had migrated was the same. Parker and Simco found it to be a nocturnal feeder, with peaks just after dark and just before dawn.

Notes

The western subspecies is apparently rare in New York and seems to be a relict species that has survived postglacial time in a few isolated pockets of favorable environment. Its nearest neighbors are in southwestern Ohio. The eastern subspecies is abundant at several localities on Long Island.

References

Forbes and Richardson, 1920 (general account). Hall and Jenkins, 1954 (age and growth). Mansueti, 1963 (development). Murdy and Wortham, 1980 (reproduction). Shepherd and Huish, 1978 (age, growth, and diet). Parker and Simco, 1975 (activity and feeding). Martin and Hubbs, 1973 (development). Moore and Burris, 1956 (lateral line).

Names

This species is named for Thomas Say, a distinguished 19th century entomologist. The subspecies name, *gibbosus*, is Latin meaning bunched or humped.

Scolopsis sayanus Gilliams, 1824: 81 Philadelphia

Scolopsoides sayanus, Ayres, 1843: 260 Long Island

Aphredoderus sayanus, Greeley, 1939: 42 Long Island

Aphredoderus gibbosus Lesueur *in* Cuvier and Valenciennes, 1833: 448-453 Lake Pontchartrain, Louisiana

Aphredoderus sayanus, Greeley, 1929: 175 Cayuga Creek, Niagara County

Aphredoderus sayanus gibbosus, Hubbs and Lagler, 1964: 99 Great Lakes

TROUT-PERCHES

PERCOPSIDAE

Trout-perches get their name from the fact that they have both an adipose fin, like the trout, and true spines in the fins, like the perches. In fact, they are members of a separate group of fishes called the Paracanthopterygii, which includes the codfishes as well as the more closely related pirate perch.

Trout-perch are terete tapering fishes with a distinctive overhanging snout. In life, they have a characteristic transparent gray color with rows of spots. The only other species in the family is the sand roller, *Percopsis transmontana,* which occurs in Washington and Oregon. Trout-perch are sometimes abundant and are important as food for larger fishes.

Percopsis

Percopsis omiscomaycus is distinguished from the related *Percopsis transmontana* of the Columbia River basin by its slender spines, well-developed lateral line, weak (or no) teeth on the preopercle, and translucent body.

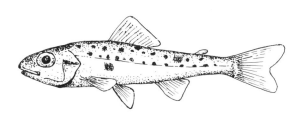

TROUT-PERCH

Percopsis omiscomaycus (Walbaum, 1792)

Identification
The trout-perch is a pale, terete fish with the unique combination of spines in the dorsal fin and an adipose fin. It has a conical snout overhanging the mouth, weakly ctenoid scales, and a forked tail. In life, it is nearly transparent with five rows of rounded spots, one in the dorsal midline and two on the upper and midsides. There is no other New York fish with which it is likely to be confused.

Description
Body elongate and terete, deepest behind the head. Dorsal profile more arched than the ventral. Dorsal origin to snout 1.4 in dorsal origin to midbase of the caudal fin. Dorsal retrogressive, its last ray about half the first ray. Dorsal margin slightly concave, its corners rounded. Adipose fin originating midway between end of dorsal base and midbase of caudal. Caudal fin moderately forked, its middle rays less than two thirds its longest upper rays. Caudal lobes rounded. Anal origin behind end of dorsal base. Anal fin retrogressive, its last ray less than half the first, its corners rounded. Anal margin straight. Pelvic fin inserted below dorsal origin, retrogressive. Pectoral rounded, its base nearly vertical. Gill membranes separate. Mouth low and horizontal. Snout conical, frenum present. Predorsal, prepectoral, isthmus, and head naked, body fully scaled. Lateral line complete, straight. Counts and proportional measurements are given in Table 27.

Color: In life, the trout-perch is quite transparent, shading from grayish dorsally to white on the belly with dark flecks above the midline in addition to the rows of rounded spots on the midsides, upper sides, and dorsal midline. The number of the spots is variable, usually 9 to 12 in the midline, 7 to 12 on the upper side, and 10 to 12 on the midside. There is a dark bar on the operculum, sloping upward from the point of the opercle to the upper end of the preopercle. Below this, there is a silver area. Top of head and snout dusky gray. Dorsal, caudal, and pectoral rays outlined, as are the bases of the anal rays. In life, the upper sides often have a brownish wash.

Juveniles and breeding adults: The trout-perch does not develop any special breeding colors nor does it have tubercles. Juveniles are miniatures of the adults.

Size: Scott and Crossman report that this species reaches 6 inches total length in Lake Ontario. Our largest New York specimen is 108.5 mm standard length.

Habitat
The trout-perch occurs in both lakes and streams. We have collected it in a swift flume in the Hoosic River and in shallow parts of West Canada Creek. It also occurs in the Great Lakes and has been taken at depths as great as 200 feet in Lake Erie. Usually, it is found over sand or fine gravel and it appears to avoid rooted aquatic vegetation. It often moves into shallow water at night.

Distribution

The trout-perch ranges across North America from Alaska to Quebec, reaching southern Illinois and Kentucky in the Mississippi drainage, and the Potomac River on the Atlantic coast.

In New York, it occurs in the Great Lakes, the Allegheny and Genesee Rivers, the St. Lawrence and Lake Champlain, and in Canandaigua, Oneida, Seneca, and Cayuga Lakes, and in the Mohawk and Hudson drainages. The Survey collected it in Rondout Creek at two localities.

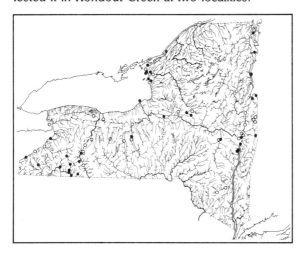

Life History

Spawning takes place in shallow water and the trout-perch make short migrations from their normal habitat in deeper water of lakes and streams to the spawning sites. In Minnesota, and probably in northern New York, the spawning begins in May and, with several peaks in June and early July, ends sometime in August.

Magnuson and Smith found that the spawning runs began after the air temperature had reached 50 F, or warmer, for about 44 days. Peak spawning occurred when the water temperature was 67 to 68 F.

Most of the spawning took place at night but, occasionally, spawning was seen during the day. There is a preponderance of males on the spawning grounds and the ratio of males to females varied from 1.8:1 early in the season to 9.5:1 near the end. In one stream tributary to the Red Lakes of Minnesota, spawning took place within 4 or 5 inches of the surface. Two, and sometimes more, males clustered around the females and the trio occasionally broke the surface as the eggs were released. The eggs were heavier than water, had a sticky surface, and adhered to the bottom wherever they settled.

The eggs are rather large, with a diameter of 1.2 to 1.75 mm, average 1.45. The number of eggs varies with the size of the females according to the formula:

Log N = −3.247 + 3.029 Log L,

where N in the number of eggs and L is the length of the female. Some of the males matured at age I and some of the females matured at age II. The maximum age was IV + .

Males averaged 50.8 mm at age I, 88.2 mm at age II, 103.5 mm at age III. Females averaged 51.4 mm at age I, 92.2 mm at age II, 108.3 mm at age III, and 114.7 mm at age IV.

Food and Feeding

Greeley noted that the trout-perch feeds on midge larvae, *Cyclops*, adult flies, and blackfly larvae. Mayflies, amphipods, and small fishes have also been reported from its stomach.

Notes

Scott and Crossman noted that the arrangement of the pyloric caeca in two rows along the gut is distinctive and often makes it possible to identify trout-perch remains in the stomachs of predators even after the rest of the fish has become unrecognizable.

References

Magnuson and Smith, 1963 (life history). Kinney, 1950 (life history). Jordan, 1917 (names). Muth and Tartar, 1975 (reproductive biology). Lawler, 1954 (ecology). House and Wells, 1973 (age, growth, fecundity).

Names

The species name is probably an Algonquian Indian name. McPhail and Lindsey (1970) suggest that it includes the word for trout.

Salmo omiscomaycus Walbaum, 1792: 65 Hudson Bay

Percopsis guttatus Agassiz, 1850: 286-289 Lake Superior

Salmoperca pellucida Thompson, 1853: 33 Lake Champlain

Percopsis omiscomaycus, Greeley, 1927: 63 Genesee drainage

CODFISHES
GADIDAE

In spite of their importance in the world's food supply, the family of the codfishes is not a large one. Worldwide, there are about 25 genera and 60 species. Most are fishes of the continental shelves and deeper waters; only one species is truly a freshwater fish.

Several species of codfishes are occasionally taken in the Hudson Estuary and the tomcod, *Microgadus tomcod*, spawns there and probably spends its entire life in or near the estuary. In addition, the freshwater species, *Lota lota* (the burbot), occurs in lakes and a few streams of the Susquehanna River system.

Cods are soft-rayed fishes. They have a peculiar kind of scales with the circuli broken into short segments and their caudal fin is highly specialized. The tomcod, like several other species, has three dorsal and two anal fins but the burbot has only one anal and two dorsal fins. Most species have a distinctive barbel at the tip of the lower jaw.

A key to the species of cods that occur in the inland waters of New York State will be found in the section on marine species.

Lota

This genus contains only one species which is the only freshwater species in the family. It is placed in the subfamily Lotinae which also contains the hake genus, *Urophycis*, along with seven other genera.

BURBOT

Lota lota (Linnaeus, 1758)

Identification
The burbot is the only strictly freshwater codfish and there is no species in our state with which it can be confused. It has an elongated body, a conspicuous single chin barbel, and two dorsal fins, the second of which is quite long as is the anal fin. The pelvic fins are inserted far forward and the tail is rounded, with its upper and lower rays short and extending forward on the body. The scales are small and deeply embedded, so the fish is quite slimy in life. Its colors are somber, predominantly dark mottlings on a slightly lighter background.

Description
Body elongate, terete, the head depressed and the caudal region compressed. First dorsal well behind the head, distance from the tip of the snout to its origin about 1.6 times in the distance from origin to the midbase of the caudal fin. First dorsal short and pointed, its middle rays longest. Second dorsal fin long and contiguous with the first dorsal, and with the caudal fin. Caudal base pointed, the caudal fin paddle shaped, its margin round, without definite corners. Anal fin slightly shorter than the second dorsal fin, its origin noticeably behind the origin of the second dorsal. Pelvic fins narrow, inserted well in advance of the pectoral base, between the gill openings. First and second pelvic rays produced into short filaments. Pectoral fin base nearly vertical. Pectoral asymmetrically rounded. Gill membranes slightly joined, free from the isthmus. Mouth subterminal, nearly horizontal, maxillary reaching to below the rear margin of the eye. Mental barbel single, median, and well developed. Anterior nostril with a low rim and a long posterior flap. Snout slightly overhanging the mouth. Eye rather small, lateral line complete. Scales embedded. Counts and proportional measurements are given in Table 27.

Color: Body generally grayish to tan, upper sides and dorsal surface marbled with darker gray, irregular marks; this pattern continued onto the fins. Margin of the vertical fins and the central part of the tail bright yellow or orange. Caudal, anal, and second dorsal with broad submarginal dark bands. Belly and head speckled but without dark marblings.

Juveniles and breeding adults: The coloration is extremely variable. Young fish are often uniformly dark and older fish lose their patterns and become uniformly light or uniformly dark.

Size: Trautman gives the maximum size of the burbot in Ohio waters of Lake Erie as 32.5 inches total length and 12 pounds 5 ounces. Ohio commercial fishermen report weights of 12 to 14 pounds. The IGFA record is 18 pounds 4 ounces from Pickford, Michigan. Scott and Crossman mention literature reports of up to 75 pounds.

Habitat

The burbot occurs in lakes and streams and has been reported to enter brackish water. Robins and Deubler provide a summary of its habits. Although it generally lives in lakes, it has stream-dwelling populations, including one in the Upper Susquehanna where it lives in cool streams that have adequate shelter such as rock slabs, trees and tunnels large enough for the fish to hide completely. In larger streams, it sometimes lives among dense *Potamogeton* plants.

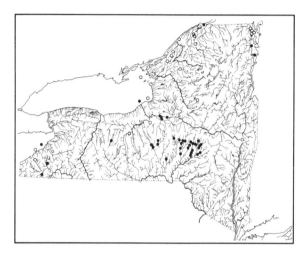

Distribution

The burbot is a circumpolar species ranging across Eurasia and North America.

In New York, it occurs sporadically in the Allegheny drainage and in Lakes Erie and Ontario and tributaries of the St. Lawrence River. The Survey reported it from the outlet of Bear Lake, and in May 1983 a specimen was taken in Conewango Creek between Jamestown and Frewsburg (Robert O. Woodward, pers. comm.). It also occurs in Canandaigua Lake, Cayuga Lake, Oneida Lake and Lake Champlain. It is absent from the Delaware, Hudson, and other coastal drainages. Stream populations occur in the Upper Susquehanna but not in the Chemung. It occurs in Canadarago and Otsego Lakes.

Robins and Deubler suggested that it invaded the Susquehanna drainage through glacial lakes and later invaded stream habitats.

Life History

Burbot are winter spawners. Robins and Deubler failed to find them in streams in December and suggested that they move downstream to larger waters in late fall and spawn between December and April. Scott and Crossman summarized life history data. Spawning occurs at temperatures of 33 to 35 F over sand and gravel shoals 1 to 4 feet deep. Some burbot may also spawn in deeper water. Spawning occurs in groups of 10 to 12 individuals moving over the bottom. Most spawning takes place at night.

The eggs are semipelagic and sink slowly in fresh water. Hatching takes 30 days at 43 F. Females produce 45,000 to more than 1 million eggs. Maturity is reached in the third or fourth year and the maximum age is about 16 years, although most of the Susquehanna stream burbot die before they reach age V, so they only spawn two or three times. In that population, the maximum age was 7 years.

Growth rates are variable. Lake fish grow faster than stream fish. In Lake Erie, they reach 616 mm standard length at age X. The Susquehanna stream fish reached 79 mm standard length at age I, 195.3 mm at age II, 234.7 mm at age III, 261 mm at age IV, and 341 mm at age VII.

Food and Feeding

Burbot less than 500 mm total length feed on insects, crayfishes, and mollusks. Young-of-the-year are almost entirely insect eaters. Larger burbot are primarily piscivores, although they will feed on invertebrates that are especially abundant, and on fish eggs. Sculpins, blacknose dace, darters, madtoms, brook trout, other salmonids, and crayfishes were reported in the stomachs of stream burbot in New York. In the winter and spring, even the larger stream fish ate mostly invertebrates.

Notes

Pivnicka studied variation in the burbot and found that there are two recognizable forms: *Lota lota lota* ranges from the Volga River eastward across Siberia, Alaska, and northern Canada to the Mackenzie River, and occurs in the Elbe and Danube Rivers in Europe. The other form, *Lota lota lacustris*, ranges through southern Canada, northern United States, and western Europe.

Lota lota lota has a long, low, caudal peduncle, and high counts for the dorsal, anal, pectoral, and pelvic fins and vertebrae. *Lota l. lacustris* has a short, deep, caudal peduncle and low meristic values.

References

Pivnicka, 1970 (systematics). Robins and Deubler, 1955 (life history in Susquehanna River). Clemens, 1951a (food); 1951b (age and growth in Lake Erie). Fish, 1930 (life history). Lawler, 1963 (biology). McCrimmon and Devitt, 1954 (winter ecology). Cahn, 1936 (breeding).

Names

Lota is from the old French (800-1300 AD) *lote*, a name for the pout, probably *Lota lota*. *Lacustris* is the genitive form of the New Latin *lacus*, lake.

  Gadus lota Linnaeus, 1758: 1172 Europe
  Mathemeg, Pennant, 1784: 191 Hudson Bay
  Gadus lacustris Walbaum, 1792: 144 (after Pennant)
  Lota lota lacustris, Speirs, 1952: 99-103 (names)
  Gadus maculosus Lesueur, 1817b: 83-84 Lake Erie
  Molva maculosa, Lesueur, 1819: 159-161 Lake Erie

Lota maculosa, Greeley, 1928: 102 Oswego drainage

Lota inornata DeKay, 1842: 283 Hudson River at Lansingburgh (doubtful locality)

Gadus compressus Lesueur, 1817b: 84

Lota compressa, DeKay, 1842: 285-286 (after Lesueur)

TABLE 27
AVERAGE PROPORTIONAL MEASUREMENTS AND COUNTS OF TROUT-PERCH, PIRATE PERCHES, AND BURBOT (*Percopsis, Aphredoderus,* and *Lota*)

All proportions are expressed in percentage of standard length.

	Percopsis omiscomaycus	*Aphredoderus* s. sayanus	s. gibbosus	*Lota* lota
ST. LENGTH (mm)	63.5	48.0	44.9	173.5
TOTAL LENGTH	127.5	130.9	124.4	106.2
FORK LENGTH	115.5	129.6	124.4	106.2
PREDORSAL	46.1	48.2	46.6	37.8
PREANAL	65.8	67.1	66.1	51.5
PREPELVIC	44.5	45.7	40.6	21.8
DORSAL BASE	18.9	24.3	27.6	53.8
ANAL BASE	8.7	12.6	13.7	40.7
BODY DEPTH	23.5	35.7	35.2	11.7
BODY WIDTH	17.3	20.5	18.0	12.0
C.PED. DEPTH	8.2	16.2	15.9	5.7
PECTORAL ALT.	16.4	21.2	21.2	5.7
HEAD LENGTH	31.0	36.7	38.0	22.1
SNOUT	12.3	11.5	11.9	6.5
EYE	7.6	9.0	6.7	3.0
MOUTH LENGTH	5.6	8.7	12.3	6.5
INTERORB	4.5	6.0	10.9	6.0
N (sample size)	5	5	4	4
COUNTS:				
DORSAL RAYS	II,10-11	IV,9-11	III,10-12	10 to 12-66 to 67
ANAL RAYS	I,6-7	III,5-6	II,6-7	65-71
PECTORAL RAYS	12-15	11-12	13-14	17-21
PELVIC RAYS	I,8-9	0-I,7-8 0-I,6-7	5-8	—
GILL RAKERS	8-13	11-14	11-12	23-25
VERTEBRAE	34-36	29	29	61-64
SCALES:				
ABOVE L.L.	5-7	8-9	8-9	Not
LATERAL LINE	43-60	41-48	46-50	counted
BELOW L.L.	7-8	9-10	9-10	

KILLIFISHES
CYPRINODONTIDAE

The killifishes are sometimes called topminnows or egg-laying toothcarps but they are not related to the true minnows. They are members of a group called the atherinomorpha which includes the silversides, the flyingfishes, the needlefishes, and their close relatives, the livebearers. Killifishes and their near relatives constitute a rather large group, with about 900 species in the warmer parts of the world. Many species are kept in home aquaria. Huver (1973) presented a bibliography of the genus *Fundulus*, and Lazara (1984) gives synonymies of all of the egg-laying killifishes.

Killifishes are soft-rayed fishes with abdominal pelvics and the dorsal and anal fins set far back, the dorsal origin a little in advance of the anal fin. The mouth is usually directed upward and there are scales on the top of the head. As killifishes go, our five species tend to be rather drab but they are sexually dimorphic and moderately colorful during their breeding season.

In an extensive recent study, Parenti (1981) re-classified the various groups of killifishes, mainly on osteological characters, and placed the genera *Cyprinodon* and *Fundulus* in separate families. Here they are treated as subfamilies.

A key to the species occurring in the inland waters of New York State will be found in the section on marine species.

Fundulus

The genus *Fundulus* is considered by Parenti to be a close relative of *Lucania*. It is defined on the basis of the structure of the upper part of the gill arches.

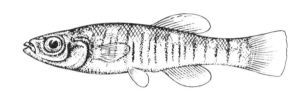

BANDED KILLIFISH
Fundulus diaphanus
(Lesueur, 1817)

Identification
The banded killifish is a freshwater species but it also enters the brackish waters of the Lower Hudson and frequently lives with the mummichog. The banded killifish is more slender than the mummichog and has a longer snout. They also differ in counts: the mummichog has five branchiostegal rays and nine or more gill rakers whereas the banded killifish has six branchiostegal rays and five or six gill rakers. In the banded killifish, the dorsal fin originates midway between the middle of the eye and the middle of the caudal base; in the mummichog, the dorsal fin origin is midway between the caudal base and the rear edge of the gill cover. The banded killifish has a shorter snout than the striped killifish.

Description
Body elongate with flat sides. Profiles symmetrical. Dorsal fin inserted well back on the body. Dorsal fin margin convex. Tail square, with its margin slightly convex. Anal fin origin below the anterior rays of the dorsal fin. Anal margin slightly convex, its middle rays longest. Pelvic fins inserted well anterior to the dorsal origin, midway between the anal origin and the gill opening in the male, midway between the anal origin and the pelvic base in the female. Pelvic fin retrogressive, with its last ray connected to the body for about one-third of its length. Pectoral base nearly vertical. Pectoral asymmetrically rounded. Gill membranes separate, free from the isthmus. Mouth strongly oblique, superior. Lower jaw protruding. Maxillary ending well in front of the eye. Premaxillary protractile. Top of head scaled, body scaled. No lateral line. Counts and proportional measurements are given in Table 28.

Color: Generally olive green to tan dorsally with

the scales conspicuously outlined with a row of melanophores. Cheeks and sides of the body silvery white, belly clear white. Fins dusky with the rays of the dorsal, anal, caudal, and anterior pectoral rays conspicuously outlined. Pelvic fins clear. Sides with 11 to 20 narrow vertical bars. These bars are much wider in males. Dorsal surface with conspicuous spots in the western form but few or no spots in the eastern form. Iris golden brown. Body quite transparent in life.

Juveniles and breeding adults: Breeding females develop a fleshy oviducal sheath around the base of the anal fin. Males become more brightly colored during the spawning season.

Size: The largest adults are about 4 inches total length. The eastern form tends to be larger than the western subspecies.

Habitat

The banded killifish lives in weedy shallows of lakes and ponds and in the slower moving parts of streams. It occurs over a variety of bottom types. Colgan noted that banded killifish burrow into sand or fine gravel when threatened. This happens less frequently in large groups. Different stocks showed different degrees of willingness to bury. Those from a quarry showed an increase in burying activities when tested in an aquarium with a sand bottom.

Melisky, Stauffer, and Hocutt reported that the final temperature preference for banded killifish from southeastern Pennsylvania was 28.6 C, whereas a population from Nova Scotia studied by Garside and Morrison had a final temperature preference of 21.0 C.

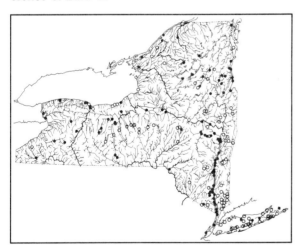

Distribution

The western banded killifish, *Fundulus diaphanus menona*, ranges from the Dakotas and Minnesota east in a curving band through the lower Great Lakes and the Upper Ohio-Allegheny system. On the Atlantic coast, the eastern subspecies, *Fundulus d. diaphanus*, occurs in the Maritime Provinces and Newfoundland south to South Carolina. Intergrades between the Atlantic coast and western subspecies occur in the Lake Ontario and St. Lawrence systems. This is the only species with eastern and western forms that intergrade in New York.

Life History

The spawning of the eastern banded killifish was described by Richardson who made his observations in a small brook tributary to the Richelieu River, Quebec. Spawning took place in pools when the water temperature reached 21 C, near the end of May. Males selected territories and defended them against other males and other species. Each male pursued a female and, during the chase, she emitted a single egg which remained attached to her body by a fine thread. This stimulated the male to an even more vigorous pursuit and eventually the pair came together in a pocket in the vegetation where they locked fins and pressed close against each other and vibrated as the female released 5 to 10 more eggs, which also remained attached for a brief time, then broke loose and sank until the threads caught in the weeds. The spawning pair then separated and, as the female started to move away, the male gave chase once more. This process was repeated until about 50 eggs had been laid in a period of about 5 minutes. The parents exhibited no awareness of the eggs. Development to the eyed stage took 3 days. Other investigators have reported hatching after 11 days and 72 F.

In Ohio, the young reach 20 to 58 mm by the end of the first summer.

Food and Feeding

Keast and Webb reported that although the mouth position would seem to indicate that the banded killifish is a surface feeder, it also feeds in midwater and near the bottom. Midge larvae, cladocerans, ostracods, and flying insects were the chief items of diet of fish up to 60 mm total length. Larger fish ate odonates, mollusks, and flatworms as well.

Notes

The two subspecies can be distinguished by the following key:

A. Scales smaller, 45 to 49 in lateral series. Dorsal rays 13 or 14, pectoral rays 16 or 17. Bars on sides narrow and regular, those of the caudal peduncle not fused into a stripe. Nine to 15 anterior bars, some extending across the dorsal surface without breaking up into spots. Commonly reaching more than 70 mm standard length.
F. d. diaphanus

A' Scales larger, 40 to 44 in lateral series. Dorsal rays 10 or 11, pectoral rays 14 or 15. Only 5 to 10 anterior bars which break into spots on the back. Bars on the caudal peduncle often fused into a median stripe. Seldom reaching lengths greater than 70 mm standard length.
F. d. menona

References

Richardson, 1939 (breeding). Keast and Webb, 1966 (feeding). Melisky, Stauffer, and Hocutt, 1980 (thermal preference). Garside and Morrison, 1977 (thermal preference). Colgan, 1974 (burying behavior). Colgan and Costeloe, 1980 (burying behavior). Baker-Dittus, 1978 (foraging patterns). Arcement and Rachlin, 1976 (karyotypes).

Names

The species name is from the Greek *dia*, through, and *phaneros*, visible or open, hence transparent. The western form, *menona*, takes its name from the lake from which it was first described.

Hydrargyra diaphana Lesueur, 1817e: 130-131 Saratoga Lake

Hydrargyra multifasciata Lesueur, 1817e:131-132 Saratoga Lake

Fundulus diaphanus, Greeley, 1930: 83-84 Champlain drainage

Fundulus diaphanus diaphanus, Greeley and Bishop, 1933: 99 Upper Hudson

Fundulus menona Jordan and Copeland, 1877: 68-69 Lake Menona, Wisconsin

Fundulus diaphanus menona, Greeley, 1927: 62-63 Genesee watershed

LIVEBEARERS
POECILIIDAE

The family Poeciliidae includes many of the favorite aquarium fishes such as the guppy and the mollies. They are generally confined to the warmer waters of the West Indies and tropical America with a few species in southern United States. As presently recognized, the family includes approximately 21 genera and at least 140 species. They are all small fishes and all but one bear their young alive. Their most conspicuous feature is the modification of the anterior part of the anal fin of the males into an intromittent organ with which sperm is transferred to the females. Most species have the mouth superior, that is, directed upward. The origin of the dorsal fin is always behind the anal fin.

Although there are no poeciliids native to New York, a hardy strain of the western mosquitofish has been introduced on Long Island. From time to time, other species are encountered where their owners have released them. This was undoubtedly the source of a thriving population of guppies that we found in a pond in Central Park. It is unlikely that these populations, for all their abundance, could survive the winter and they are not considered here.

Gambusia

Gambusia contains more than 34 species which range from eastern United States to northern Columbia and the West Indies. Most of the distinguishing features are in the anal fin which is modified for transferring sperm to the female. Males also have the upper four to six rays of the pectoral fin thickened and curved forward.

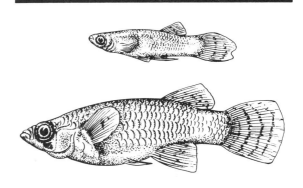

MOSQUITOFISH
Gambusia affinis
(Baird and Girard, 1853)

Identification
With its terminal or superior mouth, small size, and rounded tail, the mosquitofish resembles its relatives, the killifishes. It is, however, a livebearer and the males have the anterior rays of the anal fin modified into an elaborate intromittent organ with which sperm are transferred to the female. Mosquitofish are rather somber in color, grayish with the upper scales conspicuously outlined with dark pigment. There is a dusky teardrop mark under the eye that varies in intensity, becoming darker when the fish is alarmed. Females have a black blotch on the side of the abdomen that becomes more intense when they are carrying young. Both sexes have the dorsal fin inserted behind the anal fin and the body has a distinctive humpbacked shape with the caudal peduncle abruptly slimmer than the belly.

At first glance, the mosquitofish might be mistaken for the rainwater killifish which is similar in size and color, and somewhat similar in shape, but the rainwater killifish has its dorsal inserted in front of the anal fin.

Description
Body rather stubby, with the dorsal profile rising to the dorsal origin which is behind the midpoint of the body. Ventral profile deepest just in front of the anal fin which is farther forward than the dorsal. Caudal convex, anal bluntly pointed in the female, highly specialized as an intromittent organ in the male. Pelvics small, inserted midway between the anal origin and a point below the pectoral insertion. Pectorals

asymmetrically pointed. Gill membranes separate, free from the isthmus. Mouth superior, tip of lower jaw a continuation of the dorsal profile. Top of head scaled. Counts and proportional measurements are given in Table 28.

Color: Scales of the sides and back conspicuously outlined in dark pigment. Belly uniform white. Upper part of body, and dorsal and caudal fins, sparsely peppered with small black spots which tend to form irregular rows on the fins, two on the dorsal and two or more on the caudal. Anal fin with some dark pigment on the middle rays. Margin of the dorsal dark in some individuals. A dark teardrop mark slopes backward from the eye to the suboperculum.

Juveniles and breeding adults: In addition to the size difference, males have the striking elongation and elaboration of the anal rays and females are fatter, especially when they are gravid.

Size: Females to slightly more than 2 inches, males about 1.5 inches.

Habitat
The mosquitofish is a near-surface dweller that lives in ponds and sluggish streams. It frequently becomes extremely abundant in tiny ditches and artificial ponds with few or no predators.

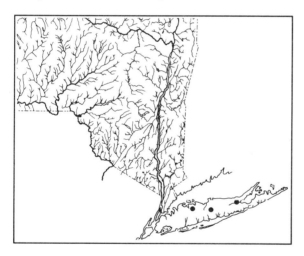

Distribution
Rosen and Bailey recognize two subspecies: *Gambusia affinis affinis* is the western form. It ranges from Veracruz in Mexico to southern Indiana and eastward to southern Alabama. It intergrades with *G. a. holbrooki*, which ranges from southern Alabama, Florida, and north on the Atlantic coast to southern New Jersey. In New York, there are introduced populations on Long Island which are apparently maintaining themselves at several locations. These are *G. a. affinis*, apparently a cold-hardy strain from the northern part of its range in the Midwest.

Life History
Mosquitofish have an extensive spawning season with each female producing two to four broods. The gestation period is 21 to 28 days. Females may

contain up to 315 embryos, usually about 40. Females mature in a matter of months when they reach 23 to 36 mm.

Food and Feeding
Mosquitofish have been introduced in many parts of the world as a method of controlling mosquitoes, which are a favorite food. They also feed on diatoms and other algae, zooplankton, and sometimes small fishes. Most of their feeding is at or near the surface.

References
Rosen and Bailey, 1963 (systematics). Krumholz, 1948 (reproduction). Harrington and Harrington, 1961 (ecology). Moyle, 1976 (California populations). Collier, 1936 (internal fertilization). Kuntz, 1914b (reproduction). Hildebrand, 1917 (life history). Rosen and Gordon, 1953 (functional anatomy).

Names
The name *affinis* is Latin for related to, a reference to its resemblance to *Heterandria holbrooki*, now called *Gambusia affinis holbrooki*, which was described later.

Heterandria affinis Baird and Girard, 1853: 390. San Antonio River drainage, Texas

Gambusia affinis affinis, Rosen and Bailey, 1963: 94-95 (systematics)

SILVERSIDES
ATHERINIDAE

Silversides are mostly small, surface or midwater fishes with two well-separated dorsal fins. The first dorsal is inconspicuous, with four slender spines. The fishes in this family get their name from a bright silver streak along the side of the body; otherwise, they are pale, straw colored or almost transparent fishes, with little dark pigment. They have abdominal pelvic fins.

The family includes approximately 29 genera and 156 species. Most of the species live in temperate coastal waters although some live in fresh water. The famed grunion of California beaches belongs to this family.

In New York State, the brook silverside lives in fresh water and three other species enter the Hudson Estuary. A key to the species in the Lower Hudson will be found in the section on marine species.

Labidesthes

The fine scales and elongate jaws distinguish this freshwater species from other members of the Atherinidae.

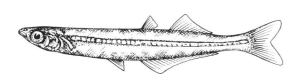

BROOK SILVERSIDE

Labidesthes sicculus (Cope, 1865)

Identification
The brook silverside is the only truly freshwater silverside in our area although species of *Menidia* and *Membras martinica* occur in the Lower Hudson. The brook silverside is a slender, transparent fish with fine scales and rather long, almost beak-like jaws. Like other silversides, it has a tiny, inconspicuous first dorsal fin and a bright silver stripe along its midside. Its long anal fin is a good recognition character. The other silversides of New York have large scales that are faintly outlined with dark pigment above the lateral band, and their jaws are much less prolonged.

Description
Body very elongate and slender, slightly compressed. Dorsal profile nearly straight, the ventral evenly curved. Origin of the first dorsal midway between caudal base and the anterior edge of the pupil. First dorsal small, with only four spines, and well separated from the second dorsal, which originates over the middle of the long anal fin. Margin of the second dorsal nearly straight. Caudal forked, its middle rays about three-fourths the longest upper rays. Anal fin with anterior rays forming a low lobe. Pelvic fins abdominal, retrogressive. No pelvic axillary process. Pectoral retrogressive, slightly falcate or bluntly pointed, its base high on the side of the body and sloping at about 45 degrees. Gill membranes separate, free from the isthmus. Jaws curved, produced into a short beak. Maxillary ending in front of the eye. Upper jaw protractile. Lateral line incomplete. Counts and proportional measurements are given in Table 28.

Color: Body transparent pale green above, transparent below so that the peritoneum can be seen through the body wall. A narrow, quite even, silvery band, bounded above by black, is the most conspicuous color feature. Cheeks and prepectoral region silvery. Jaws and top of the head dusky. Scales of the dorsum faintly outlined by dark pigment but very small.

Juveniles and breeding adults: The brook silverside does not develop breeding tubercles nor does it have special breeding colors.

Size: Brook silversides are usually about 3 inches in total length and Trautman has reported that they reach 4.2 inches in Ohio. Nelson (1968a) reported a 109-mm fork length individual from Crooked Lake, Indiana. Our largest New York specimen is 74 mm standard length.

Habitat
This species is most abundant in weedy areas of streams and lakes. It stops feeding when the water becomes temporarily turbid and apparently cannot tolerate prolonged turbidity although we have often taken it in turbid water in the Barge Canal system.

Distribution
The brook silverside ranges from the St. Lawrence River through the southern Great Lakes to Minnesota and south to Texas and along the gulf coast to peninsular Florida. On the Atlantic coast, it ranges north to South Carolina.

In New York State, it occurs in the Lake Erie drainage, the western part of the Allegheny drainage, and the Finger Lakes. It is particularly common in the old Erie Canal east of the Genesee River. The Survey obtained several records at the eastern end of the Mohawk River but we have not duplicated them.

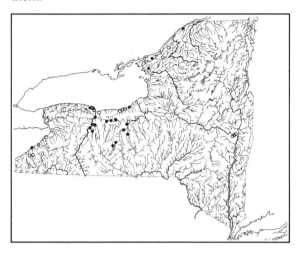

Life History

Hubbs studied the life history of the brook silverside in Portage Lake in southern Michigan. Spawning took place May to July over a washed gravel bottom where there was moderate current and the depth ranged from 1 to 3 feet. Males, which were more abundant, established rather ill-defined territories 2 to 4 meters long by 1 to 2 meters wide, driving off any invading males. When a female moved into the territory, one or more males pursued her and often she leapt clear of the water during the chase. Spawning occurred when the female allowed the male to catch her and the two glided downward, turning so their ventral surfaces were in contact. The eggs are of a special type with a long adhesive filament and several oil droplets. After being extruded well above the bottom, the egg sinks slowly and eventually the filament adheres to some object, the egg itself being nonadhesive.

Newly hatched young grow about 0.4 mm per day, reaching 70 to 80 percent of their adult size during their first summer. Ova begin to enlarge about one month after hatching indicating that the females approach maturity during their first summer, spawn when they are 1 year old, and die before the second winter. Nelson found that the annuli formed in early July.

At first, the young lived in open water and avoided shoals. Most of the time, they had their heads in contact with the surface film. They schooled only during the day. Adults, on the other hand, avoided open water and concentrated over shallows, near the surface or in midwater. They were active chiefly during the day and became quiescent at night.

Eggs and larvae: Brook silverside eggs were described by Rasmussen from the Peach River, Florida. Eggs ranged from 1.1 to 1.4 mm with two, rarely three, filaments about equal in length to the diameter of the egg, and several oil droplets. Tidewater silversides have similar eggs but with four or more filaments. Newly hatched brook silverside larvae were 4.7 to 5.6 mm long.

Food and Feeding

Most of the diet consists of adult and larval insects and surface-dwelling entomostracans. Keast and Webb noted that in Lake Opinicon, Ontario, the diet was mostly cladocerans, small flying insects, and midge larvae. Nearly all food is taken from the surface or in midwater, although Hubbs noted that they sometimes leap out of the water to catch hovering insects.

References

Hubbs, 1921b (life history). Cahn, 1927a (ecology). Nelson, 1968a (life history). Rasmussen, 1980 (eggs and development). Keast and Webb, 1966 (ecology).

Names

The name *sicculus* is from the Latin word dried because it was found in half-dry pools.

Chirostoma sicculum Cope, 1865a: 81 Detroit River, Grosse Isle, Michigan

Labidesthes sicculus, Greeley, 1928 Oswego drainage

Labidesthes sicculus sicculus, Hubbs and Lagler, 1964: 115 Great Lakes

TABLE 28
AVERAGE PROPORTIONAL MEASUREMENTS AND COUNTS OF KILLIFISH, MOSQUITOFISH, AND SILVERSIDES (*Fundulus, Gambusia, and Labidesthes*)

All proportions are expressed in percentage of standard length.

	Fundulus diaphanus	*Gambusia* affinis	*Labidesthes* sicculus
ST. LENGTH (mm)	51.4	23.2	60.6
TOTAL LENGTH	120.2	125.1	116.2
FORK LENGTH	120.2	125.1	111.4
PREDORSAL	55.9	63.5	53.6
PREANAL	61.1	52.5	52.5
PREPELVIC	45.8	43.8	40.3
DORSAL BASE	17.2	10.7	26.3
ANAL BASE	11.5	9.6	32.6
BODY DEPTH	18.1	25.5	11.5
BODY WIDTH	14.2	16.3	8.8
C.PED. DEPTH	10.2	14.4	6.0
PECTORAL ALT.	11.9	12.9	5.5
HEAD LENGTH	27.3	28.1	22.3
SNOUT	9.3	8.8	8.0
EYE	7.8	8.5	5.9
MOUTH LENGTH	8.0	8.6	8.6
INTERORB			
N (sample size)	5	5	5
COUNTS:			
DORSAL RAYS	12-15	6	IV-I,10-11
ANAL RAYS	10-13	7	25-26
PECTORAL RAYS	14-19	13	12-13
PELVIC RAYS	6	6	I,5
GILL RAKERS	4-7	11	24-29
VERTEBRAE	35-36	—	42-43
SCALES:			
TRANSVERSE	12-14	8	15
LATERAL SERIES	43-49	27	95

STICKLEBACKS

GASTEROSTEIDAE

Sticklebacks are delightful little fishes that live in weedy areas in both standing and flowing waters. With their tiny upturned mouths, slender caudal peduncles, and dorsal spines that are not connected by membrane, they can hardly be confused with any other fishes in our area.

Sticklebacks are related to the pipefishes and seahorses and are usually placed in the same order with them but recently some ichthyologists have challenged this because the evidence that both groups shared a common ancestor is weak. The family itself contains five genera and eight recog-

nized species although the threespine stickleback is exceedingly variable and is perhaps a complex of species.

These fishes have elaborate courtship and nest building habits and have been intensively studied by students of animal behavior.

Many sticklebacks show a fine disregard for salinity. The threespine and ninespine sticklebacks occur in both salt and fresh water, the fourspine enters fresh water but is more common in salt water, and the brook stickleback is strictly a freshwater species.

KEY TO THE SPECIES OF STICKLEBACKS IN NEW YORK

A. First dorsal spines 8 to 10, usually 9. Body slender and elongated.
Pungitius pungitius
Ninespine stickleback, p. 277

A'. First dorsal spines fewer than six.

B. Free dorsal spines three. Gill membranes joined to isthmus. Some populations with large vertical plates along the sides, but these may not be present in some freshwater populations.
D.

B'. Free dorsal spines usually four or five.

C. Free dorsal spines usually four, graduated in size, the first (longest) spine about equal in length to the first soft ray. First three dorsal spines close together, then a wide space between the third and fourth. Caudal peduncle long and slender. Belly with a fleshy keel on each side. Brackish and fresh water.
Apeltes quadracus
Fourspine stickleback, p. 273

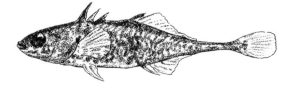

C'. Free dorsal spines usually five, evenly spaced, short, and nearly equal in length. Caudal peduncle short. A single fleshy keel along midline of belly. Fresh water.
Culaea inconstans **Brook stickleback, p. 274**

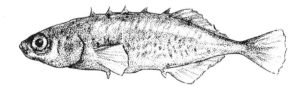

D. (B. Free dorsal spines three.) Pelvic fin with one spine and one soft ray. Caudal peduncle with a lateral keel. Body variously colored but never with conspicuous, round, black spots.
Gasterosteus aculeatus
Threespine stickleback, p. 276

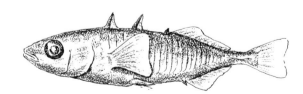

D'. Pelvic fin with two soft rays. No keel on caudal peduncle. Sides of body with conspicuous, round, black spots. Long Island; not reported from inland waters.
Gasterosteus wheatlandi
Blackspotted stickleback

Apeltes

This is a monotypic genus, characterized by four long dorsal spines, no lateral plates, and a long slender caudal peduncle without lateral keels. The pelvic skeleton has a lateral posterior process. The gill membranes are broadly united to the isthmus.

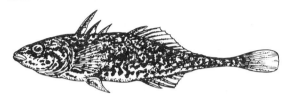

FOURSPINE STICKLEBACK

Apeltes quadracus (Mitchill, 1815)

Identification
The fourspine stickleback has four, occasionally five, rather long dorsal spines. The first and second dorsal spines and the pelvic spines are longer than the diameter of the eye. The fourspine has no bony plates on its sides and no keels on the side of the caudal peduncle. Its gill membranes are broadly joined to the isthmus. The pelvic skeleton has a lateral posterior process.

This species is probably most similar to the brook stickleback but it differs from that species in shape and in having much longer spines. This is a slender, tapering species whereas the brook stickleback tends to be more rectangular in shape.

Description
Body elongate, somewhat compressed. Caudal peduncle very slender, without lateral keels. Profiles symmetrical. Body deepest between the origins of the first and second dorsal fins. First three dorsal spines close together, graduated, each with a triangular membrane. Fourth spine separated by a greater distance and attached to the second dorsal fin by a deeply incised membrane. Caudal fin rounded. Anal origin slightly behind origin of second dorsal. Pelvics inserted below the second dorsal spine. Pelvic spine slightly serrated. Pectoral base rather high and nearly vertical. Pectoral symmetrical, its margin slightly convex or straight. Gill membranes broadly joined to the isthmus. Mouth small and terminal. No scales. Lateral line incomplete, ending below origin of second dorsal fin. Lateral posterior processes of the pelvic girdle form ventrolateral ridges on the abdomen. Counts and proportional measurements are given in Table 29.

Color: Variable. Mottled brown on the back and sides. Lower sides blotched, belly silvery white. Fin rays conspicuously outlined against clear membranes. Iris brown.

Juveniles and breeding adults: Breeding males are blotched or variegated tan to olive dorsally, creamy silvery white below and have bright red pelvic fins. The females are darker and do not have red pelvics.

Size: This is a rather small species, usually 2.0 to 2.5 inches total length.

Habitat
The fourspine is basically a nearshore marine species, but in the Lower Hudson it occurs well into freshwaters of the estuary and its tributaries. Like other sticklebacks, it is usually found in well-vegetated areas.

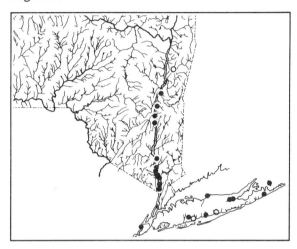

Distribution
This species ranges from Newfoundland and eastern Quebec south to Virginia. Scott and Crossman report that it is established in lakes in Nova Scotia.

Life History
The fourspine stickleback was studied by Rowland. While its courtship is generally similar to that of other sticklebacks, it differs in building a cup-shaped nest rather than a barrel-shaped one and in ventilating the nest by pumping water through the nest using its gill covers.

Males establish territories and defend them against other males. When an intruder approaches, he is greeted with a warning display in which the defender raises the pelvic spines and meets the intruder head on in a nose-down attitude. Sometimes, there is a lateral display with the defender maintaining his position with the flank exposed as the intruder moves. If the intruder enters the territory, the defender will attack, ramming and nipping until the territorial boundary is crossed.

Males build the nests by pushing and carrying bits of plant material to the base of a plant where it is cemented in place by wrapping it with an adhesive strand extruded from the ventral pore. As more material is cemented into place, the male tamps it into a cup shape. Nest building, if not interrupted, takes 2 to 4 hours. Toward the end of the nest building, the male begins fanning that will continue until the eggs hatch or even afterward.

When a female enters the territory, the male begins a display by first erecting his pelvic fins and then butting her, finally swimming in a spiral path in the horizontal plane, and ending between her and the nest. She then signals her receptiveness by assuming a head-up position and swims toward the male. She swims under his erect pelvic fins and he leads her into the nest. The male noses the nest as if to show it to her and she forces her way into the nest through the upper rim. When she is in the nest and in a head-up position, the male takes her caudal fin or peduncle in his mouth and begins to quiver. After a few seconds, the female deposits a cluster of 20 to 50 eggs, then squirms out through the other side of the nest. The male squirms through the nest, vibrating as he passes over the eggs, and fertilizes them. In a few seconds, he leaves the nest and resumes guarding the territory.

The male then proceeds to add more material to the nest, extending its sides upward and covering the eggs. The male then courts another female and this may be repeated until the nest contains as many as five clutches of eggs.

Once the nest has received eggs, the male spends more time fanning the eggs by inserting his snout into a hole in the side of the nest and drawing water over the eggs by pumping with his opercula and gill membranes. At least two holes are made for each level of eggs and the male fans each level in turn once every 10 to 30 seconds. Fanning frequency increases as the development proceeds. Hatching begins in about 6 days at 21 to 22 C. By the end of the ninth day, all of the eggs are hatched and the male ceases to care for the nest. Males may complete two nesting cycles a season.

The males usually have a 1-year life span and some females may live to spawn again at age II.

Food and Feeding

The fourspine, like other sticklebacks, feeds on plankton, cropping individual organisms with a pipetting action.

References

Rowland, 1974 (reproductive behavior). Baker, 1971 (habitat selection). Breder, 1936a (nesting). Nelson, 1968b (salinity tolerance). Reisman, 1963 (reproductive behavior). Schwartz, 1965 (life history).

Names

The name *quadracus* is from the Latin *quadr-*, fourfold, and *acus*, a needle.

Gasterosteus quadracus Mitchill, 1815: 430 New York

Apeltes quadracus, DeKay, 1842: 67 New York

Apeltes quadracus, Greeley, 1935: 101 Mohawk-Hudson drainage

Gasterosteus millipunctatus Ayres, 1842: 294 Old Man's Harbor, Long Island

Culaea

This is the only genus of sticklebacks not found in salt water. It is monotypic. It has no scales, four to six short dorsal spines, a rather short caudal peduncle, and the gill membranes are united to each other but free from the isthmus. The pelvic girdle has a narrow median posterior process.

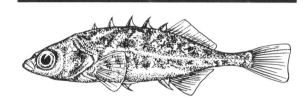

BROOK STICKLEBACK

Culaea inconstans (Kirtland, 1840)

Identification

The brook stickleback is a rectangular little fish tapering abruptly at the second dorsal fin to a very slender caudal peduncle. It has four, five, or six dorsal spines and they are rather short, usually shorter than the diameter of the eye. There are no plates along the sides of the body and the caudal peduncle is deeper than long; it is without lateral keels. There is a narrow median process on the pelvic skeleton. The gill membranes are connected to each other and form a fold across the isthmus but they are not attached to the isthmus.

Description

Body rather deep, somewhat compressed, caudal peduncle not as long and slender as in the fourspine stickleback. Dorsal profile slightly more curved than the ventral or the profiles nearly symmetrical. Dorsal spines I to IV separate, each with a triangular membrane behind it. Last dorsal spine attached to the second dorsal fin. Margin of the second dorsal straight or slightly concave. Caudal fin square or slightly lunate, its corners rounded. Anal inserted below and similar in shape to the second dorsal. Pelvics inserted below second dorsal spine. Pectoral rather high on the body, its base nearly vertical. Pectoral square, nearly symmetrical, its margin slightly convex. Gill membranes joined to each other but free from the isthmus. Mouth small, terminal, oblique. Lateral line complete. No scales. Counts and proportional measurements are given in Table 29.

Color: Extremely variable but generally olive green above with pale flecks and darker mottlings. Sometimes nearly black. Cheek, lower sides, and belly sometimes silvery white. Often, there is a suggestion of vertical bars and a pale longitudinal midlateral stripe. Fin membranes hyaline, the rays conspicuously outlined.

Juveniles and breeding adults: The breeding males are very dark, sometimes with a coppery hue above and slightly paler below. Breeding females darker than usual but not as dark as the males.

Size: Usually around 2 inches. The largest Ohio specimen was 2.7 inches total length.

Habitat

The brook stickleback inhabits clear, cool, weedy areas of lakes and ponds and the slower parts of streams wherever there is dense vegetation and a bottom of muck or organic debris. Beds of waterweed in cold creeks seem to be an ideal habitat.

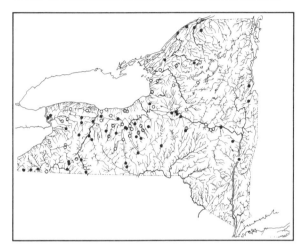

Distribution

The brook stickleback occupies a broad band across southern Canada and the northern United States from Nova Scotia, across New York, Pennsylvania, and northern Ohio to Iowa, Montana, and the southern part of the Northwest Territories. Relict populations occur in northeastern New Mexico.

Life History

The brook stickleback spawns in April or May in New York and into June or July farther north. Winn described the reproductive behavior of this species in Michigan. Water temperatures of at least 40 to 50 F and no higher than 70 F are required. Males move into shallow water before the females, establish territories, and begin to build nests. The nests are barrel-shaped or globular and constructed of bits of algae and plant debris. The nests are usually close to the bottom but sometimes on the bottom and sometimes as much as a foot above it. The nests were attached to plant stalks or sticks and both vertical and horizontal structures were used for nest sites.

A female ready to spawn became darker with a more variegated pattern. She entered the male's territory and was attacked and nipped or butted. If she remained motionless or went to the bottom, the male would move to the opening of the nest. If she did not follow, he would return and nip or butt her again until she eventually followed him to the nest and entered it. There she remained, with her head and tail protruding, while the male prodded her vent region and caudal peduncle until she responded by laying eggs, vibrating as she did so. After several spawning episodes, she moved out of the nest and the male chased her from his territory. Two or more females may spawn in one nest, each laying about 250 eggs. After the female left, the male rearranged the nest, presumably fertilizing the eggs as he did so, then remained with the nest, fanning the eggs and repairing the nest and driving off intruders that entered his territory. After the young hatched, the male herded them around the nest until they began to swim so well that he could not retrieve them.

Eggs were 1 mm in diameter, pale yellow, and adhesive. Hatching took place after 203 to 232 hours at 16 to 17 C. Newly hatched young appeared to be attached to the nest but Winn found that they hold their position by swimming against the nest, using their pectoral and caudal fins.

Brook sticklebacks mature in 1 year, some live into the second summer, and a few may survive to the third summer.

Food and Feeding

The brook stickleback feeds on aquatic insect larvae, crustaceans, snails, water mites, algae, fish eggs, and oligochaetes. Fish eggs are only a small part of their diet.

References

Winn, 1960 (life history). Jacobs, 1948 (nesting). Reisman and Cade, 1967 (reproduction). McKenzie, 1969a; 1969b (behavior). MacLean and Gee, 1971 (temperature relationships). Nelson, 1968b (salinity tolerance). Nelson, 1969 (geographic variation). Smith, 1970 (food and behavior). Thomas, 1962 (behavior).

Names

The name *inconstans* is the Latin word for inconstant, probably in reference to the variable coloration of this species.

Gasterosteus inconstans Kirtland, 1840: 273-274 Trumbull County, Ohio

Eucalia inconstans cayuga Jordan, 1876: 249 Cayuga Lake at Ithaca

Eucalia inconstans, Greeley, 1927: 63 Genesee drainage

Culaea inconstans, Bailey and Allum, 1962: 93 (nomenclature)

Gasterosteus

This genus has two species, the threespine and the blackspotted sticklebacks. Both have lateral plates (absent in some freshwater populations of the threespine), three dorsal spines, and a wide median posterior pelvic process. The gill membranes are united to the isthmus.

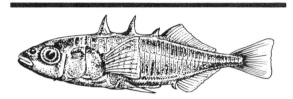

THREESPINE STICKLEBACK

Gasterosteus aculeatus
Linnaeus, 1758

Identification
The threespine stickleback usually has three spines in its dorsal fin and a few vertical bony plates along its sides. There are fewer plates in fresh water, and some freshwater populations lack the plates altogether. There are keels along side of the caudal peduncle, and gill membranes are broadly joined to the isthmus. The pelvic fin consists of one spine and one soft ray and the spine has a single pointed cusp at its base. The threespine is similar to the blackspotted stickleback, *Gasterosteus wheatlandi*, but that species has two soft rays in each pelvic fin and two cusps at the base of the pelvic spine. The blackspotted stickleback also has black spots on its lower sides and no keels on the caudal peduncle.

Description
Body rather stubby, deep and compressed. Profiles symmetrical. Caudal peduncle depressed with well-developed lateral keels. Dorsal spines well separated with triangular membranes, the first dorsal spine inserted over the pectoral base, which is a short distance behind the head. Third dorsal spine short, with its membrane connected to the base of the first dorsal soft ray. Margin of the soft dorsal straight. Caudal fin square or slightly emarginate. Anal origin inserted below fourth or fifth dorsal soft ray, similar in shape to the second dorsal fin. Pelvic spine inserted below or slightly ahead of second dorsal spine. Pectoral fin well behind head, its base vertical. Pectoral truncate, symmetrical, its margin straight. Gill membranes broadly joined to the isthmus. Mouth short and terminal, slightly oblique. Sides of body with narrow vertical plates, about 23 in Hudson River fish but absent in some populations. Lateral line high, incomplete. All spines with a locking mechanism. Counts and proportional measurements are given in Table 29.

Color: The upper sides are green to brownish with some darker mottlings, shading to silvery on the belly. The fins are pale or have a slightly reddish tint.

Juveniles and breeding adults: Breeding males become bright red on the lower sides and belly and develop bright blue eyes. The females become pinkish on the belly and throat.

Size: Our largest Hudson River specimen is 51 mm standard length.

Habitat
The threespine stickleback occurs in fresh, brackish and salt water. In the Lower Hudson, it occurs in Bowline Pond in the fall and winter but apparently moves offshore in the spring and summer. It is said to be fairly common in Lake Ontario. Weedy areas over sand or flocculent bottom are preferred.

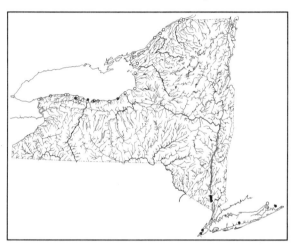

Distribution
The threespine stickleback occurs throughout Europe from Scandinavia and the Iberian Peninsula east to the Black Sea. It also occurs in Iceland, Greenland, and both coasts of North America as far south as Chesapeake Bay on the Atlantic coast and as far south as lower California on the Pacific coast. It also ranges from Korea and Japan to the Bering Strait but not on the Arctic coast of Siberia or North America.

In the Great Lakes, this species was confined to the waters below Niagara Falls until recently when it was collected in Georgian Bay of Lake Huron. In the summer of 1982, J. Nyckel discovered it in a tributary to the Straits of Mackinac. Apparently, it was able to move through the Nipissing Canal from the Ottawa River and is now spreading rapidly through the upper Great Lakes.

In New York, it occurs in Lake Ontario as well as the Lower Hudson and Long Island.

Life History
The behavior of the threespine stickleback has been studied intensively and will be reviewed only briefly here. The male establishes a territory in shallow water and builds a barrel-shaped nest on the bottom. He then entices a female by performing a ritualized courtship dance to which she responds in stylized way. Eventually, she enters the nest, deposits her eggs, and leaves. The male fertilizes the eggs and remains to guard the nest and the eggs, and later the young. Several females may deposit eggs in one nest. The adhesive eggs are yellow and opaque and

about 1.5 to 1.7 mm in diameter.

Sexual maturity is reached the first summer and they first spawn at age I + . Few fish live through the third summer.

Food and Feeding
This species, like other sticklebacks, is a pipette feeder and eats a variety of small animals including crustaceans, aquatic and terrestrial insects, and fish eggs and fry.

Notes
The threespine stickleback exhibits great variation and may actually be a complex of several species or subspecies.

References
Hynes, 1950 (food). Lewis, Walkey, and Dartsall, 1972 (effects of low oxygen tension). Manzer, 1976 (food). Perlmutter, 1963 (Long Island). Li and Owings, 1978 (sexual selection).

Names
Aculeatus is the Latin word meaning furnished with spines or prickles.

Gasterosteus aculeatus Linnaeus, 1758: 295 Europe

Gasterosteus cuvieri Girard *in* Storer, 1857: 254-260 Labrador

Gasterosteus aculeatus cuvieri, Greeley, 1927: 63 Genesee drainage

Gasterosteus aculeatus, Greeley, 1928: 102 Oswego drainage

Gasterosteus neoboracensis DeKay, 1842: 66-67 New York

Gasterosteus bispinosus (non Walbaum) Hankinson, 1924: 86 western New York

Gasterosteus biaculeatus Mitchill, 1815: 430 New York

Pungitius

The ninespine stickleback also belongs to a monotypic genus, characterized by nine short dorsal spines, a long slender caudal peduncle that is broader than deep, and lateral keels. The gill membranes are joined but free from the isthmus. The ninespine occurs in fresh and salt water in the northern parts of North America and Eurasia.

NINESPINE STICKLEBACK

Pungitius pungitius (Linnaeus, 1758)

Identification
The ninespine stickleback is more elongate and slender than the other species of sticklebacks and its caudal peduncle is wider than deep, with a distinct keel along each side. Its most distinctive feature is the number of dorsal spines, usually 9 or 10. It usually does not have bony plates along the sides.

Description
Body elongate and slender, slightly compressed. Caudal peduncle attenuate, depressed, with lateral keels. Dorsal spines short and lockable, alternately inclined left and right, with small triangular membranes. Second dorsal margin straight. Caudal fin slightly emarginate. Anal fin origin behind that of the second dorsal. Anal fin shape similar to that of the second dorsal. Pelvic fin inserted below the fourth dorsal spine. Pectoral fin base well behind head, nearly vertical. Pectoral fin symmetrical, its margin convex. Gill membranes broadly united across the isthmus. Mouth terminal, oblique. No scales but there are small, bony plates along the lateral line, at the bases of the fins, and on the caudal peduncle keels. Counts and proportional measurements are given in Table 29.

Color: The ninespine stickleback is somewhat bicolored, the dorsal half pale green with a suggestion of irregular darker gray crossbars, and the lower half silvery white. The iris is silvery, the fin rays outlined with melanophores.

Juveniles and breeding adults: Breeding males sometimes become jet black on the belly, with white pelvic fin membranes.

Size: Adults are 2 to 3 inches long. Our largest New York specimens are 61 mm standard length.

Habitat
Along the coasts, the ninespine stickleback occurs in nearshore waters and moves into fresh water to spawn. In fresh water, it lives in deeper lakes where it occurs up to 250 feet deep. It apparently moves into shallow waters to spawn.

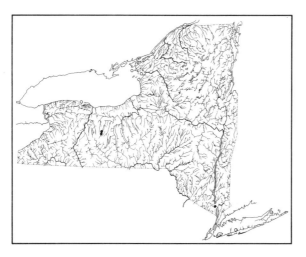

Distribution

The ninespine is a circumpolar species ranging from the British Isles across northern Eurasia to the Bering Strait and across Canada to Newfoundland, down the Atlantic coast to Long Island and New Jersey. It occurs in Alaska and the Aleutian Islands, and in eastern Asia south to Japan and China. In New York, it is known from Canandaigua Lake, Lake Ontario and eastern Long Island, where it is anadromous.

Life History

As in other sticklebacks, the male builds a barrel-shaped nest by cementing together bits of plant material using thread-like strands of a kidney secretion. The nest is usually constructed somewhat off the bottom. The male performs a courtship dance and entices the female into the nest where she lays a batch of 20 to 30 adhesive eggs. After she lays the eggs, the male chases her from the nest and swims through, fertilizing the eggs on the way. The male guards the nest and aerates the eggs by positioning himself at the entrance and fanning vigorously with his pectoral fins. After the eggs hatch, the male guards the young until they are about 2 weeks old and 15 mm long.

The young reach maturity at the end of the first summer and spawn the next year. Sometimes, they spawn more than once a season but they do not spawn in the fall. The maximum age is about 3.5 years.

Food and Feeding

The ninespine stickleback is carnivorous and feeds on immature insects, crustaceans, and the eggs and larvae of its own species.

References

McKenzie and Keenleyside, 1970 (reproductive behavior). Hynes, 1950 (food). Griswold and Smith, 1972 (growth and survival); 1973 (life history). Coad and Power, 1973 (ecology). Lindsey, 1962 (meristic variation and temperature). McPhail, 1963 (geographic variation). Morris, 1952 (homosexuality); 1958 (reproductive behavior). J. Nelson, 1968b (salinity tolerance). Lewis, Walkey, and Dartsall, 1972 (oxygen effects). Wootton, 1976 (taxonomy and biology).

Notes

McPhail found that the coastal form has more numerous dorsal spines, more lateral plates, and fewer gill rakers, but he did not believe that the two forms should be recognized as subspecies.

Names

Pungitius is Latin for pungent or sharp from *pungo*, to puncture.

Gasterosteus pungitius Linnaeus, 1758: 296 Europe

Pygosteus pungitius, Bean, 1903: 338-340 New York

Gasterosteus occidentalis Cuvier *in* Cuvier and Valenciennes, 1829: 509

Gasterosteus occidentalis, DeKay, 1842: 68 Manhattan

TABLE 29
AVERAGE PROPORTIONAL MEASUREMENTS AND COUNTS OF STICKLEBACKS
(*Apeltes, Culaea, Gasterosteus,* and *Pungitius*)

All proportions are expressed in percentage of standard length.

	Apeltes quadracus	*Culaea* inconstans	*Gasterosteus* aculeatus	*Pungitius* pungitius
ST. LENGTH (mm)	31.9	40.2	52.3	38.3
TOTAL LENGTH	116.0	116.7	115.2	114.4
FORK LENGTH	116.0	116.7	113.4	113.5
PREDORSAL	30.0	32.1	36.4	30.7
PREANAL	58.1	61.2	68.0	59.0
PREPELVIC	33.4	39.2	43.6	38.8
DORSAL BASE	27.0	25.8	25.5	30.6
ANAL BASE	24.7	28.2	20.4	23.8
BODY DEPTH	23.2	26.6	24.0	17.1
BODY WIDTH	14.2	16.1	12.0	10.1
C.PED. DEPTH	3.6	5.0	3.8	2.6
PECTORAL ALT.	11.6	15.2	11.5	9.8
HEAD LENGTH	27.9	29.3	29.5	27.6
SNOUT	8.1	7.5	8.9	8.5
EYE	7.7	7.6	8.8	8.8
MOUTH LENGTH	7.0	7.7	4.3	8.5
INTERORB	6.9	9.1	3.9	7.1
N (sample size)	5	5	5	5
COUNTS:				
DORSAL SPINES	IV-V	IV-VI	III	VIII-X
DORSAL RAYS	11-12	9-11	9-11	9-11
ANAL RAYS	I,9-11	I,10-11	I,9-11	I,8-10
PECTORAL RAYS	10	9-11	9-11	10-12
PELVIC RAYS	I,2	I,1	I,1	I,1
GILL RAKERS	4-6	11-13	18-20	12-13
VERTEBRAE	30-32	31-33	30-32	31-33

TEMPERATE BASSES
MORONIDAE

The temperate basses are rather generalized spiny-rayed fishes with ctenoid scales and strong spines in the dorsal, anal, and pelvic fins. They have 2 separate or slightly joined dorsal fins, the first consisting of all spines, the second with 1 spine and fewer than 15 soft rays. Unlike the drums and perches, they have three, rather than two, anal spines. The maxillary bone does not slip up under the suborbital bone as it does in the snappers and porgies. They have an internal bony shelf under the eyeball and a well-developed pseudobranch. Temperate basses tend to be silvery white with distinct, dark, longitudinal lines but the white perch is rather brassy, without distinct lines.

This family is represented in North America by four species, of which all but the yellow bass, *Morone mississippiensis*, occur in New York. Two closely related species occur in Europe. The striped bass and the white bass are more closely related to each other than to the white perch.

In the older literature, the species have been variously assigned to the genera *Morone*, *Roccus*, or *Lepibema* (for the white bass). There is little justification for more than a single genus, and the rules of nomenclature dictate that the name *Morone* takes precedence over the others.

These species have been placed in the family Serranidae. However, serranids are marine fishes that have three points on the opercle bone rather than two and tend to be hermaphroditic or to have the gonadal structure of hermaphrodites. Temperate basses have separate sexes and live in fresh or brackish water or are anadromous. They have also been united with certain other species in a family called the Percichthyidae, but the evidence of this relationship is not convincing and it seems preferable to revert to an older name, the Moronidae.

Morone

The relationships of this genus are currently under study by John Waldman. At present, it is the only genus in the family.

KEY TO THE SPECIES OF TEMPERATE BASSES

A. First and second dorsal fins definitely connected with membrane between all spines. No teeth on tongue. Body without dark longitudinal lines although light spots on the scales may suggest many pale longitudinal lines.
Morone americana   **White perch, p. 281**

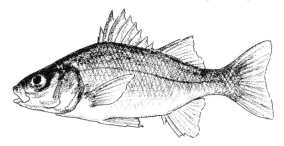

A'. First and second dorsal fins nearly separate, the membranes between the last spine of the first dorsal and the first spine of the second dorsal scarcely developed. One or two patches of teeth on the base of the tongue. Body with four to seven distinct narrow, dark, longitudinal lines.

B. Body elongate, its greatest depth distinctly less than the length of the head. Longitudinal streaks uniform and continuous although one or two may break and continue on the scale row above or below in some individuals. Young (up to about 4 inches in length) with about 10 narrow, indistinct vertical bars. Base of tongue with two patches of teeth, clearly separate and approximately equal in size.
Morone saxatilis   **Striped bass, p. 284**

B'. Body shorter and deeper, its greatest depth about equal to the length of the head. Longitudinal stripes weaker and frequently interrupted. No vertical bars, even in the young. Base of the tongue with two patches of teeth that are usually unequal in size and so close together that they appear as a single patch.

Morone chrysops **White bass, p. 282**

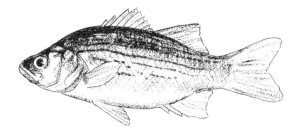

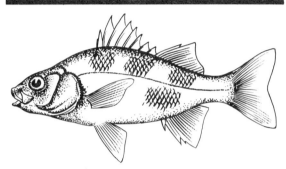

WHITE PERCH

Morone americana (Gmelin, 1789)

Identification
The white perch is the only species of temperate bass in our area that does not have definite dark longitudinal stripes on the body. It also differs in shape, being deeper and more tapered, and its dorsal fins are connected by membrane to a greater extent. It usually has 9 rays in the anal fin whereas the white bass has 11 or 12, and the striped bass has 9 to 11.

Description
Body deep and rather compressed . Dorsal profile highly arched, rising in an almost straight line to the origin of the dorsal fin. Ventral profile evenly curved. Distance from snout to dorsal origin one and one-half times in distance from dorsal origin to the caudal midbase. First dorsal rounded, its third and fourth spines longest. Dorsal fins connected by a low, but definite membrane. Spine at front of second dorsal fin about three-fourths length of the first soft ray. Last dorsal ray about half the spine length. Margin of second dorsal falcate, convex anteriorly, concave posteriorly. Caudal moderately forked, the middle ray two-thirds the longest upper rays. Caudal lobes bluntly pointed. Anal fin origin below anterior soft rays of the dorsal fin. Anal margin falcate, similar to second dorsal. First anal spine short, second and third spines longer and subequal. Pelvic fin insertion below the dorsal origin. No pelvic axillary process. Pelvic spines about two-thirds the length of the first soft ray, excluding the short filament on the latter. Pectoral base nearly vertical, pectoral asymmetrically pointed. Gill membranes separate, mouth terminal, preopercle with fine serrae on its vertical limb and the posterior part of its lower limb.

Lateral line complete, paralleling the dorsal profile. Counts and proportional measurements are given in Table 30.

Color. The dorsal surface is dark gray or olive, sometimes brownish, shading to silvery on the sides and white on the belly. Many individuals have irregular short segments of lines formed by series of darker scales on the upper sides. Light centers of the scales also form indistinct longitudinal light lines on the upper sides. Lateral line dark and conspicuous.

Juveniles and spawning adults: There is no special juvenile color pattern but the spawning adults sometimes develop a bluish cast on the head and especially the lower jaw.

Size: The maximum recorded size is 4.75 pounds and 19 inches total length. The New York record is 2 pounds 14 ounces, a fish taken in the Carmans River 27 June 1982 by John Zinkowski. In the Lower Hudson, the average weight is 0.75 pound.

Habitat
White perch can tolerate a wide range of salinities from full sea water to fresh water. They are often found in rather turbid shallow areas and at times they form dense schools. Daily migrations to shallows at night and offshore during the daylight hours have been reported.

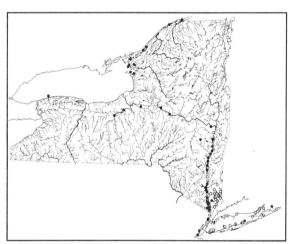

Distribution
The white perch is abundant in brackish waters along the Atlantic coast from New Brunswick to South Carolina. It is common in the Hudson River and in some landlocked lakes and ponds of the Lower Hudson drainage. During the past five decades, it has spread into the Great Lakes. Scott and Christie traced its invasion of Lake Ontario and the St. Lawrence River. In the 1930s, it was confined to the eastern end of the Mohawk River where it was taken by the Survey only as far west as Rexford. By 1948, it was in Cross Lake and must have been present in Oneida Lake as early as 1946 or 1947. It was collected in the Seneca River in 1951 and in that year a specimen was taken near Montreal. In 1952, four white perch were caught near Quebec City and since the species does not occur naturally north of the Miramichi River on the coast of New

Brunswick, Scott and Christie concluded that the St. Lawrence populations came from Lake Ontario rather than from the Atlantic Ocean. In 1952, it was first noticed in the Bay of Quinte on the north shore of Lake Ontario and by 1959 it was a dominant species there. In 1961, a small specimen was taken in the Welland Canal.

Busch, Davis and Nepszy summarized the records for Lake Erie. It was first taken in a pound net near Erie, Pennsylvania, in 1953. Later that year, two more were taken in Ohio waters near Conneaut and Fair Point. In 1973, one was caught near Port Clinton and, in 1974, three were recorded from Ohio waters of the western basin. In 1975, 34 were reported from the western half of Lake Erie. It still has not been reported from the eastern end of Lake Erie and its absence in the New York part of the lake remains unexplained.

Life History
The white perch reaches its greatest abundance in the brackish part of the Hudson River. There is evidence of an upstream migration of adults in the spring and early summer. Spawning apparently occurs in May and June when the water temperatures are 14 to 24 C and the peak of the spawning is reached at temperatures of 18 to 20 C.

Waldman reported what was apparently spawning activity in a tributary of Long Island Sound off the Hutchinson River Parkway in the Bronx. On 5 May 1980, a group of about 75 individuals were milling in an elliptical pattern over a small patch of coarse sand. The school was near the interface between fresh and salt water and the salt water was more turbid than the fresh. As the fish rolled, sunlight reflected from their sides as bright flashes. They appeared to avoid the shadow of the bridge.

White perch eggs are small, demersal, and adhesive. The water-hardened eggs are about 0.9 mm in diameter. Ovarian egg counts range from 15,740 to 247,681 according to the size of the females. Eggs hatch in 4 or 4$^{1}/_{2}$ days at 15 C, 30 hours at 20 C. Newly hatched young are 2.3 mm long and can reach 2.5 inches by the end of the first summer. The average life span is 5 to 7 years but some individuals may live 14 to 17 years.

Fritzsche and Johnson presented osteological features that can be used to distinguish white perch from striped bass at lengths as small as 7.5 mm.

Food and Feeding
Small white perch feed on such small invertebrates as copepods which are especially important foods during the first two summers. *Gammarus*, chiromomid larvae, and occasional *Cyathura* are also important foods. Fish eggs are important May through July. White perch more than 200 mm long eat mostly fish.

References
Mansueti, 1961 (population dynamics); 1964 (development). Larsen, 1954 (first record in Lake Erie). Holsapple and Foster, 1975 (reproduction in Hudson River). Toman, 1955 (summary). Raney, 1965a (summary). Sheri and Power, 1969a; 1969b (biology). Alsop and Forney, 1962 (growth and food in Oneida Lake). Fritzsche and Johnson, 1980 (larval development). Dence, 1952 (status in New York). Scott and Christie, 1963 (spread in the Great Lakes). Busch, Davis, and Nepszy, 1977 (Lake Erie). Morgan and Prince, 1978 (effects of chlorine on larvae). Thoits, 1958 (life history and ecology). Webster, 1943 (food). Woolcott, 1964 (variation). Richards, 1960 (life history in New York). Texas Instruments, 1975 (summary in Hudson). Waldman, 1981 (spawning). Bath and O'Connor, 1982 (Hudson River). Elrod et al., 1981 (food). Kellogg and Gift, 1983 (preferred temperatures).

Names
Americana refers to its distribution.

Perca americana Gmelin, 1788: 1308 New York (after Schoepf)

Morone americana, Greeley, 1937: 98 Lower Hudson

Perca immaculata Walbaum, 1792: 330 New York (after Schoepf)

Morone rufa Mitchill, 1814: 18 New York

Labrax rufus, DeKay, 1842: 9-10 New York

Morone pallida Mitchill, 1814: 19 New York

Labrax pallidus, DeKay, 1842: 11-12 New York

Perca mucronata Rafinesque, 1818b: 204 Delaware, Schuylkill and Susquehanna Rivers

Labrax nigricans DeKay, 1842: 12-13 Long Island

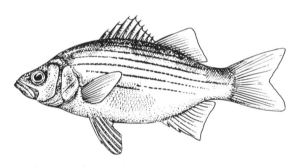

WHITE BASS

Morone chrysops
(Rafinesque, 1820)

Identification
The white bass is a silvery fish with distinct, narrow, dark, longitudinal lines and two dorsal fins that are nearly separate, although close together and connected by a low membrane. The white perch has three anal spines and its lateral line stops at the base of the tail. It has only fine serrae on the edge of the preopercle.

White bass are easily distinguished from the white perch, which lacks distinct longitudinal stripes and has 9 anal rays instead of 12 or 13. They are closely related to, and resemble, striped bass, but the striped bass is more elongate and has several dark stripes extending to the base of the tail whereas the white bass has only one full length stripe; the rest are shorter. The white bass has two patches of teeth at the base of the tongue, but they are unequal in size and close together so they appear as a single patch in whole specimens. The striped bass has two tooth patches that are clearly separate.

White bass and striped bass hybridize and the hybrids are intermediate between the two. Hybrids have two tooth patches on the tongue, but they are deep-bodied like the white bass and usually have the longitudinal lines broken into short dashes on alternating scale rows. Hybrids reach weights of 10 pounds which is larger than white bass, which seldom reach 3 pounds.

Description

Body moderately deep and compressed. Dorsal profile more curved than the ventral but not as arched as in the white perch. Caudal peduncle deeper than that of the white perch. Distance from snout to the origin of the dorsal fin contained 1.5 times in the distance from the dorsal origin to the caudal midbase. First dorsal outline rounded, its third and fourth spines longest. Second dorsal margin concave, with rounded corners. The two dorsal fins are connected by a low membrane. Caudal fin moderately forked, its middle rays 1.25 in the longest upper ray. Anal origin below anterior dorsal soft rays. Second anal spine markedly shorter than the third. Margin of anal fin concave. Pelvic fin inserted below the dorsal origin. Pelvic fin retrogressive, with straight margin. Pectoral fin asymmetrically pointed, its base oblique. Gill membranes separate and free from the isthmus. Mouth terminal. Preopercle finely serrated on its vertical limb and the posterior part of the horizontal limb. Lateral line complete and straight. Counts and proportional measurements are given in Table 30.

Color: Dusky silvery gray above, shading to silvery on the sides and white ventrally. Sides with about six (five to seven) longitudinal, narrow, dark stripes of which only the center one reaches to the base of the tail. Dorsal and caudal fins slightly dusky, pectoral and pelvic fins white, anal with melanophores on the central interradial membranes.

Juveniles and breeding adults: The juveniles are less pigmented but otherwise look like small adults. There are no special breeding colors or structures in this species.

Size: The usual size is 11 to 12 inches total length. The IGFA all-tackle record is 5 pounds 9 ounces, a fish from the Colorado River in Texas. The New York State record is a 2-pound 12-ounce fish from the Oswego River taken 4 June 1982 by Dean Myers.

Habitat

White bass are confined to large lakes and reservoirs. It moves into the lower reaches of streams for spawning and occasional juveniles are taken in streams, but in general it is a fish of big waters. The white bass is quite tolerant of turbidity. It travels in schools and often moves considerable distances.

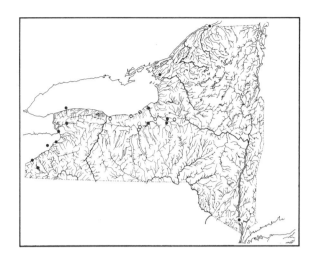

Distribution

This is a midcontinent species ranging from the St. Lawrence and the Great Lakes (few records in Lakes Superior and Huron) to the Red River of the North, and south in the Mississippi watershed to the gulf drainages and west to the Rio Grande. It has been introduced in the southeast and into some Pacific coast drainages. Recently, it has been collected in the Hudson River and this appears to be the result of some fish having moved through the Barge Canal.

Life History

White bass spawn in the spring when the water temperature reaches 55 or 60 F in May in Lake Erie and earlier farther south. The eggs are 0.8 mm in diameter, demersal, and adhesive. Spawning apparently takes place in daylight and fairly close to the surface. Ovarian egg counts of 242,000 to 933,000 have been reported. The eggs hatch in 46 hours at 60 F.

Food and Feeding

White bass are carnivorous sightfeeders. They are especially noted for feeding at the surface in groups as they pursue emerging insects or schools of small fish. During these feeding frenzies, they will strike at almost anything and even the most inept fishermen can catch white bass on almost every cast.

Small white bass feed on zooplankton and insect larvae; as they grow, the diet includes more fish including yellow perch, sunfish, minnows, and gizzard shad. They are opportunistic and even large adults feed heavily on insects.

References

Baglin and Hill, 1977 (fecundity). Riggs, 1955 (reproduction). Van Oosten, 1942 (life history). Forney and Taylor, 1963 (age and growth in Oneida Lake). Sigler, 1949 (life history). Raney, 1965a (summary in New York). Bonn, 1953 (food and growth). Dorsa and Fritsche, 1979 (larvae). Greeley, 1955b (general account). Starnes et al., 1983 (larval transport).

Names

Chrysops is from the Greek *chryos*, gold and *ops*, eye.

Perca chrysops Rafinesque, 1820a: 22 Falls of the Ohio

Labrax notatus Richardson, 1836: 8 Lower St. Lawrence River

Labrax albidus DeKay, 1842: 13 Buffalo, New York

Lepibema chrysops, Greeley, 1928: 100 Oswego watershed

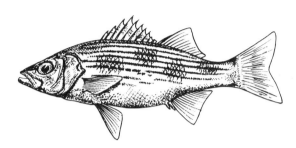

STRIPED BASS

Morone saxatilis (Walbaum, 1792)

Identification

Of the three species of temperate basses in New York State, the striper is the largest and most streamlined. It has seven to nine prominent narrow dark lines along the sides, of which two or three extend to the base of the tail. The white bass is most like the striper and has similar longitudinal dark lines, but in the white bass only one line extends from the gill opening to the base of the tail. The white perch is a smaller fish with a deeper and more arched body and no prominent dark lines.

The three species can be distinguished by the teeth on the base of the tongue: The striper has two clearly separated patches, the white bass has two patches close together so they appear to be a single patch, and the white perch has no teeth on the base of the tongue, but it does have a few teeth around the free edge of the tongue.

Description

Body elongate and somewhat compressed. Profiles about equally curved. Dorsal origin over middle of pectoral fin. First dorsal rounded, its fourth and fifth spines longest. Dorsal fins clearly separated with a scaled area between them. Second dorsal falcate with its margin concave anteriorly. Caudal fin forked, its middle rays contained 1.5 times in the longest upper ray. Anal fin inserted below the fourth dorsal soft ray. Anal spines graduated, anal fin margin concave. Third (the longest) anal spine a little more than half the first anal soft ray. Pelvic fin inserted under dorsal origin, pelvic retrogressive, its margin slightly convex. Pectoral fin shorter than the pelvic, asymmetrically pointed. Pectoral base oblique. Gill membranes separate and free from the isthmus. Mouth terminal, lower jaw protruding. Preopercles serrate. Top of head scaled forward to nostrils. Lateral line complete, straight. Counts and proportional measurements are given in Table 30.

Color: Striped bass are rather monochromatic

fishes, dusky gray to dark gray above, shading to silvery on the sides and white on the belly. Dorsal fins dusky, with the spines and rays darker than the membranes. Caudal fin dusky. Anal dusky anteriorly, white posteriorly. Pectoral fins dusky, pale along their ventral margins. Pelvic fins white. Iris silvery. Some individuals have one or more of the dark lines broken, continuing on the scale row above or below.

Juveniles and breeding adults: Striped bass less than 4 inches long have 8 to 10 dark vertical bars that dominate the longitudinal stripes. As the fish grow and the stripes become more prominent, the vertical bars disappear.

Size: Striped bass commonly reach weights of 30 pounds and the all-tackle record is a 76-pound fish from Montauk taken in 1981. The alltime record is about 125 pounds from North Carolina in 1891.

Habitat

Striped bass are anadromous, moving into rivers to spawn near the salt front. It is a coastal fish, often caught near rocks and around wrecks. This habit has earned it the local name of rockfish. Young stripers live in estuaries or bays and the adults range along the open coast, often moving into the deeper estuaries for the winter. In Lake Marion (Santee-Cooper Reservoir) in South Carolina, there is a freshwater landlocked population and this strain has been stocked in many inland waters.

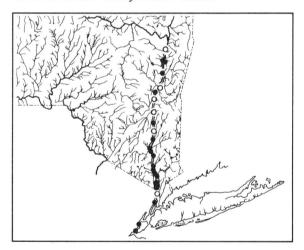

Distribution

The striped bass ranges from the Gulf of St. Lawrence to the St. Johns River in Florida. It also occurs in the Gulf of Mexico. It was introduced on the Pacific coast from the Hudson and Shrewsbury Rivers in 1874 and 1882 and now ranges from the Gulf of California north to Vancouver Island.

Life History

Striped bass move into the Hudson River in April and remain until mid-June. Temperatures at the time of migration are 11 to 21 C. Spawning takes place in fresh water near the salt front and where there is sufficient current to keep the eggs suspended. In the Hudson, most of the spawning takes place between West Point and Kingston. The spawning behavior has not been thoroughly described but it involves rolling and splashing at the surface in what are commonly termed "rock fights".

The eggs are semibuoyant and have been taken from the Tappan Zee to Kingston with the greatest concentration in mid-May from Haverstraw to Hyde Park. Yolk-sac larvae have been collected from late April to mid-June and post-yolk-sac larvae have been found from mid-May to late July. Juveniles appear in beach seine collections in late June and remain near shore until late fall, moving to deeper waters in November and December. Recently, it has been found that considerable numbers of striped bass juveniles overwinter in the pier area of lower Manhattan. It is believed that the juveniles would normally spend the winter in coastal marsh areas.

Striped bass returning to spawn for the first time are age IV to VII.

Food and Feeding

Merriman examined the stomachs of 250 striped bass from Connecticut between April and October, 1936. Forty-one percent of the stomachs were empty and the most common foods were silversides, menhaden, and shrimp (*Paleomonetes vulgaris*). Less common were gunnels, herrings, mummichogs and striped killifish, squid, sandworms, and blood worms. Sand lances, crabs, clams, snails, amphipods, and isopods were taken rarely.

Notes

The striped bass is one of the most important sport and commercial fishes of the United States. Along the Atlantic coast, three areas seem to serve as the spawning grounds for most of the striped bass. These are the Hudson River, Chesapeake Bay, and the Roanoke River. In the past few years, the Chesapeake has not produced strong year classes and the Hudson River has been contributing comparatively more to the coastal population. Because of high PCB levels, the Hudson River commercial fishery for striped bass has been closed since 1976.

References

Raney, 1952 (life history). Rathjen and Miller, 1957 (ecology). Merriman, 1937; 1941 (life history and ecology). Fritzsche and Johnson, 1980 (larvae). Morgan and Prince, 1978 (effects of chlorine on young). Trent and Hassler, 1966 (feeding). Neel, 1979 (identification of hybrids). Markle and Grant, 1970 (food of young-of-the-year). Woolcott, 1957 (osteology). Schaefer, 1970 (feeding habits, Long Island). Austin and Hickey, 1978 (predicting abundance). Hickey and Amish, 1975 (growth of jawless individual). Hickey, Young, and Bishop, 1977 (abnormalities). Kellogg and Gift, 1983 (preferred temperatures). Raney, 1957 (subpopulations); 1958 (life history summary). Raney and Woolcott, 1955a and 1955b (races). Raney, Woolcott, and Mehring, 1954 (migration). Setzler et al., 1980 (summary). Jordan, 1885a (nomenclature). Groman, 1982 (histology). Gardinier and Hoff, 1983 (food).

Names

The Latin word *saxatilis* means dwelling among rocks.

Perca saxatilis Walbaum, 1792: 33 New York

Roccus saxatilis, Greeley, 1935: 98 Lower Hudson

Sciaena lineata Bloch, 1785: pl. 304

Labrax lineatus, DeKay, 1842: 7-9 New York

Roccus lineatus, Bean, 1903: 524-527 New York

Perca septentrionalis Bloch and Schneider, 1801: 90 New York

Roccus striatus Mitchill, 1814: 24 New York

Perca mitchilli Mitchill, 1815: 413 New York

Perca mitchilli alternata Mitchill, 1815: 415 New York

Perca mitchilli interrupta Mitchill, 1815: 415 New York

TABLE 30

AVERAGE PROPORTIONAL MEASUREMENTS AND COUNTS OF TEMPERATE BASSES AND FRESHWATER DRUM (*Morone* and *Aplodinotus*)

All proportions are expressed in percentage of standard length.

| | *Morone* | | | *Aplodinotus* |
	americana	chrysops	saxatilis	grunniens
ST. LENGTH (mm)	114.1	71.3	123.4	59.2
TOTAL LENGTH	123.5	128.8	123.5	138.0
FORK LENGTH	117.2	120.1	115.9	138.0
PREDORSAL	43.3	41.6	41.0	40.5
PREANAL	71.0	68.3	69.3	66.5
PREPELVIC	40.0	38.0	38.1	36.5
DORSAL BASE	44.1	41.4	41.7	62.2
ANAL BASE	14.4	17.1	15.5	11.9
BODY DEPTH	36.3	29.2	27.9	32.4
BODY WIDTH	17.6	13.1	14.0	15.0
C.PED. DEPTH	12.2	12.4	10.7	8.7
PECTORAL ALT.	22.8	19.4	18.1	21.4
HEAD LENGTH	35.4	35.9	34.8	35.6
SNOUT	10.6	8.4	10.4	7.2
EYE	7.9	9.3	7.6	12.1
MOUTH LENGTH	11.4	13.6	12.4	13.3
INTERORB	8.4	7.9	8.2	6.9
N (sample size)	5	5	5	5
COUNTS:				
DORSAL RAYS	IX,I,11-12	IX,I,14-15	IX,I,11-14	IX-X,I,25-31
ANAL RAYS	III,9-10	III,11-13	III,11	II,7
PECTORAL RAYS	15-16	15-17	16-17	17-18
PELVIC RAYS	I,5	I,5	I,5	I,5
GILL RAKERS	20-23	25	25	26
VERTEBRAE	25	21-25	25	24-25
SCALES:				
ABOVE L. L.	7-8	8	10	10
LATERAL LINE	48-49	52-55	65	48-53
BELOW L. L.	10	13-14	14	13

SUNFISHES
CENTRARCHIDAE

This is an eastern North American family with only one species native to the area west of the Rocky Mountains. The family includes the black basses, the crappies, and the typical sunfishes; altogether 29 species in 8 genera.

Centrarchids are rather generalized, freshwater, spiny-rayed fishes, perhaps more obviously allied by the similarity of their nesting habits than by their structure. Most species are quite colorful with shades of green, brown, orange and brassy. Young sunfishes tend to look very much alike with a series of prominent vertical bars, although young large-mouth bass have a dark longitudinal stripe like that of the adult. One of the most consistent characteristics is a dark spot at the upper corner of the gill cover and in a number of species the margin of the operculum extends back as a dark flap which may be entirely black or have a colorful margin. Centrarchids have the pseudobranch poorly developed or absent and lack a suborbital shelf. Branson and Moore (1962) made a comprehensive study of the lateral line system and Mok (1981) has recently re-evaluated the classification of the family on the basis of kidney morphology.

Sunfishes are extremely important to the warm-water sport fishery of the state. The smaller species are readily caught by less experienced fishermen and the basses are worthy quarry for the expert. They are commonly stocked in ponds and reservoirs where they have a tendency to become overcrowded with poor growth and small size as a result.

Sunfishes often hybridize, especially in modified habitats of artificial water bodies. Most fish hybrids can be recognized by their combination of the characters of both parents but hybrid sunfish are often fertile and backcrosses occur, so there can be a full range of intermediate individuals. For a recent study of hybridization in sunfishes, see Childers (1967).

KEY TO THE SPECIES OF SUNFISHES AND BLACK BASSES

A. Scales large, fewer than 53 in lateral line. Body deep and compressed, its greatest depth contained 2 to 2.7 times in the length.

C.

A'. Scales small, more than 55 in lateral line. Body elongate, its depth contained 3 to 5 times in the standard length.

B. Dorsal fin with a shallow notch, its shortest spine more than half as long as the longest. Mouth smaller, the end of the maxillary bone reaching to below the middle of the pupil of the eye. Color brown or brassy, pattern uniform or consisting of one or two series of vertical bars on a lighter background. Young less than 5 or 6 inches long have an orange area at the base of the tail, separated from the clear outer part of the tail fin by a black band. *Micropterus dolomieui*

Smallmouth bass, p.306

Dorsal fins of smallmouth (top) and largemouth bass.

B'. Dorsal fin with a deep notch, its shortest spine less than half as long as the longest. Mouth large, the end of the maxillary reaching beyond the posterior border of the eye (shorter in small juveniles). Color green rather than bronze, with a prominent longitudinal stripe along the midside. Young without orange and black bands on the tail although the caudal fin sometimes has an orange or reddish wash. *Micropterus salmoides*

Largemouth bass, p. 307

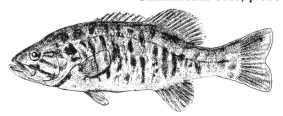

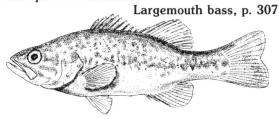

C. (A. Scales large, body deep.) Anal spines three.
                                                                        G.

C'. Anal spines five or more.

D. Dorsal spines 11 or 12.
                                                                        F.

D'. Dorsal spines 10 or fewer.

E. Dorsal spines seven or eight. Length of dorsal fin base about equal to distance from the dorsal origin to the back of the eye.
Pomoxis nigromaculatus **Black crappie, p. 311**

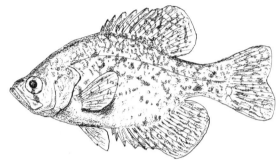

E'. Dorsal spines six or seven. Length of the dorsal base much less than the distance from the dorsal origin to the back of the eye.
Pomoxis annularis **White crappie, p. 309**

F. (D. Dorsal spines 11 or 12.) Scales ctenoid (rough to the touch). Posterior part of the ventral edge of the preopercle serrate, the vertical and horizontal margins of the preopercle meeting at an angle of about 90 degrees. Rear edge of the preorbital bones serrate.
Ambloplites rupestris **Rock bass, p. 291**

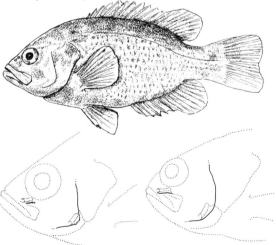

Preopercle and suborbital bones of mud sunfish (left) and rock bass.

F'. Scales cycloid (smooth). Preopercle without dentations, its vertical and horizontal edges meeting in a smooth curve. Edge of the preorbital smooth.
Acantharchus pomotis **Mud sunfish, p. 290**

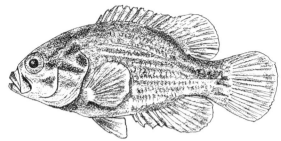

G. (C. Three anal spines.) Caudal fin forked.
                                                                        I.

G'. Caudal fin rounded.

H. Color pattern consisting of five to eight distinct bands on a pale greenish background throughout life. No blue (pale in preserved specimens) spots on sides. Opercular spot small, its diameter about equal to that of the pupil. Caudal peduncle scales small, usually 19 to 22. Pale spots on dorsal membrane not surrounded by dense melanophores. Four suborbital bones, including the lacrimal and dermosphenotic.
Enneacanthus obesus **Banded sunfish, p. 294**

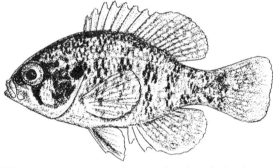

H'. Color pattern of juveniles banded, that of larger fish consisting of blue spots on a darker background. Opercular spot larger, its diameter slightly greater than that of the pupil. Caudal peduncle scales fewer, (15) 16 to 18 (19). Pale spots on interradial membranes of dorsal fin surrounded by darker rings of dense melanophores. Five suborbital bones including the lacrimal and dermosphenotic.
Enneacanthus gloriosus
                                        Bluespotted sunfish, p. 293

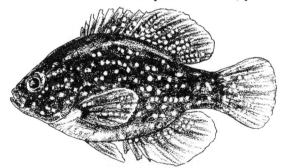

I. (G. Caudal fin forked.) Mouth large, maxillary bone ending below the posterior margin of the pu-

pil. Tongue with teeth. Supramaxillary bone longer than the widest part of the maxillary bone.
Lepomis gulosus   Warmouth, p. 300

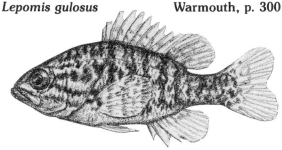

I'. Mouth smaller, maxillary ending below or in advance of the front of the eye. No teeth on tongue. Supramaxillary shorter than the maximum width of the maxillary bone or absent.

J. Pectoral fin long and pointed, its tip reaching above the lateral line when bent forward so that it is parallel to the edge of the gill cover.

                                                          M.

J'. Pectoral fin short and rounded, not reaching past the lateral line when bent upward.

K. Body short and deep, its depth contained about twice in the standard length. Edge of bony opercle, not the membrane, soft, flexible, and fimbriate (ragged). Margin of opercular flap with a red sector near its center.
Lepomis megalotis   Longear sunfish, p. 303

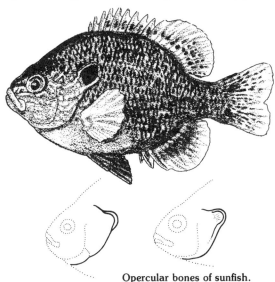

Opercular bones of sunfish.
Left: Opercle flexible at its edge.
Right: Opercle stiff to its margin.

K'. Body more elongate, contained 2.3 to 2.75 times in the standard length.

L. Mouth large, the maxillary ending below the front of the pupil. Eye small, about equal to or shorter than snout length. Gill rakers long, their tips reaching to the base of the second raker below. Opercular flap with a light margin, yellow to red in life. Opercular bone stiff to its margin. Adult males with black spots at the bases of the posterior soft rays of both the dorsal and anal fins.
Lepomis cyanellus   Green sunfish, p. 298

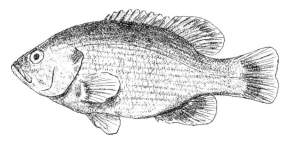

L'. Mouth smaller, the maxillary ending below front of the eye. Eye larger, longer than the snout. Gill rakers short, not reaching the second raker below. Opercular flap black, without a pale margin, very long in adults. Opercle bone flexible and fimbriate at its margin.
Lepomis auritus   Redbreast sunfish, p. 297

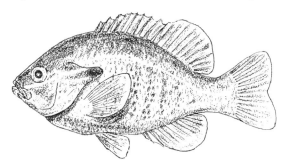

M. (J. Pectoral fin long and pointed.) Opercular flap black to its margin. A prominent black spot on the soft dorsal fin. Gill rakers long, reaching the base of the second or third raker below.*
Lepomis macrochirus   Bluegill, p. 302

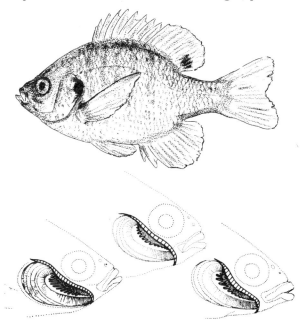

Gill rakers of sunfishes.
Left: Long gill rakers of bluegill.
Center: Short gill rakers of green sunfish.
Right: Moderately long gill rakers of pumpkinseed.

* Juveniles of these two species are quite similar. The gill rakers are good distinguishing characters but because the young pumpkinseeds have relatively longer gill rakers than older pumpkinseeds, comparisons must be made between fish of the same size.

M'. Opercular flap with a light margin. In life, there is a red sector at the lower corner of the flap. No prominent spot in the dorsal fin. Gill rakers shorter, not reaching the base of the second one below.

Lepomis gibbosus   Pumpkinseed, p. 299

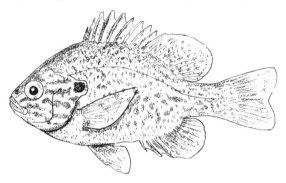

Acantharchus

This is a distinctive monotypic genus. It has six anal spines, smooth scales, and a smooth preopercle. In appearance it seems to be closest to the rock bass, *Ambloplites,* but it has a rounded, rather than forked, caudal fin.

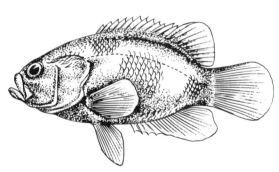

MUD SUNFISH

Acantharchus pomotis (Baird, 1855)

Identification

The mud sunfish strongly resembles the rock bass in general color and shape and, like the rock bass, has five or six spines in the anal fin. The two are readily separated by the shape of the tail, round in the mud sunfish and forked in the rock bass. The scales of the rock bass are rough and those of the mud sunfish are smooth, and the mud sunfish has a brown rather than a red eye. The preopercle of the mud sunfish is smooth and gently rounded and that of the rock bass is toothed with a noticeable angle. Young mud sunfish have wavy dark lines along the

sides whereas young rock bass have a checkerboard pattern of squarish blotches.

Crappies are the only other sunfishes in our area with more than three anal spines and they are paler, with diamond-shaped and more compressed bodies.

Description

Body rectangular, compressed. Dorsal and anal profiles about equally curved. Dorsal origin over pectoral base. Dorsal spines progressive, shorter than rays. No notch between the spiny and soft parts of dorsal. Soft dorsal rounded. Caudal convex. Anal similar to dorsal. Pelvics retrogressive, pointed anteriorly, inner ray joined to the body by membrane for about half its length. Pectorals short, rounded, slightly asymmetrical. Pectorals high on sides, their bases slightly oblique, nearly vertical. Scales ctenoid but smooth, with the denticules embedded, not cycloid as sometimes stated. Lateral line complete, arched, high on body. Opercle concave above its center, with two blunt points. Preopercle smooth, rounded. Gill membranes separate and free from the isthmus. Counts and proportional measurements are given in Table 31.

Color: Dusky reddish brown above, shading to pale brownish ventrally. Lateral line scales pale. Above this, and following the arch of the lateral line, there is a broad irregular stripe of dark scales about three scale rows wide. Below the lateral line, and not following its curve, are two straight dark bands, each two scale rows wide, and an incomplete third, lower, stripe one scale wide. Dorsal, anal, and caudal fins pale but finely peppered with melanophores and with dark edges. Fin spines and rays outlined. Pectoral fins hyaline, pelvic with dark anterior interradial membranes forming a streak behind the pale leading edge. Head with a dark spot on the operculum that is partly surrounded by a light ring, and two longitudinal streaks, one behind the eye and the other below it, the lower becoming indistinct on the operculum.

Juveniles and breeding adults: Juveniles are somewhat more contrastingly marked. Sexual dimorphism has not been reported.

Size: The maximum is about 170 mm or 6.6 inches total length.

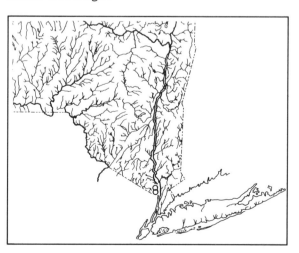

Habitat
The mud sunfish lives in darkly stained waters in sluggish lowland streams and lakes with silt or mud bottoms.

Distribution
This species ranges from the Hackensack River in New York south to extreme northern Florida and along the gulf coast to the St. Marks River. The Survey collected it at three New York locations in the Hackensack River, all west and southwest of Nyack. Impoundments upstream and downstream of this area may have destroyed some of the habitat but there is still a chance that a small population remains in a wooded wetland.

Life History
This species appears to be more secretive in its habits and there are only a few reports of its activities. Breder and Redmond were unable to find nests in northern New Jersey although they handled numerous specimens. Fowler gave a secondhand account of a nest near Willow Grove Lake, New Jersey. The nest was in a patch of spatterdock in a hole in a cranberry bog, where it was partly shaded by trees. It was being guarded by a male on June first and was about a foot in diameter in water about a foot deep. The nest had a sandy bottom but there was mud around the edge.

The species is reported to make a deep grunting sound which may have a function in reproduction. It has been suggested that it is most active at night.

Mansueti and Elser reported on age and growth from a study of 14 specimens from Maryland. The Maryland specimens ranged from 2 to 8 years old and seemed to have grown somewhat faster than the fish from New Jersey studied by Breder and Redmond.

Food and Feeding
Not reported.

Notes
Adults frequently rest head down in aquatic vegetation. Cashner noted that gulf coast specimens have slightly different scale counts and coloration. Fowler described specimens from the Suwanee River as a separate subspecies, *Acantharchus pomotis mizelli*.

References
Abbott, 1884. Breder and Redmond, 1929 (life history). Mansueti and Elser, 1953 (habitat and life history). Breder, 1936b (life history). Cashner in Lee et al., 1980 (summary). Fowler, 1945 (new species).

Names
Acantharchus is from the Greek *akantha*, thorn, and *archos*, anus, in reference to the anal spines. *Pomotis* is from the Greek *poma*, a cover and *ot*, ear, in reference to the gill cover.

Centrarchus pomotis Baird, 1855: 325 New Jersey

Acantharchus pomotis, Greeley, 1937: 103 Hackensack River

Ambloplites

This is a small genus with four species. It resembles the mud sunfish, *Acantharchus*, in shape, color, and in having more than three anal spines, but it has ctenoid scales and a serrated preopercle. It also has a slightly forked (emarginate) caudal fin.

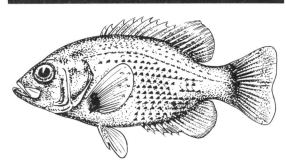

ROCK BASS

Ambloplites rupestris (Rafinesque, 1817)

Identification
The rock bass is a robust brownish-colored sunfish with five spines in the anal fin. It resembles the mud sunfish, but the mud sunfish has a rounded tail whereas the tail of the rock bass is definitely forked. Other differences between the rock bass and the mud sunfish are the shape of the preopercle, angled in the rock bass, curved in the mud sunfish, and the scales which are smooth in the mud sunfish and rough in the rock bass. The only other New York sunfishes with more than three spines in the anal fin are crappies and they have thinner, diamond-shaped bodies and short dorsal fins.

Description
Body deep, rectangular, robust but moderately compressed. Dorsal and ventral profiles about equally curved. Dorsal origin slightly behind the pectoral base. Dorsal single, the spiny part progressive, with deeply incised membranes. Last dorsal spine about two-thirds as long as the first soft ray. Soft dorsal rounded. Caudal fin slightly forked, with rounded lobes, its middle rays a little shorter than the longest upper rays. Anal origin below the ninth dorsal spine. Anal shape similar to that of the dorsal. Spiny part of the anal fin rounded, with the fourth spine longest. Anal interspinous membranes deeply notched. Soft part of the anal fin rounded, with the last anal ray connected to body by membrane for more than two-thirds its length. Pelvic fins inserted below the pectoral base, retrogressive, with convex margin. Pelvic spine a little more than half as long as the first pelvic ray, which ends in a short filament. No pelvic axillary process. Last pelvic ray connected to body for about one-half to two-thirds its length. Pectoral fins high with base oblique. Pectoral asymmetrically rounded. Mouth terminal, lower jaw projecting. Supramaxillary wider than the free end of the maxillary bone. Top of head scaled

forward to the interorbital area. Gill membranes separate and free from the isthmus. Lateral line complete, arched to the end of the dorsal base and straight on the caudal peduncle. Counts and proportional measurements are given in Table 31.

Color: Adults are generally brassy brown. The centers of the scales below the lateral line are darker, forming 11 or more lines of dark spots. Belly scarcely lighter in some specimens but bronze white in others. Vertical fins with spots and reticulations, often with pale oval or round spots. Fins usually darker at their margins. Tips of anal spines white. Pectoral fins clear, with melanophores along rays. Pelvic fins sometimes with a white leading edge. Opercle with a distinct darker spot at upper corner. Head sometimes with a blotch or bar below the eye, iris red in large individuals.

Juveniles and breeding adults: Juveniles have a striking "checkerboard" pattern of squarish blotches.

Size: As in most sunfishes, the size is extremely variable and stream fish often become stunted. In large lakes, the rock bass may reach 10 inches and Trautman reports a 14.7-inch specimen from Ohio that weighed 1 pound 15 ounces. The IGFA all-tackle record is 3 pounds from Ontario, Canada.

Habitat

The rock bass occurs in a variety of lake and stream habitats but it is probably most abundant in rocky-bottom streams of moderate size where there is abundant shelter and considerable current. In lakes, it occurs along gravelly and rocky shores. The young are frequently abundant in aquatic vegetation.

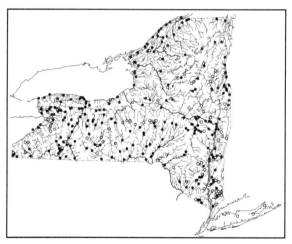

Distribution

The rock bass occurs from New England across southern Canada to the Red River of the North. West of the Appalachian Divide, it ranges south to the Tennessee system and is widespread east of the Mississippi and Missouri Rivers, with some native and many introduced populations farther west. In the south, it is replaced by the shadow bass, *Ambloplites ariommus*. There are two other species in the genus, the Roanoke bass on the Atlantic Coastal Plain and the Ozark rock bass on the Ozark Plateaus.

The rock bass is distributed throughout New York State.

Life History

The life history of the rock bass has been studied intensively in Lake Opinicon, Ontario (Gross and Nowell). Spawning took place between mid-May and mid-June. Adults moved into the shallows when temperatures reached 20 to 23 C. Males arrived 3 or 4 days before the females, established territories, and began to build dish-shaped nests by fanning and pushing gravel with the pectoral, anal, and caudal fins. The nests averaged 7.3 cm in depth and 26.6 cm in diameter, which was approximately 1.9 times the body length of the male. The water depth varied from 45 to 138 cm with gravel 0.9 to 2.4 cm in diameter. If gravel was not available, the nests were built on mud or vegetation. The nests were well separated, with distances to the nearest neighboring nest 103 cm if the neighbor was another rock bass or 78.6 cm if the neighbor was a pumpkinseed. The nests were usually completed in 1 day and the spawning began 1 to 4 days later. Spawning took place during the day with some preference for the morning over midday or evening.

Males did not court females but waited until females entered the nest and came to lie parallel with the male. Sometimes a pair circled with the male on the outside. During spawning, the male became almost black. It is suggested that this may reduce intimidation of the females by reducing contrast of the eye and fin color bands. Spawning consists of the female "dipping" (tilting her body to press her genital region against that of the male) and shaking two or three times. After spawning, the male may make an aggressive display toward the female, flaring his gills and biting her, or chasing her from the nest. The females may then return to the nest in a few minutes to spawn with other males over a 2-hour period. Gross and Nowell estimated that three to five eggs were released at each dip and that 120 dips occurred during a spawning session.

The males guarded the nests and fanned the eggs with their pectoral fins for an average of 14 days. During the time the eggs were in the nest, the male hovered with his head near the center of the nest but after the eggs hatched, he stationed himself with the center of his body at the center of the nest.

Small pumpkinseeds were persistent egg predators and the male rock bass responded to their approach by spreading their gill covers and chasing them a meter or so from the nests. About a third of the nests were vacated before the larval fishes dispersed, presumably because predators had consumed all of the eggs. Two nests contained 398 and 417 larvae.

Many males nested a second or even a third time. Females probably spawned twice, judging from the fact that early in the season the females had two size classes of oocytes in the ovaries; they had only one later.

Gross and Nowell noted that the behavior of the

rock bass differs from that of members of the genus *Lepomis*. Males use the pectoral fins more than the tail to build their nests. The darkening of the male and the irregular circling were not seen in *Lepomis*. Rock bass use the pectoral fins for fanning the eggs rather than the anal and caudal.

After nesting, the adult rock bass leave the nesting area for more suitable habitat since the shallow sites are often exposed and offer little protection.

Food and Feeding
Rock bass are extremely varied in their feeding habits. Some workers have reported that they feed only during the day with a peak of feeding activity in late afternoon but other investigators have found that they feed both day and night. They feed mostly on the bottom but may also take food in the water column or near the surface. Small rock bass feed on copepods and cladocerans, then switch to insects and crustaceans, and finally the adults feed on fish and crayfish. The diet varies with season; in the early summer adults in Oneida Lake fed on worms, crustaceans, and insect larvae but later in the season fish and crayfish dominated the diet. In the winter, amphipods make up a large part of the diet.

Notes
The rock bass has been studied intensively and there are many papers on its physiological ecology. The paper by Hile on age and growth is one of the most important early studies of the use of scales to determine growth patterns. In Pennsylvania, rock bass were not present in streams polluted by acid mine wastes when the pH was below 4.6.

References
Adams and Hankinson, 1928 (ecology). Breder, 1936b (life history). Hile, 1941 (age and growth). Hallam, 1959 (associations). Raney, 1965b (summary). Keast and Webb, 1966 (feeding). Keast and Welsh, 1968 (ecology). Gross and Nowell, 1980 (reproductive behavior). Buynak and Mohr, 1979c (larval development). Wolfert, 1980 (age and growth). Elrod et al., 1981 (food). Storr et al., 1983 (movements in Lake Ontario).

Names
Ambloplites comes from the Greek *amblys*, blunt or stupid, and *hoplon*, armor. *Rupestris* is New Latin for "living among rocks."

Bodianus rupestris Rafinesque, 1817b: 120 lakes of New York, Vermont and Canada

Ambloplites rupestris, Greeley, 1927: 63 Genesee drainage

Cichla aenea Lesueur, 1822a: 214 Lake Ontario

Centrarchus aeneus, DeKay, 1842: 27-28 Lake Champlain

Enneacanthus

This is a genus of three species of small sunfishes with nine dorsal spines, three anal spines, and rounded caudal fins. Two of the three species occur in New York, the third lives farther south on the Atlantic coast.

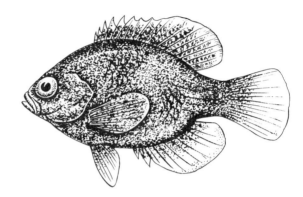

BLUESPOTTED SUNFISH

Enneacanthus gloriosus (Holbrook, 1855)

Identification
The bluespotted sunfish is a rather small species, seldom exceeding 3 inches total length, with a deep body, three anal spines, and a rounded tail. It closely resembles the banded sunfish and for many years there was some doubt that the two species were distinct. Part of the confusion is due to the fact that young bluespotted sunfish have vertical bands on the body very much like those of the banded sunfish. The adults are quite different, however, and the bands disappear in the bluespotted but not in the banded. The best feature for differentiating the two is probably the number of scale rows around the caudal peduncle. There are 16 to 18 rows in the bluespotted and 19 to 22 in the banded.

Other color differences include the smaller opercular spot in the bluespotted, and that the pale spots in the dorsal fin are surrounded by dark rings in the bluespotted but not in the banded sunfish.

Description
Body short, deep, and strongly compressed. Profiles regularly and about equally curved. Dorsal origin slightly behind the end of the operculum. Spiny part of the dorsal fin rounded, fifth and sixth spines longest. Membranes of the spiny dorsal incised. Soft dorsal rounded. Caudal rounded, its middle rays somewhat longer than the longest upper ray. Anal origin below last dorsal spine. Anal similar in shape to soft dorsal. Pelvic fin inserted below the dorsal origin. No pelvic axillary process. Pelvic spine less than two-thirds the first soft ray. Pelvic margin slightly convex. Last pelvic ray bound to the body for two-thirds its length. Pectoral base steeply oblique. Pectoral fin asymmetrically rounded. Scales ctenoid, body completely scaled. Top of

head scaled forward as far as interorbital region. Gill membranes separate and free from the isthmus. Mouth terminal, maxillary reaching to below front of eye. Preopercle smooth. Lateral line complete, arched parallel to the dorsal profile as far as the end of the dorsal fin base. Counts and proportional measurements are given in Table 31.

Color: Adults generally greenish above, slightly paler ventrally, breast a dirty white. Adult males with sides of head and body as well as bases of the vertical fins with irregularly spaced, bright turquoise spots, each surrounded by a black ring. Pelvic fins dusky, pectoral fins hyaline, with the rays outlined. Opercular spot smaller than pupil. Iris with a bronze ring around the pupil. A moderately distinct, vertical, subocular bar.

Juveniles and breeding adults: Juveniles and adult females are lighter than adult males and have pale creamy, rather than green or turquoise, spots. The young have about seven black bars on the sides and indistinct pale greenish spots. Adult males lose the bars and develop numerous pale green or blue spots.

Size: Our largest New York specimen is 75.2 mm standard length.

Habitat

The bluespotted sunfish lives in slow-moving streams and standing waters where there is dense aquatic vegetation, especially *Potamogeton* species. It usually occurs where the water is darkly stained and the bottom is muck and decaying vegetation.

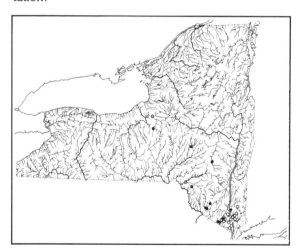

Distribution

This species ranges from southern New York, along the Atlantic coast to the southern part of peninsular Florida, and west along the gulf coast to the Florida Panhandle.

In New York, it is common in the Basher Kill in the Delaware drainage and in some lakes in southeastern New York. It has been taken in Jamesville Reservoir where it is believed to have been stocked. There is, however, a series of specimens from Oneida Lake, collected in 1916, in the archives of the College of Environmental Science and Forestry at Syracuse University. It is possible, therefore, that the Jamesville population is a relict population or that the species was introduced much earlier than is generally believed.

Life History

The life history of the bluespotted sunfish is not well known. Fowler described the nests as having a diameter of 4 or 5 inches in beds of filamentous algae. Breder stated that the nests are sometimes 12 inches in diameter in soft material. Nests have been reported in water about a foot deep. Spawning occurs in spring, May in New Jersey.

Food and Feeding

Breder reported snails, *Daphnia*, *Asellus*, amphipods, and insects in the stomachs of specimens from New Jersey. Most of their feeding is done in close proximity to plants but they learn to take food from the surface in aquaria.

Notes

The bluespotted and banded sunfishes are confused in much of the older literature.

References

Abbott, 1870 (habitat). Breder and Redmond, 1929 (life history). Breder, 1936b (life history). Casterlin and Reynolds, 1979 (thermoregulation); 1980 (diel activity). Werner, 1972 (occurrence in Lake Ontario drainage). Sweeney, 1972 (systematics).

Names

Enneacanthus is from the Greek *ennea*, nine, and *acantha*, a thorn or prickle. *Gloriosus* is Latin for superb, full of glory.

Bryttus gloriosus Holbrook, 1855: 52 Cooper River, South Carolina

Enneacanthus gloriosus, Greeley, 1936: 87 Delaware drainage

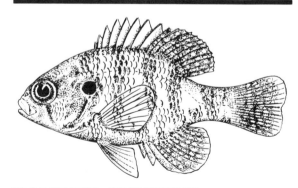

BANDED SUNFISH

Enneacanthus obesus (Girard, 1854)

Identification

The banded sunfish can be confused only with the bluespotted sunfish as these are the only New York species of sunfishes with three anal spines and rounded, rather than forked, tails. The two are very similar in appearance, however, and for a long time there was doubt that they were distinct species.

They differ in adult color pattern, in the number of scales around the caudal peduncle (19 to 22 in *obesus*, 16 to 18 in *gloriosus*), and number of circumorbital bones (5 in *gloriosus*, 4 in *obesus*). The latter feature is difficult to use as the bones are thin and deeply embedded in the skin. Color and scale count are sufficient to distinguish the two. (See account of the bluespotted sunfish for color differences).

Description

Body short and deep, compressed. Profiles symmetrical or the dorsal slightly more curved. Dorsal origin over edge of the opercle. Spiny dorsal arched, with spines V to VII longest. Interspinous membranes incised. Soft dorsal rounded. Tail rounded, longest upper ray slightly longer than middle rays. Anal origin below last dorsal spine. Anal shape similar to soft dorsal, rays 3 and 4 longest. Pelvic insertion slightly behind dorsal origin. Pelvic margin straight, last ray joined to body by membrane for two-thirds its length.

Pectoral base steep. Pectoral fin asymmetrically rounded. Gill membranes separate and free from the isthmus. Mouth terminal, maxillary reaching to below front of eye. Preopercle smooth. Lateral line arched, ending at front of caudal peduncle. Counts and proportional measurements are given in Table 31.

Color: Body generally light greenish beige with six or seven vertical lines formed by broad dark scale margins. The first of these runs from the dorsal origin to the tip of the operculum, and the top of the head ahead of this line is generally dark. Sides of head with a horizontal pale streak from the middle of the eye to the edge of the operculum. A second pale streak above this curves to connect with the pale lateral line. A dark teardrop is present. Lower jaw dusky. Spiny dorsal dusky, with the spines outlined. Soft dorsal, caudal, and anal dark, with rows of pale spots on the membranes. Pectorals hyaline. Pelvic leading edge white, the rest of the fin dark anteriorly, shading to clear posteriorly. Iris with bronze tones. Opercular spot larger than pupil, partly ringed with white.

Juveniles and breeding adults: The adult males are similar to the juveniles, not developing the high coloration of the large males of the bluespotted sunfish.

Size: This is the smallest of our species of sunfishes. Its maximum size is slightly more than 2 inches. Our largest New York specimen is about 38 mm standard length.

Habitat

This coastal plain species occurs in slow-moving and often darkly stained water where there is abundant submerged vegetation.

Distribution

Banded sunfishes are found from the northern part of peninsular Florida along the gulf coast to Alabama and north in the Atlantic drainages to New Hampshire.

In New York, the only unquestioned records are from the Peconic drainage on Long Island and in Spruce and Cranberry Lakes in the Passaic River drainage.

Life History

The life history of the banded sunfish is not well known. It is presumed to build nests in vegetation, rather than in sand or gravel.

Food and Feeding

The food habits have not been studied but it probably feeds on insects and other small invertebrates.

Notes

Because of its restricted distribution in New York, the banded sunfish is now protected. Owing to the difficulty of distinguishing it from the bluespotted sunfish, much of the older literature is unreliable.

References

Harrington, 1956 (photoperiod). Lee and Gilbert in Lee et al., 1980 (distribution).

Names

Obesus is Latin for stout, fat.

Pomotis obesus Girard, 1854b: 40 vicinity of Hingham and Charles River near Holliston, Massachusetts

Enneacanthus obesus, Greeley, 1937: 103 Spruce and Cranberry Lakes, Passaic River drainage

TABLE 31
AVERAGE PROPORTIONAL MEASUREMENTS AND COUNTS OF
SUNFISHES *(Acantharchus, Ambloplites,* and *Enneacanthus)*

All proportions are expressed in percentage of standard length.

	Acantharchus	*Ambloplites*	*Enneacanthus*	
	pomotis	rupestris	gloriosus	obesus
ST. LENGTH (mm)	69.2	64.3	43.3	29.2
TOTAL LENGTH	131.0	124.6	129.2	131.5
FORK LENGTH	131.0	122.4	129.2	131.5
PREDORSAL	45.4	45.2	43.0	45.1
PREANAL	61.8	60.4	61.7	62.2
PREPELVIC	40.6	41.0	45.1	45.0
DORSAL BASE	47.0	46.5	48.8	48.4
ANAL BASE	26.8	28.9	29.3	27.2
BODY DEPTH	38.0	42.3	49.4	46.4
BODY WIDTH	18.0	19.4	19.9	19.3
C.PED. DEPTH	16.0	15.5	16.6	15.0
PECTORAL ALT.	26.9	29.5	33.0	32.9
HEAD LENGTH	41.7	39.6	37.8	40.6
SNOUT	7.5	10.7	9.0	7.7
EYE	11.9	11.8	12.7	14.5
MOUTH LENGTH	18.4	16.4	14.2	14.5
INTERORB	7.3	10.3	10.7	8.3
N (sample size)	2	5	5	5
COUNTS:				
DORSAL SPINES	XI	XI-XII	VIII-IX	VII-IX
DORSAL RAYS	10-11	10-11	10-11	11-12
ANAL RAYS	V,10	VI,10-11	III,9-11	III,10-11
PECTORAL RAYS	14-15	14-15	11-12	11-13
PELVIC RAYS	I,5	I,5	I,5	I,5
GILL RAKERS	15-16	12	11-15	13-14
VERTEBRAE	30-31	31	27-28	27-28
SCALES:				
ABOVE L.L.	5-6	6	5	5
LATERAL LINE	38-39	38	30-33	30-33
BELOW L.L.	12-13	11	9-10	9-10

Lepomis

The genus *Lepomis* contains about 11 species. Its members have three anal spines and a forked tail. They range in shape from the bass-like green and warmouth sunfishes to the deep-bodied species like the pumpkinseed and bluegill. The warmouth was long placed in its own genus, *Chaenobryttus*, because it has teeth on the tongue and a well-developed supramaxillary bone, but because it frequently hybridizes with species of *Lepomis* it is no longer recognized as distinct.

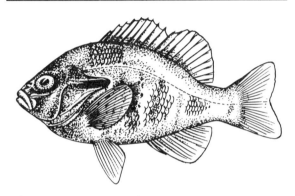

REDBREAST SUNFISH

Lepomis auritus (Linnaeus, 1758)

Identification
The redbreast sunfish is a rather elongate sunfish with a short, rounded pectoral fin, short gill rakers, and an opercular flap that is dark to its margin. It resembles the green sunfish, *Lepomis cyanellus*, most closely but the green sunfish has a larger mouth and a pale margin on the opercular flap. The warmouth differs in color pattern, in having teeth on the tongue, and in having a large supramaxillary bone. The longear and the pumpkinseed both have some red and white on the opercular flap and the bluegill has a long pointed pectral fin.

Description
Body deep and compressed but rather elongate for a *Lepomis*. Dorsal and ventral profiles about equally curved. Dorsal fin single, without a notch between the spiny and soft parts, its origin over, or slightly behind, the pectoral base. Spiny part arched, with incised membranes, soft part round with rounded corner. Caudal fin slightly forked, with round lobes. Anal similar in shape to soft dorsal, its origin below the last dorsal spine. Pelvic inserted below the dorsal origin, retrogressive, with acuminate first ray, sharp anterior, round posterior corners, and straight margin. No pelvic axillary process, last ray bound for one-half its length. Pectoral base oblique, pectoral fin asymmetrically rounded. Scales ctenoid, body completely scaled, top of head scaled to back of orbits. Operculum with long flap in adult males, margin of the bone fimbriate and flexible at its margin. Mouth terminal, maxillary reaching to below anterior edge of the eye. Gill membranes separate and free from the isthmus. Lateral line complete and arched. Villiform teeth present on the premaxillary, vomer, palatines, and dentary. Counts and proportional measurements are given in Table 32.

Color: The redbreast sunfish is a rather somber species, dark olive above, shading to paler ventrally. The scales of the sides have dark centers and paler edges. The vertical fins are dusted with melanophores, especially along the rays, and sometimes tinged with red. The pelvic fins are dusky, and pectoral fins are clear, with outlined rays. In females, the breast is yellowish and in males it is reddish, becoming brighter during the breeding season, with the red color spreading to the lower sides and underparts of the head. The iris is often reddish or bronze, and the lips of breeding males are pale blue. Some individuals have a blue line from the middle of the upper lip to below the center of the eye, occasionally continuing across the upper part of the cheek as a line of blue spots.

Juveniles and breeding adults: The juveniles are quite plain, with only a trace of vertical bars in contrast to other species of *Lepomis* which have pronounced vertical bands in the young stages.

Size: This is a small- to moderate-sized sunfish, usually 5 to 8 inches long. The maximum total length is about 9.5 inches.

Habitat
The redbreast is a fish of standing waters and the slower parts of streams. It is sometimes found in slightly brackish water. George has noted that it frequents sandy or rocky areas where it is commonly associated with rock bass and smallmouth. Scott and Crossman also mentioned that it seeks shelter under rocks.

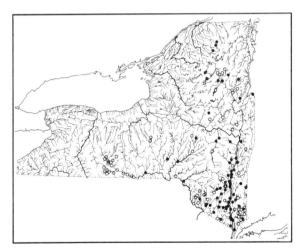

Distribution
The redbreast is essentially an Atlantic coast species. Its original range was from the Chattahoochee drainage in western Florida, east through the panhandle and peninsular Florida, north on the Atlantic Coastal Plain and Piedmont to eastern New York, and through New England to southern New Brunswick. It has been introduced in the Mobile

drainage and in other areas, including a large section of east Texas.

In New York, it is confined to the eastern part of the state in the Susquehanna, Delaware and Mohawk systems, parts of the Raquette drainage and elsewhere in the Adirondacks. George believes its presence in Lake George is long standing, probably dating from postglacial times when Lake George was connected to glacial Lake Albany.

Life History
The life history of the redbreast sunfish has not been thoroughly documented. Fragmentary reports indicate that its breeding habits are similar to those of other sunfishes. Nests are excavated in water 6 to 18 inches deep and guarded by males. The spawning season in New York ranges from early June to mid-August.

Food and Feeding
The redbreast feeds on plankton and a variety of aquatic insects and invertebrates.

References
Breder and Nigrelli, 1935 (social behavior). Roosa and Slack, 1975 (occurrence). George, 1981a (Adirondack distribution). Richmond, 1940 (spawning in tidal waters).

Names
Auritus is Latin for eared, in reference to the well-developed opercular flap.

Labrus auritus Linnaeus, 1758: 283 Philadelphia
Lepomis auritus, Greeley, 1930: 86 Lake Champlain drainage
Labrus appendix, Mitchill, 1818a: 247 New York
Pomotis appendix, DeKay, 1842: 32-33 New York

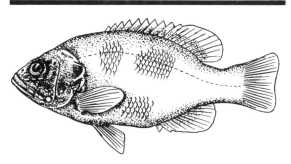

GREEN SUNFISH

Lepomis cyanellus
Rafinesque, 1819

Identification
The green sunfish is rather elongate for a *Lepomis*, with a large mouth and small scales. It resembles the warmouth in shape, but not in color, and sometimes has a few teeth on the tongue but not a definite patch of teeth like that of the warmouth. It has a short, rounded pectoral fin and a pale margin around the opercular flap. In life, the pale centers of the scales form an elusive pattern of longitudinal lines.

Description
Body compressed, rectangular, its dorsal profile slightly more curved than the ventral. Dorsal fin single, with slight notch. Dorsal origin over pectoral base. Spiny part of dorsal fin arched, with incised membranes. Soft part rounded. Caudal slightly forked, with rounded lobes. Anal origin below penultimate dorsal spine. Anal fin rounded. Pelvic inserted below third dorsal spine. Pelvic fin retrogressive, with acuminate first ray and rounded posterior corner. No pelvic axillary process. Last ray bound to body for one-half to two-thirds its length. Pectoral fin asymmetrically rounded, with oblique base. Scales ctenoid, body completely scaled. Top of head scaled to eyes, cheeks and opercles scaled. Operculum rounded, opercle stiff to its margin, not fimbriate. Preopercle and suborbital smooth. Mouth terminal, oblique, and large, reaching to below middle of eye. Gill membranes separate and free from the isthmus. Lateral line complete, arched. Counts and proportional measurements are given in Table 32.

Color: As its name implies, the green sunfish is predominantly green or olive, shading to dirty white on the belly. Its fins are generally dusky, with yellow margins on the vertical fins. The pelvics are predominantly yellow or dusky in breeding males. Pectoral clear.

The centers of the scales on the sides are pale or emerald green, forming pale lines. Sometimes there is a suggestion of 7 to 12 vague vertical bars on the body. There are greenish lines on the cheeks, one extending from the maxillary to the angle of the preopercle, others above and more or less parallel to this. A particularly prominent line extends from the middle of the maxillary toward the lower edge of the opercular spot but sometimes ends just behind the eye. The opercular spot is prominent, with a white to orange margin above, behind, and below, but not anteriorly. The last rays of the dorsal and anal fins have intense pigment that sometimes forms definite spots at the bases of these fins.

Juveniles and breeding adults: Juveniles have brighter longitudinal lines, but they do not have prominent vertical bands like the young of some other species of *Lepomis*.

Size: The size of adult green sunfish is extremely variable. Trautman records individuals up to 10.8 inches total length. Our largest New York specimens are 101 mm standard length, about 4 inches. The IGFA line class categories are open, that is, no fish have been submitted for record status.

Habitat
The green sunfish occupies a wide range of habitats from small streams and ditches to larger rivers, lakes, and ponds where there is adequate aquatic vegetation to provide shelter. Trautman notes that it does best in the absence of other species of sunfishes and it is more tolerant of silt than most other species of sunfishes, hence it often becomes abundant in perpetually turbid waters. In New York, we have found it in moderate-sized, turbid streams.

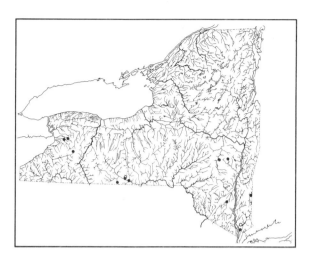

Lepomis cyanellus Rafinesque, 1819: 420 Ohio River

Lepomis cyanellus, Meek, 1889: 313 Montezuma marshes

Apomotis cyanellus, Greeley, 1928: 101 Oneida Lake

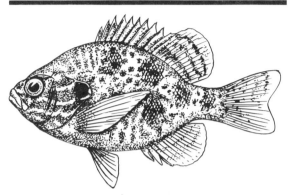

PUMPKINSEED

Lepomis gibbosus (Linnaeus, 1758)

Identification

The pumpkinseed is the most abundant and widespread species of sunfish in New York State. It is a short, deep-bodied species with a long, pointed pectoral fin and its opercular flap has a pale margin with a red sector. The opercle bone is stiff to its margin and not fimbriate. It is often taken with the bluegill but the bluegill is thinner, has no pale margin on its opercular flap, and has a distinct spot in the soft dorsal fin. The longear sunfish has a red area in the white margin of the opercular flap but it has a short rounded pectoral fin and a flexible fimbriate opercle.

Description

Body deep and compressed but somewhat streamlined. Dorsal profile slightly more arched than the ventral. Dorsal fin single, slightly notched, originating just behind the pectoral base. Spiny part of dorsal fin arched with incised membranes. Soft part rounded. Caudal fin slightly forked, its lobes blunt. Anal origin below last dorsal spine. Anal fin rounded. Pelvic insertion below second dorsal spine. Pelvic fin retrogressive, its anterior corner blunt, its posterior corner round. No axillary process. Last ray bound for two-thirds its length. Pectoral fin pointed, retrogressive. Pectoral base oblique. Scales ctenoid, body completely scaled. Top of head scaled to eyes, cheeks and opercula scaled. Opercle stiff to its margin, entire. Mouth small, terminal, maxillary ending below front of eye. Gill membranes separate and free from isthmus. Lateral line complete, arched to caudal peduncle. Gill rakers short and stubby. Counts and proportional measurements are given in Table 32.

Color: Head and body dark green, lighter ventrally. Sides with patches of dark scales, some of which are reddish brown. Breast clear white to yellow. Dorsal fin dusky mottled, sometimes with orange on the interradial membranes of the soft part.

Distribution

The original range of the green sunfish was the Mississippi Valley and the Great Lakes, from western New York to Wisconsin and southeastern South Dakota, south to New Mexico and northern Mexico. It has been widely introduced across the southern United States and on the west coast from northern Mexico to Oregon.

In New York, it apparently was originally only in the Great Lakes drainage but has been introduced in the Susquehanna and in the Lower Hudson drainage in the Wallkill, New Croton Reservoir, and Iron Mine Pond and the Webatuck River in the Housatonic drainage.

Life History

In Wisconsin, Hunter found that this species spawned from mid-May to early August when the water temperature was 68 to 82 F. Males built nests in water usually less than 1 foot deep, and often in areas sheltered by rocks or logs. Nesting was colonial: One male would start to build a nest and others would build nearby. Spawning took place over a day or two and then the male guarded the nest until the eggs hatched 3 to 5 days later. He then herded the young for an additional period. A day or two after the young dispersed, the cycle began again.

Food and Feeding

The green sunfish feeds on a variety of organisms including insects, mollusks, and small fishes.

Notes

Green sunfish are able to reproduce when they are only 3 inches long and they often become stunted in ponds. They hybridize readily with other sunfish species including longear, bluegill, orangespotted, pumpkinseed, and redbreast sunfish.

References

Greenberg, 1947 (behavior). Hunter and Hasler, 1965. Heimstra, Damkot, and Benson, 1969 (effects of turbidity). Hunter and Wisby, 1961. Hunter, 1963 (reproductive behavior). Sadzikowski and Wallace, 1976 (food). Kaya and Hasler, 1972 (photoperiod). Trautman, 1981 (Ohio).

Names

Cyanellus is from the Greek *kyaneos,* blue.

Caudal similar. Anal rays pale, anal interradial membranes dusky. Pelvics slightly dusky, pectoral clear. Sides of head with irregular narrow blue lines radiating from the eye. Opercular spot dark, opercular flap with a pale margin interrupted by a red sector. Iris with bronze tones. Lower jaw blue.

Juveniles and breeding adults: Juveniles have definite vertical bars with some spots in the pale interspaces. Breeding males are brighter than females.

Size: The pumpkinseed is a rather small species not exceeding 8 or 10 inches total length. The IGFA does not list it.

Habitat
The pumpkinseed occurs in a wide variety of habitats, from streams and small ponds to the slower parts of large rivers.

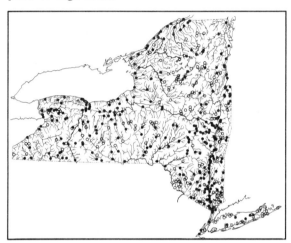

Distribution
The pumpkinseed is a northeastern species ranging from New Brunswick south along the Atlantic coast to northeastern Georgia. It ranges west through southern Ontario to Lake Winnipeg, but it is absent from the Lake Superior basin. It reaches its southern limit in northeastern Missouri, Illinois, southern Indiana and Ohio. Like most sunfishes, it has been widely introduced outside its original range. In New York State, it is essentially universal and was native to the higher parts of the Adirondacks, although apparently absent from some lakes where it now occurs.

Life History
The pumpkinseed builds its nests near shore where the water is 6 to 12 inches deep. Often, the nests are located close to aquatic vegetation and sometimes they are so close together that the nesting is described as colonial. Males begin nesting when the water temperature reaches the high 60s F and spawning may continue until August. Courtship takes place in the daytime. The female rolls against the male so that her body is at a 45-degree angle while the male remains upright. Spawning occurs repeatedly and more than one female may contribute eggs to a nest. Females lay 600 to 5,000 eggs depending on their size and presumably other factors. Hatching takes place in about 3 days and the

male guards the young for another week or more. After the young disperse, the males may build another nest and repeat the process.

Food and Feeding
The pumpkinseed is an opportunistic feeder that consumes a wide variety of prey including many kinds of insects, amphipods, mollusks, larval salamanders, and small fish.

Notes
Shoemaker reported that in a small pond, near Rensselaerville, chain pickerel fed on golden shiners that concentrated around the nests in order to feed on the sunfish eggs.

References
Creaser, 1926b (age and growth). Ingram and Odum, 1941 (nesting). Breder, 1940 (life history). Shoemaker, 1952 (homing). Greeley, 1954b (general account). Stacy and Chiszar, 1978 (behavior). Burns, 1976 (reproductive cycle). Colgan and Gross, 1977 (aggression). Shoemaker, 1952 (behavior). Sadzikowski and Wallace, 1976 (food). Domermuth and Reed, 1980 (food). Laughlin and Werner, 1980 (resource partitioning). Brown and Colgan, 1981 (juveniles). Colgan and Ealey, 1973 (nest selection).

Names
Gibbosus is Latin for hunched or humped, or shaped like the nearly full moon.

Perca gibbosa Linnaeus, 1758: 292-293 Carolinas (after Catesby)

Sparus aureus Walbaum, 1792: 290 lakes of New York

Eupomotis aureus, Mather, 1886: 7 Adirondacks

Morone maculata Mitchill, 1814: 18 New York City

Labrus anutus Mitchill, 1817: 289 Wallkill River

Pomotis vulgaris Cuvier *in* Cuvier and Valenciennes, 1829: 91

Eupomotis gibbosus, Greeley, 1927: 63 Genesee River

Lepomis gibbosus, Hubbs and Lagler, 1964: 114 (distribution)

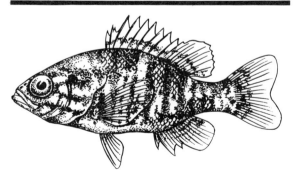

WARMOUTH

Lepomis gulosus (Cuvier, 1829)

Identification
The warmouth is somewhat similar in shape to the

rock bass but it differs in having three, not five or six, anal spines. It is a rather somber fish that lacks the bright colors of some other species of *Lepomis*, and frequently has a purplish cast in life. It has a large supramaxillary bone, longer than the greatest width of the maxillary bone, and well-developed patches of teeth on its tongue. It also has short, rounded pectoral fins.

Description
Body deep but rectangular, robust. Dorsal origin slightly behind the pectoral base. Dorsal single with shallow notch. Spiny dorsal arched, with incised membranes. Soft dorsal rounded. Caudal fin slightly forked. Anal origin below next to last or last spine. Anal rounded. Pelvic insertion below dorsal origin. No pelvic axillary process. Pelvic fin retrogressive, with pointed anterior and rounded posterior corners. Last pelvic ray bound to body for two-thirds to three-fourths its length. Pectoral base oblique. Pectoral fin asymmetrically rounded. Scales ctenoid, body completely scaled, top of head to eye, cheeks and opercula scaled. Mouth terminal, slightly oblique, large, with maxillary ending below middle or rear of eye. Supramaxillary bone well developed. Opercle, preopercle, and preorbital bones smooth. Gill membranes separate and free from the isthmus. Lateral line complete, arched to caudal peduncle. Gill rakers moderately long in small individuals. Counts and proportional measurements are given in Table 32.

Color: Generally brownish, with a purplish cast above, shading to yellowish brown on the sides and greenish yellow to dirty white below. Sides with 5 to 11 irregular, narrow, dark bars. Spiny dorsal dusky, rest of vertical fins vermiculated or dusky with pale yellow spots. Pelvic dusky, pectoral clear. Sides of head with narrow dark lines radiating from eye, and a dark streak along the edge of the maxillary and continuing to the margin of the opercle. Opercular spot black, with a pale margin. A white band along the upper margin of the operculum.

Juveniles and breeding adults: Juveniles are more contrastingly marked than the adults, with more pronounced vertical bars. Small young have transparent fins. Breeding males are said to have a bright orange spot on the base of the last three dorsal rays.

Size: The usual size of the warmouth adults is about 4 to 7 inches total length. The IGFA all-tackle record is a 2-pound 2-ounce fish from South Carolina.

Habitat
Larimore noted that, in Illinois, dense weeds and soft bottom are the two habitat characteristics with which it is most often associated. Trautman reported that, in Ohio, it is most abundant in densely vegetated, slow-moving waters with clear water and muck bottom but less common in silty areas. Our few specimens from Woodbury Creek came from deep pools without much vegetation.

Distribution
Originally, the warmouth ranged from southern Wisconsin, southern Michigan and Ohio south through the Mississippi basin to the Rio Grande drainage in Texas and New Mexico. It also occurred along the gulf coast to peninsular Florida and north on the Atlantic seaboard to Maryland and Virginia.

In New York, it is an introduced species with surviving, but apparently not spreading, populations in Woodbury Creek in Orange County and the Saw Kill in Dutchess County.

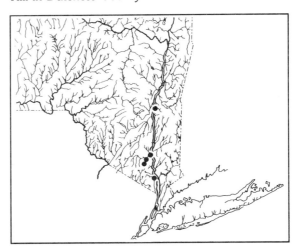

Life History
The life history of the warmouth in Illinois was thoroughly studied by Larimore. Maturity is reached at lengths between 3 and 4 inches when the fish are 1 or 2 years old. Spawning begins in early May and sometimes lasts until early August, with the peak in early June. Larger warmouth spawned over a longer period and some fish spawned several times during the season.

Males build nests in water 6 to 60 inches deep and often the nests are close together although Larimore ascribed this to a shortage of nesting sites rather than to any tendency to gregariousness. The male sweeps away the loose debris, forming a rather shapeless depression about 4 by 8 inches. One male kept working on his nest until it was symmetrical, 18 inches in diameter and 5 inches deep but this seemed to be exceptional.

When the female is ready to spawn, she allows herself to be guided into the nest by the male. Unripe females are chased and, in the confines of an aquarium, may be killed. Courting males turn bright yellow and their eyes become bright red. The male pursues the females with his opercles spread and his mouth wide open. Several females may contribute eggs to a single nest but once the eggs are being guarded, courtship ceases so that any one nest will contain eggs of approximately the same stage of development. Only a few eggs are laid during each spawning episode. At 25 to 26 C, the average time to hatching was 34 hours 30 minutes. Warmouth live 6 to 8 years.

Food and Feeding
Crayfish and insects make up the bulk of the diet, with cladocerans, ostracods, annelids, copepods, fishes, some snails, and other invertebrates being

taken less frequently. Larimore found considerable local and seasonal variation in diet.

Notes
The warmouth was formerly placed in its own genus, *Chaenobryttus*, but because it shares many features with other members of the genus *Lepomis*, and hybridizes freely with some of them, it is now placed in the latter genus. For a time, it seemed that the correct name for the species should be *coronarius*, which was the earliest name, but the author of *coronarius*, Bartram, did not consistently use binomial nomenclature and his names must be disregarded.

References
Larimore, 1957 (ecology, life history).

Names
Gulosus is the Latin word for gluttonous, from *gula*, the throat.

Pomotis gulosus Cuvier *in* Cuvier and Valenciennes, 1929: 498 Lake Pontchartrain, Louisiana

Chaenobryttus gulosus, Greeley, 1937: 103 Saw Kill near Annandale

Lepomis gulosus, Bailey et al., 1970: 75 (nomenclature)

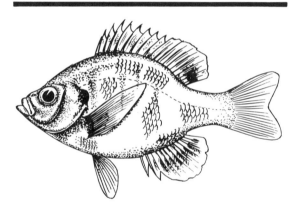

BLUEGILL

Lepomis macrochirus Rafinesque, 1818

Identification
The bluegill is a deep-bodied, highly compressed fish with a long, pointed pectoral fin and a distinct spot on the soft dorsal fin. The opercular flap is well developed but never has a pale margin; the opercle bone is flexible to its margin and fimbriate.

Juvenile bluegills and juvenile pumpkinseeds are both barred and similar in appearance but they differ in gill raker size. The comparison, however, must be made between fish of the same size because the gill rakers become shorter as the fish grow. Thus, a small pumpkinseed can have longer gill rakers than a somewhat larger bluegill, although at the same size, the gill rakers of the bluegill will be longer.

Description
Body deep and strongly compressed. Profiles about equally curved. Dorsal single with slight notch, orig-

inating over pectoral base. Spiny part arched, with incised membranes. Soft part of dorsal fin rounded. Caudal slightly forked, with rounded lobes. Anal origin below last dorsal spine. Anal fin rounded. Pelvic insertion below fourth dorsal spine. Pelvic retrogressive, with pointed anterior and rounded posterior corners. No pelvic axillary process. Last ray bound by membrane for two-thirds its length. Pectoral long and asymmetrically pointed. Its posterior corner rounded. Pectoral base oblique. Scales ctenoid, body completely scaled. Top of head scaled to eye, cheeks and opercles scaled. Opercle with fimbriate, flexible margin. Preopercle with small dentations at its angle. Mouth small, slightly oblique, maxillary ending below front of eye. Gill membranes separate and free from isthmus. Lateral line complete, arched to caudal peduncle. Counts and proportional measurements are given in Table 32.

Color: Rather greenish olive above and pale below, usually with traces of six to eight double, vertical dark bars. Vertical fins dusky, with the rays paler than the membranes. Soft dorsal with a definite spot on the lower half of the last four rays. Pelvic fin clear to slightly dusky, pectoral fins clear. Breast yellowish white except in breeding males when it takes on a red color. Opercular spot blue black, without a pale margin. Lower jaw pale blue, this color continuing backward to the gill membranes. No radiating turquoise lines on sides of head.

Juveniles and breeding adults: Juveniles have regular vertical bands with few or no spots in the interspaces. These bands tend to become double in larger fish. The dorsal spot is visible in fish as small as 1 inch total length. Breeding males become dark blue, with the breast dark red.

Size: The usual adult size is 4 to 6 inches but the IGFA all-tackle record is 4 pounds 12 ounces from Ketone Lake, Alabama, and the New York record is a 1-pound 13-ounce fish from Wilds Pond taken in May 1977.

Habitat
The bluegill occurs in standing or slow-moving water where there is vegetation or other shelter.

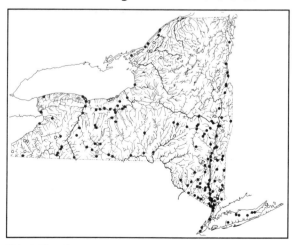

Distribution
This species is a southeastern and Mississippi Valley

fish ranging from Texas to peninsular Florida and north on the Atlantic coast to North Carolina. In the Mississippi Valley, its original range extended through the eastern parts of Oklahoma, Kansas and Nebraska to South Dakota and southern Wisconsin, into the Great Lakes drainage to the St. Lawrence watershed in New York. It now occurs throughout New York and has been introduced widely in North America and in Europe and South Africa as well.

Life History
The bluegill nests in colonies where the nests are sometimes so close that they become hexagonal rather than round. Usually, the preferred sites are on rather firm sand or mud with some debris but little vegetation. The nests are 8 to 12 inches in diameter in water 1 to 3 feet deep or shallower. Spawning occurs from May to June or July at our latitude, when air temperatures are in the high 70s F.

Bluegills have been known to live as long as 11 years. A vast amount of work has been done on their age and growth, and much of this has been summarized by Carlander. In the South, bluegills may reproduce toward the end of their first summer but in our area they do not mature until age I or II.

Dominey observed that small males unable to defend their own territories assume the coloration of the female and join in the spawning pairs on a nest, thus reproducing successfully in spite of being unable to drive the larger males from the nesting sites.

Food and Feeding
Bluegills feed during the day and most actively in the morning and afternoon. They eat a wide variety of organisms including, at times, significant amounts of plant material. Young bluegills feed on rotifers and copepod nauplii. Larger individuals eat insects and other larger particles. They feed throughout the water column.

Notes
The bluegill is frequently planted in farm ponds and other impoundments. It is also widely used in physiological studies and for toxicity tests.

Several workers have indicated that there is a fairly well-differentiated subspecies of bluegill in the Florida Peninsula, and possibly there are recognizable subdivisions in other parts of its range. The Florida form is thought to have originated when Florida was isolated from the rest of the continent during high waters of a Pleistocene interglacial period. Hubbs and Allen thought that the Florida form ranged north to North Carolina. They called it *Lepomis macrochirus purpurescens* and noted that it was distinguished by having red fins, broader lateral bars, and a modal anal ray count of 12 rather than 11. In addition, the spawning males of the southern form develop a white bar at the nape. Avise and Smith found biochemical differences at two enzyme loci, GOT-2 and Esterase-3, and were able to delimit the geographic distribution of the populations. Felly, using both morphological and genetic data,

demonstrated a zone of intergradation from southern South Carolina through central and eastern Georgia and in a narrow band across the eastern end of the Florida Panhandle to the gulf coast.

References
Breder, 1936b (life history). Hubbs and Allen, 1943 (subspecies). Snow et al., 1960 (summary). O'Hara, 1968 (temperature response). Werner, 1969 (ecology of limnetic fry). Siefert, 1972 (first food). Sadzikowski and Wallace, 1976 (food). O'Brien et al., 1976 (prey selection). Werner and Hall, 1974 (optimal foraging). Avise and Smith, 1974 (genetics). Carlander, 1977 (age and growth). Felly, 1980 (subspecies). Bain and Helfrich, 1983 (parental care). Dominey, 1980 (female mimicry). Regier, 1963a (management in farm ponds).

Names
Macrochirus is from the Greek *makros*, larger, and *cheir*, hand, in reference to the long pectoral fin.

Lepomis macrochirus Rafinesque, 1818e: 420 Ohio, Wabash, Genesee, and Licking Rivers

Helioperca macrochira, Greeley, 1936: 87 Delaware and Susquehanna watersheds

Lepomis m. macrochirus, Hubbs and Lagler, 1964: 114 (distribution)

Pomotis incisor Valenciennes *in* Cuvier and Valenciennes, 1831: 466-467 New Orleans

Helioperca incisor, Greeley, 1928: 101 Oswego drainage

Labrus pallidus Mitchill, 1815: 407 New York

Lepomis pallidus, Bean, 1903: 380 (identification uncertain)

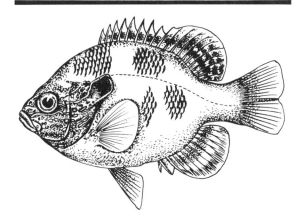

LONGEAR SUNFISH

Lepomis megalotis (Rafinesque, 1820)

Identification
The longear sunfish most resembles the pumpkinseed in that its opercular spot has a white margin with a red sector. It is, however, a stouter fish with a short, rounded pectoral fin whereas the pectoral fin of the pumpkinseed is long and pointed. The opercle of the longear has a flexible and fimbriate margin but the opercular bone of the pumpkinseed is stiff to

its margin and is smooth. There are also color differences.

Description
Body stubby and compressed but not as compressed as the pumpkinseed or bluegill. Profiles equally curved or the dorsal slightly more curved. Dorsal fin single, with a slight notch, its origin behind the pectoral base. Spiny part of the dorsal arched, with deeply incised membranes. Soft dorsal rounded. Caudal fin slightly forked, with rounded lobes. Anal origin below anterior dorsal soft rays. Anal fin rounded. Pelvic inserted below dorsal origin, retrogressive, with sharp anterior and rounded posterior corners. No pelvic axillary process. Last ray bound to body for two-thirds or more of its length. Pectoral short and asymmetrically rounded, its base oblique. Scales ctenoid, body completely scaled. Top of head scaled to eyes, cheeks and opercles scaled. Operculum with well-developed flap, opercle with flexible and fimbriate margin. Preopercle and subopercle smooth. Gill membranes separate and free from the isthmus. Lateral line complete, arched to the caudal peduncle. Counts and proportional measurements are given in Table 32.

Color: Adult males are rather uniform mottled gray above, shading to bright orange ventrally. The mottling is due to light centers on some scales and dark centers on others. The vertical fins are dusky, with orange on the membrane. Pelvic fins dusky, pectoral fins clear, with outlined rays. Sides of head with blue-green lines and rows of spots. Opercular flap dark, with a white margin that has a red sector at its middle. Caudal fin reddish brown. Females are paler and more greenish.

Juveniles and breeding adults: Breeding males are extremely colorful and many have dark reddish central spots on all of the scales on the sides of the body. The juveniles are rather plain and have only weakly developed vertical bars.

Size: The northern longear is a small species, usually only 2 to 4 inches in total length. The largest Ohio specimen reported by Trautman was 4.8 inches total length.

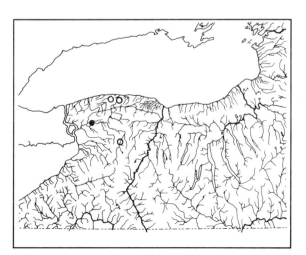

Habitat
The northern longear shows a distinct preference for dense weedy areas of larger streams.

Distribution
The longear is widely distributed from northeastern Mexico throughout the Mississippi and Great Lakes drainages to Wisconsin, Michigan and western New York and along the gulf coast to the Florida Panhandle. This species is quite variable but its subdivisions are not satisfactorily worked out. Bauer in Lee et al. (1980) noted that there may be four to six subspecies.

In New York State, it is confined to the western part of the state in Lake Erie and part of the Lake Ontario drainages. Raney mentioned its spawning in Oneida Lake, but we have found it only in Tonawanda Creek of the Lake Erie drainage.

Life History
The life history of the northern longear was studied by Hubbs and Cooper in northern Michigan where spawning takes place from late June into August. In Oneida Lake, Raney noted that it spawns in July. The nests are saucer-shaped depressions in about 1 foot of water. Hubbs and Cooper found that it matures in the third summer and that the maximum age was about 10 years. Males were about an inch longer than females.

Food and Feeding
The food habits have not been studied but it would be expected to feed on small invertebrates, especially aquatic insects.

Notes
Relatively little work has been done on the northern form, although southern populations of the longear have been studied intensively. It appears to be disappearing in New York and our few specimens were probably hybrids with the pumpkinseed. Specimens from the eastern part of the state that I first identified as this species I now believe to be hybrids between the pumpkinseed and the redbreast sunfish.

References
Hubbs and Cooper, 1935 (life history). Witt and Marzolf, 1954 (behavior of southern subspecies). Keenleyside, 1972 (nest defense). Raney, 1965b (popular account). Huck and Gunning, 1967 (behavior). Laughlin and Werner, 1980 (resource partitioning). Trautman, 1981 (Ohio). Bauer in Lee et al., 1980 (subspecies).

Names
The species name comes from the Greek *megas*, great, and *ot*, ear.

Ichthelis (Pomotis) megalotis Rafinesque, 1820a: 29 Kentucky, Licking, and Sandy Rivers, Kentucky

Lepomis peltastes Cope, 1870: 454 Huron River, Michigan

Xenotis megalotis, Greeley, 1928: 101-102 Oneida Lake

Xenotis megalotis peltastes, Greeley, 1940: 78 Lake Ontario watershed

Table 32
PROPORTIONAL MEASUREMENTS AND COUNTS OF SUNFISHES *(Lepomis)*

All proportions are expressed in percentage of standard length.

	auritus	cyanellus	gibbosus	gulosus	macro-chirus	megalotis
STANDARD LENGTH	111.7	76.6	41.1	53.1	88.5	66.4
TOTAL LENGTH	123.0	124.6	129.8	126.6	126.8	126.6
FORK LENGTH	118.1	119.2	123.9	121.8	121.3	120.9
PREDORSAL	44.9	45.5	43.8	46.3	42.1	45.5
PREANAL	65.3	65.5	64.1	63.7	63.4	65.9
PREPELVIC	41.2	44.1	44.5	41.8	42.6	42.6
DORSAL BASE	46.1	44.1	45.3	42.7	45.8	48.3
ANAL BASE	19.0	19.2	22.2	18.8	22.6	23.1
BODY DEPTH	44.7	41.9	42.3	38.0	46.4	51.5
BODY WIDTH	18.5	19.2	16.1	17.7	16.8	19.4
C. PED. DEPTH	14.6	16.2	14.2	13.6	14.3	14.9
PECTORAL ALT.	29.0	29.1	28.3	25.2	29.7	33.8
HEAD LENGTH	42.5	39.6	36.5	41.6	35.4	44.1
SNOUT LENGTH	10.8	11.4	9.3	10.0	9.6	8.7
EYE LENGTH	8.6	9.3	13.9	13.2	9.5	12.1
MOUTH LENGTH	9.4	15.6	11.5	13.0	5.9	13.2
INTERORBITAL	6.4	15.1	11.1	5.3	6.2	9.9
N (sample size)	5	5	5	1	5	5
COUNTS:						
DORSAL SPINES	X	X	X	X	X	X
DORSAL RAYS	9-12	10-12	11-12	9-10	11-12	11
ANAL RAYS	III,9-11	III,10-11	III,10-11	III,9	III,10-12	III,9-11
PECTORAL RAYS	14	13	13-14	12-13	13	12
PELVIC RAYS	I,5	I,5	I,5	I,5	I,5	I,5
GILL RAKERS	10-12	14	11	12	20	9
VERTEBRAE	30	29-30	30	28-29	29-30	30
SCALES:						
ABOVE L. L.	7	7	6	6	7	5
LATERAL LINE	41-44	43	40	39	41	36
BELOW L. L.	11-14	14	12	10	11	—

Micropterus

Although they belong to the sunfish family, members of the genus *Micropterus* are called black basses. They are elongate fishes with slightly forked tails, 3 anal spines, and more than 55 lateral line scales. They are larger and less compressed than members of the genus *Lepomis*. Six species are currently recognized.

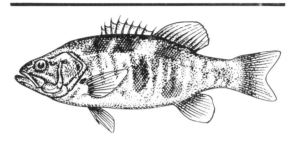

SMALLMOUTH BASS

Micropterus dolomieui
Lacepède, 1802

Identification

With its rather elongate but robust body, the smallmouth is similar in shape to the largemouth and easily differentiated from the other sunfishes in our area, all of which have deeper and more compressed bodies. While it is true that the smallmouth has a smaller mouth than the largemouth, mouth size is not always easy to judge in small individuals and color is a much easier feature to use. The smallmouth is brown or greenish bronze, plain, or with two rows of narrow vertical lines; the largemouth is greenish, with an irregular dark stripe along the middle of its side. Juvenile smallmouth have orange and black bands across the base of the tail.

The mouth of the smallmouth ends below the middle of the eye; mouth of the largemouth extends to below the back of the eye or farther. Also, the dorsal fin of the smallmouth is less deeply notched than that of the largemouth, and the pyloric caeca of the smallmouth are not branched.

Description

Body elongate, robust. Dorsal profile slightly more curved than the ventral. Dorsal origin over middle of pectoral fin. Dorsal fin notched, its margin arched, its membranes incised. Soft dorsal arched, its posterior corner rounded. Caudal slightly forked, with its middle lobes rounded. Anal fin origin under second dorsal soft ray. Anal similar in shape to soft dorsal. Pelvic fins inserted below basal one-fourth of the pectoral fin, retrogressive, with straight margin, blunt anterior corner, and rounded posterior corner. No pelvic axillary process. Last ray bound to body for one-third to one-half its length. Pectoral base oblique, pectoral fin asymmetrically rounded. Scales ctenoid. Body completely scaled, top of head scaled to eyes, cheeks and opercles scaled.

Opercle rounded, preopercle smooth, with rounded angle. Mouth terminal and slightly oblique. Gill membranes separate and free from the isthmus. Lateral line complete, arched to caudal peduncle. Counts and proportional measurements are given in Table 32.

Color: Generally greenish bronze to brown with sides lighter, shading to dirty white on belly. Sides have 8 to 11 narrow vertical bars in a row along the midside and usually a second row of similar but shorter and wider bars above, and alternating with, the first. Sometimes, there is a third series of spots on each side of the middorsal line. Sides of head with two dark lines radiating from the eye and a third line from the top of the maxillary to the operculum. Vertical fins dusky, with some pigment along the rays. Pelvic fins dusky; pectoral fins clear.

Juveniles and breeding adults: The tails of juveniles are distinctively marked with three prominent bands. The basal third of the fin is bright yellow to orange, the middle third is black, and the outer third is pale yellow or clear. Tiny fry are jet black.

Size: The IGFA all-tackle record is a fish from Kentucky that weighed 11 pounds 15 ounces. The New York State record is a 9-pound fish from Friends Lake Outlet in Warren County taken by George Tennyson in 1925.

Habitat

The smallmouth lives in streams, with slow to moderate current, and in standing water where it tends to select areas of rocky shoreline with considerable shelter. Although it tolerates a wide range of habitats, it generally occurs in cooler, clearer water than the largemouth.

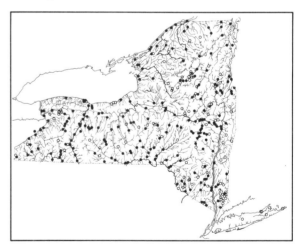

Distribution

The original distribution of the smallmouth was throughout the north-central part of the United States and southern Canada, from Minnesota and the Dakotas to the St. Lawrence drainage in southern Ontario, south in the Mississippi Valley to the Ozarks and the Tennessee drainage of northern Alabama.

Cheney did not distinguish between the largemouth and smallmouth in making the statement that the black basses were not originally found in

New York State except in waters tributary to the Great Lakes and the St. Lawrence.

The smallmouth bass has been introduced in many areas and now occurs throughout New York State. George has summarized the events that led to its distribution in the Adirondacks. According to Cheney, it entered the Mohawk system through the Erie Canal and became established in Saratoga Lake. From there it was introduced into Efner Lake of the Great Sacandaga watershed and then into the Schroon system. In 1872, Seth Green successfully introduced it into Raquette Lake and it had spread throughout most of the Adirondacks by the turn of the century.

Life History

The smallmouth is a spring spawner and begins nesting when the water temperature reaches 62 to 65 F. One nest was reported where the water temperature was 55.4 F. Nests are usually built over gravel along shores where the water is 2 to 20 feet deep, the average being about 3 feet. Usually, the diameter of the nest is roughly twice the length of the fish. The males construct and guard the nest. Females ready to spawn become more prominently marked as their dark markings become more intense and the background becomes paler. The female enters the nest and circles or hovers there. Every 2 or 3 minutes she rubs her belly against the gravel bottom. During spawning, the fish lie side by side with the male upright and the female inclined at a 45-degree angle. The eggs are laid during episodes of 4 to 6 seconds duration separated by intervals of 22 to 45 seconds. Females remain in the nest for as long as 2 hours or more. After one female leaves, another may enter the same nest, the male remaining receptive for 30 to 36 hours and usually spawning with at least three females. Males guard the nest for the entire incubation period. Hatching takes 7 to 16 days depending on temperature; at 50 to 60 F, the eggs hatched in 21 days. The newly hatched larvae remain motionless in the nest at first, then rise as a dense school that is herded by the male for a short time.

Food and Feeding

Smallmouth bass are opportunistic predators and feed on tadpoles, frogs, and almost any small animal in the water. Insects, crayfish, and fish make up most of the diet. Small individuals feed on plankton and invertebrates, switching to larger items as they become larger. In many waters, yellow perch are the prey they consume most frequently.

Notes

Smallmouth bass are among the most important game fishes in New York. However, their introduction into the Adirondacks and other areas has probably had a profound effect on other native species, including trout and some of the items trout feed on.

References

Cheney, 1897 (occurrence in New York). Hubbs and Bailey, 1938 (general account); 1940 (relationships). Tester, 1930 (spawning); 1932a (food); 1932b (growth rates). Reighard, 1906 (life history). Westman, 1941 (life history and management). Greeley, 1954 (range); 1955a (popular account). Webster, 1954a, 1954c (life history and management). Stone et al., 1954 (St. Lawrence). Raney, 1959 (young). Latta, 1963 (life history). Schneider, 1971 (SCUBA observations). Horning and Pearson, 1973 (temperature). Robbins and McCrimmon, 1974 (distribution). Tandler and Beamish, 1979 (activity). James, 1930 (spawning). Buynak and Gurzynski, 1978b (growth in polluted waters). Burdick et al., 1954 (lethal oxygen concentration). Forney, 1961, 1972 (management). George, 1981a (Adirondacks).

Names

The smallmouth bass is named for M. Dolomieu, a French geologist for whom the rock dolomite is also named.

Micropterus dolomieu Lacepède, 1802: 324-326 (no locality)

Micropterus dolomieu dolomieu, Hubbs and Bailey, 1940: 34-36 (systematics)

Bodianus achigan Rafinesque, 1817b: 120 New York

Cichla fasciata Lesueur, 1822a: 216-218 Lake Erie at Erie and Buffalo; Lake George

Centrarchus fasciatus, DeKay, 1842: 28-29 New York

Cichla minima, Lesueur, 1822a: 220-221 Lake Erie lagoons

Grystes salmoides (non Lacepède) Cuvier in Cuvier and Valenciennes, 1829: 54-58 New York and the Wabash River

Micropterus salmoides Jordan, 1876: 230

Centrarchus obscurus DeKay, 1842: 30 Onondaga Creek, New York

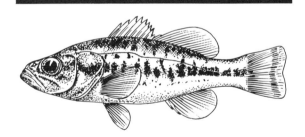

LARGEMOUTH BASS

Micropterus salmoides (Lacepède, 1802)

Identification

Compared to other members of the sunfish family, the largemouth and smallmouth bass are both elongate, robust fish, a shape that we have come to know as bass-like. As the name implies, the largemouth bass has a larger mouth, with the end of the maxillary falling below or beyond the rear margin of the eye. The largemouth also has a more deeply notched dorsal fin, larger scales, and bifurcate pyloric caeca.

The most conspicuous differences, however, are

those of color. The largemouth is a greenish fish, with a pronounced stripe running along the mid-side whereas the smallmouth is a bronze or brassy greenish color, with two rows of of narrow vertical bars on the upper side of the body. Juvenile smallmouths have black and orange bands on their caudal fins but the tail of juvenile largemouth is clear or with a faint reddish tinge.

Description

Body elongate, robust, profiles equally curved. Dorsal fin single, deeply notched, its origin over the basal one-fourth of the pectoral fin. Spiny part arched, with the membranes incised. Soft part arched, with the posterior corner rounded. Caudal slightly forked, with blunt lobes. Anal fin origin below second dorsal soft ray, its margin arched, its corners rounded. Pelvic fin inserted below the dorsal origin, retrogressive, its anterior corner pointed, its posterior corner round. No pelvic axillary process. Last pelvic ray bound to body for one-half its length. Pectoral fin asymmetrically rounded, its base oblique. Scales ctenoid, body completely scaled, top of head scaled to back of eyes, cheeks and opercles fully scaled. Operculum with two points. Preopercle rounded,smooth. Mouth terminal, oblique, maxillary reaching to or beyond the posterior margin of the eye. Supramaxillary well developed. Gill membranes separate and free from the isthmus. Lateral line complete, arched. Gill rakers short. Pyloric caeca bifurcate. Counts and proportional measurements are given in Table 33.

Color: Dark green above, shading to white ventrally, with a broad midlateral stripe that is irregular on the body and has a nearly straight upper margin on the caudal peduncle. There are patches of dark scales above and below the lateral stripe, these sometimes forming short longitudinal lines. Sides of head with dark stripes, one from the back of the eye to the dark spot above the point of the opercle, one from the lower part of the eye to the angle of the preopercle, and a short line from the upper margin of the maxillary to the edge of the lower limb of the preopercle. Vertical fins dusky, with the rays outlined. Paired fins clear.

Juveniles and breeding adults: Post-larval largemouth are clear, with weak pigment. The lateral stripe develops when they are less than an inch long. Juveniles are miniatures of the adults.

Size: The IGFA all-tackle record is 22 pounds 4 ounces from Montgomery Lake in Georgia. The New York record was a 10-pound 12-ounce fish from Chadwick Lake caught October 1975 by M. Rutkowski.

Habitat

The largemouth is a fish of warm, weedy parts of lakes, ponds, and streams.

Distribution

The original range of the largemouth is somewhat more southern than that of the smallmouth, extending from central and northern Mexico east along the gulf coast to peninsular Florida, where it is represented by a separate subspecies, and north on the Atlantic coast to South Carolina. In the Mississippi Valley, it ranged north to South Dakota, southern Wisconsin and across southern Ontario to Quebec in the Great Lakes drainage. It has been introduced into many other parts of the world.

In the 1896 report of the Commissioners of Fisheries, Game, and Forests, Cheney stated, "In nature's distribution of black bass New York State was omitted except in waters having connections with the Great Lakes or the St. Lawrence." He believed that the Erie Canal enabled it to spread to the Mohawk-Hudson drainage and that it was then stocked in New England about 1850. Its present distribution is throughout the state.

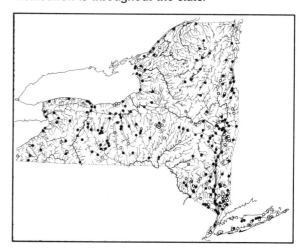

Life History

The largemouth spawns in deeper waters than the sunfishes, usually in depths of 1 to 4 feet. Males build nests 2 to 3 feet in diameter by sweeping the bottom. Usually, the nests are at least 30 feet apart. Males entice females into the nest by circling and nipping them. Once in the nest, the female tilts her body or lies alongside the male who remains upright. Eggs are emitted in small batches at intervals of about 30 seconds. After spawning, the female leaves the nest although she, or another female, may return to spawn again later. The eggs hatch in 3 or 4 days and the young remain near the nest until they are about 0.75 inch long. Maturity is achieved at age V and largemouth bass can live as long as 15 years. Females produce 2,000 to 7,000 eggs per pound of body weight. Growth rates are extremely variable.

Food and Feeding

Until they are 2 inches long, largemouth juveniles feed on plankton and miscellaneous insects and other invertebrates. As they get larger, their diet shifts to fishes and other large items and, in fact, they will try to eat almost anything that moves.

Notes

Largemouth bass from Florida reach a much larger size and are generally recognized as constituting a separate subspecies, *Micropterus salmoides floridanus*. Florida largemouth bass are currently being stocked in other parts of the country.

References

Reighard, 1906 (life history). Cheney, 1897 (distribution in New York). Hubbs and Bailey, 1940 (systematics). Lewis and Flickinger, 1967 (home range). Regier, 1963a, 1963b (management in ponds). Dudley and Eipper, 1975 (oxygen requirements). Cech et al., 1979 (temperature and respiration). Pickett, 1979 (pughead). Heimstra et al., 1969 (effects of turbidity). Nyberg, 1971 (prey capture). Heidinger, 1976 (summary). Hackney and Linkous, 1978 (striking behavior). Mraz et al., 1961 (summary).

Names

The name *salmoides* comes from *salmo*, trout and the Latin *oides*, having the form of.

Labrus salmoides Lacepède, 1802: 716-718 Charleston, South Carolina

Grystes salmoides, DeKay, 1842: 26 New York (May include more than one species.)

Grystes megastoma Garlick, 1857: 108-110 Lake Erie

Aplites salmoides, Greeley, 1927: 64 Genesee drainage

Huro salmoides, Greeley, 1939: 43 Long Island

Pomoxis

The crappies are the most specialized members of the family Centrarchidae. They have a large number of anal spines (5 or more), few dorsal spines (6 to 8), a strongly compressed body, fewer than 55 lateral line scales, and a large mouth. There are only two species in the genus, both of which live in New York.

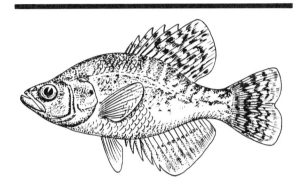

WHITE CRAPPIE

Pomoxis annularis
Rafinesque, 1818

Identification

Crappies are distinguished from other sunfishes by their compressed and rhombic bodies, long anal fins with six spines, and short dorsal fins with six to eight spines. The black and white crappies are separable by the length of the dorsal fin base. If the length of the base of the dorsal fin is stepped forward from the dorsal fin origin, it will reach the rear margin of the eye if the fish is a black crappie and only to the occiput if the fish is a white crappie. The shorter dorsal fin of the white crappie has six or seven spines rather than seven or eight. White crappies tend to be paler than black crappies but there is considerable variation and color patterns alone are not reliable for identification.

Small young-of-the-year crappies are banded and resemble juveniles of *Lepomis* species but young *Lepomis* have only three anal spines.

Description

Body rhombic, deepest at center, compressed. Dorsal and ventral profiles about equally curved. Dorsal fin origin midway between the caudal base and the tip of the snout. Dorsal fin progressive to fourth soft ray, then retrogressive. Soft dorsal rounded. Caudal weakly forked, its lobes blunt. Anal origin below third dorsal spine, similar in shape to the dorsal. Pelvic insertion below lower end of pectoral base. Pelvic retrogressive, with pointed anterior and rounded posterior corners. No pelvic axillary process, last ray bound by membrane for four-fifths of its length. Pectoral fin asymmetrically rounded, its base oblique. Body fully scaled, cheeks, opercles, and top of head forward to orbits scaled. Mouth large, maxillary reaching to below center of eye. Supramaxillary much longer than width of maxillary.

Operculum pointed, preopercle angled with fine serrations at the angle. Suborbital margin finely serrated. Gill membranes separate and free from the isthmus. Lateral line complete, arched. Counts and proportional measurements are given in Table 33.

Color: Generally, silvery white, shading to pale olive dorsally. Upper sides with patches of dark scales that tend to coalesce to form a mottled pattern, often forming irregular vertical bars. Fins mottled, with rows of pale spots across the soft parts of the vertical fins.

Juveniles and breeding adults: Juveniles are pale, nearly transparent, with pronounced vertical bars. There are no bright breeding colors.

Size: The IGFA all-tackle record is a 5-pound 3-ounce fish from Enid Dam, Mississippi.

Habitat

The white crappie occurs in lakes and ponds and slower parts of streams. It can tolerate considerable turbidity and occurs over silty bottoms as well as in vegetated areas.

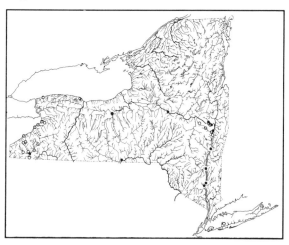

Distribution

The original range of the white crappie seems to have been from western New York and southern Ontario through southern Michigan to southern Wisconsin and South Dakota. It occurs throughout the Mississippi drainage and west to the eastern parts of Nebraska, Kansas, Oklahoma, and Texas to southern Mexico, then east along the gulf coast at least to Alabama. It may have been somewhat more widely distributed, but its original range is difficult to identify because it has been stocked in many areas across the Southwest and on the west coast as far north as southern Oregon.

Life History

Possibly, because it lives in turbid water and spawns in deeper waters, the life history of the white crappie is not as well known as that of the black crappie. Hansen described the nests along the shore of a lake in Springfield, Illinois where the sod bank had been undercut about 12 inches. The nests were 2 to 4 feet apart in water 4 to 8 inches deep, and located in sheltered areas either under the overhanging bank or where they were sheltered by an elm sapling. The bottom was hard clay, with no silt, and the

eggs were deposited on tree root fibers and other vegetation above the bottom. One nest was under a boathouse and was a small depression fanned down to clean gravel.

Siefert described the nesting and spawning in artificial ponds in South Dakota. Nests were areas swept clear of loose silt but not actual depressions. The nests were usually about 30 cm in diameter and located near some underwater objects where the bottom was gravel, rocks, or a clump of sod. Most of the sweeping was done by the males but sometimes females also exhibited the sweeping behavior. Spawning commenced with the female approaching the male on the nest. At first, he chased her but in time she refused to retreat and circled him several times before coming to lie parallel to him in the nest and facing the same direction. After remaining motionless for a few moments, they came together, moving upward and forward with their bodies quivering. Usually, the female moved under the male and pushed him upward during the 2- to 5-second episodes. The spawning acts were usually repeated after a period of 30 seconds to 2 hours. Up to 50 spawning episodes were completed in a single session lasting as long as 145 minutes. Occasionally, a second male would try to join the spawning pair but was usually chased away by the primary male. Most spawning took place between 8 am and 4 pm, usually starting before noon. Cloudy water and minor temperature variations did not interrupt the spawning. Siefert noted that the eggs were adhesive and often more eggs were on the vegetation surrounding the nest than in the nest itself. Most eggs had sand and other fine particles adhering to their surface.

Spawning began when the water temperatures were between 14 and 23 C and the hatching required 93 hours at 14.4 C, 42 hours at 22.8 C. The young fish left the nest 95 hours after hatching when they were 4.1 to 4.6 mm long.

Food and Feeding

The postlarvae fed on copepod nauplii at first, then on *Cyclops*, and still later on cladocerans. Larger white crappies fed on a variety of aquatic insects and other invertebrates as well as small fishes.

Notes

The two species of crappies sometimes hybridize with each other but not with other sunfishes.

References

Hansen, 1943 (nesting); 1951 (life history); 1965 (ecology). Morgan, 1954 (life history). Siefert, 1965 (scale development); 1968 (reproduction and feeding); 1969a (larval development); 1969b (biology). Johnson, 1945 (age and growth). Marcy, 1954 (food and growth). Mathur and Robbins, 1971 (feeding chronology). Mathur, 1972 (food habits).

Names

The species name is from the Latin *annulus*, a ring, probably in reference to the color pattern of vertical bars that partly encircle the body.

Pomoxis annularis Rafinesque 1818e: 417 Falls of the Ohio

Pomoxis annularis, Greeley, 1929: 178 Erie-Niagara drainage

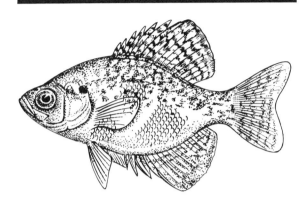

BLACK CRAPPIE

Pomoxis nigromaculatus (Lesueur, 1829)

Identification
The crappies are easily recognized by their highly compressed, diamond-shaped bodies, the presence of more than three anal spines, and their short dorsal fins with only six to eight spines. Black crappies have seven or eight dorsal spines and the base of the dorsal fin is so long that when the length of the base is stepped forward of the dorsal origin it reaches to, or close to, the back of the eye. The white crappie has six or seven dorsal spines and the base of the dorsal fin is much shorter than the distance from the dorsal origin to the eye.

Description
Body deep, rhombic and strongly compressed. Dorsal and ventral profiles equally curved. Dorsal fin single, without notch, its origin closer to snout than to caudal base. Spiny part progressive, its membranes deeply incised. Soft dorsal arched with its posterior angle rounded. Caudal fin slightly forked with blunt lobes. Anal origin below third or fourth dorsal spine, similar to dorsal in shape. Pelvic fin inserted below the upper base of the pectoral, retrogressive, with straight margin, sharp anterior and rounded posterior corners. No axillary process. Last ray bound to the body for its entire length. Pectoral fin asymmetrically rounded, its base steeply oblique. Scales ctenoid, body completely scaled. Top of head scaled to the interorbital, cheeks and opercles scaled. Operculum with two blunt points. Preopercle weakly toothed at angle, suborbital with small serrations posteriorly. Mouth terminal, oblique, maxillary reaching to below center of the eye. Gill membranes separate and free from the isthmus. Lateral line complete, arched. Counts and proportional measurements are given in Table 33.

Color: The black crappie is pale silvery white on the sides and belly, dark green dorsally with dense patches of dark scales that coalesce to form irregu-

lar blotches and marblings. There is a dark vertical bar through the eye and suborbital region. The vertical fins are dusky, with pale spots in irregular rows. The pelvic fins have a white leading edge and are otherwise lightly punctate. The pectoral fins are clear.

Juveniles and breeding adults: The juveniles are more transparent with irregular vertical bands.

Size: The IGFA record is held by a 4-pound fish from Westwego, Louisiana. The New York record weighed 3 pounds 1 ounce and was caught in Indian Lake by Albert Schuldwachter.

Habitat
Black crappies are less tolerant of silt and turbidity than white crappies and are more apt to be found in clear water where there is abundant vegetation.

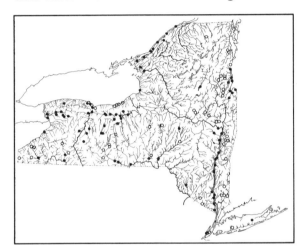

Distribution
The original range of the black crappie was from the St. Lawrence Valley of southern Quebec west to southeastern Manitoba, the eastern half of North and South Dakota, Nebraska, Kansas, Oklahoma, and east Texas. On the gulf coast, it ranged east to the tip of peninsular Florida and north to northeastern Virginia. West of the Appalachians, it reached the Great Lakes and extended eastward to western and northern New York.

It is now generally distributed through New York State but is not very common in the Adirondack Mountains.

Life History
The spawning season is May to July when the water temperatures are higher than 68 F. Nests 8 or 9 inches in diameter are constructed by fanning depressions in water 10 inches to 2 feet deep. Nests are usually built in sandy bottom in weedy areas and are generally at least 5 or 6 feet apart. The eggs are slightly less than one mm in diameter and hatch in 3 to 5 days. The maximum age is about 10 years in the North, less in the South.

Food and Feeding
Young crappies are plankton feeders but older fish feed on insects and fish. Considerable feeding takes place at night.

References

Breder, 1936b (reproductive habits). Huish, 1954 (life history in Florida). Siefert, 1969a (identification of larvae). Johnson, 1945 (age and growth).

Names

The name of the species comes from the Latin *niger*, black, and *maculatus*, spotted.

  Cantharus nigro-maculatus Lesueur *in* Cuvier and Valenciennes, 1829: 88-89

  Pomoxis nigromaculatus, Bailey, 1941: 23 (nomenclature)

  Pomoxis sparoides (non Lacepède, which is *Centrarchus macropterus*), Greeley, 1927: 63 Genesee drainage

---

TABLE 33
AVERAGE PROPORTIONAL MEASUREMENTS AND COUNTS OF BLACK BASSES AND CRAPPIES (*Micropterus* and *Pomoxis*)

All proportions are expressed in percentage of standard length.

	Micropterus		*Pomoxis*	
	dolomieui	salmoides	annularis	nigromaculatus
ST. LENGTH (mm)	71.5	102.8	46.8	67.2
TOTAL LENGTH	123.6	123.4	132.2	133.8
FORK LENGTH	119.0	120.3	126.7	125.7
PREDORSAL	44.0	41.7	50.5	48.7
PREANAL	66.2	66.1	52.0	52.5
PREPELVIC	38.3	38.6	38.3	40.5
DORSAL BASE	40.5	41.9	30.1	36.3
ANAL BASE	14.7	16.5	32.4	36.0
BODY DEPTH	29.0	31.4	34.5	40.4
BODY WIDTH	15.8	16.5	11.3	13.3
C.PED. DEPTH	11.7	12.7	12.6	13.0
PECTORAL ALT.	18.0	21.1	21.8	28.0
HEAD LENGTH	37.4	37.1	37.4	38.6
SNOUT	11.1	9.6	8.0	8.0
EYE	8.3	7.2	10.3	13.1
MOUTH LENGTH	10.3	14.8	14.2	17.2
INTERORB	10.3	7.7	7.7	7.4
N (sample size)	5	5	5	5
COUNTS:				
DORSAL SPINES	X	X-XI	VI-VII	VII-VIII
DORSAL RAYS	13-15	12-13	16-18	15-18
ANAL RAYS	III,11-12	III,10-12	VI,17-18	VI,17-18
PECTORAL RAYS	13-17	12-14	13-15	13-15
PELVIC RAYS	I,5	I,5	I,5	I,5
GILL RAKERS	8-11	8-10	28-32	27-29
VERTEBRAE	31-32	32	32	33-34
SCALES:				
ABOVE L. L.	13	7	6	7
LATERAL LINE	68-78	60-68	34-35	36-41
BELOW L.L.	18	13	13-14	12

PERCHES

PERCIDAE

The true perches are strictly freshwater fishes of the Northern Hemisphere. They are typical spiny-rayed fishes with two dorsal fins which may be quite close together, and one or two anal spines. Most are rather elongate and slender species, with strongly ctenoid scales. They have no subocular shelf.

The family is small and the species are all similar except for size. Collette (1963) reviewed the family and proposed the following classification:

Percidae
Subfamily Percinae
Tribe Percini
    Perca (North America and Europe, 3 species)
    Gymnocephalus (Europe, 3 species)
    Percarina (Europe, 1 species)
Tribe Etheostomatini (North America)
    Percina (more than 25 species)
    Ammocrypta (7 species)
    Etheostoma (more than 80 species)
Subfamily Luciopercinae
Tribe Luciopercini
    Stizostedion (North America and Europe,
        5 species)

Tribe Romanichthyini (Europe)
    Zingel (3 species)
    Romanichthys (1 species)

Both the yellow perch and the walleye are important commercial species in Lake Erie and the sauger used to be until it became commercially extinct in the late 1930s. Walleyes and perch are important sport fishes in inland lakes and streams. The darters (Etheostomatini) are too small to be of sport or commercial interest, but they are among the most colorful fishes in the world and they have an interesting variety of breeding habits. Two recent books with keys and excellent color photographs of darters in breeding colors are Page (1983) and Kuehne and Barbour (1983). A valuable study of the nomenclature of darters with a list of the known type specimens is Collette and Knapp (1966). Collette et al. (1979) present the results of a recent international symposium with papers of general interest to the student of percid biology, especially the paper on zoogeography by Collette and Banarescu (1977). Danyman (1979) studied the chromosomes of several species.

KEY TO THE SPECIES OF PERCHES IN NEW YORK

A. Margin of preopercle smooth or slightly dentate but never strongly serrated. Mouth small, maxillary not reaching to below middle of the eye. Size small, adults less than 6 inches total length, usually less than 4 inches.

                                            E.

A'. Preopercle strongly toothed. Mouth larger, mouth reaching nearly to, or beyond, a point below the middle of the eye. Adults usually longer than 7 inches total length.

B. Jaws with small teeth of uniform size and arranged in bands. Body conspicuously marked with even vertical bands. Pelvic fins close together. Pelvic fin with two spines and six to eight soft rays.
Perca flavescens   **Yellow perch, p. 337**

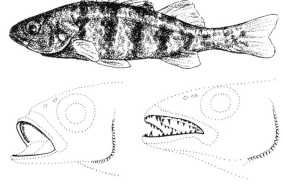

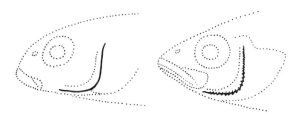

Preopercles of darters (left) and other perches.

Teeth of yellow perch (left) and walleye.

B'. Jaws with some enlarged canine teeth. Body color uniform or with indistinct, irregular and sloping saddle-shaped bands. Space between the pelvic fins wide, exceeding the length of the pelvic fin base. Anal fin II, 12 or 13.

C. Posterior end of spiny dorsal fin without a conspicuous black blotch. Usually there is no white tip on the lower lobe of the caudal fin. Dorsal fins with rows of distinct round black spots. Back crossed by three or four saddle-shaped bands, indistinct in young. Pyloric caeca usually four to six, extremes three to nine, each shorter than the stomach.
Stizostedion canadense   **Sauger, p. 347**

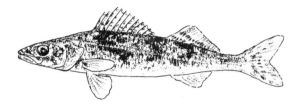

C'. Posterior end of spiny dorsal fin with a conspicuous black blotch (also present in yellow perch). Lower tip of tail fin white. Dorsal fin with various mottlings but not regular rows of round black spots. Body with irregular crossbands. Usually there are three pyloric caeca, each about the same length as the stomach.
Stizostedion vitreum   **D.**

D. Color usually yellowish or brassy, rarely pale gray. Eyes small and wide apart, the bony interorbital width contained 1.1 to 1.4 times in the eye length.
Stizostedion v. vitreum   **Walleye, p. 348**

D'. Color bluish gray, paler below. Eyes larger and closer together, bony interorbital width contained 1.4 to 2.0 times in the eye length.
Stizostedion v. glaucum   **Blue pike, p. 348**

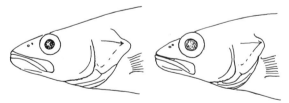

Lateral view of head of walleye (left) and blue pike.

E. (A. Small fishes with the preopercle nearly smooth.) Body very slender with large naked areas, the scales confined to a narrow row along the lateral line. Body nearly colorless except for rows of small round spots along the sides and middorsal line.
Ammocrypta pellucida
          Eastern sand darter, p. 318

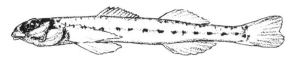

Eastern sand darter, *Ammocrypta pellucida*

E'. Body less slender with sides completely scaled. Variously pigmented but not almost colorless.

F. Space between the pelvic fin bases with at least one large star-shaped scale. Belly often with a midventral row of enlarged stellate scales.
genus *Percina*   **S.**

F'. No enlarged scales between the pelvic fin bases. Belly may be naked or scaled but never with a midventral row of modified scales.

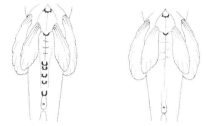

Midventral scales of *Percina* species.

G. Snout pointed or rather blunt but not conspicuously overhanging the mouth. Maxillary separated from the preorbital region for most of its length by a deep groove.
                                                      I.

G'. Snout very blunt, overhanging the mouth. Premaxillary protractile but maxillary attached to the preorbital region for most of its length with only a short groove at its posterior end.
Etheostoma blennioides
                              Greenside darter, H.

Suborbital region of greenside darter.
Only the tip of the maxillary bone is separated from the suborbital region by a groove.

H. Lateral line scales 57 to 71, average 65.4. Allegheny and Upper Genesee systems.
Etheostoma b. blennioides   **p. 319**

H'. Lateral line scales 50 to 63, average 55 to 58 depending on population. Erie, Ontario, including the Lower Genesee, and Mohawk drainages.
Etheostoma b. pholidotum   **p. 319**

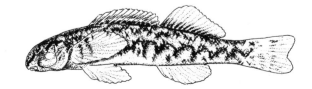

I. (G. Snout not especially overhanging the mouth, maxillary not bound to the preorbital region.) Two anal spines.

L.

I'. A single anal spine.

J. Infraorbital canal usually interrupted with four pores in the anterior section and two in the posterior. Preopercular-mandibular canal with eight or nine pores. Pectoral rays 10 or 11, sometimes 12. Mouth horizontal, profile before the eyes steeply declivous so the profile is almost vertical at the mouth. Six or more X- or W-shaped marks along the sides of the body.
Etheostoma nigrum   **Johnny darter, p. 330**

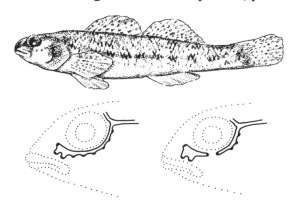

Soborbital canal of tessellated (left) and johnny darters.

J'. Infraorbital canal usually complete with eight pores. Preopercular-mandibular canal with 10 or 11 pores. Mouth somewhat oblique, snout pointed, profile sloping at the mouth. Nine to eleven X- or W-shaped marks along the midsides.
Etheostoma olmstedi   **Tessellated darter, K.**

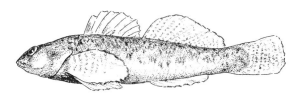

K. Nape usually naked; cheek partly to completely scaled. Breast usually naked. Belly partly scaled.
Etheostoma o. olmstedi   **p. 332**

K'. Nape, cheek, breast, and belly fully scaled. Hudson River estuary.
Etheostoma o. atromaculatum   **p. 332**

L. (I. Anal spines two.) Gill membranes separate, or at most only slightly joined anteriorly, but never broadly joined across the isthmus.

O.

L'. Gill membranes broadly joined across the isthmus.

M. Lateral line incomplete. Dorsal spines six to nine, short and often ending in fleshy knobs in mature males.
Etheostoma flabellare   **Fantail darter, p. 325**

M'. Lateral line complete, dorsal spines more than nine, longer, and without fleshy tips.

N. Dorsal spines 12. Cheeks naked. A dark band extends downward and forward across the nape to a blotch above the pectoral fin and behind the gill opening.
Etheostoma variatum   **Variegate darter, p. 333**

N'. Dorsal spines fewer than 12. Cheeks scaled but the scales are often embedded and difficult to see. No oblique band anterior to the dorsal fin but the rounded upper ends of two dark blotches almost meet in the midline, leaving a characteristic pale space just ahead of the dorsal fin.
Etheostoma zonale   **Banded darter, p. 335**

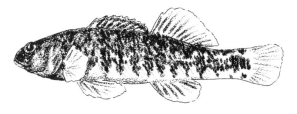

O. (L. Gill membranes separate or slightly joined across the isthmus.) Lateral line incomplete, ending below spiny or soft dorsal fin. Color pattern of sides mottled, or with bars, but never with narrow lines between the scales.

Q.

O'. Lateral line complete, or nearly so, ending near the caudal fold. Sides with narrow longitudinal lines of pigment between the scales.

P. Soft dorsal, anal, and caudal fins with a distinct black marginal band (the very edge of the fin is pale) and a pale submarginal band that is orange or red in life. Head only moderately pointed, contained about 3.5 to 3.8 times in the standard length. Tail square in young, slightly emarginate in adults. Lateral scales 50 to 60, usually about 55.
Etheostoma camurum

Bluebreast darter, p. 322

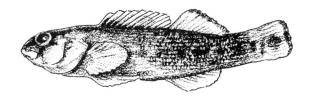

P'. Soft dorsal, anal, and caudal fins of adults without black marginal bands. Head long and pointed, about 3.2 to 3.6 times in the standard length. Tail rounded. Lateral scales 56 to 63, usually about 60.
Etheostoma maculatum **Spotted darter, p. 329**

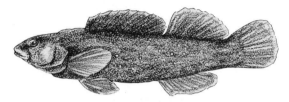

Q. (O. Lateral line quite incomplete.) Body rather deep, its greatest depth about 4 to 4.5 times in the standard length. Scales large, 40 to 50 in lateral series. Lateral line ending below the soft dorsal fin.
Etheostoma caeruleum **Rainbow darter, p. 321**

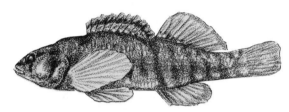

Q'. Body slender, its greatest depth 5.5 to 6.5 times in the standard length. Scales small, 47 to 62 in lateral series, usually more than 50.

R. Lateral line only slightly arched and longer, ending below the soft dorsal fin. Scales 53 to 62, 4 or more scale rows between the lateral line and the base of the spiny dorsal fin. Erie and Ontario drainages.
Etheostoma exile **Iowa darter, p. 324**

R'. Lateral line noticeably arched and shorter, ending below the spiny dorsal. Scales 47 to 53, only 3 scale rows between the lateral line and the base of the spiny dorsal fin. Eastern Long Island and coast drainages.
Etheostoma fusiforme **Swamp darter, p. 328**

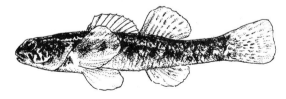

S. (F. One or more modified scales between the pelvic fins.) Snout pointed or blunt but not conical and not protruding in front of the mouth. Color pattern variable but not of alternating long and short vertical bars.

U.

S'. Snout conical and overhanging the mouth. Body pale yellowish and conspicuously marked with alternating long and short, narrow dark vertical bars.
Percina caprodes **Logperch, T.**

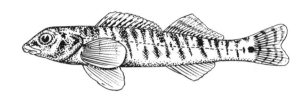

T. Nape entirely scaled. Bars uniform and regular.
Percina c. caprodes **p. 338**

T'. Nape with a triangular scaleless area. Bars less regular and often expanded at their lower ends into a midlateral row of blotches.
Percina c. semifasciata **p. 338**

U. (S. Snout not conical and not protruding in front of the mouth.) Premaxillaries protractile, the upper lip separated from the tip of the snout by a groove.
Percina copelandi **Channel darter, p. 340**

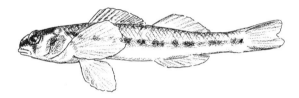

U'. Premaxillaries not protractile, the upper lip connected to the snout by a fleshy frenum (bridge) that interrupts the groove between the upper lip and the snout at the middle. (In *Percina shumardi* the frenum is sometimes crossed by a shallow groove.)

V. Belly mostly scaleless except for a patch of scales immediately in front of the anus. No midventral row of modified scales. Not definitely recorded from New York.
Percina shumardi **River darter**

V'. Belly mostly scaled. Males with a midventral row of enlarged stellate scales.

W. Back with squarish, saddle-shaped blotches that line up with the midlateral blotches to form interrupted vertical bars.
Percina evides **Gilt darter, p. 341**

W'. Saddle-shaped blotches, if present, more or less alternating with the midlateral blotches, not forming vertical bars.

X. Ventral sides of head with one to three dusky blotches, the last of which sometimes joins the sub-orbital bar to form a sickle-shaped "teardrop" mark below the eye. Head long and narrow. Midlateral blotches almost fused to form a longitudinal stripe that varies in width.
Percina macrocephala
Longhead darter, p. 342

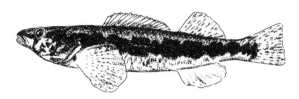

X'. Ventral side of head without blotches. Head wider, snout short. Midlateral blotches more or less separate, not forming an undulating band.

Y. Cheeks with scales.
Percina maculata   **Blackside darter, p. 343**

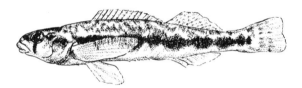

Y' Cheeks scaleless.
Percina peltata   **Shield darter, p. 344**

Ammocrypta

The genus *Ammocrypta* includes seven species of slender elongate darters with reduced scales. The preopercle is weakly serrated and there is one anal spine. Most of the species are nearly transparent. The belly and breast are without modified scales.

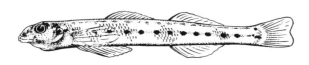

EASTERN SAND DARTER

Ammocrypta pellucida (Putnam, 1863)

Identification

The eastern sand darter is the most distinctive darter in the state. It is extremely long and slender, very pale, and has large areas of the body without scales.

Tiny young might be confused with correspondingly small johnny or tessellated darters but even when they are only a few millimeters long, the shape of the sand darter is distinctive.

Description

Body terete and very elongate. Profiles almost parallel. Dorsal origin over distal part of pectoral fin. Dorsal fins separated by a wide space. Third dorsal spine longest. Margin of spiny dorsal arched, interspinous membrane little indented. Soft dorsal low anteriorly, its rays progressively longer. Caudal emarginate, little rays equal to longest upper ray. Caudal lobes rounded. Anal origin below third dorsal soft ray. Anal rays progressively longer to antepenultimate. Pelvics inserted behind pectoral base well in advance of the dorsal origin. Pelvics pointed, no axillary process. Pectoral base vertical, pectoral pointed. Gill membranes joined anteriorly. Mouth small, horizontal, maxillary reaching to front of eye. Snout declivitous, lower jaw included. Scales on anterior part of body confined to a band along the side; caudal peduncle completely scaled. Lateral line complete. Counts and proportional measurements are given in Table 34.

Color: (from fresh specimens collected 17 August 1979) Sides with 11 to 15 oval spots that are shorter than the interspaces. These spots have their long axis horizontal and form a row just below the lateral line. Scales with sparse melanophores along their posterior margin but not completely outlined. Scales near the anal fin lack pigment. Dorsum with irregular spots that tend to be paired except along the base of the spiny dorsal fin where they alternate. On top of the caudal peduncle, these spots join to form short, irregular, crossbars. In larger specimens there are other spots and smudges on the dorsal surface, irregularly placed, but more abundant along the margin of the naked middorsal region.

Sides of snout with a dark spot in front of each eye. Tip of snout and upper lip densely pigmented. A dark line curves along the inner margin of each nostril, the two suggesting a lyre shape when the fish is viewed head on. There is a small spot at the tip of the snout.

Fresh specimens have a broad yellow stripe on the middorsal surface from the tip of the snout to the base of the tail. A bright yellow line about two scales wide extends from the gill opening to the base of the caudal rays. All fins are hyaline except that there is a bar at the base of the caudal fin formed by melanophores along the margins of the fin rays. The pelvic fins of one large individual have similar subbasal bars and bright yellow pigment on the basal half of the inner two rays. The iris has a golden ring around the pupil.

Juveniles and breeding adults: Breeding tubercles are present on the ventral surface of the pelvic spines and pelvic rays, the dorsal surface of the pelvic rays and on the anal spine and rays (Williams, 1975).

Size: The largest specimens are slightly longer than 2 inches standard length.

Habitat

The sand darter is restricted to moderate-sized streams with clean sandy bottoms. This species is apparently becoming scarce throughout much of its range, and this decline is ascribed to habitat degradation. The sand darter requires fine sand with currents slow enough to retain sand but fast enough to prevent deposition of fine silt. Clearing the land for agriculture has probably resulted in silting of many streams that were formerly suited for the sand darter.

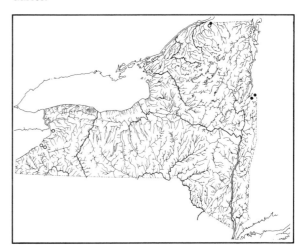

Distribution

The eastern sand darter occurs east of the Mississippi from southern Illinois and Kentucky through the Mississippi, Ohio, and Great Lakes drainages to southern Michigan and southern Ontario. It occurs in Lake Erie and its tributaries but the only New York records are from Cattaraugus Creek near Gowanda and Irving, and Cazenovia Creek near Buffalo where it was taken in 1893 by A. J. Woolman. There are no records from Lake Ontario but it is present in the St. Lawrence River near Montreal where it was reported as common as recently as 1941. The Survey collected it in the Little Salmon River near Ft. Covington and J. Platt confirmed that it still is present by collecting a single specimen in 1980. In 1935, it was taken in the Lamoille River in Vermont about four miles from Lake Champlain. In 1979, we found a breeding population (as indicated by the presence of juveniles) in the Mettawee River south of Whitehall. Recently, it has been collected in the Poultney River on the border between New York and Vermont.

The absence of this species from Lake Ontario suggests that it may have reached Lake Champlain through glacial connections in the Mohawk Valley and glacial Lake Albany, although a more northern route is possible.

Life History
Apparently, the breeding behavior of this species has not been studied.

Food and Feeding
Several authors have reported that the sand darter dives into the sandy bottom and then lies concealed with only its eyes showing. From this position it ambushes its prey, mainly midge larvae and entomostracans. Some authors have reported that it buries itself headfirst and others have stated that it enters the sand tailfirst.

References
Jordan and Copeland, 1877 (general account). Williams, 1975 (systematics). Barnes, 1979 (occurrence, Ohio). Starnes et al., 1977 (distribution).

Names
Pellucida is from the Latin *pellucidus*, clear or transparent.

  Pleurolepis pellucidus Agassiz *in* Putnam, 1863: 5 Black River, Elyria, Ohio

  Ammocrypta pellucida (Baird), Greeley, 1929: 127 Lake Erie drainage

  Ammocrypta pellucida (Putnam), Bailey et al., 1970: 75 (authorship)

  Ammocrypta pellucida (Agassiz), Williams, 1975: 17-21 (review)

The confusion in the authorship of this species stems from the fact that Baird knew of the species and had intended to describe it under the name *E. pellucidum* but had not done so when it was cited in the article by Putnam. However, it is clear that Agassiz is responsible for the description and, under the International Code of Zoological Nomenclature, is the author of the species.

Etheostoma

The genus *Etheostoma* contains more than 100 species (91 described and about 12 more known but not yet formally described). Members of this genus are diverse but lack the clear flesh of *Ammocrypta* and the modified ventral scales of *Percina*.

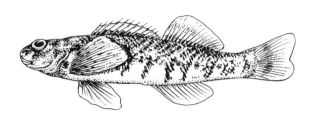

GREENSIDE DARTER

Etheostoma blennioides
Rafinesque, 1819

Identification
The greenside darter is a fairly large darter with a blunt head. The snout overhangs the mouth and the maxillaries are bound to the preorbital region for most of their length, which is to say that the groove between the maxillary and the area below the eye is present only at the posterior end of the maxillary bone.

In the field, young greenside darters resemble johnny or tessellated darters in general coloration but their markings tend to be in the shape of large W's or V's rather than X's or small W's. Greenside darters also have the caudal fin noticeably emarginate whereas the tails of the johnny and tessellated darters are nearly square or very slightly emarginate.

The two subspecies that occur in New York differ in scale size: *E. b. blennioides* from the Allegheny and Upper Genesee averages 65 or 66 lateral line scales; *E. b. pholidotum* from the Lower Genesee and Great Lakes tributaries averages 54 to 58, depending on locality.

Description
Body elongate, somewhat compressed, dorsal profile more curved than the ventral. Head blunt, snout overhanging the mouth, which is low and horizontal. Eyes high on the side of the head. First dorsal fin rectangular, last dorsal spines about as long as the first, originating over the anterior half of the pectoral fin. Dorsal fins contiguous. Second dorsal higher than the first, retrogressive, its margin slightly convex, corners rounded. Caudal emarginate with rounded lobes. Anal origin under soft dorsal origin, pelvics bluntly pointed, middle rays longest. Pelvic insertion anterior to dorsal origin. Pectorals pointed, slightly asymmetrical. Pectoral base nearly vertical. Gill membranes broadly joined across isthmus. Lateral line complete and nearly straight. Breast and prepectoral areas naked. Counts and proportional measurements are given in Table 34.

Color: Body pale tan to green, lighter ventrally. Dorsal surface with a squarish, saddle-shaped blotch in front of the dorsal origin and five or six less well developed squarish saddles along the base of the dorsal, the last of which ends at the upper procurrent caudal rays. Upper sides spotted with wavy dark lines that sometimes connect the lower ends of the saddle-shaped blotches. Sides with a longitudinal dark line interrupted by about eight V- or W-shaped marks. Upper sides of the males with scattered reddish brown spots. Dorsal fins with dark bands at their bases, the rest of the fins dusky. Caudal with four or five broad, vertical, irregular, dusky bands separated by pale spaces. Anal white, pectoral with rows of spots forming about five or six transverse dark bands. Pelvics with indistinct dark spots. Top of head dark, side of snout with a dark line connecting the anterior part of the eye with the anterior part of the upper lip. Teardrop mark sloping downward and forward. A dark spot on the opercles and another on the upper pectoral base.

Juveniles and breeding adults: In general, males of the greenside darter grow faster and reach a larger size than the females. During the breeding season, there is a marked difference in coloration and the males tend to have somewhat larger fins. Breeding color begins to develop in the fall and by January the males are quite dark. During the spawning season, both sexes are so dark that some of the blotches on the head and body are obscured. Males develop dark green vertical bands and their fins turn green. The red spots on the sides are prominent in all but the darkest males. The dorsal fin has a reddish basal bar, then a light green middle band, and a darker green outer band at the center of the fin, becoming paler toward the distal edge of the fin. The second dorsal has an orange-red basal bar that is wider at the front, a moderately dark middle band, and a light yellow or yellow-green outer band. Females tend to be predominantly yellow or greenish yellow.

Tubercles are present only in males, on the posterior part of the belly beginning about one-third of the distance from the pelvics to the anus behind the pelvics, and extending along the ventral surface of the belly and caudal peduncle to the base of the tail fin. There are three rows of scales with tubercles anteriorly, four or five rows just in front of the anus, and two rows on each side of the anal fin. There are no tubercles on the fins but the leading edge of the pelvic fin and the tips of its soft rays become swollen during the spawning period.

Size: The largest specimens are about 4.5 inches total length.

Habitat

The greenside inhabits deeper riffles with cobbles and often some algae. It is most common in moderate-sized to larger streams. Small individuals are sometimes found in somewhat slower backwater areas.

Distribution

This species lives in the Ohio and Tennessee River basins with disjunct populations in the Ozark region of Missouri and Arkansas and some populations in the Great Lakes drainage of northern Ohio, southern Michigan, and southern Ontario. Possibly it reached Lake Erie through the Wabash-Maumee connection. On the Atlantic coast, there are populations in the Potomac and a few western tributaries of the Susquehanna, which it apparently reached from the Allegheny. It also occurs in the Mohawk system.

In New York State, two subspecies are represented: *E. b. blennioides* lives in the Allegheny and Upper Genesee and *E. b. pholidotum* inhabits the Great Lakes, Lower Genesee and Mohawk systems. This indicates that the Mohawk population reached there from the Great Lakes rather than from the Susquehanna. Miller postulated that it reached the Mohawk during the Lake Warren stage or slightly later. Apparently, there are two populations in the Mohawk, one in Oriskany Creek and one in Schoharie Creek and eastward.

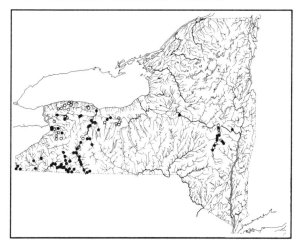

Life History

The greenside darter spawns in New York from the second week in April until June. Spawning takes place in swift riffles and the eggs are deposited on algae on rocks. Spawning is initiated when the water temperature reaches 51 F. Fahy noted that spawning takes place mostly at night and the eggs are laid in batches of 2 to 192 eggs. An individual may spawn as often as 5 times a night and the average female spawns approximately 37 times during a season. The eggs are demersal and adhesive and about 1.85 mm in diameter. Hatching takes place in 18 days at 55 to 58 F and the yolk sac is absorbed in 6 days at 60 F. Most individuals live 36 to 39 months; a few survive into the fourth or fifth growing season.

Food and Feeding

Turner reported that both large and small greenside darters fed on mayfly and midge larvae. Small young eat some entomostracans.

Notes

R. V. Miller reviewed the systematics of the greenside darter and divided it into four subspecies: *blennioides* Rafinesque, *newmani* Agassiz, *gutselli*

Hildebrand, and *pholidotum* Miller. There are slight differences between the Allegheny and Upper Genesee populations and in the Great Lakes populations as indicated by differences in lateral line scale count:

E. b. blennioides
Allegheny 57 to 72, average 65.15
Upper Genesee 60 to 71, average 65.91
E. b. pholidotum
Lake Erie 51 to 63, average 57.45
Lake Ontario 53 to 63, average 58.03
Lower Genesee 53 to 59, average 58.03
Seneca-Mohawk 50 to 58, average 54.94

In general, *E. b. pholidotum* has a fully scaled belly whereas in *E. b. blennioides* there is frequently a naked area on the anterior part of the belly.

References

Fahy, 1954 (life history). Winn, 1957 (egg site selection). Miller, R. V. 1968 (systematics). Denoncourt et al., 1977 (records in Susquehanna). Turner, 1921 (food). Ross, 1973 (chromosomes).

Names

Blennioides is a combination of the Latin *blennius*, a kind of blenny, and the New Latin *-oides*, like.

Etheostoma blennioides Rafinesque, 1819: 419 Ohio River

Diplesion blennioides, Hankinson, 1927: 484 Allegheny River

Etheostoma b. blennioides, Greeley, 1938: 71 Allegheny watershed

Etheostoma b. blennioides, Fahy, 1954 near Rochester (This is the form now called *E. b. pholidotum*.)

Etheostoma b. pholidotum Miller, 1968: 26-36 Bear Creek, Vermillion County, Illinois

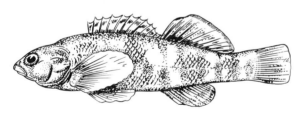

RAINBOW DARTER

Etheostoma caeruleum
Storer, 1845

Identification

The rainbow darter is a rather heavy-bodied species but it is more tapering than the spotted or bluebreast darter. Its gill membranes are narrowly joined across the isthmus, its belly is usually scaled, and its lateral line is short, with 18 to 30 pored scales out of a total count of 39 to 50. Males have some red in the fins throughout the year and become brilliant during the breeding season.

Description

Body robust, moderately compressed. Profiles nearly symmetrical. Dorsal origin over basal half of the pectoral fin. Dorsal fins contiguous, connected by a keel of membrane that is not crossed by scales. Spiny dorsal outline arched, its fourth to sixth spines longest, its membranes little incised. Soft dorsal highest anteriorly, its margin slightly convex, its last ray a little more than half the longest, its corners rounded. Caudal square to slightly emarginate, its middle rays longer than the longest upper rays, corners round. Anal round, its fourth or fifth rays longest. Pelvic insertion slightly ahead of dorsal origin. No pelvic axillary process. Pelvic fin pointed, its middle ray longest. Pectoral base slightly off vertical. Pectoral pointed, asymmetrical. Gill membranes slightly united across isthmus. Mouth moderate, slightly oblique, terminal, maxillary reaching to below the eye. Opercles scaled, cheeks, breast, and prepectoral naked. Predorsal scaled. Lateral line incomplete, ending below end of the second dorsal. Counts and proportional measurements are given in Table 34.

Color: Immatures have the body brownish or olive above, shading to pale grayish white ventrally. Dorsal midline with dark saddles immediately in front of dorsal origin, at rear of the spiny dorsal, and just behind the soft dorsal. A dark humeral scale present. Sides with dark bars, of which the last six extend to the anal base or the midventral line. The anterior, incomplete, bars are less prominent and often reduced to indistinct midlateral spots.

The spiny dorsal has a reddish-brown basal band separated by a clear area from a brownish central band. Distal to this there is a clear area with the last few interradial membranes red. Beyond this there is a broad, blue, submarginal band and a narrow clear margin. Soft dorsal dark, with two to four rows of dark spots. Caudal with a few irregular spots; anal clear. Pectorals and pelvics hyaline or slightly dusky. Lower side of head with a short, broad, subocular bar and a more distinct longitudinal bar on the side of the snout.

Juveniles and breeding adults: Juveniles are more prominently barred than adults. Breeding males develop intense blue on top of the head and body and bright orange on the vertical fins. Some of the lateral scales have red margins. The pale spaces

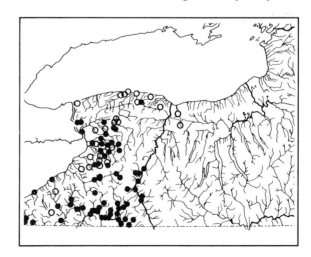

between the bars on the posterior sides of the body become bright reddish orange.

Collette found breeding tubercles on belly scales starting halfway between the pelvic and anal fins and extending four rows on each side of the anal fin. On the caudal peduncle, breeding tubercles are present on the five midventral scale rows.

Size: The maximum total length is about 68 mm.

Habitat

The rainbow darter lives in small creeks to moderate-sized rivers. It is very much a riffle species and is usually found in the gravel and cobble areas of the fastest parts of the streams.

Distribution

The rainbow darter ranges from the Ozarks of Missouri and northern Arkansas, and in the Mississippi drainage to central Minnesota, Wisconsin, and northern Illinois. It is found in the Tennessee and Ohio basins including the Wabash and other major tributaries. It occurs in Lakes Michigan, Huron, Erie, and the western part of Lake Ontario.

In New York, it is present in the Allegheny, Erie, and Ontario drainages. The Survey did not record it from the Genesee but it is now common in the region from Portageville to Caneadea and in Caneadea and Angelica Creeks. It appears to be a recent introduction in the Genesee where it is still in its explosive expansion stage.

Life History

In southern Michigan, Winn found that the males migrate to the spawning grounds in late March. Spawning takes place over fine gravel in water 4 inches to 2 feet deep. The females remain in pools below the riffles. When a female is ready to spawn, she moves onto the riffle where she is pursued by a male who drives away any competing males, thus, in effect, defending a moving territory around the female. Often a male becomes so occupied with chasing a competing male that he loses the female who is then pursued by another male or simply returns to the pool without spawning. The spawning female settles to the bottom and forces her head into the gravel and wriggles until the lower half of her body is buried. The male clasps her with his pelvic fins ahead of her depressed dorsal fin and his caudal region beside hers, with his anal and caudal fins on the same side of her body. The two vibrate rapidly and the eggs are released into the gravel. The female may spawn several times in succession with the same or other males before returning to the pool.

Rainbow darter eggs are 1.5 mm in diameter with a single oil droplet. The yolk is pale yellow. Cooper has described the developmental stages . Yolk absorption is complete by the time they reach 8 mm and the fin rays are fully formed at 9 mm total length. In this species there is no pigment around the vent until after the yolk has been absorbed. Lutterbie found that the young-of-the-year reach 37 to 42 mm by the first fall and 60 mm by the time the fourth annulus is formed.

Food and Feeding

Turner reported that young rainbow darters fed on entomostracans but that entomostracans were a negligible part of the diet of individuals more than 35 mm standard length. Fish more than 15 mm long fed on small mayfly and midge larvae while larger individuals took increasingly larger proportions of larger insect larvae, snails, and small crayfish.

Notes

The spread of this species through the Genesee Valley should be monitored carefully over the next few years.

References

Reeves, 1907 (life history but part of the observations pertain to the orangethroat darter which the author did not distinguish). Adamson and Wissing, 1977 (food and feeding). Lutterbie, 1979 (age and growth). Winn, 1957 (egg site selection); 1958a, 1958b (life history). Cooper, 1979 (development). Knapp, 1964 (systematics). Esmond and Stauffer, 1983 (populations). Ross, 1973 (chromosomes). Collette, 1965 (breeding tubercles). Turner, 1921 (food and feeding).

Names

Caeruleus is Latin for the color blue.

Etheostoma caerulea Storer, 1845: 47 Fox River, Illinois

Poecilichthys caeruleus caeruleus, Greeley, 1929: 177 Erie-Niagara drainage

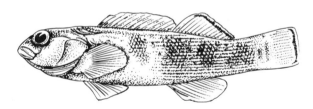

BLUEBREAST DARTER

Etheostoma camurum (Cope, 1870)

Identification

The bluebreast is a deep-bodied, rather compressed fish with a deep caudal peduncle and a moderately pointed head. It most resembles the spotted darter but differs in having conspicuous, dark, submarginal bands on the soft dorsal, anal, and caudal fins. It also has a less pointed snout and a more square or slightly convex tail than does the spotted darter.

Description

Body moderately elongate, compressed, upper profile somewhat more curved than the ventral. Caudal peduncle rather deep. Dorsal origin above basal half of pectoral fin. Dorsal fins contiguous, connected by a low keel of membrane. Spiny dorsal arched, its interspinous membranes little incised. Soft dorsal high anteriorly, its last rays about half the first, its margin nearly straight. Caudal fin square, its middle rays longer than the longest upper rays.

Anal origin under origin of second dorsal. Anal margin convex, its fourth ray longest. Pelvic pointed, its third ray longest. Pelvic insertion under origin of spiny dorsal. Pectoral asymmetrical, bluntly pointed, its base nearly vertical. Gill membranes separate. Mouth low, horizontal, maxillary reaching to below front of eye. Frenum present. Lateral line complete. Opercle scaled; breast, prepectoral, predorsal and cheek naked. Counts and proportional measurements are given in Table 34.

Color: Overall color yellowish olive, lighter below. Sides with irregular patches of one to four dark scales each. Posterior sides with lines of dark pigment in the region of overlap between the longitudinal scale rows. There are eleven of these lines which become fainter beneath the spiny dorsal and are absent from the belly. Scattered scales of the sides are bright red in life. There are two pronounced white spots, each about equal in size to the pupil, at the base of the caudal fin. Most of the scales of the upper sides are outlined by a single row of melanophores. There is a dusky teardrop band below the eye and a pronounced dark spot behind the lower posterior part of the orbit. There is another dark spot above and slightly behind the upper pectoral fin base. Paired fins whitish. First dorsal fin dusky except for a light submarginal band. Soft dorsal, anal, and caudal dusky at base with a white stripe, distal to which there is a darker marginal band, then a very narrow white edge on all three of these fins.

Juveniles and breeding adults: Juveniles are miniatures of the adults. The breeding males have the belly and ventral surface of the head bright blue black and very bright red spots on the sides. Often there are 8 to 12 more or less conspicuous vertical bands or midlateral spots. Females are less brightly colored.

Size: This is a moderate-sized darter, reaching slightly more than 3 inches total length.

Habitat
According to Trautman, the bluebreast darter inhabits larger streams with low turbidity, where it occurs in fast-flowing sections with deep riffles over large cobbles and some sandy gravel. Apparently, they migrate upstream during the breeding season

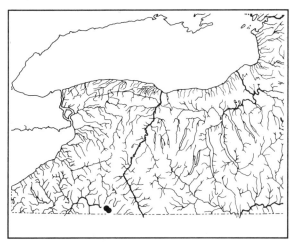

and retreat to the lower reaches in the late fall or winter.

Distribution
Zorach presented a map of the known records for the bluebreast darter. Its total range is from tributaries of the Tennessee River from southern Tennessee and North Carolina, north through Kentucky, extreme eastern Illinois, Indiana, Ohio, West Virginia, and the Allegheny River and French Creek in northwestern Pennsylvania. It has only recently been collected in New York State. So far two specimens are known: The first (AMNH 55389) was collected 20 September 1973 by Dr. Steve Eaton and students and the second (AMNH 39292) was collected 25 October 1975 by American Museum field crews. Both specimens are from the Allegheny River near Westons Mills and Portville.

Life History
Mount studied the life history of the bluebreast darter in central Ohio. He was not able to observe the spawning act in the field but he did find breeding adults in riffle areas of moderately large streams and there were indications that the eggs were laid in fine gravel that had collected downstream of large rocks. Spawning occurred during the last 2 weeks of May and the first 2 weeks of June, sometimes to the end of June, when the water temperature ranged from 21 to 24 C. Males showed brighter coloration in April when the water temperature reached 13 to 15 C.

Mount was able to get the darters to spawn in an artificial stream, a rectangular trough with a divider down the middle and a paddle wheel that moved the water around the periphery of the trough. Rocks and the corners of the trough caused eddies that approximated conditions in stream riffles. Males set up poorly defined territories and defended them against intruding males, darting at them, and ramming them, and nipping at their fins, but never causing any real damage. The limits of the territories did not seem to be sharply defined and frequently a male would move to another rock. With approach of the spawning period, females also became pugnacious, darting at each other but without actual contact. During these conflicts, both sexes developed two black bands encircling the body just behind the pectoral fin.

Females appeared to select the spawning sites and to initiate spawning. They would entice the males by swimming close to the bottom in short spurts. The males would then follow, sometimes for an hour or more, during which time the pair would occasionally swim up toward the surface. Finally, the female would bury her head in the gravel and raise her body until it was nearly perpendicular. (Mount was not sure if this was a normal display or the result of the gravel in his tank being too shallow. In any case, it stimulated the male to mount her.) Finally, the female moved to the spawning site, a riffle behind a rock where the current was swift and the gravel was about 3 inches deep. Here she buried herself until her back was level with the surface of the gravel. Then the male came to lie on top of her although the position of his lower fins could not be determined. The pair vibrated together vigorously as the eggs were released. They would frequently vibrate for 3 to 5 seconds, then rest for 3 to 5 minutes before another spawning episode. About 100 eggs were released, sometimes during a single spawning and sometimes over several episodes. Mount's studies suggested that most females spawned at least three times during the season. Spawning occurred throughout the day but most frequently during the afternoon and evening. At 21 to 24 C, the eggs hatched in about 10 days.

Food and Feeding
The food consists chiefly of benthic insects, especially dipteran larvae.

Notes.
The species is still rare in New York and it is not known if it is expanding its range or was merely missed by the Survey.

References
Zorach, 1972 (systematics). Mount, 1959 (spawning behavior). Trautman, 1981 (Ohio). Ross, 1973 (chromosomes).

Names
Camurus is Latin for blunt-headed.

Poecilichthys camurus Cope, 1870: 265 headwaters of the Cumberland River

Etheostoma camurum, Yochim, 1981: 14 Allegheny River

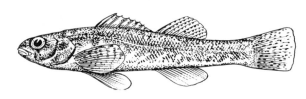

IOWA DARTER

Etheostoma exile (Girard, 1860)

Identification
The Iowa darter is a slender, nearly terete species with a blunt snout. It is generally rather dark brown with a conspicuous pale lateral line that ends below the spiny dorsal fin. The mature males have some red color in the fins and become brilliant during the breeding season.

The Iowa darter is most like the swamp darter, *Etheostoma fusiforme*, but the swamp darter is confined to the eastern part of Long Island and the Iowa darter in our state is limited to the Great Lakes drainage. Iowa darters do not have breeding tubercles, but the males are brightly colored. In the swamp darter the situation is reversed; the males do not develop bright color but they do have tubercles on the anal rays and the undersides of the pelvic fins.

Description
Body elongate, caudal peduncle slender, little compressed. Dorsal profile more arched than the ventral; body deepest ahead of the dorsal fin. Dorsal origin over basal half of the pectoral fin. Spiny dorsal arched, fourth spine longest. Dorsal fins well separated with scales crossing the interspace. Soft dorsal highest anteriorly with the last ray two-thirds the first. Interspinous membrane not deeply incised. Caudal square, its middle rays longer than the longest upper rays. Anal fin origin below third dorsal soft ray.

Anal convex, its third ray longest. Pelvic origin below dorsal origin. Pelvics pointed. Pectoral pointed, slightly asymmetrical, its base sloped. Gill membranes separate. Snout blunt, mouth low and horizontal. Frenum well developed. Maxillary reaching to below front of eye. Prepectoral and breast naked. Cheeks and opercles scaled. Lateral line ending below origin of second dorsal. Counts and proportional measurements are given in Table 34.

Color: Overall brownish, shading to yellow or white ventrally. Lateral line conspicuously pale. Midside with a row of 9 to 12 vertical bars. Middorsal region with about the same number of vague saddle-shaped blotches. Side of snout with a well-defined longitudinal stripe and a distinct teardrop mark below the eye. Spiny dorsal with ocellated blue spots on basal part of membranes. Males with a submarginal blue band. Soft dorsal, caudal, and pectoral with bands of dark spots. Anal and pelvics hyaline.

Juveniles and breeding adults: In breeding males, the bars become blue or green and the interspaces bright red, merging with a bright red streak along the lower sides below the ends of the vertical bands. Spiny dorsal with a broad orange band.

Size: Lutterbie reported Wisconsin specimens 69 mm standard length.

Habitat
The Iowa darter is a slow-water species that occurs among vegetation and often over flocculent bottom in lakes, ponds, or the slower sections of streams.

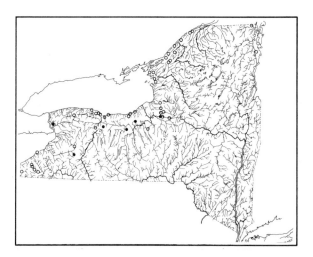

Distribution

This species occurs in a broad curving band from Alberta and Saskatchewan through southern Manitoba, southern Ontario and southern Quebec. It reaches the St. Lawrence drainage of New York and occurs in central Ohio, northern Illinois and central Nebraska. It lives in the Platte River in Wyoming and eastern Montana. In New York, there are scattered records in the western part of the state, Oneida Lake, and the St. Lawrence corridor.

Life History

In Whitmore Lake in southern Michigan, male darters established territories along undercut banks in late March or early April. Spawning occurred on fibrous roots, the females moving into the territories for spawning and then returning to deeper water. As in other darter species, the male mounted the female with his pelvic fins over her first dorsal and his caudal peduncle next to hers. Sometimes the females wriggled into the vegetation or gravel on which the eggs were to be laid; often they did not.

Food and Feeding

Turner found that young Iowa darters fed chiefly on entomostracans, and larger organisms were taken by larger fish. The diet also increased in complexity with increasing age and older individuals fed on amphipods, midge larvae, and other insect larvae.

Notes

This is a glacial species that appears to be holding its own in New York.

References

Collette, 1962 (systematics). Lutterbie, 1979 (age and growth). Gosline, 1947 (variation). Winn, 1958b (spawning). Turner, 1921 (food habits).

Names

Exile is Latin for slender.

Boleichthys exilis Girard, 1860: 103 Little Muddy River, Wisconsin

Poecilichthys exilis, Greeley, 1928: 101 Oswego drainage

Poecilichthys borealis Jordan, 1884: 477 Montreal

Etheostoma iowae Jordan and Meek, 1885: 10 Chariton River, Iowa

Poecilichthys iowae, Hankinson, 1924: 86 western New York

Boleichthys eos Jordan in Nelson, 1876: 34 Illinois

Boleichthys fusiformis eos, Bean, 1903: 521 Cape Vincent

Etheostoma boreale, Evermann and Kendall, 1902c: 240 St. Lawrence

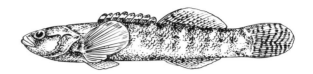

FANTAIL DARTER

Etheostoma flabellare Rafinesque, 1819

Identification

The fantail darter is a rather slender species with a pointed head, a terminal mouth, and a deep caudal peduncle. Its gill membranes are broadly joined across the isthmus; its tail is squarish or rounded; and its lateral line ends below the second dorsal fin. There is a conspicuous dark scale on the body behind the upper end of the gill opening, regular bars on the sides, and fine dark crossbands on the tail. In both sexes the dorsal spines are short and in the adult males the spines have fleshy knobs that are used to groom the eggs.

There is no other species in New York with which it is apt to be confused.

Description

Body elongate and somewhat compressed. Profiles nearly symmetrical and almost parallel. First dorsal low, arched, membrane somewhat incised between spines. Tips of spines lightly fleshy in females, decidedly so in males. Soft dorsal highest anteriorly, its fourth ray longest. Caudal rounded, its middle rays substantially longer than the longest upper rays. Anal origin below the third soft dorsal ray. Fifth or sixth anal ray longest. Pelvic insertion in advance of dorsal origin, below pectoral base. Pectoral base inclined backward. Gill membranes broadly united across isthmus. Snout pointed, mouth oblique and terminal, maxillary reaching to below the anterior edge of pupil. Lateral line straight, ending below middle of soft dorsal. Frenum present. Cheeks, opercles, breast, and prepectoral areas naked. Counts and proportional measurements are given in Table 34.

Color: Body ground color olive, shading to pale gray on the belly and ventral side of the head. Humeral scale prominent. Back with about 8 to 10 saddle-blotches between the nape and the upper caudal base. Sides with 10 to 12 or more dark vertical bars not connected with the dorsal saddles. First dorsal uniformly dusky, second dorsal with sloping rows of spots. Caudal with about five prominent, narrow, dark, vertical bars. Anal, pectorals, and pelvics pale.

Juveniles and breeding adults: Breeding males are darker with bright orange knobs on the dorsal spines and a yellowish wash over the body. In large adults of both sexes the second dorsal, caudal, anal, and pelvics are spotted.

Size: Lutterbie (1979) recorded specimens up to

74 mm total length from Wisconsin. We have New York specimens up to 3.25 inches total length.

Habitat
Fantail darters occur in riffle areas of streams where there are cobbles and gravel. They are especially abundant in streams where there are chunks or slabs of limestone or shale.

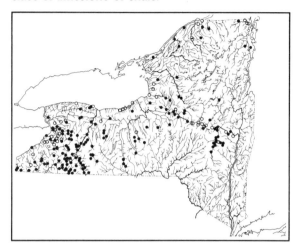

Distribution
This species occurs from southern Minnesota and Wisconsin, east through the southern Great Lakes (excluding Lake Superior) to southern Quebec and New York State. It ranges south in the Mississippi Valley to the Ozarks of eastern Kansas, eastern Oklahoma, Missouri, and northern Arkansas. In the Tennessee basin, it reaches northern Mississippi and Alabama. On the upland parts of the Atlantic slope, it ranges from northern South Carolina to southern New York. In New York, it occurs in the western and northern parts of the state but is absent from the Lower Hudson.

Life History
Lake studied the life history of the fantail darter in Black Creek, near Rochester. Spawning occurred in late April to mid-June after the water temperature reached 60 F. Males moved onto the spawning grounds, areas of moderate current above riffles, and selected their nest sites. These were usually flat rocks with a space about one-half inch high beneath them. A male cleaned his nest by wriggling his body into the crevice. Other males were chased away from the site but a female was enticed into the nest by bunting and prodding. After circling each other, the female rolled over to apply her vent region to the roof of the nest and the male assumed a head to tail position, rolling on his side and twisting the posterior part of his body to bring his vent region into proximity with that of the female. The eggs were deposited in groups of 1 to 3 at intervals of 1 to 3 minutes until about 45 eggs had been deposited. Both parents vibrated vigorously as the eggs were released and fertilized. The female remained inverted but the male turned upright between spawning episodes. After spawning the female left and the male enticed other females to spawn until the nest contained as many as 562 eggs.

The male guarded the nest, periodically grooming the eggs with the fleshy tabs on his dorsal spines, until the eggs hatched: 30 to 35 days at 63 to 68 F, 21 days at 70 F, and 14 to 16 days at 74 F.

Dissections suggested that each female spawned 5 times and that a new crop of eggs developed by November. A 33-mm female contained 128 eggs; a 49-mm female contained 422 eggs. The eggs averaged 2.3 mm in diameter.

By fall, the young averaged 30 mm and they reached sexual maturity by the following summer. Lutterbie found that Wisconsin fantail darters averaged 23.4 to 32.2 mm at age I, 39.23 to 54.78 at age II, 36 to 63.4 at age III, and 60 to 72 at age IV.

Cooper described the eggs and larvae of laboratory-reared specimens from Elk Creek, Pennsylvania, a Lake Erie tributary. The eggs were 2.3 to 2.7 mm in diameter and often somewhat elliptical, with a single oil droplet 0.7 to 0.8 mm in diameter. The yolk was pale yellow and 2 mm in diameter. Newly hatched larvae were 6.2 mm long and still retained a large yolk sac that was 31 percent of the total length. The yolk sac was retained until most of the fin rays were complete but was completely expended 7 to 10 days after hatching.

Food and Feeding
Daiber reported on the winter food of the fantail darter and the mottled sculpin in Vandermark Creek, a headwater tributary of the Genesee River in Allegheny County. Both species consumed a variety of insects, including mayflies, caddisflies and dipterans, and copepods, but the darters ate more other kinds of invertebrates including cladocerans, amphipods, isopods, hydrachnids, and gastropods. Such groups, however, made up only a small part of the diet. Medium-sized fish ate the greatest variety of food.

Turner found that young fantail darters ate mayfly and midge larvae whereas larger fish ate mayfly and midge larvae and other larger insects. In Lake Erie, they ate amphipods but he found no amphipods in the stomachs of stream-dwelling fantail darters.

References
Jaffa, 1917 (breeding). Lake, 1936 (life history). Cooper, 1979 (eggs and larvae). Adams and Wissing, 1977 (food and feeding periodicity). Lutterbie, 1979 (age and growth). Karr, 1965 (ecology). Daiber, 1956 (food). Turner, 1921 (food). Ross, 1973 (chromosomes).

Names
The species name is from the Latin *flabellaris,* like a fan, in reference to the shape of the tail.

Etheostoma flabellare Rafinesque, 1819: 419 tributaries of the Ohio River

Etheostoma linsleyi Storer, 1851: 37 Wolcott, Wayne County, New York

Catonotus fasciatus Girard, 1860: 68 Madrid, New York; Grass River

Catonotus flabellaris, Greeley, 1927: 64-65 Genesee River drainage

Catonotus flabellaris flabellaris, Greeley and Greene, 1931: 92 St. Lawrence drainage

TABLE 34
AVERAGE PROPORTIONAL MEASUREMENTS AND COUNTS OF
DARTERS *(Ammocrypta* and *Etheostoma, in part)*

All proportions are expressed in percentage of standard length.

| | Ammocrypta | | Etheostoma | | | |
	pellucida	blennioides	caeruleum	camurum	exile	flabellare
ST. LENGTH (mm)	46.3	59.5	40.3	40.4	26.5	47.2
TOTAL LENGTH	116.4	120.6	121.1	116.0	120.8	118.1
FORK LENGTH	115.0	118.5	121.0	116.0	120.8	118.1
PREDORSAL	36.8	32.2	35.7	33.4	36.2	34.4
PREANAL	63.6	60.6	63.6	65.0	62.1	63.9
PREPELVIC	27.4	27.9	33.5	33.2	33.8	29.5
DORSAL BASE	40.6	52.2	52.5	49.2	40.0	47.6
ANAL BASE	12.9	13.3	13.9	13.0	12.4	14.9
BODY DEPTH	10.6	18.5	21.6	19.8	18.2	18.1
BODY WIDTH	9.6	14.7	13.8	12.8	13.0	13.2
C.PED. DEPTH	6.1	9.8	11.4	12.1	9.6	12.5
PECTORAL ALT.	7.0	11.3	13.7	11.4	11.7	10.7
HEAD LENGTH	24.3	24.5	30.2	28.0	29.8	28.7
SNOUT	7.0	7.5	7.8	6.4	7.0	6.2
EYE	5.9	6.9	6.9	7.4	8.5	5.2
MOUTH LENGTH	6.9	6.1	8.8	8.2	9.0	8.1
INTERORB	2.6	2.1	4.1	2.8	4.7	4.9
N (sample size)	5	5	5	5	5	5
COUNTS:						
DORSAL SPINES	X	XII-XIV	X-XI	XII	VIII-XI	VII-VIII
DORSAL RAYS	8-10	12-13	13-14	12-13	10-12	11-13
ANAL RAYS	II,7-11	II,8-9	II,6-7	II,7-8	II,7	II,7-8
PECTORAL RAYS	12-16	14-15	10-15	13-14	12-14	11-13
PELVIC RAYS	I,5	I,5	I,5	I,5	I,5	I,5
GILL RAKERS	12-15	8-10	9-11	12-13	7-11	11-13
VERTEBRAE	42-44	41-42	36-37	37-38	38-39	34
SCALES:						
ABOVE L. L.	0-7	7	4-7	7	4-5	6-8
LATERAL LINE	62-84	60-70	36-57	54-59	58-59	45-60
BELOW L. L.	2-10	8-10	6-10	7-8	8-9	8-10

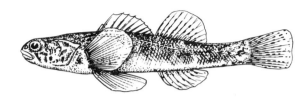

SWAMP DARTER

Etheostoma fusiforme
(Girard, 1854)

Identification

The swamp darter is a slender fish with a short, arched lateral line that ends below the spiny dorsal fin. The snout is rather blunt, the infraorbital canal is incomplete, and the breast is completely scaled. Although it is quite variable in color, this is a somber species that never develops bright breeding colors. It leaves the overall impression that its head is small for the size of its body.

The swamp darter superficially resembles the Iowa darter but their geographical distributions are quite different and there is little danger of confusion. The swamp darter is confined to the lowlands of the Atlantic coast while the Iowa darter is a midcontinent species that reaches our state only in the St. Lawrence drainage.

About 10 percent of the swamp darters have weak serrations on the preoperculum.

Description

Body elongate, little compressed. Head blunt, dorsal profile more arched than the ventral. Dorsal origin over the basal third of the pectoral fin. Dorsal fins contiguous, no scales between them. Spiny dorsal arched, the fourth through the sixth spines longest, the membranes not incised. Soft dorsal margin convex, the last ray two-thirds the second and third rays. Caudal square with rounded corners, middle rays equal to longest upper rays. Anal origin under third dorsal soft ray. Anal margin convex, its third ray longest. Pelvic insertion under dorsal origin. Pelvics pointed, third ray longest. Pectoral base oblique, pectorals paddle-like, nearly symmetrical with rounded margin. Gill membranes broadly united across isthmus. Snout blunt, mouth only slightly inclined, lower jaw included. Maxillary ending below anterior third of eye. Body fully scaled. Cheeks and opercles scaled. Lateral line incomplete, arched anteriorly and ending below spiny dorsal. Counts and proportional measurements are given in Table 35.

Color: Generally brownish with various pale marblings on the back and sides. Midventral region from the isthmus to the caudal base pale with a few dark brown spots. Edge of shoulder girdle above pectoral base with a dark bar which sometimes continues downward to the pelvic base. Midside of body with nine short, broad, indistinct bars of which the anteriormost ones are vertical, the middle ones are squarish, and posterior ones horizontal. Base of caudal with three distinct dark spots in a vertical

row, the middle one quite variable in size and shape. Cheeks and lower sides of head spotted, with a well-developed teardrop bar. A dark line around the snout.

Juveniles and breeding adults. Breeding tubercles are developed on the pelvic fins. This species does not develop bright breeding colors.

Size: To at least 2 inches total length.

Habitat

This is a species of slow-moving or still waters and rarely occurs in flowing streams and then only in low abundance. Usually, it is found over mud and detritus bottom where there is abundant aquatic vegetation, but sometimes it occurs over open sand. In aquaria, swamp darters were seen to spend much of their time resting on plants such as *Elodea*. The swamp darter appears to be quite tolerant of low oxygen and low pH and there are documented cases of it becoming more abundant as its habitat became more acid.

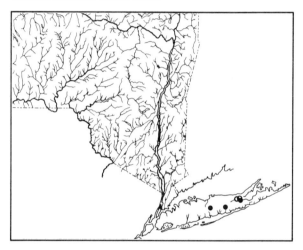

Distribution

The subspecies *E. f. fusiforme* ranges from the southeastern tip of Maine southward along the Seaboard Lowland section of New England and the Atlantic Coastal Plain to the Waccamaw River in North Carolina. South of the Waccamaw, it is replaced by the subspecies *E. f. barrati*, which continues along the southern Atlantic and Gulf Coastal Plains, peninsular Florida, and the lower Mississippi Valley as far north as southern Illinois.

In New York, its distribution is limited to the eastern two-thirds of Long Island.

Life History

Fletcher and Collette have reported on the spawning behavior of this species. Specimens collected in late April from Lake Ronkonkoma began spawning activities in the aquarium almost immediately. The male approached from the rear and came to lie on top of its mate, fanning or beating with his pelvic fins. Females would accept this but males would move away. Later, when the females were ready to spawn, they would lead the male into floating vegetation near the top of the tank. They lay side by side and the female directed her genital papilla forward and upward into the vegetation. She would then vibrate rapidly as the eggs were expelled, although the egg laying could not be seen. On Long Island and in New Jersey, the spawning occurred in early May. Only one age-class was present in fall collections and Collette concluded that most individuals do not live through their second summer.

Food and Feeding
Copepods have been found in the stomachs of swamp darters and Collette found that aquarium specimens would accept a variety of small items such as *Daphnia*, worms, and even dried food. Unfamiliar items were inspected visually, then mouthed cautiously before being swallowed or spit out.

References
Hubbs and Cannon, 1935 (systematics). Collette, 1962 (systematics). Fletcher, 1957 (spawning). Schmidt and Whitworth, 1979 (distribution and habitat).

Names
Fusiformis is a Latin word meaning spindle-shaped.

   Boleosoma fusiforme Girard, 1854b: 41 Charles River, Massachusetts

   Boleichthys fusiformis, Bean, 1903: 520-521 Long Island

   Hololepis fusiformis, Greeley, 1939: 43 Long Island

   Hololepis fusiformis fusiformis, Hubbs and Cannon, 1935: 77-81

   Etheostoma fusiformis fusiformis, Collette, 1962: 150-172 (summary account)

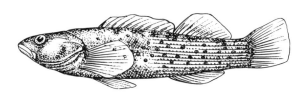

SPOTTED DARTER

Etheostoma maculatum
Kirtland, 1841

Identification
This is a heavy-bodied, compressed darter, with a deep caudal peduncle and a striking color pattern of narrow, longitudinal, dark lines on the body. The head is especially compressed and the snout is quite sharp.

The spotted darter is quite similar to the bluebreast darter but has more lateral line scales (57 to 62 as compared with 53 to 58 in the bluebreast), a more pointed head, and a rounded rather than emarginate tail. The second dorsal, anal, and caudal fins of the bluebreast have conspicuous, dusky, submarginal bands but this is not true of the spotted darter, in which these fins have pale to white margins. The males of both species have red scales, with darker margins, scattered over the sides of the body. There are similar spots in the females of the

bluebreast but the female spotted darter has no red spots.

Description
Body compressed, rather elongate, and rectangular with a deep caudal peduncle. Profiles nearly symmetrical. Dorsal origin shortly behind the pectoral axil. Spiny dorsal arched, its seventh and eighth spines longest, interspinous membranes not incised. Dorsal fins contiguous. Second dorsal highest anteriorly, its margin convex, first and last rays about four-fifths the third, longest, ray. Caudal margin convex, the middle rays noticeably longer than the longest upper rays. Anal origin slightly ahead of the origin of the soft dorsal. Anal arched, its sixth or seventh ray the longest. Pelvics inserted below origin of the spiny dorsal, pointed, their third rays longest. Pectorals bluntly rounded, their bases nearly vertical. Pectoral bluntly and asymmetrically rounded. Gill membranes separate. Frenum present. Snout long and pointed, mouth terminal. Maxillary reaching level of anterior margin of the eye. Lateral line ending under end of second dorsal, a few scales with tubes on caudal peduncle. Predorsal, cheeks, prepectoral, and breast naked. Counts and proportional measurements are given in Table 35.

Color: Females and young fish have the body generally tawny with about nine dusky saddles. Midsides with about 10 vertical bars which are short and narrow anteriorly, becoming longer and broader until the last 4 or 5 connect with the dorsal saddles and the last 2 or 3 reach the midventral line. Spiny dorsal dusky at base, somewhat spotted distally. Soft dorsal with five rows of spots formed by concentrations of melanophores along the rays. Caudal with about five, and anal with about three, similar rows of spots. Pectoral with some spots, pelvic merely dusky. Indistinct dark lines radiating from the eye. Posterior part of the body with 11 narrow dark longitudinal lines that begin just in front of the anal origin and continue to the caudal base. Caudal base with two large white spots. Sides of males with scattered small red spots.

Juveniles and breeding adults: Breeding males are dark brown without spotting on the fins. Mar-

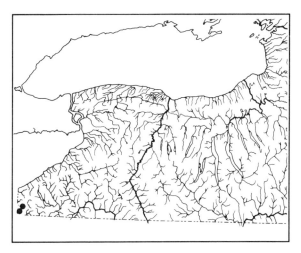

gins of fin bright greenish yellow. Red spots on sides brilliant.

Size: The spotted darter reaches lengths of approximately 4 inches total length.

Habitat
In French Creek, we collected this species only in the deepest and fastest parts of the riffles where the water was more than a foot deep and there were large rocks with abundant growths of filamentous algae.

Distribution
In New York, this species occurs only in French Creek where it was moderately common in 1975 and 1979.

The subspecies *Etheostoma maculatum maculatum* ranges southwest through the northern tributaries of the Ohio River. There is an old record from the Tippecanoe River in Indiana, but no specimens have been reported from that state since the turn of the century and it is now scarce and sporadically distributed in Ohio as well. It is present in the Green River in Kentucky but is now scarce. Zorach and Raney recognize two other subspecies: *E. m. sanguifluum* in the Cumberland River system of Kentucky and *E. m. vulneratum* in the Upper Tennessee River system in Tennessee, North Carolina, and Virginia.

Life History
The breeding habits of this colorful species were described by Raney and Lachner. Their observations were conducted in French Creek in Erie County, Pennsylvania. The spawning area was in a stream about 100 feet wide and the nests were located in water 6 inches to 2 feet deep, usually in quiet water at the head of a riffle. The minimum distance between nests was approximately 4 feet, suggesting territoriality. Breeding took place in May and early June when the water temperature had reached 17 C.

The eggs were deposited on the undersides of flat stones 3 to 9 inches in diameter. Usually the egg mass was somewhat squarish, with the eggs in 4 or 5 layers along one side and in 5 to 10 layers on the opposite side. The eggs were about 2 mm in diameter and yellow in color with a bright golden-yellow oil droplet. Most of the egg masses being guarded by males contained 288 to 352 eggs. Smaller masses usually had a female in attendance and were assumed to be incomplete.

The ovarian eggs mature in batches of about 65. Raney and Lachner suggested that females may spawn 2 to 4 times during the 5-week season. Ovaries of fish collected in March contained 200 eggs (in females 40 to 45 mm) to 400 eggs (females 50 mm).

The eggs are guarded exclusively by the males. The length of the incubation period was not determined but eyed eggs were collected in the field and kept until they hatched. The newly hatched young were 5 to 6 mm long. Spotted darters reach slightly less than 30 mm by the end of their first summer.

The sex ratio seemed to be unbalanced, 289 to 163 in favor of males, in a series of collections from various localities. Females first spawn at age II when they reach 44 mm and they average 50 mm at age III. Males reach 48 mm at age II and may live to age V. The largest male was 68 mm.

Food and Feeding
Raney and Lachner reported that 95 percent of the food of the spotted darter is aquatic insects, including dipterans (chiefly chironomids), stoneflies, mayflies, and beetles. Some water mites were eaten.

Notes
Kirtland made the following observation: "This species is readily distinguished by its flat compressed body, peculiar color, and especially its beautiful carmine maculations. It exceeds in beauty the speckled trout."

References
Zorach and Raney, 1967 (systematics). Raney and Lachner, 1939 (life history). Zorach, 1967 (systematics). Kirtland, 1841a (description).

Names
Maculatum is a Latin adjective meaning spotted.

Etheostoma maculata Kirtland, 1841a: 276 Mahoning River, Ohio

Poecilichthys maculatus, Greeley, 1938: 72 French Creek

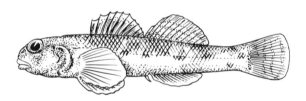

JOHNNY DARTER

Etheostoma nigrum
Rafinesque, 1820

Identification
As darters go, the johnny darter is a rather pale, slender species with a pattern of W- and X-shaped marks on the back and sides. Both the johnny and closely related tessellated darter are members of the subgenus *Boleosoma,* and characterized by the presence of only one anal fin spine. All of the other darters in New York normally have two anal spines. The johnny darter so closely resembles the tessellated darter that for a long time they were considered to be subspecies. Johnny darters, however, have blunter snouts than tessellated darters and also have the infraorbital sensory canal broken into two parts, an anterior section with four pores and a posterior segment with only two pores. In the tessellated darter, the infraorbital canal is complete.

Description
Body elongate, little compressed. Dorsal profile more arched than the ventral. Spiny dorsal fin originating over the basal third of the pectoral fin. Dorsal

fins separated by about two rows of scales. Spiny dorsal margin convex, the third or fourth spine the longest. Soft dorsal highest anteriorly, its last ray about three-fourths the second, longest, ray. Caudal margin slightly convex, the middle rays longer than the longest upper rays. Anal origin below the second or third dorsal soft ray. Pelvic insertion anterior to the dorsal origin. Pelvics pointed, the third ray the longest. Pectoral base slightly oblique. Pectoral pointed, its lower rays rather stout. Gill membranes united across the isthmus. Snout blunt, the mouth low and horizontal. Maxillary reaching to below a point between the front of the eye and the front of the pupil. Lateral line complete, nearly straight. Predorsal, breast, and prepectoral areas naked. No frenum. Counts and proportional measurements are given in Table 35.

Color: Ground color pale sandy. Dark markings at the edges of the scales grouped to form X- or W-shaped marks, about 10 along the midside. Back crossed by about six squarish, saddle-shaped blotches. Teardrop mark poorly developed or absent. Snout with a dark line on each side extending forward from the eye but not meeting on the snout. Both dorsal and caudal fins with spots along the rays forming oblique lines.   Five or six similar lines cross the caudal fin. Pectoral clear, anal and pelvics white.

Juveniles and breeding adults: Juveniles are quite hyaline with much less pigment than the adults. Breeding males become very dark, uniform gray to almost black with white knobs on the tips of the dorsal and anal spines and the lower pectoral rays.

Size: To about 3 inches total length.

Habitat

Johnny darters occur in a variety of habitats, ranging from streams with considerable current to standing waters, over a wide variety of bottom types. In general, they are darters of quieter areas rather than riffles.

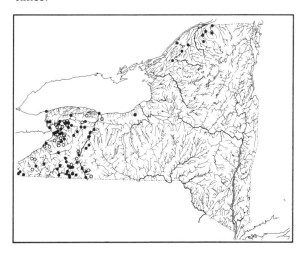

Distribution

The johnny darter ranges from the Hudson Bay drainages of Ontario, Manitoba, and Saskatchewan south throughout the eastern parts of the Dakotas,

Nebraska, and eastern Colorado. It reaches the St. Lawrence drainage in Quebec, western New York, and western Pennsylvania and ranges south in the Mississippi Valley to the Tennessee River basin. It occurs in the Mobile Bay drainage of Mississippi and Alabama and on the Atlantic coast in Virginia and North Carolina.

Life History

Like the tessellated darter, the johnny darter lays its eggs on the undersides of rocks and other objects. Males move onto the spawning ground in April in southern Michigan and establish territories around rocks with a space under them. They clear off a site for the eggs by turning upside down and sweeping it with the caudal, anal, and pelvic fins. Females remain outside the territories until they are ready to spawn. As the female approaches the rock, the male comes out to meet her, relaxing his erect fins after recognizing her as a female. The male then leads the female into the nest, turns upside down and starts to move slowly over the surface. If the female is ready to spawn, she also turns upside down and begins to move over the surface, pausing now and then to deposit one or more eggs. Occasionally the female stops, and sometimes turns upright, whereupon the male prods her until she continues. A clutch of eggs is produced in about half an hour. After the eggs are laid, the female leaves and the male remains to guard the nest, fanning the eggs with his pectoral and occasionally turning upside down to move over the eggs, thus keeping them free of silt.

Individual females lay 5 or 6 clutches, each consisting of 30 to 200 eggs. Six size groups of ova in the ovaries indicate that a female can produce 180 to 1,200 eggs depending on her size.

Lutterbie reported the following back-calculated mean sizes for johnny darters in central Wisconsin: Age I - 36.35 mm, age II - 50.51 mm, age III - 66.00 mm.

Food and Feeding

Turner found that entomostracans and small midge larvae make up the diet of young johnny darters and that larger midge larvae and mayfly larvae were added to the diet as the fish got larger. Organic and inorganic debris was present in the stomachs at all ages. Fish from lakes and streams had similar diets.

References

Turner, 1921 (food). Stone, F. 1947 (species). Lutterbie, 1979 (food). Cole, 1965 (systematics). Karr, 1964 (age and growth). Cole, 1967 (systematics, distribution). Heimberger, 1913 (habitat), Winn, 1958b (comparative life history). Speare, 1960 (growth); 1965 (fecundity). McAllister, Jolicoeur, and Tsuyuki, 1972 (comparison). Ross, 1973 (chromosomes). Kott and Humphreys, 1978 (populations). Smart and Gee, 1979 (ecology). Underhill, 1963 (distribution). Grant and Colgan, 1982 (reproductive behavior).

Names

The species name is from the Latin *niger*, black.

Etheostoma nigra Rafinesque, 1820a: 37 Green River, Kentucky

Boleosoma nigrum, Greeley, 1927: 64 Genesee drainage

Boleosoma nigrum nigrum, Greeley, 1929: 177 Erie-Niagara drainage

Etheostoma nigrum, Cole, 1965: 8-13 (systematics)

TESSELLATED DARTER

Etheostoma olmstedi Storer, 1842

Identification

The tessellated darter was formerly considered a subspecies of the johnny darter, which it greatly resembles in general appearance. Both species are rather pale with small X- or W-shaped markings on the back and upper sides. Both have only a single anal fin spine whereas all other darters in our area have two.

Tessellated darters have somewhat sharper snouts than johnny darters, more dorsal soft rays, and more pectoral fin rays (see key). The suborbital sensory canal is complete in most tessellated darters, usually broken into two sections in the johnny darter.

Description

Body elongate, little compressed. Profiles nearly symmetrical, the upper a little more arched than the ventral. First dorsal origin over basal third of pectoral. Spiny dorsal arched, its fourth and fifth spines longest. Interspinous membranes not incised. In breeding males, the spines have fleshy knobs although they are not as well developed as in the fantail darter. Second dorsal contiguous with the first, highest anteriorly, its last ray about two-thirds the first, which is slightly shorter than the second and third. Caudal square, its middle rays slightly longer than the longest upper ray. Anal fin origin below third dorsal soft ray, its sixth and seventh rays longest. Tips of anterior rays with fleshy expansions. Pelvics inserted below dorsal origin. Pectoral pointed, its lowest five rays knobbed. Gill membranes fused across the isthmus. Mouth low and horizontal, the maxillary ending below the front of the eye. Lower jaw included. Body, cheeks, opercle, prepectoral, and breast scaled. Lateral line complete and slightly decurved. No frenum. Counts and proportional measurements are given in Table 35.

Color: General ground color pale sandy, shading to whitish ventrally. Some scales of the upper sides with dark margins forming wavy bars of varying lengths and different angles. Sides with X- and W-shaped marks, of which 9 to 11 are prominent, along the midside. Dorsal fin with a dark pigment spot on the first interradial membrane, rest of the fin clear or slightly dusky. Second dorsal and caudal with spots along the rays forming irregular narrow bars, usually about nine on the tail of large adults. Some spots on the pectoral, anal and pelvics clear. Snout with a dark line from each eye to the nostrils. Teardrop usually prominent.

Juveniles and breeding adults: Unlike the johnny darter males, which become uniform dark gray to black, the tessellated darter males develop 12 or 13 rather even vertical bands along their sides while losing the wavy lines and X-shaped markings as the scales of the upper sides become completely outlined in dark pigment. The membranes of all fins except the pectoral become quite dark with pale tips on the pectoral and pelvic fins. The unpigmented areas of the second dorsal, anal, and caudal fins stand out so that the fin has the appearance of having white bands on a dark background, which is a reversal of the appearance in non-breeding adults. In this color phase, they are sometimes mistaken for a species of *Percina*.

Size: New York specimens reach a total length of about 3.6 inches.

Habitat

The tessellated darter occurs in both flowing and standing waters but it shows a preference for quieter areas and, except during the breeding season, for sand or mud bottoms.

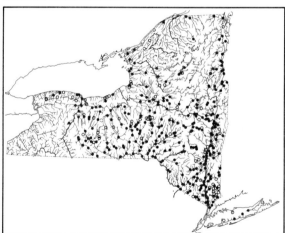

Distribution

Cole found three forms in the Hudson-Mohawk system. In the main Hudson below Troy, the species is characterized by having the nape, cheek, opercle, breast, and belly usually fully scaled. This form also occurs in the Lower Delaware and in the streams of the Chesapeake Bay drainage between the fall line and weakly brackish waters. Cole assigned these specimens to the subspecies *Etheostoma olmstedi atromaculatum*. A second form occurs in the Wallkill and in smaller tributary streams that flow directly into the ocean or are headwaters of larger streams from Cape Cod to North Carolina. Cole calls the latter form *E. o. olmstedi* and it has the nape usually naked, the cheek variously scaled, the breast usually naked, and the belly moderately scaled. In the Upper Hudson and Mohawk, as well as in Lake Ontario, Lake Champlain, the St. Lawrence drainage, Long Island, and the Delaware and Susquehanna tributaries, the fish are intermediate and Cole recognizes these as intergrades. Cole believes that this pattern suggests that the coastal fish became isolated during the Pleistocene and differentiated. With the retreat of the glaciers, the area that is now central New York was reinvaded from the south through the Susquehanna and Delaware Rivers and from the east through the Hudson.

The overall range of the tessellated darter is from the St. Lawrence drainage in southern Quebec, the southern tributaries of Lake Ontario, the Connecticut River and coastal streams from Massachusetts to the Altamaha River in Georgia. It also occurs as a disjunct population in the Oklawaha River in Florida.

Life History

Atz described the nesting and spawning of tessellated darters in the New York Aquarium, 24 May through 9 June 1939. The fish, which originally came from northern New Jersey, laid their adhesive eggs on the underside of an unusually large mussel shell that was lying with the concave side upward. The spawning pair turned upside down and the female vibrated as she deposited the eggs, which were then fertilized by the male as he moved slowly over them. Usually, the partners assumed a side-by-side position either head to tail or head to head but there was no clasping or mounting, although the male's body sometimes crossed that of the female. Spawning was frequently interrupted by the approach of another fish as the male broke away to give chase to the stranger. Spawning appeared to be triggered by one partner turning over; most often it was the male.

After spawning, the female abandoned the nest and the male remained to guard and aerate the eggs either by fanning the water with his tail while holding his position under the eggs with his pectoral fins, or by swimming upside down over the eggs and brushing them with his pectorals. Hatching took place after about 21 days at 65 F.

Usually, only one male will nest under a single stone but Raney and Lachner noted as many as three using the same stone where nesting sites were scarce. Sometimes the eggs were laid on the tops and sides of rocks in crowded conditions.

Food and Feeding

The diet of the tessellated darter is assumed to be similar to that of the johnny darter, dominated by entomostracans and small insects while the fish are small, gradually shifting to larger insects as the fish get bigger.

Notes

The distinctness of the johnny darter and the tessellated darter has been questioned by Scott and Crossman who note that the johnny darter is extremely variable and that some Canadian populations seem to be intermediate.

References

Cole, 1965 (systematics). McAllister et al.,1972 (characters), Cole, 1967 (characters, distribution). Raney and Lachner, 1943 (life history). Atz, 1940 (spawning). Stone, 1947 (two species). Layzer and Reed, 1978 (food, age and growth). Tsai, 1972 (life history). Zorach, 1971 (subspecies). Roberts and Winn, 1962 (feeding). Scott and Crossman, 1973 (status in Canada). Constanz, 1979 (social dynamics).

Names

The species was named for Charles H. Olmsted who studied the fishes of the Connecticut River in the early 1800s.

Etheostoma olmstedi Storer, 1842: 61 Hartford, Connecticut

Boleosoma tesselatum DeKay, 1842: 20 New York streams

Boleosoma nigrum olmstedi, Greeley, 1928: 101 Oswego drainage

Estrella atromaculata Girard, 1859: 66 Potomac River

Etheostoma olmstedi olmstedi, Cole, 1967: 35-59 (systematics)

Etheostoma olmstedi atromaculatum, Cole, 1967: 28 (systematics)

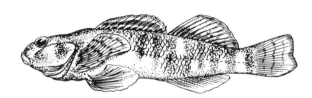

VARIEGATE DARTER

Etheostoma variatum Kirtland, 1838

Identification

The variegate darter is one of our larger and more spectacular species. In life, its ground color is a rich tawny with a sloping dark bar from the dorsal origin to the gill opening. The region behind this bar and below the dorsal fin is unmarked; the posterior part of the body is crossed by vertical bands. It has no close relatives in our state. The gill membranes are joined across the isthmus and the lateral line is complete.

Description

Body elongate, moderately compressed. Dorsal profile more arched than the ventral. Dorsal origin over basal half of the pectoral. Dorsal fin rather squarish, with spines II through X about equally long. Dorsal fins contiguous. Second dorsal margin convex with the last ray about two-thirds the longest (third) ray. Corners of the second dorsal rounded. Caudal slightly emarginate, its middle rays slightly longer than the longest rays of the upper lobe. Anal origin below or slightly behind origin of the second dorsal. Anal margin nearly straight or slightly convex, its corners rounded. Pelvic fins inserted ahead of the dorsal origin. Pelvic pointed with its third ray longest. Pectoral base sloped backward. Pectoral large, pointed. Gill membranes broadly united across the isthmus. Mouth low, reaching to below front of eye. Frenum present but narrow. Lateral line complete, slightly decurved anteriorly. Cheeks, opercles, breast, and prepectoral naked but there is a patch of scales between the pelvic bones. Counts and proportional measurements are given in Table 35.

Color: Ground color grayish above with yellow overtones, shading to tawny white ventrally. Anterior part of body nearly uniform with a dark bar sloping downward and forward from the nape to the gill opening and above the pectoral base. Conspicuous saddle-shaped marks below the last rays of the first dorsal, the middle of the second dorsal, and on the middle of the caudal peduncle. Beginning above the anal origin, there are five or six, more or less, prominent vertical bars. First dorsal of adult males with a row of dark spots along its base, then a clear area, a dusky band, a second clear area, and an orange marginal band. Second dorsal generally orange with dark pigment near its base and a dusky marginal band. Caudal orange with about four dusky crossbands. Anal with some dark pigment of the basal halves of the membranes. Cheeks tawny, teardrop and snout bars indistinct.

Juveniles and breeding adults: Breeding males are extremely colorful. Head, anterior dorsal region, and pelvic fins dark greenish to black. Upper sides dark brown, lower sides and belly red orange or salmon. Anal fin and the vertical bars green, the interspaces with a red center, flanked by white. Second dorsal greenish black. Females grayish above, tawny ventrally, with greatly enlarged genital papilla surrounded by a swollen area.

Size: According to Trautman this species reaches 4.3 inches in Ohio.

Habitat
The variegate darter is a fish of moderate-sized

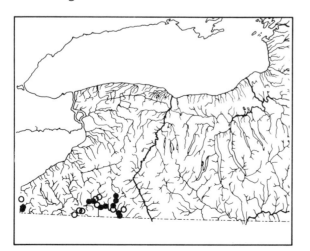

streams. In the winter, it occurs in deeper pools and in the spring it moves into riffle areas to spawn.

Distribution
The variegate darter is restricted to the Ohio River drainage, from southern Indiana, Kentucky, and West Virginia to the Allegheny system in western Pennsylvania and New York.

Life History
May found that during the colder parts of the year, when the water temperatures were below 35 F, the variegate darters moved into deeper pools. As the water warmed in late February, March, and April, the fish became sexually active, the males at about 40 F and the females at 50 F. Spawning took place in the upper parts of riffles, usually by larger rocks. In the laboratory, the males defended territories against other males and established dominance hierarchies. When a female was ready to spawn, she moved into the males' territories, swimming in short bursts, sometimes moving up in the water column to the surface. The males then followed the female who moved into an area with a sandy bottom and burrowed her head and the front of her body into the sand. The male then moved over her and clasped her with his pelvic fins anterior to her dorsal fin. The female then vibrated for up to 30 seconds. The pair then separated and the female moved away, returning later to spawn again. One female was observed to spawn four times in 2.5 hours. At each spawning, the female released 20 to 40 eggs, sometimes as many as 70. Females of age II and III contained 70 to 100 eggs.

The eggs hatched in 13 or 14 days when they were kept at 50 to 60 F for the first 10 days and at 70 F for the last 3 or 4 days.

Food and Feeding
Turner found only midge larvae in six specimens that he examined from Ohio.

Notes
Trautman (1957) noted that in some areas of Ohio the variegate darter has become extremely abundant, although it does not seem to be expanding its range. Attempts to introduce it into apparently similar habitat have been unsuccessful.

References
Hubbs and Black, 1940 (systematics). Lachner et al., 1950 (age and growth). May, 1969 (breeding behavior and development). Nemacek, 1980 (ecology). Turner, 1921 (food).

Names
Variatus is the Latin word for variegate.

Etheostoma variata Kirtland, 1838: 168, 192 Mahoning River, Ohio

Poecilichthys variatus, Greeley, 1938: 72 Allegheny drainage

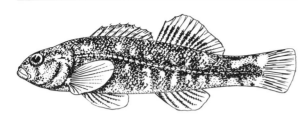

BANDED DARTER

Etheostoma zonale (Cope, 1868)

Identification
The banded darter is a rather small species with broadly joined gill membranes, a declivitous snout, and a complete lateral line with 42 to 53 scales. The ventral surface of the head is rather flat. The most conspicuous color pattern is a series of distinct vertical bands along the sides. Its most diagnostic color feature is the presence of two broad marks in front of the dorsal fin. The marks are the upper ends of vertical bars and, seen from above, they fall short of meeting in the midline so that their rounded ends suggest that the fish had been marked by two tiny thumbs pressing down on the predorsal area.

The banded darter resembles a young rainbow darter but the banded darter is more slender and the rainbow has an incomplete lateral line. The rainbow darter also lacks the thumbprint marks.

Description
Body elongate, somewhat compressed, profiles nearly symmetrical. Head blunt, snout steep. Dorsal origin over basal half of pectoral. Spiny dorsal lower than soft dorsal, its margin arched, membranes not deeply incised. Dorsal fins contiguous. Soft dorsal highest anteriorly, its margin convex, its corners rounded. Last dorsal ray a little longer than half the second longest rays. Caudal emarginate, its middle rays about equal to the longest upper rays. Anal fin origin below origin of second dorsal. Anal margin convex. Pelvic insertion anterior to dorsal origin. Pelvics pointed. Pectoral base sloping slightly backward. Pectoral pointed, nearly symmetrical, with the lower rays thicker. Gill membranes broadly united across the isthmus. Mouth low, horizontal, maxilla reaching to below the front of the eye. Lateral line complete, slightly arched anteriorly. Cheeks, opercles, and prepectoral regions scaled. Breast with a few scattered scales. Frenum present. Counts and proportional measurements are given in Table 35.

Color: The banded darter has a yellowish ground color with dark brownish to black markings. There are six or seven dark saddle-shaped dorsal blotches, the anteriormost on the nape broken at the midline. Upper sides with many irregular dark markings, midsides with 6 to 13 vertical bars, some of which encircle the caudal peduncle and the posterior part of the abdomen. Teardrop present and there is a line from the eye to the upper lip on each side of the frenum. First dorsal with reddish basal blotches on the membranes and a broad dusky submarginal band. Caudal crossed by two irregular bands, pectorals with four or five bands. Pectorals and anal dusky at the base. In females, the markings are less regular.

Juveniles and breeding adults: Juveniles are miniature adults. Breeding males become blackish green with the lower ends of the bars on the sides bright green. The spots at the base of the membrane of the spiny dorsal become bright red and this color is emphasized by the pale spines.

Size: Tsai and Raney reported the maximum size of the banded darter as 62 mm standard length for males and 54 mm for females.

Habitat
The banded darter lives in moderate-sized streams and small rivers where the current is moderate to swift. In the spring, it moves into smaller streams to spawn. It is usually found among gravel, cobbles, or boulders but sometimes it is found on mud or sand.

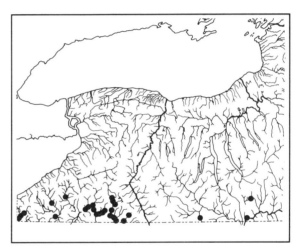

Distribution
The banded darter is widespread in the Mississippi watershed from southern Minnesota, Wisconsin and the Upper Peninsula of Michigan to northern Illinois, and from eastern Oklahoma, Arkansas, Louisiana, and Mississippi north through Ohio and Tennessee to western New York. It has been introduced into the Susquehanna and Savannah Rivers on the Atlantic coast. It spread rapidly through the Susquehanna in Pennsylvania and is now abundant in the southern part of the east branch of the Susquehanna River in New York.

Tsai and Raney recognized several races, of which the Ohio race, characterized by a naked breast and relatively low scale counts, occurs naturally in the Allegheny drainage of New York.

Life History
In spite of the wide distribution of the banded darter, its life history has received little attention. Lutterbie found banded darters in Wisconsin attained an average length of 36.5 mm at age I, 50.2 at age II, 55.1 at age III, and 61.3 at age IV.

Food and Feeding
Not reported.

References

Lachner, Westlake, and Handwerk, 1950 (age and growth). Page and Whitt, 1973 (systematics). Tsai and Raney, 1974 (systematics). Denoncourt, Hocutt, and Stauffer, 1975b (Susquehanna River). Nemacek, 1980 (ecology). Greenberg, 1983 (New York records). Lutterbie, 1979 (age and growth).

Names

The trivial name *zonale* comes from the Latin word for banded.

Poecilichthys zonalis Cope, 1868: 212 Holston River, Virginia

Poecilichthys zonalis zonalis, Greeley, 1938: 72 Allegheny drainage

Etheostoma zonale zonale, Tsai and Raney, 1974: 11-18 (systematics, distribution)

TABLE 35
AVERAGE PROPORTIONAL MEASUREMENTS AND COUNTS OF DARTERS
(*Etheostoma,* in part)

All proportions are expressed in percentage of standard length.

	fusiforme	maculatum	nigrum	olmstedi	variatum	zonale
ST. LENGTH (mm)	30.7	62.0	40.7	43.9	69.3	37.3
TOTAL LENGTH	123.5	120.2	120.8	121.6	118.8	120.5
FORK LENGTH	123.5	120.2	120.8	121.6	117.0	118.6
PREDORSAL	35.0	34.6	32.8	35.5	34.0	33.1
PREANAL	61.9	65.3	59.1	61.3	63.4	60.4
PREPELVIC	34.6	30.6	28.3	31.0	29.2	28.9
DORSAL BASE	41.2	55.6	44.9	48.9	50.7	50.0
ANAL BASE	12.0	17.0	12.2	14.0	14.5	12.6
BODY DEPTH	18.8	22.0	18.1	19.2	21.3	22.7
BODY WIDTH	11.7	12.1	14.3	16.9	15.2	16.5
C.PED. DEPTH	10.4	12.1	9.5	9.6	9.4	11.4
PECTORAL ALT.	11.6	12.1	12.4	12.9	10.9	12.2
HEAD LENGTH	30.3	29.1	25.0	27.4	27.8	25.1
SNOUT	5.8	5.6	6.6	8.7	7.6	6.4
EYE	6.9	6.5	6.6	6.9	8.0	6.8
MOUTH LENGTH	7.8	8.1	7.5	8.4	8.0	6.4
INTERORB	3.5	3.2	8.6	10.5	3.3	3.7
N (sample size)	5	2	4	5	4	5
COUNTS:						
DORSAL SPINES	IX-XI	XII-XIII	XI-XIII	XIII-XVI	XII-XIII	IX-XI
DORSAL RAYS	11	11-12	10-13	11-15	12-1	10-12
ANAL RAYS	II,7-9	II,8	II,7-8	II,6-9	II,8-9	II,6-7
PECTORAL RAYS	11-13	12-15	10-14	9-15	14-16	14-16
PELVIC RAYS	I,5	I,5	I,5	I,5	I,5	I,5
GILL RAKERS	7-8	13-14	7-8	7-8	12	8-10
VERTEBRAE	38-39	37-38	37-38	37-38	40-41	38
SCALES:						
ABOVE L. L.	3	4-9	2-7	3-7	6	4
LATERAL LINE	51-54	51-68	35-36	34-64	51-56	45-51
BELOW L. L.	7-10	8-12	4-9	6-10	6-7	4-6

Perca

The yellow perch and a similar species (or subspecies) in Europe belong to the genus *Perca*. This is a midwater species with a well-developed swim bladder and strongly serrated preopercle and well-developed anal pterygiophores. It has no large canine teeth like those of the members of the genus *Stizostedion*.

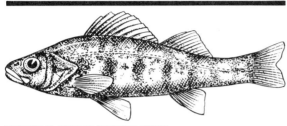

YELLOW PERCH

Perca flavescens (Mitchill, 1814)

Identification

The yellow perch is an elongate, slightly compressed fish with a bold pattern of five to nine vertical, blackish bars on a yellow or greenish-yellow background. Unlike the darters, the preopercle is strongly serrated on both limbs. Young perch develop the banded color pattern quite early, so they would not be confused with any darters. Yellow perch can be distinguished from small walleyes by shape and by color pattern. Walleyes have indistinct oblique bars in contrast to the well-defined vertical bars of the yellow perch. Also, the walleyes and saugers have conspicuous canine teeth in the jaws, and perch do not.

Description

Body elongate and somewhat compressed, its profiles symmetrical. Dorsal origin slightly behind pectoral base. Spiny dorsal larger than the second dorsal, the two fins clearly separate but close together. Third or fourth dorsal spine longest, the interspinous membranes not deeply incised. Soft dorsal highest anteriorly, its margin straight, its corners rounded. Caudal moderately forked, its middle rays four-fifths the longest upper rays. Anal origin below third dorsal soft ray. Anal margin slightly convex, corners rounded. Pelvic insertion slightly behind the dorsal origin. Pelvics larger than pectorals, second pelvic ray longest, last pelvic ray not bound to the body by membrane. Pectoral fin pointed, its base oblique. Preopercle serrate on both limbs. Gill membranes separate, overlapping at the junction. Mouth terminal, maxillary reaching to below front of eye. Body completely scaled, top of head naked. Lateral line complete, arched, parallel to dorsal profile. Counts and proportional measurements are given in Table 37.

Color: The yellow perch is generally yellowish on the sides, shading to olive or brownish above and abruptly white on the breast and belly. Sides with 7 to 10 prominent, rather even, dark, vertical bars ex-

tending from the dark dorsal region to the lower sides. First dorsal dusky with the spines darkly pigmented and with a conspicuous dark blotch on its last spines. Pectorals clear, pelvics and anal red, the color more intense on the anterior parts of the fins.

Juveniles and breeding adults: There are no special breeding colors although the males develop more intense colors during the spawning season. Juveniles tend to be more greenish, without the conspicuous red lower fins.

Size: Adults generally run 10 to 12 inches, sometimes a little larger. The IGFA all-tackle record is a 4-pound 3-ounce fish from Bordentown, New Jersey. The New York record is a 3-pound 8-ounce fish from Lake Erie taken in 1982 by George Boice.

Habitat

Yellow perch often travel in schools. They are most abundant near vegetation in lakes of moderate fertility, but they also occur in streams, sometimes in areas where there is considerable current. They feed most actively during the day and often rest motionless at night. Adult perch usually occupy deeper waters than juveniles do. Yellow perch feed throughout the year and are a popular target for ice fishermen.

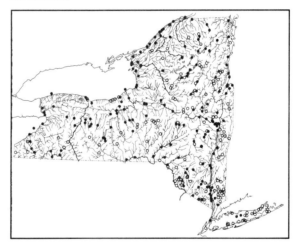

Distribution

The original range of the yellow perch was a broad curved band from the Mackenzie River basin of northwestern Canada to the Maritime Provinces. The southern limits of the band were from northeastern Nebraska and northern Missouri through southern Illinois, Indiana, and Ohio to Pennsylvania. On the Atlantic coast, it ranged south to the Santee River in South Carolina. It occurs in all parts of New York State.

Life History

Spawning takes place in the spring, April or May in our waters, when the temperature reaches 45 to 52 F. Perch spawn after walleyes and at about the same time as white suckers. Males move into the shallows before the females and remain there after the females have left. Spawning occurs in water 5 to 10 feet deep over sand, gravel, rubble, or vegetation. The eggs of the perch are laid in zigzag rows cemented together in a gelatinous band a couple of inches wide and 2 to 7 feet long. These bands are often draped over logs or vegetation. Sometimes they break loose and get washed up on shore. Hatching takes place in about 8 to 10 days, depending on temperature.

Yellow perch can live as long as 9 years. The growth rate is variable and has been studied in many areas.

Food and Feeding
Cladocerans, ostracods, and chironomid midge larvae make up much of the diet of small perch. As the fish get larger, they shift to an insect diet; large perch eat a substantial number of crayfish, small fish, and odonate nymphs. Perch are rather generalized feeders and can obtain food from the bottom as well as in midwater.

Notes
This species is an important sport fish and also the object of the commercial fishery in the Great Lakes and larger bodies of water such as Oneida Lake where they have been studied intensively by Forney and his co-workers.

Although they are an excellent panfish, perch can be extremely detrimental to trout populations. Fraser gives a case history of a lake that was monitored for 6 years before and 6 years after the introduction of perch. There was a drastic change in the food habits of the planted brook trout, splake, and rainbow trout. Brook trout switched from fish, leeches, and odonates to trichopterans. Splake switched from fish and leeches to trichopterans and rainbows changed from a broad diet to dipterans, trichopterans, and entomostracans. In the same lakes, the yellow perch became stunted. Growth rates declined and the yield per kg of brook trout, splake, and rainbow trout planted dropped from 3.3, 6.8, and 6.1 kg to 0.4, 0.9, and 0.8 kg, respectively.

References
Herman et al., 1959 (general summary). Keast and Webb, 1966 (feeding). Keast, 1977 (feeding). Forney, 1974 (interaction with walleye). Helfman, 1979 (activity cycles). Clady and Hutchinson, 1976 (food). Elrod et al., 1981 (food). Maloney and Johnson, 1957 (life history, Minnesota). Robins, 1970 (bibliography). Mansueti, 1964 (early development). Reynolds and Casterlein, 1979 (thermoregulation). Tsai and Gibson, 1971 (fecundity, Maryland). Siefert, 1972 (first food). Hart, 1933 (blue specimen). Burdick, Dean, and Harris, 1957 (lethal oxygen concentrations). Fraser, 1978 (interaction with trout). Jobes, 1952 (life history, Lake Erie). Lin, 1983 (Oneida Lake).

Names
The species name *flavescens* is Latin, meaning becoming yellow.

Morone flavescens Mitchill, 1814: 18 New York
Perca notata Rafinesque, 1818b: 205 Lake Erie
Perca serrato-granulata Cuvier *in* Cuvier and Valenciennes, 1828: 48 New York

Perca granulata Cuvier *in* Cuvier and Valenciennes, 1828: 48
Perca acuta Cuvier *in* Cuvier and Valenciennes, 1828: 49 Lake Ontario
Perca gracilis Cuvier *in* Cuvier and Valenciennes, 1828: 50 Skaneateles Lake
Perca flavescens, Greeley, 1927: 64 Genesee drainage

Percina

This genus contains 31 described species and possibly 8 more that have not been named yet. All share a common feature, the presence of large star-shaped scales on the midline of the breast of males at least and the breast of most females as well. The males of most species also have a midventral row of similarly modified scales. *Percinas* are usually not as colorful as the *Etheostomas*.

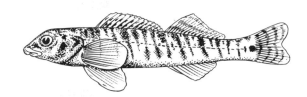

LOGPERCH

Percina caprodes (Rafinesque, 1818)

Identification
The logperch is the easiest of our darters to recognize because both its color pattern and its shape are distinctive. The color pattern is basically a series of more or less alternating long and short, narrow, vertical bars along the sides of the body. The most distinctive shape feature is its long conical snout which overhangs the mouth. There is a frenum connecting the upper lip with the snout. The logperch has small scales and is rather large for a darter, commonly reaching 5 to 6 inches.

Description
Body elongate, nearly terete. Dorsal profile a little more arched than the ventral. Dorsal fins close together, without a scaled interspace between. Margin of the dorsal arched, third dorsal spine longest, followed by progressively shorter spines. Interspinous membranes not incised. Second dorsal highest anteriorly, its margin nearly straight. Caudal emarginate with the middle rays longer than the longest upper rays. Anal origin below origin of second dorsal, anal fin margin convex. Pelvic insertion a little ahead of the dorsal origin but well behind the pectoral base. Pelvic pointed, second ray longest. No pelvic axillary process. Pectoral bluntly rounded, its base nearly vertical. Mouth low and horizontal, maxillary not reaching the front of the

eye. Snout overhanging mouth, pointed. Cheeks and opercles scaled. Gill membranes slightly joined. Prepectoral, breast, and anterior belly naked. Ventral midline with modified scales. Lateral line complete, straight. Counts and proportional measurements are given in Table 36.

Color: Body pale straw color shading to pale olive dorsally and to white ventrally. Body crossed by about 8 long, vertical, dark bars alternating with 9 or 10 shorter ones, all extending ventrally from the middorsal line. A small round, distinct spot at caudal base. Circumorbital area with a dusky expansion but no definite teardrop. Spiny dorsal with two or three dusky bands. Second dorsal with two or three, and caudal with one or two, rows of spots, the other fins clear. Lateral line paler than the background.

Juveniles and breeding adults: Juveniles have less pigment but a more conspicuous caudal spot than adults. Sometimes there is an orange tinge around the caudal spot but the species does not develop bright breeding colors.

Size: Trautman (1981) records specimens up to 7.5 inches long from Buckeye Lake, Ohio.

Habitat
The logperch inhabits slower water of streams and lakes.

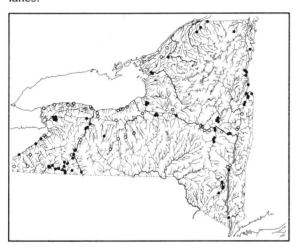

Distribution
The logperch ranges from the Hudson Bay drainage south in the Mississippi watershed to Louisiana. It occurs in the Tennessee River basin, the Great Lakes east to the Ottawa River, and Lake Champlain. Related undescribed species occur on the gulf coast.

Two subspecies are said to live in New York State: The Ohio logperch, *Percina caprodes caprodes,* and the northern logperch, *Percina c. semifasciata.* The Ohio logperch has the nape entirely scaled and the bars even throughout their length; the northern logperch has the nape naked and the bars expanded at their lower ends, almost forming a row of blotches. I have not found a consistent pattern of the occurrence of these two forms in New York.

Life History
Winn (1958b) studied two populations of logperch in Michigan. One spawned in a swift stream at the outlet of Portage Lake and the other spawned over sandy shoals in Douglas Lake. The males moved into shallow water in late June, followed soon afterward by the females. The males formed compact schools that milled around in water 4 to 12 inches deep. Some of these schools contained several hundred individuals. Females generally remained outside the group. When a female was ready to spawn, she swam through the school of males, some of which then pursued her. The female settled to the bottom and one of the males mounted her with his pelvic fins ahead of her dorsal fin and his caudal peduncle alongside her tail. Both fish vibrated vigorously, stirring up the sand. Usually, other males joined the pair and vibrated with them. After spawning, the female returned to deeper water until she was ready to spawn again. Spawning took place during the daylight hours.

In the stream population, the fish maintained themselves in swift current over boulders and gravel while the females concentrated in a pool-like area at the base of the riffle. When a female was ready to spawn, she would move up into the riffle where she was joined by a male. Together the pair moved to a gravelly area where they spawned like those in the lake.

Lutterbie (1979) calculated the following sizes at the time of annulus formation: I-64 to 76 mm, II-95 to 110 mm, III-116 to 122 mm, IV- 125 to 132 mm.

Food and Feeding
Turner found that, in Ohio, young logperch fed on entomostracans, those of intermediate size fed on insects and entomostracans and the larger fish fed mostly on insects. Several observers have reported that the logperch feeds by flipping over pebbles with its conical snout to get at the invertebrates underneath. During spawning, groups of males search out and eat the eggs as they are laid.

References
Jenkins, 1976 (systematics). Reighard, 1913 (breeding habits). Will, 1931 (age at spawning, Michigan). Cooper, 1978a (eggs and larvae). Morris and Page, 1981 (variation). Turner, 1921 (feeding).

Names
The name *caprodes* comes from the Greek *kapros* — a wild boar — and *oides,* a contraction of the Greek *o* plus *eidos,* likeness of form, in allusion to the conical (pig-like) snout.

Sciaena caprodes Rafinesque, 1818c: 354 Ohio River

Percina caprodes caprodes, Greeley, 1938: 72 Allegheny River

Pileoma semifasciatum DeKay, 1842: 16 Lake Champlain at Westport

Pileoma zebra Agassiz, 1850: 308-310 Lake Superior

Percina caprodes zebra, Greeley, 1928: 101 Oswego drainage

Percina caprodes semifasciata, Greeley and Greene, 1931: 91 St. Lawrence drainage

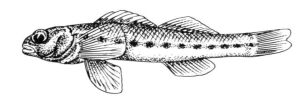

CHANNEL DARTER

Percina copelandi (Jordan, 1877)

Identification

In general appearance, the channel darter looks somewhat like a johnny darter. The two are similar in shape and in having numerous X-shaped markings on the dorsal surface. The channel darter, however, has a row of 12 to 18 elongate dark blotches along its midside and these are connected by a narrow brownish or blackish midlateral stripe. Star-shaped scales on the midventral line of males and between the pelvic fins of both sexes reveal that it is a *Percina* but, unlike most members of that genus, the channel darter has a rudimentary, rather than well-developed swim bladder.

Description

Body elongate, slightly compressed, with the dorsal profile more arched than the ventral. Dorsal origin over basal half of the pectoral fin. Dorsals separate with scales across the interspace. Membranes of the first dorsal not incised. Soft dorsal highest anteriorly, its margin nearly straight. Caudal only slightly emarginate, its middle rays longer than the longest upper rays, its lobes rounded. Anal origin slightly behind origin of second dorsal. Margin of anal fin arched, with the fourth to sixth rays longest. Pelvic insertion anterior to dorsal origin. Pelvics pointed, their third rays longest. No pelvic axillary process. Pectorals bluntly pointed, their bases nearly vertical. Gill membranes separate. Mouth horizontal, small, the maxillary reaching to below the front fourth of the eye. Snout blunt, no frenum. Breast and prepectoral naked, belly scaled, predorsal partly scaled. Lateral line complete, paralleling the dorsal outline. Counts and proportional measurements are given in Table 36.

Color: Winn described the breeding coloration of the channel darter. The females have translucent fins with some gray spots on the dorsal fins and gray at the base of the other fins. The bases of the pectorals and the posterior three or four rays of the pelvics are cream color. The lower half of the body from the chin to the caudal peduncle is white. There are 10 to 12 midlateral blotches, of which the anterior three are smaller and less distinct. The dorsal scales are outlined in black with some local intensification producing a mottled effect. There are three to six faint saddles, the most obvious ones being at the front of the first dorsal, between the fins, and at the middle of the second dorsal. There is a glistening gold spot on the lower part of the operculum, in front of which the cheek is white with gray speckles.

There is a faint gray and yellow suborbital bar and a black bar running downward and backward from the eye.

In the male, the lateral blotches are almost fused, with no creamy interspace. The lateral band has a pale blue-green cast, especially at the base of the pectorals and near the gill opening. This shades to olive green below and this color almost reaches the midline in front of the anus. The basal part of the anal fin is almost black. The pelvic membranes are very dark but the outer margin of the fin is white. The dorsal fin is dark gray, darkest basally, then a lighter band, a narrow darker band, and a white edge. The ventral part of the body is speckled gray, especially from the base of the pelvics to the tip of the lower jaw. The most highly colored males have a milky blue chin, dotted with gray, and two black spots in front of the branchiostegal membrane.

Juveniles and breeding adults: There are no special juvenile features.

Size: This is a small *Percina*, reaching a little more than 3 inches.

Habitat

The channel darter is essentially a bottom-dwelling, lake or large stream species, where it is most common over sandy or gravelly shoals off beaches. Apparently, it stays in deeper water during the day and moves into shallows at night. It spawns in the lower reaches of streams.

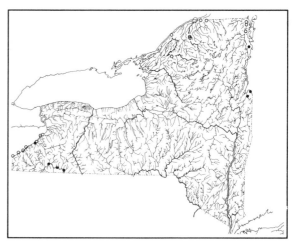

Distribution

Percina copelandi occurs from the Tennessee River, the Ohio River system and Lakes Huron, Erie, and Ontario to the St. Lawrence River and Lake Champlain. A disjunct population occurs in the Red and Arkansas Rivers in Kansas, Oklahoma, Arkansas, and northern Louisiana.

Life History

In the Cheboygan River, in the northern part of the Lower Peninsula of Michigan, Winn found channel darters spawning below a dam where the water was 18 inches to 5 feet deep. Most of the spawning took place where the water was 2 to 3 feet deep and there was a swift current (1.4 feet per second at the surface and 0.95 feet per second near the bottom). Spawning took place 9-23 July, when the temperature was between 69 and 72 F. Males established territories behind rocks about 4 inches in diameter and larger, defending them against other male channel darters but not against logperch.

Usually, males did not stray more than 3 or 4 feet from the territories and then only for brief periods. Receptive females entered the territories and were mounted by the male. The pair vibrated together vigorously in the gravel below or between the rocks. Winn thought 4 to 10 eggs were laid during each spawning episode. The eggs were slightly adhesive, demersal, somewhat flattened, with an average diameter of 1.4 mm. There was considerable variation in size. The eggs were mostly transparent with an orange-colored oil droplet.

Food and Feeding
In the eight specimens examined by Winn, chironomids dominated but caddisfly larvae were also present. Turner (1921) found midge larvae and mayfly larvae in the stomachs of channel darters from the Bass Islands in Lake Erie. The darters had also consumed appreciable amounts of algae and bottom detritus. Young and old darters ate about the same things.

References
Starnes et al., 1977 (distribution). Winn, 1953 (life history).

Names
This species was named for Herbert Edward Copeland, a close friend and colleague of David Starr Jordan, who died after falling into the White River in Indiana in January 1876.

Rheocrypta copelandi Jordan, 1877c: 9 White River near Indianapolis, Indiana

Rheocrypta copelandi, Greeley, 1929: 176 Lake Erie

Cottogaster copelandi, Greeley, 1930: 84-85 Lake Champlain

Cottogaster putnami Jordan and Gilbert, 1883: 498 Westport Brook, Lake Champlain

Cottogaster cheneyi Evermann and Kendall, 1898: 129 Raquette River near Norfolk

Hadropterus copelandi, Hubbs and Lagler, 1958: 107 (distribution)

Percina copelandi, Hubbs and Lagler, 1964: 107 (distribution)

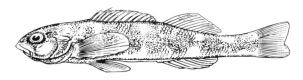

GILT DARTER

Percina evides
(Jordan and Copeland, 1877)

Identification
This is a moderate-sized darter with a well-developed frenum, a complete lateral line, narrowly connected gill membranes, and a terminal mouth. It has a distinctive "neat" appearance, with a row of squarish dorsal blotches directly over the equally square midlateral blotches. In breeding males, these unite to form a row of regular, vertical, blue-green bands. No other *Percina* in our state has red or blue breeding colors.

Description
Body elongate, slightly compressed, dorsal profile more arched than the ventral. Dorsal origin over basal half of the pectoral fin. Spiny and second dorsals separate but no scales crossing the interspace. Spiny dorsal margin arched, fifth spine the longest. Second soft dorsal ray longest, about twice the last ray. Caudal slightly forked, the middle rays about four-fifths the longest lower ray. Caudal lobes rounded. Anal origin below origin of second dorsal. Fifth and sixth anal rays longest. Pelvic insertion slightly ahead of dorsal origin. Pelvic pointed, its third ray longest, its last ray not connected to the body by membrane. No pelvic axillary process. Pectorals pointed, nearly symmetrical, their bases almost vertical. Gill membranes slightly joined anteriorly. Mouth terminal, maxillary reaching to below front of eye. Frenum present. Breast, belly, except for the specialized scales in the midline, and prepectoral regions naked. Nape partly scaled. Lateral line complete, parallel to dorsal profile. Counts and proportional measurements are given in Table 36.

Color: The pattern of the gilt darter is dominated by about eight squarish blotches along the midside, separated by somewhat shorter interspaces. These blotches are aligned with squarish dorsal saddle blotches and separated from them by a narrow pale space. Teardrop distinct; fins without prominent markings.

Juveniles and breeding adults: Breeding males are brilliant. The dark saddles become blue green and unite with similarly colored lateral blotches to form vertical bars. The interspaces and ventral parts of the body become bright red and two round orange spots develop on the caudal base. The dorsal fins are red orange and the anal and pelvics blue black. Males develop breeding tubercles over much of the ventral surface.

Size: To about 3 inches.

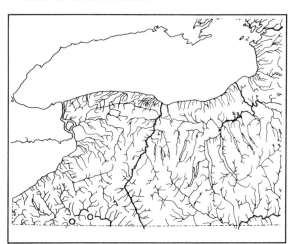

Habitat

The gilt darter is restricted to moderately-fast, deep runs and slow riffles in larger streams. It is apparently intolerant of slow water and silt and shows a preference for areas with loose gravel and boulders.

Distribution

This species occurs from Arkansas and southeastern Missouri to the Tennesee drainage. In the Mississippi Valley, it reaches eastern Minnesota. It occurs in the Wabash and in tributaries of the Ohio to the Allegheny in New York. Its only occurrence in the Great Lakes basin was in the Maumee River in Ohio.

In New York, the Survey took it from three large riffles in the Allegheny River near Carrollton.

Life History

Little is known of its life history except that it is a spring spawner. In Wisconsin, Lutterbie calculated the average size at the time of annulus formation as follows: I - 39.9 mm, II - 61.3 mm, III - 71.0 mm, IV - 75.5 mm.

Food and Feeding

Not reported.

Notes

There have been no reports of this species in New York waters since the Survey in 1937. Because it is so difficult to sample the fast deep waters of the Allegheny River it may still be present in small numbers, although the hope of its survival is diminishing each year.

References

Lutterbie, 1979 (age and growth). Page, 1974 (systematics). Page, 1976a (systematics). Page and Whitt, 1973 (systematics). Denoncourt, 1969 (systematics). Page, Retzer, and Stiles, 1982 (spawning behavior).

Names

The species name is from the Greek *evides (eueides)*, comely.

Alvordius evides Jordan and Copeland *in* Jordan, 1877b: 51 White River near Indianapolis

Hadropterus evides, Greeley, 1938: 72 Allegheny River

Percina evides Hubbs and Lagler, 1964: 107 Great Lakes

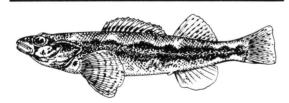

LONGHEAD DARTER

Percina macrocephala (Cope, 1869)

Identification

The longhead darter is aptly named, for its out-standing characteristics are its long head and long pointed snout. It resembles the blackside darter but differs in having smaller scales (74 to 80 in the lateral line) and in having the gill membranes united for a greater distance. A distinctive feature is the presence of one to three dusky spots on each side of the ventral surface of the head. The last of these is sometimes connected to the suborbital (teardrop) bar. Such spots are not present in the blackside darter. The longhead darter has more than 12 dorsal saddles and the blackside has fewer. In the longhead darter, the squarish midlateral blotches are somewhat connected but in the blackside they are mostly separate.

Description

Body elongate, little compressed, profiles even and symmetrical. Dorsal origin over middle of pectoral fin. Dorsal fins separate, the interspace scaled but the scales do not cross the midline. Spiny dorsal margin arched, fourth spine longest, the interspinous membrane not incised. Soft dorsal highest anteriorly, its margin straight. Caudal margin straight, longest middle rays a little longer than longest upper rays, Corners of the caudal angled. Anal origin below origin of second dorsal. Anal margin rounded, its fourth and fifth rays longest. Pelvic insertion between level of pectoral base and dorsal origin. Pelvic pointed, its last ray not bound to the body wall. Pectoral rounded, paddle shaped. Pectoral base vertical or slightly inclined backward. Gill membranes united anteriorly. Head long, mouth terminal, maxilla reaching to below front of eye. Frenum present. Predorsal scaled; breast, prepectoral, and anterior belly naked. Cheeks and opercles scaled. Lateral line complete, straight. Counts and proportional measurements are given in Table 36.

Color: The color pattern of the longhead is dominated by a midlateral stripe that alternately widens and narrows, the wider areas corresponding to the blotches on other species of *Percina*. The dorsal edge of the midlateral stripe is marked by a pale sand-colored line that grades into light olive over the back. The sides below the stripe are marbled with irregular sooty marks. The belly is white. The spiny dorsal is clear, with a basal row of dark spots on the membrane, and a dusky submarginal band. The second dorsal is clear, with three rows of dark spots, and the caudal has four rows of similar spots. The anal and pelvic fins have a few irregular dark spots, otherwise they are clear. There are six rows of dark spots crossing the pectoral fin. There is a preorbital stripe and a distinct suborbital bar. The upper lip is dark, the preopercle has dark spots, and the operculum is mostly dark. There are one to three dark spots on the lower side of the head. Some individuals have a conspicuous dark spot on the otherwise white pectoral base. There is a conspicuous basicaudal bar, with a dark bar below it.

Juveniles and breeding adults: The longhead darter does not have bright breeding colors. Young individuals have the midlateral stripe more divided into distinct blotches.

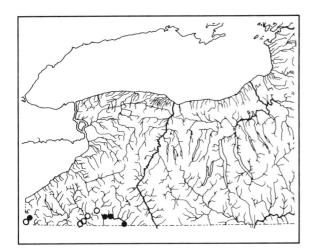

Hadropterus macrocephalus, Greeley, 1938: 72 Allegheny River

Percina macrocephala, Eaton et al., 1982: 194 Allegheny River

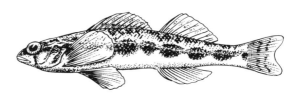

BLACKSIDE DARTER

Percina maculata (Girard, 1860)

Identification

The blackside darter is a rather typical *Percina*, with a conspicuous row of large, rectangular, black blotches along the side of the body. It resembles the longhead darter but that species has a longer, more pointed head, smaller scales, blotches that tend to fuse into a solid stripe, and characteristic spots on the underside of the head. The blackside darter looks most like the shield darter, but has scales on the cheeks which are not present in New York populations of the shield darter. The shield darter lives in the eastern part of the state, whereas the blackside is found only in the western part of the state.

Description

Body elongate, slightly compressed, dorsal profile more arched than the ventral. Dorsal origin over middle of pectoral fin. Dorsal fin completely separate, the interspace scaled. Base of second dorsal about half length of base of spiny part. Margin of first dorsal arched, the fourth through sixth spines longest. Second dorsal highest anteriorly, third and fourth rays longest. Last dorsal ray about two-thirds the longest. Margin of second dorsal straight, corners rounded. Caudal a little emarginate, the middle rays slightly shorter than the longest upper rays. Anal origin below origin of second dorsal. Fifth and sixth anal rays longest. Pelvics inserted a little ahead of the second dorsal, pointed, their second and third rays longest. Pectorals symmetrically pointed, their bases nearly vertical. Gill membranes separate. Mouth subterminal, maxillary reaching to below front of pupil. Frenum present. Cheeks and opercles scaled, breast, prepectoral and belly naked except for the stellate scales characteristic of the genus. Lateral line complete, parallel to dorsal profile. Counts and proportional measurements are given in Table 36.

Color: The ground color is pale straw yellow, shading to white ventrally. Dorsal midline with 6 to 11 quadrate, saddle-shaped blotches. A midlateral row of about eight squarish blotches more or less interconnected. A separate, vertically elongate spot at the base of the tail. Above the lateral blotches, there are short, irregular, dark lines consisting of X-shaped marks formed by pigment along the edges of the scales. Upper part of opercle black. Nasal stripe prominent, teardrop indistinct. Dorsal and

---

Size: This is a moderately large species of darter, reaching more than 4.75 inches total length. Page gives the maximum standard length as 102 mm.

Habitat

The longhead darter lives in moderate-sized to large, clear streams over gravel and cobbles. It appears to be a midwater species that is difficult to collect by the usual seining methods. Dr. Wayne Hadley and his students have had good success using a large number of people to drive the fish downstream into a seine set across the current. Page describes its habitat as pools with considerable current.

Distribution

The longhead darter has a rather restricted range in the Upper Tennessee River and the southern tributaries of the Ohio River. It occurs in the Scioto River in Ohio and the Allegheny River in New York and Pennsylvania. Recent collections have been made near Portville and Westons Mills.

Life History

Page postulated a spring spawning period; March, April, or May in the Green River in Kentucky. In New York, the season would probably be somewhat later. Page did not find clear annuli, but the scales seemed to indicate a maximum age of about 4 years.

Food and Feeding

This species is said to feed on crayfish to a greater extent than most darters. Page found only crayfish and mayflies in their stomachs.

Notes

The populations of the longnose darter should be monitored carefully. It is one of the most spectacular darters in the state but it has stringent habitat requirements.

References

Page, 1974 (systematics); 1978 (ecology).

Names

Macrocephala is from the Greek *makro,* long and *kephalos,* head.

Etheostoma macrocephala Cope, 1869b: 400 Youghiogheny River, Pennsylvania

caudal fins with rows of spots; anal, pelvics, and pectorals clear.

Juveniles and breeding adults: This species does not develop bright breeding colors. Juveniles have less pigment than adults.

Size: The blackside reaches slightly more than 4 inches total length.

Habitat

The blackside darter lives in small- to moderate-sized streams with some current and considerable shelter such as brush, vegetation, or overhanging banks, and sand or gravel bottom.

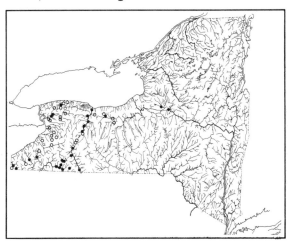

Distribution

The blackside darter ranges from southeastern Saskatchewan in a band through the southern part of the Great Lakes to western New York. It occurs south in the Mississippi Valley to eastern Oklahoma and Louisiana and east on the gulf coast to the Mobile Bay drainage.

Life History

The life history of this species was studied in central Michigan by Petravicz and confirmed by Winn. Spawning began in May when the water temperature reached 16.5 C. Spawning sites were over sand where the water was about 1 foot deep, or 2 feet in swifter raceway-like areas to which the fish migrated in March or April. Males pursue the females into the spawning areas where the female settles to the bottom. A male then comes to lie next to her with his pelvic fins across her back. The two vibrate together and press themselves into gravelly or sandy depressions where the eggs are deposited. Petravicz thought that the anal and caudal fins of the male were on opposite sides of the female but Winn doubted this. After spawning, they rest a few minutes, then spawn again. The eggs are about 2 mm in diameter. Hatching takes place in 142 hours and the newly hatched larvae are 5.75 mm long. Soon after hatching they rise to the surface and, within 3 weeks, take up a benthic existence.

Lutterbie reported the following average lengths at the time of annulus formation: I- 47.7 mm, II-70.1 mm, III-80.0 mm, IV-92.6 mm.

Food and Feeding

Apparently, the blackside is an opportunistic hunter that often feeds in midwater. Trautman reported that it occasionally leaps into the air after flying insects. Turner found midge and mayfly larvae, corixid nymphs, copepods, and small fish in the stomachs. Fish 34 mm long had approximately the same diet as those 67 mm.

References

Page, 1974 (systematics); 1976b (hybrids). Moore and Reeves, 1955 (ecology). Karr, 1964 (age, growth, food). Smart and Gee, 1979 (ecology). Lutterbie, 1979 (age and growth). Turner, 1921 (food). Trautman, 1957 (Ohio). Petravicz, 1938 (life history). Winn, 1958b (life history).

Names

Maculatus is the Latin word for spotted.

Alvordius maculatus Girard, 1860: 68 Fort Gratiot, Michigan

Hadropterus maculatus, Greeley, 1927: 64 Genesee drainage

Percina maculata, Hubbs and Lagler, 1974: 106 (distribution)

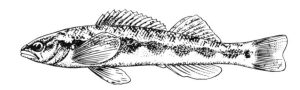

SHIELD DARTER

Percina peltata (Stauffer, 1864)

Identification

The shield darter is a rather ordinary species of *Percina* and can be recognized as such by its having a row of modified star-shaped scales on the midline of the belly, and by its conspicuous pattern of a line of partly connected, rectangular, black blotches along the side. The shield darter most resembles the blackside darter but the blackside darter has scales on the cheeks. New York populations of the shield darter do not. Furthermore, the two species have complementary ranges — the shield darter occurs only in the eastern part of the state and the blackside darter is a midwestern species living only in the western part of the state.

Description

Body elongate and slightly compressed, profiles even and symmetrical. Dorsal fin originating over middle of the pectoral fin. Dorsal fins separate, with scales in the interspace and a ridge of membrane forming a low superficial keel. Margin of the first dorsal arched, its fourth and fifth spines longest, its membrane little incised. Second dorsal highest anteriorly, its third ray longest, its margin straight. Caudal somewhat forked, its middle rays four-fifths the longest upper rays. Anal origin under origin of second dorsal. Anal margin arched, the fourth to sixth rays longest. Pelvic origin ahead of dorsal origin and behind base of pectoral fin. No pelvic axillary process. Pelvic fin pointed. Pectoral bluntly pointed, its base nearly vertical. Gill membranes separate, overlapping anteriorly. Mouth low, terminal, the maxillary reaching to below the front of the eye. Frenum present. Cheeks, opercles, prepectoral, breast and midline of belly naked (except for the row of stellate scales in males). Lateral line complete, nearly straight. Counts and proportional measurements are given in Table 36.

Color: Ground color pale straw yellow. Back crossed by blackish saddles that interconnect to enclose pale oval areas. Dark blotch on nape with pale oval center. Sides with a row of quadrate blotches of varying sizes. Caudal base with a dark spot on its lower half. First dorsal with a row of dark crescents on the basal parts of the membranes and a dark submarginal band. Second dorsal with concentrations of pigment forming irregular rows of indistinct spots. Caudal similar. Anal, pectorals, and pelvics clear, with some dark spots. Teardrop suborbital bar well developed, a dark spot behind the chin, and discrete dark spots on the breast.

Juveniles and breeding adults: The species does not develop bright breeding colors nor does it have breeding tubercles.

Size: The shield darter reaches slightly more than 3 inches total length.

Habitat

Clear moderate-sized creeks, with gravel and rubble bottom, and considerable current seem to be the requirements of the shield darter. Greeley (1936) remarked that "It is extremely agile and usually difficult to seine so that it is apt to be regarded as scarcer than it really is."

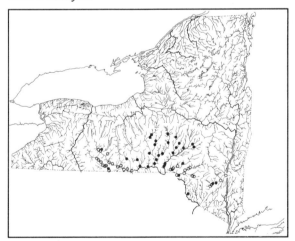

Distribution

The shield darter is an Atlantic coast species that ranges from the Hudson River to the Neuse River in North Carolina. In New York, it is found in Rondout Creek, the Delaware, and the Susquehanna systems. It occurs in Cayuta Creek, and Greeley recorded it from the Chemung drainage.

Mayden and Page compared southern population of the shield darter with its relatives, *Percina roanoka* and *Percina crassa,* and noted that southern populations of the shield darter have scales on the cheeks. They regarded the presence of scales on the cheeks, larger size, slender body, and lack of

bright colors as unspecialized features relative to the opposite conditions in the other two species.

Life History

New described the breeding behavior of this species in Otego Creek and other localities and supplemented his data with observations made on captive fish. Apparently, there is little or no migration as the year-round habitat provides the necessary spawning sites. Spawning takes place over fine gravel but large rocks must also be present. Spawning was observed in daylight and once at night. The breeding season begins around mid-April and extends through May. Males became ripe in September and spawning was earlier than in *Etheostoma olmstedi.* Males established territories on the downstream sides of rocks where there was a deposit of fine gravel. Conspecific males were driven away and chased for 2 or 3 feet, sometimes as much as 10 feet. The size of the territories was not determined but the defense seemed to be most intense within 2 feet of the sheltering rock. When intruders approached, the defender would first display, turning his body parallel to the intruder. If there was no retreat, he would strike with his mouth open and his fins erect. Fights seldom lasted more than 15 or 20 seconds, with rest periods of 3 to 5 seconds, until one fish was driven off. Sexual dimorphism is not pronounced in this species and sex recognition seems to be on the basis of behavior patterns. Frequently, males attempted to spawn with other males, particularly if the second male was lying on the bottom with the dorsal fin depressed.

When ready to spawn, a female would enter a male's territory and come to rest on the bottom with her body slightly curved. The male would mount her with his head and isthmus against her nape and his body parallel to, and over, hers. The pair would quiver vigorously for 10 to 15 seconds, ploughing through the gravel so that the eggs were released below the surface. Usually, the male's anal fin and caudal fin were on opposite sides of the female with the female's erect second dorsal on the same side as the male's anal fin.

Food and Feeding

The food habits do not seem to have been studied.

Notes

Loos and Woolcott found one hybrid between *Percina peltata* and *P. notogramma* in the York River in Virginia. Their study indicated that *P. peltata* usually spawned in faster current and was less ritualistic in its behavior than *P. notogramma,* and they suggested that this may be why hybrids are uncommon.

References

Collette, 1965 (systematics). Page, 1976a (characters). Loos and Woolcott, 1969 (hybridization). New, 1966 (reproductive behavior). Mayden and Page, 1979 (systematics). Greeley, 1936 (Delaware and Susquehanna drainages).

Names

The species name is the Latin word meaning shielded.

Etheostoma peltatum Stauffer *in* Cope, 1864: 233 Conestoga Creek, Pennsylvania

Hadropterus peltatus, Greeley, 1936: 86 Delaware and Susquehanna drainages

Percina peltata, Bailey et al., 1960: 29 (nomenclature)

TABLE 36
AVERAGE PROPORTIONAL MEASUREMENTS AND COUNTS OF DARTERS *(Percina)*

All proportions are expressed in percentage of standard length.

	caprodes	copelandi	evides	macrocephala	maculata	peltata
ST. LENGTH (mm)	61.9	36.0	44.2	62.1	47.3	67.7
TOTAL LENGTH	117.7	117.5	116.3	115.9	119.0	119.3
FORK LENGTH	116.1	116.4	113.8	113.7	116.8	115.4
PREDORSAL	32.7	33.1	34.2	37.5	36.5	34.2
PREANAL	65.1	61.9	63.9	67.3	65.1	64.5
PREPELVIC	31.1	28.6	30.4	32.9	30.3	28.0
DORSAL BASE	52.1	45.3	49.6	47.3	47.7	49.6
ANAL BASE	14.1	14.4	15.1	14.0	14.3	15.1
BODY DEPTH	17.6	15.0	17.8	16.7	17.3	17.6
BODY WIDTH	12.3	12.8	14.1	12.4	13.1	14.3
C. PED. DEPTH	8.2	8.3	8.3	7.8	8.4	8.2
PECTORAL ALT.	10.9	9.7	10.5	10.5	11.3	10.4
HEAD LENGTH	28.3	11.9	27.5	30.8	25.8	26.1
SNOUT	8.8	6.1	7.6	8.7	6.8	7.4
EYE	6.9	6.7	6.4	7.4	8.1	5.9
MOUTH LENGTH	8.1	7.2	7.9	9.1	8.2	8.0
INTERORB	4.5	2.5	4.1	3.7	8.6	4.7
N (sample size)	5	1	5	2	3	5
COUNTS:						
DORSAL SPINES	XIV-XVI	XI	XI-XIII	XIV-XV	XIV-XV	XII
DORSAL RAYS	15-16	10-12	10-14	12-13	12-14	13
ANAL RAYS	II,6-7	II,10-11	II,5-10	II,9	II,9-11	II,9-10
PECTORAL RAYS	12-16	14-15	11-16	14	13-14	14
PELVIC RAYS	I,5	I,5	I,5	I,5	I,5	I,5
GILL RAKERS	13	16-17	16	12-15	—	—
VERTEBRAE	43-45	38-39	37-42	43-44	43-44	43-44
SCALES:						
ABOVE L. L.	7-10	5	7-9	7-8	6-8	6-7
LATERAL LINE	67-100	48	55-60	75-78	65-70	53-57
BELOW L.L.	12-17	6	8-12	12-13	8-10	9-10

Stizostedion

This genus includes the sauger, walleye, and one or two European species. They are large, rather elongate fishes with toothed preopercles and large canine teeth. The anal fin supports are only weakly developed.

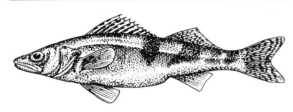

SAUGER

Stizostedion canadense
(Smith, 1834)

Identification
Sauger and walleyes are the largest members of the perch family. They both differ from the yellow perch in color and in having large canine teeth in the jaws which the perch does not have. They differ from all of the darters in their large size and in the fact that their preopercles are serrated while those of the darters are smooth, or nearly so. It is easy to confuse the sauger with the walleye, but saugers have oblique rows of definite spots on the first dorsal whereas the first dorsal of the walleye has only diffuse markings. The walleye also has a definite dark blotch at the end of the spiny dorsal which is wanting in the sauger. The sauger has five to eight pyloric caeca which are shorter than the stomach; the walleye has three that are longer than the stomach.

Description
Body elongate and slab sided, profiles even and symmetrical. Dorsal fin origin over pectoral base, spiny dorsal margin arched, its third through fifth spines longest. Dorsals separate. Second dorsal highest anteriorly, its margin straight, its corners angulate. Caudal forked, its middle rays shorter than the longest upper rays. Anal origin below anterior half of second dorsal, its third ray longest, its margin straight. Pelvics large, bluntly pointed, inserted below basal one-fourth of the pectoral. Pectoral asymmetrically pointed with its base nearly vertical. Gill membranes separate and free from the isthmus. Preopercle serrate on both limbs, the dentations of the lower limb large and antrorse. Mouth large, with strong canine teeth on the jaws, maxillary reaching to below rear of the eye. Eye large. Lateral line complete, paralleling dorsal profile. Counts and proportional measurements are given in Table 37.

Color: Generally brownish gray with yellow wash, shading to white ventrally. Body crossed by three or four irregular saddle-shaped blotches, some of which extend onto the sides as sloping bars. First dorsal with rows of distinct spots on the membranes and no black blotch at the back. Second dorsal with two or more rows of spots, its margin dusky. Caudal similar to second dorsal. Pectorals, pelvics, and anal fin light with a few dark spots, anal sometimes with a white anterior tip. Pectoral base with a dark blotch. Sides of head marbled.

Juveniles and breeding adults: Juveniles are somewhat more distinctly marked. There are no conspicuous breeding colors.

Size: Usually about 12 to 14 inches. The IGFA record is 8 pounds 12 ounces from Lake Sakajawea, North Dakota.

Habitat
The sauger is a big-water fish of lakes, reservoirs, and large rivers. It is apparently more tolerant of turbidity than the walleye.

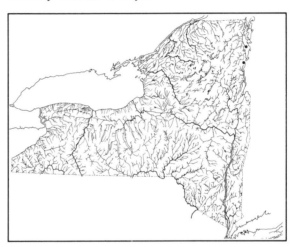

Distribution
The sauger originally ranged through the Mississippi drainage from Louisiana north to Montana and central Alberta, east to James Bay and Lake Champlain. It occurred throughout much of the Tennessee and Ohio River basins. It has now been introduced in several gulf and Atlantic coast drainages. It was formerly a commercial fish in Lake Erie but became commercially extinct there in the 1930s. It is still reasonably common in Lake Champlain.

Life History
Sauger spawn in May or June, usually after walleyes, when the temperature reaches 39 to 43 F. Males move onto the gravelly spawning shoals before the females. Spawning takes place at night in water 2 to 12 feet deep. The eggs are scattered over the gravel with no nest preparation and no parental care. Females lay 15,000 to 40,000 eggs and leave the area soon after spawning. The eggs are adhesive and stick to the gravel or rock bottom. In the laboratory, the eggs hatch in 21 days at 47 F and 9 to 14 days at 55 F.

Food and Feeding
Dendy reported that saugers in Norris Reservoir ate primarily gizzard shad, crappies, and bass. Elsewhere, they might be expected to eat other species but they are primarily piscivorous. Young-of-the-year in Lewis and Clark Reservoir fed on *Cyclops*

first, switching to *Daphnia* and *Diaptomus* later, and to fish when they reached 70 to 100 mm total length.

Notes
Recent attempts to reestablish the sauger in Lake Erie are apparently meeting with some success.

References
Dendy, 1946 (food). Greeley, 1964 (popular account). Kendall, 1978 (management). Nelson, 1968a (life history); 1968b (embryology, hybridization). Rawson and Scholl, 1978 (reestablishment in Lake Erie).

Names
The sauger is named for the country from which it was first described, Canada.

Lucioperca canadensis Smith *in* Cuvier, 1834: 275 Canada

Lucioperca grisea DeKay, 1842:19 New York

Stizostedion canadense griseum, Greeley, 1929: 176 Lake Erie

Stizostedion canadense, Greeley, 1930: 84 Lake Champlain

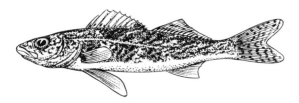

WALLEYE AND BLUE PIKE

Stizostedion vitreum vitreum (Mitchill, 1818) *and S. v. glaucum* Hubbs, 1926

Identification
The walleye is a large slender percid that differs from the yellow perch in having large caniniform jaw teeth, and in lacking the regular vertical bars of the perch although walleyes have markings that sometimes appear as rather unorganized oblique bars. Like the yellow perch, they have a dark blotch at the back of the first dorsal fin.

Walleyes are difficult to distinguish from saugers but saugers lack the black blotch at the end of the first dorsal fin and also have distinct spots on the first dorsal whereas the walleye lacks the spots and has the blotch. The walleye has three pyloric caeca that are longer than the stomach; the sauger has five to eight caeca that are shorter than the stomach.

Description
Body elongate, streamlined, little compressed. Profiles symmetrical. Dorsal origin over base of pectoral. Dorsal fins separated by a scaled space. Spiny dorsal margin arched, interspinous membrane not incised. Soft dorsal highest anteriorly, its margin straight. Caudal forked, its middle rays two-thirds the longest upper rays. Anal origin under fourth

dorsal soft ray. Anal highest anteriorly, its margin straight. Pelvic inserted below second dorsal spine. Pelvics retrogressive, last ray two-thirds the first. Pectoral fin blunt, shorter than the pelvic, pectoral base oblique. Gill membranes separate, overlapping anteriorly. Mouth terminal, maxillary reaching to below posterior edge of pupil. Preopercles strongly serrated. Body completely scaled except the breast is naked, with a triangular patch of scales in front of the pelvic fin. Prepectoral scaled. Lateral line complete, straight. Counts and proportional measurements are given in Table 37.

Color: Although its color is highly variable, the walleye is basically brownish yellow to grayish yellow, shading to white on the ventral surface. Young walleyes show vague saddle-shaped oblique bands on the body. There is a blackish spot on the pectoral base and another on the membranes at the back of the first dorsal fin. The second dorsal and the caudal base are crossed with irregular lines of spots. The tip of the lower lobe of the caudal and the tip of the anal fin are white. Pectoral, pelvic and anal fins clear, with a few dark spots.

Juveniles and breeding adults: Juveniles are more conspicuously marked. There are no special breeding colors.

Size: The IGFA record is a 25-pound fish from Old Hickory Lake in Tennessee. The New York State record is 15 pounds 3 ounces from the Chemung River.

Habitat
Walleyes occur in lakes and larger rivers. Most of the time, they hover near the bottom in loose aggregations during the day and move into shallows to feed at night. They are active during the winter.

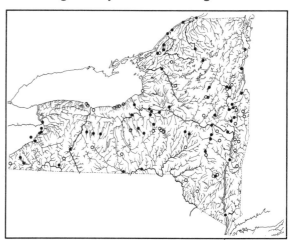

Distribution
The walleye has a wide distribution through the central part of North America from the Mackenzie River to Quebec and south to northern Texas, Alabama, and Georgia. The original range has been expanded by introductions on the Atlantic and gulf coasts and elsewhere.

Life History
Walleyes spawn in the spring just after the ice goes and the water temperatures reach 35 to 44 F. The

spawning sites are usually gravel bars in streams or shoals in lakes where there is considerable water movement over rocks, gravel, or even sand. Wall-eyes do not build nests. The males move onto the spawning area first. During the day, they remain in deep water and after dark they move into the shallows for spawning. A female accompanied by one or more males moves onto the bar and the fish vibrate and roll together as the eggs and sperm are broadcast over the gravel. Usually, the spawning site has water less than 2 feet deep and seldom more than 4 feet. Females lay 35,000 to more than 600,000 eggs. Hatching time varies according to temperature, requiring 7 days at 51 F and 26 days at 40 F. Males mature at age II or III when they are 12 to 13.5 inches long; females mature at ages IV or V when they are 17 inches long. Males tend to remain on the spawning beds longer than the females but there is no parental care.

Food and Feeding
Walleyes are opportunistic predators. Very small walleyes feed first on planktonic crustaceans, then switch to insects. By the time they are 3 inches long, they feed on fish and other larger items.

Notes
There is an enormous literature on the walleye. It is one of our most important game and commercial species and its growth rates and habits are variable, as one would expect of a widespread and successful species.

The blue pike was originally described from Lake Erie by Hubbs (1926). It was an important commercial fish as late as the early 1970s but is now probably extinct. The blue pike was distinguished from the walleye by its lack of yellow pigment and by its larger eye and narrower interorbital distance. In the walleye, the interorbital distance was contained 1.1 to 1.4 times in the eye diameter in young, about 1.0 in adults. In the blue pike, the interorbital was 1.4 to 2.0 in the eye diameter.

Bluish walleyes were also present in Lake Ontario, but several workers have expressed doubts that they were the same as the Lake Erie walleye. Overfishing and genetic swamping (interbreeding with the more abundant walleye) have been cited as reasons for the disappearance of the blue walleye.

References
Robins, 1970 (bibliography). Eschmeyer, 1950 (life history). Raney and Lachner, 1942 (ecology). Niemuth, Churchill, and Wirth, 1959 (summary). Zilliox, 1962 (Lake Champlain). Regier et al., 1969 (Lake Erie). Li and Ayles, 1981 (feeding of fingerlings). Forney, 1967, 1975, 1976, 1977a, 1977b (ecology and management in Oneida Lake). Galligan, 1960 (winter food). Wolfert, 1977 (growth). Wolfert and Van Meter, 1978 (movement). Wolfert, Busch, and Baker, 1975 (egg predation). Buynak and Gurzynski, 1978a (disease).

Names
Vitreum is the Latin word for glass, in reference to the glassy appearance of the eye.

Perca vitrea, Mitchill, 1818a: 247 Cayuga Lake
Lucioperca americana Cuvier *in* Cuvier and Valenciennes, 1828: 122 New York
Stizostedion vitreum, Greeley, 1927: 64 Genesee drainage
Stizostedion glaucum Hubbs, 1926: 58 Lake Erie
Stizostedion vitreum vitreum, Hubbs and Lagler, 1974: 106
Stizostedion vitreum glaucum, Greeley, 1940: 80 canal in Ontario drainage

TABLE 37
**AVERAGE PROPORTIONAL MEASUREMENTS AND COUNTS OF YELLOW PERCH,
SAUGER, AND WALLEYE** (*Perca* and *Stizostedion*)

All proportions are expressed in percentage of standard length.

	Perca flavescens	*Stizostedion* canadense	vitreum
ST. LENGTH (mm)	60.0	343.6	103.2
TOTAL LENGTH	123.4	117.8	120.2
FORK LENGTH	117.9	111.8	113.2
PREDORSAL	34.4	32.7	36.0
PREANAL	67.8	68.2	68.6
PREPELVIC	38.1	32.2	37.2
DORSAL BASE	30.7	54.0	50.8
ANAL BASE	11.9	13.2	12.6
BODY DEPTH	26.9	24.4	20.0
BODY WIDTH	14.1	16.5	15.0
C. PED. DEPTH	9.8	8.0	7.6
PECTORAL ALT.	18.2	13.6	13.8
HEAD LENGTH	32.9	29.7	34.8
SNOUT	8.5	8.3	10.1
EYE	9.9	4.6	7.6
MOUTH LENGTH	11.2	13.0	15.0
INTERORB	7.7	5.8	5.8
N (sample size)	5	1	2
COUNTS:			
DORSAL SPINES	XV-XVI	XIII	XIV
DORSAL RAYS	12-13	17	20-21
ANAL RAYS	II,7-8	II,12	II,11-13
PECTORAL RAYS	13-14	13-15	15
PELVIC RAYS	I,5	I,5	I,5
GILL RAKERS	19-23	19-22	21
VERTEBRAE	39-41	45	46-47
SCALES:			
ABOVE L. L.	5-6	10	12
LATERAL LINE	53-60	90-94	84
BELOW L. L.	11-13	12	15

DRUMS

SCIAENIDAE

The freshwater drum is an exception to the general rule that drums are coastal marine species. Like its marine relatives, it has a short first and long second dorsal fin and the lateral line continues out to the end of the tail fin. It also has heavy molar-like pharyngeal teeth, enlarged head canals, and the general look of some of the marine drums.

The family Sciaenidae is worldwide in temperate and warm seas. It contains about 28 genera and 160 species. Although they all share a characteristic appearance, they are, in fact, quite diverse.

Freshwater drum are not highly regarded as food fish but they can provide some sport fishing in the larger waters of our state.

A recent general study of the family, including the freshwater drum, is that of Chao (1978).

A key to the species of drums reported from the inland waters of New York State will be found in the section on marine visitors.

Aplodinotus

This genus contains only one species. It is distinguished from other sciaenids by its simple, carrot-shaped swim bladder, its heavy, fused lower pharyngeal bones, and lack of barbels.

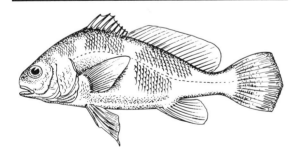

FRESHWATER DRUM

Aplodinotus grunniens
Rafinesque, 1819

Identification
The freshwater drum is a rather typical-looking member of this predominately marine family. It has a blunt head, with the snout overhanging the low horizontal mouth, and this distinctive physiognomy

has earned it its alternate name — sheepshead. The body is deepest anterior to the dorsal fin and tapers to the base of the asymmetrically pointed tail. The spiny dorsal is much shorter than the second dorsal.

One of its more distinctive sciaenid features is the enlarged sensory canals on the head. The bone covering the canals is reduced to narrow bridges and this sometimes gives the head a honeycomb appearance, although in life it is more or less masked by the dense scales covering the head. Another sciaenid feature is that the lateral line continues out to the tip of the middle caudal rays. The maxillary bone slides under the preorbital region when the mouth is closed.

Description
Body moderately elongate and somewhat compressed, deepest just behind the head. Dorsal profile rising steeply, then sloping evenly to the caudal peduncle. Ventral profile almost straight. Body compressed dorsally, less so ventrally, producing a somewhat triangular cross section. Snout blunt, overhanging the almost horizontal mouth. Top of head scaly to a line in front of the eyes. Cheeks, preopercles, and opercles scaly, bases of vertical fins and pectorals scaly. Dorsal fins continuous, the first spine short, the second and third subequal, the rest graduated, except the last which is longer than the preceding and closely connected to the first soft ray. Soft dorsal long, its margin evenly convex, rounded posteriorly. Anal high, rounded. Caudal asymmetrically rounded or bluntly pointed, its longest rays below the center. Pelvics inserted slightly behind the pectoral base, retrogressive, rounded posteriorly. First pelvic ray with a short filament. Gill membranes separate, free from the isthmus. Lateral line complete, parallel to the dorsal profile anteriorly, straight on the caudal peduncle, continuing to the end of the caudal rays. Head bones cavernous. Gill rakers short and blunt. Counts and proportional measurements are given in Table 30.

Color: Silvery gray to brownish above, shading to silvery on the lower sides and white on the belly. Pelvic fins white, sometimes with an orange tinge distally. Pectoral clear.

Juveniles and breeding adults: Juveniles have longer and more pointed tails but otherwise are miniatures of the adults. There are no special breeding colors or structures in this species.

Size: The drum can reach weights of 25 pounds or more although they are seldom over 10 pounds. Statements that bones from Indian middens indicate weights of 100 pounds, or more, are probably in error. The New York State angling record is a 15-pound 6-ounce drum from the Barge Canal caught May 1981 by Paul Donovan.

Habitat
Drums are limited to big rivers and lakes. The species is generally restricted to shallow water and is quite tolerant of turbidity.

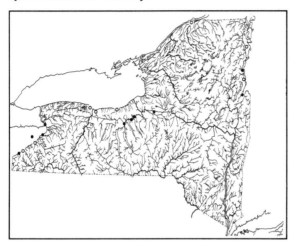

Distribution
The freshwater drum ranges from the gulf coast drainages between Yucatan and Mobile Bay. It occurs throughout the Mississippi and Missouri basins to Montana and east to the Hudson Bay drainage and the estuarine part of the St. Lawrence River. In New York, it is common in Lakes Erie, Ontario and Champlain.

Life History
The drum is one of the few freshwater fishes that produces a planktonic egg. It has a protracted breeding season, spawning from July to September in Lake Erie. Its spawning behavior has not been described and, indeed, it is not known exactly where spawning takes place, but it is presumed that it spawns in midwater or near the surface.

The drum is a long-lived species, reaching at least age XII. Ovarian egg counts of more than $1/2$ million have been reported.

Foods and Feeding
Young drum eat plankton and midge larvae, switching to midges, entomostracans, and larger insect larvae as they grow. Fish and crayfish are prominent in the diet of larger drums.

Notes
The otoliths of drums are large, nearly an inch in diameter in larger individuals. They make fine curios; an angled groove on one side forms an L (for luck). The drum also has very large molariform teeth that appear to be adapted for crushing molluscan prey, although Lake Erie drum were found to be feeding on insects and soft-bodied organisms even in areas where snails were abundant.

References
Barney, 1926 (ecology). Daiber, 1952 (food habits). Edsall, 1967 (ecology). Witt, 1960 (size of ancient fish). Swedberg and Walberg, 1970 (spawning and life history). Burkett and Jackson, 1971 (eye lens as indicator of age). Green, 1941 (osteology). Price, 1963 (food).

Names
The trivial name *grunniens* is the Latin word for grunting like a pig. This species is a notorious sound producer.

Aplodinotus grunniens Rafinesque, 1819: 418 Ohio River

Sciaena oscula Lesueur, 1822b: 252 Lake Ontario

Corvina oscula DeKay, 1842: 73-74 Lakes Erie and Ontario

SCULPINS

COTTIDAE

Sculpins and their relatives belong to a group called the mail-cheeked fishes because they have a bony bar connecting the circumorbital bones with the preopercle. In sculpins, this bar is covered with skin but it can be felt with a little probing. This is a rather large family with more than 300 species in about 67 genera. Most of the species are marine but a few live in fresh water. There are four freshwater species in New York, and two marine strays have been reported from the Lower Hudson.

All of our species are scaleless, although they may have a few prickly remnants of scales. Sculpins have broad, somewhat depressed, heads and large fan-like pectoral fins. The pelvic fins have a small spine and usually three or four soft rays. There are no spines in the anal fin but there is a separate spiny dorsal fin with slender, weak spines.

Sculpins are sometimes abundant in small, cold streams where they are often associated with trout. They are accused of preying on trout eggs but apparently they eat only those not covered during the spawning process. Their role as competitors of trout is less clear.

KEY TO THE SPECIES OF SCULPINS IN THE INLAND WATERS OF NEW YORK

A. Gill membranes free from the isthmus.
$\qquad$ **E.**

A'. Gill membranes broadly attached to the isthmus.

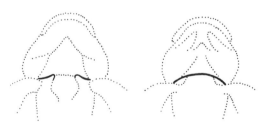

Gill membranes free from (left) and joined to the isthmus.

B. Lateral line complete. Upper preopercular spine strongly curved upward and forward, its length greater than two-thirds the diameter of the eye.
Cottus ricei   Spoonhead sculpin, p. 358

B'. Lateral line incomplete. Upper preopercular spine curved but not hooked upward and forward, shorter, its length less than two-thirds the diameter of the eye.

C. Pelvic rays typically I,3. Palatine teeth usually absent. Anal fin interradial membranes deeply notched between the rays. Caudal peduncle always shorter than the postorbital head length.
Cottus cognatus   Slimy sculpin, p. 356

Pelvic rays of slimy sculpin.

The caudal peduncle of the slimy sculpin is shorter than the postorbital head length. In the mottled sculpin it is longer.

C'. Pelvic rays typically I,4. Palatine teeth usually present. Anal interradial membranes less deeply notched. Caudal peduncle always shorter than the postorbital head length.
Cottus bairdi **Mottled sculpin, D.**

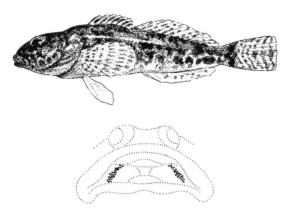

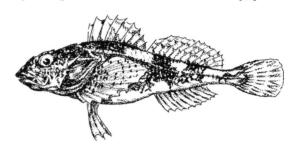

F'. Uppermost preopercular spine at most twice as long as spine below it, its tip not reaching the margin of the gill cover. Origin of first dorsal ahead of a vertical line through the tip of the gill cover.
Myoxocephalus aenaeus **Grubby, p. 449**

Palatine teeth of mottled sculpin.

D. Distance between tip of snout and anus when measured backward from the anus extending to a point nearer the base than the tip of the caudal fin. Body with definite dark bars.
Cottus b. bairdi **p. 355**

D'. Distance from tip of snout to anus when stepped backward from anus reaching a point nearer the tip than the base of the caudal fin. Body rather slender with less definite dark bars.
Cottus b. kumlieni **p. 355**

E. (A. Gill membranes free from the isthmus.) Preopercle with four spines. Dorsal fins separated by a distinct gap. Great Lakes.
Myoxocephalus thompsoni
Deepwater sculpin, p. 359

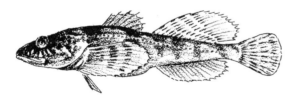

E'. Preopercle with three spines. Dorsal fins close together. Marine.

F. Uppermost preopercular spine long, about four times as long as the spine below it, its tip reaching the margin of the gill cover.
Myoxocephalus octodecemspinosus
Longhorn sculpin, p. 450

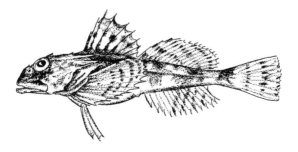

Cottus

There are about 25 species of *Cottus* of which 3 occur in New York waters. They are scaleless freshwater fishes with three or four pelvic rays and contiguous dorsal fins. The gill membranes are joined to the isthmus.

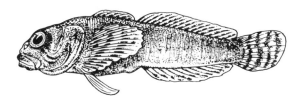

MOTTLED SCULPIN

Cottus bairdi Girard, 1850

Identification

The three New York species of *Cottus* are quite similar and easily confused. All three have the same general shape and color and all have the gill membranes broadly joined to the isthmus whereas in the related genus, *Myoxocephalus,* the gill membranes are joined to each other but free from the isthmus. The mottled sculpin and the slimy sculpin both have two pores at the tip of the chin where the spoonhead has only one. The spoonhead also has a flatter head, and the upper spine on its preopercle is curved almost into a semicircle. In New York, the slimy and the mottled sculpins can be told apart by the number of pelvic fin rays, nearly always four in *C. bairdi* and nearly always three in *C. cognatus.* Farther west, the two species vary more and this feature becomes unreliable. McAllister noted that the caudal peduncle length, the distance from the posterior end of the anal fin base to the middle of the caudal fold, is greater than the distance from the rear margin of the eye to the tip of the opercular membrane in the slimy sculpin, but less in the mottled sculpin. The membranes between the anal fin rays are deeply incised in the slimy sculpin and less so in the mottled sculpin. Palatine teeth are usually present in *C. bairdi,* usually absent in *C. cognatus.* The last ray of the dorsal fin is usually double in *bairdi,* usually single in *cognatus,* and the bands on the pectoral fin are wider than the pupil in *cognatus,* narrower in *bairdi.*

Description

Body short and robust, head and anterior body depressed. Caudal peduncle slightly compressed. Dorsal profile much more curved than the ventral, which is nearly straight. Head flattened ventrally, rounded above. Eyes dorsolateral. Dorsal fins close together, spiny dorsal convex, soft dorsal with spines increasing in length to the fourth or fifth, then becoming shorter. Caudal rounded. Anal similar to the soft dorsal,inserted below the fourth dorsal soft ray, its fourth through sixth spines longest. Membranes of anal fin slightly indented between the rays. Pelvic fin inserted behind the anterior, lower end of the pectoral base. Pelvic pointed, with its second and third rays subequal. Pectoral large and asymmetrically rounded, its lower membranes incised and lower rays somewhat thickened. Gill membranes broadly joined to the isthmus. Preopercular spines four, the uppermost longest, stout and slightly curved. Maxillary reaching to below the anterior third of the eye. Lips prominent. Lateral line ending below the posterior third of the dorsal fin. Two chin pores. Last two anal elements close together. Counts and proportional measurements are given in Table 38.

Color: Upper surface generally brownish, belly clear white in front of the anal fin. Dorsal surface with traces of four saddles, rather small and indistinct, the first at the beginning of the dorsal fin, the second under the last dorsal spine, the third under the anterior third of the second dorsal, and the fourth near the end of the soft dorsal. There is an irregular bar at the caudal base. The caudal fin has spots on its proximal third, then three vertical bars. Margin of the caudal fin clear.

The lower sides of the body are punctate, with irregular marbling and blotches on the back extending to slightly below the lateral line. Dorsal and anal fins with relatively clear membranes. Intensification of the pigment along the rays forms irregular oblique bands across the dorsal fin. Anal fin with similar rows of spots. Pectoral with seven or eight narrow bands of spots. Interradial membranes of the fin punctate. Dorsal surface of the head dark, lower side and ventral surface merely punctate back to, and including, the pelvic fin.

Juveniles and breeding adults: Breeding males have the margin of the spiny dorsal fin orange with a submarginal dark band. In nonbreeding males and females, this submarginal band is represented by dark spots at each end of the fin.

Size: The largest specimen reported by Scott and Crossman (1973) measured 5.2 inches total length.

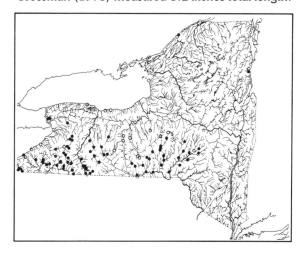

Habitat

The mottled sculpin lives in lakes and cooler streams. Specimens from the Great Lakes and other larger lakes are said to have shorter caudal regions and have been recognized as a separate subspecies, *C. b. kumlieni.* The distance from the tip of the snout to the anus, projected backward, reaches to near the end of the caudal fin in *kumlieni,* and only to the base of the caudal in *C. b. bairdi.*

Distribution
The mottled sculpin ranges from eastern Canada south to the Tennessee, Alabama and Mobile drainages of the gulf coast. There are disjunct populations in the Ozark region and the Columbia River system in southern Canada, Utah, Montana, Idaho, and Washington. This is a variable species but some of those populations may be different species. It occurs across the southern part of New York State.

Life History
The mottled sculpin is a spring spawner and its breeding season begins when the water temperature reaches approximately 50 F. Males set up territories near a shelter site, a rock or overhanging ledge. Savage reported on the breeding behavior in aquaria where the shelter was a sloping piece of brick or slate. When a female was placed in the aquarium, the male turned black and responded to the female with one of four movements: Shaking the head, nodding the head, expanding the gill covers, or undulating the body. If the female responded, the male bit her cheeks or pectoral fin and enticed her into the shelter site where the courtship continued, sometimes for several hours. Spawning took place when the female turned upside down. The eggs were emitted in an initial burst, then additional eggs were added more slowly. During the spawning, the male's body gradually turned paler but his fins remained black.

Bailey studied reproduction in southwestern Montana. Spawning occurred 5 June through 30 June when the water temperature was 46 to 63 F. Hatching took 21 to 28 days. Each female produced 69 to 406 eggs (average 203) and nests contained 54 to 1,587 eggs, indicating that there was some polygamy.

The newly hatched larvae were 5.8 to 8.1 mm long and the yolk sac was absorbed in 2 weeks when the larvae were 9.0 to 9.9 mm long. Age I fish ranged from 29.6 to 56.7 mm, age II - 64.4 to 79.3 mm, age III - 80.5 to 98.0 mm, age IV - 84 to 118.8 mm, and age V - 93 to 110.3 mm.

Food and Feeding
Food habits of the mottled sculpin were studied in streams near Ithaca and in Cayuga Lake by Koster. Mayflies, caddisflies, and dipteran larvae were the most important items and together made up about 90 percent of the diet of the stream form (called *C. b. bairdi* by Koster). The smallest fish ate mostly dipterans and the larger fish ate mostly caddisflies. The lake form, *Cottus b. kumlieni,* ate more mayflies and crustaceans which probably reflected the abundance of these items in the environment. Daiber studied the winter food habits of this species and the fantail darter in a small headwater tributary of the Genesee River. The food of both was primarily

insects with some copepods. Occasionally, a small sculpin was eaten by a larger one. Larger fish ate larger items and the sculpins ate fewer items than the darters did, possibly a reflection of the sculpin's sedentary feeding by ambush.

Notes
The subspecies *kumlieni* is said to be a Great Lakes form that lives in Lakes Superior, Michigan, Huron, Ontario, and the eastern basin of Lake Erie. It also occurs in the Finger Lakes and the St. Lawrence River and a few inland lakes in Michigan. In view of the variability of this species, the distinctions are doubtful, and the subspecies are not recognized here.

References
McAllister, 1964 (identification). McAllister and Lindsey, 1961 (systematics). Smith, 1923 (nesting). Savage, 1963 (behavior). Dineen, 1951 (food habits). Bailey, 1952 (life history). Robins, 1955 (taxonomy). Gage, 1878 (Cayuga Lake). Koster, 1936, 1937 (life history and feeding), Ludwig and Norden, 1969 (life history). Ludwig and Lange, 1975 (fecundity). Gilson and Bensen, 1979 (prey selection). Daiber, 1956 (winter feeding). Godkin, Christie, and McAllister, 1982 (identification).

Names
The mottled sculpin is named for Spencer Fullerton Baird, the first United States Commissioner of Fisheries.

Cottus bairdii Girard, 1850: 410 Mahoning River, Ohio

Cottus bairdii Greeley, 1927: 65 Genesee drainage

Pegedictis ictalops Rafinesque, 1820a: 85 Lexington, Kentucky

Cottus ictalops, Bean, 1903: 635-637 New York

Cottus ictalops bairdii, Meek, 1889: 315 Cayuga Lake

Cottus bairdii bairdii, Greeley, 1929: 178 Erie-Niagara drainage

Uranidea kumlieni Hoy *in* Nelson, 1876: 41 Lake Michigan

Cottus bairdii kumlieni, Greeley, 1928: 102 Oswego drainage.

SLIMY SCULPIN

Cottus cognatus
Richardson, 1836

Identification
The slimy sculpin closely resembles the mottled sculpin, but the two can usually be told apart in our area by the number of pelvic fin rays: three in the

slimy sculpin and four in the mottled sculpin. (Both species have a tiny spine that cannot be seen without dissection.) Other useful characters are as follows: No palatine teeth in the slimy sculpin; the last rays of the dorsal and anal fins are single in the slimy sculpin but double in the mottled sculpin, that is, they are closer to each other than the rest of the rays in those fins. McAllister (1964) also noted that while most of these features are variable and occasionally overlap, the caudal peduncle of the slimy sculpin is always longer than the postorbital distance, and the interradial membranes of the anal fin are more deeply incised in the slimy sculpin. Color differences include narrower and more distinct bands on fins of the mottled sculpin.

The slimy sculpin differs from the spoonhead in having a less flattened head and a gently curved, rather than strongly hooked, upper preopercular spine. Also, the spoonhead has a single pore at the tip of the lower jaw where the slimy and mottled sculpins have two. Members of the genus *Myoxocephalus* have the gill membranes free from the isthmus.

Description

Body stout and short, round or slightly depressed anteriorly. Dorsal profile arched, ventral profile nearly straight. First dorsal strongly arched, second dorsal convex, the fifth ray longest. Caudal fin rounded. Anal similar to the second dorsal, its last two rays not closer than the other rays. Anal and lower pectoral interradial membranes deeply incised. Pectoral fin large and fan-shaped, its base sloping downward and forward. Pelvic inserted behind the lower end of the pectoral base. Head triangular in dorsal view, eyes rather close together. Maxillary reaching to below anterior third of the eye, head and mouth generally shorter than in the mottled sculpin. Pelvic fins progressive, third rays the longest. Preopercle with four spines, the upper long and gently curved upward. The other spines are embedded in the skin. Dorsal surface with prickles, lateral line ending below middle of the second dorsal fin. Counts and proportional measurements are given in Table 38.

Color: Mottled brown to pinkish above with indistinct dorsal saddle-shaped darker blotches. Sides marbled to punctate above a line between the middle of the pectoral base and the anal fin origin. Belly and lower surface of the caudal peduncle white. Few melanophores on the pelvic and anal fins. Pectoral fin with five wide, irregular, and indistinct bands. Spiny dorsal with three or four oblique bands. Second dorsal with about nine similar bands. Caudal with a few spots forming weak bands.

Juveniles and breeding adults: Breeding males tend to be darker and have a bright orange margin on the first dorsal fin.

Size: The largest specimens are about 5 inches total length.

Habitat

This is a northern species. In our area, it is limited to cold creeks where there is some shelter and to lakes. It occurs at depths of 18 to 270 feet in Lake Michigan, 300 to 350 feet in Lake Superior.

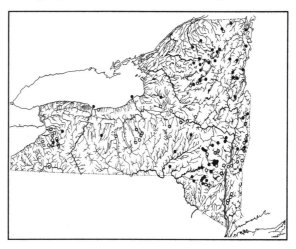

Distribution

Slimy sculpins range from northeastern Siberia throughout much of Canada and south on the Atlantic coast to Virginia. On the west coast, they reach British Columbia, Washington, and Montana. In New York State, it is widely distributed but absent from the Genesee and Chemung drainages and sporadic in the Ontario and St. Lawrence corridors.

Life History

Koster studied the reproduction of the slimy sculpin in a tributary of Fall Creek near Ithaca. Spawning took place in the spring when water temperatures reached 40 to 60 F and at somewhat lower temperatures in Cayuga Lake. Males established territories that included a nesting site, usually a crevice under a log, rock, or tree root. Females were enticed into the nest and deposited the eggs on the roof of the cavity. After spawning, the female left and the male often courted other females so that a single nest usually contained the eggs of more than one female. Males kept guard over the nest and the young until they began to feed.

In Saskatchewan (Van Vleit as quoted by Scott and Crossman, 1973), the eggs were 2.3 to 2.6 mm in diameter and females age III produced 1,400 eggs. The eggs hatched in about 4 weeks.

Food and Feeding

Sculpins frequently occur with trout and, because of the potential for interacting with the game species, their food habits have been studied rather intensively. Koster investigated the food of slimy and mottled sculpins near Ithaca and in Cayuga Lake. Insects made up most of the diet. Mayflies contributed 35 percent of the volume, caddisflies 18.4 percent and dipterans 32 percent. Smaller sculpins ate more dipterans and the larger fish ate more caddisflies. The largest individuals ate a few fish and fish eggs but this was not considered significant. The smallest individuals frequently fed on entomostracans. Plant materials, worms, mollusks, and spiders were rare in the stomachs.

Notes

In New York, the slimy and mottled sculpins have quite consistent characteristics and can usually be identified with little difficulty. In the northwestern parts of their range, the species are more variable and most of the distinguishing features overlap.

References

McAllister, 1964 (identification). McAllister and Lindsey, 1961 (systematics). Koster, 1936 (life history); 1937 (feeding). Symons, Metcalf, and Harding, 1976 (temperature requirements). Otto and O'Hara Rice, 1977 (temperature). Godkin, Christie, and McAllister, 1982 (identification).

Names

The name *cognatus* is the Latin word meaning related. It is a reference to the similarity of the slimy sculpin to a European species.

Cottus cognatus Richardson, 1836: 40 Great Bear Lake

Cottus cognatus, Greeley, 1928: 102 Oswego drainage

Cottus gracilis Heckel, 1840: 148 New York

Cottus gracilis cayuga Meek, 1889: 315 Cayuga Lake

Uranidea gracilis, Evermann and Kendall, 1902c: 240 St. Lawrence

Cottus viscosus Haldemann, 1840: 3 Susquehanna River

Uranidea gracilis viscosa (Haldeman), Greeley, 1927: 65 (not taken in Genesee)

Uranidea quiescens DeKay, 1842: 61 Adirondacks

Cottus formosus Girard, 1852: 587 Lake Ontario

Uranidea formosa, Bean, 1903: 638 New York (after Girard)

Cottus meridionalis Girard, 1850: 410 James River, Virginia

Cottus meridionalis, Hankinson, 1924: 87 western New York

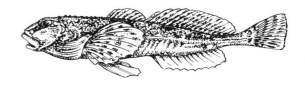

SPOONHEAD SCULPIN

Cottus ricei (Nelson, 1876)

Identification

The spoonhead is the most distinctive of the three species of the genus *Cottus* that occur, or did occur, in New York State. These three species are quite similar in appearance and a close look is often necessary to determine their identification. The spoonhead is the most distinctive. It has a flattened depressed head, a single pore at the tip of the chin (two in the others), and the upper spine on its preopercle is curved, almost forming a semicircle. It also has a complete lateral line, four pelvic rays, and prominent prickles over most of its body.

Description

Body rather slender, profiles about equally curved. Head flattened, the preorbital area expanded forward so as to appear as lobes on either side of the snout and giving the posterior margin of the premaxillary groove a trilobed appearance. Preopercular spines two, three, or four. Dorsal fins contiguous, the spiny dorsal rounded, the soft dorsal gently convex. Caudal fin truncate. Anal fin similar to the second dorsal, its rays increasing slightly in length posteriorly. Pectoral fins long and rounded, their bases sloping so the lower rays are farther forward. No scales, but the body has small prickles. Lateral line complete. Gill membranes broadly joined to the isthmus. Maxillary reaching to below the eye. Counts and proportional measurements are given in Table 38.

Color: Light brown or tan with indistinct saddle-shaped blotches and various speckling on head, body, and fins. Ventral surface generally unmarked, pelvic fins white. Anal fin pale with faint groups of melanophores. Small specimens sometimes have a vertical bar at the caudal base.

Juveniles and breeding adults: No sexual or juvenile characters have been reported.

Size: The largest known specimen was 5.3 inches total length. Most specimens are 1.6 to 2.4 inches but specimens more than 3 inches long are not uncommon.

Habitat

In the Great Lakes, the spoonhead is known from moderately deep water from the shore to 450 feet. Scott and Crossman suggested that its optimum depth is about 200 feet. Farther north it occurs in larger rivers and sometimes even in swift streams.

Distribution

The range of the spoonhead is a broad area from the Great Lakes and the St. Lawrence River to the

Lower Mackenzie River and to the Peace and Upper Missouri Rivers in Alberta. It is now apparently extinct in Lake Ontario and possibly also in Lake Erie. Fish reported it from off Dunkirk, New York. Trautman notes that there have been no Lake Erie records since 1950.

Life History
According to Scott and Crossman, females taken in August have larger eggs than those taken in June or July, which suggests a summer or fall spawning season. Otherwise, its life history is unknown.

Food and Feeding
Its diet has not been reported.

Notes
Most of the lake specimens of this species are from the stomachs of larger fish such as burbot and lake trout.

References
McAllister and Lindsey, 1961 (systematics). Delisle and Van Vliet, 1968 (life history). Scott and Crossman, 1973 (Canada). Trautman, 1981 (Ohio). Fish, 1932 (larvae).

Names
This species is named in honor of M. L. Rice who discovered the first specimen.

Cottopsis ricei Nelson, 1876: 40 Lake Michigan off Evanston, Illinois

Cottus ricei, Greeley, 1929: 179 Lake Erie

Myoxocephalus

This genus includes the larger cottid fishes of marine and deep-lake waters. Members of this genus have well-separated dorsal fins and gill membranes that are not joined to the isthmus.

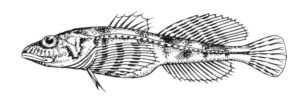

DEEPWATER SCULPIN

Myoxocephalus thompsoni (Girard, 1852)

Identification
Members of the genus *Myoxocephalus* are rather large sculpins with well-separated dorsal fins and gill membranes that are joined to each other but free from the isthmus. Three species occur in New York waters: Two are marine strays occasionally reported from the Hudson Estuary, but the deepwater sculpin is a true freshwater species occurring in the Great Lakes and in some smaller lakes in Canada and Michigan. It is often cited as a glacial relict on the assumption that its present disjunct distribution pattern must have resulted from its moving along the glacial margin as the Wisconsin ice sheet receded.

The preopercular margin of the deepwater sculpin has four strong spines, of which the upper two are close together and similar in size, so that they appear to be a single bifurcate spine. The two marine species have three preopercular spines with the second much larger than the other two.

All members of the genus *Cottus* have the gill membranes joined to the isthmus.

Description
Body rather elongate, tapering, and terete. Head depressed. Snout blunt, rising sharply and flat on top, slightly concave between and behind the orbits. Epaxial muscles prominent behind the occiput. All fin rays unbranched. Spiny dorsal short, separated from the second dorsal by a wide space. Dorsal spines slender. Spiny dorsal outline rounded. Second dorsal with the rays increasing in length to the sixth, and the posterior part of the fin rounded. Caudal square. Anal fin with short rays at the front, most of the rays about equal in length. Pelvic fins paddle shaped with the third ray longest. Pectoral fins large, asymmetrically rounded, with exserted rays, their bases sloping backward. Preopercle with four spines, the first directed upward, the second backward, the third downward, and the fourth separated from the others and directed anteriorly. Skin of dorsal surface with weak prickles. Mouth large, maxillary reaching to below rear edge of pupil.

Lower jaw with a distinct symphyseal knob. Lateral line prominent, nearly complete, dipping low on the caudal peduncle and ending behind the end of the dorsal base. Counts and proportional measurements are given in Table 38.

Color: (from Lake Michigan specimens) Generally pale grayish to tan above, sharply delimited along sides and white ventrally. Body somewhat blotched but no regular markings. First dorsal peppered with melanophores, a little heavier along the rays. Second dorsal with an intensification of pigment along the base and at the middle third of the fin. Caudal with traces of three irregular, equally spaced bands, and an indistinct marginal band. Anal fin white. Pelvics white. Pectoral fins with three irregular bands alternating with rows of spots, becoming paler ventrally where the melanophores are confined to the rays. Iris with golden bronze ring at edge of pupil.

Juveniles and breeding adults: The sexes are about the same color, but the adult males have the dorsal, anal, and upper pectoral rays extending beyond the membrane as short filaments. These extensions have approximately four points on each segment so that they are quite rough. The points are less well developed on the anal fins.

Size: Deepwater sculpins from the northern parts of their range are said to be smaller than those from the Great Lakes. It is reported to have reached lengths of 9.2 inches total length in Lake Ontario.

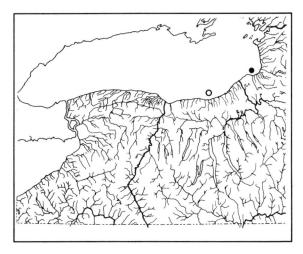

Habitat

True to its name, the deepwater sculpin lives in deeper parts of freshwater lakes where the summer maximum temperatures are always below 8 C. Preferred temperatures are between 0 and 5 C. Most of the lakes from which the species is known are clear and slightly acidic (pH 6.5 to 6.7). Deepwater sculpins are most abundant at depths of 73 to 91 meters but they have been taken from 25 meters to 366 meters, the deepest record being from Lake Superior.

Distribution

The deepwater sculpin occurs in North America from Great Bear Lake in the Canadian Northwest Territories, south and east in a curving band to the Great Lakes. It has received considerable attention as an example of a glacially distributed fish (Dadswell, 1974). It is apparently extinct in Lake Ontario where no specimens have been reported in nearly 20 years, but it remains abundant in Lakes Huron, Michigan, and Superior. Its present status in Lake Erie is not known.

Life History

The life history of the deepwater sculpin is unknown. Reports suggest that spawning occurs in summer or perhaps early fall but the exact dates undoubtedly vary with latitude. Fish illustrated specimens 12.5 and 16.2 mm long taken in Lake Erie in July and mid-August so spawning must have occurred there in June or July. One Lake Ontario specimen has eggs in its mouth but it is not known if this was accidental or if the species is an oral brooder.

Foods and Feeding

Midges, *Pontoporeia*, mysids, and copepods have been reported from the stomachs of deepwater sculpins.

Notes

This species was formerly considered a subspecies of the marine fourhorn sculpin, *Myoxocephalus quadricornis,* but there is evidence that it is a distinct species and the two are sometimes found together in the brackish waters of the Hudson Bay region. Larval pigment and other structural differences support its being accorded full species rank. Champagne, Harrington, and McAllister reported a fossil from the Champlain sea clays east of Ottawa, Canada. The specimen was thought to be late Wisconsin of postglacial age.

References

Dadswell, 1974 (origin and distribution). Cowan, 1971 (morphology). McAllister, 1961 (systematics). McAllister and Aniskowicz, 1976 (vertebral numbers). McPhail and Lindsey, 1970 (general account). Fish, 1932 (juvenile stages). Champagne, Harrington, and McAllister, 1979 (fossil record). Delisle and Van Vliet, 1968 (Canadian records).

Names

The species is named in honor of Zadock Thompson who published on the fishes of Lake Champlain.

Triglopsis thompsonii Girard, 1852: 65, 66, 67, 71 Lake Ontario

Triglopsis thompsonii, Girard, 1854a: 19 Lake Ontario off Oswego, New York

Triglopsis thompsonii, Greeley, 1929: 178 Lake Erie

Myoxocephalus quadricornis thompsonii, Hubbs and Lagler, 1964: 118 (distribution)

TABLE 38
AVERAGE PROPORTIONAL MEASUREMENTS AND COUNTS OF FRESHWATER SCULPINS (*Cottus* and *Myoxocephalus*)

All proportions are expressed in percentage of standard length.

	Cottus bairdi	cognatus	ricei	*Myoxocephalus* thompsoni
ST. LENGTH (mm)	44.3	64.9	43.6	96.8
TOTAL LENGTH	124.3	123.4	122.5	118.7
FORK LENGTH	124.3	123.4	121.6	118.7
PREDORSAL	36.0	34.2	35.3	38.3
PREANAL	57.0	55.7	54.5	61.5
PREPELVIC	30.5	30.8	30.3	31.6
DORSAL BASE	55.9	58.9	54.8	48.9
ANAL BASE	28.4	29.1	29.9	24.5
BODY DEPTH	18.8	20.1	15.8	19.1
BODY WIDTH	18.3	17.8	16.5	21.0
C.PED. DEPTH	8.9	9.2	5.3	4.9
PECTORAL ALT.	12.2	11.8	9.4	11.5
HEAD LENGTH	32.7	33.6	31.8	30.5
SNOUT	8.8	9.4	9.0	10.2
EYE	9.6	6.9	6.9	7.7
MOUTH LENGTH	12.0	13.0	11.5	15.5
INTERORB	2.5	2.9	3.7	5.2
N (sample size)	5	5	5	10
COUNTS:				
DORSAL SPINES	VII-VIII	VI-IX	VIII-IX	VII-X
DORSAL RAYS	16-18	14-19	13-14	13-16
ANAL RAYS	11-13	10-14	13-14	13-16
PECTORAL RAYS	13-17	12-16	14-16	15-18
PELVIC RAYS	I,4	I,3	(4)	I,3 or 4
GILL RAKERS	Rudimentary	Rudimentary	?	8-13
VERTEBRAE	31-33	31-35	34-35	37-39

Vertebral counts for *C. ricei* from Scott and Crossman, (1973); other counts
and measurements from USNM specimens from Glacier Park, Montana.

FRESHWATER AND DIADROMOUS FISHES OF NEW YORK

PETROMYZONTIDAE

1. *Ichthyomyzon bdellium* (Jordan, 1885), Ohio lamprey
2. *Ichthyomyzon fossor* Reighard and Cummins, 1916, northern brook lamprey
3. *Ichthyomyzon greeleyi* Hubbs and Trautman, 1937, mountain brook lamprey
4. *Ichthyomyzon unicuspis* Hubbs and Trautman, 1937, silver lamprey
5. *Lampetra appendix* (DeKay, 1842), American brook lamprey
6. *Petromyzon marinus* Linnaeus, 1758, sea lamprey

ACIPENSERIDAE

7. *Acipenser brevirostrum* Lesueur, 1818, shortnose sturgeon
8. *Acipenser fulvescens* Rafinesque, 1817, lake sturgeon
9. *Acipenser oxyrhynchus* Mitchill, 1815, Atlantic sturgeon

POLYODONTIDAE

10. *Polyodon spathula* (Walbaum, 1792), paddlefish

LEPISOSTEIDAE

11. *Lepisosteus osseus* (Linnaeus, 1758), longnose gar
12. *Lepisosteus platostomus* (Rafinesque, 1820), shortnose gar
    Lepisosteus oculatus (Winchell, 1864), spotted gar (hypothetical)

AMIIDAE

13. *Amia calva* Linnaeus, 1766, bowfin

ANGUILLIDAE

14. *Anguilla rostrata* (Lesueur, 1817), American eel

CLUPEIDAE

15. *Alosa aestivalis* (Mitchill, 1814), blueback herring
16. *Alosa mediocris* (Mitchill, 1815), hickory shad
17. *Alosa pseudoharengus* (Wilson, 1811?), alewife
18. *Alosa sapidissima* (Wilson, 1811?), American shad
19. *Dorosoma cepedianum* (Lesueur, 1818), gizzard shad

HIODONTIDAE

20. *Hiodon tergisus* Lesueur, 1818, mooneye

ICTALURIDAE

21. *Ictalurus catus* (Linnaeus, 1758), white catfish
22. *Ictalurus melas* (Rafinesque, 1820), black bullhead
23. *Ictalurus natalis* (Lesueur, 1819), yellow bullhead
24. *Ictalurus nebulosus* (Lesueur, 1819), brown bullhead
25. *Ictalurus punctatus* (Rafinesque, 1818), channel catfish
26. *Noturus flavus* Rafinesque, 1818, stonecat
27. *Noturus gyrinus* (Mitchill, 1817), tadpole madtom
28. *Noturus insignis* (Richardson, 1836), margined madtom
29. *Noturus miurus* Jordan, 1877, brindled madtom

CATOSTOMIDAE

30. *Carpiodes cyprinus* (Lesueur, 1817), quillback
31. *Catostomus catostomus* (Forster, 1773), longnose sucker
32. *Catostomus commersoni* (Lacepède, 1803), white sucker
33. *Erimyzon oblongus* (Mitchill, 1815), creek chubsucker
34. *Erimyzon sucetta* (Lacepède, 1803), lake chubsucker
35. *Hypentelium nigricans* (Lesueur, 1817), northern hog sucker
36. *Moxostoma anisurum* (Rafinesque, 1820), silver redhorse
37. *Moxostoma carinatum* (Cope, 1870), river redhorse
38. *Moxostoma duquesnei* (Lesueur, 1817), black redhorse
39. *Moxostoma erythrurum* (Rafinesque, 1818), golden redhorse
40. *Moxostoma macrolepidotum* (Lesueur, 1817), shorthead redhorse
    M. m. macrolepidotum (Lesueur, 1817)
    M. m. breviceps (Cope, 1870)
41. *Moxostoma valenciennesi* Jordan, 1885, greater redhorse

CYPRINIDAE

42. *Carassius auratus* (Linnaeus, 1758), goldfish
43. *Ctenopharyngodon idella* (Valenciennes, 1844), grass carp
44. *Cyprinus carpio* Linnaeus, 1758, common carp
45. *Rhodeus sericeus* (Pallas, 1776), bitterling
46. *Scardinius erythrophthalmus* (Linnaeus, 1785), rudd
47. *Campostoma anomalum* (Rafinesque, 1820), central stoneroller
48. *Ericymba buccata* Cope, 1865, silverjaw minnow
49. *Exoglossum laurae* (Hubbs, 1931), tonguetied minnow
50. *Exoglossum maxillingua* (Lesueur, 1818), cutlips minnow
51. *Notemigonus crysoleucas* (Mitchill, 1814), golden shiner
52. *Couesius plumbeus* (Agassiz, 1850), lake chub
53. *Hybopsis amblops* (Rafinesque, 1820), bigeye chub
54. *Hybopsis dissimilis* (Kirtland, 1840), streamline chub
55. *Hybopsis storeriana* (Kirtland, 1844), silver chub
56. *Hybopsis x-punctata* Hubbs and Crowe, 1956, gravel chub
57. *Nocomis biguttatus* (Kirtland, 1840), hornyhead chub
58. *Nocomis micropogon* (Cope, 1865), river chub
59. *Rhinichthys atratulus* (Hermann, 1804), eastern blacknose dace
60. *Rhinichthys cataractae* (Valenciennes, 1842), longnose dace
61. *Rhinichthys meleagris* Agassiz, 1854, western blacknose dace
62. *Semotilus atromaculatus* (Mitchill, 1818), creek chub
63. *Semotilus corporalis* (Mitchill, 1817), fallfish
64. *Semotilus margarita* (Cope, 1868), pearl dace
    S. m. margarita (Cope, 1868)
    S. m. nachtriebi (Cox, 1896)
65. *Clinostomus elongatus* (Kirtland, 1838), redside dace
66. *Hybognathus hankinsoni* Hubbs, 1929, brassy minnow
67. *Hybognathus regius* Girard, 1857, eastern silvery minnow
68. *Notropis amoenus* (Abbott, 1874), comely shiner
69. *Notropis atherinoides* Rafinesque, 1818, emerald shiner
70. *Notropis photogenis* (Cope, 1865), silver shiner
71. *Notropis rubellus* (Agassiz, 1850), rosyface shiner
72. *Notropis analostanus* (Girard, 1860), satinfin shiner
73. *Notropis chrysocephalus* (Rafinesque, 1820), striped shiner
74. *Notropis cornutus* (Mitchill, 1817), common shiner
75. *Notropis spilopterus* (Cope, 1868), spotfin shiner
76. *Notropis umbratilis* (Girard, 1857), redfin shiner
77. *Notropis anogenus* Forbes, 1885, pugnose shiner
78. *Notropis bifrenatus* (Cope, 1869), bridle shiner
79. *Notropis chalybaeus* (Cope, 1869), ironcolor shiner
80. *Notropis heterodon* (Cope, 1865), blackchin shiner
81. *Notropis heterolepis* Eigenmann and Eigenmann, 1893, blacknose shiner
82. *Notropis procne* (Cope, 1865), swallowtail shiner
83. *Notropis dorsalis* (Agassiz, 1854), bigmouth shiner
84. *Notropis hudsonius* (Clinton, 1824), spottail shiner
85. *Notropis stramineus* (Cope, 1865), sand shiner

86. *Notropis volucellus* (Cope, 1865), mimic shiner
87. *Phoxinus eos* (Cope, 1862), northern redbelly dace
88. *Phoxinus neogaeus* Cope, 1868, finescale dace
89. *Pimephales notatus* (Rafinesque, 1820), bluntnose minnow
90. *Pimephales promelas* Rafinesque, 1820, fathead minnow

SALMONIDAE
91. *Coregonus alpenae* (Koelz, 1924), longjaw cisco
92. *Coregonus artedii* Lesueur, 1818, cisco or lake herring
93. *Coregonus clupeaformis* (Mitchill, 1818), lake whitefish
94. *Coregonus hoyi* (Gill, 1872), bloater
95. *Coregonus kiyi* (Koelz, 1921), kiyi
96. *Coregonus reighardi* (Koelz, 1924), shortnose cisco
97. *Coregonus zenithicus* (Jordan and Evermann, 1909), shortjaw cisco
98. *Prosopium cylindraceum* (Pallas, 1784), round whitefish
99. *Oncorhynchus kisutch* (Walbaum, 1792), coho salmon
100. *Oncorhynchus nerka* (Walbaum, 1792), kokanee
101. *Oncorhynchus tshawytscha* (Walbaum, 1792), chinook salmon
102. *Oncorhynchus gorbuscha* (Walbaum, 1792), pink salmon
103. *Salmo gairdneri* Richardson, 1836, rainbow trout
104. *Salmo salar* Linnaeus, 1758, Atlantic salmon
105. *Salmo trutta* Linnaeus, 1758, brown trout
106. *Salvelinus fontinalis* (Mitchill, 1815), brook trout
107. *Salvelinus namaycush* (Walbaum, 1792), lake trout

OSMERIDAE
108. *Osmerus mordax* (Mitchill, 1815), rainbow smelt

UMBRIDAE
109. *Umbra limi* (Kirtland, 1841), central mudminnow
110. *Umbra pygmaea* (DeKay, 1842), eastern mudminnow

ESOCIDAE
111. *Esox americanus* Gmelin, 1788
     E. a. americanus Gmelin, 1788, redfin pickerel
     E. a. vermiculatus Lesueur, 1846, grass pickerel
112. *Esox lucius* Linnaeus, 1758, northern pike
113. *Esox masquinongy* Mitchill, 1824, muskellunge
114. *Esox niger* Lesueur, 1818, chain pickerel

APHREDODERIDAE
115. *Aphredoderus sayanus* (Gilliams, 1824), pirate perch
     A. s.sayanus (Gilliams, 1824)
     A. s. gibbosus Lesueur, 1833

PERCOPSIDAE
116. *Percopsis omiscomaycus* (Walbaum, 1792), trout-perch

GADIDAE
117. *Lota lota* (Linnaeus, 1758), burbot

CYPRINODONTIDAE
118. *Fundulus diaphanus* (Lesueur, 1817), banded killifish

POECILIIDAE
119. *Gambusia affinis* (Baird and Girard, 1853), mosquitofish

ATHERINIDAE
120. *Labidesthes sicculus* (Cope, 1865), brook silverside

GASTEROSTEIDAE
121. *Apeltes quadracus* (Mitchill, 1815), fourspine stickleback
122. *Culaea inconstans* (Kirtland, 1840), brook stickleback
123. *Gasterosteus aculeatus* Linnaeus, 1758, threespine stickleback
124. *Pungitius pungitius* (Linnaeus, 1758), ninespine stickleback

MORONIDAE
125. *Morone americana* (Gmelin, 1789), white perch
126. *Morone chrysops* (Rafinesque, 1820), white bass
127. *Morone saxatilis* (Walbaum, 1792), striped bass

CENTRARCHIDAE
128. *Acantharchus pomotis* (Baird, 1855), mud sunfish
129. *Ambloplites rupestris* (Rafinesque, 1817), rock bass
130. *Enneacanthus gloriosus* (Holbrook, 1855), bluespotted sunfish
131. *Enneacanthus obesus* (Girard, 1854), banded sunfish
132. *Lepomis auritus* (Linnaeus, 1758), redbreast sunfish
133. *Lepomis cyanellus* Rafinesque, 1819, green sunfish
134. *Lepomis gibbosus* (Linnaeus, 1758), pumpkinseed
135. *Lepomis gulosus* (Cuvier, 1829), warmouth
136. *Lepomis macrochirus* Rafinesque, 1818, bluegill
137. *Lepomis megalotis* (Rafinesque, 1820), longear sunfish
138. *Micropterus dolomieui* Lacepède, 1802, smallmouth bass
139. *Micropterus salmoides* (Lacepède, 1802), largemouth bass
140. *Pomoxis annularis* Rafinesque, 1818, white crappie
141. *Pomoxis nigromaculatus* (Lesueur, 1829), black crappie

PERCIDAE
142. *Ammocrypta pellucida* (Putnam, 1863), eastern sand darter
143. *Etheostoma blennioides* Rafinesque, 1819, greenside darter
144. *Etheostoma caeruleum* Storer, 1845, rainbow darter
145. *Etheostoma camurum* (Cope, 1870), bluebreast darter
146. *Etheostoma exile* (Girard, 1860), Iowa darter
147. *Etheostoma flabellare* Rafinesque,1819, fantail darter
148. *Etheostoma fusiforme* (Girard, 1854), swamp darter
149. *Etheostoma maculatum* Kirtland, 1841, spotted darter
150. *Etheostoma nigrum* Rafinesque, 1820, johnny darter
151. *Etheostoma olmstedi* Storer, 1842, tessellated darter
152. *Etheostoma variatum* Kirtland, 1838, variegate darter
153. *Etheostoma zonale* (Cope, 1868), banded darter
154. *Perca flavescens* (Mitchill, 1814), yellow perch
155. *Percina caprodes* (Rafinesque, 1818), logperch
156. *Percina copelandi* (Jordan, 1877), channel darter
157. *Percina evides* (Jordan and Copeland, 1877), gilt darter
158. *Percina macrocephala* (Cope, 1869), longhead darter
159. *Percina maculata* (Girard, 1860), blackside darter
160. *Percina peltata* (Stauffer, 1864), shield darter
161. *Stizostedion canadense* (Smith, 1834), sauger
162. *Stizostedion vitreum* (Mitchill, 1818)
     S. v. vitreum (Mitchill, 1818), walleye
     S. v. glaucum Hubbs, 1926, blue pike

SCIAENIDAE
163. *Aplodinotus grunniens* Rafinesque, 1819, freshwater drum

COTTIDAE
164. *Cottus bairdi* Girard, 1850, mottled sculpin
165. *Cottus cognatus* Richardson, 1836, slimy sculpin
166. *Cottus ricei* (Nelson, 1876), spoonhead sculpin
167. *Myoxocephalus thompsoni* (Girard, 1852), deepwater sculpin

BROOK TROUT   *Salvelinus fontinalis*

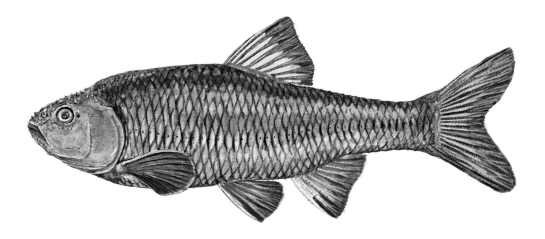

COMMON SHINER   *Notropis cornutus*

SPOTFIN SHINER   *Notropis spilopterus*

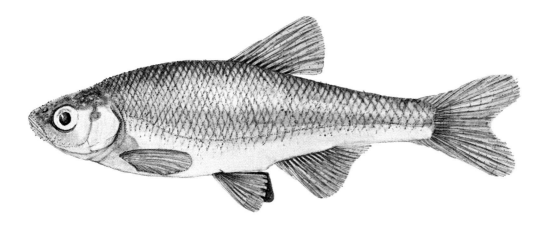

REDFIN SHINER   *Notropis umbratilis*

ROSYFACE SHINER   *Notropis rubellus*

EASTERN BLACKNOSE DACE   *Rhinichthys atratulus* male

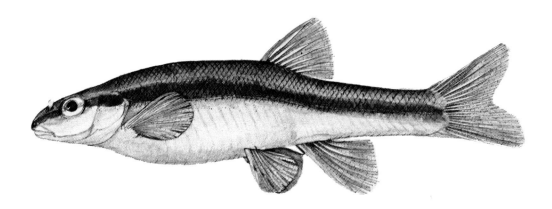

EASTERN BLACKNOSE DACE   *Rhinichthys atratulus* female

WESTERN BLACKNOSE DACE   *Rhinichthys meleagris* male

REDSIDE DACE   *Clinostomus elongatus*

NORTHERN REDBELLY DACE   *Phoxinus eos* female

PEARL DACE   *Semotilus margarita*

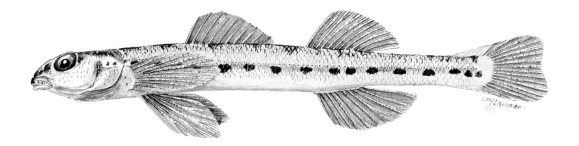

EASTERN SAND DARTER   *Ammocrypta pellucida*

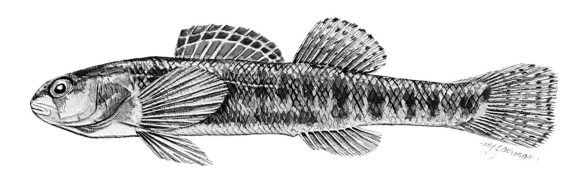

IOWA DARTER   *Etheostoma exile*

SPOTTED DARTER   *Etheostoma maculatum*

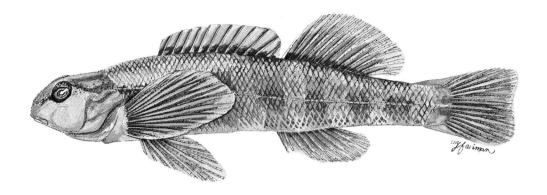

VII

GREENSIDE DARTER *Etheostoma blennioides*

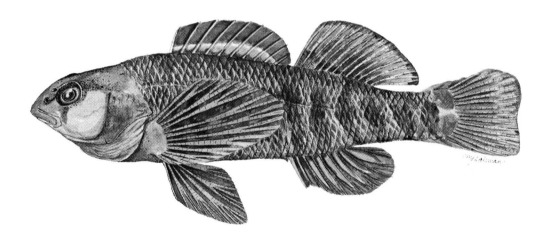

RAINBOW DARTER *Etheostoma caeruleum*

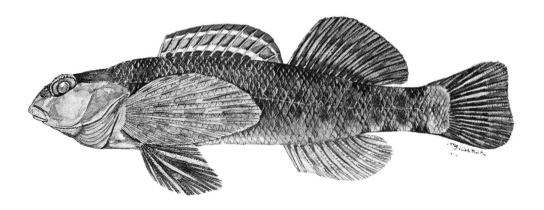

VARIEGATE DARTER *Etheostoma variatum*

VIII

TESSELLATED DARTER   *Etheostoma olmstedi*

BANDED DARTER   *Etheostoma zonale*

CHANNEL DARTER   *Percina copelandi*

MARINE FISHES IN THE INLAND WATERS OF NEW YORK

Because the Hudson River is open to the sea with no physical barriers below the Troy dam and lock at River Mile 153 (153 miles above Battery Park), almost any species that occurs in the nearby Atlantic Ocean could enter the estuary. In order to simplify the identification of inland fishes, the marine species found inland only in the Hudson River estuary are treated separately. The species listed here are those known to have been collected in, or reliably reported from, the river through 1982. Species from the North River (the area off Manhattan) are included but species that have only been reported from the Arthur Kill (between Staten Island and New Jersey) are not (Figure 10).

The Hudson River is a complex estuarine ecosystem with a correspondingly complex fish fauna. Normally, the salt water intrudes as far upstream as the region between Poughkeepsie and Newburgh but this varies with the amount of rainfall in the upper parts of the river basin. Furthermore, the salt front has rather vague limits under most conditions because there is considerable mixing due to wind and flow currents, and to the effects of the propellers of tugs and large ships as they travel up the Hudson. Thus, the distance that marine fishes travel upstream varies with the season and with the climatic conditions of each particular year. A number of the marine fishes reported from the Hudson are tropical species that normally live in the West Indies. These apparently were carried northward by the Gulf Stream when they were larvae and were able to survive, at least for the summer, in our waters.

The decisions as to which species to include in this section have not always been easy because there is a gradation from strictly freshwater fishes to strictly marine forms with several families containing species that are not clearly one or the other. Species that have only been reported from the Hudson Estuary a few times are generally considered to be marine strays. Most of the tropical species fall into this category. There are some other species regularly found in the river but only during certain parts of the year. I consider these to be seasonal resident marine species. The bay anchovy, tomcod, and hogchoker are examples of estuarine species that spend protracted periods in fresh water. They are included here with the marine species. The fourspine stickleback, on the other hand, has been included with the freshwater fishes because the other three members of its family have both marine and freshwater populations. Truly anadromous species, those that move into the river to spawn, and the catadromous American eel are treated with the freshwater species but I have chosen to separate the marine herrings (family Clupeidae) from the freshwater gizzard shad and the anadromous river shads. I have done the same with the mummichog, although with less conviction.

Most of the families in this section have such distinctive shapes that they can easily be identified by direct comparison with the key drawings. The keys will supplement the drawings and present precise anatomical distinctions between similar families. For identification of species, however, the reader should refer to the family keys and species accounts where characteristics will be found that will separate similar species that either have been found or might be expected in the inland waters of the Hudson Estuary. As with the freshwater species, it is important to compare all specimens with the descriptions as well as with the illustrations.

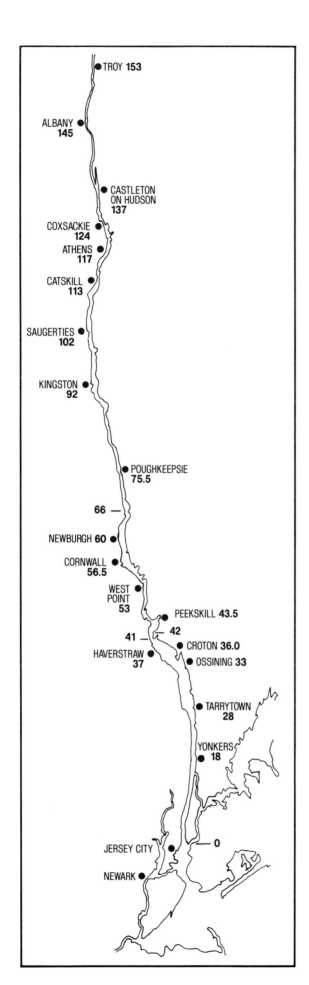

Figure 10. Hudson River Locations in River Miles above Battery Park

KEY TO FAMILIES

Anadromous species such as the sea lamprey, the sturgeons, the river herrings including the American shad, and the temperate basses are in the freshwater and anadromous keys beginning on page 25. When you are in doubt as to which key to use, try them both.

A. Gills covered with a bony plate so that there is only a single pair of gill openings, which may be completely separate or joined across the ventral side of the head.

C.

A'. Head with five pairs of gill openings.

B. Body nearly round in cross section. Gill openings in front of, and mostly above the level of, the pectoral fins.

Requiem sharks, p. 390

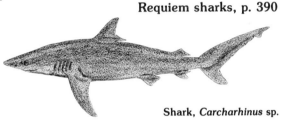

Shark, *Carcharhinus* sp.

B'. Body flat and diamond shaped. Gill openings on the underside of the head.
Rajidae   **Skates, p. 391**

Barndoor skate, *Raja laevis*

C. (A. A single pair of gill openings.) Both eyes on the same side of the head.

SS.

C'. One eye on each side of the head.

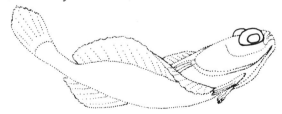

Flatfish showing both eyes on the same side of the body.

D. Pelvic fins present although sometimes small, fused into a sucker-like disk or reduced to a pair of double filaments inserted on the underside of the head.

L.

D'. Pelvic fins absent.

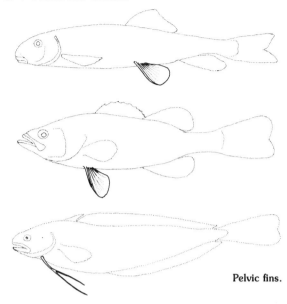

Pelvic fins.

E. Body not extremely flexible, not eel-like, tail separate from dorsal and anal fins.

G.

E'. Body extremely flexible, eel-like. Tail pointed and joined to the dorsal and anal fins.

F. Dorsal origin well forward, over the ends of the pectoral fins.
Congridae   **Conger eels, p. 393**

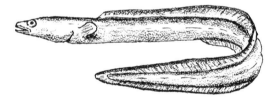

Conger eel, *Conger oceanicus*

F'. Dorsal fin origin farther back, well behind the tips of the pectoral fins.
Anguillidae   **Freshwater eels, p. 60**

American eel, *Anguilla rostrata*

G. (E. Body not eel-like.) Mouth not at the end of a tube.

I.

G'. Mouth at the end of a tube-like face.

H. Body encased in bony rings.
Syngnathidae   **Pipefishes, p. 418**

Tube-like snout of pipefish, note bony rings encircling body.

Northern pipefish, *Syngnathus fuscus*

Lined seahorse, *Hippocampus erectus*

H'. Body not encased in bony rings, tail with a long filament formed by extensions of its central rays.
Fistulariidae **Cornetfishes, p. 417**

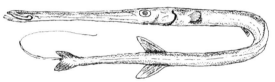

Bluespotted cornetfish, *Fistularia tabacaria*

I. (G. Face not tube-like.) Body elongate and slender, lower jaw projecting. Skin with diagonal folds.
Ammodytidae **Sand lances, p. 441**

American sand lance, *Ammodytes americanus*

I'. Body not elongate

J. Body not strongly compressed but nearly terete and inflatable. Teeth fused into beak-like structures.
UU.

J'. Body strongly compressed.

K. Dorsal fin with a stout spine, color gray to brownish yellow.
Balistidae **Leatherjackets, p. 459**

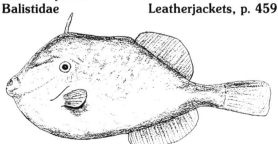

Orange filefish, *Aluterus schoepfi*

K'. Dorsal fin without large spines. Color silvery.
Stromateidae **Butterfishes, p. 446**

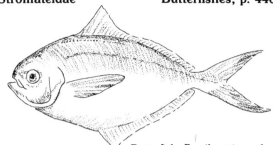

Butterfish, *Peprilus triacanthus*

L. (D. Pelvic fins present.) Pelvic fins thoracic or jugular.
U.

L'. Pelvic fins abdominal.

M. Gular plate present.
Elopidae **Tarpons, p. 392**

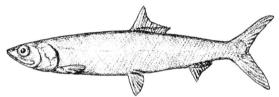

Ladyfish, *Elops saurus*

M'. Gular plate absent.

N. No adipose dorsal fin.
P.

N'. Adipose dorsal fin present.

O. Body terete, head pointed.
Synodontidae **Lizardfishes, p. 399**

Inshore lizardfish, *Synodus foetens*

O'. Body slightly compressed, head not especially pointed.
Osmeridae **Smelts, p. 239**

Rainbow smelt, *Osmerus mordax*

P. (N. No adipose dorsal fin.) Two dorsal fins, well separated, the first with four slender spines.
Atherinidae **Silversides, p. 414**

Atlantic silverside, *Menidia menidia*

P'. A single dorsal fin.

Q. Body robust or elongated but not strongly compressed, not especially silvery, head canals simple.

S.

Q'. Body compressed, silvery or with a silvery stripe, head canals dendritic.

R. Mouth smaller, not reaching to preopercle. At least one and usually several ventral scutes are present but if there is only one it may be deeply embedded in the skin.
Clupeidae   **Herrings, p. 394**

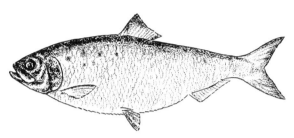

American shad, *Alosa sapidissima*

R'. Mouth large, maxillary bone reaching past the edge of the preoperculum. No ventral scutes.
Engraulidae   **Anchovies, p. 397**

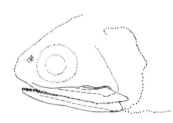

Anchovy, showing long maxillary bone.

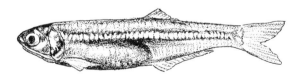

Bay anchovy, *Anchoa mitchilli*

S. (Q. Head canals simple.) Body long and slender. Jaws elongate with needlelike teeth.
Belonidae   **Needlefishes, p. 408**

Atlantic needlefish, *Strongylura marina*

S'. Body not especially elongate. Jaws short, mouth superior or termino-superior.
Cyprinodontidae   **Killifishes, T.**

T. Body stubby.
subfamily Cyprinodontinae   **Pupfishes, p. 409**

Sheepshead minnow, *Cyprinodon variegatus*

T'. Body somewhat elongate.
subfamily Fundulinae   **Killifishes, p. 409**

Mummichog, *Fundulus heteroclitus*

U. (L. Pelvic fins thoracic or jugular.) Top of head with a complex sucker which is a modified first dorsal fin.
Echeneidae   **Remoras, p. 423**

Sharksucker, *Echeneis naucrates*

U'. No sucker on top of head..

V. Dorsal fin with true spines although they may be slender and flexible.

X.

V'. Dorsal fin without true spines.

W. Body elongate, eel shaped. Dorsal and anal fins joined to the tail. Pelvic fins reduced to a double filament on each side of the isthmus.
Ophidiidae   **Cusk-eels, p. 407**

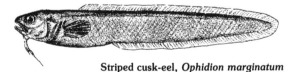

Striped cusk-eel, *Ophidion marginatum*

W'. Body not eel shaped. Tail fin separate. Pelvic fins thoracic.
Gadidae   **Codfishes, p. 401**

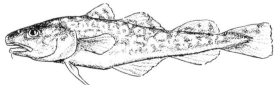

Atlantic tomcod, *Microgadus tomcod*

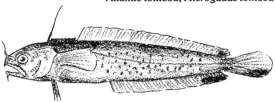

Fourbeard rockling, *Enchelyopus cimbrius*

X. (V. Dorsal fin with true spines.) All dorsal spines connected by membrane.

AA.

X'. Some dorsal spines not fully connected by membrane, although usually there is a triangular membrane behind each separate spine.

Y. Only the first three dorsal spines unconnected, the first with a specialized fishing lure. Head and body depressed, Head very large with a huge mouth. No scales but body and lips with fleshy tabs.
Lophiidae   **Goosefishes, p. 400**

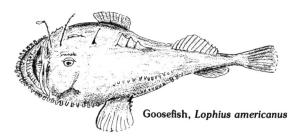

Goosefish, *Lophius americanus*

Y'. All dorsal spines unconnected.

Z. Small fishes with a slender caudal peduncle and one or two pelvic soft rays.
Gasterosteidae   **Sticklebacks, p. 272**

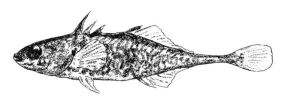

Fourspine stickleback, *Apeltes quadracus*

Z'. Large fish with five pelvic rays.
Rachycentridae   **Cobias, p. 422**

Cobia, *Rachycentron canadum*

AA. (X. Dorsal spines connected.) Dorsal fins separated into a spiny first dorsal and a second dorsal which may or may not have one spine at its front. Bases of the first and second dorsal fins separated by a space at least as wide as the length of the base of the first dorsal fin.

RR.

AA'. Spiny and soft dorsal fins contiguous or nearly so, sometimes separated by a deep notch.

BB. Head covered with skin or scales but not with sculptured plates.

EE.

BB'. Head covered with sculptured bony plates. Pectoral fins very large.

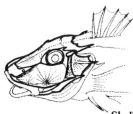

Skull plates of searobin.

CC. Head cuboidal, mouth nearly vertical. Top of head with smooth areas behind the eyes.
Uranoscopidae   **Stargazers, p. 439**

Northern stargazer, *Astroscopus guttatus*

CC'. Head tapering, mouth inferior, top of head without smooth areas.

DD. Lower pectoral rays free, finger-like.
Triglidae   **Searobins, p. 447**

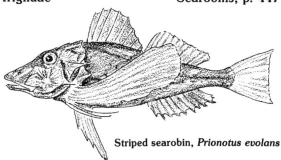

Striped searobin, *Prionotus evolans*

DD'. Lower pectoral rays not separate. Upper five or six pectoral rays form a separate fin. Preopercle with a large backward spine.
Dactylopteridae   **Flying gurnards, p. 452**

Flying gurnard, *Dactylopterus volitans*

EE. (BB. Head not covered with bony plates.) Skin with large or small scales.

GG.

EE'. Skin naked.

FF. Ventral fins modified into a sucker.
Cyclopteridae   **Snailfishes, p. 451**

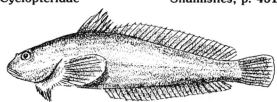

Seasnail, *Liparis atlanticus*

FF'. Ventral fins not modified. Preopercle with prominent spines.
Cottidae   Sculpins, p. 449

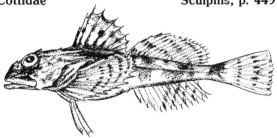

Longhorn sculpin, *Myoxocephalus octodecemspinosus*

GG. (EE. Skin with scales.) Anal fin with fewer than 13 rays.
                                                    JJ.

GG'. Anal fin with more than 15 rays.

HH. Dorsal fin consisting of all spines and no rays. Body elongate, eel shaped, caudal fin rounded.
Pholidae   Gunnels, p. 440

Rock gunnel, *Pholis gunnellus*

HH'. Dorsal fin with some soft rays. Body not eel shaped, caudal fin deeply forked. First two anal spines well separated from the rest of the fin.

II. First two anal spines large and conspicuous. Jaw teeth small, in bands. No teeth on basibranchial bones.
Carangidae   Jacks, p. 424

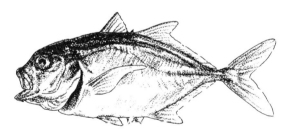

Crevalle jack, *Caranx hippos*

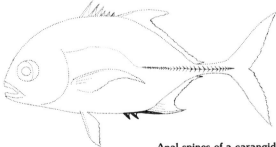

Anal spines of a carangid.

II'. First two anal spines small, almost totally embedded in skin. Jaws with large, flattened conical teeth. Teeth present on basibranchial bones.
Pomatomidae   Bluefishes, p. 421

Bluefish, *Pomatomus saltatrix*

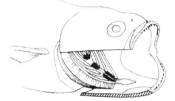

Basibranchial teeth of bluefish.

JJ. (GG. Anal fin with fewer than 13 rays.) Dorsal fin with 16 to 18 spines. Caudal fin squarish or rounded.
Labridae   Wrasses, p. 435

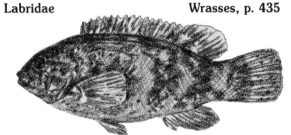

Tautog, *Tautoga onitis*

JJ'. Dorsal fin with 12 or fewer spines.

KK. Anal spines three.
                                                    NN.

KK'. Anal spines zero to two.

LL. Anal spines one or two in adult.
Sciaenidae   Drums, p. 431

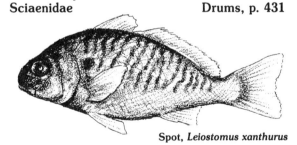

Spot, *Leiostomus xanthurus*

LL'. No anal spines.

MM. Pelvic fins united by membrane forming a cup-shaped, sucker-like disk.
Gobiidae   Gobies, p. 443

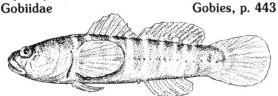

Naked goby, *Gobiosoma bosci*

United pelvic fins.

MM'. Pelvic fins separate.
Eleotridae   **Sleepers, p. 442**

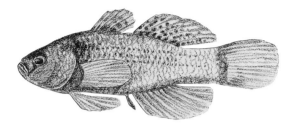

Fat sleeper, *Dormitator maculatus*

NN. (KK. Anal spines three.) Mouth extremely protrusible, capable of being extended forward into a tube. Body diamond shaped, chin profile concave.
Gerreidae   **Mojarras, p. 428**

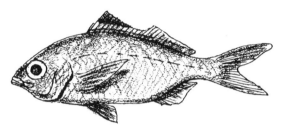

Spotfin mojarra, *Eucinostomus argenteus*

NN'. Mouth only slightly or not at all protrusible.

OO. Maxillary bone exposed for its entire length.

QQ.

OO'. Maxillary bone slipping under the preorbital region, exposed only at its posterior end when the mouth is closed.

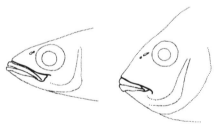

Exposed (left) and concealed maxillary bones.

PP. Teeth conical. Some anterior teeth enlarged, caniniform.
Lutjanidae   **Snappers, p. 427**

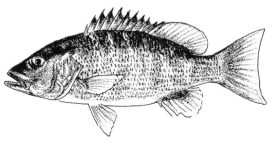

Gray snapper, *Lutjanus griseus*

PP'. Anterior jaw teeth incisiform, lateral jaw teeth molariform.
Sparidae   **Porgies, p. 429**

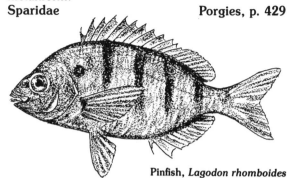

Pinfish, *Lagodon rhomboides*

QQ. (OO. Maxillary exposed.) Body color silvery, dorsal fins nearly separate. Opercle with two spines.
Moronidae   **Temperate basses, p. 280**

Striped bass, *Morone saxatilis*

QQ'. Body color not silvery. Dorsal fins with only a shallow notch. Opercle with three spines.
Serranidae   **Sea basses, p. 420**

Black sea bass, *Centropristis striata*

RR. (AA. Dorsal fins separated by a wide space.) Scales small, finlets present behind the dorsal and anal fins.
Scombridae   **Mackerels, p. 445**

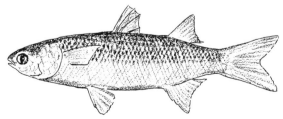

Atlantic mackerel, *Scomber scombrus*

RR'. Scales larger, no finlets.
Mugilidae   **Mullets, p. 437**

Striped mullet, *Mugil cephalus*

SS. (C. Both eyes on the same side of the head.) Both eyes on the left side of the head.

Bothidae   **Lefteye flounders, p. 453**

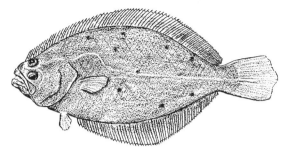

Summer flounder (Fluke), *Paralichthys dentatus*

SS'. Both eyes on the right side of the head.

TT. Body oval, no pectoral fins.

Soleidae   **Soles, p. 458**

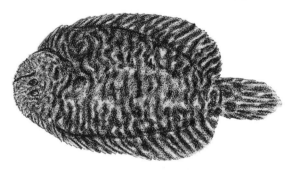

Hogchoker, *Trinectes maculatus*

TT'. Body diamond shaped, pectoral fin present at least on the eyed side.

Pleuronectidae   **Righteye flounders, p. 456**

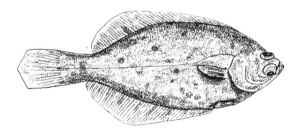

Winter flounder, *Pseudopleuronectes americanus*

UU. (J. Teeth fused into beak-like structures.) Upper and lower jaws each with a single tooth plate.

Diodontidae   **Porcupinefishes, p. 461**

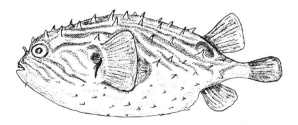

Striped burrfish, *Chilomycterus schoepfi*

UU'. Upper and lower jaws each with two tooth plates.

Tetraodontidae   **Puffers, p. 460**

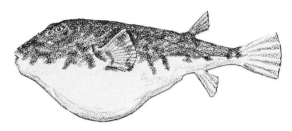

Northern puffer, *Sphoeroides maculatus*

REQUIEM SHARKS

CARCHARHINIDAE

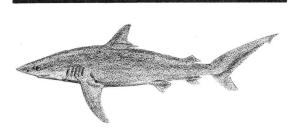

SHARKS

Carcharhinidae; Sphyrnidae

Identification
Recognizing a shark, with its distinctive heterocercal tail, five gill openings and undershot mouth, is no particular problem, but identifying sharks to species is quite difficult and in many cases requires close examination of specimens in hand. Only an expert should attempt to identify sharks at a distance. Because of the problem of accurate identification, it is not at all certain which species of sharks have been reported from the inland waters of New York.

Occurrence
Mearns (1898) listed the dusky shark, *Carcharhinus obscurus*, from the area of the Hudson Highlands: "Several were taken in the lower part of the Hudson in the summer of 1881, and one up the river as far as Peekskill." Since Mearns did not give any distinguishing characteristics, this record must be regarded as questionable. The dusky shark is an open-ocean species of the tropical parts of the Atlantic and the Mediterranean Sea. It is much more likely that the Hudson River sharks were bull sharks, *Carcharhinus leucas*, which frequently enter fresh water in many parts of the world. Bull sharks and dusky sharks are quite similar in shape but the dusky shark has a definite keel between the dorsal fins which is lacking in the bull shark.

Mearns also mentioned a hammerhead caught between West Point and Cornwall "about 1876" but this could also have been one of several species.

Notes
Sharks are exciting animals and somehow seem to be irresistible to pranksters who catch them in the ocean and bring them home to plant in places where they are likely to be found by friends. A blue shark, *Prionace glauca*, reported from Yonkers in June 1979 was such a hoax as, no doubt, was the one found in Chittenango Creek in October 1982.

Any specimens of sharks captured in the Hudson River estuary should be examined by a specialist. If it is not possible to freeze the entire shark, a series of photographs showing a good side view of the entire body and details of the fins and the underside of the head may serve. Many species have distinctive teeth and the jaws can be carefully dissected out and frozen or preserved in formalin or isopropyl (rubbing) alcohol.

References
Bigelow and Schroeder, 1948 (general account, a standard reference on sharks). Gilbert, 1967 (hammerheads). Lineaweaver and Backus, 1970 (excellent popular account of the natural history of sharks). Ellis, 1975 (popular text on sharks).

SKATES
RAJIDAE

Skates are cartilaginous fishes somewhat related to sharks. Both groups have five pairs of gill slits, a cartilaginous skeleton, and primitive jaw and fin structure. Sharks have the gill openings on the sides of the head, in front of and above the pectoral fins, but in the skates and their relatives, the rays, the gill openings are on the underside of the head below the pectoral fins. Most rays and skates are very flat and diamond shaped but some are elongate and quite shark-like.

Skates and rays have a conspicuous opening called the spiracle behind the eye. Water is taken in through the spiracle, passed over the gills, and expelled through the gill slits. Nearly all other fishes take in water for breathing through the mouth. Many skates have specialized scales on the surfaces of the body and tail. The distribution of these prickles is important for recognizing species. Rays bear their young alive but skates lay eggs in horny, squarish cases with tendrils at the corners. These are the familiar "mermaids' purses" so often seen on Long Island beaches. Skate teeth are flat and fit together like floor tiles to form a surface for crushing their prey. One species is doubtfully recorded from the Hudson River.

BARNDOOR SKATE
Raja laevis Mitchill, 1818

Identification
The barndoor skate differs from similar species in having no large thorny scales in the midline of the back from the spiracles to the level of the ends of the bases of the pectoral fins. It has three rows of prickles on the tail and in all but the smallest individuals there is black pigment around the sensory pores of the head and body. This is a large species, reaching a length of 5 feet.

Occurrence
The only inland record for the Hudson River is a specimen in the New York State Museum. This specimen was contributed on 4 August 1932 although the date of capture is not stated. The fisherman claimed to have caught it at North Albany on hook and line but in view of the absence of other records, and since this is a species that seldom comes into fresh water, we must regard this record as dubious. The specimen was not located in 1979. The barndoor skate ranges along the Atlantic coast from the Grand Banks to North Carolina.

Notes
The egg capsules of the barndoor skate are larger than those of other species in the area, measuring 68 to 72 mm by 124 to 132 mm. They have short tapering tendrils about 13 to 19 mm long. The barndoor skate is a bottom feeder whose diet consists mostly of large crustaceans including crabs, spider crabs, lobsters, and shrimp. It also takes squids and worms and a variety of fishes including sand lances, cunners, tautogs, butterfish, herring, and flatfishes.

References
Bigelow, H.B. and W.C. Schroeder, 1953a (general account). Greeley, 1936 (Albany record).

Names
Laevis is a Latin word meaning smooth.
   Raja laevis Mitchill, 1818a: 327 New York

TARPONS
ELOPIDAE

The ladyfish is a close relative of the tarpon and the two are now placed in a single family, the Elopidae. They are also related to the bonefish, *Albula*, and more distantly to the eels. The chief characteristic that unites these rather different fishes is the specialized larval stage, the leptocephalus. This is a transparent, ribbon-like, pelagic (free-swimming) stage that is found in no other fishes. There are also some unique anatomical features that unite the group.

The genus *Elops* has five or six species.

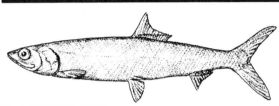

LADYFISH
Elops saurus Linnaeus, 1766

Identification
The ladyfish is a slender, streamlined fish with a deeply forked tail, small scales and a short dorsal fin situated well back on the body. The eye is large, the mouth large, oblique and terminal. Its pectoral fins are low and horizontal and the pelvics originate just slightly ahead of the dorsal fin. Both the pelvic and pectoral fins have large scaly axillary processes and the dorsal and anal fins have scaly sheaths at their bases. The single most important characteristic of the ladyfish is its gular plate, a superficial bone in the midline of the lower jaw between the gill membranes. A similar gular plate occurs in the bowfin but in that species it is broad whereas in the ladyfish it is slender.

Occurrence
A single specimen about 12 inches long was collected at Bowline Pond by LMS in 1979, and Tom Lake caught another at River Mile 66.5 in October 1982. Mr. Lake's specimen was 13 inches total length.

Notes
Although the ladyfish looks something like a herring, it is a close relative of the bonefish and the tarpon and a distant relative of the eels, sharing with that group the very specialized larval form called a leptocephalus. Because no other fishes have such larvae, its presence is considered evidence of close relationship.

Recent studies have revealed the existence of several closely similar species instead of one worldwide form.

References
Hildebrand, 1963a: 124-131 (general account).

Names
Saurus is a Greek word meaning lizard.
Elops saurus Linnaeus, 1766: 518 Carolinas

CONGER EELS

CONGRIDAE

The relationships of eels are not well understood and the present arrangement of nineteen families and nearly 600 species must be considered tentative. The family Congridae is one of the larger families with about 38 genera and 100 species. This is strictly a marine family and the one species that strays into the Lower Hudson is definitely a visitor.

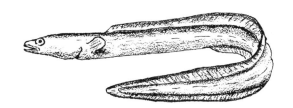

CONGER EEL

Conger oceanicus (Mitchill, 1818)

Identification

Eels, unless they are brightly colored, tend to look alike and the conger is likely to be mistaken for an American eel which it resembles in color and shape. The two are easily told apart, however, by the position of the origin of the dorsal fin. In the conger, the dorsal origin is at the level of the tip of the pectoral fins whereas in the American eel the dorsal fin begins much farther back, closer to the origin of the anal fin than to the tip of the pectoral. Congers also have larger eyes than American eels. Congers have no scales but those of American eels are deeply embedded in the skin and arranged in a herringbone pattern. Congers are generally grayish, somewhat lighter ventrally, with dark margins on the dorsal and anal fins. They are said to reach a weight of 22 pounds and a length of 7 feet in American waters, and in England they may weigh more than 100 pounds. In June 1982, a world record for 30-pound-test line was set by an 87-pound conger eel that was 7.5 feet long.

Occurrence

Congers are occasionally taken in the Hudson Estuary. AMNH 48297 is a specimen 544 mm total length that was collected at River Mile 42 on 1 December 1978 by Texas Instruments personnel.

References

Bigelow and Schroeder, 1953b: 154-157(general account).

Names

The species name refers to its habitat in salt water.
   Anguilla oceanica Mitchill, 1818b: 407 New York

HERRINGS
CLUPEIDAE

Herrings are silvery soft-rayed fishes with abdominal pelvics, forked tails and deciduous, sometimes fimbriate, cycloid scales. They have a single pair of nostrils and their lateral line is reduced to a short branched tube in the shoulder region or altogether absent. The head canals are greatly elaborated, with many branches. The head is scaleless, the mouth is variable and the teeth are small or absent. Most herrings have strongly compressed bodies, often with a row of modified scales forming a saw-toothed keel along the ventral edge of the breast and belly. The eyes are partially covered with adipose tissue and the swim bladder is connected to the ear by a hollow tube.

Most herrings are marine or anadromous but some are confined to fresh water. Herrings are worldwide in distribution but reach their greatest diversity in the tropics. At present, about 50 genera and 180 species are recognized.

The round herrings are recognized by some ichthyologists as a separate family because they do not have the row of scutes (modified scales) along the edge of the belly. They do, however, have one or two scutes embedded in the skin around the base of the pelvic fins and are otherwise similar to the herrings. Whitehead (1963) recognized 7 genera and 10 species of round herrings, mostly from the Indo-Pacific region with a few species along our Atlantic and Pacific coasts.

The New York fauna includes freshwater, marine, and estuarine species. A key to all of the local species will be found in the freshwater section. The three species that are treated here, the menhaden, the Atlantic herring, and the round herring are marine strays in the Hudson Estuary.

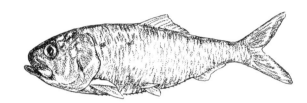

ATLANTIC MENHADEN
Brevoortia tyrannus (Latrobe, 1802)

Identification

The menhaden is a deep-bodied, compressed fish, with a very large head and a double row of modified scales in the middorsal line in front of the dorsal fin. Menhaden scales have nearly straight vertical edges that are toothed (pectinate) so that the surface of the fish has a distinctive appearance. Like other herrings, the menhaden is generally silvery with a row of sharp scutes along the ventral midline. The peritoneum is black and the intestine has extra loops. The back is dusky olive to bluish, and the sides of the head and body sometimes have a brassy or iridescent cast. There is a large spot followed by a band of smaller spots, not necessarily in rows, behind the gill opening. In life, the fins have a yellowish cast.

The maximum size is around 18 to 20 inches but the usual size of adults is 12 to 14 inches.

Occurrence

Menhaden are coastal marine fishes and usually stay within 10 or 15 miles of shore. From May to September, they move into estuaries. Fishermen say that arrival of menhaden signals the end of shad fishing season. Young menhaden are common in the river in late summer. In the Hudson, the menhaden is found as far upstream as Newburgh.

Atlantic menhaden range from Nova Scotia to Florida and they are taken commercially from Maine to Florida. A similar and closely related species, *Brevoortia patronus*, replaces the Atlantic menhaden in the Gulf of Mexico.

Notes

Unlike the river herrings that come into fresh water to spawn, the menhaden is a species that moves into the river after spawning offshore. The peak in spawning in our area seems to be in June. Females lay 38,000 to 631,000 eggs, each about 1.3 to 2.0 mm in diameter. Hatching requires 42 to 54 hours at water temperatures of 15 to 20 C.

Menhaden are filter feeders. They strain small particles from the water with their gill rakers. They have a muscular stomach that is used for grinding food and the intestine is about 4.5 times as long as the body.

Menhaden are extremely valuable commercial fishes. Large commercial vessels use purse seines to surround the schools after they are spotted from light planes. Most of the catch is used for oil and meal and they are not considered a desirable food fish.

References
Hildebrand, 1963c (general review). Reintjes, 1964 (bibliography). Dietrich, 1979 (fecundity). Jones, Martin, and Hardy, 1978 (larval stages). Ferraro, 1980 (embryology). Edgar and Hoff, 1976 (feeding). Hildebrand, 1948 (systematics). Higham and Nicholson, 1964 (reproduction). Goode, 1878a, 1878b, (systematics). Jeffries, 1975 (food habits). Westman and Nigrelli, 1955 (mortality).

Names
Tyrannus is Latin for tyrant. In the New York area, menhaden are usually called mossbunkers or simply bunkers. They are also known as pogies.

Clupea tyrannus Latrobe, 1802: 77 Chesapeake Bay

Alosa tyrannus, DeKay, 1842: 258 New York

Clupea menhaden Mitchill, 1815: 453 New York

Clupea neglecta Rafinesque, 1818b: 206 Long Island

Alosa sadina DeKay, 1842: 263 (not of Mitchill)

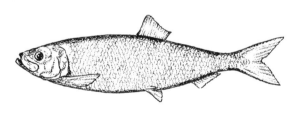

ATLANTIC HERRING

Clupea harengus Linnaeus, 1758

Identification
The Atlantic herring is easily recognized as a herring by its silvery color, compressed shape, ventral scutes, and its lack of a lateral line, adipose fin, and gular plate. It differs from the menhaden in that it has a shorter head, a more slender body, and no modified scales in front of the dorsal fin. It has neither the dorsal filament nor the bulbous snout of the gizzard shad. The Atlantic herring differs from the river herrings of the genus *Alosa* in that its dorsal fin originates about midway between the tip of the snout and the base of the tail. In the river shads, the dorsal origin is much farther forward. The presence of teeth on the vomer is a distinctive feature of the herring.

The usual size of the herring is about 12 inches total length, maximum about 18 inches.

In life, the herring is blue or greenish on the back with the change from the dark back to the pale sides often marked by a greenish band. The gill covers often have brassy or golden tones.

Occurrence
The Atlantic herring is a fish of open seas that seldom ventures into fresh water. There are a few records of juveniles from the Hudson River as far upstream as River Mile 42. The subspecies *Clupea harengus harengus* is found on both sides of the Atlantic. In Europe, it ranges from the Straits of Gibraltar to Spitzbergen, and on the American coast it is found from Greenland to North Carolina. A Pacific subspecies, *C. h. pallasi*, ranges from southern California to the Aleutian Islands, Siberia, and Japan.

Notes
The herring has been studied intensively because of its great commercial importance. There are several discrete stocks with slightly different morphological characteristics. Herrings are plankton feeders. They spawn along the coasts, usually in waters 2 to 20 feet deep but sometimes in water so shallow that the eggs wash ashore, and sometimes 15 to 20 miles offshore. Spawning takes place in the spring, summer, and fall, and in some stocks there are both spring and fall runs. Females lay 20,000 to 40,000 sticky eggs.

References
Hildebrand, 1963c: 275-293 (general account). Jones, Martin, and Hardy, 1978 (life history).

Names
Harengus is Middle Latin for herring.

Clupea harengus Linnaeus, 1758: 317 seas of Europe

Clupea halec Mitchill, 1815: 451 New York

Clupea vittata Mitchill, 1815: 456 New York

Clupea elongata (Lesueur), DeKay, 1842: 250-251 New York

Clupea caerulea Mitchill, 1815: 457 New York

Clupea minima, DeKay, 1842: 253-254 New York

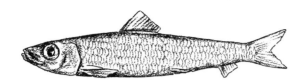

ROUND HERRING

Etrumeus teres (DeKay, 1842)

Identification

The round herring differs from other herrings in that its body is nearly round in cross section rather than compressed and its belly does not have a saw-toothed edge. Unlike other herrings in our area, the round herring has only one ventral scute and that is deeply embedded in the skin around the pelvic fins. It is more slender and less compressed than the river shads, it lacks the deep body and the modified predorsal scales of the menhaden, and it has neither the dorsal filament nor the overhanging snout of the gizzard shad. Otherwise, it shares with the herrings the following characteristics: all fin rays soft, no gular plate, no adipose dorsal fin, no lateral line on the body, a single pair of nostrils. Body silvery, scales deciduous.

The color in life is greenish olive above, shading to silvery on the sides. The maximum size is 380 mm (15 inches) total length but most specimens are 8 to 10 inches total length.

Occurrence

Round herring occur from the Bay of Fundy to Florida and the Gulf of Mexico. There are a few records from the Hudson Estuary.

References

Hildebrand, 1963c (general account). Jones, Martin and Hardy, 1978 (life history). Bath et al., 1977 (Hudson River). Whitehead, 1963: 321 (nomenclature)

Names

Teres means terete, round in cross section.
   Clupea sadina Mitchill, 1815: 457 New York
   Alosa teres DeKay, 1842: 262 New York

ANCHOVIES

ENGRAULIDAE

Anchovies are usually small, transparent fishes with a conical, transparent snout that extends in front of a very large mouth. The maxillary bone extends well behind the eye, even beyond the gill opening in some species. The preopercle and the bones supporting the lower jaw slope backward to accommodate the large mouth and this gives anchovies an unmistakable physiognomy. Most species have fine gill rakers, usually more than 50 on the lower limb of the first arch. There are no fin spines and the dorsal fin is short and usually placed about mid-body. They have very little pigment and are nearly transparent with a broad silvery stripe along their midside. About 20 genera and more than 100 species are known, some of which are important commercial species. Anchovies are near relatives of the herrings and are classified with them in the order Clupeiformes.

The bay anchovy is a resident in the Hudson Estuary and the striped anchovy is a stray.

KEY TO THE SPECIES OF ANCHOVIES IN NEW YORK

A. Anal fin originates below the anterior third of the dorsal fin. Anal rays 24 to 27. Lateral silvery stripe somewhat diffuse.
Anchoa mitchilli   **Bay anchovy, p. 397**

A'. Anal fin originates below the posterior part of the dorsal fin. Anal rays usually 20 or 21. Lateral silvery stripe sharply defined.
Anchoa hepsetus   **Striped anchovy, p. 398**

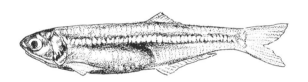

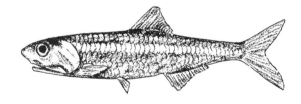

BAY ANCHOVY

Anchoa mitchilli
(Valenciennes, 1848)

Identification

Anchovies are distinctive in having a snout that overhangs the mouth and a very long maxillary bone reaching at least to near the margin of the preopercle and usually beyond. This places the corner of the mouth well behind the back of the eye and gives the head a distinctive appearance. The bay anchovy is similar in appearance to the striped anchovy, but the anal fin originates farther forward (under or just behind the dorsal origin) in the bay anchovy. In the striped anchovy, it originates under the middle of the dorsal fin. The bay anchovy has a more prominent snout and a longer anal fin with 24 to 30, rather than 18 to 23 rays. This is a pale species, nearly transparent in life. It is slightly greenish with a prominent silvery band along the midside. The peritoneum is silvery and shows through the body muscles. There are a few melanophores scattered on the upper surface and around and behind the anal fin base. The usual size is 3 to 4 inches total length.

The bay anchovy is usually found along ocean beaches and in the saltwater part of the Hudson Estuary, sometimes moving into fresh water. In the ocean, it has been taken at depths of up to 30 or 40 meters.

Occurrence

Bay anchovies occur from Yucatan, Mexico, north to Cape Cod with occasional individuals reaching the Gulf of Maine. In New York, it occurs along the coast of Long Island and in the lower reaches of the Hudson Estuary. In the spring of 1983, Walter Keller of the New York Department of Environmental Conservation, collected several adults at the Troy dam at River Mile 151.5 but the usual range seems to be below Croton Point, sometimes as far upstream as Kingston. Young-of-the-year are common in Piermont Marsh.

Notes

The spawning season is listed as June to September in Long Island Sound. Spawning seems to take place in the early evening hours. Incubation requires 24 hours at 27.2 to 27.8 C. Newly hatched larvae are about 1.8 to 2.7 mm. The larvae are transparent and pelagic until they reach about 225 mm when they are completely transformed and resemble miniature adults. According to Hildebrand, the bay anchovy feeds extensively on mysid shrimps and copepods. Small fish, gastropods, and isopods are also taken.

Anchovies are considered an important link in the food chains of the Hudson Estuary.

References

Hildebrand, 1963b (general account). Jones, Martin, and Hardy, 1978 (life history summary). Kuntz, 1914a (development).

Names

The trivial name *mitchilli* is in honor of Samuel L. Mitchill, the first naturalist to write extensively on the fishes of New York.

Engraulis Mitchilli Valenciennes *in* Cuvier and Valenciennes, 1848: 50 New York, Carolina, Lake Pontchartrain

Anchoviella mitchilli, Greeley, 1937: 91 Hudson River

Stolephorus mitchilli, Bean, 1903: 218-219 New York

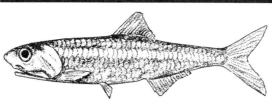

STRIPED ANCHOVY

Anchoa hepsetus (Linnaeus, 1758)

Identification

The slender, compressed shape and the conical snout with long maxillary bone reaching to the gill opening brand the striped anchovy as a member of the Engraulidae. In our area, the only other anchovy is the bay anchovy, *Anchoa mitchilli,* and while the two species are quite similar, they differ in number of anal fin rays (18 to 23 in the striped anchovy, 24 to 30 in the bay anchovy) and in the fact that the anal fin originates just behind the dorsal origin in the bay anchovy and under the posterior part of the dorsal base in the striped anchovy.

The striped anchovy is nearly transparent in life with a striking silver stripe along the side. The stripe is somewhat variable — in some individuals it is

only slightly wider than the diameter of the pupil and in others it is four-fifths of the eye diameter.

Most striped anchovy adults are 100 to 125 mm total length. One specimen 153 mm long has been reported.

Occurrence

The striped anchovy ranges from Nova Scotia to Uruguay. There are a few records from the Lower Hudson, but in general the striped anchovy rarely strays into brackish water. Its occurrence north of the Chesapeake is variable; some years it is abundant, other years it is quite rare.

Notes

Striped anchovies are plankton feeders and eat mostly copepods.

References

Hildebrand, 1963b: 194-200 (general account); 1943 (systematics). Bath et al., 1977: 1 (listed for the Lower Hudson). Jones, Martin, and Hardy, 1978: 154-157 (life history).

Names

The species name *hepsetus* is from the New Latin *epsetus,* which is an old name for anchovies.

Esox hepsetus Linnaeus, 1758: 314 America

Clupea vittata Mitchill, 1815: 456-459 New York

Engraulis brownii Valenciennes *in* Cuvier and Valenciennes, 1848: 41-49

Stolephorus brownii, Bean, 1903: 214-215 New York

LIZARDFISHES

SYNODONTIDAE

This is a rather small family with about 4 genera and 34 species. They are related to a number of deep-sea families although most lizardfishes occur on the continental slopes of tropical and temperate seas.

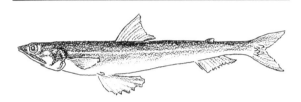

INSHORE LIZARDFISH

Synodus foetens (Linnaeus, 1766)

Identification
The inshore lizardfish is a slender, terete fish with a tiny adipose dorsal fin. It gets its name from its distinctive physiognomy — its cheeks and opercles are scaly and its head is pointed with bands of pointed teeth that give it a definite reptilian appearance. The fins of the lizardfish are also distinctive. The pelvics are larger than the pectorals and their inner rays are longer than the outer ones. The pelvics are sub-thoracic, having their origin between the ends of the pectorals and the beginning of the dorsal. There is a large pelvic axillary process. The pectorals are high on the side of the body. The scales are thin and cycloid. The lateral line is incomplete. The top of the head is scaleless, the branchiostegal rays are numerous, and the upper jaw is bounded by the premaxillary alone.

The larvae of lizardfishes are planktonic with a distinctive series of black spots formed by pigment in the lining of the body cavity. The extreme transparency of the body wall makes these spots visible externally.

Occurrence
Larval lizardfishes are occasionally carried into the Hudson Estuary. Specimens were collected by Texas Instruments personnel on 27 September 1976 at River Mile 27 and on 8 September 1980 at River Mile 30. Tabery et al. (1978) recorded it from River Miles 17 to 26.

Notes
Lizardfishes have a mixture of primitive and advanced features that confused the early ichthyologists. This resulted in their being placed with the trouts by Linnaeus (1766) (owing, no doubt, to the presence of an adipose dorsal fin) and with the pikes by Mitchill (1815) (presumably because of their numerous strong teeth). Rosen (1973) places them in the order Aulopiformes.

References
Gibbs, 1959 (larval stage identification). Anderson, Gehringer, and Berry, 1966 (general account).

Names
The species name is a Latin word meaning *odorous*, having a bad smell.

Salmo foetens Linnaeus, 1766: 513-514 South Carolina

Esox salmoneus Mitchill, 1815: 442-443 New York

GOOSEFISHES

LOPHIIDAE

The goosefishes are bizarre creatures that have been described as animated fish traps. The goosefish is a large, shallow-water species that sometimes wanders into the mouths of estuaries. The first impression is that the fish is mostly head, and the head is mostly mouth, with long sharp caniniform teeth. A closer look reveals that the first spine of the dorsal fin is separate and has a wormlike appendage at its tip, and that the chin bears a fringe of feathery, fleshy tabs.

The entire fish is flattened and the pectoral fins are almost arm-like. The gill opening is restricted to a small hole at the "elbow" of the pectoral fin base. Fishes of this family occur on both sides of the Atlantic and in the Indian and Western Pacific Oceans. It is a small group with about five genera and a dozen species.

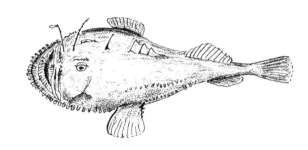

GOOSEFISH

Lophius americanus
Valenciennes, 1837

Identification

If a fish ever deserved to be called a monster, this one does. It is a large species reaching nearly 3 feet in length. It is a depressed fish that is mostly head, and its head is mostly mouth. The lower jaw projects so that the long sharp teeth are exposed even when the mouth is closed. Its skin is smooth with a row of fleshy flaps on the lower jaws and smaller flaps along the sides. The pectoral fins are arm-like, and the gill openings reduced to small pores at the elbows of the pectoral fins. The first dorsal spine has a fleshy lure at its tip. The second and third spines have small triangular membranes and there are two small dorsal fins that are well separated, the first with only three spines.

They are also known as anglerfish because they attract their prey with a lure-like modification of the first dorsal spine.

Occurrence

Goosefish are marine but they are occasionally taken in the Lower Hudson about as far north as the George Washington Bridge.

References

Bigelow and Schroeder, 1953b (general account).

Names

Americanus is in reference to its range — America. A similar species occurs in European Atlantic waters.

Lophius piscatorius Linnaeus, 1766: 402 Europe
Lophius americanus Valenciennes *in* Cuvier and Valenciennes, 1837: 380 Philadelphia

CODFISHES

GADIDAE

The codfishes and their allies constitute a rather diverse group of about 55 species of temperate and coldwater fishes. They are presently classified in a group called the Paracanthopterygii which is characterized by the presence of a specialized subdivision of the jaw muscles and certain peculiarities of the caudal fin skeleton.

The limits of the family are in some question. Some authorities regard the silver hake as a member of the Gadidae; others assign it and its near relatives to a separate family, the Merlucciidae. Silver hakes are slender fishes with rather large mouths and strong teeth. Their pelvic fins are not reduced to filaments. Their unifying character is a V-shaped ridge on the top of a rather flattened head. Otherwise, they are quite similar to the rest of the cods.

Without the silver hake, the family includes two subfamilies, the Gadidinae which includes such forms as the cod, tomcod, pollock, haddock and others that have three dorsal and two anal fins. The other subfamily, the Lotinae, have two dorsals and one anal fin and this group includes the red and spotted hakes and the only freshwater cod, the burbot, *Lota lota*.

Cods have no spines in their fins. The pelvic fins are usually inserted anterior to the pectoral fins and sometimes reduced to filaments. The scales are small and of a special type with the circuli broken into short segments. Many cods have barbels on the chin or snout.

Codfishes are extremely important in the commercial fishery of the north temperate regions because of their size, abundance, and high quality as food fishes.

KEY TO THE SPECIES OF CODFISHES IN THE INLAND WATERS OF NEW YORK

A. One or two dorsal fins and one anal fin.

D.

A'. Three dorsal fins and two anal fins.

B. Pelvic fins wide, with the second ray extended as a short filament less than one-third as long as the rest of the ray. Maximum length more than 3 feet.

C.

B'. Pelvic fins narrow, the second ray protruding as a long filament about as long as the rest of the ray. Maximum size less than 15 inches.
Microgadus tomcod

Atlantic tomcod, p. 404

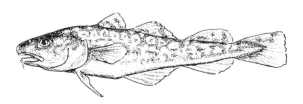

C. (B. Pelvic fins wide, with short filament.) Lower jaw longer than the upper jaw. Chin barbel small or sometimes absent.
Pollachius virens   Pollock, p. 404

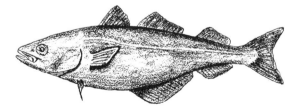

C'. Lower jaw shorter than the upper. Chin barbel well developed.
Gadus morhua   Atlantic cod, p. 403

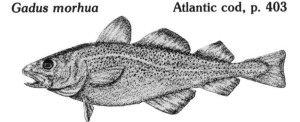

D. (A. Dorsal fins one or two.) Dorsal fin single, preceded by a fringe of short rays and one long ray. Three barbels at the tip of the snout and one on the chin.

Enchelyopus cimbrius

Fourbeard rockling, p. 403

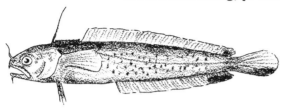

D'. Two dorsal fins, no separate dorsal fin rays.

E. Pelvic fins long and feeler-like, consisting of two filaments and inserted well forward, almost on the edge of the gill openings.

G.

E'. Pelvic fins of the normal type, not long and feeler-like but consisting of several soft rays, inserted below or slightly ahead of the pectoral fins.

F. A chin barbel is present. First dorsal fin originating behind the tips of the pectorals. No notch in second dorsal or anal fins. Fresh water. See freshwater section.

Lota lota

Burbot, p. 261

F'. No chin barbel. First dorsal originating just behind base of pectoral fins. Second dorsal and anal fins with a notch, followed by longer rays giving the appearance of two fins joined together.

Merluccius bilinearis

Silver hake, p. 406

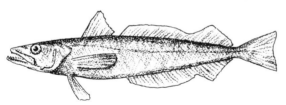

G. (E. Pelvic fins feeler-like.) First dorsal fin without prolonged filamentous rays. Outer half of first dorsal fin black with a whitish margin. Pectoral fins reaching to origin of anal fin. Lateral line dark but interrupted by a series of whitish spots.

Urophycis regia

Spotted hake, p. 405

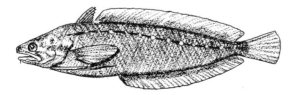

G'. Third ray of first dorsal fin prolonged into a filament that is three to five times as long as the rest of the fin. Pectoral fins not reaching to anal origin. Lateral line not dark with white spots.

Urophycis chuss

Red hake, p. 405

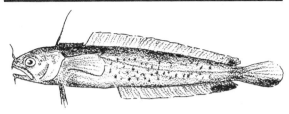

FOURBEARD ROCKLING

Enchelyopus cimbrius (Linnaeus,1766)

Identification
The fourbeard rockling gets its name from its conspicuous barbels — one in front of the nostril on each side, one at the tip of the snout, and one at the tip of the chin. The fourbeard is a peculiar fish in other ways, too. The first dorsal fin consists of a single long ray followed by about 50 short hairlike rays that are not interconnected by membrane. The second dorsal fin is elongate with 45 to 53 rays. The anal fin has 39 to 43 rays. It has a rounded tail and the pectorals are high on the sides with their bases almost vertical. The pelvic fins begin in front of the pectorals. In general shape, the fourbeard resembles the hakes — tapering, round in front of the anal, and compressed behind. The fourbeard is a rather somber fish with conspicuous spots at the ends of the dorsal and anal fins and on the base of the tail. There are some scattered spots on the sides of the body. The maximum size is about 12 inches total length.

Occurrence
Fourbeard rocklings have been taken in the Lower Hudson as far upstream as Indian Point where Wayne Ahlmer collected a specimen in the winter of 1973.

Notes
Cohen and Russo studied variation in this species and found that southern populations have more dark pigment and frequently have four dark blotches in the dorsal fin rather than one. Southern fish also have more dark pigment at the base of the short rays of the dorsal fin. There is clinal variation in dorsal, anal, and pectoral fin ray counts, gill raker number and vertebral number. These authors consider the fourbeard to be a single species not divisible into subspecies.

References
Bath, Beebe, Dew, Reider, and Hecht, 1977 (Hudson River). Cohen and Russo, 1979 (relationships and variation).

Names
According to Jordan and Evermann *cimbrius* is Latin for Welsh

Gadus cimbrius Linnaeus, 1766: 440 Atlantic Ocean

Rhinonemus cimbrius, Goode and Bean, 1895: 384-385 New York

Enchelyopus cimbrius, Bean, 1903: 710-711

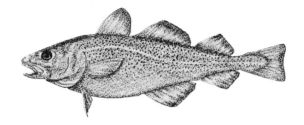

ATLANTIC COD

Gadus morhua Linnaeus, 1758

Identification
The Atlantic cod is an ordinary codfish which is to say that it has three dorsal fins, two anal fins, and rather normal pelvic fins. In the inland waters of New York, it could only be confused with the tomcod which is a much smaller species and differs in the following ways: 1) The Atlantic cod has a square tail whereas that of the tomcod is rounded. 2) The anterior rays of the pelvic fin of the tomcod are prolonged into a filament which is about as long as the rest of the fin, but in the Atlantic cod the filament is only about a fourth as long as the rest of the fin. 3) The dorsal fin originates over the base of the pectoral in the Atlantic cod and the pectoral extends beyond the rear of the base of the first dorsal fin. In the tomcod, the dorsal originates farther back and the end of the pectoral is below the rear third of the first dorsal. 4) The eye of the cod is large, about four times in the head length, but in the tomcod it is small, about six times in the head length.

The color pattern of the Atlantic cod is one of darker spots on a lighter background which can be either green or red. In contrast to some other similar codfishes, the lateral line is pale.

Codfish are large, reaching weights of more than 200 pounds. The all-tackle record is 98 pounds 12 ounces from the Isle of Shoals, New Hampshire. Fish weighing 50 to 60 pounds are still caught on occasion.

Occurrence
Boyle reported that Atlantic cods are sometimes taken by commercial fishermen in Haverstraw Bay. Mr. Tom Lake picked up the skull of a cod estimated to have been about 2 feet long on the beach at Haverstraw Bay in the winter of 1983.

Notes
The Atlantic cod occurs on both sides of the Atlantic from the Bay of Biscay and Novaya Zemlya to Greenland and south to Cape Hatteras.

References
Bigelow and Schroeder, 1953b: 182-196. Boyle, 1969 (Hudson River).

Names
Morhua is a Middle Latin name for the cod.

Gadus morhua Linnaeus, 1758: 252 off Europe

Gadus arenosus Mitchill, 1815: 368 New York

Gadus rupestris Mitchill, 1815: 368 New York

Morrhua minuta (Linnaeus), DeKay, 1842: 277 New York

Morrhua americana, DeKay, l842: 274-276 New York (not *M. americana* of Storer which is *Microgadus*)

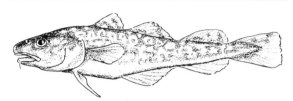

ATLANTIC TOMCOD

Microgadus tomcod (Walbaum, 1792)

Identification
At first glance, the tomcod with its three dorsal fins, two anal fins, and prominent chin barbel, looks like a small version of the Atlantic cod. The two are easy to distinguish, however, because the tomcod has a smaller eye, a rounded rather than square tail, and filaments on the pelvic fins that are as long as the rest of the fin. The tomcod is a much smaller species than the cod and its dorsal fin originates farther back, over the middle of the pectoral rather than over its base. The color varies from olive to green without definite color phases and the pattern is mottled rather than spotted. Its size is usually 10 to 12 inches, rarely 15 inches, total length.

Occurrence
Tomcod are fish of the inshore coastal areas. They are almost anadromous, moving upstream to brackish water to spawn. In Canada, there are landlocked populations in a few lakes. Tomcod range from insular Newfoundland to Chesapeake Bay. It apparently does not spawn south of the Hudson River.

In the Hudson, most of the spawning takes place between West Point and Poughkeepsie.

Notes
The tomcod spawns from November to February in tidal waters. The demersal and somewhat adhesive eggs are deposited on sand or gravel shoals at temperatures of 0 to 2.5 C. Growth is rapid and individuals seldom live more than 2 years. Ninety percent mature 1 year after they are hatched. Each female lays 14,000 to 20,000 eggs. After spawning, they move downstream to the Lower Hudson and ocean bays. The eggs hatch in 5 or 6 weeks and the yolk-sac larvae drift for another week or two. The larvae spend March to May feeding on zooplankton and drifting downstream, reaching Croton by May or June and feeding more and more on benthic organisms. They spend July through September in the lower estuary, sometimes moving into the deep waters near West Point and downstream again to the ocean bays. Their growth is rapid and by December they begin to move upstream toward the spawning grounds.

Bigelow and Schroeder report that tomcod feed on small crustaceans, mollusks, and fish fry. They feed near the bottom and depend largely on chemical senses for finding their food.

This species is tremendously abundant in the lower estuary and it is potentially an important sport fish during the colder months. Because of its short life span, its abundance is an excellent index of environmental conditions in the estuary.

References
Bigelow and Schroeder, 1953b: 196-199 (general account). Grabe, 1978 (food of juveniles); 1980 (food of age I and age II fish). Smith et al., 1979 (hepatoma in Hudson River fish). Hecht and Dew, n.d. (ecology and population dynamics). Peterson et al., 1980 (early life history stages). Schaner and Sherman, 1960 (fecundity).

Names
The trivial name is taken directly from the English common name.

Gadus tomcod Walbaum, 1792: 133
Gadus tomcodus pruinosus Mitchill, 1815: 369
Morrhua pruinosa, DeKay, 1842: 278 Albany
Gadus tomcodus fuscus Mitchill, 1815: 369
Gadus tomcodus luteus Mitchill, 1815: 369
Gadus tomcodus luteo-pallidus Mitchill, 1815: 369
Gadus tomcodus mixtus Mitchill, 1815: 369
Gadus polymorphus Mitchill, 1815: 369
Microgadus tomcod, Greeley, 1935: 101

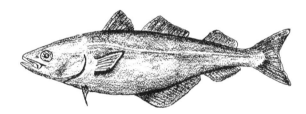

POLLOCK

Pollachius virens (Linnaeus, 1758)

Identification
The pollock resembles the Atlantic cod in having three dorsal fins, two anal fins, and a pale lateral line. It differs from the cod in that its lower jaw projects beyond the upper and in the fact that its chin barbel is small or absent whereas in the cod it is quite prominent. The cod is spotted but the pollock is a uniform olive green. The tail of the pollock is more deeply forked with sharper angles than that of the cod.

Occurrence
The pollock is included here on the basis of a 53-mm specimen collected 28 October l980 at River Mile 42 by J. Reichle of Texas Instruments. This specimen is now AMNH 48283.

Names
Virens is the past participle of the Latin word meaning to be green.

Gadus virens Linnaeus, 1758: 253 oceans of Europe

Gadus purpureus Mitchill, 1815: 370 New York

Merlangus leptocephalus DeKay, 1842: 288 Long Island

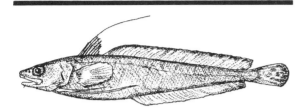

RED HAKE

Urophycis chuss (Walbaum, 1792)

Identification

In the red hake and the spotted hake, *Urophycis regia*, the pelvic fins are reduced to long filaments inserted on the side of the isthmus between the gill covers. The body is long and tapering, the caudal fin rounded, and there are two dorsal fins in both species. The red hake differs from the spotted hake in lacking spots along the lateral line and in having the third ray of the dorsal fin prolonged into a filament three to five times as long as the rest of the dorsal rays. There is no such prolongation in the spotted hake. The red hake is also difficult to distinguish from the white hake, *Urophycis tenuis*, which has been reported from the Arthur Kill but not from the Hudson Estuary. The white hake has smaller scales (119 to 148 in the lateral line, 12 rows between the lateral line and the base of the dorsal fin; the red hake has 95 to 117 lateral line scales and 9 rows between the lateral line and the dorsal fin). It has been stated that the upper jaw reaches to below the rear margin of the pupil in the red hake, to the rear margin of the eye in the white hake and well beyond the the rear of the eye in the spotted hake but Musick found that this feature did not work for separating the red hake and the white hake. A much better characteristic, according to Musick, is that the red hake has three gill rakers on the upper part of the gill arch and the white hake has two (not counting rudiments).

The red hake reaches a maximum weight of about 6 pounds.

Occurrence

Juvenile red hake are inquilines, that is, they live in the mantle cavities of scallops. As they get too large for the scallop shells they become free-living.

The red hake sometimes moves up the Hudson River as far as Indian Point (River Mile 42) where it was reported by Texas Instruments personnel in 1975.

References

Hildebrand and Cable, 1938: 612-618 (development). Musick, 1973 (identification); 1974 (distribution). Miller and Marak, 1959 (larval stages). Markle et al., 1982 (habitat). Texas Instruments Report to Consolidated Edison, 1975. Bigelow and Schroeder, 1953b (general summary). Svetovidov, 1982 (recognition). Pearson and Miller, 1980 (feeding).

Names

Chuss is an old vernacular name, probably derived from cusk.

Blennius chuss Walbaum, 1792: 186 Long Island

Gadus longipes Mitchill, 1815: 372 New York

Urophycis chuss, Bean, 1903: 704-708 New York

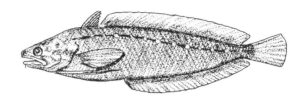

SPOTTED HAKE

Urophycis regia (Walbaum, 1792)

Identification

The spotted hake, with its tapering body, two dorsal fins and filamentous pelvic fins resembles the red hake and the white hake. It differs, however, in not having the third ray of the dorsal fin prolonged into a filament, in having larger scales (90 to 95 in the lateral line of the spotted hake; 100 to 110 in the lateral line of the red hake), and a larger mouth with the end of the maxillary behind the level of the back of the eye. The coloration of the spotted hake is distinctive. The distal half of the dorsal fin is black with a narrow white margin. The lateral line is black but interrupted by a series of white spots. The pelvic fins are white.

Occurrence

Bath et al. (1977) listed the spotted hake from the Hudson Estuary. On 2 June 1980 a 111-mm specimen was collected at River Mile 20 by H.M. Woodward. This specimen is AMNH 48283.

References

Bigelow and Schroeder, 1953b (summary account). Barans and Barans, 1972 (larval stages).

Names

Regia is Latin for royal.

Blennius regius Walbaum, 1792: 186 Long Island (after Schoepf)

Enchelyopus regalis Bloch and Schneider, 1801: 53 Long Island

Gadus punctatus Mitchill, 1815: 372 New York

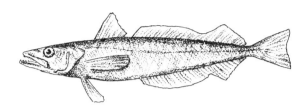

SILVER HAKE

Merluccius bilinearis
(Mitchill, 1814)

Identification
The silver hake is quite different from other cods. It is a long, slender fish with a projecting lower jaw, strong teeth and two dorsal fins, although the second has a notch that suggests the division into two, the second and third fins. The anal is similar to the second dorsal fin and has a similar notch. The pelvic fins are of the usual form, that is not reduced to filaments, and are inserted slightly ahead of the pectorals. There are no chin barbels. The tail is emarginate.

The silver hake is indeed iridescent silvery, somewhat darker above, with a slight reddish or purplish cast. There are about 13 indistinct dusky rose blotches along the side. The usual size is about 14 inches; the maximum is about 30 inches.

Occurrence
The silver hake is a marine species that occasionally strays into the Hudson Estuary. Boyle reported that commercial fishermen sometimes get it in Haverstraw Bay in November and December. One fisherman reported catching one in a muskrat trap set in a tidal marsh.

Notes
Schaefer noted that in the inshore areas of the New York Bight the silver hake feeds on invertebrates, especially amphipods, and sand shrimps and about as frequently on small fishes. Blueback herring and Atlantic silversides are the most frequent fish species eaten in inshore areas whereas offshore the most frequent item in the stomachs was other members of their own species. Schaefer also found that female whiting (silver hake) grew more rapidly and to a larger size than the males.

References
Cohen, 1980 (names). Schaefer, 1960 (growth and feeding). Boyle, 1969 (Hudson River).

Names
The silver hake is also called whiting in the New York area. *Bilinearis* is Latin for two lines.

Stomodon bilinearis Mitchill, 1814: 7 New York

Gadus albidus Mitchill, 1818b: 409 New York

Merluccius albidus, DeKay, 1842: 280-282 New York

Merluccius bilinearis, Boyle, 1969: 260 Verplanck

CUSK-EELS
OPHIDIIDAE

The cusk-eels are slender, eel-like fishes closely allied to the codfishes. They resemble eels in shape and in having the dorsal and anal fins long and continuous with the tail fin but they differ superficially in that they have pelvic fins. These fins, however, are reduced to two slender rays each and they are inserted far forward in the throat region, in fact, directly below the eye.

Cusk-eels are bottom dwellers in coastal waters. The family is rather a small one; worldwide, there are about 10 genera and some 35 species. One species has been recorded from the Hudson River as a marine stray.

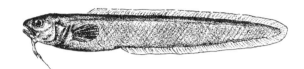

STRIPED CUSK-EEL

Ophidion marginatum
(DeKay, 1842)

Identification
The cusk-eel resembles an eel but the filament-like pelvic fins on the sides of the isthmus are distinctive. The longer of the two filaments on each side is slightly shorter that the head. The lateral line stops a little before the base of the tail and is darker than the pale grayish-green ground color. The dorsal fin has a distinct dark marginal line that continues around the tail and forward to about the middle of the anal fin.

Occurrence
The striped cusk-eel is a marine species reported from the Arthur Kill and from the Lower Hudson. Specimens 224 and 287 mm long were collected at River Mile 42 in 1980. These are AMNH 48292 and 48293, respectively.

Notes
Studies in progress show that there are at least 10 species of *Ophidion* in the Western North Atlantic.

References
Bath et al., 1977 (in list of Hudson River fishes). Cohen and Nielson, 1978 (systematics).

Names
The name *marginatum* apparently refers to the dark margins on the vertical fins.

Ophidium marginatum DeKay, 1842: 315 New York Harbor

Rissola marginata, Bath et al., 1977 Hudson River

NEEDLEFISHES

BELONIDAE

The needlefishes are related to the flyingfishes and halfbeaks. Most needlefishes are marine but a few live in fresh water. One species is a summer resident in the Hudson Estuary. There are about 10 genera and nearly 30 species.

Sometimes, the needlefishes are called sea gars because of their elongated jaws and slender bodies. They are not at all related to the true gars which are primitive freshwater fishes with thick diamond-shaped bony scales.

ATLANTIC NEEDLEFISH

Strongylura marina
(Walbaum, 1792)

Identification
The Atlantic needlefish is distinguished by its very elongate, slender and terete body. There are only soft rays in the fins and the dorsal and anal fins are placed far back on the body, the dorsal origin somewhat behind the origin of the anal. The tail is only slightly forked, with the lower lobe a little larger; the pelvic fins are abdominal.

In needlefishes, as in their relatives, the flyingfishes, the lateral line runs low on the side of the body. Living fish are conspicuously green above and silvery below with a narrow dark line along the side and another in the middorsal line. The jaws are extremely elongate and narrow and armed with sharply pointed teeth. In this species, only the right gonad develops whereas in its southern relative, the very similar *Strongylura timucu*, both gonads are functional. *Strongylura marina* has 213 to 214 scales (average 256) and *S. timucu* has 120 to 185 (average 156).

Occurrence
The Atlantic needlefish is a consistent summer resident in the Hudson Estuary where is occurs as far north as Ulster Park. In the summer of 1984, it was taken at Kingston Point Beach (River Mile 91) by Steve Stanne and John Mylod of the Hudson River Sloop Clearwater.

Notes
Tom Lake and Christopher Letts report that although they are hard to hook, needlefish readily strike artificial lures and provide some interesting late summer fishing.

References
Collette, 1968 (systematics). Lake, 1982 (fishing for needlefish in the Hudson River).

Names
The species name *marina* refers to its habitat. It is a Latin word meaning of the sea.

Esox marinus Walbaum, 1792: 88 off New York (after Schoepf)

Tylosurus marinus, Bean, 1903: 317-319

Strongylura marina, Greeley, 1937: 98 Lower Hudson

Esox longirostris Mitchill, 1818a: 322 Hudson River

Belone truncata Lesueur, 1821: 126 New York Bay

KILLIFISHES
CYPRINODONTIDAE

The killifishes are generally small fishes and some species are called topminnows or toothcarps although they have no Weberian apparatus and are not related to the true minnows. Killifishes live in fresh and marine waters and some can even tolerate the hypersaline conditions of drying tide pools. This is a rather large family with about 50 genera and more than 300 species. Recently, Parenti has divided the family, placing *Fundulus* and *Lucania* in the Fundulidae and *Cyprinodon* in the family Cyprinodontidae. Other ichthyologists believe that the relationships between the two groups are best expressed by calling them subfamilies of the family Cyprinodontidae.

In the New York fauna, the banded killifish occurs in truly fresh water as well as in brackish water, the mummichog lives in marine and brackish water, and the rest of the species treated here are primarily marine species that sometimes wander into brackish or fresh water.

KEY TO THE SPECIES OF KILLIFISHES IN THE INLAND WATERS OF NEW YORK

A. Jaw teeth each with two or more points. Body short and deep, its depth contained about 2 times in the standard length.
Cyprinodon variegatus
    Sheepshead minnow, p. 411

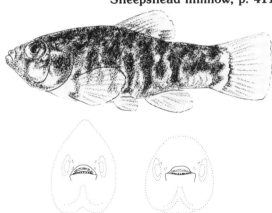

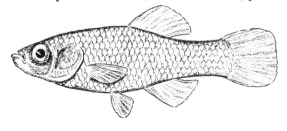

Teeth of *Fundulus* (left) and *Cyprinodon*.

A'. Jaw teeth with single points. Body more elongate, depth at least 3 times in the standard length.

B. Jaw teeth in a single series.
Lucania parva **Rainwater killifish, p. 413**

B'. Jaw teeth in a band of more than one row.

C. Scales 35 to 55. Caudal peduncle slender, its least depth contained more than 7 times in the standard length.
Fundulus diaphanus **Banded killifish, F.**

C'. Scales 31 to 35. Caudal peduncle deep, its least depth less than 7 times in standard length.

D. Dorsal fin of males originating slightly behind the origin of the anal fin. Scales 31 or 32. Male with a distinct ocellus on the last few rays of the dorsal fin. Sides of males with 10 to 12 heavy darker bars. Females unbarred or with numerous delicate bars. A small species not exceeding 40 mm in length.
Fundulus luciae **Spotfin killifish, p. 412**

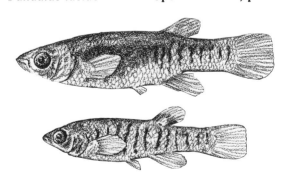

D'. Dorsal fin of males originating over or slightly ahead of the origin of the anal fin.

E. Snout blunt, its length slightly longer than eye. Eye contained 1.5 to 2 times in the postorbital head length. Color pattern dark, without longitudinal lines. Males with vertical bars on the body and an ocellus on the back of the dorsal fin.
Fundulus heteroclitus   **Mummichog, p. 411**

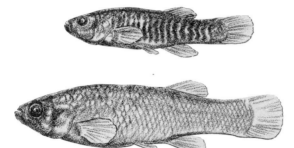

E'. Snout long, its length nearly twice the eye diameter. Eye 2 to 3 times in the postorbital head length. Color pattern of both sexes pale, males with vertical bars and females with two or three longitudinal lines.
Fundulus majalis   **Striped killifish, p. 413**

F. (C. Scales 35 to 55.) Scales usually 45 to 49. Dorsal rays usually 13 or 14. Anal rays usually 11 or 12. Pectoral rays usually 16 or 17. Scales with sharp dark outlines. Bars on the sides of the body continue across the back. Bars on caudal peduncle short but distinct. Commonly reaching more than 70 mm standard length.
Fundulus diaphanus diaphanus   **p. 264**

F'. Scales usually 40 to 44. Dorsal rays usually 11 to 13. Anal rays usually 10 or 11. Pectoral rays usually 14 or 15. Scales with diffuse dark outlines. Bars on the side of the body broken into spots across the back. Bars on caudal peduncle more or less fused into a median lengthwise stripe. Seldom more than 70 mm standard length.
Fundulus d. menona   **p. 264**

SHEEPSHEAD MINNOW

Cyprinodon variegatus
Lacepède, 1803

Identification

Although not a true minnow, this species is minnow-sized, the largest individuals being about 2 inches in total length. The sheepshead minnow (really a killifish) differs from true minnows in having teeth on the jaws and in lacking a Weberian apparatus. Its rather flat head with scales on the top, large scales on the body, and saltwater habitat also differentiate it from the true minnows. This is the most distinctive of our killifishes for it is the only one that has a short deep shape. Its greatest depth is approximately half the standard length. It is also moderately compressed. The jaw teeth are tricuspid and wedge shaped rather than conical. The pelvic fins are small and abdominal in position and dwarfed by the much larger pectorals. The tail is square. The sheepshead minnow has a rather bold pattern of irregular bars. Breeding males have salmon-colored bellies and the pelvic and anal fin edges and the leading edge of the dorsal fin are bright orange contrasting with the steel-blue wash of the anterior dorsal part of the body and the greenish sheen behind the dorsal fin.

Occurrence

The sheepshead minnow is a coastal fish that ranges from Cape Cod to Mexico in brackish, marine, or hypersaline environments. It is common in bays and estuaries of Long Island and there is one record from the Hudson River at Newburgh.

Notes

The record from Newburgh is puzzling. Since sheepshead minnows are easily caught in shallow estuarine habitats and keep well in aquaria it is possible that this specimen was a discarded aquarium pet.

References

Hildebrand, 1917 (life history). Raney, Backus, Crawford, and Robins, 1953 (breeding behavior). Parenti, 1981 (systematics).

Names

The name *variegatus* is from the Latin *vario*, change, referring to the color pattern which varies on different parts of the body.

Cyprinodon variegatus Lacepède, 1803: 486 South Carolina

Esox ovinus Mitchill, 1815: 441 New York

Lebias ovinus, DeKay, 1842: 215-216 New York

MUMMICHOG

Fundulus heteroclitus
(Linnaeus, 1766)

Identification

The mummichog is easily recognized as a killifish by its general shape. The dorsal and anal fins are far back, the top of the head is scaly, and the upper jaw is protractile. It differs from the banded killifish and the striped killifish in that its snout is short and its body is shorter and deeper. It is also darker in color, the males with white or yellow spots on the scales and indistinct blue or silver bars. Males have an ocellus on the back of the dorsal fin. Females are lighter and more uniform in color. In general appearance, it is most like the spotfin killifish, *Fundulus luciae,* but that species has only 8 dorsal rays where the mummichog has 11 or 12. Young striped killifish, a more brackish water species, resemble small mummichogs but they have scales on the area in front of the eye. The mummichog has a scaleless preorbital.

The dorsal fin of the males is marbled and has a large posterior spot that is absent in the females. Adult males also have a yellow spot at the origin of the dorsal fin. Breeding males are intense yellow on the lower sides, the belly, head, and the lower fins. The blotch in the dorsal fin is surrounded by a yellow ring. Breeding males are also blue dorsally and the vertical bars become quite bright. The dorsal and anal fins of the males are larger than those of the females with small pearl organs along the fin rays.

The maximum size is about 130 mm. We have a 99-mm (standard length) specimen from Haverstraw Bay.

Occurrence

The mummichog is an estuarine species that can tolerate a wide range of salinities. It frequently occurs together with the banded killifish in fresh water and areas of low salinity. It can tolerate rather high temperatures, up to 93 F at 14 ppt salinity. Freshwater populations have growth rates similar to those of brackish water populations (Samaritan and Schmidt, 1982).

The general range of the mummichog is from northeastern Florida to the Gulf of St. Lawrence. Current studies by Able and others suggest that there is a northern form, *F. h. macrolepidotus,* which appears to intergrade with the typical mummichog, *F. h. heteroclitus,* in New Jersey. Both forms have been taken on Long Island. They are distinguished by egg structure (number of filaments and oil droplets) and in their spawning behavior.

In the Hudson River, there seem to be no records between Newburgh and Claverack, but the status of the populations above and below this stretch has yet to be determined.

Notes

In Delaware, where it has been studied rather thoroughly, the mummichog spawns between April and the end of August. Spawning is cyclical and correlated with high tides associated with the times of the new and full moon. The eggs are laid at levels reached only by high spring tides. Eggs are deposited in clutches of 10 to 300 and are hidden in leaves or empty mussel shells. In these situations, the eggs are protected from drying, and hatching can be delayed for at least 2 weeks until the eggs are again reached by the tides. Apparently, most of the spawning occurs on the night tide because females collected at night had ovulated eggs in the ovary and those collected during the day did not. Morin and Able have described variation in spawning habits.

The mummichog consumes a variety of plant and animal matter including diatoms, amphipods, mollusks, crustaceans, small fishes, fish eggs, and sea grass fragments. It is widely used as an experimental animal, especially for studies of endocrinology.

References

Newman, 1907 (spawning). Mast, 1915 (behavior in tide pools). Bigelow and Schroeder, 1953b (general summary). Perlmutter, 1958 (popular account). Butner and Brattstrom, 1960 (movements). Richards and McBean, 1966 (larvae). Garside and Morrison, 1977 (thermal preference). Meredith and Lotrich, 1979 (population dynamics). Taylor et. al., 1979 (lunar spawning cycle). Lotrich, 1975 (movements and home range). Fritz et al., 1975 (movements). Able and Castagna, 1975 (reproductive behavior). Baker-Dittus, 1978 (foraging patterns). Samaritan and Schmidt, 1982 (life history in fresh water). Morin and Able, 1983 (spawning). Taylor and DiMichele, 1983 (spawning sites). Relyea, 1983 (systematics).

Names

Heteroclitus is from the Greek *hetero*, different, and *klitos*, a slope or hillside, the lower part of a place. In combination this is taken to mean irregular or unusual.

Cobitis heteroclitus Linnaeus, 1766: 500 Charleston, South Carolina

Fundulus heteroclitus, Greeley, 1935: 97 Hudson River

Cobitis macrolepidota Walbaum, 1792: 11 (after Schoepf)

Fundulus heteroclitus macrolepidota, Greeley, 1937: 98 Lower Hudson

Esox pisiculus Mitchill, 1815: 440 New York

Esox pisculentis Mitchill, 1815: 441 New York

Hydrargyra nigrofasciata Lesueur, 1817e: 133-134 Rhode Island

Fundulus viridescens DeKay, 1842: 217 New York

Fundulus zebra DeKay, 1842: 218 New York

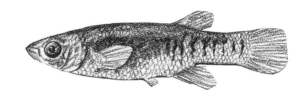

SPOTFIN KILLIFISH
Fundulus luciae (Baird, 1855)

Identification

The spotfin closely resembles the mummichog in shape and coloration but the two species can be distinguished by dorsal ray count: 8 in the spotfin, 11 or 12 in the mummichog. The dorsal fin of the spotfin originates farther back, over or slightly behind the anal and about equidistant between the tip of the tail and the anterior half of the eye. In the mummichog, it is about equidistant between the tip of the tail and the tip of the snout in males, somewhat nearer to the tip of the tail than to the tip of the snout in adult females. The base of the dorsal fin is shorter than the base of the anal fin.

There is a pronounced ocellus (a black spot surrounded by a pale ring) on the back of the dorsal fin of males.

This is a small species, seldom attaining 50 mm in total length.

Occurrence

The Survey obtained this species on Long Island (Suffolk County). Its overall range is Long Island to Georgia.

Notes

Dr. Kenneth Able of Rutgers University has found this species to be common in pools in tidal marshes along the New Jersey coast.

References

Richards and Bailey, 1967. Kneib, 1978 (ecology). Byrne, 1978 (life history).

Names

This species was named for Lucy Baird, the daughter of Spencer Fullerton Baird.

Hydrargyra luciae Baird, 1855: 344 Beesleys Point, New Jersey

Fundulus luciae, Greeley, 1939: 41 Long Island

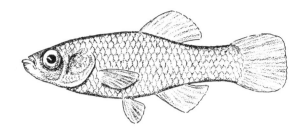

STRIPED KILLIFISH
Fundulus majalis (Walbaum, 1792)

Identification
The striped killifish is more slender than the mummichog and has a much longer snout than any other killifish in our area. It differs from the mummichog in having scales on the preorbital region.

The striped killifish is a pale fish with a bold pattern of darker stripes: vertical lines in the males, and at least a trace of longitudinal lines in females. In fully mature females, a long narrow stripe runs from the gill opening to the tail with one or two interrupted stripes below this, and one or two vertical bars at the base of the tail. Juveniles of both sexes are barred.

Occurrence
The striped killifish is more of a saltwater fish than is the mummichog. The Survey did not get it in the Hudson River estuary, and I have been unable to find records of its occurrence there. It is abundant in the bays and estuaries of Long Island and the Survey collected it in the mouths of streams tributary to Long Island Sound.

References
Rosen, 1973a (identification). Able, 1976 (cleaning symbiosis). Clemmer and Schwartz, 1964 (age and growth). Richards and McBean, 1966 (larvae). Relyea, 1983 (systematics).

Names
Majalis is from the New Latin, pertaining to the month of May, i.e. Mayfish.

Cobitis majalis Walbaum, 1792: 12 Long Island
Esox flavulus Mitchill, 1815: 439 New York
Esox zonatus Mitchill, 1815: 443 New York
Fundulus majalis, Greeley, 1937: 98 Long Island Sound (not Lower Hudson)

RAINWATER KILLIFISH
Lucania parva (Baird, 1855)

Identification
This is a small, rather undistinguished killifish that is more apt to be confused with the mosquitofish than with members of its own family. It is a stubby little fish with large scales conspicuously outlined with dark pigment. There is a dark middorsal streak in front of the dorsal fin. During the breeding season, the males develop a dark leading edge on the dorsal and anal fins, and the anal and pelvic fins become slightly red. The maximum size is about 2 inches total length.

The teeth of the rainwater killifish are pointed and in a single irregular row rather than in a band as in species of *Fundulus*, or tricuspid and incisor-like as in *Cyprinodon*.

Occurrence
Greeley (1939) reported this species from the lower parts of streams in Suffolk County, Long Island. He noted that while it is not a typical freshwater fish, it can tolerate fresh water at least temporarily. Its range is Cape Cod to Tampico, Mexico.

Notes
This species has been introduced into California.

References
Hubbs and Miller, 1965 (taxonomy). McCoid and St. Amant, 1980 (established in California).

Names
Parva is Latin for small.

Cyprinodon parvus Baird, 1855: 345. Long Island
Lucania parva, Greeley, 1939: 41-42. Long Island

SILVERSIDES

ATHERINIDAE

The silversides are usually small slender fishes with two dorsal fins and a pronounced silver stripe along the sides. There are about 30 genera and more than 150 species living in fresh and salt water. In New York, there is one freshwater species and three others that live in brackish and salt water. Silversides are distantly related to the killifishes.

KEY TO THE SPECIES OF SILVERSIDES IN NEW YORK

A. Edges of the scales scalloped or undulating.
Membras martinica   **Rough silverside, p. 415**

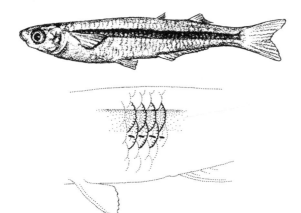

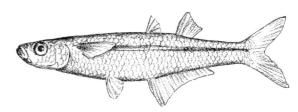

Atlantic silverside, *Menidia menidia*

Laciniate scale of rough silverside.

A'. Edges of scales smooth.

B. Jaws prolonged into a short beak-like structure. Scales small, 76 to 80 in lateral series. Freshwater species.
Labidesthes sicculus   **Brook silverside, p. 269**

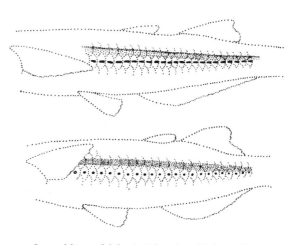

Lateral lines of Atlantic (above) and inland silversides.

C'. Lateral line consisting of pits in the face of each scale. Anal rays (15) 16 to 18.
Menidia beryllina   **Inland silverside, p. 415**

B'. Jaws short, not forming a beak. Scales larger, fewer than 50 in lateral series. Marine and estuarine species.

C. Lateral line consisting of tubes passing through the scale. Anal rays about 24.
Menidia menidia   **Atlantic silverside, p. 415**

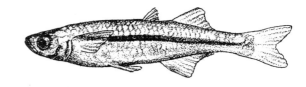

ROUGH SILVERSIDE

Membras martinica (Valenciennes, 1835)

Identification
The rough silverside differs from the brook silverside in having short jaws and large scales. It closely resembles the two species of *Menidia* in our area but differs from them in that its scales are laciniate, that is, with scalloped edges that make the fish slightly rough to the touch. It also differs from *Menidia* in that it has sheaths of scales at the bases of the dorsal and anal fins. These sheaths consist of single rows of large scales that are rather easily dislodged.

Occurrence
Rough silversides are apparently resident in the Lower Hudson and they may be more common than is usually realized because they closely resemble the Atlantic and tidewater silversides. Boyle reported it first from Haverstraw Bay.

Notes
This is a coastal species generally restricted to areas of high salinity.

References
Boyle, 1969.

Names
This species is named for the island of Martinique in the West Indies where it was first collected.
Atherina martinica Valenciennes *in* Cuvier and Valenciennes, 1835: 40 Martinique
Membras martinica, Boyle, 1969: 227-228 Senasqua Beach
Kirtlandia vagrans, Bean, 1903: 359-361 Mecox Bay, Long Island

INLAND SILVERSIDE

Menidia beryllina (Cope, 1869)

Identification
The inland silverside differs from the brook silverside in having large scales and short jaws. It differs from the rough silverside in that its scales are, at most, only slightly scalloped and there are no scaly sheaths at the bases of the dorsal and anal fins. The difficulty in identifying the inland silverside is distinguishing between it and the Atlantic silverside.

While superficially very similar, these two species differ in lateral scale count (37 to 41 in *M. beryllina*, 44 to 50 in *M. menidia*), in the number of oblique scale rows between the upper end of the gill opening and the origin of the spiny dorsal fin (12 to 14 in tidewater, and 15 to 18 in Atlantic), and anal ray count (I,14 to 20 in *beryllina*, I,20 to 26 in *menidia*). In *M. beryllina*, the end of the dorsal fin is directly above the end of the anal fin, but in *M. menidia*, the end of the dorsal fin is conspicuously in front of the end of the anal fin. In the inland silverside, the lateral line consists of a series of pits in the scales but in the Atlantic silverside each lateral line scale has a definite tube. Finally, in the Atlantic silverside, the peritoneum is dark but in the inland silverside the peritoneum is silvery with well-spaced, small, black spots.

Occurrence
Greeley reported this species from Peekskill and from a Long Island Sound tributary near Mamaroneck. The Survey also found it to be common on Long Island in streams where it occurred in waters of lower salinity than did the Atlantic silverside. The Survey found it in one pond on Staten Island. It ranges from Massachusetts to Veracruz.

Notes
The inland form formerly known as *Menidia audens* has recently been shown to be indistinguishable from *Menidia beryllina*.

References
Johnson, 1975 (systematics). Chernoff et al., 1981 (systematics). Greeley, 1939 (Long Island).

Names
Beryllina is the Latin word for green-colored.
Chirostoma beryllinum Cope, 1869b: 403 Potomac River
Menidia beryllina cerea Kendall, 1902: 261 Waquoit Bay, Massachusetts
Menidia beryllina cerea, Greeley, 1937: 99 Lower Hudson

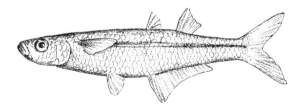

ATLANTIC SILVERSIDE

Menidia menidia (Linnaeus, 1766)

Identification
With its short snout, large, nearly smooth-edged scales, and dorsal and anal fins without scaly sheaths, the Atlantic silverside can only be confused with the inland silverside, *Menidia beryllina*. Characters for separating the two species have been given under that species. Possibly the best differ-

ence is the presence of tubes in the lateral line scales of the Atlantic silverside and of pits only in the inland silverside.

Occurrence

Greeley noted that Atlantic silversides were fairly common in the Lower Hudson and in tributaries of Long Island Sound in August and September. On Long Island, the Survey found that it was less inclined to enter fresh water than was the inland silverside. Its overall range is Newfoundland to Florida.

Notes

Middaugh et al. studied the reproductive behavior of this species in the Edisto River estuary in South Carolina. Spawning occurred in the upper intertidal zone in April or May through July at northern latitudes, March through July farther south. About an hour before spawning, the fish began swimming in schools parallel to, and about 30 to 60 meters off the shoreline. Approximately 15 minutes before spawning, they moved to within 2 or 3 meters of the shoreline and continued to pass back and forth along a 100-meter section. Females deposited the eggs on stems of *Spartina alterniflora*, passing between the stems and releasing the eggs while fluttering the rear part of the body against the stems. Males followed close behind and released sperm in the same area. The eggs adhere to the plants by fine threads that form as the eggs are ovulated. Sometimes, groups of 6 to 15 males moved to a single plant and positioned their heads close to the plant, forming a rosette through which a dozen or so females swam, depositing their eggs as their heads broke through the surface of the water. Eggs were also deposited on detrital mats and in crab burrows, along the walls of the mats, 2 or 3 cm below the water surface. The eggs were deposited at average heights of 1.5 to 1.8 meters above mean low water so that they were exposed to the atmosphere for about 10 hours between high tides.

References

Hildebrand and Schroeder, 1928 (general account). Middaugh et al., 1981 (life history) Middaugh, 1981 (reproductive ecology). Conover and Ross, 1982 (population dynamics). Greeley, 1939 (Long Island).

Names

Menidia is an old fish name from New Latin.

Atherina menidia Linnaeus, 1766: 519 Charleston, South Carolina

Atherina notata Mitchill, 1815: 446 New York

Atherina viridescens Mitchill, 1815: 447 New York

Menidia menidia notata, Greeley, 1937: 99 Lower Hudson

CORNETFISHES

FISTULARIIDAE

The cornetfishes are distant relatives of the pipe-fishes. They are long and slender, with a tubular face and a relatively small, oblique, terminal mouth. They are quite large fishes, some reaching 2 yards or more in length. Unlike the pipefishes, they are not encased in bony rings. In fact, they have no scales although they do have parts of the lateral line surrounded by bony tubes that are sharply pointed in some species. They are somewhat flattened in cross section. There are no fin spines. The dorsal and anal fins are far back on the body and short with about 14 rays in the dorsal. The tail is forked but the middle rays are drawn out into a long fila-ment. The pectorals are small with a broad base, the pelvics abdominal with six rays. The anus is shortly behind the pelvics. Cornetfishes have 76 to 88 ver-tebrae of which the first four are greatly elongated. There are no gill rakers. Cornetfishes live in warm seas, occasionally drifting into temperate waters. Two species occur in the Western Atlantic; one has been recorded as a marine stray in the Hudson Es-tuary.

The color is variable, greenish brown above with many pale blue spots and lines. One other species occurs in the Western Atlantic, *Fistularia petimba*, the red cornetfish. The red cornetfish lacks blue spots and has pronounced points on the bony ossi-fications along the lateral line. The corresponding ossifications in the bluespotted cornetfish are quite smooth.

Occurrence
During the summer of 1981, members of the De-partment of Environmental Conservation collected a specimen of this species in the Lower Hudson.

Notes
This is a coastal marine species that is generally found in tropical waters. Its presence in the Hudson is surely the result of its planktonic larval stage hav-ing been carried north by currents associated with the Gulf Stream.

References
Fritzsche, 1978 (identification).

Names
Tabacaria refers to tobacco, probably in reference to the shape of the fish which resembles a tobacco pipe.

    Fistularia tabacaria Linnaeus, 1758: 312-313 tropical America

    Fistularia neo-boracensis Mitchill, 1815: 437 New York

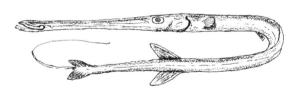

BLUESPOTTED CORNETFISH

Fistularia tabacaria
Linnaeus, 1758

Identification
The cornetfish is an extremely elongate fish with a rather stiff body, a long filament extending from the middle of the tail, and a small mouth at the end of a long tubular face. From a distance, the cornetfish might be confused with a needlefish but the needle-fish has long jaws whereas the cornetfish has short jaws but a long face. The head of the cornetfish is about one-third of the body length and the snout constitutes about three-fourths of the head length.

PIPEFISHES
SYNGNATHIDAE

Pipefishes and seahorses are highly specialized fishes that have the body enclosed in bony rings. They have tiny mouths at the tip of a long tubular facial region and this gives them the name tube snouts. A few species live in fresh water but both of our species are confined to salt water of the ocean and the lower reaches of the Hudson Estuary.

KEY TO THE SPECIES OF SEAHORSES AND PIPEFISHES IN NEW YORK

A. Body straight, tail not prehensile, caudal fin present.
Syngnathus fuscus   **Northern pipefish, p. 419**

A'. "Neck" bent so that the head is at right angles to the body. Tail prehensile, without a developed caudal fin.
Hippocampus erectus   **Lined seahorse, p. 418**

LINED SEAHORSE

Hippocampus erectus Perry, 1810

Identification
Looking like a marine version of a chess knight, the seahorse is one of the most bizarre fishes in existence. There is nothing but another seahorse with which it can be confused. The head is bent at a right angle to the body, the tail prehensile and curved under most circumstances, and there is no tail fin. Its posture is upright and the dorsal fin is the main propulsion unit. Like the pipefish, the body and tail are encased in bony rings, about 12 on the body and 33 to 36 on the tail. The dorsal fin has 18 or 19 unbranched rays. The tiny mouth is at the end of a long tubular face. The egg pouch is on the abdomen and nearly completely enclosed.

There are three North Atlantic species but only the lined seahorse occurs in our area. The only other species that might stray into our area is the longsnout seahorse, *Hippocampus reidi*, which is a more southern (Cape Hatteras to Rio de Janeiro) species with a bold pattern of spots and an even longer snout (snout length 0.41 to 0.49 of the head length in *reidi*, 0.33 to 0.46 in *erectus*).

Occurrence

The seahorse is not uncommon in the Lower Hudson in the vicinity of George Washington Bridge. Mearns (1898) reported it from Consook (now Con Hook) during the summers of 1895 and 1896. Texas Instruments personnel collected a specimen at River Mile 42 on 27 April 1980.

References

Vari, 1982 (general account).

Names

The species name is Latin meaning erect.

Hippocampus erectus Perry, 1810, pl. XLV American seas

Hippocampus hudsonius DeKay, 1842: 322 Hudson River

NORTHERN PIPEFISH

Syngnathus fuscus Storer, 1839

Identification

The pipefish looks first like a piece of twig and second like a straightened-out seahorse. Its body is long and slender but stiff, because it is encased in bony rings: 10 on the trunk and 35 to 38 on the tail. It is polygonal in cross section because there are keel-like ridges running along the body and tail. Its strongly oblique mouth is tiny and at the end of an elongate face. Pipefishes have no pelvic fins but they do have well-developed pectoral and dorsal fins (with 13 or 14 and 33 to 49 rays, respectively). There is a conspicuous caudal fin and a minute anal fin that lies just behind the vent. In males, the anal fin is within the egg pouch located on the ventral side of the first 15 tail rings.

Occurrence

This species, which ranges from Prince Edward Island to Jupiter Inlet in Florida, is reasonably common in the Hudson at least as far north as Indian Point.

Notes

The Survey found males from Haverstraw Bay with eggs in their brood pouches on 25 August. On 16 July 1936, males with eyed eggs were taken at the mouth of a stream in Mamaroneck.

References

Dawson, 1982 (general account).

Names

The species name, *fuscus* is the Latin word for brown, dark, or dusky.

Syngnathus typhle (not of Linnaeus), Mitchill, 1814: 475 New York

Syngnathus peckii Storer, 1839: 162 (nomen nudum)

Syngnathus fuscus Storer, 1839: 162 Massachusetts

Syngnathus peckianus Storer, 1839: 163 Woods Hole

Syngnathus fasciatus (not of Risso, 1818), DeKay, 1842: 319

Syngnathus viridescens DeKay, 1842: 321

Syngnathus pechianus, DeKay, 1842: 321 (misspelling)

Syngnathus DeKayi Dumeril, 1870: 568-569 (replacement for *S. fasciatus* DeKay, preoccupied)

Syngnathus Milbertianus Dumeril, 1870: 568,573 (replacement name for New York specimens of *S. fasciatus* Kaup)

Syngnathus peckianus, Ayres, 1843: 282 Long Island Sound

Siphostoma fuscum Bean, 1903: 347-472

Syrictes fuscus Breder, 1938: 26,28 Lower Hudson

Syngnathus pekianus, Greeley, 1937: 98 Lower Hudson (misspelling)

SEA BASSES

SERRANIDAE

The sea basses are often considered to be the typical spiny-rayed fishes. They have thoracic pelvic fins and a single dorsal fin with 9 to 11 spines and no, or a very shallow, notch between the spines and rays. There are 3 anal fin spines and 9 or 10 anal rays. The maxillary is exposed, that is, it is not covered by the preorbital bone when the mouth is closed. Most sea basses are tropical but a few live in temperate waters. The family includes the giant groupers as well as a large number of smaller species. Many, including some populations of the black sea bass, are hermaphroditic, beginning life as females and transforming to males after they have spawned as females. Other sea basses are male and female at the same time. At present, about 370 species are placed here but their relationships are poorly understood.

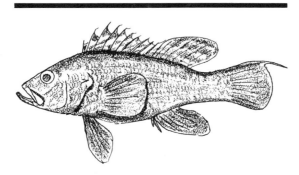

BLACK SEA BASS

Centropristis striata (Linnaeus, 1758)

Identification
The black sea bass is a rather somber fish with the spiny and soft parts of the dorsal fin continuous. The caudal fin of adults is distinctive; there is a short filament at the upper corner. Smaller teeth and 10 spines in the dorsal fin serve to differentiate the black sea bass from the blackfish (tautog), which has 16 or 17 spines and 7 or 8 soft rays in its dorsal fin. Adult sea bass are nearly black with pale gray centers on the scales and a white margin on the tail. Older males develop a pronounced hump behind the head. The pelvic fins are large and originate in front of the pectorals, which are high on the sides and have vertical bases.

Occurrence
The black sea bass apparently has not been reported from the Hudson River above the George Washington Bridge, but it has been taken in the Arthur Kill and in New York Harbor.

Notes
Black sea bass are protogynous hermaphrodites. They begin life as females and transform into males after they have spawned as females.

References
Kendall, 1972, 1979 (larvae). Bigelow and Schroeder, 1953b (general summary). Briggs, 1960 (nomenclature).

Names
Striatus is New Latin for striped.

Labrus striatus Linnaeus, 1758: 285 America

Perca fulva Walbaum, 1792: 336 New York (after Schoepf)

Coryphaena nigrescens Bloch and Schneider, 1801: 297 New York

Perca varia Mitchill, 1815: 415 New York

Centropristes striatus, Bigelow and Schroeder, 1953b: 407-409

Centropristis striata, Briggs, 1960: 358 (correct spelling of name)

BLUEFISHES
POMATOMIDAE

This is a small family of about three species. They occur worldwide in tropical and temperate oceans. The bluefish is a silvery, streamlined, spiny-rayed fish with small scales, a rather small spiny dorsal fin, and a long soft dorsal. The preopercle has a flap that overlaps the operculum. Bluefish have very efficient jaw teeth and are legendary for their voraciousness.

BLUEFISH

Pomatomus saltatrix
(Linnaeus, 1758)

Identification
Bluefish are overall silvery with a bluish or greenish cast dorsally and a black, smudge-like spot at the base of the pectoral fin. The body is compressed and moderately elongate with a deeply forked tail and a rather deep caudal peduncle. The spiny dorsal fin has 7 or 8 short spines, the second dorsal has 23 to 26 soft rays, and the anal has 2 very short spines that are separated from the rest of the fin which has one spine and 25 to 27 rays. The bluefish is remarkable for its teeth. The jaws are armed with a single series of flattened, pointed teeth and there are patches of fine villiform teeth on the floor of the mouth between the ends of the gill slits. Bluefish have small deciduous scales and the bases of the dorsal and anal fins are densely scaled. Its lateral line is nearly straight.

Occurrence
Snapper blues (juveniles up to 10 inches long) are quite common in the Lower Hudson each summer and larger fish are sometimes found as far upstream as Haverstraw Bay.

Notes
Bluefish are notorious carnivores and are said to feed on smaller fishes, often continuing to strike and slash after their stomachs are full. Apparently, bluefish winter off Florida and return to the New York area each April or May.

References
Bigelow and Schroeder, 1953b (general account). Lund, 1961 (races). Kendall and Walford, 1979 (distribution of larvae). Richards, 1976 (age and growth).

Names
Saltatrix comes from the Latin *salto,* to dance, and means dancing girl.

> *Perca saltatrix* Linnaeus, 1758: 293 Carolinas
> *Temnodon saltator* DeKay, 1842: 130-132
> *Pomatomus saltatrix,* Greeley, 1937: 100 Lower Hudson

COBIAS

RACHYCENTRIDAE

The cobia is placed in its own family which is usually considered closely related to the remoras to which it bears a remarkable resemblance except that it does not have the suctorial modification of the dorsal fin. It has rather small smooth scales and its dorsal spines are short and not connected by membrane. It occurs in the Atlantic, Pacific, and Indian Oceans.

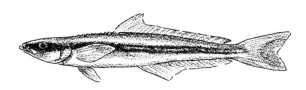

COBIA

Rachycentron canadum
(Linnaeus, 1766)

Identification
The cobia is a rugged, heavy-bodied, elongate fish with a projecting lower jaw and a broad flat head. The spiny dorsal consists of a series of short, stout spines that are not connected by membrane. The second dorsal has one spine and about 30 rays, with a blunt lobe anteriorly. The anal is also long and contains 1 spine and about 23 rays. The tail is forked in adults but pointed in juveniles less than 4 or 5 inches long.

Cobias are grayish brown, paler below, with a broad, dark, lateral stripe from the tip of the snout to the base of the tail. A lighter stripe above this sets it off from the darker middorsal region. In shape and coloration, this species bears a remarkable resemblence to the sharksucker, *Echeneis naucrates*.

Occurrence
The cobia is a widespread species sought as a game fish along our southern Atlantic and gulf coasts. It is included in the inland fauna on the basis of a single specimen, a 95-mm juvenile collected in Croton River Cove about 1 mile north of Sing Sing in June 1876.

Notes
This is a circumtropical species. The IGFA all-tackle record is a 110-pound 5-ounce fish from Mombasa, Kenya.

References
Fisher, 1891 (Hudson River). Bigelow and Schroeder, 1953b (general account).

Names
Jordan and Evermann point out that the name is for Canada where the species is not found.

Gasterosteus canadus Linnaeus, l766: 491 Carolinas

Centronotus spinosus Mitchill, 1815: 490-492 New York

Elecate atlantica Cuvier *in* Cuvier and Valenciennes, 1834: 334

Elecate canada, Fisher, 1891: 195 Hudson River

Rachycentron canadum, Greeley, 1937: 100 Lower Hudson

REMORAS
ECHENEIDAE

Remoras are highly specialized fishes that have the first dorsal fin modified into a sucking disk with which they attach to other fish and sometimes to boats and swimmers. Some species are host-specific and found only on certain whales, but the sharksucker is less particular and sometimes clings to boats or swimmers. The family is currently divided into seven genera and seven or eight species. They are circumtropical in warm and temperate seas.

SHARKSUCKER

Echeneis naucrates
Linnaeus, 1758

Identification
The sharksucker is a slender terete fish with a pointed to lunate tail (sharper in young), long symmetrical dorsal and anal fins, and a conspicuously projecting lower jaw. Its most outstanding characteristic is the sucking disk on top of the head. This is an oval structure with about 20 pairs of transverse plates that suggest a venetian blind. This disk is a modified dorsal fin.

Other remoras occur off our coast but they have shorter disks and lack the bold, striped pattern of the sharksucker. In the present species, there is a broad dark lateral stripe from the snout through the eye and the base of the pectoral fin to the tail. White stripes above and below this midlateral stripe separate it from the dark pigment of the belly and the back. There are white corners on the tail that contrast sharply with its otherwise dark color.

Occurrence
Allen Beebe has called my attention to an old record of the sharksucker in the Hudson River. De-Kay (1842) mentions one that "had ascended a considerable distance up the Hudson River."

Notes
If this species still enters the river, it must do so only rarely, because there are no recent records. Although the sharksucker leaves its host for extended periods, it is unlikely that it would ascend far up the river by itself. Hence, its presence would depend upon larger fish, especially sharks.

References
Cressy and Lachner, 1970 (hosts and food habits). Maul, 1956 (systematics).

Names
Naucrates is Latin for pilot, from the Greek *naus*, a ship, and *krates*, to guide.

Echeneis neucrates Linnaeus, 1758: 261 (misprint for *naucrates*)

Echeneis albicauda Mitchill: 1817: 244 New York

JACKS
CARANGIDAE

Jacks are a rather diverse family of fast-swimming marine species with a few species that spend part of the year in brackish water. They are spiny-rayed fishes with the the first two anal spines separated from the rest of the anal fin. Most jacks are strongly compressed, silvery fishes with deeply forked tails and some enlarged scales (scutes) along the lateral line. Some are quite bizarre in their shapes. The family also includes the somewhat less-specialized amberjacks which are more torpedo-shaped and lack the lateral line scutes. There are about 24 genera and 200 species.

KEY TO THE SPECIES OF JACKS IN THE INLAND WATERS OF NEW YORK

A. Lateral line with a series of greatly enlarged scutes on its posterior part. Back and belly rounded.

C.

A'. Lateral line without greatly enlarged scutes. Caudal peduncle may have a few slightly enlarged scales along the lateral line. Back and belly sharp edged.

B. Second dorsal and anal fins with high lobes in front. Caudal peduncle without enlarged scales in the lateral line.
Selene vomer Lookdown, p. 426

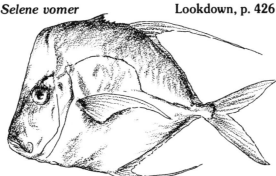

B'. Second dorsal and anal fins without high lobes. Lateral line on caudal peduncle with slightly enlarged scales.
Selene setapinnis Atlantic moonfish, p. 425

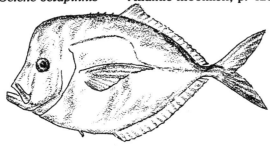

C. (A. Lateral line with enlarged scutes.) Last rays of dorsal and anal fin detached as separate finlets. Lateral line with about 30 scutes on the caudal peduncle.
Decapterus macarellus * Mackerel scad

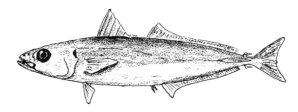

C'. No detached finlets behind dorsal and anal fins.

D. Shoulder girdle (under gill cover and behind the gills) with a deep transverse furrow near its ventral end and a fleshy knob above this. Body rather elongate and forehead sloping, only moderately steep.
Selar crumenophthalmus * Bigeye scad

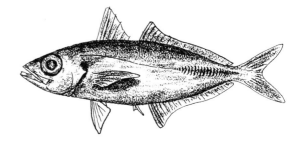

D'. Shoulder girdle without transverse furrow and

*The presence of the mackerel scad and/or the bigeye scad has not been verified and these species are not treated here.

fleshy knob. Body deep, compressed, the forehead very steep.

Caranx hippos   Crevalle jack, p. 425

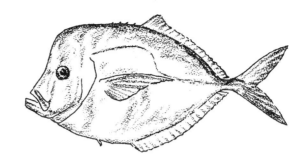

ATLANTIC MOONFISH

Selene setapinnis (Mitchill, 1815)

Identification
The moonfish rather resembles the lookdown in that both species are deep-bodied, highly compressed fishes with deeply forked tails and slender caudal peduncles. The moonfish is not quite as deep bodied as the lookdown, however, and it lacks the high lobes at the front of the dorsal and anal fins although the anterior rays of those fins are slightly longer than the rest of the rays. The moonfish also has small scutes along the posterior straight part of the lateral line. Scutes are not present in the lookdown and they are much larger in all of the other species of jacks in our area. Like the lookdown, the moonfish has a very small spiny dorsal fin and minute pelvics. Its facial profile is somewhat concave and the part above the eye is nearly vertical.

Occurrence
The moonfish ranges from Cape Cod to Uruguay and occasionally strays to Nova Scotia. It is, however, a fish of warmer waters and is not common north of Chesapeake Bay. Allen Beebe reports that there is a specimen in the New York State Museum from River Mile 15.

References
Ginsburg, 1952b (systematics). Bigelow and Schroeder, l953b: 378-379 (general account).

Names
Setapinnis is from Latin *seta*, bristle, and *pinna*, a wing or fin.
   Zeus setapinnis Mitchill, 1815: 384-385 New York
   Vomer brownii Cuvier *in* Cuvier and Valenciennes, 1833: 189 New York
   Vomer setapinnis, Ginsburg, 1952b: 109-112

CREVALLE JACK

Caranx hippos (Linnaeus, 1766)

Identification
The crevalle jack is a highly compressed fish with a blunt face, a deeply forked tail, and an extremely slender caudal peduncle with strong scutes (modified, plate-like scales) along the posterior part of the lateral line. Its pectoral fin is long and scythe shaped. It has a large black spot at the upper corner of the gill cover and another on the upper pectoral fin rays. The shape of the crevalle jack is distinctive and it can be separated from similar species that might stray into our area by the lack of scales on its breast.

Occurrence
Crevalle jacks are common summer residents of the Lower Hudson. Mr. Tom Lake has informed me that in 1982 they were especially abundant as far upstream as River Mile 68 in early October and were still present at River Mile 66 in early November.

References
Ginsburg, l952b (systematics). Lake, 1982 (sport fishery in Hudson River).

Names
Hippos is Greek for horse.
   Scomber hippos Linnaeus, 1766: 494 Charleston, South Carolina
   Caranx defensor DeKay, 1842:120 New York
   Caranx hippos, Greeley, 1937:100 Haverstraw Bay

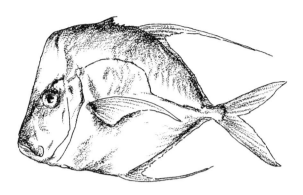

LOOKDOWN

Selene vomer (Linnaeus, 1758)

Identification
The lookdown is one of the more improbable fishes. Its body is short and very deep, almost diamond shaped and extremely compressed. The front of the head is nearly vertical. The anterior rays of both the dorsal and the anal fins extend into long slender lobes. The first dorsal fin is very small and the pelvic fins are tiny in adults although in the juveniles they are prolonged into filaments that are longer than the body. The anterior half of the lateral line is arched and the posterior half is quite straight. Unlike other jacks in our area there are no scutes along the lateral line.

Occurrence
Lookdowns are much more common south of Chesapeake Bay, but they occasionally are found as far north as Cape Cod. It has been recorded several times from the Hudson River as far north as Indian Point (River Mile 42).

References
Ginsburg, 1952b (systematics). Aleveras, 1973 (Hudson River).

Names
Vomer is Latin for plowshare, an obvious reference to the shape of the lookdown.

Zeus vomer Linnaeus, 1758: 266 America

Argyreiosus vomer, DeKay, 1842: 124-125 New York

Zeus capillaris Mitchill, 1815: 383 New York

Zeus rostratus Mitchill, 1815: 384 New York

Zeus geometricus Mitchill, 1818a: 245 New York

Argyriosus mitchilli DeKay, 1842: 126 New York

SNAPPERS
LUTJANIDAE

The snappers are closely related to the sea basses but they differ in having most of the maxillary covered by the preorbital region when the mouth is closed. Members of the genus *Lutjanus* have a characteristic shape and large canine teeth near the tip of the upper jaw. The rest of the teeth are villiform or caniniform.

Snappers are a tropical family but one species occasionally strays into the Lower Hudson. Worldwide, there are more than 230 species.

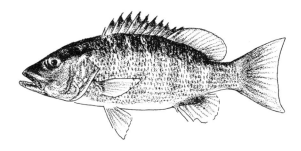

GRAY SNAPPER

Lutjanus griseus (Linnaeus, 1758)

Identification
Snappers are bass-like marine fishes with a rather pointed head (at least in this genus), 10 or 11 dorsal spines, and the maxillary bone almost hidden by suborbital bones when the mouth is closed. The upper jaw has strong canine teeth anteriorly. The dorsal fin is continuous with only a shallow notch between the spines and rays. The preopercle is finely serrated with a notch above its angle that receives a point of the subopercular bone. There are three spines and seven rays in the anal fin.

The general color of the gray snapper is indeed gray, often with purplish or reddish-brown overtones. The scales of the upper sides are spotted and these spots form definite longitudinal lines. There is a prominent bar from the tip of the snout through the eye to just below the origin of the dorsal fin. The margin of the dorsal is black as far back as the middle of the soft dorsal. The caudal and anal fins have dusky margins with a narrow white edge. In small specimens, there is a narrow pale blue line (dark in preserved specimens) from the center of the upper jaw to the point of the operculum and another be- low this from the upper jaw to below the rear margin of the eye.

Occurrence
The gray snapper has a planktonic larval stage and occasionally the young drift as far north as the New York Bight. Records from the Hudson River include a juvenile from near Tarrytown (Boyle, 1969), one specimen collected by LMS at Bowline Pond, and three collected by Texas Instruments (two from River Mile 42 and one from River Mile 28).

References
Starck and Schroeder, 1970 (life history and food habits).

Names
Griseus is a Middle Latin word meaning gray.

Labrus griseus Linnaeus, 1758: 283 Carolinas (after Catesby)

Neomanis griseus, Bean, 1903: 548-550 New York

Lutjanus griseus, Boyle, 1969: 229-230 Hudson River

MOJARRAS
GERREIDAE

Mojarras are also tropical fishes but one or two species occasionally stray into the Hudson Estuary. They are rather diamond-shaped, silvery fishes with smooth scales. The head is scaled and there are pronounced scaly sheaths along the bases of the dorsal and anal fins. Their outstanding characteristic is the mouth, which can be extended into a short tube. The lower jaw has a distinctive concave profile. This is a small group of about 40 species.

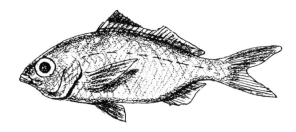

SPOTFIN MOJARRA

Eucinostomus argenteus
Baird, 1855

Identification
The outstanding feature of the mojarra is its mouth, which can be extended downward and forward into a tube. Mojarras are rather silvery, diamond-shaped fishes with strong anal spines and moderately forked tails. The dorsal fin is single with the spines becoming progressively shorter and the last spine is considerably shorter than the first soft ray. There are scaly sheaths along the bases of the dorsal and anal fins and a large pelvic axillary process. In the spotfin mojarra, there is a scaleless groove on top of the snout; the head is otherwise covered with scales. This species is somewhat more slender than some other species of mojarras and has a conspicuous black blotch on the anterior part of the dorsal fin. There are traces of inclined, irregular bars on the upper sides of the body.

Occurrence
Mojarras are tropical species and only a few juvenile specimens have been taken in the Lower Hudson at Bowline Pond and Indian Point.

Notes
Mojarras are distinctive fishes but the species are difficult to distinguish especially when they are small. The identification of this species is accepted with reservation. Although they are tropical, the type of *E. argenteus* was collected in New Jersey.

Hubbs and Miller noted that although the description of the species *argenteus* is usually attributed to Baird and Girard, it is clear that Baird alone is the describer.

References
Bohlke and Chaplin, 1968: 394 (identification). Hubbs and Miller, 1965 (nomenclature).

Names
Argenteus is Latin for silvery.

Eucinostomus argenteus Baird, 1855: 335 Beesleys Point, New Jersey

PORGIES

SPARIDAE

The porgies are also a family of about 100 species of rather typical spiny-rayed fishes. Porgies characteristically have a rather deep head which gives them a distinctive, somewhat vacuous look. The anterior teeth of the lower jaw are chisel-like, while those at the back of the jaw are molar-like. Some species are hermaphroditic.

KEY TO THE SPECIES OF PORGIES IN NEW YORK

A. Front teeth deeply notched. Color pattern consisting of a prominent spot behind the gill covers followed by four or five vertical, dark bands, each narrower than the interspaces.
Lagodon rhomboides   Pinfish, p. 429

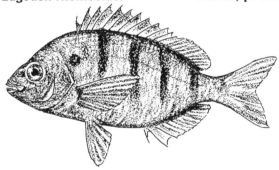

A'. Front teeth not notched. Color pattern plain in the adults, young with about six vague dark crossbars. No prominent spot behind the gill covers.
Stenotomus chrysops   Scup, p. 430

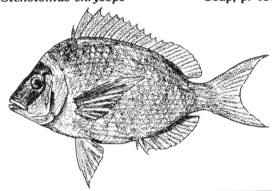

PINFISH

Lagodon rhomboides (Linnaeus, 1766)

Identification
The pinfish is a rather deep-bodied, compressed fish with a long dorsal fin and a moderately forked tail. The mouth is low and almost horizontal and the dorsal profile is highly arched. The premaxillaries are protractile and the maxillary is almost covered by the suborbital region when the mouth is closed. There are three anal spines.

The teeth at the front of the jaw of the pinfish are flat and chisel-like with a deep notch in each. There are eight incisors followed by a double row of blunt molariform teeth on the sides of the jaws.

Pinfish are dusky greenish, shading to silvery ventrally with four to six darker crossbars. There is a conspicuous round dark spot nearly as large as the eye behind the gill openings. In life, the body has narrow light blue and yellow longitudinal lines.

Occurrence
The pinfish is another tropical stray that occasionally makes its way into the Hudson Estuary. Bath et al. (1977) list it from the Hudson, and Mr. Allen Beebe has informed me that this record is based on a specimen collected at Tompkins Cove 15 September 1969.

References
Caldwell, 1957 (life history). Hildebrand and Cable, 1938 (development). Stoner, 1980 (feeding ecology). Hansen, 1969 (ecology). Kjelson and Johnson, 1976 (feeding ecology of young).

Names
Rhomboides probably refers to the shape of the body but it comes from a Greek word *rhombos*, which means whorling or turning.

Sparus rhomboides Linnaeus, 1766: 470-471 Charleston, South Carolina

Lagodon rhomboides, Holbrook, 1855: 56 Charleston, South Carolina

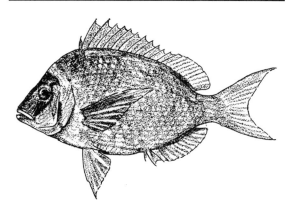

SCUP

Stenotomus chrysops
(Linnaeus, 1766)

Identification
Although the scup resembles the pinfish in general appearance, its back is even more highly arched and its incisor teeth are not notched. The scup is plain bluish silvery above, sometimes with a pinkish cast, and silvery white below. There is no spot behind the gill opening although the axil of the pectoral fin is dark. Young scup sometimes have a few dusky crossbars.

Occurrence
Scup are rather common along the coast where they are a valued sport and food fish. Allen Beebe (M.S.) lists two specimens, one from River Mile 29, the other from River Mile 31, both taken on 26 July 1976.

References
Bigelow and Schroeder, 1953b: 411-416 (general account). Finkelstein, 1969a (life history); 1969b (age at maturity). Briggs, 1968 (sport fishery).

Names
Chrysops is from the Greek *chrysos*, gold and *ops*, eye.

Sparus chrysops Linnaeus, 1766: 471 Charleston, South Carolina

Labrus versicolor Mitchill, 1815: 404 New York

Sargus ambassis Gunther, 1859: 449-452 New York

DRUMS
SCIAENIDAE

This family includes a large number of species that live in marine and estuarine habitats and on the continental slopes. Most of the species live in temperate waters but a few are found in the tropics. There is one truly freshwater drum in our area.

Most drums have highly specialized swim bladders that serve as sound-producing organs, and this has led to the common name of croakers. The kingfish, however, has lost the ability to produce sound and, in fact, its swim bladder disappears as it reaches adulthood.

Drums characteristically have the soft dorsal longer than the spiny dorsal and two spines in the anal fin. The lateral line continues out to the tip of the caudal fin rays, and some species have pointed tails. They also have very large sensory canals on the head.

KEY TO THE SPECIES OF DRUMS IN NEW YORK

A. A conspicuous dark spot behind the upper part of the gill opening. Upper sides with 12 or more narrow, dark, not quite vertical lines.
Leiostomus xanthurus **Spot, p. 433**

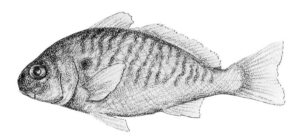

A'. No dark spot behind the gill openings and no dark vertical bars, except that some species have more or less distinct broad saddle-shaped marks or rows of spots that tend to form vertical lines.

B. Lower jaw without barbels.

D.

B'. Lower jaw with one or more barbels.

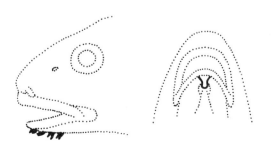

Barbels of croaker (left) and kingfish.

C. Lower jaw with a single prominent peg-like barbel at the front.
Menticirrhus saxatilis
Northern kingfish, p. 434

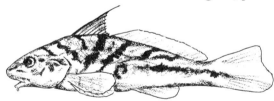

C'. Lower jaw with a row of small but distinct barbels on each side.
Micropogonias undulatus
Atlantic croaker, p. 434

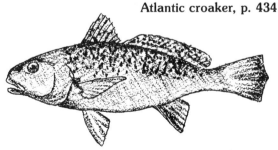

D. (B. No barbels.) Upper jaw with two large canine teeth at the front
Cynoscion regalis **Weakfish, p. 433**

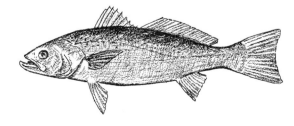

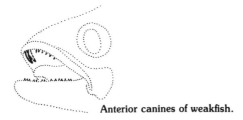

Anterior canines of weakfish.

D'. No large canine teeth at the front of the upper jaw.

E. Dorsal spines 11 or 12, dorsal soft rays 19 to 21. Mouth terminal. Marine, entering Hudson Estuary.
Bairdiella chrysoura   Silver perch, p. 432

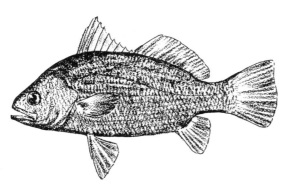

E'. Dorsal spines 8 or 9, dorsal soft rays 24 to 32. Mouth subterminal, the snout projecting beyond the upper jaw. Fresh water.
Aplodinotus grunniens

Freshwater drum, p. 351

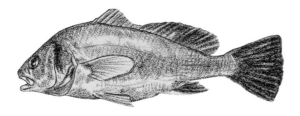

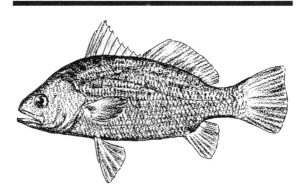

SILVER PERCH

Bairdiella chrysoura
(Lacepède, 1803)

Identification
In general appearance, the silver perch most resembles the freshwater drum, *Aplodinotus grunniens*, in shape, in lacking barbels, and in the size and position of the mouth. The silver perch, however, differs from the freshwater drum in that the snout is shorter so that it does not overhang the mouth, in having a serrate preopercle, and in having a shorter second dorsal fin (19 to 21 rays in the silver perch, 27 to 33 in the freshwater drum).

Occurrence
Juvenile silver perch are not uncommon in the Hudson in the summer, and they have been collected at Indian Point by Texas Instruments.

Notes
In this genus and its near relatives, the swim bladder is divided into two chambers by a constriction. The anterior one is transversely elongate; the posterior is a simple tapering shape.

References
Chao, 1978 (systematics). Kuntz, 1914a (embryology). Welsch and Breder, 1923 (life history). Hildebrand and Cable, 1930 (development). Powles, 1980 (larvae). Chao and Musick, 1977 (ecology of juveniles).

Names
The species name is from the Greek *chrysos*, gold, and *oura*, tail.

    Perca punctatus Linnaeus, 1766: 482 South Carolina (preoccupied)

    Dipterodon chrysourus Lacepède, 1803: 166 South Carolina

    Bodianus argyro-leucas Mitchill, 1815: 417 New York

    Bodianus exiguus Mitchill, 1815: 419 New York
    Bodianus pallidus Mitchill, 1815: 420 New York
    Corvina argyroleuca, DeKay, 1842: 74 New York

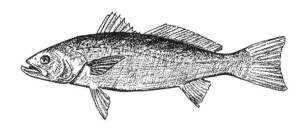

WEAKFISH

Cynoscion regalis
(Bloch and Schneider, 1801)

Identification
The weakfish is rather long and slender for a drum and that is probably why some members of the genus are called sea trout. There are no barbels and the mouth is large and somewhat oblique with a pair of large canine teeth, at least twice as large as the other teeth, at the tip of the upper jaw. The preopercle is not serrated. The anterior and posterior dorsal fins are separate but close together. Weakfish have ctenoid scales and the scales extend onto the basal one-third of the second dorsal and anal fins. There are 11 or 12 anal soft rays and the pectoral fins are longer than the pelvics. The weakfish and their close allies are characterized by having the swim bladder with a pair of anterolateral diverticula tapering forward from the anterior corners of the main chamber to the back of the skull. Weakfish are gray above and silvery below with small spots forming wavy oblique lines on the upper sides. The tail is pointed in juveniles but becomes emarginate or lunate in adults.

Occurrence
The weakfish is a common summer resident in the Lower Hudson, where it has been taken as far north as Indian Point. Boyle reported it from Haverstraw Bay. It was not listed by the 1936 Survey.

References
Welsch and Breder, 1923 (life history). Chao, 1978 (systematics). Pearson, 1941 (ecology of young). Merriner, 1975 (food); 1976 (reproductive biology). Perlmutter, 1953 (summary). Perlmutter, Miller, and Poole, 1956 (ecology). Nesbit, 1939 (ecology, fishery). Massmann, 1963 (annulus formation). Hildebrand and Cable, 1934 (reproduction). Chao and Musick, 1977 (ecology of juveniles). Boyle, 1969 (Hudson River).

Names
Regalis is Latin for royal.
Johnius regalis Bloch and Schneider, 1801: 75 New York
Otolithus regalis DeKay, 1842: 71-72 New York
Roccus comes Mitchill, 1814: 25- 26 New York
Labrus squeteague Mitchill, 1815: 396- 398 New York
Cynoscion regalis Boyle, 1969

SPOT

Leiostomus xanthurus
Lacepède, 1802

Identification
The spot is a rather small, compressed fish with the dorsal profile strongly arched and the ventral outline nearly straight. There are no barbels and the mouth is small, almost horizontal, and slightly overhung by the snout. The body is silvery with faint oblique bars on the upper sides and a pronounced black spot above the upper angle of the gill opening. The teeth are small and those of the lower jaw become obsolescent in adults. The dorsal fins are continuous, the first rather high with 10 spines. The tail is square in young and concave in adults.

Occurrence
The spot has a wide distribution in the Northwestern Atlantic in coastal and estuarine waters. Some years, it is quite common in the Hudson at least as far north as Haverstraw Bay.

Notes
The spot is commonly called Lafayette in our area. According to Boyle, this name came about because there was a great run of them in the river when General Lafayette visited New York in 1824. They were said to have been absent for many years; then they became quite abundant in the summer of 1975.

References
Chao, 1978: 29 (systematics). Boyle, 1969 (presence in Hudson River). Welsch and Breder, 1923 (life history). Hildebrand and Cable, 1930 (development). Kjelson and Johnson, 1976 (feeding ecology). Pacheco, 1962 (age and growth in Chesapeake Bay). Chao and Musick, 1977 (life history).

Names
Xanthurus is from the Greek, *xanthos*, yellow and *oura*, tail.
Leiostomus xanthurus Lacepède, 1802: 439 Carolina (Types in the MNHN, Paris.)
Mugil obliquus Mitchill, 1815: 405 New York
Leiostomus obliquus, DeKay, 1842: 69-70 New York
Leiostomus humeralis Cuvier *in* Cuvier and Valenciennes, 1830: 105 New York (Types in the MNHN, Paris.)
Leiostomus xanthurus, Greeley, 1937: 103 Lower Hudson

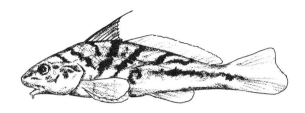

NORTHERN KINGFISH

Menticirrhus saxatilis
(Bloch and Schneider, 1801)

Identification

The kingfish is a rangy, elongate fish with a single stout peg-like barbel at the tip of the chin. The anal fin has a single spine and eight soft rays, and the swim bladder is absent or rudimentary in adults. In this species, the third dorsal spine is prolonged into a filament that reaches well beyond the origin of the second dorsal. The caudal fin is asymmetrical, with the upper lobe angular and the lower lobe rounded. The upper jaw is longer than the lower and the snout overhangs the mouth. There are no canine teeth.

The northern kingfish is a boldly marked species, dark gray above and silvery below, with irregular dark crossbars. The first slopes downward and backward, the rest slope downward and forward so there is a V-shaped configuration on the body below the dorsal fin. Usually, there is a dark longitudinal streak below the lateral line posteriorly.

Occurrence

The northern kingfish occurs along the Atlantic and gulf coasts to Yucatan, Mexico. There are a few records of juveniles as far upstream as Croton Bay (Beebe, M.S.).

Notes

Unlike other sciaenids, members of this genus lack sonic muscles.

References

Chao, 1978: 31 (systematics). Schaefer, 1965a (age and growth); 1965b (swim bladder present in juveniles). Chao and Musick, 1977 (ecology of juveniles). Welsch and Breder, 1923 (life history).

Names

Saxatilis is Latin, meaning dwelling among rocks.

Johnius saxatilis Bloch and Schneider, 1801: 75. New York. (The holotype is a stuffed skin in the Humboldt-Universitat, Berlin.)

Sciaena nebulosa Mitchill, 1815: 408-409 New York

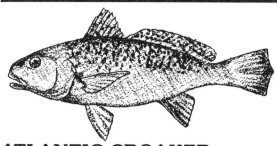

ATLANTIC CROAKER

Micropogonias undulatus
(Linnaeus, 1766)

Identification

This species somewhat resembles the kingfish and the weakfish but, unlike them, it has a row of small barbels along the inside edge of each side of the lower jaw. It also has strong serrations on the preopercle. There are 50 to 56 pored scales in the lateral line and 2 anal spines. The body is silvery with a pinkish cast in life and the back has numerous brassy or brownish spots arranged in rows to form oblique wavy lines. The young are merely spotted.

The swim bladder of this species is highly specialized, this no doubt associated with its well-known ability to produce croaking sounds. There are slender diverticula, one on each side, arising near the middle of the swim bladder and curving forward. The posterior end of the swim bladder tapers to a tail-like point. The lateral diverticula extend forward as far as the transverse septum but do not reach the skull before curving backward again toward the front of the swim bladder.

Occurrence

Small croakers, most less than 21 mm standard length, were collected between River Miles 29 and 38 by Texas Instruments personnel in 1973 and 1976.

Notes

This species has long been known as *Micropogon undulatus,* but Chao noted that the genus *Micropogon* is preoccupied in birds and that Bonaparte proposed *Micropogonias* as a substitute name in 1831.

References

Chao, 1978 (systematics and anatomy). Morse, 1980a (reproduction). Hansen, 1969 (ecology). White and Chittenden, 1977 (age and growth). Chao and Musick, 1977 (juvenile ecology). Welsch and Breder, 1923 (life history). Hildebrand and Cable, 1930 (development).

Names

The name *undulatus* is the Latin word for wavy, in reference to the color pattern.

Perca undulata Linnaeus, 1766: 483 South Carolina

Bodianus costatus Mitchill, 1815: 417-418 New York

Micropogon lineatus Cuvier *in* Cuvier and Valenciennes, 1830: 160 New York

Micropogon undulatus, Bath et al., 1977: 4 Hudson River

WRASSES

LABRIDAE

The wrasses are essentially a tropical family with a few species in temperate waters. They have a single dorsal fin with more spines than rays, and they are characterized by their dentition which includes both caniniform teeth in the jaws and molariform teeth on the pharyngeal bones which are fused into a single solid, triangular plate. The family is extremely diverse and contains about 400 species.

KEY TO THE SPECIES OF WRASSES IN NEW YORK

A. Scales small, about 70 in lateral line. Margin of preopercle smooth, without dentations. Cheeks and gill covers with only a few scales. Forehead profile steep.

Tautoga onitis   Tautog, p. 435

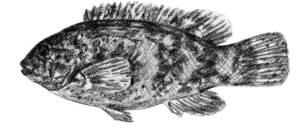

A'. Scales larger, about 40 in lateral line. Margin of preopercle serrated. Cheeks and opercles nearly covered with scales. Head pointed, profile of forehead not so steep.

Tautogolabrus adspersus   Cunner, p. 436

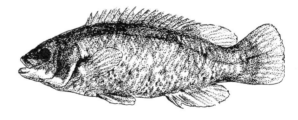

TAUTOG

Tautoga onitis (Linnaeus, 1758)

Identification
The tautog is a rather rectangular fish with a deep, moderately compressed body, a steep forehead, and a single long dorsal fin with 16 to 18 spines and 11 rays. The tail is rounded with only 12 branched rays. The pharyngeal bones of the tautog are fused and pharyngeal teeth are bluntly conical or molariform in larger specimens. The lateral line is high anteriorly and parallels the dorsal profile, then drops suddenly to the midside of the caudal peduncle.

Tautogs differ from cunners, the only other northern wrasse, in having a blunter head, deeper and more compressed body, and finer scales (about 70 in the lateral line). The cheeks and opercles of the tautog are naked or with only a few scales. The preopercular margin is smooth.

Occurrence
Tautogs have been taken in the river as far upstream as Indian Point. Mr. John Cronin has informed me that during the exceptionally dry summer of 1981 tautogs were quite common as far north as the Tappan Zee Bridge.

Notes
The tautog is a shelter-loving fish of rocky reefs. They are active during the day and quiescent at night. Individuals less than 10 inches long feed near their nocturnal homes, but larger fish may travel as much as 500 meters from their resting sites. When the temperature drops below 10 C in the fall, the large tautog move offshore but small fish become inactive in their normal shelter sites.

Tautog feed principally on blue mussels, selecting smaller shells because they are apparently unable to crush the larger ones. Tautogs are long-lived fish, some reaching as much as 34 years. At age XXII, males averaged 548 mm; females 501 mm. Females, however, were somewhat heavier than males at the same lengths.

References
Olla, Bejda, and Martin, 1974 (activity and movements); 1975 (ecology and behavior); 1979 (dispersal and habitat selection). Olla et al., 1980 (temperature). Cooper, 1966 (migration); 1967 (age and growth). Olla and Samet, 1977 (courtship).

Names
The derivation of the species name is unexplained. *Onitis* is a kind of plant.

Labrus onitis Linnaeus, 1758: 286 (no locality)

Labrus americanus Bloch and Schneider, 1801: 261

Labrus tautoga Mitchill, 1815: 399-402 Long Island

Tautoga fusca Mitchill, 1814: 24 New York
Tautoga rubens Mitchill, 1814: 24 New York
Tautoga alius Mitchill, 1814: 24 New York
Tautoga niger Mitchill, 1814: 23 New York
Tautoga americana DeKay, 1842: 175-176 New York

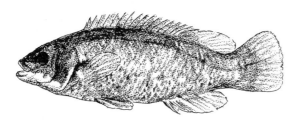

CUNNER

Tautogolabrus adspersus
(Walbaum, 1792)

Identification
The cunner is also a wrasse with a single long dorsal fin with 16 to 18 spines and 9 to 11 soft rays. The cunner is a more elongate fish than the tautog and has a more pointed head. It also has larger scales, about 40 in the lateral line. The cheeks and opercles of the cunner are mostly scaled and the margin of the preopercle is serrated.

Occurrence
The cunner was reported from the Arthur Kill by Howells (1981) and it occasionally strays into the Hudson River. Texas Instruments personnel collected a 73-mm specimen at River Mile 42 on 29 February 1980.

Notes
The cunner is also very much a reef fish and seldom ventures more than a few meters from some shelter, be it natural outcrops or manmade structures such as wrecks, pilings, or boat docks. Cunners are active during the day but during the hours of darkness they are quiescent and lie against objects or in crevices. In the winter, when the temperature is below 5

or 6 C, they remain inactive all the time and sometimes even become covered with a layer of silt.

Cunners feed both on the bottom and in the water column. There is some social facilitation of feeding. One or two individuals will start to feed and the intensity of their feeding activity will increase as they are joined by others. Although they feed at various levels in the water column, cunners tend to maintain their orientation facing into the current. Cunners feed on a variety of organisms including mussels, isopods, microcrustaceans, barnacles, crabs, fish remains, fish eggs, and carideans, but the diet is dominated by the mussel, *Mytilis edulis*, and the isopod, *Idotea baltica*.

References
Olla et al., 1975 (habits, ecology). Johansen, 1925 (natural history). Shumway and Stickney, 1975 (food habits). Serchuk and Frame, 1973 (bibliography). Chao, 1973 (food habits). Dew, 1976 (life history, ecology). Green and Farewell, 1971 (winter habits).

Names
Adspersus is a Latin word meaning a sprinkling upon.

Labrus adspersus Walbaum, 1792: 254-255 (after Schoepf)

Tautoga coerulea Mitchill, 1814: 24 New York
Labrus chogset Mitchill, 1815: 403 New York
Labrus chogset fulva Mitchill, 1815: 403 New York

Ctenolabrus uninotus Valenciennes *in* Cuvier and Valenciennes, 1839: 174 (239) New York

MULLETS

MUGILIDAE

Mullets are silvery, bullet-shaped fishes with a small spiny dorsal fin with four spines. The dorsal fins are separated by a wide space. Their pelvic fins are sub-abdominal (well behind the pectoral girdle), with one spine and five rays. Most species have a rather flat head and a thick adipose layer that almost covers the eye. Marine mullets often have gizzards similar to those of the gizzard shad. There are about 13 genera and between 70 and 100 species.

KEY TO THE SPECIES OF MULLETS IN NEW YORK

A. Anal fin with 3 spines and 2 soft rays or 2 spines and 9 rays in very small individuals. Second dorsal and anal fins with only a few scales on their interradial membranes. Scales on sides of body with dark spots that form longitudinal stripes.
Mugil cephalus   **Striped mullet, p. 437**

A'. Anal fin with 3 spines and 9 soft rays or 2 spines and 10 rays in small individuals. Second dorsal and anal fins densely covered with scales. Color uniform, without stripes.
Mugil curema   **White mullet, p. 438**

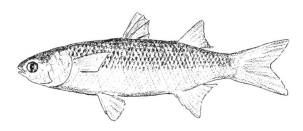

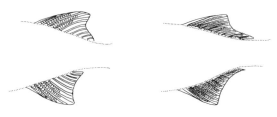

Scales at the base of the dorsal and anal fins of the striped (left) and white mullets.

STRIPED MULLET

Mugil cephalus Linnaeus, 1758

Identification
Mullets are cigar-shaped fishes with two well-separated dorsal fins, large scales and a forked tail. The body is nearly round in cross section, becoming compressed toward the tail. The head is bluntly pointed and more or less triangular in cross section. Each eye is nearly covered with a fatty tissue with a vertical, lenticular opening in the center. The pectoral fins are high on the sides and the pelvic fins are well behind them.

The striped mullet is easy to separate from the white mullet by its pattern of dark lines formed by dark centers on the scales of the sides, and by the anal count of III,8 rather than III,9. Striped mullet have few scales on the membranes of the second dorsal and anal fins.

Occurrence
The following specimens from the Hudson River are in the collections of the American Museum of Natural History: AMNH 35957, 212 mm, River Mile 36, collected 23 September 1976 by Lander and Texas Instruments field crew. AMNH 43062 (2), 114 to 121 mm, Bowline Point, 29 July 1977 by LMS personnel.

Names
Cephalus is an old name from the Greek *kephale*, head.

Mugil cephalus Linnaeus, 1758: 316 European oceans

Mugil albula Linnaeus, 1766: 520 Charleston, South Carolina

Mugil lineatus Mitchill *in* Cuvier and Valenciennes, 1836: 96 New York

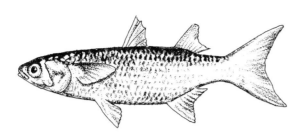

WHITE MULLET

Mugil curema Valenciennes, 1836

Identification

The elongate shape, silvery color, two well-separated dorsal fins, conspicuous adipose eyelid, and abdominal pelvic fins all identify the white mullet as a member of the Mugilidae. The white mullet closely resembles the striped mullet but it differs in color (lacking conspicuous stripes), in having dense scales on the bases of the membranes of the second dorsal and anal fins, and in having more anal fin rays.

Young mullets are compressed and bright silvery. This juvenile stage is called a querimana. During development, the third element of the anal fin changes from a ray to a spine. In the white mullet, the young have 2 spines and 10 rays and the adults have 3 spines and 9 rays. In the striped mullet, the young have two spines and nine rays, the adults three spines and eight rays.

Occurrence

Two specimens from the Hudson River are in the American Museum. AMNH 37243 is from River Mile 15 and was collected 2 October 1975. AMNH 37244 is from River Mile 15 and was collected 17 October 1975, both by Texas Instruments personnel.

Names

Curema is a Portuguese name used by Marcgrave, and is probably related to the Spanish name Queriman.

Mugil curema Valenciennes *in* Cuvier and Valenciennes, 1836: 87 Brazil, Martinique, Cuba

STARGAZERS

URANOSCOPIDAE

The stargazers get their name from their ability to produce a noticeable electric shock. This is done by special organs derived from eye muscles and located on the top of the head behind the rather small eyes. These fishes spend much of their time buried in sand just below the surface of the bottom, waiting to ambush their prey. Their mouth is large and nearly vertical and the lips have a fringe of tentacles that apparently aids in keeping the sand out of the mouth. They also have venomous spines on the shoulder girdle.

This is a small family of 8 genera and 25 species. They occur in all of the major oceans.

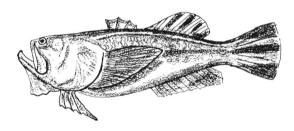

NORTHERN STARGAZER

Astroscopus guttatus
Abbott, 1860

Identification
The northern stargazer is a bizarre fish with a large, almost vertical mouth surrounded by fringed lips. Its head is broad and flat on top with a smooth flat space behind each of its tiny eyes. These smooth areas are separated by a Y-shaped bony ridge and they cover electric organs that can produce a noticeable shock when the fish is 8 or 10 inches long.

Occurrence
The northern stargazer ranges from New York to Virginia and it is included in the inland fauna on the basis of a few juveniles collected in the estuary by Texas Instruments personnel as far upstream as River Mile 24.

Names
Guttatus is a Latin word meaning spotted, as with raindrops.

Astroscopus guttatus Abbott, 1860: 365 Cape May, New Jersey

GUNNELS

PHOLIDAE

Gunnels are compressed, ribbon-shaped fishes with tiny pelvic fins. The dorsal and anal fins are long and separated from the tail fin. The dorsal fin has no soft rays, only spines. The anal fin has 2 spines and 37 to 44 rays.

This family name is sometimes spelled Pholidi-dae. Pholids are referred to as northern blennies, indicating their relationship to the blennies of tropical waters.

ROCK GUNNEL

Pholis gunnellus (Linnaeus, 1758)

Identification

The rock gunnel is sometimes called rock eel but it is actually related to the tropical blennies. It is quite elongate, its body 8 to 10 times as long as deep, with a long dorsal fin that contains 73 to 86 spines and no soft rays. The anal fin is correspondingly elongate, with 2 spines and 37 to 44 soft rays. Both the dorsal and the anal are joined to the rather small, squarish caudal fin. The pectorals are paddle-shaped and about half as long as the body is deep. The pelvics are well forward and tiny, with one spine and one ray each. The head is short, the mouth large and obliquely terminal. The body is covered with small, inconspicuous scales, the head naked. Rock gunnels can attain a length of 12 inches but most are smaller.

The color of the gunnel varies from yellow to greenish to red. There are 10 to 14 dark spots along the base of the dorsal fin and about 15 indistinct vertical bars across the anal fin. A dark vertical bar extends from the top of the head through the eye to the angle of the mouth.

Occurrence

Rock gunnels have been taken a few times in the Lower Hudson.

References

Bigelow and Schroeder, 1953b: 492-494. Sawyer, 1967 (life history).

Names

The name *gunnellus* is a Latinization of the English name for this or a similar species and is thought to be a corruption of gunwale.

Blennius gunnellus Linnaeus, 1758: 257 Atlantic Ocean

Ophidium mucronatum Mitchill, 1815: 361-362 New York

SAND LANCES
AMMODYTIDAE

Sand lances are small, elongate, and compressed fishes with no teeth, usually no pelvic fins, no fin spines, and a forked tail. The body has oblique fleshy folds, and there is a longitudinal fleshy ridge on each side of the belly. The lateral line is close to the base of the dorsal fin.

Sand lances occur in temperate and colder parts of the Atlantic and Pacific Oceans and in the Indian Ocean. There are three genera, one of which has pelvic fins.

AMERICAN SAND LANCE

Ammodytes americanus DeKay, 1842

Identification

The species of sand lances are incompletely known. There is a general trend for the sand lances from northern and offshore waters to be more slender (body depth 6.1 to 10.5 percent of the standard length, mode 8.3) and to have more dorsal fin rays (60 to 69, mode 64), vertebrae (70-78, mode 73), and anal rays (30-37, mode 34). In contrast, the sand lances from southern and inshore waters have deeper bodies (8.2 to 14.4, average 12.3 percent of the standard length), fewer dorsal rays (52 to 60), fewer vertebrae (63 to 72), and fewer anal rays (25-33). Some studies have cast doubt on these differences and it has been suggested that there is only a single variable inshore species that is possibly conspecific with another nominal form, *A. marinus*, from Greenland.

Occurrence

Sand lances are not uncommon in the lower part of the Hudson, although there have been few published records of its occurrence there. Texas Instruments crews have collected the following specimens from River Mile 42: AMNH 48285, 130 mm, collected 26 January 1979; and AMNH 48205, 107 mm, collected 13 April 1979.

References

Richards and Kendall, 1973 (larval distribution). Meyer, Cooper, and Langston, 1979 (abundance, behavior and food in the Gulf of Maine). Scott, 1972 (variation). Winters, 1970 (variation). Westin et al., 1979 (biology).

Names

Americanus means of America.

Ammodytes americanus DeKay, 1842: 317-318 Connecticut

Ammodytes vittatus DeKay, 1842: 318 New York

SLEEPERS
ELEOTRIDAE

Sleepers are closely related to the gobies but they do not have the inner rays of the pelvic fins joined by membranes as most (but not all) gobies do. The fat sleeper is a stray in the Hudson River; it is normally found in Central America and the Caribbean where it occurs in fresh as well as salt water.

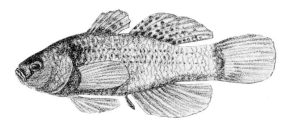

FAT SLEEPER

Dormitator maculatus
(Bloch, 1785)

Identification
The fat sleeper is a stubby little fish with two separate dorsal fins and a conspicuously flat head covered with scales. In general appearance, it resembles the gobies but the gobies of our area have no scales and their pelvic fins are fused into a disk. The sleeper has separate pelvic fins and a rounded tail. The entire fish is a somber brown, with lighter spots in life, and a large darker blotch above the pectoral fin.

Occurrence
The fat sleeper has been taken from the Hudson River at River Mile 52 and River Mile 47 (Beebe, M.S.).

Names
Maculatus is Latin for spotted.
   Sciaena maculata Bloch, 1785: 299 West Indies

GOBIES

GOBIIDAE

Gobies are small fishes that usually have the inner rays of the pelvic fins connected by membrane so that they form a cup-like sucker. This, however, is quite different from the highly developed sucker of the snailfishes as the pelvic fins of the gobies are otherwise unmodified. Gobies have two separate dorsal fins and our species have no scales.

The family is a large one with an estimated 800 species. Most of them are tropical and new species are still being discovered.

KEY TO THE SPECIES OF GOBIES IN NEW YORK

A. Pelvic disk short, reaching about halfway from its base to the anus. Second dorsal usually with 13 rays. Body deep, its depth contained 3.9 to 4.8 times in the standard length.
Gobiosoma bosci   Naked goby, p. 443

A'. Pelvic disk longer, reaching two-thirds of the way from its base to the anus. Second dorsal fin usually with 12 rays. Body slender, its depth 6 to 7.2 in length.
Gobiosoma ginsburgi   Seaboard goby, p. 444

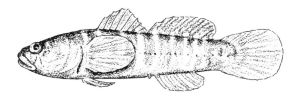
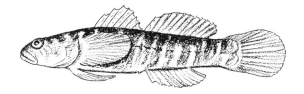

NAKED GOBY

Gobiosoma bosci (Lacepède, 1798)

Identification
The naked goby is a small fish, rarely reaching 2 inches total length. Both the naked goby and the seaboard goby lack scales. In general appearance, they are quite similar but they differ in body proportions. The naked goby is deeper, its greatest depth contained about 4 or 5 times in the standard length (6 to more than 7 in the seaboard) and the pelvic disk is shorter (reaching halfway to the vent in the naked goby, three-fourths of the way in the sea-

board). Also, the dorsal rays are modally 13 in the naked goby, 12 in the seaboard goby.

Occurrence
The naked goby was listed for the Lower Hudson by Bath et al. (1977).

Reference
Dahlberg and Conyers, 1973 (ecology).

Names
This species is named in honor of M. Bosc, French consul at Charleston in the 18th century, an ardent naturalist.

  Gobius bosci Lacepède, 1798: 555

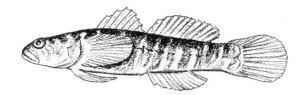

SEABOARD GOBY

Gobiosoma ginsburgi
Hildebrand and Schroeder, 1928

Identification

The seaboard goby is more slender than the naked goby, its greatest body depth contained about 6 to more than 7 times in the standard length. The pelvic disk is longer, reaching about three-fourths of the way from its origin to the vent. Its dorsal soft rays are modally 12 and the fins are somewhat higher than those of the naked goby.

Occurrence

The seaboard goby was recorded from the Lower Hudson by Bath et al. (1977).

References

Dahlberg and Conyers, 1973 (ecology). Hoff, 1976 (biology).

Names

The seaboard goby is named in honor of Isaac Ginsburg, a leading student of gobies of the Atlantic coast.

   Gobiosoma ginsburgi Hildebrand and Schroeder, 1928: 324-325 Cape Charles, Virginia

MACKERELS

SCOMBRIDAE

Mackerels are graceful torpedo-shaped fishes with two well-separated dorsal fins and seven or eight detached finlets behind the dorsal and anal fins. The color is generally blue, in keeping with their open ocean habitat, and they often have wavy stripes on the upper sides. The mouth is terminal but not protractile. The caudal peduncle is very slender and the tail deeply forked. This family includes the tunas. There are about 45 species.

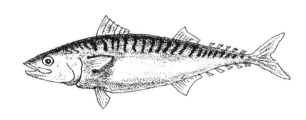

ATLANTIC MACKEREL

Scomber scombrus
Linnaeus, 1758

Identification
The Atlantic mackerel is a slender torpedo-shaped fish, blue above with diagonal, wavy, dark lines crossing the back. The sides below the midline are silvery without definite dark spots. There are two dorsal fins, separated by a space longer than the base of the first dorsal. There are five separate finlets behind the dorsal fin and five behind the anal fin. There are two short, longitudinal keels on each side of the slender caudal peduncle. The entire body is covered with small scales. Atlantic mackerel reach a length of nearly 22 inches but the usual size is about 14 inches.

Occurrence
A specimen 440 mm in total length was taken at River Mile 44 on 16 July 1977 by Texas Instruments personnel.

Notes
Mackerel are important commercial fish on the east coast.

References
Sette, 1943; 1950 (general account, migration patterns). Bigelow and Schroeder, 1953b (general account). Morse, 1980a, 1980b (spawning and fecundity). Berrien, 1975 (eggs and larvae).

Names
Both the genus and species come from the Greek *skombros* and Latin *scomber,* mackerel.

Scomber scombrus Linnaeus, 1758: 297 Atlantic Ocean

Scomber vernalis Mitchill, 1815: 423 Sandy Hook, New Jersey

BUTTERFISHES
STROMATEIDAE

The butterfishes are deep-bodied, compressed fishes with a specialized outpocketing of the esophagus. This is a small family with three genera and a dozen or so species. Our butterfish is rather specialized with no pelvic fin and a row of pores along the back near the base of the dorsal fin.

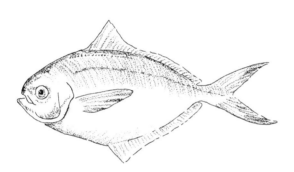

BUTTERFISH
Peprilus triacanthus (Peck, 1804)

Identification
The butterfish, a silvery, compressed, teardrop-shaped fish with a blunt head, a forked tail and long dorsal and anal fins, has been described as looking like a flounder swimming on edge. Its two outstanding features are the absence of pelvic fins and the presence of a conspicuous row of pores on the upper sides of the body. In life, the butterfish has dark spots but these fade soon after death. The maximum size is around 12 inches; most are smaller.

Occurrence
Mearns reported that it was quite common at West Point in the summers of 1882 and 1883. It is still taken occasionally in the Lower Hudson, and Dr. Joseph O'Connor (pers comm.) has reported that it was common in trawl samples taken between Bowline Point and the Tappan Zee Bridge from late July to early September 1984. Dr. O'Connor's specimens were small, ranging from early postlarval to about 3.5 inches total length. The smallest specimens were found farthest upstream.

The butterfish ranges from Nova Scotia and Prince Edward Island to peninsular Florida. It is re-placed in the Gulf of Mexico by another species, *Peprilus burti*. There is a gap around Florida where neither species occurs. Butterfish appear to prefer sandy bottoms but they are not closely associated with the bottom, at least when they are inshore during the summer. There is some indication that they remain near the bottom during the day and move upward at night.

Notes
There are at least two populations of the butterfish, one north and the other south of Cape Hatteras. The northern population shows a definite migratory pattern, moving inshore and northward in the spring and summer, and offshore to the edge of the continental shelf in late autumn and winter. Spawning takes place May to July with the peak in June. Growth is rapid and some fish mature by the end of their first year, the rest during the second year although in Chesapeake Bay spawning may be delayed another year. The maximum age is about 6 years.

Butterfish feed on a variety of invertebrates, including tunicates, crustaceans, chaetognaths, polychaetes, ctenophores, and cnidarians. They are eaten by such larger fishes as haddock, silver hake, swordfish, bluefish, and weakfish.

The butterfish is an important commercial species and they are taken in pound nets and trapnets, gill nets, otter trawls and haul seines. A considerable number are caught incidental to the squid fishery.

References
Mearns, 1898 (Hudson River). Murawski and Waring, 1979 (fishery, life history, ecology). Oviatt and Kremer, 1973 (feed on ctenophores). Caldwell, 1961 (populations). Honey, 1963 (eggs and larvae). Colton and Honey, 1963 (eggs and larvae). DuPaul and McEachran, 1973 (age and growth).

Names
Triacanthus is from the Greek *treis*, three, and *akantha*, horn or spine.

Stromateus triacanthus Peck, 1804: 48 Piscataqua

Rhombus triacanthus, Mearns, 1898: 319 Hudson Highlands

Poronotus triacanthus, Greeley, 1937: 100 Lower Hudson (after Mearns)

Stromateus cryptosus, Mitchill, 1815: 365 New York Bay

SEAROBINS

TRIGLIDAE

Searobins have greatly enlarged, wing-like pectoral fins although they do not fly. Some of the head bones are superficial and exquisitely sculptured plates, and the lower rays of the pectoral fins are separate fingers not connected by membrane. There are two dorsal fins and no free spines. About 10 genera and 70 species occur in warm and temperate seas.

KEY TO THE SPECIES OF SEAROBINS IN NEW YORK

A. Sides of body with two dark longitudinal lines. Pectoral fin long, extending back to about the ninth ray of the second dorsal fin when folded.
Prionotus evolans   **Striped searobin, p. 448**

A'. Sides of body without dark lines, plain or with indistinct mottlings. Pectoral fin shorter, reaching only to the sixth ray of the second dorsal fin when folded.
Prionotus carolinus   **Northern searobin, p. 447**

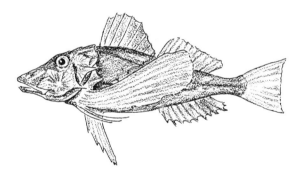

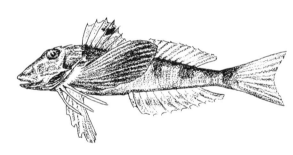

NORTHERN SEAROBIN

Prionotus carolinus (Linnaeus, 1771)

Identification
The northern searobin differs from the striped searobin in having a shorter head, two dark bars across the pectoral fin instead of one, and in lacking a prominent brown line along the side of the body. There is a black spot between the fourth and fifth dorsal spines.

Occurrence
The range of this species is from the Bay of Fundy to South Carolina, but it is uncommon north of Cape Cod. In the Hudson, it has been taken at least as far north as River Mile 15 off Bergen County, New Jersey.

References
Bigelow and Schroeder, 1953b: 467-470. Marshall, 1946 (comparative ecology). Richards, Mann, and Walker, 1979 (spawning and growth).

Names
The species name is for the Carolinas where Linnaeus' specimens were collected.
Trigla carolina Linnaeus, 1771: 528 Carolina
Trigla palmipes Mitchill, 1815: 431 New York

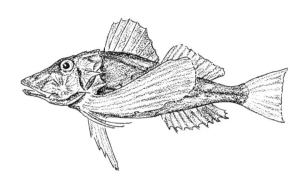

STRIPED SEAROBIN

Prionotus evolans (Linnaeus, 1766)

Identification

The striped searobin resembles the northern sea-robin but differs in having a larger head, larger mouth, and longer pectoral fins. In this species, the pectoral fins reach to the rear third of the second dorsal fin, but in the northern searobin they extend only to the front third. The tail is more square in the striped searobin, and the free pectoral rays taper toward their tips (in the northern searobin they are somewhat club-shaped). These filaments are banded in the striped searobin, plain in the northern searobin. As the name implies, the striped searobin has a conspicuous narrow reddish-brown stripe along the side below the lateral line. There is only one dark bar crossing the pectoral fin and usually it is so diffuse as to be a mere darkening of the center of the fin rather than a definite pattern.

Occurrence

This species has about the same range as the northern searobin —Carolina to the Gulf of Maine—, except that it is rare north of Cape Cod. It is known from the Hudson Estuary where two specimens have been taken at the Indian Point power plant at River Mile 42 by Texas Instruments personnel. One of these is AMNH 37279 and the other is New York State Museum 33451.

References

Bigelow and Schroeder, 1953b: 470-471. (general account). Marshall, 1946 (comparative ecology). McEachran and Davis, 1970 (age and growth). Richards, Mann, and Walker, 1979 (spawning and growth).

Names

Evolans is the Latin word meaning flying, apparently a reference to the wing-like pectoral fins although, of course, the searobin does not fly.

Trigla evolans Linnaeus, 1766: 498 Carolinas

SCULPINS
COTTIDAE

Sculpins are bottom-dwelling fishes with large pectoral fins and naked or prickly skins. Their relationships are in doubt; some features of the jaw muscles are similar to those of codfishes and this has led some classifiers to regard them as rather primitive spiny-rayed fishes. In other respects, they are quite advanced, having lost their scales and having modified pectoral fins. Because they have a bony strut connecting the bones around the eye with the preopercle, they are placed with the mail-cheeked fishes, but this arrangement is not entirely satisfactory. Worldwide, the family has about 67 genera and perhaps 300 species. In our fauna, there are four freshwater species and two marine species that are frequently taken in the Lower Hudson.

A key to all of the species of sculpins from the inland waters of New York will be found in the freshwater section.

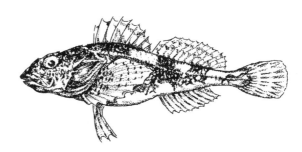

GRUBBY

Myoxocephalus aenaeus
(Mitchill, 1814)

Identification

The grubby differs from the fourhorn sculpin in having only three spines along the preopercular margin and in having the dorsal fins close together. Both of these features are also shared by the longhorn sculpin. The most conspicuous difference between the grubby and the longhorn sculpin is the length of the upper preopercular spine, which is about twice as long as the spine below it in the grubby, but more than four times as long in the longhorn. The anal fin of the grubby has 10 or 11 rays, that of the longhorn has about 14.

All of the species of *Myoxocephalus* differ from members of the genus *Cottus* in having the gill membranes free from the isthmus and from each other.

Occurrence

The grubby is a northern species that ranges from New Jersey to Nova Scotia and the Gulf of St. Lawrence. In the Hudson, it is occasionally taken by commercial fishermen in Haverstraw Bay and there are specimens in the AMNH and the New York State Museum from Indian Point. It is quite common in the North River (the upper part of New York Harbor) where it spawns in late winter.

Notes

This is the smallest of the common sculpins of the Atlantic coast. It seldom reaches more than 6 or 7 inches.

References

Bigelow and Schroeder, 1953b: 443-445 (general account). Lund and Marcy, 1975 (development).

Names

Aeneus is a Latin word meaning of bronze or copper.

    Cottus aenaeus Mitchill, 1814: 8 New York

    Cottus anceps Sauvage, 1878: 145 New York

    Acanthocottus aeneus, Jordan, Evermann, and Clark, 1930: 386 (nomenclature)

refers to the spines on the head, of which there are 20, not 18.

    Cottus octodecim-spinosus Mitchill, 1815: 380 New York

    Myoxocephalus octodecemspinosus Boyle, 1969: 210 Verplanck

    Acanthocottus octodecemspinosus, Jordan, Evermann, and Clark, 1930: 386

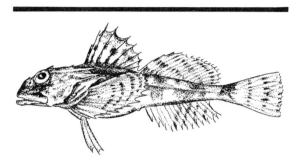

LONGHORN SCULPIN

Myoxocephalus octodecemspinosus (Mitchill, 1815)

Identification

The longhorn sculpin is quite similar to the grubby, sharing with it the general shape and color and the presence of three, rather than four, spines along the edge of the preopercle. It differs from the grubby in that the upper preopercular spine is much longer (about 4 times) than the second spine. It also has 14 rather than 10 or 11 anal rays, and is a considerably larger species, reaching nearly 18 inches total length.

The longhorn sculpin also resembles the shorthorn sculpin, *Myoxocephalus scorpius*, which has not yet been reported from inland waters but it can be distinguished from that species by the position of the anal fin origin which is below the second or third ray of the second dorsal rather than below the fourth or fifth. Furthermore, in the longhorn sculpin, there is a series of cartilaginous plates along the lateral line whereas the shorthorn sculpin has prickly scales in its lateral line.

The one feature that distinguishes the longhorn sculpin is the extremely long upper preopercular spine. The outer part of this spine is not covered with skin.

Occurrence

The longhorn sculpin is a northern species ranging from Newfoundland to New Jersey and occasionally south to Virginia. It is sometimes taken in the Lower Hudson in Haverstraw Bay.

References

Boyle, 1969 (taken by commercial fishermen in Haverstraw Bay). Bigelow and Schroeder, 1953b: 449-452 (general account). Morrow, 1951 (biology).

Names

The specific name is Latin for eighteen-spined and

SNAILFISHES

CYCLOPTERIDAE

Members of this family are characterized by having the pelvic fins joined into a sucking disk. They are quite varied, some species globose with rows of bony plates, others elongate and sometimes gelatinous. They are all marine and tend to occur in the colder oceans, especially the Arctic.

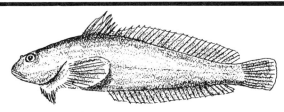

SEASNAIL

Liparis atlanticus
(Jordan and Evermann, 1898)

Identification

Seasnails are small tadpole-like fishes with soft scaleless bodies and a complex ventral sucker that is formed partly by the modified pelvic fins.

They have a single dorsal fin with about six spines differentiated from the soft rays by a slight notch. This species reaches a maximum length of about 5 inches.

Occurrence

Seasnails are marine fishes ranging from Newfoundland to New Jersey. This species has been taken in the Lower Hudson a few times.

Notes

Although this species has been reported to live in the mantle cavities of sea scallops, Able found that more than 6,000 specimens of seasnail from scallops were a distinct species, *Liparis inquilinus*, not *Liparis atlanticus*.

References

Able, 1973 (characters distinguishing *L. atlanticus* and *L. inquilinus*).

Names

Atlanticus refers to its geographic distribution.

Neoliparis atlanticus Jordan and Evermann, 1898: 2107 Godbout, Quebec (Type USNM 37215.)

Liparis atlanticus, Able, 1973

FLYING GURNARDS

DACTYLOPTERIDAE

The flying gurnard rather resembles the searobins in having expanded pectoral fins and sculptured superficial head bones. It does not, however, have free lower pectoral rays although there is a separate dorsal section of the pectoral fin. There is a large spine-like expansion of the head bones above the pectoral fin and a large spine at the angle of the preopercle that extends past the gill opening to below the pectoral fin. The first two spines of the first dorsal fin are not connected by membrane. There are prominent keels on the scales of the body. This is a small group with about four monotypic genera.

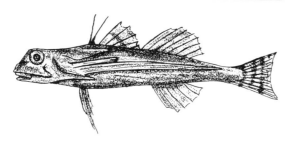

FLYING GURNARD

Dactylopterus volitans
(Linnaeus, 1758)

Identification
With its armored head and greatly expanded pectoral fins, the flying gurnard resembles a searobin but it does not have the free, fingerlike pectoral rays of searobins and closer inspection will soon reveal a number of other important differences. Not only are the pectoral fins huge, they are divided with the first (upper) six rays forming a separate small lobe. The dorsal fin is also divided with the first two spines separate from each other and from the rest of the fin. The pelvic fins have one spine and four rather than five, rays.

The head of the gurnard is covered with sculptured superficial bones and is noticeably concave between the eyes. At the back of the skull, a long blade-like extension of the dorsal head armour reaches to below the dorsal fin. The angle of the preopercle also extends backward as a strong, flat spine that reaches to below the pectoral fin. The scales of the dorsal surface of the terete body are armed with keels that end in sharp points.

The pectoral fins are dark but conspicuously marked with spots and streaks that are blue in life. The body is grayish brown, a little lighter ventrally.

Occurrence
One specimen of this species was taken in the Hudson River in 1981. The flying gurnard is a tropical species that commonly strays north to the Carolinas and occasionally as far north as Massachusetts.

References
Bigelow and Schroeder, 1953b: 472-473 (general account).

Names
Volitans is Latin for flying.

Trigla volitans Linnaeus, 1758: 302 Mediterranean

Polynemus sexradiatus Mitchill, 1815: pl.4, fig.10 New York

LEFTEYE FLOUNDERS

BOTHIDAE

As the name implies, the lefteye flounders normally have their eyes on the left side of the body. This is a fairly large family with more than 200 species. The summer flounder, commonly called fluke in the New York area, is an important game fish.

KEY TO THE SPECIES OF LEFTEYE FLOUNDERS IN THE INLAND WATERS OF NEW YORK

A. Lateral line nearly straight, scales large, about 40 to 45 in lateral line.

B.

A'. Lateral line with a definite arch over the pectoral fin. Scales small, more than 50 in the lateral line.

C.

B. Mouth moderately small, maxillary contained 1.75 to 3.3 times in the head. Jaws about equally curved (in the frontal plane). Teeth about equally developed on both sides, becoming somewhat larger anteriorly. Tip of snout with a bony knob.
Citharichthys arctifrons

Gulf Stream flounder, p. 454

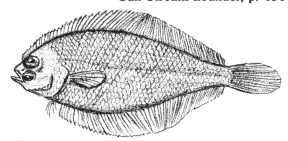

B'. Mouth small, maxillary 3.5 to 4.2 times in head length. Jaw of the blind side more strongly curved. Teeth better developed on the blind side, not larger anteriorly. Snout without bony knob.
Etropus microstomus

Smallmouth flounder, p. 454

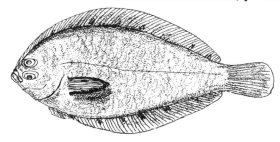

C. Left pelvic fin continous with the anal fin, right pelvic fin separate. Body deep, its outline nearly round. Upper surface with many diffuse spots. Anterior rays of the dorsal fin branched and free at their tips.
Scophthalmus aquosus   **Windowpane, p. 455**

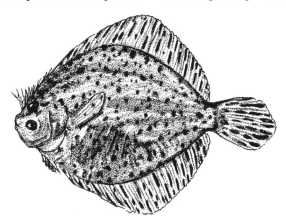

C'. Both pelvic fins separate from the anal fin. Shape more elongate, not nearly round. Upper surface with distinct black spots. Anterior dorsal rays neither branched nor free at their tips.
Paralichthys dentatus

Summer flounder (Fluke), p. 454

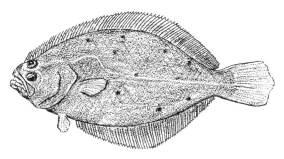

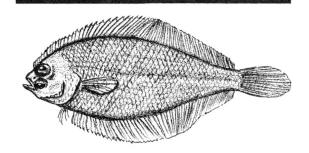

GULF STREAM FLOUNDER

Citharichthys arctifrons
Goode, 1880

Identification
The lefteyed Gulf Stream flounder has a tapering body with a rather small head. Its mouth reaches as far back as the level of the eyes. Its most characteristic feature is the large scales, about 40 in the nearly straight lateral line. Both pectoral fins are developed but the left is considerably longer. The left pelvic fin is on the midline, the right slightly up on the blind side. In females, the pelvic fins are about the same size but in males the right pelvic is longer. The species is rather plain brownish above and white on the blind side. The Gulf Stream flounder differs from other members of the genus *Citharichthys* in having a bony protuberance on its snout, its upper jaw less than one third the head length, and its body depth usually less than 40 percent of the standard length.

Occurrence
This species was listed from the Lower Hudson by Bath et al. (1977).

References
Gutherz and Blackman, 1970 (systematics).

Names
The species name means narrow forehead, from the Latin *arctus*, narrow, confined, and *frons*, forehead.

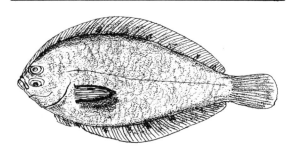

SMALLMOUTH FLOUNDER

Etropus microstomus (Gill, 1865)

Identification
This lefteyed species has a small head and an even smaller mouth. Its eyes are close together with only a narrow ridge separating them. Its lateral line is nearly straight with 41 to 45 scales. There is no anal spine. The left pelvic fin is on the edge of the abdomen and the right is on the blind side. The smallmouth flounder differs from its near relative, *Etropus crossotus*, in that it has about 13 rakers on the lower limb of the first gill arch whereas *crossotus* has only 8. The smallmouth is also more slender, with its greatest body depth less than half the standard length.

Occurrence
Texas Instruments personnel collected specimens at River Mile 42 on 10 December 1972 and at River Mile 16 on 3 September 1980. These are cataloged as AMNH 48300 and 48301, respectively. The species ranges from New York to Virginia and perhaps farther south.

References
Scherer and Bourne, 1980 (eggs and early larvae).

Names
The species name means smallmouth from the Greek *mikros*, small, and *stoma*, mouth.
   Citharichthys microstomus Gill, 1865: 223 Beesleys Point, New Jersey

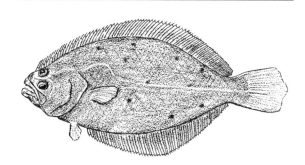

SUMMER FLOUNDER (FLUKE)

Paralichthys dentatus
(Linnaeus, 1766)

Identification
Flukes are lefteyed with a large mouth and a prominent arch in the anterior part of the lateral line. The jaws are somewhat curved. The eyes are separated by a distance equal to three-fourths the eye diameter in large specimens. The gill rakers are rather long and slender, 14 to 18 on the lower limb of the first arch. The tail is round in young, but in older fish it tends to become pointed (concave above and below the center). The pelvic fins are symmetrical. There are pectoral fins on both sides but the left is slightly larger.

   Most individuals have round black spots surrounded by light rings scattered over a brownish background. Three prominent spots form a triangle on the back of the body with the anteriormost apex on the lateral line.

Occurrence

This species is fairly common in the Lower Hudson from the George Washington Bridge to the Tappan Zee Bridge. The Survey collected it in Croton Bay.

References

Ginsburg, 1952a (systematics). Poole, 1961 (age and growth); 1962 (sport fishery); 1964 (feeding). Hildebrand and Cable, 1930 (development). Smith and Daiber, 1977 (Delaware Bay). Powell and Schwartz, 1979 (food habits). Scarlett, 1982 (bibliography).

Names

The species name, *dentatus*, is the Latin word for toothed.

Pleuronectes dentatus Linnaeus, 1766: 458-459 Carolinas

Platessa dentata, DeKay, 1842: 298 New York

Pleuronectes melanogaster Mitchill, 1815: 390-391 New York

Platessa ocellaris DeKay, 1842: 300 New York

Paralichthys dentatus, Greeley, 1937: 99 Croton Bay

Occurrence

This species was listed from the Lower Hudson by Bath et al. (1977).

References

Bigelow and Schroeder, 1953b: 290-294 (general account under the name *Lophopsetta maculata*, sand flounder). Hickey, 1975 (feeding habits).

Names

The name *aquosus* is from the Latin *aqua*, water and *-osus*, full of, possibly in reference to its transparent or translucent flesh.

Pleuronectes maculatus Mitchill, 1814: 9 New York

Pleuronectes aquosus Mitchill, 1815: 389 New York

Lophopsetta maculata, Gill, 1865: 220 (classification)

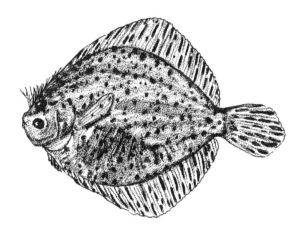

WINDOWPANE

Scophthalmus aquosus (Mitchill, 1814)

Identification

The windowpane is more deep bodied and diamond shaped than most of the other flounders of our area. The anterior dorsal fin rays are branched and free at their outer ends so they look like a decorative fringe. The lateral line is strongly arched over the pectoral fin. Pectoral fins are present on both sides with the left slightly larger. The left pelvic fin is on the midline of the abdomen, but the right one is off center on the blind side. The bases of the pelvics are as wide as their tips. The rays of both the dorsal and anal fins are longest near the middle of the fins and this enhances the diamond shape of the fish. The tail is rounded.

The eyed left side is translucent olive or greenish, sometimes tinged with reddish brown, and has darker mottlings and small spots.

RIGHTEYE FLOUNDERS

PLEURONECTIDAE

Although occasional individuals have the eyes on the left, the occurrence of reversed individuals is quite rare and most individuals have their eyes on the right. The winter flounder is one of the most common inshore flatfishes in the New York area and frequently moves into the Lower Hudson. The other species reported from the estuary are encountered less frequently.

KEY TO THE SPECIES OF RIGHTEYE FLOUNDERS IN THE INLAND WATERS OF NEW YORK

A. Lateral line nearly straight, without a definite arch over the pectoral fin. No sharp bony projection in front of the anal fin. Snout rather blunt, body fairly thick.
Pseudopleuronectes americanus
Winter flounder, p. 457

A'. Lateral line with a distinct arch over the pectoral fin. A definite spine-like bony projection in front of the anal fin. Snout relatively pointed, body thin.
Limanda ferruginea **Yellowtail flounder, p. 457**

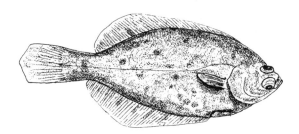

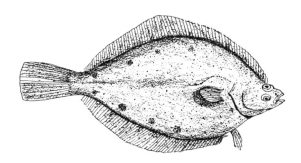

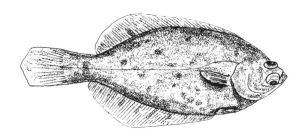

WINTER FLOUNDER

Pseudopleuronectes americanus (Walbaum, 1792)

Identification
In the New York area, this species is the plain "flounder", whereas the names of other flatfishes have some modifying term to specify which flounder is meant or do not contain the word flounder. The flounder is a righteyed species with a small asymmetrical mouth and teeth only on the left side. Its lateral line is nearly straight and the caudal fin is convex. The pelvic fins are symmetrical and originate below the pectorals. They reach to or beyond the anal origin. The left pectoral fin is present but smaller than the right. The scales of the eyed side are strongly ctenoid, and there are rows of scales along the fin rays.

Occurrence
Winter flounders are not uncommon in the Lower Hudson and the Survey collected them in August. The species is found from Ungava Bay, Labrador, south to Georgia.

Notes
The winter flounder is one of the most important sport and commercial species in the northeast. Breder described the spawning of this species in tanks at Woods Hole, Massachusetts. Although there were other flounders in the tank at the time, three males and two females participated in the spawning which took place at 3:00 to 3:30 am in spite of the lights that were shining on the tank. Each of the five fish swam in a tight circle about one foot in diameter at a slight upward angle so they gradually rose in the water column. The movement was counterclockwise so the vent was at the outside of the circle. As the fish swam in intersecting circles, the eggs were extruded and ran along the upper side of the anal fin and on out over the edge of the caudal fin. The motion of the fish seemed to fling the eggs outward so the spawning fish resembled a spinning Fourth of July pinwheel.

References
Sullivan, 1915 (young). Breder, 1922 (spawning). Bigelow and Schroeder, 1953b: 276-283 (general account). Wells et al., 1973 (feeding). Rogers, 1976 (temperature, salinity, and survival). Lux, 1973 (age and growth). Olla, Wicklund, and Wilk, 1969 (behavior).

Names
The species name reflects the country where it was first collected.

Pleuronectes americanus Walbaum, 1792: 113 (after Schoepf)

Pleuronectes planus Mitchill, 1815: 387-388 New York

Platessa plana, DeKay, 1842: 295-296 New York

Platessa pusilla DeKay, 1842: 296 New York

Pseudopleuronectes americanus, Greeley, 1937: 99 New York

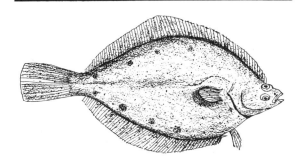

YELLOWTAIL FLOUNDER

Limanda ferruginea (Storer, 1839)

Identification
The yellowtail is a righteyed flounder with 76 to 85 dorsal rays and 56 to 63 anal rays. There is a small but sharp anteriorly directed spine just in front of the anal fin.

Adults are rather diamond shaped with the dorsal profile of the frontal region somewhat concave so that the head is rather pointed. The interorbital region is scaly and the lateral line is arched anteriorly. It somewhat resembles the witch flounder, *Glyptocephalus cynoglossus,* but that species has large mucus pits on the blind side that are not present in the yellowtail.

Occurrence
A juvenile 11 mm in total length was collected at River Mile 16 on 8 May 1974 by Texas Instruments personnel. It is in the AMNH where it bears the number 48288.

References
Bigelow and Schroeder, 1953b: 271-275 (general account). Lux, 1963 (stocks). Howell and Kessler, 1977 (fecundity). Royce, Buller, and Premetz, 1959 (fishery).

Names
The species name is from the Latin *ferrugo* meaning iron rust.

Platessa ferruginea Storer, 1839: 141 Cape Ann

SOLES

SOLEIDAE

Soles are rather specialized flatfishes with their eyes on the right side of the head. Their jaws and pelvic fins are asymmetrical and their general shape is a broad oval.

One species, the hogchoker, *Trinectes maculatus*, lives in the Lower Hudson where it is quite abundant and apparently occurs year-round. It often occurs in fresh water although never far from saltwater influence.

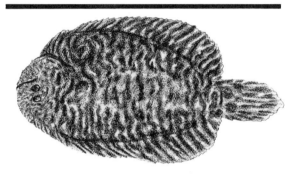

HOGCHOKER

Trinectes maculatus (Bloch and Schneider, 1801)

Identification

The hogchoker is a stubby little sole with its eyes on the right side, no pectoral fins, and no obvious snout. Its body is almost oval and its dorsal fin extends to the tip of the snout. The pelvic fins are asymmetrical with the right one on the midline and more or less continuous with the anal fin. The tail is short and rounded but separate from the dorsal and anal fins. The eyes of the hogchoker are tiny and close together and its mouth is curved and quite asymmetrical with teeth only on the blind side. The skin has fine fleshy papillae which are longest on the head and the front of the body, giving the hogchoker a definite furry appearance.

Its color is variable, the eyed side brownish with 7 to 11 narrow crosslines, or with a variegated pattern of transverse lines and irregular marblings. The dorsal fin has 15 or more bold lines formed by dark interradial membranes alternating with pale ones. The fin rays themselves are generally pale. The anal, right pelvic, and caudal fins have similar bars, the left pelvic is white. The blind side is creamy white with dark spots varying from indistinct flecks and smudges to large circular spots.

In the Hudson, the hogchoker reaches about 5.5 inches. The maximum length for the species is about 8 inches.

Occurrence

The hogchoker lives along the coast and is most abundant in bays and estuaries where the water is brackish. It frequently occurs in fresh water. Juveniles can be taken in seines in late summer and make delightful aquarium fish.

In the Hudson River, the hogchoker occurs as far upstream as Newburgh. It ranges from Massachusetts to Panama, but there are few records north of Cape Cod.

Notes

The spawning season is May to October with the peak in July and early August. Koski studied the growth of the hogchoker in the Hudson. Scales are valid for age determination but some individuals had false annuli. Females were slightly heavier than males and lived longer; the oldest females were age VI and the oldest males age IV. In general, the hogchoker matures at age II but some males may spawn at age I.

Hildebrand and Schroeder reported that the hoghoker feeds on annelids and small crustaceans.

In aquaria, the juveniles an inch or so long are able to travel up the sides of the tank and upside-down on the surface film as if it were a solid surface.

References

Hildebrand and Schoeder, 1928 (general account). Koski, 1974 (sinistrality and albinism in the Hudson River); 1978 (age, growth, and maturity in the Hudson River). Dovel, Mihursky, and McErlean, 1969 (life history).

Names

The name *maculatus* is the Latin word for spotted, in reference to the color pattern of the blind side.

Pleuronectes maculatus Bloch and Schneider, 1801: 157

Achirus fasciatus Lacepède, 1803: 659 Charleston, South Carolina

Achirus fasciatus, Greeley, 1937: 99 Lower Hudson drainage

Pleuronectes lineatus Schoepf, 1788: 148 Long Island

Pleuronectes mollis Mitchill, 1814: 9

Achirus mollis, DeKay, 1842: 303-304

LEATHERJACKETS

BALISTIDAE

This family includes the filefishes and triggerfishes which are too closely related to be placed in separate families. They have rather modified scales. Those of the triggerfishes are hard and plate-like; those of the filefishes are small and bristly. Filefishes have only one or two dorsal spines and no pelvic fins. The mouth is small with prominent teeth. The gill opening is reduced to a small slit in front of the pectoral fin base. Filefishes are rather inflexible fishes that swim with a peculiar motion of the dorsal and anal fins.

ORANGE FILEFISH

Aluterus schoepfi (Walbaum, 1792)

Identification

The orange filefish is a highly compressed paddle-shaped fish with two dorsal spines (the first much larger than the second) and no pelvic fin remnant. There are 32 to 39 soft rays in the second dorsal fin and 35 to 41 in the anal fin. In small specimens, the tail is very large, more than half the standard length.

Occurrence

In the Hudson Estuary, the species is known from one specimen, now a dry skeleton AMNH 21552SD. It was collected in the North River 21 August 1966. The species ranges from Nova Scotia to Brazil.

References

Berry and Vogele, 1961 (systematics).

Names

This species is named for Johann Schoepf, a physician who worked on Long Island during the Revolutionary War and wrote several papers on the fishes of New York.

Balistes schoepfii Walbaum, 1792: 461 Long Island (after Schoepf)

Balistes aurantiacus Mitchill, 1815: 468-470 New York

Aluterus cuspicauda DeKay, 1842: 338 New York

Aluterus cultrifrons Hollard, 1855: 8 New York and Bahia

Ceratacanthus schoepfii Jordan, Evermann, and Clark, 1930: 495 (nomenclature)

460

PUFFERS
TETRAODONTIDAE

Puffers are rather terete fishes with no pelvic fins and two beak-like teeth in each jaw. They are related to the balistids but have lost the dorsal spines completely and have also developed the capacity to inflate themselves with air or water. They have no scales but there are small prickles in the skin.

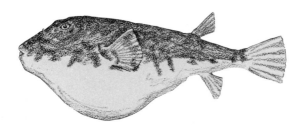

NORTHERN PUFFER

Sphoeroides maculatus
(Bloch and Schneider, 1801)

Identification
Sometimes called blowfish, the puffer has the ability to inflate itself with air or water until it resembles a ball with a tail. Its eyes are rather small and can be partially closed. The puffer has no fin spines and no pelvic fins. The dorsal and anal fins are set far back on the body; the tail is slightly convex. Although puffers have no regular scales, the body is covered with fine prickles so that it feels bristly. The gill openings are mere small slits in front of the base of the pectoral fins. The nostrils are small double openings at the tip of a Y-shaped tube that is set in a shallow pit. Puffers have two large teeth in each jaw. Together they form beak-like structures. In life, the northern puffer is dusky to greenish olive above with darker spots and mottlings. The belly is pure white. There are partial vertical bars of irregular length and width along the boundary between the dark back and the pale belly. There is an especially prominent blotch behind the pectoral fin.

Occurrence
Specimens were collected by Texas Instruments personnel at Haverstraw Bay 7 April 1980 and at River Mile 30 on 4 September 1980.

References
Shipp and Yerger, 1969 (systematics). Welsch and Breder, 1922 (life history). Laroche and Davis, 1973 (age, growth, and reproduction). Merriner and Laroche, 1977 (fecundity).

Names
Maculatus is the Latin word for spotted.

Tetrodon hispidus var. maculatus Bloch and Schneider, 1801: 504 Rhode Island

Tetrodon turgidus Mitchill, 1815: 473-474 New York

PORCUPINEFISHES

DIODONTIDAE

Porcupinefishes resemble puffers in their ability to inflate themselves with air or water but differ in that there is only a single tooth plate in each jaw and the scales are modified as large spines that erect as the body is inflated. There are about 5 genera and 15 species.

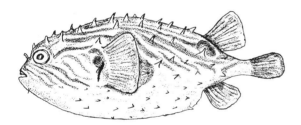

STRIPED BURRFISH

Chilomycterus schoepfi (Walbaum,1792)

Identification

The burrfish is a small football-shaped fish with short stout spines over most of its head and body. Its dorsal and anal fins are far back, the dorsal directly over the anal. The tail is rounded and the pectorals are broad and paddle shaped and high on the side of the body. It has no pelvic fins. Each jaw has a single beak-like tooth plate. The nostrils are tubular.

The burrfish is strikingly marked with broad wavy lines running lengthwise on the back and on the sides of the head. Large black spots are present: one below the base of the dorsal fin and another above the base of the anal fin; one above and one behind the pectoral fin. The usual length of the burrfish is less than 10 inches.

Occurrence

The burrfish is a coastal species ranging from Florida to New York and occasionally strays a little farther north. A specimen was reported from the Hudson Estuary in 1981.

References
Bigelow and Schroeder, 1953b: 527-528.

Names

This is another species named for J. Schoepf, an early student of fishes.

Diodon schoepfii Walbaum, 1792: 601 Long Island (after Schoepf)

Diodon geometricus lineatus Bloch and Schneider, 1801: 513 New York

Diodon maculato striatus Mitchill, 1814: 470 New York

Diodon rivulatus Cuvier, 1818: 129 New York

Diodon nigrolineatus Ayres, 1843: 68 Brookhaven, Long Island

Diodon verrucosus DeKay, 1842: 325 (after Mitchill)

SPECIES LIST

MARINE FISHES IN THE INLAND WATERS OF NEW YORK

CARCHARHINIDAE
1. *Carcharhinus* species

RAJIDAE
2. *Raja laevis* Mitchill, barndoor skate

ELOPIDAE
3. *Elops saurus* Linnaeus, ladyfish

CONGRIDAE
4. *Conger oceanicus* (Mitchill), conger eel

CLUPEIDAE
5. *Brevoortia tyrannus* (Latrobe), Atlantic menhaden
6. *Clupea harengus* Linnaeus, Atlantic herring
7. *Etrumeus teres* (DeKay), round herring

ENGRAULIDAE
8. *Anchoa mitchilli* (Valenciennes), bay anchovy
9. *Anchoa hepsetus* (Linnaeus), striped anchovy

SYNODONTIDAE
10. *Synodus foetens* (Linnaeus), inshore lizardfish

LOPHIIDAE
11. *Lophius americanus* Valenciennes, goosefish

GADIDAE
12. *Enchelyopus cimbrius* (Linnaeus), fourbeard rockling
13. *Gadus morhua* Linnaeus, Atlantic cod
14. *Microgadus tomcod* (Walbaum), Atlantic tomcod
15. *Pollachius virens* (Linnaeus), pollock
16. *Urophycis chuss* (Walbaum), red hake
17. *Urophycis regia* (Walbaum), spotted hake
18. *Merluccius bilinearis* (Mitchill), silver hake

OPHIDIIDAE
19. *Ophidion marginatum* (DeKay), striped cusk-eel

BELONIDAE
20. *Strongylura marina* (Walbaum), Atlantic needlefish

CYPRINODONTIDAE
21. *Cyprinodon variegatus* Lacepède, sheepshead minnow
22. *Fundulus heteroclitus* (Linnaeus), mummichog
23. *Fundulus luciae* (Baird), spotfin killifish
24. *Fundulus majalis* (Walbaum), striped killifish
25. *Lucania parva* (Baird), rainwater killifish

ATHERINIDAE
26. *Membras martinica* (Valenciennes), rough silverside
27. *Menidia beryllina* (Cope), inland silverside
28. *Menidia menidia* (Linnaeus), Atlantic silverside

SYNGNATHIDAE
29. *Hippocampus erectus* Perry, lined seahorse
30. *Syngnathus fuscus* Storer, northern pipefish

FISTULARIIDAE
31. *Fistularia tabacaria* Linnaeus, bluespotted cornetfish

SERRANIDAE
32. *Centropristis striata* (Linnaeus), black sea bass

POMATOMIDAE
33. *Pomatomus saltatrix* (Linnaeus), bluefish

RACHYCENTRIDAE
34. *Rachycentron canadum* (Linnaeus), cobia

CARANGIDAE
35. *Caranx hippos* (Linnaeus), crevalle jack
36. *Selene setapinnis* (Mitchill), Atlantic moonfish
37. *Selene vomer* (Linnaeus), lookdown

ECHENEIDAE
38. *Echeneis naucrates* Linnaeus, sharksucker

LUTJANIDAE
39. *Lutjanus griseus* (Linnaeus), gray snapper

GERREIDAE
40. *Eucinostomus argenteus* Baird, spotfin mojarra

SPARIDAE
41. *Lagodon rhomboides* (Linnaeus), pinfish
42. *Stenotomus chrysops* (Linnaeus), scup

SCIAENIDAE
43. *Bairdiella chrysoura* (Lacepède), silver perch
44. *Cynoscion regalis* (Bloch and Schneider), weakfish
45. *Leiostomus xanthurus* Lacepède, spot
46. *Menticirrhus saxatilis* (Bloch and Schneider), northern kingfish
47. *Micropogonias undulatus* (Linnaeus), Atlantic croaker

LABRIDAE
48. *Tautoga onitis* (Linnaeus), tautog
49. *Tautogolabrus adspersus* (Walbaum), cunner

MUGILIDAE
50. *Mugil cephalus* Linnaeus, striped mullet
51. *Mugil curema* Valenciennes, white mullet

URANOSCOPIDAE
52. *Astroscopus guttatus* Abbott, northern stargazer

PHOLIDAE
53. *Pholis gunnellus* (Linnaeus), rock gunnel

AMMODYTIDAE
54. *Ammodytes americanus* DeKay, American sand lance

ELEOTRIDAE
55. *Dormitator maculatus* (Bloch), fat sleeper

GOBIIDAE
56. *Gobiosoma bosci* (Lacepède), naked goby
57. *Gobiosoma ginsburgi* Hildebrand and Schroeder, seaboard goby

SCOMBRIDAE
58. *Scomber scombrus* Linnaeus, Atlantic mackerel

STROMATEIDAE
59. *Peprilus triacanthus* (Peck), butterfish

TRIGLIDAE
60. *Prionotus carolinus* (Linnaeus), northern searobin
61. *Prionotus evolans* (Linnaeus), striped searobin

COTTIDAE
62. *Myoxocephalus aenaeus* (Mitchill), grubby
63. *Myoxocephalus octodecemspinosus* (Mitchill), longhorn sculpin

CYCLOPTERIDAE
64. *Liparis atlanticus* (Jordan and Evermann), seasnail

DACTYLOPTERIDAE
65. *Dactylopterus volitans* (Linnaeus), flying gurnard

BOTHIDAE
66. *Citharichthys arctifrons* Goode, Gulf Stream flounder
67. *Etropus microstomus* (Gill), smallmouth flounder
68. *Paralichthys dentatus* (Linnaeus), summer flounder
69. *Scophthalmus aquosus* (Mitchill), windowpane

PLEURONECTIDAE
70. *Limanda ferruginea* (Storer), yellowtail flounder
71. *Pseudopleuronectes americanus* (Walbaum), winter flounder

SOLEIDAE
72. *Trinectes maculatus* (Bloch and Schneider), hogchoker

BALISTIDAE
73. *Aluterus schoepfi* (Walbaum), orange filefish

TETRAODONTIDAE
74. *Sphoeroides maculatus* (Bloch and Schneider), northern puffer

DIODONTIDAE
75. *Chilomycterus schoepfi* (Walbaum), striped burrfish

Abbreviate heterocercal — The tail fin of gars and bowfins has the vertebral column bent upward but the fin itself is externally only slightly asymmetrical with the upper part of the base longer.

Adipose fin — Small fatty fin on the middorsal line behind the dorsal fin. Adipose fins occur in catfishes, salmonids, lizardfishes and pirate perches. In catfishes they are either keel-like (adnate) or flag-like (adnexed); the others have adnexed adipose fins.

Adnate — Keel-like. See adipose fin.

Adnexed — Flag-like. See adipose fin.

Age — The age of fishes is usually given as its age group which is usually the number of annual rings on its hard parts. Thus a II + fish has two annuli and is in its third summer.

Anadromous — Fishes that spend most of their life in the ocean but come into fresh water to spawn are said to be anadromous.

Anal fin — Unpaired fin on the midventral line behind the anus. Anal fins are characterized by their length (the distance between the bases of the first and last rays), height (length of the longest rays), and shape. They are described as deltoid if the height is about equal to or longer than the length, trapezoid if the length is greater than the height and the last ray is more than half the longest. Anal fins sometime have the anterior rays distinctly longer than the rest of rays forming a definite lobe, in which case the fin is said to be lobate or falcate. The shape can also be described according to whether the margin of the fin (when erect) is straight, concave, or convex and whether the front and rear corners are sharply angled or rounded.

Antrorse — Directed forward. Often used for spines on the lower limb of the preopercle.

Aufwuchs — Organisms growing on underwater surfaces that project above the bottom such as stones or rooted plants.

Barbels — Thin fleshy projections on the head of catfishes, and some codfishes and minnows. While the barbels are prominent in the catfishes, they can be extremely small in some minnows. Their number and location is important in classification and identification.

Base of the caudal fin (Caudal base) — The base of the caudal fin is marked by a fold that forms when the tail is gently flexed. It marks the line where the bases of the caudal rays overlap the bony supports, the "hypural plate." The standard length and other measurements are taken to the middle of the caudal base, that is, the point on the fold halfway between the dorsal and ventral margins of the caudal peduncle.

Benthic — Pertaining to or living on the bottom.

Body shape — The configuration of the body of a fish is characteristic and consists of descriptors for its cross section: terete, slab sided, compressed or depressed, its general profile: elongate, robust, stubby, rhombic or rectangular, the comparison of the curvature of the dorsal and ventral profiles, whether they are curved evenly, whether they are curved equally and where the greatest depth of the body lies.

Branchiostegal rays — Thin bony rods that support the gill membranes.

Catadromous — Running out to sea to spawn. In our area the American eel is catadromous.

Caudal fin — The tail fin. Caudal fins vary in shape. Pointed, asymmetrically pointed, rounded, squarish, lunate, forked, and deeply forked are commonly used descriptive terms.

Caudal peduncle — The region of the body between the end of the anal fin and the beginning of the caudal fin. Its shape is described as the relation of its depth to its length and its cross section.

Circuli — Bony ridges on fish scales. Not to be confused with year marks or annuli.

Classification — Arranging things in an orderly scheme. See identification.

Compressed — Flattened from side to side.

Center — In describing color patterns on fins the center is the third of the fin that is midway between the anterior and posterior edges.

Clinal — Showing a trend in variation of some feature. Often individual fish from the northern part of the species' range have more scales. If there is a trend without sharp breaks, the variation is said to be clinal. Normally, populations showing clinal variation are not named even though specimens from the extreme ends of the range may be as different as some full species.

Decurved — Dipping downward. The lateral line of the golden shiner is strongly decurved, almost parallel to the ventral profile of the body.

Depressed — Flattened from dorsal to ventral.

Described — When an ichthyologist discovers a species that is new to science and gives it a name in a formal announcement, he is describing the species and the name will be recognized as of the date of publication. To be valid, a description must meet rigid conditions set forth by the International Commission on Zoological Nomenclature.

Diadromous — Moving into water of a different salinity to spawn. Anadromous fishes move from salt to fresh water and catadromous fishes move from fresh to salt. Diadromous is the general term that includes both.

Dorsal fin — Dorsal fins are median, unpaired, fins. In lower fishes, they are supported by soft rays only and in more advanced fishes the anterior supporting elements may be spines. Sometimes, the spiny and soft parts are separated as two fins and sometimes they are joined into a single continuous fin where they may be partly separated by a notch. The same descriptive terms used for the anal fin are applied to describe the shape of the dorsal fin.

Emarginate — With a slight notch. Usually used for caudal fins in which the central rays are slightly shorter so that the outline of the fin has a slight concavity.

Epilimnion — The upper layer of warm water in a lake or pond that is thermally stratified. That part of the water mass that is above the thermocline.

Exserted — Fin rays that extend beyond the connecting membrane are said to be exserted.

Eyed eggs — Eggs in which the eyes of the developing embryo are clearly visible. This is a stage that is resistant to shock and eggs are commonly shipped after they reach the eyed stage.

Eyes — Eyes are described according to size, position, and shape of the pupil.

Fimbriate — Fringed. The opercular bone of sunfishes is said to be fimbriate if its margin has finger-like projections along its edge.

Fin rays (rays and spines) — Bony supporting elements of fins. Soft rays are jointed, branched, and have right and left halves. Spines are solid, never branched, and single.

Fin position — The pectoral fin is supported by the bones of the pectoral girdle. Therefore, its base is nearly always close behind the gill opening. The position of the dorsal fin can be described in relation to the pectoral fin, whether the dorsal begins over the base, the middle, the tip, or behind the pectoral, or it can be described in terms of the distance to the base of the tail compared with the distance to the tip of the snout or some other definite point. The anal fin position can be described by the relation of its beginning to the dorsal fin base. The position of the

pelvic can also be described in relation to the dorsal origin (under, in front of, or behind). If the pelvics are far forward, they can be placed in relation to the pelvic fin or the gill opening.

Fulcra — Hard, short, modified scales along the leading edges of the dorsal, anal, and caudal fins of gars (Lepisosteidae).

Fusiform — Spindle-shaped, i.e., slender, evenly tapered and thickest near the middle.

Gill arch — The bones and associated structures that support the gill filaments. Most modern fishes have four pairs of gill arches, each supporting two rows of filaments on its posterior side.

Gill cover — The gill cover is the flat structure that covers the gill chamber. It is supported by four bones, the upper, triangular opercle that sometimes bears spines, and the narrow subopercle. Other bones that support the gill cover are the interopercle that is just behind the lower jaw and the preopercle or cheek bone.

Gill membrane (opercular membrane or branchiostegal membrane) — The membrane that extends beyond the bones of the gill cover and forms a flexible edge and acts as a seal between the operculum and the body. The gill membrane is itself supported by bony rods, the branchiostegal rays.

Gill opening — The round or slit-like openings behind the head. Lampreys have seven pairs of round gill openings, sharks have five or six, and all other fishes have a single gill opening. Water that has been taken through the mouth and passed over the gills exits through the gill opening.

Gill rakers — Bony, finger-like projections on the front of the gill arches. They vary in number and shape and are useful taxonomic characters. Counts are often given as: number on the upper section + 1 at the angle + number on the lower section of the gill arch. Usually, rudimentary gill rakers are included in the count. Because it is sometimes difficult to distinguish between those of the upper limb and those of the lower limb, counts are usually given here as total counts, unless there is a compelling reason to do otherwise.

Gular plate — An unpaired superficial bone on the midline of the lower jaw of the bowfin and ladyfish.

Head canals — Tubular sensory organs that run beneath the surface of the head or in grooves in some fishes. The main branches are the lateral canal, which is a forward continuation of the lateral line on the body, and a temporal canal that extends from the lateral canal toward the dorsal midline across the occipital region of the head. A preopercular-mandibular canal runs in the cheek bone and continues out toward the tip of the lower jaw; supraorbital and suborbital canals run above and below the eye. The form of the canals is variable and is useful for identification of some species.

Homocercal — The advanced type of fish tail that is externally symmetrical at its base but internally asymmetrical. It is supported by a complex of specialized bones.

Humeral scale — An enlarged scale over or just behind the shoulder girdle.

Head shape — The shape of the head can be described as blunt or pointed, narrow or broad (relative to the body width) and flat dorsally or ventrally.

Hypolimnion — That part of a thermally stratified body of water that is below the thermocline.

Identification — Determining that a specimen belongs to a species that is already known. See classification.

Incised — A fin membrane that is notched between the rays or spines is said to be incised.

Isthmus — The triangular area of the body that extends forward between the lower ends of the gill covers.

Lateral line — A tubular sensory organ that runs along the side of the body. Typically, it extends from the shoulder girdle to the base of the tail but in some species it is shorter or even lacking, or it can continue on to the tip of the tail fin.

Length (of a fish) — The length can be measured as total length from the extreme front of the head to the extreme end of the tail, fork length from the extreme front of the head to the end of the middle caudal rays, or standard length from the tip of the upper jaw to the fold at the base of the tail.

Margin (of fins) — The margin of the fin is the edge formed by the ends of the rays, the distal edge of the fin. The anterior and posterior limits of the fin are its edges.

Maxilla — The main bone of the upper jaw. In lower fishes, it forms part of the edge of the upper jaw but in advanced fishes a process of the premaxillary bone runs along its ventral side and takes its place as the margin of the upper jaw.

Middle — In describing color pattern on fins, the middle is the third of the fin that is midway between the base of the fin and its margin. The center is the third of the fin between the front and back.

Myomeres — Body muscle segments.

Myosepta — The connective tissue walls between successive myomeres.

Nauplii — Larval stages of crustaceans.

Nomen nudum — A name that was published without an accompanying description. Such names have no standing in nomenclature although they can be used later, in which case the name dates from the date of publication of the description.

Outlined — When fin rays or scales have a row of melanophore pigment cells along their margins, they are said to be outlined.

Pectoral fin — Paired fins that are supported by the shoulder girdle (the pectoral girdle). Paired fins may be low or high on the body with their bases horizontal, oblique, vertical, or sloped backward. Their shape is described as asymmetrical if the upper rays are longer than the lower rays or if the longest rays are above the middle of the fin. The distal margin of the fin can be pointed, rounded, square, or emarginate. Some fishes have pectoral fins with the upper rays prolonged giving the fin a sickle shape. Such fins are called falcate.

Palynology — The study of pollen in sediments. Palynologists are thus able to tell what kind of vegetation occurred in the region in the past.

Pelvic fins — Paired fins on the ventral surface. Pelvic fins are described by position: abdominal, thoracic, jugular, or mental; number of rays; and shape. If the rays become shorter posteriorly, the fin is said to be retrogressive; if the rays are longer posteriorly, it is said to be progressive. The fin is pointed if the middle rays are the longest. Sometimes, the posteriormost ray is joined to the body by a membrane for some part of its length.

Pigmentation — In the descriptions, considerable emphasis is placed on describing the patterns of melanophores that are retained after the specimens are preserved.

Pod — A tight school of fish in which the individuals swim in actual physical contact with each other.

Premaxilla — The anteriormost bones of the upper jaw. In advanced fishes, the premaxilla send a process backward that excludes the maxilla from the margin of the upper jaw.

Preoccupied — A name that has been previously used for another organism is said to be preoccupied and is therefore not available for the second organism.

Preopercle — The cheekbone. A superficial, L-shaped bone on the side of the head. Its free edge marks the beginning of the gill cover and consists of a vertical and a horizontal lower limb. Many fishes have serrations along the edge of the preopercle.

Profiles — The outline of the fish as seen in silhouette. A comparison of the the upper and lower profiles is a good measure of the shape of the fish.

Procurrent rays — In most fishes, the short unbranched rays at the front of the caudal fin.

Pseudobranchium — A remnant of a gill on the inside of the gill cover.

Pyloric caeca — Finger-like appendages of the digestive tract arising at the beginning of the intestine.

Rays — see fin rays.

Retrorse — Pointing backward. Opposite of antrorse.

River Mile — In the Hudson River, locations are specified by river miles above the Battery. For example, the Tappan Zee bridge is at River Mile 24.

Salt front — Because salt water is more dense than fresh water, it pushes upstream beneath the fresh water as a saltwater wedge. The upper limit of the saline intrusion is the salt front.

Scales — Scales are classified as placoid, the tooth-like scales of sharks and rays; cycloid, the smooth scales; and ctenoid, the rough scales that have tooth-like points on their exposed parts.

Slab sided — Somewhat compressed. A slab-sided fish is nearly oval in cross section with the sides flattened.

Sonic muscles — Specialized muscles, usually associated with the swim bladder, that enable a fish to produce sounds.

Subocular shelf — A bony flange that extends inward from the circumoral bones beneath the eyeball. Not visible externally.

Substitute name — A name that is proposed to replace a name that is not available for some strictly legalistic reason, for example, a name that is preoccupied, having been used previously for a different organism.

Supramaxillary — A small bone lying along the upper edge of the rear part of the maxillary bone. Usually, the supramaxillary appears to be separated from the maxillary bone by a shallow, externally visible groove.

Survey — Used here to refer to the New York State Conservation Department watershed surveys conducted between 1926 and 1939. Specimens collected in the course of these surveys are simply listed as having been collected by "the Survey".

Sympatric — Occurring in the same geographic region.

Syntopic — Occurring together in the same habitat.

Teardrop — A dark bar below the eye of a fish. Also called the subocular bar.

Teeth — Teeth can occur on several bones: the premaxillary, the maxillary, the vomer, the palatines, the pterygoids, the tongue, the dentary, and the basibranchials. Teeth themselves can be blunt in patches (cardiform or villiform), pointed (caniniform), molar-like (molariform), chisel-like (incisiform) or triple-pointed (tricuspid). Fish also have upper and lower pharyngeal teeth above and behind the gills.

Thermocline — In a thermally stratified body of water, the layer of rapid change is the thermocline. Warm water above the thermocline is the epilimnion and water below is the hypolimnion.

Trass — A volcanic rock used in the manufacture of hydraulic cement used in the construction of canal locks.

Trinomial — A name consisting of three words: the genus name, the species name (trivial name), and the name of a subspecies.

Trivial name — The name of the species. A scientific name must consist of a genus name and a species name to to be specific. Hence, it is not correct to refer to the species name as the specific name.

Unbranched ray — Soft fin rays are either branched or unbranched. Branched rays divide one or more times toward the margin of the fin; unbranched rays do not divide but they are segmented and have right and left halves.

Vermiculations — Worm-shaped marks, especially those of the upper surface of the brook trout.

Villiform — Teeth that are slender and blunt so they resemble the intestinal villi are said to be villiform.

Vomer — A median bone in the roof of the mouth just behind the upper jaw. In many fishes, the vomer bears teeth. Anatomically, the correct name of the tooth-bearing bone is prevomer.

Weberian apparatus — A chain of bones derived from the vertebral column and connecting the swim bladder with the ear in minnows, suckers, catfishes, and their relatives.

Yolk-sac larvae — Most fishes hatch while they still have a considerable amount of yolk remaining. At this stage, they are sometimes referred to as yolk-sac larvae.

Abbott, Charles C.
1860 Description of a new species of *Astroscopus*, Brev., in the museum of the Academy of Natural Sciences of Philadelphia. Proc. Acad. Nat. Sci. Phila. 12: 365, 1 pl.
1870 Mud-loving fishes. Am. Nat. 4(7): 385-391.
1874 Notes of the cyprinoids of central New Jersey. Am. Nat. 8: 326-338.
1884 On the habits of certain sunfish. Am. Nat. 17: 1254-1257.

Able, Kenneth W.
1973 A new cyclopterid fish, *Liparis inquilinus*, associated with the scallop, *Placopecten magellanicus*, in the western North Atlantic, with notes on the *Liparis liparis* complex. Copeia (4): 787-794.
1976 Cleaning behavior in the cyprinodontid fishes: *Fundulus majalis*, *Cyprinodon variegatus*, and *Lucania parva*. Chesapeake Sci. 17 (1): 35-39.

Able, Kenneth W. and M. Castagna
1975 Aspects of an undescribed reproductive behavior in *Fundulus heteroclitus* (Pisces: Cyprinodontidae) from Virginia. Chesapeake Sci. 16 (4): 282-284.

Adams, C. C. and T. L. Hankinson
1916 Notes on Oneida Lake fish and fisheries. Trans. Am. Fish. Soc. 45(3): 154-169.
1928 The ecology and economics of Oneida Lake fish. Roos. Wildl. Ann. 1(3/4): 239-548, map 16.

Adams, C. C., T. L. Hankinson, and W. C. Kendall
1919 A preliminary report on a fish cultural policy for the Palisades Interstate Park. Trans. Am. Fish. Soc. 48(4): 193-204.

Adams, Leverett A.
1942 Age determination and rate of growth of *Polyodon spathula*, by means of the growth rings of the otoliths and dentary bone. Am. Midl. Nat. 28 (3): 617-630.

Adamson, Scott W. and Thomas E. Wissing
1977 Food habits and feeding periodicity of the rainbow, fantail, and banded darters in Four Mile Creek. Ohio J. Sci. 77(4): 164-169.

Agassiz, Alexander
1878 The development of *Lepidosteus*. Proc. Am. Acad. Arts, Sci. 13: 65-76, 5 pls.

Agassiz, J. Louis R.
1850 Lake Superior. Its physical character, vegetation and animals compared with those of other and similar regions. Gould, Kendall and Lincoln, Boston. 438 pp.
1854 Notice of a collection of fishes from the southern bend of the Tennessee River "In the state of" Alabama. Am. J. Sci. Arts. ser. 2, 17: 297-308, 353-369.
1855 Synopsis of the ichthyological fauna of the Pacific slope of North America, chiefly from the collections made by the U. S. Expl. Expedition under the command of Capt. C. Wilkes, with recent additions and comparisons with eastern types. Am. Jour. Sci. Arts. ser. 2, 19: 71-79, 215-231.

Aleveras, Ronald A.
1973 Occurrence of a lookdown in the Hudson River. N. Y. Fish Game J. 20 (1): 76.

Allen, Wm. F.
1911 Notes on the breeding season and young of *Polyodon spathula*. J. Washington Acad. Sci. 1: 280-282.

Alpaugh, Walter C.
1972 High lethal temperatures of golden shiners (*Notemigonus crysoleucas*). Copeia (1): 185.

Alsop, R. G. and J. L. Forney
1962 Growth and food of white perch in Oneida Lake. N. Y. Fish Game J. 9 (2): 133-136.

Anderson, R. C. and Dan Brazo
1978 Abundance, feeding habits and degree of segregation of the spottail shiner (*Notropis hudsonius*) and longnose dace (*Rhinichthys cataractae*) in a Lake Michigan surge zone near Ludington, Michigan. Mich. Acad. 10(3): 337-346.

Anderson, William W., Jack W. Gehringer and Frederick H. Berry
1966 Field guide to the Synodontidae (lizardfishes) of the Western Atlantic Ocean. U. S. Fish Wildl. Serv. Circ. 245, 12 pp.

Applegate, Vernon C.
1943 Partial analysis of growth in a population of mudminnows, *Umbra limi* (Kirtland). Copeia (2): 92-96.

1950 Natural history of the sea lamprey, *Petromyzon marinus*, in Michigan. U. S. Fish and Wildl. Serv. Spec. Sci. Rept. 55, 237 p.
1951 The sea lamprey in the Great Lakes. Sci. Monthly 72(5): 275-281.

Applegate, Vernon C. and J. W. Moffett
1955 Sea lamprey and lake trout. Twentieth Century Bestiary. Simon and Schuster, New York. pp. 9-16.

Arcement, Reese J. and Joseph W. Rachlin
1976 A study of the karyotype of a population of the banded killifish (*Fundulus diaphanus*) from the Hudson River. J. Fish. Biol. 8: 119-125

Armstrong, John W., Charles R. Liston, Peter I. Tack, and Robert C. Anderson
1977 Age, growth, maturity and seasonal food habits of round whitefish, *Prosopium cylindraceum*, in Lake Michigan near Ludington, Michigan. Trans. Am. Fish. Soc. 106(2): 151-155.

Aron, William I. and Stanford H. Smith
1971 Ship canals and aquatic ecosystems. Science 174: 13-20.

Atkins, C. G.
1905 Culture of the fallfish or chub. Am. Fish Cult. 2: 189.

Atkinson, C. E.
1951 Feeding Habits of adult shad (*Alosa sapidissima*) in fresh water. Ecology 32(3): 556-557.

Atz, James W.
1940 Reproductive behavior in the eastern johnny darter, *Boleosoma nigrum olmstedi* (Storer). Copeia (2): 100-106.

Atz, James W. and C. L. Smith
1976 Hermaphroditism and gonadal teratoma-like growths in sturgeon (*Acipenser*). Bull. South. Calif. Acad. Sci. 75(2): 119-126.

Auer, Nancy A. (ed.)
1982 Identification of larval fishes of the Great Lakes with emphasis on the Lake Michigan drainage. Great Lakes Fish Comm. Spec. Publ. 82-3, 744 pp.

Austin, Herbert M. and Clarence R. Hickey, Jr.
1978 Predicting abundance of striped bass, *Morone saxatilis*, in New York waters from modal lengths. Fish. Bull. 76(2): 467- 473.

Avery, Ed L.
1983 A bibliography of beaver, trout, wildlife, and forest relationships with special reference to beaver and trout. Wis. Conserv. Dept. Tech. Bull. 137, 23 pp.

Avise, John C. and Michael H. Smith
1974 Biochemical genetics of sunfish. I. Geographic variation and subspecific intergradation in the bluegill, *Lepomis macrochirus*. Evolution 28 (1): 42-56.

Ayres, William O.
1842 Description of four species of fishes from Brookhaven, Long Island, two of which are believed to be new. Proc. Boston Soc. Nat. Hist. 1841-1844, 1: 67-68
1843 Description of four species of fish from Brookhaven, Long Island, all of which are believed to be new. Boston J. Nat. Hist. 4: 293.

Bacon, Edward H.
1954 Field characters of prolarvae and alevins of brook, brown and rainbow trout in Michigan. Copeia (3): 232, 1 pl.

Bade, E.
1926 The central European bitterling found in the States. Bull. N. Y. Zool. Soc., 29 (6): 188, 205-206.

Baglin, R. E., Jr. and Loren G. Hill
1977 Fecundity of the white bass, *Morone chrysops* (Rafinesque), in Lake Texoma. Amer. Midl. Nat. 98(1): 233-238.

Bailey, Jack E.
1952 Life history and ecology of the sculpin *Cottus bairdi punctulatus* in southwestern Montana. Copeia (4): 243-255.

Bailey, M. M.
1964 Age, growth, maturity, and sex composition of the American smelt, *Osmerus mordax* (Mitchill), of western Lake Superior. Trans. Am. Fish. Soc. 93(4): 382-395.
1969 Age, growth, and maturity of the longnose sucker *Catostomus catostomus*, of Western Lake Superior. J. Fish. Res. Board Can. 26(5): 1289-1299.

Bailey, Reeve M.
1938 The fishes of the Merrimack drainage. New Hampshire Fish and Game Department Survey Report 3: 149-185.
1941 The scientific name of the black crappie. Copeia (1): 21-23.
1951 A check-list of the fishes of Iowa, with keys for identification. pp. 185-238 in: Iowa Fish and Fishing by J. R. Harlan and Everett B. Speaker. Ames, Iowa. 238 pp.
1954 Distribution of the American cyprinid fish, *Hybognathus hankinsoni* with comments on its original description. Copeia (4): 289-291.
1959 Distribution of the American cyprinid fish, *Notropis anogenus*. Copeia (2): 119-123.

Bailey, Reeve M. and Marvin O. Allum
1962 Fishes of South Dakota. Misc. Publ. Mus. Zool. Univ. Mich. 119: 1-131, 1 pl.

Bailey, Reeve M. and G. R. Smith
1981 Origin and geography of the fish fauna of the Laurentian Great Lakes Basin. Can. J. Fish. Aquat. Sci. 38(12): 1539-1561.

Bailey, Reeve M. et al.
1960, 1970 (revised edition) A list of common and scientific names of fishes from the United States and Canada. Second edition. Amer. Fish. Soc. Spec. Publ. 2 Ann Arbor, 102 pp. Third Edition Spec. Publ. No. 6, 149 pp.

Bailey, Reeve M., Howard Elliott Winn and C. Lavett Smith
1954 Fishes from the Escambia River, Alabama and Florida, with ecologic and taxonomic notes. Proc. Acad. Nat. Sci. Phila. 106: 109-164.

Bain, Mark B. and Louis A. Helfrich
1983 Role of male parental care in survival of larval bluegills. Trans. Am. Fish. Soc. 112(1): 47-52.

Baird, Spencer F.
1855 Report on fishes observed on the coasts of New Jersey and Long Island during the summer of 1854. Smithson. Inst. 9th Ann. Rept. (1854): 317-352.

Baird, Spencer F. and Charles Girard
1853 Descriptions of new species of fishes collected by Mr. John H. Clark, on the U. S. and Mexican boundary survey, under Lt. Col. Jas. D. Graham. Proc. Acad. Nat. Sci. Phila. 6: 387-390.

Baker, J. A. and S. T. Ross
1981 Spatial and temporal resource utilization by southeastern cyprinids. Copeia (1): 178-189.

Baker, M. C.
1971 Habitat selection in fourspine sticklebacks (*Apeltes quadracus*). Amer. Midl. Nat. 85(1): 239-242.

Baker-Dittus, Anne M.
1978 Foraging patterns of three sympatric killifish. Copeia (3): 383-389.

Balon, Eugene K.
1974 Domestication of the carp, *Cyprinus carpio* L. Misc. Publ. Roy. Ontario Mus. Life Sci. 37 pp.

Barans, Charles A. and Allene C. Barans
1972 Eggs and early larval stages of the spotted hake *Urophycis regius*. Copeia (1): 188-190.

Barber, Willard E. and W. L. Minckley
1971 Summer foods of the cyprinid fish (*Semotilus atromaculatus*). Trans. Am. Fish. Soc. 100(2): 283-289.

Barbour, Thomas
1911 The smallest *Polyodon*. Biol. Bull. 21(4): 207-215.

Bardach, John E. and J. J. Bernstein
1957 Extreme temperatures for growth and survival of fish. Table for Handbook of Biological Data. 7 pp.

Barnes, Mark D.
1979 Eastern sand darter, *Ammocrypta pellucida* and other fishes from the streams of the Wayne National Forest. Ohio J. Sci. 79: 92-94.

Barney, R. L.
1926 The distribution of the fresh-water sheepshead, *Aplodinotus grunniens* Rafinesque, in respect to the glacial history of North America. Ecology 7(3): 351-364.

Bartnik, Victor G.
1970 Reproductive isolation between two sympatric dace, *Rhinichthys atratulus* and *R. cataractae*, in Manitoba. J. Fish. Res. Board Can. 27(12): 2125-2141.

Bath, Dale W., C. Allen Beebe, C. Braxton Dew, Robert H. Reider, and Jack H. Hecht.
1977 A list of common and scientific names of fishes collected from the Hudson River, 1976. Fourth Symposium on Hudson River Ecology. Hudson River Environmental Society. 6 pp.

Bath, Dale W. and J. M. O'Connor
1982 The biology of the white perch, *Morone americana*, in the Hudson River Estuary. Fish. Bull. 80(3): 599-610.

Battle, Helen I.
1940 The embryology and larval development of the goldfish (*Carassius auratus* L.) from Lake Erie. Ohio J. Sci. 40(2): 82-93.

Baur, Richard J.
1970 Digestion rate of the Clear Lake black bullhead. Proc. Iowa Acad. Sci. 77: 112-121.

Beamish, F. William H.
1979 Migration and spawning energetics of the anadromous sea lamprey, *Petromyzon marinus*. Environ. Biol. Fish. 4(1): 3-7.

Beamish, Richard J.
1972 Lethal pH for the white sucker, *Catostomus commersoni* (Lacepède). Trans. Am. Fish. Soc. 101(2): 355-358.
1973 Determination of age and growth of populations of the white sucker (*Catostomus commersoni*) exhibiting a wide range of size at maturity. J. Fish. Res. Board Can. 30: 607-616.
1974 Growth and survival of white suckers (*Catostomus commersoni*) in an acidified lake. J. Fish. Res. Board Can. 31(1): 49-54.

Beamish, Richard J. and E. J. Crossman
1977 Validity of the subspecies designation for the dwarf white sucker (*Catostomus commersoni utawana*). J. Fish. Res. Board Can. 34(3): 371-378.

Beamish, Richard J. and H. H. Harvey
1969 Age determination in the white sucker. J. Fish. Res. Board Can. 26 (3): 633- 638.

Bean, Tarleton H.
1891 Observations upon fishes of Great South Bay, Long Island, New York. Rept. Comm. Fish. State N. Y. 19: 237-281, pls, 1-26.
1899 Fishes of the south shore of Long Island. Science 9(211): 52-55.
1902 Catalog of the fishes of Long Island. Ann. Rept. Forest, Fish Game Comm. State N. Y. 6 (1901): 373-478.
1903 Catalogue of the fishes of New York. Bull. N. Y. State Museum 60, Zoology 9, 784 pp.
1916 Description of a new cisco from Lake Erie. Proc. Biol. Soc. Wash. 29: 25-26.

Becker, Lewis R. Jr.
1982 Fishes of the Allegheny River and its tributaries between Salamanca and Allegany, Cattaraugus County, New York. M.S. Thesis, St. Bonaventure University. 132 pp.

Belding, David L.
1940 The number of eggs and pyloric appendages as criteria of river varieties of the Atlantic Salmon (*Salmo salar*). Trans. Am. Fish. Soc. 69: 285-289.

Berg, L. S.
1962 Freshwater fishes of the U. S. S. R. and adjacent countries Vol 1, 4th ed. (1948). Israel Prog. Sci. Transl. Jerusalem. 514 pp.

Berner, Lester M.
1948 The intestinal convolutions: new generic characters for the separation of *Carpiodes* and *Ictiobus*. Copeia (2): 140-141.

Berrien, Peter L.
1975 A description of Atlantic mackerel, *Scomber scombrus*, eggs and early larvae. Fish. Bull. 73(1): 186-192.

Berry, Frederick H. and Louis E. Vogele
1961 Filefishes (Monacanthidae) of the Western North Atlantic. Fish. Bull. 61: 61-109.

Berst, Alfred H., Alan R. Emery, and George R. Spangler
1981 Reproductive behavior of hybrid charr (*Salvelinus fontinalis* x *S. namaycush*). Can. J. Fish. Aquat. Sci. 38(4): 432-440.

Bigelow, Henry B. and William C. Schroeder
1948 Sharks. In : Fishes of the Western North Atlantic. Mem. Sears Found. Mar. Res. No.1, part 1: 59-576.
1953a Sawfishes, guitarfishes, skates and rays. Mem. Sears Found. Mar. Res. No. 1, part 2: 1-514.
1953b Fishes of the Gulf of Maine. First revision. Fishery Bull. 74, Bull. U. S. Fish and Wildl. Serv. vol 53: viii + 577.

Bigelow, N. K.
1923 The food of young suckers (*Catostomus commersonii*) in Lake Nipigon. Univ. Toronto Stud. Bio. ser. 24. Publ. Ont. Fish. Res. Lab. 21: 83-115.

Bimber, David L.
1983 Longevity, growth, and mortality of muskellunge in Chautauqua Lake, New York. N. Y. Fish Game J. 29(2)(1982): 134-141.

Black, John D.
1945 Natural history of the northern mimic shiner, *Notropis volucellus volucellus* Cope. Invest. Indiana Lakes Streams 2(16): 449-469.

Black, John D. and Lyman G. Williamson
1947 Artificial hybrids between muskellunge and northern pike. Trans. Wis. Acad. Sci., Arts, and Lett. 38 (1946): 299-314.

Bloch, Marc Elieser
1797 Ichthyologie ou histoire naturelle des poissons. 10: 65, pl. 343.
1782 Oeconomische Naturgeschichte der Fische Deutschlands. Berlin (1782-1785): 3 pts. and 108 col. pls.
1785 Ichthyologie ou histoire naturelle général et particulière des poissons avec des figures enluminées dissinées d'après nature. 12 vols.

Bloch, M. E. and J. G. Schneider
1801 Systema Ichthyologiae. Berolini. Facsimile edition J. Cramer, 1967.

Bodola, A.
1966 Life history of the gizzard shad, *Dorosoma cepedianum* (LeSueur), in western Lake Erie. Fish. Bull. 65(2): 391-425.

Bohlke, James E. and Charles C. G. Chaplin
1968 Fishes of the Bahamas and adjacent tropical waters. Livingston Publishing Co. Wynnewood, Pa. xxiii + 771 pp.

Bonn, Edward
1953 The food and growth rate of young white bass (*Morone chrysops*) in Lake Texoma. Trans. Am. Fish. Soc. 82 (1952): 213-221.

Booke, Henry E.
1974 A cytotaxonomic study of the round whitefishes, genus *Prosopium*. Copeia (1): 115-119.

Boreske, John R. Jr.
1974 A review of the North American fossil amiid fishes. Bull. Mus. Comp. Zool. 146(1): 1-87.

Bornholdt, David Parshall
1979 A literature review of the Chinese grass carp (*Ctenopharyngodon idella* (Val.)); its biology and possible application for aquatic weed control. M. S. Thesis, Long Island University. 63 pp.

Boreman, John
1981 Characteristics of fall and spring migrant rainbow trout in Cayuga Inlet, New York. N. Y. Fish Game J. 28(1): 100-107.

Bowen, Edith
1931 The role of the sense organs in aggregation of *Ameiurus melas*. Ecol. Monogr. 1(1): 1-35.

Bowman, H. B.
1932 A descriptive and ecological study of the margined madtom *Rabida insignis* (Richardson). M. S. Thesis, Cornell University.
1936 Further notes on the margined madtom *Rabida insignis*

REFERENCES

(Richardson) and notes on a kindred species *Noturus flavus* Rafinesque. Ph. D. Thesis, Cornell University.

Bowman, Milton L.
1970 Life history of the black redhorse, *Moxostoma duquesnei* (Lesueur), in Missouri. Trans. Am. Fish. Soc. 99(3): 546-559.

Boyle, Robert H.
1968 Notes on fishes of the lower Hudson River. Underwater Nat. 5(2): 32-33, 40.
1969 The Hudson River. A natural and unnatural history. W. W. Norton and Company, New York. 304 pp.

Branson, Branley A. and George A. Moore
1962 The lateralis components of the acoustico-lateralis system in the sunfish family Centrarchidae. Copeia (1): 1-108.

Brasch, John G., James M. McFadden, and Stanley Kmiotek
1958 The eastern brook trout: its life history, ecology, and management. Publ. Wis. Conserv. Dept. 226, 11 pp.

Brazo, Dan C., Charles R. Liston, and Robert C. Anderson.
1978 Life History of the longnose dace, *Rhinichthys cataractae,* in the surge zone of eastern Lake Michigan, near Ludington, Michigan. Trans. Am. Fish. Soc. 107(4): 550-556.

Breder, Charles M., Jr.
1922 Description of the spawning habits of *Pseudopleuronectes americanus* in captivity. Copeia 102: 3-4.
1933a The development of the urostyle in *Umbra pygmaea* (DeKay). Am. Mus. Novit. 610, 5 pp.
1933b *Rhodeus amarus* spawning in American mussels. Copeia (3): 147-148.
1936a "All modern conveniences" A note on the nest architecture of the four-spined stickleback. Bull. N. Y. Zool. Soc. 39(2): 72-76.
1936b The reproductive habits of the North American sunfishes (Family Centrarchidae). Zoologica 21(1): 1-48, 7 pls.
1938 The species of fish in New York Harbor. Bull. N. Y. Zool. Soc. 41(1): 23-29.
1940 The nesting behavior of *Eupomotis gibbosus* (Linnaeus) in a small pond. Zoologica 25(3): 353-360, pls. 1-2.

Breder, Charles M. Jr. and D. R. Crawford
1922 Food of certain minnows. Zoologica 2: 287-327.

Breder, Charles M. Jr. and R. F. Nigrelli
1935 The influence of temperature and other factors on the winter aggregation of the sunfish, *Lepomis auritus,* with critical remarks on the social behavior of fishes. Ecology 16(1): 33-47.

Breder, Charles M. Jr. and A. C. Redmond
1929 The bluespotted sunfish. A contribution to the life history and habits of *Enneacanthus* with notes on other Lepominae. Zoologica 9(10): 379-401.

Breder, Charles M. Jr. and Donn E. Rosen
1966 Modes of reproduction in fishes. The Natural History Press. xv + 941 pp.

Brett, J. R.
1944 Some lethal temperature relations of Algonquin Park fishes. Publ. Ontario Fish. Res. Lab. 63 Univ. Toronto Stud. Biol. Ser. 52, 49 pp.
1956 Some principles of the thermal requirements of fishes. Quart. Rev. Biol. 31(2): 75-87.

Briggs, John C.
1960 The nomenclature of *Centropristis,* Cuvier, 1829. Copeia (4): 358.

Briggs, Philip T.
1968 The sport fishery for scup in the inshore waters of eastern Long Island. N. Y. Fish Game J. 15(2): 165-185.

Bridges, C. H. and J. W. Miller
1958 A compendium of the life history and ecology of the

eastern brook trout, *Salvelinus fontinalis* (Mitchill). Bull. Mass. Div. Fish and Game 23, 37 pp.

Brigham, E. D.
1932 The life history, ecology, and intestinal histology of the minnow, *Notropis atherinoides.* M. S. Thesis, Syracuse University.

Brinley, Floyd J. and R. E. Bowen
1935 Some feeding habits of the common eel (*Anguilla bostoniensis*). Copeia (3): 140.

Brown, Bradford E.
1961 Behavior of splake and brook trout fingerlings. Trans. Am. Fish. Soc. 90(3): 328-329.

Brown, C. J. D. and J. W. Moffett
1942 Observations on the number of eggs and feeding habits of the cisco (*Leucichthys artedi*) in Swains Lake, Jackson County, Michigan. Copeia (3): 149-152

Brown, Edward H. Jr.
1968 Population characteristics and physical condition of alewives, *Alosa pseudoharengus,* in a massive dieoff in Lake Michigan, 1967. Great Lakes Fish. Comm. Tech. Rept. 13, 20 pp.
1972 Population biology of alewives, *Alosa pseudoharengus,* in Lake Michigan, 1949-1970. J. Fish. Res. Board Can. 29(5): 477-500.

Brown, J. A. and P. W. Colgan
1981 The use of lateral body bar markings in identification of young-of-year sunfish (*Lepomis*) in Lake Opinicon, Ontario. Can. J. Zool. 59: 1852-1855.

Brown, Joseph H., V. Theodore Hammer, and Gordon D. Koshinsky
1970 Breeding biology of the lake chub, *Couesius plumbeus,* at Lac la Ronge, Saskatchewan. J. Fish. Res. Board Can. 27(6): 1005-1015.

Brown, Tommy L.
1975 The 1973 salmonid run: New York's Salmon River sport fishery, angler activity, and economic impact. New York Sea Grant Inst. NYSSGP-RS-75-024, 26 pp.

Browne, Robert A.
1981 Lakes as islands: biogeographic distribution, turnover rates, and species composition in the lakes of central New York. J. Biogeogr. 8: 75-83.

Brundage, Harold M. and Robert E. Meadows
1982 The Atlantic sturgeon, *Acipenser oxyrhynchus,* in the Delaware River estuary, Fish. Bull. 80(2): 337-343.

Brynildson, Oscar M., Vernon A. Hacker, and Thomas A. Klick
1963 Brown trout. Its life history, ecology and management. Publ. Wis. Conserv. Dept. 234, 14 pp.

Burdick, G. E.
1954 An analysis of the factors, including pollution, having possible influence on the abundance of shad in the Hudson River. N. Y. Fish Game J. 1(2): 188-205.

Burdick, G. E., Howard J. Dean, and Earl J. Harris
1957 Lethal oxygen concentration for yellow perch. N. Y. Fish Game J. 4(1): 92-101.

Burdick, G. E., Morris Lipschuetz, Howard J. Dean, and Earl J. Harris
1954 Lethal oxygen concentrations for trout and smallmouth bass. N. Y. Fish Game J. 1(1): 84-97.

Burkett, Robert D. and William B. Jackson
1971 The eye lens as an age indicator in freshwater drum. Amer. Midl. Nat. 85(1): 222-225.

Burkhead, Noel M., Robert E. Jenkins, and Eugene G. Maurakis
1980 New records, distribution and diagnostic characteristics of Virginia ictalurid catfishes with an adnexed adipose fin. Brimleyana 4: 75-93.

Burns, John R.
1976 The reproductive cycle and its environmental control in the pumpkinseed, *Lepomis gibbosus* (Pisces: Centrarchidae). Copeia (3): 449-455.

Burr, Brooks M. and Richard L. Mayden
1982 Life history of the brindled madtom *Noturus miurus* in Mill Creek, Illinois (Pisces: Ictaluridae). Amer. Midl. Nat. 107(1): 25-41.

Burr, Brooks M. and Michael A. Morris
1977 Spawning behavior of the shorthead redhorse, *Moxostoma macrolepidotum*, in Big Rock Creek, Illinois. Trans. Am. Fish. Soc. 106(1): 80-82.

Busch, Wolf-Dieter N., David H. Davies, and Stephen J. Nepszy
1977 Establishment of white perch, *Morone americana*, in Lake Erie. J. Fish. Res. Board Can. 34(7): 1039-1041.

Buss, K.
1957 The kokanee. Pennsylvania Fish Commission Special Purpose Report. 13 pp. mimeogr.
1961a Record northern pike -- fact or fiction. Pennsylvania Angler 30 (10): 6-7.
1961b A literature survey of the life history and culture of the northern pike. Pennsylvania Fish Commission Benner Spring Fisheries Research Station Special Purpose Report. 58 pp.
1962 A literature survey of the life history of the redfin and grass pickerels. Pennsylvania Fish Commission Benner Spring Fisheries Research Station Special purpose Report. 12 pp. mimeo.

Buss, Keen and Jack Miller
1967 Interspecific hybridization of esocids: hatching success, pattern development and fertility of some F$_1$ hybrids. U. S. Bur. Sport Fish. Wildl. Tech. Pap. 14, 30 pp.

Buss, Keen and James E. Wright
1958 Appearance and fertility of trout hybrids. Trans. Am. Fish. Soc. 87: 172-181.

Buth, Donald G.
1979 Biochemical systematics of the cyprinid genus *Notropis*. I. the subgenus *Luxilus*. Biochem. Syst. Ecol. 7(1): 69-79.
1980 Evolutionary genetics and systematic relationships in the catostomid genus *Hypentelium*. Copeia (2): 280-290.

Buth, Donald G. and Brooks M. Burr
1978 Isozyme variability in the cyprinid genus *Campostoma*. Copeia (2): 298-311.

Butner, Alfred and Bayard H. Brattstrom
1960 Local movements in *Menidia* and *Fundulus*. Copeia (2): 139-141.

Buynak, Gerard L. and Andrew J. Gurzynski
1978a Lymphocystis disease in walleye (*Stizostedion vitreum*) captured in the Susquehanna River. Proc. Pa. Acad. Sci. 52(1): 49-50.
1978b Age and growth of smallmouth bass (*Micropterus dolomieui*) in a large river polluted by acid mine drainages. Proc. Pa. Acad. Sci. 52: 176-178.

Buynak, Gerard L. and Harold W. Mohr, Jr.
1978a Larval development of the northern hog sucker (*Hypentelium nigricans*), from the Susquehanna River. Trans. Am. Fish. Soc. 107(4): 595-599.
1978b Larval development of the white sucker (*Catostomus commersoni*) from the Susquehanna River. Proc. Pa. Acad. Sci. 52(2): 143-145.
1979a Larval development of creek chub and fallfish from two Susquehanna River tributaries. Prog. Fish-Cult. 41(3): 124-129.
1979b Larval development of the shorthead redhorse (*Moxostoma macrolepidotum*) from the Susquehanna River. Trans. Am. Fish. Soc. 108(2): 161-165.
1979c Larval development of rock bass from the Susquehanna River. Prog. Fish-Cult. 41(1): 39-42.
1980a Larval development of stoneroller, cutlips minnow, and river chub with diagnostic keys, including four additional cyprinids. Prog. Fish-Cult. 42 (3): 127-135.
1980b Larval development of the common shiner (*Notropis cornutus*) from northeast Pennsylvania. Proc. Pa. Acad. Sci. 54(2): 165-168.
1980c Key to the identification of sucker larvae in the Susquehanna River near Berwick, Pennsylvania. Proc. Pa. Acad. Sci. 54(2): 161-164.

Byrne, Donald M.
1978 Life history of the spotfin killifish, *Fundulus luciae* (Pisces: Cyprinodontidae), in Fox Creek marsh, Virginia. Estuaries 1(4): 211-227.

Cahn, Alvin R.
1927a An ecological study of southern Wisconsin fishes; the brook silverside (*Labidesthes sicculus*) and the cisco (*Leucichthys artedi*) in their relations to the region. Ill. Biol. Monogr. 11(1): 1-151.
1927b The European rudd (*Scardinius*) in Wisconsin. Copeia 162: 5.
1936 Observations on the breeding of the lawyer, *Lota maculosa*. Copeia (3): 163-165.

Caldwell, David K.
1957 The biology and systematics of the pinfish *Lagodon rhomboides* (Linnaeus). Bull. Fla. State Mus. 2(6): 77-173.
1961 Populations of the butterfish, *Poronotus triacanthus* (Peck), with systematic comments. Bull. South. Calif. Acad. Sci. 60(1): 19-31.

Calhoun, Alex (ed.)
1966 Inland fisheries management. State of California Dept. Fish and Game. vi + 546 pp.

Cameron, G. S.
1948 An unusual maskinonge from Little Vermillion Lake, Ontario. Canadian Jour. Res. D, 26: 223-229.

Campbell, J. S. and H. R. MacCrimmon
1970 Biology of the emerald shiner, *Notropis atherinoides* Rafinesque in Lake Simcoe, Can. Jour. Fish. Biol. 2(3): 259-273.

Carbine, W. F.
1942 Observations on the life history of the northern pike, *Esox lucius* L., in Houghton Lake, Michigan. Trans. Am. Fish. Soc. 71(1941): 149-164.

Carlander, Kenneth D.
1969 Handbook of freshwater fishery biology. Vol.1. Iowa State University Press. vi + 752 pp.
1977 Handbook of freshwater fishery biology. Vol. 2. Iowa State University Press. vii + 431 pp.

Carlson, Douglas M. and Patrick S. Bronislawsky
1981 The paddlefish (*Polyodon spathula*) fisheries of the midwestern United States. Fisheries 6(2): 17-22, 26-27.

Carnes, W. C. Jr.
1958 Contributions to the biology of the eastern creek chubsucker, *Erimyzon oblongus oblongus* (Mitchill). M. S. Thesis, North Carolina State University. 69 pp.

Carscadden, James E. and William C. Leggett
1975 Meristic differences in spawning populations of American shad, *Alosa sapidissima*: evidence for homing to tributaries in the St. John River, New Brunswick. J. Fish. Res. Board Can. 32: 653-660.

Casterlin, Martha E. and William W. Reynolds
1979 Thermoregulatory behavior of the bluespotted sunfish, *Enneacanthus gloriosus*. Hydrobiologia 64(1): 3-4.
1980 Diel activity of the bluespotted sunfish, *Enneacanthus gloriosus*. Copeia (2): 344-345.

Cating, James P.
1953 Determining age of Atlantic shad from their scales. Fish. Bull. 85, vol. 54: 187-199.

Cech, Joseph J. Jr., Clain G. Campagna, and Stephen J. Mitchill
1979 Respiratory responses of largemouth bass (*Micropterus salmoides*) to environmental changes in temperature and dissolved oxygen. Trans. Am. Fish. Soc. 108(2): 166-171.

Chambers, E. T. D.
1904 Maskinonge or mascalonge. Forest and Stream 62: 316.

Chambers, J. P., J. A. Musick and J. Davis
1976 Methods of distinguishing larval alewife from larval blueback herring. Chesapeake Sci. 17(2): 93-100.

Champagne, Donald E., C. R. Harington, and Don E. McAllister
1979 Deepwater sculpin, *Myoxocephalus thompsoni* (Girard), from a Pleistocene nodule, Green Creek, Ontario, Canada. Can. J. Earth Sci. 16(8): 1621-1628.

Chang, Chang-Hwa
1979 Food habits and feeding chronology of the redfin pickerel, *Esox americanus* Gmelin, in Woodbury Creek, New York. M. S. Thesis, City College, CUNY.

Chao, Labbish Ning
1973 Digestive system and feeding habits of the cunner, *Tautogolabrus adspersus*, a stomachless fish. Fish. Bull. 71(2): 565-586.
1978 A basis for classifying western Atlantic Sciaenidae (Teleostei: Perciformes). NOAA Tech. Rept. NMFS Tech. Circ. 415: 1-64.

Chao, Labbish Ning and John A. Musick
1977 Life history, feeding habits, and functional morphology of juvenile sciaenid fishes in the York River Estuary, Virginia. Fish. Bull. 75(4): 657-702.

Cheek, R. P.
1968 The American shad. U. S. Fish Wildl. Serv. Fish Leaflet 614.

Cheney, A. Nelson
1897 Black bass and their distribution in the waters of New York State. Ann. Rep. Forest Fish Game Comm. State N. Y. 2 (1896): 176-184.
1898 The Hudson River as a salmon stream. Bull. U. S. Fish. Comm. (1897) 17: 247-251.

Chernoff, Barry, John V. Conner, and Charles F. Bryan
1981 Systematics of the *Menidia beryllina* complex (Pisces:Atherinidae) from the Gulf of Mexico and its tributaries. Copeia (2): 319-336.

Childers, William F.
1967 Hybridization of four species of sunfishes (Centrarchidae). Bull. Ill. Nat. Hist. Surv. 29(3): 159-214

Chittenden, Mark E. Jr.
1973 Salinity tolerance of young American shad, *Alosa sapidissima*. Chesapeake Sci. 14(3): 207-210.
1974 Trends in the abundance of American shad, *Alosa sapidissima*, in the Delaware River basin. Chesapeake Sci. 15(2): 96-103.
1976a Weight loss, mortality, feeding, and duration of residence of adult American shad, *Alosa sapidissima*, in fresh water. Fish. Bull. 74: 151-157.
1976b Present and historical spawning grounds and nurseries of American shad, *Alosa sapidissima* in the Delaware River. Fish. Bull. 74: 343-352.

Christie, W. J.
1973 A review of the changes in the fish species composition of Lake Ontario. Great Lakes Fish. Comm. Tech. Rept. 23, v + 65 pp.
1974 Changes in the fish species composition of the Great Lakes. J. Fish. Res. Board Can. 31: 827-854.

Cianci, John Martin
1969 Larval development of the alewife *Alosa pseudo-*

harengus Wilson and the glut herring, *Alosa aestivalis* Mitchill. M. S. Thesis, University of Connecticut.

Clady, Michael D
1976a Changes in abundance of inshore fishes in Oneida Lake, 1916 to 1970. N. Y. Fish Game J. 23(1): 73-81.
1976b Distribution and abundance of larval ciscoes, *Coregonus artedii* and burbot, *Lota lota*, in Oneida Lake. J. Great Lakes Res. 2: 234-247.

Clady, Michael and Brendan Hutchinson
1976 Food of the yellow perch, *Perca flavescens*, following a decline of the burrowing mayfly, *Hexagenia limbata*. Ohio J. Sci. 76(3): 133-138.

Clark, C. F.
1950 Observations on the spawning habits of the northern pike, *Esox lucius*, in northwestern Ohio. Copeia (4): 285-288.

Clary, James Robert
1972 Predation on the brown trout by the slimy sculpin. Prog. Fish-Cult. 34(2): 91-95.

Clemens, Howard P.
1951a The food of the burbot *Lota lota maculosa* (Le Sueur) in Lake Erie. Trans. Am. Fish. Soc. 80 (1950): 56-66.
1951b The growth of the burbot, *Lota lota maculosa* (LeSueur) in Lake Erie. Trans. Am. Fish. Soc. 80(1950): 163-173.

Clemens, Howard P. and Kermit E. Sneed
1957 The spawning behavior of the channel catfish *Ictalurus punctatus*. U. S. Fish Wildl. Serv. Spec. Sci. Rept. 219, 11 pp.

Clemens, Wilbert A.
1928 The food of trout from the streams of Oneida County, New York State. Trans. Am. Fish. Soc. 58: 183-195.

Clemmer, Glenn H. and Frank J. Schwartz
1964 Age, growth, and weight relationships of the striped killifish, *Fundulus majalis*, near Solomons, Maryland. Trans. Am. Fish. Soc. 93(2): 197-198.

Clinton, De Witt
1815 Some remarks on the fishes of the western waters of the state of New York in a letter to Samuel L. Mitchill. Trans. Lit. Philos. Soc. 1: 493-501.
1822a Letters on the natural history and internal resources of the state of New York. Bliss and White, New York. 224 pp.
1822b Account of the *Salmo otsego* or the Otsego basse in a letter to John W. Francis, M. D. New York - C.S. Van Winkle. 6 pp.
1824 Description of a new species of fish from the Hudson River. Ann. Lyceum Nat. Hist. N. Y. 1: 49-50.

Clugston, James P. and Edwin L. Cooper
1960 Growth of the common eastern madtom, *Noturus insignis*, in central Pennsylvania. Copeia (1): 9-16.

Coad, Brian W.
1981 A bibliography of the sticklebacks. Syllogeus 35: 1-142.

Coad, Brian W. and G. Power
1973 Observations on the ecology and meristic variation of the ninespine stickleback, *Pungitius pungitius* (L., 1758) of the Metawek River system, Quebec. Amer. Midl. Nat. 90(2): 498-503.

Cobb, John N.
1904 The commercial fisheries of the interior lakes and rivers of New York and Vermont. Rept. U. S. Fish Comm. (1903): 225-246.

Cohen, Daniel M.
1980 Names of hakes. Marine Fisheries Review January, 1980: 2-3.

Cohen, Daniel M. and Jorgen G. Nielson
1978 Guide to the identification of genera of the fish order

Ophidiiformes with a tentative classification of the order. NOAA Tech. Rept. NMFS Circ. 417, vii + 72 pp.

Cohen, Daniel M. and Joseph L. Russo
1979 Variation in the fourbeard rockling, *Enchelyopus cimbrius*, a north Atlantic gadid fish, with comments on the genera of rocklings. Fish. Bull. 77(1): 91-104.

Coker, R. E.
1923 Methuselah of the Mississippi (Paddlefish). Sci. Monthly 16(1): 89-103.

Colby, Peter J. and L. T. Brooke
1973 Effects of temperature on embryonic development of lake herring (*Coregonus artedii*). J. Fish. Res. Board Can. 30: 799-810.

Cole, Charles F.
1965 Additional evidence for separation of *Etheostoma olmstedi* Storer from *Etheostoma nigrum* Rafinesque. Copeia (1): 8-13.
1967 A study of the eastern Johnny darter, *Etheostoma olmstedi* Storer (Teleostei, Percidae). Chesapeake Sci. 8(1): 28-51.

Colgan, Patrick
1974 Burying experiments with the banded killifish, *Fundulus diaphanus*. Copeia (1): 258-259.

Colgan, Patrick and David Ealey
1973 Role of woody debris in nest site selection by pumpkinseed sunfish, *Lepomis gibbosus*. J. Fish. Res. Board Can. 30: 853-856.

Colgan, Patrick and Nigel Costeloe
1980 Plasticity of burying behavior by the banded killifish, *Fundulus diaphanus*. Copeia (2): 349-351.

Colgan, P. W. and M. R. Gross
1977 Dynamics of aggression in male pumpkinseed sunfish (*Lepomis gibbosus*) over the reproduction phase. Z. Tierpsychol. 43: 139-151.

Collette, Bruce B.
1962 The swamp darters of the subgenus *Hololepis* (Pisces, Percidae). Tulane Stud. Zool. Bot. 9(4): 115-211.
1963 The subfamilies, tribes, and genera of the Percidae (Teleostei). Copeia (4): 615-623.
1965 Systematic significance of breeding tubercles in fishes of the family Percidae. Proc. U. S. Natl. Mus. 117(3518): 567-614.
1968 *Strongylura timucu* (Walbaum): a valid species of western Atlantic needlefish. Copeia (1): 189-192.

Collette, Bruce B. and Leslie W. Knapp
1966 Catalog of type specimens of the darters (Pisces, Percidae, Etheostomatini). Proc. U. S. Natl. Mus. 119 (3550): 1-88.

Collette, Bruce B., M. A. Ali, K. E. F. Hokanson, Maria Nagiec, S. A. Smirnov, J. E. Thorpe, A. H. Weatherly, and J. Willemsen
1979 Biology of Percids. J. Fish. Res. Board Can. 34(10): 1890-1899.

Collette, Bruce B. and Petru Banarescu
1977 Systematics and zoogeography of the fishes of the family Percidae. J. Fish. Res. Board Can. 34 (10): 1450-1463.

Collier, Albert
1936 The mechanism of internal fertilization in *Gambusia*. Copeia (1): 45-53.

Colton, John B. Jr. and Kenneth A. Honey
1963 The eggs and larval stages of the butterfish, *Poronotus triacanthus*. Copeia(2): 447-450.

Conover, David O. and Michael R. Ross
1982 Patterns in seasonal abundance, growth, and biomass of the Atlantic silverside, *Menidia menidia*, in a New England estuary. Estuaries 5(4): 275-286.

Constanz, George D.
1979 Social dynamics and parental care in the tessellated darter (Pisces: Percidae). Proc. Acad. Nat. Sci. Phila. 131: 131-138.

Cooper, A. L.
1960 Lethal oxygen concentrations for the northern common shiner. N. Y. Fish Game J. 7(1): 72-76.

Cooper, Edwin L.
1983 Fishes of Pennsylvania and the northeastern United States. Pennsylvania State University Press. 243 pp.

Cooper, Gerald P.
1936a Some results of forage fish investigations in Michigan. Trans. Am. Fish. Soc. 65(1935): 132-142.
1936b Age and growth of the golden shiner (*Notemigonus crysoleucas auratus*) and its suitability for propagation. Pap. Mich. Acad. Sci., Arts, Lett. 21 (1935): 587-597.

Cooper, John E.
1978a Eggs and larvae of the logperch, *Percina caprodes* (Rafinesque). Am. Midl. Nat. 99(2): 257-269.
1978b Identification of eggs, larvae, and juveniles of the rainbow smelt, *Osmerus mordax*, with comparisons to larval alewife, *Alosa pseudoharengus*, and gizzard shad, *Dorosoma cepedianum*. Trans. Am. Fish. Soc. 107(1): 56-62.
1979 Description of eggs and larvae of fantail (*Etheostoma flabellare*) and rainbow (*E. caeruleum*) darters from Lake Erie tributaries. Trans. Am. Fish. Soc. 108(1): 46-56.
1980 Egg, larval and juvenile development of longnose dace, *Rhinichthys cataractae*, and river chub, *Nocomis micropogon*, with notes on their hybridization. Copeia (3): 469-478.

Cooper, Richard A.
1966 Migration and population estimation of the tautog, *Tautoga onitis* (Linnaeus), from Rhode Island. Trans. Am. Fish. Soc. 95(3): 239-247.
1967 Age and growth of the tautog, *Tautoga onitis* (Linnaeus) from Rhode Island. Trans. Am. Fish. Soc. 96: 134-142.

Cope, Edward Drinker
1862 (Observations upon certain cyprinoid fish in Pennsylvania). Proc. Acad. Nat. Sci. Phila. (1861): 13: 522-524.
1864 On a blind silurid from Pennsylvania, Proc. Acad. Nat. Sci. Phila. 16:231-233.
1865a Partial catalogue of the cold-blooded vertebrata of Michigan. Part 1. Proc. Acad. Nat. Sci. Phila. (1864) 16: 276-285.
1865b Note on fishes brought from the Platte River, near Fort Riley, by Dr. Wm. A. Hammond. Proc. Acad. Nat. Sci. Phila. (1865)17: 85-88.
1868 On the distribution of fresh-water fishes in the Allegheny region of southwestern Virginia. Jour. Acad. Nat. Sci. Phila., 2 ser, 6: 207-247.
1869a Synopsis of the Cyprinidae of Pennsylvania. Trans. Am. Philos. Soc. 13(13): 351-399.
1869b On some new species of American and African Fishes. Trans. Am. Philos. Soc. 13: 400-407.
1870a On some etheostomine perch from Tennessee and North Carolina. Proc. Am. Philos. Soc. 11: 261-274.
1870b A partial synopsis of the fishes of the fresh waters of North Carolina. Proc. Am. Philos. Soc. 11: 448-495.

Copeman, Douglas G. and Don E. McAllister
1978 Analysis of the effect of transplantation on morphometric and meristic characters in lake populations of the rainbow smelt, *Osmerus mordax* (Mitchill). Environ. Biol. Fish 3(3): 253-259.

Copes, Frederick A.
1975 Ecology of the brassy minnow, *Hybognathus hankinsoni* (Cyprinidae). Repts. Fauna and Flora Wis. 10. Contrib. Ichthyol. Univ. Wisconsin at Stevens Point. pp. 45-72.

Coventry, A. F.
1922 Breeding habits of the land-locked sea lamprey (*Petromyzon marinus* var. *dorsatus* Wilder). Univ. Toronto Stud.

Biol. ser no.20. Publ. Ont. Fish Res. Lab. 9: 129-136, figs.1-3.

Cowan, G.
1971 Comparative morphology of the cottid genus *Myoxocephalus* based on meristic, morphometric, and other anatomical characters. Can. J. Zool. 49(1): 1479-1496.

Cox, Ulysses O.
1896 A report upon the fishes of southwestern Minnesota. Rept. U. S. Fish Comm. 20 (1894): 605-616.

Coyle, Elizabeth E.
1930 The algal food of *Pimephales promelas* (fathead minnow). Ohio J. Sci. 30(1): 23-35.

Creaser, Charles W.
1926a The establishment of the Atlantic smelt in the upper waters of the Great Lakes. Pap. Mich. Acad. Sci., Arts, Lett. 5: 405-424, pls. 24-27.
1926b The structure and growth of the scales of fishes in relation to the interpretation of their life-history, with special reference to the sunfish *Eupomotis gibbosus*. Misc. Publ. Mus. Zool. Univ. Mich. 17, 82 pp., 1 pl.
1932 Atlantic smelt in the Great Lakes. The Fisherman 1 (9): 3-4,11.

Creaser, Charles W. and Clare S. Hann
1929 The food of larval lampreys. Pap. Mich. Acad. Sci., Arts, Lett. 10 (1928): 433-437.

Cressy, Roger F. and Ernest A. Lachner
1970 The parasitic copepod diet and life history of diskfishes (Echeneidae). Copeia (2): 310-318.

Crossman, Edwin J.
1962a The redfin pickerel, *Esox a. americanus* in North Carolina. Copeia (1): 114-123.
1962b The grass pickerel *Esox americanus vermiculatus* Le-Sueur in Canada. Contribution 55, Life Sciences Division Royal Ontario Museum University Toronto. 29pp.
1966 A taxonomic study of *Esox americanus* and its subspecies in eastern North America. Copeia (1): 1-20.
1977 Displacement, and home range movements of muskellunge determined by ultrasonic tracking. Environ. Biol. Fish. 1(2): 145-158.
1978 Taxonomy and distribution of North American esocids. Am. Fish. Soc. Spec. Publ. 11: 13-26.

Crossman, Edwin J. and C. D. Goodchild
1978 An annotated bibliography of the Muskellunge, *Esox masquinongy*. Misc. Publ. Roy. Ont.Mus. Life Sci. 131 pp.

Crossman, Edwin J. and G. E. Lewis
1973 An annotated bibliography of the chain pickerel, *Esox niger* (Osteichthys: Salmoniformes). Misc. Publ. R. Ont. Mus. Life Sci. pp. 1-87.

Crossman, Edwin J. and Harry D. Van Meter
1979 Annotated list of the fishes of the Lake Ontario watershed. Great Lakes Fish. Comm. Tech. Rept. 36, 25 pp.

Crowe, Walter P.
1975 Great Lakes Fishery Commission. History, program, progress. Great Lakes Fishery Comm. 21 pp.

Cuerrier, Jean Paul and George Roussow
1957 Age and growth of lake sturgeon from Lake St. Francis, St. Lawrence River. Report on material collected in 1947. Can. Fish Cult. 10: 17-29.

Cuvier, G. L. C. F. D.
1819 Sur les *Diodons*, vulgairement orbes épineux. Mem. Mus. Nat. Hist. Paris 4: 121-138.
1834 The animal kingdom arranged in conformity with its organization with supplementary additions to each order by Edward Griffith. Vol. the tenth. The class Pisces arranged by the Baron Cuvier. London, Whittaker and Co.

Cuvier, G. L. C. F. D., and A. Valenciennes
1828-1850 Histoire Naturelle des Poissons 22 vols. Strasbourg. V. Leverault.

Dadswell, Michael J.
1974 Distribution, ecology, and postglacial dispersal of certain crustaceans and fishes in eastern North America. National Museum of Canada Publications in Zoology 11, xviii + 110 pp.
1979 Biology and population characteristics of the shortnose sturgeon, *Acipenser brevirostrum* Lesueur, 1818 (Osteichthys, Acipenseridae) in the St. John estuary, New Brunswick, Canada. Can. J. Zool. 57: 2186-2210.

Dahlberg, Michael D. and James C. Conyers
1973 An ecological study of *Gobiosoma bosci* and *G. ginsburgi* (Pisces, Gobiidae) on the Georgia coast. Fish. Bull. 71 (1): 279-288.

Daiber, F. C.
1952 The food and feeding relationships of the freshwater drum *Aplodinotus grunniens* Rafinesque in western Lake Erie. Ohio J. Sci. 52(1): 35-46.
1956 A comparative analysis of the winter feeding habits of two benthic stream fishes. Copeia (3): 141-151.

Daly, Russell, Vernon A. Hacker, and Lawrence Wiegert
1962 The lake trout. Its life history, ecology and management. Wis. Conserv. Dept. Publ. 223, 14pp.

Danymann, Roy G.
1979 The karyology of eight species of fish belonging to the family Percidae. Can. J. Zool. 57: 2055-2060.

Darnell, Rezneat M. and Richard R. Meierotto
1965 Diurnal periodicity in the black bullhead, *Ictalurus melas* (Rafinesque). Trans. Am. Fish Soc. 94(1): 1-8.

Davis, Billy J. and Rudolph J. Miller
1967 Brain patterns in minnows of the genus *Hybopsis* in relation to feeding habits and habitat. Copeia (1): 1-39.

Dawson, C. E.
1982 Subfamilies Doryrhamphinae and Syngnathinae. Mem. Sears Found. Mar. Res. 1(8): 4-182.

Dean, Bashford
1896 On the larval development of *Amia calva*. Zool. Jahrbuch. 9: 639-672, pls. 9-11.

Dean, B. and F. B. Sumner
1898 Notes on the spawning habits of the brook lamprey (*Petromyzon wilderi*). Trans. N. Y. Acad. Sci. (16): 321-324.

Dean, Howard J., James R. Colquhoun and Howard A. Simonin
1977 Toxicity of methoxychlor and naled to several life stages of landlocked Atlantic salmon. N. Y. Fish Game J. 24(2): 144-153.

Dean, Howard J., Jack C. Skea, James R. Colquhoun, and Howard A. Simonin
1979 Reproduction of lake trout in Lake George. N. Y. Fish Game Jr. 26(2): 188-191.

Deason, Hilary J. and Ralph Hile
1947 Age and growth of the kiyi, *Leucichthys kiyi* Koelz in Lake Michigan. Trans. Am. Fish. Soc. 74 (1944): 88-142.

Decker, Daniel J., Ronald A. Howard, Jr. and W. Harry Everhart
1978 Identifying New York's salmon and trout. N. Y. College of Agriculture and Life Sciences Conservation Circular 16(4), 11 pp + append.

Decker,Daniel J., Ronald A. Howard, Jr. W. Harry Everhart, and John W. Kelley
n.d. Guide to the freshwater fishes of New York. . Department of Natural Resources New York State College of Agriculture and Life Sciences Miscellaneous Bulletin 108, 140 pp.

DeKay, James E.
1842 Zoology of New York or the New York fauna; part IV.

Fishes. W. and A. White and J. Visscher, Albany. xv + 415 pp. 79 pls.

1855 Catalogue of the fishes inhabiting the state of New York and described in part IV of the New York fauna. Eighth Annual Report Regents University of the State of New York on the condition of the State Cabinet of Natural History. pp. 49-69.

Delisle, Claude and W. Van Vliet
1968 First records of the sculpins *Myoxocephalus thompsonii* and *Cottus ricei* from the Ottawa Valley, Southwestern Quebec. J. Fish. Res. Board Can. 25 (12): 2733-2737.

DeMonte, David J.
1982 Use of *Lepomis macrochirus* Rafinesque nests by spawning *Notemigonus crysoleucas* (Mitchill) (Pisces: Centrarchidae and Cyprinidae). Brimleyana 8: 61-63.

Dence, W. A.
1925 Bitter carp (*Rhodeus amarus*) from New York State waters. Copeia 142: 33.

1928 A preliminary report on the trout streams of southwestern Cattaraugus Co. New York. Roos. Wildl. Bull. 5(1): 145-210.

1933 Notes on a large bowfin (*Amia calva*) living in a mudpuddle. Copeia (1): 35.

1948 Life history, ecology and habits of the dwarf sucker, *Catostomus commersoni utawana* Mather, at the Huntington Wildlife Station. Roos. Wildl. Bull. 8(4): 81-150.

1952 Establishment of the white perch *Morone americana* in central New York. Copeia (3): 200-201.

1956 Concretions of the alewife, *Pomolobus pseudoharengus* (Wilson) at Onondaga Lake, New York. Copeia (3): 155-158.

Dendy, Jack S.
1946 Food of several species of fish, Norris Reservoir, Tennessee. J. Tenn. Acad. Sci. 21(1): 105-127.

Denoncourt, Robert F.
1969 A systematic study of the gilt darter (*Percina evides*). Ph.D. Thesis, Cornell University. 209 pp.

Denoncourt, Robert F. and Edwin L. Cooper
1975 A review of the literature and checklist of the fishes of the Susquehanna River drainage above Conowingo Dam. Proc. Pa. Acad. Sci. 49(2): 121-125.

Denoncourt, Robert F., Charles H. Hocutt and Jay R. Stauffer, Jr.
1975a Additions to the Pennsylvania ichthyofauna of the Susquehanna River drainage. Proc. Acad. Nat. Sci. Phila. 127(9): 67-69.

1975b Extensions of the known ranges of *Ericymba buccata* Cope and *Etheostoma zonale* (Cope) in the Susquehanna River Drainage. Proc. Pa. Acad. Sci. 49: 45-46.

Denoncourt, Robert F., W. A. Potter, and Jay R. Stauffer, Jr.
1977 Records of the greenside darter, *Etheostoma blennioides* from the Susquehanna River drainage in Pennsylvania. Ohio J. Sci. 77(1): 38-42.

Denoncourt, Robert F., Timothy W. Robins, and Robert Hesser
1975 Recent introduction and reintroductions to the Pennsylvania fish fauna of the Susquehanna River drainage above Conowingo Dam. Proc. Pa. Acad. Sci. 49(1): 57-58.

Dew, C. Braxton
1973 Comments on the recent incidence of the gizzard shad, *Dorosoma cepedianum*, in the lower Hudson River. Proc. Third Hudson River Symposium, Hudson River Environmental Society.

1976 A contribution to the life history of the cunner, *Tautogolabrus adspersus*, in Fishers Island Sound, Connecticut. Chesapeake Sci. 17(2): 101-113.

Diana, James S.
1979 The feeding patterns and daily ration of a top carnivore, the northern pike (*Esox lucius*). Can. J. Zool. 57: 2121-2127.

Dietrich, Charles S., Jr.
1979 Fecundity of the Atlantic menhaden, *Brevoortia tyrannus*. Fish. Bull. 77(1): 308-311.

Dineen, Clarence F.
1951 A comparative study of the food habits of *Cottus bairdii* and associated species of salmonidae. Am. Midl. Nat. 46 (3): 640-645.

Dineen, Clarence F. and Paul S. Stokely
1954 Osteology of the central mudminnow, *Umbra limi*. Copeia (3): 169-179.

Dingerkus, Guido and W. Mike Howell
1976 Karyotypic analysis and evidence of tetraploidy in the North American paddlefish, *Polyodon spathula*. Science 194: 842-844.

Dinsmore, James J.
1962 Life history of the creek chub, with emphasis on growth. Proc. Iowa Acad. Sci. 69: 296-301.

Dobie, J. R., O. L. Meehan and G. N. Washburn
1956 Raising bait fishes. U. S. Fish Wildl. Serv. Circ. 35, 123 pp.

Dodson, Julian J. and William C. Leggett
1973 Behavior of adult American shad (*Alosa sapidissima*) homing to the Connecticut River from Long Island Sound. J. Fish. Res. Board Can. 30(12): 1847-1860.

1974 Role of olfaction and vision in the behavior of American shad (*Alosa sapidissima*) homing to the Connecticut River from Long Island Sound. J. Fish Res. Board Can. 31(10): 1607-1619.

Domermuth, Robert B. and Roger J. Reed
1980 Food of juvenile american shad, *Alosa sapidissima*, juvenile blueback herring, *Alosa aestivalis*, and pumpkinseed, *Lepomis gibbosus*, in the Connecticut River below Holyoke Dam, Massachusetts. Estuaries 3(1): 65-68.

Dominey, Wallace J.
1980 Female mimicry in male bluegill sunfish — a genetic polymorphism? Nature 284 (5756): 546-548.

Dorsa, Warren J. and Ronald A. Fritzsche
1979 Characters of newly hatched larvae of *Morone chrysops* (Pisces, Percichthyidae), from Yocona River, Mississippi. J. Miss. Acad. Sci. 24: 37-41.

Dovel, William L.
1978 Biology and management of Atlantic sturgeons (*Acipenser oxyrhynchus*) Mitchill, and shortnose sturgeons (*Acipenser brevirostrum*) Lesueur, of the Hudson Estuary. Wapora Inc. 181pp.

1981a Ichthyoplankton of the Lower Hudson estuary, New York. N. Y. Fish Game J. 28(1): 21-39.

1981b The endangered shortnose sturgeon of the Hudson Estuary: Its life history and vulnerability to the activities of man. Report submitted to the Federal Energy Regulatory Commission by the Oceanic Society. 139 pp.

Dovel, William L., J. A. Mihursky and A. J. McErlean
1969 Life history aspects of the hogchoker, *Trinectes maculatus*, in the Patuxent River Estuary, Maryland. Chesapeake Sci. 10(2): 104-119.

Drahos, Nick
1968 Fish with a future. The silver (coho) salmon. Conservationist 22 (5): 2-3.

Dryer, W. R. and J. Beil
1964 Life history of the lake herring in Lake Superior. Fish. Bull. 63 (3): 493-530.

Dudley, Richard G. and A. W. Eipper
1975 Survival of largemouth bass embryos at low-dissolved oxygen concentrations. Trans. Am. Fish. Soc. 104 (1): 122-128.

REFERENCES

Dumas, Richard F.
1961 Effect of light, diet, and age of spawning of brown trout upon certain characteristics of their eggs and fry. N. Y. Fish Game J. 8(1): 49-56.

Dumeril, A. H. A.
1867 Prodrome d'une monographie des esturgeons et description des espèces de l'Amérique du Nord que appartiennent au sous-genre *Antaceus*. Nouv. Arch. Mus. Hist. Nat. Paris 3: 131-188, 6 pls.
1870 Histoire Naturelle des poissons ou Ichthyologie générale. Tome second. Ganoids, Dipnes, Lophobranches. Paris Librairie Ency. de Roret. 624 pp.

Dunson, William A. and Ronald R. Martin
1973 Survival of brook trout in a bog-derived acidity gradient. Ecology 54(6): 1370-1376.

DuPaul, William D. and John D. McEachran
1973 Age and growth of the butterfish, *Peprilus triacanthus*, in the lower York River. Chesapeake Sci. 14(7): 205-207.

Durbin, Ann Gall, Scott W. Nixon, and Candace A. Oviatt
1979 Effects of spawning migration of the alewife, *Alosa pseudoharengus*, on freshwater ecosystems. Ecology 60(1): 8-17.

Dymond, J. R.
1926 The fishes of Lake Nipigon. Univ. Toronto Stud. Biol. Ser. 27, Publ. Ont. Fish. Res. Lab. 27: 1-108, pls 1-11.

Dymond, J. R., J. L. Hart, and A. L. Pritchard
1929 The fishes of the Canadian waters of Lake Ontario. Univ. Toronto Stud. Biol. Ser. 33 Publ. Ont. Fish. Res. Lab. 37: 1-35.

Eastman, Joseph T.
1977 The pharyngeal bones and teeth of catostomid fishes. Am. Midl. Nat. 97: 68-88.

Eastman, Joseph T. and James C. Underhill
1973 Intraspecific variation in the pharyngeal tooth formula of some cyprinid fishes. Copeia (1): 45-53.

Eaton, Stephen W. and Larry P. Kardos
1972 The fishes of Canandaigua Lake, 1971. Sci. Stud. 28: 23-43, figs 1-14.

Eaton, S. W. and L. J. Moffett
1971 A preliminary study of Canandaigua Lake in 1970. Sci. Stud. 27: 69-85.

Eaton, Stephen, Russell J. Nemacek, and Mark M. Kozubowski
1982 Fishes of the Allegheny River above Kinzua Dam. N. Y. Fish Game J. 29(2): 189-198.

Echelle, Anthony A. and Carl D. Riggs
1972 Aspects of the early life history of gars (*Lepisosteus*). Trans. Am. Fish. Soc. 101(1): 106-112

Eddy, Samuel
1944 Hybridization between northern pike (*Esox lucius*) and muskellunge (*Esox masquinongy*). Proc. Minn. Acad. Sci. 12: 38-43.
1957 How to know the freshwater fishes. W.C. Brown Company Dubuque, Iowa. iv + 253 pp.

Edgar, Robert K. and James G. Hoff
1976 Grazing of freshwater and estuarine benthic diatoms by adult Atlantic menhaden, *Brevoortia tyrannus*. Fish. Bull. 74: 689-693.

Edsall, Thomas A.
1967 Biology of the freshwater drum in western Lake Erie. Ohio J. Sci. 67(6): 321-340.

Edsall, Thomas A. and Donald V. Rottiers
1976 Temperature tolerance of young-of-the-year lake whitefish, *Coregonus clupeaformis*. J. Fish. Res. Board Can. 33(1): 177-180.

Edsall, Thomas A., Donald V. Rottiers, and Edward H. Brown
1970 Temperature tolerance of bloater (*Coregonus hoyi*). J. Fish. Res. Board Can. 27(11): 2047-2052.

Edsall, Thomas Henry
1882 Something about fish, fisheries, and fishermen in New York in the seventeenth century. Privately printed. Trow's printing and Bookbinding Co. New York. 22 pp.

Eigenmann, Carl H. and R. S. Eigenmann
1893 Preliminary description of new fishes from the northwest. Am. Nat. 27: 151-154.

Ellis, Richard
1975 The book of sharks. Grosset and Dunlap, New York. 320 pp.

Elrod, Joseph H., Wolf-Dieter Busch, Bernard L. Griswold, Clifford P. Schneider, and David R. Wolfert
1981 Food of white perch, rock bass, and yellow perch in eastern Lake Ontario. N. Y. Fish Game J. 28(2): 191-201.

Embody, G. C.
1910 The ecology, habits, and growth of the pike, *Esox lucius*. Ph.D. Thesis, Cornell University.

Emery, Alan R.
1973 Preliminary comparisons of day and night habits of freshwater fish in Ontario Lakes. J. Fish. Res. Board Can. 30(6): 761-774.

Emery, Lee
1981 Range extension of pink salmon, (*Oncorhynchus gorbuscha*) into the lower Great Lakes. Fisheries 6(2): 7-10.

Emery, Lee and Edward H. Brown, Jr.
1978 Fecundity of the bloater (*Coregonus hoyi*) in Lake Michigan. Trans. Am. Fish. Soc. 107(6): 785-789.

Emery, Lee and Dale C. Wallace
1974 The age and growth of the blacknose shiner, *Notropis heterolepis* Eigenmann and Eigenmann. Am. Midl. Nat. 91(1): 242-243.

Engel, Sandy
1976 Food habits and prey selection of coho salmon (*Oncorhynchus kisutch*) and cisco (*Coregonus artedii*) in relation to zooplankton dynamics in Pallette Lake, Wisconsin. Trans. Am. Fish. Soc. 105(5): 607-614.

Eschmeyer, Paul H.
1950 The life history of the walleye, *Stizostedion vitreum* (Mitchill), in Michigan. Bull. Inst. Fish. Res. Mich. Dept. Conserv. (3): 1-99.
1955 The reproduction of the lake trout in southern Lake Superior. Trans. Am. Fish. Soc. 84(1954): 47-74.

Esmond, Edward F. and Jay R. Stauffer, Jr.
1983 Taxometric comparison of the Atlantic slope and Ohio River populations of *Etheostoma caeruleum* Storer. Am. Midl. Nat. 109(2): 390-397.

Estes, R. Don, ed.
1983 Bibliography of the eastern brook trout *Salvelinus fontinalis*. Southeastern Division, American Fisheries Society, Cookeville, Tennessee. 33 pp.

Evans, H. E.
1952 The correlation of brain pattern and feeding habits in four species of cyprinid fishes. J. Comp. Neurol. 97(1): 133-142.

Evans, H. E. and E. E. Deubler
1955 Pharyngeal tooth replacement in *Semotilus atromaculatus* and *Clinostomus elongatus*, two species of cyprinid fishes. Copeia (1): 31-41.

Everhart, W. H.
1950 Fishes of Maine. Maine Department of Inland Fish and Game. 53 pp.

Evermann, Barton Warren and E. E. Goldsborough
1902 Notes on the fishes and mollusks of Lake Chautauqua, New York. Rept. U. S. Comm. Fish and Fish. 27(1901): 169-175.

Evermann, Barton Warren and William Converse Kendall
1898 Descriptions of new or little-known genera and species of fishes from the United States. Bull. U.S. Fish Comm. 17(5) (1897): 125-133, pls 6-9.
1901 Notes on the fishes of Lake Ontario. Ann. Rep. Forest Fish Game Comm. State N. Y. (1900): 479-488.
1902a Notes on the fishes of Lake Ontario. Rept. U. S. Comm. Fish and Fish. (1901): 209-216.
1902b An annotated list of the fishes known to occur in Lake Champlain and its tributary waters. Rept. U. S. Fish Comm. (1901): 217-225.
1902c An annotated list of the fishes known to occur in the St. Lawrence River. Rept. U.S. Comm. Fish and Fish. (1901): 227-240.

Evermann, Barton Warren and Hugh M. Smith
1896 The whitefishes of North America. Rept. U.S. Fish Comm. 20(1894): 283-324, pls. 12-28.

Facey, Douglas E. and George W. Labar
1981 Biology of American eels in Lake Champlain, Vermont. Trans. Am. Fish. Soc. 110(3): 396-402.

Farmer, G. J. and F. W. H. Beamish
1973 Sea lamprey (*Petromyzon marinus*) predation on freshwater teleosts. J. Fish. Res. Board Can. 30(5): 601-605.

Fahy, William E.
1954 The life history of the northern greenside darter, *Etheostoma blennioides blennioides* Rafinesque. J. Elisha Mitchell Sci. Soc. 70(2): 139-205.

Fava, James A., Jr. and Chu-Fa Tsai
1974 The life history of the pearl dace, *Semotilus margarita*, in Maryland. Chesapeake Sci. 15(3): 159-162.

Fee, Everett
1965 Life history of the northern common shiner, *Notropis cornutus frontalis*, in Boone County, Iowa. Proc. Iowa Acad. Sci. 72: 272-281.

Felley, James
1980 Analysis of morphology and asymmetry in bluegill sunfish (*Lepomis macrochirus*) in the southeastern United States. Copeia (1): 18-29.

Ferguson, Moira M. and David L. G. Noakes
1981 Social groupings and genetic variation in common shiners, Notropis cornutus (Pisces, Cyprinidae). Environ. Biol. Fish. 6 (3/4): 357-360.

Ferraro, Steven P.
1980 Embryonic development of Atlantic menhaden, *Brevoortia tyrannus*, and a fish embryo age estimation method. Fish. Bull. 77(4): 943-949.

Finger, T. R.
1982 Fish community habitat relations in a central New York stream. Jour. Freshwater Ecol. 1(4): 343-352

Finkelstein, Samuel L.
1969a Age and growth of the scup in the waters of eastern Long Island. N. Y. Fish Game J. 16(1): 84-110.
1969b Age at maturity of scup from New York waters. N. Y. Fish Game J. 16(2): 224-237.

Fish, Marie Poland
1927 Contribution to the embryology of the American eel (*Anguilla rostrata* LeSueur). Zoologica 8(5): 289-324.
1930 Contribution to the natural history of the burbot, *Lota maculosa* (LeSueur). Bull. Buffalo Soc. Nat. Sci. 14(3): 1-20.
1932 Contributions to the early life histories of sixty-two species of fishes from Lake Erie and its tributary waters. Bull. U. S. Bur. Fish. 10, vol. 47(1931-33): 293-398, figs.

Fisher, A. K.
1891 Notes on the occurrence of a young crab eater (*Elacate canadum*) from the lower Hudson Valley, New York. Proc. U. S. Natl. Mus. (1890) 13(811): 195.

Flemmer, David A. and William S. Woolcott
1966 Food habits and distribution of the fishes of Tuckahoe Creek, Virginia, with special emphasis on the bluegill, *Lepomis macrochirus* Rafinesque. Chesapeake Sci. 7(2): 75-89.

Fletcher, Alan M.
1957 A rare darter-spawning. The Aquarium, June, 26(6): 202-203.

Flick, William A. and Dwight A. Webster
1975 Movement, growth, and survival in a stream population of wild brook trout (*Salvelinus fontinalis*) during a period of removal of non-trout species. J. Fish. Res. Board Can. 32(8): 1359-1367.
1976 Production of wild, domestic, and interstrain hybrids of brook trout (*Salvelinus fontinalis*) in natural ponds. J. Fish. Res. Board Can. 33(7): 1525-1539.

Flickinger, Stephen A.
1969 Determination of sexes in the fathead minnow. Trans. Am. Fish. Soc. 98 (3): 526-527.

Flittner, Glenn A.
1964 Morphometry and life history of the emerald shiner, *Notropis atherinoides* Rafinesque. Ph.D. Thesis, University of Michigan.

Foerster, R. E.
1968 The sockeye salmon, *Oncorhynchus nerka*. Bull. Fish. Res. Board Can. 162, xv + 422 pp.

Foltz, Jeffrey W. and Carroll R. Norden
1977 Food habits and feeding chronology of rainbow smelt, *Osmerus mordax*, in Lake Michigan. Fish. Bull. 75(3): 637-640.

Forbes, S. A.
1885 Description of new Illinois fishes. Bull. Ill. State Lab. Nat. Hist. 2: 135-139.

Forbes, S. A. and R. E. Richardson
1920 The fishes of Illinois. State of Illinois, Natural History Survey Division. 357 pp.

Forney, John L.
1955 Life history of the black bullhead *Ameiurus melas* (Rafinesque), of Clear Lake, Iowa. Iowa State College Journal Science 30(1): 145-162.
1957 Bait fish production in New York ponds. N. Y. Fish Game J. 4(2): 150-194.
1961 Growth, movements and survival of smallmouth bass (*Micropterus dolomieui*) in Oneida Lake, New York. N. Y. Fish Game J. 8(2): 88-105.
1967 Estimates of biomass and mortality rates in a walleye population. N. Y. Fish Game J. 14(2): 176-192.
1968 Raising baitfish and crayfish in New York ponds. New York State College of Agriculture Bulletin 986, 31 pp.
1972 Biology and management of smallmouth bass in Oneida Lake, New York. N. Y. Fish Game J. 19(2): 132-154.
1974 Interactions between yellow perch abundance, walleye predation, and survival of alternate prey in Oneida Lake, New York. Trans. Am. Fish. Soc. 103(1): 15-24.
1975 Contribution of stocked fry to walleye fry populations in New York lakes. Prog. Fish.-Cult. 37(1): 20-24.
1976 Year-class formation in the walleye (*Stizostedion vitreum vitreum*) population of Oneida Lake, New York, 1966-1973. J. Fish. Res. Board Can. 33(4): 783-792.
1977a Evidence of inter- and intraspecific competition as factors regulating walleye (*Stizostedion vitreum vitreum*) biomass in Oneida Lake, New York. J. Fish. Res. Board Can. 34: 1812-1820.
1977b Reconstruction of yellow perch (*Perca flavescens*) cohorts from examination of walleye (*Stizostedion vitreum vitreum*) stomachs. J. Fish. Res. Board Can. 34(7): 925-932.

Forney, John L. and C. B. Taylor
1963 Age and growth of the white bass in Oneida Lake, New York. N. Y. Fish Game J. 10(2): 194-200.

Forster, J. R.
1773 An account of some curious fishes, sent fron Hudson's Bay. By Mr. John R. Forster F.R.S. in a letter to Thomas Pennant, Esq., F.R.S.. Philos. Trans. Roy. Soc. London 63(1): 149-160.

Fowler, Henry W.
1909 A synopsis of the cyprinidae of Pennsylvania. Proc. Acad. Nat. Sci. Phila. 60: 517-553, pl. 27.
1917 Some notes on the breeding habits of local catfishes. Copeia 42: 32-36.
1945 A study of the fishes of the southern piedmont and coastal plains. Monogr. Acad. Nat. Sci. Phila. 7: vi + 1-408, figs 1-313.

Franklin, D. R. and Lloyd L. Smith Jr.
1963 Early life history of the northern pike, Esox lucius L., with special reference to the factors influencing the numerical strength of year classes. Trans. Am. Fish. Soc. 92(2): 91-110.

Fraser, J. M.
1978 The effect of competition with yellow perch on the survival and growth of planted brook trout, splake, and rainbow trout in a small Ontario Lake. Trans. Am. Fish. Soc. 107(4): 505-517.

Fried, Stephen M. and James D. McCleave
1973 Occurrence of the shortnose sturgeon (Acipenser brevirostrum), an endangered species, in Montsweag Bay, Maine. J. Fish. Res. Board Can. 30(4): 563-564.

Fritzsche, Ronald A.
1978 Fistulariidae. FAO Species Identification Sheets Fishing Area 31, West Central Atlantic. FAO Rome vol. II, 2 pp.

Fritzsche, Ronald A. and G. David Johnson
1980 Early osteological development of white perch and striped bass with emphasis on identification of their larvae. Trans. Am. Fish. Soc. 109(4): 387-406.

Fritz, E. S., W. H. Meredith, and V. A. Lotrich
1975 Fall and winter movements and activity level of the mummichog, Fundulus heteroclitus, in a tidal creek. Chesapeake Sci. 16(3): 211-215.

Fuchs, Everett H.
1967 Life history of the emerald shiner, Notropis atherinoides in Lewis and Clark Lake, South Dakota. Trans. Am. Fish. Soc. 96(3): 247-256.

Fuiman, Lee A., and Joan P. Baker
1981 Larval stages of the lake chub, Couesius plumbeus. Can. J. Zool. 59(2): 218-224.

Fuiman, Lee A. and Jules J. Loos
1977 Identifying characters of the early development of the daces Rhinichthys atratulus and R. cataractae (Osteichthys: Cyprinidae). Proc. Acad. Nat. Sci. Phila. 129 (2): 23-32.

Fuiman, Lee A., and John R. Trojnar
1980 Factors affecting egg diameter of white suckers (Catostomus commersoni). Copeia (4): 699-704.

Gabriel, W. L., W. C. Leggett, J. E. Carscadden, and B. D. Glebe
1976 Origin and characteristics of "fall-run" American shad (Alosa sapidissima) from the St. John River, New Brunswick. J. Fish. Res. Board Can. 33(8): 1764-1770.

Gage, Simon Henry
1878 Notes on the Cayuga Lake stargazer. The Cornell Review 6(2): 91-94.
1928 The lampreys of New York state--life history and economics. In: A Biological Survey of the Oswego River System. Supp. 17th Ann. Rept. N. Y. Conserv. Dept. (1927): 158-191.
1929 Lampreys and their ways. Sci. Monthly 28: 401-416.

Galat, D. L. and A. W. Eipper
1975 Presence of food organisms in the prolarval environment as a factor in the growth and mortality of larval muskellunge (Esox masquinongy). Trans. Am. Fish. Soc. 104(2): 338-341.

Gale, William F.
1983 Fecundity and spawning frequency of caged bluntnose minnows — fractional spawners. Trans. Am. Fish. Soc. 112(3): 398-402.

Gale, William F. and Gerard L. Buynak
1978 Spawning frequency and fecundity of satinfin shiner (Notropis analostanus) — a fractional, crevice spawner. Trans. Am. Fish. Soc. 107(3): 460-463.

Gale, William F. and Cynthia A. Gale
1976 Selection of artificial spawning sites by the spotfin shiner (Notropis spilopterus). J. Fish. Res. Board Can. 33(9): 1906-1913.
1977 Spawning habits of spotfin shiner (Notropis spilopterus)— a fractional, crevice spawner. Trans. Am. Fish. Soc. 106(2): 170-177.

Galligan, James P.
1960 Winter food habits of pikeperch in Oneida Lake. N. Y. Fish Game J. 7(2): 156-157.
1962 Depth distribution of lake trout and associated species in Cayuga Lake, New York. N. Y. Fish Game J. 9(1): 44-68.

Gardinier, Marcia and Thomas B. Hoff
1983 Diet of striped bass in the Hudson River estuary. N. Y. Fish Game J. 29(2)(1982): 152-165.

Garlick, Theodatus
1857 A treatise on the artificial propagation of certain kinds of fish with the description and habits of such kinds as are most suitable for pisciculture. Cleveland. 141 pp., 21 figs.

Garside, E. T. and G. C. Morrison
1977 Thermal preference of mummichog, Fundulus heteroclitus L., and banded killifish, F. diaphanus (Lesueur), (Cyprinodontidae) in relation to thermal acclimation and salinity. Can. J. Zool. 55: 1190-1194.

Gee, John H.
1972 Adaptive variation in swim-bladder length and volume in dace, genus Rhinichthys. J. Fish. Res. Board Can. 29(2): 119-127.
1980 Respiratory patterns and antipredator responses in the central mudminnow, Umbra limi, a continuous, facultative, air-breathing fish. Can. J. Zool. 58(5): 819-827.

Gee, John H. and Kazimierz Machniak
1972 Ecological notes on a lake dwelling population of longnose dace (Rhinichthys cataractae). J. Fish. Res. Board Can. 29(3): 330-332.

Gee, John H. and T. G. Northcote
1963 Comparative ecology of two sympatric species of dace (Rhinichthys) in the Fraser River System, British Columbia. J. Fish. Res. Board Can. 20(1): 105-118.

Geen, G. H., T. G. Northcote, G. F. Hartman and C. C. Lindsey
1966 Life histories of two species of catostomid fishes in Sixteenmile Lake, British Columbia, with particular reference to inlet stream spawning. J. Fish. Res. Board Can. 23(11): 1761-1788.

George, Carl J.
1981a The fishes of the Adirondack Park. New York State Dept. Env. Conserv. mimeo. 94 pp.
1981b The fishes of the Lake George watershed. pp. 257-284 in The Lake George Ecosystem, Charles W. Boylan, ed. The Lake George Association.
1983 Occurrence of the gizzard shad in the lower Mohawk Valley. N. Y. Fish Game J. 30(1): 113-114.

George, Carl J. and John H. Gordon II
1976 Observations on the rainbow smelt in Lake George, New York. N. Y. Fish Game J. 23(1): 13-19.

Gerald, Jerry W.
1966 Food habits of longnose dace, *Rhinichthys cataractae*. Copeia (3): 478-485.

Gerking, Shelby D.
1947 The use of minor postglacial connections by fishes in Indiana. Copeia (2): 89-91.

Gerlach, Jane M.
1983 Characters for distinguishing larvae of carp, *Cyprinus carpio* and goldfish, *Carassius auratus*. Copeia (1): 116-121.

Gibbons, John R. H. and John H. Gee
1972 Ecological segregation between longnose and blacknose dace (Genus *Rhinichthys*) in the Mink River, Manitoba. J. Fish. Res. Board Can. 29(9): 1245-1252.

Gibbons, W. P.
1855 Description of a new trout, *Salmo iridio*. Proc. Calif. Acad. Sci. 2: 35-36.

Gibbs, Robert H. Jr.
1957 Cyprinid fishes of the subgenus *Cyprinella* of *Notropis*. II. Distribution and variation of *Notropis spilopterus* with the description of a new subspecies. Lloydia 20(3): 186-211.
1959 A synopsis of the postlarvae of western Atlantic lizardfishes (Synodontidae). Copeia (3): 232-236.
1963 Cyprinid fishes of the subgenus *Cyprinella* of *Notropis*. The *Notropis whipplei-analostanus-chloristius* complex. Copeia (3): 511-528.

Gibson, R. John and G. Power
1975 Selection by brook trout (*Salvelinus fontinalis*) and juvenile Atlantic salmon (*Salmo salar*) of shade related to water depth. J. Fish. Res. Board Can. 32(9): 1652-1656.

Gilbert, Carter R.
1953 Age and growth of the yellow stone catfish, *Noturus flavus* (Rafinesque). M. S. Thesis, Ohio State University. 67 pp.
1961 Hybridization versus intergradation. An inquiry into the relationships of two cyprinid fishes. Copeia (2): 181-192.
1964 The American cyprinid fishes of the subgenus *Luxilus* (genus *Notropis*). Bull. Fla. State Mus. 8(2): 95-194.
1967 A revision of the hammerhead sharks (Family Sphyrnidae). Proc. U. S. Natl. Mus. 119 (3539): 1-88, 10 pls.
1971 Emended publication dates for certain fish species described by E. D. Cope with notes on the type material of *Notropis photogenis*. Copeia (3): 474-479.
1978 Type catalog of the North American cyprinid fish genus *Notropis*. Bull. Florida State Mus., Biol. Sci. 23(1): 1-104.

Gilbert, Carter R. and Reeve M. Bailey
1972 Systematics and Zoogeography of the American cyprinid fish *Notropis* (*Opsopoeodus*) *emiliae*. Occas. Pap. Mus. Zool. Univ. Mich. 664, 35 pp.

Gill, Theodore
1865 Synopsis of the pleuronectids of the eastern coast of North America. Proc. Acad. Nat. Sci. Phila. 16(1864): 214-224.

Gillen, Alan L. and Thomas Hart
1980 Feeding interrelationships between the sand shiner and the striped shiner. Ohio J. Sci. 80(2): 71-76.

Gilliams, J.
1824 Description of a new species of fish of the Linnaean genus *Perca*. Jour. Acad. Nat. Sci. Phila. n.s. 4(1): 80-82.

Gilson, Ricardo F. and Arnold Bensen
1979 Prey preference and size selected predation by the mottled sculpin (*Cottus bairdi bairdi* Girard). Proc. Pa. Acad. Sci. 53: 135-138.

Ginsburg, Isaac
1952a Flounders of the genus *Paralichthys* and related genera in American waters. Fish. Bull. 71, vol. 52, pp. 267-351.
1952b Fishes of the family Carangidae of the northern Gulf of Mexico and three related species. Publ. Inst. Mar. Sci. 2(2): 43-117.

Girard, Charles F.
1850 A monograph of the fresh water *Cottus* of North America. Proc. Am. Assoc. Adv. Sci. 2: 409-411.
1852 Contribution to the natural history of the fresh water fishes of North America I. A monograph of the cottoids. Smithson. Contrib. Know. 3(3): 80 pp., 3 pls.
1854a no title. Proc. Boston Soc. Nat. Hist. 4: 18-19.
1854b "On a new species of the genus *Salmo*" Proc. Acad. Nat. Sci. Phila. 6(1853): 380.
1854c Descriptions of some new species of fish from the state of Massachusetts. Proc. Boston Soc. Nat. Hist. 5(1854): 40-42.
1857 Researches upon the cyprinoid fishes inhabiting the fresh waters of the United States of America, west of the Mississippi Valley, from specimens in the museum of the Smithsonian Institution. Proc. Acad. Nat. Sci. Phila. 8(1856): 165-213.
1859 Ichthyology of the Boundary. U. S. and Mexico Boundary Survey. 2: 1-85.
1860 Ichthyological notices. Proc. Acad. Nat. Sci. Phila. 11(1859): 56-68, 100-104, 113-122, 157-161.

Glenn, C. L.
1978 Seasonal growth and diets of young-of-the-year mooneye (*Hiodon tergisus*) from the Assiniboine River, Manitoba. Trans. Am. Fish. Soc. 107(4): 587-589.

Gmelin, Johann Frederich
1788 Amphibia, Pisces. In: Carolia Linne Systema Naturae per regna tria naturae secondum classes, ordines, genera, species cum characteribus, differentiis synonymis locis. Tome I, Pars III. Edition decimo tertia pp. 1033-1125

Godkin, C.M., W. J. Christie, and D. E. McAllister
1982 Problems of species identity in the Lake Ontario sculpins *Cottus bairdi* and *Cottus cognatus*. Can. J. Fish. Aquat. Sci. 39(10): 1373-1382.

Goode, G. Brown
1878a The *Clupea tyrannus* of Latrobe. Proc. U. S. Natl. Mus. 1: 5-6.
1878b A revision of the American species of the genus *Brevoortia*, with a description of a new species from the Gulf of Mexico. Proc. U. S. Natl. Mus. 1: 30-42.
1880 Descriptions of seven new species from deep soundings on the southern New England coast, with diagnoses of two undescribed genera of flounders and a new genus related to *Merluccius*. Proc. U. S. Natl. Mus. 3(1880): 337-350.

Goode, George Brown and Tarleton H. Bean
1895 Oceanic Ichthyology. Smithsonian Inst. U. S. Natl. Mus. Spec. Bull. Washington. 2 vols. 553 pp. + plates.

Gorham, Stanley W. and Don E. McAllister
1974 The shortnose sturgeon, *Acipenser brevirostrum*, in the Saint John River, New Brunswick, Canada, a rare and possibly endangered species. Syllogeus no. 5, 18 pp.

Gosline, W. A.
1947 Some meristic characters in a population of the fish *Poecilichthys exilis*: their variation and correlation. Occas. Pap. Mus. Zoo. Univ. Mich. 500: 23 pp, 2 pls.

Gould, W. R. and C. J. D. Brown.
1967 The distribution of *Hybognathus* (Cyprinidae) in Montana. Proc. Mont. Acad. Sci. 26: 54-56.

Grabe, Stephen A.
1978 Food and feeding habits of juvenile Atlantic tomcod, *Microgadus tomcod*, from Haverstraw Bay, Hudson River. Fish. Bull. 76(1): 89-94.
1980 Food of age 1 and 2 Atlantic tomcod, *Microgadus tomcod*, from Haverstraw Bay, Hudson River, New York. Fish. Bull. 77(4): 1003-1006.

Graham, J.J.
1956 Observations on the alewife, *Pomolobus pseudoharengus* (Wilson), in fresh water. Univ. Toronto Stud. Biol. Ser. 62. Publ Ontario Fish. Res. Lab. 74: vii + 43 pp.

Grant, James W. A. and Patrick W. Colgan
1982 Reproductive success and mate choice in the johnny darter, *Etheostoma nigrum* (Pisces: Percidae). Can. J. Zool. 61: 437-446.

Greeley, John R.
1927 Fishes of the Genesee region with annotated list. In: A biological survey of the Genesee River system. Suppl. Sixteenth Ann. Rept. New York State Conserv. Dept. (1926): 47-66, 8 pls.
1928 Fishes of the Oswego watershed. In: A biological survey of the Oswego River system. Suppl. Seventeenth Ann. Rept. New York State Conserv. Dept. (1927): 84-107, 12 pls.
1929 Fishes of the Erie-Niagara watershed. In: A biological survey of the Erie-Niagara system. Suppl. Eighteenth Ann. Rept. New York State Conserv Dept. (1928): 150-179, 8 pls.
1930 Fishes of the Champlain watershed. In: A biological survey of the Champlain watershed. Suppl. Nineteenth Ann. Rept. New York State Conserv. Dept. (1929): 44-87, 16 pls.
1932 The spawning habits of the brook, brown, and rainbow trout and the problem of egg predators. Trans. Am. Fish. Soc. 62 (1932): 239-248.
1934 Fishes of the Raquette watershed with an annotated list. In: A biological survey of the Raquette watershed. Suppl. Twenty-third Ann. Rept. New York State Conserv. Dept. (1933): 53-108, 12 pls.
1935 Fishes of the watershed with an annotated list. In: A biological survey of the Mohawk-Hudson watershed. Suppl. Twenty-fourth Ann. Rept. New York State Conserv. Dept. (1934): 63-101, 4 pls.
1936 Fishes of the area with annotated list. In: A biological survey of the Delaware and Susquehanna watersheds. Suppl. Twenty-fifth Ann. Rept. New York State Conserv. Dept. (1935): 45-88, 4 pls.
1937 Fishes of the area with annotated list. In: A biological survey of the Lower Hudson watershed. Suppl. Twenty-sixth Ann. Rept. New York State Conserv. Dept. (1926): 45-103, 4 pls.
1938 Fishes of the area with annotated list. In: A biological survey of the Allegheny and Chemung watersheds. Suppl. Twenty-seventh Ann. Rept. New York State. Conserv. Dept. (1937): 48-73, 2 pls.
1939 The fresh-water fishes of Long Island and Staten Island with annotated list. In: A biological survey of the fresh waters of Long Island. Suppl. Twenty-eighth Ann. Rept. New York State Conserv. Dept. (1938): 29-44.
1940 Fishes of the watershed with annotated list. In: A biological survey of the Lake Ontario watershed. Suppl. Twenty-ninth Ann. Rept. New York State Conserv. Dept. (1939): 42-81, 4 pls.
1952 Cats and madtoms. Conservationist 6(6): 33 and back cover.
1954a The spread of the black bass. Conservationist 8(6): 17-18.
1954b Sunfishes are bright. Conservationist 9(1): 17, 24, and back cover.
1955a Our black basses. Conservationist 9(6): 28-29.
1955b White Bass. Conservationist 10(1): 29.
1955c Chubs. Conservationist 10(1): 32-33.
1955d Survival of planted Atlantic salmon in Lake George. N. Y. Fish Game J. 2(1): 1-12.
1956a Landlocked Atlantic salmon. Conservationist 10(6): 28-30.
1956b The lamprey in New York waters. Conservationist 11(1): 18-21.
1962 Our stake in the Great Lakes fisheries. Conservationist 16(3): 14-15.
1964 Some warm-water game fishes of New York. Conservationist 19(1): 15-19.

Greeley, John R. and Sherman C. Bishop
1932 Fishes of the watershed with annotated list. In: A biological survey of the Oswegatchie and Black River systems. Suppl. Twenty-first Ann. Rept. New York State Conserv. Dept. (1931): 54-92, 12 pls.
1933 Fishes of the Upper Hudson watershed with annotated list. In: A biological survey of the Upper Hudson watershed. Suppl. Twenty-second Ann. Rept. New York State Conserv. Dept. (1932): 64-101, 12 pls.

Greeley, John R. and Fred Everett
1952 Coarse fish of New York. Conservationist. 6(6): 24-25.

Greeley, John R. and C. Willard Greene
1931 Fishes of the area with annotated list. In: A biological survey of the St. Lawrence watershed. Suppl. Twentieth Ann. Rept. New York State Conserv. Dept. (1930): 44-94, 12 pls.

Green, Morton
1941 The cranial and appendicular osteology of *Aplodinotus grunniens* Rafinesque. Trans. Kans. Acad. Sci. 44: 400-413.

Green, John M. and Morley Farwell
1971 Winter habits of the cunner, *Tautogolabrus adspersus* (Walbaum 1792), in Newfoundland. Can. J. Zool. 49(12): 1497-1499.

Greenberg, Bernard
1947 Some relations between territory, social hierarchy, and leadership in the green sunfish (*Lepomis cyanellus*). Physiol. Zool. 20(3): 267-299.

Greenberg, Larry A.
1983 First record of the banded darter in the New York part of the Susquehanna River drainage. N. Y. Fish Game J. 29(2)(1982): 215-216.

Greene, C. Willard
1930 The smelts of Lake Champlain. Pp. 105-129 *in* A biological Survey of the Champlain Watershed. Suppl 19th Ann. Rept. N. Y. State Conserv. Dept. (1929).
1935 The distribution of Wisconsin Fishes. Wis. Conser. Comm. Madison. 235 pp.

Greenfield, David W.
1973 An evaluation of the advisability of the release of the grass carp, *Ctenopharyngodon idella*, into the natural waters of the United States. Trans. Ill. Acad. Sci. 66(1/2): 47-53.

Greenfield, David W., Fathi Abdel-Hameed, Gary Deckert, and Ronald R. Flinn
1973 Hybridization between *Chrosomus erythrogaster* and *Notropis cornutus* (Pisces: Cyprinidae). Copeia (1): 54-60.

Greenwood, P. H.
1977 Notes on the anatomy and classification of elopomorph fishes. Bull. Br. Mus. (Nat. Hist.) Zool. 32(4): 65-102.

Griswold, Bernard L.
1963 Food and growth of spottail shiners and other forage fishes of Clear Lake, Iowa. Proc. Iowa Acad. Sci. 70: 215-223.

Griswold, Bernard L. and Lloyd L. Smith, Jr.
1972 Early survival and growth of the ninespine stickleback, *Pungitius pungitius*. Trans Am. Fish. Soc. 101(2): 350-352.
1973 The life history and trophic relationships of ninespined stickleback, *Pungitius pungitius* in the Apostle Islands area of Lake Superior. Fish. Bull. 71(4): 1039-1060.

Groman, D. B.
1982 Histology of the striped bass. Am. Fish. Soc. Monogr. 3, 120 pp.

Gross, Mart R. and William A. Nowell
1980 The reproductive biology of rock bass, *Ambloplites rupestris* (Centrarchidae), in Lake Opinicon, Ontario. Copeia(3): 482-494.

Grossman, Gary D., Peter B. Moyle, and John O. Whitaker, Jr.
1982 Stochasticity in structural and functional characteristics of an Indiana stream fish assemblage: a test of community theory. Am. Nat. 120(4): 423-454.

Gruchy, C. G., R. H. Bowen, and I. M. Gruchy
1973 First records of the silver shiner, *Notropis photogenis*, from Canada. J. Fish. Res. Board Can. 30(9): 1379-1382.

Gundarson, Jeffrey
197-? Fish tails, trout and salmon. Minnesota Sea Grant Extension.

Gunning, Gerald E. and William M. Lewis
1956 Age and growth of two important bait species in a cold-water stream in southern Illinois. Am. Midl. Nat. 55(1): 118-120.

Gunning, G. E. and C. R. Shoop
1962 Restricted movements of the American eel, *Anguilla rostrata* (Lesueur), in freshwater streams with comments on growth rates. Tulane Stud. Zool. Bot. 9(5): 265-272.

Gunther, A.
1859 Catalog of the acanthopterygian fishes in the collection of the British Museum. 1, xxxi + 1-524.
1868 Catalog of the physostomi in the British Museum. vol 7. Taylor and Francis, London. xx + 512 pp.

Gutherz, Elmer J.
1967 Field guide to the flatfishes of the family Bothidae in the western North Atlantic. U. S. Fish Wildl. Circ. 263, 47 pp.

Gutherz, Elmer J. and Robbin R. Blackman
1970 Two new species of the flatfish genus *Citharichthys* (Bothidae) from the Western North Atlantic. Copeia (2): 340-348.

Haase, Ruthann and Bruce L. Haase
1975 Feeding ecology of the cutlips minnow, *Exoglossum maxillingua*, in the Delaware River at Bushkill, Pennsylvania. Proc. Pa. Acad. Sci. 49: 67-72.

Hackney, Peter A. and Thomas E. Linkous
1978 Striking behavior of the largemouth bass and use of the binomial distribution for its analysis. Trans. Am. Fish. Soc. 107(5): 682-688.

Hackney, Peter A., W. M. Tatum, and S. L. Spencer
1968 Life history study of the river redhorse, *Moxostoma carinatum* Cope, in the Cahaba River, Alabama, with notes on the management of the species as a sportfish. Proc. 21st. Ann. Conf. Southeast. Assoc. Game and Fish. Comm. pp. 324-332.

Hadley, Wayne F., and Kent Clulow
1979 First record of the fallfish from the Lake Erie drainage of New York. N. Y. Fish Game J. 26(2): 192-193.

Haldemann, S. S.
1840 Supplement to No. 1 of "A monograph of the limniades, or freshwater univalve shells of N. America." containing descriptions of apparent new animals in different classes, and the names and characters of the subgenera in *Paludina* and *Anculosa*. Philadelphia, E. G. Dorsey. 3 pp.

Hall, Gordon E and Robert M. Jenkins
1954 Notes on the age and growth of the pirate perch, *Aphredoderus sayanus*, in Oklahoma. Copeia (4): 69.

Hallam, J. C.
1959 Habitat and associated fauna of four species of fish in Ontario Streams. J. Fish. Res. Board Can. 16(2): 147-173.

Hankinson, T. L.
1919 Notes on life-histories of Illinois fish. Trans. Ill. State Acad. Sci. 12: 132-150.
1922 Nest of the cut-lips minnow *Exoglossum maxillingua* (LeSueur). Copeia 102: 1-3.
1923 The creek fish of Western New York. Copeia 115: 29-33.
1924 A preliminary report on a fish survey in Western New York. Bull. Buffalo Soc. Nat. Sci. 13(3): 57-87.
1927 A preliminary survey of the fish life of Allegany State Park in 1921. Roos. Wildl. Bull. 4(3): 483-490.
1930 Breeding behavior of the silverfin minnow *Notropis whipplei spilopterus* (Cope). Copeia (3): 73-74.
1932 Observations on the breeding behavior and habitats of fishes in southern Michigan. Pap. Mich. Acad. Sci. Arts Lett. 15 (1931): 411-425, pls. 33-34.

Hankinson, T. L. and C. L. Hubbs
1922 The establishment of smelt in the Great Lakes waters. Copeia 109: 57-59.

Hansen, David J.
1969 Food, growth, migration, reproduction and abundance of the pinfish, *Lagodon rhomboides*, and Atlantic croaker, *Micropogon undulatus*, near Pensacola, Florida, 1963-65. Fish. Bull. 68(1): 135-146.

Hansen, Donald F.
1943 On nesting of the white crappie, *Pomoxis annularis*. Copeia (4): 259-260.
1951 Biology of the white crappie in Illinois. Bull. Ill. Nat. Hist. Surv. 25: 211-265.
1965 Further observation on nesting of the white crappie, *Pomoxis annularis*. Trans. Am. Fish. Soc. 94(2): 182-184.

Harkness, W. J. K. and J. R. Dymond
1961 The lake sturgeon. The history of its fishery and problems of conservation. Ont. Dept. Lands and Forests, Fish and Wildl Br. 121 pp.

Harney, Margaret A. and Carroll R. Norden
1972 Food habits of the coho salmon, *Oncorhynchus kisutch*, in Lake Michigan. Trans. Wis. Acad. Sci., Arts, Lett. 60: 79-85.

Harrington, Robert W. Jr.
1947a The early life history of the bridled shiner, *Notropis bifrenatus* (Cope). Copeia (2): 97-102.
1947b The breeding behavior of the bridled shiner, *Notropis bifrenatus*. Copeia (3): 186-192.
1948a The life cycle and fertility of the bridled shiner, *Notropis bifrenatus* (Cope). Am. Midl. Nat. 39: 83-92.
1948b The food of the bridled shiner, *Notropis bifrenatus* (Cope). Am. Midl. Nat. 40(2): 353-361.
1955 The osteocranium of the American cyprinid fish, *Notropis bifrenatus*, with an annotated synonymy of teleost skull bones. Copeia (4): 267-290.
1956 An experiment on the effects of contrasting daily photoperiods on gametogenesis and reproduction in the centrarchid fish *Enneacanthus obesus* (Girard). J. Exp. Zool. 131(2): 203-223.

Harrington, Robert W. Jr. and Eleanor S. Harrington
1961 Food selection among fishes invading a high subtropical salt marsh: from onset of flooding through the progress of a mosquito brood. Ecology 42(4): 646-666.

Harris, Roy H. D.
1962 Growth and reproduction of the longnose sucker *Catostomus catostomus* (Forster), in Great Slave Lake. J. Fish. Res. Board Can. 19(1): 113-126.

Harrison, Edward J. and Wayne F. Hadley
1978 Ecologic separation of sympatric muskellunge and northern pike. pp. 129-134 in Special publ. 11, American Fisheries Soc., Robert L. Kendall, ed.
1983 Biology of the northern pike in the upper Niagara River watershed. N. Y. Fish Game J. 30(1): 57-66.

Hart, J. L.
1930 The spawning and early life history of the whitefish, *Coregonus clupeaformis* (Mitchill) in the Bay of Quinte, Ontario. Contrib. Can. Biol. Fish. 6(7): 165-214.
1933 Another blue perch. Copeia (1): 34.

Hartman, Wilbur L.
1959 Biology and vital statistics of rainbow trout in the Finger Lakes region, New York. N. Y. Fish Game J. 6(2): 121-178.
1973 Effects of exploitation, environmental changes, and new species on the fish habitats and resources of Lake Erie. Great Lakes Fish. Comm. Tech. Rep. 22, v +43 pp.

Harvey, K. A. and K. Warner
1970 The landlocked salmon (*Salmo salar*). Its life history and management in Maine. Sport Fishery Institute, Washington, and Maine Department Inland Fish and Game. 129pp.

Hassler, Thomas J.
1969 Biology of the northern pike in Oahe reservoir, 1959-1965. U.S. Bur. Sport Fish. Wildl. Tech. Paper 29, 13 pp.

Hatch, R. W.
1957 Success of natural spawning of rainbow trout in the Finger Lakes region of New York, N. Y. Fish Game J. 4(1): 69-87.

Hay, John
1979 The run. W. W. Norton and Co. 184 pp.

Haynes, James M. and David C. Nettles
1983 Fall movements of brown trout in Lake Ontario and a tributary. N. Y. Fish Game J. 30(1): 39-56.

Heacox, C. E.
1974 The compleat brown trout. Winchester Press, New York.

Hecht, J. H. and C. B. Dew
n.d. Ecology and population dynamics of Atlantic tomcod (*Microgadus tomcod*) in the Hudson River Estuary. Lawler, Matusky and Skelly Engineers, Tappan, New York.

Heckel, J. J.
1840 Ichthyologische Beitrage zu den Familien der Cottoiden, Scorpaenoiden, Gobioiden, und Cyprinoiden. Ann. Wien Mus. Natur. 2: 143-164.

Heidinger, Roy C.
1976 Synopsis of biological data on the largemouth bass, *Micropterus salmoides* (Lacepède) 1802. FAO Fisheries Synopsis no. 115: viii + 85 pp.

Heimburger, H. V.
1913 The factors that determine the distribution of *Boleosoma nigrum* in Douglas Lake, Cheboygan County, Michigan. Rept. Mich. Acad. Sci. 15: 120.

Heimstra, Norman W., David K. Damkot and Norman G. Benson
1969 Some effects of silt turbidity on behavior of juvenile largemouth bass and green sunfish. U. S. Bur. Sport Fish. Wildl. Tech. Paper 20: 9 pp.

Helfman, Gene S.
1979 Twilight activities of yellow perch, *Perca flavescens*. J. Fish. Res. Board Can. 36(2): 173-179.

Herman, Elmer, Warren Wisby, Lawrence Wiegert, and Milton Burdick
1959 The yellow perch. Its life history, ecology, and management. Wis. Conserv. Dept. Publ. 228, 14 pp.

Hermann, Johannes
1804 Observationis zoologicae quibus novae compluris, aliaeque animalium species discribuntur et illustrantur IV. Pisces: 290-328. (Opus posthumum edidit Fredricus Ludovivius Hammb) Argentoratiun and Paris amandus Koenig. viii + 332 pp.

Hervey, G. F. and J. Hems
1968 The goldfish. Faber and Faber, London. 271 pp.

Hickey, Clarence R., Jr.
1975 Fish behavior as revealed through stomach content analysis. N. Y. Fish Game J. 22(2): 148-155.

Hickey, Clarence R., Jr. and Richard A. Amish
1975 Stunted growth of a jawless striped bass, *Morone saxatilis*. Trans. Am. Fish. Soc. 104(2): 410-412.

Hickey, Clarence R. Jr. and Thomas E. Lester
1976 First record of a gizzard shad from Long Island, New York. N. Y. Fish Game J. 23(2): 188-189.

Hickey, Clarence R., Jr, Byron H. Young, and R. David Bishop
1977 Skeletal abnormalities in striped bass. N. Y. Fish Game J. 24(1): 69-85.

Higham, Joseph R. and William R. Nicholson
1964 Sexual maturation and spawning of Atlantic menhaden. Fish. Bull. 63(2): 255-271.

Hildebrand, Samuel F.
1917 Notes on the life history of the minnows *Gambusia affinis* and *Cyprinodon variegatus*. Rept. U. S. Comm. Fish. (1917) Append. VI: 3-15.
1943 A review of the American anchovies (Family Engraulidae). Bull. Bingham Oceanogr. Coll. 8(2): 1-165.
1948 A review of the American menhaden, genus *Brevoortia*, with a description of a new species. Smithsonian Misc. Coll. 107(18): 1-39.
1963a Family Elopidae. In: Fishes of the Western North Atlantic. Mem. Sears Found. Mar. Res. number 1, part 3: 111-147.
1963b Family Engraulidae. In: Fishes of the Western North Atlantic. Mem. Sears Found. Mar. Res. number 1, part 3: 152-249.
1963c Family Clupeidae. In: Fishes of the Western North Atlantic. Mem. Sears Found. Mar. Res. number 1, part 3: 257-454.

Hildebrand, Samuel F. and Louella E. Cable
1930 Development and life histories of fourteen teleostean fishes at Beaufort, North Carolina. Bull. U. S. Bur. Fish. 46 (1093): 383-488.
1934 Reproduction and development of whitings or kingfishes, drums, spot, croaker, and weakfishes or sea trouts, family Sciaenidae of the Atlantic coast of the United States. Bull. U. S. Bur. Fish. 48(16): 41-117.
1938 Further notes on the development and life history of some teleosts at Beaufort, North Carolina. Bull U. S. Bur. Fish. 48(24): 505-642.

Hildebrand, Samuel F. and William C. Schroeder
1928 Fishes of Chesapeake Bay. Bull. U. S. Bur. Fish. 43(1927)(1): 366 pp.

Hile, Ralph
1941 Age and growth of the rock bass, *Ambloplites rupestris* (Rafinesque), in Nebish Lake, Wisconsin. Trans. Wis. Acad. Sci. Arts Lett. 33: 189-337.

Hile, Ralph and Hilary J. Deason
1947 Distribution, abundance, and spawning season and grounds of the kiyi, *Leucichthys kiyi* Koelz, in Lake Michigan. Trans. Am. Fish. Soc. 74 (1944): 143-165.

Hinricks, Michael A. and Henry E. Booke
1975 Egg development and larval feeding of the lake herring, *Coregonus artedii* Lesueur. Repts. Fauna Flora Wis. 10. Contrib. to Ichthyol. 4: 75-86, 21 figs.

Hoff, J. G.
1976 Contribution to the biology of the seaboard goby, *Gobiosoma ginsburgi*. Copeia (2): 385-386.

Holbrook, John Edward
1855 An account of several species of fish observed in Florida, Georgia, etc. J. Acad. Nat. Sci. Phila. ser. 2, 3: 47-58, pls. V-VI.

Hollard, H. L. G. M.
1855 Monographie de la famille des balistides. Ann. Sci. Nat. (Zool.) ser. 4, 4: 5-27.

Holsapple, John G. and Lynn E. Foster
1975 Reproduction of white perch in the lower Hudson River. N. Y. Fish Game J. 22(2): 122-127.

Honey, K. A.
1963 The eggs and larval stages of the butterfish, *Poronotus triacanthus*. Copeia (2): 447-450.

Hooper, Frank F.
1949 Age analysis of a population of the ameiurid fish, *Schilbeodes mollis*. Copeia (1): 34-38.

Hoover, Earl E.
1936a The spawning activities of freshwater smelt, with spe-

cial reference to the sex ratio. Copeia (2): 85-91.
1936b Contribution to the life history of the chinook and landlocked salmon in New Hampshire. Copeia (4): 193-198.

Horning, W. B. II, and R. E. Pearson.
1973 Growth, temperature requirements and lower lethal temperatures for juvenile smallmouth bass (*Micropterus dolomieui*). J. Fish. Res. Board Can. 30(8): 1226-1230.

Hough, Franklin B.
1852 Fifth annual report of the regents of the university of the state of New York on the condition of the state cabinet of natural history and the historical and antiquarian collection annexed thereto. Albany.

Hough, Jack L.
1958 Geology of the Great Lakes. University of Illinois Press, Urbana. xviii + 313 pp.

Hourston, A. S.
1955 A study of variations in the maskinonge from three regions in Canada. Contrib. Roy. Ont. Mus. Zool. Paleontol. 40: 13pp, 16pls.

House, Robert and LaRue Wells
1973 Age, growth, spawning season and fecundity of the trout-perch (*Percopsis omiscomaycus*) in southeastern Lake Michigan. J. Fish. Res. Board Can. 30(8): 1221-1225.

Houser, Albert and Michael G. Bross
1959 Observations on growth and reproduction of the paddlefish. Trans. Am. Fish. Soc. 88(1): 50-52.

Howells, Robert G.
1981 An annotated list of the fishes of the Arthur Kill. Proc. State Island Inst. Arts Sci. 31(1): 18-21.

Howell, W. Hunting and David H. Kessler
1977 Fecundity of the southern New England stock of yellowtail flounder, *Limanda ferruginea*. Fish. Bull. 75(4): 877-880.

Hoy, P. R.
1872 Deep-water fauna of Lake Michigan. Trans. Wis. Acad. Sci., Arts, Lett. 1: 98-101.

Hoyt, Robert D.
1971a The reproductive biology of the silverjaw minnow, *Ericymba buccata* Cope, in Kentucky. Trans. Am. Fish. Soc. 100(3): 510-519.
1971b Age and growth of the silverjaw minnow *Ericymba buccata* Cope, in Kentucky. Am. Midl. Nat. 86(2): 257-275.

Hubbs, Carl L.
1921a Geographical variation of *Notemigonus crysoleucas* — an American minnow. Trans. Ill. State Acad. Sci. 11 (1918): 147-151.
1921b An ecological study of the life-history of the freshwater atherine fish *Labidesthes sicculus*. Ecology 2(4): 262-276.
1925 The life cycle and growth of lampreys. Pap. Mich. Acad. Sci., Arts, Lett. 4(1924): 587-603.
1926 A check-list of the fishes of the Great Lakes and tributary waters, with nomenclatorial notes and analytical keys. Misc. Publ. Univ. Mich. Mus. Zool. 15, 77 pp., 3 pls.
1930a Further additions and corrections to the list of the fishes of the Great Lakes and tributary waters. Pap. Mich. Acad. Sci., Arts, Lett. 11(1929): 425-436.
1930b Materials for a revision of the catostomid fishes of eastern North America. Misc. Publ. Univ. Mich. Mus. Zool. 20: 47pp.
1931 *Parexoglossum laurae*, a new cyprinid fish from the upper Kanawha River system. Occas. Pap. Mus. Zool. Univ. Mich. 234: 1-12, pls. I-II.
1936 An older name for the black-nose dace. Copeia (2): 124-125.
1942 Sexual dimorphism in the cyprinid fishes *Margariscus* and *Couesius*, and alleged hybridization between these genera. Occas. Pap. Mus. Zool. Univ. Mich. 468: 1-6.
1951 The American cyprinid fish *Notropis garmanus* Hay,

interpreted as an intergeneric hybrid. Am. Midl. Nat. 45(2): 446-454.
1955 Hybridization between fish species in nature. Syst. Zool. 4(1): 1-20.

Hubbs, Carl L. and E. Ross Allen
1943 Fishes of Silver Springs, Florida. Proc. Fla. Acad. Sci. 6(3/4): 110-130.

Hubbs, Carl L. and Reeve M. Bailey
1938 The small-mouthed bass. Cranbrook Inst. Sci. Bull. 10: 92 pp.
1940 A revision of the black basses (*Micropterus and Huro*) with descriptions of four new forms. Misc. Publ. Mus. Zool. Univ. Mich. 48: 51 pp., 6 pls. 2 maps.

Hubbs, Carl L. and John D. Black
1940 Percid fishes related to *Poecilichthys variatus*, with descriptions of new forms. Occas. Pap. Mus. Zool. Univ. Mich. 416: 1-30, 2 pls.

Hubbs, Carl L. and D. E. S. Brown
1929 Materials for a distributional study of Ontario Fish. Trans. Roy. Can. Inst. 17(1): 1-56.

Hubbs, Carl L. and Mott Dwight Cannon
1935 The darters of the genera *Hololepis* and *Villora*. Misc. Publ. Univ. Mich. Mus. Zool. 30: 1-93, 3 pls.

Hubbs, Carl L. and Gerald P. Cooper
1935 Age and growth of the long-eared and the green sunfishes in Michigan, Pap. Mich. Acad. Sci., Arts Lett. 20 (1934): 669-696, pl. 104-107.
1936 Minnows of Michigan. Cranbrook Inst. Sci. Bull. 8: 1-95.

Hubbs, Carl L. and Walter R. Crowe
1956 Preliminary analysis of the American cyprinid fishes, seven new, referred to the genus *Hybopsis*, subgenus *Erimystax*. Occas. Pap. Mus. Zool. Univ. Mich. 578: 1-8.

Hubbs, Carl L. and C. Willard Greene
1928 Further notes on the fishes of the Great Lakes and tributary waters. Pap. Mich. Acad. Sci., Arts Lett. 8(1927): 371-392.

Hubbs Carl L. and Karl F. Lagler
1964 Fishes of the Great Lakes region with a new preface. University of Michigan Press. xv +213 pp., pls 1-44. (editions of 1947, 1958, 1964. Fourth printing 1974).

Hubbs, Carl L. and Robert Rush Miller
1965 Studies on Cyprinodont fishes XXII. Variation in *Lucania parva*, its establishment in Western United States, and description of a new species from an interior basin in Coahuila, Mexico. Misc. Publ. Mus. Zool. Univ. Mich. 127: 104 pp., 3 pls.

Hubbs, Carl L. and T. E. B. Pope
1937 The spread of the sea lamprey through the Great Lakes. Trans. Am. Fish. Soc. 66(1937): 172-176.

Hubbs, Carl L. and I. C. Potter
1971 Distribution, phylogeny, and taxonomy. In: The Biology of Lampreys, M. W. Hardisty and I. C. Potter, eds. Academic Press, London and New York. pp. 1-65.

Hubbs, Carl L. and Edward C. Raney
1944 Systematic notes on North American siluroid fishes of the genus *Schilbeodes*. Occas. Papers Mus. Zool. Univ. Mich. 487: 1-36, 1 pl.
1947 *Notropis alborus*, a new cyprinid fish from North Carolina and Virginia. Occas. Papers Mus. Zool. Univ. Mich. 498: 17 pp. + 1 pl.
1948 Subspecies of *Notropis altipinnis*, a cyprinid fish of the eastern United States. Occas. Papers. Mus. Zool. Univ. Mich. 506: 1-20, 1 pl.

Hubbs, Carl L. and M. B. Trautman
1937 A revision of the lamprey genus *Ichthyomyzon*. Misc. Publ. Univ. Mich. Mus. Zool. 35: 1-109, 2 pls.

Huck, L. L. and G. E. Gunning
1967 Behavior of the longear sunfish *Lepomis megalotis* (Rafinesque). Tulane Stud. Zool. Bot. 4(3): 121-131.

Huish, Melvin T.
1954 Life history of the black crappie of Lake George, Florida. Trans. Am. Fish. Soc. 83: 176-193.

Hunter, John R.
1963 The reproductive behavior of the green sunfish, *Lepomis cyanellus*. Zoologica 48(2): 13-24.

Hunter, John R. and Arthur D. Hasler
1965 Spawning association of the redfin shiner, *Notropis umbratilis* and the green sunfish *Lepomis cyanellus*. Copeia (3): 265-281.

Hunter, J. R. and W. J. Wisby
1961 Utilization of the nests of green sunfish (*Lepomis cyanellus*) by the redfin shiner (*Notropis umbratilis cyanocephalus*). Copeia (1): 113-115.

Huntsman, Gene R.
1967 Nuptial tubercles in carpsuckers *(Carpiodes)*. Copeia (2): 457-458.

Hurley, Donald A.
1972 The American eel (*Anguilla rostrata*) in eastern Lake Ontario. J. Fish. Res. Board Can. 29(5): 535-543.

Huver, Charles W.
1973 A bibliography of the genus *Fundulus*. G. K. Hall and Co. Boston. v + 138 pp.

Hynes, H. B. N.
1950 The food of the fresh-water sticklebacks (*Gasterosteus aculeatus* and *Pygosteus pungitius*), with a review of methods used in studies of the food of fishes. J. Anim. Ecol. 19(1): 36-58.

Ingram, William Marcus and Eugene Pleasants Odum
1941 Nests and behavior of *Lepomis gibbosus* (Linnaeus) in Lincoln Pond, Rensselaerville, New York. Am. Midl. Nat. 26(1): 182-193.

International Game Fish Association
1983 World Record Game Fishes. 328 pp.

Isaak, Daniel
1961 The ecological life history of the fathead minnow, *Pimephales promelas* (Rafinesque). Ph.D. Thesis, University of Minnesota.

Jablonski, David
1974 The evolution of the Hudson Valley. New York Paleont. Soc. Notes. 4(5): 1-12.

Jacobs, D. L. 1
1948 Nesting of the brook stickleback. Proc. Minn. Acad. Sci. 16: 33-34.

Jaeger, Edmund C.
1950 A source-book of biological names and terms, second ed. Charles C. Thomas. Springfield, Illinois. xxxv + 287 pp.

Jaffa, B. B.
1917 Notes on the breeding and incubation periods of the Iowa darter, *Etheostoma iowae* Jordan and Meek. Copeia (47): 71-72.

James, M. C.
1930 Spawning reactions of small-mouthed bass. Trans. Am. Fish. Soc. 60: 62-63.

Janssen, John
1978 Will alewives (*Alosa pseudoharengus*) feed in the dark? Environ. Biol. Fish 3(2): 239-240.

Jeffries, H. Perry
1975 Diets of juvenile Atlantic menhaden (*Brevoortia tyrannus*) in three estuarine habitats as determined from fatty acid composition of gut contents. J. Fish. Res. Board Can. 32: 587-592.

Jenkins, Robert E.
1970 Systematic studies of the catostomid fish tribe Moxostomatini. Ph.D. Dissertation, Cornell University, 800 pp.
1971 Behavioral and morphological evidence of monophyly of nest building cyprinid fishes. ASB Bull. 18(2): 40.
1976 A list of undescribed freshwater fishes of continental United States and Canada, with additions to the 1970 checklist. Copeia (3): 642-644.

Jenkins, R. E. and E. A. Lachner
1971 Criteria for analysis and interpretation of the American fish genera *Nocomis* Girard and *Hybopsis* Agassiz. Smithson. Contrib. Zool. 90: 15pp.

Jenkins, Robert E. and Timothy Zorach
1970 Zoogeography and characters of the American cyprinid fish *Notropis bifrenatus*. Chesapeake Sci. 11(3): 174-182.

Jessop, B. M. and G. Power
1973 Age, growth and maturity of round whitefish (*Prosopium cylindraceum*) from the Leaf River, Ungava, Quebec. J. Fish. Res. Board Can. 30: 299-304.

Jobes, Frank W.
1949a The age, growth and distribution of the longjaw cisco, *Leucichthys alpenae* Koelz in Lake Michigan. Trans. Am. Fish. Soc. 76(1946): 215-247.
1949b The age, growth, and bathymetric distribution of the bloater, *Leucichthys hoyi* (Gill) in Lake Michigan. Pap. Mich. Acad. Sci. Arts Lett. 33 (1947): 135-172.
1952 Age, growth, and production of yellow perch in Lake Erie. Fish. Bull. 70 (52): 205-266.

Johansen, F.
1925 Natural history of the cunner. Contrib. Can. Biol. 2: 423-468.

Johnson, David W. and Dwight A. Webster
1977 Avoidance of low pH in selection of spawning sites by brook trout (*Salvelinus fontinalis*). J. Fish. Res. Board Can. 34(11): 2215-2218.

Johnson, G. H.
1951 An investigation of the mooneye (*Hiodon tergisus*). Abst. 5th Tech. Sess. Res. Council Ontario. 16.

Johnson, James H.
1980 Production and growth of subyearling coho salmon, *Oncorhynchus kisutch*, chinook salmon, *Oncorhynchus tshawytscha*, and steelhead, *Salmo gairdneri*, in Orwell Brook, tributary of the Salmon River, N. Y. Fish. Bull. 78(2): 549-554.
1981 Comparative food selection by coexisting coho salmon, chinook salmon, and rainbow trout in a tributary of Lake Ontario. N. Y. Fish Game J. 28(2): 150-161.
1982 Summer feeding ecology of the blacknose dace, *Rhinichthys atratulus*, in a tributary of Lake Ontario. Can. Field-Nat. 96(3): 282-286.
1983a Summer diet of juvenile fishes in the St. Lawrence River. N. Y. Fish Game J. 30(1): 91-99.
1983b Food of recently stocked subyearling chinook salmon in Lake Ontario. N. Y. Fish Game J. 30(1): 115-116.

Johnson, James H. and Emily Z. Johnson
1982a Observations on the eye-picking behavior of the cutlips minnow, *Exoglossum maxillingua*. Copeia (3): 711-712.
1982b Diel foraging in relation to available prey in an Adirondack mountain stream fish community. Hydrobiologia 96: 97-104.

Johnson, James H. and Neil H. Ringler
1981 Natural reproduction and juvenile ecology of Pacific salmon and rainbow trout in tributaries of the Salmon River, New York. N. Y. Fish Game J. 28(1): 49-60.

Johnson, Michael S.
1975 Biochemical systematics of the atherinid genus *Menidia*. Copeia (4): 662-691.

Johnson, Wendell L.
1945 Age and growth of the black and white crappies of Greenwood Lake. Invest. Indiana Lakes Streams 2(15): 297-324.

Jones, Philip W., F. Douglas Martin, and Jerry D. Hardy, Jr.
1978 Development of fishes of the Mid-Atlantic Bight. An atlas of egg, larval and juvenile stages. Vol. 1. Acipenseridae through Ictaluridae. U.S.D.I. Fish and Wildl. Serv. 366 pp.

Jordan, David Starr
1876 A manual of the vertebrates of the northern United States. ed I., Class V. Pisces. Chicago.
1877a On the fishes of northern Indiana. Proc. Acad. Nat. Sci. Phila. 29: 42-104.
1877b A partial synopsis of the fishes of upper Georgia with supplementary papers on fishes of Tennessee, Kentucky, and Indiana. Ann Lyc. Nat. Hist. New York. 11: 307-377.
1877c Notes on Cottidae, Etheostomatidae, Percidae, Centrarchidae, Aphredoderidae, Dorysomatidae and Cyprinidae with revisions of genera and descriptions of new or little known species. Bull. U. S. Natl. Mus. 10(A): 1-68, pl.45.
1877d Synopsis of the Siluridae of the fresh waters of North America. Bull. U.S. Natl. Mus. 10(B): 69-120.,pls.1-44.
1884 Description of four new species of *Poecilichthys* in the U. S. National Museum. Proc. U. S. Natl. Mus. 7(1884): 477-480.
1885a Note on the scientific name of the yellow perch, the striped bass, and other North American fishes. Proc. U. S. Natl. Mus. 8: 72-73.
1885b A catalogue of the fishes known to inhabit the waters of North America, north of the Tropic of Cancer, with notes on species discovered in 1883 and 1884. U. S. Fish Comm. Document 94, 185pp.
1894 Descriptions of new varieties of trout. Calif. St. Bd. Fish. Comm. 13th Biennial Rept. for 1893-1894: 142-143.
1917 Changes in names of American fishes. Copeia 49: 85-89.
1929 Manual of the vertebrate animals of the northeastern United States, inclusive of marine species. 13th ed. xxxi + 446 pp. World Book Co. New York.

Jordan, David Starr and H. E. Copeland
1877 The sand darter. Am. Nat. 11: 86-88.

Jordan, David Starr and Barton Warren Evermann
1896 The fishes of North and Middle America.... Bull. U. S. Natl. Mus. 47(1): xl + 1240 pp.
1909 Descriptions on three new species of cisco or lake herring (*Argyrosomus*), from the Great Lakes of America with a note on the species of whitefish. Proc. U. S. Natl. Mus. 36(1662): 165-172.
1911 A review of the salmonid fishes of the Great Lakes, with notes on the whitefishes of other regions. Bull. U. S. Bur. Fish. 29(1909): 1-41.

Jordan, David Starr, Barton Warren Evermann and Howard Walton Clark
1930 Check list of the fishes and fishlike vertebrates of North and Middle America north of the northern boundary of Venezuela and Colombia. Rept. U. S. Comm. Fish. (1928) pt. II: iv + 1-670.

Jordan, David Starr and C. H. Gilbert
1883 Synopsis of the fishes of North America. Bull. U. S. Natl. Mus. 16(1882), lvi + 1018 pp.

Jordan, David Starr and S. E. Meek
1885 List of fishes collected in Iowa and Missouri in August 1884, with descriptions of three new species. Proc. U. S. Natl. Mus. 8(1): 1-16.

Joswiak, Gerard R. and William S. Moore
1982 Discriminant analysis of two cyprinid fishes, *Phoxinus eos* and *Phoxinus erythrogaster* (Pisces: Cyprinidae). Am. Midl. Nat. 108(2): 398-401.

June, Fred C.
1977 Reproductive patterns in seventeen species of warm-water fishes in a Missouri River Reservoir. Env. Biol. Fish. 2(3): 285-296.

Karr, James R.
1964 Age, growth, and food habits of johnny, slenderhead, and blackside darters of Boone County, Iowa. Proc. Iowa Acad. Sci. 70: 228-236.
1965 Age, growth, fecundity and food habits of fantail darters in Boone County, Iowa. Proc. Iowa Acad. Sci. 71: 274-280.

Kaup, J. J.
1856 Catalogue of apodal fish in the collection of the British Museum. London. viii + 163, 19 pls.

Kaya, Calvin M. and Arthur D. Hasler
1972 Photoperiod and temperature effects on the gonads of green sunfish, *Lepomis cyanellus* (Rafinesque) during the quiescent, winter phase of its annual sexual cycle. Trans. Am. Fish. Soc. 101(2): 270-275.

Keast, Allen
1966 Trophic interrelationships in the fish fauna of a small stream. Great Lakes Res. Div. Univ. Mich. Publ. 15: 51-79.
1977 Diet overlaps and feeding relationships between the year classes in the yellow perch (*Perca flavescens*). Env. Biol. Fish. 2(1): 53-70.

Keast, Allen and Deirdre Webb
1966 Mouth and body form relative to feeding ecology in the fish fauna of a small lake, Lake Opinicon, Ontario. J. Fish. Res. Board Can. 23(12): 1845-1874.

Keast, Allen and Linda Welsh
1968 Daily feeding periodicities, food uptake rates, and dietary changes with hour of day in some lake fishes. J. Fish. Res. Board Can. 25(6): 1133-1144.

Keenleyside, Miles H. A.
1972 Intraspecific intrusions into nests of spawning longear sunfish (Pisces: Centrarchidae). Copeia (2): 272-278.

Keller, Walter T.
1979 Management of wild and hybrid brook trout in New York lakes, ponds, and coastal streams. New York State Dept. Env. Conserv. Bur. Fish. iv + 1-40.

Kellogg, Robert L. and James J. Gift
1983 Relationship between optimum temperatures for growth and preferred temperatures for the young of four fish species. Trans. Am. Fish. Soc. 112(3): 424-430.

Kendall, Arthur W. Jr.
1972 Description of black sea bass, *Centropristes striata* (Linnaeus), larvae and their occurrence north of Cape Lookout, North Carolina, in 1966. Fish. Bull. 70(4): 1243-1259.
1979 Morphological comparisons of North American sea bass larvae (Pisces: Serranidae). NOAA Tech. Rept. NMFS Circ. 428: iv + 1-50.

Kendall, Arthur W. Jr. and Lionel W. Walford
1979 Sources and distribution of bluefish, *Pomatomus saltatrix*, larvae and juveniles on the east coast of the United States. Fish. Bull. 77(1):213-228.

Kendall, Robert L., editor.
1978 Selected coolwater fishes of North America. American Fisheries Society Publication no. 11, xii + 437.

Kendall, William Converse
1902 Notes on the silversides of the genus *Menidia* of the east coast of the United States, with descriptions of two new subspecies. Rept. U. S. Fish Comm. (1901)27: 241-267.
1927 The smelts. Bull. U. S. Bur. Fish. 41(1926): 217-375, 25 figs.

Kendall, William C. and Wilford Albert Dence
1922 A trout survey of Allegany State Park in 1922. Roos. Wildl. Bull. 4(3): 291-482, 1 map.
1929 The fishes of the Cranberry Lake Region. Roos. Wildl. Bull. 5(2): 219-309, figs. 63-92.

Kenyon, Roger B.
1979 Changes in the fish populations of Lakes Erie and Ontario 1970-1979. Bull. Buffalo Soc. Nat. Sci. 25(4): xi + 120 pp.

Kinney, E. C.
1950 The life history of the trout-perch *Percopsis omiscomaycus* (Walbaum) in western Lake Erie. M. S. Thesis, Ohio State University. 75 pp.
1954 A life history study of the silver chub, *Hybopsis storeriana* (Kirtland), in western Lake Erie, with notes on associated species. Ph.D. Thesis, Ohio State Univ. 99 pp.

Kirtland, Jared P.
1838 Report on the zoology of Ohio. A catalog of the mammalia, birds, reptiles, fishes, testacea and crustacea in Ohio. Second Annual Report Geological Survey State of Ohio. pp. 155-200, (Fishes 168-170, 190-197).
1841a Description of four new species of fishes. J. Nat. Hist. Boston Soc. Nat. Hist. (1840-41), 3: 273-277.
1841b Descriptions of the fishes of the Ohio River and its tributaries. Boston J. Nat. Hist. 3(10): 338-352.
1844a Description of *Acipenser rubicundus, A. platyrhynchus,* and *Rutilis storerianus.* Proc. Boston Soc. Nat. Hist. 1(1841-1844): 71.
1844b Description of *Leuciscus storerianus,* sp. nov. from Ohio. Proc. Boston Soc. Nat. Hist.(1841-1844)1: 199-200.
1845 Descriptions of the fishes of the Ohio River and its tributaries. J. Nat. Hist. Boston Soc. Nat. Hist. 5(1845-1847)(2): 21-32.
1854a *Alburnus nitidus* (Silvery minnow). Ann. Sci. 2: 44-45.
1854b Revision of the species belonging to the genus *Esox* inhabiting Lake Erie and the Ohio River. Ann. Sci. including Trans. Cleveland Acad. Nat. Sci. 2(3): 78-79.

Kjelson. Martin A. and G. N. Johnson
1976 Further observations on the feeding ecology of postlarval pinfish, *Lagodon rhomboides,* and spot, *Leiostomus xanthurus.* Fish. Bull. 74(2): 423-432.

Kleinert, S. J. and D. Mraz
1966 Life history of the grass pickerel *Esox americanus vermiculatus,* in southeastern Wisconsin. Wis. Conserv. Dept. Tech. Bull. 37, 40 pp.

Knapp, L. W.
1964 Systematic studies of the rainbow darter, *Etheostoma caeruleum* (Storer) and the subgenus *Hadropterus* (Pisces, Percidae). Ph.D. Thesis, Cornell Univ.

Kneib, R. T.
1978 Habitat, diet, reproduction and growth of the spotfin killifish, *Fundulus luciae* from a North Carolina salt marsh. Copeia (1): 164-168.

Koelz, W.
1921 Description of a new cisco from the Great Lakes. Occas. Pap. Mus. Zool. Univ. Mich. (104): 1-4.
1924 Two new species of cisco from the Great Lakes. Occas. Pap. Mus. Zool. Univ. Mich. (146): 1-8.
1929 Coregonid fishes of the Great Lakes. Bull. U. S. Bur. Fish. 43(1927)(2): 297-643.
1931 The coregonid fishes of northeastern America Pap. Mich. Acad. Sci. Arts Lett. 13: 303-432.

Kofoid, Charles A.
1900 Notes on the natural history of *Polyodon.* Science n.s. 11(268): 252.

Koski, Robert T.
1974 Sinistrality and albinism among hogchokers in the Hudson River. N. Y. Fish Game J. 21(2): 186-187.
1978 Age, growth, and maturity of the hogchoker, *Trinectes maculatus,* in the Hudson River, New York. Trans. Am. Fish. Soc. 107(3): 449-453.

Koski, Robert T., Edward C. Kelley, and Brian E. Turnbaugh
1971 A record-sized shortnose sturgeon from the Hudson River. N. Y. Fish Game J. 18(1): 75.

Koster, W. J.
1936 The life history and ecology of sculpins in central New York. Ph. D. Thesis, Cornell University.
1937 The food of sculpins (Cottidae) in central New York. Trans. Am. Fish. Soc. 66(1936): 374-382.
1939 Some phases of the life history and relationships of the cyprinid *Clinostomus elongatus* (Kirtland). Copeia (4): 201-208.

Kott, Edward and Gregory Humphreys
1978 A comparison between two populations of the johnny darter, *Etheostoma nigrum nigrum* (Percidae) from Ontario, with notes on other populations. Can. J. Zool. 56(5): 1043-1051.

Kott, Edward, Robert E. Jenkins, and Gregory Humphreys
1979 Recent collections of the black redhorse, *Moxostoma duquesnei,* from Ontario. Can. Field-Nat. 93(1): 63-66.

Kott, Edward, Robert W. McCauley, and Gregory Humphreys
1980 Morphological and physiological comparisons between *Notropis cornutus* Mitchill and *N. chrysocephalus* (Rafinesque) from Grand River, Ontario. Can. J. Zool. 58(11): 2096-2102.

Kraatz, Walter C.
1923 A study of the food of the minnow *Campostoma anomalum.* Ohio J. Sci. 23(6): 265-283.
1924 The intestine of the minnow *Campostoma anomalum* (Rafinesque), with special reference to the development of its coiling. Ohio J. Sci. 24(6): 265-298.
1928 Study of the food of the blunt-nosed minnow, *Pimephales notatus.* Ohio J. Sci. 28(2): 86-98.

Krumholz, Louis A.
1948 Reproduction in the western mosquitofish, *Gambusia affinis affinis* (Baird & Girard), and its use in mosquito control. Ecol. Monogr. 18(1): 1-43.

Kuehne, Robert A.
1962 A classification of streams illustrated by fish distribution in an eastern Kentucky creek. Ecology 43(4): 608-614.

Kuehne, Robert A. and Roger W. Barbour
1983 The American darters. Univ. Press of Kentucky. Lexington. 177 pp.

Kuntz, Albert
1914a The embryology and larval development of *Bairdiella chrysura* and *Anchovia mitchilli.* Bull. U. S. Bur. Fish. 33 (1913): 1-19.
1914b Notes on the habits, morphology of the reproductive organs and embryology of the viviparous fish *Gambusia affinis.* Bull. U. S. Bur. Fish. 33(1913): 177-190, pls.16-19.

Kwain, Wen-Hwa
1975a Embryonic development, early growth, and meristic variation in rainbow trout (*Salmo gairdneri*) exposed to combinations of light intensity and temperature. J. Fish. Res. Board Can. 32(3): 397-402.
1975b Effects of temperature on development and survival of rainbow trout, *Salmo gairdneri,* in acid waters. J. Fish. Res. Board Can.. 32(4): 493-497.
1982 Spawning behavior and early life history of pink salmon (*Oncorhynchus gorbuscha*) in the Great Lakes. Can. Jour. Fish. Aquat. Sci. 39(10): 1353-1360.

Kwain, Wen-Hwa and Andrew H. Laurie
1981 Pink salmon in the Great Lakes. Fisheries 6(2): 2-6.

LaBar, George W. and Douglas E. Facey
1983 Local movements and inshore population sizes of american eels in Lake Champlain, Vermont. Trans. Am. Fish. Soc. 112(1): 111-116.

Lacepède, B. G.
1798-1803 Histoire Naturelle des Poissons. Vols 1-4, Paris.

Lachner, Ernest A.
1950 The comparative food habits of the cyprinid fishes *Nocomis biguttatus* and *Nocomis micropogon* in western New York. J. Wash. Acad. Sci. 40(7): 229-236.
1952 Studies of the biology of the cyprinid fishes of the chub genus *Nocomis* of northeastern United States. Am. Midl. Nat. 48(2): 433-466.

Lachner, Ernest A. and Robert E. Jenkins
1967 Systematics, distribution, and evolution of the chub genus *Nocomis* (Cyprinidae) in the southwestern Ohio River basin, with the description of a new species. Copeia (3): 557-580.
1971a Systematics, distribution and evolution of the chub genus *Nocomis* Girard (Pisces, Cyprinidae) of eastern United States, with descriptions of new species. Smithson. Contrib. Zool. 85: 97 pp.
1971b Systematics, distribution, and evolution of the *Nocomis biguttatus* species group (Family Cyprinidae: Pisces) with a description of a new species from the Ozark Upland. Smithson. Contrib. Zool. 91: 28 pp.

Lachner, Ernest A., Edward. F. Westlake, and Paul S. Handwerk
1950 Studies on the biology of some percid fishes from western Pennsylvania. Am. Midl. Nat. 43(1): 92-111.

Lagler, K. F. and F. V. Hubbs
1940 Food of the long-nosed gar (*Lepisosteus osseus oxyurus*) and the bowfin (*Amia calva*) in southern Michigan. Copeia (4): 239-241.

Lagler, K. F., D. B. Obrecht and G. V. Harry
1942 The food and habits of gars (*Lepisosteus* spp.) considered in relation to fish management. Invest. Indiana Lakes Streams 2: 118-135.

Lake, C. T.
1936 The life history of the fan-tailed darter *Catonotus flabellaris flabellaris* (Rafinesque). Am. Midl. Nat. 17(5): 816-830.

Lake, Tom
1982 Fall fishing. Hudson River Fisherman, Autumn, 1982, p. 3, 5.

Langlois, T. H.
1929 Breeding habits of the northern dace. Ecology 10(1): 161-163.
1935 Notes on the spawning habits of the Atlantic smelt. Copeia (3): 141-142.
1954 The western end of Lake Erie and its ecology. Edward Brothers Inc. Ann Arbor. 479 pp.

Larimore, R. Weldon
1957 Ecological life history of the warmouth (Centrarchidae). Bull. Ill. Nat. Hist. Surv. 27 (1): 83 pp.

Lark, John G. I.
1973 An early record of the sea lamprey (*Petromyzon marinus*) from Lake Ontario. J. Fish. Res. Board Can. 30(1): 131-133.

Laroche, J. L. and J. Davis
1973 Age, growth, and reproduction of the northern puffer, *Sphoeroides maculatus*. Fish. Bull. 71: 955-963.

Larsen, Alfred
1954 First record of the white perch (*Morone americana*) in Lake Erie. Copeia (2): 154.

Latta, W. C.
1963 The life history of the smallmouth *Micropterus d. dolomieui* at Waugoshance Point, Lake Michigan. Mich. Dept. Conserv. Bull. Inst. Fish. Res. 5: 1-56.

Latrobe, Benjamin Henry
1802 A drawing and description of *Clupea tyrannus* and *Oniscus praegustator*. Trans. Am. Philos. Soc. 5(1802): 77-81.

Laughlin, Dennis R. and Earl R. Werner
1980 Resource partitioning in two coexisting sunfish: pump-

kinseed (*Lepomis gibbosus*) and northern longear sunfish (*Lepomis megalotis peltastes*). Can. J. Fish. Aquat. Sci. 37(9): 1411-1420.

Lawler, G. H.
1954 Observations on the trout-perch, *Percopsis omiscomaycus* (Walbaum) at Heming Lake, Manitoba. J. Fish. Res. Board Can. 11(1): 1-4.
1963 The biology and taxonomy of the burbot, *Lota lota*, in Heming Lake, Manitoba. J. Fish. Res. Board Can. 20(2): 417-433.

Lawrie, A. H.
1970 The sea lamprey in the Great Lakes. Trans. Am. Fish. Soc 99(4): 766-775.

Layzer, James B. and Roger J. Reed
1978 Food, age and growth of the tessellated darter, *Etheostoma olmstedi*, in Massachusetts. Am. Midl. Nat. 100(2): 459-462.

Lazara, Kenneth J.
1984 The killifish master index. A checklist of ovoviviparous cyprinodontiform fishes. Third Ed. The American Killifish Association Cincinnati. 295 pp.

Leach, J. H. and S. J. Nepszy
1976 The fish community in Lake Erie. J. Fish. Res. Board Can. 33(3): 622-638.

Leach, W. James
1940 Occurrence and life history of the northern brook lamprey, *Ichthyomyzon fossor* in Indiana. Copeia (1): 21-34.

Lee, David S., Carter R. Gilbert, Charles H. Hocutt, Robert E. Jenkins, Don E. McAllister, and Jay R. Stauffer, Jr.
1980 et seq. Atlas of North American freshwater fishes. North Carolina State Mus. Nat. Hist. Raleigh. x + 854 pp.

Legendre, P.
1970 The bearing of *Phoxinus* (Cyprinidae) hybridity on the classification of its North American species. Can. J. Zool. 48(6): 1167-1177.

Legendre, Vianney
1942 Rédécouverte après un siècle et réclassification d'une espèce de catostomide. Nat. Can. 69 (10/11): 227-233.

Leggett, W. C. and R. R. Whitney
1972 Water temperature and the migrations of American shad. Fish. Bull. 70: 659-670.

Le Grande, W. H.
1981 Chromosomal evolution in North American catfish (Siluriformes, Ictaluridae) with particular emphasis on madtoms, *Noturus*. Copeia (1): 33-52.

Leim, A. H.
1924 The life history of the shad (*Alosa sapidissima* (Wilson)) with special reference to the factors limiting its abundance. Contrib. Can. Biol. n.s. 2(1): 163-284.

Leim, A. H. and W. B. Scott
1966 Fishes of the Atlantic Coast of Canada. Bull. Fish. Res. Board Can. 155, 485 pp.

Leonard, A. K.
1927 The rate of growth and the food of the horned dace (*Semotilus atromaculatus*) in Quebec, with some data on the food of the common shiner (*Notropis cornutus*) and of the brook trout (*Salvelinus fontinalis*) from the same region. Univ. Toronto Stud. Biol. Ser. 29. Publ. Ont. Fish. Res. Lab. 30: 35-44.

Lennon, Robert E.
1954 Feeding mechanisms of the sea lamprey and its effect on host fishes. Fish. Bull. 98, vol. 56: 247-293.

Lesueur, C. A.
1817a A short description of five (supposed) new species of the genus *Muraena*, discovered by Mr. Le Sueur in the year

490

REFERENCES

1816. J. Acad. Nat. Sci. Phila. 1(1): 81-83.

1817b Description of two new species of the genus *Gadus*. J. Acad. Nat. Sci. Phila. 1(1): 83-85.

1817c Description of a new species of the genus *Cyprinus*. J. Acad. Nat. Sci. Phila. n.s. 1(1): 85-86.

1817d A new genus of fishes, of the order Abdominales, proposed, under the name of *Catostomus*; and the characters of this species, with those of its species indicated. J. Acad. Nat. Sci. Phila. 1(1/2): 88-96, 102-111.

1817e Descriptions of four new species, and two varieties, of the genus *Hydrargira*. J. Acad. Nat. Sci. Phila. n.s. 1, pt.1. no. 6: 126-134.

1818a Description of several species of chondropterygious fishes of North America, with their varieties. Trans. Am. Philos. Soc. n.s. 1:383-394.

1818b Description of several new species of North American fishes. J. Acad. Nat. Sci. Phila. 1(2): 222-235, 359-368.

1818c Description of several new species of the genus *Esox*, of North America. J. Acad. Nat. Sci. Phila. 1(2): 413-417.

1819 Notice de quelques poissons découvert dans les lac du Haut Canada, durant l'été de 1816. Mem. Mus. Hist Nat. 5: 148-161.

1821 Observations on several genera and species of fish belonging to the natural family of the Esoces. J. Acad. Nat. Sci. Phila. 1821 2(1): 124-138.

1822a Descriptions of five new species of the genus *Cichla* of Cuvier. J. Acad. Nat. Sci. Phila. 2(2): 214-221, 1 fig.

1822b Description of three new species of the genus *Sciaena*. J. Acad. Nat. Sci. Phila.. 2: 251-256.

1827 American ichthyology or, natural history of the fishes of North America; with coloured figures from drawings executed from nature. Indiana: New Harmony. Unnumbered.

Levesque, Raymond C. and Roger J. Reed
1972 Food availability and consumption by young Connecticut River shad *Alosa sapidissima*. J. Fish. Res. Board Can. 29(10): 1495-1499.

Lewis, David B., M. Walker, and H. J. G. Dartsall
1972 Some effects of low oxygen tensions on the distribution of the three-spined *Gasterosteus aculeatus* L. and nine-spined stickleback *Pungitius pungitius* (L.). J. Fish. Biol. 4(1): 103-108.

Lewis, Gerald E.
1976 Summer food of channel catfish in a West Virginia flood control reservoir. Prog. Fish.-Cult. 38(4): 177-178.

Lewis, Michael
1977 New sexual dimorphism and biological characteristics for *Pimephales promelas* (Cyprinidae) Maricopa County, Arizona. J. Ariz. Acad. Sci. 12(2): 79-80.

Lewis William M. and Stephen Flickinger
1967 Home range tendency of the largemouth bass (*Micropterus salmoides*). Ecology 48(6): 1020-1023.

Li, S. K. and D. H. Owings
1978 Sexual selection in the three-spined stickleback. II. Nest raiding during the courtship phase. Behaviour 64: 298-304.

Li, Sifa and G. G. Ayles
1981 An investigation of feeding habits of walleye (*Stizostedion v. vitreum*) fingerlings in constructed earthen ponds in the Canadian prairies. Can. Tech. Rep. Fish. Aquat. Sci. 1040: iv + 10 pp.

Liegy, F., E. H. Donahue and S. W. Eaton
1955 The fishes of Olean Creek, Cattaraugus County., New York. Sci. Stud. 17: 5-25.

Lin, Yao-Sung
1983 Studies on factors controlling transition of young yellow perch (*Perca flavescens*) in Oneida Lake. Bull. Inst. Zool. Acad. Sinica (Taipei) 22(1): 13-24.

Lineaweaver, Thomas H. III and Richard H. Backus
1970 The natural history of sharks. J. B. Lippincott Co. Phila. and New York. 256 pp.

Lindsey, C. C.
1956 Distribution and taxonomy of fishes in the Mackenzie drainage of British Columbia. J. Fish. Res. Board Can. 13(6): 759-789.

1962 Observations on meristic variation in ninespine stickleback, *Pungitius pungitius*, reared at different temperatures. Can. J. Zool. 40(7): 1237-1247.

Lindsey, C. C. and C. S. Woods
1970 Biology of coregonid fishes. Univ. Manitoba Press. Winnipeg. 560 pp.

Linne, Caroli A.
1758 Systema naturae sivi regna tria naturae, systematici proposita per classes, ordines, genera et species, cum characteribus differentis, synonymis, locis, etc. Editio decima, reformata. Tome i. Regnum animale. 824 pp.

1766 Systema naturae per regna tria naturae secundum classes, ordines, genera, species cum characteribus differentii, synonymis, locis. Tome l. Editio duodecimum reformata. Holmiae Impenses dirict Laurentii Sabii.

1771 Mantissa plantarum altera generum editionis VI et Specierum editionis II. 528-529 Regni Animalis appendix. Holmiae.

Lippman, Michael and Clark Hubbs
1969 A karyological analysis of two cyprinid fishes, *Notemigonus crysoleucas* and *Notropis lutrensis*. Tex. Rept. Biol. Med. 27(2): 427-435.

Lock, J. S.
1974 Phenotypic variation in the lake whitefish, *Coregonus clupeaformis*, induced by introduction into a new environment. J. Fish. Res. Board Can. 31(1): 55-62.

Loeb, Howard A.
1962 Effect of lysergic acid diethylamide (LSD-25) on the surfacing behavior of laboratory carp. N. Y. Fish Game J. 9(2): 127-132.

1964 Submergence of brown bullheads in bottom sediments. N. Y. Fish Game J. 11(2): 119-124.

Loesch, Joseph G. and William A. Lund, Jr.
1977 A contribution to the life history of the blueback herring, *Alosa aestivalis*. Trans. Am. Fish. Soc. 106(6): 583-589.

Loos, Jules J. and W. S. Woolcott
1969 Hybridization and behavior in two species of *Percina* (Percidae). Copeia (2): 374-385.

Lord, Russell F. Jr.
1927 Notes on the use of the blackhead minnow, *Pimephales promelas promelas*, as a forage fish. Trans. Am. Fish. Soc. 92-99.

Lotrich, Victor A.
1973 Growth, production, and community composition of fishes inhabiting a first, second and third order stream of eastern Kentucky. Ecol. Monogr. 43(3): 377-397.

1975 Summer home range and movements of *Fundulus heteroclitus* (Pisces: Cyprinodontidae). Ecology 56(1): 191-198.

Ludwig, Gerald M. and Eugene L. Lange
1975 The relationship of length, age, and age-length interaction to the fecundity of the northern mottled sculpin, *Cottus b. bairdi*. Trans. Am. Fish. Soc. 104(1): 64-67.

Ludwig, Gerald M. and C. R. Norden
1969 Age, growth and reproduction of the northern mottled sculpin (*Cottus bairdi bairdi*) in Mt. Vernon Creek, Wisconsin. Milwaukee Publ. Mus. Occas. Pap. Nat. Hist. 2, 67pp.

Lund, W. A.
1961 A racial investigation of the bluefish, *Pomatomus saltatrix* (Linnaeus) of the Atlantic coast of North America. Bolet. Inst. Oceangr. (1): 3-59.

Lund, W. A. and B. C. Marcy
1975 Early development of the grubby, *Myoxocephalus aenaeus*. Biol. Bull. 149: 373-383.

Lutterbie, Gary W.
1979 Reproduction and age and growth in Wisconsin darters (Osteichthyes: Percidae). Repts. Flora Fauna Wis. 15, 44 pp.

Lux, Fred E.
1963 Identification of New England yellowtail flounder groups. Fish. Bull. 63(1): 1-10.
1973 Age and growth of the winter flounder, *Pseudopleuronectes americanus* on Georges Bank. Fish. Bull. 71: 505-512.

MacCallum, Wayne R. and Henry A. Regier
1970 Distribution of smelt, *Osmerus mordax,* and the smelt fishery in Lake Erie in the early 1960's. J. Fish. Res. Board Can. 27(10): 1823-1846.

MacClintock, Paul and Earl T. Apfel
1944 Correlation of the drifts of the Salamanca Re-entrant, New York. Bull. Geol. Soc. Am. 55: 1143-1164.

MacCrimmon, Hugh R.
1971 World distribution of rainbow trout (*Salmo gairdneri*). J. Fish. Res. Board Can. 28(5): 663-704.
1972 World distribution of rainbow trout (*Salmo gairdneri*): further observations. J. Fish. Res. Board Can. 29(12): 1788-1791.

MacCrimmon, Hugh R. and T. L. Marshall
1968 World distribution of brown trout, *Salmo trutta.* J. Fish. Res. Board Can. 25(12): 2527-2548.

MacCrimmon, Hugh R., Barra L. Gots, and Ross R. Clayton
1983 Examination of possible taxonomic differences within Lake Erie rainbow smelt, *Osmerus mordax* (Mitchill). Can. J. Zool. 61(2): 326-338.

MacCrimmon, Hugh R., T. Larry Marshall and Barra L. Gots
1970 World distribution of brown trout, *Salmo trutta*: further observations. J. Fish. Res. Board Can. 27(4): 811-818.

MacKay, H. H.
1963 Fishes of Ontario. Ontario Dept. Lands and Forests, Toronto. 300 pp.

MacLean, J. A. and John H. Gee
1971 Effects of temperature on movements of prespawning brook sticklebacks, *Culaea inconstans,* in the Roseau River, Manitoba. J. Fish. Res. Board Can. 28(6): 919-923.

MacLellan, Patricia G., E. (Buck) Newsome, and Peter A. Dill
1981 Discrimination by external features between alewife (*Alosa pseudoharengus*) and blueback herring (*A. aestivalis*). Can. J. Fish. Aquat. Sci. 38(5): 544-546.

MacWatters, Robert C.
1983 The fishes of Otsego Lake. second edition. Occas. Papers Biol. Field Station, Cooperstown, New York. 59 pp. (unpublished).

Magnan, Pierre and Gerard J. FitzGerald
1982 Resource partitioning between brook trout (*Salvelinus fontinalis* Mitchill) and creek chub (*Semotilus atromaculatus* Mitchill) in selected oligotrophic lakes of southern Quebec. Can. J. Zool. 60(7): 1612-1617.

Magnin, Étienne
1963 Notes sur la répartition, la biologie et particulièrement la croissance de l' *Acipenser brevirostris* Lesueur, 1817. Nat. Can. 90(3): 87-96.

Magnin, Étienne and Gérard Beaulieu
1966 Divers aspects de la biologie et de l'écologie de la barbue *Ictalurus punctatus* (Rafinesque) du fleuve Saint Laurent d'a-près les données du marquage. Trav. Pêcheries Que. 92(12): 277-291.

Magnuson, John J. and Lloyd L. Smith, Jr.
1963 Some phases of the life history of the trout-perch. Ecology 44(1): 83-95.

Maher, F. P. and P. A. Larkin
1955 Life history of the steelhead trout of the Chilliwack River, British Columbia. Trans. Am. Fish. Soc. 84 (1954): 27-38.

Mahon, Robin
1977 Age and fecundity of the tadpole madtom, *Noturus gyrinus* on Long Point, Lake Erie. Can. Field-Nat. 91(3): 292-294.

Mahy, Gerard J. D.
1972 Osteology of the North American species of the genus *Chrosomus* and their Eurasian relative *Phoxinus phoxinus* (Pisces, Cyprinidae). Amer. Zool. 12(4): 728-729.

Malick, Robert W. Jr.
1978 The mimic shiner, *Notropis volucellus* (Cope), in the Susquehanna River drainage of Pennsylvania. Proc. Pa. Acad. Sci. 52(12): 199-200.

Malick, Robert W. Jr., Philip C. Ritson, and Janet L. Polk
1978 First records of the silvery minnow, *Hybognathus nuchalis* Agassiz, in the Susquehanna River drainage of Pennsylvania. Proc. Acad. Nat. Sci. Phila. 129(5): 83-85.

Maloney, J. E. and F. H. Johnson
1957 Life histories and interrelationships of walleye and yellow perch, especially during their first summer, in two Minnesota lakes. Trans. Am. Fish. Soc. 85: 191-202.

Manion, Patrick J. and H. A. Purvis
1971 Giant American brook lampreys, *Lampetra lamottei,* in the upper Great Lakes. J. Fish. Res. Board Can. 28: 616-620.

Manion, Patrick J. and Bernard R. Smith
1978 Biology of larval and metamorphosing sea lampreys, *Petromyzon marinus,* of the 1960 year class in the Big Garlic River, Michigan, Part II, 1966-1972. Great Lakes Fishery Comm. Tech. Rept. 30, 35 pp.

Manion, Patrick J. and Thomas M. Stauffer
1970 Metamorphosis of the landlocked sea lamprey, *Petromyzon marinus.* J. Fish. Res. Board Can.. 27(10): 1735-1746.

Mansfield, Pamela J., David L. Jude, David T. Michaud, Dan C. Brazo, and John Gulvas
1983 Distribution and abundance of larval burbot and deepwater sculpin in Lake Michigan. Trans. Am. Fish. Soc. 112 (2a): 162-172.

Mansueti, Alice Jane
1963 Some changes in morphology during ontogeny in the pirate perch, *Aphredoderus s. sayanus.* Copeia (3): 546-557.
1964 Early development of the yellow perch, *Perca flavescens.* Chesapeake Sci. 5(1/2):46-66.

Mansueti, Romeo J.
1961 Movements, reproduction and mortality of the white perch, *Roccus americanus,* in the Patuxent Estuary, Maryland. Chesapeake Sci. 2 (3/4): 142-205.
1962 Eggs, larvae, and young of the hickory shad, *Alosa mediocris,* with comments on its ecology in the estuary. Chesapeake Sci. 3(3): 173-205.
1964 Eggs, larvae, and young of the white perch, *Roccus americanus,* with comments on its ecology in the estuary. Chesapeake Sci. 5(1/2): 3-45.

Mansueti, Romeo J. and H. J. Elser
1953 Ecology and growth of the mud sunfish, *Acantharchus pomotis* in Maryland. Copeia (2): 117-119.

Mansueti, Romeo and Haven Kolb
1953 A historical review of the shad fisheries of North America. Publ. 97. Chesapeake Biol. Lab. vi + 293 pp.

Manzer, J. I.
1976 Distribution, food, and feeding of the threespine stickleback, *Gasterosteus aculeatus*, in Great Central Lake, Vancouver Island, with comments on competition for food with juvenile sockeye salmon, *Oncorhynchus nerka*. Fish. Bull. 74: 647-668.

Marcy, Barton C. Jr.
1969 Age determination from scales of *Alosa pseudoharengus* (Wilson) and *Alosa aestivalis* (Mitchill) in Connecticut waters. Trans. Am. Fish. Soc. 98(4): 622-630.

Marcy, D. E.
1954 The food and growth of the white crappie, *Pomoxis annularis*, in Pymatuning Lake, Pennsylvania and Ohio. Copeia (3): 236-239.

Mark, E. L.
1890 Studies on *Lepidosteus*. Bull. Mus. Comp. Zool. Harvard Univ. 19(1): 1-127, pls. 1-9.

Markle, D. F. and G. C. Grant
1970 The summer food habits of young-of-year striped bass in three Virginia Rivers. Chesapeake Sci. 11(1): 50-54.

Markle, Douglas F., David A. Methven and Linda J. Coates-Markle
1982 Aspects of spatial and temporal co-occurrence in the life history stages of the sibling hakes, *Urophycis chuss* (Walbaum, 1792) and *Urophycis tenuis* (Mitchill, 1815) (Pisces: Gadidae). Can. Jour. Zool. 60(9): 2057-2078.

Markus, H. C.
1934 Life history of the blackhead minnow (*Pimephales promelas*). Copeia (3): 116-122.

Marshall, Nelson
1939 Annulus formation in scales of the common shiner, *Notropis cornutus chrysocephalus* (Rafinesque). Copeia (3): 148-154.
1946 Observations on the comparative ecology and life history of two sea robins, *Prionotus carolinus* and *Prionotus evolans strigatus*. Copeia (3): 118-144.
1947 Studies on the life history and ecology of *Notropis chalybaeus* (Cope). Quart. J. Fla. Acad. Sci. 9(3/4) (1946): 163-188.

Martin, F. Douglas and Clark Hubbs
1973 Observations on the development of pirate perch, *Aphredoderus sayanus* (Pisces: Aphredoderidae) with comments on yolk circulation patterns as a possible taxonomic tool. Copeia (2): 377-379.

Massmann, William H.
1963 Annulus formation on the scales of weakfish, *Cynoscion regalis*, of Chesapeake Bay. Chesapeake Sci. 4(1): 54-56.

Mast, S. O.
1915 The behavior of *Fundulus* with especial reference to overland escape from tidal pools and locomotion on land. J. Anim. Behavior. 5: 341-350.

Mather, Fred
1886 Memoranda relating to Adirondack fishes with descriptions of new species from researches made in 1882. State of New York Adirondack Survey from appendix to the twelfth report. (Zoology) 1886: 1- 56.

Mathewson, Robert F.
1959 Fresh-water fish of Staten Island. Proc. Staten Island Inst. Arts Sci. 21(2): 43-51.

Mathur, Dilip
1972 Seasonal food habits of adult white crappie, *Pomoxis annularis* Rafinesque, in Conowingo Reservoir. Am. Midl. Nat. 87(1): 236-241.

Mathur, Dilip and Timothy W. Robbins
1971 Food habits and feeding chronology of young white crappie, *Pomoxis annularis* Rafinesque, in Conowingo Reservoir. Trans. Am. Fish. Soc. 100(2): 307-311.

Maul, G. E.
1956 Monografia dos Peixes do Museu Municipal do Funchal. Ordem Discocephali. Bol. Mus. Municipal do Funchal 9(23): 5-75.

May, Bruce
1969 Observations on the biology of the variegated darter, *Etheostoma variatum* Kirtland. Ohio. J. Sci. 69: 85-92.

Mayden, Richard L. and Lawrence M. Page
1979 Systematics of *Percina roanoka* and *P. crassa*, with comparison to *P. peltata* and *P. notogramma* (Pisces: Percidae). Copeia (3): 413-426.

McAllister, Don E.
1961 The origin and status of the deepwater sculpin, *Myoxocephalus thompsonii*, a nearctic glacial relict. Bull. Natl. Mus. Canada 172, Contrib. to Zool.: 44-65.
1963 A revision of the smelt family, Osmeridae. Bull. Natl. Mus. Canada 191, Biol Ser. 71: iv + 53 pp.
1964 Distinguishing characters for the sculpins *Cottus bairdii* and *C. cognatus* in eastern Canada. J. Fish. Res. Board Can. 21(5): 1339-1342.

McAllister, Don E. and Jadwiga Aniskowicz
1976 Vertebral number in North American sculpins of the *Myoxocephalus quadricornis* complex. J. Fish. Res. Board Can. 33(12): 2792-2799.

McAllister, Don E., Pierre Jolicoeur, and Hiroshi Tsuyuki
1972 Morphological and myogen comparison of johnny and tessellated darters and their hybrids, genus *Etheostoma* near Ottawa, Canada. J. Fish. Res. Board Can. 29(8): 1173-1180.

McAllister, D. E. and C. C. Lindsey
1961 Systematics of the freshwater sculpins (*Cottus*) of British Columbia. Bull. Natl. Mus. Can. Contrib. Zool. (1959) 172: 66-89.

McCabe, B. C.
1943 An analysis of the distribution of fishes in the streams of western Massachusetts. Copeia (2): 85-89.
1958 *Esox niger* LeSueur. Tabular treatment of the life history and ecology of the chain pickerel. Nat. Acad. Sci. Comm. Handb. Biol. Data. 45 pp. mimeo.

McCann, J. A.
1959 Life history studies of the spottail shiner of Clear Lake, Iowa, with particular reference to some sampling problems. Trans. Am. Fish. Soc. 88(4): 336-343.

McCarraher, D. B.
1960 Pike hybrids (*Esox lucius* x *Esox vermiculatus*) in a sand hill lake, Nebraska. Trans. Am. Fish. Soc. 89 (1): 82-83.

McCauley, R. W. and J. S. Tait
1970 Preferred temperature of yearling lake trout *Salvelinus namaycush*. J. Fish. Res. Board Can.. 27(10): 1729-1733.

McCleave, James D., Steven M. Freed, and Andrew Towt

1977 Daily movements of shortnose sturgeon, *Acipenser brevirostrum,* in a Maine estuary. Copeia (1): 149-157.

McCoid, Michael and James A. St. Amant

1980 Notes on the establishment of the rainwater killifish, *Lucania parva,* in California. Calif. Fish Game 66(2): 124-125.

McCormick, J. Howard, and Charles F. Kleiner

1976 Growth and survival of young-of-the-year emerald shiners (*Notropis atherinoides*) at different temperatures. J. Fish. Res. Board Can. 33(4): 839-842.

McCormick, J. Howard, K. E. F. Hokanson, and B. R. Jones

1972 Effects of temperature on growth and survival of young brook trout, *Salvelinus fontinalis.* J. Fish. Res. Board Can.. 29: 1107-1112.

McCormick, J. Howard, Bernard R. Jones, and Roll F. Syrett

1971 Temperature requirements for growth and survival of larval ciscos (*Coregonus artedii*). J. Fish. Res. Board Can.. 28(6): 924-927.

McCrimmon, Hugh R.

1968 Carp in Canada. Bull. Fish. Res. Bd. Can. 165: ix + 93 pp.

McCrimmon, Hugh R. and O. E. Devitt

1954 Winter studies on the burbot, *Lota lota lacustris,* of Lake Simcoe, Ontario. Can. Fish. Cult. 16: 34-41.

McEachran, John D. and Jackson Davis

1970 Age and growth of the striped searobin. Trans. Am. Fish. Soc. 99(2): 343-352.

McKenzie, R. A.

1964 Smelt life history and fishery in the Miramichi River, New Brunswick. Bull. Fish. Res. Bd. Can. 144, 77 pp.

McKenzie, Joseph A.

1969a A descriptive analysis of the aggressive behavior of the male brook stickleback, *Culaea inconstans.* Can. J. Zool. 47(6): 1275-1279.

1969b The courtship of the male stickleback, *Culaea inconstans.* Can. J. Zool. 47(6): 1281-1286.

McKenzie, Joseph A. and M. H. Keenleyside

1970 Reproductive behavior of ninespine stickleback in south bay, Manitoulin Island, Ontario. Can. J. Zool. 48: 55-61.

McNamara, Fred

1937 Breeding and food habits of the pikes (*Esox lucius* and *Esox vermiculatus*). Trans. Am. Fish. Soc. 66 (1936): 372-373.

McPhail, J. D.

1963 Geographic variation in North American ninespine sticklebacks, *Pungitius pungitius.* J. Fish. Res. Board Can. 20(1); 27-44.

McPhail, J. D. and C. C. Lindsey

1970 Freshwater fishes of northwestern Canada and Alaska. Bull. Fish. Res. Bd. Can. 173: 381 pp.

Mearns, Edgar A.

1898 A study of the vertebrate fauna of the Hudson Highlands, with observations on the Mollusca, Crustacea, Lepidoptera, and the flora of the region. Bull. Am. Mus. Nat. Hist. 10(16): 303-352.

Medeiros, W. H.

1974 The Hudson River shad fishery: background, management, problems, and recommendations. N. Y. Sea Grant NYSSGP-RS-75-011: 53pp.

Meek, Seth E.

1889 Notes on fishes of Cayuga Lake basin. Ann. New York Acad. Sci. 4: 297-316.

Mehrle, Paul M. and Foster L. Mayer, Jr.

1975 Toxaphene effects on growth and bone composition of fathead minnows, *Pimephales promelas.* J. Fish. Res. Board Can. 32: 593-598.

Melisky, Edward L., J. R. Stauffer, Jr. and Charles H. Hocutt

1980 Temperature preference of banded killifish, *Fundulus diaphanus,* from southwestern Pennsylvania. Copeia (2): 346-349.

Mendelson, Jon

1975 Feeding relationships among species of *Notropis* (Pisces: Cyprinidae) in a Wisconsin Stream. Ecol. Monogr. 45(3): 199-230.

Menz, Fredric C. and Donald P. Wilton

1983 An economic study of the muskellunge fishery in New York. N. Y. Fish Game J. 30(1): 12-29.

Menzel, Bruce W.

1976 Biochemical systematics and evolutionary genetics of the common shiner species group. Biochem. Syst. Ecol. 4: 281-293.

1978 Three hybrid combinations of minnows (Cyprinidae) involving members of the common shiner species complex (genus *Notropis,* subgenus *Luxilus*). Am. Midl. Nat. 99(1): 249-256.

Menzel, Bruce W. and David M. Green, Jr.

1972 A color mutant of the chain pickerel, *Esox niger* LeSueur. Trans. Am. Fish. Soc. 101(2): 370-372.

Menzel, Bruce W. and Edward C. Raney

1973 Hybrid madtom catfish, *Noturus gyrinus* x *Noturus miurus* from Cayuga Lake, New York. Am. Midl. Nat. 90(1): 165-176.

Menzel, R. Winston

1945 The catfish fishery of Virginia. Trans. Am. Fish. Soc. 73: 374-372.

Meredith, William H. and Victor A. Lotrich

1979 Production dynamics of a tidal creek population of *Fundulus heteroclitus.* Estuarine and Coastal Marine Science 8: 99-118.

Merriman, Daniel

1937 Notes on the life history of the striped bass (*Roccus lineatus*). Copeia (1): 15-36.

1941 Studies on the striped bass (*Roccus saxatilis*) of the Atlantic coast. Fish. Bull. 35, vol. 50: 1-77.

Merriner, John V.

1975 Food habits of the weakfish, *Cynoscion regalis,* in North Carolina waters. Chesapeake Sci. 16(1): 74-76.

1976 Aspects of the reproductive biology of the weakfish, *Cynoscion regalis* (Sciaenidae), in North Carolina. Fish. Bull. 74(1): 18-26.

Merriner, John V. and Joanne L. Laroche

1977 Fecundity of the northern puffer, *Sphoeroides maculatus,* from Chesapeake Bay. Chesapeake Sci. 18(1): 81-83.

Merritt, Robert B.

1972 Geographic distribution and enzymatic properties of lactate dehydrogenase allozymes in the fathead minnow, *Pimephales promelas.* Amer. Nat. 106(948): 173-184.

Metcalf, Artie L.
1966 Fishes of the Kansas River system in relation to zoogeography of the Great Plains. Bull. Univ. Kansas Mus. Nat. Hist. 17(3): 23-189.

Meyer, Thomas L., Richard A. Cooper, and Richard W. Langston
1979 Relative abundance, behavior and food habits of the American sand lance, *Ammodytes americanus* from the Gulf of Maine. Fish. Bull. 77(1): 243-253.

Meyer, William H.
1962 Life history of three species of redhorse (*Moxostoma*) in the Des Moines River, Iowa. Trans. Am. Fish. Soc. 91(4): 412-419.

Middaugh, Douglas P.
1981 Reproductive ecology and spawning periodicity of the Atlantic silverside, *Menidia menidia* (Pisces: Atherinidae). Copeia (4): 766-776.

Middaugh, Douglas P., Geoffrey I. Scott, and John M. Dean
1981 Reproductive behavior of the Atlantic silverside, *Menidia menidia* (Pisces: Atherinidae). Environ. Biol. Fish. 6(3/4): 269-276.

Mikol, Gerald F. and Wayne F. Hadley
1979 Evidence of successful reproduction of coho salmon in a New York tributary of Lake Erie. N. Y. Fish Game J. 21(1): 97-98.

Miller, David and Robert R. Marak
1959 The early larval stages of the red hake, *Urophycis chuss*. Copeia (3): 248-250.

Miller, H. C.
1962 The behavior of *Lepomis gibbosus* (Linnaeus) with notes on the behavior of other species of *Lepomis, Elassoma evergladei,* and *Enneacanthus gloriosus*. Behavior 22(1/2): 88-151.

Miller, J. G.
1962 Occurrence of ripe chain pickerel in the fall. Trans. Am. Fish. Soc. 91(3): 323.

Miller, Robert Rush
1957 Origin and dispersal of the alewife *Alosa pseudoharengus,* and the gizzard shad, *Dorosoma cepedianum,* in the Great Lakes. Trans. Am. Fish. Soc. 86(1956): 97-111.
1960 Systematics and biology of the gizzard shad *Dorosoma cepedianum* and related fishes. Fish. Bull. 60(173): iv + 371-392.
1965 Quaternary freshwater fishes of North America. Pp. 569-581 in H.E. Wright and David G. Frey, (eds.) The quaternary of the United States. Princeton Univ. Press.

Miller, Robert Victor
1968 A systematic study of the greenside darter *Etheostoma blennioides* Rafinesque (Pisces: Percidae). Copeia (1): 1-40.

Miller, Rudolph J.
1962 Reproductive behavior of the stoneroller minnow, *Campostoma anomalum pullum*. Copeia (2): 407-417.
1963 Comparative morphology of three cyprinid fishes: *Notropis cornutus, Notropis rubellus,* and the hybrid, *Notropis cornutus* x *N. rubellus*. Am. Midl. Nat. 69(1): 1-33.
1964 Behavior and ecology of some North American cyprinid fishes. Amer. Midl. Nat. 72(2): 313-357.
1968 Speciation in the common shiner: an alternate view. Copeia (3): 642-647.

Minckley, W. L.
1963 The ecology of a spring stream, Doe Run, Meade County, Kentucky. Wildl. Monogr. 11: 1-124.

Ming, A. D.
1968 Life history of the grass pickerel, *Esox americanus vermiculatus* in Oklahoma. Bull. Okla. Fish. Res. Lab. 8: 66 pp.

Mitchill, Samuel Latham
1814 Report in part of Samuel L. Mitchill, M. D., Professor of Natural History &c., on the fishes of New York. New York, Printed by D. Carlisle. 28 pp. (facsimile edited by T. Gill, 1898, Washington).
1815 The fishes of New York, described and arranged. Trans. Lit. Phil. Soc. (1814) 1: 355-492, 6 pls.
1817 "Report on the ichthyology of the Wallkill, from specimens presented to the society (Lyceum of Natural History) by Dr. B. Ackerly." Am. Month. Mag. Crit. Rev. 1: 289-290.
1818a Memoir on ichthyology. The fishes of New York, described and arranged. In a supplement to the memoir on the same subject, printed in the New York Literary and Philosophical Transactions, 1815. Am. Month. Mag. Crit. Rev. 2: 241-248, 321-328.
1818b Description of three species of fish. J. Acad. Nat. Sci. Phila. (1818) n.s. 1(2): 407-412.
1824 "Articles in Mirror" p. 297 (not seen; reference from DeKay, 1842).

Mok, Hin-Kiu
1981 The phylogenetic implications of centrarchid kidneys. Bull. Instit. Zool. Acad. Sinica (Taipei) 20(2): 59-67.

Mooradian, Stephen and William L. Shepherd
1973 Management of muskellunge in Chautauqua Lake. N. Y. Fish Game J. 20(2): 152-157.

Moore, George A.
1944 Notes on the early life history of *Notropis girardi*. Copeia (4): 209-214.
1957 Fishes Pp. 31-210 in Vertebrates of the United States by W. Frank Blair, Albert P. Blair, Pierce Brodkorb, Fred A. Cagle and George A. Moore. McGraw-Hill Book Co. New York, Toronto, London. vii + 819 pp.

Moore, George A. and William E. Burris
1956 Description of the lateral-line system of the pirate perch, *Aphredoderus sayanus*. Copeia (1): 18-20.

Moore, George A. and Jones D. Reeves
1955 *Hadropterus pantherinus,* a new percid fish from Oklahoma and Arkansas. Copeia (2): 89-92.

Moore, J. W. and F. W. H. Beamish
1973 Food of larval sea lamprey (*Petromyzon marinus*) and American brook lamprey (*Lampetra lamottei*). J. Fish. Res. Board Can.. 30(1): 7-15.

Morgan, G. D.
1954 Life history of the white crappie, *Pomoxis annularis* of Buckeye Lake, Ohio. J. Sci. Lab. Denison Univ. 43: 113-144.

Morgan, Raymond P. II and Robert D. Prince
1978 Chlorine effects on larval development of striped bass (*Morone saxatilis*), white perch (*M. americana*) and blueback herring (*Alosa aestivalis*). Trans. Am. Fish. Soc. 107(4): 636-641.

Morin, Richard P. and Kenneth W. Able
1983 Patterns of geographic variation in the egg morphology of the fundulid fish, *Fundulus heteroclitus*. Copeia (3): 726-740.

Morris, Desmond
1952 Homosexuality in the tenspine stickleback. Behavior 4: 233-261.
1958 The reproductive behavior of the ten-spined stickleback (*Pygosteus pungitius* L.). Behavior Suppl 6: 1-154.

Morris, Michael and Lawrence M. Page
1981 Variation in western logperches (Pisces: Percidae), with description of a new subspecies from the Ozarks. Copeia (1): 95-108.

Morrow, James E.
1951 Studies on the marine resources of southern New England. VIII. The biology of the longhorn sculpin, *Myoxocephalus octodecemspinosus* Mitchill, with a discussion of the southern New England "trash" fishery. Bull. Bingham. Oceanogr. Coll. Yale Univ. 13: 1-89.

Morse, Wallace W.
1980a Maturity, spawning, and fecundity of Atlantic croaker, *Micropogonias undulatus,* occurring north of Cape Hatteras, North Carolina. Fish. Bull. 78(1): 190-195.
1980b Spawning and fecundity of Atlantic mackerel, *Scomber scombrus,* in the middle Atlantic Bight. Fish. Bull. 78(1): 103-108.

Morsell, J. W. and C. R. Norden
1968 Food habits of the alewife, *Alosa pseudoharengus* (Wilson), in Lake Michigan. Proc. 11th Conf. Great Lakes Res. 96-102.

Moshenko, Robert W. and John H. Gee
1973 Diet, time, and place of spawning and environments occupied by creek chub (*Semotilus atromaculatus*) in the Mink River, Manitoba. J. Fish. Res. Board Can.. 30(3): 357- 362.

Mount, Donald I.
1959 Spawning behavior of the bluebreast darter, *Etheostoma camurum* (Cope). Copeia (3): 240-243.

Moyle, Peter B.
1973 Ecological separation among three species of minnows (Cyprinidae) in a Minnesota Lake. Trans. Am. Fish. Soc. 102(4): 794-805.
1976 Inland fishes of California. Univ. California Press, Berkeley. 405 pp.

Mraz, Donald, Stanley Kmiotek, and Ludwig Frankenberger
1961 The largemouth bass. Its life history, ecology and management. Wisc. Conserv. Dept. Publ. 232, 13 pp.

Murai, T. and J. W. Andrews
1977 Effects of salinity on the eggs and fry of the golden shiner and goldfish. Prog. Fish-Cult. 39(3): 121-122.

Murawski, Steven A. and Gordon T. Waring
1979 A population assessment of butterfish, *Peprilus triacanthus,* in the northwestern Atlantic Ocean. Trans. Am. Fish. Soc. 108(5): 427-439.

Murdy, Edward O. and J. W. Edward Wortham, Jr.
1980 Contributions to the reproductive biology of the eastern pirateperch, *Aphredoderus sayanus.* Va. J. Sci. 31 (1/2): 20-27.

Musick, J. A.
1973 A meristic and morphometric comparison of the hakes, *Urophycis chuss* and *U. tenuis* (Pisces: Gadidae). Fish. Bull. 71 (2): 479-488.
1974 Seasonal distribution of sibling hakes, *Urophycis chuss* and *U. tenuis* (Pisces: Gadidae) in New England. Fish. Bull. 2 (2): 481-495.

Muth, S. E. and D. C. Tarter
1975 Reproductive biology of the trout perch, *Percopsis omiscomaycus* (Walbaum), in Beech Fork of Twelvepole Creek, Wayne County, West Virginia. Am. Midl. Nat. 93(2): 434-439.

Myers, G. S.
1925 Introduction of the European bitterling (*Rhodeus*) in New York and of the rudd (*Scardinius*) in New Jersey. Copeia 140: 20-21.

Neel, Annette Morris
1979 Stripers, hybrids, and whites: How to identify them. Texas Parks and Wildlife 37(4): 6-7.

Nelson, Edward M.
1959 The embryology of the swim bladder in the common sucker, *Catostomus commersoni* (Lacepède). Am. Midl. Nat. 61(1): 245-252.

Nelson, Edward William
1876 A partial catalog of the fishes of Illinois. Bull. Ill. Mus. Nat. Hist. 1: 33-52.

Nelson, Gareth and M. Norma Rothman
1973 The species of gizzard shads (Dorosomatinae) with particular reference to the Indo-Pacific region. Bull. Am. Mus. Nat. Hist. 150(2): 131-206.

Nelson, Joseph S.
1968a Life history of the brook silverside, *Labidesthes sicculus,* in Crooked Lake, Indiana. Trans. Am. Fish. Soc. 97(3): 293-296.
1968b Salinity tolerance of brook stickleback, *Culaea inconstans,* freshwater ninespine stickleback, *Pungitius pungitius,* and freshwater fourspine stickleback, *Apeltes quadracus.* Can. J. Sci. 46(4): 663-667.
1969 Geographic variation in the brook stickleback, *Culaea inconstans* and notes on nomenclature and distribution. J. Fish. Res. Board Can. 26(9): 2431-2447.
1973 Occurrence of hybrids between longnose sucker (*Catostomus catostomus*) and white sucker (*C. commersoni*) in upper Kananaskis Reservoir. J. Fish. Res. Board Can. 30(4):557-560.
1976 Fishes of the world. John Wiley and Sons, New York. xiii + 416 pp.

Nelson, W. P.
1968a Embryo and larval characteristics of sauger, walleye, and their reciprocal hybrids. Trans. Am. Fish. Soc. 97(2): 147-152.
1968b Reproduction and early life history of sauger, *Stizostedion canadense,* in Lewis and Clark Lake. Trans. Am. Fish. Soc. 97(2): 159-166.

Nemecek, Russell John
1980 The comparative ecology of three species of darters in the genus *Etheostoma: Etheostoma variatum* (Kirtland), *Etheostoma caeruleum* (Storer) and *Etheostoma zonale* (Cope) in the Allegheny River drainage of western New York. Ph. D. Thesis, St. Bonaventure University. 175 pp.

Nesbit, Robert A.
1939 Weakfish (*Cynoscion regalis*). pp 97-106 In: A biological survey of the salt waters of Long Island. 1938 Part. 1. Suppl. 28th Ann. Rept. New York State Conserv. Dept.

Netboy, Anthony
1968 The Atlantic salmon, A vanishing species. Faber and Faber, London. 457 pp.

Neth, Paul C. and Thomas Jolliff
1984 Sea lamprey in New York State. Conservationist 38(4): 42-47; 38(5): 40-45.

Netsch, Lt. Norval F. and Arthur Witt, Jr.
1962 Contributions to the life history of the longnose gar (*Lepisosteus osseus*) in Missouri. Trans. Am. Fish. Soc. 91(3): 251-262.

496

New, John G.
1962 Hybridization between two cyprinids, *Chrosomus eos* and *Chrosomus neogaeus*. Copeia (1): 147-152.
1966 Reproductive behavior of the shield darter, *Percina peltata peltata*, in New York. Copeia (1): 20-28.

Newell, Arthur J.
1976 The relationships of age, growth, and food habits to the relative success of the whitefish (*Coregonus clupeaformis*) and the cisco (*C. artedii*) in Otsego Lake, New York. Occas. Pap. Biol. Field Sta. (Cooperstown, N. Y.) 2, vii + 68 pp.

Newman, H. N.
1907 Spawning behavior and sexual dimorphism in *Fundulus heteroclitus* and allied fish. Biol. Bull. 12: 314-346.

Newsome, G. E. (Buck) and J. H. Gee
1978 Preference and selection of prey by creek chub (*Semotilus atromaculatus*) inhabiting the Mink River, Manitoba. Can. J. Zool 56(12): 2486-2497.

New York State Department of Environmental Conservation
no date. Fish and Fishing in New York. 36 pp.

Nichols, John Treadwell
1913 A list of the fishes known to have occurred within fifty miles of New York City. Abstract of the Proceedings of the Linnaean Society of New York 20-23 (1907-1911): 90-106.
1920 Notes on marine fishes of New York. Copeia (88): 95-97.

Niemuth, Wallace, Warren Churchill, and Thomas Wirth
1959 The walleye. Its life history, ecology and management. Wis. Conserv. Dept. Publ. 227, 14 pp.

Noble, Richard L.
1967 Life history and ecology of the western blacknose dace, Boone County, Iowa. Proc. Iowa Acad. Sci. 72(1965): 82-293.

Norden, Carroll R.
1961 Comparative osteology of representative salmonid fishes, with particular reference to the grayling, (*Thymallus arcticus*) and its phylogeny. J. Fish. Res. Board Can. 18(5): 679-791.

Normandeau, Donald A.
1969 Life history and ecology of the round whitefish *Prosopium cylindraceum* (Pallas) of Newfound Lake, Bristol, New Hampshire. Trans. Am. Fish. Soc. 98(1): 7-13.

Norris, Thaddeus
1865 The American angler's book. ed. 2. Philadelphia. 701 pp.
1868 Remarks on a new species of *Osmerus*. Proc. Acad. Nat. Sci. Phila. (1868): 93-94.

Nursall, J. R.
1973 Some behavioral interactions of spottail shiners (*Notropis hudsonius*), yellow perch (*Perca flavescens*) and northern pike (*Esox lucius*). J. Fish. Res. Board Can. 30(8): 1161-1178.

Nyberg, Dennis Wayne
1971 Prey capture in the largemouth bass. Am. Midl. Nat. 86(1): 128-144.

O'Brien, W. John, Norman A. Slade, and Gary L. Vinyard
1976 Apparent size as the determinant of prey selection by bluegill sunfish. Ecology 57(6): 1304-1310.

Odell, T. T.
1934 The life history and ecological relationships of the alewife (*Pomolobus pseudoharengus* [Wilson]) in Senaca Lake, New York. Trans. Am. Fish. Soc. 14: 118-126.

Ogden, John C.
1970 Relative abundance, food habits and age of the American eel, *Anguilla rostrata* (LeSueur) in certain New Jersey streams. Trans. Am. Fish. Soc. 99(1): 54-59.

O'Gorman, R.
1974 Predation by rainbow smelt (*Osmerus mordax*) on young of the year alewives (*Alosa pseudoharengus*). Prog. Fish-Cult. 36: 223-224.

O'Hara, James
1968 The influence of weight and temperature on the metabolic rate of sunfish. Ecology 49(1): 159-161.

Okkelberg, Peter
1922 Notes on the life-history of the brook lamprey *Ichthyomyzon unicolor*. Occas. Pap. Univ. Mich. Mus. Zool. 125, 14pp. 4 figs.

Olla, Bori L., Allen J. Bejda, and A. Dale Martin
1974 Daily activity, movements, and seasonal occurrence in the tautog, *Tautoga onitis*. Fish. Bull. 72(1): 27-35.
1975 Activity, movements, and feeding behavior of the cunner, *Tautogolabrus adspersus*, and comparison of food habits with young tautog, *Tautoga onitis* off Long Island, New York. Fish. Bull. 73(4): 895-900.
1979 Seasonal dispersal and habitat selection of the cunner, *Tautogolabrus adspersus*, and young tautog, *Tautoga onitis*, in Fire Island Inlet, Long Island, New York. Fish. Bull. 77(1): 255-263.

Olla, Bori L. and Carol Samet
1977 Courtship and spawning behavior of the tautog, *Tautoga onitis* (Pisces: Labridae), under laboratory conditions. Fish. Bull. 75: 585-599.

Olla, Bori, A. L Studholme, A. J. Bejda, and Carol Samet
1980 Role of temperature in triggering migratory behavior of the adult tautog *Tautoga onitis* under laboratory conditions. Mar. Biol. (Berl.) 59: 23-30.

Olla, Bori L., Robert Wicklund, and Stuart Wilk
1969 Behavior of winter flounder in a natural habitat. Trans. Am. Fish. Soc. 98(4): 717-720.

Olmsted, Luke R., Sandra Krater, George E. Williams, and Robert G. Jaeger.
1979 Foraging tactics of the mimic shiner in a two-prey system. Copeia (3): 437-441.

Otto, Robert G., Max A. Kitchel and John O'Hara Rice
1976 Lethal and preferred temperatures of the alewife (*Alosa pseudoharengus*) in Lake Michigan. Trans. Am. Fish. Soc. 105(1): 96-106.

Otto, Robert G. and John O'Hara Rice
1977 Responses of a freshwater sculpin (*Cottus cognatus gracilis*) to temperature. Trans. Am. Fish. Soc. 106(1): 89-94.

Oviatt, Candace A. and Patricia M. Kremer
1973 Predation on the ctenophore, *Mnemiopsis leidyi*, by butterfish, *Peprilus triacanthus*, in Narragansett Bay, Rhode Island. Chesapeake Sci. 18(2): 236-240.

Pacheco, Anthony L.
1962 Age and growth of spot in lower Chesapeake Bay, with

notes on distribution and abundance of juveniles in the York River system. Chesapeake Sci. 3(1): 18-28.

Page, Gladys and Étienne Magnin
1978 Quelques aspects de la biologie du mene à nageoires rouge *Notropis cornutus* (Mitchill) d'un lac des Laurentides au Quebec. Nat. Can. 105(5): 301-308.

Page, Lawrence M.
1974 The subgenera of *Percina* (Percidae: Etheostomidae). Copeia (1): 66-86.
1976a The modified midventral scales of *Percina* (Osteichthyes: Percidae). J. Morphol. 148(2): 255-264.
1976b Natural darter hybrids: *Etheostoma gracile* x *Percina maculata*, *Percina caprodes* x *Percina maculata*, and *Percina phoxocephala* x *Percina maculata*. Southwest. Nat. 21(2): 161-168.
1978 Redescription, description, variation and life history notes on *Percina macrocephala* (Percidae). Copeia (4): 655-664.
1983 Handbook of darters. TFH Publications, Inc. Ltd. Neptune City N. J. 271 pp.

Page, Lawrence M., Michael E. Retzer, and Robert A. Stiles
1982 Spawning behavior in seven species of darters (Pisces: Percidae). Brimleyana 8: 135-143.

Page, Lawrence M. and G. S. Whitt
1973 Lactate dehydrogenase isozymes of darters and the inclusiveness of the genus *Percina*. Ill. Nat. Hist. Surv. Biol. Notes 2: 7pp.

Pallas, Peter Simon
1776 Reise durch verschiedene Provinzen des Russischen Reiches vol. 3.

Panek, Frank Michael
1980 Strategic plan for management of the muskellunge population and sport fishery of the St. Lawrence River. N. Y. DEC mimeo. 13 pp.
1981 The life history and ecology of the eastern mudminnow (*Umbra pygmaea*) with notes on ecological and zoogeographic relationships with the central mudminnow (*Umbra limi*). Dissert. Abst. 42(04): 1351-1352 B.

Pappantoniou, Antonius and George W. Dale
1982 Comparative food habits of two minnow species: Blacknose dace, *Rhinichthys atratulus* and longnose dace, *Rhinichthys cataractae*. J. Freshwater Ecol. 1(4): 361-364.

Parenti, Lynne R.
1981 A phylogenetic and biogeographic analysis of cyprinodontiform fishes (Teleostei, Atherinomorpha). Bull. Am. Mus. Nat. Hist. 168(4): 335-557.

Parker, N. C. and B. A. Simco
1975 Activity patterns, feeding and behavior of the pirate perch, *Aphredoderus sayanus*. Copeia (3): 572-574.

Parsons, J. W.
1973 History of salmon in the Great Lakes, 1850-1970. U. S. Fish and Wildl. Serv. Tech. Pap. 68, 80 pp.

Pasko, Donald G.
1957 Carry Falls Reservoir investigation. N. Y. Fish Game J. 4(1): 1-31.

Pearson, John C.
1941 The young of some marine fishes taken in lower Chesapeake Bay, Virginia, with special reference to the gray sea trout, *Cynoscion regalis* (Bloch). Fish. Bull. 36, vol. 50: 79-102.

Pearson, Walter H. and Stephen E. Miller
1980 Chemoreception in the food-searching and feeding behavior of the red hake, *Urophycis chuss* (Walbaum). J. Exp. Mar. Biol. 48: 139-150.

Pearson, William D., Gregory A. Thomas and Aron L. Clark
1979 Early piscivory and timing of the critical period in postlarval longnose gar at mile 571 of the Ohio River. Trans. Ky. Acad. Sci. 40(3/4): 122-128.

Peck, William D.
1804 Description of four remarkable fishes taken near the Piscataqua in New Hampshire. Mem. Am. Acad. Sci. 2(2): 46-57.

Peckham, Richard S. and Clarence F. Dineen
1957 Ecology of the central mudminnow, *Umbra limi* (Kirtland). Am. Midl. Nat. 58(1): 222-231.

Peer, D. L.
1966 Relationship between size and maturity in the spottail shiner, *Notropis hudsonius*. J. Fish. Res. Bd. Canada 23(3): 455-457.

Pennant, T.
1784 Arctic zoology. Henry Hughes, London. Vol. 1, cc + 185pp.

Perlmutter, Alfred
1953 Weakfish study on Long Island. Conservationist 7(6): 6-7.
1958 Small marine fishes of New York. Part 1. The forage fishes. Conservationist 13(2): 23-26, 36.
1963 Observations on fishes of the genus *Gasterosteus* in the waters of Long Island, New York. Copeia (1): 168-173.

Perlmutter, Alfred, William S. Miller, and John C. Poole
1956 The weakfish (*Cynoscion*) in New York waters. N. Y. Fish Game J. 3(1): 1-43.

Perlmutter, Alfred, Eugene E. Schmidt, and Eugene Leff
1967 Distribution and abundance of fish along the shores of the lower Hudson River during the summer of 1965. N.Y. Fish Game J. 14(1): 47-75.

Perry, George
1810 Arcana: or the Museum of Natural History. London, 1810-1811. 84 col. pls.

Peters, Charles E. and George W. LaBar
1980 Fecundity of an unexploited population of ciscoes in three areas of Lake Champlain. N. Y. Fish Game J. 27(1): 72-78.

Peterson, R, H., P. H. Johansen, and J. L. Metcalfe
1980 Observations on early life stages of Atlantic tomcod, *Microgadus tomcod*. Fish. Bull. 78(1): 147-158.

Petravicz, W. P.
1938 The breeding habits of the blackside darter, *Hadropterus maculatus* Girard. Copeia (1): 40-44.

Pfeiffer, Rev. R. A.
1955 Studies on the life history of the rosyface shiner, *Notropis rubellus*. Copeia (2): 95-104.

Pfleiger, William L.
1965 Reproductive behavior of the minnows, *Notropis spilopterus* and *Notropis whipplei*. Copeia (1): 1-7.
1971 A distributional study of Missouri Fishes. Publ. Univ. Kansas Mus. Nat. Hist. 20(3): 225-570, 15 figs., 193 maps.
1975 The Fishes of Missouri. Missouri Department of Conservation. 343 pp.

REFERENCES

Phillips, Gary L.

1969 Morphology and variation of the American cyprinid fishes *Chrosomus erythrogaster* and *Chrosomus eos*. Copeia (3): 501-509.

Pickett Joseph F.

1979 Pugheadedness in a largemouth bass. N. Y. Fish Game J. 26(1): 98-99.

Pivnicka, Karel

1970 Morphological variation in the burbot (*Lota lota*) and recognition of the subspecies: a review. J. Fish. Res. Bd. Canada 27(10): 1757-1765.

Plosila, Daniel S.

1977a Relationship between strain and size at stocking to survival of lake trout in Adirondack lakes. N. Y. Fish Game J. 24(1): 1-24.

1977b A lake trout management plan for New York State. N. Y. DEC mimeo. 68 pp.

Plosila, Daniel S. and George W. Labar

1981 Occurrence of juvenile blueback herring in Lake Champlain. N. Y. Fish Game J. 28(1): 118.

Poll, Max

1949 L'introduction en Belgique et l'acclimatation dans la nature d'un poisson Americain supplementaire *Umbra pygmaea* (DeKay). Inst. R. Sci. Nat. Belg. Bull. 22(35).

Poole, John C.

1961 Age and growth of the fluke in Great South Bay and their significance to the sport fishery. N. Y. Fish Game J. 8(1): 1-18.

1962 The fluke population of Great South Bay in relation to the sport fishery. N. Y. Fish Game J. 9(2): 93-117.

1964 Feeding habits of the summer flounder in Great South Bay. N. Y. Fish Game J. 11(1): 28-34.

Potter, George E.

1926 Ecological studies of the short-nosed gar-pike *Lepidosteus platystomus*. Univ. Iowa Stud. Nat. Hist. 11(9): 17-27.

Potter, I. C. and F. W. H. Beamish

1977 The freshwater biology of adult anadromous sea lampreys, *Petromyzon marinus*. J. Zool. London 181: 113-130.

Potter, I. C., F. W. H. Beamish, and B. G. H. Johnson

1974 Sex ratios and lengths of adult sea lamprey (*Petromyzon marinus*) from a Lake Ontario tributary. J. Fish. Res. Bd. Canada 31(1): 122-124.

Powell, Allyn B. and Frank J. Schwartz

1979 Food of *Paralichthys dentatus* and *P. lethostigma* (Pisces: Bothidae) in North Carolina estuaries. Estuaries 2(4): 276-279.

Powles, Howard

1980 Descriptions of larval silver perch, *Bairdiella chrysoura,* banded drum, *Larimus fasciatus,* and star drum, *Stellifer lanceolatus* (Sciaenidae). Fish. Bull. 78(1): 119-136.

Powles, P. M., Douglas Parker, and Ronald Reid

1977 Growth, maturation, and apparent and absolute fecundity of creek chub *Semotilus atromaculatus* (Mitchill) in the Kawartha Lake region, Ontario. Can. J. Zool. 55(5): 843-846.

Prescott, William

1851 Descriptions of new species of fishes. Am. J. Sci. ser. 2 11: 340-345.

Price, J. W.

1940 Time-temperature relations in the incubation of the whitefish, *Coregonus clupeaformis* (Mitchill). J. Gen. Physiol. 23: 449-468.

Price, John W.

1963 A study of the food habits of some Lake Erie fish. Bull. Ohio Biol. Surv. n.s. 2(1): x + 89 pp.

Price, Wm. Stephen

1978 Otolith comparison of *Alosa pseudoharengus* (Wilson) and *Alosa aestivalis* (Mitchill). Can. J. Zool. 56: 1216-1218.

Priegel, Gordon R.

1963 Dispersal of the shortnose gar, *Lepisosteus platostomus* in the Great Lakes drainage. Trans. Am. Fish. Soc. 92(2): 178.

1973 Lake sturgeon management on the Menominee River. Wis. Dept. Nat. Res. Tech. Bull. 67. 20 pp.

Priegel, Gordon R, and T. L. Wirth

1971 The lake sturgeon. Its life history, ecology and management. Wis. Dept. Nat. 1. 240-70. 19 pp.

1975 Lake sturgeon harvest, growth, and recruitment in Lake Winnebago, Wisconsin. Wis. Dept. Nat. Res. Tech. Bull. 83. 25 pp.

1978 Lake sturgeon populations, growth, and exploitation in Lakes Poygan, Winneconne, and Lake Butte des Morts, Wisconsin. Wis. Dept. Nat. Res. Tech. Bull. 107. 23 pp.

Pritchard, A. L.

1929 The alewife (*Pomolobus pseudoharengus*) in Lake Ontario. Univ. Toronto Stud., Publ. Ontario Fish. Res. Lab. 38: 37-54.

1930 Spawning habits and fry of the cisco (*Leucichthys artedi*) in Lake Ontario. Contrib. Can. Biol. Fish. n.s. 6(9): 225-240.

1931 Taxonomic and life history studies of the ciscoes of Lake Ontario. Univ. Toronto Stud. Biol. Ser. 35, Publ. Ontario Fish. Res. Lab. 41: 78 pp.

Probst, R. T. and E. L. Cooper

1954 Age, growth, and production of the lake sturgeon (*Acipenser fulvescens*) in the Lake Winnebago region, Wisconsin. Trans. Am. Fish. Soc. 84: 207-227.

Purkett, Charles A. Jr.

1958 Growth rate of Missouri stream fishes. Missouri Cons. Comm., Fish and Game Div. D-J Series no. 1, 46 pp.

1961 Reproduction and early development of the paddlefish. Trans. Am. Fish. Soc. 90(2): 125-129.

Purvis, Harold A.

1970 Growth, age at metamorphosis, and sex ratio of the northern brook lamprey in a tributary of southern Lake Superior. Copeia (2): 326-332.

Putnam, Frederick

1863 List of fishes sent by the museum to different institutions, in exchange for other specimens, with annotations. Bull. Mus. Comp. Zool. 1(1): 2-16.

Radforth, I.

1944 Some considerations on the distribution of fishes in Ontario. Contr. R. Ont. Mus. Zool. 25: 1-116.

Rafinesque, C. S.

1817a Additions to the observations on the sturgeons of North America. Am. Month. Mag. 1: 288.

1817b First decade of new North American fishes. Am. Month. Mag. Crit. Rev. 2(2): 120-121.

1818a Descriptions of two new genera of North American fishes, *Opsanus* and *Notropis*. Am. Month. Mag. Crit. Rev. 2(2): 203-204.

1818b Second decade of new North American fishes. Am. Month. Mag. Crit. Rev. 2(2): 204-206.

1818c Discoveries in natural history made during a journey through the western region of the United States. Am. Month. Mag. Crit. Rev. 3(5): 354-356.

1818d Further account of discoveries in natural history, in the western states, by Constantine Samuel Rafinesque, Esq. Communicated in a letter from that gentleman to the editor. Am. Month. Mag. Crit. Rev. 4: 39-42.

1818e Description of three new genera of fluviatile fish, *Pomoxis, Sarchirus,* and *Exoglossum.* Jour. Acad. Nat. Sci. Phila. 1(2): 417-422.

1819 Prodrome de 70 nouveaux genres d'animaux découverts dans l'intérieur des États-Unis d'Amérique durant l'année 1818. Jour. Physique 88: 417-429.

1820a Ichthyologia Ohiensis, or natural history of the fishes inhabiting the River Ohio and its tributary streams, preceded by a physical description of the Ohio and its branches. Lexington, Kentucky. 90 pp.

1820b Annals of Nature or annual synopsis of new genera and species of animals, plants, etc. discovered in North America. First Annual Number for 1820 pp. 1-16, British Museum, London.

1820c Description of the silures or catfishes of the river Ohio. Quart. J. Sci. Lit. Arts Roy. Inst. London 9:48-52.

1820d The fishes of the River Ohio. Western Reserve and Miscellaneous Magazine 2 (4/5): 235-242, 299-307.

Rainboth, W. I. and G. S. Whitt

1978 Analysis of evolutionary relationships among shiners of the subgenus *Luxilus* (Teleostei: Cypriniformes, *Notropis*) with lactate dehydrogenase and malate dehydrogenase isozyme systems. Comp. Biochem. Physiol. 49b: 241-252.

Raney, Edward C.

1939a The breeding habits of *Ichthyomyzon greeleyi* Hubbs and Trautman. Copeia (2): 111-112.

1939b The breeding habits of the silvery minnow, *Hybognathus regius* Girard. Am. Midl. Nat. 21(3): 674-680.

1939c Observations on the nesting habits of *Parexoglossum laurae* Hubbs. Copeia (2): 112-113.

1940a Comparison of the breeding habits of two subspecies of black-nosed dace, *Rhinichthys atratulus* (Hermann). Am. Midl. Nat. 23(2): 399-403.

1940b The breeding behavior of the common shiner, *Notropis cornutus* (Mitchill). Zoologica 25(1): 1-14, 4 pls.

1940c Reproductive activities of a hybrid minnow, *Notropis cornutus* x *Notropis rubellus.* Zoologica 25(24): 361-367.

1941 Range extension and remarks on the distribution of *Parexoglossum laurae* Hubbs. Copeia (4): 272.

1942a The summer food and habits of the chain pickerel (*Esox niger*) of a small New York pond. Jour. Wildl. Managt. 6(1): 58-66.

1942b Propagation of the silvery minnow (*Hybognathus nuchalis regius* Girard) in ponds. Trans. Am. Fish. Soc. 71(1941): 215-218.

1943 Unusual spawning habitat for the common white sucker *Catostomus commersonnii.* Copeia (4): 256.

1947a Subspecies and breeding behavior of the cyprinid fish *Notropis procne* (Cope). Copeia (2): 103-109.

1947b *Nocomis* nests used by other breeding cyprinid fishes in Virginia. Zoologica 32(15): 125-132, 1 pl.

1949 Nests under the water. Can. Nat. 11(3) 71-78.

1952a The life history of the striped bass *Roccus saxatilis* (Walbaum) Bull. Bingham Oceanogr. Coll. 14(1): 5-97.

1952b A new lamprey, *Ichthyomyzon hubbsi,* from the upper Tennessee River system. Copeia (2): 93-99.

1955 Natural hybrids between two species of pickerel (*Esox*) in Stearns Pond, Massachusetts. Suppl. Fisheries Rept. for some central, eastern, and western Mass. lakes, ponds and reservoirs 1951-1952. Mass. Div. Fish Game. 15 pp.

1957 Subpopulations of the striped bass *Roccus saxatilis* (Walbaum), in tributaries of Chesapeake Bay. pp. 85-107 in Contributions to the study of subpopulations of fishes. Special Scientific Reports United States Fish Wildlife Serv. Fisheries No. 208.

1958 Striped bass. Fishery Leaflet No. 451 United States Fish and Wildlife Service. 6 pp.

1959 Some young fresh-water fishes of New York. Conservationist Aug-Sept. pp. 22-28.

1965a Some panfishes of New York — yellow perch, white perch, white bass, freshwater drum. Conservationist 19(5): 22-28.

1965b Some pan fishes of New York — rock bass, crappies, and other sunfishes. Conservationist 19(6): 21-29.

1967 Some catfishes of New York. Conservationist 21(6): 20-25.

1969 Minnows of New York. Part 1: facts about some of our chubs and dace. Conservationist 23(5): 22-29. Part 2: the shiners. Conservationist 23(6): 21-29.

Raney Edward C., Richard H. Backus,
Ronald W. Crawford, and C. Richard Robins

1953 Reproductive behavior in *Cyprinodon variegatus* Lacepède, in Florida. Zoologica 38(6): 97-104, pls. I-II.

Raney, Edward C. and Ernest A. Lachner

1939 Observations on the life history of the spotted darter *Poecilichthys maculatus* (Kirtland). Copeia (3): 157-165.

1942 Studies of the summer food, growth, and movements of young yellow pikeperch *Stizostedion v. vitreum* in Oneida Lake, New York. Jour. Wildl. Managt. 6(1): 1-16.

1943 Age and growth of johnny darters, *Boleosoma nigrum olmstedi* (Storer) and *Boleosoma longimanum* (Jordan). Am. Midl. Nat. 29(1): 229-238.

1946 Age, growth and habits of the hog sucker, *Hypentelium nigricans* (LeSueur), in New York. Am. Midl. Nat. 36(1): 76-86.

Raney, Edward C. and Dwight A. Webster

1940 The food and growth of the young of the common bullhead, *Ameiurus nebulosus nebulosus* (LeSueur), in Cayuga Lake, New York. Trans. Am. Fish. Soc. 69(1939): 205-209.

1942 The spring migration of the common white sucker, *Catostomus commersoni* (Lacepède), in Skaneateles Lake Inlet, New York. Copeia (3): 139-148.

Raney, Edward C. and William S. Woolcott

1955a Races of the striped bass, "*Roccus saxatilis*" (Walbaum) in southeastern United States. Proc. Southeastern Association of Game and Fish Commissioners (1954): 60-64.

1955b Races of the striped bass, *Roccus saxatilis* (Walbaum) in southeastern United States. Jour. Wildl. Management 19 (4): 444-450.

Raney, Edward C., William S. Woolcott, and
Albert G. Mehring

1954 Migratory patterns and racial structure of Atlantic coast striped bass. Transactions 19th North American Wildlife Conference (1954): 376-396.

Rasmussen, Ross P.

1980 Egg and larva development of brook silversides from the Peace River, Florida. Trans. Am. Fish. Soc. 109(4): 407-416.

Rawson, Michael R. and Russell L. Scholl

1978 Reestablishment of sauger in western Lake Erie. Pp. 261-265 in R.L. Kendall ed., Selected coolwater fishes of North America. Am. Fish. Soc. Spec. Publ. 11.

Rathjen, Warren F. and Lewis C. Miller

1957 Aspects of the early life history of the striped bass (*Roccus saxatilis*) in the Hudson River. N. Y. Fish Game J. 4: 43-60.

Reed, Hugh Daniel

1907 The poison glands of *Noturus* and *Schilbeodes.* Am. Nat. 41(489): 553-566.

Reed, H. D. and A. H. Wright

1909 The vertebrates of the Cayuga Lake basin, New York. Proc. Am. Philos. Soc. 48(193): 370-459, pls 17-20.

Reed, Roger J.

1954 Hermaphroditism in the rosyface shiner, *Notropis rubellus*. Copeia (4): 293-294.

1957 Phases of the life history of the rosyface shiner, *Notropis rubellus*, in northwestern Pennsylvania. Copeia (4): 286-290.

1958 The early life history of two cyprinids, *Notropis rubellus* and *Campostoma anomalum pullum*. Copeia (4): 325-327.

1959 Age, growth, and food of the longnose dace, *Rhinichthys cataractae*, in northwestern Pennsylvania. Copeia (2): 160-162.

1971 Biology of the fallfish, *Semotilus corporalis* (Pisces: Cyprinidae). Trans. Am. Fish. Soc. 100(4): 717-725.

Reed, Roger J. and James C. Moulton

1973 Age and growth of blacknose date, *Rhinichthys atratulus* and longnose dace, *R. cataractae* in Massachusetts. Am. Midl. Nat. 90(1): 206-210.

Reeves, C. D.

1907 The breeding habits of the rainbow darter (*Etheostoma caeruleum* Storer). Biol. Bull. 14: 35-39.

Regier, Henry A.

1963a Ecology and management of largemouth bass and bluegills in farm ponds in New York. N. Y. Fish Game J. 10(1): 1-89.

1963b Ecology and management of largemouth bass and golden shiners in farm ponds in New York. N. Y. Fish Game J. 10(2): 139-169.

1963c Ecology and management of channel catfish in farm ponds in New York. N. Y. Fish Game J. 10(2): 170-185.

Regier, Henry A., Vernon C. Applegate, and Richard A. Ryder

1969 The ecology and management of the walleye in western Lake Erie. Great Lakes Fishery Comm. Tech. Rept. 15: vii + 101 pp.

Reider, Robert H.

1979a Occurrence of the silver lamprey in the Hudson River. N. Y. Fish Game J. 26(1): 93.

1979b Occurrence of a kokanee in the Hudson River. N. Y. Fish Game J. 26(1): 94.

Reighard, Jacob E.

1902 The breeding habits of certain fishes. Science n.s. 15(380): 574-575.

1904 The natural history of *Amia calva Linnaeus*. no 4, pp. 57-109 in Mark Anniversary Volume, New York.

1906 The breeding habits, development, and propagation of the black bass (*Micropterus dolomieu* Lacepède and *Micropterus salmoides* Lacepède). Bull. Michigan Fish. Comm. 7, 73 pp., figs. A-K, 1-29.

1910 Methods of studying the habits of fishes, with an account of the breeding habits of the horned dace. Bull. U. S. Bur. Fish. 28(2): 1111-1146, pls. 114-120.

1913 The breeding habits of the log-perch (*Percina caprodes*). Rept. Mich. Acad. Sci. 15: 104-105.

1920 The breeding behavior of the suckers and minnows. Biol. Bull. 38(1): 1-32, figs. 1-7.

1943 The breeding habits of the river chub, *Nocomis micropogon* (Cope). Pap. Mich. Acad. Sci. Arts Lett. 28 (1942): 397-423.

Reighard Jacob E. and Harold Cummins

1916 Description of a new species of lamprey of the genus *Ichthyomyzon*. Occas. Pap. Mus. Zool. Univ. Mich. 31: 1-12, pls. 1-2.

Reintjes, John W.

1964 Annotated bibliography on biology of menhadens and menhaden-like fishes of the world. Fish. Bull. 63(3): 531-549.

Reisman, Howard M.

1963 Reproductive behavior of *Apeltes quadracus*, including some comparisons with other gasterosteid fishes. Copeia (1): 191-192.

Reisman, Howard M. and Tom J. Cade

1967 Physiological and behavioral aspects of reproduction in the brook stickleback (*Culaea inconstans*). Am. Midl. Nat. 77(2): 257-295.

Reisman, Howard H. and William Nicol

1973 The fishes of Gardiner's Island, New York. N. Y. Fish Game J. 20(1): 25-31.

Relyea, Kenneth

1983 A systematic study of two species complexes of the genus *Fundulus* (Pisces: Cyprinodontidae). Bull. Fla. State Mus. Biol. Sci. 29(1): 1-64.

Reno, Harley W.

1969 Cephalic lateral-line system of the cyprinid genus *Hybopsis*. Copeia (4): 736-773.

1971 The lateral-line system of the silverjaw minnow, *Ericymba buccata* Cope. Southwest. Nat. 15(3): 347-358.

Reynolds, William Wallace and Martha Elizabeth Casterlin

1977 Diel activity in the yellow bullhead. Prog. Fish-Cult. 39(3): 132-133.

1979 Thermoregulatory behavior of brown trout, *Salmo trutta*. Hydrobiologia 62(1): 79-80.

Rhode, Fred C., Rudolf G. Arndt, and Johnson C. S. Wang

1976 Life history of the freshwater lampreys *Okkelbergia aepyptera* and *Lampetra lamottenii* (Pisces: Petromyzontidae), on the Delmarva Peninsula (East Coast, United States). Bull. South. Calif. Acad. Sci. 75(2): 99-111.

Richards, C. E. and Richard L. Bailey

1967 Occurrence of *Fundulus luciae*, spotfin killifish, on the seaside of Virginia's eastern shore. Chesapeake Sci. 8(3): 204-205.

Richards, Sarah W.

1976 Age, growth, and food of bluefish (*Pomatomus saltatrix*) from east central Long Island Sound from July through November 1975. Trans. Am. Fish. Soc. 105(4): 523-525.

Richards, Sarah W. and Arthur W. Kendall, Jr.

1973 Distribution of sand lance *Ammodytes* sp. larvae on the continental shelf from Cape Cod to Cape Hatteras, from R/ V Dolphin surveys in 1966. Fish. Bull. 71(2): 371-386.

Richards, Sarah W., Jack M. Mann, and Joseph A. Walker

1979 Comparison of spawning seasons, age, growth rates and food of two sympatric species of searobins, *Prionotus carolinus* and *Prionotus evolans*, from Long Island Sound. Estuaries 2(4): 255-268.

Richards, Sarah W. and A. Marshall McBean

1966 Comparison of postlarvae and juveniles of *Fundulus heteroclitus* and *Fundulus majalis* (Pisces: Cyprinodontidae). Trans. Am. Fish. Soc. 95(2): 218-226.

Richards, W. J.

1960 The life history, habits and ecology of the white perch *Roccus americanus* (Gmelin) in Cross Lake, New York. M. S. Thesis, Syracuse University.

Richardson, John
1823a Notice of the fishes. In: Narrative of a journey to the shores of the polar seas in the years 1819, 1820, 1821, 1822 by John Franklin. London. pp. 705-728.
1823b Account of some fishes observed during Capt. Franklin's and Dr. Richardson's journey to the polar sea. Mem. Wern. Nat. Hist. Soc. Edinburgh, 1823-1824 5: 509-522.
1836 Fauna boreali — Americana; or the Zoology of the Northern parts of British America. part third. The Fish. London, Richard Bently. xv + 327 pp., 97 pls.

Richardson, L. R.
1939 The spawning behavior of *Fundulus diaphanus* (Le Sueur). Copeia (3): 165-167.

Richmond, N. D.
1940 Nesting of the sunfish, *Lepomis auritus* (Linnaeus), in tidal waters. Zoologica 25(3): 329-330.

Ricker, W. E.
1932 Studies of speckled trout (*Salvelinus fontinalis*) in Ontario. Univ. Toronto Stud. Biol. Publ. Ont. Fish. Res. Lab. 44: 67-110.
1966 Salmon of the North Pacific ocean. Part 3. A review of the life history of North Pacific salmon. 4. Sockeye salmon in British Columbia. Int. North Pac. Fish. Comm. Bull. 18: 59-70.

Riggs, C. D.
1955 Reproduction of the white bass *Morone chrysops*. Invest. Indiana Lakes Streams 4(3): 87-110.

Rigley, Louis and John Muir
1979 The role of sound production by the brown bullhead *Ictalurus nebulosus*. Proc. Pa. Acad. Sci. 53: 132-134.

Rimsky-Korsakoff, V. N.
1930 The food of certain fishes of the Lake Champlain watershed. Pp. 88-104 in: A Biological Survey of the Lake Champlain watershed. N. Y. Conserv. Dept. Suppl. 19th Ann. Rept. (1929).

Robbins, W. H. and H. R. McCrimmon
1974 The blackbass in America and overseas. Ontario Canada Biomanagement and Research Enterprises. 196 pp.

Roberts, Nicholas J. and Howard E. Winn
1962 Utilization of the senses in feeding behavior of the johnny darter *Etheostoma nigrum*. Copeia (3): 567-570.

Robins, C. R.
1955 A taxonomic revision of the *Cottus bairdi* and *Cottus carolinae* species groups in eastern North America (Pisces: Cottidae). Dissert. Absts. XV(2): 302-303.

Robins, C. R. and E. E, Deubler Jr.
1955 The life history and systematic status of the burbot, *Lota lota lacustris* (Walbaum), in the Susquehanna River system. N. Y. State Mus. Sci. Serv. Circ. 39: 1-49.

Robins, C. R. (ed.)
1980 A list of common and scientific names of fishes from the United States and Canada. Fourth Edition. Am. Fish. Soc. Publ. 12, 174 pp.

Robins, G. L.
1970 A bibliography of the pike perch of the genus *Stizostedion* (including the genus known as *Lucioperca*). Fish. Res. Board Can. Tech. Rept. 161: 67 pp.

Robinson, John Wesley
1967 Observations on the life history, movement, and harvest of the paddlefish, *Polyodon spathula*, in Montana. Proc. Mont. Acad. Sci. 26: 33-44.

Roecker, Robert M.
1961 *Osmerus mordax* — the smelt. Conservationist 15(5): 16-18.

Rogers, C. A.
1976 Effects of temperature and salinity on the survival of winter flounder embryos. Fish. Bull. 74: 52-58.

Rollwagon, J. and D. Stainken
1980 Ectoparasites and feeding behavior of the blacknose dace, *Rhinichthys atratulus* Hermann (Cyprinidae: Cypriniformes). Am. Midl. Nat. 103(1): 185-190.

Roosa, Peter and Margaret J. Slack
1975 An ichthyology of four Adirondack Lakes. Rensselaer Freshwater Inst. Lake George. Rept. 75-7: 39 pp.

Rosen, Donn Eric
1973a Suborder Cyprinodontoidei, Superfamily Cyprinodontoidea, Families Cyprinodontidae, Poeciliidae, Anablepidae. Mem. Sears Found. Mar. Res. 1(6): 229-262.
1973b Interrelationships of higher euteleostean fishes. Pp. 397-513 in Interrelationships of Fishes. P.H. Greenwood, R. S. Miles, and Colin Patterson, Eds. Suppl. 1 to Jour. Linnaean Soc. London. 53.

Rosen, Donn Eric and Reeve M. Bailey
1963 The poeciliid fishes (Cyprinodontiformes), their structure, zoogeography, and systematics. Bull. Am. Mus. Nat. Hist. 126 (1): 1-176.

Rosen, Donn Eric and Myron Gordon
1953 Functional anatomy and evolution of male genitalia in poeciliid fishes. Zoologica 38(1): 1-47, 4 pls.

Rosen, Donn Eric and Colin Patterson
1969 The structure and relationships of the paracanthopterygian fishes. Bull. Am. Mus. Nat. Hist. 141(3): 357-474, pls. 52-78.

Rosen, R. A. and D. C. Hales
1981 Feeding of paddlefish, *Polyodon spathula*. Copeia (2): 441-455.

Ross, David F.
1974 Tuberculation of the silverjaw minnow *Ericymba buccata*. Copeia (1): 271-272.

Ross, Michael R.
1973 A chromosome study of five species of etheostomine fishes (Percidae). Copeia (1): 163-165.
1976 Nest-entry behavior of female creek chubs (*Semotilus atromaculatus*) in different habitats. Copeia (2): 378-380.
1977a Aggression as a social mechanism in the creek chub (*Semotilus atromaculatus*). Copeia (2): 393-397.
1977b Function of creek chub (*Semotilus atromaculatus*) nest-building. Ohio J. Sci. 77(1): 36-37.
1983 The frequency of nest construction and satellite male behavior in the fallfish minnow. Environ. Biol. Fishes 9(1): 65-70.

Ross, Michael R. and Ted M. Cavender
1981 Morphological analyses of four experimental intergeneric cyprinid hybrid crosses. Copeia (2): 377-387.

Ross, Michael R. and Roger J. Reed
1978 The reproductive behavior of the fallfish *Semotilus corporalis*. Copeia (2): 215-221.

Ross, Robert D.
1958 Races of the cyprinid fish *Campostoma anomalum pullum* Agassiz in eastern United States. Va. Agric. Exp. Sta. Tech. Bull. 136, 20 pp.

REFERENCES

Rostlund, Eckard
1953 Henry Hudson's comment on salmon in the Hudson River, September, 1609. Copeia (3): 192-193.

Rothschild, Brian J.
1962 Aspects of the population dynamics of the alewife *Alosa pseudoharengus* (Wilson), in Cayuga Lake, New York. Am. Midl. Nat. 74(2): 479-496.
1966 Observations on the alewife (*Alosa pseudoharengus*) in Cayuga Lake. N. Y. Fish Game J. 13(2): 188-195.

Rowland, William J.
1974 Reproductive behavior of the fourspine stickleback, *Apeltes quadracus*. Copeia (1): 183-194.

Royce, W. F.
1951 Breeding habits of the lake trout in New York. Fish. Bull. 59: 59-76.

Royce, W. F., R. J. Buller, and E. D. Premetz
1959 Decline of the yellowtail flounder (*Limanda ferruginea*) off New England. Fish. Bull. 146, vol 59: 169-267.

Rubec, P. J. and B. W. Coad
1974 First record of the margined madtom, (*Noturus insignis*) from Canada. J. Fish. Res. Board Can. 31(8): 1430-1431.

Rupp, R. S.
1965 Shore-spawning and survival of eggs of the American smelt. Trans. Am. Fish. Soc. 94(2): 160-168.

Ryder, John A.
1886 The development of the mudminnow. Am. Nat. 20(9): 823-824.
1888 On the development of the common sturgeon, *Acipenser sturio*. Am. Nat. 22(259): 659-660.

Ryer, Robert, III
1938 Contribution to the life history of *Notropis cornutus cornutus* (Mitchill). M.S. Thesis, Cornell University. 41 pp.

Sadzikowski, Mark R. and Dale C. Wallace
1976 A comparison of the food habits of size classes of three sunfishes (*Lepomis macrochirus* Rafinesque, *L. gibbosus* (Linnaeus), and *L. cyanellus* Rafinesque). Am. Midl. Nat. 95(1): 220-225.

Samaritan, Jeanette M. and Robert E. Schmidt
1982 Aspects of the life history of a freshwater population of the mummichog, *Fundulus heteroclitus* (Pisces: Cyprinodontidae), in the Bronx River, New York, U. S. A. Hydrobiologia 94: 149-154.

Sauvage, Henri Émile
1878 Description de poissons nouveaux ou imparfaitement connus de la collection du Muséum d'Histoire Naturelle; famille des scorpénidés, des platycephalidés et des triglidés. Nouv. Arch. Mus. Hist. Nat. Paris ser. 1 no. 2: 107-158, 2 pls.

Savage, T.
1963 Reproductive behavior of the mottled sculpin, *Cottus bairdi* Girard. Copeia (2): 317-325.

Sawyer, Philip J.
1967 Intertidal life-history of the rock gunnel, *Pholis gunnellus*, in the western Atlantic. Copeia (1): 55-61.

Scarlett, Paul G.
1982 Annotated bibliography and subject index on the summer flounder, *Paralichthys dentatus*. NOAA Tech. Rept. NMFS SSRF-775, 12 pp.

Scarola, John F.
1973 Freshwater fishes of New Hampshire. N. H. Fish Game Dept. 131 pp.

Schaefer, Richard H.
1960 Growth and feeding habits of the whiting or silver hake in the New York Bight. N. Y. Fish Game J. 7(2): 85-98.
1965a Age and growth of the northern kingfish in New York waters. N. Y. Fish Game J. 12(2): 191-216.
1965b Presence of a swimbladder in northern kingfish. N. Y. Fish Game J. 12(2): 242-243.
1970 Feeding habits of striped bass from the surf waters of Long Island. N. Y. Fish Game J. 17(1): 1-17.

Schaffer, William M. and Paul F. Elson
1975 The adaptive significance of variations in life history among local populations of Atlantic salmon in North America. Ecology 56(3): 577-590.

Schaner, Everett and Kenneth Sherman
1960 Observations on the fecundity of the tomcod, *Microgadus tomcod* (Walbaum). Copeia (4): 347-348.

Schemske, Douglas W.
1974 Age, length and fecundity of the creek chub, *Semotilus atromaculatus* (Mitchill), in central Illinois. Am. Midl Nat. 92(2): 505-509.

Scherer, Michael D. and Donald W. Bourne
1980 Eggs and early larvae of smallmouth flounder, *Etropus microstomus*. Fish. Bull. 77(3): 708-712.

Schiavone, Albert, Jr.
1983 The Black Lake fish community: 1931 to 1979. N. Y. Fish Game J. 30(1): 78-90.

Schmidt, Robert E. and J. McGurk
1982 Biology of the European bitterling *Rhodeus sericeus* (Pisces: Cyprinidae) in the Bronx River, New York, U.S.A.: an apparently benign exotic species. Biol. Conserv. 24: 157-162.

Schmidt, Robert E. and Jeanette M. Samaritan
1984 Fishes of an urban stream: the Bronx River, New York. Northeast. Environ. Sci. 3(1): 3-7.

Schmidt, Robert E., Jeanette M. Samaritan, and Antonio Pappantoniou
1981 Status of the bitterling, *Rhodeus sericeus* in southeastern New York. Copeia (2): 481-482.

Schmidt, Robert E. and Walter R. Whitworth
1979 Distribution and habitat of the swamp darter. (*Etheostoma fusiforme*), in southern New England. Am. Midl. Nat. 102(2): 408-413.

Schmidt, Johs.
1922 The breeding places of the eel. Phil. Trans. Roy. Soc. London ser. B. 211: 179-208.
1925 The breeding places of the eel. Ann. Rept. Smithsonian Inst. (1924): 279-316, 7 pls.

Schmitz, E. H. and C. D. Baker
1969 Digestive anatomy of the gizzard shad, *Dorosoma cepedianum*, and the threadfin shad, *D. petenense*. Trans. Am. Micr. Soc. 88: 525-546.

Schneider, Clifford P.
1971 SCUBA observations of spawning smallmouth bass. N. Y. Fish Game J. 18(2): 112-116.

Schoepf, Johann David
1784a Der Gemeine Hecht In Amerika. Naturforscher 20: 26-31.
1784b Vom nordamerikanischen Pertsch. Naturforscher 20: 17-25.
1788 Beschreibung einiger nordamerikanischen Fische vorzuglich aus den neu-yorkischen Gewassern. Schrift. Ges. Naturf. Freunde Berlin 8: 138-194.

Schuck, Howard A.
1945 Survival, population density, growth, and movement of the wild brown trout in Crystal Creek. Trans. Am. Fish. Soc. 73(1943): 209-230.

Schultz, Leonard P.
1927 Temperature-controlled variation in the golden shiner, *Notemigonus crysoleucas*. Pap. Mich. Acad. Sci. Arts Lett. 7: 417-432.

Schwartz, Frank J.
1963 The fresh-water minnows of Maryland. Maryland Conservationist 40(2): 19-29, key.
1965 Age, growth, and egg complement of the stickleback *Apeltes quadracus*, at Solomons, Maryland. Chesapeake Sci. 6(2): 116-118.
1972 World literature of fish hybrids with an analysis by family, species and hybrid. Publ. Gulf Coast Res. Lab. Mus. 3: 328 pp.

Schwartz, Frank J. and John Norvall
1958 Food, growth and sexual dimorphism of the redside dace, *Clinostomus elongatus* (Kirtland) in Linesville Creek, Crawford County, Pennsylvania. Ohio J. Sci. 58(5): 311-316.

Scott, J. S.
1972 Morphological and meristic variation in northwest Atlantic sand lance (*Ammodytes*). J. Fish. Res. Board Can. 29(12): 1673-1678.

Scott, W. B. and W. J. Christie
1963 The invasion of the lower Great Lakes by the white perch, *Roccus americanus* (Gmelin). J. Fish. Res. Board Can. 20(5): 1189-1195.

Scott, W. B. and E. J. Crossman
1973 Freshwater fishes of Canada. Bull. Fish. Res. Board Can. 184: xi + 966 pp.

Scott, W. B. and Stanford H. Smith
1962 The occurrence of the longjaw cisco, *Leucichthys alpenae*, in Lake Erie. J. Fish. Res. Board Can. 19(6): 1013-1023.

Seaman, W. Jr.
1968 Distribution and variation of the American cyprinid fish, *Notropis hudsonius* (Clinton). M. S. Thesis, University of Florida.

Serchuk, F. M. and D. W. Frame
1973 An annotated bibliography of the cunner, *Tautogolabrus adspersus* (Walbaum). U. S. Natl. Mar. Fish. Serv. Spec. Sci. Rept. Fish. 668.

Sette, Oscar Elton
1943 Biology of the Atlantic mackerel (*Scomber scombrus*) Part I. Early life history, including the growth, drift, and mortality of the egg and larval populations. Bull. U. S. Fish Wildl. Serv. 38, vol. 50: 149-237.
1950 Biology of the Atlantic mackerel (*Scomber scombrus*) of North America. II. Migration and habits. Fish. Bull. 49. vol. 51: 251-358.

Setzler, Eileen, Walter R. Boynton, Kathryn V. Wood, Henry H. Zion, Lawrence Lubbers, Nancy K. Mountford, Phyllis Fueri, Luther Tucker, and Joseph A. Mihursky.
1980 Synopsis of biological data on striped bass, *Morone saxatilis* (Walbaum). NOAA Tech. Rept. NMFS Circular 433. FAO Synopsis 121, 69 pp.

Shapiro, S. M.
1975 A bibliography of the spottail shiner, *Notropis hudsonius* (Clinton) (Pisces: Cyprinidae). Mass. Coop. Fish. Res. Unit Publ. no. 43. Univ. Massachusetts, Amherst. 47 pp.

Shapovalov, L. and A. C. Taft
1954 The life histories of the steelhead rainbow trout (*Salmo gairdnerii gairdnerii*) and silver salmon (*Oncorhynchus kisutch*) with special reference to Waddell Creek, California, and recommendations for their management. Calif. Dep. Fish Game Fish. Bull. 98: 375 pp.

Shepherd, Marsha E. and Melvin T. Huish
1978 Age, growth, and diet of the pirate perch in a coastal plain stream of North Carolina. Trans. Am. Fish. Soc. 107(3): 457-459.

Sheppard, J. D.
1969 Some aspects of the life histories of the golden shiner, *Notemigonus crysoleucas* (Mitchill), and the common shiner, *Notropis cornutus* (Mitchill), in eastern Ontario with particular reference to growth. M. Sc. Thesis, Queen's University. 324 pp.

Sheri, A. N. and G. Power
1969a Annulus formation on scales of the white perch, *Morone americanus* (Gmelin), in the Bay of Quinte, Lake Ontario. Trans. Am. Fish. Soc. 98 (2): 322-326.
1969b Vertical distribution of the white perch, *Roccus americanus*, modified by light. Can. Field-Nat. 83(2): 160-161.

Shipp, R. L. and R. W. Yerger
1969 Status, character, and distribution of the northern and southern puffers of the genus *Sphoeroides*. Copeia (3): 425-433.

Shirvell, C. S. and R. G. Dungey
1983 Microhabitats chosen by brown trout for feeding and spawning in rivers. Trans. Am. Fish. Soc. 112(3): 355-367.

Shoemaker, Hurst H.
1952 Fish home areas of Lake Myosotis, New York. Copeia (2): 83-87.

Shumway, Sandra and Robert R. Stickney
1975 Notes on the biology and food habits of the cunner. N. Y. Fish Game J. 22(1): 71-79.

Siefert, Richard E.
1965 Early scale development in the white crappie. Trans. Am. Fish. Soc. 94(2): 182.
1968 Reproductive behavior, incubation and mortality of eggs, and postlarval food selection in the white crappie. Trans. Am. Fish. Soc. 97(3): 252-259.
1969a Characteristics for separation of white and black crappie larvae. Trans. Am. Fish Soc. 98(2): 326-328.
1969b Biology of the white crappie in Lewis and Clark Lake. U. S. Bur. Sportfish. and Wildl. Tech. Paper 22, 16 pp.
1972 First food of larval yellow perch, white sucker, bluegill, emerald shiner, and rainbow smelt. Trans. Am. Fish. Soc. 101(2): 219-225.

Siefert, Richard E., William A. Spoor, and Roll F. Syrett
1973 Effects of reduced oxygen concentration on northern pike (*Esox lucius*) embryos and larvae. J. Fish. Res. Board Can.. 30: 849-852.

Sigler, W. F.
1949 Life history of the white bass *Lepibema chrysops* (Rafinesque), of Spirit Lake, Iowa. Iowa State College Agr. Med. Arts, Res. Bull. 366: 203-244.

Sisk, Morgan E.
1966 Unusual spawning behavior of the northern creek chub, *Semotilus atromaculatus* (Mitchill). Trans. Ky. Acad. Sci. 27(1/2): 3-4.

Small, James W. Jr.
1975 Energy dynamics of benthic fishes in a small Kentucky stream. Ecology 56(4): 827-840.

Smart, Heather J. and John H. Gee
1979 Coexistence and resource partitioning in two species of darters (Percidae), *Etheostoma nigrum* and *Percina maculata*. Can. Jour. Zool. 57: 2061-2071.

Smith, Bernard R.
1971 Sea lampreys in the Great Lakes of North America. Pp. 207-247 in Hardisty M. W. and I. C. Potter (eds.) The Biology of Lampreys vol.1. Academic Press, New York. xiv + 1-423.

Smith, Bertram G.
1908 The spawning habits of *Chrosomus erythrogaster* Rafinesque. Biol. Bull. 15(1): 9-18.

1923 Notes on the nesting habits of *Cottus*. Pap. Mich. Acad. Sci. Arts Lett. 2(1922): 221-224, pl. 11.

Smith, C. E., T. H. Peck, R. J. Klauda and J. B. McLaren
1979 Hepatomas in Atlantic tomcod *Microgadus tomcod* (Walbaum) collected in the Hudson River Estuary in New York. Jour. Fish. Diseases 2(4): 313-319.

Smith, David B.
1972 Age and growth of the cisco in Oneida Lake, New York. N. Y. Fish Game J. 19(1): 83-91.

Smith, Eugene
1898 The fishes of the fresh and brackish waters in the vicinity of New York City. Proc. Linn. Soc. New York 9(1897): 9-51.

Smith, Hugh M.
1895 Notes on two hitherto unrecognized species of American whitefishes. Bull. U. S. Fish Comm. 14(1894)(1): 1-13, pl. 1.

Smith, Hugh M. and L. G. Harron
1903 Breeding habits of the yellow cat-fish. Bull. U. S. Fish. Comm. 22(1902): 149-154.

Smith, Lloyd L. Jr. and Robert H. Kramer
1964 The spottail shiner in lower Red Lake, Minnesota. Trans. Am. Fish. Soc. 93(1): 35-45.

Smith, Osgood R.
1935 The breeding habits of the stone roller minnow, (*Campostoma anomalum* Rafinesque) Trans. Am. Fish. Soc. 65: 148-151.

Smith, R. J. F.
1970 Effects of food availability on aggression and nest building in brook stickleback (*Culaea inconstans*). J. Fish. Res. Board Can. 27(12): 2350-2355.
1978 Seasonal changes in the histology of the gonads and dorsal skin of the fathead minnow, *Pimephales promelas*. Can. Jour. Zool. 56(10): 2103-2109.

Smith, R. J. F. and B. D. Murphy
1974 Functional morphology of the dorsal pad in fathead minnows (*Pimephales promelas* Rafinesque). Trans. Am. Fish. Soc. 103(1): 65-72.

Smith, Stanford H.
1957 Life history of the herring of Green Bay, Lake Michigan. Fish. Bull. 57, vol. 109: 87-138.
1964 Status of the deepwater cisco population of Lake Michigan. Trans. Am. Fish. Soc. 93(2): 155-163.
1968 That little pest the alewife. Limnos: 12-20.
1970 Species interactions of the alewife in the Great Lakes. Trans. Am. Fish. Soc. 99(4): 754-765.
1972 The future of salmonid communities in the Laurentian Great Lakes. J. Fish. Res. Board Can. 29(6): 951-957.

Smith, T. I. J., E. K. Dingley, and D. E. Marchette
1980. Induced spawning and culture of Atlantic sturgeon. Prog. Fish-Cult. 42 (3): 147-151.

Smith, Ronald W. and Franklin C. Daiber
1977 Biology of the summer flounder, *Paralichthys dentatus*, in Delaware Bay. Fish. Bull. 75(4): 823-830.

Snelson, Franklin F. Jr.
1968 Systematics of the cyprinid fish *Notropis amoenus*, with comments on the subgenus *Notropis*. Copeia (4): 776-802.
1971 *Notropis mekistocholas*, a new herbivorous cyprinid fish endemic to the Cape Fear River basin, North Carolina. Copeia (3): 449-462.
1972 Systematics of the subgenus *Lythrurus*, Genus *Notropis* (Pisces: Cyprinidae). Bull. Fla. State Mus. Biol. Sci. 17(1): 1-92.

Snelson, Franklin F. Jr. and William L. Pfleiger
1975 Redescription of the redfin shiner, *Notropis umbratilis*, and its subspecies in the central Mississippi River basin. Copeia (2): 231-249.

Snow, Howard, Arthur Ensign, and John Klingbiel
1960 The bluegill, Its life history, ecology, and management. Publ. Wis. Conserv. Dep. 230, 14 pp.

Snyder, Darrell E., M. B. M. Snyder, and S. C. Douglas
1977 Identification of golden shiner, *Notemigonus crysoleucas*, spotfin shiner, *Notropis spilopterus*, and fathead minnow, *Pimephales promelas* larvae. J. Fish. Res. Board Can. 34: 1397-1409.

Snyder, Darrel E. and Susan C. Douglas
1978 Description and identification of mooneye, *Hiodon tergisus*, protolarvae. Trans. Am. Fish. Soc. 107(4): 590-594.

Sosiak, A. J., R. G. Randall, and J. A. McKenzie
1979 Feeding by hatchery-reared and wild Atlantic salmon (*Salmo salar*) parr in streams. J. Fish. Res. Board Can.. 36(11): 1408-1412.

Sopuck, R. D.
1978 Emigration of juvenile rainbow trout in Cayuga Inlet, New York. N. Y. Fish Game J. 25(2): 108-120.

Speare, Edward P.
1960 Growth of central johnny darter (*Etheostoma nigrum nigrum*) in Augusta Creek, Michigan. Copeia (3): 241-243.
1965 Fecundity and egg survival of central johnny darter (*Etheostoma nigrum nigrum*) in southern Michigan. Copeia 1965: 308-314.

Speirs, J. Murray
1952 Nomenclature of the channel catfish, and the burbot of North America. Copeia (2): 99-103.

Stacy, P. B. and D. Chiazar
1978 Body color pattern and the aggressive behavior of male pumpkinseed sunfish (*Lepomis gibbosus*) during the reproductive season. Behaviour 64: 271-297.

Stanley Jon G., W. Woodward Miley II and David L. Sutton
1978 Reproductive requirements and likelihood for naturalization of escaped grass carp in the United States. Trans. Am. Fish. Soc. 107(1): 119-128.

Starck, Walter A. II and Robert E. Schroeder
1970 Investigations on the gray snapper, *Lutjanus griseus*. Stud. Trop. Oceanogr. Miami 10: 224 pp., 44 figs.

Starnes, Lynn B., Peter A. Hackney, and Thomas A. McDonough
1983 Larval fish transport: a case study of white bass. Trans. Am. Fish. Soc. 112(3): 390-397.

Starnes, Wayne, David A. Etnier, Lynn B. Starnes and Neil H. Douglas
1977 Zoogeographic implications of the rediscovery of the percid genus *Ammocrypta* in the Tennessee River drainage. Copeia (4): 783-786.

Starrett, W. C.
1950 Food relationships of the minnows of the Des Moines River, Iowa. Ecology 31: 216-233.

Stasiak, Richard H.
1977 Morphology and variation in the finescale dace *Chrosomus neogaeus*. Copeia (4): 771-774.
1978a Reproduction, age and growth of the finescale dace *Chrosomus neogaeus*, in Minnesota. Trans. Am. Fish. Soc. 107(5): 720-723.
1978b Food, age, and growth of the pearl dace, *Semotilus margarita*, in Nebraska. Am. Midl. Nat. 100(2): 463-466.

Stauffer, Jay. R., Charles H. Hocutt, and Robert F. Denencourt
1979 Status and distribution of the hybrid *Nocomis micropogon* x *Rhinichthys cataractae*, with a discussion of hybridization as a viable mode of vertebrate speciation. Am. Midl. Nat. 101(2): 355-365.

Stenton, J. E.
1951 Eastern brook trout eggs taken by longnose suckers in Banff National Park, Canada. Copeia (2): 171-172.

Stewart, Kenneth W. and Casimir C. Lindsey
1983 Postglacial dispersal of lower vertebrates in the Lake Agassiz region. Pp. 391-409 in J. T. Teller and Lee Clayton, eds. Glacial Lake Agassiz. Spec. Pap. Geol. Assoc. Can. 26, v + 451 pp.

Stewart, Norman Hamilton
1926 Development, growth, and food habits of the white sucker, Catostomus commersonii Lesueur. Bull. U. S. Bur. Fish. 42, Doc. 1007: 147-184.

Stockard, Charles R.
1907 Observations on the natural history of Polyodon spathula. Am. Nat. 41: 753-766.

Stone, Frederick L.
1947 Notes on two darters of the genus Boleosoma. Copeia (2): 92-96.

Stone, Udell Bennett
1940 Studies on the biology of the satinfin minnows, Notropis analostanus and Notropis spilopterus. Ph. D. Thesis, Cornell University. 98 pp.
1947 A study of the deep-water cisco fishery of Lake Ontario with particular reference to the bloater Leucichthys hoyi (Gill). Trans. Am. Fish. Soc. 74(1944): 230-249.

Stone, Udell B., Donald G. Pasko, and Robert M. Roecker
1954 A study of Lake Ontario- St. Lawrence River smallmouth bass. N. Y. Fish Game J. 1(1): 1-26.

Stoner, Allan W.
1980 Feeding ecology of Lagodon rhomboides (Pisces: Sparidae): Variation and functional responses. Fish. Bull. 78(2): 337-352.

Stoneking, Mark, Daniel J. Wagner, and Ann C. Hildebrand
1981 Genetic evidence suggesting subspecific difference between northern and southern populations of brook trout (Salvelinus fontinalis) Copeia (4): 810-819.

Storer, David Humphreys
1839 Report on the fishes, reptiles, and birds of Massachusetts. Boston. 426 pp., 4 pls.
1842 Descriptions of two new species of fishes. J. Boston Soc. Nat. Hist. 4(1): 58-62.
1845 Descriptions of hitherto undescribed fishes. Proc. Boston Soc. Nat. Hist. 2: 47-49.
1848 Descriptions of two new species of Alosa and one of Platessa. Proc. Boston Soc. Nat. Hist. 10(2): 242-243.

Storer, Horatio Robinson
1851 A description of a new species of Etheostoma, under the name of Etheostoma Linsleyi. Proc. Boston Soc. Nat. Hist. 4: 37-39.
1857 Observations on the fishes of Nova Scotia and Labrador, with descriptions of new species. Proc. Boston Nat. Hist. Soc. 3: 247-270.

Storr, John F., Patricia J. Hadden-Carter, and Julian M. Myers
1983 Dispersion of rock bass along the south shore of Lake Ontario. Trans. Am. Fish. Soc. 112(5): 618-628.

Stout, John F.
1975 Sound communication during the reproductive behavior of Notropis analostanus (Pisces: Cyprinidae). Am. Midl. Nat. 94(2): 296-325.

Sullivan, W. E.
1915 A description of the young stages of the winter flounder (Pseudopleuronectes americanus Walbaum). Trans. Am. Fish. Soc. 44(2): 125-136.

Summerfelt, Robert C. and Charles O. Minckley
1969 Aspects of the life history of the sand shiner, Notropis

stramineus (Cope), in the Smoky Hill River, Kansas. Trans. Am. Fish. Soc. 98(3): 444-453.

Surface, A. H.
1898 The lampreys of central New York. Bull. U. S. Fish Comm. 17 (1897): 209-215.

Suttkus, Royal D.
1958 Status of the nominal cyprinid species Moniana deliciosa Girard and Cyprinella texana Girard. Copeia (4): 307-318.
1963 Order Lepisostei. Mem. Sears Found. Mar. Res. 1(3): 61-88.

Svetovidov, A. N.
1982 Taxonomic differences between red hake, Urophycis chuss and U. tenuis, Gadidae. Jour. Ichthyol. (3): 150-153.

Swarts, Frederick A., William A. Dunson, and James E. Wright.
1978 Genetic and environmental factors involved in increased resistance of brook trout to sulfuric acid solutions and mine acid polluted waters. Trans. Am. Fish. Soc. 107(5) 651-677.

Swedberg, Donald V. and Charles H. Walburg
1970 Spawning and early life history of the freshwater drum in Lewis and Clark Lake, Missouri River. Trans. Am. Fish. Soc. 99(3): 560-570.

Swee, U. B. and H. R. McCrimmon
1966 Reproductive biology of the carp, Cyprinus carpio L., in Lake St. Lawrence, Ontario. Trans. Am. Fish. Soc. 95(4): 372-380.

Sweeney, Edward Francis
1972 The systematics and distribution of the centrarchid fish tribe Enneacanthini. Ph. D. Thesis, Boston University. 221 pp.

Swenson, William A. and Melvin L. Matson
1976 Influence of turbidity on survival, growth, and distribution of larval lake herring (Coregonus artedii). Trans. Am. Fish. Soc. 105 (4): 541-545.

Symons, P. E. K., James L. Metcalf, and G. D. Harding
1976 Upper lethal and preferred temperatures of the slimy sculpin, Cottus cognatus. J. Fish. Res. Board Can. 33(1): 180-183.

Tabery, Michael A., Arthur Ricciardi, and Theodore J. Chambers
1978 Occurrence of larval inshore lizardfish in the Hudson River estuary. N. Y. Fish Game J. 25(1): 87-89.

Talbot, George B.
1954 Factors associated with fluctuation in abundance of the Hudson River shad. Fish. Bull. 101, vol. 56: 373-413.

Tandler, A. and F. W. H. Beamish
1979 Mechanical and biochemical components of apparent specific dynamic action in largemouth bass, Micropterus salmoides Lacepède. J. Fish. Biol. 14(4): 343-350.

Tanyolac, Julide
1973 Morphometric variation and life history of the cyprinid fish, Notropis stramineus (Cope). Occas. Pap. Mus. Nat. Hist. Univ. Kansas 12, 28 pp.

Tarter, Donald C.
1969 Some aspects of reproduction in the western blacknose dace, Rhinichthys atratulus meleagris Agassiz, in Doe Run, Meade County, Kentucky. Trans. Am. Fish. Soc. 98(3): 454-459.
1970 Food and feeding habits of the western blacknose dace, Rhinichthys atratulus meleagris Agassiz, in Doe Run, Meade County, Kentucky. Am. Midl. Nat. 83(1): 134-159.

Taubert, B. D.
1980 Reproduction of shortnose sturgeon (Acipenser brevirostrum) in Holyoke Pool, Connecticut River, Massachusetts. Copeia (1): 114-117.

Taylor, Jane and Robin Mahon
1977 Hybridization of *Cyprinus carpio* and *Carassius aura-tus*, the first two exotic species in the lower Laurentian Great Lakes. Environ. Biol. Fish. 1(2): 205-208.

Taylor, Malcolm H., Glenn J. Leach, Leonard DiMichele, William M. Levitan, and William F. Jacob
1979 Lunar spawning cycle in the mummichog, *Fundulus heteroclitus* (Pisces: Cyprinodontidae). Copeia (2): 291-297.

Taylor, Malcolm H. and Leonard Di Michele
1983 Spawning site utilization in a Delaware population of *Fundulus heteroclitus* (Pisces: Cyprinodontidae). Copeia (3): 719-725.

Taylor, William Ralph
1954 Records of fishes in the John N. Lowe collection from the upper penninsula of Michigan. Misc. Publ. Mus. Zool. Univ. Mich. 87: 50 pp.
1969 A revision of the catfish genus *Noturus* Rafinesque with an analysis of higher groups in the Ictaluridae. Bull. U. S. Natl. Mus. 282, vi + 315 pp., 21 pls.

Tester, Albert L.
1930 Spawning habits of the small-mouthed black bass in Ontario waters. Trans. Am. Fish. Soc. 60(1930): 53-61.
1932a Food of the small-mouthed black bass (*Micropterus dolomieu*) in some Ontario waters. Univ. Toronto Stud. Biol. Ser. 36: 169-203. (Publ. Ontario Fish. Res. Lab. no. 46).
1932b Rate of growth of the small-mouthed black bass (*Micropterus dolomieu*) in some Ontario waters. Univ. Toronto Stud. Biol. Ser. 36: 205-221 (Publ. Ontario Fish. Res. Lab. no. 47).

Texas Instruments Inc. Ecological Services
1975 First annual report for the multiplant impact study of the Hudson River Estuary vol. 1.

Thoits, C. F., III
1958 A compendium of the life history and ecology of the white perch, *Morone americana* (Gmelin). Mass. Div. Fish Game Fish. Bull. 24, 16 pp. mimeo.

Thomas, B. O.
1962 Behavioral studies of the brook stickleback, *Eucalia inconstans* (Kirtland). Am. Zool. 2 (3): 452.

Thompson, David H.
1933 The finding of very young *Polyodon*. Copeia (1): 31-33.

Thompson, John H. (ed.)
1977 Geography of New York State. Syracuse Univ. Press. 543 pp.

Thompson, Zadock
1842 History of Vermont, natural, civil, and statistical. Burlington, 1842.
1850 Description of a new species of *Esox* (*Esox nobilior*). Proc. Boston Soc. Nat. Hist. (1848-1851) 3: 163,305.
1853 Appendix to: Natural History of Vermont. 224pp.

Thomson, Keith Stewart, W. H. Weed III, and Algis G. Taruski
1971 Saltwater Fishes of Connecticut. Bull. State Geological and Natural History Survey of Connecticut. 105: vii + 165 pp.

Thorgaard, Gary H.
1983 Chromosomal differences among rainbow trout populations. Copeia (3): 650-652.

Threinen, C. W., C. Wistrom, B. Apelgren, and H. Snow
1966 The northern pike, its life history, ecology, and management. Wis. Conserv. Dept. Publ. 235, 16 pp.

Todd, J. H.
1971 The chemical language of fishes. Sci. Am. 224: 98-108.

Todd, Thomas N.
1981 *Coregonus prognathus* Smith: a nomen dubium. Copeia (2): 489-490.

Toman, Frank A.
1955 White perch. Conservationist 10(1): 28.

Trautman, Milton B.
1931 *Parexoglossum hubbsi*, a new cyprinid fish from western Ohio. Occas. Pap. Mus. Zool. Univ. Mich. 235, 11 pp., 1 pl.
1957 The fishes of Ohio with illustrated keys. The Ohio State Univ. Press. Columbus. xviii + 683 pp.
1981 The fishes of Ohio with illustrated keys. Revised Edition. Ohio State Univ. Press, Columbus. xxvi + 782 pp.

Traver, Jay R.
1929 The habits of the black-nosed dace, *Rhinichthys atronasus* (Mitchill). J. Elisha Mitchell Sci. Soc. 45 (1): 101-129.

Trembley, F. J.
1930 The gar-pike of Lake Champlain. Pp. 139-145 in: A Biol. Survey of the Champlain watershed. Suppl. Nineteenth Ann. Rept. N. Y. State Conserv. Dept. (1929).

Trent, Lee, and William W. Hassler
1966 Feeding behavior of adult striped bass, *Roccus saxatilis*, in relation to stages of sexual maturity. Chesapeake Sci. 7(4): 189-192.

Trojnar, John R.
1977 Egg and larval survival of white suckers (*Catostomus commersoni*) at low pH. J. Fish. Res. Board Can. 34(2): 262-266.

Tsai, Chu-Fa
1971 Occurrence of the fathead minnow, *Pimephales promelas* (Pisces: Cyprinidae), in the Chesapeake Atlantic slope drainages. Chesapeake Sci. 12(4): 274-275.
1972 Life history of the eastern johnny darter, *Etheostoma olmstedi* Storer, in cold tailwater and sewage-polluted water. Trans. Am. Fish. Soc. 101(1): 80-88.

Tsai, Chu-Fa and George R. Gibson, Jr.
1971 Fecundity of the yellow perch, *Perca flavescens* Mitchill, in the Patuxent River, Maryland. Chesapeake Sci. 12 (4): 270-274.

Tsai, Chu-Fa and Edward C. Raney
1974 Systematics of the banded darter, *Etheostoma zonale* (Pisces: Percidae). Copeia (1): 1-24.

Turner, Clarence L.
1921 Food of the common Ohio darters. Ohio J. Sci. 22(2): 41-62.

Tyler, Albert V.
1966 Some lethal temperature relations of two minnows of the genus *Chrosomus*. Can. J. Zool. 44(3): 349-364.

Ulvestad, Dennis A. and Jerrold H. Zar
1977 Preferred temperature of the common shiner, *Notropis cornutus*, in relation to age, size, season, and nutritional state. Ohio. J. Sci. 77(4): 170-173.

Underhill, A. H.
1949 Studies on the development, growth, maturity of the chain pickerel, *Esox niger* (Lesueur). J. Wildl. Managt. 13(4): 377-391.

Underhill, James C.
1963 Distribution in Minnesota of the subspecies of the percid fish *Etheostoma nigrum*, and of their intergrades. Am. Midl. Nat. 70(2): 470-478.

Underhill, James C. and David J. Merrell
1959 Intra-specific variation in the bigmouth shiner (*Notropis dorsalis*). Am. Midl. Nat. 61(1): 133-147.

Van Cleave, Harley J. and Henry C. Markus
1929 Studies on the life history of the blunt-nosed minnow. Am. Nat. 63(689): 530-539.

Vandermeer, John H.
1966 Statistical analysis of geographic variation of the fathead minnow, *Pimephales promelas*. Copeia (3): 457-466.

Van Duzer, Evelyn May
1939 Observations on the breeding habits of the cutlips minnow, *Exoglossum maxillingua*. Copeia (2): 65-75.

Vanicek, C. David
1961 Life history of the quillback and highfin carpsuckers in the Des Moines River. Proc. Iowa Acad. Sci. 68: 238-246.

Van Meter, Harry D. and Milton B. Trautman
1970 An annotated list of the fishes of Lake Erie and its tributary waters exclusive of the Detroit River. Ohio J. Sci. 70(2): 65-78.

Van Oosten, John
1929 Life history of the lake herring (*Leucichthys artedi* Le Sueur) of Lake Huron as revealed by its scales, with a critique of the scale method. Bull. U. S. Bur. Fish. 44 (Document 1053): 265-428, figs. 15, 17-36.
1937a The age, growth, and sex ratio of the Lake Superior longjaw, *Leucichthys zenithicus* (Jordan and Evermann). Pap. Mich. Acad. Sci., Arts Lett. 22 (1936): 691-711.
1937b First record of the smelt *Osmerus mordax* in Lake Erie. Copeia (1):64-65.
1937c The dispersal of smelt, *Osmerus mordax* (Mitchill), in the Great Lakes region.Trans. Am. Fish. Soc. 66: 160-171.
1942 The age and growth of the Lake Erie white bass, *Lepibema chrysops* (Rafinesque). Pap. Mich. Acad. Sci. Arts Lett. 27(2): 307-334.
1961 Records, ages, and growth of the mooneye, *Hiodon tergisus*, of the Great Lakes. Trans. Am. Fish. Soc. 90(2): 170-174.

Van Oosten, John J. and Hilary J. Deason
1938 The food of the lake trout (*Cristivomer namaycush namaycush*) and of the lawyer, (*Lota maculosa*) of Lake Michigan. Trans. Am. Fish. Soc. 67(1937): 157-177.
1939 The age, growth, and feeding habits of the whitefish, *Coregonus clupeaformis* (Mitchill) of Lake Champlain. Trans. Am. Fish. Soc. 68(1938): 152-162.

Vari, Richard P.
1982 The seahorses (Subfamily Hippocampinae). Mem. Sears Found. Mar. Res. no. 1, part 8: 173-189.

Vasetskiy, S. G.
1971 Fishes of the family Polyodontidae. J. Ichthyol. 11(1): 18-25.

Victor, B. C. and E. B. Brothers
1982 Age and growth of the fallfish *Semotilus corporalis* with daily otolith increments as a method of annulus verification. Can. J. Zool. 60: 2543- 2550.

Vladykov, Vadim D.
1949 Quebec lampreys (Petromyzonidae). I. List of species and their economical importance. Dept. Fish. Prov. Quebec Contrib. 26, 67 pp.
1960 Description of young ammocoetes belonging to two species of lampreys: *Petromyzon marinus* and *Entosphenus lamottenii*. J. Fish. Res. Board Can. 17(27): 267-288.

Vladykov, Vadim D. and Gérard Beaulieu
1946 Études sur l'Esturgeon (*Acipenser*) de la Province de Quebec. Nat. Can. 73(6-8): 143-204.

Vladykov, Vadim D. and John R. Greeley
1963 Order Acipenseroidei. Mem. Sears Found. Mar. Res. 1(3): 24-60.

Vladykov, Vadim D. and Edward Kott
1982 Correct scientific names for the least brook lamprey and the American brook lamprey (Petromyzontidae). Can. J. Zool. 60: 856-864.

Vladykov, Vadim D. and J. M. Roy
1948 Biologie de la lamproie d'eau douce (*Ichthyomyzon unicuspis*) après la métamorphose (Résumé). Rev. Can. Biol. 7(3): 483-485.

Wagner, Charles C. and Edwin L. Cooper
1963 Population density, growth, and fecundity of the creek chubsucker, *Erimyzon oblongus*. Copeia (2): 350-357.

Wagner, Wilbert C. and Thomas M. Stauffer
1980 Three-year-old pink salmon in Lake Superior tributaries. Trans. Am. Fish. Soc. 109(4): 458-460.

Walbaum, Johanne Julio
1792 Petri Artedi sueci genera piscium in quibus systema totum ichthyologiae proponitur cum classibus ordinibus, generum characteribus, specierum differentiis observationibus plurimus, Redactis speciebus. 242 ad genera 52. Ichthyologiae, pars III. Emendata et aucta a Johanne Hulio Walbaum. Grypeswaldia 1793. 723 pp., 3 pls.

Walburg, Charles H.
1975 Food of young-of-year channel catfish in Lewis and Clark Lake, a Missouri River reservoir. Am. Midl. Nat. 93(1): 218-221.

Waldman, John
1981 White perch on the run. Underwater Nat. 13(2): 22-23.

Wallace, C. R.
1967 Observations on the reproductive behavior of the black bullhead (*Ictalurus melas*). Copeia (4): 852-853.

Wallace, Dale C.
1971 The age and growth of the silverjaw minnow, *Ericymba buccata*. Am. Midl. Nat. 86(1): 116-127.
1972 The ecology of the silverjaw minnow, *Ericymba buccata* Cope. Am. Midl. Nat. 87: 172-190.
1973 Reproduction of the silverjaw minnow, *Ericymba buccata* Cope. Trans. Am. Fish. Soc. 102 (4):786-793.
1976 Feeding behavior and developmental, seasonal and diel changes in the food of the silverjaw minnow, *Ericymba buccata* Cope. Am. Midl. Nat. 95(2): 361-376.

Warner, Kendall
1973 Spring food of the chain pickerel (*Esox niger*) in Maine lakes. Trans. Am. Fish. Soc. 102(1): 149-151.

Washburn, George N.
1948 Propagation of the creek chub in ponds with artificial raceways. Trans. Am. Fish. Soc. 75(1945): 336-350.

Webster, Dwight A.
1942 The life histories of some Connecticut fishes. In: A fishery survey of important Connecticut Lakes. Connecticut State Geol. Nat. Hist. Surv. Bull. 63: 122-227, 60 figs.
1943 Food progression in young white perch *Morone americana* (Gmelin) from Bantam Lake, Connecticut. Trans. Am. Fish. Soc. 72: 136-144.
1954a Smallmouth bass, *Micropterus dolomieu*, in Cayuga Lake (Part 1. Life history and management). Mem. Agric. Exp. Sta. Cornell Univ. 327, 39 pp.
1954b A survival experiment and an example of selective sampling of brook trout (*Salvelinus fontinalis*) by angling and rotenone in an Adirondack pond. N. Y. Fish Game J. 1(2): 214-219.
1954c Smallmouth bass, *Micropterus dolomieui*, in Cayuga Lake. Part 1. Life History and environment. Cornell Univ. Mem. 327.
1980 De Witt Clinton's ". . . .Fishes of the western waters of the State of New York" reexamined. Fisheries 5(2): 5-12.
1982 Early history of the Atlantic salmon in New York. N. Y. Fish Game J. 29(1): 26-44.

Webster, Dwight A. and Gudny Eiriksdottir
1976 Upwelling water as a factor influencing choice of spawning sites by brook trout (*Salvelinus fontinalis*). Trans. Am. Fish. Soc. 105(3): 416-421.

Webster, Dwight A. and William Flick
1960 Brandon Park fish management report summary, 1950-1959. 71 pp.

Wedemeyer, Gary
1973 Some physiological aspects of sublethal heat stress in

the juvenile steelhead trout (*Salmo gairdneri*) and coho salmon (*Oncorhynchus kisutch*). J. Fish. Res. Board Can. 30: 831-834.

Weed, Alfred C.
1927 Pike, pickerel, and muskalonge. Field Mus. Nat. Hist. Zool. Leaflet 9, 52 pp.

Weisel, George F.
1962 Comparative study of the digestive tract of a sucker, *Catostomus catostomus*, and a predaceous minnow, *Ptychocheilus oregonense*. Am. Midl. Nat. 68(2): 334-346.
1966 Young salmonid fishes of western Montana. Proc. Mont. Acad. Sci. 26: 1-21.

Wells, Barbara, D. H. Steele, and A. V. Tyler
1973 Intertidal feeding of winter flounder (*Pseudopleuronectes americanus*) in the Bay of Fundy. J. Fish. Res. Board Can. 30(9): 1374-1378.

Wells, LaRue
1969 Fishery survey of the U. S. waters of Lake Ontario. Pp. 51-57 in Limnological Survey of Lake Ontario, 1964. Great Lakes Fish. Comm. Tech Rept. 14.

Wells, LaRue and Alfred M. Beeton
1963 Food of the bloater, *Coregonus hoyi*, in Lake Michigan. Trans. Am. Fish. Soc. 92(3): 245-255.

Wells, LaRue and Robert House
1974 Life history of the spottail shiner (*Notropis hudsonius*) in southeastern Lake Michigan, the Kalamazoo River and western Lake Erie. Bur. Sport Fish. Wildl. Res. Rept. 78:iv + 10 pp.

Welsch, William W. and C. M. Breder Jr.
1922 A contribution to the life history of the puffer, *Sphoeroides maculatus* (Schneider). Zoologica 2 (12): 261-276, 1 fig.
1923 Contributions to life histories of Sciaenidae of the eastern United States coast. Bull. U. S. Bur. Fish. 39 (document 945): 141-201.

Wenner, Charles A.
1973 Occurrence of American eel, *Anguilla rostrata*, in waters overlying the eastern North American continental shelf. J. Fish. Res. Board Can. 30: 1752-1755.

Wenner, Charles A. and J. A. Musick
1974 Fecundity and gonad observations of the American eel, *Anguilla rostrata*, migrating from Chesapeake Bay, Virginia. J. Fish. Res. Board Can. 31(8): 1387-1391.
1975 Food habits and seasonal abundance of the American eel, *Anguilla rostrata*, from the lower Cheaspeake Bay. Chesapeake Sci. 16(1): 62-66.

Werner, Earl E. and Donald J. Hall
1974 Optimal foraging and the size selection of prey by the bluegill sunfish (*Lepomis macrochirus*). Ecology 55(5): 1042-1052.
1976 Niche shifts in sunfishes: experimental evidence and significance. Science 191: 404-406.
1977 Competition and habitat shift in two sunfishes (Centrarchidae). Ecology 58(4): 869-876.
1979 Foraging efficiency and habitat switching in competing sunfishes. Ecology 60(2): 256-264.

Werner, Robert G.
1969 Ecology of limnetic bluegill fry (*Lepomis macrochirus*) in Crane Lake, Indiana. Am. Midl. Nat. 81(1): 164-181.
1972 Bluespotted sunfish, *Enneacanthus gloriosus*, in Lake Ontario drainage. Copeia (4): 878-879.
1979 Homing mechanism of spawning white suckers in Wolf Lake, New York. N. Y. Fish Game J. 26(1): 48-58.
1980 Freshwater fishes of New York State, a field guide. Syracuse Univ. Press. viii + 186 pp.

Westin, D. T., K. J. Abernathy, L. E. Meller and B. A. Rogers
1979 Some aspects of biology of the American sand lance, *Ammodytes americanus*. Trans. Am. Fish. Soc. 108(3): 328-331.

Westman, James R.
1938 Studies on the reproduction and growth of the blunt-nosed minnow, *Hyborhynchus notatus* (Rafinesque). Copeia (2): 57-61.
1941 A consideration of population life history studies in relation to the problems of fish management research with special reference to the small mouthed bass *Micropterus dolomieu* Lacepède, the lake trout *Cristivomer namaycush* (Walbaum) and the mudminnow *Umbra limi* (Kirtland). Ph. D. Thesis, Cornell University. 182 pp.

Westman, James R. and Ross F. Nigrelli
1955 Preliminary studies of menhaden and their mass mortalities in Long Island and New Jersey waters. N. Y. Fish Game J. 2(2): 142-153.

Westman, James R., William Kelly, Mark Chittenden Jr. and Howard Loeb
1965 Return of another native — The American shad of the Delaware River. Conservationist 19(4): 16-19.

Whitaker, John O. Jr.
1977 Seasonal changes in food habits of some cyprinid fishes from the White River at Petersburg, Indiana. Am. Midl. Nat. 97(2): 411-419.

White, Michael L. and Mark E. Chittenden
1977 Age determination, reproduction, and population dynamics of the Atlantic croaker, *Micropogonias undulatus*. Fish. Bull. 75(1): 109-123.

White, Steven T. and Dale C. Wallace
1973 Diel changes in the feeding activity and food habits of the spotfin shiner, *Notropis spilopterus* (Cope). Am. Midl. Nat. 90 (1): 200-205.

Whitehead, P. J. P.
1963 A revision of recent round herrings (Pisces: Dussumieriidae). Bull. Br. Museum (Nat. Hist.) 10(6): 307-380.

Whitford, M. E.
1914 History of the canal system of the State of New York. Albany, Brandon Printing Company.

Whitworth, Walter R., Peter L. Berrern, and Walter T. Keller
1968 Freshwater fishes of Connecticut. Bull. State Geological and Natural History Survey of Connecticut. 101: vi + 134 pp.

Wich, K. and J. W. Mullan
1958 A compendium of the life history and ecology of the chain pickerel, *Esox niger* (LeSueur). Contrib. Nat. Acad. Sci. Comm. Handb. Biol. Data 22, 23 pp. + bibliogr.

Wigley, R. L.
1959 Life history of the sea lamprey of Cayuga Lake, New York. Fish. Bull. 154, vol. 59: 561-617.

Wilcox, Douglas and Steven W. Effler
1981 Formation of alewife concretions in polluted Onondaga Lake. Environmental Pollution (Series B.) 2: 203-215.

Wilder, Burt G.
1877 Gar-pikes, old and young. Popular Sci. Monthly 11.

Wilder, D. G.
1947 A comparative study of the Atlantic salmon, *Salmo salar* Linnaeus, and the lake salmon, *Salmo salar sebago* (Girard). Can. J. Res. D. 25: 175-189.
1952 A comparative study of the anadromous and freshwater populations of the brook trout, (*Salvelinus fontinalis* (Mitchill)). J. Fish. Res. Board Can.. 9(4): 169-203.

Wiley, E. O.
1976 The phylogeny and biogeography of fossil and recent gars (Actinopterygii: Lepisosteidae). Univ. Kansas Mus. Nat. Hist. Misc. Publ. 64: 1-111.

Wiley, Martin L. and Bruce B. Collette
1970 Breeding tubercles and contact organs in fishes: their occurrence, structure, and significance. Bull. Am. Mus. Nat. Hist. 143(3): 143-216.

Will, Homer C.
1931 Age of the spawning groups of northern log-perch, *Percina caprodes semifasciata* (DeKay), of Douglas Lake, Michigan, as revealed by their scales. Proc. Pa. Acad. Sci. 5: 82-88.

Williams, James D.
1975 Systematics of the percid fishes of the subgenus *Ammocrypta*, genus *Ammocrypta*, with descriptions of two new species. Bull. Ala. Mus. Nat. Hist. 1, 56 pp.

Williamson, Lyman O.
1942 Spawning habits of muskellunge, northern pike. Wis. Conserv. Bull. 7(5): 10-11.

Wilsmann, Leni Ann
1979 Resource partitioning and mechanisms of coexistence of blackchin and blacknose shiners (*Notropis*: Cyprinidae). Ph.D. Thesis, Michigan State University. 130 pp.

Wilson, Alfred W. G.
1907 Chub's nests. Am. Nat. 41(485): 323-327.

? Wilson, Alexander
ca. 1811 *Clupea pseudoharengus* and *C. sapidissima*. In: Rees' New Cyclopedia IX, no pagination.

Wilson, F. W.
1955 Lampreys in the Lake Champlain basin. Am. Midl. Nat. 54(1): 168-172.

Winchell, Alexander
1864 Description of a gar-pike, supposed to be new- *Lepidosteus* (*Cylindrosteus*) *oculatus*. Proc. Acad. Nat. Sci. Phila. 16: 183-185.

Winn, Howard E.
1953 Breeding habits of the percid fish *Hadropterus copelandi* in Michigan. Copeia (1): 26-30.
1957 Egg site selection by three species of darters (Pisces-Percidae). Br. J. Anim. Behav. 5(1): 25-28.
1958a Observations on the reproductive habits of darters (Pisces-Percidae). Am. Midl. Nat. 59(1): 190-212.
1958b Comparative reproductive behavior and ecology of fourteen species of darters (Pisces- Percidae). Ecol. Monogr. 28(2): 155-191.
1960 Biology of the brook stickleback, *Eucalia inconstans* (Kirtland). Am. Midl. Nat. 63(2): 424-438.

Winn, Howard E. and John F. Stout
1960 Sound production by the satinfin shiner, *Notropis analostanus*, and related fishes. Science 132: 222-223.

Winters, G. H.
1970 Meristics and morphometrics of sand launce in the Newfoundland area. J. Fish. Res. Board Can. 27(11): 2104-2108.

Witt, A. Jr.
1960 Length and weight of ancient freshwater drum, *Aplodinotus grunniens*, calculated from otoliths found in Indian middens. Copeia (3): 181-185.

Witt, A. Jr. and R. C. Marzolf
1954 Spawning and behavior of the longear sunfish, *Lepomis megalotis megalotis*. Copeia (3): 188-190.

Wolfert, David R.
1977 Age and growth of the walleye in Lake Erie, 1963-1968. Trans. Am. Fish. Soc. 106(6): 569-577.
1980 Age and growth of rock bass in eastern Lake Ontario. N. Y. Fish Game J. 27(1): 88-90.

Wolfert, David R., Wolf-Dieter N. Busch, and Carl T. Baker
1975 Predation by fish on walleye eggs on a spawning reef in western Lake Erie. Ohio. J. Sci. 75(3): 118-125.

Wolfert, David R. and Terence J. Miller
1978 Age, growth, and food of the northern pike in eastern Lake Ontario. Trans. Am. Fish. Soc. 107(5): 696-702.

Wolfert, David R. and Harry D. Van Meter
1978 Movements of tagged walleyes in eastern Lake Erie. N. Y. Fish Game J. 25(1): 16-22.

Woolcott, William S.
1957 Comparative osteology of serranid fishes of the genus *Roccus* (Mitchill). Copeia (1): 1-10.
1964 Infraspecific variation in the white perch. Chesapeake Sci. 3(2): 94-113.

Wootton, R. J.
1976 The biology of the sticklebacks. Academic Press, London. x + 387 pp.

Wynne-Edwards, V. C.
1932 The breeding habits of the black-headed minnow (*Pimephales promelas* Rafinesque). Trans. Am. Fish. Soc.62: 382-383, 2 figs.

Yochim, William D.
1981 Distribution of darters (*Etheostoma* and *Percina*) in the major riffles of the Allegheny River, upstream of the Allegheny reservoir. M.S. Thesis, St. Bonaventure University. 96 pp.

Young, Robert T. and Leon J. Cole
1900 On the nesting habits of the brook lamprey (*Lampetra wilderi*). Am. Nat. 34 (404): 617-620.

Youngs, W. D.
1972 An estimation of lamprey-induced mortality on a lake trout population. Ph.D. Thesis, Cornell University.

Youngs, William D. and Ray T. Oglesby
1972 Cayuga Lake: effects of exploitation and introduction on the salmonid community. J. Fish. Res. Board Can. 29(6): 787-794.

Zilliox, Robert G.
1962 The walleyes of Lake Champlain. Conservationist 16(5): 10-11,34.

Zilliox, Robert G. and William D. Youngs
1958 Further studies on the smelt of Lake Champlain. N. Y. Fish Game J. 5(2): 164-174.

Zorach, Timothy
1964 Systematic studies of *Etheostoma microlepidotum* and *E. maculatum*, percid fishes of the subgenus *Nothonotus* (Etheostomatini). M. S. Thesis, Cornell University.
1967 Systematics of the darters of the subgenus *Nothonotus* (*Etheostoma*: Percidae). Ph.D. Thesis, Cornell University.
1971 Taxonomic status of the subspecies of the tessellated darter, *Etheostoma olmstedi* Storer, in southeastern Virginia. Chesapeake Sci. 11(4): 254-263.
1972 Systematics of the percid fishes, *Etheostoma camurum* and *E. chlorobranchium* new species, with a discussion of the subgenus *Nothonotus*. Copeia (3): 427-447.

Zorach, Timothy and Edward C. Raney
1967 Systematics of the percid fish, *Etheostoma maculatum* Kirtland, and related species of the subgenus *Nothonotus*. Am. Midl. Nat. 77(2): 296-322.

9

Alphabetical Serials Index

Am. Fish Cult. — American Fish Culturist

Am. Fish. Soc. Spec. Publ. — American Fisheries Society Special Publication

Am. Jour. Sci. Arts — American Journal of Science and Arts

Am. Midl. Nat. — The American Midland Naturalist

Am. Month. Mag. — The American Monthly Magazine

Am. Month. Mag. Crit. Rev. — The American Monthly Magazine and Critical Review (New York)

Am. Mus. Novit. — American Museum Novitiates

Am. Nat. — The American Naturalist

Am. Zool. — American Zoologist

Ann. Lyc. Nat. Hist. N.Y. — Annals of the Lyceum of Natural History (New York)

Ann. N. Y. Acad. Sci. — Annals of the New York Academy of Science

Ann. Rep. Forest Fish Game Comm State N. Y. — Annual Report of the Forest, Fish and Game Commission of the State of New York

Ann. Science — Annals of Science

Ann. Wien. Mus. Natur. — Annalen des Naturhistorischen Museums in Wien

ASB Bull. — Association of Southeastern Biologists Bulletin

Biochem. Syst. Ecol. — Biochemical Systematics and Ecology

Biol. Bull. — The Biological Bulletin (Woods Hole, Mass.)

Biol. Conserv. — Biological Conservation

Boston J. Nat. Hist. — Boston Journal of Natural History

Brimleyana — Brimleyana

Bol. Inst. Oceanogr. — Boletim do Instituto Oceanografico (Sao Paolo)

Bol. Mus. Municipal do Funchal — Boletin Museo Municipal do Funchal

Br. J. Anim. Behav. — British Journal of Animal Behavior

Bull. Am. Mus. Nat. Hist. — Bulletin of the American Museum of Natural History

Bull. Ala. Mus. Nat. Hist. — Bulletin of the Alabama Museum of Natural History

Bull. Bingham Oceanogr. Coll. — Bulletin of the Bingham Oceanographic Collection of Yale University

Bull. Br. Mus. (Nat. Hist.) Zool. — Bulletin of the British Museum (Natural History) Zoology

Bull. Buffalo Soc. Nat. Sci. — Bulletin of the Buffalo Society of Natural Sciences

Bull. Fish. Res. Board Can. — Bulletin of the Fisheries Research Board of Canada

Bull. Fla. State Mus. Biol. Sci. — Bulletin of the Florida State Museum of Biological Sciences

Bull. Ill. Nat. Hist. Surv. — Bulletin of the Illinois Natural History Survey

Bull. Ill. State Lab. Nat. Hist. — Bulletin of the Illinois State Laboratory of Natural History

Bull. Inst. Fish. Res. Michigan Dept. Conserv. — Bulletin of the Institute for Fisheries Research of the Michigan Department of Conservation

Bull. Inst. Zool. Acad. Sinica (Taipei) — Bulletin of the Institute of Zoology, Academia Sinica (Taipei)

Bull. Mass. Div. Fish Game — Bulletin of the Massachusetts Division of Fish and Game

Bull. Mich. Dept. Conser. Inst. Fish. Res. — Bulletin of the Michigan Department of Conservation Institute for Fisheries Research

Bull. Mich. Fish Comm. — Bulletin of the Michigan Fish Commission

Bull. Mus. Comp. Zool. — Bulletin of the Museum of Comparative Zoology (Harvard University)

Bull. Nat. Mus. Can. — Bulletin of the National Museum of Canada

Bull. N. Y. Zool. Soc. — Bulletin of the New York Zoological Society

Bull. N. Y. State Mus. — Bulletin of the New York State Museum

Bull. Ohio Biol. Surv. — Bulletin of the Ohio Biological Survey

Bull. Okla. Fish. Res. Lab. — Bulletin of the Oklahoma Fisheries Research Laboratory

Bull. South. Calif. Acad. Sci. — Bulletin of the Southern California Academy of Science

Bull. U. S. Bur. Fish. — Bulletin of the United States Bureau of Fisheries

Bull. U. S. Fish Comm. — Bulletin of the United States Fish Commission

Bull. U. S. Natl. Mus. — Bulletin of the United States National Museum

Bull. Univ. Kans. Mus. Nat. Hist. — Bulletin of the University of Kansas Museum of Natural History

Calif. Dep. Fish Game Fish. Bull. — California Department of Fish and Game Fishery Bulletin

Calif. Fish Game — California Fish and Game

Can. Field-Nat. — Canadian Field-Naturalist

Can. Fish Cult. — Canadian Fish Culturist

Can. J. Earth Sci. — Canadian Journal of Earth Sciences

Can. J. Fish Aquat. Sci. — Canadian Journal of Fisheries and Aquatic Science

Can. J. Fish Biol. — Canadian Journal of Fish Biology

Can. J. Res. — Canadian Journal of Research

Can. J. Zool. — Canadian Journal of Zoology

Can. Nature — Canadian Nature

Can. Tech. Rept. Fish. Aquat. Sci. — Canadian Technical Report of Fisheries and Aquatic Sciences

Chesapeake Sci. — Chesapeake Science

Comp. Biochem. Physiol. — Comparative Biochemistry and Physiology

Conservationist — The Conservationist (Albany, New York)

Copeia — Copeia

Contrib. Can. Biol. — Contributions to Canadian Biology

Contrib. Can. Biol. Fish. — Contribution to Canadian Biology of Fishes

Contrib. Ichthyol. — Contributions to Ichthyology

Cont. Roy. Ont. Mus. Paleont. — Contributions of the Royal

Ontario Museum of Paleontology

Cranbrook Inst. Sci. Bull. — Cranbrook Institute of Science Bulletin

Dept. Fish. Prov. Quebec Contrib. — Department of Fisheries of the Province of Quebec Contributions

Diss. Abstr. — Dissertation Abstracts B. The Sciences and Engineering

Ecology — Ecology

Ecol. Monogr. — Ecological Monographs

Environ. Biol. — Environmental Biology

Environ. Biol. Fish. — Environmental Biology of Fishes

Estuaries — Estuaries

FAO Fish. Synopsis. — Food and Agricultural Organization of the United Nations Fishery Synopsis

Fish. Bull. — U. S. Fish and Wildlife Service Fishery Bulletin (continued as National Marine Fisheries Service Fishery Bulletin)

Fisheries — Fisheries (Bethesda)

Geol. Assoc. Can. Spec. Pap. — Geological Association of Canada Special Paper

Great Lakes Fish. Comm. Spec. Publ. — Great Lakes Fishery Commission Special Publication

Great Lakes Fish. Comm. Tech. Rept. — Great Lakes Fishery Commission Technical Report.

Great Lakes Res. Div. Univ. Mich. Publ. — Publication of the Great Lakes Research Division of the University of Michigan

Ill. Biol. Monogr. — Illinois Biological Monographs

Iowa State Coll. J. Sci. — Iowa State College Journal of Science

Inst. R. Sci. Nat. Belg. Bull. — Institute Royal Science Natural Belgique Bulletin

Invest. Indiana Lakes Streams — Investigations of Indiana Lakes and Streams

J. Acad. Nat. Sci. Phila. — The Journal of the Academy of Natural Sciences of Philadelphia

J. Anim. Behav. — The Journal of Animal Behaviour

J. Anim. Ecol. — The Journal of Animal Ecology

J. Ariz. Acad. Sci. — Journal of the Arizona Academy of Sciences

J. Biogeogr. — Journal of Biogeography

J. Comp. Neurol. — The Journal of Comparative Neurology

J. Elisha Mitchell Sci. Soc. — Journal of the Elisha Mitchell Scientific Society

J. Exp. Mar. Biol. — Journal of Experimental Marine Biology

J. Exp. Zool. — The Journal of Experimental Zoology

J. Fish Biol. — Journal of Fish Biology

J. Fish Diseases — Journal of Fish Diseases

J. Fish. Res. Board Can. — Journal of the Fisheries Research Board of Canada

J. Freshwater Ecol. — Journal of Freshwater Ecology

J. Gen. Physiol. — Journal of General Physiology

J. Ichthyol. — Journal of Ichthyology (English translation of Voprosy Ikhtiologii)

J. Linn. Soc. London Zoology — The Journal of the Linnaean Society of London Zoology

J. Miss. Acad. Sci. — Journal of the Mississippi Academy of Science

J. Morphol. — The Journal of Morphology

J. Nat. Hist. Boston Soc. Nat. Hist. — Journal of Natural History of the Boston Society of Natural History

J. Physique — Journal du Physique

J. Sci. Lab. Denison Univ. — Journal of the Science Laboratory of Denison University

J. Wash. Acad. Sci. — Journal of the Washington Academy of Science

J. Wildl. Manage. — The Journal of Wildlife Management

J. Zool. (Lond.) — Journal of Zoology (London)

Limnos — Limnos

Lloydia — Lloydia (Cincinnati)

Mar. Biol. (Berl.) — Marine Biology International Journal on Life in the Oceans and Coastal Waters (Berlin)

Mem. Amer. Acad. Sci. — Memoirs of the American Academy of Sciences

Mem. Amer. Acad. Arts Sci. — Memoirs of the American Academy of Arts and Sciences

Mem. Mus. Nat. Hist. — Memoirs of the Museum of Natural History

Mem. Sears Found. Mar. Res. — Memoirs of the Sears Foundation for Marine Research

Mich. Acad. — Michigan Academician

Milwaukee Publ. Mus. Occas. Pap. Nat. Hist. — Milwaukee Public Museum Occasional Papers in Natural History

Misc. Publ. Mus. Zool. Univ. Mich. — Miscellaneous Publication of the Museum of Zoology of the University of Michigan

Misc. Publ. Roy. Ont. Mus. Life. Sci. — Miscellaneous Publication of the Royal Ontario Museum of Life Sciences

Monogr. Acad. Nat. Sci. Phila. — Monograph of the Academy of Natural Science of Philadelphia

Nat. Can. — Le Naturaliste Canadienne Biologie Aquatique

N. Y. DEC mimeo. — Mimeographed report of the New York Department of Environmental Conservation

N. Y. Fish. Bull. — New York Fishery Bulletin

N. Y. Fish Game J. — New York Fish and Game Journal

N. Y. Paleontol. Soc. Notes — New York Paleontological Society Notes

N. H. Fish Game Dept. Surv. Rept. — New Hampshire Fish and Game Department Survey Report

NOAA Tech. Rept. NMFS Tech. Circ. (United States) — National Oceanic and Atmospheric Administration Technical Report National Marine Fisheries Service Technical Report

Nouv. Arch. Mus. Hist. Nat. Paris — Nouvelle Archives Museum d'Histoire Naturelle de Paris

Northeast. Environ. Sci. — Northeastern Environmental Science

Occas. Pap. Biol. Field Sta. — Occasional Papers of the Biological Field Station at Cooperstown

Occas. Pap. Mus. Nat. Hist Univ. Kansas — Occasional Papers of the Museum of Natural History of the University of Kansas

Occas. Pap. Mus. Zool. Univ. Mich. — Occasional Papers of the Museum of Zoology of the University of Michigan

Ohio J. Sci. — Ohio Journal of Science

Okla. Fish. Res. Lab. Bull. — Oklahoma Fisheries Research Laboratory Bulletin

Ont. Mus. Life Sci. Misc. Publ. — Ontario Museum of Life Sciences Miscellaneous Publication

Pap. Mich. Acad. Sci. Arts Lett. — Papers of the Michigan Academy of Science, Arts and Letters

Physiol. Zool. — Physiological Zoology

Proc. Acad. Nat. Sci. Phila. — Proceedings of the Academy of Natural Sciences of Philadelphia

Proc. Amer. Acad. Arts Sci. — Proceedings of the American Academy of Arts and Sciences

Proc. Am. Assoc. Adv. Sci. — Proceedings of the American Association for the Advancement of Science

Proc. Am. Philos. Soc. — Proceedings of the American Philosophical Society

Proc. Ann. Conf. Southeast. Assoc. Game Fish. Comm. — Proceedings of the Annual Conference of the Southeastern Association of Game and Fish Commissioners

Proc. Biol. Soc. Wash. — Proceedings of the Biological Society of Washington

Proc. Boston Soc. Nat. Hist. — Proceedings of the Boston Society of Natural History

Proc. Calif. Acad. Sci. — Proceedings of the California Academy of Sciences

Proc. Fla. Acad. Sci. — Proceedings of the Florida Academy of Science

Proc. Iowa Acad. Sci. — Proceedings of the Iowa Academy of Science

Proc. Linnaean Soc. London — Proceedings of the Linnaean Society of London

Proc. Minn. Acad. Sci. — Proceedings of the Minnesota Academy of Science

Proc. Mont. Acad. Sci. — Proceedings of the Montana Academy of Sciences

Proc. Pa. Acad. Sci. — Proceedings of the Pennsylvania Academy of Science

Proc. Staten Island Inst. Arts Sci. — Proceedings of the Staten Island Academy of Arts and Sciences

Proc. U. S. Natl. Mus. — Proceedings of the United States National Museum

Prog. Fish-Cult. — Progressive Fish-Culturist, U.S. Fish and Wildlife Service

Publ. Chesapeake Biol. Lab. — Publications of the Chesapeake Biological Laboratory

Publ. Inst. Mar. Sci. — Publications of the Institute of Marine Science

Publ. Ont. Fish. Res. Lab. — Publications of the Ontario Fishery Research Laboratory

Publ. Univ. Kans. Mus. Nat. Hist. — Publications of the University of Kansas Museum of Natural History

Publ. Wis. Conserv. Dep. — Publications of the Wisconsin Conservation Department

Quart. J. Fla. Acad. Sci. — Quarterly Journal of the Florida Academy of Sciences

Quart. J. Sci. Lit. Arts Roy. Inst. London — Quarterly Journal of Science Literature and Arts of the Royal Institute of London

Quart. Rev. Biol. — Quarterly Review of Biology

Repts. Flora Fauna Wis. — Reports on the Flora and Fauna of Wisconsin

Rept. Comm. Fish. State N. Y. — Report of the Commissioners of Fisheries of the State of New York

Rept. Mich. Acad. Sci. — Report of the Michigan Academy of Sciences

Rept. U. S. Comm. Fish. — Report of the United States Commissioner of Fisheries

Rept. U. S. Comm. Fish Fish. — Report of the United States Commissioner of Fish and Fisheries

Rept. U. S. Fish. Comm. — Report of the United States Fish Commission.

Rev. Can. Biol. — Revue Canadienne de Biologie

Roos. Wildl. Ann. — Roosevelt Wildlife Annals

Roos. Wildl. Bull. — Roosevelt Wildlife Bulletin

Schritt. Ges. Naturf. Freunde Berlin — Schriften der Berlinischen Gesellschaft Naturforschender Freunde. Berlin

Science — Science (Washington, D.C.)

Sci. Stud. — Science Studies St. Bonaventure University

Sci. Amer. — Scientific American

Sci. Monthly — Scientific Monthly

Smithson. Contrib. Know. — Smithsonian Contributions to Knowledge

Smithson. Contrib. Zool. — Smithsonian Contributions to Zoology

Smithson. Misc. Coll. — Smithsonian Miscellaneous Collections

Smithson. Inst. Ann. Rept. — Smithsonian Institution Annual Report

Southwest. Nat. — Southwestern Naturalist

Stud. Trop. Oceanogr. Miami — Studies in Tropical Oceanography University of Miami

Suppl. Ann. Rept. N.Y. State Conserv. Dept. — Supplement to the Annual Report of the New York State Conservation Department

Syllogeus — Syllogeus

Syst. Zool. — Systematic Zoology

Tech. Bull. Dept. Nat. Res. Wis. — Technical Bulletin of the Wisconsin Department of Natural Resources, Madison

Tex. Rept. Biol. Med. — Texas Reports on Biology and Medicine

Tex. Parks Wildl. — Texas Parks and Wildlife

Trans. Am. Fish. Soc. — Transactions of the American Fisheries Society

Trans. Am. Philos Soc. — Transactions of the American Philosophical Society

Trans. Am. Micr. Soc. — Transactions of the American Microscopical Society

Trans. Cleveland Acad. Nat. Sci. — Transactions of the Cleveland Academy of Natural Science

Trans. Ill. State Acad. Sci. — Transactions of the Illinois State Academy of Science

Trans. Kan. Acad. Sci. — Transactions of the Kansas Academy of Science

Trans. Ky. Acad. Sci. — Transactions of the Kentucky Academy of Science

Trans. Lit. Philos. Soc. — Transactions of the Literary and Philosophical Society of New York

Trans. Roy. Can. Inst. — Transactions of the Royal Canadian Institute

Trans. Roy. Soc. London — Transactions of the Royal Society of London

Trans. Wis. Acad. Sci. Arts Lett. — Transactions of the Wisconsin Academy of Science, Arts and Letters

Trav. Pecheries Que. — Travaux sur les Pecheries du Quebec

Tulane Stud. Zool. Bot. — Tulane Studies in Zoology and Botany

Underwater Nat. — Underwater Naturalist

Univ. Iowa Stud. Nat. Hist. — University of Iowa Studies in Natural History

Univ. Kans. Bull. Mus. Nat. Hist. — University of Kansas Museum of Natural History Bulletin

Univ. Toronto Stud. Biol Ser. — University of Toronto Studies. Biological Series

U. S. Bur. Sport Fish. Wildl. Tech. Pap. — United States Bureau of Sport Fisheries and Wildlife Technical Papers

U. S. Fish Wildl. Serv. Circ. — United States Fish and Wildlife Service Circular (U. S. Dept. Interior, Fish and Wildlife Service Bureau of Commercial Fisheries Circular)

U. S. Fish Wildl. Serv. Spec. Sci. Rept. — United States Fish and Wildlife Service Special Scientific Report

U. S. Natl. Mar. Fish. Serv. Spec. Sci. Rept. — United States National Marine Fisheries Service Special Scientific Report

Va. Agric. Exp. Stn. Tech. Bull. — Virginia Agricultural Experiment Station Technical Bulletin

Va. J. Sci. — Virginia Journal of Science

Wildl. Monogr. — Wildlife Monograph

Wis. Acad. Sci. Arts Lett. — Wisconsin Academy of Science, Arts, and Letters

Wis. Conserv. Dep. Tech. Bull. — Wisconsin Conservation Department Technical Bulletin

Wis. Conserv. Dept. Publ. — Wisconsin Conservation Department Publication

Wis. Dept. Nat. Res. Tech. Bull. — Wisconsin Department of Natural Resources Technical Bulletin

Z. Tierpsychol. — Zeitschrift fur Tierpsychologie

Zool. Jahrbuch — Zoologische Jahrbuch

Zoologica — Zoologica. Scientific Contributions of the New York Zoological Society

Common and Scientific Names Index *

* The principal reference directly follows each entry. Page references in boldface include an illustration.

Geographic Names Index *

* Page references in boldface include an illustration.

* Page references in boldface include an illustration.